Collins Canadian Discovery World Atlas

Collins
An imprint of HarperCollins*Publishers*
2 Bloor St. E. 20th Floor
Toronto
Ontario
M4W 1A8

Collins Discovery World Atlas
First Published 2004

Canadian Edition 2004

Copyright © HarperCollins*Publishers* 2004
Maps © Collins Bartholomew Ltd 2004

Collins ® is a registered trademark of
HarperCollins*Publishers* Ltd

Printed and bound in Singapore by Imago

British Library Cataloguing in Publication Data.
A catalogue record for this book is available from
the British Library.

ISBN 0 00 639590 2

RF 11839 Imp 001

All mapping in this atlas is generated from Collins
Bartholomew digital databases. Collins Bartholomew,
the UK's leading independent geographical information
supplier, can provide a digital, custom, and premium
mapping service to a variety of markets.
For further information:
Tel: 416.975.9334

We also offer a choice of books, atlases and maps that
can be customized to suit a customer's own
requirements. For further information:
Tel: 416.975.9334

everything clicks at www.harpercollins.ca

Collins

Collins Canadian
Discovery World Atlas

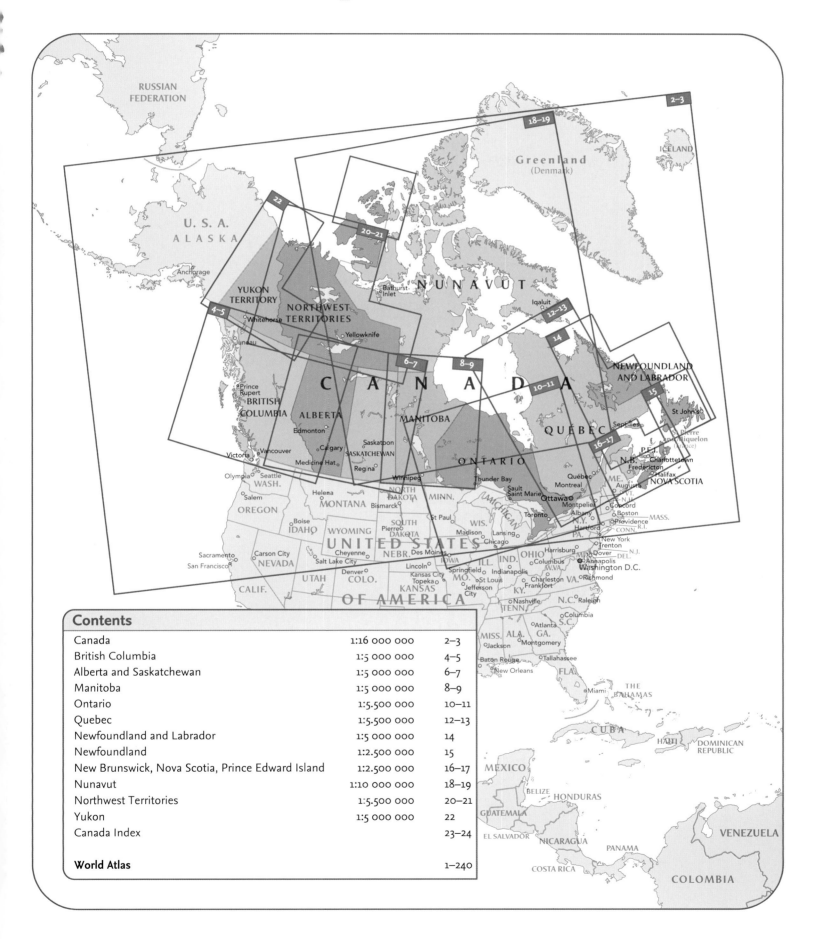

Contents

Lambert Conformal Conic Projection

1:16 000 000

| 0 | 200 | 400 | miles |

| 0 | 200 | 400 | 600 | 800 | km |

Canada

States in the U.S.A.
numbered on the map:

1. CONNECTICUT (K5)
2. MASSACHUSETTS (K5)
3. NEW HAMPSHIRE (K5)
4. RHODE ISLAND (K5)
5. VERMONT (K5)

British Columbia

Date entered Confederation	July 20 1871
Capital	Victoria
Area (sq km)	944 735 km²
Population	3 907 738
Provincial Code	BC
Main settlements (population)	
Vancouver (Metropolitan Area)	1 986 965
Kelowna	96 288
Kamloops	77 281
Victoria	74 125
Nanaimo	73 000

British Columbia

Canada's most mountainous province, containing the Rocky, the Columbia and the Coast Mountains. The highest peak is Mount Fairweather (4 670 m). There are over two million hectares of lakes and rivers, and numerous national parks and nature reserves. The largest river is the Fraser River. The main industries are forestry, fishing, farming, hydroelectric power and tourism. Rich mineral resources include coal, oil and gas.

Internet Links

● Government of British Columbia	**www.gov.bc.ca**
● Victoria	**www.city.victoria.bc.ca**
● NASA Visible Earth	**visibleearth.nasa.gov**

Vancouver Island and the Coast Mountains, British Columbia.
Image courtesy of SeaWiFS Project NASA/GSFC ORBIMAGE.

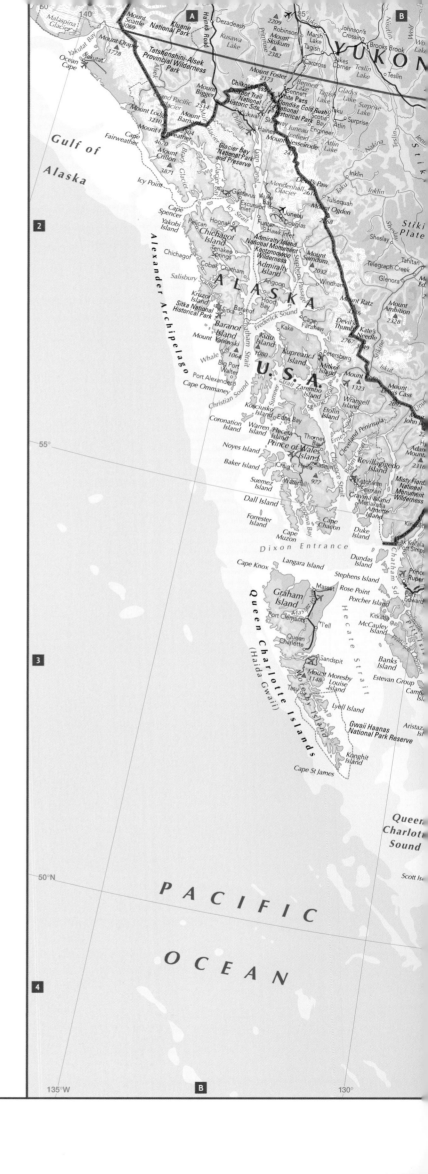

Conic Equidistant Projection

1:5 000 000

```
0        50       100      150    miles
|----|----|----|----|----|----|----|
0   50   100  150  200  250 km
```

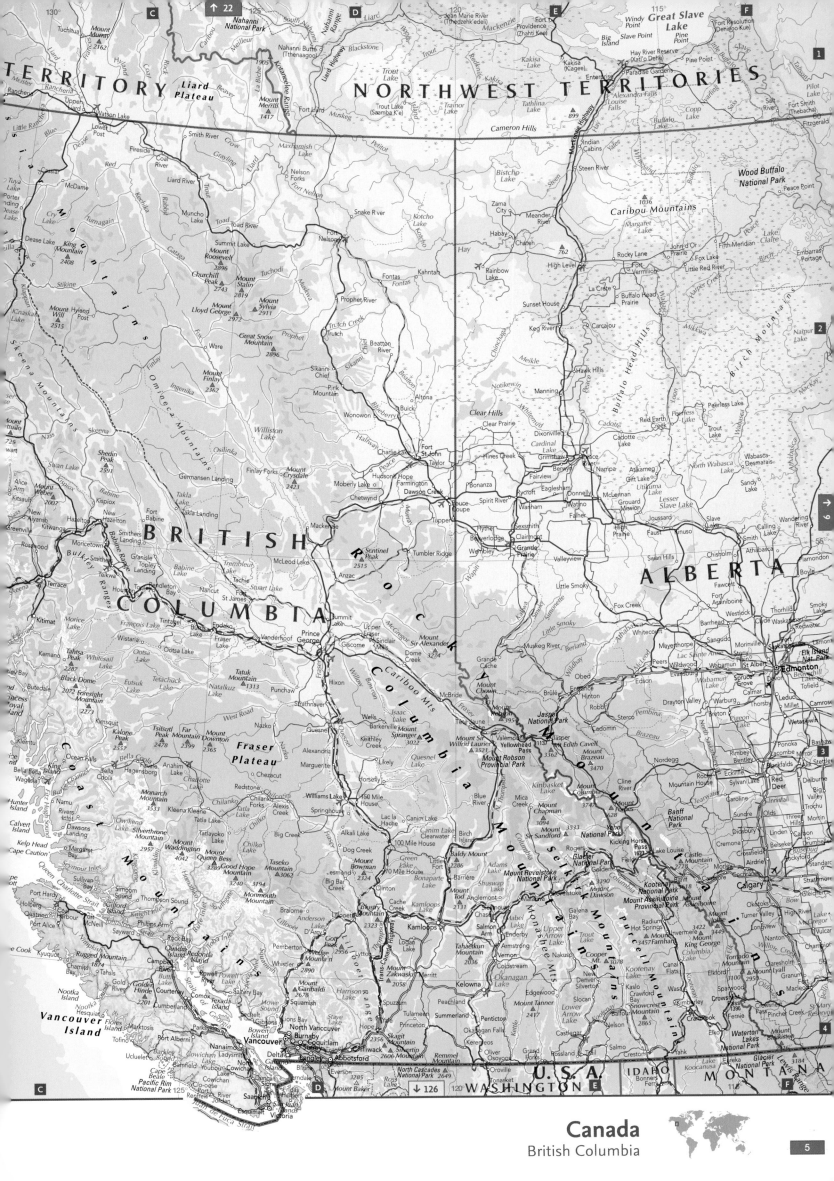

Canada
British Columbia

Alberta

Date entered Confederation	Sept 1 1905
Capital	Edmonton
Area (sq km)	661 848 km²
Population	2 974 807
Provincial Code	AB
Main settlements (population)	
Calgary	922 315
Edmonton	666 104
Red Deer	72 691
Lethbridge	72 717
St Albert	54 588
Medicine Hat	51 249

Alberta

The most westerly of Canada's Prairie Provinces, with the Rocky Mountains to the west and the USA to the south. The highest mountain is Mount Columbia (3 747 m). The main rivers include the Athabaska, Peace, North Saskatchewan and South Saskatchewan. Principal industries include grain, livestock, forestry, oil, gas, information technology and tourism. Alberta contains seventy per cent of Canada's coal reserves.

Internet Links

● Government of Alberta	**www.gov.ab.ca**
● Edmonton	**www.gov.edmonton.ab.ca**
● NASA Earth Observatory	**earthobservatory.nasa.gov**

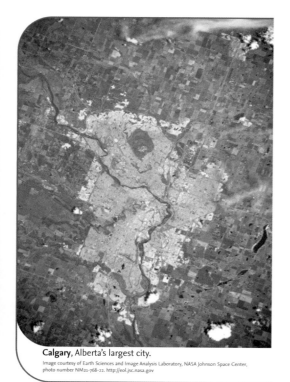

Calgary, Alberta's largest city.

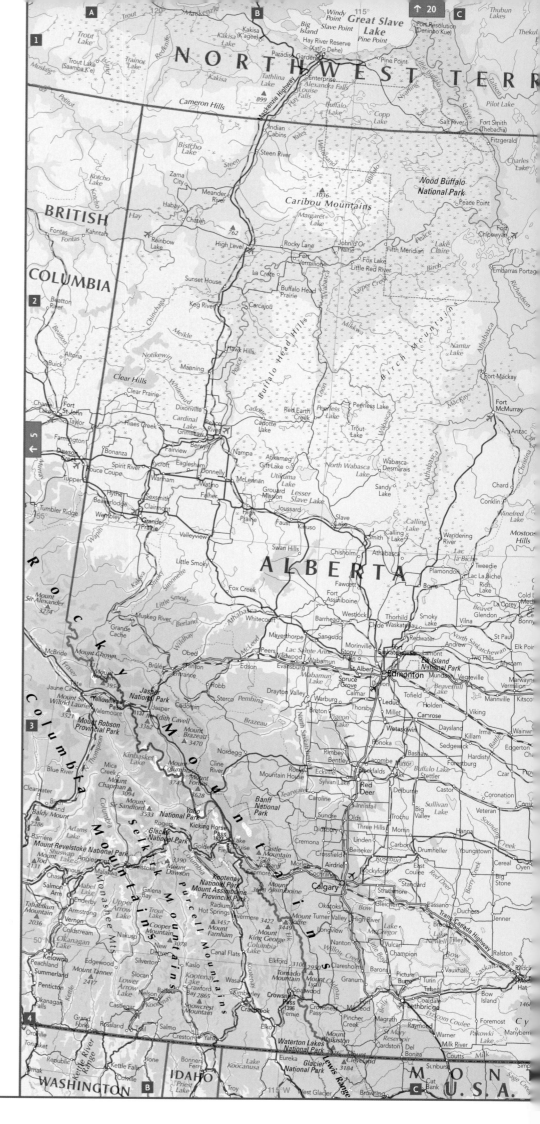

Conic Equidistant Projection

1:5 000 000

0	50	100	150	miles
0	50	100	150	200	250	km

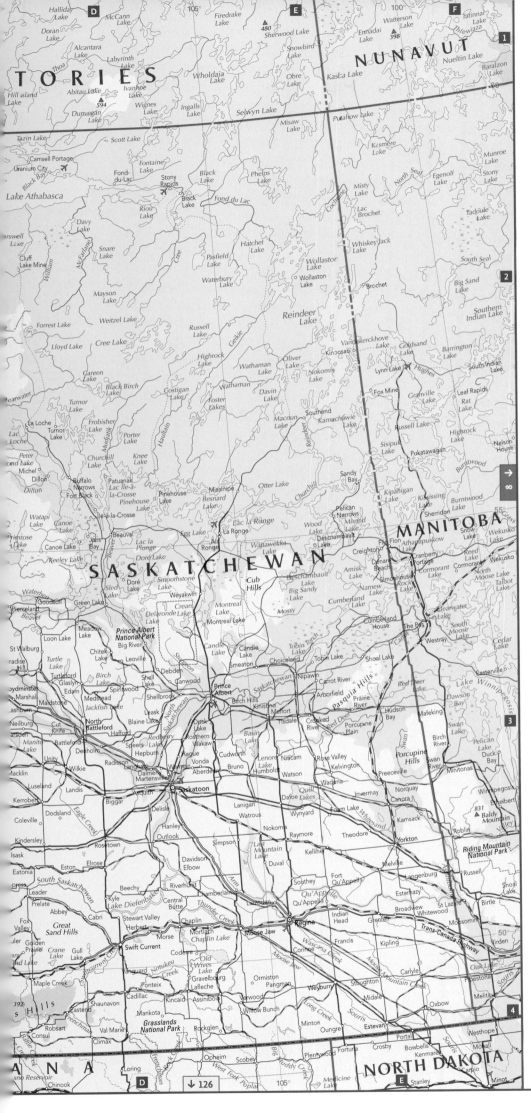

Lake Diefenbaker, Saskatchewan, on the South Saskatchewan river.

Image courtesy of Earth Sciences and Image Analysis Laboratory, NASA Johnson Space Center, photo number STS066-154-114. http://eol.jsc.nasa.gov

Saskatchewan	
Date entered Confederation	Sept 1 1905
Capital	Regina
Area (sq km)	651 036 km²
Population	978 933
Provincial Code	SK
Main settlements (population)	
Saskatoon	196 811
Regina	178 225
Prince Albert	34 291
Moose Jaw	32131

Saskatchewan

Canada's largest wheat producer and the central Prairie Province. Lakes and swamps lie to the north, with prairie to the south. The highest point (1 392 m) is within the Cypress Hills. The main rivers include the Churchill, Saskatchewan and the Qu' Appelle. The economy is based chiefly on agriculture (including wheat, rapeseed and oats) and mineral resources (including copper, zinc and coal).

Internet Links	
● Government of Saskatchewan	www.gov.sk.ca
● City of Regina	www.cityregina.com
● NASA Earth Observatory	earthobservatory.nasa.gov

Canada
Alberta and Saskatchewan

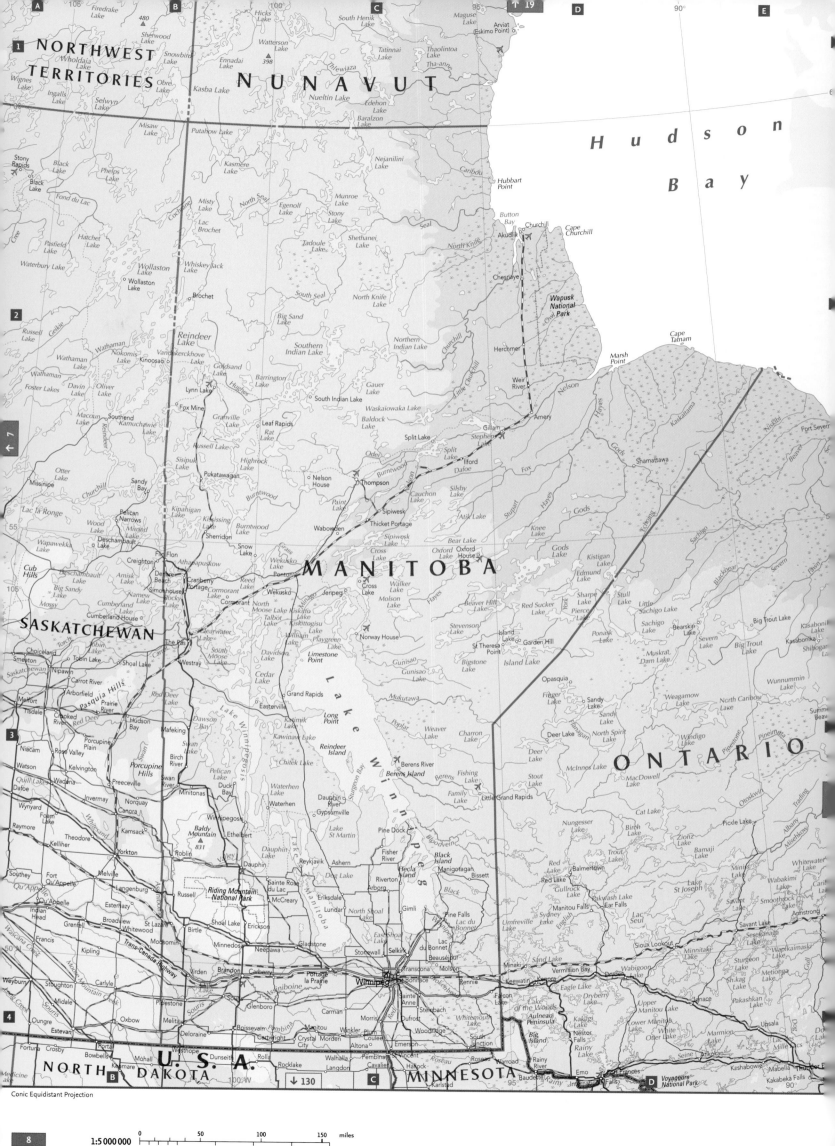

NORTHWEST
TERRITORIES

N U N A V U T

Hudson

Bay

MANITOBA

SASKATCHEWAN

ONTARIO

U.S.A.
NORTH DAKOTA
MINNESOTA

Conic Equidistant Projection

1:5 000 000

| 0 | 50 | 100 | 150 | miles |
| 0 | 50 | 100 | 150 | 200 | 250 | km |

← 7

↓ 130

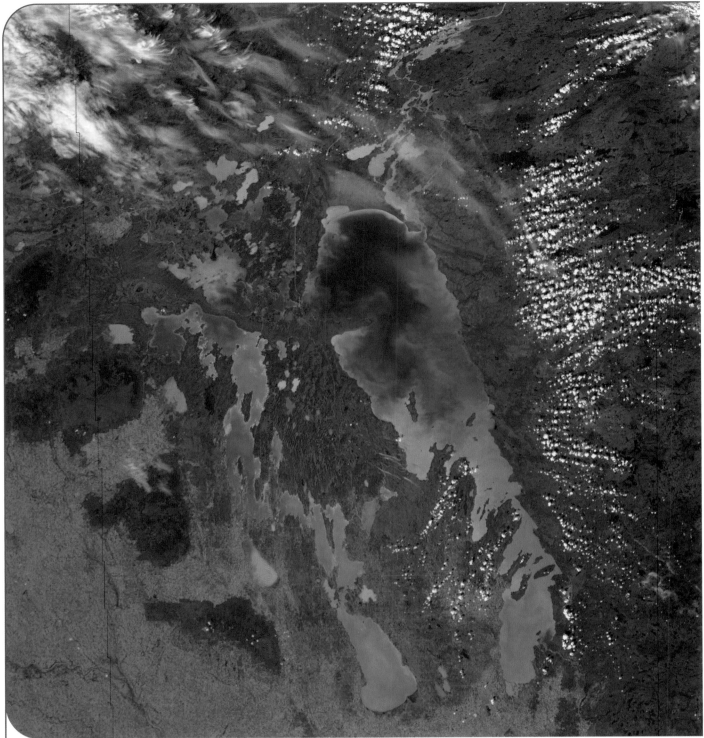

Lake Winnipeg, Manitoba is in the centre of this image, with Lakes Winnipegosis and Manitoba to the left.
Image courtesy of MODIS Rapid Response Project at NASA/GSFC.

Manitoba	
Date entered Confederation	July 15 1870
Capital	Winnipeg
Area (sq km)	647 797 km²
Population	1 119 583
Provincial Code	MB
Main settlements (population)	
Winnipeg	619 544
Brandon	39 716
Thompson	13 256
Portage la Prairie	12 976

Internet Links

● Province of Manitoba	**www.gov.mb.ca**
● Winnipeg	**winnipeg.ca**
● MODIS Satellite Imagery	**modis.gsfc.nasa.gov**

Manitoba

The easternmost Prairie Province, with prairie in the southwest, extensive forests in the north and tundra near Hudson Bay in the northeast. The highest point is Baldy Mountain (831 m). Numerous lakes and rivers include lakes Winnipeg, Winnipegosis and Manitoba and the Churchill, Nelson and Hayes rivers. The economy relies on agriculture, food and machinery manufacturing, hydroelectric power and mineral resources.

Conic Equidistant Projection

1:5 500 000

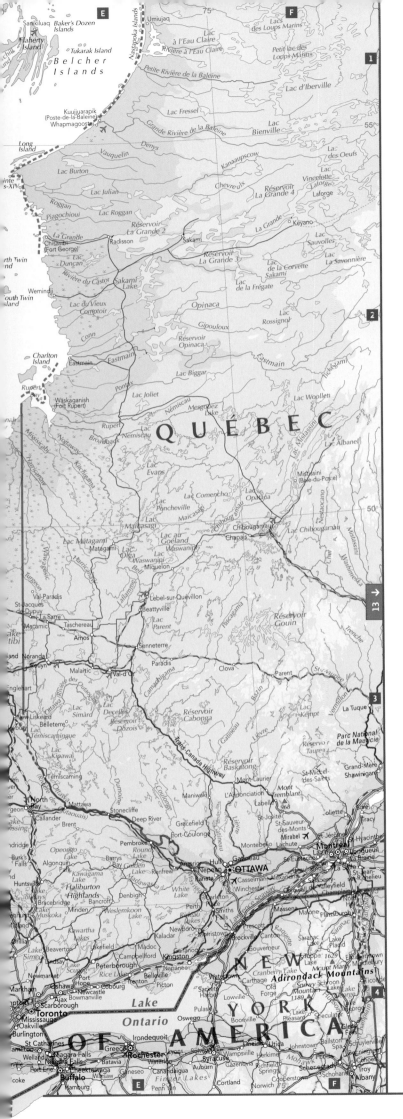

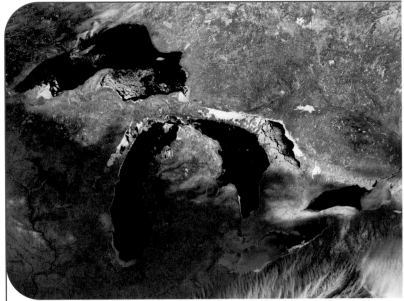

The Great Lakes straddling the border between Canada (top) and the USA (bottom).
Image courtesy of MODIS Rapid Response Project at NASA/GSFC

Ontario	
Date entered Confederation	July 1 1867
Capital	Toronto
Area (sq km)	1 076 395 km²
Population	11 410 046
Provincial Code	ON
Main settlements (population)	
Toronto	2 481 494
Ottawa	774 072
Mississauga	612 925
Hamilton	490 268
London	336 539
Brampton	325 428

Ontario

The second-largest Canadian province, containing the fertile plain of the lower Great Lakes and the St Lawrence River. The region is one of the world's leading industrial areas. The highest point is Batchawana Mountain (653 m). There are over 250 000 lakes in Ontario, containing approximately one-third of the world's fresh water. The economy is based chiefly on mineral production, finance and service industries, agriculture and manufacturing.

Internet Links	
Government of Ontario	**www.gov.on.ca**
Toronto	**www.city.toronto.on.ca**
Ottawa National Capital Commission	**www.canadascapital.gc.ca**
MODIS Satellite Imagery	**modis.gsfc.nasa.gov**

Canada
Ontario

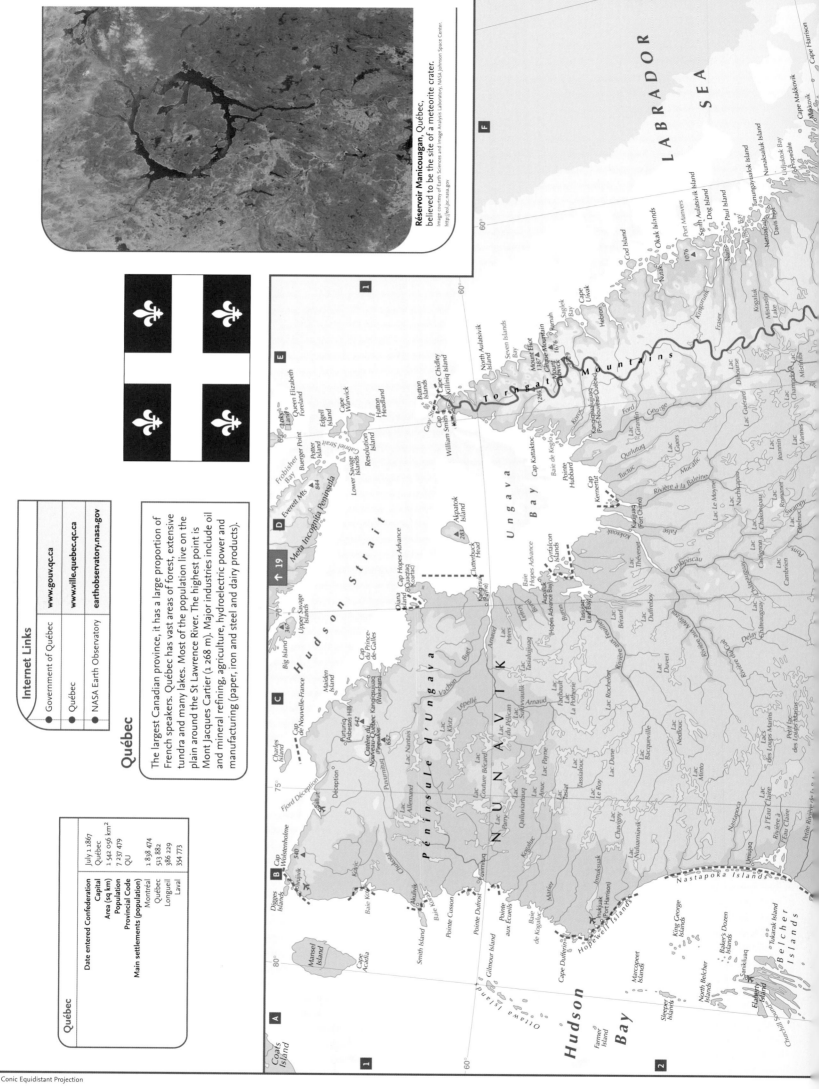

Internet Links

● Government of Québec	**www.gouv.qc.ca**
● Québec	**www.ville.quebec.qc.ca**
● NASA Earth Observatory	**earthobservatory.nasa.gov**

Québec

The largest Canadian province, it has a large proportion of French speakers. Québec has vast areas of forest, extensive tundra and many lakes. Most of the population live on the plain around the St Lawrence River. The highest point is Mont Jacques Cartier (1 268 m). Major industries include oil and mineral refining, agriculture, hydroelectric power and manufacturing (paper, iron and steel and dairy products).

Québec

Date entered Confederation	July 1 1867
Capital	Québec
Area (sq km)	1 542 056 km²
Population	7 237 479
Provincial Code	QU
Main settlements (population)	
Montréal	1 838 474
Québec	513 882
Longueil	386 229
Laval	354 773

Conic Equidistant Projection

1:5 500 000

0	50	100	150	miles
0	50	100	150	200	250	km

Canada

Québec

Space shuttle image showing part of the **Newfoundland and Labrador coastline.**
Digital Image © 1996 CORBIS; original image courtesy of NASA/Corbis.

Canada
Newfoundland and Labrador

Conic Equidistant Projection

1:5 500 000

Newfoundland and Labrador	
Date entered Confederation	March 31 1949
Capital	St John's
Area (sq km)	405 212 km²
Population	512 930
Provincial Code	NL
Main settlements (population)	
St John's	99 182
Mount Pearl	24 964
Corner Brook	20 103
Conception Bay South	19 772

Newfoundland and Labrador

Canada's most easterly province comprising the island of Newfoundland on the Gulf of St Lawrence, and sparsely populated Labrador on the mainland. The highest point is Mount Caubvick (1 729 m) in Labrador. Major rivers include the Churchill, Exploits and Gander. The economy is based on oil, fishing, mining, logging and newsprint production. Tourism and business and computer services are growing in importance.

Internet Links

● Government of Newfoundland and Labrador	www.gov.nf.ca
● St John's	www.stjohns.ca
● NASA Visible Earth	visibleearth.nasa.gov

Conic Equidistant Projection

1:2 500 000

0   25   50   75   miles
0   25   50   75   100   125   km

Canada
Newfoundland

QUEBEC

Détroit d'Honguedo

Île d'Anticosti

Péninsule de Gaspé

Monts Chic-Chocs

Monts Notre Dame

Gulf of St Lawrence

NEW BRUNSWICK

PRINCE EDWARD ISLAND

Chaleur Bay

Northumberland Strait

U.S.A.

MAINE

NOVA SCOTIA

Bay of Fundy

Chignecto Bay

Minas Channel

Minas Basin

Cobequid Mountains

Cobequid Bay

Gulf of Maine

Conic Equidistant Projection

1:2 500 000

0   25   50   75 miles

0   25   50   75 100 125 km

Maritime Provinces

New Brunswick
The largest of Canada's three Maritime Provinces, situated on the Gulf of St Lawrence and the Bay of Fundy. The highest point is Mount Carleton (820 m). Major rivers include the St John, Miramichi, Restigouche and Nepisiguit. Approximately one-third of the population are French-speaking. The economy is based on farming (potato and dairy), fishing, forestry, mining and tourism.

Nova Scotia
One of the Maritime Provinces, comprising the Nova Scotia peninsula and Cape Breton Island. The highest point is White Hill (532 m). Major rivers include the Shubenacadie and the Annapolis. The Minas Basin has one of the world's highest tide reaches, averaging 12 m. Economic activity relies on mining, agriculture, fishing, forestry and manufacturing. Offshore reserves of natural gas are being exploited.

Prince Edward Island
The smallest Canadian province, located in the Gulf of St Lawrence and separated from New Brunswick by the Northumberland Strait. The highest point is only 152 m. The economy is based on agriculture (the chief crop is potato), tourism, fishing (lobsters constitute half the fishing income) and forestry. No place on Prince Edward Island is more than 16 km from the sea.

New Brunswick	
Date entered Confederation	July 1 1867
Capital	Fredericton
Area (sq km)	72 908 km²
Population	729 498
Provincial Code	NB
Main settlements (population)	
Saint John	69 661
Moncton	61 046
Fredericton	47 560

Nova Scotia	
Date entered Confederation	July 1 1867
Capital	Halifax
Area (sq km)	55 284 km²
Population	908 007
Provincial Code	NS
Main settlements (population)	
Halifax (metropolitan area)	359 183
New Glasgow	21 102
Kentville	13 121

Prince Edward Island	
Date entered Confederation	July 1 1873
Capital	Charlottetown
Area (sq km)	5 660 km²
Population	135 294
Provincial Code	PE
Main settlements (population)	
Charlottetown	32 245
Summerside	14 654
Stratford	6 314

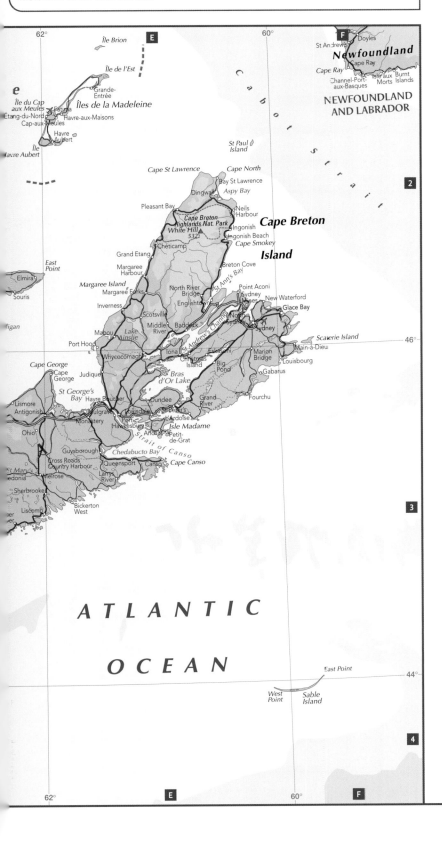

Internet Links	
Government of New Brunswick	www.gnb.ca
Fredericton	www.city.fredericton.nb.ca
Government of Nova Scotia	www.gov.ns.ca
Halifax	www.region.halifax.ns.ca
Government of Prince Edward Island	www.gov.pe.ca
Charlottetown	www.city.charlottetown.pe.ca
Natural Resources of Canada	www.nrcan-mcan.gc.ca/inter
Geological Survey of Canada	www.nrcan.gc.ca/gsc

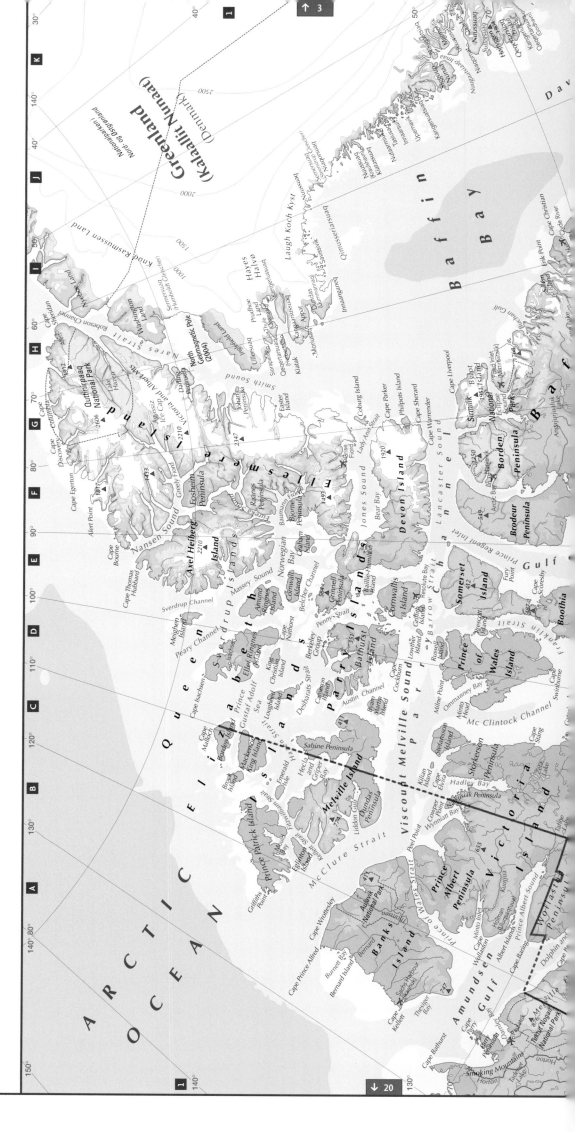

Greenland
(Kalaallit Nunaat)
(Denmark)

B a f f i n   B a y

A R C T I C

O C E A N

Nunavut

Created from part of the Northwest Territories as an autonomous region for the Inuit people, the territory occupies one-fifth of Canada's land area. The highest point is in Quttinirpaaq National Park (2 606 m). Economic activity has largely been confined to subsistence hunting and fishing. However, new jobs are emerging in mineral exploration and extraction, tourism and the exploitation of oil and gas reserves.

Nunavut

Date entered Confederation	April 1 1999
Capital	Iqaluit
Area (sq km)	2 093 190 km²
Population	26 745
Provincial Code	NU
Main settlements (population)	Iqaluit 5 236
	Rankin Inlet 2 177

Internet Links

● Government of Nunavut	www.gov.nu.ca
● Iqaluit	www.city.iqaluit.nu.ca
● Natural Resources of Canada	www.nrcan-mcan.gc.ca/inter

Conic Equidistant Projection

18

1:10 000 000

0   100   200   300   400 miles

0 100 200 300 400 500 600 km

ARCTIC OCEAN

Beaufort Sea

Banks Island

Prince Albert Peninsula

Victoria Island

Amundsen Gulf

Wollaston Peninsula

Colville Mountains

NUNAVUT

Great Bear Lake

NORTHWEST TERRITORIES

YUKON TERRITORY

Mackenzie Mountains

Selwyn Mountains

Backbone Ranges

Canyon Ranges

Nahanni National Park

Great Slave Lake

Yellowknife (Sombak'e)

Hay River

BRITISH COLUMBIA

Liard Plateau

Cassiar Mountains

ALBERTA

Wood Buffalo National Park

Conic Equidistant Projection

1:5 500 000

0   50   100   150   miles
0   50   100   150   200   250   km

Northwest Territories

Canada's third largest territory comprises many lakes and islands and vast areas of sparsely inhabited forest and tundra. The Mackenzie River is Canada's longest. The highest point is Tungsten in the Mackenzie Mountains (2 773 m). Economic activity has been largely traditional and based on subsistence agriculture but there is great potential for mineral extraction and the development of oil and gas exploration, forestry and agriculture.

Internet Links	
● Government of the Northwest Territories	www.gov.nt.ca
● City of Yellowknife	city.yellowknife.nt.ca
● Geological Survey of Canada	www.nrcan.gc.ca/gsc

Mackenzie River Delta, Northwest Territories, looking towards the Richardson Mountains.
Image © Lowell Georgia/CORBIS.

Continued from the top of page 20.

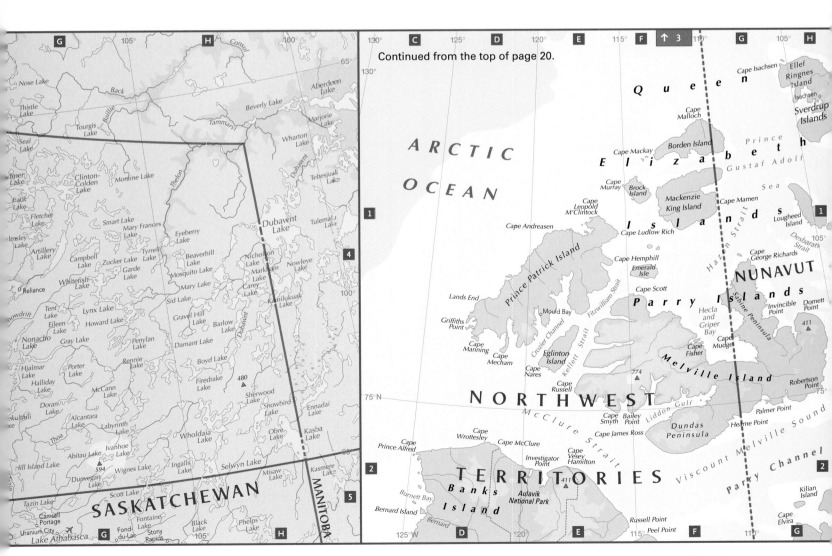

Canada
Northwest Territories

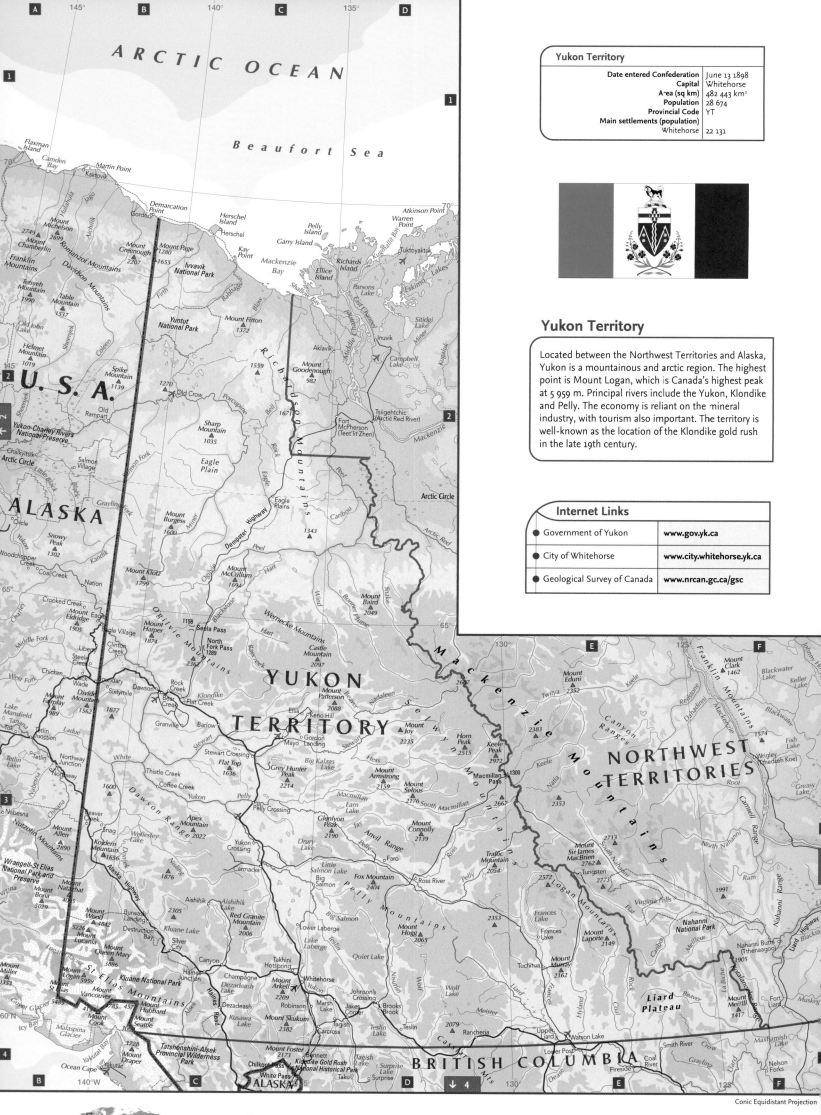

Yukon Territory

Date entered Confederation	June 13 1898
Capital	Whitehorse
Area (sq km)	482 443 km²
Population	28 674
Provincial Code	YT
Main settlements (population)	
Whitehorse	22 131

Yukon Territory

Located between the Northwest Territories and Alaska, Yukon is a mountainous and arctic region. The highest point is Mount Logan, which is Canada's highest peak at 5 959 m. Principal rivers include the Yukon, Klondike and Pelly. The economy is reliant on the mineral industry, with tourism also important. The territory is well-known as the location of the Klondike gold rush in the late 19th century.

Internet Links

● Government of Yukon	www.gov.yk.ca
● City of Whitehorse	www.city.whitehorse.yk.ca
● Geological Survey of Canada	www.nrcan.gc.ca/gsc

Conic Equidistant Projection

Canada
Yukon Territory

1:5 000 000

0 50 100 150 miles
0 50 100 150 200 250 km

This index includes the names of the most significant places and physical features in Canada. Names are indexed to the Canadian regional maps in the Atlas of Canada section. Provinces are identified by their Provincial Code. For an explanation of any other abbreviations used in this index, refer to page 161 of the main index to the world atlas.

Abbey *SK* 7 D3
Abbotsford *BC* 5 D4
Abitibi, Lake *ON/QC* 3 J5
Acadie Siding *NB* 16 C2
Admiralty Island *NU* 19 D3
Advocate Harbour *NS* 16 C3
Agate *ON* 10 D3
Aguathuna *NL* 15 A2
Airdrie *AB* 6 C3
Akimiski Island *NU* 19 F4
Aklavik *NT* 20 A3
Akpatok Island *NU* 19 H3
Akudlik *MB* 8 D2
Akulivik *QC* 12 B1
Alberta *prov.* 6 C3
Alert *NU* 18 H1
Alexandria *BC* 5 D3
Alexis Creek *BC* 5 D3
Algonquin Park *ON* 11 E3
Alice Arm *BC* 5 C2
Alix *AB* 6 C3
Alkali Lake *BC* 5 D3
Alma *NB* 16 C3
Alma *QC* 13 C4
Alsask *SK* 7 D3
Altona *BC* 5 D2
Ambition, Mount *BC* 4 B2
Amery *MB* 8 D2
Amos *QC* 13 B4
Amund Ringnes Island *NU* 18 E2
Amundsen Gulf *NT* 20 D2
Anahim Lake *BC* 5 C3
Angels Cove *NL* 15 C3
Annapolis *r. NS* 16 C3
Annapolis Royal *NS* 16 C3
Anzac *AB* 6 C2
Anzac *BC* 5 D3
Apex Mountain *YT* 22 C3
Arborfield *SK* 7 E3
Arctic Bay *NU* 18 F2
Arctic Red River *NT see* **Tsiigehtchic**
Argentia *NL* 15 C3
Arichat *NS* 17 E3
Arkell, Mount *YT* 22 C3
Armstrong *ON* 10 C2
Armstrong, Mount *YT* 22 D3
Aroland *ON* 10 C2
Aroostook *NB* 16 B2
Asbestos Hill *QC see* **Purtuniq**
Ashern *MB* 8 C3
Asquith *SK* 7 D3
Assiniboine *r. MB/SK* 2 F4
Assiniboine, Mount *AB/BC* 2 G4
Athabasca *r. AB* 6 C2
Athabasca, Lake *AB/SK* 7 D2
Atikameg *AB* 6 B2
Atlin *BC* 4 B2
Atlin Lake *BC/YT* 4 B2
Auden *ON* 10 C2
Aulavik National Park *NT* 21 [inset] E2
Aupaluk *QC* 12 D2
Avalon Peninsula *NL* 15 D3
Avalon Wilderness *NL* 15 D3
Axel Heiberg Island *NU* 18 E2
Baddeck *NS* 17 E2
Badger *NL* 15 C2
Badger's Quay *NL* 15 D2
Baffin Bay *Can./Greenland* 3 L2
Baffin Island *NU* 18 H3
Baie-Comeau *QC* 13 D4
Baie-du-Poste *QC see* **Mistissini**
Baie-Johan-Beetz *QC* 13 E3
Baie-Trinite *QC* 13 D4
Baird, Mount *YT* 22 D2
Baker Lake *NU* 19 E2
Bakers Brook *NL* 15 B2
Baldy Mount *BC* 5 E3
Baldy Mountain *MB* 8 B3
Balmertown *ON* 10 B2
Barnfield *BC* 5 C4
Banff National Park *AB* 6 B3
Banks Island *NT* 21 [inset] D2
Barkerville *BC* 5 D3
Barlow *YT* 22 C3
Barnard, Mount *AK/BC Can./U.S.A.* 4 A2
Barnes Icecap *NU* 19 G2
Barons *AB* 6 C4
Barr'd Harbour *NL* 15 B1
Barrie *ON* 11 E4
Barrière *BC* 5 D3
Barrington *NS* 16 C4
Barrington Passage *NS* 16 C4
Bartletts Harbour *NL* 15 B1
Bashaw *AB* 6 C3
Bass River *NB* 16 C2
Batchawana Mountain *ON* 10 D3
Bath *NB* 16 B2
Bathurst *NB* 16 C2
Bathurst, Cape *NT* 20 C2
Bathurst Island *NU* 18 E1
Bay de Verde *NL* 15 D2
Bay L'Argent *NL* 15 C3
Bay St Lawrence *NS* 17 E2
Bear Cove *NL* 15 B2
Bear Creek *YT* 22 C3
Beardmore *ON* 10 C3
Bear River *NS* 16 C3
Bearskin Lake *ON* 10 B2
Beatton River *BC* 5 D2
Beattyville *QC* 13 B4
Beaufort Sea *Can./U.S.A.* 2 D2
Beauval *SK* 7 D2
Beaver Creek *YT* 22 B3
Bedford *NS* 16 D3
Beechy *SK* 7 D3
Beiseker *AB* 6 C3
Belcher Islands *NU* 19 G3
Bella Coola *BC* 5 C3
Bellburns *NL* 15 B1
Belleoram *NL* 15 C3
Belle Isle, Strait of *sea chan. NL* 15 B1
Belleterre *QC* 13 B4
Belleville *ON* 11 E4
Benedict, Mount *NL* 14 C3
Benjamin River *NB* 16 B2
Bennett *BC* 4 B2
Bentley *AB* 6 C3
Benton *NB* 16 B3
Benton *NL* 15 C2
Berwick *NB* 16 C3
Berwyn *AB* 6 B2
Betsiamites *QC* 13 D4
Bickerton West *NS* 17 E3
Big Bar Creek *BC* 5 D3
Big Brook *NL* 15 B1
Bigger, Mount *BC* 4 A2
Big Pond *NS* 17 E3
Big River *SK* 7 D3
Big Salmon *YT* 22 D3
Big Stone *AB* 6 C3
Big Trout Lake *ON* 10 C2
Big Valley *AB* 6 C3
Birch Hills *SK* 7 D3
Birch Island *BC* 5 E3
Birch River *MB* 8 B3
Birchy Bay *NL* 15 C2
Bird Cove *NL* 15 B1
Birtle *MB* 8 B3
Biscotasing *ON* 10 D3
Bissett *MB* 8 C3
Black Dome *BC* 5 C3
Black Duck *NL* 15 A2
Black Lake *SK* 7 D2
Black Tickle *NL* 14 C3
Blaikiston, Mount *BC* 5 F4
Blanc-Sablon *QC* 13 F3
Blissville *NB* 16 B3
Blue Mountain *NL* 15 B1
Blue River *BC* 5 E3
Boiestown *NB* 16 B2
Bonny River *NB* 16 B3
Boothia, Gulf of *NU* 18 E1
Boothia Peninsula *NU* 18 E1
Borden-Carleton *PE* 16 D2
Bow *r. AB* 6 C4
Bowman, Mount *BC* 5 D3
Boyle *AB* 6 C3
Bralorne *BC* 5 D3
Brampton *ON* 11 E4
Branch *NL* 15 D3
Brandon *MB* 8 C4
Brantford *ON* 10 D4
Brent *ON* 11 E3
Breton *AB* 6 C3
Breton Cove *NS* 17 E2
Bristol *NB* 16 B2
British Columbia *prov.* 5 D3
Broadview *SK* 7 E3
Brochet *MB* 8 B2
Brockville *ON* 11 E4
Brockway *NB* 16 B3
Brookfield *NS* 16 D3
Brooks Brook *YT* 22 D3
Broughton Island *NU see* **Qikiqtarjuaq**
Browns Cove *NL* 15 B2
Bruce Peninsula National Park *ON* 10 D3
Brûlé *AB* 6 B3
Bruno *SK* 7 D3
Buchans Junction *NL* 15 B2
Buffalo Head Prairie *AB* 6 B2
Buick *BC* 5 D2
Burgess, Mount *YT* 22 C2
Burk's Falls *ON* 11 E3
Burlington *NL* 15 B2
Burnaby *BC* 5 D4
Burns Lake *BC* 5 C3
Burnt Islands *NL* 15 A3
Burtts Corner *NB* 16 B2
Burwash Landing *YT* 22 B3
Butedale *BC* 5 C3
Cabot Strait *NL/NS* 17 E2
Cabri *SK* 7 D3
Cadillac *SK* 7 D4
Cadomin *AB* 6 B3
Cadotte Lake *AB* 6 B2
Caledonia *NS* 16 C3
Caledonia *NS* 17 D3
Calgary *AB* 6 C3
Calling Lake *AB* 6 C2
Calstock *ON* 10 D3
Cambridge *NS* 16 C3
Campbell River *BC* 5 C3
Campbellton *NL* 15 C2
Camrose *AB* 6 C3
Camsell Portage *SK* 7 D2
Canaan *NB* 16 C2
Canal Flats *BC* 5 E3
Candle Lake *SK* 7 D3
Caniapiscau *QC* 13 D3
Caniapiscau *r. QC* 13 D2
Canim Lake *BC* 5 D3
Canning *NS* 16 C3
Canoe Lake *SK* 7 D2
Canwood *SK* 7 D3
Canyon *YT* 22 C3
Cap-de-la-Madeleine *QC* 13 C4
Cape Anguille *NL* 15 A3
Cape Breton Highlands National Park *NS* 17 E2
Cape Breton Island *NS* 17 E2
Cape Charles *NL* 14 C3
Cape George *NS* 17 E3
Cape Race *NL* 15 D3
Cape Ray *NL* 15 A3
Cape Sable Island *NS* 16 C4
Cape St George *NL* 15 A2
Cape Tormentine *NB* 16 D2
Cape Wolfe *PE* 16 C2
Cappahayden *NL* 15 D3
Carberry *MB* 8 C4
Carcajou *AB* 6 B2
Carcross *YT* 22 D3
Cariboo Mountains *BC* 5 D3
Caribou Mountains *AB* 6 B2
Carleton, Mount *NB* 16 B2
Carmacks *YT* 22 C3
Carmanville *NL* 15 C2
Caroline *AB* 6 C3
Cartwright *MB* 8 C4
Cartwright *NL* 14 C3
Cascade Range *Can./U.S.A.* 2 F5
Castle Mountain *YT* 22 C3
Castor *AB* 6 C3
Caubvick, Mount *NL* 14 B2
Central Butte *SK* 7 D3
Cereal *AB* 6 C3
Chamberlain *SK* 7 D3
Champion *AB* 6 C3
Champlain, Lake *Can./U.S.A.* 3 K5
Chance Cove *NL* 15 D3
Change Islands *NL* 15 C2
Chapel Arm *NL* 15 D3
Chaplin *SK* 7 D3
Chapman, Mount *BC* 5 E3
Chard *AB* 6 C2
Charlie Lake *BC* 5 D2
Charlottetown *PE* 16 D2
Chateh *AB* 6 B2
Chatham *ON* 10 D4
Chatham Sound *sea chan. BC* 4 B3
Chauvin *AB* 6 C3
Chelsea *NS* 16 C3
Chesterfield Inlet *NU* 19 E2
Chéticamp *NS* 17 E2
Chezacut *BC* 5 D3
Chicoutimi 3 K5
Chidley, Cape *NU* 19 H2
Chilanko Forks *BC* 5 D3
Chilkoot Pass *AK/BC Can./U.S.A.* 4 A2
Chilliwack *BC* 5 D4
Chimney Cove *NL* 15 A2
Chisasibi *QC* 13 B3
Chisholm *AB* 6 C3
Chitek Lake *SK* 7 D3
Choiceland *SK* 7 E3
Chown, Mount *AB* 6 B3
Christmas Island *NS* 17 E3
Churchill *r. NL* 14 B3
Churchill *r. SK* 7 E2
Churchill, Cape *MB* 8 D2
Churchill Falls *NL* 14 B3
Churchill Peak *BC* 5 C2
Church Point *NS* 16 B3
Chute-des-Passes *QC* 13 C4
Cirque Mountain *NL* 14 B2
Clairmont *AB* 6 B2
Clark, Mount *NT* 20 D4
Clarke's Head *NL* 15 C2
Clearwater *BC* 5 E3
Clementsport *NS* 16 C3
Clifton *NL* 15 D2
Climax *SK* 7 D4
Cline River *AB* 6 B3
Clinton *BC* 5 D3
Clinton Creek *YT* 22 B3
Clo-oose *BC* 5 D4
Clova *QC* 13 B4
Cluff Lake Mine *SK* 7 D2
Clyde *AB* 6 C3
Clyde River *NS* 16 C4
Clyde River *NU* 18 H1
Coachman's Cove *NL* 15 B1
Coal Branch *NB* 16 C2
Coal River *BC* 5 C2
Coast Mountains *BC* 5 C3
Coderre *SK* 7 D3
Codroy Pond *NL* 15 A2
Coffee Creek *YT* 22 C3
Cole Harbour *NS* 16 D3
Coleville *SK* 7 D3
Collingwood *ON* 10 D4
Columbia, Mount *AB/BC* 5 E3
Columbia Mountains *BC* 5 D3
Colville Lake *NT* 20 C3
Conception Bay South *NL* 15 D3
Conche *NL* 15 C1
Conklin *AB* 6 C2
Connolly, Mount *YT* 22 D3
Consort *AB* 6 C3
Consul *SK* 7 D4
Cook, Mount *Can./U.S.A.* 22 C3
Cook's Harbour *NL* 15 C1
Coomb's Cove *NL* 15 C3
Copper Cliff *ON* 10 D3
Coppermine *r. NT/NU* 19 C2
Coral Harbour *NU* 19 F2
Corberrie *NS* 16 C3
Corinne *SK* 7 E3
Coronation Gulf *NU* 2 G3
Cormack *NL* 15 B2
Corner Brook *NL* 15 B2
Cornwall *ON* 11 F3
Courtenay *BC* 5 D4
Cow Head *NL* 15 B2
Cox's Cove *NL* 15 A2
Cranberry Portage *MB* 8 B3
Cranbrook *BC* 5 E4
Cremona *AB* 6 C3
Crooked River *SK* 7 E3
Cross Creek *NB* 16 B2
Cross Lake *MB* 8 C3
Cross Roads Country Harbour *NS* 17 E3
Crowsnest Pass *AB/BC* 5 F4
Crysdale, Mount *BC* 5 D2
Crystal City *MB* 8 C4
Cudworth *SK* 7 D3
Cumberland House *SK* 7 E3
Cumberland Peninsula *NU* 15 H2
Cut Knife *SK* 7 D3
Cypress Hills *AB/SK* 6 C4
Czar *AB* 6 C3
Dafoe *SK* 7 E3
Dalton *ON* 10 D3
Daniel's Harbour *NL* 15 B1
D'Arcy *BC* 5 D3
Dark Cove *NL* 15 C2
Darnley *PE* 16 D2
Dartmouth *NS* 16 D3
Davis Cove *NL* 15 C3
Davis Inlet *NL* 14 B2
Davis Strait *Can./Greenland* 3 M3
Dawson *YT* 2 E3
Dawson, Mount *BC* 5 E3
Dawson Creek *BC* 5 D2
Dawsons Landing *BC* 5 C3
Daysland *AB* 6 C3
Dayton *NS* 16 B4
Dease Lake 2 F4
Debden *SK* 7 D3
Déception *QC* 12 C1
Deer Lake *ON* 10 B2
De Grau *NL* 15 A2
Del Bonita *AB* 6 C4
Delburne *AB* 6 C3
Déljne *NT* 20 D3
Delisle *SK* 7 D3
Denare Beach *SK* 7 E3
Denbigh *ON* 11 E3
Denholm *SK* 7 D3
Deschambault Lake *SK* 7 E3
Destruction Bay *YT* 22 C3
Detah *NT* 20 F4
Devil's Thumb *AK/BC Can./U.S.A.* 4 B2
Devon Island *NU* 18 F1
Dezadeash *YT* 22 C3
Diefenbaker, Lake *SK* 7 D3
Dieppe *NB* 16 C2
Dildo *NL* 15 D3
Dillon *SK* 7 D2
Dingwall *NS* 17 E2
Dipper Harbour *NB* 16 B3
Dixon Entrance *sea chan. Can./U.S.A.* 2 E4
Dixonville *AB* 6 B2
Dodsland *SK* 7 D3
Dog Creek *BC* 5 D3
Dolphin and Union Strait *NT/NU* 2 G3
Dome Creek *BC* 5 D3
Dorchester *NB* 16 C3
Doré Lake *SK* 7 D3
Dove Brook *NL* 14 C3
Downton, Mount *BC* 5 D3
Doyles *NL* 15 A3
Drummondville *QC* 13 C4
Dryberry Lake *ON* 10 B3
Duchess *AB* 6 C3
Duck Bay *MB* 8 B3
Duck Lake *SK* 7 D3
Dufferin, Cape *NU* 19 G3
Duncan *BC* 5 D4
Dundee *NS* 17 E3
Dunnville *ON* 11 E4
Dunville *NL* 15 D3
Durham Bridge *NB* 16 B2
Duval *SK* 7 E3
Eagle Plains *YT* 22 C2
Eaglesham *AB* 6 B2
Earltown *NS* 16 D3
East Coulee *AB* 6 C3
Eastend *SK* 7 D4
Easterville *MB* 8 C3
East Ferry *NS* 16 B3
Eastmain *QC* 13 B3
Eastport *NL* 15 D2
Eatonia *SK* 7 D3
Echo Bay *NT* 20 E3
Echo Bay *ON* 10 D3
Eckville *AB* 6 C3
Economy *NS* 16 D3
Edam *SK* 7 D3
Eddies Cove *NL* 15 B1
Eddies Cove West *NL* 15 B1
Edgerton *AB* 6 C3
Edgewood *BC* 5 E4
Edmonton *AB* 6 C3
Edmundston *NB* 16 A2
Eduni, Mount *NT* 20 C4
Edziza, Mount *BC* 4 B2
Elbow *SK* 7 D3
Elderbank *NS* 16 D3
Elgin *NB* 16 C3
Eliot, Mount *NL* 14 B2
Elizabeth, Mount *NB* 16 B2
Elk Lake *ON* 10 D3
Elko *BC* 5 E4
Ellesmere Island *NU* 18 F1
Elliot Lake *ON* 10 D3
Elmira *PE* 17 D2
Elmsvale *NS* 16 D3
Elsa *YT* 22 C3
Embarras Portage *AB* 6 C2
Emeril *NL* 14 A3
Emerson *MB* 8 C4
Emo *ON* 10 B3
Empress *AB* 7 C3
Endako *BC* 5 C3
Englee *NL* 15 C1
Englehart *ON* 11 E3
English Harbour East *NL* 15 C3
Englishtown *NS* 17 E2
Enterprise *NT* 20 E4
Erickson *MB* 8 C3
Erie, Lake *Can./U.S.A.* 3 J5
Eriksdale *MB* 8 C3
Esker *NL* 14 A3
Estevan *SK* 7 E4
Etamamiou *QC* 13 F3
Ethelbert *MB* 8 B3
Evansburg *AB* 6 B3
Evansville *ON* 10 D3
Everett *NB* 16 B2
Exploits *r. NL* 15 C2
Fairweather, Mount *AK/BC Can./U.S.A.* 4 A2
Falcon Lake *MB* 8 C4
Farewell *NL* 15 C2
Far Mountain *BC* 5 C3
Farnham, Mount *BC* 5 E3
Faro *YT* 22 D3
Fathom Five National Marine Park *ON* 10 D3
Fawcett *AB* 6 C3
Fermont *QC* 13 D3
Ferryland *NL* 15 D3
Field *BC* 5 E3
Fifth Meridian *AB* 6 C2
Finlay, Mount *BC* 5 C2
Finlay Forks *BC* 5 D2
Fireside *BC* 5 C2
Firvale *BC* 5 C3
Fischells *NL* 15 A2
Fisher River *MB* 8 C3
Fitton, Mount *YT* 22 C2
Fitzgerald *AB* 6 C2
Flat Top *YT* 22 C3
Fleur de Lys *NL* 15 B1
Flin Flon *MB* 8 B3
Florenceville *NB* 16 B2
Flowers Cove *NL* 15 B1
Fogo *NL* 15 C2
Foleyet *ON* 10 D3
Fond-du-Lac *SK* 7 D2
Fontanges *QC* 13 C3
Fontas *BC* 5 D2
Foremost *AB* 6 C4
Foresight Mountain *BC* 5 C3
Forestburg *AB* 5 C3
Fort Assiniboine *AB* 6 C3
Fort Babine *BC* 5 C2
Fort Black *SK* 7 D2
Fort Chipewyan *AB* 6 C2
Forteau *NL* 15 B1
Fort Erie *ON* 11 E4
Fort Franklin *NT see* **Déljne**
Fort George *QC* 13 B3 *see* **Chisasibi**
Fort Good Hope *NT* 20 C3
Fort Liard *NT* 2 F3
Fort Mackay *AB* 6 C2
Fort McMurray *AB* 6 C2
Fort McPherson *NT* 20 B3
Fort Nelson *BC* 5 D2
Fort Norman *NT see* **Tulít'a**
Fort Providence *NT* 20 E4
Fort Qu'Appelle *SK* 7 E3
Fort Resolution *NT* 20 F4
Fort Rupert *QC* 13 B3 *see* **Waskaganish**
Fort Saskatchewan *AB* 2 G4
Fort Severn *ON* 10 C1
Fort St John *BC* 5 D2
Fortune Harbour *NL* 15 C2
Fort Vermilion *AB* 6 B2
Foster Lakes *SK* 7 D2
Foster, Mount *AK/BC Can./U.S.A.* 4 A2
Fosterville *NB* 16 B3
Fourchu *NS* 17 E3
Foxe Basin *NU* 19 G2
Foxe Peninsula *NU* 19 G2
Fox Island River *NL* 15 A2
Fox Lake *AB* 6 B2
Fox Mine *MB* 8 B2
Fox Mountain *YT* 22 D3
Fox Valley *SK* 7 D3
Frances Lake *YT* 22 E3
Francis *SK* 7 E3
Francois *NL* 15 B3
Franklin Mountains *NT* 20 D4
Franz *ON* 10 D3
Fraser *r. BC* 5 B4
Fraserdale *ON* 10 D3
Fraser Plateau *BC* 5 D3
Fredericton *NB* 16 B3
Fredericton Junction *NB* 16 B3
Freeport *NS* 16 B3
Frenchman's Cove *NL* 15 A2
Frobisher Bay *NU see* **Iqaluit**
Fundy, Bay of *NB/NS* 16 B3
Fundy National Park *NB* 16 C3
Fury and Hecla Strait *NU* 19 F2
Gabarouse *see* **Gabarus**
Gabarus *NS* 17 E3
Gagetown *NB* 16 B3
Gagnon *QC* 13 D3
Gallants *NL* 15 A2
Gander *NL* 15 C2
Garden Hill *MB* 8 D3
Garibaldi, Mount *BC* 5 D4
Garibaldi Provincial Park *BC* 5 D4
Garnish *NL* 15 C3
Gaspé *QC* 13 E4
Gaspé, Cap c. *QC* 13 E4
Gaspé, Péninsule de *QC* 13 D4
Gaspereau Forks *NB* 16 C2
Gaultois *NL* 15 C3
Georgetown *PE* 16 D2
Georgian Bay *ON* 10 D3
Georgian Bay Islands National Park *ON* 10 E4
Germansen Landing *BC* 5 D2
Gift Lake *AB* 6 B2
Giscome *BC* 5 D3
Gjoa Haven *NU* 19 E2
Glace Bay *NS* 17 F2
Glacier National Park *BC* 5 E3
Glaslyn *SK* 7 D3
Gleichen *AB* 6 C3
Glenboro *MB* 8 C4
Glendon *AB* 6 C3
Glenlyon Peak *YT* 22 D3
Glenora *BC* 4 B2
Glenwood *NB* 16 B3
Glenwood *NL* 15 C2
Godbout *QC* 13 D4
Gods *r. MB* 3 D2
Gogama *ON* 10 D3
Golden Hinde *BC* 5 C4
Golden Prairie *SK* 7 D3
Goodenough, Mount *NT* 20 A3
Good Hope Mountain *BC* 5 D3
Goose Arm *NL* 15 B2
Goose Cove *NL* 15 C1
Gordon Landing *YT* 22 C3
Gott Peak *BC* 5 D3
Gouin, Réservoir *QC* 13 C4
Grainfield *NB* 16 C2
Granby *QC* 13 C4
Grand Bend *ON* 10 D4
Grand Bruit *NL* 15 A3
Grande-Entree *QC* 13 E4
Grande Prairie *AB* 6 B2
Grand Etang *NS* 17 E2
Grande-Vallée *QC* 13 D4
Grand Harbour *NB* 16 B3
Grand Pacific Glacier *BC* 4 A2
Grand Rapids *MB* 8 C3
Grand River *NS* 17 E3
Granisle *BC* 5 C3
Granum *AB* 6 C4
Granville *YT* 22 C3
Granville Ferry *NS* 16 C3
Grasslands National Park *SK* 7 D4
Grates Cove *NL* 15 D2
Great Bear Lake *NT* 20 E3
Great Brehat *NL* 15 C1
Great Harbour Deep *NL* 15 B1
Great Plain of the Koukdjuak *NU* 19 G2
Great Slave Lake *NT* 20 F4
Great Snow Mountain *BC* 5 D2
Great Village *NS* 16 D3
Green Island Cove *NL* 15 B1
Green Lake *SK* 7 D3
Greenville *BC* 5 C2
Grey Hunter Peak *YT* 22 C3
Grey River *NL* 15 B3
Grise Fiord *NU* 18 F1
Grizzly Bear Mountain *NT* 20 D3
Gros Morne *NL* 15 B2
Gros Morne National Park *NL* 15 B2
Grouard Mission *AB* 6 B2
Guysborough *NS* 17 E3
Gwaii Haanas National Park Reserve *BC* 4 B3
Habay *AB* 6 B2
Hafford *SK* 7 D3
Hagensborg *BC* 5 C3
Hague *SK* 7 D3
Haida Gwaii *is BC see* **Queen Charlotte Islands**
Haines Junction 2 E3
Halfway Point *NL* 15 A2
Halifax *NS* 16 D3
Haliburton Highlands *ON* 11 E3
Hall Beach *NU* 19 F2
Hamilton *ON* 11 E4
Hampden *NL* 15 B2
Hampstead *NB* 16 B3
Hampton *NS* 16 C3
Happy Valley-Goose Bay *NL* 14 B3
Harbour Main *NL* 15 D3
Harbourville *NS* 16 C3
Harcourt *NB* 16 C2
Hardisty *AB* 6 C3
Harper, Mount *YT* 22 C3
Harrington Harbour *QC* 13 F3
Harry's Harbour *NL* 15 C2
Hartland *NB* 16 B2
Hartley Bay *BC* 2 F4
Harvey *NB* 16 B3
Havelock *NB* 16 C3
Havre Aubert *QC* 13 E4
Havre Boucher *NS* 17 E3
Hawkes Bay *NL* 15 B1
Hawkshaw *NB* 16 B3
Hayes *r. MB* 8 D2
Hay River *NT* 20 E4
Hazelton *BC* 5 C2
Head of Bay d'Espoir *NL* 15 C3
Heart's Content *NL* 15 D3
Heart's Delight *NL* 15 D3
Heath Steele *NB* 16 B2
Hebron *NL* 14 B2
Hecate Strait *BC* 4 B3
Hectanooga *NS* 16 B3
Henley Harbour *NL* 15 C1
Henrietta Maria, Cape *NU* 19 F3
Herbert *SK* 7 D3
Hermitage-Sandyville *NL* 15 C3
Herschel *YT* 22 C2
Hesquiat *BC* 5 C4
Hickman's Harbour *NL* 15 D2
Highlands *NL* 15 A2
Hillsport *ON* 10 C3
Hines Creek *AB* 6 B2
Hixon *BC* 5 D3
Hogg, Mount *YT* 22 D3
Holberg *BC* 5 C3
Holden *AB* 6 C3
Holman *NT* 20 E2
Hopedale *NL* 14 B2
Hopes Advance Bay *QC see* **Aupaluk**
Hopewell *NS* 16 D3
Horn Peak *YT* 22 D3
Horsefly *BC* 5 D3
Horwood *NL* 15 C2
Howley *NL* 15 B2
Hubbard, Mount *Can./U.S.A.* 22 C3
Hubbards *NS* 16 C3
Hudson, Baie d' *see* **Hudson Bay**
Hudson, Détroit d' *strait see* **Hudson Strait**
Hudson Bay *NU* 3 J4
Hudson Strait *NU* 3 K3
Hull *QC* 13 B4
100 Mile House *BC* 5 D3
150 Mile House *BC* 5 D3
Hunter River *PE* 16 D2
Huntsville *ON* 11 E3
Huron, Lake *Can./U.S.A.* 3 J5
Hyland Post *BC* 5 C2
Igloolik *NU* 19 F2
Igluligaarjuk *NU see* **Chesterfield Inlet**
Ikaahuk *NT see* **Sachs Harbour**
Îles de la Madeleine *is QC* 13 E4
Ilford *MB* 8 C2
Indian Cabins *AB* 6 B2
Indian Harbour *NL* 14 C3
Ingonish *NS* 17 E2
Ingonish Beach *NS* 17 E2
Inklin *BC* 4 B2
Inuvik *NT* 20 B3
Invermay *SK* 7 E3
Iona *NS* 17 E3
Iqaluit *NU* 19 H2
Iroquois Falls *ON* 10 D3
Isachsen *NU* 18 D1
Island Lake *MB* 8 D3
Isle aux Morts *NL* 15 A3
Ivvavik National Park *YT* 22 C2
Jackson's Arm *NL* 15 B2
Jacques Cartier, Mont *QC* 13 D4
Jacquet River *NB* 16 B2
James Bay *NU* J4
Jans Bay *SK* 7 D2
Jasper National Park *AB* 6 B3
Jean Marie River *NT* 20 D4
Jellicoe *ON* 10 C3
Jenner *AB* 6 C3
Jenpeg *MB* 8 C3
Joe Batt's Arm *NL* 15 C2
Joggins *NS* 16 C3
John d'Or Prairie *AB* 6 B2
John Jay, Mount *AK/BC Can./U.S.A.* 4 B2
Joliette *QC* 13 C4
Jonquière *QC* 13 C4
Joussard *AB* 6 B2
Joy, Mount *YT* 22 D3
Juan de Fuca Strait *Can./U.S.A.* 2 F5
Judique *NS* 17 E3
Juniper *NB* 16 B2
Kahntah *BC* 5 D2
Kakabeka Falls *ON* 10 C3
Kakisa *NT* 20 E4
Kaladar *ON* 11 E4
Kalone Peak *BC* 5 C3
Kamloops *BC* 5 D3
Kangiqsualujjuaq *QC* 12 D2
Kangiqsujuaq *QC* 12 C1
Kangirsuk *QC* 12 C1
Kapuskasing *ON* 10 D3
Kasabonika *ON* 10 C2
Kashabowie *ON* 10 B3
Kashechewan *ON* 10 D2
Kate's Needle *AK/BC Can./U.S.A.* 4 B2
Kawawachikamach *QC* 13 D2
Kedgwick River *NB* 16 B2
Keele Peak *YT* 22 D3
Keg River *AB* 6 B2
Keithley Creek *BC* 5 D3
Kejimkujik National Park *NS* 16 C3
Kelliher *SK* 7 E3
Kelowna *BC* 5 E4
Kemano *BC* 5 C3
Kennetcook *NS* 16 D3
Kent Junction *NB* 16 C2
Kentville *NS* 16 C3
Keyano *QC* 13 C3
Key Harbour *ON* 10 D3
Kicking Horse Pass 2 G4
Killarney *ON* 10 D3
Killiniq *QC* 12 E1
Kimmirut *NU* 19 H2
Kimsquit *BC* 5 C3
Kincaid *SK* 7 D4
Kincolith *BC* 4 C3
King George, Mount *BC* 5 E3
King Mountain *BC* 5 C2
King's Point *NL* 15 B2
Kingston *ON* 11 E4
Kingwell *NL* 15 C3
Kinistino *SK* 7 D3
Kinoosao *SK* 7 E2
Kinuso *AB* 6 B2
Kirkland Lake *ON* 11 D3
Kispiox *BC* 5 C2
Kitchener *ON* 10 D4
Kitimat *BC* 5 C3
Kitkatla *BC* 4 B3
Kitsault *BC* 5 C2
Kitwanga *BC* 5 C2
Kleena Kleene *BC* 5 D3
Klemtu *BC* 5 C3
Klondike *r. YT* 22 C3
Klotz, Mount *YT* 22 B2
Kluane National Park *YT* 22 C3
Koartac *QC see* **Quaqtaq**
Koidern Mountain *YT* 22 B3
Kootenay Lake *BC* 5 E4
Kootenay National Park *BC* 5 E3
Kouchibouguac National Park *NB* 16 C2
Koukdjuak *r. NU* 19 G2
Kuujjuarapik *QC* 13 B2
Kyle *SK* 7 D3
Kyuquot *BC* 5 C3
La Baie *QC* 13 C4
Labelle *QC* 13 C4
Labrador *reg. NL* 14 B3
Labrador City *NL* 14 A3
Labrador Sea *Can./Greenland* 3 M4
Lac Allard *QC* 13 E3
Lac-Baker *NB* 16 A2
Lachute *QC* 3 K5
Lac la Hache *BC* 5 D3
Lac la Martre *NT see* **Wha Ti**
Lac-Mégantic *QC* 13 C4
La Crete *AB* 6 B2
Lafleche *SK* 7 D4
Laforge *QC* 13 C3
La Grande 4, Réservoir *QC* 3 K4
Lake Harbour *NU see* **Kimmirut**
Lake Louise *AB* 6 B3
Lake of the Woods *Can./U.S.A.* 3 I5
Lake River *ON* 10 D2
Lamaline *NL* 15 C3
Landis *SK* 7 D3
Langley *BC* 5 D4
L'Anse-au-Loup *NL* 15 B1
Laporte, Mount *YT* 22 E3
L'Ardoise *NS* 17 E3
Lark Harbour *NL* 15 A2
Larrys River *NS* 17 E3
La Tabatière *QC* 13 F3
La Tuque *QC* 13 C4
Laurenceton *NL* 15 C2
Laval *QC* 13 C4
Lavillette *NB* 16 C2
Lawn *NL* 15 C3
Lawrence Station *NB* 16 B3
Lax Kw'alaams *BC* 4 B3
Leader *SK* 7 D3
Leading Tickles *NL* 15 C2
Leaf Bay *QC see* **Tasiujaq**
Leask *SK* 7 D3
Leduc *AB* 6 C3
Leoville *SK* 7 D3
Les Méchins *QC* 13 D4
Lesser Slave Lake *AB* 6 B2
Lethbridge *AB* 6 C4
Lethbridge *NL* 15 D2
Lévis *QC* 13 C4
Lewis Cass, Mount *AK/BC Can./U.S.A.* 4 B2
Lewis Hills *NL* 15 A2
Liard Plateau *YT* 22 E3
Liard River *BC* 5 C2
Likely *BC* 5 D3

Collins Discovery World Atlas

Contents

Map Symbols

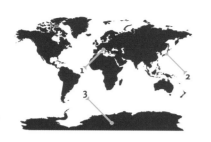

Southern Europe   1

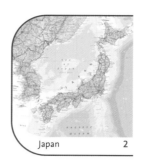
Japan   2

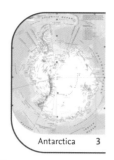
Antarctica   3

Settlements

Population	National capital	Administrative capital	Other city or town
over 10 million	**BEIJING** ✹	**Karachi** ◉	**New York** ◉
5 million to 10 million	**JAKARTA** ✶	**Tianjin** ◉	**Nova Iguaçu** ◉
1 million to 5 million	**KĀBUL** ✷	**Sydney** ◉	**Kaohsiung** ◉
500 000 to 1 million	BANGUI ✵	Trujillo ◎	Jeddah ◎
100 000 to 500 000	WELLINGTON ✵	Mansa ⊙	Apucarana ⊙
50 000 to 100 000	PORT OF SPAIN ✿	Potenza ○	Arecibo ○
10 000 to 50 000	MALABO ✿	Chinhoyi ○	Ceres ○
under 10 000	VALLETTA ✿	Ati ○	Venta ○

Built-up area

Boundaries

▪▬▪▬▪   International boundary

▪▮▪▮▪   Disputed international boundary
or alignment unconfirmed

─────   Administrative boundary

●●●●●   Ceasefire line

Miscellaneous

----------   National park

············   Reserve or
Regional park

✳   Site of specific interest

⊂⊃⊂⊃⊂⊃   Wall

Land and sea features

Desert

Oasis

Lava field

1234
△   Volcano
height in metres

Marsh

Ice cap or Glacier

Escarpment

Coral reef

1234
Pass
height in metres

Lakes and rivers

Lake

Impermanent lake

Salt lake or lagoon

Impermanent salt lake

Dry salt lake or salt pan

123   Lake height
surface height above
sea level, in metres

─────   River

─────   Impermanent river
or watercourse

ǁ   Waterfall

─   Dam

│   Barrage

Relief

Contour intervals and layer colours

Height
metres

6000
5000
4000
3000
2000
1000
500
200
0
below sea level

0
200
2000
4000
6000

Depth

1234
▲   Summit
height in metres

-123
·   Spot height
height in metres

123
·   Ocean deep
depth in metres

Transport

━━━▷ ▪▪▪▪   Motorway (tunnel; under construction)

━━━▷ ─────   Main road (tunnel; under construction)

───▷ ─────   Secondary road (tunnel; under construction)

·············   Track

▪━▪━▪ ▪▪▪▪   Main railway (tunnel; under construction)

───── ─────   Secondary railway (tunnel; under construction)

───── ─────   Other railway (tunnel; under construction)

─────   Canal

✈   Main airport

✈   Regional airport

SPOT

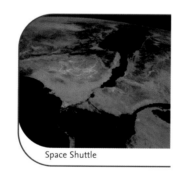
Space Shuttle

IKONOS

Satellite imagery - The thematic pages in the atlas contain a wide variety of photographs and images. These are a mixture of terrestrial and aerial photographs and satellite imagery. All are used to illustrate specific themes and to give an indication of the variety of imagery available today. The main types of imagery used in the atlas are described in the table below. The sensor for each satellite image is detailed on the acknowledgements page.

Main satellites/sensors

Satellite/sensor name	Launch dates	Owner	Aims and applications	Internet links	Additional internet links
Landsat 4, 5, 7	July 1972–April 1999	National Aeronautics and Space Administration (NASA), USA	The first satellite to be designed specifically for observing the Earth's surface. Originally set up to produce images of use for agriculture and geology. Today is of use for numerous environmental and scientific applications.	geo.arc.nasa.gov landsat.gsfc.nasa.gov	asterweb.jpl.nasa.gov earth.jsc.nasa.gov earthnet.esrin.esa.it
SPOT 1, 2, 3, 4, 5 (Satellite Pour l'Observation de la Terre)	February 1986–March 1998	Centre National d'Etudes Spatiales (CNES) and Spot Image, France	Particularly useful for monitoring land use, water resources research, coastal studies and cartography.	www.cnes.fr www.spotimage.fr	earthobservatory.nasa.gov eol.jsc.nasa.gov modis.gsfc.nasa.gov
Space Shuttle	Regular launches from 1981	NASA, USA	Each shuttle mission has separate aims. Astronauts take photographs with high specification hand held cameras. The Shuttle Radar Topography Mission (SRTM) in 2000 obtained the most complete near-global high-resolution database of the earth's topography.	science.ksc.nasa.gov/shuttle/countdown www.jpl.nasa.gov/srtm	seawifs.gsfc.nasa.gov topex-www.jpl.nasa.gov visibleearth.nasa.gov
IKONOS	September 1999	Space Imaging	First commercial high-resolution satellite. Useful for a variety of applications mainly Cartography, Defence, Urban Planning, Agriculture, Forestry and Insurance.	www.spaceimaging.com	www.rsi.ca www.usgs.gov

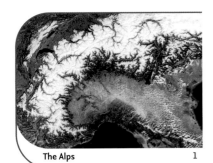

The Alps   1

Amsterdam, Netherlands   2

Italy   3

Europe		Area sq km	Area sq miles	Population	Capital	Languages	Religions	Currency
ALBANIA		28 748	11 100	3 166 000	Tirana	Albanian, Greek	Sunni Muslim, Albanian Orthodox, Roman Catholic	Lek
ANDORRA		465	180	71 000	Andorra la Vella	Spanish, Catalan, French	Roman Catholic	Euro
AUSTRIA		83 855	32 377	8 116 000	Vienna	German, Croatian, Turkish	Roman Catholic, Protestant	Euro
BELARUS		207 600	80 155	9 895 000	Minsk	Belorussian, Russian	Belorussian Orthodox, Roman Catholic	Belarus rouble
BELGIUM		30 520	11 784	10 318 000	Brussels	Dutch (Flemish), French (Walloon), German	Roman Catholic, Protestant	Euro
BOSNIA-HERZEGOVINA		51 130	19 741	4 161 000	Sarajevo	Bosnian, Serbian, Croatian	Sunni Muslim, Serbian Orthodox, Roman Catholic, Protestant	Marka
BULGARIA		110 994	42 855	7 897 000	Sofia	Bulgarian, Turkish, Romany, Macedonian	Bulgarian Orthodox, Sunni Muslim	Lev
CROATIA		56 538	21 829	4 428 000	Zagreb	Croatian, Serbian	Roman Catholic, Serbian Orthodox, Sunni Muslim	Kuna
CZECH REPUBLIC		78 864	30 450	10 236 000	Prague	Czech, Moravian, Slovak	Roman Catholic, Protestant	Czech koruna
DENMARK		43 075	16 631	5 364 000	Copenhagen	Danish	Protestant	Danish krone
ESTONIA		45 200	17 452	1 332 000	Tallinn	Estonian, Russian	Protestant, Estonian and Russian Orthodox	Kroon
FINLAND		338 145	130 559	5 207 000	Helsinki	Finnish, Swedish	Protestant, Greek Orthodox	Euro
FRANCE		543 965	210 026	60 144 000	Paris	French, Arabic	Roman Catholic, Protestant, Sunni Muslim	Euro
GERMANY		357 022	137 849	82 476 000	Berlin	German, Turkish	Protestant, Roman Catholic	Euro
GREECE		131 957	50 949	10 976 000	Athens	Greek	Greek Orthodox, Sunni Muslim	Euro
HUNGARY		93 030	35 919	9 877 000	Budapest	Hungarian	Roman Catholic, Protestant	Forint
ICELAND		102 820	39 699	290 000	Reykjavík	Icelandic	Protestant	Icelandic króna
IRELAND, REPUBLIC OF		70 282	27 136	3 956 000	Dublin	English, Irish	Roman Catholic, Protestant	Euro
ITALY		301 245	116 311	57 423 000	Rome	Italian	Roman Catholic	Euro
LATVIA		63 700	24 595	2 307 000	Rīga	Latvian, Russian	Protestant, Roman Catholic, Russian Orthodox	Lats
LIECHTENSTEIN		160	62	34 000	Vaduz	German	Roman Catholic, Protestant	Swiss franc
LITHUANIA		65 200	25 174	3 444 000	Vilnius	Lithuanian, Russian, Polish	Roman Catholic, Protestant, Russian Orthodox	Litas
LUXEMBOURG		2 586	998	453 000	Luxembourg	Letzeburgish, German, French	Roman Catholic	Euro
MACEDONIA (F.Y.R.O.M.)		25 713	9 928	2 056 000	Skopje	Macedonian, Albanian, Turkish	Macedonian Orthodox, Sunni Muslim	Macedonian denar
MALTA		316	122	394 000	Valletta	Maltese, English	Roman Catholic	Maltese lira
MOLDOVA		33 700	13 012	4 267 000	Chişinău	Romanian, Ukrainian, Gagauz, Russian	Romanian Orthodox, Russian Orthodox	Moldovan leu
MONACO		2	1	34 000	Monaco-Ville	French, Monegasque, Italian	Roman Catholic	Euro
NETHERLANDS		41 526	16 033	16 149 000	Amsterdam/The Hague	Dutch, Frisian	Roman Catholic, Protestant, Sunni Muslim	Euro
NORWAY		323 878	125 050	4 533 000	Oslo	Norwegian	Protestant, Roman Catholic	Norwegian krone
POLAND		312 683	120 728	38 587 000	Warsaw	Polish, German	Roman Catholic, Polish Orthodox	Złoty
PORTUGAL		88 940	34 340	10 062 000	Lisbon	Portuguese	Roman Catholic, Protestant	Euro
ROMANIA		237 500	91 699	22 334 000	Bucharest	Romanian, Hungarian	Romanian Orthodox, Protestant, Roman Catholic	Romanian leu
RUSSIAN FEDERATION		17 075 400	6 592 849	143 246 000	Moscow	Russian, Tatar, Ukrainian, local languages	Russian Orthodox, Sunni Muslim, Protestant	Russian rouble
SAN MARINO		61	24	28 000	San Marino	Italian	Roman Catholic	Euro
SERBIA AND MONTENEGRO		102 173	39 449	10 527 000	Belgrade	Serbian, Albanian, Hungarian	Serbian Orthodox, Montenegrin Orthodox, Sunni Muslim	Serbian dinar, Euro
SLOVAKIA		49 035	18 933	5 402 000	Bratislava	Slovak, Hungarian, Czech	Roman Catholic, Protestant, Orthodox	Slovakian koruna
SLOVENIA		20 251	7 819	1 984 000	Ljubljana	Slovene, Croatian, Serbian	Roman Catholic, Protestant	Tólar
SPAIN		504 782	194 897	41 060 000	Madrid	Castilian, Catalan, Galician, Basque	Roman Catholic	Euro
SWEDEN		449 964	173 732	8 876 000	Stockholm	Swedish	Protestant, Roman Catholic	Swedish krona
SWITZERLAND		41 293	15 943	7 169 000	Bern	German, French, Italian, Romansch	Roman Catholic, Protestant	Swiss franc
UKRAINE		603 700	233 090	48 523 000	Kiev	Ukrainian, Russian	Ukrainian Orthodox, Ukrainian Catholic, Roman Catholic	Hryvnia
UNITED KINGDOM		243 609	94 058	58 789 194	London	English, Welsh, Gaelic	Protestant, Roman Catholic, Muslim	Pound sterling
VATICAN CITY		0.5	0.2	472	Vatican City	Italian	Roman Catholic	Euro

Dependent territories		Territorial status	Area sq km	Area sq miles	Population	Capital	Languages	Religions	Currency
Azores		Autonomous Region of Portugal	2 300	888	242 073	Ponta Delgada	Portuguese	Roman Catholic, Protestant	Euro
Faroe Islands		Self-governing Danish Territory	1 399	540	47 000	Tórshavn	Faroese, Danish	Protestant	Danish krone
Gibraltar		United Kingdom Overseas Territory	7	3	27 000	Gibraltar	English, Spanish	Roman Catholic, Protestant, Sunni Muslim	Gibraltar pound
Guernsey		United Kingdom Crown Dependency	78	30	62 701	St Peter Port	English, French	Protestant, Roman Catholic	Pound sterling
Isle of Man		United Kingdom Crown Dependency	572	221	75 000	Douglas	English	Protestant, Roman Catholic	Pound sterling
Jersey		United Kingdom Crown Dependency	116	45	87 186	St Helier	English, French	Protestant, Roman Catholic	Pound sterling

Ganges Delta, India   1

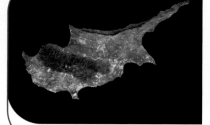

Cyprus, eastern Mediterranean   2

Indian subcontinent   3

Asia

	Area sq km	Area sq miles	Population	Capital	Languages	Religions	Currency
AFGHANISTAN	652 225	251 825	23 897 000	Kābul	Dari, Pushtu, Uzbek, Turkmen	Sunni Muslim, Shi'a Muslim	Afghani
ARMENIA	29 800	11 506	3 061 000	Yerevan	Armenian, Azeri	Armenian Orthodox	Dram
AZERBAIJAN	86 600	33 436	8 370 000	Baku	Azeri, Armenian, Russian, Lezgian	Shi'a Muslim, Sunni Muslim, Russian and Armenian Orthodox	Azerbaijani manat
BAHRAIN	691	267	724 000	Manama	Arabic, English	Shi'a Muslim, Sunni Muslim, Christian	Bahrain dinar
BANGLADESH	143 998	55 598	146 736 000	Dhaka	Bengali, English	Sunni Muslim, Hindu	Taka
BHUTAN	46 620	18 000	2 257 000	Thimphu	Dzongkha, Nepali, Assamese	Buddhist, Hindu	Ngultrum, Indian rupee
BRUNEI	5 765	2 226	358 000	Bandar Seri Begawan	Malay, English, Chinese	Sunni Muslim, Buddhist, Christian	Brunei dollar
CAMBODIA	181 035	69 884	14 144 000	Phnom Penh	Khmer, Vietnamese	Buddhist, Roman Catholic, Sunni Muslim	Riel
CHINA	9 584 492	3 700 593	1 289 161 000	Beijing	Mandarin, Wu, Cantonese, Hsiang, regional languages	Confucian, Taoist, Buddhist, Christian, Sunni Muslim	Yuan, HK dollar*, Macau pataca
CYPRUS	9 251	3 572	802 000	Nicosia	Greek, Turkish, English	Greek Orthodox, Sunni Muslim	Cyprus pound
EAST TIMOR	14 874	5 743	778 000	Dili	Portuguese, Tetun, English	Roman Catholic	United States dollar
GEORGIA	69 700	26 911	5 126 000	T'bilisi	Georgian, Russian, Armenian, Azeri, Ossetian, Abkhaz	Georgian Orthodox, Russian Orthodox, Sunni Muslim	Lari
INDIA	3 064 898	1 183 364	1 065 462 000	New Delhi	Hindi, English, many regional languages	Hindu, Sunni Muslim, Shi'a Muslim, Sikh, Christian	Indian rupee
INDONESIA	1 919 445	741 102	219 883 000	Jakarta	Indonesian, local languages	Sunni Muslim, Protestant, Roman Catholic, Hindu, Buddhist	Rupiah
IRAN	1 648 000	636 296	68 920 000	Tehrān	Farsi, Azeri, Kurdish, regional languages	Shi'a Muslim, Sunni Muslim	Iranian rial
IRAQ	438 317	169 235	25 175 000	Baghdād	Arabic, Kurdish, Turkmen	Shi'a Muslim, Sunni Muslim, Christian	Iraqi dinar
ISRAEL	20 770	8 019	6 433 000	Jerusalem (De facto capital. Disputed)	Hebrew, Arabic	Jewish, Sunni Muslim, Christian, Druze	Shekel
JAPAN	377 727	145 841	127 654 000	Tōkyō	Japanese	Shintoist, Buddhist, Christian	Yen
JORDAN	89 206	34 443	5 473 000	'Ammān	Arabic	Sunni Muslim, Christian	Jordanian dinar
KAZAKHSTAN	2 717 300	1 049 155	15 433 000	Astana	Kazakh, Russian, Ukrainian, German, Uzbek, Tatar	Sunni Muslim, Russian Orthodox, Protestant	Tenge
KUWAIT	17 818	6 880	2 521 000	Kuwait	Arabic	Sunni Muslim, Shi'a Muslim, Christian, Hindu	Kuwaiti dinar
KYRGYZSTAN	198 500	76 641	5 138 000	Bishkek	Kyrgyz, Russian, Uzbek	Sunni Muslim, Russian Orthodox	Kyrgyz som
LAOS	236 800	91 429	5 657 000	Vientiane	Lao, local languages	Buddhist, traditional beliefs	Kip
LEBANON	10 452	4 036	3 653 000	Beirut	Arabic, Armenian, French	Shi'a Muslim, Sunni Muslim, Christian	Lebanese pound
MALAYSIA	332 965	128 559	24 425 000	Kuala Lumpur/Putrajaya	Malay, English, Chinese, Tamil, local languages	Sunni Muslim, Buddhist, Hindu, Christian, traditional beliefs	Ringgit
MALDIVES	298	115	318 000	Male	Divehi (Maldivian)	Sunni Muslim	Rufiyaa
MONGOLIA	1 565 000	604 250	2 594 000	Ulan Bator	Khalka (Mongolian), Kazakh, local languages	Buddhist, Sunni Muslim	Tugrik (tögrög)
MYANMAR	676 577	261 228	49 485 000	Rangoon	Burmese, Shan, Karen, local languages	Buddhist, Christian, Sunni Muslim	Kyat
NEPAL	147 181	56 827	25 164 000	Kathmandu	Nepali, Maithili, Bhojpuri, English, local languages	Hindu, Buddhist, Sunni Muslim	Nepalese rupee
NORTH KOREA	120 538	46 540	22 664 000	P'yŏngyang	Korean	Traditional beliefs, Chondoist, Buddhist	North Korean won
OMAN	309 500	119 499	2 851 000	Muscat	Arabic, Baluchi, Indian languages	Ibadhi Muslim, Sunni Muslim	Omani riyal
PAKISTAN	803 940	310 403	153 578 000	Islamabad	Urdu, Punjabi, Sindhi, Pushtu, English	Sunni Muslim, Shi'a Muslim, Christian, Hindu	Pakistani rupee
PALAU	497	192	20 000	Koror	Palauan, English	Roman Catholic, Protestant, traditional beliefs	United States dollar
PHILIPPINES	300 000	115 831	79 999 000	Manila	English, Pilipino, Cebuano, local languages	Roman Catholic, Protestant, Sunni Muslim, Aglipayan	Philippine peso
QATAR	11 437	4 416	610 000	Doha	Arabic	Sunni Muslim	Qatari riyal
RUSSIAN FEDERATION	17 075 400	6 592 849	143 246 000	Moscow	Russian, Tatar, Ukrainian, local languages	Russian Orthodox, Sunni Muslim, Protestant	Russian rouble
SAUDI ARABIA	2 200 000	849 425	24 217 000	Riyadh	Arabic	Sunni Muslim, Shi'a Muslim	Saudi Arabian riyal
SINGAPORE	639	247	4 253 000	Singapore	Chinese, English, Malay, Tamil	Buddhist, Taoist, Sunni Muslim, Christian, Hindu	Singapore dollar
SOUTH KOREA	99 274	38 330	47 700 000	Seoul	Korean	Buddhist, Protestant, Roman Catholic	South Korean won
SRI LANKA	65 610	25 332	19 065 000	Sri Jayewardenepura Kotte	Sinhalese, Tamil, English	Buddhist, Hindu, Sunni Muslim, Roman Catholic	Sri Lankan rupee
SYRIA	185 180	71 498	17 800 000	Damascus	Arabic, Kurdish, Armenian	Sunni Muslim, Shi'a Muslim, Christian	Syrian pound
TAIWAN	36 179	13 969	22 548 000	T'aipei	Mandarin, Min, Hakka, local languages	Buddhist, Taoist, Confucian, Christian	Taiwan dollar
TAJIKISTAN	143 100	55 251	6 245 000	Dushanbe	Tajik, Uzbek, Russian	Sunni Muslim	Somoni
THAILAND	513 115	198 115	62 833 000	Bangkok	Thai, Lao, Chinese, Malay, Mon-Khmer languages	Buddhist, Sunni Muslim	Baht
TURKEY	779 452	300 948	71 325 000	Ankara	Turkish, Kurdish	Sunni Muslim, Shi'a Muslim	Turkish lira
TURKMENISTAN	488 100	188 456	4 867 000	Ashgabat	Turkmen, Uzbek, Russian	Sunni Muslim, Russian Orthodox	Turkmen manat
UNITED ARAB EMIRATES	77 700	30 000	2 995 000	Abu Dhabi	Arabic, English	Sunni Muslim, Shi'a Muslim	United Arab Emirates dirham
UZBEKISTAN	447 400	172 742	26 093 000	Tashkent	Uzbek, Russian, Tajik, Kazakh	Sunni Muslim, Russian Orthodox	Uzbek som
VIETNAM	329 565	127 246	81 377 000	Ha Nôi	Vietnamese, Thai, Khmer, Chinese, local languages	Buddhist, Taoist, Roman Catholic, Cao Dai, Hoa Hao	Dong
YEMEN	527 968	203 850	20 010 000	San'ā'	Arabic	Sunni Muslim, Shi'a Muslim	Yemeni rial

Dependent and disputed territories	Territorial status	Area sq km	Area sq miles	Population	Capital	Languages	Religions	Currency
Christmas Island	Australian External Territory	135	52	1 560	The Settlement	English	Buddhist, Sunni Muslim, Protestant, Roman Catholic	Australian dollar
Cocos Islands	Australian External Territory	14	5	632	West Island	English	Sunni Muslim, Christian	Australian dollar
Gaza	Semi-autonomous region	363	140	1 203 591	Gaza	Arabic	Sunni Muslim, Shi'a Muslim	Israeli shekel
Jammu and Kashmir	Disputed territory (India/Pakistan)	222 236	85 806	13 000 000	Srinagar			
West Bank	Disputed territory	5 860	2 263	2 303 660		Arabic, Hebrew	Sunni Muslim, Jewish, Shi'a Muslim, Christian	Jordanian dinar, Israeli shekel

*Hong Kong dollar

Victoria Falls 1

Sinai Peninsula, Egypt 2

Africa		Area sq km	Area sq miles	Population	Capital	Languages	Religions	Currency
ALGERIA		2 381 741	919 595	31 800 000	Algiers	Arabic, French, Berber	Sunni Muslim	Algerian dinar
ANGOLA		1 246 700	481 354	13 625 000	Luanda	Portuguese, Bantu, local languages	Roman Catholic, Protestant, traditional beliefs	Kwanza
BENIN		112 620	43 483	6 736 000	Porto-Novo	French, Fon, Yoruba, Adja, local languages	Traditional beliefs, Roman Catholic, Sunni Muslim	CFA franc*
BOTSWANA		581 370	224 468	1 785 000	Gaborone	English, Setswana, Shona, local languages	Traditional beliefs, Protestant, Roman Catholic	Pula
BURKINA		274 200	105 869	13 002 000	Ouagadougou	French, Moore (Mossi), Fulani, local languages	Sunni Muslim, traditional beliefs, Roman Catholic	CFA franc*
BURUNDI		27 835	10 747	6 825 000	Bujumbura	Kirundi (Hutu, Tutsi), French	Roman Catholic, traditional beliefs, Protestant	Burundian franc
CAMEROON		475 442	183 569	16 018 000	Yaoundé	French, English, Fang, Bamileke, local languages	Roman Catholic, traditional beliefs, Sunni Muslim, Protestant	CFA franc*
CAPE VERDE		4 033	1 557	463 000	Praia	Portuguese, creole	Roman Catholic, Protestant	Cape Verde escudo
CENTRAL AFRICAN REPUBLIC		622 436	240 324	3 865 000	Bangui	French, Sango, Banda, Baya, local languages	Protestant, Roman Catholic, traditional beliefs, Sunni Muslim	CFA franc*
CHAD		1 284 000	495 755	8 598 000	Ndjamena	Arabic, French, Sara, local languages	Sunni Muslim, Roman Catholic, Protestant, traditional beliefs	CFA franc*
COMOROS		1 862	719	768 000	Moroni	Comorian, French, Arabic	Sunni Muslim, Roman Catholic	Comoros franc
CONGO		342 000	132 047	3 724 000	Brazzaville	French, Kongo, Monokutuba, local languages	Roman Catholic, Protestant, traditional beliefs, Sunni Muslim	CFA franc*
CONGO, DEMOCRATIC REP. OF		2 345 410	905 568	52 771 000	Kinshasa	French, Lingala, Swahili, Kongo, local languages	Christian, Sunni Muslim	Congolese franc
CÔTE D'IVOIRE		322 463	124 504	16 631 000	Yamoussoukro	French, creole, Akan, local languages	Sunni Muslim, Roman Catholic, traditional beliefs, Protestant	CFA franc*
DJIBOUTI		23 200	8 958	703 000	Djibouti	Somali, Afar, French, Arabic	Sunni Muslim, Christian	Djibouti franc
EGYPT		1 000 250	386 199	71 931 000	Cairo	Arabic	Sunni Muslim, Coptic Christian	Egyptian pound
EQUATORIAL GUINEA		28 051	10 831	494 000	Malabo	Spanish, French, Fang	Roman Catholic, traditional beliefs	CFA franc*
ERITREA		117 400	45 328	4 141 000	Asmara	Tigrinya, Tigre	Sunni Muslim, Coptic Christian	Nakfa
ETHIOPIA		1 133 880	437 794	70 678 000	Addis Ababa	Oromo, Amharic, Tigrinya, local languages	Ethiopian Orthodox, Sunni Muslim, traditional beliefs	Birr
GABON		267 667	103 347	1 329 000	Libreville	French, Fang, local languages	Roman Catholic, Protestant, traditional beliefs	CFA franc*
THE GAMBIA		11 295	4 361	1 426 000	Banjul	English, Malinke, Fulani, Wolof	Sunni Muslim, Protestant	Dalasi
GHANA		238 537	92 100	20 922 000	Accra	English, Hausa, Akan, local languages	Christian, Sunni Muslim, traditional beliefs	Cedi
GUINEA		245 857	94 926	8 480 000	Conakry	French, Fulani, Malinke, local languages	Sunni Muslim, traditional beliefs, Christian	Guinea franc
GUINEA-BISSAU		36 125	13 948	1 493 000	Bissau	Portuguese, crioulo, local languages	Traditional beliefs, Sunni Muslim, Christian	CFA franc*
KENYA		582 646	224 961	31 987 000	Nairobi	Swahili, English, local languages	Christian, traditional beliefs	Kenyan shilling
LESOTHO		30 355	11 720	1 802 000	Maseru	Sesotho, English, Zulu	Christian, traditional beliefs	Loti, S. African rand
LIBERIA		111 369	43 000	3 367 000	Monrovia	English, creole, local languages	Traditional beliefs, Christian, Sunni Muslim	Liberian dollar
LIBYA		1 759 540	679 362	5 551 000	Tripoli	Arabic, Berber	Sunni Muslim	Libyan dinar
MADAGASCAR		587 041	226 658	17 404 000	Antananarivo	Malagasy, French	Traditional beliefs, Christian, Sunni Muslim	Malagasy franc
MALAWI		118 484	45 747	12 105 000	Lilongwe	Chichewa, English, local languages	Christian, traditional beliefs, Sunni Muslim	Malawian kwacha
MALI		1 240 140	478 821	13 007 000	Bamako	French, Bambara, local languages	Sunni Muslim, traditional beliefs, Christian	CFA franc*
MAURITANIA		1 030 700	397 955	2 893 000	Nouakchott	Arabic, French, local languages	Sunni Muslim	Ouguiya
MAURITIUS		2 040	788	1 221 000	Port Louis	English, creole, Hindi, Bhojpuri, French	Hindu, Roman Catholic, Sunni Muslim	Mauritius rupee
MOROCCO		446 550	172 414	30 566 000	Rabat	Arabic, Berber, French	Sunni Muslim	Moroccan dirham
MOZAMBIQUE		799 380	308 642	18 863 000	Maputo	Portuguese, Makua, Tsonga, local languages	Traditional beliefs, Roman Catholic, Sunni Muslim	Metical
NAMIBIA		824 292	318 261	1 987 000	Windhoek	English, Afrikaans, German, Ovambo, local languages	Protestant, Roman Catholic	Namibian dollar
NIGER		1 267 000	489 191	11 972 000	Niamey	French, Hausa, Fulani, local languages	Sunni Muslim, traditional beliefs	CFA franc*
NIGERIA		923 768	356 669	124 009 000	Abuja	English, Hausa, Yoruba, Ibo, Fulani, local languages	Sunni Muslim, Christian, traditional beliefs	Naira
RWANDA		26 338	10 169	8 387 000	Kigali	Kinyarwanda, French, English	Roman Catholic, traditional beliefs, Protestant	Rwandan franc
SÃO TOMÉ AND PRÍNCIPE		964	372	161 000	São Tomé	Portuguese, creole	Roman Catholic, Protestant	Dobra
SENEGAL		196 720	75 954	10 095 000	Dakar	French, Wolof, Fulani, local languages	Sunni Muslim, Roman Catholic, traditional beliefs	CFA franc*
SEYCHELLES		455	176	81 000	Victoria	English, French, creole	Roman Catholic, Protestant	Seychelles rupee
SIERRA LEONE		71 740	27 699	4 971 000	Freetown	English, creole, Mende, Temne, local languages	Sunni Muslim, traditional beliefs	Leone
SOMALIA		637 657	246 201	9 890 000	Mogadishu	Somali, Arabic	Sunni Muslim	Somali shilling
SOUTH AFRICA, REPUBLIC OF		1 219 090	470 693	45 026 000	Pretoria/Cape Town	Afrikaans, English, nine official local languages	Protestant, Roman Catholic, Sunni Muslim, Hindu	Rand
SUDAN		2 505 813	967 500	33 610 000	Khartoum	Arabic, Dinka, Nubian, Beja, Nuer, local languages	Sunni Muslim, traditional beliefs, Christian	Sudanese dinar
SWAZILAND		17 364	6 704	1 077 000	Mbabane	Swazi, English	Christian, traditional beliefs	Emalangeni, South African rand
TANZANIA		945 087	364 900	36 977 000	Dodoma	Swahili, English, Nyamwezi, local languages	Shi'a Muslim, Sunni Muslim, traditional beliefs, Christian	Tanzanian shilling
TOGO		56 785	21 925	4 909 000	Lomé	French, Ewe, Kabre, local languages	Traditional beliefs, Christian, Sunni Muslim	CFA franc*
TUNISIA		164 150	63 379	9 832 000	Tunis	Arabic, French	Sunni Muslim	Tunisian dinar
UGANDA		241 038	93 065	25 827 000	Kampala	English, Swahili, Luganda, local languages	Roman Catholic, Protestant, Sunni Muslim, traditional beliefs	Ugandan shilling
ZAMBIA		752 614	290 586	10 812 000	Lusaka	English, Bemba, Nyanja, Tonga, local languages	Christian, traditional beliefs	Zambian kwacha
ZIMBABWE		390 759	150 873	12 891 000	Harare	English, Shona, Ndebele	Christian, traditional beliefs	Zimbabwean dollar

Dependent and disputed territories		Territorial status	Area sq km	Area sq km	Population	Capital	Languages	Religions	Currency
Canary Islands		Autonomous Community of Spain	7 447	2 875	1 694 477	Santa Cruz de Tenerife, Las Palmas	Spanish	Roman Catholic	Euro
Madeira		Autonomous Region of Portugal	779	301	242 603	Funchal	Portuguese	Roman Catholic, Protestant	Euro
Mayotte		French Territorial Collectivity	373	144	171 000	Dzaoudzi	French, Mahorian	Sunni Muslim, Christian	Euro
Réunion		French Overseas Department	2 551	985	756 000	St-Denis	French, creole	Roman Catholic	Euro
St Helena and Dependencies		United Kingdom Overseas Territory	121	47	5 644	Jamestown	English	Protestant, Roman Catholic	St Helena pound
Western Sahara		Disputed territory (Morocco)	266 000	102 703	308 000	Laâyoune	Arabic	Sunni Muslim	Moroccan dirham

*Communauté Financière Africaine franc

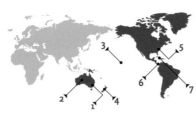

Sydney, Australia 1

Uluṟu (Ayers Rock), Australia 2

Oceania		Area sq km	Area sq miles	Population	Capital	Languages	Religions	Currency
AUSTRALIA		7 692 024	2 969 907	19 731 000	Canberra	English, Italian, Greek	Protestant, Roman Catholic, Orthodox	Australian dollar
FIJI		18 330	7 077	839 000	Suva	English, Fijian, Hindi	Christian, Hindu, Sunni Muslim	Fiji dollar
KIRIBATI		717	277	88 000	Bairiki	Gilbertese, English	Roman Catholic, Protestant	Australian dollar
MARSHALL ISLANDS		181	70	53 000	Delap-Uliga-Djarrit	English, Marshallese	Protestant, Roman Catholic	United States dollar
MICRONESIA, FEDERATED STATES OF		701	271	109 000	Palikir	English, Chuukese, Pohnpeian, local languages	Roman Catholic, Protestant	United States dollar
NAURU		21	8	13 000	Yaren	Nauruan, English	Protestant, Roman Catholic	Australian dollar
NEW ZEALAND		270 534	104 454	3 875 000	Wellington	English, Maori	Protestant, Roman Catholic	New Zealand dollar
PAPUA NEW GUINEA		462 840	178 704	5 711 000	Port Moresby	English, Tok Pisin (creole), local languages	Protestant, Roman Catholic, traditional beliefs	Kina
SAMOA		2 831	1 093	178 000	Apia	Samoan, English	Protestant, Roman Catholic	Tala
SOLOMON ISLANDS		28 370	10 954	477 000	Honiara	English, creole, local languages	Protestant, Roman Catholic	Solomon Islands dollar
TONGA		748	289	104 000	Nuku'alofa	Tongan, English	Protestant, Roman Catholic	Pa'anga
TUVALU		25	10	11 000	Vaiaku	Tuvaluan, English	Protestant	Australian dollar
VANUATU		12 190	4 707	212 000	Port Vila	English, Bislama (creole), French	Protestant, Roman Catholic, traditional beliefs	Vatu

Dependent territories		Territorial status	Area sq km	Area sq miles	Population	Capital	Languages	Religions	Currency
American Samoa		United States Unincorporated Territory	197	76	67 000	Fagatoga	Samoan, English	Protestant, Roman Catholic	United States dollar
Cook Islands		Self-governing New Zealand Territory	293	113	18 000	Avarua	English, Maori	Protestant, Roman Catholic	New Zealand dollar
French Polynesia		French Overseas Territory	3 265	1 261	244 000	Papeete	French, Tahitian, Polynesian languages	Protestant, Roman Catholic	CFP franc*
Guam		United States Unincorporated Territory	541	209	163 000	Hagåtña	Chamorro, English, Tapalog	Roman Catholic	United States dollar
New Caledonia		French Overseas Territory	19 058	7 358	228 000	Nouméa	French, local languages	Roman Catholic, Protestant, Sunni Muslim	CFP franc*
Niue		Self-governing New Zealand Territory	258	100	2 000	Alofi	English, Polynesian	Christian	New Zealand dollar
Norfolk Island		Australian External Territory	35	14	2 037	Kingston	English	Protestant, Roman Catholic	Australian Dollar
Northern Mariana Islands		United States Commonwealth	477	184	79 000	Capitol Hill	English, Chamorro, local languages	Roman Catholic	United States dollar
Pitcairn Islands		United Kingdom Overseas Territory	45	17	51	Adamstown	English	Protestant	New Zealand dollar
Tokelau		New Zealand Overseas Territory	10	4	2 000		English, Tokelauan	Christian	New Zealand dollar
Wallis and Futuna Islands		French Overseas Territory	274	106	15 000	Matā'utu	French, Wallisian, Futunian	Roman Catholic	CFP franc*

*Franc des Comptoirs Français du Pacifique

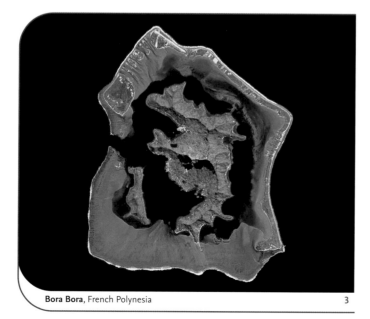

Bora Bora, French Polynesia 3

Mount Cook, New Zealand 4

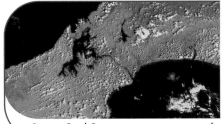

The Pentagon, Washington DC, USA   5

Panama Canal, Panama   6

Cuba, Caribbean Sea   7

North America		Area sq km	Area sq miles	Population	Capital	Languages	Religions	Currency
ANTIGUA AND BARBUDA		442	171	73 000	St John's	English, creole	Protestant, Roman Catholic	East Caribbean dollar
THE BAHAMAS		13 939	5 382	314 000	Nassau	English, creole	Protestant, Roman Catholic	Bahamian dollar
BARBADOS		430	166	270 000	Bridgetown	English, creole	Protestant, Roman Catholic	Barbados dollar
BELIZE		22 965	8 867	256 000	Belmopan	English, Spanish, Mayan, creole	Roman Catholic, Protestant	Belize dollar
CANADA		9 984 670	3 855 103	31 510 000	Ottawa	English, French	Roman Catholic, Protestant, Eastern Orthodox, Jewish	Canadian dollar
COSTA RICA		51 100	19 730	4 173 000	San José	Spanish	Roman Catholic, Protestant	Costa Rican colón
CUBA		110 860	42 803	11 300 000	Havana	Spanish	Roman Catholic, Protestant	Cuban peso
DOMINICA		750	290	79 000	Roseau	English, creole	Roman Catholic, Protestant	East Caribbean dollar
DOMINICAN REPUBLIC		48 442	18 704	8 745 000	Santo Domingo	Spanish, creole	Roman Catholic, Protestant	Dominican peso
EL SALVADOR		21 041	8 124	6 515 000	San Salvador	Spanish	Roman Catholic, Protestant	El Salvador colón, United States dollar
GRENADA		378	146	80 000	St George's	English, creole	Roman Catholic, Protestant	East Caribbean dollar
GUATEMALA		108 890	42 043	12 347 000	Guatemala City	Spanish, Mayan languages	Roman Catholic, Protestant	Quetzal, United States dollar
HAITI		27 750	10 714	8 326 000	Port-au-Prince	French, creole	Roman Catholic, Protestant, Voodoo	Gourde
HONDURAS		112 088	43 277	6 941 000	Tegucigalpa	Spanish, Amerindian languages	Roman Catholic, Protestant	Lempira
JAMAICA		10 991	4 244	2 651 000	Kingston	English, creole	Protestant, Roman Catholic	Jamaican dollar
MEXICO		1 972 545	761 604	103 457 000	Mexico City	Spanish, Amerindian languages	Roman Catholic, Protestant	Mexican peso
NICARAGUA		130 000	50 193	5 466 000	Managua	Spanish, Amerindian languages	Roman Catholic, Protestant	Córdoba
PANAMA		77 082	29 762	3 120 000	Panama City	Spanish, English, Amerindian languages	Roman Catholic, Protestant, Sunni Muslim	Balboa
ST KITTS AND NEVIS		261	101	42 000	Basseterre	English, creole	Protestant, Roman Catholic	East Caribbean dollar
ST LUCIA		616	238	149 000	Castries	English, creole	Roman Catholic, Protestant	East Caribbean dollar
ST VINCENT AND THE GRENADINES		389	150	120 000	Kingstown	English, creole	Protestant, Roman Catholic	East Caribbean dollar
TRINIDAD AND TOBAGO		5 130	1 981	1 303 000	Port of Spain	English, creole, Hindi	Roman Catholic, Hindu, Protestant, Sunni Muslim	Trinidad and Tobago dollar
UNITED STATES OF AMERICA		9 826 635	3 794 085	294 043 000	Washington DC	English, Spanish	Protestant, Roman Catholic, Sunni Muslim, Jewish	United States dollar

Dependent territories		Territorial status	Area sq km	Area sq miles	Population	Capital	Languages	Religions	Currency
Anguilla		United Kingdom Overseas Territory	155	60	12 000	The Valley	English	Protestant, Roman Catholic	East Caribbean dollar
Aruba		Self-governing Netherlands Territory	193	75	100 000	Oranjestad	Papiamento, Dutch, English	Roman Catholic, Protestant	Arubian florin
Bermuda		United Kingdom Overseas Territory	54	21	82 000	Hamilton	English	Protestant, Roman Catholic	Bermuda dollar
Cayman Islands		United Kingdom Overseas Territory	259	100	40 000	George Town	English	Protestant, Roman Catholic	Cayman Islands dollar
Greenland		Self-governing Danish Territory	2 175 600	840 004	57 000	Nuuk	Greenlandic, Danish	Protestant	Danish krone
Guadeloupe		French Overseas Department	1 780	687	440 000	Basse-Terre	French, creole	Roman Catholic	Euro
Martinique		French Overseas Department	1 079	417	393 000	Fort-de-France	French, creole	Roman Catholic, traditional beliefs	Euro
Montserrat		United Kingdom Overseas Territory	100	39	4 000	Plymouth	English	Protestant, Roman Catholic	East Caribbean dollar
Netherlands Antilles		Self-governing Netherlands Territory	800	309	221 000	Willemstad	Dutch, Papiamento English	Roman Catholic, Protestant	Netherlands guilder
Puerto Rico		United States Commonwealth	9 104	3 515	3 879 000	San Juan	Spanish, English	Roman Catholic, Protestant	United States dollar
St Pierre and Miquelon		French Territorial Collectivity	242	93	6 000	St-Pierre	French	Roman Catholic	Euro
Turks and Caicos Islands		United Kingdom Overseas Territory	430	166	21 000	Grand Turk	English	Protestant	United States dollar
Virgin Islands (U.K.)		United Kingdom Overseas Territory	153	59	21 000	Road Town	English	Protestant, Roman Catholic	United States dollar
Virgin Islands (U.S.A.)		United States Unincorporated Territory	352	136	111 000	Charlotte Amalie	English, Spanish	Protestant, Roman Catholic	United States dollar

South America		Area sq km	Area sq miles	Population	Capital	Languages	Religions	Currency
ARGENTINA		2 766 889	1 068 302	38 428 000	Buenos Aires	Spanish, Italian, Amerindian languages	Roman Catholic, Protestant	Argentinian peso
BOLIVIA		1 098 581	424 164	8 808 000	La Paz/Sucre	Spanish, Quechua, Aymara	Roman Catholic, Protestant, Baha'i	Boliviano
BRAZIL		8 514 879	3 287 613	178 470 000	Brasília	Portuguese	Roman Catholic, Protestant	Real
CHILE		756 945	292 258	15 805 000	Santiago	Spanish, Amerindian languages	Roman Catholic, Protestant	Chilean peso
COLOMBIA		1 141 748	440 831	44 222 000	Bogotá	Spanish, Amerindian languages	Roman Catholic, Protestant	Colombian peso
ECUADOR		272 045	105 037	13 003 000	Quito	Spanish, Quechua, other Amerindian languages	Roman Catholic	US dollar
GUYANA		214 969	83 000	765 000	Georgetown	English, creole, Amerindian languages	Protestant, Hindu, Roman Catholic, Sunni Muslim	Guyana dollar
PARAGUAY		406 752	157 048	5 878 000	Asunción	Spanish, Guaraní	Roman Catholic, Protestant	Guaraní
PERU		1 285 216	496 225	27 167 000	Lima	Spanish, Quechua, Aymara	Roman Catholic, Protestant	Sol
SURINAME		163 820	63 251	436 000	Paramaribo	Dutch, Surinamese, English, Hindi	Hindu, Roman Catholic, Protestant, Sunni Muslim	Suriname guilder
URUGUAY		176 215	68 037	3 415 000	Montevideo	Spanish	Roman Catholic, Protestant, Jewish	Uruguayan peso
VENEZUELA		912 050	352 144	25 699 000	Caracas	Spanish, Amerindian languages	Roman Catholic, Protestant	Bolívar

Dependent territories		Territorial status	Area sq km	Area sq miles	Population	Capital	Languages	Religions	Currency
Falkland Islands		United Kingdom Overseas Territory	12 170	4 699	3 000	Stanley	English	Protestant, Roman Catholic	Falkland Islands pound
French Guiana		French Overseas Department	90 000	34 749	178 000	Cayenne	French, creole	Roman Catholic	Euro

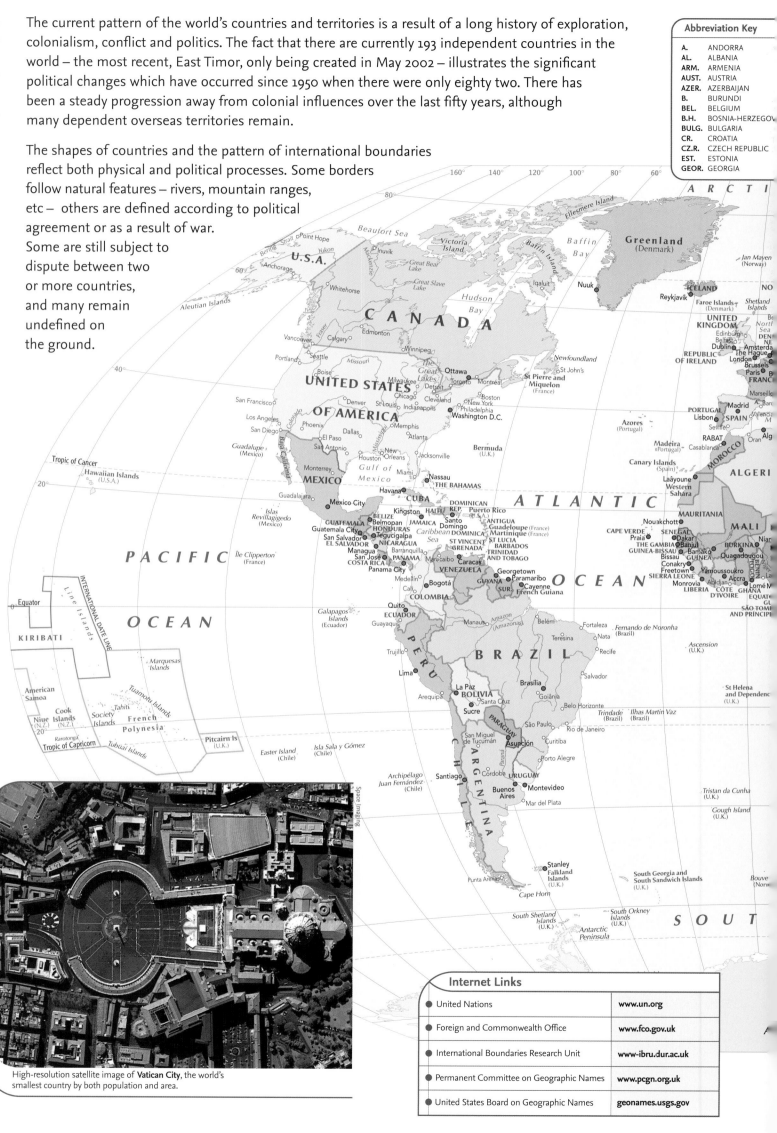

World Countries

The current pattern of the world's countries and territories is a result of a long history of exploration, colonialism, conflict and politics. The fact that there are currently 193 independent countries in the world – the most recent, East Timor, only being created in May 2002 – illustrates the significant political changes which have occurred since 1950 when there were only eighty two. There has been a steady progression away from colonial influences over the last fifty years, although many dependent overseas territories remain.

The shapes of countries and the pattern of international boundaries reflect both physical and political processes. Some borders follow natural features – rivers, mountain ranges, etc – others are defined according to political agreement or as a result of war. Some are still subject to dispute between two or more countries, and many remain undefined on the ground.

High-resolution satellite image of **Vatican City**, the world's smallest country by both population and area.

Internet Links	
United Nations	www.un.org
Foreign and Commonwealth Office	www.fco.gov.uk
International Boundaries Research Unit	www-ibru.dur.ac.uk
Permanent Committee on Geographic Names	www.pcgn.org.uk
United States Board on Geographic Names	geonames.usgs.gov

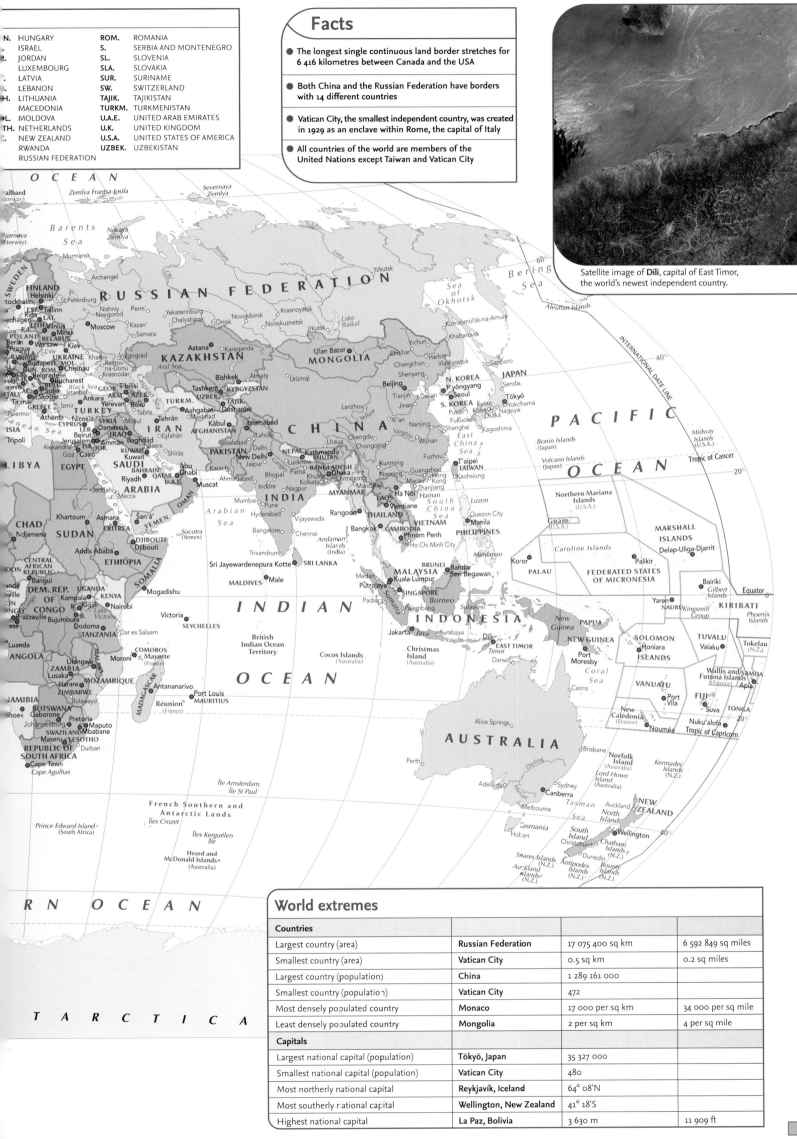

Facts

- The longest single continuous land border stretches for 6 416 kilometres between Canada and the USA

- Both China and the Russian Federation have borders with 14 different countries

- Vatican City, the smallest independent country, was created in 1929 as an enclave within Rome, the capital of Italy

- All countries of the world are members of the United Nations except Taiwan and Vatican City

Satellite image of **Dili**, capital of East Timor, the world's newest independent country.

World extremes

Countries			
Largest country (area)	**Russian Federation**	17 075 400 sq km	6 592 849 sq miles
Smallest country (area)	**Vatican City**	0.5 sq km	0.2 sq miles
Largest country (population)	**China**	1 289 161 000	
Smallest country (population)	**Vatican City**	472	
Most densely populated country	**Monaco**	17 000 per sq km	34 000 per sq mile
Least densely populated country	**Mongolia**	2 per sq km	4 per sq mile
Capitals			
Largest national capital (population)	**Tōkyō, Japan**	35 327 000	
Smallest national capital (population)	**Vatican City**	480	
Most northerly national capital	**Reykjavík, Iceland**	64° 08'N	
Most southerly national capital	**Wellington, New Zealand**	41° 18'S	
Highest national capital	**La Paz, Bolivia**	3 630 m	11 909 ft

The earth's physical features, both on land and on the sea bed, closely reflect its geological structure. The current shapes of the continents and oceans have evolved over millions of years. Movements of the tectonic plates which make up the earth's crust have created some of the best-known and most spectacular features. The processes which have shaped the earth continue today with earthquakes, volcanoes, erosion, climatic variations and man's activities all affecting the earth's landscapes.

The total topographic range of the earth's surface is nearly 20 000 metres, from the highest point Mount Everest, to the lowest point in the Mariana Trench. Major mountain ranges include the Himalaya, the Andes and the Rocky Mountains, each of which give rise to some of the world's greatest rivers. In contrast, the deserts of the Sahara, Australia, the Arabian Peninsula and the Gobi cover vast areas and each provide unique landscapes.

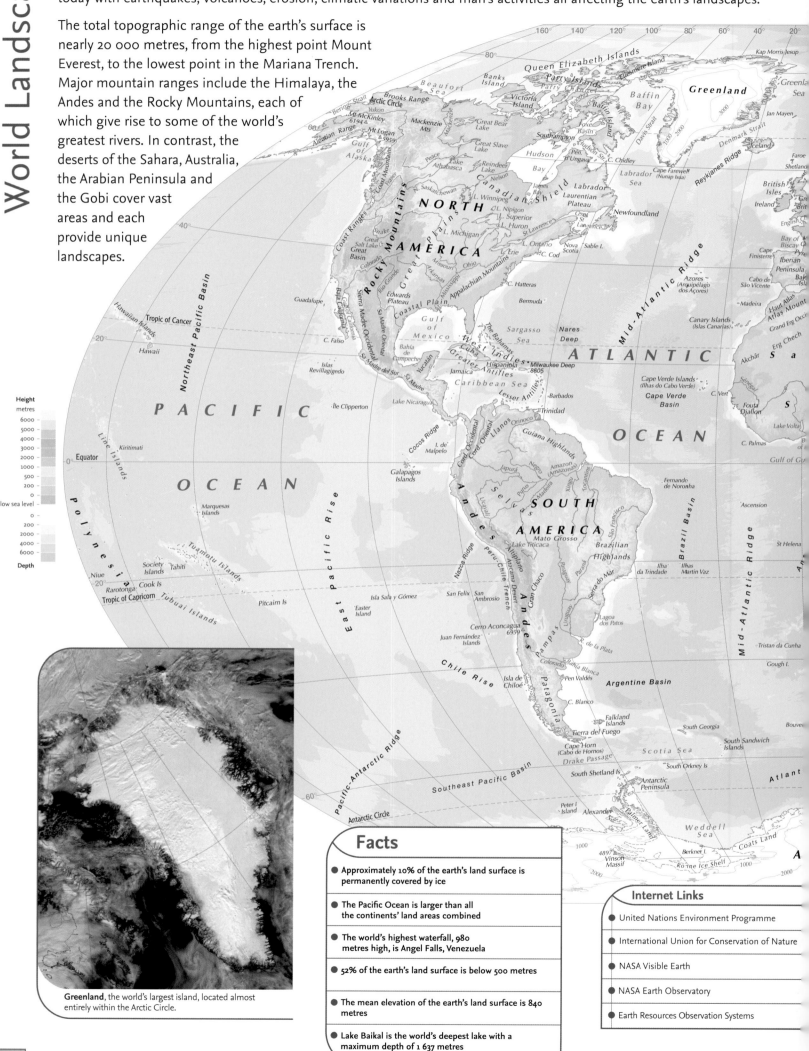

Greenland, the world's largest island, located almost entirely within the Arctic Circle.

Facts

- Approximately 10% of the earth's land surface is permanently covered by ice

- The Pacific Ocean is larger than all the continents' land areas combined

- The world's highest waterfall, 980 metres high, is Angel Falls, Venezuela

- 52% of the earth's land surface is below 500 metres

- The mean elevation of the earth's land surface is 840 metres

- Lake Baikal is the world's deepest lake with a maximum depth of 1 637 metres

Internet Links

- United Nations Environment Programme

- International Union for Conservation of Nature

- NASA Visible Earth

- NASA Earth Observatory

- Earth Resources Observation Systems

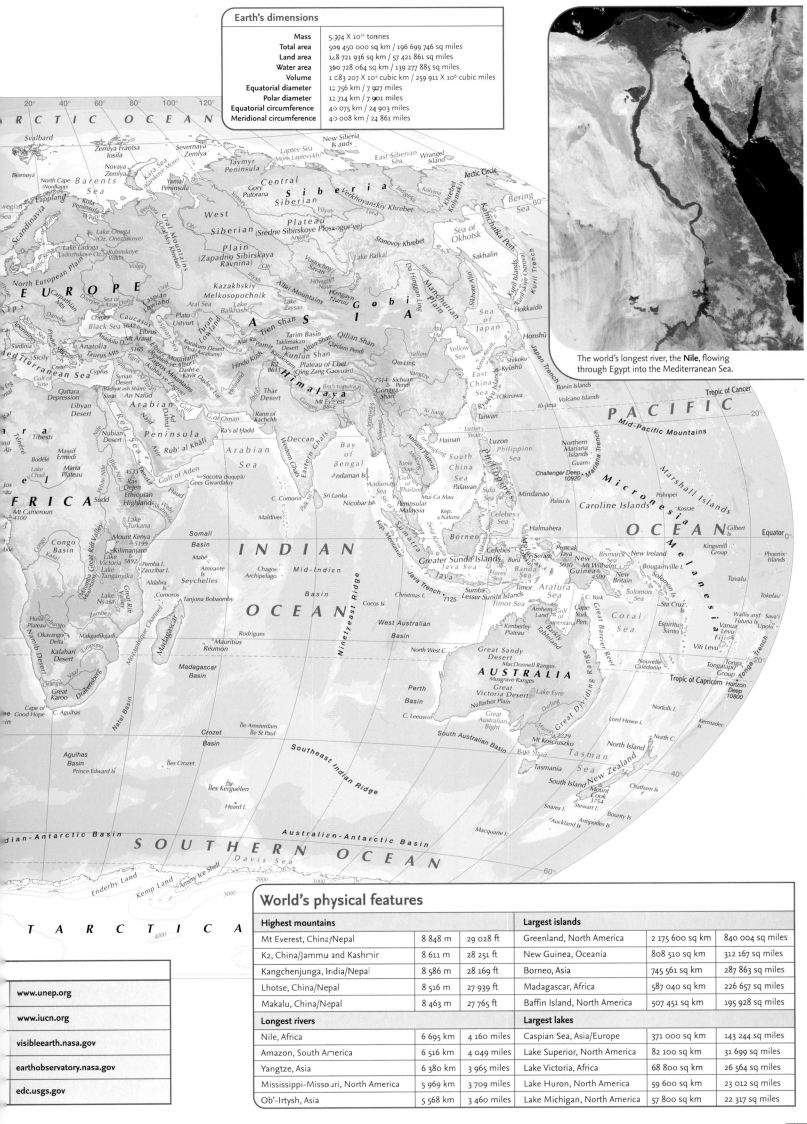

Earth's dimensions

Mass	5.974 X 10²¹ tonnes
Total area	509 450 000 sq km / 196 699 746 sq miles
Land area	148 721 936 sq km / 57 421 861 sq miles
Water area	360 728 064 sq km / 139 277 885 sq miles
Volume	1 083 207 X 10⁹ cubic km / 259 911 X 10⁶ cubic miles
Equatorial diameter	12 756 km / 7 927 miles
Polar diameter	12 714 km / 7 901 miles
Equatorial circumference	40 075 km / 24 903 miles
Meridional circumference	40 008 km / 24 861 miles

The world's longest river, the **Nile**, flowing through Egypt into the Mediterranean Sea.

World's physical features

Highest mountains			Largest islands		
Mt Everest, China/Nepal	8 848 m	29 028 ft	Greenland, North America	2 175 600 sq km	840 004 sq miles
K2, China/Jammu and Kashmir	8 611 m	28 251 ft	New Guinea, Oceania	808 510 sq km	312 167 sq miles
Kangchenjunga, India/Nepal	8 586 m	28 169 ft	Borneo, Asia	745 561 sq km	287 863 sq miles
Lhotse, China/Nepal	8 516 m	27 939 ft	Madagascar, Africa	587 040 sq km	226 657 sq miles
Makalu, China/Nepal	8 463 m	27 765 ft	Baffin Island, North America	507 451 sq km	195 928 sq miles
Longest rivers			**Largest lakes**		
Nile, Africa	6 695 km	4 160 miles	Caspian Sea, Asia/Europe	371 000 sq km	143 244 sq miles
Amazon, South America	6 516 km	4 049 miles	Lake Superior, North America	82 100 sq km	31 699 sq miles
Yangtze, Asia	6 380 km	3 965 miles	Lake Victoria, Africa	68 800 sq km	26 564 sq miles
Mississippi-Missouri, North America	5 969 km	3 709 miles	Lake Huron, North America	59 600 sq km	23 012 sq miles
Ob'-Irtysh, Asia	5 568 km	3 460 miles	Lake Michigan, North America	57 800 sq km	22 317 sq miles

www.unep.org

www.iucn.org

visibleearth.nasa.gov

earthobservatory.nasa.gov

edc.usgs.gov

Earthquakes and volcanoes hold a constant fascination because of their power, their beauty, and the fact that they cannot be controlled or accurately predicted. Our understanding of these phenomena relies mainly on the theory of plate tectonics. This defines the earth's surface as a series of 'plates' which are constantly moving relative to each other, at rates of a few centimetres per year. As plates move against each other enormous pressure builds up and when the rocks can no longer bear this pressure they fracture, and energy is released as an earthquake. The pressures involved can also melt the rock to form magma which then rises to the earth's surface to form a volcano.

The distribution of earthquakes and volcanoes therefore relates closely to plate boundaries. In particular, most active volcanoes and much of the earth's seismic activity are centred on the 'Ring of Fire' around the Pacific Ocean.

Facts

● Over 900 earthquakes of magnitude 5.0 or greater occur every year

● An earthquake of magnitude 8.0 releases energy equivalent to 1 billion tons of TNT explosive

● Ground shaking during an earthquake in Alaska in 1964 lasted for 3 minutes

● Indonesia has more than 120 volcanoes and over 30% of the world's active volcanoes

● Volcanoes can produce very fertile soil and important industrial materials and chemicals

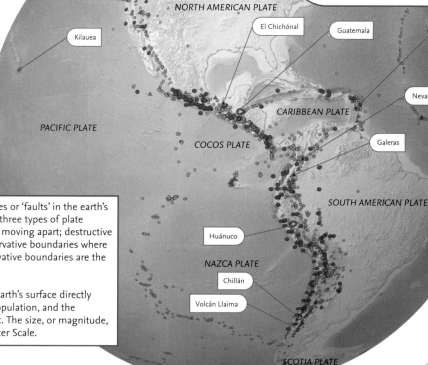

Earthquakes

Earthquakes are caused by movement along fractures or 'faults' in the earth's crust, particularly along plate boundaries. There are three types of plate boundary: constructive boundaries where plates are moving apart; destructive boundaries where two or more plates collide; conservative boundaries where plates slide past each other. Destructive and conservative boundaries are the main sources of earthquake activity.

The epicentre of an earthquake is the point on the earth's surface directly above its source. If this is near to large centres of population, and the earthquake is powerful, major devastation can result. The size, or magnitude, of an earthquake is generally measured on the Richter Scale.

Deadliest earthquakes, 1900–2003

Year	Location	Deaths
1905	**Kangra**, India	19 000
1907	west of **Dushanbe**, Tajikistan	12 000
1908	**Messina**, Italy	110 000
1915	**Abruzzo**, Italy	35 000
1917	**Bali**, Indonesia	15 000
1920	**Ningxia Province**, China	200 000
1923	**Tōkyō**, Japan	142 807
1927	**Qinghai Province**, China	200 000
1932	**Gansu Province**, China	70 000
1933	**Sichuan Province**, China	10 000
1934	**Nepal/India**	10 700
1935	**Quetta**, Pakistan	30 000
1939	**Chillán**, Chile	28 000
1939	**Erzincan**, Turkey	32 700
1948	**Ashgabat**, Turkmenistan	19 800
1962	**Northwest Iran**	12 225
1970	**Huánuco Province**, Peru	66 794
1974	**Yunnan** and **Sichuan Provinces**, China	20 000
1975	**Liaoning Province**, China	10 000
1976	central **Guatemala**	22 778
1976	**Hebei Province**, China	255 000
1978	**Khorāsan Province**, Iran	20 000
1980	**Ech Chélif**, Algeria	11 000
1988	**Spitak**, Armenia	25 000
1990	**Manjil**, Iran	50 000
1999	**Kocaeli (İzmit)**, Turkey	17 000
2001	**Gujarat**, India	20 000
2003	**Bam**, Iran	26 271

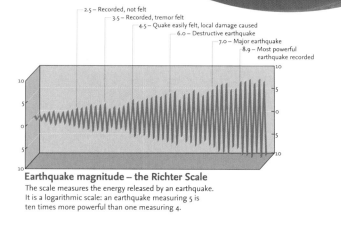

2.5 – Recorded, not felt
3.5 – Recorded, tremor felt
4.5 – Quake easily felt, local damage caused
6.0 – Destructive earthquake
7.0 – Major earthquake
8.9 – Most powerful earthquake recorded

Earthquake magnitude – the Richter Scale

The scale measures the energy released by an earthquake. It is a logarithmic scale: an earthquake measuring 5 is ten times more powerful than one measuring 4.

Extensive damage caused by major earthquake centred on **Bam, Iran** in December 2003.

Deadliest earthquake

Earthquake of magnitude 7.5 or greater

Earthquake of magnitude 5.5 – 7.4

Major volcano

Other volcano

Volcanoes

The majority of volcanoes occur along destructive plate boundaries in the 'subduction zone' where one plate passes under another. The friction and pressure causes the rock to melt and to form magma which is forced upwards to the earth's surface where it erupts as molten rock (lava) or as particles of ash or cinder. This process created the numerous volcanoes in the Andes, where the Nazca Plate is passing under the South American Plate. Volcanoes can be defined by the nature of the material they emit. 'Shield' volcanoes have extensive, gentle slopes formed from free-flowing lava, while steep-sided 'continental' volcanoes are created from thicker, slow-flowing lava and ash.

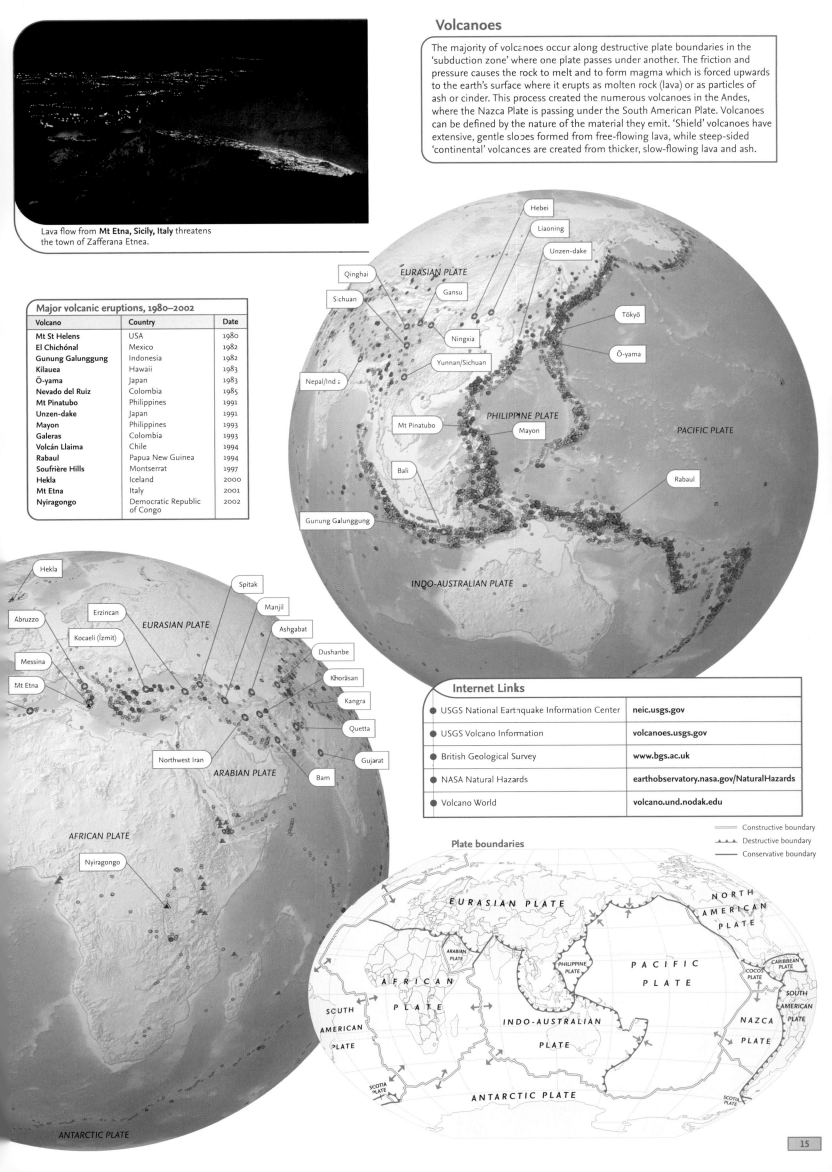

Lava flow from **Mt Etna, Sicily, Italy** threatens the town of Zafferana Etnea.

Major volcanic eruptions, 1980–2002

Volcano	Country	Date
Mt St Helens	USA	1980
El Chichónal	Mexico	1982
Gunung Galunggung	Indonesia	1982
Kilauea	Hawaii	1983
Ō-yama	Japan	1983
Nevado del Ruiz	Colombia	1985
Mt Pinatubo	Philippines	1991
Unzen-dake	Japan	1991
Mayon	Philippines	1993
Galeras	Colombia	1993
Volcán Llaima	Chile	1994
Rabaul	Papua New Guinea	1994
Soufrière Hills	Montserrat	1997
Hekla	Iceland	2000
Mt Etna	Italy	2001
Nyiragongo	Democratic Republic of Congo	2002

Internet Links

USGS National Earthquake Information Center	neic.usgs.gov
USGS Volcano Information	volcanoes.usgs.gov
British Geological Survey	www.bgs.ac.uk
NASA Natural Hazards	earthobservatory.nasa.gov/NaturalHazards
Volcano World	volcano.und.nodak.edu

Plate boundaries

——— Constructive boundary
▲▲▲ Destructive boundary
——— Conservative boundary

15

The climate of a region is defined by its long-term prevailing weather conditions. Classification of Climate Types is based on the relationship between temperature and humidity and how these factors are affected by latitude, altitude, ocean currents and winds. Weather is the specific short term condition which occurs locally and consists of events such as thunderstorms, hurricanes, blizzards and heat waves. Temperature and rainfall data recorded at weather stations can be plotted graphically and the graphs shown here, typical of each climate region, illustrate the various combinations of temperature and rainfall which exist worldwide for each month of the year. Data used for climate graphs are based on average monthly figures recorded over a minimum period of thirty years.

World Statistics: see pages **154–160**

Tropical storm Dina, January 2002, northeast of Mauritius and Réunion, Indian Ocean.

Weather extremes

Highest recorded temperature	**57.8°C/136°F** Al'Azīzīyah, Libya (September 1922)
Hottest place - annual mean	**34.4°C/93.6°F** Dalol, Ethiopia
Driest place - annual mean	**0.1mm/0.004 inches** Atacama Desert, Chile
Most sunshine - annual mean	**90%** Yuma, Arizona, USA (over 4000 hours)
Lowest recorded temperature	**-89.2°C/-128.6°F** Vostok Station, Antarctica (July 1983)
Coldest place - annual mean	**-56.6°C/-69.9°F** Plateau Station, Antarctica
Wettest place annual mean	**11 873 mm/467.4 inches** Meghalaya, India
Greatest snowfall	**31 102 mm/1 224.5 inches** Mount Rainier, Washington, USA (February 1971 – February 1972)
Windiest place	**322 km per hour/200 miles per hour** (in gales) Commonwealth Bay, Antarctica

Facts

- Arctic Sea ice thickness has declined 4% in the last 40 years

- 2001 marked the end of the La Niña episode

- Sea levels are rising by one centimetre per decade

- Precipitation in the northern hemisphere is increasing

- Droughts have increased in frequency and intensity in parts of Asia and Africa

Climate change

In 2001 the global mean temperature was 0.63°C higher than that at the end of the nineteenth century. Most of this warming is caused by human activities which result in a build-up of greenhouse gases, mainly carbon dioxide, allowing heat to be trapped within the atmosphere. Carbon dioxide emissions have increased since the beginning of the industrial revolution due to burning of fossil fuels, increased urbanization, population growth, deforestation and industrial pollution. Annual climate indicators such as number of frost-free days, length of growing season, heat wave frequency, number of wet days, length of dry spells and frequency of weather extremes are used to monitor climate change. The map highlights some events of 2001 which indicate climate change. Until carbon dioxide emissions are reduced it is likely that this trend will continue.

1. Warmest winter recorded in **Alaska and Yukon.**
2. Third warmest year on record in **Canada.**
3. Severe rainfall deficit in **northwest USA.**
4. Costliest storm in US history was tropical storm **Alison.**
5. Extreme summer drought in **Central America.**
6. Strongest hurricane to hit Cuba since 1952 was **Michelle.**

14. Continued drought in area around **Horn of Africa.**
15. Widespread minimum winter temperatures near -60°C in **Siberia and Mongolia.**
16. 1998 drought continues in **Southern Asia.**
17. Severe drought and water shortages in **Northern China, Korean Peninsula and Japan.**
18. Extensive flooding in September caused by Typhoon **Nari.**
19. Severe flooding August to October in **Vietnam and Cambodia.**

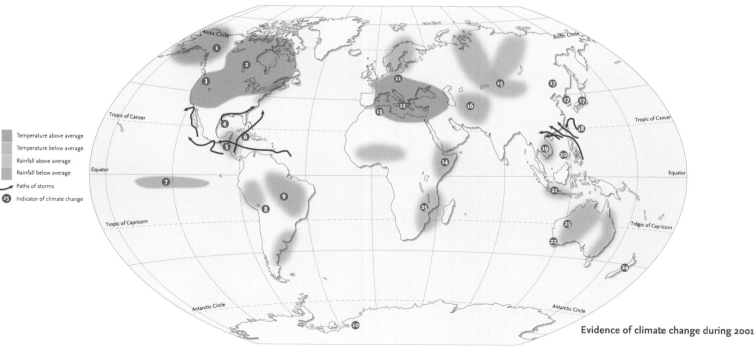

▮	Temperature above average
▮	Temperature below average
▮	Rainfall above average
▮	Rainfall below average
	Paths of storms
25	Indicator of climate change

Evidence of climate change during 2001

7. End of **La Niña** episode.
8. Severe flooding in **Bolivia.**
9. Normal rainy season hit by drought in **Brazil.**
10. Longer lasting ozone hole than previous years in **Antarctica.**
11. Worst flooding since 1997 in **southwest Poland and Czech Republic.**
12. Temperatures 1°–2°C above average for 2001 in **Europe and Middle East.**
13. Severe November flooding in **Algeria.**

20. Severe flooding causes more than 400 deaths when four tropical cyclones, **Durian, Yutu, Ulor and Toraji** made landfall in July.
21. Major flooding in February on **Java.**
22. Driest summer on record in **Perth.**
23. Cooler and wetter than normal in **Western Australia.**
24. One of the driest summers recorded in **New Zealand.**
25. Severe flooding February to April in **Mozambique, Zambia, Malawi and Zimbabwe.**

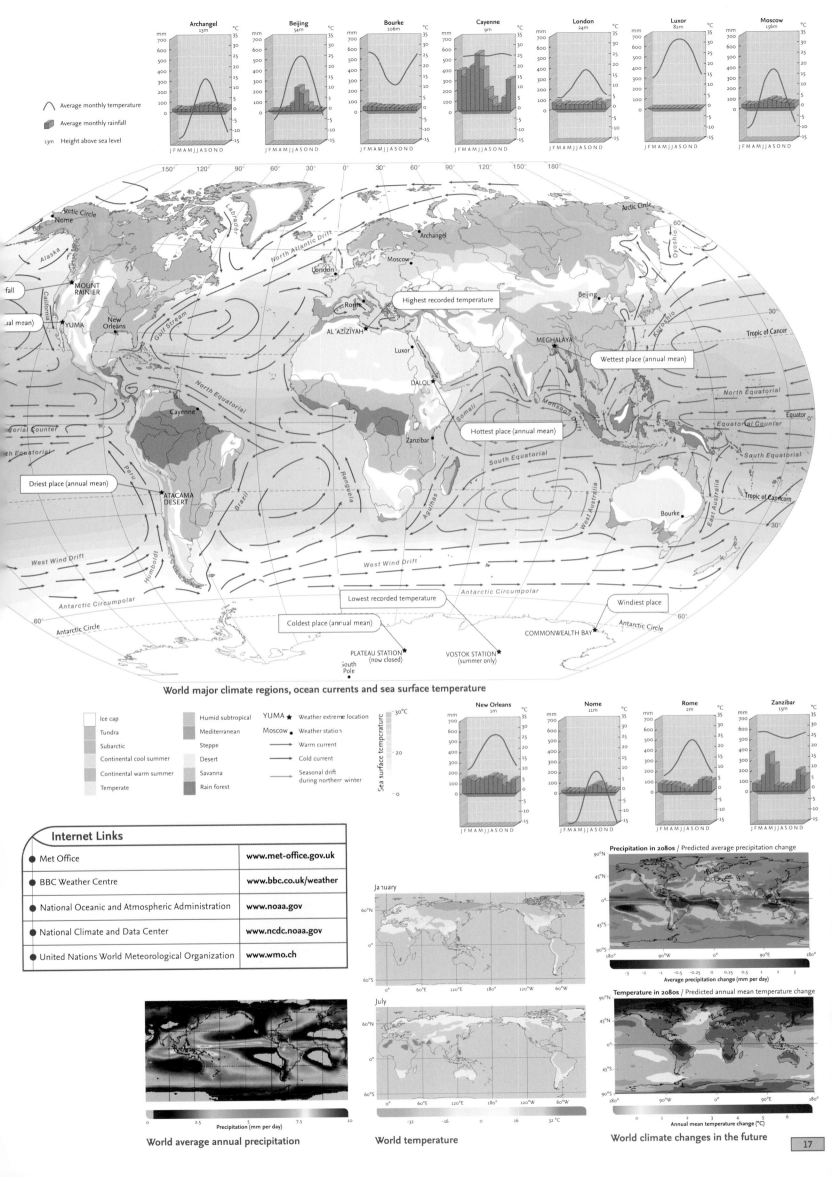

Archangel 13m
Beijing 54m
Bourke 106m
Cayenne 9m
London 24m
Luxor 82m
Moscow 156m

Average monthly temperature
Average monthly rainfall
13m Height above sea level

World major climate regions, ocean currents and sea surface temperature

Ice cap
Tundra
Subarctic
Continental cool summer
Continental warm summer
Temperate

Humid subtropical
Mediterranean
Steppe
Desert
Savanna
Rain forest

YUMA ★ Weather extreme location
Moscow ● Weather station
→ Warm current
→ Cold current
→ Seasonal drift during northern winter

Sea surface temperature

New Orleans 1m
Nome 11m
Rome 2m
Zanzibar 15m

January

July

Precipitation in 2080s / Predicted average precipitation change

Average precipitation change (mm per day)

Temperature in 2080s / Predicted annual mean temperature change

Annual mean temperature change (°C)

Precipitation (mm per day)

World average annual precipitation

World temperature

World climate changes in the future

17

The oxygen- and water- rich environment of the earth has helped create a wide range of habitats. Forest and woodland ecosystems form the predominant natural land cover over most of the earth's surface. Tropical rainforests are part of an intricate land-atmosphere relationship that is disturbed by land cover changes. Forests in the tropics are believed to hold most of the world's bird, animal, and plant species. Grassland, shrubland and deserts collectively cover most of the unwooded land surface, with tundra on frozen subsoil at high northern latitudes. These areas tend to have lower species diversity than most forests, with the notable exception of Mediterranean shrublands, which support some of the most diverse floras on the earth. Humans have extensively altered most grassland and shrubland areas, usually through conversion to agriculture, burning and introduction of domestic livestock. They have had less immediate impact on tundra and true desert regions, although these remain vulnerable to global climate change.

Evergreen needleleaf forest
Evergreen broadleaf forest
Deciduous needleleaf forest
Deciduous broadleaf forest
Mixed forest
Closed shrubland
Open shrubland
Woody savanna
Savanna
Grassland
Permanent wetland
Cropland
Urban and built-up
Cropland/Natural vegetation mosaic
Snow and Ice
Barren or sparsely vegetated
Water bodies

Snow and ice, Spitsbergen, Svalbard, inside the Arctic Circle.

World land cover
Map courtesy of IGBP, JRC and USGS

Urban, La Paz, Bolivia.

Land cover

The land cover map shown here was derived from data aquired by the Advanced Very High Resolution Radiometer sensor on board the polar orbiting satellites of the US National Oceanic and Atmospheric Administration. The high resolution (ground resolution of 1km) of the imagery used to compile the data set and map allows detailed interpretation of land cover patterns across the world. Important uses include managing forest resources, improving estimates of the earth's water and energy cycles, and modelling climate change.

Internet Links

World Resources Institute	**www.wri.org**
World Conservation Monitoring Centre	**www.unep-wcmc.org**
United Nations Environment Programme (UNEP)	**www.unep.org**
IUCN The World Conservation Union	**www.iucn.org**
Land Cover at Boston University	**geography.bu.edu/landcover/index.html**

Top 20 protected areas by size

Rank	Protected area	Country	Size (sq km)	Designation
1	Greenland	Greenland	972 000	National Park
2	Rub' al Khālī	Saudi Arabia	640 000	Wildlife Management Area
3	Great Barrier Reef Marine Park	Australia	344 360	Marine Park
4	Northwestern Hawaiian Islands	United States	341 362	Coral Reef Ecosystem Reserve
5	Amazonia	Colombia	326 329	Forest Reserve
6	Qiangtang	China	298 000	Nature Reserve
7	Macquarie Island	Australia	162 060	Marine Park
8	Sanjiangyuan	China	152 300	Nature Reserve
9	Cape Churchill	Canada	137 072	Wildlife Management Area
10	Galapagos Islands	Ecuador	133 000	Marine Reserve
11	Northern Wildlife Management Zone	Saudi Arabia	100 875	Wildlife Management Area
12	Ngaanyatjarra Lands	Australia	98 129	Indigeneous Protected Area
13	Alto Orinoco-Casiquiare	Venezuela	84 000	Biosphere Reserve
14	Vale do Javari	Brazil	83 380	Indigenous Area
15	Ouadi Rimé-Ouadi Achim	Chad	80 000	Faunal Reserve
16	Arctic	United States	78 049	National Wildlife Refuge
17	Yanomami	Brazil	77 519	Indigenous Park
18	Yukon Delta	United States	77 425	National Wildlife Refuge
19	Aïr and Ténéré	Niger	77 360	National Nature Reserve
20	Pacifico	Colombia	73 981	Forest Reserve

Great Barrier Reef, Australia, the world's 3rd largest protected area.

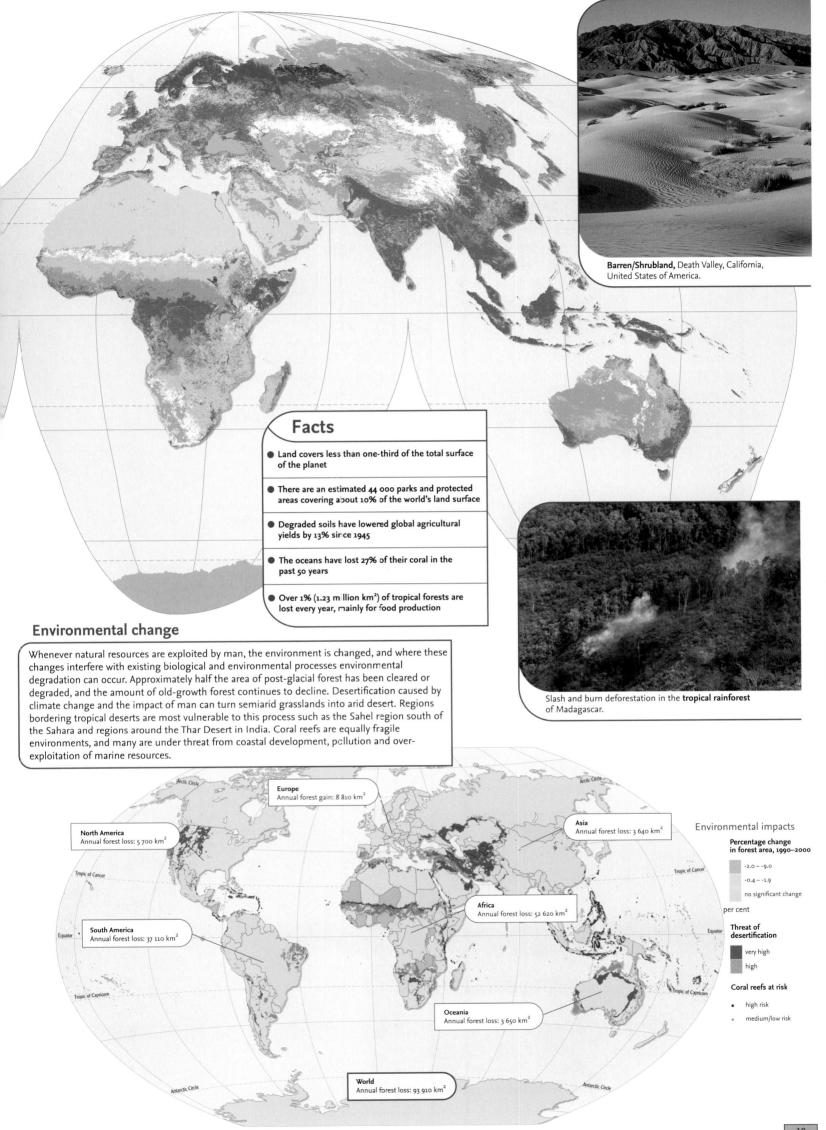

Barren/Shrubland, Death Valley, California, United States of America.

Facts

- Land covers less than one-third of the total surface of the planet

- There are an estimated 44 000 parks and protected areas covering about 10% of the world's land surface

- Degraded soils have lowered global agricultural yields by 13% since 1945

- The oceans have lost 27% of their coral in the past 50 years

- Over 1% (1.23 million km²) of tropical forests are lost every year, mainly for food production

Environmental change

Whenever natural resources are exploited by man, the environment is changed, and where these changes interfere with existing biological and environmental processes environmental degradation can occur. Approximately half the area of post-glacial forest has been cleared or degraded, and the amount of old-growth forest continues to decline. Desertification caused by climate change and the impact of man can turn semiarid grasslands into arid desert. Regions bordering tropical deserts are most vulnerable to this process such as the Sahel region south of the Sahara and regions around the Thar Desert in India. Coral reefs are equally fragile environments, and many are under threat from coastal development, pollution and over-exploitation of marine resources.

Slash and burn deforestation in the **tropical rainforest** of Madagascar.

Europe
Annual forest gain: 8 810 km²

North America
Annual forest loss: 5 700 km²

Asia
Annual forest loss: 3 640 km²

Africa
Annual forest loss: 52 620 km²

South America
Annual forest loss: 37 110 km²

Oceania
Annual forest loss: 3 650 km²

World
Annual forest loss: 93 910 km²

Environmental impacts

Percentage change in forest area, 1990–2000

- -2.0 – -9.0
- -0.4 – -1.9
- no significant change

per cent

Threat of desertification

- very high
- high

Coral reefs at risk

- high risk
- medium/low risk

After increasing very slowly for most of human history, world population more than doubled in the last half century. Whereas world population did not pass the one billion mark until 1804 and took another 123 years to reach two billion in 1927, it then added the third billion in 33 years, the fourth in 14 years and the fifth in 13 years. Just twelve years later on October 12, 1999 the United Nations announced that the global population had reached the six billion mark. It is expected that another three billion people will have been added to the world's population by 2050.

world statistics: see pages **154–160**

Facts

- The world's population is growing at an annual rate of 76 million people per year

- Today's population is only 5.7% of the total number of people who ever lived on the earth

- It is expected that in 2050 there will be more people aged over 60 than children aged less than 14

- More than 90% of the 70 million inhabitants of Egypt are located around the River Nile

- India's population reached 1 billion in August 1999

Top 20 countries by population density, 2003
(persons per square kilometre)

Rank	Country	Population density
1	Monaco	17 000
2	Singapore	6 656
3	Malta	1 247
4	Malcives	1 067
5	Bahrain	1 048
6	Bangladesh	1 019
7	Vatican City	944
8	Barbados	628
9	Taiwan	623
10	Nauru	612
11	Mauritius	593
12	South Korea	480
13	San Marino	459
14	Tuvalu	440
15	Comoros	412
16	Netherlands	383
17	Lebanon	350
18	India	343
19	Belgium	338
20	Japan	338

Top 20 countries by population, 2003

Rank	Country	Population
1	China	1 289 161 000
2	India	1 065 462 000
3	United States of America	294 043 000
4	Indonesia	219 883 000
5	Brazil	178 470 000
6	Pakistan	153 578 000
7	Bangladesh	146 736 000
8	Russian Federation	143 246 000
9	Japan	127 654 000
10	Nigeria	124 009 000
11	Mexico	103 457 000
12	Germany	82 476 000
13	Vietnam	81 377 000
14	Philippines	79 999 000
15	Egypt	71 931 000
16	Turkey	71 325 000
17	Ethiopia	70 678 000
18	Iran	68 920 000
19	Thailand	62 833 000
20	France	60 144 000

Population distribution

The world's population in mid-2003 had reached 6 301 million, over half of which live in six countries: China, India, USA, Indonesia, Brazil and Pakistan. Over 80% (5 098 million) of the total population live in less developed regions. As shown on the population distribution map, over a quarter of the land area is uninhabited or has extremely low population density. Barely a quarter of the land area is occupied at densities of 25 or more persons per square km, with the three largest concentrations in east Asia, the Indian subcontinent and Europe accounting for over half the world total.

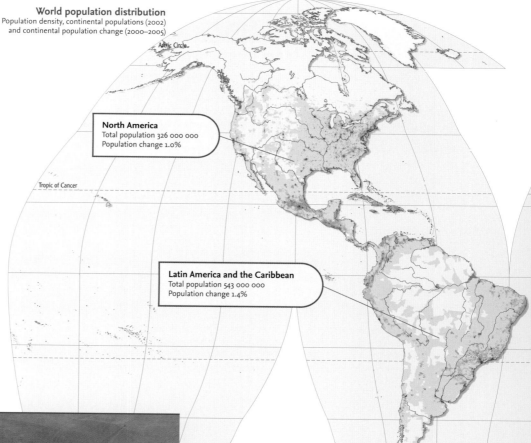

World population distribution
Population density, continental populations (2002) and continental population change (2000–2005)

Arctic Circle

North America
Total population 326 000 000
Population change 1.0%

Tropic of Cancer

Latin America and the Caribbean
Total population 543 000 000
Population change 1.4%

over 2 500	over 1 000
1 250 – 2 500	500 – 1 000
625 – 1 250	250 – 500
250 – 625	100 – 250
125 – 250	50 – 100
62.5 – 125	25 – 50
12.5 – 62.5	5 – 25
2.5 – 12.5	1 – 5
0 – 2.5	0 – 1
Uninhabited	Uninhabited
Inhabitants (per sq mile)	**Inhabitants** (per sq km)

Kuna Indians inhabit this congested island off the north coast of Panama.

Population change by country, 2000–2005
Average annual rate of population change (per cent) and the top ten contributors to world population growth (net annual addition)

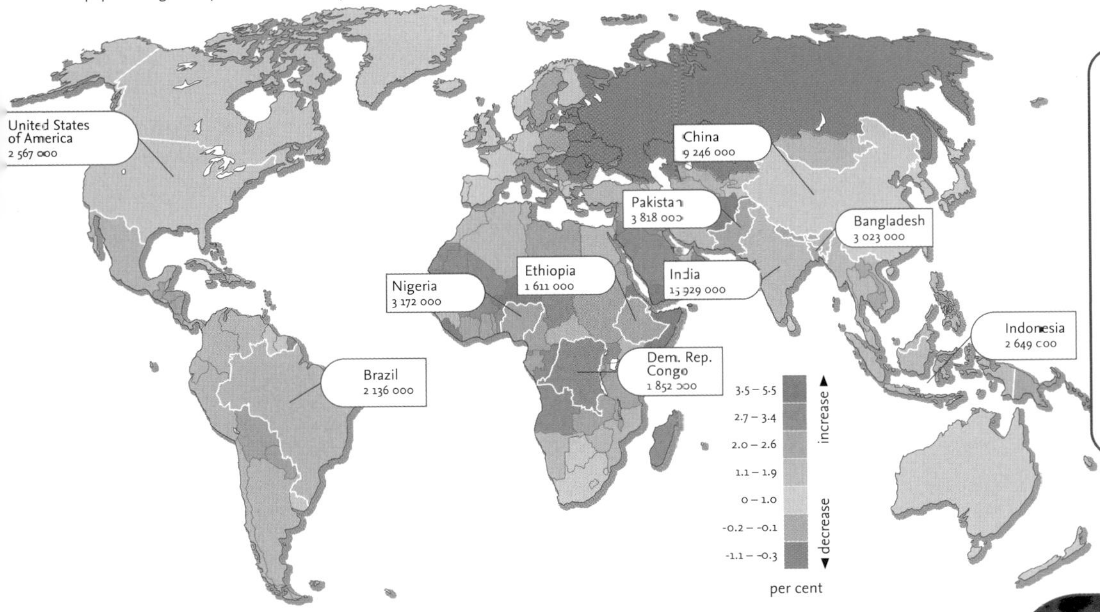
United States of America 2 567 000
China 9 246 000
Pakistan 3 818 000
Bangladesh 3 023 000
Nigeria 3 172 000
Ethiopia 1 611 000
India 15 929 000
Indonesia 2 649 000
Brazil 2 136 000
Dem. Rep. Congo 1 852 000
3.5 – 5.5
2.7 – 3.4
2.0 – 2.6
1.1 – 1.9
0 – 1.0
-0.2 – -0.1
-1.1 – -0.3
increase
decrease
per cent

World population change

Population growth since 1950 has been spread very unevenly between the continents. While overall numbers have been growing rapidly since 1950, a massive 89 per cent increase has taken place in the less developed regions, especially southern and eastern Asia. In contrast, Europe's population level has been almost stationary and is expected to decrease in the future. India and China alone are responsible for over one-third of current growth. But most of the highest rates of growth are to be found in Sub-Saharan Africa with Liberia and Sierra Leone experiencing the highest percentage increases in population between 2000 and 2005. Until population growth is brought under tighter control, the developing world in particular will continue to face enormous problems of supporting a rising population.

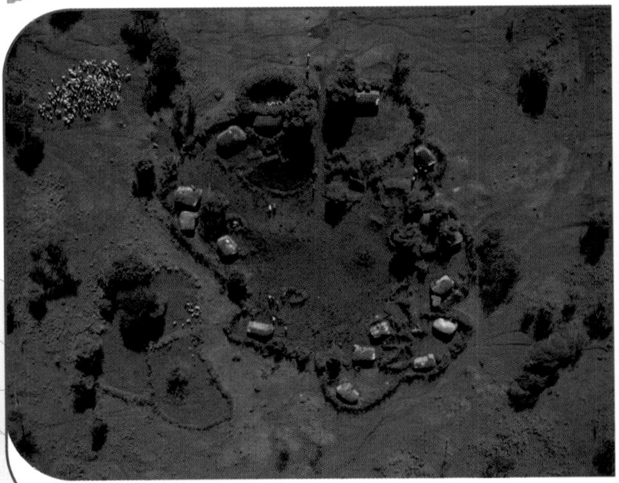

Masai village in sparsely populated southwest Kenya.

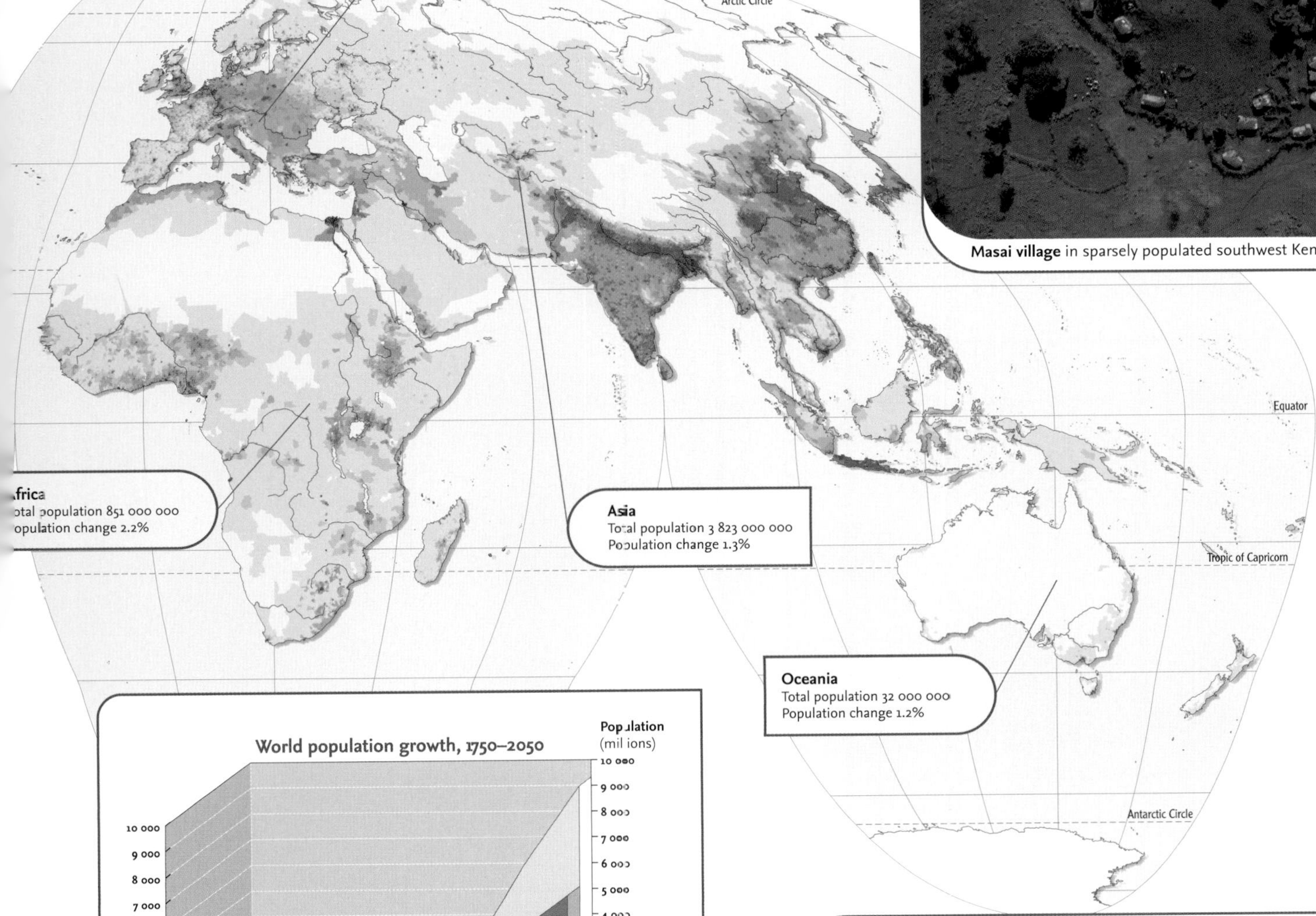
Europe
Total population 726 000 000
Population change -0.1%
World
Total population 6 301 000 000
Population change 1.2%
Arctic Circle
Africa
Total population 851 000 000
Population change 2.2%
Asia
Total population 3 823 000 000
Population change 1.3%
Equator
Tropic of Capricorn
Oceania
Total population 32 000 000
Population change 1.2%
Antarctic Circle

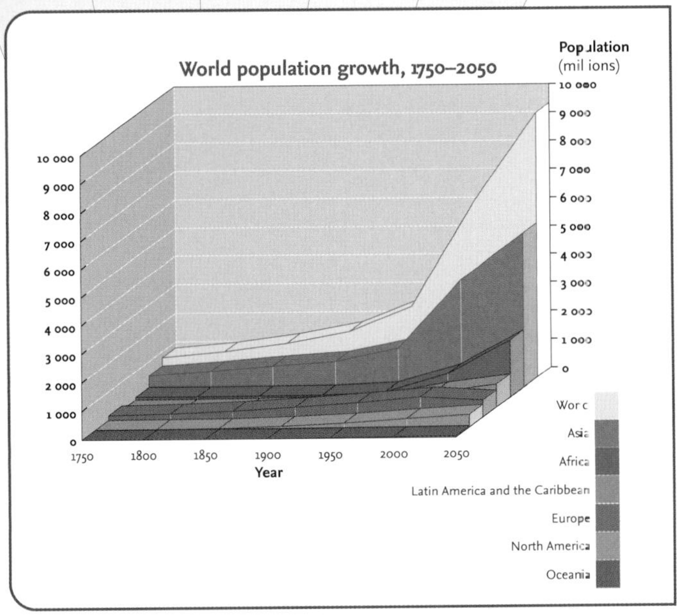
World population growth, 1750–2050
Population (millions)
10 000
9 000
8 000
7 000
6 000
5 000
4 000
3 000
2 000
1 000
0
1750
1800
1850
1900
1950
2000
2050
Year
World
Asia
Africa
Latin America and the Caribbean
Europe
North America
Oceania

Internet Links

United Nations Population Information Network	www.un.org/popin
US Census Bureau	www.census.gov
UK Census	www.statistics.gov.uk/census2001
Population Reference Bureau Pop Net	www.popnet.org
Socioeconomic Data and Applications Center	sedac.ciesin.columbia.edu

World Urbanization and Cities

The world is becoming increasingly urban but the level of urbanization varies greatly between and within continents. At the beginning of the twentieth century only fourteen per cent of the world's population was urban and by 1950 this had increased to thirty per cent. In the more developed regions and in Latin America and the Caribbean seventy per cent of the population is urban while in Africa and Asia the figure is less than one third. In recent decades urban growth has increased rapidly to nearly fifty per cent and there are now 387 cities with over 1 000 000 inhabitants. It is in the developing regions that the most rapid increases are taking place and it is expected that by 2030 over half of urban dwellers worldwide will live in Asia. Migration from the countryside to the city in the search for better job opportunities is the main factor in urban growth.

World Statistics: see pages 154–160

Facts

- Cities occupy less than 2% of the earth's land surface but house almost half of the human population

- Urban growth rates in Africa are the highest in the world

- Antarctica is uninhabited and most settlements in the Arctic regions have less than 5 000 inhabitants

- India has 32 cities with over one million inhabitants; by 2015 there will be 50

- London was the first city to reach a population of over 5 million

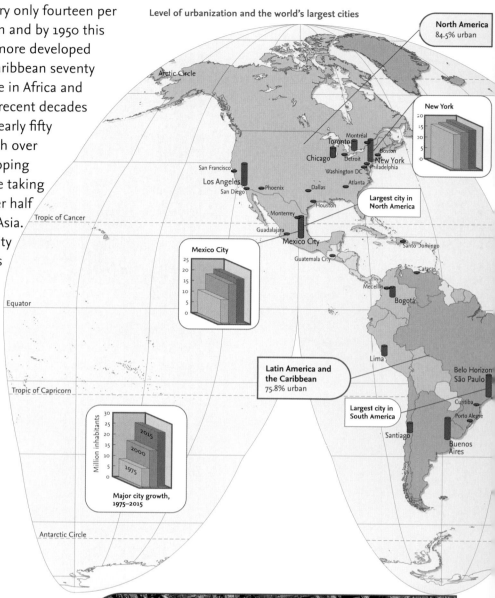

Level of urbanization and the world's largest cities

North America
84.5% urban

New York

Largest city in North America

Mexico City

Largest city in South America

Latin America and the Caribbean
75.8% urban

Major city growth, 1975–2015

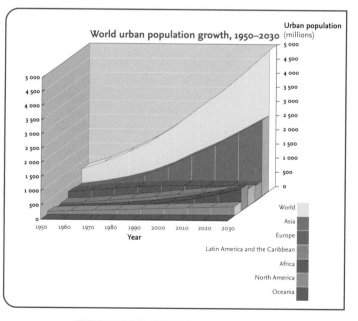

World urban population growth, 1950–2030

Urban population (millions)

World
Asia
Europe
Latin America and the Caribbean
Africa
North America
Oceania

Characteristic high-rise development and densely packed low-rise buildings in Tōkyō, the world's largest city.

Internet Links

United Nations Population Division	www.un.org/esa/population/unpop.htm
United Nations World Urbanization Prospects	www.un.org/esa/population/publications/wup2003/2003WUP.htm
United Nations Population Information Network	www.un.org/popin
The World Bank - Urban Development	www.worldbank.org/urban/
City Populations	www.citypopulation.de

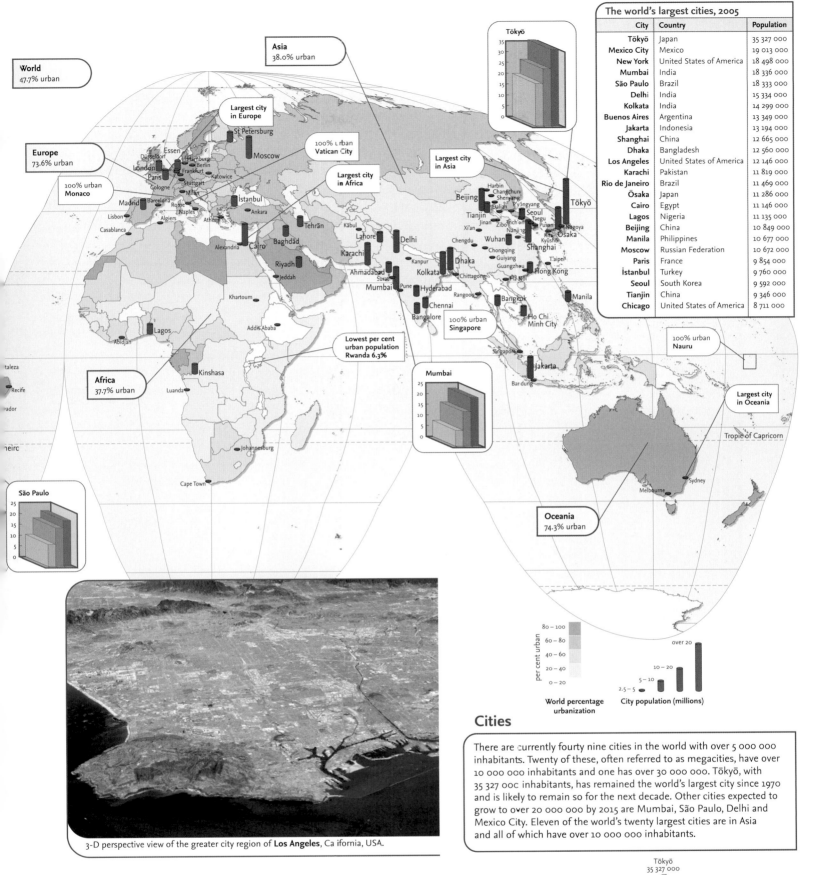

World 47.7% urban

Europe 73.6% urban

100% urban **Monaco**

Africa 37.7% urban

Asia 38.0% urban

Largest city in Europe

100% urban **Vatican City**

Largest city in Africa

Largest city in Asia

Tōkyō

Lowest per cent urban population Rwanda 6.3%

100% urban **Singapore**

Mumbai

100% urban **Nauru**

Largest city in Oceania

São Paulo

Oceania 74.3% urban

Tropic of Capricorn

City labels on map: St Petersburg, Moscow, Düsseldorf, Essen, Hamburg, Berlin, London, Frankfurt, Paris, Cologne, Stuttgart, Katowice, Milan, Madrid, Barcelona, Rome, Naples, İstanbul, Ankara, Lisbon, Algiers, Athens, Casablanca, Alexandria, Cairo, Baghdad, Tehrān, Kābul, Lahore, Delhi, Riyadh, Jeddah, Karachi, Kanpur, Ahmadabad, Surat, Kolkata, Mumbai, Pune, Hyderabad, Chittagong, Chennai, Bangalore, Dhaka, Khartoum, Addis Ababa, Lagos, Abidjan, Kinshasa, Luanda, Johannesburg, Cape Town, Harbin, Changchun, Shenyang, Dalian, Beijing, Pyŏngyang, Tianjin, Jinan, Zibo, Inch'on, Seoul, Taegu, Pusan, Xi'an, Nanjing, Nagoya, Tōkyō, Ōsaka, Kyūshū, Chengdu, Wuhan, Shanghai, Chongqing, Guiyang, Guangzhou, T'aipei, Hong Kong, Hà Nôi, Rangoon, Bangkok, Ho Chi Minh City, Manila, Singapore, Jakarta, Bandung, Sydney, Melbourne, Recife, Fortaleza, Salvador, heiro

The world's largest cities, 2005

City	Country	Population
Tōkyō	Japan	35 327 000
Mexico City	Mexico	19 013 000
New York	United States of America	18 498 000
Mumbai	India	18 336 000
São Paulo	Brazil	18 333 000
Delhi	India	15 334 000
Kolkata	India	14 299 000
Buenos Aires	Argentina	13 349 000
Jakarta	Indonesia	13 194 000
Shanghai	China	12 665 000
Dhaka	Bangladesh	12 560 000
Los Angeles	United States of America	12 146 000
Karachi	Pakistan	11 819 000
Rio de Janeiro	Brazil	11 469 000
Ōsaka	Japan	11 286 000
Cairo	Egypt	11 146 000
Lagos	Nigeria	11 135 000
Beijing	China	10 849 000
Manila	Philippines	10 677 000
Moscow	Russian Federation	10 672 000
Paris	France	9 854 000
İstanbul	Turkey	9 760 000
Seoul	South Korea	9 592 000
Tianjin	China	9 346 000
Chicago	United States of America	8 711 000

per cent urban
80 — 100
60 — 80
40 — 60
20 — 40
0 — 20

World percentage urbanization

City population (millions)
over 20
10 – 20
5 – 10
2.5 – 5

City population (millions)

Cities

There are currently fourty nine cities in the world with over 5 000 000 inhabitants. Twenty of these, often referred to as megacities, have over 10 000 000 inhabitants and one has over 30 000 000. Tōkyō, with 35 327 000 inhabitants, has remained the world's largest city since 1970 and is likely to remain so for the next decade. Other cities expected to grow to over 20 000 000 by 2015 are Mumbai, São Paulo, Delhi and Mexico City. Eleven of the world's twenty largest cities are in Asia and all of which have over 10 000 000 inhabitants.

3-D perspective view of the greater city region of **Los Angeles**, California, USA.

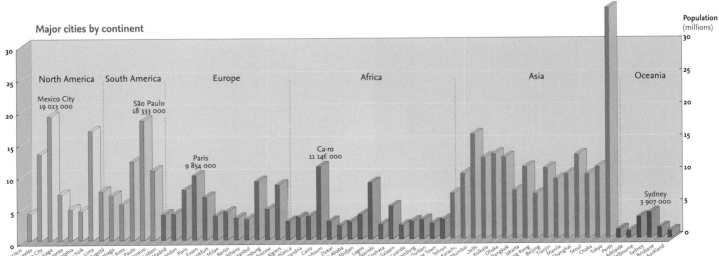

Major cities by continent

Population (millions)

North America — South America — Europe — Africa — Asia — Oceania

Mexico City 19 013 000

São Paulo 18 333 000

Paris 9 854 000

Cairo 11 146 000

Tōkyō 35 327 000

Sydney 3 907 000

City axis labels: San Francisco, Los Angeles, Mexico City, Chicago, Toronto, Philadelphia, New York, Lima, Bogotá, Santiago, Buenos Aires, São Paulo, Rio de Janeiro, Lisbon, Madrid, London, Paris, Essen, Frankfurt, Milan, Berlin, Athens, İstanbul, St Petersburg, Moscow, Algiers, Casablanca, Alexandria, Cairo, Khartoum, Addis Ababa, Abidjan, Lagos, Nairobi, Kinshasa, Luanda, Dar es Salaam, Durban, Johannesburg, Cape Town, Tehran, Karachi, Mumbai, Delhi, Kolkata, Dhaka, Bangkok, Hong Kong, Jakarta, Beijing, Tianjin, Manila, Shanghai, Seoul, Ōsaka, Tokyo, Perth, Adelaide, Melbourne, Sydney, Brisbane, Auckland

Increased availability and ownership of telecommunications equipment since the beginning of the 1970s has aided the globalization of the world economy. Over half of the world's fixed telephone lines have been installed since the mid-1980s and the majority of the world's internet hosts have come on line since 1997. There are now over one billion fixed telephone lines in the world. The number of mobile cellular subscribers has grown dramatically from sixteen million in 1991 to well over one billion today.

The internet is the fastest growing communications network of all time. It is relatively cheap and now links over 140 million host computers globally. Its growth has resulted in the emergence of hundreds of Internet Service Providers (ISPs) and internet traffic is now doubling every six months. In 1993 the number of internet users was estimated to be just under ten million, there are now over half a billion.

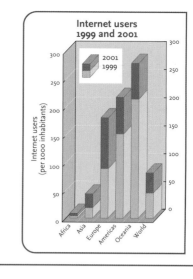

Internet users 1999 and 2001

Internet Links

● OECD Information and Communication Technologies	**www.oecd.org**
● Telegeography Inc.	**www.telegeography.com**
● International Telecommunication Union	**www.itu.int**

Internet users per 1 000 inhabitants

- over 200
- 150 – 200
- 100 – 149
- 10 – 99
- 0 – 9
- no data

- 0.0 – 0.3
- 1.0 – 4.5
- 5.0 – 24.9
- 25.0 – 125.0

Major interregional internet routes

○ London

Internet hub cities, 2001

Internet users and major Internet routes

The Internet

The Internet is a global network of millions of computers around the world, all capable of being connected to each other. Internet Service Providers (ISPs) provide access via 'host' computers, of which there are now over 140 million. It has become a vital means of communication and data transfer for businesses, governments and financial and academic institutions, with a steadily increasing proportion of business transactions being carried out on-line.

A visualization of **global internet traffic**. Each line represents the path of a data probe sent to specific internet locations.

Top 20 Internet Service Providers (ISPs)

Internet Service	Web Address	Subscribers (000s)
AOL (USA)	www.aol.com	20 500
T-Online (Germany)	www.t-online.de	4 151
Nifty-Serve (Japan)	www.nifty.com	3 500
EarthLink (USA)	www.earthlink.com	3 122
Biglobe (Japan)	www.biglobe.ne.jp	2 720
MSN (USA)	www.msn.com	2 700
Chollian (South Korea)	www.chollian.net	2 000
Tin.it (Italy)	www.tin.it	1 990
Freeserve (UK)	www.freeserve.com	1 575
AT&T WorldNet (USA)	www.att.net	1 500
Prodigy (USA)	www.prodigy.com	1 502
NetZero (USA)	www.netzero.com	1 450
Terra Networks (Spain)	www.terra.es	1 317
HiNet (Taiwan-China)	www.hinet.net	1 200
Wanadoo (France)	www.wanadoo.fr	1 124
AltaVista	www.microav.com	750
Freei (USA)	www.freei.com	750
SBC Internet Services	www.sbc.com	720
Telia Internet (Sweden)	www.telia.se	613
Netvigator (Hongkong SAR)	www.netvigator.com	561

Satellite communications

International telecommunications use either fibre-optic cables or satellites as transmission media. Although cables carry the vast majority of traffic around the world, communications satellites are important for person-to-person communication, including cellular telephones, and for broadcasting. The positions of communications satellites are critical to their use, and reflect the demand for such communications in each part of the world. Such satellites are placed in 'geostationary' orbit 36 000 km above the equator. This means that they move at the same speed as the earth and remain fixed above a single point on the earth's surface.

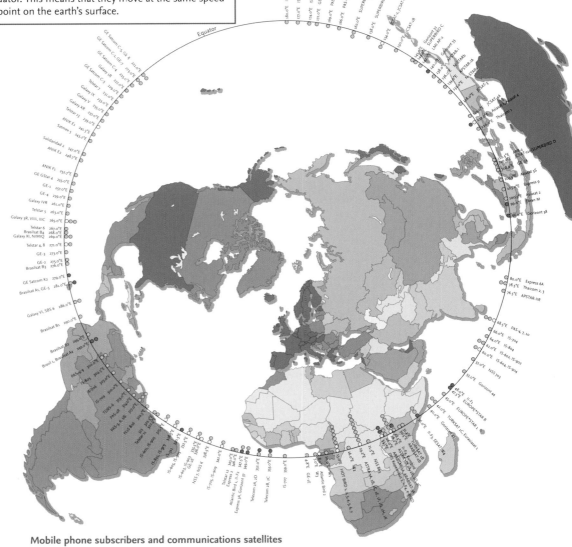

Cellular mobile subscribers per 100 inhabitants

- over 40
- 15 – 39.9
- 5 – 14.9
- 1.5 – 4.9
- 0.5 – 1.4
- 0 – 0.4
- no data

Geostationary communications satellites
- ◉ In service
- ● Inclined orbit
- ○ Planned

Facts

- Luxembourg has the world's highest density of telephone lines per person with more telephones than Bangladesh – a country with more than 300 times as many people.

- Fibre-optic cables can now carry approximately 20 million simultaneous telephone calls

- The first transatlantic telegraph cable came into operation in 1858

- The internet is the fastest growing communications network of all time and now has over 140 million host computers

- Sputnik, the world's first artificial satellite, was launched in 1957

Mobile phone subscribers and communications satellites

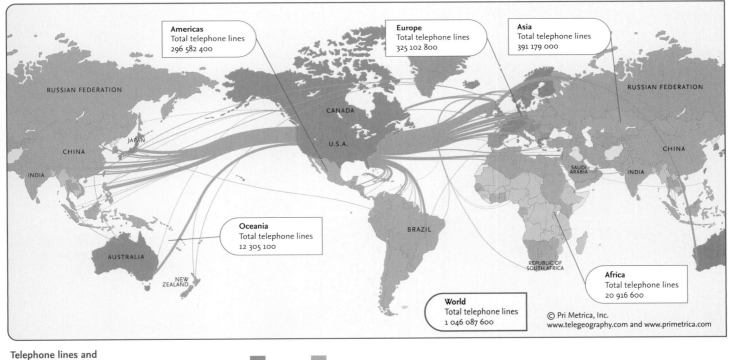

Americas
Total telephone lines
296 582 400

Europe
Total telephone lines
325 102 800

Asia
Total telephone lines
391 179 000

Oceania
Total telephone lines
12 305 100

Africa
Total telephone lines
20 916 600

World
Total telephone lines
1 046 087 600

© Pri Metrica, Inc.
www.telegeography.com and www.primetrica.com

Telephone lines and telecommunications traffic

Telephone lines per 100 inhabitants
- over 50.0
- 35.0 – 50.0
- 15.0 – 34.9
- 10.0 – 14.9
- 5.0 – 9.9
- 1.0 – 4.9
- 0 – 0.9
- no data

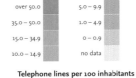

Traffic flows

Million minutes of telecommunications traffic (mMiTTs)
5 000   2 500   1 000   100

25

Countries are often judged on their level of economic development, but national and personal wealth are not the only measures of a country's status. Numerous other indicators can give a better picture of the overall level of development and standard of living achieved by a country. The availability and standard of health services, levels of educational provision and attainment, levels of nutrition, water supply, life expectancy and mortality rates are just some of the factors which can be measured to assess and compare countries.

While nations strive to improve their economies, and hopefully also to improve the standard of living of their citizens, the measurement of such indicators often exposes great discrepancies between the countries of the 'developed' world and those of the 'less developed' world. They also show great variations within continents and regions and at the same time can hide great inequalities within countries.

World Statistics: see pages 154–160

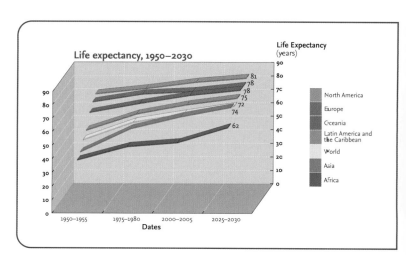

Life expectancy, 1950–2030

Life Expectancy (years)

- North America
- Europe
- Oceania
- Latin America and the Caribbean
- World
- Asia
- Africa

Internet Links	
● United Nation Development Programme	**www.undp.org**
● World Health Organization	**www.who.int**
● United Nations Statistics Division	**unstats.un.org**
● United Nations Millennium Development Goals	**millenniumindicators.un.org**

UN Millennium Development Goals
From the Millennium Declaration, 2000

Goal 1	Eradicate extreme poverty and hunger
Goal 2	Achieve universal primary education
Goal 3	Promote gender equality and empower women
Goal 4	Reduce child mortality
Goal 5	Improve maternal health
Goal 6	Combat HIV/AIDS, malaria and other diseases
Goal 7	Ensure environmental sustainability
Goal 8	Develop a global partnership for development

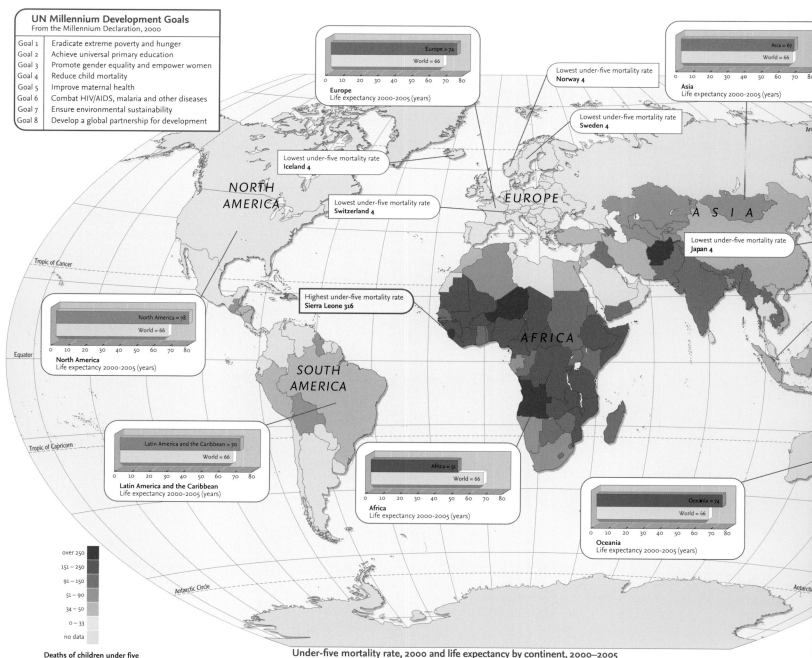

Europe = 74
World = 66

Europe
Life expectancy 2000-2005 (years)

Asia = 67
World = 66

Asia
Life expectancy 2000-2005 (years)

Lowest under-five mortality rate
Norway 4

Lowest under-five mortality rate
Sweden 4

Lowest under-five mortality rate
Iceland 4

Lowest under-five mortality rate
Switzerland 4

Lowest under-five mortality rate
Japan 4

NORTH AMERICA

EUROPE

ASIA

Highest under-five mortality rate
Sierra Leone 316

AFRICA

North America = 78
World = 66

North America
Life expectancy 2000-2005 (years)

SOUTH AMERICA

Latin America and the Caribbean = 70
World = 66

Latin America and the Caribbean
Life expectancy 2000-2005 (years)

Africa = 51
World = 66

Africa
Life expectancy 2000-2005 (years)

Oceania = 74
World = 66

Oceania
Life expectancy 2000-2005 (years)

Tropic of Cancer

Equator

Tropic of Capricorn

Antarctic Circle

- over 250
- 151 – 250
- 91 – 150
- 51 – 90
- 34 – 50
- 0 – 33
- no data

Deaths of children under five per 1 000 live births

Under-five mortality rate, 2000 and life expectancy by continent, 2000–2005

Outdoor education at a school in Bahia state, northeast Brazil.

Measuring development

Measuring the extent to which a country is 'developed' is difficult, and although there have been many attempts to standardize techniques there is no universally accepted method. One commonly used measure is the Human Development Index (HDI), which is based on a combination of statistics relating to life expectancy, education (literacy and school enrolment) and wealth (Gross Domestic Product – GDP).

At the Millennium Summit in September 2000, the United Nations identified eight Millennium Development Goals (MDGs) which aim to combat poverty, hunger, disease, illiteracy, environmental degradation and discrimination against women. Forty eight indicators have been identified which will measure the progress each country is making towards achieving these goals.

Facts

● Of the 10 countries with under-5 mortality rates of more than 200, 9 are in Africa

● Many western countries believe they have achieved satisfactory levels of education and no longer closely monitor levels of literacy

● Children born in Nepal have only a 12% chance of their birth being attended by trained health personnel, for most European countries the figure is 100%

● The illiteracy rate among young women in the Middle East and north Africa is almost twice the rate for young men.

Lowest under-five mortality rate
Singapore 4

Tropic of Cancer

Equator

Tropic of Capricorn

OCEANIA

Literacy rate, 2002
Percentage of population aged 15–24 with at least a basic ability to read and write

per cent
96 – 100
86 – 95
66 – 85
41 – 65
0 – 40
no data

Doctors per 100 000 people
Number of trained doctors per 100 000 people

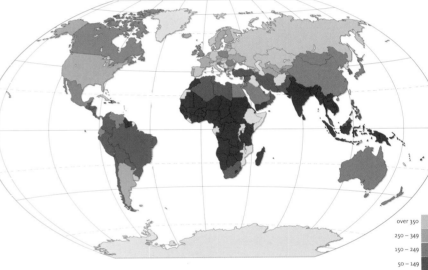

over 350
250 – 349
150 – 249
50 – 149
0 – 49
no data

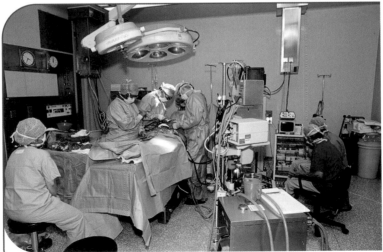
High class **health care facilities** such as these are not available in many parts of the world.

Health and education

Perhaps the most important indicators used for measuring the level of national development are those relating to health and education. Both of these key areas are vital to the future development of a country, and if there are concerns in standards attained in either (or worse, in both) of these, then they may indicate fundamental problems within the country concerned. The ability to read and write (literacy) is seen as vital in educating people and encouraging development, while easy access to appropriate health services and specialists is an important requirement in maintaining satisfactory levels of basic health.

Human Development Index (HDI), 2002	
Top 10	
Rank	Country
1	Norway
2	Sweden
3	Canada
4	Belgium
5	Australia
6	USA
7	Iceland
8	Netherlands
9	Japan
10	Finland
Bottom 10	
Rank	Country
164	Mali
165	Central African Republic
166	Chad
167	Guinea-Bissau
168	Ethiopia
169	Burkina
170	Mozambique
171	Burundi
172	Niger
173	Sierra Leone

World Economy and Wealth

The globalization of the economy is making the world appear a smaller place. However, this shrinkage is an uneven process. Countries are being included in and excluded from the global economy to differing degrees. The wealthy countries of the developed world, with their market-led economies, access to productive new technologies and international markets, dominate the world economic system. Great inequalities exist between and also within countries. There may also be discrepancies between social groups within countries due to gender and ethnic divisions. Differences between countries are evident by looking at overall wealth on a national and individual level.

World Statistics: see pages 154–160

The City, London, the world's largest financial centre.

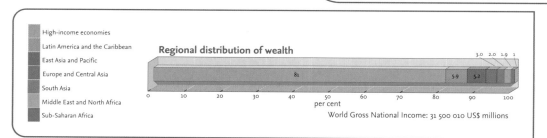

Regional distribution of wealth

High-income economies
Latin America and the Caribbean
East Asia and Pacific
Europe and Central Asia
South Asia
Middle East and North Africa
Sub-Saharan Africa

World Gross National Income: 31 500 010 US$ millions

Facts

- The City, one of 33 London boroughs, is the world's largest financial centre and contains Europe's biggest stock market

- Half the world's population earns only 5% of the world's wealth

- During the second half of the 20th century rich countries gave over US$1 trillion in aid

- For every £1 in grant aid to developing countries, more than £13 comes back in debt repayments

- On average, The World Bank distributes US$30 billion each year between 100 countries

Personal wealth

A poverty line set at $1 a day has been accepted as the working definition of extreme poverty in low-income countries. It is estimated that a total of 1.2 billion people live below that poverty line. This indicator has also been adopted by the United Nations in relation to their Millennium Development Goals. The United Nations goal is to halve the proportion of people living on less than $1 a day in 1990 to 14.5 per cent by 2015. Today, over 80 per cent of the total population of Ethiopia, Uganda and Nicaragua live on less than this amount.

Percentage of population living on less than $1 a day

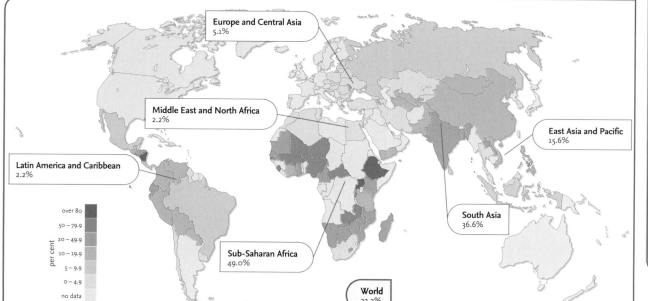

Europe and Central Asia
5.1%

Middle East and North Africa
2.2%

East Asia and Pacific
15.6%

Latin America and Caribbean
2.2%

South Asia
36.6%

Sub-Saharan Africa
49.0%

World
23.2%

per cent
- over 80
- 50 – 79.9
- 20 – 49.9
- 10 – 19.9
- 5 – 9.9
- 0 – 4.9
- no data

Gross National Income per capita

Highest

Rank	Country	US$ 2001
1	Luxembourg	41 770
2	Switzerland	36 970
3	Japan	35 990
4	Norway	35 530
5	United States	34 870
6	Denmark	31 090
7	Iceland	28 880
8	Sweden	25 400
9	United Kingdom	24 230
10	Netherlands	24 040

Lowest

Rank	Country	US$ 2001
150	Mozambique	210
151	Chad	200
152	Eritrea	190
153	Tajikistan	170
154	Malawi	170
155	Niger	170
156	Guinea-Bissau	160
157	Sierra Leone	140
158	Burundi	100
159	Ethiopia	100

Key economic indicators by region

	World	High-income economies	East Asia and Pacific	Europe and Central Asia	Latin America and The Caribbean	Middle East and North Africa	South Asia	Sub-Saharan Africa
Gross National Income (US$ millions)	31 500 010	25 506 410	1 649 435	930 455	1 861 820	601 270	615 596	317 045
Gross National Income per capita (US$)	5 170	27 680	1 060	2 010	3 670	2 090	440	470
Gross Domestic Product (US$ millions)	31 283 840	25 103 680	1 664 211	986 652	1 943 350	no data	615 307	315 269
Gross Domestic Product growth (annual %, US$ millions)	1.41	1.07	5.49	2.50	0.42	no data	4.39	3.00
Aid per capita received (US$)	9.64	1.99	4.68	22.91	9.67	15.63	3.13	20.42
External debt, total (US$ millions)	no data	no data	632 953	499 344	774 418	203 785	164 375	215 794
Official development assistance and official aid received (US$ millions)	58 369	1 387	8 463	10 867	4 987	4 609	4 241	13 453
Total debt service (US$ millions)	no data	no data	92 730	74 902	179 221	24 921	14 517	12 342

Gross National Income per capita

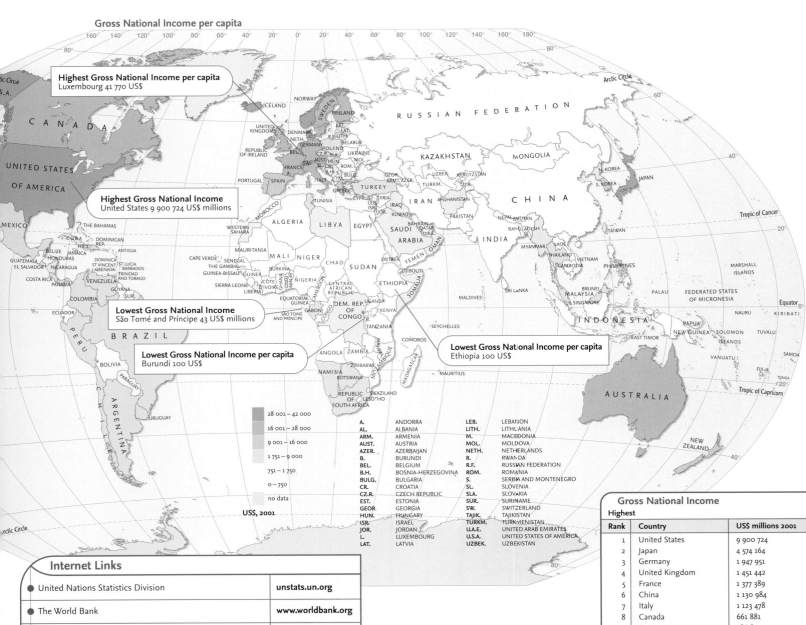

Highest Gross National Income per capita
Luxembourg 41 770 US$

Highest Gross National Income
United States 9 900 724 US$ millions

Lowest Gross National Income
São Tomé and Príncipe 43 US$ millions

Lowest Gross National Income per capita
Burundi 100 US$

Lowest Gross National Income per capita
Ethiopia 100 US$

28 001 – 42 000
16 001 – 28 000
9 001 – 16 000
1 751 – 9 000
751 – 1 750
0 – 750
no data

US$, 2001

A.	ANDORRA	LEB.	LEBANON
AL.	ALBANIA	LITH.	LITHUANIA
ARM.	ARMENIA	M.	MACEDONIA
AUST.	AUSTRIA	MOL.	MOLDOVA
AZER.	AZERBAIJAN	NETH.	NETHERLANDS
B.	BURUNDI	R.	RWANDA
BEL.	BELGIUM	R.F.	RUSSIAN FEDERATION
B.H.	BOSNIA-HERZEGOVINA	ROM.	ROMANIA
BULG.	BULGARIA	S.	SERBIA AND MONTENEGRO
CR.	CROATIA	SLA.	SLOVENIA
CZ.R.	CZECH REPUBLIC	SLA.	SLOVAKIA
EST.	ESTONIA	SUR.	SURINAME
GEOR.	GEORGIA	SW.	SWITZERLAND
HUN.	HUNGARY	TAJIK.	TAJIKISTAN
ISR.	ISRAEL	TURKM.	TURKMENISTAN
JOR.	JORDAN	U.A.E.	UNITED ARAB EMIRATES
L.	LUXEMBOURG	U.S.A.	UNITED STATES OF AMERICA
LAT.	LATVIA	UZBEK.	UZBEKISTAN

Internet Links

United Nations Statistics Division	unstats.un.org
The World Bank	www.worldbank.org
International Monetary Fund	www.imf.org
Organisation for Economic Co-operation and Development	www.oecd.org

Measuring wealth

One of the indicators used to determine a country's wealth is its Gross National Income (GNI). This gives a broad measure of an economy's performance. This is the value of the final output of goods and services produced by a country plus net income from non-resident sources. The total GNI is divided by the country's population to give an average figure of the GNI per capita. From this it is evident that the developed countries dominate the world economy with the United States having the highest GNI. China is a growing world economic player with the sixth highest GNI figure and a relatively high GNI per capita (US$890) in proportion to its huge population.

Rural homesteads, **Sudan** – most of the world's poorest countries are in Africa.

Gross National Income

Highest

Rank	Country	US$ millions 2001
1	United States	9 900 724
2	Japan	4 574 164
3	Germany	1 947 951
4	United Kingdom	1 451 442
5	France	1 377 389
6	China	1 130 984
7	Italy	1 123 478
8	Canada	661 881
9	Spain	586 874
10	Mexico	550 456

Lowest

Rank	Country	US$ millions 2001
150	Solomon Islands	253
151	Dominica	224
152	Comoros	217
153	Vanuatu	212
154	Guinea-bissau	202
155	Tonga	154
156	Palau	132
157	Marshall Islands	115
158	Kiribati	77
159	São Tomé and Príncipe	43

The world's biggest companies

Rank	Name	Sales (US$ millions)
1	Wal-Mart Stores	256 330
2	BP	232 570
3	ExxonMobil	222 880
4	General Motors	185 520
5	Ford Motor	164 200
6	DaimlerChrysler	157 130
7	Toyota Motor	135 820
8	General Electric	134 190
9	Royal Dutch/Shell Group	133 500
10	Total	131 640

World Conflict

Geo-political issues shape the countries of the world and the current political situation in many parts of the world reflects a long history of armed conflict. Since the Second World War conflicts have been fairly localized, but there are numerous 'flash points' where factors such as territorial claims, ideology, religion, ethnicity and access to resources can cause friction between two or more countries. Such factors also lie behind the recent growth in global terrorism.

Military expenditure can take up a disproportionate amount of a country's wealth – Eritrea, with a Gross National Income (GNI) per capita of only US$190 spends over twenty seven per cent of its total GNI on military activity. There is an encouraging trend towards wider international cooperation, mainly through the United Nations (UN) and the North Atlantic Treaty Organization (NATO), to prevent escalation of conflicts and on peacekeeping missions.

Facts

- There have been nearly 70 civil or internal wars throughout the world since 1945
- The Iran-Iraq war in the 1980s is estimated to have cost half a million lives
- The UN are currently involved in 15 peacekeeping operations
- It is estimated that there are nearly 20 million refugees throughout the world
- Over 1 600 UN peacekeepers have been killed since 1948

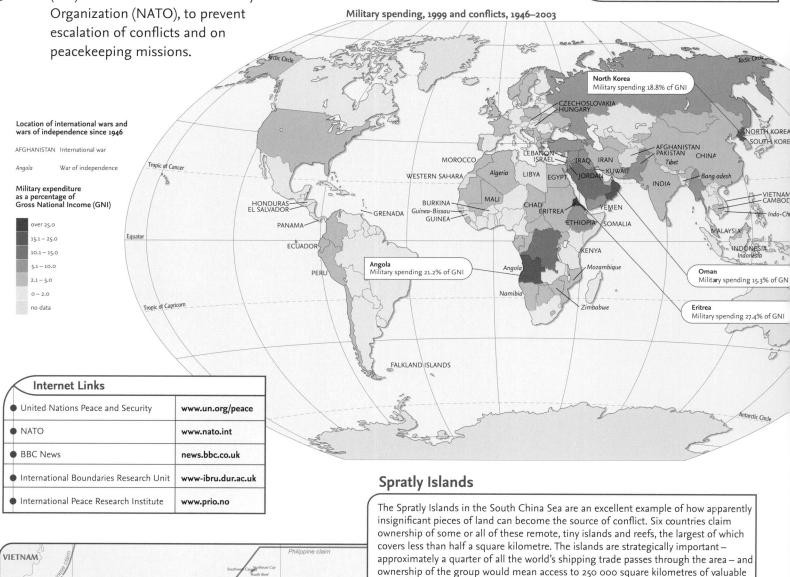

Military spending, 1999 and conflicts, 1946–2003

North Korea Military spending 18.8% cf GNI

Angola Military spending 21.2% of GNI

Oman Military spending 15.3% of GN

Eritrea Military spending 27.4% of GNI

Location of international wars and wars of independence since 1946

AFGHANISTAN   International war

Angola   War of independence

Military expenditure as a percentage of Gross National Income (GNI)

- over 25.0
- 15.1 – 25.0
- 10.1 – 15.0
- 5.1 – 10.0
- 2.1 – 5.0
- 0 – 2.0
- no data

Internet Links

United Nations Peace and Security	www.un.org/peace
NATO	www.nato.int
BBC News	news.bbc.co.uk
International Boundaries Research Unit	www.ibru.dur.ac.uk
International Peace Research Institute	www.prio.no

Spratly Islands

The Spratly Islands in the South China Sea are an excellent example of how apparently insignificant pieces of land can become the source of conflict. Six countries claim ownership of some or all of these remote, tiny islands and reefs, the largest of which covers less than half a square kilometre. The islands are strategically important – approximately a quarter of all the world's shipping trade passes through the area – and ownership of the group would mean access to 250 000 square kilometres of valuable fishing grounds and sea bed believed to be rich in oil and gas reserves. Five of the claimant countries have occupied individual islands to endorse their claims, although there appears little prospect of international agreement on ownership.

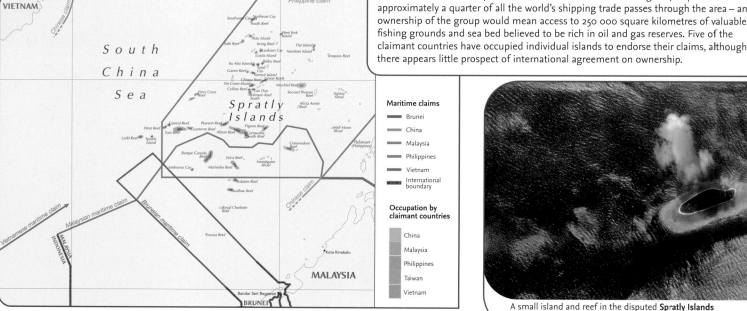

Maritime claims
- Brunei
- China
- Malaysia
- Philippines
- Vietnam
- International boundary

Occupation by claimant countries
- China
- Malaysia
- Philippines
- Taiwan
- Vietnam

A small island and reef in the disputed **Spratly Islands** in the South China Sea.

Terrorist incidents, 1998–2003

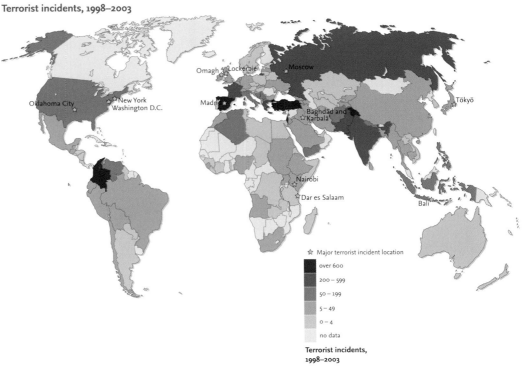

⭐ Major terrorist incident location

- over 600
- 200 – 599
- 50 – 199
- 5 – 49
- 0 – 4
- no data

Terrorist incidents, 1998–2003

Investigators inspect wreckage outside the Neve Shalom synagogue, **Istanbul, Turkey** after car bombs killed 20 people and injured more than 250.

Global terrorism

Terrorism is defined by the United Nations as "All criminal acts directed against a State and intended or calculated to create a state of terror in the minds of particular persons or a group of persons or the general public". The world has become increasingly concerned about terrorism and the possibility that terrorists could acquire and use nuclear, chemical and biological weapons. One common form of terrorist attack is suicide bombing. Pioneered by Tamil secessionists in Sri Lanka, it has been widely used by Palestinian groups fighting against Israeli occupation of the West Bank and Gaza. In recent years it has also been used by the Al Qaida network in its attacks on the western world.

Major terrorist incidents

Date	Location	Summary	Killed	Injured
December 1988	Lockerbie, Scotland	Airline bombing	270	5
March 1995	Tōkyō, Japan	Sarin gas attack on subway	12	5700
April 1995	Oklahoma City, USA	Bomb in the Federal building	168	over 500
August 1998	Nairobi, Kenya and Dar es Salaam, Tanzania	US Embassy bombings	257	over 4000
August 1998	Omagh, Northern Ireland	Town centre bombing	29	330
September 2001	New York and Washington D.C., USA	Airline hijacking and crashing	2752	4300
October 2002	Bali, Indonesia	Car bomb outside nightclub	202	300
October 2002	Moscow, Russian Federation	Theatre siege	170	over 600
March 2004	Bāghdad and Karbalā', Iraq	Suicide bombing of pilgrims	181	over 400
March 2004	Madrid, Spain	Train bombings	191	1800

Middle East politics
Changing boundaries in Israel/Palestine, 1922–2003

West Bank
Population
97% Palestinian Arab
610 000 refugees

West Bank
Security
13% of land under Palestinian control
23% of land under Palestinian civil control and joint security control
59% of land under Israeli control

Gaza
Population
98% Palestinian Arab
865 000 refugees

Gaza
Security
60% of land under Palestinian control
40% of land under Israeli control or settlement

—·—·—	International boundary
—×—×—	Disputed International boundary
··········	Ceasefire line
▬▬▬	British Mandate Boundary 1922–1948
▬▬▬	Israel Boundary 1948
▨	Land occupied by Israel 1967
Jenin ☐	Main Palestinian towns

Security fence along the **Egypt/Gaza** border near Rafiah.

The Middle East

The on-going Israeli/Palestinian conflict reflects decades of unrest in the region of Palestine which, after the First World War, was placed under British control. In 1947 the United Nations (UN) proposed a partitioning into separate Jewish and Arab states – a plan which was rejected by the Palestinians and by the Arab states in the region. When Britain withdrew in 1948, Israel declared its independence. This led to an Arab-Israeli war which left Israel with more land than originally proposed under the UN plan. Hundreds of thousands of Palestinians were forced out of their homeland and became refugees, mainly in Jordan and Lebanon. The 6-Day War in 1967 resulted in Israel taking possession of Sinai and Gaza from Egypt, West Bank from Jordan, and the Golan Heights from Syria. These territories (except Sinai which was subsequently returned to Egypt) remain occupied by Israel – the main reason for the Palestinian uprising or 'Intifada' against Israel. The situation remains complex, with poor prospects for peace and for mutually acceptable independent states being established.

With the process of globalization has come an increased awareness of, and direct interest in, issues which have global implications. Social issues can now affect large parts of the world and can impact on large sections of society. Perhaps the current issues of greatest concern are those of national security, including the problem of international terrorism (see World Conflict pages 30–31), health, crime and natural resources. The three issues highlighted here reflect this and are of immediate concern.

The international drugs trade, and the crimes commonly associated with it, can impact society and individuals in devastating ways; scarcity of water resources and lack of access to safe drinking water can have major economic implications and causes severe health problems; and the AIDS epidemic is having disastrous consequences in large parts of the world, particularly in sub-Saharan Africa.

Internet Links	
● UNESCO	**www.unesco.org**
● UNAIDS	**www.unaids.org**
● WaterAid	**www.wateraid.org.uk**
● World Health Organization	**www.who.int**
● United Nations Office on Drugs and Crime	**www.unodc.org**

The drugs trade

The international trade in illegal drugs is estimated to be worth over US$400 billion. While it may be a lucrative business for the criminals involved, the effects of the drugs on individual users and on society in general can be devastating. Patterns of drug production and abuse vary, but there are clear centres for the production of the most harmful drugs – the opiates (opium, morphine and heroin) and cocaine. The 'Golden Triangle' of Laos, Myanmar and Thailand, and western South America respectively are the main producing areas for these drugs. Significant efforts are expended to counter the drugs trade, and there have been signs recently of downward trends in the production of heroin and cocaine.

Soldiers in **Colombia**, a major producer of cocaine, destroy an illegal drug processing laboratory.

The international drugs trade
Main producers and trafficking routes for opiates (opium, morphine, heroin) and cocaine

■ Cocaine producer
■ Opiate producer

→ Cocaine trafficking route
→ Opiate trafficking route

Afghanistan
Opiate production 2002:
3 400 metric tonnes

Myanmar
Opiate production 2002:
828 metric tonnes

Colombia
Cocaine production 2002:
580 metric tonnes

Peru
Cocaine production 2002:
160 metric tonnes

World
Opiate production 2002: 4 491 metric tonnes
Cocaine production 2002: 800 metric tonnes

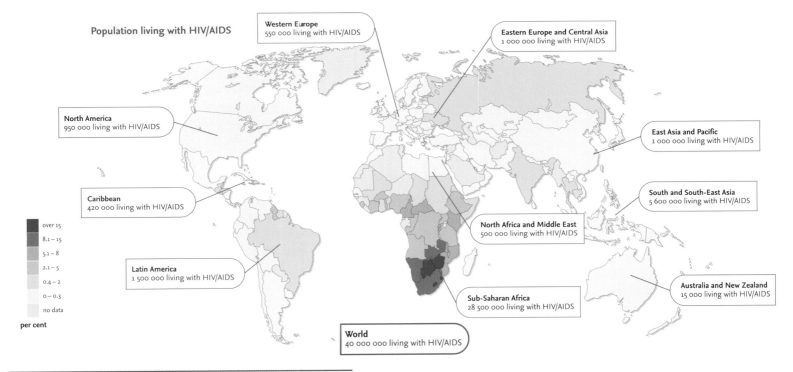

Population living with HIV/AIDS

Western Europe
550 000 living with HIV/AIDS

Eastern Europe and Central Asia
1 000 000 living with HIV/AIDS

North America
950 000 living with HIV/AIDS

East Asia and Pacific
1 000 000 living with HIV/AIDS

Caribbean
420 000 living with HIV/AIDS

South and South-East Asia
5 600 000 living with HIV/AIDS

North Africa and Middle East
500 000 living with HIV/AIDS

Latin America
1 500 000 living with HIV/AIDS

Australia and New Zealand
15 000 living with HIV/AIDS

Sub-Saharan Africa
28 500 000 living with HIV/AIDS

World
40 000 000 living with HIV/AIDS

over 15
8.1 – 15
5.1 – 8
2.1 – 5
0.4 – 2
0 – 0.3
no data

per cent

AIDS poster in **Zambia**, one of the countries worst affected by the AIDS epidemic.

Aids epidemic

With over 40 million people living with HIV/AIDS (Human Immunodeficiency Virus/Acquired Immune Deficiency Syndrome) and more than 20 million deaths from the disease, the AIDS epidemic poses one of the biggest threats to public health. The UNAIDS project estimated that 5 million people were newly infected in 2003 and that 3 million AIDS sufferers died. Estimates into the future look bleak, especially for poorer developing countries where an additional 45 million people are likely to become infected by 2010. The human cost is huge. As well as the death count itself, more than 11 million African children, half of whom are between the ages of 10 and 14, have been orphaned as a result of the disease.

Access to safe water, 2000
Percentage of population with access to improved drinking water

91 – 100
66 – 90
51 – 65
31 – 50
0 – 30
no data

per cent

Facts

- The majority of people infected with **HIV**, if not treated, develop signs of AIDS within 8 to 10 years

- One in five developing countries will face water shortages by 2030

- Over 5 million people die each year from water-related diseases such as cholera and dysentery

- Estimates suggest that 200 million people consume illegal drugs around the world

Water resources

Water is one of the fundamental requirements of life, and yet in some countries it is becoming more scarce due to increasing population and climate change. Safe drinking water, basic hygiene, health education and sanitation facilities are often virtually nonexistent for impoverished people in developing countries throughout the world. WHO/UNICEF estimate that the combination of these conditions results in 6 000 deaths every day, most of these being children. Currently over 1.2 billion people drink unclean water and expose themselves to serious health risks, while political struggles over diminishing water resources are increasingly likely to be the cause of international conflict.

Domestic use of **untreated water** in Kathmandu, Nepal.

Many parts of the world are undergoing significant changes which can have widespread and long-lasting effects. The principal causes of change are environmental – particularly climatic – factors and the influence of man. However, it is often difficult to separate these causes because man's activities can influence and exaggerate environmental change. Changes, whatever their cause, can have significant effects on the local population, on the wider region and even on a global scale. Major social, economic and environmental impacts can result from often irreversible changes – land reclamation can destroy fragile marine ecosystems, major dams and drainage schemes can affect whole drainage basins, and local communities can be changed beyond recognition through such projects.

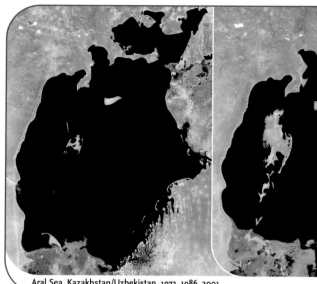

Aral Sea, Kazakhstan/Uzbekistan, 1973, 1986, 2001.

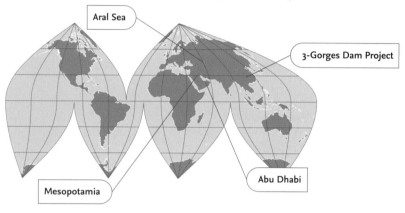

Aral Sea

3-Gorges Dam Project

Mesopotamia

Abu Dhabi

Internet Links	
● NASA Visible Earth	visibleearth.nasa.gov
● NASA Earth Observatory	earthobservatory.nasa.gov
● USGS Earthshots	earthshots.usgs.gov

Man-made change

Human activity has irreversibly changed the environment in many parts of the world. Major engineering projects and the expansion of towns and cities create completely new environments and have major social and economic impacts. The 3-Gorges Dam project in China will control the flow of the Yangtze river and generate enormous amounts of hydro-electric power. During its construction, millions of people were relocated as over 100 towns and villages were inundated by the new reservoir.

The city of Abu Dhabi, capital of the United Arab Emirates, has been built largely on land reclaimed from The Gulf. From a small fishing village it has grown, through a dramatic re-modelling of the coastline, into a major city.

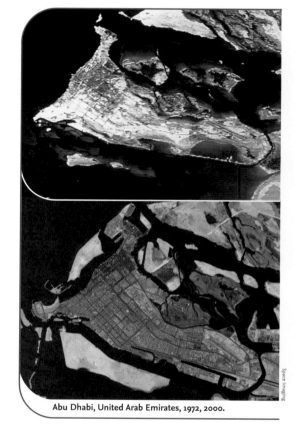

Abu Dhabi, United Arab Emirates, 1972, 2000.

Part of the **Yangtze** river, China, in the region of the 3-Gorges, before construction of the new reservoir.

The **3-Gorges Dam** under construction.

Environmental change

Water resources in certain parts of the world are becoming increasingly scarce. The Aral Sea in central Asia was once the world's fourth largest lake but it now ranks only tenth after shrinking by almost 40 000 square kilometres. This shrinkage has been due to climatic change and to the diversion, for farming purposes, of the major rivers which feed the lake. The change has had a devastating effect on the local fishing industry and has caused health problems for the local population.

The marshlands of Mesopotamia in Iraq have also undergone significant change. It is estimated that only 7 per cent of these ecologically valuable wetlands now remain after systematic drainage of the area and upstream diversion of the Tigris and Euphrates rivers.

Facts

- Earth-observing satellites can now detect land detail, and therefore changes in land cover, of less than 1 metre extent

- Over 90 000 square kilometres of precious tropical forest and wetland habitats are lost each year

- The surface level of the Dead Sea has fallen by 16 metres over the last 30 years

- Hong Kong International Airport, opened in 1998 and covering an area of over 12 square kilometres, was built almost entirely on reclaimed land

Mesopotamian marshlands, Iraq, 1973. Large areas of dense marsh vegetation show as dark red.

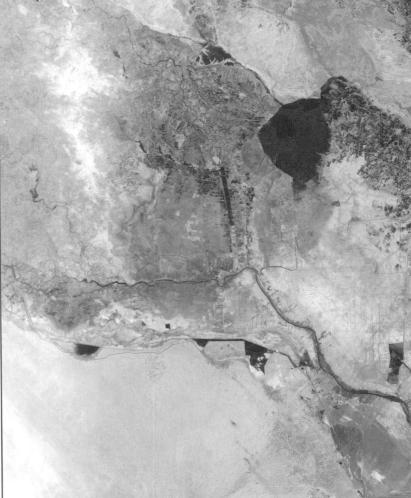

Mesopotamian marshlands, Iraq, 2000. Vast areas of former marshland now appear as grey-green areas of sparse vegetation or bare ground.

Europe Landscapes

Europe, the westward extension of the Asian continent and the second smallest of the world's continents, has a remarkable variety of physical features and landscapes. The continent is bounded by mountain ranges of varying character – the highlands of Scandinavia and northwest Britain, the Pyrenees, the Alps, the Carpathian Mountains, the Caucasus and the Ural Mountains. Two of these, the Caucasus and Ural Mountains define the eastern limits of Europe, with the Black Sea and the Bosporus defining its southeastern boundary with Asia.

Across the centre of the continent stretches the North European Plain, broken by some of Europe's greatest rivers, including the Volga and the Dnieper and containing some of its largest lakes. To the south, the Mediterranean Sea divides Europe from Africa. The Mediterranean region itself has a very distinct climate and landscape.

Iceland in winter, one of Europe's largest islands.

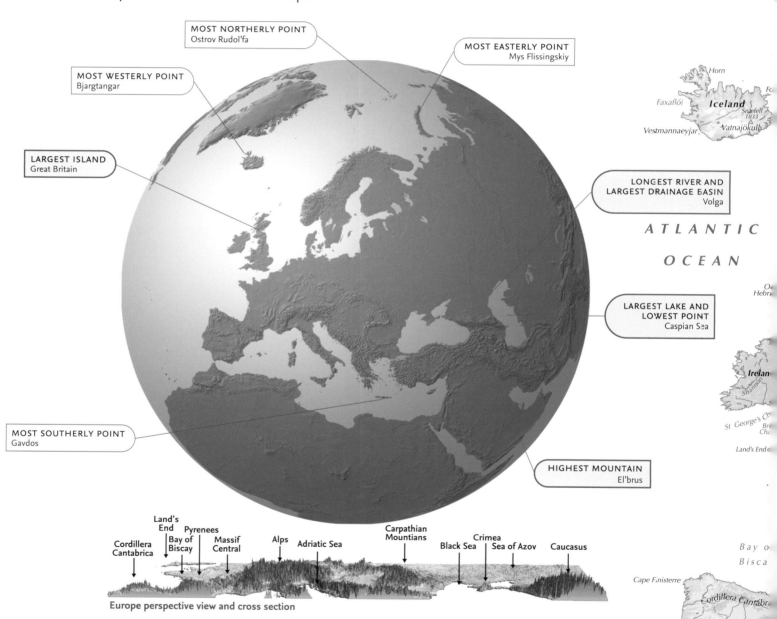

MOST NORTHERLY POINT
Ostrov Rudol'fa

MOST EASTERLY POINT
Mys Flissingskiy

MOST WESTERLY POINT
Bjargtangar

LARGEST ISLAND
Great Britain

LONGEST RIVER AND LARGEST DRAINAGE BASIN
Volga

LARGEST LAKE AND LOWEST POINT
Caspian Sea

MOST SOUTHERLY POINT
Gavdos

HIGHEST MOUNTAIN
El'brus

Cordillera Cantabrica · Land's End · Bay of Biscay · Pyrenees · Massif Central · Alps · Adriatic Sea · Carpathian Mountians · Black Sea · Crimea · Sea of Azov · Caucasus

Europe perspective view and cross section

Europe's greatest physical features

Highest mountain	El'brus, Russian Federation	5 642 metres	18 510 feet
Longest river	Volga, Russian Federation	3 688 km	2 292 miles
Largest lake	Caspian Sea	371 000 sq km	143 243 sq miles
Largest island	Great Britain, United Kingdom	218 476 sq km	84 354 sq miles
Largest drainage basin	Volga, Russian Federation	1 380 000 sq km	532 818 sq miles

Europe's extent

Total Land Area	9 908 599 sq km / 3 825 710 sq miles
Most northerly point	Ostrov Rudol'fa, Russian Federation
Most southerly point	Gavdos, Crete, Greece
Most westerly point	Bjargtangar, Iceland
Most easterly point	Mys Flissingskiy, Russian Federation

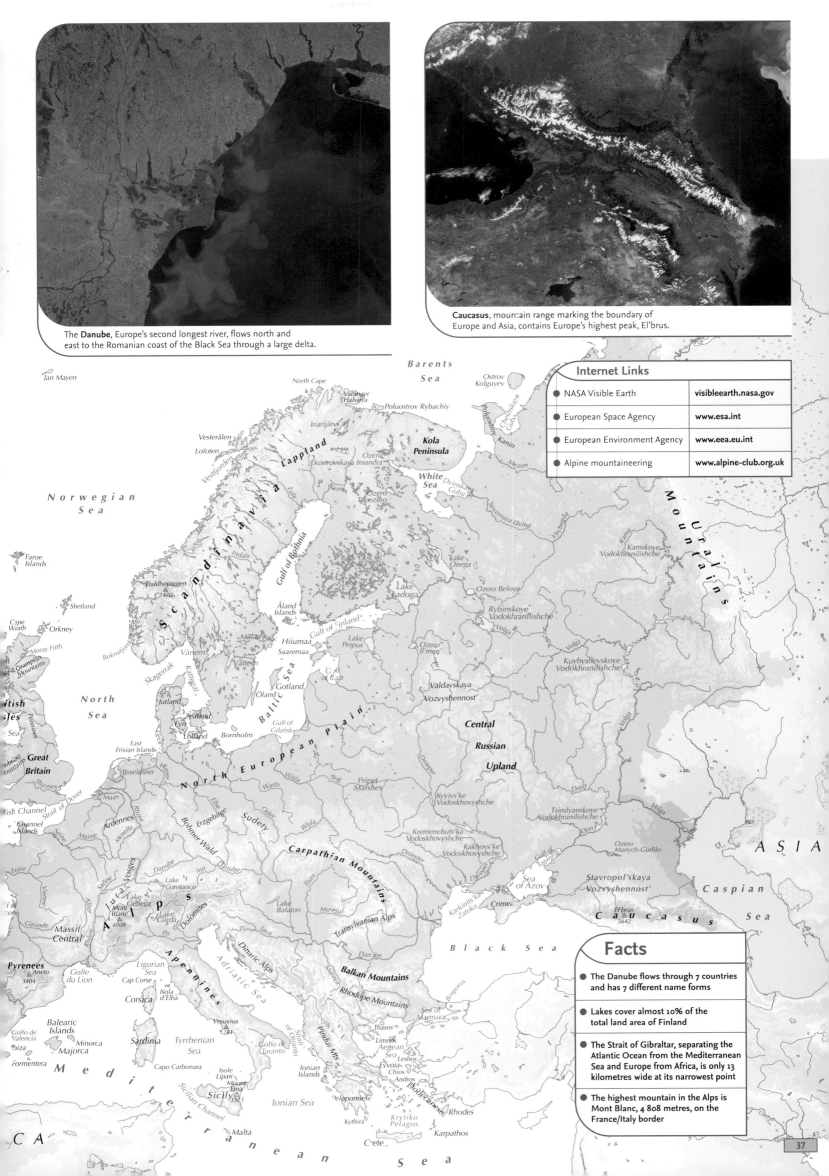

The **Danube**, Europe's second longest river, flows north and east to the Romanian coast of the Black Sea through a large delta.

Caucasus, mountain range marking the boundary of Europe and Asia, contains Europe's highest peak, El'brus.

Internet Links

● NASA Visible Earth	**visibleearth.nasa.gov**
● European Space Agency	**www.esa.int**
● European Environment Agency	**www.eea.eu.int**
● Alpine mountaineering	**www.alpine-club.org.uk**

Facts

- The Danube flows through 7 countries and has 7 different name forms
- Lakes cover almost 10% of the total land area of Finland
- The Strait of Gibraltar, separating the Atlantic Ocean from the Mediterranean Sea and Europe from Africa, is only 13 kilometres wide at its narrowest point
- The highest mountain in the Alps is Mont Blanc, 4 808 metres, on the France/Italy border

Jan Mayen

Barents Sea

North Cape
Varanger Halvøya
Poluostrov Rybachiy
Ostrov Kolguyev
Inarijärvi
Vesterålen
Lofoten
Kola Peninsula
Ozero Imandra
Ekostrovskaya Imandra
Vestfjorden
White Sea
Dvinskaya Guba
Poluostrov Kanin
Ozero Topozero
Mezen

Norwegian Sea

Galdhøpiggen 2470
Shetland
Faroe Islands

Kem'
Lule
Ume
Indals
Gulf of Bothnia
Åland Islands
Lake Onega
Ozero Beloye
Severnaya Dvina
Vychegda
Kama
Kamskoye Vodokhranilishche
Lake Ladoga
Lake Onega

Cape Wrath
Orkney
Moray Firth
Grampian Mountains

North Sea

Boknafjorden
Vänern
Kattegat
Vättern
Öland
Gotland
Hiiumaa
Saaremaa
Lake Peipus
Gulf of Riga
Gulf of Finland
Rybinskoye Vodokhranilishche
Volga
Kuybyshevskoye Vodokhranilishche

Baltic Sea

Ozero Il'men'
Valdayskaya Vozvyshennost'
Volga

Central Russian Upland

Jutland
Zealand
Fyn
Lolland
Bornholm
Gulf of Gdańsk
East Frisian Islands

North European Plain

Great Britain
Pennines
Thames
ish Channel
Channel Islands

Ijsselmeer
Weser
Elbe
Wisła
Warta
Bug
Pripet Marshes
Dniester
Kyyivs'ke Vodoskhovyshche
Don

Rhine
Ardennes
Maas
Seine
Marne
Moselle
Bohmer Wald
Erzgebirge
Sudety
Dnieper
Kremenchuts'ka Vodoskhovyshche
Kakhovs'ke Vodoskhovyshche
Tsimlyanskoye Vodokhranilishche
Don
Volga

Carpathian Mountains

Loire
Vienne
Saône
Vosges
Jura
Danube
Lake Constance
Inn
Danube
Tisza
Dniester
Mureșul

Gulf of Taganrog
Sea of Azov
Ozero Manych-Gudilo

ASIA

Massif Central
Rhône
Alps
Mont Blanc 4808
Lake Geneva
Dolomites
Lake Garda
Po
Lake Balaton
Sava
Transylvanian Alps

Karkinits'ka Zatoka
Crimea
Stavropol'skaya Vozvyshennost'
El'brus 5642
Caucasus
Caspian Sea

Pyrenees
Aneto 3404
Golfe du Lion
Cap Corse
Ligurian Sea
Corsica
Isola d'Elba
Dinaric Alps
Adriatic Sea
Danube
Balkan Mountains
Rhodope Mountains
Black Sea

Balearic Islands
Golfo de Valencia
Ibiza
Minorca
Majorca
Formentera
Sardinia
Apennines
Tyrrhenian Sea
Vesuvius 1281
Golfo di Taranto
Pindus Mts
Thasos
Sea of Marmara
Bosporus

Capo Carbonara
Isole Lipari
Mount Etna 3323
Sicily
Sicilian Channel
Ionian Sea
Isole Egadi
Peloponnese
Aegean Sea
Limnos
Lesbos
Chios
Evvoia
Andros
Dodecanese
Rhodes
Karpathos

M e d i t e r r a n e a n   S e a

Malta
Krytiko Pelagos
Kythira
Crete
Ionian Islands

CA

The predominantly temperate climate of Europe has led to it becoming the most densely populated of the continents. It is highly industrialized, and has exploited its great wealth of natural resources and agricultural land to become one of the most powerful economic regions in the world.

The current pattern of countries within Europe is a result of numerous and complicated changes throughout its history. Ethnic, religious and linguistic differences have often been the cause of conflict, particularly in the Balkan region which has a very complex ethnic pattern. Current boundaries reflect, to some extent, these divisions which continue to be a source of tension. The historic distinction between 'Eastern' and 'Western' Europe is no longer made, following the collapse of Communism and the break up of the Soviet Union in 1991.

Paris, the capital of France and Europe's largest capital city with 9 630 000 residents.

Facts

- The European Union was founded by six countries: Belgium, France, Germany, Italy, Luxembourg, and the Netherlands. It now has 25 members

- The newest members of the European Union joined in 2004: Cyprus, Czech Republic, Estonia, Hungary, Latvia, Lithuania, Malta, Poland, Slovakia, and Slovenia

- Europe has the 2 smallest independent countries in the world – Vatican City and Monaco

- Vatican City is an independent country entirely within the city of Rome, and is the centre of the Roman Catholic Church

LEAST DENSELY POPULATED COUNTRY
Iceland

MOST NORTHERLY CAPITAL
Reykjavík

LARGEST CAPITAL
Paris

SMALLEST COUNTRY
(AREA AND POPULATION)
Vatican City

LARGEST COUNTR
(AREA AND POPULATION
Russian Federatio

HIGHEST CAPITAL
Andorra la Vella

SMALLEST CAPITAL
Vatican City

MOST SOUTHERLY CAPITAL
Valletta

MOST DENSELY POPULATED COUNTRY
Monaco

Reykjavík ICELAND

ATLANTIC

OCEAN

REPUBL
OF Du
IRELAND

Bre

Bay
Bisca

Azores
(Portugal)

Cape Finisterre   A Coruña
Bilba

Oporto   Douro
Salamanca

PORTUGAL   Madrid

Lisbon   SPAIN
Tagus

Cabo de   Sevilla   Córdoba
São Vicente
Cádiz   Málaga   Cartac
Str. of   Gibraltar
Gibraltar

A

Bosporus, Turkey, a narrow strait of water which separates Europe from Asia.

Europe's capitals

Largest capital (population)	Paris, France	9 854 000
Smallest capital (population)	Vatican City	480
Most northerly capital	Reykjavík, Iceland	64° 39'N
Most southerly capital	Valletta, Malta	35° 54'N
Highest capital	Andorra la Vella, Andorra	1 029 metres 3 376 feet

Europe (excluding Russian Federation) percentage of total population and land area

Legend:
- Population
- Land area

(x-axis labels): Ukraine, France, Spain, Sweden, Germany, Finland, Norway, Poland, Italy, UK, Romania, Belarus, Greece, Bulgaria, Iceland, Serb. and Mont., Hungary, Portugal, Austria, Czech Rep., Rep. of Ireland, Lithuania, Latvia, Croatia, Bosnia-Herz., Slovakia, Estonia, Denmark, Netherlands, Switzerland, Moldova, Belgium, Albania, Macedonia, Slovenia, Luxembourg, Andorra, Malta, Liechtenstein, San Marino, Monaco, Vatican City

Europe's countries

Largest country (area)	Russian Federation	17 075 400 sq km	6 592 812 sq miles
Smallest country (area)	Vatican City	0.5 sq km	0.2 sq miles
Largest country (population)	Russian Federation	143 246 000	
Smallest country (population)	Vatican City	472	
Most densely populated country	Monaco	17 000 per sq km	34 000 per sq mile
Least densely populated country	Iceland	3 per sq km	7 per sq mile

Belgrade, the capital of Serbia and Montenegro, stands at the junction of the Danube, Europe's second longest river, and the Sava river.

Internet Links

● European Union	europa.eu.int
● UK Foreign and Commonwealth Office	www.fco.gov.uk
● CIA World Factbook	www.cia.gov/cia/publications/factbook

Conic Equidistant Projection

1:7 500 000

Conic Equidistant Projection

1:5 000 000

| 0 | 50 | 100 | 150 | miles |

| 0 | 50 | 100 | 150 | 200 | 250 | km |

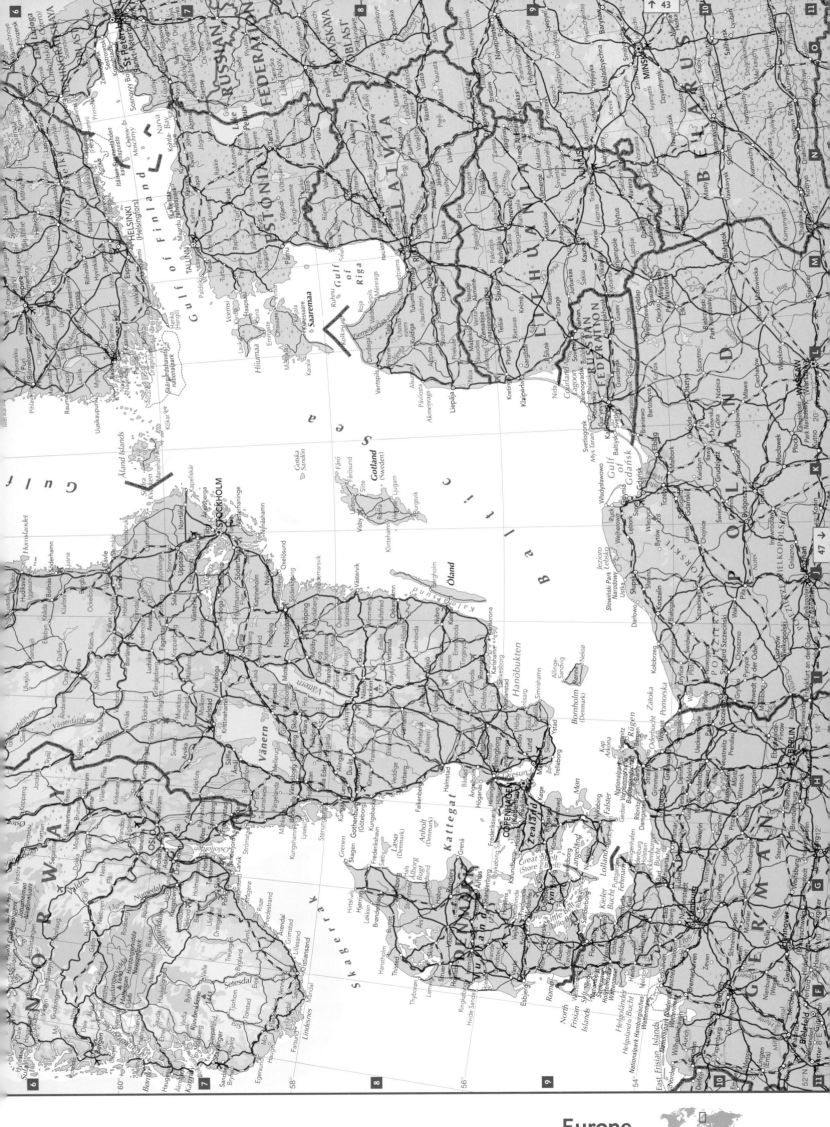

↗ 47

Europe

Scandinavia and the Baltic States

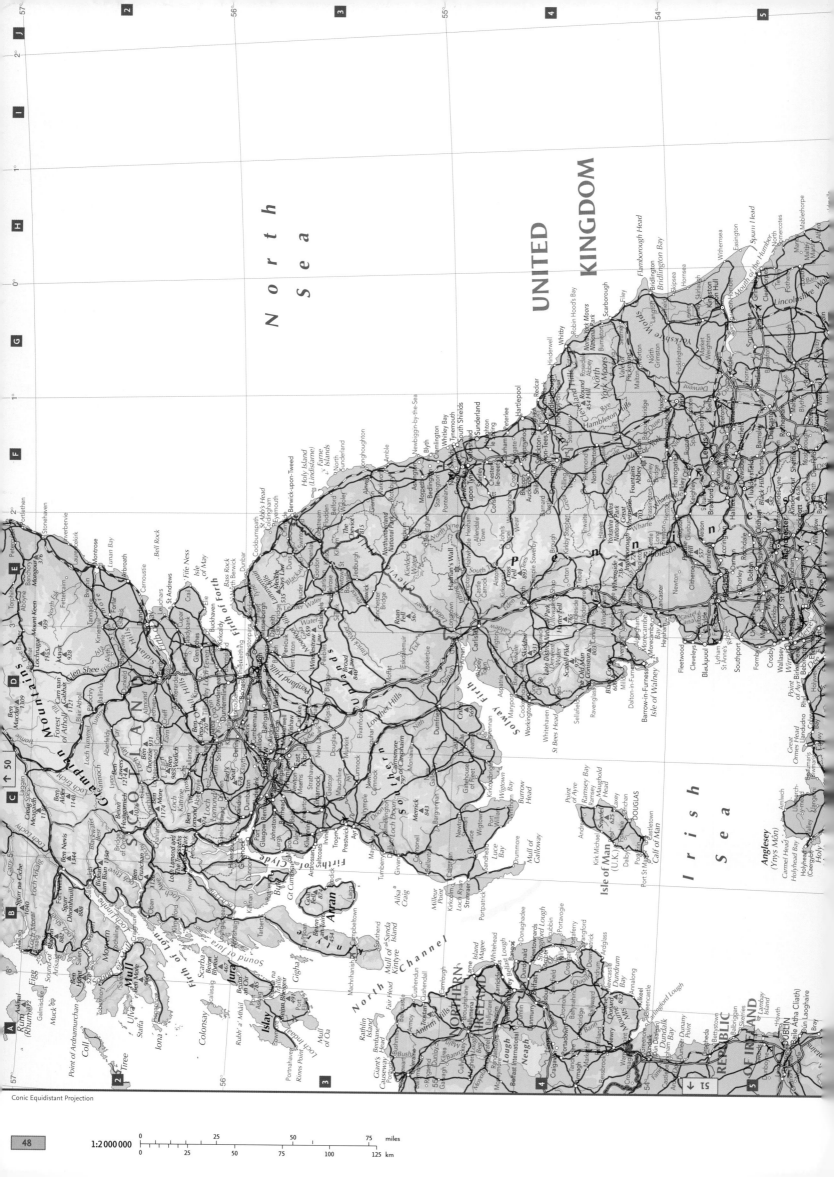

North Sea

UNITED

KINGDOM

Irish Sea

North Channel

SCOTLAND

NORTHERN IRELAND

REPUBLIC OF IRELAND

Conic Equidistant Projection

1:2 000 000

miles
0   25   50   75

km
0   25   50   75   100   125

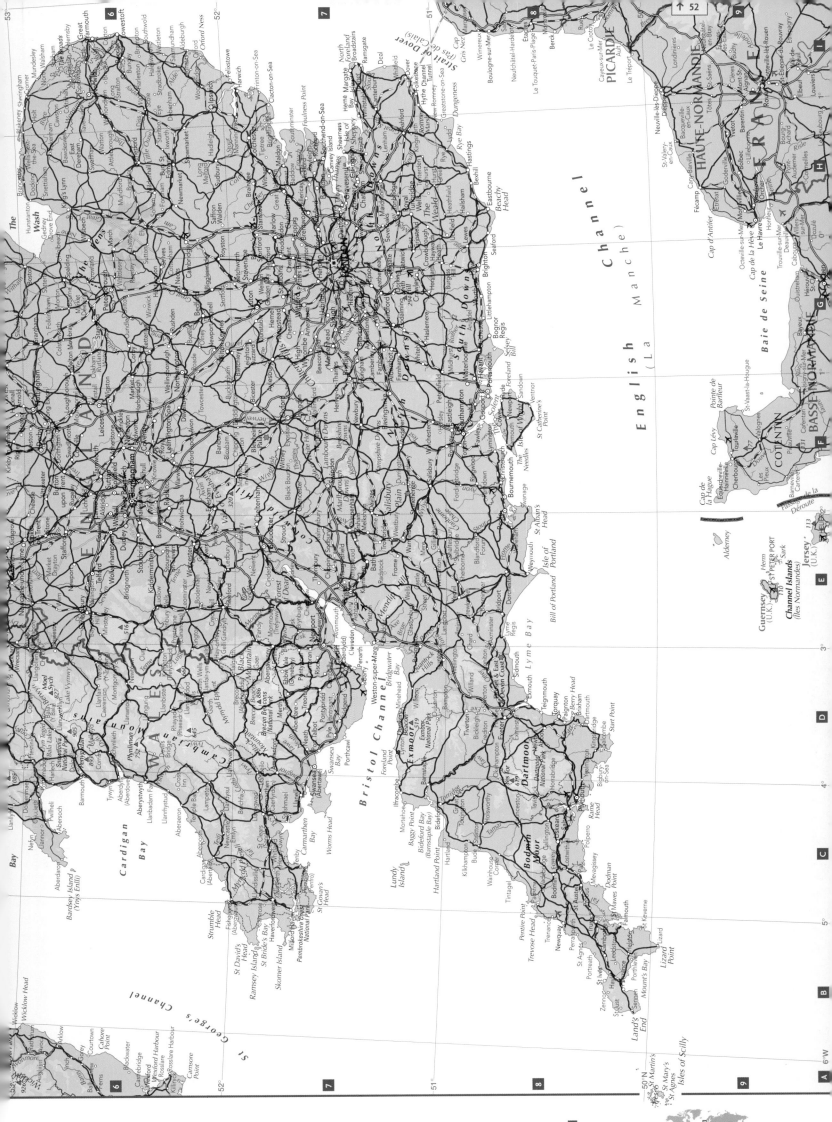

Europe
England and Wales

Europe
Scotland

Conic Equidistant Projection

1:2 000 000

Conic Equidistant Projection

1:2 000 000

Conic Equidistant Projection

Europe
France

1:5 000 000

onic Equidistant Projection

1:5 000 000

0   50   100   150   miles
0   50   100   150   200   250   km

Conic Equidistant Projection

1:5 000 000

| 0 | 50 | 100 | 150 miles |
| 0 | 50 | 100 | 150 | 200 | 250 km |

Asia Landscapes

Asia is the world's largest continent and occupies almost one-third of the world's total land area. Stretching across approximately 165° of longitude from the Mediterranean Sea to the easternmost point of the Russian Federation on the Bering Strait, it contains the world's highest and lowest points and some of the world's greatest physical features. Its mountain ranges include the Himalaya, Hindu Kush, Karakoram and the Ural Mountains and its major rivers – including the Yangtze, Tigris-Euphrates, Indus, Ganges and Mekong – are equally well-known and evocative.

Asia's deserts include the Gobi, the Taklimakan, and those on the Arabian Peninsula, and significant areas of volcanic and tectonic activity are present on the Kamchatka Peninsula, in Japan, and on Indonesia's numerous islands. The continent's landscapes are greatly influenced by climatic variations, with great contrasts between the islands of the Arctic Ocean and the vast Siberian plains in the north, and the tropical islands of Indonesia.

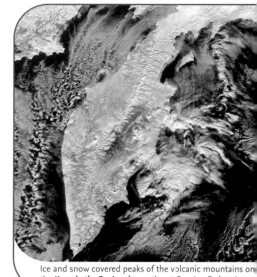
Ice and snow covered peaks of the volcanic mountains on the **Kamchatka Peninsula**, northeast Russian Federation.

Facts

- 90 of the world's 100 highest mountains are in Asia
- The Indonesian archipelago is made up of over 13 500 islands
- The height of the land in Nepal ranges from 60 metres to 8 848 metres
- The deepest lake in the world is Lake Baikal, Russian Federation, which is over 1 600 metres deep

Asia's physical features

Highest mountain	Mt Everest, China/Nepal	8 848 metres	29 028 feet
Longest river	Yangtze, China	6 330 km	3 965 miles
Largest lake	Caspian Sea	371 000 sq km	143 243 sq miles
Largest island	Borneo	745 561 sq km	287 861 sq miles
Largest drainage basin	Ob'-Irtysh, Kazakhstan/Russian Federation	2 990 000 sq km	1 154 439 sq miles
Lowest point	Dead Sea	-398 metres	-1 306 feet

Internet Links	
● NASA Visible Earth	visibleearth.nasa.gov
● NASA Earth Observatory	earthobservatory.nasa.gov
● Peakware World Mountain Encyclopedia	www.peakware.com
● The Himalaya	himalaya.alpine-club.org.uk

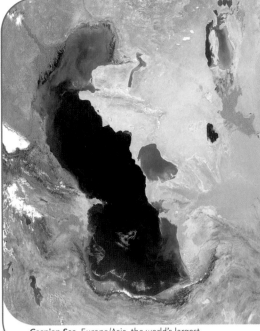

Caspian Sea, Europe/Asia, the world's largest expanse of inland water.

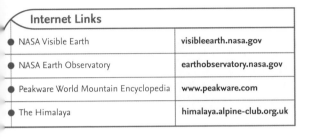

MOST EASTERLY POINT
Mys Dezhneva

MOST NORTHERLY POINT
Mys Arkticheskiy

LARGEST DRAINAGE BASIN
Ob'-Irtysh

LARGEST LAKE
Caspian Sea

MOST WESTERLY POINT
Bozcaada

HIGHEST MOUNTAIN
Mt Everest

LONGEST RIVER
Yangtze

LOWEST POINT
Dead Sea

LARGEST ISLAND
Borneo

MOST SOUTHERLY POINT
Pamana

Mediterranean Sea
Cyprus
Caucasus
Caspian Sea
Turan Lowlands
Tien Shan
Tarim Basin
Plateau of Tibet
Gobi
Yellow Sea
Sea of Japan
Honshu

Asia perspective view and cross section

Hahajima-rettō
Bonin Islands
cano lands

IFIC
EAN

Asia's extent

TOTAL LAND AREA	45 036 492 sq km / 17 388 686 sq miles
Most northerly point	Mys Arkticheskiy, Russian Federation
Most southerly point	Pamana, Indonesia
Most westerly point	Bozcaada, Turkey
Most easterly point	Mys Dezhneva, Russian Federation

Palau
slands

rah
berg
Puncak Jaya
5030
New Guinea

Kepulauan Aru
pulauan
nimbar
afura Sea

The **Yangtze**, China, Asia's longest river, flowing into the East China Sea near Shanghai.

Asia Countries

With approximately sixty per cent of the world's population, Asia is home to numerous cultures, people groups and lifestyles. Several of the world's earliest civilizations were established in Asia, including those of Sumeria, Babylonia and Assyria. Cultural and historical differences have led to a complex political pattern, and the continent has been, and continues to be, subject to numerous territorial and political conflicts – including the current disputes in the Middle East and in Jammu and Kashmir.

Separate regions within Asia can be defined by the cultural, economic and political systems they support. The major regions are: the arid, oil-rich, mainly Islamic southwest; southern Asia with its distinct cultures, isolated from the rest of Asia by major mountain ranges; the Indian- and Chinese-influenced monsoon region of southeast Asia; the mainly Chinese-influenced industrialized areas of eastern Asia; and Soviet Asia, made up of most of the former Soviet Union.

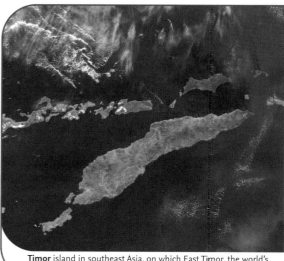

Timor island in southeast Asia, on which East Timor, the world's newest independent state, is located.

Facts

- Over 60% of the world's population live in Asia
- Asia has 11 of the world's 20 largest cities
- East Timor is Asia's newest independent country – founded in May 2002
- The Korean peninsula was divided into North Korea and South Korea in 1948 approximately along the 38th parallel

Asia's countries

Largest country (area)	Russian Federation	17 075 400 sq km	6 592 812 sq miles
Smallest country (area)	Maldives	298 sq km	115 sq miles
Largest country (population)	China	1 289 161 000	
Smallest country (population)	Palau	20 000	
Most densely populated country	Singapore	6 656 per sq km	17 219 per sq mile
Least densely populated country	Mongolia	2 per sq km	4 per sq mile

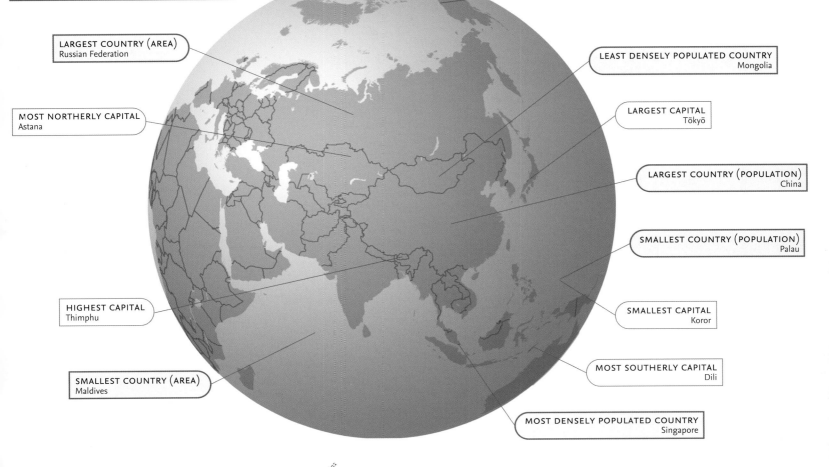

LARGEST COUNTRY (AREA) Russian Federation

MOST NORTHERLY CAPITAL Astana

HIGHEST CAPITAL Thimphu

SMALLEST COUNTRY (AREA) Maldives

LEAST DENSELY POPULATED COUNTRY Mongolia

LARGEST CAPITAL Tōkyō

LARGEST COUNTRY (POPULATION) China

SMALLEST COUNTRY (POPULATION) Palau

SMALLEST CAPITAL Koror

MOST SOUTHERLY CAPITAL Dili

MOST DENSELY POPULATED COUNTRY Singapore

Different land use patterns help identify the borders between **Egypt**, **Israel** and **Gaza** in this space shuttle photograph.

Asia (excluding Russian Federation) percentage of total population and land area

Asia's capitals

Largest capital (population)	Tōkyō, Japan	35 327 000
Smallest capital (population)	Koror, Palau	14 000
Most northerly capital	Astana, Kazakhstan	51° 10'N
Most southerly capital	Dili, East Timor	3° 35'S
Highest capital	Thimphu, Bhutan	2 423 metres 7 949 feet

Beijing, capital of China, the most populous country in the world.

63

Conic Equidistant Projection

1:20 000 000

| 0 | 200 | 400 | 600 | miles |
| 0 | 200 | 400 | 600 | 800 | 1000 | km |

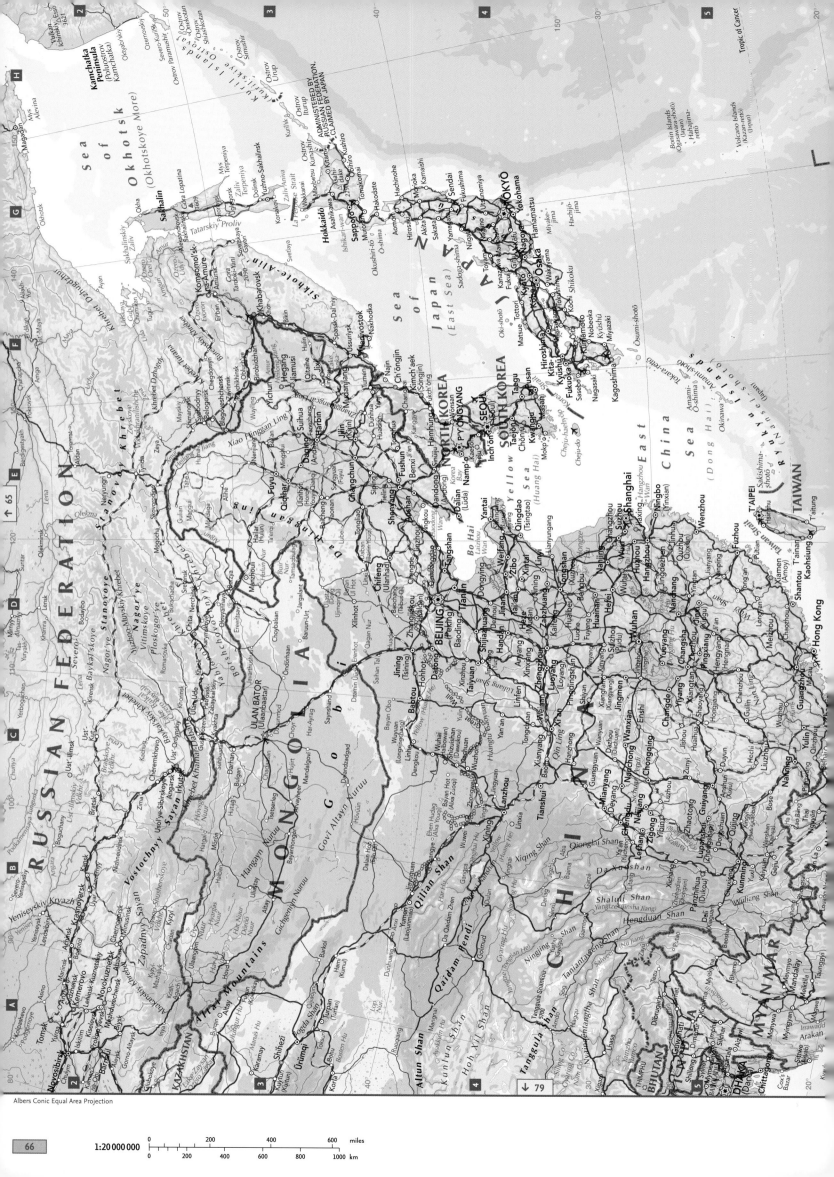

Albers Conic Equal Area Projection

1:20 000 000

Asia
Eastern and Southeast Asia

Asia
Southeast Asia

Mercator Projection

1:7 000 000

miles
0   100   200

km
0   100   200   300   400

Asia

Myanmar, Thailand, Peninsular Malaysia and Indo-China

Albers Conic Equal Area Projection

72

1:15 000 000

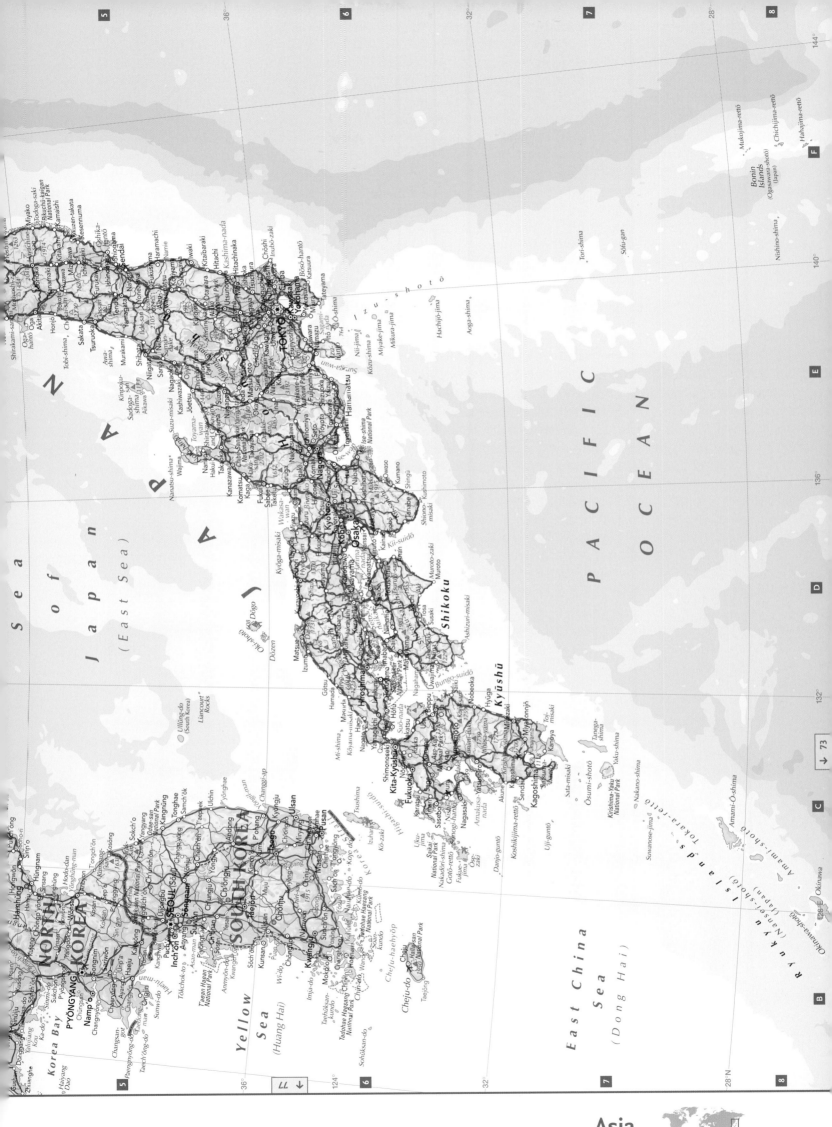

Conic Equidistant Projection

1:7 000 000

Asia
Southeast China

Albers Conic Equal Area Projection

1:20 000 000

| | | 200 | 400 | 600 | miles |
| 0 | 200 | 400 | 600 | 800 | 1000 km |

Albers Equal Area Conic Projection

1:13 000 000

0		100		200		300		400		500 miles
0	100	200	300	400	500	600	700	800 km

Conic Equidistant Projection

Administrative divisions in India
numbered on the map:

1. DADRA AND NAGAR HAVELI (C5)
2. DAMAN AND DIU (B5, C5)

1:7 000 000

| 0 | 100 | 200 | miles |

| 0 | 100 | 200 | 300 | 400 | km |

Asia
Northern India, Nepal, Bhutan and Bangladesh

Asia
Southern India and Sri Lanka

1:7 000 000

Conic Equidistant Projection

Administrative divisions in India
numbered on the map:

1. DADRA AND NAGAR HAVELI (B1)
2. DAMAN AND DIU (A1, B1)
3. PONDICHERRY (C4)

Albers Conic Equal Area Projection

1:13 000 000

0	100	200	300	400	500 miles
0	100	200	300	400	500	600	700	800 km

Conic Equidistant Projection

1:7 000 000

0   100   200   miles

0   100   200   300   400 km

Asia
The Gulf, Iran, Afghanistan and Pakistan

Administrative divisions in Russian Federation
numbered on the map:

1. RESPUBLI-KA KALMYKIYA - KHALM'G-TANGCH (G1)
2. RESPUBLI-KA DAGESTAN (G2)
3. CHECHENSKAYA RESPUBLIKA (G2)
4. RESPUBLIKA INGUSHETIYA (G2)
5. RESPUBLIKA SEVERNAYA OSETIYA - ALANIYA (G2)
6. KABARDINO-BALKARSKAYA RESPUBLIKA (F2)
7. KARACHAYEVO-CHERKESSKAYA RESPUBLIKA (F2)
8. RESPUBLIKA ADYGEYA (F1)

Black Sea

Mediterranean Sea

GREECE

CYPRUS

LIBYA

EGYPT

ROMANIA

BULGARIA

UKRAINE

TURKEY

SYRIA

LEBANON

ISRAEL

JORDAN

SERBIA AND MONTENEGRO

MACEDONIA

Conic Equidistant Projection

1:7 000 000

0   100   200   miles
0   100 200 300 400 km

Some of the world's greatest physical features are in Africa, the world's second largest continent. Variations in climate and elevation give rise to the continent's great variety of landscapes. The Sahara, the world's largest desert, extends across the whole continent from west to east, and covers an area of over nine million square kilometres. Other significant African deserts are the Kalahari and the Namib. In contrast, some of the world's greatest rivers flow in Africa, including the Nile, the world's longest, and the Congo.

The Great Rift Valley is perhaps Africa's most notable geological feature. It stretches for nearly 3 000 kilometres from Jordan, through the Red Sea and south to Mozambique, and contains many of Africa's largest lakes. Significant mountain ranges on the continent are the Atlas Mountains and the Ethiopian Highlands in the north, the Ruwenzori in east central Africa, and the Drakensberg in the far southeast.

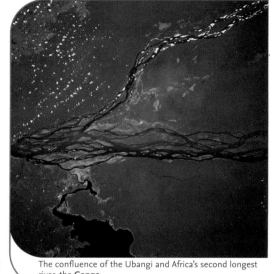

The confluence of the Ubangi and Africa's second longest river, the **Congo**.

Africa's extent

TOTAL LAND AREA	30 343 578 sq km / 11 715 655 sq miles
Most northerly point	La Galite, Tunisia
Most southerly point	Cape Agulhas, South Africa
Most westerly point	Santo Antão, Cape Verde
Most easterly point	Raas Xaafuun, Somalia

Internet Links	
● NASA Visible Earth	**visibleearth.nasa.gov**
● NASA Astronaut Photography	**eol.jsc.nasa.gov**
● Peace Parks Foundation	**www.peaceparks.org**

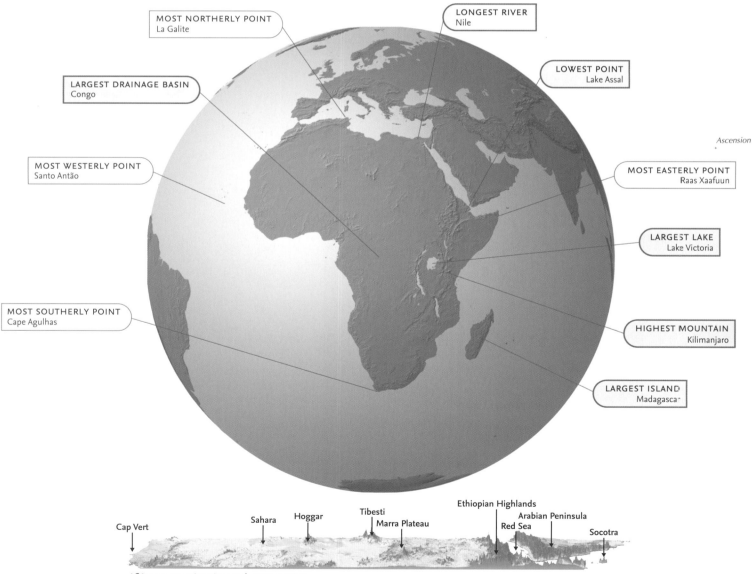

MOST NORTHERLY POINT
La Galite

LONGEST RIVER
Nile

LARGEST DRAINAGE BASIN
Congo

LOWEST POINT
Lake Assal

MOST WESTERLY POINT
Santo Antão

MOST EASTERLY POINT
Raas Xaafuun

LARGEST LAKE
Lake Victoria

MOST SOUTHERLY POINT
Cape Agulhas

HIGHEST MOUNTAIN
Kilimanjaro

LARGEST ISLAND
Madagascar

Cap Vert   Sahara   Hoggar   Tibesti   Marra Plateau   Ethiopian Highlands   Arabian Peninsula   Red Sea   Socotra

Africa perspective view and cross section

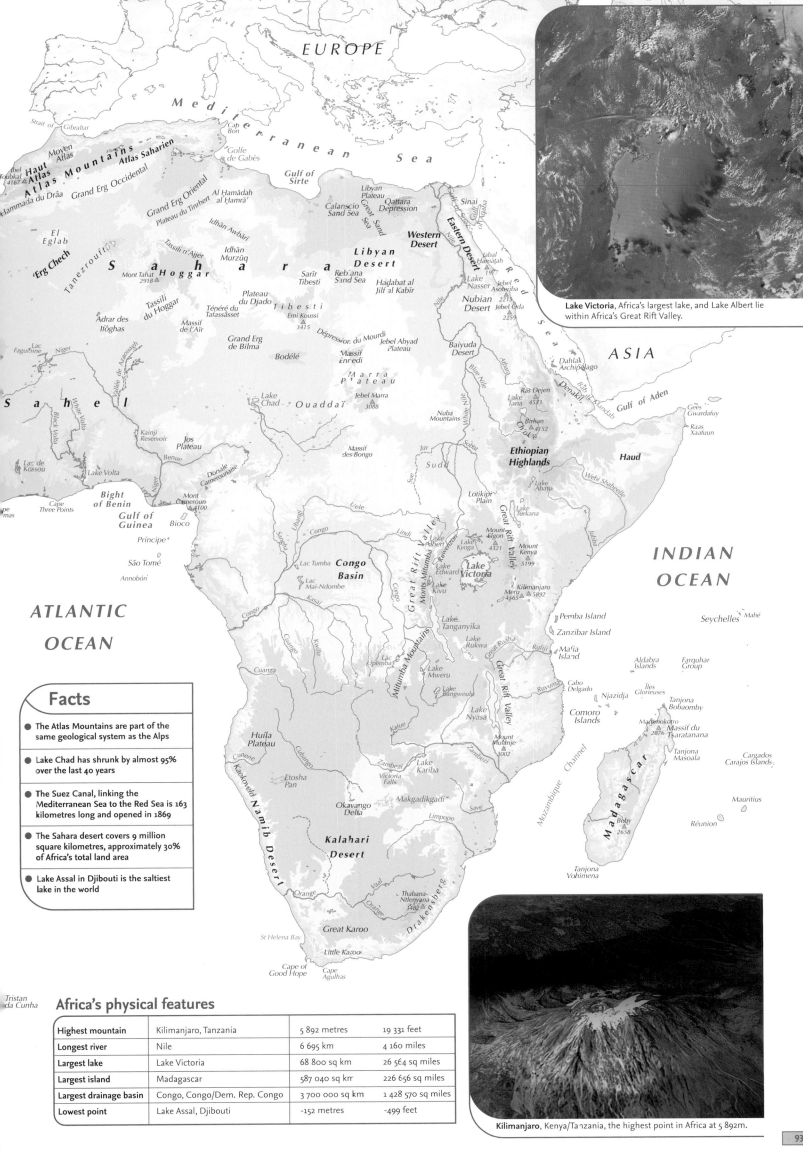

EUROPE

Mediterranean Sea

Strait of Gibraltar
Cap Bon
Golfe de Gabès
Gulf of Sirte

Moyen Atlas
Jebel Toubkal 4167
Haut Atlas
Atlas Mountains
Atlas Saharien
Hammada du Drâa
Grand Erg Occidental
Grand Erg Oriental
Plateau du Tinrhert
Al Hamādah al Hamrā'
Libyan Plateau
Calanscio Sand Sea
Qattara Depression
Sinai

El Eglab
'Erg Chech
Tanezrouft
Idhān Awbāri
S a h a r a
Idhān Murzūq
Tassili n'Ajjer
Mont Tahat 2918
H o g g a r
Sarīr Tibesti
Rebiana Sand Sea
Hadabat al Jilf al Kabīr
Western Desert
Eastern Desert
Jabal Hamātah 1977

Libyan Desert

Adrar des Ifôghas
Tassili du Hoggar
Ténéré du Tafassâsset
Massif de l'Aïr
Plateau du Djado
T i b e s t i
Emi Koussi 3415
Dépression du Mourdi
Jebel Abyad Plateau
Massif Enredi
Lake Nasser
Jebel Asoteriba 2215
Jebel Oda 2259

Lac Faguibine
Niger
Vallée de Azaouagh
Grand Erg de Bilma
Bodélé
Marra Plateau
Baiyuda Desert
Dahlak Archipelago
ASIA

S a h e l
Lake Chad
Ouaddaï
Jebel Marra 3088
Nubian Desert
Nuba Mountains
Lake Tana
Ras Dejen 4533
Gees Gwardafuy
Gulf of Aden

White Volta
Black Volta
Kainji Reservoir
Jos Plateau
Benue
Jebel Marra
Jur
Sue
Sudd
Ethiopian Highlands
Birhan 4152
Choke
Lake Abaya
Haud
Raas Xaafuun
Webi Shabeelle

Lac de Kossou
Lake Volta
Dorsale Camerounaise
Massif des Bongo
Lotikipi Plain
Lake Turkana

Bight of Benin
Cape Three Points
Gulf of Guinea
Mont Cameroun 4100
Bioco
Uele
Ubangi
Lindi
Mount Elgon 4321
Mount Kenya 5199

Príncipe
São Tomé
Annobón
Congo
Sangha
Lac Tumba
Congo Basin
Lac Mai-Ndombe
Kasai
Lake Albert
Monts Mitumba
Lake Kyoga
Lake Edward
Lake Victoria
Lake Kivu
Ruwenzori
Kilimanjaro 5892
Meru 4565

ATLANTIC OCEAN

Great Rift Valley
Congo
Cuango
Kwilu
Lac Upemba
Lake Tanganyika
Lake Rukwa
Great Ruaha
Rufiji
INDIAN OCEAN

Pemba Island
Zanzibar Island
Mafia Island
Seychelles · Mahé

Cuanza
Kafue
Lake Mweru
Lake Bangweulu
Mitumba Mountains
Lake Mweru
Great Rift Valley

Cabo Delgado
Njazidja
Comoro Islands
Aldabra Islands
Îles Glorieuses
Farquhar Group
Tanjona Bobaomby

Ruvuma
Lake Nyasa

Maromokotro 2876
Massif du Tsaratanana
Tanjona Masoala
Cargados Carajos Islands

Huíla Plateau
Cunene
Cubango
Zambezi
Lake Kariba
Mount Mulanje 3002
Mozambique Channel
Tanjona Masoala
Mauritius

Etosha Pan
Zambezi
Victoria Falls
Makgadikgadi
Savé
M a d a g a s c a r
Réunion

Kapoveld
Okavango Delta
Limpopo
Boby 2658

Namib Desert
Kalahari Desert
Tanjona Vohimena

Orange
Vaal
Thabana-Ntlenyana 3482
Drakensberg
Great Karoo
Little Karoo

St Helena Bay
Cape of Good Hope
Cape Agulhas

Tristan da Cunha

Facts

- The Atlas Mountains are part of the same geological system as the Alps

- Lake Chad has shrunk by almost 95% over the last 40 years

- The Suez Canal, linking the Mediterranean Sea to the Red Sea is 163 kilometres long and opened in 1869

- The Sahara desert covers 9 million square kilometres, approximately 30% of Africa's total land area

- Lake Assal in Djibouti is the saltiest lake in the world

Lake Victoria, Africa's largest lake, and Lake Albert lie within Africa's Great Rift Valley.

Africa's physical features

Highest mountain	Kilimanjaro, Tanzania	5 892 metres	19 331 feet
Longest river	Nile	6 695 km	4 160 miles
Largest lake	Lake Victoria	68 800 sq km	26 564 sq miles
Largest island	Madagascar	587 040 sq km	226 656 sq miles
Largest drainage basin	Congo, Congo/Dem. Rep. Congo	3 700 000 sq km	1 428 570 sq miles
Lowest point	Lake Assal, Djibouti	-152 metres	-499 feet

Kilimanjaro, Kenya/Tanzania, the highest point in Africa at 5 892m.

Africa Countries

Africa is a complex continent, with over fifty independent countries and a long history of political change. It supports a great variety of ethnic groups, with the Sahara creating the major divide between Arab and Berber groups in the north and a diverse range of groups, including the Yoruba and Masai, in the south.

The current pattern of countries in Africa is a product of a long and complex history, including the colonial period, which saw European control of the vast majority of the continent from the fifteenth century until widespread moves to independence began in the 1950s. Despite its great wealth of natural resources, Africa is by far the world's poorest continent. Many of its countries are heavily dependent upon foreign aid and many are also subject to serious political instability.

Cape Verde, North Atlantic Ocean, a small group of islands lying 500 kilometres off the coast of west Africa.

Madeira (Portugal)

Canary Islands (Spain)

Laâyoune

WESTERN SAHARA

Nouâdhibou

MAURITANI

Nouakchott

CAPE VERDE

St-Louis

Dakar

Praia

SENEGAL

Banjul   Kaolack   Kaye

THE GAMBIA

GUINEA-BISSAU   Bissau

GUINEA

Conakry   Kar

Freetown

SIERRA LEONE

Monrovia

LIBER

MOST NORTHERLY CAPITAL
Tunis

LARGEST CAPITAL
Cairo

LARGEST COUNTRY (AREA)
Sudan

LARGEST COUNTRY (POPULATION)
Nigeria

HIGHEST CAPITAL
Addis Ababa

SMALLEST CAPITAL
Victoria

Ascension (U.K.)

SMALLEST COUNTRY (AREA AND POPULATION)
Seychelles

LEAST DENSELY POPULATED COUNTRY
Namibia

MOST DENSELY POPULATED COUNTRY
Mauritius

MOST SOUTHERLY CAPITAL
Cape Town

Internet Links

● UK Foreign and Commonwealth Office	**www.fco.gov.uk**
● CIA World Factbook	**www.odci.gov/cia/publications/factbook**
● Southern African Development Community	**www.sadc.int**
● Satellite imagery	**www.spaceimaging.com**

Facts

- Africa has over 1 000 linguistic and cultural groups
- Only Liberia and Ethiopia have remained free from colonial rule throughout their history
- Over 30% of the world's minerals, and over 50% of the world's diamonds, come from Africa
- 9 of the 10 poorest countries in the world are in Africa

Africa percentage of total population and land area

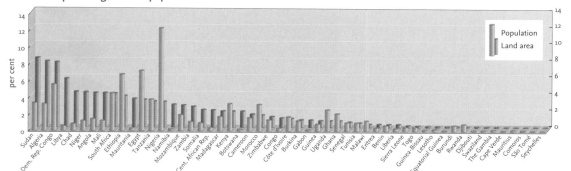

per cent

Population
Land area

Sudan, Algeria, Dem. Rep. Congo, Libya, Chad, Niger, Angola, Mali, South Africa, Ethiopia, Mauritania, Egypt, Tanzania, Nigeria, Namibia, Mozambique, Zambia, Somalia, Cent. African Rep., Madagascar, Kenya, Botswana, Cameroon, Morocco, Zimbabwe, Congo, Côte d'Ivoire, Burkina, Gabon, Guinea, Uganda, Ghana, Senegal, Tunisia, Malawi, Eritrea, Benin, Liberia, Sierra Leone, Togo, Guinea-Bissau, Lesotho, Equatorial Guinea, Burundi, Rwanda, Djibouti, Swaziland, The Gambia, Cape Verde, Mauritius, Comoros, São Tomé, Seychelles

EUROPE

Mediterranean Sea

MOROCCO
Strait of Tangier
Gibraltar
Casablanca
Rabat
Beni Mellal
arrakech
Fès
Oran
Algiers
Sidi Bel Abbès
Ech Chélif
Béchar
Laghouat

Atlas Mountains

ALGERIA

Skikda Annaba
Bejaïa Constantine Tunis
TUNISIA Tripoli
Sfax
Gabès
Miṣrātah
Gulf of Sirte
Benghazi

LIBYA

Libyan Desert

Al Baydā'

S a h a r a

Alexandria
Tanta Cairo
Giza
Suez
Al Minyā
Asyūṭ
EGYPT
Qina
Luxor
Aswān
Lake Nasser

Nile

Port Said

Red Sea

Space Imaging

Cairo, capital of Egypt and the largest city in Africa with 11 146 000 inhabitants.

ASIA

Port Sudan

MALI
Niger
Gao
Mopti
gou
amako
o-Dioulasso

Niamey
BURKINA
Ouagadougou
Tamale
BENIN

NIGER
Agadez
Zinder
Sokoto
Kano
Maiduguri
Zaria
Maroua
NIGERIA Kumo
Ogbomosho
Abuja

CHAD
Abéché
Lake Chad Ndjamena
Moundou
Sarh
Bossangoa
Bouar

SUDAN
Omdurman
Khartoum Wad Medani
Gedaref
El Obeid

Blue Nile
White Nile

ERITREA
Asmara
Mek'elē
Bahir Dar

DJIBOUTI
Djibouti
Dirē Dawa
Addis Ababa

Berbera
Hargeysa

Gulf of Aden

CÔTE
Bouaké
moussoukro
GHANA
Kumasi
D'IVOIRE
Abidjan

Ibadan
Lake Volta Lagos
TOGO
Parakou
Lomé
Accra
Cape Coast
Porto-Novo

Onitsha
Warri
Uyo
CAMEROON
Port Harcourt
Douala
Malabo
Nkongsamba
Yaoundé

Ngaoundéré

CENTRAL AFRICAN REPUBLIC
Bangui

Wau

Juba

ETHIOPIA

SOMALIA
Mogadishu

Gulf of Guinea
EQUATORIAL GUINEA
São Tomé
SÃO TOMÉ AND PRÍNCIPE
Libreville
Port-Gentil
GABON
Franceville

CONGO
Mbandaka
Bandundu
Brazzaville
Pointe-Noire
CABINDA (Angola)
Kinshasa
Matadi

DEMOCRATIC REPUBLIC OF CONGO
Kisangani
Congo
Kikwit
Kasai
Kananga
Mbuji-Mayi
Kamina

UGANDA
Kampala
RWANDA
Bukavu Kigali
BURUNDI
Bujumbura
Kigoma

Congo

Kisumu
Nakuru
Lake Victoria
Mwanza
Arusha

KENYA
Mount Kenya 5199
Nairobi

Kilimanjaro 5895

Kismaayo

Mombasa

Tanga

INDIAN OCEAN

Victoria

SEYCHELLES

ATLANTIC OCEAN

Luanda
Cuanza
Lobito
Benguela
ANGOLA
Huambo
Namibe
Lubango

St Helena and Dependencies (U.K.)

Cubango

Tabora
Dodoma
TANZANIA
Iringa
Mbeya
Kasama
Mansa
Likasi
Lubumbashi
Solwezi
Ndola
Chingola
Kabwe
ZAMBIA
Mongu
Lusaka

MALAWI
Lake Nyasa
Chipata
Lilongwe
Blantyre
Nampula

Kalemie
Lake Tanganyika
Zanzibar
Zanzibar Island
Dar es Salaam

Pemba
Nacala

COMOROS
Moroni
Mayotte (France)

Antsirañana

Aldabra Islands

Pemba

Tete
Quelimane
MOZAMBIQUE

Mozambique Channel

Mahajanga

MADAGASCAR
Antananarivo

Toamasina

MAURITIUS
Port Louis

Réunion (France)

Fianarantsoa

Etosha Pan
NAMIBIA
Okavango Delta
Windhoek
Namib Desert

Livingstone
Chitungwiza
Harare
ZIMBABWE
Gweru
Bulawayo
Francistown
BOTSWANA
Gaborone

Mutare
Beira

Inhambane

Toliara

Zambezi

Orange

Johannesburg
Carletonville
Soweto
Pretoria
Xai-Xai
Maputo
Mbabane
SWAZILAND

Kimberley
LESOTHO
Bloemfontein Maseru
REPUBLIC OF SOUTH AFRICA
Cape Town Khayelitsha
Cape of Good Hope
Cape Agulhas
Durban
East London
Port Elizabeth

Space Imaging

Cape Town, legislative capital of the Republic of South Africa and the most southerly African capital city.

Africa's countries

Largest country (area)	Sudan	2 505 813 sq km	967 494 sq miles
Smallest country (area)	Seychelles	455 sq km	176 sq miles
Largest country (population)	Nigeria	124 009 000	
Smallest country (population)	Seychelles	81 000	
Most densely populated country	Mauritius	599 per sq km	1 549 per sq mile
Least densely populated country	Namibia	2 per sq km	6 per sq mile

Africa's capitals

Largest capital (population)	Cairo, Egypt	11 146 000	
Smallest capital (population)	Victoria, Seychelles	30 000	
Most northerly capital	Tunis, Tunisia	36° 46'N	
Most southerly capital	Cape Town, Republic of South Africa	33° 57'S	
Highest capital	Addis Ababa, Ethiopia	2 408 metres	7 900 feet

Lambert Azimuthal Equal Area Projection

1:16 000 000

miles
0   200   400
0   200   400   600   800 km

Africa
Republic of South Africa

Oceania comprises Australia, New Zealand, New Guinea and the islands of the Pacific Ocean. It is the smallest of the world's continents by land area. Its dominating feature is Australia, which is mainly flat and very dry. Australia's western half consists of a low plateau, broken in places by higher mountain ranges, which has very few permanent rivers or lakes. The narrow, fertile coastal plain of the east coast is separated from the interior by the Great Dividing Range, which includes the highest mountain in Australia.

The numerous Pacific islands of Oceania are generally either volcanic in origin or consist of coral. They can be divided into three main regions of Micronesia, north of the equator between Palau and the Gilbert islands; Melanesia, stretching from mountainous New Guinea to Fiji; and Polynesia, covering a vast area of the eastern and central Pacific Ocean.

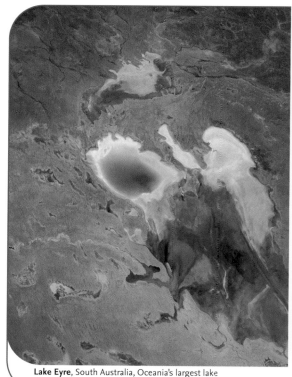

Lake Eyre, South Australia, Oceania's largest lake and the lowest point in Australia.

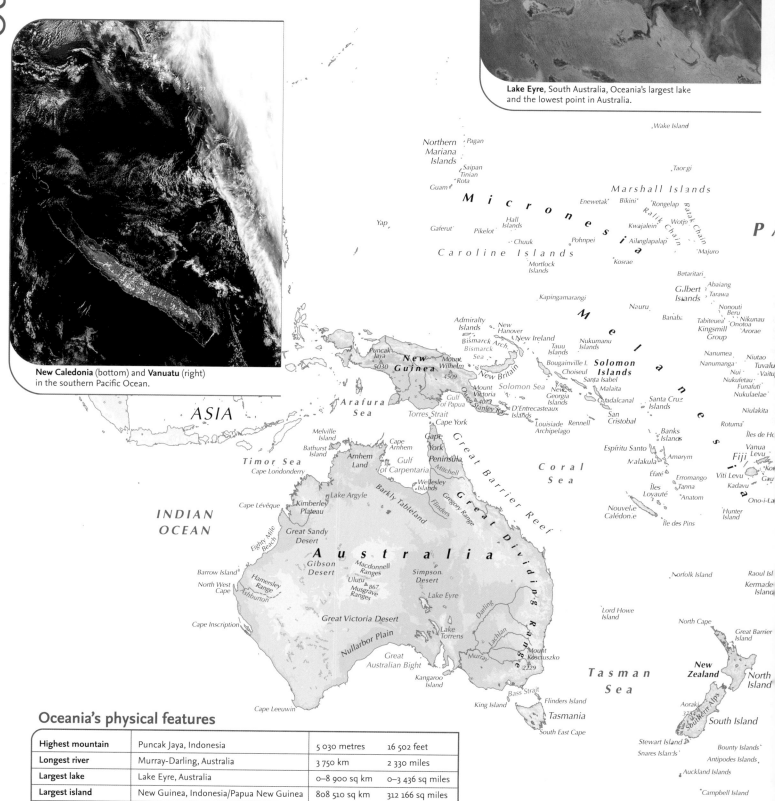

New Caledonia (bottom) and **Vanuatu** (right) in the southern Pacific Ocean.

Oceania's physical features

Highest mountain	Puncak Jaya, Indonesia	5 030 metres	16 502 feet
Longest river	Murray-Darling, Australia	3 750 km	2 330 miles
Largest lake	Lake Eyre, Australia	0–8 900 sq km	0–3 436 sq miles
Largest island	New Guinea, Indonesia/Papua New Guinea	808 510 sq km	312 166 sq miles
Largest drainage basin	Murray-Darling, Australia	1 058 000 sq km	408 494 sq miles
Lowest point	Lake Eyre, Australia	-16 metres	-53 feet

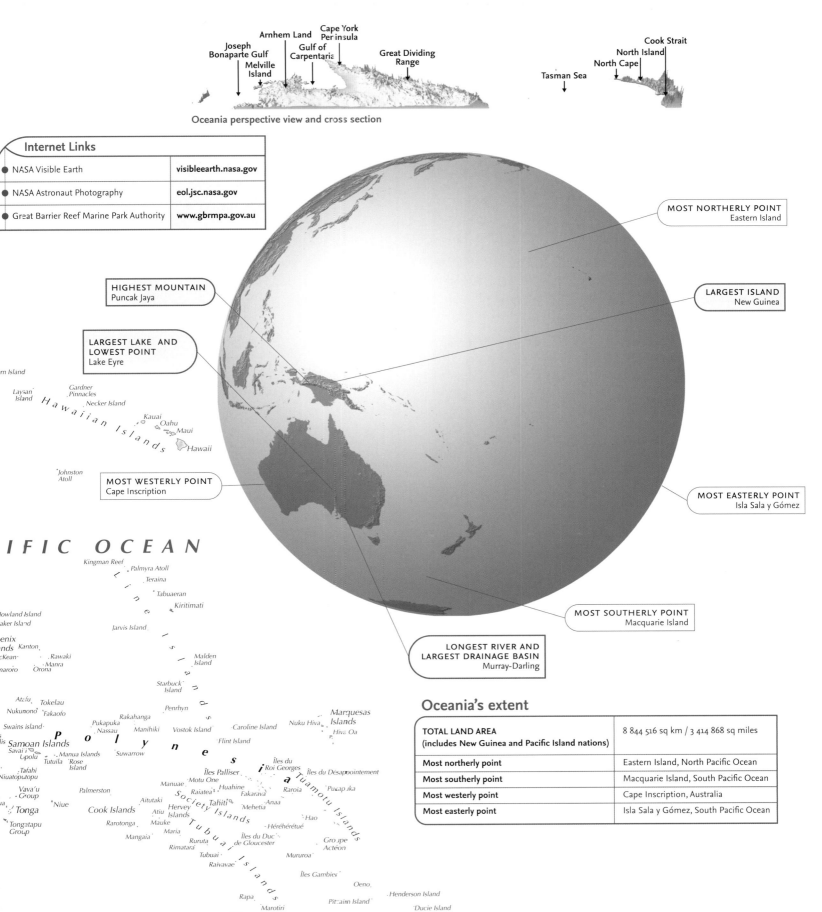

Oceania perspective view and cross section

Joseph Bonaparte Gulf
Melville Island
Arnhem Land
Gulf of Carpentaria
Cape York Peninsula
Great Dividing Range

Cook Strait
North Island
North Cape
Tasman Sea

MOST NORTHERLY POINT
Eastern Island

LARGEST ISLAND
New Guinea

HIGHEST MOUNTAIN
Puncak Jaya

LARGEST LAKE AND LOWEST POINT
Lake Eyre

MOST WESTERLY POINT
Cape Inscription

MOST EASTERLY POINT
Isla Sala y Gómez

MOST SOUTHERLY POINT
Macquarie Island

LONGEST RIVER AND LARGEST DRAINAGE BASIN
Murray-Darling

ern Island

Laysan Island
Gardner Pinnacles
Necker Island
Hawaiian Islands
Kauai
Oahu
Maui
Hawaii
Johnston Atoll

IFIC OCEAN

Kingman Reef
Palmyra Atoll
Teraina
Tabuaeran
Kiritimati
Line Islands
Howland Island
Baker Island
Jarvis Island
enix ands
Kanton
cKean
Rawaki
Manra
maroro
Orona
Malden Island
Starbuck Island
Atafu
Tokelau
Nukunono
Fakaofo
Penrhyn
Rakahanga
Pukapuka
Nassau
Manihiki
Vostok Island
Caroline Island
Marquesas Islands
Nuku Hiva
Hiva Oa
Swains island
Polynesia
lis
Samoan Islands
Savai'i
Upolu
Manua Islands
Rose Island
Suwarrow
Flint Island
Tafahi
Niuatoputopu
Vava'u Group
Palmerston
Niue
Manuae
Motu One
Îles Palliser
Raiatea
Tahiti
Huahine
Mehetia
Anaa
Raroia
Pukapuka
Îles du Roi Georges
Îles du Désappointement
Society Islands
Aitutaki
Atiu
Hervey Islands
Hao
Tuamotu Islands
Tonga
Cook Islands
Mauke
Rarotonga
Maria
Ruruta
Rimatara
Mangaia
Îles du Duc de Gloucester
Héréhérétué
Groupe Actéon
Tubuai Islands
Tubuai
Mururoa
Raivavae
Îles Gambier
Oeno
Rapa
Marotiri
Pitcairn Island
Henderson Island
Ducie Island
Tongatapu Group
ua

Oceania's extent

TOTAL LAND AREA (includes New Guinea and Pacific Island nations)	8 844 516 sq km / 3 414 868 sq miles
Most northerly point	Eastern Island, North Pacific Ocean
Most southerly point	Macquarie Island, South Pacific Ocean
Most westerly point	Cape Inscription, Australia
Most easterly point	Isla Sala y Gómez, South Pacific Ocean

Facts

- Australia's Great Barrier Reef is the world's largest coral reef and stretches for over 2 000 kilometres

- The highest point of Tuvalu is only 5 metres above sea level

- New Zealand lies directly on the boundary between the Pacific and Indo-Australian tectonic plates

- The Mariana Trench in the Pacific Ocean contains the earth's deepest point – Challenger Deep, 10 920 metres below sea level

atham Islands
Island

The spectacular **Banks Peninsula**, South Island, New Zealand, formed by two overlapping volcanic centres.

HERN OCEAN

Oceania Countries

Stretching across almost the whole width of the Pacific Ocean, Oceania has a great variety of cultures and an enormously diverse range of countries and territories. Australia, by far the largest and most industrialized country in the continent, contrasts with the numerous tiny Pacific island nations which have smaller, and more fragile economies based largely on agriculture, fishing and the exploitation of natural resources.

The division of the Pacific island groups into the main regions of Micronesia, Melanesia and Polynesia – often referred to as the South Sea islands – broadly reflects the ethnological differences across the continent. There is a long history of colonial influence in the region, which still contains dependent territories belonging to Australia, France, New Zealand, the UK and the USA.

Wellington, capital of New Zealand and the most southerly national capital in the world.

Tasmania, a small Australian island state, separated from the mainland by the Bass Strait.

Facts

- Over 91% of Australia's population live in urban areas

- The Maori name for New Zealand is Aotearoa, meaning 'land of the long white cloud'

- Auckland, New Zealand, has the largest Polynesian population of any city in Oceania

- Over 800 different languages are spoken in Papua New Guinea

Internet Links

UK Foreign and Commonwealth Office	www.fco.gov.uk
CIA World Factbook	www.odci.gov/cia/publications/factbook
Geoscience Australia	www.ga.gov.au

SOUTHERN

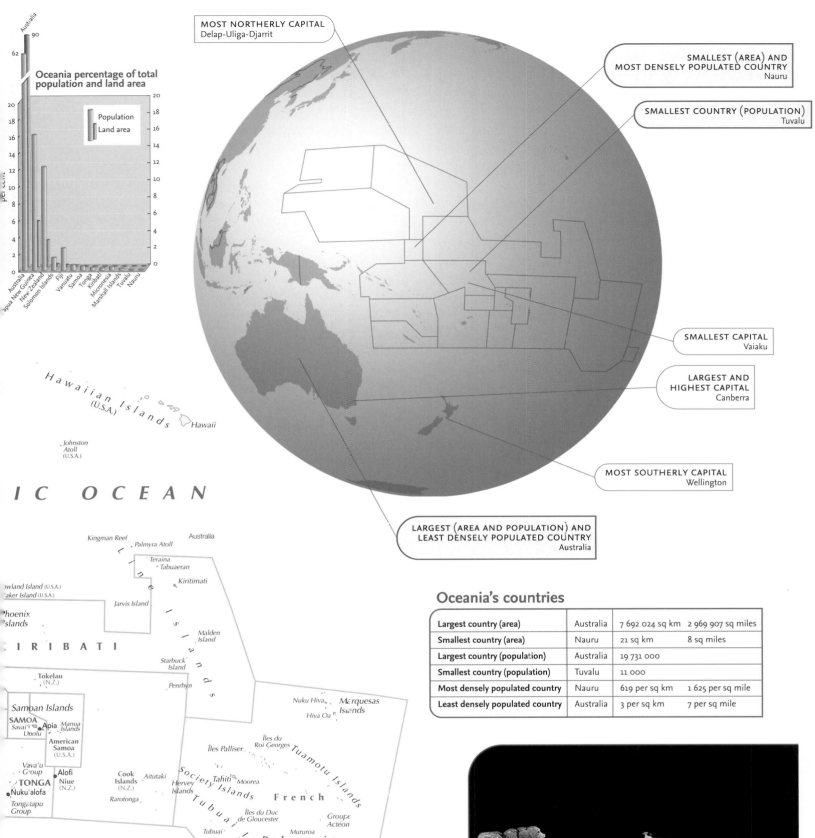

Oceania percentage of total population and land area

per cent

Australia 90
62

20
18
16
14
12
10
8
6
4
2
0

Population
Land area

Australia
Papua New Guinea
New Zealand
Solomon Islands
Fiji
Vanuatu
Samoa
Tonga
Kiribati
Micronesia
Marshall Islands
Tuvalu
Nauru

MOST NORTHERLY CAPITAL
Delap-Uliga-Djarrit

SMALLEST (AREA) AND
MOST DENSELY POPULATED COUNTRY
Nauru

SMALLEST COUNTRY (POPULATION)
Tuvalu

SMALLEST CAPITAL
Vaiaku

LARGEST AND
HIGHEST CAPITAL
Canberra

MOST SOUTHERLY CAPITAL
Wellington

LARGEST (AREA AND POPULATION) AND
LEAST DENSELY POPULATED COUNTRY
Australia

IC   OCEAN

Hawaiian Islands
(U.S.A.)
Hawaii

Johnston
Atoll
(U.S.A.)

Kingman Reef
Palmyra Atoll
Australia

Teraina
Tabuaeran
Kiritimati

owland Island (U.S.A.)
aker Island (U.S.A.)

Jarvis Island

hoenix
slands

Malden
Island

K I R I B A T I

Starbuck
Island

Tokelau
(N.Z.)

Penrhyn

Line Islands

Nuku Hiva
Hiva Oa

Marquesas
Islands

Samoan Islands

SAMOA   Apia   Manua
Savai'i   Islands
Upolu

American
Samoa
(U.S.A.)

Îles Palliser

Îles du
Roi Georges

Vava'u
Group

Alofi
Niue
(N.Z.)

Cook
Islands
(N.Z.)

Aitutaki

Tahiti
Moorea

Tuamotu Islands

TONGA

Nuku'alofa

Hervey
Islands

Society Islands

French

Tongatapu
Group

Rarotonga

Tubuai Islands

Îles du Duc
de Gloucester

Groupe
Actéon

Tubuai

Mururoa

Polynesia

Îles Gambier

Pitcairn Is
(U.K.)   Henderson Island

Rapa

Pitcairn Island

atham Islands
Z.)

Oceania's countries

Largest country (area)	Australia	7 692 024 sq km	2 969 907 sq miles
Smallest country (area)	Nauru	21 sq km	8 sq miles
Largest country (population)	Australia	19 731 000	
Smallest country (population)	Tuvalu	11 000	
Most densely populated country	Nauru	619 per sq km	1 625 per sq mile
Least densely populated country	Australia	3 per sq km	7 per sq mile

Oceania's capitals

Largest capital (population)	Canberra, Australia	387 000
Smallest capital (population)	Vaiaku, Tuvalu	5 100
Most northerly capital	Delap-Uliga-Djarrit, Marshall Islands	7° 7'N
Most southerly capital	Wellington, New Zealand	41° 18'S
Highest capital	Canberra, Australia	581 metres 1 906 feet

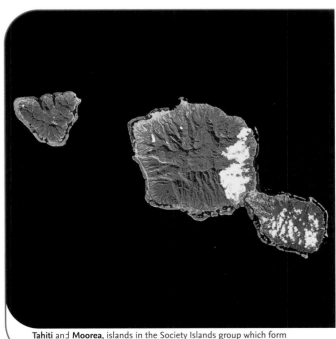

Tahiti and **Moorea**, islands in the Society Islands group which form part of the dependent territory of French Polynesia.

C E A N

Lambert Azimuthal Equal Area Projection

1:20 000 000

| 0 | 200 | 400 | 600 | miles |

| 0 | 200 | 400 | 600 | 800 | 1000 | km |

Oceania
Australia, New Zealand and Southwest Pacific

Lambert Azimuthal Equal Area Projection

1:8 000 000

Oceania
Western Australia

Lambert Azimuthal Equal Area Projection

1:8 000 000

0	100	200	300	miles

| 0 | 100 | 200 | 300 | 400 | 500 | km |

Oceania
Eastern Australia

Oceania
Southeast Australia

Lambert Azimuthal Equal Area Projection

1:5 000 000

Tasman
Sea

NEW
ZEALAND

North
Island

South
Island

Tasman Sea

PACIFIC
OCEAN

Conic Equidistant Projection

1:5 250 000

0   50   100   150 miles
0   50   100   150   200   250 km

North America Landscapes

North America, the world's third largest continent, supports a wide range of landscapes from the Arctic north to sub-tropical Central America. The main physiographic regions of the continent are the mountains of the west coast, stretching from Alaska in the north to Mexico and Central America in the south; the vast, relatively flat Canadian Shield; the Great Plains which make up the majority of the interior; the Appalachian Mountains in the east; and the Atlantic coastal plain.

These regions contain some significant physical features, including the Rocky Mountains, the Great Lakes – three of which are amongst the five largest lakes in the world – and the Mississippi-Missouri river system which is the world's fourth longest river. The Caribbean Sea contains a complex pattern of islands, many volcanic in origin, and the continent is joined to South America by the narrow Isthmus of Panama.

Internet Links

NASA Visible Earth	visibleearth.nasa.gov
U.S. Geological Survey	www.usgs.gov
Natural Resources Canada	www.nrcan-rncan.gc.ca
SPOT Image satellite imagery	www.spotimage.fr

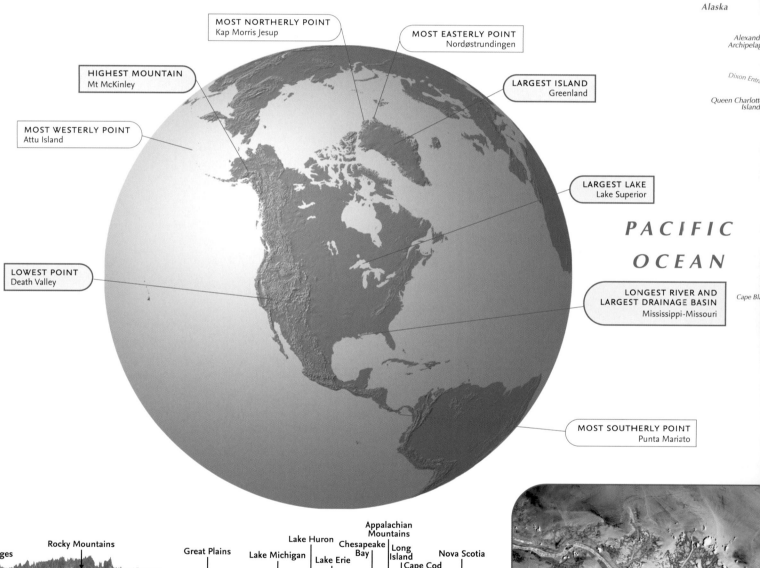

MOST NORTHERLY POINT — Kap Morris Jesup
MOST EASTERLY POINT — Nordøstrundingen
HIGHEST MOUNTAIN — Mt McKinley
LARGEST ISLAND — Greenland
MOST WESTERLY POINT — Attu Island
LARGEST LAKE — Lake Superior
LOWEST POINT — Death Valley
LONGEST RIVER AND LARGEST DRAINAGE BASIN — Mississippi-Missouri
MOST SOUTHERLY POINT — Punta Mariato

PACIFIC OCEAN

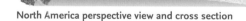

North America perspective view and cross section

North America's physical features

Highest mountain	Mt McKinley, USA	6 194 metres	20 321 feet
Longest river	Mississippi-Missouri, USA	5 969 km	3 709 miles
Largest lake	Lake Superior, Canada/USA	82 100 sq km	31 699 sq miles
Largest island	Greenland	2 175 600 sq km	839 999 sq miles
Largest drainage basin	Mississippi-Missouri, USA	3 250 000 sq km	1 254 825 sq miles
Lowest point	Death Valley, USA	-86 metres	-282 feet

North America's longest river system, the Mississippi-Missouri, flows into the Gulf of Mexico through the **Mississippi Delta**.

114

North America's extent

TOTAL LAND AREA (including Hawaiian Islands)	24 680 331 sq km / 9 529 076 sq miles
Most northerly point	Kap Morris Jesup, Greenland
Most southerly point	Punta Mariato, Panama
Most westerly point	Attu Island, USA
Most easterly point	Nordostrundingen, Greenland

The **Grand Canyon**, Arizona, USA, the world's largest and most spectacular land canyon.

Facts

- Devon Island, Canada, is the world's largest uninhabited island
- Canada has the longest coastline of any country in the world
- Lake Superior is the world's largest freshwater lake
- Over 320 000 square kilometres of the USA is protected for conservation purposes

The **Yucatán peninsula**, Mexico, divides the Gulf of Mexico from the Caribbean Sea.

ARCTIC OCEAN

Greenland Sea

Kap Morris Jesup

Shannon Ø

Kong Frederik VIII Land

Kong Oscars Fjord

Kangertittivaq

Ellesmere Island

Axel Heiberg Island

Kong Christian X Land

Denmark Strait

Ellef Ringnes Island

Borden Island

Queen Elizabeth Islands

Greenland

Point Barrow

Prince Patrick Island

Parry Islands

Melville Island

Devon Island

Kong Christian IX Land

Beaufort Sea

Banks Island

Parry Channel

Eylot Island

Baffin Bay

Qimusseriarsuaq

Porcupine

Somerset Island

Prince of Wales Island

Brodeur Peninsula

Baffin Island

Davis Strait

Kong Frederik VI Kyst

Yukon

Victoria Island

Boothia Peninsula

Home Bay

Cape Farewell

Mackenzie Mountains

King William Island

Gulf of Boothia

Prince Charles Island

Qeqertarsuaq

Selwyn Mountains

Great Bear Lake

Queen Maud Gulf

Nettilling Lake

Cumberland Peninsula

Cassiar Mountains

Liard

Southampton Island

Foxe Basin

Cumberland Sound

Labrador Sea

Coast Mountains

Caribou Mountains

Great Slave Lake

Dubawnt Lake

Foxe Pen

Amadjuak Lake

Frobisher Bay

Peace

Lake Athabasca

Wollaston Lake

Coats Island

Mansel Island

Hudson Strait

C. Chidley

Rocky Mountains

Mount Robson 3954

Reindeer Lake

Hudson Bay

Péninsule d'Ungava

Ungava Bay

Labrador

Vancouver Island

North Saskatchewan

Southern Indian Lake

Nelson

Belcher islands

Lac Caniapiscau

Smallwood Reservoir

Fraser

Saskatchewan

Severn

Laurentian Plateau

Mount Rainier 4392

F. D. Roosevelt Lake

South Saskatchewan

Lake Winnipeg

Canadian Shield

James Bay

Reservoir La Grande 2

Lac Bienville

Newfoundland

Cape Race

Columbia

Cascade Range

Bitterroot Range

Lake Winnipegosis

Albany

Île d'Anticosti

Gulf of St Lawrence

Cabot Strait

Missouri

Fort Peck Reservoir

Lake Sakakawea

Lake of the Woods

Lake Nipigon

Great Lakes

Cape Breton Island

ATLANTIC OCEAN

Nova Scotia

Sable Island

Yellowstone

Great Plains

Lake Superior

Lake Huron

St Lawrence

Ottawa

Bay of Fundy

Cape Sable

Snake

Lake Oahe

Missouri

Lake Michigan

Massachusetts Bay

Cape Cod

Columbia

Platte

Illinois

Lake Ontario

Hudson

Sierra Nevada

San Joaquin

Great Salt Lake

Sangre de Cristo Range

Lake Erie

Long Island

Great Basin

Mount Elbert 4398

Lake of the Ozarks

Ohio

Allegheny Mountains

Chesapeake Bay

Death Valley

Grand Canyon

Colorado Plateau

Colorado

Arkansas

Ozark Plateau

Appalachian Mountains

Mount Mitchell 2037

Cape Hatteras

Gila

Canadian

Mississippi

Tennessee

Alabama

Cape Fear

Guadalupe

Rio Grande

Llano Estacado

Pecos

Edwards Plateau

Brazos

Red

Coastal Plain

Cape Canaveral

Baja California

Gulf of California

Conchos

Rio Grande

Sierra Madre Oriental

Mississippi Delta

Grand Bahama

The Bahamas

Great Abaco

West Indies

Yaqui

Padre Island

Gulf of Mexico

Andros

Acklins Island

Turks and Caicos Islands

Virgin Islands

Anguilla

Cabo Falso

Sierra Madre Occidental

Great Inagua

Straits of Florida

Cuba

Puerto Rico

Guadaloupe

Cabo Corrientes

Cayman Islands

Greater Antilles

Hispaniola

Dominica

Martinique

St Lucia

Islas Revillagigedo

Volcán Popocatépetl 5452

Yucatán

Jamaica

Barbados

Sierra Madre del Sur

Bahía de Campeche

Yucatán Channel

Caribbean Sea

Lesser Antilles

Tobago

Islas de la Bahía

Aruba

Netherlands Antilles

Trinidad

Île Clipperton

Gulf of Tehuantepec

Sierra Madre

Golfo de Fonseca

Lago Nicaragua

Panama Canal

Golfo del Darién

SOUTH AMERICA

Península de Nicoya

Cordillera Central

Isthmus of Panama

Gulf of Panamá

North America Countries

North America has been dominated economically and politically by the USA since the nineteenth century. Before that, the continent was subject to colonial influences, particularly of Spain in the south and of Britain and France in the east. The nineteenth century saw the steady development of the western half of the continent. The wealth of natural resources and the generally temperate climate were an excellent basis for settlement, agriculture and industrial development which has led to the USA being the richest nation in the world today.

Although there are twenty three independent countries and fourteen dependent territories in North America, Canada, Mexico and the USA have approximately eighty five per cent of the continent's population and eighty eight per cent of its land area. Large parts of the north remain sparsely populated, while the most densely populated areas are in the northeast USA, and the Caribbean.

Washington DC, a leading international political centre and capital city of the United States.

LARGEST (AREA) AND
LEAST DENSELY POPULATED COUNTRY
Canada

LARGEST COUNTRY (POPULATION)
United States of America

MOST NORTHERLY CAPITAL
Ottawa

LARGEST AND
HIGHEST CAPITAL
Mexico City

SMALLEST COUNTRY
(AREA AND POPULATION)
St Kitts and Nevis

MOST DENSELY POPULATED COUNTRY
Barbados

SMALLEST CAPITAL
Belmopan

MOST SOUTHERLY CAPITAL
Panama City

North America's capitals

Largest capital (population)	Mexico City, Mexico	19 013 000	
Smallest capital (population)	Belmopan, Belize	9 000	
Most northerly capital	Ottawa, Canada	45° 25'N	
Most southerly capital	Panama City, Panama	8° 56'N	
Highest capital	Mexico City, Mexico	2 300 metres	7 546 feet

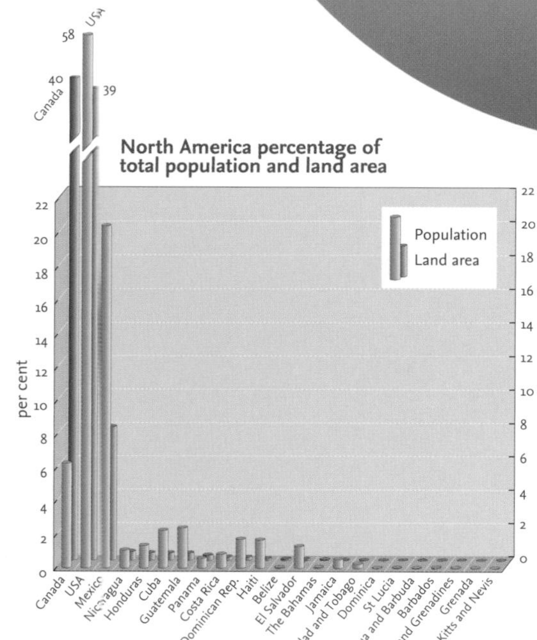

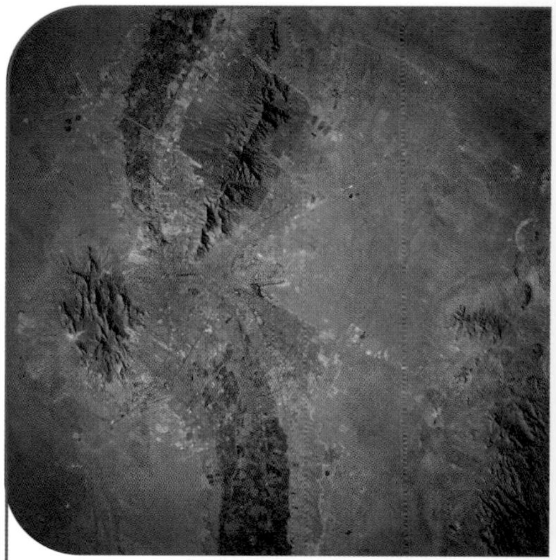

North America percentage of total population and land area

Population
Land area

The cities of **El Paso**, USA, and **Ciudad Juarez**, Mexico, are located on the Rio Grande which forms part of the USA/Mexico border.

North America's countries

Largest country (area)	Canada	9 984 670 sq km	3 855 103 sq miles
Smallest country (area)	St Kitts and Nevis	261 sq km	101 sq miles
Largest country (population)	United States of America	294 043 000	
Smallest country (population)	St Kitts and Nevis	42 000	
Most densely populated country	Barbados	628 per sq km	1 627 per sq mile
Least densely populated country	Canada	3 per sq km	8 per sq mile

Internet Links	
UK Foreign and Commonwealth Office	www.fco.gov.uk
CIA World Factbook	www.odci.gov/cia/publications/factbook
U.S. Board on Geographic Names	geonames.usgs.gov
NASA Astronaut Photography	eol.jsc.nasa.gov

The Bahamas, a chain of islands in the North Atlantic Ocean, lying southeast of Florida, USA.

Facts

- The Panama Canal, opened in 1914, cut the journey between the Atlantic and the Pacific by over 14 000 km

- Mexico City is the highest city in North America and houses approximately 18% of Mexico's population

- The state of Alaska was bought by the USA from Russia in 1867

- The territory of Nunavut is Canada's newest administrative division, created in 1999 from the eastern part of Northwest Territories

Lambert Conformal Conic Projection

1:16 000 000

States in the U.S.A.
numbered on the map:

1. CONNECTICUT (K5)
2. MASSACHUSETTS (K5)
3. NEW HAMPSHIRE (K5)
4. RHODE ISLAND (K5)
5. VERMONT (K5)

Conic Equidistant Projection

1:7 000 000

North America
Western Canada

Labrador Sea

VIK
du
can
s u l e
a v a

Ungava
Bay

Torngat Mountains

NEWFOUNDLAND AND LABRADOR

Labrador

NEWFOUNDLAND
AND LABRADOR
Newfoundland

QUÉBEC

Gulf of St Lawrence

Île d'Anticosti

QUÉBEC

Péninsule de Gaspé

Monts Notre Dame

NEW BRUNSWICK

MAINE

NOVA SCOTIA

PRINCE EDWARD ISLAND

St Pierre and Miquelon (France)

Cabot Strait

ATLANTIC OCEAN

Bay of Fundy

Gulf of Maine

VERMONT

NEW HAMPSHIRE

ICA

Lambert Conformal Conic Projection

1:12 000 000

0   100   200   300   400   miles
0   100   200   300   400   500   600   700   km

North America
Western United States

Lambert Conformal Conic Projection

1:7 000 000

G

Tropic of Cancer

F

E

D

C

G u l f   o f   M e x i c o

5

6

7

North America
Central United States

States in the U.S.A.
numbered on the map:
1. CONNECTICUT (F3)
2. DELAWARE (F4)
3. MASSACHUSETTS (F3)
4. RHODE ISLAND (G3)

Lambert Conformal Conic Projection

1:7 000 000

0   100   200   miles
0   100   200   300   400   km

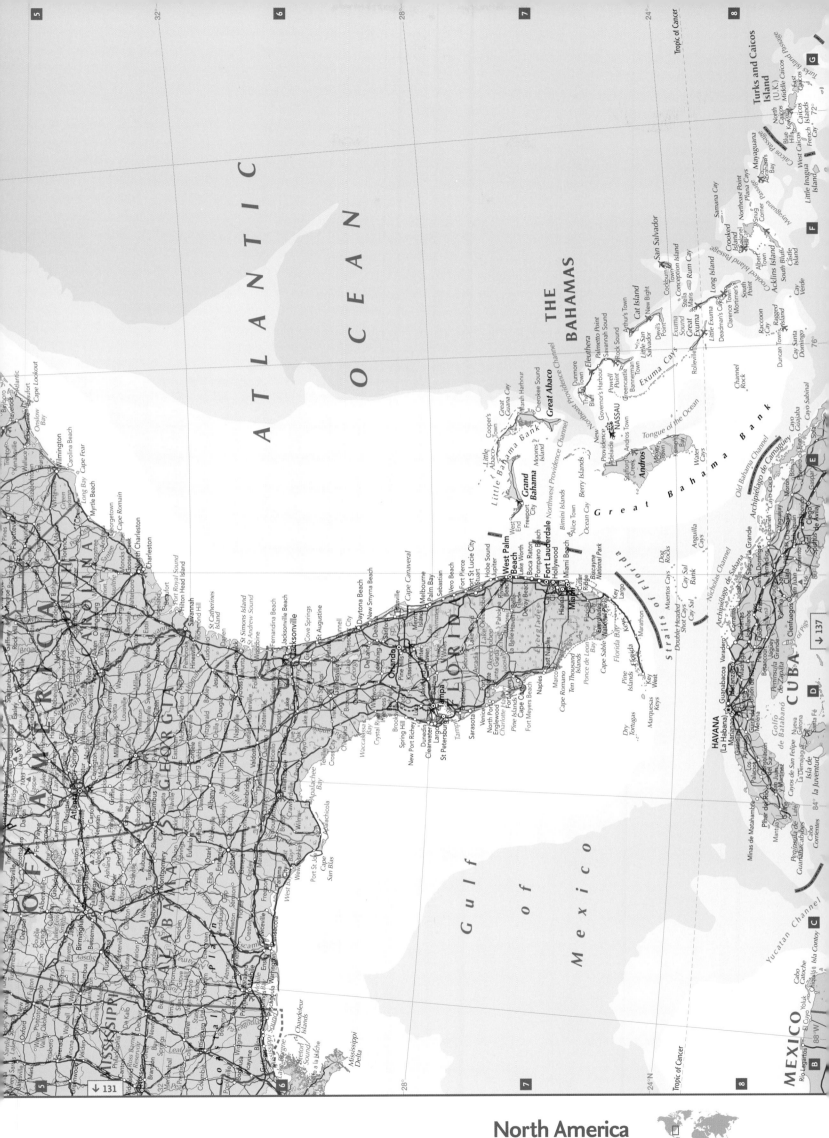

ATLANTIC

OCEAN

Gulf

of

Mexico

THE
BAHAMAS

Tropic of Cancer

NORTH CAROLINA

SOUTH CAROLINA

GEORGIA

ALABAMA

MISSISSIPPI

FLORIDA

CUBA

MEXICO

Turks and Caicos
Island

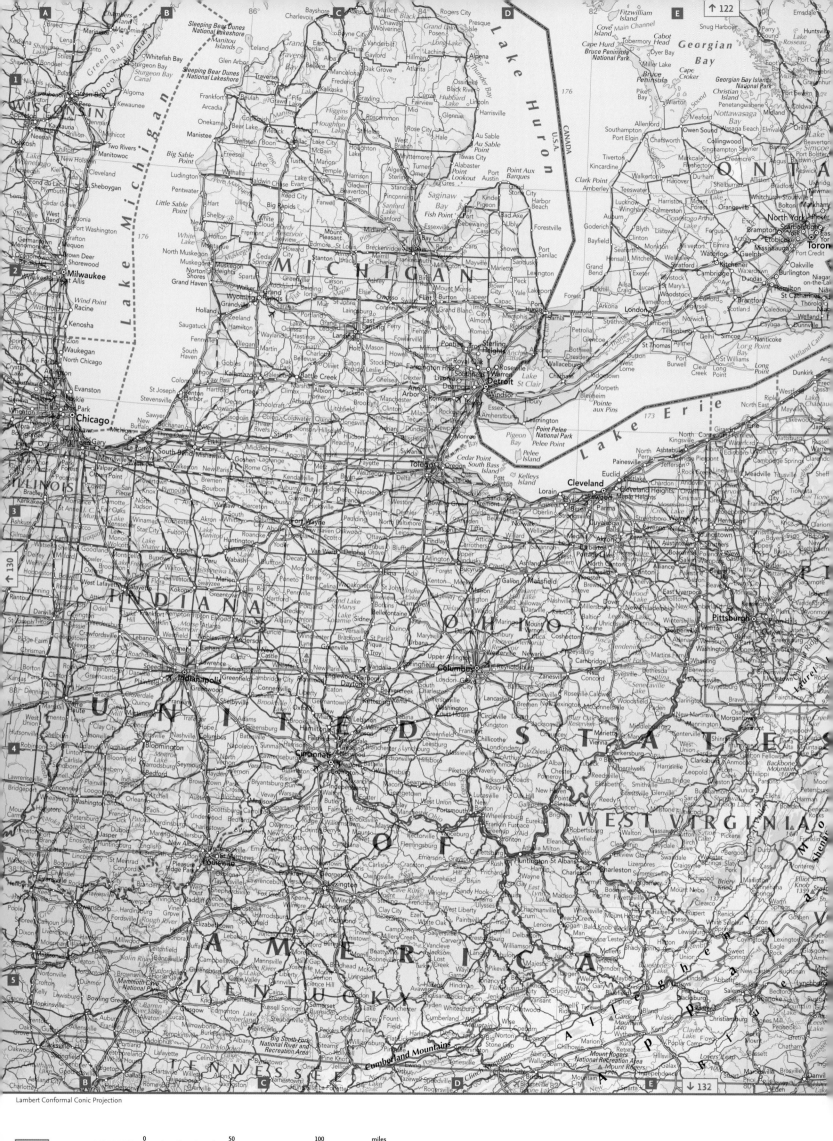

North America
Northeast United States

Lambert Conformal Conic Projection

1:14 000 000

| 0 | | 200 | | 400 | miles |

| 0 | 200 | 400 | 600 | 800 | km |

VIRGINIA 75°

WEST VIRGINIA

Charlottesville · Richmond
Lynchburg · Petersburg · Newport News
Danville · Virginia Beach
Chesapeake · Norfolk

NORTH CAROLINA

Cape Hatteras

SOUTH CAROLINA

Cape Lookout

GEORGIA

Cape Fear

Myrtle Beach
Georgetown

ATLANTIC

Charleston

Hilton Head Island
Savannah

HAMILTON · Bermuda (U.K.)

OCEAN

FLORIDA

Jacksonville
St Augustine

Ocala · Daytona Beach

Orlando · Titusville · Cape Canaveral

Melbourne

Lakeland
Clearwater · Tampa · Vero Beach
St Petersburg · Sebring · Fort Pierce
Bradenton · Sarasota
Venice · Okeechobee · West Palm Beach

Little Abaco
Marsh Harbour
Grand Bahama

Tropic of Cancer

Fort Myers
Fort Lauderdale · Hollywood · Miami
Naples

Cape Sable · Key Largo
Florida Keys
Key West

Straits of Florida

Freeport · Grand Bahama
Bimini Islands

Great Abaco

Eleuthera

Governor's Harbour

NASSAU

THE BAHAMAS

Andros Town · Cat Island
Andros · San Salvador
Rum Cay

Great Exuma
Exuma Cays
Long Island

Crooked Island
Mayaguana

HAVANA
(La Habana) · Cárdenas
Matanzas · Sagua la Grande
Pinar del Río · Santa Clara · Sancti Spíritus
Guane · Cienfuegos · Ciego de Ávila
Golfo de Batabanó · Trinidad · Camagüey
Nueva Gerona · Las Tunas
Isla de la Juventud

Ackins Island
Crooked Island Passage

Great Inagua
Matthew Town

Turks and Caicos Islands
Caicos Islands (U.K.)

GRAND TURK
(Cockburn Town)
Turks Islands

CUBA

Archipiélago de los Jardines de la Reina
Santa Cruz del Sur · Holguín
Golfo de Guacanayabo · Bayamo
Manzanillo · Santiago de Cuba

Cabo Lucrecia · Banes
Nuevitas

Cabo Cruz
Guantánamo
Port-de-Paix · Monte Cristi · Puerto Plata
Cap-Haïtien · Santiago

Hispaniola

Virgin Islands (U.K.)

Leeward Islands

Anguilla (U.K.)
THE VALLEY
St-Martin (France)
St-Barthélemy (France)

Little Cayman
Grand Cayman
Cayman Brac

St Ann's Bay

Cayman Islands (U.K.)
GEORGE TOWN

Montego Bay
Savanna-la-Mar · Mandeville
Spanish Town

JAMAICA · KINGSTON

Jérémie
Île de la Gonâve
PORT-AU-PRINCE

HAITI
St-Marc · Gonaïves

Pico Duarte
Elías Piña · La Vega · San Pedro de Macorís
Barahona

Navassa Island (U.S.A.)
Les Cayes · Jacmel

Cabo Beata

DOMINICAN REPUBLIC
SANTO DOMINGO

Pedernales

Higüey · Aguadilla
Mayagüez · SAN JUAN

ROAD TOWN

CHARLOTTE AMALIE

Virgin Islands (U.S.A.)

Ponce · La Romana
Vieques

Puerto Rico (U.S.A.)

Basseterre
ST KITTS AND NEVIS
Montserrat (U.K.)
PLYMOUTH

St Maarten (Neth.)
St Eustatius (Neth.)

ANTIGUA AND BARBUDA
ST JOHN'S
Antigua · Barbuda

Guadeloupe (France)
BASSE-TERRE
Pointe-à-Pitre
Marie-Galante

DOMINICA
ROSEAU

Morne Diablotins

Dominica Passage

FORT-DE-FRANCE
Martinique (France)
CASTRIES
Soufrière

ST LUCIA

St Vincent Passage

BARBADOS
BRIDGETOWN

ST VINCENT AND THE GRENADINES
KINGSTOWN
The Grenadines

GRENADA
ST GEORGE'S

Lesser Antilles

Tobago
Scarborough
TRINIDAD AND TOBAGO
PORT OF SPAIN
Arima · Trinidad
San Fernando

Caribbean Sea

HONDURAS

Roatán
Trujillo
La Ceiba

Punta Patuca
Laguna de Caratasca

Wampusirpi

Cayos Miskitos

NICARAGUA
MANAGUA

Puerto Cabezas

Isla de Providencia (Colombia)

Punta de Perlas
Islas del Maíz (Corn Islands) (Nicaragua)

Isla de San Andrés (Colombia)

Aruba (Neth.)
ORANJESTAD

Netherlands Antilles
Curaçao
WILLEMSTAD
Bonaire

Lesser Antilles

Islas Los Roques

Isla Blanquilla

Isla la Tortuga
Los Testigos
Isla de Margarita
Porlamar
Carúpano
Gulf of Paria

Bluefields

Granada · Lake Nicaragua
Rivas

COSTA RICA

Puerto Limón

SAN JOSÉ

Bahía de Coronado
Península de Osa

Bocas del Toro
Golfo de los Mosquitos

David
PANAMA
Santiago · Penonomé
Las Tablas · Chitré
PANAMA CITY
Colón · El Porvenir
Gulf of Panama
Golfo de Chiriquí
Isla de Coiba
Punta Mariato · Punta Mala

Santa Marta
Ciénaga
Riohacha
Maicao
Punta Gallinas
Península de la Guajira

Barranquilla · Valledupar
Cartagena · Plato

Golfo de Morrosquillo
Sincelejo · Magangué

Golfo del Darién
Acandí

Maracaibo · Cabimas
Golfo de Venezuela
Coro
Paraguaná

Puerto Cabello
CARACAS
Valencia · Maracay · Los Teques
San Carlos · Barcelona
Barquisimeto · Maturín
San Juan de los Morros
Valle de la Pascua
Zaraza

Orinoco Delta
Tucupita
Mariusa
Waini Point

Turbo · Caucasia
Montería

Acarigua
Guanare · El Baúl

El Tigre
Ciudad Guayana

Barinas · San Fernando de Apure
Calabozo

Serranía de Imataca

Mompós
Convención
Ocaña

Mérida
Trujillo · Valera
Guasdualito
Achaguas

El Callao

Bucaramanga
Cúcuta · San Cristóbal
Pamplona

Guárico

Ciudad Bolívar

Maripa

VENEZUELA

Socorro

Arauca

La Paragua

El Dorado
Tramén Tepui

GUYANA

Tumeremo

Medellín

Manizales
Pereira
Armenia
Ibagué

BOGOTÁ
Villavicencio

Quibdó
Cabo Corrientes

Puerto Carreño

San Fernando de Atabapo
Cerro Yaví

Tuluá
Sevilla
Buga

Cali
Buenaventura

Neiva

San José del Guaviare

Puerto Inírida

Serra Parima

Boa Vista

Isla Gorgona
Guapi
Popayán

COLOMBIA

Puerto Ayacucho

BRAZIL

North America
Central America and the Caribbean

South America is a continent of great contrasts, with landscapes varying from the tropical rainforests of the Amazon Basin, to the Atacama Desert, the driest place on earth, and the sub-Antarctic regions of southern Chile and Argentina. The dominant physical features are the Andes, stretching along the entire west coast of the continent and containing numerous mountains over 6 000 metres high, and the Amazon, which is the second longest river in the world and has the world's largest drainage basin.

The Altiplano is a high plateau lying between two of the Andes ranges. It contains Lake Titicaca, the world's highest navigable lake. By contrast, large lowland areas dominate the centre of the continent, lying between the Andes and the Guiana and Brazilian Highlands. These vast grasslands stretch from the Llanos of the north through the Selvas and the Gran Chaco to the Pampas of Argentina.

South America's largest lake, **Lake Titicaca**, high in the Andes on the border between Bolivia and Peru.

South America perspective view and cross section

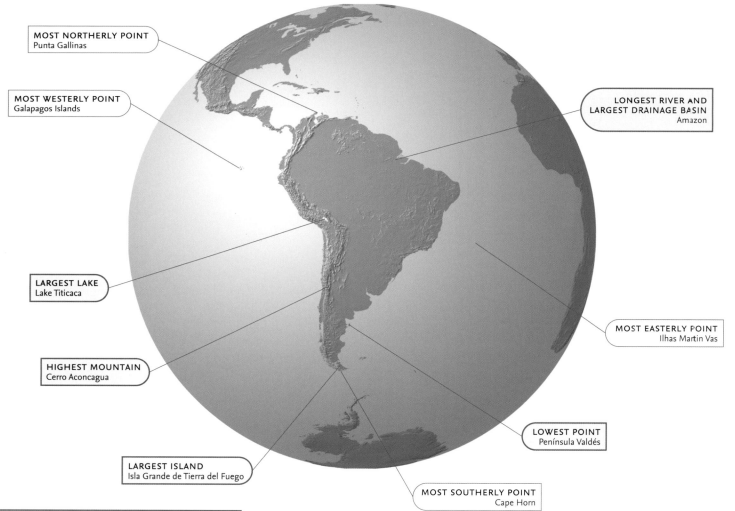

MOST NORTHERLY POINT
Punta Gallinas

MOST WESTERLY POINT
Galapagos Islands

LONGEST RIVER AND
LARGEST DRAINAGE BASIN
Amazon

LARGEST LAKE
Lake Titicaca

MOST EASTERLY POINT
Ilhas Martin Vas

HIGHEST MOUNTAIN
Cerro Aconcagua

LOWEST POINT
Península Valdés

LARGEST ISLAND
Isla Grande de Tierra del Fuego

MOST SOUTHERLY POINT
Cape Horn

Internet Links

NASA Visible Earth	visibleearth.nasa.gov
NASA Astronaut Photography	eol.jsc.nasa.gov
World Rainforest Information Portal	www.rainforestweb.org
Peakware World Mountain Encyclopedia	www.peakware.com

South America's physical features

Highest mountain	Cerro Aconcagua, Argentina	6 959 metres	22 831 feet
Longest river	Amazon	6 516 km	4 049 miles
Largest lake	Lake Titicaca, Bolivia/Peru	8 340 sq km	3 220 sq miles
Largest island	Isla Grande de Tierra del Fuego, Argentina/Chile	47 000 sq km	18 147 sq miles
Largest drainage basin	Amazon	7 050 000 sq km	2 722 005 sq miles
Lowest point	Península Valdés, Argentina	-40 metres	-131 feet

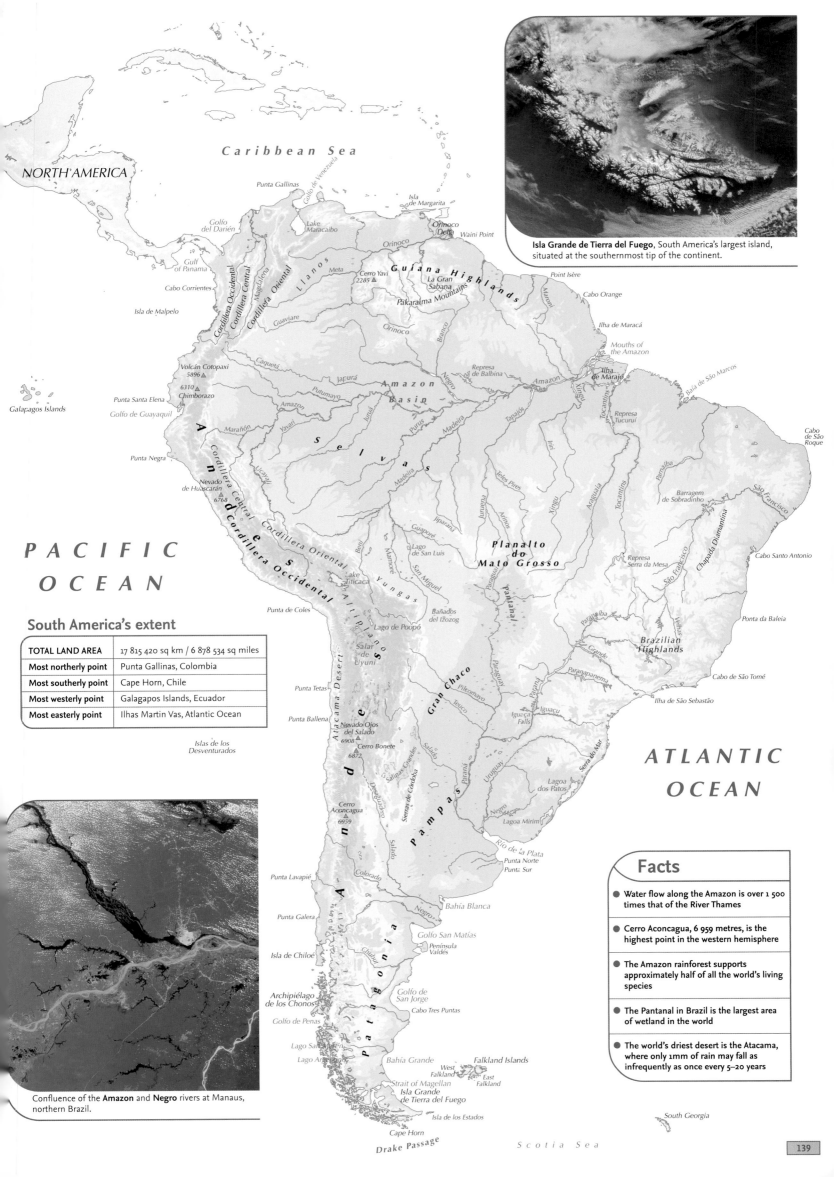

NORTH AMERICA

Caribbean Sea

Punta Gallinas

Golfo del Darién

Gulf of Panama

Cabo Corrientes

Isla de Malpelo

Punta Santa Elena

Galapagos Islands

Punta Negra

Golfo de Venezuela
Lake Maracaibo
Isla de Margarita
Orinoco
Orinoco Delta
Waini Point
Point Isère
Cabo Orange

Cordillera Occidental
Cordillera Central
Cordillera Oriental
Magdalena
L l a n o s
Meta
Cerro Yavi 2285
G u i a n a   H i g h l a n d s
La Gran Sabana
Pakaraima Mountains
Maroni
Ilha de Maracá

Guaviare
Orinoco
Branco
Represa de Balbina
Amazon
Mouths of the Amazon
Ilha de Marajó
Baía de São Marcos

Volcán Cotopaxi 5896
6310 Chimborazo
Caquetá
Japurá
Negro
A m a z o n   B a s i n
Xingu

Golfo de Guayaquil
Amazon
Putumayo
Juruá
Purus
Madeira
Tapajós
Represa Tucuruí
Cabo de São Roque

Marañón
Yavari
S   e   l   v   a   s
Iriri
Tocantins

Punta Negra

Nevado de Huascarán 6768
Ucayali
Madeira
Juruena
Teles Pires
Arinos
Xingu
Araguaia
Tocantins
São Francisco
Barragem de Sobradinho

A n d e s

PACIFIC

OCEAN

Cordillera Central
Cordillera Oriental
Cordillera Occidental
Beni
Guaporé
Lago de San Luis
Mamoré
Juparaná
Planalto do Mato Grosso
Represa Serra da Mesa
São Francisco
Chapada Diamantina
Cabo Santo Antonio

Altiplano
Lake Titicaca
Yungas
San Miguel
Paraguai
Pantanal
Brazilian Highlands
Velhas

South America's extent

TOTAL LAND AREA	17 815 420 sq km / 6 878 534 sq miles
Most northerly point	Punta Gallinas, Colombia
Most southerly point	Cape Horn, Chile
Most westerly point	Galagapos Islands, Ecuador
Most easterly point	Ilhas Martin Vas, Atlantic Ocean

Punta de Coles
Bañados del Izozog
Lago de Poopó
Salar de Uyuni
Gran Chaco
Paraguay
Parnaíba
Ponta da Baleia

Punta Tetas
Atacama Desert
Teuco
Pilcomayo
Grande
Paranapanema
Cabo de São Tomé

Punta Ballena
Nevado Ojos del Salado 6908
Cerro Bonete 6872
Salado
Salinas Grandes
Sierras de Córdoba
Iguaçu Falls
Iguaçu
Uruguay
Paraná
Ilha de São Sebastião

ATLANTIC

OCEAN

Islas de los Desventurados

Salado
Desaguadero
Negro
Lagoa dos Patos
Serra do Mar

Cerro Aconcagua 6959
P a m p a s
Uruguay
Río de la Plata
Punta Norte
Punta Sur
Lagoa Mirim

Punta Lavapié
Salado
Colorado
Bahía Blanca

Punta Galera
Negro
Golfo San Matías
Península Valdés

Isla de Chiloé
P a t a g o n i a
Chubut
Golfo de San Jorge
Cabo Tres Puntas

Archipiélago de los Chonos
Golfo de Peñas
Lago San Martín
Lago Argentino
Bahía Grande
West Falkland
East Falkland
Falkland Islands

Strait of Magellan
Isla Grande de Tierra del Fuego
Isla de los Estados
South Georgia

Cape Horn
Drake Passage
Scotia Sea

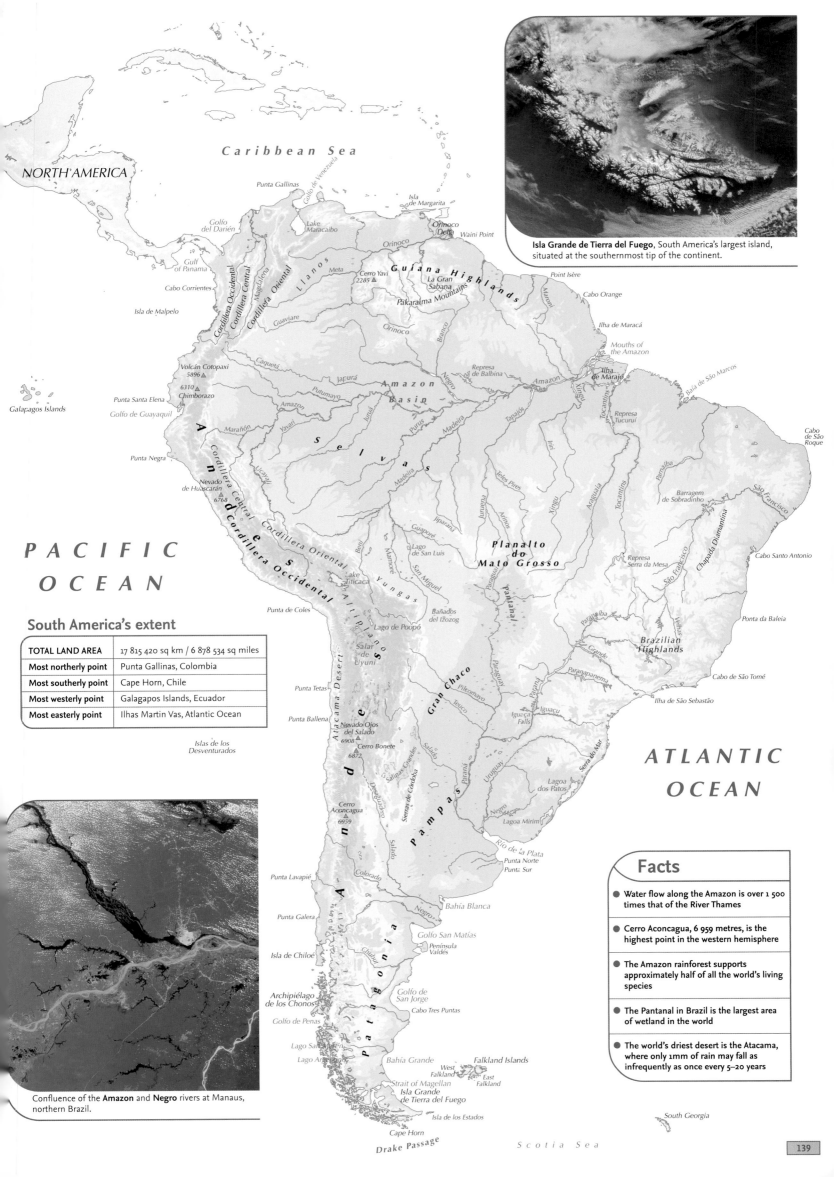

Isla Grande de Tierra del Fuego, South America's largest island, situated at the southernmost tip of the continent.

Confluence of the **Amazon** and **Negro** rivers at Manaus, northern Brazil.

Facts

- Water flow along the Amazon is over 1 500 times that of the River Thames

- Cerro Aconcagua, 6 959 metres, is the highest point in the western hemisphere

- The Amazon rainforest supports approximately half of all the world's living species

- The Pantanal in Brazil is the largest area of wetland in the world

- The world's driest desert is the Atacama, where only 1mm of rain may fall as infrequently as once every 5–20 years

French Guiana, a French Department, is the only remaining territory under overseas control on a continent which has seen a long colonial history. Much of South America was colonized by Spain in the sixteenth century, with Britain, Portugal and the Netherlands each claiming territory in the northeast of the continent. This colonization led to the conquering of ancient civilizations, including the Incas in Peru. Most countries became independent from Spain and Portugal in the early nineteenth century.

The population of the continent reflects its history, being composed primarily of indigenous Indian peoples and mestizos – reflecting the long Hispanic influence. There has been a steady process of urbanization within the continent, with major movements of the population from rural to urban areas. The majority of the population now live in the major cities and within 300 kilometres of the coast.

Rio de Janeiro, third largest city in Brazil and the capital until 1960 when the status of capital was transferred to Brasília.

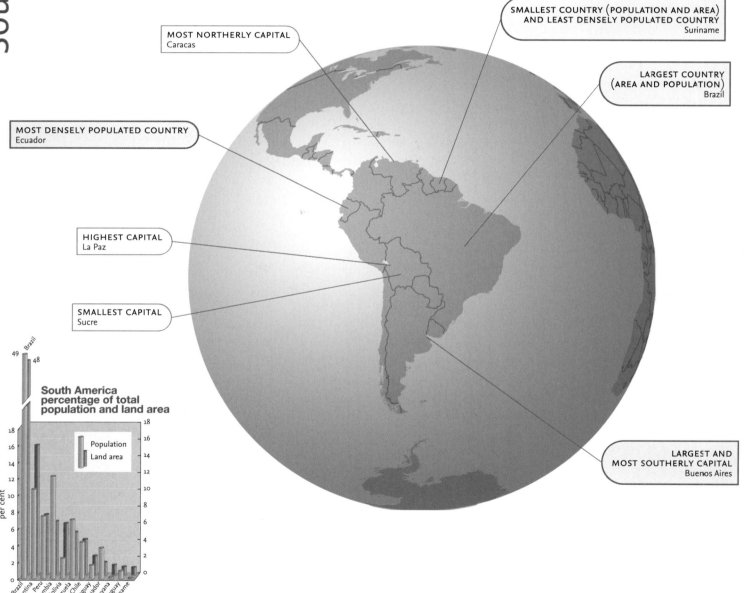

MOST NORTHERLY CAPITAL
Caracas

SMALLEST COUNTRY (POPULATION AND AREA) AND LEAST DENSELY POPULATED COUNTRY
Suriname

LARGEST COUNTRY (AREA AND POPULATION)
Brazil

MOST DENSELY POPULATED COUNTRY
Ecuador

HIGHEST CAPITAL
La Paz

SMALLEST CAPITAL
Sucre

LARGEST AND MOST SOUTHERLY CAPITAL
Buenos Aires

South America percentage of total population and land area

Population
Land area

per cent

Brazil 49 / 48

Brazil Argentina Peru Colombia Bolivia Venezuela Chile Paraguay Ecuador Guyana Uruguay Suriname

South America's countries

Largest country (area)	Brazil	8 514 879 sq km	3 287 613 sq miles
Smallest country (area)	Suriname	163 820 sq km	63 251 sq miles
Largest country (population)	Brazil	178 470 000	
Smallest country (population)	Suriname	436 000	
Most densely populated country	Ecuador	48 per sq km	124 per sq mile
Least densely populated country	Suriname	3 per sq km	7 per sq mile

Internet Links

UK Foreign and Commonwealth Office	www.fco.gov.uk
CIA World Factbook	www.odci.gov/cia/publications/factbook
Caribbean Community (Caricom)	www.caricom.org
Latin American Network Information Center	lanic.utexas.edu

South America's capitals

Largest capital (population)	Buenos Aires, Argentina	13 349 000
Smallest capital (population)	Sucre, Bolivia	183 000
Most northerly capital	Caracas, Venezuela	10° 28'N
Most southerly capital	Buenos Aires, Argentina	34° 36'S
Highest capital	La Paz, Bolivia	3 630 metres 11 909 feet

Caribbean Sea

NORTH AMERICA

Punta Gallinas

Barranquilla
Cartagena
Maracaibo
Cabimas
Maracay
Caracas
Cumaná
Barquisimeto
Valencia
Monteria
San Cristóbal
Ciudad Bolívar
VENEZUELA
Georgetown
Paramaribo
GUYANA
Cayenne
Medellín
Tunja
Puerto Ayacucho
SURINAME
French Guiana
Ibagué
Bogotá
Orinoco
Meta
COLOMBIA
Cali
Neiva
Guaviare
Boa Vista
Mouths of the Amazon
Isla de Malpelo
(Colombia)
Orinoco
Caquetá
Esmeraldas
Pasto
Negro
Japurá
Represa de Balbina
Belém
Quito
Manta
Putumayo
Tonantins
Amazon
Manaus
Santarém
São Luis
Parnaíba
ECUADOR
Guayaquil
Cuenca
Marañón
Iquitos
Amazon
Yavari
Carauari
Purus
Madeira
Tapajós
Xingu
Tocantins
Maraba
Fortaleza
Teresina
Galapagos Islands
(Ecuador)
Sullana
Tarapoto
Juruá
Iriri
Natal
Chiclayo
Pucallpa
Cruzeiro do Sul
Teles Pires
João Pessoa
Floresta
Recife
Trujillo
Ucayali
Rio Branco
Porto Velho
B R A Z I L
São Francisco
Juàzeiro
Maceió
PERU
Huancayo
Puerto Maldonado
Madeira
Jiparaná
Arinos
Araguaia
Tocantins
Aracaju
Guaporé
Callao
Lima
Cusco
Beni
Lago de San Luis
Cuiabá
Brasília
Ilhéus
Salvador
Ica
Juliaca
Mamoré
Trinidad
Goiânia
São Francisco
Teófilo Otôni
Arequipa
Lake Titicaca
BOLIVIA
Pantanal
Patos de Minas
La Paz
Cochabamba
Santa Cruz
Campo Grande
Uberaba
Belo Horizonte
Vitória
Arica
Sucre
Araçatuba
Ribeirão Preto
Iquique
Potosí
Paranaíba
Nova Iguaçu
Tarija
Grande
Campinas
Rio de Janeiro
Antofagasta
PARAGUAY
Pedro Juan Caballero
Paranapanema
Maringá
São Paulo
San Salvador de Jujuy
Paraguay
Teuco
Asunción
Iguaçu
Foz do Iguaçu
Curitiba
San Miguel de Tucumán
Pilcomayo
Formosa
Encarnación
Copiapó
Resistencia
Corrientes
Posadas
Florianópolis
Catamarca
Salado
Santa Maria
Porto Alegre
La Rioja
Paraná
Uruguay
Lagoa dos Patos
San Juan
Córdoba
Santa Fé
Concordia
Paysandú
Cerro Aconcagua 6959
Paraná
Rio Grande
Valparaíso
Mendoza
San Luis
Rosario
URUGUAY
Santiago
San Rafael
Buenos Aires
La Plata
Montevideo
Talca
Rio de la Plata
Concepción
Chillán
Colorado
Santa Rosa
Bahía Blanca
Mar del Plata
ARGENTINA
Neuquén
Valdivia
Negro
Puerto Montt
Viedma
Isla de Chiloé
Trelew
Patagonia
Comodoro Rivadavia
Golfo de San Jorge
Archipiélago de los Chonos
Punta Medanosa
Puerto Natales
Bahía Grande
Río Gallegos
Stanley
Punta Arenas
Isla Grande de Tierra del Fuego
Ushuaia
Cape Horn

PACIFIC OCEAN

ATLANTIC OCEAN

Galapagos Islands, an island territory of Ecuador which lies on the equator in the eastern Pacific Ocean over 900 kilometres west of the coast of Ecuador.

Facts

- South America is often referred to as 'Latin America', reflecting the historic influences of Spain and Portugal

- The largest city in each South American country is the capital, except in Brazil and Ecuador

- South America has only 2 landlocked countries – Bolivia and Paraguay

- Chile is over 4 000 kilometres long but has an average width of only 177 kilometres

Falkland Islands
(U.K.)

Falkland Islands, an overseas UK territory in the South Atlantic Ocean.

South Georgia
(U.K.)

South America
Southern South America

1:14 000 000

Lambert Azimutha Equal Area Projection

South America
Southeast Brazil

Between them, the world's oceans and polar regions cover approximately seventy per cent of the earth's surface. The oceans contain ninety six per cent of the earth's water and a vast range of flora and fauna. They are a major influence on the world's climate, particularly through ocean currents. The Arctic and Antarctica are the coldest and most inhospitable places on the earth. They both have vast amounts of ice which, if global warming continues, could have a major influence on sea level across the globe.

Our understanding of the oceans and polar regions has increased enormously over the last twenty years through the development of new technologies, particularly that of satellite remote sensing, which can generate vast amounts of data relating to, for example, topography (both on land and the seafloor), land cover and sea surface temperature.

The Oceans

The world's major oceans are the Pacific, the Atlantic and the Indian Oceans. The Arctic Ocean is generally considered as part of the Atlantic, and the Southern Ocean, which stretches around the whole of Antarctica is usually treated as an extension of each of the three major oceans.

One of the most important factors affecting the earth's climate is the circulation of water within and between the oceans. Differences in temperature and surface winds create ocean currents which move enormous quantities of water around the globe. These currents re-distribute heat which the oceans have absorbed from the sun, and so have a major effect on the world's climate system. El Niño is one climatic phenomenon directly influenced by these ocean processes.

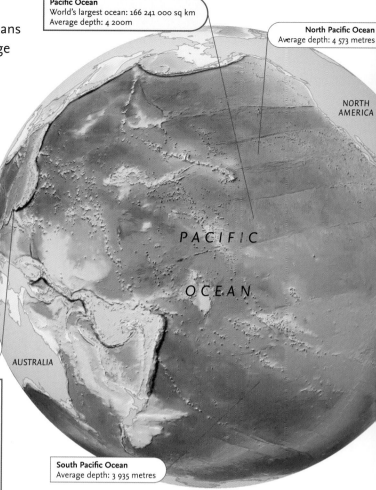

Pacific Ocean
World's largest ocean: 166 241 000 sq km
Average depth: 4 200m

North Pacific Ocean
Average depth: 4 573 metres

NORTH AMERICA

PACIFIC OCEAN

AUSTRALIA

Challenger Deep: 10 920 metres
Mariana Trench
Deepest point

South Pacific Ocean
Average depth: 3 935 metres

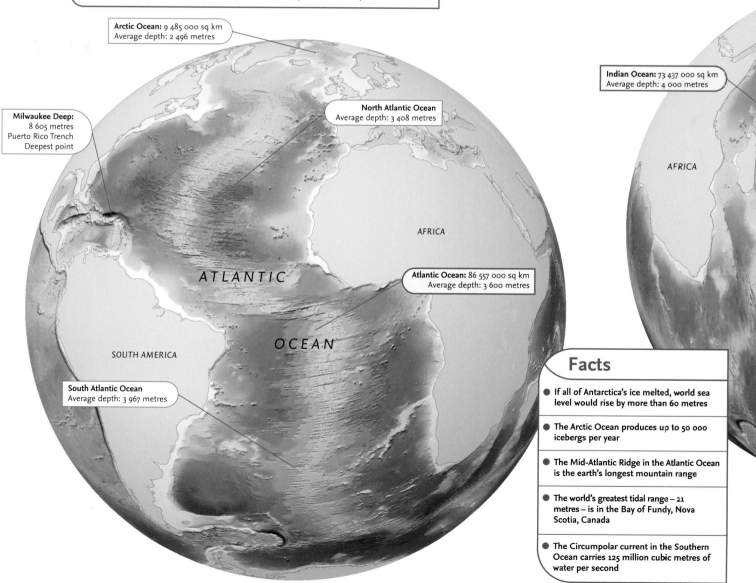

Arctic Ocean: 9 485 000 sq km
Average depth: 2 496 metres

Milwaukee Deep:
8 605 metres
Puerto Rico Trench
Deepest point

North Atlantic Ocean
Average depth: 3 408 metres

Indian Ocean: 73 437 000 sq km
Average depth: 4 000 metres

AFRICA

ATLANTIC

AFRICA

Atlantic Ocean: 86 557 000 sq km
Average depth: 3 600 metres

SOUTH AMERICA

OCEAN

South Atlantic Ocean
Average depth: 3 967 metres

Facts

- If all of Antarctica's ice melted, world sea level would rise by more than 60 metres

- The Arctic Ocean produces up to 50 000 icebergs per year

- The Mid-Atlantic Ridge in the Atlantic Ocean is the earth's longest mountain range

- The world's greatest tidal range – 21 metres – is in the Bay of Fundy, Nova Scotia, Canada

- The Circumpolar current in the Southern Ocean carries 125 million cubic metres of water per second

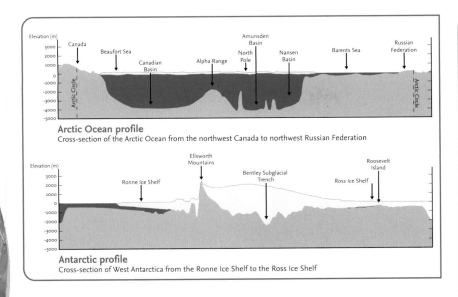

Arctic Ocean profile
Cross-section of the Arctic Ocean from the northwest Canada to northwest Russian Federation

Antarctic profile
Cross-section of West Antarctica from the Ronne Ice Shelf to the Ross Ice Shelf

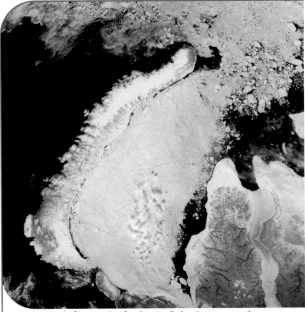

The island of **Novaya Zemlya**, Russian Federation, prevents the Kara Sea (right) from being affected by the warming influence of the Gulf Stream in the Atlantic Ocean and the Barents Sea (left).

Internet Links

● National Oceanic and Atmospheric Administration	**www.noaa.gov**
● Southampton Oceanography Centre	**www.soc.soton.ac.uk**
● British Antarctic Survey	**www.bas.ac.uk**
● Scott Polar Research Institute (SPRI)	**www.spri.cam.ac.uk**
● The National Snow and Ice Data Center (NSIDC)	**nsidc.org**

Polar Regions

Although a harsh climate is common to the two polar regions, there are major differences between the Arctic and Antarctica. The North Pole is surrounded by the Arctic Ocean, much of which is permanently covered by sea ice, while the South Pole lies on the huge land mass of Antarctica. This is covered by a permanent ice cap which reaches a maximum thickness of over four kilometres. Antarctica has no permanent population, but Europe, Asia and North America all stretch into the Arctic region which is populated by numerous ethnic groups. Antarctica is subject to the Antarctic Treaty of 1959 which does not recognize individual land claims and protects the continent in the interests of international scientific cooperation.

Java Trench: 7 125 metres
Deepest point

Southern Ocean
Average depth: 3 239 metres

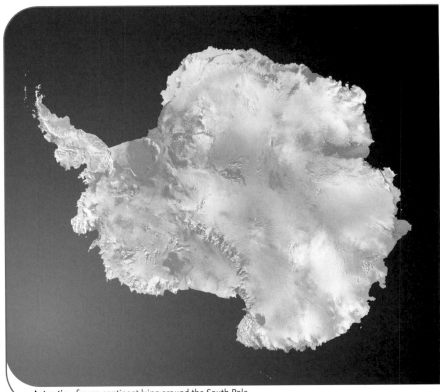

Antarctica, frozen continent lying around the South Pole.

Antarctica's physical features

Highest mountain: Vinson Massif	4 897 m	16 066 ft
Total land area (excluding ice shelves)	12 093 000 sq km	4 669 292 sq miles
Ice shelves	1 559 000 sq km	601 954 sq miles
Exposed rock	49 000 sq km	18 920 sq miles
Lowest bedrock elevation (Bentley Subglacial Trench)	2 496 m below sea level	8 189 ft below sea level
Maximum ice thickness (Astrolabe Subglacial Basin)	4 776 m	15 669 ft
Mean ice thickness (including ice shelves)	1 859 m	6 099 ft
Volume of ice sheet (including ice shelves)	25 400 000 cubic km	10 160 000 cubic miles

Atlantic Ocean
Indian Ocean

149

Pacific Ocean

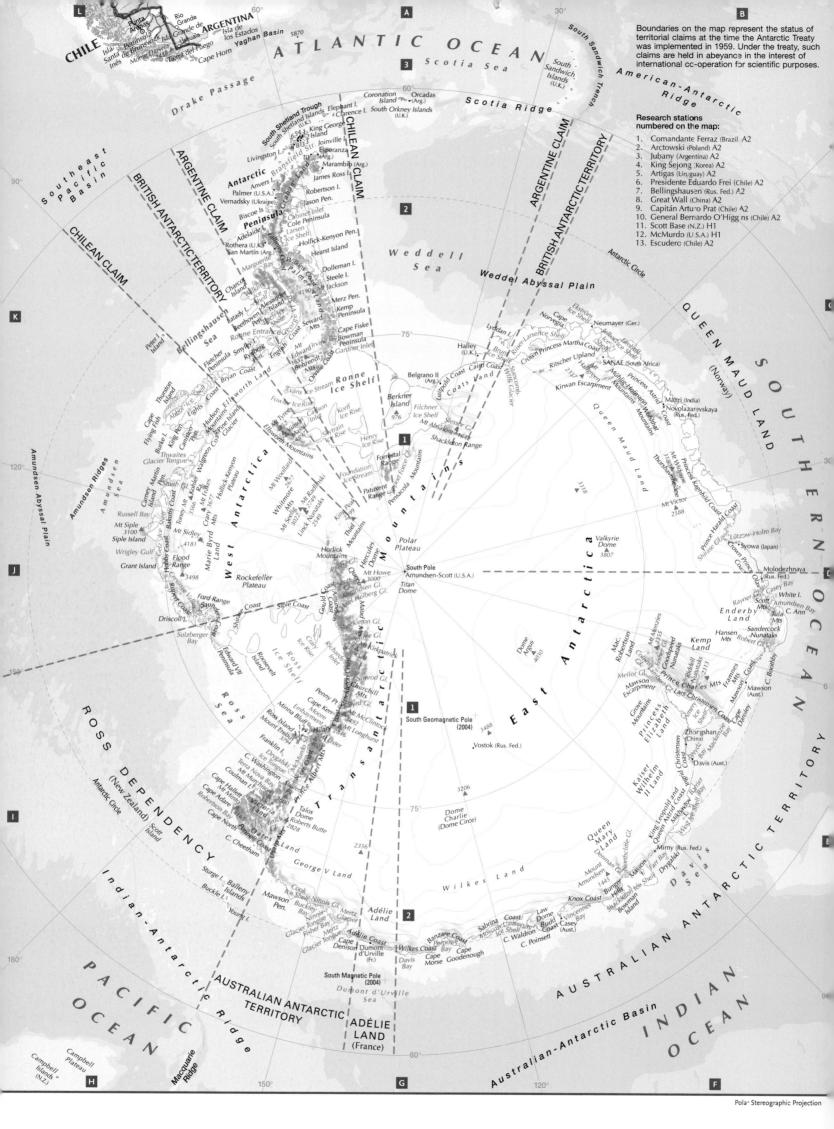

Research stations numbered on the map:

1. Comandante Ferraz (Brazil) A2
2. Arctowski (Poland) A2
3. Jubany (Argentina) A2
4. King Sejong (Korea) A2
5. Artigas (Uruguay) A2
6. Presidente Eduardo Frei (Chile) A2
7. Bellingshausen (Rus. Fed.) A2
8. Great Wall (China) A2
9. Capitán Arturo Prat (Chile) A2
10. General Bernardo O'Higgins (Chile) A2
11. Scott Base (N.Z.) H1
12. McMurdo (U.S.A.) H1
13. Escudero (Chile) A2

Antarctica

1:26 000 000

| 0 | 200 | 400 | 600 | 800 | 1000 miles |

| 0 | 200 | 400 | 600 | 800 | 1000 | 1200 | 1400 | 1600 km |

Polar Stereographic Projection

The Arctic

153

Polar Stereographic Projection

1:26 000 000

World Statistics

	Population						Economy					
	Total population	Population change (%)	% urban	Total fertility	Population by age (000s) 0–14	65 or over	2050 projected population	Total Gross National Income (GNI) (US$M)	GNI per capita (US$)	Total debt service (US$)	Debt service ratio (% GNI)	Aid receipts (% GNI)	Military spending (% GNI)
WORLD	6 301 000 000	1.2	47.7	2.7	1 814 525	418 420	9 322 251 000	31 500 010	5 170	...	...	...	2.3
AFGHANISTAN	23 897 000	3.7	22.3	6.8	9 466	619	72 267 000	...	...	...	...	...	...
ALBANIA	3 166 000	0.6	42.9	2.3	939	184	3 905 000	4 236	1 230	27 000 000	0.7	8.5	1.3
ALGERIA	31 800 000	1.8	57.5	2.8	10 554	1 248	51 180 000	50 355	1 630	4 466 500 096	8.8	0.3	4.0
ANDORRA	71 000	4.1	92.2	...	...	...	193 000	...	...	...	...	...	...
ANGOLA	13 625 000	3.0	34.9	7.2	6 326	373	53 328 000	6 707	500	1 204 499 968	25.4	8.1	21.2
ANTIGUA AND BARBUDA	73 000	0.3	37.1	...	...	...	73 000	621	9 070	...	...	1.5	...
ARGENTINA	38 428 000	1.2	88.3	2.4	10 265	3 592	54 522 000	260 994	6 960	27 345 100 800	9.9	...	1.6
ARMENIA	3 061 000	0.1	67.2	1.1	898	327	3 150 000	2 127	560	43 000 000	2.2	11.2	5.8
AUSTRALIA	19 731 000	1.0	91.2	1.8	3 927	2 346	26 502 000	383 291	19 770	...	...	...	1.8
AUSTRIA	8 116 000	-0.1	67.4	1.2	1 343	1 256	6 452 000	194 463	23 940	...	...	...	0.8
AZERBAIJAN	8 370 000	0.6	51.8	1.5	2 330	546	8 897 000	5 283	650	180 900 000	3.7	2.9	6.6
THE BAHAMAS	314 000	1.2	88.9	2.3	90	16	449 000	...	...	...	...	0.1	...
BAHRAIN	724 000	1.7	92.5	2.3	180	19	1 008 000	...	...	...	...	...	8.1
BANGLADESH	146 736 000	2.1	25.6	3.6	53 190	4 291	265 432 000	49 882	370	789 699 968	1.7	2.4	1.3
BARBADOS	270 000	0.4	50.5	1.5	55	28	263 000	...	...	...	...	...	0.5
BELARUS	9 895 000	-0.4	69.6	1.2	1 904	1 357	8 305 000	11 892	1 190	232 200 000	0.8	0.1	1.3
BELGIUM	10 318 000	0.1	97.4	1.5	1 771	1 744	9 583 000	239 779	23 340	...	...	...	1.4
BELIZE	256 000	1.9	48.1	2.9	87	10	392 000	718	2 910	66 100 000	8.6	1.9	1.6
BENIN	6 736 000	2.8	43.0	5.7	2 907	172	18 070 000	2 349	360	76 700 000	3.6	10.6	1.4
BHUTAN	2 257 000	2.6	7.4	5.1	891	88	5 569 000	529	640	6 600 000	1.3	11.6	...
BOLIVIA	8 808 000	2.2	62.9	3.9	3 300	334	16 966 000	8 044	940	661 600 000	8.2	5.8	1.8
BOSNIA-HERZEGOVINA	4 161 000	1.1	43.4	1.3	753	393	3 458 000	5 037	1 240	334 000 000	7.2	16.2	4.5
BOTSWANA	1 785 000	0.5	49.4	3.9	649	44	2 109 000	5 863	3 630	68 000 000	1.3	0.6	4.7
BRAZIL	178 470 000	1.2	81.7	2.2	49 077	8 760	247 244 000	528 503	3 060	62 787 600 384	11.0	0.1	1.9
BRUNEI	358 000	1.8	72.8	2.5	105	11	565 000	...	...	...	...	...	4.0
BULGARIA	7 897 000	-1.0	67.4	1.1	1 252	1 282	4 531 000	12 644	1 560	1 189 200 000	10.2	2.7	3.0
BURKINA	13 002 000	3.0	16.9	6.8	5 617	375	46 304 000	2 395	210	54 700 000	2.5	14.0	1.6
BURUNDI	6 825 000	3.0	9.3	6.8	3 023	182	20 219 000	692	100	21 400 000	3.2	13.8	7.0
CAMBODIA	14 144 000	2.4	17.5	4.8	5 749	367	29 883 000	3 329	270	31 400 000	1.0	12.6	4.0
CAMEROON	16 018 000	2.1	49.7	4.7	6 411	545	32 284 000	8 723	570	561 900 032	6.8	4.7	1.8
CANADA	31 510 000	0.8	78.9	1.6	5 882	3 875	40 407 000	661 881	21 340	...	...	...	1.4
CAPE VERDE	463 000	2.1	63.5	3.2	168	20	807 000	596	1 310	16 100 000	2.9	17.0	0.9
CENTRAL AFRICAN REPUBLIC	3 865 000	1.6	41.7	4.9	1 599	150	8 195 000	1 006	270	14 100 000	1.5	7.9	2.8
CHAD	8 598 000	3.1	24.1	6.7	3 663	247	27 732 000	1 597	200	26 300 000	1.9	9.6	2.4
CHILE	15 805 000	1.2	86.1	2.4	4 328	1 090	22 215 000	66 915	4 350	6 162 599 936	9.0	0.1	3.0
CHINA	1 289 161 000	0.7	36.7	1.8	316 838	87 428	1 462 058 000	1 130 984	890	21 728 299 008	2.0	0.2	2.3
COLOMBIA	44 222 000	1.6	75.5	2.6	13 806	1 993	70 862 000	82 017	1 910	5 170 599 936	6.6	0.2	3.2
COMOROS	768 000	2.9	33.8	5.0	304	19	1 900 000	217	380	2 700 000	1.3	9.3	...
CONGO	3 724 000	3.0	66.1	6.3	1 396	101	10 744 000	2 171	700	42 800 000	1.9	1.5	3.5
CONGO, DEMOCRATIC REPUBLIC OF	52 771 000	3.3	30.7	6.7	24 846	1 465	203 527 000	...	...	24 800 000	...	...	14.4
COSTA RICA	4 173 000	2.0	59.5	2.7	1 302	205	7 195 000	15 332	3 950	649 900 032	4.4	0.1	0.5
CÔTE D'IVOIRE	16 631 000	2.1	44.0	4.6	6 745	495	32 185 000	10 259	630	1 020 300 032	11.8	3.7	0.8
CROATIA	4 428 000	0.0	58.1	1.7	840	658	4 180 000	20 366	4 550	2 437 400 064	13.0	0.3	3.3
CUBA	11 300 000	0.3	75.5	1.6	2 377	1 072	10 764 000	...	...	...	...	...	1.9
CYPRUS	802 000	0.8	70.2	1.9	181	90	910 000	...	...	...	...	...	3.4
CZECH REPUBLIC	10 236 000	-0.1	74.5	1.2	1 686	1 421	8 429 000	54 108	5 270	4 773 499 904	9.5	0.9	2.3
DENMARK	5 364 000	0.2	85.1	1.7	971	798	5 080 000	166 345	31 090	...	...	...	1.6
DJIBOUTI	703 000	1.0	84.2	5.8	273	20	1 068 000	572	890	13 500 000	2.4	12.5	4.3
DOMINICA	79 000	-0.1	71.4	...	...	...	72 000	224	3 060	10 200 000	4.3	6.4	...
DOMINICAN REPUBLIC	8 745 000	1.5	66.0	2.7	2 805	359	11 960 000	18 955	2 230	520 800 000	2.8	0.3	0.7
EAST TIMOR	778 000	3.9	7.5	3.9	317	20	1 410 000	...	...	...	...	...	...
ECUADOR	13 003 000	1.7	63.4	2.8	4 278	594	21 190 000	15 952	1 240	1 276 099 968	10.3	1.2	3.7
EGYPT	71 931 000	1.7	42.7	2.9	24 004	2 808	113 840 000	99 406	1 530	1 813 400 064	1.8	1.3	2.7
EL SALVADOR	6 515 000	1.8	61.5	2.9	2 235	312	10 855 000	13 088	2 050	373 700 000	2.9	1.4	0.9
EQUATORIAL GUINEA	494 000	2.8	49.3	5.9	200	18	1 378 000	327	700	5 300 000	1.1	...	3.2
ERITREA	4 141 000	4.2	19.1	5.3	1 608	106	10 028 000	792	190	3 300 000	0.5	25.3	27.4
ESTONIA	1 323 000	-1.1	69.4	1.2	247	200	752 000	5 255	3 810	427 600 000	9.3	1.4	1.5
ETHIOPIA	70 678 000	2.4	15.9	6.8	28 414	1 859	186 452 000	6 767	100	139 400 000	2.2	11.1	8.8
FIJI	839 000	1.1	50.2	3.0	271	28	916 000	1 755	2 130	30 100 000	2.1	2.0	2.0
FINLAND	5 207 000	0.1	58.5	1.6	933	773	4 693 000	124 171	23 940	...	...	...	1.4
FRANCE	60 144 000	0.4	75.5	1.8	11 098	9 462	61 833 000	1 377 389	22 690	...	...	...	2.7
GABON	1 329 000	2.5	82.3	5.4	494	72	3 164 000	3 990	3 160	467 900 000	11.0	0.3	2.4
THE GAMBIA	1 426 000	2.4	31.3	4.8	525	40	2 605 000	440	330	18 600 000	4.5	12.4	1.3
GEORGIA	5 126 000	-0.5	56.5	1.4	1 077	680	3 219 000	3 097	620	116 900 000	3.8	5.3	1.2

Social Indicators						Environment				Communications				
Infant mortality rate	Life expectancy M	Life expectancy F	Literacy rate (%)	Access to safe water (%)	Doctors per 100 000 people	Forest area (%)	Annual change in forest area (%)	Protected land area (%)	CO_2 emissions	Telephone lines per 100 people	Cellular phones per 100 people	Internet connections per 1 000 people	International dialling code	Time zone
83	**63.9**	**68.1**	**...**	**82**	**...**	**29.6**	**-0.2**	**6.4**	**...**	**17.2**	**15.6**	**82.3**	**...**	**...**
257	43.0	43.5	...	13	...	2.1	..	0.3	0.0	...	...	...	...	+4.5
31	70.9	76.7	98.2	97	129	36.2	-0.8	2.9	0.5	5.0	8.8	2.5	355	+1
65	69.9	73.3	90.4	89	85	0.9	1.3	2.5	3.6	6.0	0.3	1.9	213	+1
7	...	...	...	100	...	...	...	...	...	43.8	30.2	89.7	376	+1
295	44.5	47.1	...	38	8	56.0	-0.2	6.6	0.5	0.6	0.6	4.4	244	+1
15	...	...	...	91	114	20.5	..	...	5.0	47.4	31.8	65.2	1 268	-4
21	70.6	77.7	98.6	...	268	12.7	-0.8	1.8	3.8	21.6	18.6	80.0	54	-3
30	70.3	76.2	99.8	...	316	12.4	1.3	7.6	0.9	14.0	0.7	142.1	374	+4
6	76.4	82.0	...	100	240	20.1	-0.2	7.0	17.7	52.0	57.8	372.3	61	+8 to +10.5
5	75.4	81.5	...	100	302	47.0	0.2	29.2	7.9	46.8	80.7	319.4	43	+1
105	68.7	75.5	...	78	360	13.1	1.3	5.5	4.9	11.1	8.0	3.2	994	+4
18	65.2	73.9	97.4	97	152	84.1	..	...	6.1	40.0	19.7	55.0	1 242	-5
16	72.1	76.3	98.6	...	100	...	14.9	...	29.1	24.7	42.5	198.9	973	+3
82	60.6	60.8	52.1	97	20	10.2	1.3	0.7	0.2	0.4	0.4	1.1	880	+6
14	74.5	79.5	...	100	125	4.7	..	...	5.9	46.3	10.6	37.4	1 246	-4
20	62.8	74.4	99.8	100	443	45.3	3.2	6.3	6.0	27.9	1.4	41.2	375	+2
6	75.7	81.9	...	...	395	22.2	-0.2	2.8	9.9	49.3	74.7	280.0	32	+1
41	73.0	75.9	98.2	92	55	59.1	-2.3	20.9	1.8	14.4	11.6	73.8	501	-6
154	52.5	55.7	55.5	63	6	24.0	-2.3	6.9	0.1	0.9	1.9	3.9	229	+1
100	62.0	64.5	...	62	16	64.2	...	21.2	0.5	2.0	...	3.6	975	+6
30	61.9	65.3	96.3	83	130	48.9	-0.3	14.2	1.5	6.2	9.0	14.6	591	-4
18	71.3	76.7	...	...	...	44.6	..	0.5	1.2	11.1	5.7	11.1	387	+1
101	38.7	37.4	89.1	95	24	21.9	-0.9	18.0	2.4	9.3	16.7	15.4	267	+2
38	64.7	72.6	93.0	87	127	64.3	-0.4	4.4	1.8	21.8	16.7	46.6	55	-2 to -5
7	74.2	78.9	99.5	...	85	83.9	-0.2	...	17.1	24.5	28.9	104.5	673	+8
16	67.1	74.8	99.7	100	345	33.4	0.6	4.5	5.7	35.9	19.1	74.6	359	+2
198	47.0	49.0	36.9	42	3	25.9	-0.2	10.4	0.1	0.5	0.6	1.7	226	GMT
190	39.8	41.4	66.1	78	...	3.7	-9.0	5.3	0.0	0.3	0.3	0.9	257	+2
135	53.6	58.6	80.1	30	30	52.9	-0.6	15.8	0.1	0.3	1.7	0.7	855	+7
154	49.3	50.6	94.4	58	7	51.3	-0.9	4.4	0.1	0.7	2.0	3.0	237	+1
6	76.2	81.8	...	100	229	26.5	..	9.1	15.5	65.5	32.0	435.3	1	-3.5 to -8
40	67.0	72.8	89.2	74	17	21.1	9.3	...	0.3	14.3	7.2	27.5	238	-1
130	42.7	46.0	69.9	70	4	36.8	-0.2	8.2	0.1	0.3	0.3	0.5	236	+1
138	45.1	47.5	69.9	27	3	10.1	-0.6	9.0	0.0	0.1	0.3	0.5	235	+1
12	73.0	79.0	99.0	93	110	20.7	-0.1	18.7	4.1	23.9	34.0	200.2	56	-4
40	69.1	73.5	98.2	75	162	17.5	1.2	6.2	2.5	13.8	11.2	26.0	86	+8
30	69.2	75.3	97.2	91	116	47.8	-0.4	8.2	1.7	17.1	7.6	27.0	57	-5
82	59.4	62.2	59.0	96	7	4.3	-4.3	...	0.1	1.2	...	3.4	269	+3
108	49.6	53.7	97.8	51	25	64.6	-0.1	4.5	0.6	0.7	4.8	0.2	242	+1
207	51.0	53.3	83.7	45	7	59.6	-0.4	4.3	0.1	0.0	0.3	0.1	243	+1 to +2
12	75.0	79.7	98.4	95	141	38.5	-0.8	14.2	1.4	23.0	7.6	93.4	506	-6
173	47.7	48.1	67.6	81	9	22.4	-3.1	5.2	0.9	1.8	4.5	4.3	225	GMT
9	70.3	78.1	99.8	...	229	31.9	0.1	7.4	4.5	36.5	37.7	55.9	385	+1
9	74.8	78.7	99.8	91	530	21.4	1.3	17.2	2.2	5.1	0.1	10.7	53	-5
7	76.0	80.5	99.8	100	255	18.6	3.7	...	7.9	64.3	46.4	221.6	357	+2
5	72.1	78.7	...	...	303	34.1	..	15.8	11.5	37.4	65.9	136.3	420	+1
5	74.2	79.1	...	100	290	10.7	0.2	32.0	10.1	72.3	73.7	447.2	45	+1
146	...	...	85.7	100	14	0.3	..	...	0.6	1.5	0.5	5.1	253	+3
16	...	...	...	97	49	61.3	-0.7	...	...	29.1	1.6	77.8	1 767	-4
48	64.4	70.1	91.7	86	216	28.4	..	31.3	2.5	11.0	14.7	21.5	1 809	-4
...	49.2	50.9	...	...	...	34.3	-0.5	...	...	...	...	...	670	+9
32	68.3	73.5	97.5	85	170	38.1	-1.2	42.6	2.2	10.4	6.7	25.4	593	-5
43	68.2	71.9	71.3	97	202	0.1	3.3	0.8	1.7	10.3	4.3	9.3	20	+2
40	67.7	73.7	89.0	77	107	5.8	-4.5	0.2	1.0	9.3	12.5	8.0	503	-6
156	52.4	55.6	97.4	44	25	62.5	-0.5	0.0	0.6	1.5	3.2	1.9	240	+1
114	51.1	53.7	72.0	46	3	13.5	-0.3	4.3	...	0.8	...	2.6	291	+3
21	65.8	76.4	99.8	...	297	48.7	0.5	11.1	12.1	35.2	45.5	300.5	372	+2
174	42.8	43.8	57.2	24	...	4.2	-0.8	5.0	0.0	0.5	0.0	0.4	251	+3
22	68.1	71.5	99.2	47	48	44.6	-0.2	1.1	0.9	11.0	9.3	18.3	679	+12
5	74.4	81.5	...	100	299	72.0	..	5.5	10.4	54.8	77.8	430.3	358	+2
5	75.2	82.8	...	...	303	27.9	0.4	13.5	6.3	57.4	60.5	263.8	33	+1
90	53.1	55.1	...	86	...	84.7	..	2.7	2.4	3.0	20.5	13.5	241	+1
128	45.7	48.5	60.0	62	4	48.1	1.0	2.0	0.2	2.6	3.2	13.5	220	GMT
29	69.5	77.6	...	79	436	43.7	..	2.8	1.0	15.9	5.4	4.6	995	+4

See page 160 for explanatory table and sources

	Population						Economy					
	Total population	Population change (%)	% urban	Total fertility	Population by age (000s) 0 – 14	65 or over	2050 projected population	Total Gross National Income (GNI) (US$M)	GNI per capita (US$)	Total debt service (US$)	Debt service ratio (% GNI)	Aid receipts (% GNI)	Military spending (% GNI)
GERMANY	82 476 000	0.0	87.7	1.3	12 739	13 453	70 805 000	1 947 951	23 700	...	...	...	1.6
GHANA	20 922 000	2.2	36.4	4.2	7 901	627	40 056 000	5 731	290	471 800 000	9.4	11.5	0.8
GREECE	10 976 000	0.0	60.3	1.2	1 598	1 862	8 983 000	124 553	11 780	...	...	...	4.7
GRENADA	80 000	0.3	38.4	...	...	...	105 000	368	3 720	12 000 000	3.2	4.7	...
GUATEMALA	12 347 000	2.6	39.9	4.4	4 965	404	26 551 000	19 559	1 670	438 000 000	2.3	1.4	0.7
GUINEA	8 480 000	1.5	27.9	5.8	3 592	226	20 711 000	3 043	400	133 000 000	4.5	5.0	1.6
GUINEA-BISSAU	1 493 000	2.4	32.3	6.0	521	43	3 276 000	202	160	6 200 000	3.1	37.7	2.7
GUYANA	765 000	0.2	36.7	2.3	233	38	504 000	641	840	115 600 000	17.5	16.3	0.8
HAITI	8 326 000	1.6	36.3	4.0	3 305	302	13 982 000	3 887	480	41 700 000	1.0	5.4	...
HONDURAS	6 941 000	2.3	53.7	3.7	2 682	216	12 845 000	5 922	900	578 099 968	10.0	7.8	0.7
HUNGARY	9 877 000	-0.5	64.8	1.2	1 689	1 460	7 486 000	48 924	4 800	7 945 900 032	18.0	0.6	1.7
ICELAND	290 000	0.7	92.7	1.9	65	33	333 000	8 201	28 880	...	...	...	...
INDIA	1 065 462 000	1.5	27.9	3.0	337 921	50 096	1 572 055 000	474 323	460	9 694 000 128	2.1	...	2.5
INDONESIA	219 883 000	1.2	42.1	2.3	65 232	10 221	311 335 000	144 731	680	18 771 900 416	13.2	1.2	1.1
IRAN	68 920 000	1.4	64.7	2.8	26 302	2 364	121 424 000	112 855	1 750	3 438 200 064	3.3	0.1	2.9
IRAQ	25 175 000	2.7	67.4	4.8	9 554	659	53 574 000	...	...	...	...	...	5.5
IRELAND, REPUBLIC OF	3 956 000	1.0	59.3	2.0	820	431	5 366 000	88 385	23 060	...	...	...	1.0
ISRAEL	6 433 000	2.0	91.8	2.7	1 706	596	10 065 000	...	...	...	...	...	8.8
ITALY	57 423 000	-0.1	67.1	1.2	8 216	10 396	42 962 000	1 123 478	19 470	...	...	...	2.0
JAMAICA	2 651 000	0.9	56.6	2.4	810	186	3 816 000	7 264	2 720	643 400 000	9.2	0.2	0.8
JAPAN	127 654 000	0.1	78.9	1.3	18 694	21 826	109 220 000	4 574 164	35 990	...	...	...	1.0
JORDAN	5 473 000	2.8	78.7	4.3	1 968	137	11 709 000	8 786	1 750	669 200 000	8.0	6.8	9.2
KAZAKHSTAN	15 433 000	-0.4	55.8	2.0	4 364	1 109	15 302 000	20 146	1 360	1 839 500 032	10.8	1.2	0.9
KENYA	31 987 000	1.9	34.4	4.2	13 331	869	55 368 000	10 309	340	481 000 000	4.7	5.0	1.9
KIRIBATI	88 000	1.3	38.6	...	...	...	138 000	77	830	...	...	21.8	...
KUWAIT	2 521 000	2.6	96.1	2.7	599	42	4 001 000	...	...	...	...	...	7.7
KYRGYZSTAN	5 138 000	1.2	34.3	2.3	1 670	297	7 538 000	1 386	280	173 200 000	14.2	17.8	2.4
LAOS	5 657 000	2.3	19.7	4.8	2 256	184	11 438 000	1 650	310	41 900 000	2.5	17.1	2.0
LATVIA	2 307 000	-0.6	59.8	1.1	421	357	1 744 000	7 719	3 260	561 600 000	7.8	1.3	0.9
LEBANON	3 653 000	1.6	90.1	2.2	1 089	212	5 018 000	17 585	4 010	1 821 200 000	10.5	1.2	4.0
LESOTHO	1 802 000	0.7	28.8	4.5	799	85	2 478 000	1 127	550	65 800 000	5.7	3.7	2.6
LIBERIA	3 367 000	5.5	45.5	6.8	1 244	83	14 370 000	...	...	700 000	...	...	1.2
LIBYA	5 551 000	2.2	88.0	3.3	1 795	179	9 969 000	...	...	...	...	...	...
LIECHTENSTEIN	34 000	1.1	21.5	...	...	...	39 000	...	...	...	...	...	...
LITHUANIA	3 444 000	-0.2	68.6	1.2	719	494	2 989 000	11 401	3 270	906 000 000	8.1	0.9	1.3
LUXEMBOURG	453 000	1.2	91.9	1.8	81	63	715 000	18 550	41 770	...	...	...	0.8
MACEDONIA (F.Y.R.O.M.)	2 056 000	0.3	59.4	1.5	460	203	1 894 000	3 445	1 690	161 300 000	4.6	7.7	2.5
MADAGASCAR	17 404 000	2.8	30.1	5.7	7 143	481	47 030 000	4 170	260	92 700 000	2.4	8.1	1.2
MALAWI	12 105 000	2.2	15.1	6.3	5 239	332	31 114 000	1 778	170	58 700 000	3.5	24.9	0.6
MALAYSIA	24 425 000	1.7	58.1	2.9	7 575	918	37 850 000	86 510	3 640	5 967 200 256	7.2	0.1	2.3
MALDIVES	318 000	3.0	28.0	5.4	127	10	868 000	578	2 040	19 900 000	3.8	4.7	...
MALI	13 007 000	2.9	30.9	7.0	5 235	454	41 724 000	2 280	210	97 200 000	4.3	15.6	2.3
MALTA	394 000	0.4	91.2	1.8	79	48	400 000	...	...	...	...	...	0.8
MARSHALL ISLANDS	53 000	...	66.0	...	...	...	85 000	115	2 190	...	...	56.6	...
MAURITANIA	2 893 000	3.0	59.1	6.0	1 176	84	8 452 000	974	350	100 300 000	11.0	23.3	4.0
MAURITIUS	1 221 000	0.8	41.6	1.9	298	72	1 426 000	4 592	3 830	553 299 968	12.7	0.5	0.2
MEXICO	103 457 000	1.4	74.6	2.5	32 770	4 671	146 652 000	550 456	5 540	58 258 698 240	10.4	...	0.6
MICRONESIA, FEDERATED STATES OF	109 000	2.4	28.6	...	...	...	269 000	258	2 150	...	...	39.5	...
MOLDOVA	4 267 000	-0.3	41.4	1.4	993	400	3 577 000	1 399	380	135 400 000	10.0	9.1	0.5
MONACO	34 000	0.9	100.0	...	...	...	38 000	...	...	...	...	...	...
MONGOLIA	2 594 000	1.1	56.5	2.3	892	96	4 146 000	962	400	29 200 000	3.1	23.7	2.1
MOROCCO	30 566 000	1.8	56.1	3.0	10 355	1 238	50 361 000	34 555	1 180	3 332 699 904	10.3	1.3	4.3
MOZAMBIQUE	18 863 000	1.8	33.3	5.9	8 037	591	38 837 000	3 747	210	87 500 000	2.5	24.8	2.5
MYANMAR	49 485 000	1.2	28.1	2.8	15 806	2 193	68 546 000	...	...	87 000 000	...	...	7.8
NAMIBIA	1 987 000	1.7	31.4	4.9	768	66	3 663 000	3 520	1 960	...	...	4.4	2.9
NAURU	13 000	2.3	100.0	...	...	...	26 000	...	...	...	...	...	...
NEPAL	25 164 000	2.3	12.2	4.5	9 455	859	52 415 000	5 879	250	99 700 000	1.8	7.2	0.8
NETHERLANDS	16 149 000	0.3	89.6	1.5	2 902	2 165	15 845 000	385 401	24 040	...	...	...	1.8
NEW ZEALAND	3 875 000	0.7	85.9	2.0	867	441	4 439 000	47 632	12 380	...	...	...	1.2
NICARAGUA	5 466 000	2.6	56.5	3.8	2 162	155	11 477 000	...	...	300 200 000	14.2	25.7	1.2
NIGER	11 972 000	3.6	21.1	8.0	5 401	218	51 872 000	1 953	170	28 300 000	1.6	21.5	1.2
NIGERIA	124 009 000	2.6	44.9	5.4	51 300	3 471	278 788 000	37 116	290	1 009 299 968	2.7	0.5	1.6
NORTH KOREA	22 664 000	0.7	60.5	2.1	5 902	1 315	28 038 000	...	...	...	...	...	18.8
NORWAY	4 533 000	0.4	75.0	1.7	883	687	4 880 000	160 577	35 530	...	...	...	2.2
OMAN	2 851 000	3.3	76.5	5.5	1 119	63	8 751 000	...	...	864 099 968	...	...	15.3

	Socal Indicators					Environment				Communications				
Infant mortality rate	Life expectancy M	Life expectancy F	Literacy rate (%)	Access to safe water (%)	Doctors per 100 000 people	Forest area (%)	Annual change in forest area (%)	Protected land area (%)	CO_2 emissions	Telephone lines per 100 people	Cellular phones per 100 people	Internet connections per 1 000 people	International dialling code	Time zone
5	75.0	81.1	...	...	350	30.7	...	26.9	10.1	63.5	68.3	364.3	49	+1
102	56.0	58.5	92.1	73	6	27.8	-1.7	4.6	0.2	1.2	0.9	1.9	233	GMT
6	75.9	81.2	99.8	...	392	27.9	0.9	3.6	8.1	52.9	75.1	132.1	30	+2
26	...	...	...	95	50	14.7	0.9	...	1.9	32.8	6.4	52.0	1 473	-4
59	63.0	68.9	80.3	92	93	26.3	-1.7	16.8	0.9	6.5	9.7	17.1	502	-6
175	48.0	49.0	...	48	13	28.2	-0.5	0.7	0.2	0.3	0.7	1.9	224	GMT
215	44.0	46.9	60.9	56	17	60.5	-0.9	0.0	...	1.0	...	3.3	245	GMT
74	58.0	66.9	99.8	94	18	78.5	-0.3	0.3	2.2	9.2	8.7	109.2	592	-4
125	50.2	56.5	66.2	46	8	3.2	-5.7	0.3	0.2	1.0	1.1	3.6	509	-5
40	63.2	69.1	84.2	88	83	48.1	-1.0	6.0	0.8	4.7	3.6	6.2	504	-6
9	67.8	76.1	99.8	99	357	19.9	0.4	7.0	5.8	37.4	49.8	148.4	36	+1
4	77.1	81.8	...	...	326	0.3	2.2	9.5	7.6	66.4	82.0	679.4	354	GMT
96	63.6	64.9	74.1	84	48	21.6	0.1	4.4	1.1	3.4	0.6	6.8	91	+5.5
48	65.3	69.3	98.0	78	16	58.0	-1.7	10.1	1.2	3.7	2.5	18.6	62	+7 to +9
44	68.8	70.8	94.8	92	85	4.5	...	5.1	4.7	16.0	2.7	6.2	98	+3.5
130	63.5	66.5	45.3	85	...	1.8	...	<0.1	3.7	...	...	...	964	+3
6	74.4	79.6	...	...	219	9.6	3.0	0.9	10.3	48.5	72.9	233.1	353	GMT
6	77.1	81.0	99.5	...	385	6.4	4.9	15.5	10.1	47.6	80.8	230.5	972	+2
6	75.5	81.9	99.8	...	554	34.0	0.3	7.3	7.2	47.1	83.9	275.8	39	+1
20	73.7	77.8	94.5	92	140	30.0	-1.5	0.1	4.3	19.7	26.9	38.5	1 876	-5
4	77.8	85.0	...	...	193	64.0	...	6.8	9.0	59.7	58.8	454.7	81	+9
34	69.7	72.5	99.5	96	166	1.0	...	3.3	3.0	12.7	14.4	40.9	962	+2
75	59.6	70.7	...	91	353	4.5	2.2	2.7	8.2	11.3	3.6	6.2	7	+4 to +6
120	48.7	49.9	95.8	57	13	30.0	-0.5	6.0	0.3	1.0	1.6	16.0	254	+3
70	...	...	...	48	...	38.4	...	...	0.3	4.0	0.5	25.0	686	+12 to +14
10	74.9	79.0	93.1	...	189	0.3	3.5	1.5	26.3	24.0	24.8	101.5	965	+3
63	64.8	72.3	...	77	301	5.2	2.6	3.5	1.3	7.7	0.5	10.6	996	+5
105	53.3	55.8	73.3	37	24	54.4	-0.4	0.0	0.1	0.9	0.5	1.8	856	+7
21	65.7	76.2	99.8	...	282	47.1	0.4	12.5	3.2	30.8	27.9	72.3	371	+2
32	71.9	75.1	95.6	100	210	3.5	-0.4	0.5	3.9	19.5	21.3	85.8	961	+2
133	37.5	35.1	91.1	78	5	0.5	...	0.2	...	1.0	1.5	2.3	266	+2
235	54.6	56.7	71.7	...	...	31.3	-2.0	1.2	0.1	...	...	...	231	GMT
20	70.7	74.8	97.0	72	128	0.2	1.4	0.1	7.2	10.9	0.9	3.6	218	+2
11	...	...	...	...	...	46.7	1.2	...	...	...	...	...	423	+1
21	67.6	77.7	99.8	...	395	31.9	0.2	9.9	4.2	31.3	25.3	67.9	370	+2
5	74.6	80.9	...	...	272	...	...	...	18.0	78.3	96.7	226.6	352	+1
26	71.4	75.8	...	...	204	35.6	...	7.1	6.1	26.4	10.9	34.3	389	+1
139	52.5	54.8	81.5	47	11	20.2	-0.9	1.9	0.1	0.4	0.9	2.1	261	+3
188	39.6	39.0	72.5	57	...	27.2	-2.4	8.9	0.1	0.5	0.5	1.7	265	+2
9	70.6	75.5	97.9	...	66	58.7	-1.2	4.6	5.4	19.9	30.0	239.5	60	+8
80	68.3	67.0	99.2	100	40	3.3	...	...	1.3	10.1	6.8	37.0	960	+5
233	51.1	53.0	69.9	65	5	10.8	-0.7	3.7	0.1	0.4	0.4	2.6	223	GMT
6	75.9	81.0	98.7	100	261	n.s.	...	...	4.7	53.0	35.4	252.6	356	+1
68	...	...	...	...	...	...	...	...	...	6.0	0.1	12.9	692	+12
183	50.9	54.1	49.6	37	14	43.9	...	1.7	1.2	0.7	0.3	2.6	222	GMT
20	68.4	75.8	94.3	100	85	7.9	-0.6	...	1.5	25.6	25.0	131.7	230	+4
30	70.4	76.4	97.2	88	186	28.9	-1.1	3.4	3.9	13.7	21.7	36.2	52	-6 to -8
24	...	...	...	...	...	21.7	-4.5	...	...	8.3	...	33.8	691	+10 to +11
33	62.8	70.3	99.8	92	350	9.9	0.2	1.4	2.3	15.4	4.8	13.7	373	+2
5	...	...	...	100	...	...	...	...	...	...	...	...	377	+1
78	61.9	65.9	99.6	60	243	6.8	-0.5	11.5	3.3	4.8	7.6	15.6	976	+8
46	68.3	72.0	69.6	80	46	6.8	...	0.7	1.2	3.9	15.7	13.2	212	GMT
200	37.3	38.6	62.8	57	...	39.0	-0.2	6.0	0.1	0.4	0.8	0.7	258	+2
110	53.8	58.8	91.4	72	30	52.3	-1.4	0.3	0.2	0.6	0.0	0.2	95	+6.5
69	48.9	49.0	92.3	77	30	9.8	-0.9	12.9	0.0	6.6	5.6	25.2	264	+2
30	...	...	...	...	...	...	...	...	...	...	...	...	674	+12
100	60.1	59.6	62.8	88	4	27.3	-1.8	7.6	0.1	1.3	0.1	2.5	977	+5.75
5	75.6	81.0	98.3	100	251	11.1	0.3	5.7	10.4	62.1	73.9	329.2	31	+1
6	75.3	80.7	...	...	218	29.7	0.5	23.4	7.9	47.1	62.1	280.7	64	+12
45	67.2	71.9	72.3	77	86	27.0	-3.0	7.0	0.7	3.1	3.0	9.9	505	-6
270	45.9	46.5	24.4	59	4	1.0	-3.7	7.7	0.1	0.2	0.0	1.1	227	+1
184	52.0	52.2	88.5	62	18	14.8	-2.6	3.3	0.7	0.4	0.3	1.8	234	+1
30	62.5	68.0	...	100	...	68.2	...	2.6	10.3	...	...	...	850	+9
4	76.0	81.9	...	100	413	28.9	0.4	6.5	7.6	72.0	82.5	596.3	47	+1
14	70.2	73.2	98.5	39	133	0.0	5.3	16.1	8.8	9.0	12.4	45.8	968	+4

See page 160 for explanatory table and sources

	Population							Economy					
	Total population	Population change (%)	% urban	Total fertility	Population by age (ooos) 0 – 14	Population by age (ooos) 65 or over	2050 projected population	Total Gross National Income (GNI) (US$M)	GNI per capita (US$)	Total debt service (US$)	Debt service ratio (% GNI)	Aid receipts (% GNI)	Military spending (% GNI)
PAKISTAN	153 578 000	2.5	33.4	5.1	59 021	5 195	344 170 000	59 637	420	2 856 600 064	4.8	1.1	5.9
PALAU	20 000	2.1	69.3	...	...	...	39 000	131	6 730	...	...	...	...
PANAMA	3 120 000	1.4	56.5	2.4	...	...	4 262 000	9 532	3 290	928 400 000	9.9	0.2	1.4
PAPUA NEW GUINEA	5 711 000	2.2	17.6	4.3	1 929	117	10 980 000	3 026	580	304 500 000	8.3	7.2	1.1
PARAGUAY	5 878 000	2.5	56.7	3.8	2 173	191	12 565 000	7 345	1 300	330 000 000	4.4	1.1	1.1
PERU	27 167 000	1.6	73.1	2.6	8 567	1 238	42 122 000	52 147	2 000	4 305 299 968	8.3	0.8	2.4
PHILIPPINES	79 999 000	1.9	59.4	3.2	28 395	2 670	128 383 000	80 845	1 050	6 736 699 904	8.5	0.7	1.4
POLAND	38 587 000	-0.1	62.5	1.3	7 395	4 685	33 370 000	163 907	4 240	10 290 299 904	6.6	0.9	2.1
PORTUGAL	10 062 000	0.1	65.8	1.5	1 672	1 563	9 006 000	109 156	10 670	...	...	...	2.1
QATAR	610 000	1.5	92.9	3.3	151	9	831 000	...	...	...	...	...	10.0
ROMANIA	22 334 000	-0.3	55.2	1.3	4 095	2 986	18 150 000	38 388	1 710	2 340 800 000	6.4	1.2	1.6
RUSSIAN FEDERATION	143 246 000	-0.6	72.9	1.1	26 123	18 170	104 259 000	253 413	1 750	11 670 700 032	4.9	0.7	5.6
RWANDA	8 387 000	2.1	6.3	5.8	3 370	200	18 523 000	1 884	220	35 000 000	2.0	13.3	4.5
SAMOA	178 000	0.3	22.3	4.2	65	7	223 000	260	1 520	8 500 000	3.6	11.6	...
SAN MARINO	28 000	1.1	90.4	...	...	...	30 000	...	...	...	...	...	...
SÃO TOMÉ AND PRÍNCIPE	161 000	1.8	47.7	...	...	...	294 000	43	280	4 400 000	10.1	79.5	1.0
SAUDI ARABIA	24 217 000	3.1	86.7	5.5	8 735	602	59 683 000	...	...	...	...	...	14.9
SENEGAL	10 095 000	2.5	48.2	5.1	4 176	236	22 711 000	4 726	480	228 000 000	5.3	9.8	1.7
SERBIA AND MONTENEGRO	10 527 000	-0.1	51.7	1.6	2 113	1 381	9 030 000	...	...	177 400 000	2.1	...	5.0
SEYCHELLES	81 000	1.3	64.6	...	...	...	145 000	...	...	17 400 000	3.0	3.0	...
SIERRA LEONE	4 971 000	4.5	37.3	6.5	1 949	128	14 351 000	726	140	42 600 000	6.9	25.0	3.0
SINGAPORE	4 253 000	1.7	100.0	1.5	878	291	4 620 000	...	...	...	...	...	4.8
SLOVAKIA	5 402 000	0.1	57.6	1.3	1 054	615	4 674 000	20 028	3 700	2 590 000 128	13.8	0.6	1.8
SLOVENIA	1 984 000	-0.1	49.1	1.1	316	277	1 527 000	19 447	9 780	...	...	0.3	1.4
SOLOMON ISLANDS	477 000	3.3	20.2	5.3	200	12	1 458 000	253	580	9 100 000	3.2	24.0	...
SOMALIA	9 890 000	4.2	27.9	7.3	4 209	211	40 936 000	...	...	...	...	...	...
SOUTH AFRICA, REPUBLIC OF	45 026 000	0.8	57.7	2.9	14 734	1 545	47 301 000	125 486	2 900	3 859 599 872	3.1	0.4	1.5
SOUTH KOREA	47 700 000	0.7	82.5	1.5	9 740	3 305	51 561 000	447 698	9 400	23 204 999 168	5.1	...	2.9
SPAIN	41 060 000	0.0	77.8	1.1	5 874	6 767	31 282 000	586 874	14 860	...	...	...	1.3
SRI LANKA	19 065 000	0.9	23.1	2.1	4 976	1 186	23 066 000	16 294	830	737 500 032	4.6	1.7	4.7
ST KITTS AND NEVIS	42 000	-0.7	34.2	...	...	...	34 000	283	6 880	19 600 000	7.1	1.4	...
ST LUCIA	149 000	1.1	38.0	2.5	47	8	189 000	628	3 970	40 300 000	6.0	1.5	...
ST VINCENT AND THE GRENADINES	120 000	0.6	56.0	...	...	...	138 000	312	2 690	15 400 000	4.9	2.0	...
SUDAN	33 610 000	2.3	37.1	4.5	12 474	1 071	63 530 000	10 346	330	61 000 000	0.6	2.3	4.8
SURINAME	436 000	0.4	74.8	2.1	127	23	418 000	709	1 690	...	...	...	1.8
SWAZILAND	1 077 000	0.9	26.7	4.4	385	32	1 391 000	1 388	1 300	23 600 000	1.6	1.0	1.5
SWEDEN	8 876 000	-0.1	83.3	1.3	1 609	1 541	7 777 000	225 894	25 400	...	...	...	2.3
SWITZERLAND	7 169 000	-0.1	67.3	1.4	1 194	1 147	5 607 000	266 503	36 970	...	...	...	1.2
SYRIA	17 800 000	2.5	51.8	3.7	6 612	507	36 345 000	16 608	1 000	343 600 000	2.2	1.0	7.0
TAIWAN	22 548 000	0.7	36.7	...	...	...	...	...	...	...	...	...	...
TAJIKISTAN	6 245 000	0.7	27.7	2.9	2 397	279	9 763 000	1 051	170	87 500 000	9.3	15.3	1.3
TANZANIA	36 977 000	2.3	33.3	5.0	15 800	857	82 740 000	9 198	270	216 700 000	2.4	11.2	1.4
THAILAND	62 833 000	1.1	20.0	2.0	16 742	3 282	82 491 000	120 872	1 970	14 016 499 712	11.6	0.5	1.7
TOGO	4 909 000	2.6	33.9	5.4	2 004	142	11 832 000	1 279	270	29 600 000	2.5	5.5	1.8
TONGA	104 000	0.4	33.0	...	...	...	125 000	154	1 530	4 100 000	2.6	12.1	...
TRINIDAD AND TOBAGO	1 303 000	0.5	74.5	1.5	323	86	1 378 000	7 249	5 540	500 200 000	7.5	...	1.4
TUNISIA	9 832 000	1.1	66.2	2.1	2 809	554	14 076 000	20 051	2 070	1 900 000 000	10.2	1.2	1.8
TURKEY	71 325 000	1.3	66.2	2.3	20 021	3 847	98 818 000	168 335	2 540	21 135 800 320	10.5	0.2	5.3
TURKMENISTAN	4 867 000	1.9	44.9	3.2	1 783	202	8 401 000	5 236	950	...	...	0.7	3.4
TUVALU	11 000	1.3	53.2	...	...	...	16 000	...	...	...	...	...	...
UGANDA	25 827 000	3.2	14.5	7.1	11 466	586	101 524 000	6 286	280	159 300 000	2.6	13.1	2.3
UKRAINE	48 523 000	-0.9	68.0	1.1	8 840	6 849	29 959 000	35 185	720	3 660 699 904	11.9	1.7	3.0
UNITED ARAB EMIRATES	2 995 000	1.7	87.2	2.9	678	71	3 709 000	...	...	...	...	...	4.1
UNITED KINGDOM	58 789 194	0.2	89.5	1.6	11 272	9 359	58 933 000	1 451 442	24 230	...	...	...	2.5
UNITED STATES OF AMERICA	294 043 000	0.9	77.4	1.9	61 507	34 831	397 063 000	9 900 724	34 870	...	...	...	3.0
URUGUAY	3 415 000	0.7	92.1	2.3	827	430	4 249 000	19 036	5 670	1 313 100 032	6.8	0.1	1.3
UZBEKISTAN	26 093 000	1.4	36.6	2.3	9 022	1 163	40 513 000	13 780	550	898 700 032	12.1	1.4	1.7
VANUATU	212 000	2.5	22.1	4.3	83	6	462 000	212	1 050	2 200 000	1.0	20.4	...
VATICAN CITY	472	...	100.0	...	...	...	1 000	...	...	...	...	...	...
VENEZUELA	25 699 000	1.8	87.2	2.7	8 227	1 075	42 152 000	117 169	4 760	5 846 099 968	4.9	0.1	1.4
VIETNAM	81 377 000	1.3	24.5	2.3	26 070	4 178	123 782 000	32 578	410	1 303 200 000	4.2	5.4	...
YEMEN	20 010 000	4.1	25.0	7.6	9 188	423	102 379 000	8 304	460	221 400 000	3.0	3.5	6.1
ZAMBIA	10 812 000	2.1	39.8	5.7	4 850	307	29 262 000	3 336	320	185 600 000	6.7	28.7	1.0
ZIMBABWE	12 891 000	1.7	36.0	4.5	5 709	403	23 546 000	6 164	480	471 400 000	6.6	2.6	5.0

Socal Indicators					Environment				Communications				
Infant mortality rate	Life expectancy		Literacy rate (%)	Access to safe water (%)	Doctors per 100 000 people	Forest area (%)	Annual change in forest area (%)	Protected land area (%)	CO₂ emissions	Telephone lines per 100 people	Cellular phones per 100 people	Internet connections per 1 000 people	International dialling code	Time zone
	M	F												
110	61.2	60.9	58.7	90	57	3.1	-1.5	4.7	0.7	2.4	0.6	3.5	92	+5
29	...	...	...	79	...	76.1	..	...	...	...	...	...	680	+9
26	...	...	97.0	90	167	38.6	-1.6	18.8	2.1	14.8	20.7	31.7	507	-5
112	56.8	58.7	76.9	42	7	67.6	-0.4	<0.1	0.5	1.4	0.2	28.1	675	+10
31	68.6	73.1	97.3	78	110	58.8	-0.5	3.4	0.9	5.1	20.4	10.6	595	-4
50	67.3	72.4	97.1	80	93	50.9	-0.4	2.7	1.1	7.8	5.9	115.0	51	-5
40	68.0	72.0	98.8	86	123	19.4	-1.4	4.8	1.0	4.0	13.7	25.9	63	+8
10	69.8	78.0	99.8	...	236	29.7	0.2	9.1	8.3	29.5	26.0	98.4	48	+1
6	72.6	79.6	99.8	...	312	40.1	1.7	6.6	5.5	42.7	77.4	349.4	351	GMT
16	69.4	72.1	95.3	...	126	0.1	9.5	...	85.7	27.5	29.3	65.6	974	+3
22	66.5	73.3	99.7	58	184	28.0	0.2	4.6	4.1	18.3	17.2	44.7	40	+2
22	60.0	72.5	99.8	99	421	50.4	...	3.1	9.8	24.3	3.8	29.3	7	+2 to +12
187	40.2	41.7	84.9	41	...	12.4	-3.9	13.8	0.1	0.3	0.8	2.5	250	+2
26	66.9	73.5	99.8	99	34	37.2	-2.1	...	0.8	5.6	1.7	16.7	685	-11
6	...	...	...	...	...	...	...	...	...	...	...	...	378	+1
75	...	...	...	...	47	28.3	.	...	0.5	3.6	...	60.0	239	GMT
29	71.1	73.7	93.6	95	166	0.7	..	2.3	14.4	14.5	11.3	13.4	966	+3
139	52.5	56.2	52.9	78	8	32.2	-0.7	11.1	0.4	2.5	4.0	10.4	221	GMT
20	70.9	75.6	...	98	...	28.3	-0.1	3.3	...	22.9	18.7	56.2	381	+1
17	...	...	...	...	132	66.7	...	...	2.5	26.7	55.2	112.5	248	+4
316	39.2	41.8	...	57	7	14.7	-2.9	1.1	0.1	0.5	0.6	1.4	232	GMT
4	75.9	80.3	99.8	100	163	3.3	..	4.7	21.0	47.1	72.4	605.2	65	+8
9	69.8	77.6	...	100	353	45.3	0.9	22.1	7.1	28.8	39.7	120.3	421	+1
5	72.3	79.6	99.8	100	228	55.0	0.2	5.9	7.4	40.1	76.0	300.8	386	+1
25	67.9	70.7	...	71	14	88.8	-0.2	0.0	0.4	1.6	0.2	4.3	677	+11
225	47.4	50.5	...	...	...	12.0	-1.0	0.3	0.0	...	...	...	252	+3
70	42.5	42.3	91.8	86	56	7.3	-0.1	5.4	8.3	11.4	21.0	70.1	27	+2
5	71.8	79.1	99.8	92	136	63.3	-0.1	6.9	7.8	47.6	60.8	510.7	82	+9
5	75.4	82.3	99.8	...	424	28.8	0.6	8.4	6.3	43.1	65.5	182.8	34	+1
19	69.9	75.9	97.1	77	36	30.0	-1.6	13.3	0.4	4.3	3.8	7.9	94	+6
25	...	...	...	98	117	11.1	-0.6	...	2.5	56.9	3.1	51.6	1 869	-4
19	71.1	76.4	...	98	47	14.8	-4.9	...	1.3	...	...	...	1 758	-4
25	...	...	...	93	88	15.4	-1.4	...	1.4	22.0	2.1	30.9	1 784	-4
108	57.6	60.6	79.1	75	9	25.9	-1.4	3.4	0.1	1.4	0.3	1.8	249	+3
33	68.5	73.7	...	82	25	90.5	...	4.5	5.2	17.6	19.1	33.0	597	-3
142	35.8	34.8	91.2	...	15	30.3	1.2	...	0.4	3.1	6.5	13.7	268	+2
4	77.6	82.6	...	100	311	65.9	...	8.1	5.5	73.9	79.0	516.3	46	+1
4	75.9	82.3	...	100	323	30.3	0.4	25.7	5.9	71.8	72.4	404.0	41	+1
29	70.6	73.1	88.3	80	144	2.5	...	0.0	3.3	10.9	1.2	3.6	963	+2
...	...	...	...	...	...	...	...	...	...	57.3	96.6	349.0	886	+8
73	65.2	70.8	99.8	60	201	2.8	0.5	4.1	0.8	3.6	0.0	0.5	992	+5
165	50.1	52.0	91.6	68	4	43.9	-0.2	14.6	0.1	0.4	1.2	8.3	255	+3
29	67.9	73.8	99.0	84	24	28.9	-0.7	13.8	3.2	9.4	11.9	55.6	66	+7
142	51.1	53.3	77.4	54	8	9.4	-3.4	7.6	0.2	1.0	2.0	10.7	228	GMT
21	...	...	...	100	...	5.5	...	...	1.2	9.9	0.1	10.2	676	+13
20	72.5	77.2	99.8	90	79	50.5	-0.8	6.0	17.4	24.0	17.3	92.3	1 868	-4
28	70.8	73.7	94.3	80	70	3.1	0.2	0.3	2.4	10.9	4.0	41.2	216	+1
45	68.0	73.2	96.9	82	121	13.3	0.2	1.3	3.2	28.5	30.2	37.7	90	+2
70	63.9	70.4	...	...	300	8.0	...	4.1	5.7	8.0	0.2	1.7	993	+5
53	...	...	...	...	...	...	...	...	...	...	...	...	688	+12
127	45.3	46.8	80.3	52	...	21.0	-2.0	7.9	0.1	0.3	1.4	2.7	256	+3
21	62.7	73.5	99.9	98	299	16.5	0.3	1.6	7.0	21.2	4.4	11.9	380	+2
9	74.1	78.4	91.5	...	181	3.8	2.8	...	32.4	39.7	72.0	339.2	971	+4
6	75.7	80.7	...	100	164	11.6	0.6	20.4	9.2	58.8	78.3	399.5	44	GMT
8	74.6	80.4	...	100	279	24.7	0.2	13.1	19.8	66.5	44.4	499.5	1	-5 to -10
17	71.6	78.9	99.3	98	370	7.4	5.0	0.3	1.8	28.3	15.5	119.0	598	-3
67	66.8	72.5	99.7	85	309	4.8	0.2	1.8	4.5	6.6	0.3	5.9	998	+5
44	67.5	70.5	...	88	12	36.7	0.1	...	0.3	3.4	0.2	27.4	678	+11
...	...	...	...	...	...	...	...	...	...	...	...	...	39	+1
23	70.9	76.7	98.2	83	236	56.1	-0.4	35.4	6.7	11.2	26.4	52.8	58	-4
39	66.9	71.6	97.3	77	48	30.2	0.5	3.0	0.6	3.8	1.5	4.9	84	+7
117	60.7	62.9	67.8	69	23	0.9	-1.9	0.0	0.9	2.2	0.8	0.9	967	+3
202	42.6	41.7	89.1	64	7	42.0	-2.4	8.5	0.2	0.8	0.9	2.4	260	+2
117	43.3	42.4	97.6	83	14	49.2	-1.5	7.9	1.2	1.9	2.4	7.3	263	+2

Definitions

Indicator	Definition
Population	
Total population	Interpolated mid-year population, 2003.
Population change	Percentage annual rate of change, 2000–2005.
% urban	Urban population as a percentage of the total population, 2001.
Total fertility	Average number of children a women will have during her child-bearing years, 2000–2005.
Population by age	Population in age groups 0–14 and 65 or over, in thousands, 2000.
2050 projected population	Projected total population for the year 2050.
Economy	
Total Gross National Income (GNI)	The sum of value added to the economy by all resident producers plus taxes, less subsidies, plus net receipts of primary income from abroad. Data are in U.S. dollars (millions), 2001. Formerly known as Gross National Product (GNP).
GNI per capita	Gross National Income per person in U.S. dollars using the World Bank Atlas method, 2001.
Total debt service	Sum of principal repayments and interest paid on long-term debt, interest paid on short-term debt and repayments to the International Monetary Fund (IMF), 2000.
Debt service ratio	Debt service as a percentage of GNI, 2000.
Aid receipts	Aid received as a percentage of GNI from the Development Assistance Committee (DAC) of the Organization for Economic Co-operation and Development (OECD), 2000.
Military spending	Military-related spending, including recruiting, training, construction, and the purchase of military supplies and equipment, as a percentage of Gross National Income, 1999.
Social Indicators	
Infant mortality rate	Number of deaths of children aged under 5 per 1 000 live births, 2000.
Life expectancy	Average life expectancy, at birth in years, male and female, 2000–2005.
Literacy rate	Percentage of population aged 15–24 with at least a basic ability to read and write, 2002.
Access to safe water	Percentage of the population with sustainable access to sources of improved drinking water, 2000.
Doctors	Number of trained doctors per 100 000 people, most recent year figures obtained.
Environment	
Forest area	Percentage of total land area covered by forest.
Change in forest area	Average annual percentage change in forest area, 1990–2000.
Protected land area	Percentage of total land area designated as protected land.
CO_2 emissions	Emissions of carbon dioxide from the burning of fossil fuels and the manufacture of cement, divided by the population, expressed in metric tons, 1998.
Communications	
Telephone lines	Main telephone lines per 100 inhabitants, 2001.
Cellular phones	Cellular mobile subscribers per 100 inhabitants, 2001.
Internet connections	Internet users per 1 000 inhabitants, 2001.
International dialling code	The country code prefix to be used when dialling from another country.
Time zone	Time difference in hours between local standard time and Greenwich Mean Time.

Main Statistical Sources	Internet Links
United Nations Statistics Division	unstats.un.org/unsd
World Population Prospects: The 2002 Revision and World Urbanization Prospects: The 2001 Revision, United Nations Population Division	www.un.org/esa/population/unpop
United Nations Population Information Network	www.un.org/popin
United Nations Development Programme	www.undp.org
Organisation for Economic Cooperation and Development	www.oecd.org
State of the World's Forests 2001, Food and Agriculture Organization of the United Nations	www.fao.org
World Development Indicators 2002, World Bank	www.worldbank.org/data
World Resources 2000–2001, World Resources Institute	www.wri.org
International Telecommunication Union	www.itu.int

Introduction to the index

The index includes all names shown on the reference maps in the atlas. Each entry includes the country or geographical area in which the feature is located, a page number and an alphanumeric reference. Additional entry details and aspects of the index are explained below.

Name forms

The names policy in this atlas is generally to use local name forms which are officially recognized by the governments of the countries concerned. Rules established by the Permanent Committee on Geographical Names for British Official Use (PCGN) are applied to the conversion of non-roman alphabet names, for example in the Russian Federation, into the roman alphabet used in English.

However, English conventional name forms are used for the most well-known places for which such a form is in common use. In these cases, the local form is included in brackets on the map and appears as a cross-reference in the index. Other alternative names, such as well-known historical names or those in other languages, may also be included in brackets on the map and as cross-references in the index. All country names and those for international physical features appear in their English forms. Names appear in full in the index, although they may appear in abbreviated form on the maps.

Referencing

Names are referenced by page number and by grid reference. The grid reference relates to the alphanumeric values which appear on the edges of each map. These reflect the graticule on the map – the letter relates to longitude divisions, the number to latitude divisions. Names are generally referenced to the largest scale map page on which they appear. For large geographical features, including countries, the reference is to the largest scale map on which the feature appears in its entirety, or on which the majority of it appears.

Rivers are referenced to their lowest downstream point – either their mouth or their confluence with another river. The river name will generally be positioned as close to this point as possible.

Alternative names

Alternative names appear as cross-references and refer the user to the index entry for the form of the name used on the map.

For rivers with multiple names - for example those which flow through several countries - all alternative name forms are included within the main index entries, with details of the countries in which each form applies.

Administrative qualifiers

Administrative divisions are included in entries to differentiate duplicate names - entries of exactly the same name and feature type within the one country - where these division names are shown on the maps. In such cases, duplicate names are alphabetized in the order of the administrative division names.

Additional qualifiers are included for names within selected geographical areas, to indicate more clearly their location.

Descriptors

Entries, other than those for towns and cities, include a descriptor indicating the type of geographical feature. Descriptors are not included where the type of feature is implicit in the name itself, unless there is a town or city of exactly the same name.

Insets

Where relevant, the index clearly indicates [inset] if a feature appears on an inset map.

Alphabetical order

The Icelandic characters Ð and þ are transliterated and alphabetized as 'Th' and 'th'. The German character ß is alphabetized as 'ss'. Names beginning with Mac or Mc are alphabetized exactly as they appear. The terms Saint, Sainte, etc, are abbreviated to St, Ste, etc, but alphabetized as if in the full form.

Numerical entries

Entries beginning with numerals appear at the beginning of the index, in numerical order. Elsewhere, numerals are alphabetized before 'a'.

Permuted terms

Names beginning with generic geographical terms are permuted - the descriptive term is placed after, and the index alphabetized by, the main part of the name. For example, Mount Everest is indexed as Everest, Mount; Lake Superior as Superior, Lake. This policy is applied to all languages. Permuting has not been applied to names of towns, cities or administrative divisions beginning with such geographical terms. These remain in their full form, for example, Lake Isabella, USA.

Gazetteer entries and connections

Selected entries have been extended to include gazetteer-style information. Important geographical facts which relate specifically to the entry are included within the entry in coloured type.

Entries for features which also appear on, or which have a topical link to, the thematic pages of the atlas include a reference to those pages.

Abbreviations

admin. dist.	administrative district	IL	Illinois	plat.	plateau		
admin. div.	administrative division	imp. l.	impermanent lake	P.N.G.	Papua New Guinea		
admin. reg.	administrative region	IN	Indiana	Port.	Portugal		
Afgh.	Afghanistan	Indon.	Indonesia	pref.	prefecture		
AK	Alaska	Kazakh.	Kazakhstan	prov.	province		
AL	Alabama	KS	Kansas	pt	point		
Alg.	Algeria	KY	Kentucky	Qld	Queensland		
AR	Arkansas	Kyrg.	Kyrgyzstan	Que.	Québec		
Arg.	Argentina	l.	lake	r.	river		
aut. comm.	autonomous community	LA	Louisiana	reg	region		
aut. reg.	autonomous region	lag.	lagoon	res.	reserve		
aut. rep.	autonomous republic	Lith.	Lithuania	resr	reservoir		
AZ	Arizona	Lux.	Luxembourg	RI	Rhode Island		
Azer.	Azerbaijan	MA	Massachusetts	Rus. Fed.	Russian Federation		
b.	bay	Madag.	Madagascar	S.	South, Southern		
Bangl.	Bangladesh	Man.	Manitoba	S.A.	South Australia		
B.C.	British Columbia	MD	Maryland	salt l.	salt lake		
Bol.	Bolivia	ME	Maine	Sask.	Saskatchewan		
Bos.-Herz.	Bosnia-Herzegovina	Mex.	Mexico	SC	South Carolina		
Bulg.	Bulgaria	MI	Michigan	SD	South Dakota		
c.	cape	MN	Minnesota	sea chan.	sea channel		
CA	California	MO	Missouri	Serb. and Mont.	Serbia and Montenegro		
Cent. Afr. Rep.	Central African Republic	Moz.	Mozambique	Sing.	Singapore		
CO	Colorado	MS	Mississippi	Switz.	Switzerland		
Col.	Colombia	MT	Montana	Tajik.	Tajikistan		
CT	Connecticut	mt.	mountain	Tanz.	Tanzania		
Czech Rep.	Czech Republic	mts	mountains	Tas.	Tasmania		
DC	District of Columbia	N.	North, Northern	terr.	territory		
DE	Delaware	nat. park	national park	Thai.	Thailand		
Dem. Rep. Congo	Democratic Republic of Congo	N.B.	New Brunswick	TN	Tennessee		
depr.	depression	NC	North Carolina	Trin. and Tob.	Trinidad and Tobago		
des.	desert	ND	North Dakota	Turkm.	Turkmenistan		
Dom. Rep.	Dominican Republic	NE	Nebraska	TX	Texas		
E.	East, Eastern	Neth.	Netherlands	U.A.E.	United Arab Emirates		
Equat. Guinea	Equatorial Guinea	NH	New Hampshire	U.K.	United Kingdom		
esc.	escarpment	NJ	New Jersey	Ukr.	Ukraine		
est.	estuary	NM	New Mexico	U.S.A.	United States of America		
Eth.	Ethiopia	N.S.	Nova Scotia	UT	Utah		
Fin.	Finland	N.S.W.	New South Wales	Uzbek.	Uzbekistan		
FL	Florida	N.T.	Northern Territory	VA	Virginia		
for.	forest	NV	Nevada	Venez.	Venezuela		
Fr. Guiana	French Guiana	N.W.T.	Northwest Territories	Vic.	Victoria		
F.Y.R.O.M.	Former Yugoslav Republic of Macedonia	NY	New York	vol.	volcano		
g.	gulf	N.Z.	New Zealand	vol. crater	volcanic crater		
GA	Georgia	OH	Ohio	VT	Vermont		
Guat.	Guatemala	OK	Oklahoma	W.	West, Western		
HI	Hawaii	OR	Oregon	WA	Washington		
H.K.	Hong Kong	PA	Pennsylvania	W.A.	Western Australia		
Hond.	Honduras	Para.	Paraguay	WI	Wisconsin		
i.	island	P.E.I.	Prince Edward Island	WV	West Virginia		
IA	Iowa	pen.	peninsula	WY	Wyoming		
ID	Idaho	Phil.	Philippines	Y.T.	Yukon Territory		

1

3-y Severnyy Rus. Fed. 41 S3
5 de Outubro Angola see Xá-Muteba
9 de Julio Arg. 144 D5
25 de Mayo Buenos Aires Arg. 144 D5
25 de Mayo La Pampa Arg. 140 C5
26 Bakı Komissarı Azer. 91 H3
70 Mile House Canada 120 F5
100 Mile House Canada 120 F5
150 Mile House Canada 120 F4

A

Aabenraa Denmark see Åbenrå
Aachen Germany 52 G4
Aalborg Denmark see Ålborg
Aalborg Bugt b. Denmark see Ålborg Bugt
Aalen Germany 53 K6
Aalesund Norway see Ålesund
Aaley Lebanon see Aley
Aalst Belgium 52 E4
Aanaar Fin. see Inari
Aarhus Denmark see Århus
Aarlen Belgium see Arlon
Aars Denmark see Års
Aarschot Belgium 52 E4
Aasiaat Greenland 119 M3
Aath Belgium see Ath
Aba China 76 D1
Aba Dem. Rep. Congo 98 D3
Aba Nigeria 96 D4
Abacaxis r. Brazil 143 G4
Ābādān Iran 88 C4
Ābādeh Iran 88 D4
Ābādeh Ṭashk Iran 88 D4
Abadla Alg. 54 D5
Abaeté Brazil 145 B2
Abaetetuba Brazil 143 I4
Abagnar Qi China see Xilinhot
Abaiang atoll Kiribati 150 H5
Abajo Peak U.S.A. 129 I3
Abakaliki Nigeria 96 D4
Abakan Rus. Fed. 72 G2
Abakanskiy Khrebet mts Rus. Fed. 72 F2
Abalak Niger 96 D3
Abana Turkey 90 D2
Abancay Peru 142 D6
Abariringa atoll Kiribati see Kanton
Abarkūh, Kavīr-e des. Iran 88 D4
Abarqū Iran 88 D4
Abarshahr Iran see Neyshābūr
Abashiri Japan 74 G3
Abashiri-wan b. Japan 74 G3
Abasolo Mex. 131 D7
Abau P.N.G. 110 E1
Abaya, Lake Eth. 98 D3
Ābaya Hāyk' l. Eth. see Abaya, Lake
Ābay Wenz r. Eth. 98 D2 see Blue Nile
Abaza Rus. Fed. 72 G2
Abba Cent. Afr. Rep. 98 B3
Abbasabad Iran 88 D3
'Abbāsābād Iran 88 E2
Abbasanta Sardinia Italy 58 C4
Abbatis Villa France see Abbeville
Abbe, Lake Djibouti/Eth. 86 F7
Abbeville France 52 B4
Abbeville AL U.S.A. 133 C6
Abbeville GA U.S.A. 133 D6
Abbeville LA U.S.A. 131 E6
Abbeville SC U.S.A. 133 D5
Abbey Canada 121 I5
Abbeyfeale Rep. of Ireland 51 C5
Abbey Town U.K. 48 D4
Abborrträsk Sweden 44 K4
Abbot, Mount Australia 110 D4
Abbot Ice Shelf Antarctica 152 K2
Abbotsford Canada 120 F5
Abbott NM U.S.A. 127 G5
Abbott VA U.S.A. 134 E5
Abbottabad Pak. 89 I3
'Abd al 'Azīz, Jabal hill Syria 87 F3
'Abd al Kūrī i. Yemen 86 H7
'Abd Allah, Khawr sea chan. Iraq/Kuwait 88 C4
Abd al Ma'asīr well Saudi Arabia 85 D4
Ābdānān Iran 88 B3
Abdollāhābād Iran 88 D3
Abdulino Rus. Fed. 41 Q5
Abéché Chad 97 F3
Abellinum Italy see Avellino
Abel Tasman National Park N.Z. 113 D5
Abengourou Côte d'Ivoire 96 C4
Åbenrå Denmark 45 F9
Abensberg Germany 53 L6
Abeokuta Nigeria 96 D4
Aberaeron U.K. 49 C6
Aberchirder U.K. 50 G3
Abercorn Zambia see Mbala
Abercrombie r. Australia 112 D4
Aberdare U.K. 49 D7
Aberdaron U.K. 49 C6
Aberdaugleddau U.K. see Milford Haven
Aberdeen Australia 112 E4
Aberdeen Hong Kong China 77 [inset]
Aberdeen S. Africa 100 G7
Aberdeen U.K. 50 G3
Aberdeen U.S.A. 130 D2
Aberdeen Lake Canada 121 L1
Aberdovey U.K. see Aberdyfi
Aberdyfi U.K. 49 C6
Aberfeldy U.K. 50 F4
Aberford U.K. 48 F5
Aberfoyle U.K. 50 E4
Abergavenny U.K. 49 D7
Abergwaun U.K. see Fishguard
Aberhonddu U.K. see Brecon
Abermaw U.K. see Barmouth
Abernathy U.S.A. 131 C5
Aberporth U.K. 49 C6
Abersoch U.K. 49 C6
Abertawe U.K. see Swansea
Aberteifi U.K. see Cardigan
Aberystwyth U.K. 49 C6
Abeshr Chad see Abéché
Abez' Rus. Fed. 41 S2
Āb Gāh Iran 89 E5
Abhā Saudi Arabia 86 F6
Abhar Iran 88 C2
Abiad, Bahr el r. Sudan/Uganda 86 D6 see White Nile

▶Abidjan Côte d'Ivoire 96 C4
Former capital of Côte d'Ivoire. 4th most populous city in Africa.

Abijatta-Shalla National Park Eth. 98 D3
Ab-i-Kavīr salt flat Iran 88 E3
Abilene KS U.S.A. 130 D4
Abilene TX U.S.A. 131 D5
Abingdon U.K. 49 F7
Abingdon U.S.A. 134 D5
Abington Reef Australia 110 E3
Abinsk Rus. Fed. 90 E1
Abiseo, Parque Nacional nat. park Peru 142 C5
Abitau Lake Canada 121 J2
Abitibi, Lake Canada 122 E4
Ab Khūr Iran 88 E3
Abminga Australia 109 F6
Abnūb Egypt 90 C6
Åbo Fin. see Turku
Abohar India 82 C3
Aboisso Côte d'Ivoire 96 C4
Aboite U.S.A. 134 C3
Abomey Benin 96 D4
Abongabong, Gunung mt. Indon. 71 B6
Abong Mbang Cameroon 96 E4
Abou Déia Chad 97 E3
Abovyan Armenia 91 G2
Aboyne U.K. 50 G3
Abqaiq Saudi Arabia 88 C5
Abraham's Bay Bahamas 133 F8
Abramov, Mys pt Rus. Fed. 42 I2
Abrantes Port. 57 B4
Abra Pampa Arg. 144 C2
Abreojos, Punta pt Mex. 127 E8
'Abri Sudan 86 D5
Abrolhos Bank sea feature S. Atlantic Ocean 148 F7
Abruzzo, Parco Nazionale d' nat. park Italy 58 E4
Absalom, Mount Antarctica 152 B1
Absaroka Range mts U.S.A. 126 F3
Abtar, Jabal al hills Syria 85 C2
Abtsgmünd Germany 53 J6
Abū aḍ Ḍuhūr Syria 85 C2
Abū al Ḥusayn, Qā' imp. l. Jordan 85 D3
Abū 'Alī i. Saudi Arabia 88 C5
Abū al Jirāb i. U.A.E. 88 D5
Abū 'Āmūd, Wādī watercourse Jordan 85 C4
Abū 'Arīsh Saudi Arabia 86 F6
Abu 'Aweigīla well Egypt see Abū 'Uwayqilah
Abu Deleiq Sudan 86 D6

▶Abu Dhabi U.A.E. 88 D5
Capital of the United Arab Emirates.

Abū Du'ān Syria 85 D1
Abu Gubeiha Sudan 86 D7
Abū Ḥafnah, Wādī watercourse Jordan 85 D3
Abu Haggag Egypt see Ra's al Ḥikmah
Abū Ḥallūfah, Jabal hill Jordan 85 C4
Abu Hamed Sudan 86 D6

▶Abuja Nigeria 96 D4
Capital of Nigeria.

Abū Jifān well Saudi Arabia 88 B5
Abū Jurdhān Jordan 85 B4
Abū Kamāl Syria 91 F4
Abu Matariq Sudan 97 F3
Abumombazi Dem. Rep. Congo 98 C3
Abu Musa i. The Gulf 88 D5
Abū Mūsá, Jazīreh-ye i. The Gulf see Abu Musa
Abunā r. Bol. 142 E5
Abunā Brazil 142 E5
Ābune Yosēf mt. Eth. 86 E7
Abū Nujaym Libya 97 E1
Abū Qa'ṭūr Syria 85 C2
Abū Rawthah, Jabal mt. Egypt 85 B5
Aburo mt. Dem. Rep. Congo 98 D3
Abu Road India 79 G4
Abū Rujmayn, Jabal mts Syria 85 D2
Abu Rûtha, Gebel mt. Egypt see Abū Rawthah, Jabal
Abū Sawādah well Saudi Arabia 88 C5
Abu Simbil Egypt see Abū Sunbul
Abū Sunbul Egypt 86 D5
Abū Ṭarfā', Wādī watercourse Egypt 85 A5
Abut Head hd N.Z. 113 C6
Abū 'Uwayqilah well Egypt 85 B4
Abu Zabad Sudan 86 C7
Abū Ẓabī U.A.E. see Abu Dhabi
Abūzam Iran 88 C4
Abū Zanīmah Egypt 90 D5
Abu Zenîma Egypt see Abū Zanīmah
Abyad Sudan 86 C7
Abyaḍ, Jabal al mts Syria 85 C2
Abyār al Hakīm well Libya 90 A5
Abydos Australia 108 B5
Abyei Sudan 86 C8
Abyssinia country Africa see Ethiopia
Academician Vernadskiy research station Antarctica see Vernadsky
Academy Bay Rus. Fed. see Akademii, Zaliv
Acadia prov. Canada see Nova Scotia
Acadia National Park U.S.A. 132 G2
Açailândia Brazil 143 I5
Acamarachi mt. Chile see Pili, Cerro
Acampamento de Caça do Mucusso Angola 99 C5
Acandí Col. 142 C2
A Cañiza Spain 57 B2
Acaponeta Mex. 136 C4
Acapulco Mex. 136 E5
Acapulco de Juárez Mex. see Acapulco
Acará Brazil 143 I4
Acaraú Brazil 143 J4
Acaray, Represa de resr Para. 144 E3
Acari, Serra hills Brazil/Guyana 143 G3
Acarigua Venez. 142 E2
Acatlan Mex. 136 E5
Accho Israel see 'Akko
Accomac U.S.A. 135 H5
Accomack U.S.A. see Accomac

▶Accra Ghana 96 C4
Capital of Ghana.

Accrington U.K. 48 E5
Ach r. Germany 53 L6
Achacachi Bol. 142 E7
Achaguas Venez. 142 E2
Achalpur India 82 D5
Achampet India 84 C2
Achan Rus. Fed. 74 E2
Achayvayam Rus. Fed. 65 S3
Acheng China 74 B3
Achhota India 84 D1
Achicourt France 52 C4
Achill Rep. of Ireland 51 C4
Achillbeg Island Rep. of Ireland 51 C4
Achill Island Rep. of Ireland 51 B4
Achiltibuie U.K. 50 D2
Achim Germany 53 J1
Achinsk Rus. Fed. 64 K4
Achit Rus. Fed. 41 R4
Achit Nuur l. Mongolia 80 H2
Achkhoy-Martan Rus. Fed. 91 G2
Achna Cyprus 85 A2
Achnasheen U.K. 50 D3
Acıgöl l. Turkey 59 M6
Acıpayam Turkey 59 M6
Acireale Sicily Italy 58 F6
Ackerman U.S.A. 131 F5
Ackley U.S.A. 130 E3
Acklins Island Bahamas 133 F8
Acle U.K. 49 I6

▶Aconcagua, Cerro mt. Arg. 144 B4
Highest mountain in South America. South America 138–139

Acopiara Brazil 143 K5
A Coruña Spain 57 B2
Acqui Terme Italy 58 C2
Acra U.S.A. 135 H2
Acragas Sicily Italy see Agrigento
Acraman, Lake salt flat Australia 111 A7
Acre r. Brazil 142 E6
Acre Israel see 'Akko
Acre, Bay of Israel see Haifa, Bay of
Acri Italy 58 G5
Ács Hungary 47 Q7
Actaeon Group is Fr. Polynesia see Actéon, Groupe
Actéon, Groupe is Fr. Polynesia 151 K7
Acton Canada 134 E2
Acton U.S.A. 128 D4
Acungui Brazil 145 A4
Acunum Acusio France see Montélimar
Ada MN U.S.A. 130 D2
Ada OH U.S.A. 134 D3
Ada OK U.S.A. 131 D5
Ada WI U.S.A. 134 B2
Adabazar Turkey see Sakarya
Adaja r. Spain 57 D3
Adalia Turkey see Antalya
Adam Oman 87 I5
Adam, Mount hill Falkland Is 144 E8
Adamantina Brazil 145 A3
Adams IN U.S.A. 134 C4
Adams KY U.S.A. 134 D4
Adams MA U.S.A. 135 I2
Adams NY U.S.A. 135 G2
Adams, Mount U.S.A. 126 C3
Adams Center U.S.A. 135 G2
Adams Lake Canada 120 G5
Adams Mountain U.S.A. 120 D4
Adam's Peak Sri Lanka 84 D5
Adams Peak U.S.A. 128 C2

▶Adamstown Pitcairn Is 151 L7
Capital of the Pitcairn Islands.

'Adan Yemen see Aden
Adana Turkey 85 B1
Adana prov. Turkey 85 B1
Adana Yemen see Aden
Adapazarı Turkey see Sakarya
Adare Rep. of Ireland 51 D5
Adare, Cape Antarctica 152 H2
Adavale Australia 111 D5
Adban Afgh. 89 H2
Ad Dabbah Sudan see Ed Debba
Ad Ḍabbīyah well Saudi Arabia 88 C5
Ad Dafinah Saudi Arabia 86 F5
Ad Dahnā' des. Saudi Arabia 86 G5
Ad Dakhla W. Sahara 96 B2
Ad Damir Sudan see Ed Damer
Ad Dammām Saudi Arabia see Dammam
Addanki India 84 C3
Ad Dār al Ḥamrā' Saudi Arabia 86 E4
Ad Darb Saudi Arabia 86 F6
Ad Dawādimī Saudi Arabia 86 F5
Ad Dawḥah Qatar see Doha
Ad Dawr Iraq 91 F4
Ad Daww plain Syria 85 C2
Ad Dayr Iraq 91 G5
Ad Dibdibah plain Saudi Arabia 88 B5
Aḍ Ḍiffah plat. Egypt see Libyan Plateau

▶Addis Ababa Eth. 98 D3
Capital of Ethiopia.

Addison U.S.A. 135 G2
Ad Dīwānīyah Iraq 91 G5
Addlestone U.K. 49 G7
Addo Elephant National Park S. Africa 101 G7
Addoo Atoll Maldives see Addu Atoll
Addu Atoll Maldives 81 D12
Ad Duwayd well Saudi Arabia 91 F5
Ad Duwaym Sudan see Ed Dueim
Ad Duwayris well Saudi Arabia 88 C6
Adegaon India 82 D5
Adel GA U.S.A. 133 D6
Adel IA U.S.A. 130 E3

▶Adelaide Australia 111 B7
State capital of South Australia.

Adelaide r. Australia 108 E3
Adelaide Bahamas 133 E7
Adelaide Island Antarctica 152 L2
Adelaide River Australia 108 E3
Adele Island Australia 108 C3
Adélie Coast Antarctica 152 G2
Adélie Land reg. Antarctica 152 G2
Adelong Australia 112 D5
Aden Yemen 86 F7
Aden, Gulf of Somalia/Yemen 86 G7
Adena U.S.A. 134 E3
Adenau Germany 52 G4
Adendorf Germany 53 K1
Aderbissinat Niger 96 D3
Aderno Sicily Italy see Adrano
Adesar India 82 B5
Adhan, Jabal mt. U.A.E. 88 E5
Adh Dhāyūf well Saudi Arabia 91 G6
'Adhfā' well Saudi Arabia 91 F5
'Ādhirīyāt, Jibāl al mts Jordan 85 C4
Adi i. Indon. 69 I7
Ādī Ārk'ay Eth. 86 E7
Adige r. Italy 58 E2
Ādīgrat Eth. 98 D2
Adilabad India 84 C2
Adilcevaz Turkey 91 F3
Adin U.S.A. 126 C4
Adīrī Libya 97 E2
Adirondack Mountains U.S.A. 135 H1
Ādīs Ābeba Eth. see Addis Ababa
Adi Ugri Eritrea see Mendefera
Adıyaman Turkey 90 E3
Adjud Romania 59 L1
Adlavik Islands Canada 123 K3
Admiralty Island Canada 119 H3
Admiralty Island U.S.A. 120 C3
Admiralty Island National Monument - Kootznoowoo Wilderness nat. park U.S.A. 120 C3
Admiralty Islands P.N.G. 69 L7
Ado-Ekiti Nigeria 96 D4
Adok Sudan 86 D8
Adolfo L. Mateos Mex. 127 E8
Adolphus U.S.A. 134 B5
Adonara i. Indon. 108 C2
Adoni India 84 C3
Adorf Germany 53 M4
Adorf (Diemelsee) Germany 53 I3
Ado-Tymovo Rus. Fed. 74 F2
Adour r. France 56 D5
Adra Spain 57 E5
Adramyttium Turkey see Edremit
Adramyttium, Gulf of Turkey see Edremit Körfezi
Adrano Sicily Italy 58 F6
Adrar Alg. 96 C2
Adrar hills Mali see Ifôghas, Adrar des
Adraskand r. Afgh. 89 F3
Adré Chad 97 F3
Adrian MI U.S.A. 134 C3
Adrian TX U.S.A. 131 C5
Adrianople Turkey see Edirne
Adrianopolis Turkey see Edirne
Adriatic Sea Europe 58 E2
Adua Eth. see Ādwa
Adunara i. Indon. see Adonara
Adusa Dem. Rep. Congo 98 C3
Aduwa Eth. see Ādwa
Adverse Well Australia 108 C5
Ādwa Eth. 98 D2
Adycha r. Rus. Fed. 65 O3
Adyk Rus. Fed. 43 J7
Adzhiyan Turkm. 88 D2
Adzopé Côte d'Ivoire 96 C4
Aegean Sea Greece/Turkey 59 K5
Aegina i. Greece see Aigina
Aegyptus country Africa see Egypt
Aela Jordan see Al 'Aqabah
Aelana Jordan see Al 'Aqabah
Aelia Capitolina Israel/West Bank see Jerusalem
Aelōnlaplap atoll Marshall Is see Ailinglapalap
Aenus Turkey see Enez
Aerzen Germany 53 J2
Aesernia Italy see Isernia
A Estrada Spain 57 B2
Afabet Eritrea 86 E6
Afanas'yevo Rus. Fed. 42 L4
Affreville Alg. see Khemis Miliana
Afghānestān country Asia see Afghanistan
▶Afghanistan country Asia 89 G3
Asia 6, 62–63
Afgooye Somalia 98 E3
'Afif Saudi Arabia 86 F5
Afiun Karahissar Turkey see Afyon
Åfjord Norway 44 G5
Aflou Alg. 54 E5
Afmadow Somalia 98 E3
Afogados da Ingazoira Brazil 143 K5
A Fonsagrada Spain 57 C2
Afonso Cláudio Brazil 145 C3
Āfrēra Terara vol. Eth. 86 F7
Africa Nova country Africa see Tunisia
'Afrīn Syria 85 C1
'Afrīn, Nahr r. Syria/Turkey 85 C1
Afşin Turkey 90 E3
Afsluitdijk barrage Neth. 52 F2
Afton U.S.A. 126 F4
Afuá Brazil 143 H4
'Afula Israel 85 B3
Afyon Turkey 59 N5
Afyonkarahisar Turkey see Afyon
Aga Germany 53 M4
Agadès Niger see Agadez
Agadez Niger 96 D3
Agadir Morocco 96 C1
Agadyr' Kazakh. 80 D2
Agalega Islands Mauritius 149 L6
Agana Guam see Hagåtña
Agara Georgia 91 F2
Agartala India 83 G5
Agashi India 84 B2
Agate Canada 122 E4
Agathe France see Agde
Agathonisi i. Greece 59 L6
Agats Indon. 69 J8
Agatti i. India 84 B4
Agboville Côte d'Ivoire 96 C4
Ağcabädi Azer. 91 G2
Ağdam Azer. 91 G3
Ağdaş Azer. 91 G2
Agdash Azer. see Ağdaş
Agde France 56 F5
Agdzhabedi Azer. see Ağcabädi
Agedabia Libya see Ajdābiyā
Agen France 56 E4
Aggeneys S. Africa 100 D5
Aggteleki nat. park Hungary 47 R6
Aghil Pass China/Jammu and Kashmir 82 D1
Agiabampo Mex. 127 F8
Agiguan i. N. Mariana Is see Aguijan
Ağın Turkey 90 E3
Aginskoye Rus. Fed. 72 G1
Aginum France see Agen
Agios Dimitrios Greece 59 J6
Agios Efstratios i. Greece 59 K5
Agios Georgios i. Greece 59 J6
Agios Nikolaos Greece 59 K7
Agios Theodoros Cyprus 85 B2
Agiou Orous, Kolpos b. Greece 59 J4
Agirwat Hills Sudan 86 E6
Agisanang S. Africa 101 G4
Agnes, Mount hill Australia 109 E6
Agnew Australia 109 C6
Agnibilékrou Côte d'Ivoire 96 C4
Agnita Romania 59 K2
Agniye-Afanas'yevsk Rus. Fed. 74 E2
Agra India 82 D4
Agrakhanskiy Poluostrov pen. Rus. Fed. 91 G2
Agram Croatia see Zagreb
Ağrı Turkey 91 F3
Agria Gramvousa i. Greece 59 J7
Agrigan i. N. Mariana Is see Agrihan
Agrigento Sicily Italy 58 E6
Agrigentum Sicily Italy see Agrigento
Agrihan i. N. Mariana Is 69 L3
Agrinio Greece 59 I5
Agropoli Italy 58 F4
Agryz Rus. Fed. 41 Q4
Ağsu Azer. 91 H2
Agua, Volcán de vol. Guat. 136 F6
Água Clara Brazil 144 F2
Aguadilla Puerto Rico 137 K5
Agua Escondida Arg. 144 C5
Agua Fria r. U.S.A. 129 G5
Agua Fria National Monument nat. park U.S.A. 129 G4
Aguanaval r. Mex. 131 C7
Aguanga U.S.A. 128 E5
Aguanus r. Canada 123 J4
Aguapeí r. Brazil 145 A3
Agua Prieta Mex. 127 F7
Aguaro-Guariquito, Parque Nacional nat. park Venez. 142 E2
Aguascalientes Mex. 136 D4
Agudos Brazil 145 A3
Águeda Port. 57 B3
Aguemour reg. Alg. 96 D2
Aguié Niger 96 D3
Aguijan i. N. Mariana Is 69 L4
Aguilar U.S.A. 127 G5
Aguilar de Campóo Spain 57 D2
Águilas Spain 57 F5

▶Agulhas, Cape S. Africa 100 E8
Most southerly point of Africa.

Agulhas Basin sea feature Southern Ocean 149 J9
Agulhas Negras mt. Brazil 145 B3
Agulhas Plateau sea feature Southern Ocean 149 J8
Agulhas Ridge sea feature S. Atlantic Ocean 148 I8
Ağva Turkey 59 M4
Agvali Rus. Fed. 91 G2
Ahaggar plat. Alg. see Hoggar
Āhangarān Iran 89 F3
Ahar Iran 88 B2
Ahaura N.Z. 113 C6
Ahaus Germany 52 H2
Ahipara Bay N.Z. 113 D2
Ahiri India 84 D2
Ahklun Mountains U.S.A. 118 B4
Ahlen Germany 53 H3
Ahmadabad India 82 C5
Aḥmadābād Iran 89 E3
Aḥmad al Bāqir, Jabal mt. Jordan 85 B5
Ahmadī Iran 88 E5
Ahmadnagar India 84 B2
Ahmadpur East Pak. 89 H4
Ahmar mts Eth. 98 E3
Ahmar Mountains Eth. see Ahmar
Ahmedabad India see Ahmadabad
Ahmednagar India see Ahmadnagar
Ahorn Germany 53 K4
Ahr r. Germany 52 H4
Ahram Iran 88 C4
Ahrensburg Germany 53 K1
Āhtäri Fin. 44 N5
Ahtme Estonia 45 O7
Ahu China 77 H1
Āhū Iran 88 C4
Ahun France 56 F3
Ahuzhen China see Ahu
Ahvāz Iran 88 C4
Ahwa India 84 B1
Ahwāz Iran see Ahvāz
Ai-Ais Namibia 100 C4
Ai-Ais Hot Springs and Fish River Canyon Park nature res. Namibia 100 C4
Aichwara India 82 D4
Aid U.S.A. 134 D4
Aidin Turkm. 88 D2
Aigialousa Cyprus 85 B2
Aigina i. Greece 59 J6
Aigio Greece 59 J5
Aigle de Chambeyron mt. France 56 H4
Aigües Tortes i Estany de Sant Maurici, Parc Nacional d' nat. park Spain 57 G2
Ai He r. China 74 B4
Aihua China see Yunxian
Aihui China see Heihe
Aijal India see Aizawl
Aikawa Japan 75 E5
Aiken U.S.A. 133 D5
Ailao Shan mts China 76 D3
Aileron Australia 108 F5
Ailinglabelab atoll Marshall Is see Ailinglapalap
Ailinglapalap atoll Marshall Is 150 H5
Ailly-sur-Noye France 52 C5
Ailsa Craig Canada 134 E2
Ailsa Craig i. U.K. 50 D5
Aimangala India 84 C3
Aimorés, Serra dos hills Brazil 145 C2
Aïn Beïda Alg. 58 B7
'Aïn Ben Tili Mauritania 96 C2
'Aïn Dâlla spring Egypt see 'Ayn Dāllah
Aïn Defla Alg. 57 H5
Aïn Deheb Alg. 57 G6
Aïn el Hadjel Alg. 57 H6
'Ain el Maqfi spring Egypt see 'Ayn al Maqfī
Aïn el Melh Alg. 57 I6
Aïn Mdila well Alg. 58 B7
Aïn-M'Lila Alg. 54 F4
Aïn Oussera Alg. 57 H6
Ain Salah Alg. see In Salah
Aïn Sefra Alg. 54 D5
Ainsworth U.S.A. 130 D3
Aintab Turkey see Gaziantep
Aïn Taya Alg. 57 H5
Aïn Tédélès Alg. 57 G5
Aïn Temouchent Alg. 57 F6
'Ain Tibaghbagh spring Egypt see 'Ayn Tabaghbugh
'Ain Timeira spring Egypt see 'Ayn Tumayrah
'Ain Zeitûn Egypt see 'Ayn Zaytūn
Aiquile Bol. 142 E7
Air i. Indon. 71 D7
Airaines France 52 B5
Airdrie Canada 120 H5
Airdrie U.K. 50 F5
Aire r. France 52 E5
Aire, Canal d' France 52 C4
Aire-sur-l'Adour France 56 D5
Air Force Island Canada 119 K3
Airpanas Indon. 108 D1
Aisatung Mountain Myanmar 70 A2
Aisch r. Germany 53 L5
Aishihik Canada 120 B2
Aishihik Lake Canada 120 B2
Aisne r. France 52 C5
Aïssa, Djebel mt. Alg. 54 D5
Aitamännikkö Fin. 44 N3
Aitana mt. Spain 57 F4
Aït Benhaddou tourist site Morocco 54 C5
Aiterach r. Germany 53 M6
Aitkin U.S.A. 130 E2
Aiud Romania 59 J1
Aix France see Aix-en-Provence
Aix-en-Provence France 56 G5
Aix-la-Chapelle Germany see Aachen
Aix-les-Bains France 56 G4
Aiyina i. Greece see Aigina
Aíyion Greece see Aigio
Aizawl India 83 H5
Aizkraukle Latvia 45 N8
Aizpute Latvia 45 L8
Aizu-wakamatsu Japan 75 E5
Ajaccio Corsica France 56 I6
Ajanta India 84 B1
Ajanta Range hills India see Sahyadriparvat Range
Ajaureforsen Sweden 44 I4
Ajax Canada 134 F2
Ajayameru India see Ajmer
Ajban U.A.E. 88 D5
Aj Bogd Uul mt. Mongolia 80 I3
Ajdābiyā Libya 97 F1
a-Jiddét des. Oman see Ḥarāsīs, Jiddat al
'Ajlūn Jordan 85 B3
'Ajman U.A.E. 88 D5
Ajmer India 82 C4
Ajmer-Merwara India see Ajmer
Ajnala India 82 C3
Ajo U.S.A. 129 G5
Ajo, Mount U.S.A. 129 G5
Ajrestan Afgh. 89 G3
Akademii, Zaliv b. Rus. Fed. 74 E1
Akademii Nauk, Khrebet mt. Tajik. see Akademiyai Fanho, Qatorkŭhi
Akademiyai Fanho, Qatorkŭhi mt. Tajik. 89 H2
Akagera National Park Rwanda 98 D4
Akalkot India 84 C2
Akama, Akra c. Cyprus see Arnauti, Cape
Akamagaseki Japan see Shimonoseki
Akan National Park Japan 74 G4
Akaroa N.Z. 113 D6
Akas reg. India 76 B3
Akāshat Iraq 91 E4
Akbarābād Iran 91 I5
Akbarpur Uttar Pradesh India 82 E4
Akbarpur Uttar Pradesh India 83 E4
Akbaytal, Pereval pass Tajik. 89 I2
Akbaytal Pass Tajik. see Akbaytal, Pereval
Akbez Turkey 85 C1
Akçadağ Turkey 90 E3
Akçakale Turkey 85 D1
Akçakoca Turkey 59 N4
Akçakoca Dağları mts Turkey 55 N4
Akçakoyunlu Turkey 85 C1
Akçalı Dağları mts Turkey 85 A1
Akchâr reg. Mauritania 96 B3
Akchi Kazakh. see Akshiy
Akdağlar mts Turkey 59 M6
Akdağmadeni Turkey 90 D3
Akdere Turkey 85 A1
Akelamo Indon. 69 H6
Åkersberga Sweden 45 K7
Akersloot Neth. 52 E2
Aketi Dem. Rep. Congo 98 C3
Akgyr Erezi hills Turkm. see Akkyr, Gory
Akhali-Afoni Georgia see Akhali Ap'oni
Akhali Ap'oni Georgia 91 F2
Akhḍar, Al Jabal al mts Libya 97 F1
Akhḍar, Jabal mts Oman 88 E6
Akhisar Turkey 59 L5
Akhnoor Jammu and Kashmir 82 C2
Akhsu Azer. see Ağsu
Akhta Armenia see Hrazdan
Akhtarīn Syria 85 C1
Akhtubinsk Rus. Fed. 43 J6
Akhty Rus. Fed. 91 G2
Akhtyrka Ukr. see Okhtyrka
Aki Japan 75 D6
Akiéni Gabon 98 B4
Akimiski Island Canada 122 E3
Akishma r. Rus. Fed. 74 D1

Akita Japan 75 F5
Akjoujt Mauritania 96 B3
Akkajaure l. Sweden 44 J3
Akkerman Ukr. see Bilhorod-Dnistrovs'kyy
Akkeshi Japan 74 G4
'Akko Israel 85 B3
Akkol' Akmolinskaya Oblast' Kazakh. 80 D1
Akkol' Atyrauskaya Oblast' Kazakh. 43 K7
Akku Kazakh. 80 E1
Akkul' Kazakh. see Akkol'
Akkuş Turkey 90 E2
Akkyr, Gory hills Turkm. 88 D1
Aklavik Canada 118 E3
Aklera India 82 D4
Ak-Mechet Kazakh. see Kyzylorda
Akmenrags pt Latvia 45 L8
Akmeqit China 82 D1
Akmola Kazakh. see Astana
Akmolinsk Kazakh. see Astana
Akobo Sudan 97 G4
Akobo Wenz r. Eth./Sudan 98 D3
Akokan Niger 96 D3
Akola India 84 C1
Akom II Cameroon 96 E4
Akonolinga Cameroon 96 E4
Akordat Eritrea 86 E6
Akören Turkey 90 D3
Akot India 82 D5
Akpatok Island Canada 123 I1
Akqi China 80 E3
Akra, Jabal mt. Syria/Turkey see Aqra', Jabal al
Akranes Iceland 44 [inset]
Åkrehamn Norway 45 D7
Akrérèb Niger 96 D3
Akron CO U.S.A. 130 C3
Akron IN U.S.A. 134 B3
Akron OH U.S.A. 134 E3
Akrotiri Bay Cyprus 85 A2
Akrotirion Bay Cyprus see Akrotiri Bay
Akrotiriou, Kolpos b. Cyprus see Akrotiri Bay
Akrotiri Sovereign Base Area military base Cyprus 85 A2

▶Aksai Chin terr. Asia 82 D2
Disputed territory (China/India).

Aksaray Turkey 90 D3
Aksay China 80 H4
Aksay Kazakh. 41 Q5
Ak-Say r. Kyrg. 87 M1
Aksay Rus. Fed. 43 H7
Akşehir Turkey 59 N5
Akşehir Gölü l. Turkey 59 N5
Akseki Turkey 90 C3
Aksha Rus. Fed. 73 K2
Akshiganak Kazakh. 80 B2
Akshiy Kazakh. 80 E3
Akshukur Kazakh. 91 H2
Aksu China 80 F3
Aksu Kazakh. 80 E1
Aksu r. Tajik. see Oqsu
Aksu r. Turkey 59 N6
Aksuat Kazakh. 80 F2
Aksu-Ayuly Kazakh. 80 D2
Aksubayevo Rus. Fed. 43 K5
Āksum Eth. 86 E7
Aktag mt. China 83 F1
Aktas Dağı mt. Turkey 91 G3
Aktau Kazakh. 78 E2
Akto China 89 J2
Aktobe Kazakh. 78 E1
Aktogay Karagandinskaya Oblast' Kazakh. 80 E2
Aktogay Vostochnyy Kazakhstan Kazakh. 80 E2
Aktsyabrski Belarus 43 F5
Aktyubinsk Kazakh. see Aktobe
Akulivik Canada 119 K3
Akune Japan 75 C6
Akure Nigeria 96 D4
Akuressa Sri Lanka 84 D5
Akureyri Iceland 44 [inset]
Akusha Rus. Fed. 43 J8
Akwanga Nigeria 96 D4
Akxokesay China 83 G1
Akyab Myanmar see Sittwe
Akyatan Gölü salt l. Turkey 85 B1
Akyazı Turkey 59 N4
Akzhaykyn, Ozero salt l. Kazakh. 80 C3
Ål Norway 45 F6
'Alā, Jabal al hills Syria 85 C2
Alabama r. U.S.A. 133 C6
Alabama state U.S.A. 133 C5
Alabaster AL U.S.A. 133 C5
Alabaster MI U.S.A. 134 D1
Al 'Abṭīyah well Iraq 91 G5
Alaca Turkey 90 D2
Alacahan Turkey 90 E3
Alaçam Turkey 90 D2
Alaçam Dağları mts Turkey 59 M5
Alacant Spain see Alicante-Alacant
Alaçatı Turkey 59 L5
Aladağ Turkey 90 D3
Ala Dağlar mts Turkey 91 F3
Ala Dağları mts Turkey 90 D3
Al 'Adam Libya 90 A5
Al Aflāj reg. Saudi Arabia 88 B6
Alag Hu l. China 76 C1
Alagir Rus. Fed. 91 G2
Alagoinhas Brazil 145 D1
Alahärmä Fin. 44 M5
Al Aḥmadī Kuwait 88 C4
Alai Range mts Asia 89 H2
Alaivān Iran 88 D3
Alājah Syria 85 B2
Alajärvi Fin. 44 M5
Al 'Ajrūd well Egypt 85 B4
Alakanuk U.S.A. 118 B3
Al Akhḍar Saudi Arabia 90 E5
Alakol', Ozero salt l. Kazakh. 80 F2
Ala Kul salt l. Kazakh. see Alakol', Ozero
Alakurtti Rus. Fed. 44 Q3
Al 'Alamayn Egypt 90 C5
Al 'Alayyah Saudi Arabia 86 F6
Alama Somalia 98 E3
Al 'Amādīyah Iraq 91 F3
Alamagan i. N. Mariana Is 69 L3
Alamaguan i. N. Mariana Is see Alamagan
Al 'Amārah Iraq 91 G5
'Alam ar Rūm, Ra's pt Egypt 90 B5
'Alāmarvdasht watercourse Iran 88 D4
Alamdo China 76 B2
Alameda U.S.A. 128 B3
'Alam el Rûm, Râs pt Egypt see 'Alam ar Rūm, Ra's
Al Amghar waterhole Iraq 91 G5
Al 'Āmirīyah Egypt 90 C5
Alamo GA U.S.A. 133 D5
Alamo NV U.S.A. 129 F3
Alamo Dam U.S.A. 129 G4
Alamogordo U.S.A. 127 G6
Alamo Heights U.S.A. 131 D6
Alamos Sonora Mex. 127 F7
Alamos Sonora Mex. 127 F8
Alamos r. Mex. 131 C7
Alamos, Sierra mts Mex. 127 F8
Alamosa U.S.A. 127 G5
Alamos de Peña Mex. 127 G7
Alampur India 84 C3
Alan Myanmar see Myede
Alanäs Sweden 44 I4
Åland is Fin. see Åland Islands
Aland r. Germany 53 L1
Aland India 84 C2
Al Andarīn Syria 85 C2
Åland Islands Fin. 45 K6
Alandur India 84 D3
Alanson U.S.A. 134 C1
Alanya Turkey 90 D3
Alapli Turkey 59 N4
Alappuzha India see Alleppey
Alapuzha India see Alleppey
Al 'Aqabah Jordan 85 B5
Al 'Aqīq Saudi Arabia 86 F5
Al 'Arabīyah as Sa'ūdīyah country Asia see Saudi Arabia
Alarcón, Embalse de resr Spain 57 E4
Al 'Arīsh Egypt 85 A4
Al Arṭāwīyah Saudi Arabia 86 G4
Alas, Selat sea chan. Indon. 108 B2
Alaşehir Turkey 59 M5
Alashiya country Asia see Cyprus
Al Ashmūnayn Egypt 90 C6
Alaska state U.S.A. 118 D3
Alaska, Gulf of U.S.A. 118 D4
Alaska Highway Canada/U.S.A. 120 A2
Alaska Peninsula U.S.A. 118 B4
Alaska Range mts U.S.A. 118 D3
Älät Azer. 91 H3
Alat Uzbek. 89 F2
Alataw Shankou pass China/Kazakh. see Dzungarian Gate
Al Atwā' well Saudi Arabia 91 F5
Alatyr' Rus. Fed. 43 J5
Alatyr' r. Rus. Fed. 43 J5
Alausí Ecuador 142 C4
Alaverdi Armenia 91 G2
'Alavī Iran 88 C3
Alavieska Fin. 44 N4
Alavus Fin. 44 M5
Alawbum Myanmar 70 B1
Alawoona Australia 111 C7
Alay Kyrka Toosu mts Asia see Alai Range
Al 'Ayn Oman 88 E6
Al 'Ayn U.A.E. 88 D5
Alayskiy Khrebet mts Asia see Alai Range
Al 'Azīzīyah Iraq 91 G4

▶Al 'Azīzīyah Libya 55 G5
Highest recorded shade temperature in the world.

Al Azraq al Janūbī Jordan 85 C4
Alba Italy 58 C2
Alba U.S.A. 134 C1
Al Bāb Syria 85 C1
Albacete Spain 57 F4
Al Badī' Saudi Arabia 88 B6
Al Bādiyah al Janūbīyah hill Iraq 91 G5
Al Bahrayn country Asia see Bahrain
Alba Iulia Romania 59 J1
Al Bajā' well U.A.E. 88 C5
Albājī Iran 88 C4
Al Bakhrā well Saudi Arabia 88 B5
Albanel, Lac l. Canada 123 G4
▶Albania country Europe 59 H4
Europe 5, 38–39
Albany Australia 109 B8
Albany r. Canada 122 E3
Albany GA U.S.A. 133 C6
Albany IN U.S.A. 134 C3
Albany KY U.S.A. 134 C5
Albany MO U.S.A. 130 E3

▶Albany NY U.S.A. 135 I2
State capital of New York.

Albany OH U.S.A. 134 D4
Albany OR U.S.A. 126 C3
Albany TX U.S.A. 131 D5
Albany Downs Australia 112 D1
Albardão do João Maria coastal area Brazil 144 F4
Al Bardī Libya 90 B5
Al Bāridah hills Saudi Arabia 85 D5
Al Baṣrah Iraq see Basra
Al Baṭḥa' marsh Iraq 91 G5
Al Bāṭinah reg. Oman 88 E5
Albatross Bay Australia 110 C2
Albatross Island Australia 111 [inset]
Al Bawītī Egypt 90 C5
Al Bayḍā' Libya 86 B3
Al Bayḍā' Yemen 86 G7
Albemarle U.S.A. 133 D5
Albemarle Island Galápagos Ecuador see Isabela, Isla
Albemarle Sound sea chan. U.S.A. 132 E5
Albenga Italy 58 C2
Alberche r. Spain 57 D4
Alberga Australia 111 A5
Alberga watercourse Australia 111 A5
Albergaria-a-Velha Port. 57 B3
Albert Australia 112 C4
Albert France 52 C5
Albert, Lake Dem. Rep. Congo/Uganda 98 D3
Albert, Parc National nat. park Dem. Rep. Congo see Virunga, Parc National des
Alberta prov. Canada 120 H4
Alberta U.S.A. 135 G5
Albert Kanaal canal Belgium 52 F4
Albert Lea U.S.A. 130 E3
Albert Nile r. Sudan/Uganda 97 G4
Alberto de Agostini, Parque Nacional nat. park Chile 144 B8
Alberton S. Africa 101 I4
Alberton U.S.A. 126 E3
Albert Town Bahamas 133 F8
Albertville Dem. Rep. Congo see Kalemie
Albertville France 56 H4
Albertville U.S.A. 133 C5
Albestroff France 52 G6
Albi France 56 F5
Albia U.S.A. 130 E3
Al Biḍah des. Saudi Arabia 88 C5
Albina Suriname 143 H2
Albino Italy 58 C2
Albion CA U.S.A. 128 B2
Albion IL U.S.A. 130 F4
Albion IN U.S.A. 134 C3
Albion MI U.S.A. 134 C2
Albion NE U.S.A. 130 D3
Albion NY U.S.A. 135 F2
Albion PA U.S.A. 134 E3
Al Biqā' valley Lebanon see El Béqaa
Al Bi'r Saudi Arabia 90 E5
Al Birk Saudi Arabia 86 F5
Al Biyāḍh reg. Saudi Arabia 86 G5
Alborán, Isla de i. Spain 57 E6
Ålborg Denmark 45 F8
Ålborg Bugt b. Denmark 45 G8
Albro Australia 110 D4
Al Budayyi Bahrain 88 C5
Albufeira Port. 57 B5
Al Buḥayrāt al Murrah lakes Egypt see Bitter Lakes
Albuquerque U.S.A. 127 G6
Al Burayj Syria 85 C2
Al Buraymī Oman 88 D5
Al Burj Jordan 85 B5
Alburquerque Spain 57 C4
Albury Australia 112 C6
Al Buşayrah Syria 91 F4
Al Busayṭā' plain Saudi Arabia 85 D4
Al Bushūk well Saudi Arabia 88 B4
Alcácer do Sal Port. 57 B4
Alcalá de Henares Spain 57 E3
Alcalá la Real Spain 57 E5
Alcamo Sicily Italy 58 E6
Alcañiz Spain 57 F3
Alcántara Spain 57 C4
Alcantara Lake Canada 121 I2
Alcaraz Spain 57 E4
Alcázar de San Juan Spain 57 E4
Alcazarquivir Morocco see Ksar el Kebir
Alchevs'k Ukr. 43 H6
Alcobaça Brazil 145 D2
Alcoi Spain see Alcoy-Alcoi
Alcoota Australia 108 F5
Alcora Spain 57 F3
Alcova U.S.A. 126 G4
Alcoy Spain see Alcoy-Alcoi
Alcoy-Alcoi Spain 57 F4
Alcúdia Spain 57 H4
Aldabra Islands Seychelles 99 E4
Aldan Rus. Fed. 65 N4
Aldan r. Rus. Fed. 65 N3
Alde r. U.K. 49 I6
Aldeboarn Neth. see Oldeboorn
Aldeburgh U.K. 49 I6
Alder Creek U.S.A. 135 H2
Alderney i. Channel Is 49 E9
Alder Peak U.S.A. 128 C4
Aldershot U.K. 49 G7
Al Dhafrah reg. U.A.E. 88 D6
Aldingham U.K. 48 D4
Aldridge U.K. 49 F6
Aleg Mauritania 96 B3
Alegre Espírito Santo Brazil 145 C3
Alegre Minas Gerais Brazil 145 B2
Alegrete Brazil 144 E3
Alegros Mountain U.S.A. 129 I4
Aleksandra, Mys hd Rus. Fed. 70 E1
Aleksandriya Ukr. see Oleksandriya
Aleksandro-Nevskiy Rus. Fed. 39 I5
Aleksandropol Armenia see Gyumri
Aleksandrov Rus. Fed. 42 H4
Aleksandrov Gay Rus. Fed. 43 K6
Aleksandrovsk Rus. Fed. 41 R4
Aleksandrovsk Ukr. see Zaporizhzhya
Aleksandrovskiy Rus. Fed. see Aleksandrovsk
Aleksandrovskoye Rus. Fed. 91 F1
Aleksandrovsk-Sakhalinskiy Rus. Fed. 74 F2
Aleksandry, Zemlya i. Rus. Fed. 64 F1
Alekseyevka Akmolinskaya Oblast' Kazakh. see Akkol'
Alekseyevka Vostochnyy Kazakhstan Kazakh. see Terekty
Alekseyevka Amurskaya Oblast' Rus. Fed. 74 B1
Alekseyevka Belgorodskaya Oblast' Rus. Fed. 43 H6
Alekseyevka Belgorodskaya Oblast' Rus. Fed. 43 H6
Alekseyevskaya Rus. Fed. 43 I6
Alekseyevskoye Rus. Fed. 42 K5
Aleksin Rus. Fed. 43 H5
Aleksinac Serb. and Mont. 59 I3
Alèmbé Gabon 98 B4
Ålen Norway 44 G5
Alençon France 56 E2
Alenquer Brazil 143 H4
Alenuihaha Channel HI U.S.A. 127 [inset]
Alep Syria see Aleppo
Aleppo Syria 85 C1
Alert Canada 119 L1
Alerta Peru 142 D6
Alès France 56 G4
Aleşd Romania 59 J1
Aleshki Ukr. see Tsyurupyns'k
Aleşkirt Turkey see Eleşkirt
Alessandria Italy 58 C2
Alessio Albania see Lezhë
Ålesund Norway 44 E5
Aleutian Basin sea feature Bering Sea 150 H2
Aleutian Islands U.S.A. 118 A4
Aleutian Range mts U.S.A. 118 C4
Aleutian Trench sea feature N. Pacific Ocean 150 I2
Alevina, Mys c. Rus. Fed. 65 Q4
Alevişik Turkey see Samandağı
Alexander U.S.A. 130 C2
Alexander, Kap c. Greenland see Ullersuaq
Alexander, Mount hill Australia 110 B2
Alexander Archipelago is U.S.A. 120 B3
Alexander Bay b. Namibia/S. Africa 100 C5
Alexander Bay S. Africa 100 C5
Alexander City U.S.A. 133 C5
Alexander Island Antarctica 148 L2
Alexandra Australia 112 B6
Alexandra N.Z. 113 B7
Alexandra, Cape S. Georgia 144 I8
Alexandra Channel India 71 A4
Alexandra Land i. Rus. Fed. see Aleksandry, Zemlya
Alexandreia Greece 59 J4
Alexandretta Turkey see İskenderun
Alexandria Afgh. see Ghaznī
Alexandria Canada 135 H1

▶Alexandria Egypt 90 C5
5th most populous city in Africa.

Alexandria Romania 59 K3
Alexandria S. Africa 101 H7
Alexandria Turkm. see Mary
Alexandria U.K. 50 E5
Alexandria IN U.S.A. 134 C3
Alexandria KY U.S.A. 134 C4
Alexandria LA U.S.A. 131 E6
Alexandria VA U.S.A. 135 G4
Alexandria Arachoton Afgh. see Kandahār
Alexandria Areion Afgh. see Herāt
Alexandria Bay U.S.A. 135 H1
Alexandria Prophthasia Afgh. see Farāh
Alexandrina, Lake Australia 107 B7
Alexandroupoli Greece 59 K4
Alexis r. Canada 123 K3
Alexis Creek Canada 120 F4
Aley Lebanon 85 B3
Aleyak Iran 88 E2
Aleysk Rus. Fed. 72 E2
Alf Germany 52 H4
Al Farwānīyah Kuwait 88 B4
Al Fas Morocco see Fès
Al Fatḥah Iraq 91 F4
Al Fāw Iraq 91 H5
Al Fayyūm Egypt 90 C5
Alfeld (Leine) Germany 53 J3
Alfenas Brazil 145 B3
Alford U.K. 48 H5
Alfred ME U.S.A. 135 J2
Alfred NY U.S.A. 135 G2
Alfred and Marie Range hills Australia 109 D6
Al Fujayrah U.A.E. see Fujairah
Al Fuqahā' Libya 97 E2
Al Furāt r. Iraq/Syria 85 D2 see Euphrates
Alga Kazakh. 80 A2
Ålgård Norway 45 D7
Algarrobo del Aguilla Arg. 144 C5
Algarve reg. Port. 57 B5
Algeciras Spain 57 D5
Algemesí Spain 57 F4
Algena Eritrea 86 E6
Alger Alg. see Algiers
Alger U.S.A. 134 C1

▶Algeria country Africa 96 C2
2nd largest country in Africa.
Africa 7, 94–95

Algérie country Africa see Algeria
Algermissen Germany 53 J2
Algha Kazakh. see Alga
Al Ghāfāt Oman 88 E6
Al Ghammās Iraq 91 G5
Al Ghardaqah Egypt see Al Ghurdaqah
Al Ghawr plain Jordan/West Bank 85 B4
Al Ghayḍah Yemen 86 H6
Alghero Sardinia Italy 58 C4
Al Ghurdaqah Egypt 86 D4
Al Ghuwayr well Qatar 88 C5

▶Algiers Alg. 57 H5
Capital of Algeria.

Algoa Bay S. Africa 101 G7
Algoma U.S.A. 134 B1
Algona U.S.A. 130 E3
Algonac U.S.A. 134 D2
Algonquin Park Canada 135 F1
Algonquin Provincial Park Canada 135 F1
Algorta Spain 57 E2
Algueirao Moz. see Hacufera
Al Habakah well Saudi Arabia 91 F5
Al Ḥabbānīyah Iraq 91 F4
Al Ḥadaqah well Saudi Arabia 88 B4
Al Ḥadd Bahrain 88 C5
Al Hadhālīl plat. Saudi Arabia 91 F5
Al Ḥadīdīyah Syria 85 C2
Al Ḥadīthah Iraq 91 F4
Al Hadīthah Saudi Arabia 85 C4
Al Ḥaḍr Iraq see Hatra
Al Ḥafār well Saudi Arabia 91 F5
Al Ḥaffah Syria 85 C2
Al Haggounia W. Sahara 96 B2
Al Ḥajar al Gharbī mts Oman 88 E5
Al Ḥajar ash Sharqī mts Oman 88 E6
Al Ḥamād plain Asia 90 E5
Al Ḥamādah al Ḥamrā' plat. Libya 96 E2
Alhama de Murcia Spain 57 F5
Al Ḥamar Saudi Arabia 88 B6
Al Ḥamīdīyah Syria 85 B2
Al Ḥammām Egypt 90 C5
Al Ḥanākīyah Saudi Arabia 86 F5
Al Ḥanīsh al Kabīr i. Yemen 86 F7
Al Haniyah esc. Iraq 91 G5
Al Hariq Saudi Arabia 88 B6
Al Ḥarrah Egypt 90 C5
Al Harūj al Aswad hills Libya 97 E2
Al Hasa reg. Saudi Arabia 88 C5
Al Ḥasakah Syria 91 F3
Al Hawi salt pan Saudi Arabia 85 D5
Al Hawjā' Saudi Arabia 90 E5
Al Ḥawṭah reg. Saudi Arabia 88 B6
Al Ḥayy Iraq 91 G4
Al Ḥayz Egypt 90 C5
Al Hazīm Jordan 85 C4
Al Ḥazm Saudi Arabia 90 E5
Al Ḥazm al Jawf Yemen 86 F6
Al Ḥibāk des. Saudi Arabia 87 H6
Al Hījānah Syria 85 C3
Al Ḥillah Iraq see Hillah
Al Ḥillah Saudi Arabia 86 G5
Al Ḥinnāh Saudi Arabia 98 E1
Al Ḥinw mt. Saudi Arabia 85 D4
Al Hirrah well Saudi Arabia 88 C6
Al Hishah Syria 85 D1
Al Ḥismā plain Saudi Arabia 90 D5
Al Ḥiṣn Jordan 85 B3
Al Hoceima Morocco 57 E6
Al Ḥudaydah Yemen see Hodeidah
Al Ḥufrah reg. Saudi Arabia 90 E5
Al Hufūf Saudi Arabia 86 G4
Al Hūj hills Saudi Arabia 90 E5
Al Husayfin Oman 88 E5
Al Huwwah Saudi Arabia 88 B6
Ali China 82 D2
'Alīābād Afgh. 89 H2
'Alīābād Golestān Iran 88 D2
'Alīābād Hormozgan Iran 88 D4
'Alīābād Khorāsān Iran 89 F4
'Alīābād Kordestān Iran 88 B2
Alīābād, Kūh-e mt. Iran 88 C3
Aliağa Turkey 59 L5
Aliakmonas r. Greece 59 J4
Alibag India 84 B2
Äli Bayramlı Azer. 91 H3
Alicante Spain see Alicante-Alacant
Alicante-Alacant Spain 57 F4
Alice r. Australia 110 C2
Alice watercourse Australia 110 D5
Alice U.S.A. 131 D7
Alice, Punta pt Italy 58 G5
Alice Springs Australia 109 F5
Alice Town Bahamas 133 E7
Aliceville U.S.A. 131 F5
Alichur Tajik. 89 I2
Alichur r. Tajik. 89 I2
Alick Creek r. Australia 110 C4
Alifu Atoll Maldives see Ari Atoll
Al Ifẓi'iyyah i. U.A.E. 88 C5
Aliganj India 82 D4
Aligarh Rajasthan India 82 D4
Aligarh Uttar Pradesh India 82 D4
Alīgūdarz Iran 88 C3
Alihe China 74 A2
Alījūq, Kūh-e mt. Iran 88 C4
'Alī Kheyl Afgh. 89 H3
Al Imārāt al 'Arabīyah at Muttaḥidah country Asia see United Arab Emirates
Alimia i. Greece 59 L6
Alindao Cent. Afr. Rep. 98 C3
Alingsås Sweden 45 H8
Aliova r. Turkey 59 M5
Alipura India 82 D4
Alipur Duar India 83 G4
Alirajpur India 82 C5
Al 'Irāq country Asia see Iraq
Al 'Īsāwīyah Saudi Arabia 85 C4
Al Iskandarīyah Egypt see Alexandria
Al Iskandarīyah Iraq 91 G4
Al Ismā'īlīyah Egypt 90 D5
Aliveri Greece 59 K5
Aliwal North S. Africa 101 H6
Alix Canada 120 H4
Al Jafr Jordan 85 C4
Al Jāfūrah des. Saudi Arabia 88 C5
Al Jaghbūb Libya 90 B5
Al Jahrah Kuwait 88 B4
Al Jamalīyah Qatar 88 C5
Al Jarāwī well Saudi Arabia 85 D4
Al Jauf Saudi Arabia see Al Jawf
Al Jawb reg. Saudi Arabia 88 C6
Al Jawf Libya 97 F2
Al Jawf Saudi Arabia 91 E5
Al Jawsh Libya 96 E1
Al Jaza'ir country Africa see Algeria
Al Jaza'ir Alg. see Algiers
Aljezur Port. 57 B5
Al Jībān reg. Saudi Arabia 88 C5
Al Jil well Iraq 91 F5
Al Jilh esc. Saudi Arabia 88 B5
Al Jithāmīyah Saudi Arabia 91 F6
Al Jīzah Egypt see Giza
Al Jīzah Jordan 85 B4
Al Jubayl hills Saudi Arabia 88 B5
Al Jubaylah Saudi Arabia 88 B5
Al Jufra Oasis Libya 97 E2
Al Julayqah well Saudi Arabia 88 C5
Aljustrel Port. 57 B5
Al Juwayf depr. Syria 85 C3
Al Kahfah Al Qaṣīm Saudi Arabia 86 F4
Al Kahfah Ash Sharqīyah Saudi Arabia 88 C5
Alkali Lake Canada 120 F5
Al Karak Jordan 85 B4
Al Kāẓimīyah Iraq 91 G4
Al Khābūrah Oman 88 E6
Al Khalīl West Bank see Hebron
Al Khāliṣ Iraq 91 G4
Al Khārijah Egypt 86 D4
Al Kharj reg. Saudi Arabia 88 B6
Al Kharrārah Qatar 88 C5
Al Kharrūbah Egypt 85 A4
Al Khaṣab Oman 88 E5
Al Khatam reg. U.A.E. 88 D5
Al Khawkhah Yemen 86 F7
Al Khawr Qatar 88 C5
Al Khizāmī well Saudi Arabia 88 C5
Al Khums Libya 97 E1
Al Khunfah sand area Saudi Arabia 90 E5
Al Khunn Saudi Arabia 98 E1
Al Kifl Iraq 91 G4
Al Kir'ānah Qatar 88 C5
Al Kiswah Syria 85 C3
Alkmaar Neth. 52 E2
Al Kūbrī Egypt 85 A4
Al Kūfah Iraq 91 G4
Al Kumayt Iraq 91 G4
Al Kuntillah Egypt 85 B5
Al Kusūr hills Saudi Arabia 85 D4
Al Kūt Iraq 91 G4
Al Kuwayt country Asia see Kuwait
Al Kuwayt Kuwait see Kuwait
Al Labbah plain Saudi Arabia 91 F5
Al Lādhiqīyah Syria see Latakia
Allagadda India 84 C3
Allahabad India 83 E4
Al Lajā lava field Syria 85 C3
Allakaket U.S.A. 118 C3
Allakh-Yun' Rus. Fed. 65 O3
Allanmyo Myanmar see Myede
Allanridge S. Africa 101 H4
Allapalli India 84 D2
'Allāqī, Wādī al watercourse Egypt 86 D5
'Allâqi, Wâdi el watercourse Egypt see 'Allāqī, Wādī al
Allardville Canada 123 I5
Alldays S. Africa 101 I2
Allegan U.S.A. 134 C2
Allegheny r. U.S.A. 134 F3
Allegheny Mountains U.S.A. 130 D5
Allegheny Reservoir U.S.A. 135 F3
Allen, Lough l. Rep. of Ireland 51 D3
Allendale U.S.A. 133 D5
Allendale Town U.K. 48 E4
Allende Coahuila Mex. 131 C6
Allende Nuevo León Mex. 131 C7
Allendorf (Lumda) Germany 53 I4
Allenford Canada 134 E1
Allenstein Poland see Olsztyn
Allensville U.S.A. 134 B5
Allentown U.S.A. 135 H3
Alleppey India 84 C4
Aller r. Germany 53 J2
Alliance NE U.S.A. 130 C3
Alliance OH U.S.A. 134 E3
Al Lībīyah country Africa see Libya
Allier r. France 56 F3
Al Liḥābah well Saudi Arabia 88 B5
Allinge-Sandvig Denmark 45 I9
Al Liṣāfah well Saudi Arabia 88 B5
Al Lisān pen. Jordan 85 B4
Alliston Canada 134 F1
Al Līth Saudi Arabia 86 F5
Al Liwā' oasis U.A.E. 88 D6
Alloa U.K. 50 F4
Allons U.S.A. 134 C5
Allora Australia 112 F2
Allur India 84 D3
Alluru Kottapatnam India 84 D3
Al Lussuf well Iraq 91 F5
Alma Canada 123 H4
Alma MI U.S.A. 134 C2
Alma NE U.S.A. 130 D3
Alma WI U.S.A. 130 F2
Al Ma'ānīyah Iraq 91 F5
Alma-Ata Kazakh. see Almaty
Almada Port. 57 B4
Al Madāfi' plat. Saudi Arabia 90 E5
Al Ma'danīyāt well Iraq 91 G5
Almaden Australia 110 D3
Almadén Spain 57 D4
Al Madīnah Saudi Arabia see Medina
Al Mafraq Jordan 85 C3
Al Maghrib country Africa see Morocco
Al Maghrib reg. U.A.E. 88 D6
Al Mahākik reg. Saudi Arabia 88 C6
Al Mahdum Syria 85 C1
Al Maḥiā depr. Saudi Arabia 90 E6
Al Maḥwīt Yemen 86 F6
Al Malsūnīyah reg. Saudi Arabia 88 C5
Almalyk Uzbek. 80 C3
Al Manadir reg. Oman 88 D6
Al Manāmah Bahrain see Manama
Al Manjūr well Saudi Arabia 88 B6
Almanor, Lake U.S.A. 128 C1
Almansa Spain 57 F4
Al Manṣūrah Egypt 90 C5
Almanzor mt. Spain 57 D3
Al Mariyyah U.A.E. 88 D6
Al Marj Libya 97 F1
Almas, Rio das r. Brazil 145 A1
Al Maṭarīyah Egypt 90 D5

▶Almaty Kazakh. 80 E3
Former capital of Kazakhstan.

Al Mawşil Iraq see Mosul
Al Mayādīn Syria 91 F4
Al Mazār Egypt 85 A4
Almaznyy Rus. Fed. 65 M3
Almeirim Brazil 143 H4
Almeirim Port. 57 B4
Almelo Neth. 52 G2
Almenara Brazil 145 C2
Almendra, Embalse de resr Spain 57 C3
Almendralejo Spain 57 C4
Almere Neth. 52 F2
Almería Spain 57 E5
Almería, Golfo de b. Spain 57 E5
Al'met'yevsk Rus. Fed. see Al'met'yevsk
Al'met'yevsk Rus. Fed. 41 Q5
Älmhult Sweden 45 I8
Almina, Punta pt Spain 57 D6
Al Mindak Saudi Arabia 86 F5
Al Minyā Egypt 90 C5
Almirós Greece see Almyros
Al Mish'āb Saudi Arabia 88 C4
Almodôvar Port. 57 B5
Almond r. U.K. 50 F4
Almont U.S.A. 134 D2
Almonte Spain 57 C5
Almora India 82 D3
Al Mu'ayzilah hill Saudi Arabia 85 D5
Al Mubarrez Saudi Arabia 86 G4
Al Muḍaibī Oman 87 I5
Al Muḍairib Oman 88 E6
Al Muḥarraq Bahrain 88 C5
Al Mukallā Yemen see Mukalla
Al Mukhā Yemen see Mocha
Al Mukhaylī Libya 86 B3
Al Munbaṭiḥ des. Saudi Arabia 88 C6
Almuñécar Spain 57 E5
Al Muqdādīyah Iraq 91 G4
Al Mūrītānīyah country Africa see Mauritania
Al Murūt well Saudi Arabia 91 E5
Almus Turkey 90 E2
Al Musannāh ridge Saudi Arabia 88 B4
Al Musayyib Iraq 88 B3
Al Muwaqqar Jordan 85 C4
Almyros Greece 59 J5
Almyrou, Ormos b. Greece 59 K7
Alnwick U.K. 48 F3

▶Alofi Niue 107 J3
Capital of Niue.
Oceania 8, 104–105

Aloja Latvia 45 N8

Alon Myanmar 70 A2
Along India 83 H3
Alongshan China 74 A2
Alonnisos *i.* Greece 59 J5
Alor *i.* Indon. 108 D2
Alor, Kepulauan *is* Indon. 108 D2
Alor Setar Malaysia 71 C6
Alor Star Malaysia *see* Alor Setar
Alost Belgium *see* Aalst
Aloysius, Mount Australia 109 E6
Alozero Rus. Fed. 44 Q4
Alpen Germany 52 G3
Alpena U.S.A. 134 D1
Alpercatas, Serra das *hills* Brazil 143 J5
Alpha Australia 110 D4
Alpha Ridge *sea feature* Arctic Ocean 153 A1
Alpine *AZ* U.S.A. 129 I5
Alpine *NY* U.S.A. 135 G2
Alpine *TX* U.S.A. 131 C6
Alpine *WY* U.S.A. 126 F4
Alpine National Park Australia 112 C6
Alps *mts* Europe 56 H4
Al Qa'āmīyāt *reg.* Saudi Arabia 86 G6
Al Qaddāḩīyah Libya 97 E1
Al Qadmūs Syria 85 C2
Al Qaffāy *i.* U.A.E. 88 D5
Al Qāhirah Egypt *see* Cairo
Al Qā'īyah Saudi Arabia 86 F5
Al Qā'īyah *well* Saudi Arabia 88 B5
Al Qalībah Saudi Arabia 90 E5
Al Qāmishlī Syria 91 F3
Al Qar'ah Libya 90 B5
Al Qar'ah *well* Saudi Arabia 88 B5
Al Qar'ah *lava field* Syria 85 C3
Al Qardāḩah Syria 85 C2
Al Qarqar Saudi Arabia 85 C4
Al Qaryatayn Syria 85 C2
Al Qaşab *Ar Riyāḑ* Saudi Arabia 88 B5
Al Qaşab *Ash Sharqīyah* Saudi Arabia 88 C6
Al Qaţīf Saudi Arabia 88 C5
Al Qaţn Yemen 86 G6
Al Qaţrānah Jordan 85 C4
Al Qaţrūn Libya 97 E2
Al Qāyşūmah *well* Saudi Arabia 91 F5
Al Qumur *country* Africa *see* Comoros
Al Qunayţirah Syria 85 B3
Al Qunfidhah Saudi Arabia 86 F6
Al Qurayyāt Saudi Arabia 85 C4
Al Qurnah Iraq 91 G5
Al Quşaymah Egypt 85 B4
Al Quşayr Egypt 86 D4
Al Quşayr Syria 85 C2
Al Qūşīyah Egypt 90 C6
Al Qūşūrīyah Saudi Arabia 88 B6
Al Quţayfah Syria 85 C3
Al Quwayi' Saudi Arabia 88 B6
Al Quwayīyah Saudi Arabia 86 G5
Al Quwayrah Jordan 85 B5
Al Rabbād *reg.* U.A.E. 88 D6
Alroy Downs Australia 110 B3
Alsace *admin. reg.* France 53 H6
Alsace *reg.* France 56 H2
Alsager U.K. 49 E5
Al Samīt *well* Iraq 91 F5
Alsask Canada 121 I5
Alsatia *reg.* France *see* Alsace
Alsek *r.* U.S.A. 120 B3
Alsfeld Germany 53 J4
Alsleben (Saale) Germany 53 L3
Alston U.K. 48 E4
Alstonville Australia 112 F2
Alsunga Latvia 45 L8
Alta Norway 44 M2
Alta, Mount N.Z. 113 B7
Altaelva *r.* Norway 44 M2
Altafjorden *sea chan.* Norway 44 M1
Alta Floresta Brazil 143 G5
Altai Mountains Asia 72 F3
Altamaha *r.* U.S.A. 133 D6
Altamira Brazil 143 H4
Altamura Italy 58 G4
Altan Shiret China 73 J5
Altan Xiret China *see* Altan Shiret
Alta Paraiso de Goiás Brazil 145 B1
Altar *r.* Mex. 127 F7
Altar, Desierto de *des.* Mex. 125 F6
Altavista U.S.A. 134 F5
Altay China 80 G2
Altay Mongolia 80 I2
Altayskiy Rus. Fed. 80 G1
Altayskiy Khrebet *mts* Asia *see* Altai Mountains
Altdorf Switz. 56 I3
Altea Spain 57 F4
Alteidet Norway 44 M1
Altenahr Germany 52 G4
Altenberge Germany 53 H2
Altenburg Germany 53 M4
Altenkirchen (Westerwald) Germany 53 H4
Altenqoke China 83 H1
Altin Köprü Iraq 91 G4
Altınoluk Turkey 59 L5
Altınözü Turkey 85 C1
Altıntaş Turkey 59 N5
Altiplano *plain* Bol. 142 E7
Altmark *reg.* Germany 53 L2
Altmühl *r.* Germany 53 L6
Alto, Monte *hill* Italy 58 D2
Alto Chicapa Angola 99 B5
Alto del Moncayo *mt.* Spain 57 F3
Alto de Pencoso *hills* Arg. 144 C4
Alto Garças Brazil 143 H7
Alto Madidi, Parque Nacional *nat. park* Bol. 142 E6
Alton *CA* U.S.A. 128 A1
Alton *IL* U.S.A. 130 F4
Alton *MO* U.S.A. 131 F4
Alton *NH* U.S.A. 135 J2
Altona Canada 120 F3
Altoona U.S.A. 135 F3
Alto Parnaíba Brazil 143 I5
Altötting Germany 47 N6
Altrincham U.K. 48 E5
Alt Schwerin Germany 53 M1
Altūn Kūbrī Iraq *see* Altin Köprü
Altun Shan *mts* China 80 G4
Alturas U.S.A. 126 C4
Altus U.S.A. 131 D5
Al Ubaylah Saudi Arabia 98 F1
Alucra Turkey 90 E2
Alūksne Latvia 45 O8
Alūm Iran 88 C3
Alum Bridge U.S.A. 134 E4
Al 'Uqaylah Libya 97 E1
Al 'Uqaylah Saudi Arabia *see* An Nabk
Al Uqşur Egypt *see* Luxor
Alur India 84 C3
Al Urayq *des.* Saudi Arabia 90 E5
Al 'Urdun *country* Asia *see* Jordan
Alur Setar Malaysia *see* Alor Setar
'Ālūt Iran 88 B3
Aluva India *see* Alwaye
Al 'Uwayjā' *well* Saudi Arabia 88 C6
Al 'Uwaynāt Libya 86 B5
Al 'Uwayqīlah Saudi Arabia 91 F5
Al 'Uzayr Iraq 91 G5
Alva U.S.A. 131 D4
Alvand, Kūh-e *mt.* Iran 88 C3
Alvarães Brazil 142 F4
Alvaton U.S.A. 134 B5
Alvdal Norway 44 G5
Älvdalen Sweden 45 I6
Alvesta Sweden 45 I8
Ålvik Norway 45 E6
Alvik Sweden 44 J5
Alvin U.S.A. 131 E6
Alvorada do Norte Brazil 145 B1
Älvsbyn Sweden 44 L4
Al Wafrah Kuwait 88 B4
Al Wajh Saudi Arabia 86 E4
Al Wakrah Qatar 88 C5
Al Waqbá *well* Saudi Arabia 88 B4
Alwar India 82 D4
Al Warī'ah Saudi Arabia 86 G4
Al Wāţiyah *well* Egypt 90 B5
Alwaye India 84 C4
Al Widyān *plat.* Iraq/Saudi Arabia 91 F4
Al Wusayţ *well* Saudi Arabia 88 B4
Alxa Youqi China *see* Ehen Hudag
Alxa Zuoqi China *see* Bayan Hot
Al Yamāmah Saudi Arabia 88 B5
Al Yaman *country* Asia *see* Yemen
Alyangula Australia 110 B2
Al Yāsāt *i.* U.A.E. 88 C5
Alyth U.K. 50 F4
Alytus Lith. 45 N9
Alzette *r.* Lux. 52 G5
Alzey Germany 53 I5
Amacayacu, Parque Nacional *nat. park* Col. 142 D4
Amadeus, Lake *salt flat* Australia 109 E6
Amadjuak Lake Canada 119 K3
Amadora Port. 57 B4
Amakusa-nada *b.* Japan 75 C6
Åmål Sweden 45 H7
Amalia S. Africa 101 G4
Amaliada Greece 59 I6
Amalner India 82 C5
Amamapare Indon. 69 J7
Amambaí Brazil 144 E2
Amambaí, Serra de *hills* Brazil/Para. 144 E2
Amami-Ō-shima *i.* Japan 75 C7
Amami-shotō *is* Japan 75 C8
Amamula Dem. Rep. Congo 98 C4
Amanab P.N.G. 69 K7
Amangel'dy Kazakh. 80 C1
Amankeldi Kazakh. *see* Amangel'dy
Amantea Italy 58 G5
Amanzimtoti S. Africa 101 J6
Amapá Brazil 143 H3
Amarante Brazil 143 J5
Amarapura Myanmar 70 B2
Amareleja Port. 57 C4
Amargosa Brazil 145 D1
Amargosa *watercourse* U.S.A. 128 E3
Amargosa Desert U.S.A. 128 E3
Amargosa Range *mts* U.S.A. 128 E3
Amargosa Valley U.S.A. 128 E3
Amarillo U.S.A. 131 C5
Amarillo, Cerro *mt.* Arg. 144 C4
Amarkantak India 83 E5
Amasia Turkey *see* Amasya
Amasine W. Sahara 96 B2
Amasra Turkey 90 D2
Amasya Turkey 90 D2
Amata Australia 109 E6
Amatulla India 83 H4
Amau P.N.G. 110 E1
Amay Belgium 52 F4
Amazar Rus. Fed. 74 A1
Amazar *r.* Rus. Fed. 74 A1

▶Amazon *r.* S. America 142 F4
Longest river and largest drainage basin in South America and 2nd longest river in the world.
Also known as Amazonas or Solimões.
South America 138–139
World 12–13

Amazon, Mouths of the Brazil 143 I3
Amazonas *r.* S. America 142 F4 *see* Amazon
Amazon Cone *sea feature* S. Atlantic Ocean 148 E5
Amazónia, Parque Nacional *nat. park* Brazil 143 G4
Ambajogai India 84 C2
Ambala India 82 D3
Ambalangoda Sri Lanka 84 D5
Ambalavao Madag. 99 E6
Ambam Cameroon 98 B3
Ambar Iran 88 E4
Ambarchik Rus. Fed. 65 R3
Ambarnyy Rus. Fed. 44 R4
Ambasa India *see* Ambassa
Ambasamudram India 84 C4
Ambassa India 83 G5
Ambathala Australia 111 D5
Ambato Ecuador 142 C4
Ambato Boeny Madag. 99 E5
Ambato Finandrahana Madag. 99 E6
Ambatolampy Madag. 99 E5
Ambatomainty Madag. 99 E5
Ambatondrazaka Madag. 99 E5
Ambejogai India *see* Ambajogai
Ambelau *i.* Indon. 69 H7
Ambeno *enclave* East Timor *see* Ocussi
Amberg Germany 53 L5
Ambergris Cay *i.* Belize 136 G5
Ambérieu-en-Bugey France 56 G4
Amberley Canada 134 E1
Ambgaon India 84 D1
Ambianum France *see* Amiens
Ambikapur India 83 E5
Ambilobe Madag. 99 E5
Ambition, Mount Canada 120 D3
Amble U.K. 48 F3
Ambler U.S.A. 118 C3
Ambleside U.K. 48 E4
Amblève *r.* Belgium 52 F4
Ambo India 83 F5
Amboasary Madag. 99 E6
Ambodifotatra Madag. 99 E5
Ambohimahasoa Madag. 99 E6
Ambohitra *mt.* Madag. 99 E5
Amboina Indon. *see* Ambon
Ambon Indon. 69 H7
Ambon *i.* Indon. 69 H7
Amboró, Parque Nacional *nat. park* Bol. 142 F7
Ambositra Madag. 99 E6
Ambovombe Madag. 99 E6
Amboy U.S.A. 129 F4
Ambre, Cap d' *c.* Madag. *see* Bobaomby, Tanjona
Ambrim *i.* Vanuatu *see* Ambrym
Ambriz Angola 99 B4
Ambrizete Angola *see* N'zeto
Ambrosia Lake U.S.A. 129 J4
Ambrym *i.* Vanuatu 107 G3
Ambunti P.N.G. 69 K7
Ambur India 84 C3
Am-Dam Chad 97 F3
Amded, Oued *watercourse* Alg. 96 D2
Amdo China 83 G2
Ameland *i.* Neth. 52 F1
Amelia Court House U.S.A. 135 G5
Amenia U.S.A. 135 I3
Amer, Erg d' *des.* Alg. 98 A1
Amereli India *see* Amreli
American, North Fork *r.* U.S.A. 128 C2
Americana Brazil 145 B3
American-Antarctic Ridge *sea feature* S. Atlantic Ocean 148 G9
American Falls U.S.A. 126 E4
American Falls Reservoir U.S.A. 126 E4
American Fork U.S.A. 129 H1

▶American Samoa *terr.* S. Pacific Ocean 107 J3
United States Unincorporated Territory.
Oceania 8, 104–105

Americus U.S.A. 133 C5
Amersfoort Neth. 52 F2
Amersfoort S. Africa 101 I4
Amersham U.K. 49 G7
Amery Canada 121 M3
Amery Ice Shelf Antarctica 152 E2
Ames U.S.A. 130 E3
Amesbury U.K. 49 F7
Amesbury U.S.A. 135 J2
Amet India 82 C4
Amethi India 83 E4
Amfissa Greece 59 J5
Amga Rus. Fed. 65 O3
Amgalang China 73 L3
Amgu Rus. Fed. 74 E3
Amguid Alg. 96 D2
Amgun' *r.* Rus. Fed. 74 E1
Amherst Canada 123 I5
Amherst Myanmar *see* Kyaikkami
Amherst *MA* U.S.A. 135 I2
Amherst *OH* U.S.A. 134 D3
Amherst *VA* U.S.A. 134 F5
Amherstburg Canada 134 D2
Amherst Island Canada 135 G1
Amiata, Monte *mt.* Italy 58 D3
Amida Turkey *see* Diyarbakır
Amidon U.S.A. 130 C2
Amiens France 52 C5
'Amīj, Wādī *watercourse* Iraq 91 F4
Amik Ovası *marsh* Turkey 85 C1
'Amīnābād Iran 88 D4
Amindivi *atoll* India *see* Amini
Amindivi Islands India 84 B4
Amini *atoll* India 84 B4
Amino Eth. 98 E3
Aminuis Namibia 100 D2
Amīrābād Iran 88 B3
Amirante Islands Seychelles 149 L6
Amirante Trench *sea feature* Indian Ocean 149 L6
Amisk Lake Canada 121 K4
Amistad, Represa de *resr* Mex./U.S.A. *see* Amistad Reservoir
Amistad Reservoir Mex./U.S.A. 131 C6
Amisus Turkey *see* Samsun
Amite U.S.A. 131 F6
Amity Point Australia 112 F1
Amla India 82 D5
Amlapura Indon. *see* Karangasem
Amlash Iran 88 C2
Amlekhganj Nepal 83 F4
Åmli Norway 45 F7
Amlia Island U.S.A. 118 A4
Amlwch U.K. 48 C5

▶'Ammān Jordan 85 B4
Capital of Jordan.

Ammanazar Turkm. 88 D2
Ammanford U.K. 49 D7
Ämmänsaari Fin. 44 P4
'Ammār, Tall *hill* Syria 85 C3
Ammarnäs Sweden 44 J4
Ammaroo Australia 110 A4
Ammassalik Greenland 153 J2
Ammerland *reg.* Germany 53 H1
Ammern Germany 53 K3
Ammochostos Cyprus *see* Famagusta
Ammochostos Bay Cyprus 85 B2
Am Nābiyah Yemen 86 F7
Amne Machin Range *mts* China *see* A'nyêmaqên Shan
Amnok-kang *r.* China/N. Korea *see* Yalu Jiang
Amo Jiang *r.* China 76 D4
Amol Iran 88 D2
Amorbach Germany 53 J5
Amorgos *i.* Greece 59 K6
Amory U.S.A. 131 F5
Amos Canada 122 F4
Amourj Mauritania 96 C3
Amoy China *see* Xiamen
Ampani India 84 D2
Ampanihy Madag. 99 E6
Amparai Sri Lanka 84 D5
Amparo Brazil 145 B3
Ampasimanolotra Madag. 99 E5
Amphitheatre Australia 112 A6
Amphitrite Group *is* Paracel Is 68 E3
Ampoa Indon. 69 G7
Amraoti India *see* Amravati
Amravati India 84 C1
Amrawad India 82 D5
Amreli India 82 B5
Amri Pak. 89 H5
Amring India 83 H4
'Amrīt Syria 85 B2
Amritsar India 82 C3
Amroha India 82 D3
Amsden U.S.A. 134 D3
Åmsele Sweden 44 K4
Amstelveen Neth. 52 E2

▶Amsterdam Neth. 52 E2
Official capital of the Netherlands.

Amsterdam S. Africa 101 J4
Amsterdam U.S.A. 135 H2
Amsterdam, Île *i.* Indian Ocean 149 N8
Amstetten Austria 47 O6
Am Timan Chad 97 F3
Amudar'ya *r.* Asia 89 F2
Amudaryo *r.* Asia *see* Amudar'ya
Amund Ringnes Island Canada 119 I2
Amundsen, Mount Antarctica 152 F2
Amundsen Abyssal Plain *sea feature* Southern Ocean 152 J2
Amundsen Basin *sea feature* Arctic Ocean 153 H1
Amundsen Bay Antarctica 152 D2
Amundsen Coast Antarctica 152 J1
Amundsen Glacier Antarctica 152 I1
Amundsen Gulf Canada 118 F2
Amundsen Ridges *sea feature* Southern Ocean 152 J2
Amundsen-Scott *research station* Antarctica 152 C1
Amundsen Sea Antarctica 152 K2
Amuntai Indon. 68 F7
Amur *r.* China 74 D2 *also known as* Heilong Jiang (China)
Amur *r.* Rus. Fed. 74 F1
'Amur, Wadi *watercourse* Sudan 86 D6
Amur Oblast *admin. div.* Rus. Fed. *see* Amurskaya Oblast'
Amursk Rus. Fed. 74 E2
Amurskaya Oblast' *admin. div.* Rus. Fed. 74 C1
Amurskiy liman *strait* Rus. Fed. 74 F1
Amurzet Rus. Fed. 74 C3
Amvrosiyivka Ukr. 43 H7
Amyderya *r.* Asia *see* Amudar'ya
Am-Zoer Chad 97 F3
An Myanmar 70 A3
Anaa *atoll* Fr. Polynesia 151 K7
Anabanua Indon. 69 G7
Anabar *r.* Rus. Fed. 65 M2
Anacapa Islands U.S.A. 128 D4
Anaconda U.S.A. 126 E3
Anacortes U.S.A. 126 C2
Anadarko U.S.A. 131 D5
Anadolu Dağları *mts* Turkey 90 E2
Anadyr' Rus. Fed. 65 S3
Anadyr, Gulf of Rus. Fed. *see* Anadyrskiy Zaliv
Anadyrskiy Zaliv *b.* Rus. Fed. 65 T3
Anafi *i.* Greece 59 K6
Anagé Brazil 145 C1
'Ānah Iraq 91 F4
Anaheim U.S.A. 128 E5
Anahim Lake Canada 120 E4
Anáhuac Mex. 131 C7
Anahuac U.S.A. 131 E6
Anaimalai Hills India 84 C4
Anaiteum *i.* Vanuatu *see* Anatom
Anajás Brazil 143 I4
Anakie Australia 110 D4
Analalava Madag. 99 E5
Anamã Brazil 142 F4
Anambas, Kepulauan *is* Indon. 71 D7
Anamosa U.S.A. 130 F3
Anamur Turkey 85 A1
Anan Japan 75 D6
Anand India 82 C5
Anandapur India 83 F5
Anantapur India 84 C3
Ananthapur India *see* Anantapur
Anantnag India 82 C2
Anant Peth India 82 D4
Anantpur India *see* Anantapur
Ananyev Ukr. *see* Anan'yiv
Anan'yiv Ukr. 43 F7
Anapa Rus. Fed. 90 E1
Anápolis Brazil 145 A2
Anár Fin. *see* Inari
Anār Iran 88 D4
Anardara Afgh. 89 F3
Anatahan *i.* N. Mariana Is 69 L3
Anatajan *i.* N. Mariana Is *see* Anatahan
Anatolia *reg.* Turkey 90 D3
Anatom *i.* Vanuatu 107 G4
Añatuya Arg. 144 D3
Anaypazari Turkey *see* Gülnar
An Biên Vietnam 71 D5
Anbūr-e Kālārī Iran 88 D5
Anbyon N. Korea 75 B5
Ancenis France 56 D3
Anchorage U.S.A. 118 D3
Anchorage Island *atoll* Cook Is *see* Suwarrow
Anchor Bay U.S.A. 134 D2
Anchuthengu India *see* Anjengo
Anci China *see* Langfang
An Cóbh Rep. of Ireland *see* Cóbh
Ancona Italy 58 E3
Ancud, Golfo de *g.* Chile 144 B6
Ancyra Turkey *see* Ankara
Anda *Heilong.* China 74 B3
Anda *Heilong.* China *see* Daqing
Andacollo Chile 144 B4
Andado Australia 110 A5
Andahuaylas Peru 142 D6
Andal India 83 F5
Åndalsnes Norway 44 E5
Andalucía *aut. comm.* Spain 53 D5
Andalusia *aut. comm.* Spain *see* Andalucía
Andalusia U.S.A. 133 C6
Andaman Basin *sea feature* Indian Ocean 149 O5
Andaman Islands India 71 A4
Andaman Sea Indian Ocean 71 A5
Andaman Strait India 71 A4
Andamooka Australia 111 B6
Andapa Madag. 99 E5
Andarāb *reg.* Afgh. 89 H3
Ande China 76 E4
Andegavum France *see* Angers
Andelle *r.* France 52 B5
Andenes Norway 44 J2
Andenne Belgium 52 F4
Andéramboukane Mali 96 D3
Anderlecht Belgium 52 E4
Andermatt Switz. 56 I3
Andernos-les-Bains France 56 D4
Anderson *r.* Canada 118 F3
Anderson *AK* U.S.A. 118 D3
Anderson *IN* U.S.A. 134 C3
Anderson *SC* U.S.A. 133 D5
Anderson *TX* U.S.A. 131 E6
Anderson Bay Australia 111 [inset]
Anderson Lake Canada 120 F5
Andes *mts* S. America 144 C4
Andfjorden *sea chan.* Norway 40 J2
Andhíparos *i.* Greece *see* Antiparos
Andhra Lake India 84 B2
Andhra Pradesh *state* India 84 C2
Andijon Uzbek. *see* Andizhan
Andikithira *i.* Greece *see* Antikythira
Andilamena Madag. 99 E5
Andilanatoby Madag. 99 E5
Andīmeshk Iran 88 C3
Andímilos *i.* Greece *see* Antimilos
Andípsara *i.* Greece *see* Antipsara
Andırın Turkey 90 E3
Andirlangar China 83 E1
Andizhan Uzbek. 80 D3
Andkhvoy Afgh. 89 G2
Andoany Madag. 99 E5
Andoas Peru 142 C4
Andogskaya Gryada *hills* Rus. Fed. 42 H4
Andol India 84 C2
Andong China *see* Dandong
Andong S. Korea 75 C5
Andongwei China 77 H1
Andoom Australia 110 C2
▶Andorra *country* Europe 57 G2
Europe 5, 38–39

▶Andorra la Vella Andorra 57 G2
Capital of Andorra.

Andorra la Vieja Andorra *see* Andorra la Vella
Andover U.K. 49 F7
Andover *NY* U.S.A. 135 G2
Andover *OH* U.S.A. 134 E3
Andøya *i.* Norway 44 I2
Andrade U.S.A. 129 F5
Andradina Brazil 145 A3
Andranomavo Madag. 99 E5
Andranopasy Madag. 99 E6
Andreanof Islands U.S.A. 150 I2
Andreapol' Rus. Fed. 42 G4
Andreas Isle of Man 48 C4
André Félix, Parc National de *nat. park* Cent. Afr. Rep. 98 C3
Andrelândia Brazil 145 B3
Andrew Canada 121 H4
Andrew Bay Myanmar 70 A3
Andrews *SC* U.S.A. 133 E5
Andrews *TX* U.S.A. 131 C5
Andreyevka Kazakh. 80 F2
Andria Italy 58 G4
Androka Madag. 99 E6
Andropov Rus. Fed. *see* Rybinsk
Andros *i.* Bahamas 133 E7
Andros *i.* Greece 59 K6
Androscoggin *r.* U.S.A. 135 K2
Andros Town Bahamas 133 E7
Andrott *i.* India 84 B4
Andselv Norway 44 K2
Andújar Spain 57 D4
Andulo Angola 99 B5
Anec, Lake *salt flat* Australia 105 E5
Āneen-Kio *terr.* N. Pacific Ocean *see* Wake Island
Anéfis Mali 96 D3
Anegada, Bahía *b.* Arg. 144 D6
Anegada Passage Virgin Is (U.K.) 137 L5
Aného Togo 96 D4
Aneityum *i.* Vanuatu *see* Anatom
'Aneiza, Jabal *hill* Iraq *see* 'Unayzah, Jabal
Anemourion *tourist site* Turkey 85 A1
Anepmete P.N.G. 69 L8
Anet France 52 B6
Anetchom, Île *i.* Vanuatu *see* Anatom
Aneto *mt.* Spain 57 G2
Ānewetak *atoll* Marshall Is *see* Enewetak
Aney Niger 96 E3
Aneytioum, Île *i.* Vanuatu *see* Anatom
Anfu China 77 G3
Angalarri *r.* Australia 108 E3
Angamos, Punta *pt* Chile 144 B2
Ang'angxi China 74 A3

▶Angara *r.* Rus. Fed. 72 G1
Part of the Yenisey-Angara-Selenga, 3rd longest river in Asia.

Angarsk Rus. Fed. 72 I2
Angas Downs Australia 109 F6
Angatuba Brazil 145 A3
Angaur *i.* Palau 69 I5
Ånge Sweden 44 I5
Angel, Salto *waterfall* Venez. *see* Angel Falls
Ángel de la Guarda, Isla *i.* Mex. 127 E7

▶Angel Falls *waterfall* Venez. 142 F2
Highest waterfall in the world.

Ängelholm Sweden 45 H8
Angellala Creek *r.* Australia 112 C1
Angels Camp U.S.A. 128 C2
Ångermanälven *r.* Sweden 44 J5
Angers France 56 D3
Angikuni Lake Canada 121 L2
Angiola U.S.A. 128 D4
Angkor *tourist site* Cambodia 71 C4
Anglesea Australia 112 B7
Anglesey *i.* U.K. 48 C5
Angleton U.S.A. 131 E6
Anglo-Egyptian Sudan *country* Africa *see* Sudan
Angmagssalik Greenland *see* Ammassalik
Ang Mo Kio Sing. 71 [inset]
Ango Dem. Rep. Congo 98 C3
Angoche Moz. 99 D5
Angohrān Iran 88 E5
Angol Chile 144 B5
▶Angola *country* Africa 99 B5
Africa 7, 94–95
Angola *IN* U.S.A. 134 C3
Angola *NY* U.S.A. 134 F2
Angola Basin *sea feature* S. Atlantic Ocean 148 H7
Angora Turkey *see* Ankara
Angostura Mex. 127 F8
Angoulême France 56 E4
Angra dos Reis Brazil 145 B3
Angren Uzbek. 80 D3
Ang Thong Thai. 71 C4
Anguang China 74 A3

▶Anguilla *terr.* West Indies 137 L5
United Kingdom Overseas Territory.
North America 9, 116–117

Anguilla Cays *is* Bahamas 133 E8
Anguille, Cape Canada 123 K5
Angul India 84 E1
Angus Canada 134 F1
Angutia Char *i.* Bangl. 83 G5
Anholt *i.* Denmark 45 G8
Anhua China 77 F2
Anhui *prov.* China 77 H1
Anhumas Brazil 143 H7
Anhwei *prov.* China *see* Anhui
Aniak U.S.A. 113 C3
Aniakchak National Monument and Preserve *nat. park* U.S.A. 118 C4
Anin Myanmar 70 B4
Anitápolis Brazil 145 A4
Anıtlı Turkey 85 A1
Aniva Rus. Fed. 74 F3
Aniva, Mys *c.* Rus. Fed. 74 F3
Aniva, Zaliv *b.* Rus. Fed. 74 F3
Anizy-le-Château France 52 D5
Anjadip *i.* India 84 B3
Anjalankoski Fin. 45 O6
Anjar *tourist site* Lebanon 85 B3
Anjengo India 84 C4
Anji China 77 H2
Anjir Avand Iran 88 D3
Anjoman Iran 88 E3
Anjou *reg.* France 56 D3
Anjouan *i.* Comoros *see* Nzwani
Anjozorobe Madag. 99 E5
Anjuman *reg.* Afgh. 89 H3
Anjuthengu India *see* Anjengo
Ankang China 77 F1

▶Ankara Turkey 90 D3
Capital of Turkey.

Ankaratra *mt.* Madag. 99 E5
Ankazoabo Madag. 99 E6
Ankeny U.S.A. 130 E3
An Khê Vietnam 71 E4
Ankleshwar India 82 C5
Anklesvar India *see* Ankleshwar
Ankola India 84 B3
Ankouzhen China 76 E1
Anlong China 76 E3
Anlu China 77 G2
Anmoore U.S.A. 134 E4
An Muileann gCearr Rep. of Ireland *see* Mullingar
Anmyŏn-do *i.* S. Korea 75 B5
Ann, Cape Antarctica 152 D2
Ann, Cape U.S.A. 135 J2
Anna Rus. Fed. 43 I6
Anna, Lake U.S.A. 135 G4
Annaba Alg. 58 B6
Annaberg-Buchholtz Germany 53 N4
An Nabk Saudi Arabia 85 C4
An Nabk Syria 85 C2
An Nafūd *des.* Saudi Arabia 91 F5
An Najaf Iraq 91 G5
Annalee *r.* Rep. of Ireland 51 E3
Annalong U.K. 51 G3
Annam *reg.* Vietnam 68 D3
Annam Highlands *mts* Laos/Vietnam 70 D3
Annan U.K. 50 F6
Annan *r.* U.K. 50 F6
'Annān, Wādī al *watercourse* Syria 85 D2
Annandale U.S.A. 135 G4
Anna Plains Australia 108 C4

▶Annapolis U.S.A. 135 G4
State capital of Maryland.

Annapurna Conservation Area *nature res.* Nepal 83 F3
Annapurna I *mt.* Nepal 83 E3
Ann Arbor U.S.A. 134 D2
Anna Regina Guyana 143 G2
An Nás Rep. of Ireland *see* Naas
An Nāşirīyah Iraq 91 G5
An Naşrānī, Jabal *mts* Syria 81 C3
Annean, Lake *salt flat* Australia 109 B6
Anne Arundel Town U.S.A. *see* Annapolis
Annecy France 56 H4
Anne Marie Lake Canada 123 J3
Annen Neth. 52 G1
Annette Island U.S.A. 120 D4
An Nimārah Syria 85 C3
An Nimāş Saudi Arabia 86 F6
Anning China 76 D3
Anniston U.S.A. 133 C5
Annobón *i.* Equat. Guinea 96 D5
Annonay France 56 G4
An Nu'mānīyah Iraq 91 G4

An Nuşayrīyah, Jabal mts Syria 85 C2
Anonima atoll Micronesia see Namonuito
Anoón de Sardinas, Bahía de b. Col. 142 C3
Anorontany, Tanjona hd Madag. 99 E5
Ano Viannos Greece 59 K7
Anpu Gang b. China 77 F4
Anqing China 77 H2
Anren China 77 G3
Ans Belgium 52 F4
Ansbach Germany 53 K5
Anser Group is Australia 112 C7
Anshan China 74 A4
Anshun China 76 E3
Anshunchang China 76 D2
An Sirhān, Wādī watercourse Saudi Arabia 90 E5
Ansley U.S.A. 130 D3
Anson U.S.A. 131 D5
Anson Bay Australia 108 E3
Ansongo Mali 96 D3
Ansonville Canada 122 E4
Ansted U.S.A. 134 E4
Ansudu Indon. 69 J7
Antabamba Peru 142 D6
Antakya Turkey 85 C1
Antalaha Madag. 99 F5
Antalya Turkey 59 N6
Antalya prov. Turkey 85 A1
Antalya Körfezi g. Turkey 59 N6

▶Antananarivo Madag. 99 E5
Capital of Madagascar.

An tAonach Rep. of Ireland see Nenagh

▶Antarctica 152
Most southerly and coldest continent, and the continent with the highest average elevation.
Poles 146–147

Antarctic Peninsula Antarctica 152 L2
Antas r. Brazil 145 A5
An Teallach mt. U.K. 50 D3
Antelope Island U.S.A. 129 G1
Antelope Range mts U.S.A. 128 E2
Antequera Spain 57 D5
Anthony Lagoon Australia 110 A3
Anti Atlas mts Morocco 54 C6
Antibes France 56 H5
Anticosti, Île d' i. Canada 123 J4
Anticosti Island Canada see Anticosti, Île d'
Antifer, Cap d' c. France 49 H9
Antigo U.S.A. 130 F2
Antigonish Canada 123 J5
Antigua i. Antigua and Barbuda 137 L5
Antigua country West Indies see Antigua and Barbuda
▶Antigua and Barbuda country West Indies 137 L5
North America 9, 116–117
Antikythira i. Greece 59 J7
Antikythiro, Steno sea chan. Greece 59 J7
Anti Lebanon mts Lebanon/Syria see Sharqī, Jabal ash
Antimilos i. Greece 59 K6
Antimony U.S.A. 129 H2
An tInbhear Mór Rep. of Ireland see Arklow
Antioch Turkey see Antakya
Antioch U.S.A. 128 C2
Antiocheia ad Cragum tourist site Turkey 85 A1
Antiochia Turkey see Antakya
Antiparos i. Greece 59 K6
Antipodes Islands N.Z. 107 H6
Antipsara i. Greece 59 K5
Antium Italy see Anzio
Antlers U.S.A. 131 E5
Antofagasta Chile 144 B2
Antofagasta de la Sierra Arg. 144 C3
Antofalla, Volcán vol. Arg. 144 C3
Antoing Belgium 52 D4
António Enes Moz. see Angoche
Antri India 82 D4
Antrim U.K. 51 F3
Antrim Hills U.K. 51 F2
Antrim Plateau Australia 108 E4
Antropovo Rus. Fed. 42 I4
Antsalova Madag. 99 E5
Antseranana Madag. see Antsirañana
Antsirabe Madag. 99 E5
Antsirañana Madag. 99 E5
Antsla Estonia 45 O8
Antsohihy Madag. 99 E5
Anttis Sweden 44 M3
Anttola Fin. 45 O6
An Tuc Vietnam see An Khê
Antwerp Belgium 52 E3
Antwerp U.S.A. 135 H1
Antwerpen Belgium see Antwerp
An Uaimh Rep. of Ireland see Navan
Anuc, Lac l. Canada 122 G2
Anuchino Rus. Fed. 74 D4
Anugul India see Angul
Anupgarh India 82 C3
Anuradhapura Sri Lanka 84 D4
Anveh Iran 88 D5
Anvers Island Antarctica 152 L2
Anvik U.S.A. 118 B3
Anvil Range mts Canada 120 C2
Anxi Fujian China 77 H3
Anxi Gansu China 80 I3
Anxiang China 77 G2
Anxious Bay Australia 109 F8
Anyang Guangxi China see Du'an
Anyang Henan China 73 K5
Anyang S. Korea 75 B5
A'nyêmaqên Shan mts China 76 C1
Anyuan Jiangxi China 77 G3
Anyuan Jiangxi China 77 G3
Anyue China 76 E2
Anyuy r. Rus. Fed. 74 E2
Anyuysk Rus. Fed. 65 R3
Anzac Alta Canada 121 I3
Anzac B.C. Canada 120 F4
Anzhero-Sudzhensk Rus. Fed. 64 J4
Anzi Dem. Rep. Congo 98 C4
Anzio Italy 58 E4
Aoba i. Vanuatu 107 G3
Aoga-shima i. Japan 75 E6
Aokal Afgh. 89 F3
Ao Kham, Laem pt Thai. 71 B5
Aomen China see Macau
Aomen Tebie Xingzhengqu aut. reg. China see Macau
Aomori Japan 74 F4
Ao Phang Nga National Park Thai. 71 B5

▶Aoraki mt. N.Z. 113 C6
Highest mountain in New Zealand.

Aôral, Phnum mt. Cambodia 71 D4
Aorangi mt. N.Z. see Aoraki
Aosta Italy 58 B2
Aotearoa country Oceania see New Zealand
Aouk, Bahr r. Cent. Afr. Rep./Chad 97 E4
Aoukâr reg. Mali/Mauritania 96 C2
Aoulef Alg. 96 D2
Aozou Chad 97 E2
Apa r. Brazil 144 E2
Apache Creek U.S.A. 129 I5
Apache Junction U.S.A. 129 H5
Apaiang atoll Kiribati see Abaiang
Apalachee Bay U.S.A. 133 C6
Apalachicola U.S.A. 133 C6
Apalachicola r. U.S.A. 133 C6
Apalachin U.S.A. 135 G2
Apamea Turkey see Dinar
Apaporis r. Col. 142 E4
Aparecida do Tabuado Brazil 145 A3
Aparima N.Z. see Riverton
Aparri Phil. 150 E4
Apatity Rus. Fed. 44 R3
Apatzingán Mex. 136 D5
Ape Latvia 45 O8
Apeldoorn Neth. 52 F2
Apelern Germany 53 J2
Apennines mts Italy 58 C2
Apensen Germany 53 J1
Apex Mountain Canada 120 B2
Api mt. Nepal 82 E3
Api i. Vanuatu see Epi
Apia atoll Kiribati see Abaiang

▶Apia Samoa 107 I3
Capital of Samoa.

Apiacas, Serra dos hills Brazil 143 G6
Apiaí Brazil 145 A4
Apishapa r. U.S.A. 130 C4
Apiti N.Z. 113 E4
Apizolaya Mex. 131 C7
Aplao Peru 142 D7
Apo, Mount vol. Phil. 69 H5
Apoera Suriname 143 G2
Apolda Germany 53 L3
Apollo Bay Australia 112 A7
Apollonia Bulg. see Sozopol
Apolo Bol. 142 E6
Aporé Brazil 145 A2
Aporé r. Brazil 145 A2
Apostle Islands U.S.A. 130 F2
Apostolens Tommelfinger mt. Greenland 119 N3
Apostolos Andreas, Cape Cyprus 85 B2
Apoteri Guyana 143 G3
Apozai Pak. 89 H4
Appalachian Mountains U.S.A. 134 D5
Appalla i. Fiji see Kabara
Appennino mts Italy see Apennines
Appennino Abruzzese mts Italy 58 E3
Appennino Tosco-Emiliano mts Italy 58 D3
Appennino Umbro-Marchigiano mts Italy 58 E3
Appingedam Neth. 52 G1
Applecross U.K. 50 D3
Appleton MN U.S.A. 130 D2
Appleton WI U.S.A. 134 A1
Apple Valley U.S.A. 128 E4
Appomattox U.S.A. 135 F5
Aprilia Italy 58 E4
Aprunyi India 76 B2
Apsheronsk Rus. Fed. 91 E1
Apsheronskaya Rus. Fed. see Apsheronsk
Apsley Canada 135 F1
Apt France 56 G5
Apucarana Brazil 145 A3
Apucarana, Serra da hills Brazil 145 A3
Apulum Romania see Alba Iulia
Aq"a Georgia see Sokhumi
'Aqaba Jordan see Al 'Aqabah
Aqaba, Gulf of Asia 90 D5
'Aqaba, Wâdi el watercourse Egypt see 'Aqabah, Wādī al
'Aqabah, Birkat al well Iraq 88 A4
'Aqabah, Wādī al watercourse Egypt 85 A4
Aqadyr Kazakh. see Agadyr'
Aqdoghmish r. Iran 88 B2
Aqköl Akmolinskaya Oblast' Kazakh. see Akkol'
Aqköl Atyrauskaya Oblast' Kazakh. see Akkol'
Aqmola Kazakh. see Astana
Aqqan China 83 F1
Aqqikkol Hu salt l. China 83 G1
Aqra', Jabal al mt. Syria/Turkey 85 B2
'Aqran hill Saudi Arabia 85 D4
Aqsay Kazakh. see Aksay
Aqsayqin Hit terr. Asia see Aksai Chin
Aqshī Kazakh. see Akshiy
Aqshuqyr Kazakh. see Akshukur
Aqsū Kazakh. see Aksu
Aqsūat Kazakh. see Aksuat
Aqsū-Ayuly Kazakh. see Aksu-Ayuly
Aqtaū Kazakh. see Aktau
Aqtöbe Kazakh. see Aktobe
Aqtoghay Kazakh. see Aktogay
Aquae Grani Germany see Aachen
Aquae Gratianae France see Aix-les-Bains
Aquae Sextiae France see Aix-en-Provence
Aquae Statiellae Italy see Acqui Terme
Aquarius Mountains U.S.A. 129 G4
Aquarius Plateau U.S.A. 129 H3
Aquaviva delle Fonti Italy 58 G4
Aquidauana Brazil 144 E2
Aquiles Mex. 127 G7
Aquincum Hungary see Budapest
Aquiry r. Brazil see Acre
Aquisgranum Germany see Aachen
Aquitaine reg. France 56 D5
Aquitania reg. France see Aquitaine
Aqzhayqyn Köli salt l. Kazakh. see Akzhaykyn, Ozero
Ara India 83 F4
Āra Ārba Eth. 98 E3
Arab Afgh. 89 G4
Arab, Bahr el watercourse Sudan 97 F4
'Arab, Khalīg el b. Egypt see 'Arab, Khalīj al
'Arab, Khalīj al b. Egypt 90 C5
'Arabah, Wādī al watercourse Israel/Jordan 85 B5
Arabian Basin sea feature Indian Ocean 149 M5
Arabian Gulf Asia see The Gulf
Arabian Peninsula Asia 86 G5
Arabian Sea Indian Ocean 87 K6
Araç Turkey 90 D2
Araça r. Brazil 142 F4
Aracaju Brazil 143 K6
Aracati Brazil 143 K4
Aracatu Brazil 145 C1
Araçatuba Brazil 145 A3
Aracena Spain 57 C5
Aracruz Brazil 145 C2
Araçuaí Brazil 145 C2
Araçuaí r. Brazil 145 C2
'Arad Israel 85 B4
Arad Romania 59 I1
'Arādah U.A.E. 88 D6
Arafura Sea Australia/Indon. 106 D2
Arafura Shelf sea feature Australia/Indon. 150 E6
Aragarças Brazil 143 H7
Aragón r. Spain 57 F2
Araguaçu Brazil 145 A1
Araguaia r. Brazil 145 A1
Araguaia, Parque Nacional de nat. park Brazil 143 H6
Araguaiana Brazil 145 A1
Araguaína Brazil 143 I5
Araguari Brazil 145 A2
Araguari r. Brazil 143 H3
Araguatins Brazil 143 I5
Araí Brazil 145 B1
'Araîf el Naga, Gebel hill Egypt see 'Urayf an Nāqah, Jabal
Araiosos Brazil 143 J4
Arak Alg. 96 D2
Arāk Iran 88 C3
Arak Syria 85 D2
Arakan reg. Myanmar 70 A2
Arakan Yoma mts Myanmar 70 A2
Arakkonam India 84 C3
Araks r. Armenia see Araz
Araku India 84 D2
Aral China 80 F3
Aral Kazakh. see Aral'sk
Aral Tajik. see Vose

▶Aral Sea salt l. Kazakh./Uzbek. 80 B2
3rd largest lake in Asia.

Aral'sk Kazakh. 80 B2
Aral'skoye More salt l. Kazakh./Uzbek. see Aral Sea
Aralsor, Ozero l. Kazakh. 43 K6
Aral Tengizi salt l. Kazakh./Uzbek. see Aral Sea
Aramac Australia 110 D4
Aramac Creek watercourse Australia 110 D4
Aramah plat. Saudi Arabia 88 B5
Aramberri Mex. 131 D7
Aramia r. P.N.G. 69 K8
Aran r. India 84 C2
Aranda de Duero Spain 57 E3
Arandai Indon. 69 I7
Aranđelovac Serb. and Mont. 59 I2
Arandis Namibia 100 B2
Arang India 83 E5
Arani India 84 C3
Aran Island Rep. of Ireland 51 D3
Aran Islands Rep. of Ireland 51 C4
Aranjuez Spain 57 E3
Aranos Namibia 100 D3
Aransas Pass U.S.A. 131 D7
Arantangi India 84 C4
Aranuka atoll Kiribati 107 H1
Aranyaprathet Thai. 71 C4
Arao Japan 75 C6
Araouane Mali 96 C3
Arapaho U.S.A. 131 D5
Arapgir Turkey 90 E3
Arapiraca Brazil 143 K5
Arapis, Akra pt Greece 59 K4
Arapkir Turkey see Arapgir
Arapongas Brazil 145 A3
Araquari Brazil 145 A4
'Ar'ar Saudi Arabia 91 F5
Araracuara Col. 142 D4
Araranguá Brazil 145 A5
Araraquara Brazil 145 A3
Araras Brazil 143 H5
Ararat Armenia 91 G3
Ararat Australia 112 A6
Ararat, Mount Turkey 91 G3
Araria India 83 F4
Araripina Brazil 143 J5
Aras Turkey 91 F3
Aras r. Turkey see Araz
Arataca Brazil 145 D1
Arauca Col. 142 D2
Arauca r. Venez. 142 E2
Aravalli Range mts India 82 C4
Aravete Estonia 45 N7
Arawa P.N.G. 106 F2
Araxá Brazil 145 B2
Araxes r. Asia see Araz
Arayıt Dağı mt. Turkey 59 N5
Araz r. Azer. 91 H2
also spelt Araks (Armenia), Aras (Turkey), formerly known as Araxes
Arbailu Iraq see Arbīl
Arbat Iraq 91 G4
Arbela Iraq see Arbīl
Arberth U.K. see Narberth
Arbīl Iraq 91 G3
Arboga Sweden 45 I7
Arborfield Canada 121 K4
Arborg Canada 121 L5
Arbroath U.K. 50 G4
Arbuckle U.S.A. 128 B2
Arbu Lut, Dasht-e des. Afgh. 89 F4
Arcachon France 56 D4
Arcade U.S.A. 135 F2
Arcadia FL U.S.A. 133 D7
Arcadia LA U.S.A. 131 E5
Arcadia MI U.S.A. 134 B1
Arcanum U.S.A. 134 C4
Arcata U.S.A. 126 B4
Arc Dome mt. U.S.A. 128 E2
Arcelia Mex. 136 D5
Archangel Rus. Fed. 42 I2
Archer r. Australia 67 G9
Archer Bend National Park Australia 110 C2
Archer City U.S.A. 131 D5
Arches National Park U.S.A. 129 I2
Archipiélago Los Roques nat. park Venez. 142 E1
Ärçivan Azer. 91 H3
Arckaringa watercourse Australia 111 A6
Arco U.S.A. 126 E4
Arcos Brazil 145 B3
Arcos de la Frontera Spain 57 D5
Arctic Bay Canada 119 J2
Arctic Institute Islands Rus. Fed. see Arkticheskogo Instituta, Ostrova
Arctic Mid-Ocean Ridge sea feature Arctic Ocean 153 H1
▶Arctic Ocean 153 B1
Poles 146–147
Arctic Red r. Canada 118 E3
Arctowski research station Antarctica 152 A2
Arda r. Bulg. 59 L4
also known as Ardas (Greece)
Ardabīl Iran 88 C2
Ardahan Turkey 91 F2
Ardakān Iran 88 D3
Årdalstangen Norway 45 E6
Ardara Rep. of Ireland 51 D3
Ardas r. Bulg. see Arda
Ard aş Şawwān plain Jordan 85 C4
Ardatov Nizhegorodskaya Oblast' Rus. Fed. 43 I5
Ardatov Respublika Mordoviya Rus. Fed. 43 J5
Ardee Rep. of Ireland 51 F4
Ardennes plat. Belgium 52 E5
Ardennes, Canal des France 52 E5
Arden Town U.S.A. 128 C2
Arderin hill Rep. of Ireland 51 E4
Ardestān Iran 88 D3
Ardglass U.K. 51 G3
Ardila r. Port. 57 C4
Ardlethan Australia 112 C5
Ardmore U.S.A. 131 D5
Ardnamurchan, Point of U.K. 50 C4
Ardon Rus. Fed. 91 G2
Ardrishaig U.K. 50 D4
Ardrossan U.K. 50 E5
Ardvasar U.K. 50 D3
Areia Branca Brazil 143 K4
Arel Belgium see Arlon
Arelas France see Arles
Arelate France see Arles
Aremberg hill Germany 52 G4
Arena, Point U.S.A. 128 B2
Arenas de San Pedro Spain 57 D3
Arendal Norway 45 F7
Arendsee (Altmark) Germany 53 L2
Areopoli Greece 59 J6
Arequipa Peru 142 D7
Arere Brazil 143 H4
Arévalo Spain 57 D3
Arezzo Italy 58 D3
'Arfajah well Saudi Arabia 85 D4
Argadargada Australia 110 B4
Arganda Spain 57 E3
Argel Alg. see Algiers
Argentan France 56 D2
Argentario, Monte hill Italy 58 D3
Argentera, Cima dell' mt. Italy 58 B2
Argenthal Germany 53 H5

▶Argentina country S. America 144 C5
2nd largest country in South America. 3rd most populous country in South America.
South America 9, 140–141

Argentine Abyssal Plain sea feature S. Atlantic Ocean 148 E9
Argentine Basin sea feature S. Atlantic Ocean 148 F8
Argentine Republic country S. America see Argentina
Argentine Rise sea feature S. Atlantic Ocean 148 E8
Argentino, Lago l. Arg. 144 B8
Argenton-sur-Creuse France 56 E3
Argentoratum France see Strasbourg
Argeş r. Romania 59 L2
Arghandab r. Afgh. 89 G4
Argi r. Rus. Fed. 74 C1
Argolikos Kolpos b. Greece 59 J6
Argos Greece 59 J6
Argos U.S.A. 134 B3
Argostoli Greece 59 I5
Arguís Spain 57 F2
Argun' r. China/Rus. Fed. 73 M2
Argun Rus. Fed. 91 G2
Argungu Nigeria 96 D3
Argus Range mts U.S.A. 128 E4
Argyle Canada 123 I6
Argyle, Lake Australia 108 E4
Argyrokastron Albania see Gjirokastër
Ar Horqin Qi China see Tianshan
Århus Denmark 45 G8
Ariah Park Australia 112 C5
Ariamsvlei Namibia 100 D5
Ariana Tunisia see L'Ariana
Ariano Irpino Italy 58 F4
Ari Atoll Maldives 81 D11
Aribinda Burkina 96 C3
Arica Chile 142 D7
Arid, Cape Australia 109 C8
Arigza China 76 C1
Arīḩā Syria 85 C2
Arīḩā West Bank see Jericho
Arikaree r. U.S.A. 130 C3
Arima Trin. and Tob. 137 L6
Ariminum Italy see Rimini
Arinos Brazil 145 B1
Aripuanã Brazil 143 G6
Aripuanã r. Brazil 142 F5
Ariquemes Brazil 142 F5
Aris Namibia 100 C2
Arisaig U.K. 50 D4
Arisaig, Sound of sea chan. U.K. 50 D4
'Arīsh, Wādī al watercourse Egypt 85 A4
Aristazabal Island Canada 120 D4
Arixang China see Wenquan
Ariyalur India 84 C4
Arizaro, Salar de salt flat Arg. 144 C2
Arizona Arg. 144 C5
Arizona state U.S.A. 127 F6
Arizpe Mex. 127 F7
'Arjah Saudi Arabia 86 F5
Arjasa Indon. 68 F8
Arjeplog Sweden 44 J3
Arjuni India 82 E5
Arkadak Rus. Fed. 43 I6
Arkadelphia U.S.A. 131 E5
Arkaig, Loch l. U.K. 50 D4
Arkalyk Kazakh. 80 C1
Arkansas r. U.S.A. 131 F5
Arkansas state U.S.A. 131 E5
Arkansas City AR U.S.A. 131 F5
Arkansas City KS U.S.A. 131 D4
Arkatag Shan mts China 83 G1
Arkell, Mount Canada 120 C2
Arkenu, Jabal mt. Libya 86 B5
Arkhangel'sk Rus. Fed. see Archangel
Arkhara Rus. Fed. 74 C2
Arkhipovka Rus. Fed. 74 D4
Arki i. Greece see Arkoi
Arklow Rep. of Ireland 51 F5
Arkoi i. Greece 59 L6
Arkona Canada 134 E2
Arkona, Kap c. Germany 47 N3
Arkonam India see Arakkonam
Arkport U.S.A. 135 G2
Arkticheskogo Instituta, Ostrova is Rus. Fed. 64 J2
Arkul' Rus. Fed. 42 K4
Arlang, Gora mt. Turkm. 88 D2
Arles France 56 G5
Arlington S. Africa 101 H5
Arlington NY U.S.A. 135 I3
Arlington OH U.S.A. 134 D3
Arlington SD U.S.A. 130 D2
Arlington VA U.S.A. 135 G4
Arlington Heights U.S.A. 134 A2
Arlit Niger 96 D3
Arlon Belgium 52 F5
Arm r. Canada 121 J5
Armadale Australia 109 A8
Armagh U.K. 51 F3
Armant Egypt 86 D4
Armavir Rus. Fed. 91 F1
▶Armenia country Asia 91 G2
Asia 6, 62–63
Armenia Col. 142 C3
Armenopolis Romania see Gherla
Armeria Mex. 136 D5
Armidale Australia 112 E3
Armington U.S.A. 126 F3
Armit Lake Canada 121 N1
Armori India 84 D1
Armour U.S.A. 130 D3
Armoy U.K. 51 F2
Armstrong r. Australia 108 E4
Armstrong Canada 122 C4
Armstrong, Mount Canada 120 C2
Armstrong Island Cook Is see Rarotonga
Armu r. Rus. Fed. 74 E3
Armur India 84 C2
Armutçuk Dağı mts Turkey 59 L5
Armyanskaya S.S.R. country Asia see Armenia
Arnaoutis, Cape Cyprus see Arnauti, Cape
Arnaud r. Canada 123 H2
Arnauti, Cape Cyprus 85 A2
Årnes Norway 45 G6
Arnett U.S.A. 131 D4
Arnhem Neth. 52 F3
Arnhem, Cape Australia 110 B2
Arnhem Land reg. Australia 108 F3
Arno r. Italy 58 D3
Arno Bay Australia 111 B7
Arnold U.K. 49 F5
Arnold's Cove Canada 123 L5
Arnon r. Jordan see Mawjib, Wādī al
Arnprior Canada 135 G1
Arnsberg Germany 53 I3
Arnstadt Germany 53 K4
Arnstein Germany 53 J5
Arnstorf Germany 53 M6
Aroab Namibia 100 D4
Aroland Canada 122 D4
Arolsen Germany 53 J3
Aroma Sudan 86 E6
Arona Italy 58 C2
Arorae i. Kiribati 107 H2
Arore i. Kiribati see Arorae
Aros r. Mex. 127 F7
Arossi i. Solomon Is see San Cristobal
Arqalyq Kazakh. see Arkalyk
Arquipélago da Madeira aut. reg. Port. 96 B1
Arrabury Australia 111 C5
Arrah India see Ara
Arraias Brazil 145 B1
Arraias, Serra de hills Brazil 145 B1
Ar Ramādī Iraq 91 F4
Ar Ramlah Jordan 85 B5
Ar Ramthā Jordan 85 C3
Arran i. U.K. 50 D5
Ar Raqqah Syria 85 D2
Arras France 52 C4
Ar Rass Saudi Arabia 86 F4
Ar Rastān Syria 85 C2
Ar Rayyān Qatar 88 C5
Arrecife Canary Is 96 B2
Arretium Italy see Arezzo
Arriagá Mex. 136 F5
Ar Rifā'ī Iraq 91 G5
Ar Rihāb salt flat Iraq 91 G5
Ar Rimāl reg. Saudi Arabia 98 F1
Arrington U.S.A. 135 F5
Ar Riyāḑ Saudi Arabia see Riyadh
Arrochar U.K. 50 E4
Arrojado r. Brazil 145 B1
Arrow, Lough l. Rep. of Ireland 51 D3
Arrowsmith, Mount N.Z. 113 C6
Arroyo Grande U.S.A. 128 C4
Ar Rubay'iyah Saudi Arabia 88 B5
Ar Rummān Jordan 85 B3
Ar Ruq'ī well Saudi Arabia 88 B4
Ar Ruşāfah Syria 85 D2
Ar Ruşayfah Jordan 85 C3
Ar Rustāq Oman 88 E6
Ar Ruţbah Iraq 91 F4
Ar Ruwayḑah Saudi Arabia 88 B5
Ar Ruwayḑah Saudi Arabia 88 B6
Ar Ruwayḑah Syria 85 C2
Års Denmark 45 F8
Ars Iran 88 B2
Arseno Lake Canada 120 H1
Arsen'yev Rus. Fed. 74 D3
Arsk Rus. Fed. 42 K4
Arta Greece 59 I5
Artem Rus. Fed. 74 D4
Artemisa Cuba 133 D8
Artemivs'k Ukr. 43 H6
Artemovsk Ukr. see Artemivs'k
Artenay France 56 E2
Artesia AZ U.S.A. 129 I5
Artesia NM U.S.A. 127 G6
Arthur Canada 134 E2
Arthur NE U.S.A. 130 C3
Arthur TN U.S.A. 134 D5
Arthur, Lake U.S.A. 134 E3
Arthur's Pass National Park N.Z. 113 C6
Arthur's Town Bahamas 133 F7
Arti Rus. Fed. 41 R4
Artigas research station Antarctica 152 A2
Artigas Uruguay 144 E4
Art'ik Armenia 91 F2
Artillery Lake Canada 121 I2
Artisia Botswana 101 H3
Artois reg. France 52 B4
Artois, Collines d' hills France 52 B4
Artos Dağı mt. Turkey 91 F3
Artova Turkey 90 E2
Artsakh aut. reg. Azer. see Dağlıq Qarabağ
Artsiz Ukr. see Artsyz
Artsyz Ukr. 59 M2
Artur de Paiva Angola see Kuvango
Artux China 80 E4
Artvin Turkey 91 F2
Artyk Turkm. 88 E2
Aru, Kepulauan is Indon. 108 F1
Arua Uganda 98 D3
Aruanã Brazil 145 A1

▶Aruba terr. West Indies 137 K6
Self-governing Netherlands Territory.
North America 9, 116–117

Arumã Brazil 142 F4
Arunachal Pradesh state India 83 H4
Arundel U.K. 49 G8
Arun Gol r. China 74 B3
Arun He r. China see Arun Gol
Arun Qi China see Naji
Aruppukkottai India 84 C4
Arusha Tanz. 98 D4
Aruwimi r. Dem. Rep. Congo 98 C3
Arvada U.S.A. 126 G5
Arvagh Rep. of Ireland 51 E4
Arvayheer Mongolia 80 J2
Arviat Canada 121 M2
Arvidsjaur Sweden 44 K4
Arvika Sweden 45 H7
Arvonia U.S.A. 135 F5
Arwā' Saudi Arabia 88 B6
Arwād i. Syria 85 B2
Arwala Indon. 108 D1
Arxan China 73 L3
Aryanah Tunisia see L'Ariana
Arys' Kazakh. 80 C3
Arzamas Rus. Fed. 43 I5
Arzanah i. U.A.E. 88 D5
Arzberg Germany 53 M4
Arzew Alg. 57 F6
Arzgir Rus. Fed. 91 G1
Arzila Morocco see Asilah
Aš Czech Rep. 53 M4
Asaba Nigeria 96 D4
Asad, Buḩayrat al resr Syria 85 D1
Asadābād Afgh. 89 H3
Asadābād Iran 88 C3
Asahi-dake vol. Japan 74 F4
Asahikawa Japan 74 F4
'Asal Egypt 85 A5
Āsalē l. Eth. 98 E2
Asālem Iran 88 C2
'Asalūyeh Iran 88 D5
Asan-man b. S. Korea 75 B5
Asansol India 83 F5
Āsayita Eth. 98 E2
Asbach Germany 53 H4
Asbestos Mountains S. Africa 100 F5
Asbury Park U.S.A. 135 H3
Ascalon Israel see Ashqelon
Ascea Italy 58 F4
Ascensión Bol. 142 F7
Ascensión Mex. 127 G7
Ascension atoll Micronesia see Pohnpei

▶Ascension i. S. Atlantic Ocean 148 H6
Dependency of St Helena.

Aschaffenburg Germany 53 J5
Ascheberg Germany 53 H3
Aschersleben Germany 53 L3
Ascoli Piceno Italy 58 E3
Asculum Italy see Ascoli Piceno
Asculum Picenum Italy see Ascoli Piceno
Ascutney U.S.A. 135 I2
Āseb Eritrea see Assab
Åseda Sweden 45 I8
Åsele Sweden 44 J4
Asenovgrad Bulg. 59 K3
Aşfar, Jabal al mt. Jordan 85 C3
Aşfar, Tall al hill Syria 85 C3
Aşgabat Turkm. see Ashgabat
Asha Rus. Fed. 41 R5
Ashburn U.S.A. 133 D6
Ashburton watercourse Australia 108 A5
Ashburton N.Z. 113 C6
Ashburton Range hills Australia 108 F4
Ashdod Israel 85 B4
Ashdown U.S.A. 131 E5

Asheboro U.S.A. 132 E5
Asher U.S.A. 131 D5
Ashern Canada 121 L5
Asheville U.S.A. 132 D5
Asheweig r. Canada 122 D3
Ashford Australia 112 E2
Ashford U.K. 49 H7
Ash Fork U.S.A. 129 G4

▶Ashgabat Turkm. 88 E2
Capital of Turkmenistan.

Ashibetsu Japan 74 F4
Ashikaga Japan 75 E5
Ashington U.K. 48 F3
Ashizuri-misaki pt Japan 75 D6
Ashkelon Israel see Ashqelon
Ashkhabad Turkm. see Ashgabat
Ashkum U.S.A. 134 B3
Ashkun reg. Afgh. 89 H3
Ashland AL U.S.A. 133 C5
Ashland ME U.S.A. 132 G2
Ashland NH U.S.A. 135 J2
Ashland OH U.S.A. 134 D3
Ashland OR U.S.A. 126 C4
Ashland VA U.S.A. 135 G5
Ashland WI U.S.A. 130 F2
Ashland City U.S.A. 134 B5
Ashley Australia 112 D2
Ashley MI U.S.A. 134 C2
Ashley ND U.S.A. 130 D2

▶Ashmore and Cartier Islands terr. Australia 108 C3
Australian External Territory.

Ashmore Reef Australia 108 C3
Ashmore Reefs Australia 110 D1
Ashmyany Belarus 45 N9
Ashqelon Israel 85 B4
Ash Shabakah Iraq 91 F5
Ash Shaddādah Syria 91 F3
Ash Shallūfah Egypt 85 A4
Ash Sham Syria see Damascus
Ash Shanāfiyah Iraq 91 G5
Ash Shaqīq well Saudi Arabia 91 F5
Ash Sharawrah Saudi Arabia 86 G6
Ash Shāriqah U.A.E. see Sharjah
Ash Sharqāṭ Iraq 91 F4
Ash Shaṭrah Iraq 91 G5
Ash Shaṭṭ Egypt 85 A5
Ash Shawbak Jordan 85 B4
Ash Shaybānī well Saudi Arabia 91 F5
Ash Shaykh Ibrāhīm Syria 85 D2
Ash Shiblīyāt hill Saudi Arabia 85 C5
Ash Shiḥr Yemen 86 G7
Ash Shu'aybah Saudi Arabia 91 F6
Ash Shu'bah Saudi Arabia 86 F4
Ash Shurayf Saudi Arabia see Khaybar
Ashta India 82 D5
Ashtabula U.S.A. 134 E3
Ashtarak Armenia 91 G2
Ashti Maharashtra India 82 D5
Ashti Maharashtra India 84 B2
Ashti Maharashtra India 84 C2
Āshtīān Iran 88 C3
Ashton S. Africa 100 E7
Ashton U.S.A. 126 F3
Ashton-under-Lyne U.K. 48 E5
Ashuanipi r. Canada 123 I3
Ashuanipi Lake Canada 123 I3
Ashur Iraq see Ash Sharqāṭ
Ashville U.S.A. 133 C5
Ashwaubenon U.S.A. 134 A1
Asi r. Asia 90 E3 see 'Āṣī, Nahr al
'Āṣī r. Lebanon/Syria see Orontes
'Āṣī, Nahr al r. Asia 90 E3
also known as Asi or Orontes
Āsīā Bak Iran 88 C3
Asifabad India 84 C2
Asika India 84 E2
Asilah Morocco 57 C6
Asinara, Golfo dell' b. Sardinia Italy 58 C4
Asino Rus. Fed. 64 J4
Asipovichy Belarus 43 F5
Asīr Iran 88 D5
'Asīr reg. Saudi Arabia 86 F5
Asisium Italy see Assisi
Askale Jammu and Kashmir 82 C2
Aşkale Turkey 91 F3
Asker Norway 45 G7
Askersund Sweden 45 I7
Askim Norway 45 G7
Askino Rus. Fed. 41 R4
Askival hill U.K. 50 C4
Asl Egypt see 'Asal
Aslanköy r. Turkey 85 B1
Asmar reg. Afgh. 89 H3

▶Asmara Eritrea 86 E6
Capital of Eritrea.

Āsmera Eritrea see Asmara
Åsnen l. Sweden 45 I8
Aso-Kuju National Park Japan 75 C6
Asonli India 76 B2
Asop India 82 C4
Asori Indon. 69 J7
Āsosa Eth. 98 D2
Asotin U.S.A. 126 D3
Aspang-Markt Austria 47 P7
Aspatria U.K. 48 D4
Aspen U.S.A. 126 G5
Asperg Germany 53 J6
Aspermont U.S.A. 131 C5
Aspiring, Mount N.Z. 113 B7
Aspro, Cape Cyprus 85 A2
Aspromonte, Parco Nazionale dell' nat. park Italy 58 F5
Aspron, Cape Cyprus see Aspro, Cape
Aspur India 89 I6
Asquith Canada 121 J4
As Sa'an Syria 85 C2
Assab Eritrea 86 F7
As Sabsab well Saudi Arabia 88 C5
Assad, Lake resr Syria see Asad, Buḥayrat al
Aş Şadr U.A.E. 88 D5
Aş Şafā lava field Syria 85 C3
Aş Şafāqis Tunisia see Sfax
Aş Şaff Egypt 90 C5
As Safīrah Syria 85 C1
Aş Şaḥrā' al Gharbīyah des. Egypt see Western Desert
Aş Şaḥrā' ash Sharqīyah des. Egypt see Eastern Desert
Assake-Audan, Vpadina depr. Kazakh./Uzbek. 91 J2
'Assal, Lac l. Djibouti see Assal, Lake

▶Assal, Lake Djibouti 86 F7
Lowest point in Africa.
Africa 92–93

Aş Şāliḥīyah Syria 91 F4
As Sallūm Egypt 90 B5
As Salmān Iraq 91 G5
As Salṭ Jordan 85 B3
Assam state India 83 G4
Assamakka Niger 96 D3
As Samāwah Iraq 91 G5
As Samrā' Jordan 85 C3
Aş Şanām reg. Saudi Arabia 86 H5
As Sarīr reg. Libya 97 F2
Assateague Island U.S.A. 135 H4
As Sawādah reg. Saudi Arabia 88 B6
Assayeta Eth. see Āsayita
As Sayḥ Saudi Arabia 88 B6
Assen Neth. 52 G1
Assenede Belgium 52 D3
Assesse Belgium 52 F4
As Sidrah Libya 97 E1
As Sīfah Oman 88 E6
Assigny, Lac l. Canada 123 I3
As Sikak Saudi Arabia 88 C5
Assiniboia Canada 121 J5
Assiniboine r. Canada 121 L5
Assiniboine, Mount Canada 118 G4
Assis Brazil 145 A3
Assisi Italy 58 E3
Aßlar Germany 53 I4
Aş Şubayḥīyah Kuwait 88 B4
Aş Şufayrī well Saudi Arabia 88 B4
As Sukhnah Syria 85 D2
As Sulaymānīyah Iraq 91 G4
As Sulaymī Saudi Arabia 86 F4
Aş Şulb reg. Saudi Arabia 88 C5
Aş Şummān plat. Saudi Arabia 88 B5
Aş Şummān plat. Saudi Arabia 88 C6
As Sūq Saudi Arabia 86 F5
As Sūrīyah country Asia see Syria
Aş Şuwar Syria 91 F4
As Suwaydā' Syria 85 C3
As Suways Egypt see Suez
As Suways governorate Egypt 81 A4
Assynt, Loch l. U.K. 50 D2
Astakida i. Greece 59 L7
Astakos Greece 59 I5
Astalu Island Pak. see Astola Island

▶Astana Kazakh. 80 D1
Capital of Kazakhstan.

Astaneh Iran 88 C2
Astara Azer. 91 H3
Āstārā Iran 86 G2
Asterabad Iran see Gorgān
Asti Italy 58 C2
Astillero Peru 142 E6
Astin Tag mts China see Altun Shan
Astipálaia i. Greece see Astypalaia
Astola Island Pak. 89 F5
Astor r. Pak. 89 I3
Astorga Spain 57 C2
Astoria U.S.A. 126 C3
Åstorp Sweden 45 H8
Astrabad Iran see Gorgān
Astrakhan' Rus. Fed. 43 K7
Astrakhan' Bazar Azer. see Cälilabad
Astravyets Belarus 45 N9
Astrida Rwanda see Butare
Asturias aut. comm. Spain 57 C2
Asturias, Principado de aut. comm. Spain see Asturias
Asturica Augusta Spain see Astorga
Astypalaia i. Greece 59 L6
Asuncion i. N. Mariana Is 69 L3

▶Asunción Para. 144 E3
Capital of Paraguay.

Aswad Oman 88 E5
Aswān Egypt see Aswān
Aswān Egypt 86 D5
Asyūt Egypt see Asyūṭ
Asyūṭ Egypt 90 C6
Ata i. Tonga 107 I4
Atacama, Desierto de des. Chile see Atacama Desert
Atacama, Salar de salt flat Chile 144 C2

▶Atacama Desert Chile 144 C3
Driest place in the world.

Atafu atoll Tokelau 107 I2
Atafu i. Tokelau 150 I6
'Aṭā'iṭah, Jabal al mt. Jordan 85 B4
Atakent Turkey 85 B1
Atakpamé Togo 96 D4
Atalándi Greece see Atalanti
Atalanti Greece 59 J5
Atalaya Peru 142 D6
Ataléia Brazil 145 C2
Atambua Indon. 108 D2
Ataniya Turkey see Adana
'Ataq Yemen 86 G7
Atâr Mauritania 96 B2
Atari Pak. 89 I4
Atascadero U.S.A. 128 C4
Atasu Kazakh. 80 D2
Ataúro, Ilha de i. East Timor 108 D2
Atáviros mt. Greece see Attavyros
Atayurt Turkey 85 A1
Atbara Sudan 86 D6
Atbara r. Sudan 86 D6
Atbasar Kazakh. 80 D1
Atchison U.S.A. 130 E4
Atebubu Ghana 96 C4
Ateransk Kazakh. see Atyrau
Āteshān Iran 88 D3
Āteshkhāneh, Kūh-e hill Afgh. 89 F3
Atessa Italy 58 F3
Ath Belgium 52 D4
Athabasca r. Canada 121 I3
Athabasca, Lake Canada 121 I3
Athalia U.S.A. 134 D4
'Athāmīn, Birkat al well Iraq 88 A4
Atharan Hazari Pak. 89 I4
Athboy Rep. of Ireland 51 F4
Athenae Greece see Athens
Athenry Rep. of Ireland 51 D4
Athens Canada 135 H1

▶Athens Greece 59 J6
Capital of Greece.

Athens AL U.S.A. 133 C5
Athens GA U.S.A. 133 D5
Athens MI U.S.A. 134 C2
Athens OH U.S.A. 134 D4
Athens PA U.S.A. 135 G3
Athens TN U.S.A. 132 C5
Athens TX U.S.A. 131 E5
Atherstone U.K. 49 F6
Atherton Australia 110 D3
Athies France 52 C5
Athina Greece see Athens
Athínai Greece see Athens
Athleague Rep. of Ireland 51 D4
Athlone Rep. of Ireland 51 E4
Athnā', Wādī al watercourse Jordan 85 D3
Athni India 84 B2
Athol N.Z. 113 B7
Athol U.S.A. 135 I2
Atholl, Forest of reg. U.K. 50 E4
Athos mt. Greece 59 K4
Ath Thamad Egypt 85 B5
Ath Thāyat mt. Saudi Arabia 85 C5
Ath Thumāmī well Saudi Arabia 88 B5
Athy Rep. of Ireland 51 F5
Ati Chad 97 E3
Aṭīābād Iran 88 E3
Atico Peru 142 D7
Atikameg Canada 120 H4
Atikameg r. Canada 122 E3
Atik Lake Canada 121 M4
Atikokan Canada 119 I5
Atikonak Lake Canada 123 I3
Atka Rus. Fed. 65 Q3
Atka Island U.S.A. 118 A4
Atkarsk Rus. Fed. 43 J6
Atkri Indon. 69 I7

▶Atlanta GA U.S.A. 133 C5
State capital of Georgia.

Atlanta IN U.S.A. 134 B3
Atlanta MI U.S.A. 134 C1
Atlantic IA U.S.A. 130 E3
Atlantic NC U.S.A. 133 E5
Atlantic City U.S.A. 135 H4
Atlantic-Indian-Antarctic Basin sea feature S. Atlantic Ocean 148 H10
Atlantic-Indian Ridge sea feature Southern Ocean 148 H9

▶Atlantic Ocean 148
2nd largest ocean in the world.

Atlantic Peak U.S.A. 126 F4
Atlantis S. Africa 100 D7
Atlas Méditerranéen mts Alg. see Atlas Tellien
Atlas Mountains Africa 54 C5
Atlas Saharien mts Alg. 54 E5
Atlas Tellien mts Alg. 57 H6
Atlin Lake Canada 120 C3
Atmakur India 84 C3
Atmore U.S.A. 133 C6
Atnur India 84 C2
Atocha Bol. 142 E8
Atoka U.S.A. 131 D5
Atouat mt. Laos 70 D3
Atouila, Erg des. Mali 96 C2
Atqan China see Aqqan
Atrak r. Iran/Turkm. see Atrek
Atrak, Rūd-e r. Iran/Turkm. 88 D2
Atrato r. Col. 142 C2
Atrek r. Iran/Turkm. 88 D2
also known as Atrak, alt. Etrek
Atropatene country Asia see Azerbaijan
Atsonupuri vol. Rus. Fed. 74 G3
Aṭ Ṭafīlah Jordan 85 B4
Aṭ Ṭā'if Saudi Arabia 86 F5
Attalea Turkey see Antalya
Attalia Turkey see Antalya
At Tamīmī Libya 90 A4
Attapu Laos 70 D4
Attavyros mt. Greece 59 L6
Attawapiskat Canada 122 E3
Attawapiskat r. Canada 122 E3
Attawapiskat Lake Canada 122 D3
Aṭ Ṭawīl mts Saudi Arabia 91 E5
At Taysīyah plat. Saudi Arabia 91 F5
Attendorn Germany 53 H3
Attersee l. Austria 47 N7
Attica IN U.S.A. 134 B3
Attica NY U.S.A. 135 F2
Attica OH U.S.A. 134 D3
Attigny France 52 E5
Attikamagen Lake Canada 123 I3
Attila Line Cyprus 85 A2
Attleborough U.K. 49 I6
Attopeu Laos see Attapu
Attu Greenland 119 M3
Aṭ Ṭubayq reg. Saudi Arabia 85 C5

▶Attu Island U.S.A. 65 S4
Most westerly point of North America.

At Tūnisīyah country Africa see Tunisia
Aṭ Ṭūr Egypt 90 D5
Attur India 84 C4
Aṭ Ṭuwayyah well Saudi Arabia 91 F6
Atuk Mountain hill U.S.A. 118 A3
Åtvidaberg Sweden 45 I7
Atwater U.S.A. 128 C3
Atwood U.S.A. 130 C4
Atwood Lake U.S.A. 134 E3
Atyashevo Rus. Fed. 43 J5
Atyrau Kazakh. 78 E2
Atyraū admin. div. Kazakh. see Atyrauskaya Oblast'
Atyrau Oblast admin. div. Kazakh. see Atyrauskaya Oblast'
Atyrauskaya Oblast' admin. div. Kazakh. 41 Q6
Aua Island P.N.G. 69 K7
Aub Germany 53 K5
Aubagne France 56 G5
Aubange Belgium 52 F5
Aubenas France 56 G4
Aubergenville France 52 B6
Auboué France 52 F5
Aubrey Cliffs mts U.S.A. 129 G4
Aubry Lake Canada 118 F3
Auburn r. Australia 111 E5
Auburn Canada 134 E2
Auburn AL U.S.A. 133 C5
Auburn CA U.S.A. 128 C2
Auburn IN U.S.A. 134 C3
Auburn KY U.S.A. 134 B5
Auburn ME U.S.A. 135 J1
Auburn NE U.S.A. 130 E3
Auburn NY U.S.A. 135 G2
Auburn Range hills Australia 110 E5
Aubusson France 56 F4
Auch France 56 E5
Auche Myanmar 70 B1
Auchterarder U.K. 50 F4

▶Auckland N.Z. 113 E3
5th most populous city in Oceania.

Auckland Islands N.Z. 107 G7
Auden Canada 122 D4
Audenarde Belgium see Oudenaarde
Audo mts Eth. 98 E3
Audo Range mts Eth. see Audo
Audruicq France 52 C4
Audubon U.S.A. 130 E3
Aue Germany 53 M4
Auerbach Germany 53 M4
Auerbach in der Oberpfalz Germany 53 L5
Auersberg mt. Germany 53 M4
Augathella Australia 111 D5
Augher U.K. 51 E3
Aughnacloy U.K. 51 F3
Aughrim Rep. of Ireland 51 F5
Augrabies S. Africa 100 E5
Augrabies Falls S. Africa 100 E5
Augrabies Falls National Park S. Africa 100 E5
Au Gres U.S.A. 134 D1
Augsburg Germany 47 M6
Augusta Australia 109 A8
Augusta Sicily Italy 58 F6
Augusta AR U.S.A. 131 F5
Augusta GA U.S.A. 133 D5
Augusta KY U.S.A. 134 C4

▶Augusta ME U.S.A. 135 K1
State capital of Maine.

Augusta MT U.S.A. 126 E3
Augusta Auscorum France see Auch
Augusta Taurinorum Italy see Turin
Augusta Treverorum Germany see Trier
Augusta Vindelicorum Germany see Augsburg
Augusto de Lima Brazil 145 B2
Augustus, Mount Australia 109 B6
Auke Bay U.S.A. 120 C3
Aukštaitijos nacionalinis parkas nat. park Lith. 45 O9
Aulavik National Park Canada 118 G2
Auld, Lake salt flat Australia 108 C5
Auliye Ata Kazakh. see Taraz
Aulnoye-Aymeries France 52 D4
Aulon Albania see Vlorë
Ault France 52 B4
Aumale Alg. see Sour el Ghozlane
Aumale France 52 B5
Aundh India 84 B2
Aundhi India 84 D1
Aunglan Myanmar see Myede
Auob watercourse Namibia/S. Africa 100 E4
Aupaluk Canada 123 H2
Aur i. Malaysia 71 D7
Aura Fin. 45 M6
Auraiya India 82 D4
Aurangabad Bihar India 83 F4
Aurangabad Maharashtra India 84 B2
Aure r. France 49 F9
Aurich Germany 53 H1
Aurigny i. Channel Is see Alderney
Aurilândia Brazil 145 A2
Aurillac France 56 F4
Aurora CO U.S.A. 126 G5
Aurora IL U.S.A. 134 A3
Aurora MO U.S.A. 131 E4
Aurora NE U.S.A. 130 D3
Aurora UT U.S.A. 129 H2
Aurora Island Vanuatu see Maéwo
Aurukun Australia 110 C2
Aus Namibia 100 C4
Au Sable U.S.A. 134 D1
Au Sable Point U.S.A. 134 D1
Auskerry i. U.K. 50 G1
Austin IN U.S.A. 134 C4
Austin MN U.S.A. 130 E3
Austin NV U.S.A. 128 E2

▶Austin TX U.S.A. 131 D6
State capital of Texas.

Austin, Lake salt flat Australia 109 B6
Austintown U.S.A. 134 E3
Austral Downs Australia 110 B4
Australes, Îles is Fr. Polynesia see Tubuai Islands

▶Australia country Oceania 106 C4
Largest country in Oceania. Most populous country in Oceania.
Oceania 8, 104–105

Australian - Antarctic Basin sea feature Southern Ocean 150 C9
Australian Antarctic Territory reg. Antarctica 152 G2
Australian Capital Territory admin. div. Australia 112 D5
▶Austria country Europe 47 N7
Europe 5, 38–39
Austvågøy i. Norway 44 I2
Autazes Brazil 143 G4
Autesiodorum France see Auxerre
Authie r. France 52 B4
Autti Fin. 44 O3
Auvergne reg. France 56 F4
Auvergne, Monts d' mts France 56 F4
Auxerre France 56 F3
Auxi-le-Château France 52 C4
Auxonne France 56 G3
Auyuittuq National Park Canada 119 L3
Auzangate, Nevado mt. Peru 142 D6
Ava MO U.S.A. 131 E4
Ava NY U.S.A. 135 H2
Avallon France 56 F3
Avalon U.S.A. 128 D5
Avalon Peninsula Canada 123 L5
Avān Iran 91 G3
Avarau atoll Cook Is see Palmerston
Avaré Brazil 145 A3
Avaricum France see Bourges

▶Avarua Cook Is 151 J7
Capital of the Cook Islands, on Rarotonga island.

Avawam U.S.A. 134 D5
Avaz Iran 89 F3
Aveiro Port. 57 B3
Aveiro, Ria de est. Port. 57 B3
Āvej Iran 88 C3
Avellino Italy 58 F4
Avenal U.S.A. 128 C3
Avenhorn Neth. 52 E2
Avenio France see Avignon
Aversa Italy 58 F4
Avesnes-sur-Helpe France 52 D4
Avesta Sweden 45 J6
Aveyron r. France 56 E4
Avezzano Italy 58 E3
Aviemore U.K. 50 F3
Avignon France 56 G5
Ávila Spain 57 D3
Avilés Spain 57 D2
Avion France 52 C4
Avis U.S.A. 135 G3
Avlama Dağı mt. Turkey 85 A1
Avlama Dağı mt. Turkey 85 A1
Avlona Albania see Vlorë
Avnyugskiy Rus. Fed. 42 J3
Avoca Australia 112 A6
Avoca r. Australia 109 A5
Avoca Rep. of Ireland 51 F5
Avoca IA U.S.A. 130 E3
Avoca NY U.S.A. 135 G2
Avola Sicily Italy 58 F6
Avon r. England U.K. 49 E6
Avon r. England U.K. 49 E7
Avon r. England U.K. 49 F8
Avon r. Scotland U.K. 50 F3
Avon U.S.A. 135 G2
Avondale U.S.A. 129 G5
Avonmore r. Rep. of Ireland 51 F5
Avonmore U.S.A. 134 F3
Avonmouth U.K. 49 E7
Avranches France 56 D2
Avre r. France 52 C5
Avsuyu Turkey 85 C1
Avuavu Solomon Is 107 G2
Avveel Fin. see Ivalo
Avvil Fin. see Ivalo
A'waj r. Syria 85 B3
Awakino N.Z. 113 E4
Awālī Bahrain 88 C5
Awanui N.Z. 113 D2
Āwarē Eth. 98 E3
'Awārid, Wādī al watercourse Syria 85 D2
Awarua Point N.Z. 113 B7
Āwash Eth. 98 E3
Āwash r. Eth. 98 E2
Awa-shima i. Japan 75 E5
Āwash National Park Eth. 98 D3
Awasib Mountains Namibia 100 B3
Awat China 80 F3
Awatere r. N.Z. 113 E5
Awbārī Libya 96 E2
Awbeg r. Rep. of Ireland 51 D5
'Awdah well Saudi Arabia 88 C6
'Awdah, Hawr al imp. l. Iraq 91 G5
Aw Dheegle Somalia 97 H4
Awe, Loch l. U.K. 50 D4
Aweil Sudan 97 F4
Awka Nigeria 96 D4
Awserd W. Sahara 96 B2
Axe r. England U.K. 49 D8
Axe r. England U.K. 49 E7
Axedale Australia 112 B6
Axel Heiberg Glacier Antarctica 152 I1
Axel Heiberg Island Canada 119 I2
Axim Ghana 96 C4
Axminster U.K. 49 E8
Axum Eth. see Āksum
Ay France 52 E5
Ayachi, Jbel mt. Morocco 54 D5
Ayacucho Arg. 144 E5
Ayacucho Peru 142 D6
Ayadaw Myanmar 70 A2
Ayagoz Kazakh. 80 F2
Ayaguz Kazakh. see Ayagoz
Ayakkum Hu salt l. China 83 G1
Ayaköz Kazakh. see Ayagoz
Ayan Rus. Fed. 65 O4
Ayancık Turkey 90 D2
Ayang N. Korea 75 B5
Ayaş Turkey 90 D2
Āybak Afgh. 89 H2
Aybas Kazakh. 43 K7
Aydar r. Ukr. 43 H6
Aydarkul', Ozero l. Uzbek. 80 C3
Aydın Turkey 59 L6
Aydıncık Turkey 85 A1
Aydın Dağları mts Turkey 59 L5
Āyelu Terara vol. Eth. 86 F7
Ayer U.S.A. 135 J2
Ayers Rock hill Australia see Uluru
Ayeyarwady r. Myanmar see Irrawaddy
Ayila Ri'gyü mts China 82 D2
Áyios Dhimítrios Greece see Agios Dimitrios
Áyios Evstrátios i. Greece see Agios Efstratios
Áyios Nikólaos Greece see Agios Nikolaos
Áyios Yeóryios i. Greece see Agios Georgios
Aylesbury N.Z. 113 D6
Aylesbury U.K. 49 G7
Aylett U.S.A. 135 G5
Ayllón Spain 57 E3
Aylmer Ont. Canada 134 E2
Aylmer Que. Canada 135 H1
Aylmer Lake Canada 121 I1
'Ayn al 'Abd well Saudi Arabia 84 C4
'Ayn al Baidā' Saudi Arabia 85 C4
'Ayn al Bayḍā' well Syria 85 C2
'Ayn al Ghazālah well Libya 90 A4
'Ayn al Maqfī spring Egypt 90 C6
'Ayn Dāllah spring Egypt 90 B6
Ayní Tajik. 89 H2
'Ayn 'Īsá Syria 85 D1
'Ayn Tabaghbugh spring Egypt 90 B5
'Ayn Tumayrah spring Egypt 90 B5
'Ayn Zaytūn Egypt 90 B5
Ayod Sudan 86 D8
Ayon, Ostrov i. Rus. Fed. 65 R3
'Ayoûn el 'Atroûs Mauritania 96 C3
Ayr Australia 110 D3
Ayr Canada 134 E2
Ayr U.K. 50 E5
Ayr r. U.K. 50 E5
Ayr, Point of U.K. 48 D5
Ayrancı Turkey 90 D3
Ayre, Point of Isle of Man 48 C4
Aytos Bulg. 59 L3
Ayuthia Thai. see Ayutthaya
Ayutthaya Thai. 71 C4
Ayvacık Turkey 59 L5
Ayvalı Turkey 90 E3
Ayvalık Turkey 59 L5
Azak Rus. Fed. see Azov
Azalia U.S.A. 134 C4
Azamgarh India 83 E4
Azaouâd reg. Mali 96 C3
Azaouagh, Vallée de watercourse Mali/Niger 96 D3
Azaran Iran see Hashtrud
Azärbaycan country Asia see Azerbaijan
Azärbayjan country Asia see Azerbaijan
Azare Nigeria 96 E3
A'zāz Syria 85 C1
Azbine mts Niger see L'Aïr, Massif de
Azdavay Turkey 90 D2
▶Azerbaijan country Asia 91 G2
Asia 6, 62–63
Azerbaydzhanskaya S.S.R. country Asia see Azerbaijan
Azhikal India 84 B4
Aziscohos Lake U.S.A. 135 J1
'Azīzābād Iran 88 E4
Aziziye Turkey see Pınarbaşı
Azogues Ecuador 142 C4

▶Azores terr. N. Atlantic Ocean 148 G3
Autonomous region of Portugal.
Europe 5, 38–39

Azores-Biscay Rise sea feature N. Atlantic Ocean 148 G3
Azotus Israel see Ashdod
Azov Rus. Fed. 43 H7
Azov, Sea of Rus. Fed./Ukr. 43 H7
Azovs'ke More sea Rus. Fed./Ukr. see Azov, Sea of
Azovskoye More sea Rus. Fed./Ukr. see Azov, Sea of
Azraq, Bahr el r. Sudan 86 D6 see Blue Nile
Azraq ash Shishān Jordan 85 C4
Azrou Morocco 54 C5
Aztec U.S.A. 129 I3
Azuaga Spain 57 D4
Azuero, Península de pen. Panama 137 H7
Azul, Cordillera mts Peru 142 C5
Azuma-san vol. Japan 75 F5
'Azza Gaza see Gaza
Azzaba Alg. 58 B6
Az Ẓahrān Saudi Arabia see Dhahran
Az Zaqāzīq Egypt 90 C5
Az Zarbah Syria 85 C1
Az Zarqā' Jordan 85 C3
Az Zawr, Ra's pt Saudi Arabia 91 H6
Azzeffâl hills Mauritania/W. Sahara 96 B2
Az Zubayr Iraq 91 G5
Az Zuqur i. Yemen 86 F7

B

Baa Indon. 108 C2
Baabda Lebanon 85 B3
Ba'albek Lebanon 85 C2
Ba'al Hazor mt. West Bank 85 B4
Baan Baa Australia 112 D3
Baardheere Somalia 98 E3
Bab India 82 D4
Bābā, Kūh-e mts Afgh. 89 H3
Baba Burnu pt Turkey 59 L5
Babadağ mt. Azer. 91 H2
Babadag Romania 59 M2
Babadaykhan Turkm. 89 F2
Babadurmaz Turkm. 88 E2
Babaeski Turkey 59 L4
Babahoyo Ecuador 142 C4
Babai India 82 D5
Babai r. Nepal 83 E3
Bābā Kalān Iran 88 C4
Bāb al Mandab strait Africa/Asia 86 F7
Babanusa Sudan 86 C7
Babao Qinghai China see Qilian
Babao Yunnan China 76 E4
Babar i. Indon. 108 E1
Babar, Kepulauan is Indon. 108 E1
Babati Tanz. 99 D4
Babayevo Rus. Fed. 42 G4
Babayurt Rus. Fed. 91 G2
B'abdā Lebanon see Baabda
Bab el Mandeb, Straits of Africa/Asia see Bāb al Mandab
Babi, Pulau i. Indon. 71 B7
Babian Jiang r. China 76 D4
Babine r. Canada 120 E4
Babine Lake Canada 120 E4
Babine Range mts Canada 120 E4

Bābol Iran 88 D2
Bābol Sar Iran 88 D2
Babongo Cameroon 97 E4
Baboon Point S. Africa 100 D7
Baboua Cent. Afr. Rep. 98 B3
Babruysk Belarus 43 F5
Babstovo Rus. Fed. 74 D2
Babu China see Hezhou
Babuhri India 82 B4
Babusar Pass Pak. 89 I3
Babuyan i. Phil. 69 G3
Babuyan Channel Phil. 69 G3
Babuyan Islands Phil. 69 G3
Bacaadweyn Somalia 98 E3
Bacabal Brazil 143 J4
Bacan i. Indon. 69 H7
Bacanora Mex. 127 F7
Bacău Romania 59 L1
Baccaro Point Canada 123 I6
Bắc Giang Vietnam 70 D2
Bacha China 74 D2
Bach Ice Shelf Antarctica 152 L2
Bach Long Vi, Đao i. Vietnam 70 D2
Bachu China 80 E4
Bachuan China see Tongliang
Back r. Australia 110 C3
Back r. Canada 121 M1
Bačka Palanka Serb. and Mont. 59 H2
Backbone Mountain U.S.A. 134 F4
Backbone Ranges mts Canada 120 D2
Backe Sweden 44 J5
Backstairs Passage Australia 111 B7
Bac Lac Vietnam 70 D2
Bac Liêu Vietnam 71 D5
Bắc Ninh Vietnam 70 D2
Bacoachi Mex. 127 F7
Bacoachi watercourse Mex. 127 F7
Bacobampo Mex. 127 F8
Bacolod Phil. 69 G4
Bắc Quang Vietnam 70 D2
Bacqueville, Lac l. Canada 122 G2
Bacqueville-en-Caux France 49 H9
Bacubirito Mex. 127 G8
Bād Iran 88 D3
Bada China see Xilin
Bada mt. Eth. 98 D3
Bada i. Myanmar 71 B5
Bad Abbach Germany 53 M6
Badagara India 84 B4
Badain Jaran Shamo des. China 80 J3
Badajoz Spain 57 C4
Badami India 84 B3
Badampaharh India 83 F5
Badanah Saudi Arabia 91 F5
Badanjilin Shamo des. China see Badain Jaran Shamo
Badaojiang China see Baishan
Badarpur India 83 H4
Badaun India see Budaun
Bad Axe U.S.A. 134 D2
Bad Bergzabern Germany 53 H5
Bad Berleburg Germany 53 I3
Bad Bevensen Germany 53 K1
Bad Blankenburg Germany 53 L4
Bad Camberg Germany 53 I4
Badderen Norway 44 M2
Bad Driburg Germany 53 J3
Bad Düben Germany 53 M3
Bad Dürkheim Germany 53 I5
Bad Dürrenberg Germany 53 M3
Bademli Turkey see Aladağ
Bademli Geçidi pass Turkey 90 C3
Bad Ems Germany 53 H4
Baden Austria 47 P6
Baden Switz. 56 I3
Baden-Baden Germany 53 I6
Baden-Württemberg land Germany 53 I6
Bad Essen Germany 53 I2
Bad Grund (Harz) Germany 53 K3
Bad Harzburg Germany 53 K3
Bad Hersfeld Germany 53 J4
Bad Hofgastein Austria 47 N7
Bad Homburg vor der Höhe Germany 53 I4
Badia Polesine Italy 58 D2
Badin Pak. 89 H5
Bad Ischl Austria 47 N7
Bādiyat ash Shām des. Asia see Syrian Desert
Badkhyzskiy Zapovednik nature res. Turkm. 89 F3
Bad Kissingen Germany 53 K4
Bad Königsdorff Poland see Jastrzębie-Zdrój
Bad Kösen Germany 53 L3
Bad Kreuznach Germany 53 H5
Bad Laasphe Germany 53 I4
Badlands reg. ND U.S.A. 130 C2
Badlands reg. SD U.S.A. 130 C3
Badlands National Park U.S.A. 130 C3
Bad Langensalza Germany 53 K3
Bad Lauterberg im Harz Germany 53 K3
Bad Liebenwerda Germany 53 N3
Bad Lippspringe Germany 53 I3
Bad Marienberg (Westerwald) Germany 53 H4
Bad Mergentheim Germany 53 J5
Bad Nauheim Germany 53 I4
Badnawar India 82 C5
Badnera India 84 C1
Bad Neuenahr-Ahrweiler Germany 52 H4
Bad Neustadt an der Saale Germany 53 K4
Badnor India 82 C4
Badong China 77 F2
Ba Đông Vietnam 71 D5
Badou Togo 96 D4
Bad Pyrmont Germany 53 J3
Badrah Iraq 91 G4
Bad Reichenhall Germany 47 N7
Badr Ḥunayn Saudi Arabia 86 E5
Bad Sachsa Germany 53 K3
Bad Salzdetfurth Germany 53 K2
Bad Salzuflen Germany 53 I2
Bad Salzungen Germany 53 K4
Bad Schwalbach Germany 53 I4
Bad Schwartau Germany 47 M4
Bad Segeberg Germany 47 M4
Badu Island Australia 110 C1
Badulla Sri Lanka 84 D5
Bad Vilbel Germany 53 I4
Bad Wilsnack Germany 53 L2
Bad Windsheim Germany 53 K5
Badzhal Rus. Fed. 74 D2
Badzhal'skiy Khrebet mts Rus. Fed. 74 D2
Bad Zwischenahn Germany 53 I1
Bae Colwyn U.K. see Colwyn Bay
Baesweiler Germany 52 G4
Baeza Spain 57 E5
Bafatá Guinea-Bissau 96 B3
Baffa Pak. 89 I3
Baffin Bay sea Canada/Greenland 119 L2

▶Baffin Island Canada 119 L3
2nd largest island in North America and 5th in the world.
World 12–13

Bafia Cameroon 96 E4
Bafilo Togo 96 D4
Bafing r. Africa 96 B3
Bafoulabé Mali 96 B3
Bafoussam Cameroon 96 E4
Bāfq Iran 88 D4
Bafra Turkey 90 D2
Bafra Burnu pt Turkey 90 D2
Bāft Iran 88 E4
Bafwaboli Dem. Rep. Congo 98 C3
Bafwasende Dem. Rep. Congo 98 C3
Bagaha India 83 F4
Bagalkot India 84 B2
Bagalkote India see Bagalkot
Bagamoyo Tanz. 99 D4
Bagan China 76 C1
Bagan Datoh Malaysia see Bagan Datuk
Bagan Datuk Malaysia 71 C7
Bagansiapiapi Indon. 71 C7
Bagata Dem. Rep. Congo 98 B4
Bagdad U.S.A. 129 G4
Bagdarin Rus. Fed. 73 K2
Bagé Brazil 144 F4
Bagerhat Bangl. 83 G5
Bageshwar India 82 D3
Baggs U.S.A. 126 G4
Baggy Point U.K. 49 C7
Bagh India 82 C5
Bàgh a' Chaisteil U.K. see Castlebay
Baghak Pak. 89 G4
Baghbaghū Iran 89 F2

▶Baghdād Iraq 91 G4
Capital of Iraq.

Bāgh-e Malek Iran 88 C4
Bagherhat Bangl. see Bagerhat
Bāghīn Iran 88 E4
Baghlān Afgh. 89 H2
Baghrān Afgh. 89 G3
Bağırsak r. Turkey 85 C1
Bağırsak Deresi r. Syria/Turkey see Sājūr, Nahr
Bagley U.S.A. 130 E2
Baglung Nepal 83 E3
Bagnères-de-Luchon France 56 E5
Bago Myanmar see Pegu
Bago Phil. 69 G4
Bagong China see Sansui
Bagor India 89 I5
Bagrationovsk Rus. Fed. 45 L9
Bagrax China see Bohu
Bagrax Hu l. China see Bosten Hu
Baguio Phil. 69 G3
Bagur, Cabo c. Spain see Begur, Cap de
Bagzane, Monts mts Niger 96 D3
Bahādorābād-e Bālā Iran 88 E4
Bahalda India 83 F5
Bahāmabād Iran see Rafsanjān
▶Bahamas, The country West Indies 133 E7
North America 9, 116–117
Bahara Pak. 89 G5
Baharampur India 83 G4
Bahardipur Pak. 89 H5
Bahariya Oasis oasis Egypt see Baḥrīyah, Wāḥāt al
Bahau Malaysia 71 C7
Bahawalnagar Pak. 89 I4
Bahawalpur Pak. 89 H4
Bahçe Adana Turkey 85 B1
Bahçe Osmaniye Turkey 90 E3
Baher Dar Eth. see Bahir Dar
Baheri India 82 D3
Bahia Brazil see Salvador
Bahia state Brazil 145 C1
Bahía Asunción Mex. 127 E8
Bahía Blanca Arg. 144 D5
Bahía Kino Mex. 127 F7
Bahía Laura Arg. 144 C7
Bahía Negra Para. 144 E2
Bahía Tortugas Mex. 127 E8
Bahir Dar Eth. 98 D2
Bahl India 82 C3
Bahlā Oman 88 E6
Bahomonte Indon. 69 G7
Bahraich India 83 E4
▶Bahrain country Asia 88 C5
Asia 6, 62–63
Bahrain, Gulf of Asia 88 C5
Bahrām Beyg Iran 88 C2
Bahrāmjerd Iran 88 E4
Baḥrīyah, Wāḥāt al oasis Egypt 90 C6
Bahuaja-Sonene, Parque Nacional nat. park Peru 142 E6
Baia Mare Romania 59 J1
Baiazeh Iran 88 D3
Baicang China 83 G3
Bai Canh, Hon i. Vietnam 71 D5
Baicheng Henan China see Xiping
Baicheng Jilin China 74 A3
Baicheng Xinjiang China 80 F3
Baidoa Somalia see Baydhabo
Baidoi Co l. China 83 F2
Baidu China 77 H3
Baie-aux-Feuilles Canada see Tasiujaq
Baie-Comeau Canada 123 H4
Baie-du-Poste Canada see Mistissini
Baie-St-Paul Canada 123 H5
Baie-Trinite Canada 123 I4
Baie Verte Canada 123 K4
Baiguan China see Shangyu
Baiguo Hubei China 77 G2
Baiguo Hunan China 77 G3
Baihanchang China 76 C3
Baihar India 82 E5
Baihe Jilin China 74 C4
Baihe Shaanxi China 77 F1
Baiji Iraq see Bayjī

▶Baikal, Lake Rus. Fed. 72 J2
Deepest lake in the world and in Asia. 3rd largest lake in Asia.

Baikunthpur India 83 E5
Baile Átha Cliath Rep. of Ireland see Dublin
Baile Átha Luain Rep. of Ireland see Athlone
Baile Mhartainn U.K. 50 B3
Băileşti Romania 59 J2
Bailey Range hills Australia 109 C7
Bailianhe Shuiku resr China 77 G2
Bailieborough Rep. of Ireland 51 F4
Bailleul France 52 C4
Baillie r. Canada 121 J1
Bailong China see Hadapu
Bailong Jiang r. China 76 E1
Baima Qinghai China 76 D1
Baima Xizang China see Baxoi
Baima Jian mt. China 77 H2
Baimuru P.N.G. 69 K8
Bain r. U.K. 48 G5
Bainang China 83 G3
Bainbridge GA U.S.A. 133 C6
Bainbridge IN U.S.A. 134 B4
Bainbridge NY U.S.A. 135 H2
Bainduru India 84 B3
Baingoin China 83 G3
Baini China see Yuqing
Baiona Spain 57 B2
Baiqên China 76 D1
Baiquan China 74 B3
Bā'ir Jordan 85 C4
Bā'ir, Wādī watercourse Jordan/Saudi Arabia 85 C4
Bairab Co l. China 83 E2
Bairat India 82 D4
Baird U.S.A. 131 D5
Baird Mountains U.S.A. 118 C3

▶Bairiki Kiribati 150 H5
Capital of Kiribati, on Tarawa atoll.

Bairin Youqi China see Daban
Bairnsdale Australia 112 C6
Baisha Chongqing China 76 E2
Baisha Hainan China 77 F5
Baisha Sichuan China 77 F2
Baishan Guangxi China see Mashan
Baishan Jilin China 74 B4
Baishan Jilin China see Baishanzhen
Baishanzhen China 74 B4
Baishui Shaanxi China 77 F1
Baishui Sichuan China 75 E1
Baishui Jiang r. China 76 E1
Baisogala Lith. 45 M9
Baitadi Nepal 82 E3
Baitang China 76 C1
Bai Thương Vietnam 70 D3
Baixi China see Yibin
Baiyashi China see Dong'an
Baiyin China 72 I5
Baiyü China 76 C2
Baiyuda Desert Sudan 86 D6
Baja Hungary 58 H1
Baja, Punta pt Mex. 127 E7
Baja California pen. Mex. 127 E7
Baja California state Mex. 127 E7
Baja California Norte state Mex. see Baja California
Baja California Sur state Mex. 127 E8
Bajan Mex. 131 C7
Bajau i. Indon. 71 D7
Bajaur reg. Pak. 89 H3
Bajawa Indon. 108 C2
Baj Baj India 83 G5
Bājgīrān Iran 88 E2
Bājil Yemen 86 F7
Bajo Caracoles Arg. 144 B7
Bajoga Nigeria 96 E3
Bajoi China 76 D2
Bajrakot India 83 F5
Bakala Cent. Afr. Rep. 97 F4
Bakanas Kazakh. 80 E3
Bakar Pak. 89 H5
Bakel Senegal 96 B3
Baker CA U.S.A. 128 E4
Baker ID U.S.A. 126 E3
Baker LA U.S.A. 131 F6
Baker MT U.S.A. 126 G3
Baker NV U.S.A. 129 F2
Baker OR U.S.A. 126 D3
Baker WV U.S.A. 135 F4
Baker, Mount vol. U.S.A. 126 C2
Baker Butte mt. U.S.A. 129 H4

▶Baker Island terr. N. Pacific Ocean 107 I1
United States Unincorporated Territory.

Baker Island U.S.A. 120 C4
Baker Lake salt flat Australia 109 D6
Baker Lake Canada 121 M1
Baker Lake l. Canada 121 M1
Baker's Dozen Islands Canada 122 F2
Bakersfield U.S.A. 128 D4
Bakersville U.S.A. 132 D4
Bå Kêv Cambodia 71 D4
Bakhardok Turkm. 88 E2
Bākharz mts Iran 89 F3
Bakhasar India 82 B4
Bakhirevo Rus. Fed. 74 C2
Bakhmach Ukr. 43 G6
Bakhma Dam Iraq see Bēkma, Sadd
Bakhmut Ukr. see Artemivs'k
Bākhtarān Iran see Kermānshāh
Bakhtegan, Daryācheh-ye l. Iran 88 D4
Bakhtiari Country reg. Iran 88 C3
Bakı Azer. see Baku
Bakırköy Turkey 59 M4
Bakkejord Norway 44 K2
Bakloh India 82 C2
Bako Eth. 98 D3
Bakongan Indon. 71 B7
Bakouma Cent. Afr. Rep. 98 C3
Baksan Rus. Fed. 91 F2

▶Baku Azer. 91 H2
Capital of Azerbaijan.

Baku Dem. Rep. Congo 98 D3
Bakutis Coast Antarctica 152 J2
Baky Azer. see Baku
Balâ Turkey 90 D3
Bala U.K. 49 D6
Bala, Cerros de mts Bol. 142 E6
Balabac i. Phil. 68 F5
Balabac Strait Malaysia/Phil. 68 F5
Baladeh Māzandarān Iran 88 C2
Baladeh Māzandarān Iran 88 C2
Baladek Rus. Fed. 74 D1
Balaghat India 82 E5
Balaghat Range hills India 84 B2
Bālā Ḥowẓ Iran 88 E4
Balaka Malawi 99 D5
Balakän Azer. 91 G2
Balakhna Rus. Fed. 42 I4
Balakhta Rus. Fed. 72 G1
Balaklava Australia 111 B7
Balaklava Ukr. 90 D1
Balakleya Ukr. see Balakliya
Balakliya Ukr. 43 H6
Balakovo Rus. Fed. 43 J5
Bala Lake U.K. see Tegid, Llyn
Balaman India 82 E4
Balan India 82 B4
Balanda Rus. Fed. see Kalininsk
Balanda r. Rus. Fed. 43 J6
Balan Dağı hill Turkey 59 M6
Balanga Phil. 69 G4
Balangir India see Bolangir
Balaözen r. Kazakh./Rus. Fed. see Malyy Uzen'
Balarampur India see Balrampur
Balashov Rus. Fed. 43 I6
Balasore India see Baleshwar
Balaton, Lake Hungary 58 G1
Balatonboglár Hungary 58 G1
Balatonfüred Hungary 58 G1
Balbina Brazil 143 G4
Balbina, Represa de resr Brazil 143 G4
Balbriggan Rep. of Ireland 51 F4
Balchik Bulg. 59 M3
Balclutha N.Z. 113 B8
Balcones Escarpment U.S.A. 131 C6
Bald Knob U.S.A. 134 E5
Bald Mountain U.S.A. 129 F3
Baldock Lake Canada 121 L3
Baldwin Canada 134 F1
Baldwin FL U.S.A. 133 D6
Baldwin MI U.S.A. 134 C2
Baldwin PA U.S.A. 134 F3
Baldy Mount Canada 126 D2
Baldy Mountain hill Canada 121 K5
Baldy Peak U.S.A. 129 I5
Bale Indon. 68 C7
Bâle Switz. see Basel
Baléa Mali 96 B3
Baleares is Spain see Balearic Islands
Baleares, Islas is Spain see Balearic Islands
Baleares Insulae is Spain see Balearic Islands
Balearic Islands is Spain 57 G4
Balears is Spain see Balearic Islands
Balears, Illes is Spain see Balearic Islands
Baleia, Ponta da pt Brazil 145 D2
Bale Mountains National Park Eth. 98 D3
Baler Phil. 69 G3
Baleshwar India 83 F5
Balestrand Norway 45 E6
Baléyara Niger 96 D3
Balezino Rus. Fed. 41 Q4
Balfe's Creek Australia 110 D4
Balfour Downs Australia 108 C5
Balgo Australia 108 D5
Balguntay China 80 G3
Bali India 82 C4
Bali i. Indon. 108 A2
Bali, Laut sea Indon. 108 A1
Balia India see Ballia
Baliapal India 83 F5
Balige Indon. 71 B7
Baliguda India 84 D1
Balıkesir Turkey 59 L5
Balīkh r. Syria/Turkey 85 D2
Balikpapan Indon. 68 F7
Balimila Reservoir India 84 D2
Balimo P.N.G. 69 K8
Balin China 74 A2
Baling Malaysia 71 C6
Balingen Germany 47 L6
Balintore U.K. 50 F3
Bali Sea Indon. see Bali, Laut
Balk Neth. 52 F2
Balkan Mountains Bulg./Serb. and Mont. 59 J3
Balkassar Pak. 89 I3
Balkhash Kazakh. 80 D2

▶Balkhash, Lake Kazakh. 80 D2
4th largest lake in Asia.

Balkhash, Ozero l. Kazakh. see Balkhash, Lake
Balkuduk Kazakh. 43 J7
Ballachulish U.K. 50 D4
Balladonia Australia 109 C8
Balladoran Australia 112 D3
Ballaghaderreen Rep. of Ireland 51 D4
Ballan Australia 112 B6
Ballangen Norway 44 J2
Ballantine U.S.A. 126 F3
Ballantrae U.K. 50 E5
Ballarat Australia 112 A6
Ballard, Lake salt flat Australia 105 C7
Ballarpur India 84 C2
Ballater U.K. 50 F3
Ballé Mali 96 C3
Ballena, Punta pt Chile 144 B3
Balleny Islands Antarctica 152 H2
Ballia India 83 F4
Ballina Australia 112 F2
Ballina Rep. of Ireland 51 C3
Ballinafad Rep. of Ireland 51 D3
Ballinalack Rep. of Ireland 51 E4
Ballinamore Rep. of Ireland 51 E3
Ballinasloe Rep. of Ireland 51 D4
Ballindine Rep. of Ireland 51 D4
Ballinger U.S.A. 131 D6
Ballinluig U.K. 50 F4
Ballinrobe Rep. of Ireland 51 C4
Ballon d'Alsace mt. France 47 K7
Ballston Spa U.S.A. 135 I2
Ballybay Rep. of Ireland 51 F3
Ballybrack Rep. of Ireland 51 B6
Ballybunnion Rep. of Ireland 51 C5
Ballycanew Rep. of Ireland 51 F5
Ballycastle Rep. of Ireland 51 C3
Ballycastle U.K. 51 F2
Ballyclare U.K. 51 G3
Ballyconnell Rep. of Ireland 51 E3
Ballygar Rep. of Ireland 51 D4
Ballygawley U.K. 51 E3
Ballygorman Rep. of Ireland 51 E2
Ballyhaunis Rep. of Ireland 51 D4
Ballyheigue Rep. of Ireland 51 C5
Ballykelly U.K. 51 E2
Ballylynan Rep. of Ireland 51 E5
Ballymacmague Rep. of Ireland 51 E5
Ballymahon Rep. of Ireland 51 E4
Ballymena U.K. 51 F3
Ballymoney U.K. 51 F2
Ballymote Rep. of Ireland 51 D3
Ballynahinch U.K. 51 G3
Ballyshannon Rep. of Ireland 51 D3
Ballyteige Bay Rep. of Ireland 51 F5
Ballyvaughan Rep. of Ireland 51 C4
Ballyward U.K. 51 F3
Balmartin U.K. see Baile Mhartainn
Balmer India see Barmer
Balmertown Canada 121 M5
Balmorhea U.S.A. 131 C6
Balochistan prov. Pak. 89 G4
Balombo Angola 99 B5
Balonne r. Australia 112 D2
Balotra India 82 C4
Balqash Kazakh. see Balkhash
Balqash Köli l. Kazakh. see Balkhash, Lake
Balrampur India 83 E4
Balranald Australia 112 A5
Balş Romania 59 K2
Balsam Lake Canada 135 F1
Balsas Brazil 143 I5
Balta Ukr. 43 F7
Baltasound U.K. 50 [inset]
Baltay Rus. Fed. 43 J5
Bălţi Moldova 43 E7
Baltic U.S.A. 134 E3
Baltic Sea g. Europe 45 J9
Balṭīm Egypt see Balṭīm
Balṭīm Egypt 90 C5
Baltimore S. Africa 101 I2
Baltimore MD U.S.A. 135 G4
Baltimore OH U.S.A. 134 D4
Baltinglass Rep. of Ireland 51 F5
Baltistan reg. Jammu and Kashmir 82 C2
Baltiysk Rus. Fed. 45 K9
Balu India 76 B3
Baluarte, Arroyo watercourse U.S.A. 131 D7
Baluch Ab well Iran 88 E4
Balumundam Indon. 71 B7
Balurghat India 83 G4
Balve Germany 53 H3
Balvi Latvia 45 O8
Balya Turkey 59 L5
Balykchy Kyrg. 80 E3
Balykshi Kazakh. 78 E2
Balyqshy Kazakh. see Balykshi
Bam Iran 88 E4
Bām Iran 88 E2
Bama China 76 E3

▶Bamako Mali 96 C3
Capital of Mali.

Bamba Mali 96 C3
Bambari Cent. Afr. Rep. 98 C3
Bambel Indon. 71 B7
Bamberg Germany 53 K5
Bamberg U.S.A. 133 D5
Bambili Dem. Rep. Congo 98 C3
Bambio Cent. Afr. Rep. 98 B3
Bamboesberg mts S. Africa 101 H6
Bamboo Creek Australia 108 C5
Bambouti Cent. Afr. Rep. 98 C3
Bambuí Brazil 145 B3
Bamda China 76 C2
Bamenda Cameroon 96 E4
Bāmīān Afgh. 89 G3
Bamiantong China see Muling
Bamingui Cent. Afr. Rep. 98 C3
Bamingui-Bangoran, Parc National du nat. park Cent. Afr. Rep. 98 B3
Bâmnak Cambodia 71 D4
Bamnet Narong Thai. 70 C4
Bamor India 82 D4
Bamori India 84 C1
Bam Posht reg. Iran 89 F5
Bam Posht, Kūh-e mts Iran 89 F5
Bampton U.K. 49 D8
Bampūr Iran 89 F5
Bampūr watercourse Iran 89 E5
Bamrūd Iran 89 F3
Bam Tso l. China 83 G3
Bamyili Australia 108 F3
Banaba i. Kiribati 107 G2
Banabuiu, Açude resr Brazil 139 K5
Bañados del Izozog swamp Bol. 142 F7
Banagher Rep. of Ireland 51 E4
Banalia Dem. Rep. Congo 98 C3
Banamana, Lagoa l. Moz. 101 K2
Banamba Mali 96 C3
Banámichi Mex. 127 F7
Banana Australia 110 E5
Bananal, Ilha do i. Brazil 143 H6
Bananga India 71 A6
Banapur India 84 E2
Banas r. India 82 D4
Banaz Turkey 59 M5
Ban Ban Laos 70 C3
Banbar China 76 B2
Ban Bo Laos 70 C3
Banbridge U.K. 51 F3
Ban Bua Chum Thai. 70 C4
Ban Bua Yai Thai. 70 C4
Ban Bungxai Laos 70 D4
Banbury U.K. 49 F6
Ban Cang Vietnam 70 C2
Banc d'Arguin, Parc National du nat. park Mauritania 96 B2
Ban Channabot Thai. 70 C3
Banchory U.K. 50 G3
Bancroft Canada 135 G1
Bancroft Zambia see Chililabombwe
Banda Dem. Rep. Congo 98 C3
Banda India 82 E4
Banda, Kepulauan is Indon. 69 H7
Banda, Laut sea Indon. 69 H8
Banda Aceh Indon. 71 A6
Banda Banda, Mount Australia 112 F3
Banda Daud Shah Pak. 89 H3
Bandahara, Gunung mt. Indon. 71 B7
Bandama r. Côte d'Ivoire 96 C4
Bandān Kūh mts Iran 89 F4
Bandar India see Machilipatnam
Bandar Moz. 99 D5
Bandar Abbas Iran see Bandar-e 'Abbās
Bandarban Bangl. 83 H5
Bandar-e 'Abbās Iran 88 E5
Bandar-e Anzalī Iran 88 C2
Bandar-e Deylam Iran 88 C4
Bandar-e Emām Khomeynī Iran 88 C4
Bandar-e Lengeh Iran 88 D5
Bandar-e Ma'shur Iran 88 C4
Bandar-e Nakhīlū Iran 88 D5
Bandar-e Pahlavī Iran see Bandar-e Anzalī
Bandar-e Shāh Iran see Bandar-e Torkeman
Bandar-e Shāhpūr Iran see Bandar-e Emām Khomeynī
Bandar-e Shīū' Iran 88 D5
Bandar-e Torkeman Iran 88 D2
Bandar Labuan Malaysia see Labuan
Bandar Lampung Indon. 68 D8
Bandarpunch mt. India 82 D3

▶Bandar Seri Begawan Brunei 68 E6
Capital of Brunei.

Banda Sea sea Indon. see Banda, Laut
Band-e Amīr l. Afgh. 89 G3
Band-e Amīr, Daryā-ye r. Afgh. 89 G2
Band-e Bābā mts Afgh. 89 F3
Bandeira Brazil 145 C1
Bandeirante Brazil 145 A1
Bandeiras, Pico de mt. Brazil 145 C3
Bandelierkop S. Africa 101 I2
Banderas Mex. 131 B6
Banderas, Bahía de b. Mex. 136 C4
Band-e Sar Qom Iran 88 C3
Band-e Torkestān mts Afgh. 89 F3
Bandhi Pak. 89 H5
Bandhogarh India 82 E5
Bandi r. India 82 C4
Bandiagara Mali 96 C3
Bandikui India 82 D4
Bandipur National Park India 84 C4
Bandırma Turkey 59 L4
Bandjarmasin Indon. see Banjarmasin
Bandon Rep. of Ireland 51 D6
Bandon r. Rep. of Ireland 51 D6
Ban Don Thai. see Surat Thani
Bandon U.S.A. 126 B4
Band Qīr Iran 88 C4
Bandra India 84 B2
Bandundu Dem. Rep. Congo 98 B4
Bandung Indon. 68 D8
Bandya Australia 109 C6
Bāneh Iran 88 B3
Banera India 82 C4
Banes Cuba 137 I4
Banff Canada 120 H5
Banff U.K. 50 G3
Banff National Park Canada 120 G5
Banfora Burkina 96 C3
Banga Dem. Rep. Congo 99 C4
Bangalore India 84 C3
Bangalow Australia 112 F2
Bangaon India 83 G5
Bangar Brunei 68 F6
Bangassou Cent. Afr. Rep. 98 C3
Bangdag Co salt l. China 83 E2
Banggai Indon. 69 G7
Banggai, Kepulauan is Indon. 69 G7
Banggi i. Malaysia 68 F5
Banghāzī Libya see Benghazi
Banghiang, Xé r. Laos 70 D3
Bangka i. Indon. 68 D7
Bangka, Selat sea chan. Indon. 68 D7
Bangkalan Indon. 68 E8
Bangkaru i. Indon. 71 B7
Bangko Indon. 68 C7

▶Bangkok Thai. 71 C4
Capital of Thailand.

Bangkok, Bight of b. Thai. 71 C4
Bangkor China 83 F3
Bangla state India see West Bengal
▶Bangladesh country Asia 83 G4
Asia 6, 62–63
Bangma Shan mts China 76 C4
Bang Mun Nak Thai. 70 C3
Bangolo Côte d'Ivoire 96 C4
Bangong Co salt l. China/Jammu and Kashmir 82 D2
Bangor Northern Ireland U.K. 51 G3
Bangor Wales U.K. 48 C5
Bangor ME U.S.A. 132 G2
Bangor MI U.S.A. 134 B2
Bangor PA U.S.A. 135 H3
Bangor Erris Rep. of Ireland 51 C3
Bangs, Mount U.S.A. 129 G3
Bang Saphan Yai Thai. 71 B5
Bangsund Norway 44 G4
Bangued Phil. 69 G3

▶Bangui Cent. Afr. Rep. 98 B3
Capital of Central African Republic.

Bangweulu, Lake Zambia 99 C5
Banhā Egypt 90 C5
Banhine, Parque Nacional de nat. park Moz. 101 K2
Ban Hin Heup Laos 70 C3
Ban Houayxay Laos 70 C2
Ban Houei Sai Laos see Ban Houayxay
Ban Huai Khon Thai. 70 C3
Ban Huai Yang Thai. 71 B5
Bani, Jbel ridge Morocco 54 C6
Bania Cent. Afr. Rep. 98 B3
Bani-Bangou Niger 96 D3
Banifing r. Mali 96 C3
Banī Forūr, Jazīreh-ye i. Iran 88 D5

Beaverton Canada 134 F1
Beaverton MI U.S.A. 134 C2
Beaverton OR U.S.A. 126 C3
Beawar India 82 C4
Beazley Arg. 144 C4
Bebedouro Brazil 145 A3
Bebington U.K. 48 D5
Bebra Germany 53 J4
Bêca China 76 C2
Bécard, Lac l. Canada 123 G1
Beccles U.K. 49 I6
Bečej Serb. and Mont. 59 I2
Becerreá Spain 57 C2
Béchar Alg. 54 D5
Bechhofen Germany 53 K5
Bechuanaland country Africa see Botswana
Beckley U.S.A. 134 E5
Beckum Germany 53 I3
Becky Peak U.S.A. 129 F2
Bečov nad Teplou Czech Rep. 53 M4
Bedale U.K. 48 F4
Bedburg Germany 52 G4
Bedelē Eth. 98 D3
Bederkesa Germany 53 I1
Bedford N.S. Canada 123 J5
Bedford Que. Canada 135 I1
Bedford E. Cape S. Africa 101 H7
Bedford Kwazulu-Natal S. Africa 101 J5
Bedford U.K. 49 G6
Bedford IN U.S.A. 134 B4
Bedford KY U.S.A. 134 C4
Bedford PA U.S.A. 135 F3
Bedford VA U.S.A. 134 F5
Bedford, Cape Australia 110 D2
Bedford Downs Australia 108 D4
Bedgerebong Australia 112 C4
Bedi India 82 B5
Bedla India 82 C4
Bedlington U.K. 48 F3
Bedok Sing. 71 [inset]
Bedok Jetty Sing. 71 [inset]
Bedok Reservoir Sing. 71 [inset]
Bedou China 77 F3
Bedourie Australia 110 B5
Bedum Neth. 52 G1
Bedworth U.K. 49 F6
Beechworth Australia 112 C6
Beechy Canada 121 J5
Beecroft Peninsula Australia 112 E5
Beed India see Bid
Beelitz Germany 53 M2
Beenleigh Australia 112 F1
Beernem Belgium 52 D3
Beersheba Israel 85 B4
Be'ér Sheva' Israel see Beersheba
Be'ér Sheva' watercourse Israel 85 B4
Beervlei Dam S. Africa 100 F7
Beerwah Australia 112 F1
Beetaloo Australia 108 F4
Beethoven Peninsula Antarctica 152 L2
Beeville U.S.A. 131 D6
Befori Dem. Rep. Congo 98 C3
Beg, Lough l. U.K. 51 F3
Bega Australia 112 D6
Begari r. Pak. 89 H4
Begicheva, Ostrov i. Rus. Fed. see Bol'shoy Begichev, Ostrov
Begur, Cap de c. Spain 57 H3
Begusarai India 83 F4
Béhague, Pointe pt Fr. Guiana 143 H3
Behbehān Iran 88 C4
Behrendt Mountains Antarctica 152 L2
Behrūsī Iran 88 D4
Behshahr Iran 88 D2
Behsūd Afgh. 89 G3
Bei'an China 74 B2
Bei'ao China see Dongtou
Beibei China 76 E2
Beichuan China 76 E2
Beida Libya see Al Bayḍā'
Beigang Taiwan see Peikang
Beiguan China see Anyang
Beihai China 77 F4
Bei Hulsan Hu salt l. China 83 H1

▶Beijing China 73 L5
Capital of China.

Beijing municipality China 73 L4
Beik Myanmar see Mergui
Beilen Neth. 52 G2
Beiliu China 77 F4
Beilngries Germany 53 L5
Beiluheyan China 76 B1
Beinn an Oir hill U.K. 50 D5
Beinn an Tuirc hill U.K. 50 D5
Beinn Bheigeir hill U.K. 50 C5
Beinn Bhreac hill U.K. 50 D4
Beinn Dearg mt. U.K. 50 G3
Beinn Heasgarnich mt. U.K. 50 E4
Beinn Mholach hill U.K. 50 C2
Beinn Mhòr hill U.K. 50 B3
Beinn na Faoghlia i. U.K. see Benbecula
Beipan Jiang r. China 76 E3
Beipiao China 73 M4
Beira Moz. 99 D5

▶Beirut Lebanon 85 B3
Capital of Lebanon.

Bei Shan mts China 80 I3
Beitbridge Zimbabwe 99 C6
Beith U.K. 50 E5
Beit Jālā West Bank 85 B4
Beja Port. 57 C4
Béja Tunisia 58 C6
Bejaïa Alg. 57 I5
Béjar Spain 57 D3
Beji r. Pak. 80 C6
Bekaa valley Lebanon see El Béqaa
Bekdash Turkm. 91 I2
Békés Hungary 59 I1
Békéscsaba Hungary 59 I1
Bekily Madag. 99 E6
Bekkai Japan 74 G4
Bēkma, Sadd dam Iraq 91 G3
Bekovo Rus. Fed. 43 I5
Bekwai Ghana 96 C4
Bela India 83 E4
Bela Pak. 89 G5
Belab r. Pak. 89 H4
Bela-Bela S. Africa 101 I3
Bélabo Cameroon 96 E4
Bela Crkva Serb. and Mont. 59 I2
Bel Air U.S.A. 135 G4
Belalcázar Spain 57 D4
Bělá nad Radbuzou Czech Rep. 53 M5
Belapur India 84 B2
Belaraboon Australia 112 B4
▶Belarus country Europe 43 E5
Europe 5, 38–39
Belau country N. Pacific Ocean see Palau
Bela Vista Brazil 144 E2
Bela Vista Moz. 101 K4
Bela Vista de Goiás Brazil 145 A2
Belawan Indon. 71 B7
Belaya r. Rus. Fed. 65 S3
also known as Bila
Belaya Glina Rus. Fed. 43 I7
Belaya Kalitva Rus. Fed. 43 I6
Belaya Kholunitsa Rus. Fed. 42 K4
Belaya Tserkva Ukr. see Bila Tserkva
Belbédji Niger 96 D3
Bełchatów Poland 47 Q5
Belcher U.S.A. 134 D5
Belcher Islands Canada 122 F2
Belchiragh Afgh. 89 G3
Belcoo U.K. 51 E3
Belden U.S.A. 128 C1
Belding U.S.A. 134 C2
Beleapani reef India see Cherbaniani Reef
Belebey Rus. Fed. 41 Q5
Beledweyne Somalia 98 E3
Belém Brazil 143 I4
Belém Novo Brazil 145 A5
Belén Arg. 144 C3
Belen Antalya Turkey 85 A1
Belen Hatay Turkey 85 C1
Belen U.S.A. 127 G6
Belep, Îles is New Caledonia 107 G3
Belev Rus. Fed. 43 H5
Belfast S. Africa 101 J3

▶Belfast U.K. 51 G3
Capital of Northern Ireland.

Belfast U.S.A. 132 G2
Belfast Lough inlet U.K. 51 G3
Bēlfodiyo Eth. 98 D2
Belford U.K. 48 F3
Belfort France 56 H3
Belgaum India 84 B3
Belgern Germany 53 N3
Belgian Congo country Africa see Congo, Democratic Republic of
België country Europe see Belgium
Belgique country Europe see Belgium
▶Belgium country Europe 52 E4
Europe 5, 38–39
Belgorod Rus. Fed. 43 H6
Belgorod-Dnestrovskyy Ukr. see Bilhorod-Dnistrovs'kyy
Belgrade ME U.S.A. 135 K1
Belgrade MT U.S.A. 126 F3

▶Belgrade Serb. and Mont. 59 I2
Capital of Serbia and Montenegro.

Belgrano II research station Antarctica 152 A1
Belice r. Sicily Italy 58 E6
Belinskiy Rus. Fed. 43 I5
Belinyu Indon. 68 D7
Belitung i. Indon. 68 D7
Belize Angola 99 B4

▶Belize Belize 136 G5
Former capital of Belize.

▶Belize country Central America 136 G5
North America 9, 116–117
Beljak Austria see Villach
Belkina, Mys pt Rus. Fed. 74 E3
Bel'kovskiy, Ostrov i. Rus. Fed. 65 O2
Bell Australia 112 E1
Bell r. Australia 112 D4
Bell r. Canada 122 F4
Bella Bella Canada 120 D4
Bellac France 56 E3
Bella Coola Canada 120 E4
Bellaire U.S.A. 134 C1
Bellary India 84 C3
Bellata Australia 112 D2
Bella Unión Uruguay 144 E4
Bella Vista U.S.A. 128 B1
Bellbrook Australia 112 F3
Bell Cay reef Australia 110 E4
Belledonne mts France 56 G4
Bellefontaine U.S.A. 134 D3
Bellefonte U.S.A. 135 G3
Belle Fourche U.S.A. 130 C2
Belle Fourche r. U.S.A. 130 C2
Belle Glade U.S.A. 133 D7
Belle-Île i. France 56 C3
Belle Isle i. Canada 123 L4
Belle Isle, Strait of Canada 123 K4
Belleville Canada 135 G1
Belleville IL U.S.A. 130 F4
Belleville KS U.S.A. 130 D4
Bellevue IA U.S.A. 130 F3
Bellevue MI U.S.A. 134 C2
Bellevue OH U.S.A. 134 D3
Bellevue WA U.S.A. 126 C3
Bellin Canada see Kangirsuk
Bellingham U.K. 48 E3
Bellingham U.S.A. 126 C2
Bellingshausen research station Antarctica 152 A2
Bellingshausen Sea Antarctica 152 L2
Bellinzona Switz. 56 I3
Bellows Falls U.S.A. 135 I2
Bellpat Pak. 89 H4
Belluno Italy 58 E1
Belluru India 84 C3
Bell Ville Arg. 144 D4
Bellville S. Africa 100 D7
Belm Germany 53 I2
Belmont Australia 112 E4
Belmont U.K. 50 [inset]
Belmont U.S.A. 135 F2
Belmonte Brazil 145 D1

▶Belmopan Belize 136 G5
Capital of Belize.

Belmore, Mount hill Australia 112 F2
Belmullet Rep. of Ireland 51 C3
Belo Madag. 99 E6
Belo Campo Brazil 145 C1
Belœil Belgium 52 D4
Belogorsk Rus. Fed. 74 C2
Belogorsk Ukr. see Bilohirs'k
Beloha Madag. 99 E6
Belo Horizonte Brazil 145 C2
Beloit KS U.S.A. 130 D4
Beloit WI U.S.A. 130 F3
Belokurikha Rus. Fed. 80 F1
Belo Monte Brazil 143 H4
Belomorsk Rus. Fed. 42 G2
Belonia India 83 G5
Belorechensk Rus. Fed. 91 E1
Belorechenskaya Rus. Fed. see Belorechensk
Belören Turkey 90 D3
Beloretsk Rus. Fed. 64 G4
Belorussia country Europe see Belarus
Belorusskaya S.S.R. country Europe see Belarus
Belostok Poland see Białystok
Belot, Lac l. Canada 118 F3
Belo Tsiribihina Madag. 99 E5
Belovo Rus. Fed. 72 F2
Beloyarskiy Rus. Fed. 41 T3
Beloye, Ozero l. Rus. Fed. 42 H3
Beloye More sea Rus. Fed. see White Sea
Belozersk Rus. Fed. 42 H3
Belpre U.S.A. 134 E4
Beltana Australia 111 B6
Belted Range mts U.S.A. 128 E3
Belton U.S.A. 131 D6
Bel'ts' Moldova see Bălţi
Bel'tsy Moldova see Bălţi
Belukha, Gora mt. Kazakh./Rus. Fed. 80 G2
Belush'ye Rus. Fed. 42 J2
Belvidere IL U.S.A. 130 F3
Belvidere NJ U.S.A. 135 H3
Belyando r. Australia 110 D4
Belyayevka Ukr. see Bilyayivka
Belyy Rus. Fed. 42 G5
Belyy, Ostrov i. Rus. Fed. 64 I2
Belzig Germany 53 M2
Belzoni U.S.A. 131 F5
Bemaraha, Plateau du Madag. 99 E5
Bembe Angola 99 B4
Bemidji U.S.A. 130 E2
Béna Burkina 96 C3
Bena Dibele Dem. Rep. Congo 98 C4
Ben Alder mt. U.K. 50 E4
Benalla Australia 112 B6
Benares India see Varanasi
Ben Arous Tunisia 58 D6
Benavente Spain 57 D2
Ben Avon mt. U.K. 50 F3
Benbane Head hd U.K. 51 F2
Benbecula i. U.K. 50 B3
Ben Boyd National Park Australia 112 E6
Benburb U.K. 51 F3
Bên Cat Vietnam 71 D5
Bencha China 77 I1
Ben Chonzie hill U.K. 50 F4
Ben Cleuch hill U.K. 50 F4
Ben Cruachan mt. U.K. 50 D4
Bend U.S.A. 126 C3
Bendearg mt. S. Africa 101 H6
Bender Moldova see Tighina
Bender-Bayla Somalia 98 F3
Bendery Moldova see Tighina
Bendigo Australia 112 B6
Bendoc Australia 112 D6
Bene Moz. 99 D5
Benedict, Mount hill Canada 123 K3
Benenitra Madag. 99 E6
Benešov Czech Rep. 47 O6
Bénestroff France 52 G6
Benevento Italy 58 F4
Beneventum Italy see Benevento
Benezette U.S.A. 135 F3
Beng, Nam r. Laos 70 C3
Bengal, Bay of sea Indian Ocean 81 G8
Bengamisa Dem. Rep. Congo 98 C3
Bengbu China 77 H1
Benghazi Libya 97 F1
Bengkalis Indon. 71 C7
Bengkalis i. Indon. 71 C7
Bengkulu Indon. 68 C7
Bengtsfors Sweden 45 H7
Benguela Angola 99 B5
Benha Egypt see Banhā
Ben Hiant hill U.K. 50 C4
Ben Hope hill U.K. 50 E2
Ben Horn hill U.K. 50 E2
Beni r. Bol. 142 E6
Beni Dem. Rep. Congo 98 C3
Beni Nepal 83 E3
Beni-Abbès Alg. 54 D5
Beniah Lake Canada 121 H2
Benidorm Spain 57 F4
Beni Mellal Morocco 54 C5
▶Benin country Africa 96 D4
Africa 7, 94–95
Benin, Bight of g. Africa 96 D4
Benin City Nigeria 96 D4
Beni-Saf Alg. 57 F6
Beni Snassen, Monts des mts Morocco 57 E6
Beni Suef Egypt see Banī Suwayf
Benito, Islas is Mex. 127 E7
Benito Juárez Arg. 144 E5
Benito Juárez Mex. 129 F5
Benjamim Constant Brazil 142 E4
Benjamin U.S.A. 131 D5
Benjamín Hill Mex. 127 F7
Benjina Indon. 69 I8
Benkelman U.S.A. 130 C3
Ben Klibreck hill U.K. 50 E2
Ben Lavin Nature Reserve S. Africa 101 I2
Ben Lawers mt. U.K. 50 E4
Ben Lomond mt. Australia 112 E3
Ben Lomond hill U.K. 50 E4
Ben Lomond National Park Australia 111 [inset]
Ben Macdui mt. U.K. 50 F3
Benmara Australia 110 B3
Ben More hill U.K. 50 C4
Ben More mt. U.K. 50 E4
Benmore, Lake N.Z. 113 C7
Ben More Assynt hill U.K. 50 E2
Bennetta, Ostrov i. Rus. Fed. 65 P2
Bennett Island Rus. Fed. see Bennetta, Ostrov
Bennett Lake Canada 120 C3
Bennettsville U.S.A. 133 E5
Ben Nevis mt. U.K. 50 D4
Bennington NH U.S.A. 135 J2
Bennington VT U.S.A. 135 I2
Benoni S. Africa 101 I4
Ben Rinnes hill U.K. 50 F3
Bensheim Germany 53 I5
Benson AZ U.S.A. 129 H6
Benson MN U.S.A. 130 E2
Benta Seberang Malaysia 71 C6
Benteng Indon. 69 G8
Bentinck Island Myanmar 71 B5
Bentiu Sudan 86 C8
Bent Jbaïl Lebanon 85 B3
Bentley U.K. 48 F5
Bento Gonçalves Brazil 145 A5
Benton AR U.S.A. 131 E5
Benton CA U.S.A. 128 D3
Benton IL U.S.A. 130 F4
Benton KY U.S.A. 131 F4
Benton LA U.S.A. 131 E5
Benton MO U.S.A. 131 F4
Benton PA U.S.A. 135 G3
Bentong Malaysia see Bentung
Benton Harbor U.S.A. 134 B2
Bentonville U.S.A. 131 E4
Bên Tre Vietnam 71 D5
Bentuang Karimun National Park Indon. 68 E6
Bentung Malaysia 71 C7
Benue r. Nigeria 96 D4
Benum, Gunung mt. Malaysia 71 C7
Ben Vorlich hill U.K. 50 E4
Benwee Head hd Rep. of Ireland 51 C3
Benwood U.S.A. 134 E3
Ben Wyvis mt. U.K. 50 E3
Benxi Liaoning China 74 A4
Benxi Liaoning China 74 B4
Beograd Serb. and Mont. see Belgrade
Béoumi Côte d'Ivoire 96 C4
Beppu Japan 75 C6
Béqaa valley Lebanon see El Béqaa
Berach r. India 82 C4
Beraketa Madag. 99 E6
Bérard, Lac l. Canada 123 H2
Berasia India 82 D5
Berat Albania 59 H4
Beravina Madag. 99 E5
Berbak National Park Indon. 68 C7
Berber Sudan 86 D6
Berbera Somalia 98 E2
Berbérati Cent. Afr. Rep. 98 B3
Berchtesgaden, Nationalpark nat. park Germany 47 N7
Berck France 52 B4
Berdichev Ukr. see Berdychiv
Berdigestyakh Rus. Fed. 65 N3
Berdyans'k Ukr. 43 H7
Berdychiv Ukr. 43 F6
Berea KY U.S.A. 134 C5
Berea OH U.S.A. 134 E3
Beregovo Ukr. see Berehove
Beregovoy Rus. Fed. 74 B1
Berehove Ukr. 43 D6
Bereina P.N.G. 69 L8
Bereket Turkm. see Gazandzhyk
Berekum Ghana 96 C4
Berenice Egypt see Baranīs
Berenice Libya see Benghazi
Berens r. Canada 121 L4
Berens Island Canada 121 L4
Berens River Canada 121 L4
Beresford U.S.A. 130 D3
Bereza Belarus see Byaroza
Berezino Belarus see Byerazino
Berezivka Ukr. 43 F7
Berezne Ukr. 43 E6
Bereznik Rus. Fed. 42 I3
Berezniki Rus. Fed. 41 R4
Berezov Rus. Fed. see Berezovo
Berezovka Rus. Fed. 74 B2
Berezovka Ukr. see Berezivka
Berezovo Rus. Fed. 41 T3
Berezovyy Rus. Fed. 74 D2
Berga Germany 53 L3
Berga Spain 57 G2
Bergama Turkey 59 L5
Bergamo Italy 58 C2
Bergby Sweden 45 J6
Bergen Mecklenburg-Vorpommern Germany 47 N3
Bergen Niedersachsen Germany 49 J2
Bergen Norway 45 D6
Bergen U.S.A. 135 G2
Bergen op Zoom Neth. 52 E3
Bergerac France 56 E4
Bergères-lès-Vertus France 52 E6
Bergheim (Erft) Germany 52 G4
Bergisches Land reg. Germany 53 H4
Bergisch Gladbach Germany 52 H4
Bergland Namibia 100 C2
Bergomum Italy see Bergamo
Bergoo U.S.A. 134 E4
Bergsjö Sweden 45 J6
Bergsviken Sweden 44 L4
Bergtheim Germany 53 K5
Bergues France 52 C4
Bergum Neth. 52 G1
Bergville S. Africa 101 I5
Berhampur India see Baharampur
Beringa, Ostrov i. Rus. Fed. 65 R4
Beringen Belgium 52 F3
Beringovskiy Rus. Fed. 65 S3
Bering Sea N. Pacific Ocean 65 S4
Bering Strait Rus. Fed./U.S.A. 65 U3
Beris, Ra's pt Iran 89 F5
Berislav Ukr. see Beryslav
Berkåk Norway 44 G5
Berkane Morocco 57 E6
Berkel r. Neth. 52 G2
Berkeley U.S.A. 128 B3
Berkeley Springs U.S.A. 135 F4
Berkhout Neth. 52 F2
Berkner Island Antarctica 152 A1
Berkovitsa Bulg. 59 J3
Berkshire Downs hills U.K. 49 F7
Berkshire Hills U.S.A. 135 I2
Berland r. Canada 120 G4
Berlare Belgium 52 E3
Berlevåg Norway 44 P1

▶Berlin Germany 53 N2
Capital of Germany.

Berlin land Germany 53 N2
Berlin MD U.S.A. 135 H4
Berlin NH U.S.A. 135 J1
Berlin PA U.S.A. 135 F4
Berlin Lake U.S.A. 134 E3
Bermagui Australia 112 E6
Bermejo r. Arg./Bol. 144 E3
Bermejo Bol. 142 F8
Bermen, Lac l. Canada 123 H3

▶Bermuda terr. N. Atlantic Ocean 137 L2
United Kingdom Overseas Territory.
North America 9, 116–117

Bermuda Rise sea feature N. Atlantic Ocean 148 D4

▶Bern Switz. 56 H3
Capital of Switzerland.

Bernalillo U.S.A. 127 G6
Bernardino de Campos Brazil 145 A3
Bernardo O'Higgins, Parque Nacional nat. park Chile 144 B7
Bernasconi Arg. 144 D5
Bernau Germany 53 N2
Bernburg (Saale) Germany 53 L3
Berne Germany 53 I1
Berne Switz. see Bern
Berne U.S.A. 134 C3
Berner Alpen mts Switz. 56 H3
Berneray i. Scotland U.K. 50 B3
Berneray i. Scotland U.K. 50 B4
Bernier Island Australia 109 A6
Bernina Pass Switz. 56 J3
Bernkastel-Kues Germany 52 H5
Beroea Greece see Veroia
Beroea Syria see Aleppo
Beroroha Madag. 99 E6
Beroun Czech Rep. 47 O6
Berounka r. Czech Rep. 47 O6
Berovina Madag. see Beravina
Berri Australia 111 C7
Berriane Alg. 54 E5
Berridale Australia 112 D6
Berriedale U.K. 50 F2
Berrigan Australia 112 B5
Berrima Australia 112 E5
Berrouaghia Alg. 57 H5
Berry Australia 112 E5
Berry U.S.A. 134 C4
Berryessa, Lake U.S.A. 128 B2
Berry Head hd U.K. 49 D8
Berry Islands Bahamas 133 E7
Berryville U.S.A. 135 G4
Berseba Namibia 100 C4
Bersenbrück Germany 53 H2
Bertam Malaysia 71 C6
Berté, Lac l. Canada 123 H4
Berthoud Pass U.S.A. 126 G5
Bertolínia Brazil 143 J5
Bertoua Cameroon 96 E4
Bertraghboy Bay Rep. of Ireland 51 C4
Beru atoll Kiribati 107 H2
Beruri Brazil 142 F4
Beruwala Sri Lanka 84 C5
Berwick Australia 112 B7
Berwick U.S.A. 135 G3
Berwick-upon-Tweed U.K. 48 E3
Berwyn hills U.K. 49 D6
Beryslav Ukr. 59 O1
Berytus Lebanon see Beirut
Besalampy Madag. 99 E5
Besançon France 56 H3
Besar, Gunung mt. Malaysia 71 C7
Besbay Kazakh. 80 A2
Beserah Malaysia 71 C7
Beshkent Uzbek. 89 G2
Beshneh Iran 88 D4
Besikama Indon. 108 D2
Besitang Indon. 71 B6
Beskra Alg. see Biskra
Beslan Rus. Fed. 91 G2
Besnard Lake Canada 121 J4
Besni Turkey 90 E3
Besor watercourse Israel 85 B4
Beşparmak Dağları mts Cyprus see Pentadaktylos Range
Bessbrook U.K. 51 F3
Bessemer U.S.A. 133 C5
Besshoky, Gora hill Kazakh. 91 I1
Besskorbnaya Rus. Fed. 43 I7
Bessonovka Rus. Fed. 43 J5
Betanzos Spain 57 B2
Bethal S. Africa 101 I4
Bethanie Namibia 100 C4
Bethany U.S.A. 130 E3
Bethel U.S.A. 123 H5
Bethel Park U.S.A. 134 E3
Bethesda U.K. 48 C5
Bethesda MD U.S.A. 135 G4
Bethesda OH U.S.A. 134 E3
Bethlehem S. Africa 101 I5
Bethlehem U.S.A. 135 H3
Bethlehem West Bank 85 B4
Bethulie S. Africa 101 G6
Béthune France 52 C4
Beti Pak. 89 H4
Betim Brazil 145 B2
Bet Lehem West Bank see Bethlehem
Betma India 82 C5
Betong Thai. 71 C6
Betoota Australia 110 C5
Betpak-Dala plain Kazakh. 80 D2
Betroka Madag. 99 E6
Bet She'an Israel 85 B3
Betsiamites Canada 123 H4
Betsiamites r. Canada 123 H4
Bettiah India 83 F4
Bettyhill U.K. 50 E2
Bettystown Rep. of Ireland 51 F4
Betul India 82 D5
Betwa r. India 82 D4
Betws-y-coed U.K. 49 D5
Betzdorf Germany 53 H4
Beulah Australia 111 C7
Beulah MI U.S.A. 134 B1
Beulah ND U.S.A. 130 C2
Beult r. U.K. 49 H7
Beuthen Poland see Bytom
Bever r. Germany 53 H2
Beverley U.K. 48 G5
Beverly MA U.S.A. 135 J2
Beverly OH U.S.A. 134 E4
Beverly Hills U.S.A. 128 D4
Beverly Lake Canada 121 K1
Beverstedt Germany 53 I1
Beverungen Germany 53 J3
Beverwijk Neth. 52 E2
Bewani P.N.G. 69 K7
Bexbach Germany 53 H5
Bexhill U.K. 49 H8
Bexley, Cape Canada 118 G3
Beyānlū Iran 88 B3
Beyce Turkey see Orhaneli
Bey Dağları mts Turkey 59 N6
Beykoz Turkey 59 M4
Beyla Guinea 96 C4
Beylagan Azer. see Beyläqan
Beyläqan Azer. 91 G3
Beyneu Kazakh. 78 E2
Beypazarı Turkey 59 N4
Beypınarı Turkey 90 E3
Beypore India 84 B4
Beyrouth Lebanon see Beirut
Beyşehir Turkey 90 C3
Beyşehir Gölü l. Turkey 90 C3
Beytonovo Rus. Fed. 74 B1
Beytüşşebap Turkey 91 F3
Bezameh Iran 88 E3
Bezbozhnik Rus. Fed. 42 K4
Bezhanitsy Rus. Fed. 42 F4
Bezhetsk Rus. Fed. 42 H4
Béziers France 56 F5
Bezmein Turkm. see Byuzmeyin
Bezwada India see Vijayawada
Bhabha India see Bhabhua
Bhabhar India 82 B4
Bhabhua India 83 E4
Bhabua India see Bhabhua
Bhachau India 82 B5
Bhachbhar India 82 B4
Bhadgaon Nepal see Bhaktapur
Bhadohi India 83 E4
Bhadra India 82 C3
Bhadrachalam Road Station India see Kottagudem
Bhadrak India 83 F5
Bhadrakh India see Bhadrak
Bhadravati India 84 B3
Bhag Pak. 89 G4
Bhagalpur India 83 F4
Bhainsa India 84 C2
Bhainsdehi India 82 D5
Bhairab Bazar Bangl. 83 G4
Bhairi Hol mt. Pak. 89 G5
Bhaktapur Nepal 83 F4
Bhalki India 84 C2
Bhamo Myanmar 70 B1
Bhamragarh India 84 D2
Bhandara India 82 D5
Bhanjanagar India 84 E2
Bhanrer Range hills India 82 D5
Bhaptiahi India 83 F4
Bharat country Asia see India
Bharatpur India 82 D4
Bhareli r. India 83 H4
Bharuch India 82 C5
Bhatapara India 83 E5
Bhatarsaigh i. U.K. see Vatersay
Bhatghar Lake India 84 B2
Bhatinda India see Bathinda
Bhatnair India see Hanumangarh
Bhatpara India 83 G5
Bhaunagar India see Bhavnagar
Bhavani r. India 84 C4
Bhavani Sagar l. India 84 C4
Bhavnagar India 82 C5
Bhawana Pak. 89 I4
Bhawanipatna India 84 D2
Bhearnaraigh, Eilean i. U.K. see Berneray
Bheemavaram India see Bhimavaram
Bhekuzulu S. Africa 101 J4
Bhera Pak. 89 I3
Bhikhna Thori Nepal 83 F4
Bhilai India 82 E5
Bhildi India 82 C4
Bhilwara India 82 C4
Bhima r. India 84 C2
Bhimar India 82 B4
Bhimavaram India 84 D2
Bhimlath India 82 E5
Bhind India 82 D4
Bhinga India 83 E4
Bhiwandi India 84 B2
Bhiwani India 82 D3
Bhogaipur India 82 D4
Bhojpur Nepal 83 F4
Bhola Bangl. 83 G5
Bhongweni S. Africa 101 I6
Bhopal India 82 D5
Bhopalpatnam India 84 D2
Bhrigukaccha India see Bharuch
Bhuban India 84 E1
Bhubaneshwar India 84 E1
Bhubaneswar India see Bhubaneshwar
Bhuj India 82 B5
Bhumiphol Dam Thai. 70 B3
Bhusawal India 82 C5
▶Bhutan country Asia 83 G4
Asia 6, 62–63
Bhuttewala India 82 B4
Bia r. Ghana 96 C4
Bia, Phou mt. Laos 70 C3
Biābān mts Iran 88 E5
Biafo Glacier Jammu and Kashmir 82 C2
Biafra, Bight of g. Africa see Benin, Bight of
Biak Indon. 69 J7
Biak i. Indon. 69 J7
Biała Podlaska Poland 43 D5
Białogard Poland 47 O4
Białystok Poland 43 D5

Bianco, Monte mt. France/Italy see Blanc, Mont
Biandangang Kou r. mouth China 77 I1
Bianzhao China 74 A3
Bianzhuang China see Cangshan
Biaora India 82 D5
Biarritz France 56 D5
Bi'ār Tabrāk well Saudi Arabia 88 B5
Bibai Japan 74 F4
Bibbenluke Australia 112 D6
Bibbiena Italy 58 D3
Bibby Island Canada 121 M2
Biberach an der Riß Germany 47 L6
Bibile Sri Lanka 84 D5
Biblis Germany 53 I5
Biblos Lebanon see Jbail
Bicas Brazil 145 C3
Biçer Turkey 59 N5
Bicester U.K. 49 F7
Bichabhera India 82 C4
Bicheng China see Bishan
Bichevaya Rus. Fed. 74 D3
Bichi r. Rus. Fed. 74 E1
Bickerton Island Australia 110 B2
Bickleigh U.K. 49 D8
Bicknell U.S.A. 134 B4
Bicuari, Parque Nacional do nat. park Angola 99 B5
Bid India 84 B2
Bida Nigeria 96 D4
Bidar India 84 C2
Biddeford U.S.A. 135 J2
Biddinghuizen Neth. 52 F2
Bidean nam Bian mt. U.K. 50 D4
Bideford U.K. 49 C7
Bideford Bay U.K. 49 C7
Bidokht Iran 88 E3
Bidzhan Rus. Fed. 74 C3
Bié Angola see Kuito
Biedenkopf Germany 53 I4
Biel Switz. 56 H3
Bielawa Poland 47 P5
Bielefeld Germany 53 I2
Bielitz Poland see Bielsko-Biała
Biella Italy 58 C2
Bielsko-Biała Poland 47 Q6
Bielstein hill Germany 53 J3
Bienenbüttel Germany 53 K1
Biên Hoa Vietnam 71 D5
Bienne Switz. see Biel
Bienville, Lac l. Canada 123 G3
Bié Plateau Angola 99 B5
Bierbank Australia 112 B1
Biesiesvlei S. Africa 101 G4
Bietigheim-Bissingen Germany 53 J6
Bièvre Belgium 52 F5
Bifoun Gabon 98 B4
Big r. Canada 123 K3
Biga Turkey 59 L4
Bigadiç Turkey 59 M5
Biga Yarımadası pen. Turkey 59 L5
Big Baldy Mountain U.S.A. 126 F3
Big Bar Creek Canada 120 F5
Big Bear Lake U.S.A. 128 E4
Big Belt Mountains U.S.A. 126 F3
Big Bend Swaziland 101 J4
Big Bend National Park U.S.A. 131 C6
Bigbury-on-Sea U.K. 49 D8
Big Canyon watercourse U.S.A. 131 C6
Biger Nuur salt l. Mongolia 80 I2
Big Falls U.S.A. 130 E1
Big Fork r. U.S.A. 130 E1
Biggar Canada 121 J4
Biggar U.K. 50 F5
Biggar, Lac l. Canada 122 G4
Bigge Island Australia 108 D3
Biggenden Australia 111 F5
Bigger, Mount Canada 120 B3
Biggesee l. Germany 53 H3
Biggleswade U.K. 49 G6
Biggs CA U.S.A. 128 C2
Biggs OR U.S.A. 126 C3
Big Hole r. U.S.A. 126 E3
Bighorn r. U.S.A. 126 G3
Bighorn Mountains U.S.A. 126 G3
Big Island Nunavut Canada 119 K3
Big Island N.W.T. Canada 120 G2
Big Island Ont. Canada 121 M5
Big Kalzas Lake Canada 120 C2
Big Lake l. Canada 121 H1
Big Lake U.S.A. 131 C6
Bignona Senegal 96 B3
Big Pine U.S.A. 128 D3
Big Pine Peak U.S.A. 128 D4
Big Raccoon r. U.S.A. 134 B4
Big Rapids U.S.A. 134 C2
Big River Canada 121 J4
Big Sable Point U.S.A. 134 B1
Big Salmon r. Canada 120 C2
Big Sand Lake Canada 121 L3
Big Sandy r. U.S.A. 126 F4
Big Sandy Lake Canada 121 J4
Big Smokey Valley U.S.A. 128 E2
Big South Fork National River and Recreation Area park U.S.A. 134 C5
Big Spring U.S.A. 131 C5
Big Stone Canada 121 I5
Big Stone Gap U.S.A. 134 D5
Bigstone Lake Canada 121 M4
Big Timber U.S.A. 126 F3
Big Trout Lake Canada 121 N4
Big Trout Lake l. Canada 121 N4
Big Valley Canada 121 H4
Big Water U.S.A. 129 H3
Bihać Bos.-Herz. 58 F2
Bihar state India 83 F4
Bihariganj India 83 F4
Bihar Sharif India 83 F4
Bihor, Vârful mt. Romania 59 J1
Bihoro Japan 74 G4
Bijagós, Arquipélago dos is Guinea-Bissau 96 B3
Bijapur India 82 D4
Bijapur India 84 B2
Bījār Iran 88 B3
Bijbehara Jammu and Kashmir 82 C2
Bijeljina Bos.-Herz. 59 H2
Bijelo Polje Serb. and Mont. 59 H3
Bijeraghogarh India 82 E5
Bijiang China see Zhiziluo
Bijie China 76 E3
Bijji India 84 D2
Bijnor India 82 D3
Bijnore India see Bijnor
Bijnot Pak. 89 H4
Bijrān well Saudi Arabia 88 C5
Bijrān, Khashm hill Saudi Arabia 88 C5
Bikampur India 82 C4
Bikaner India 82 C3
Bīkhūyeh Iran 88 D5
Bikin Rus. Fed. 74 D3
Bikin r. Rus. Fed. 74 D3
Bikini atoll Marshall Is 150 H5
Bikori Sudan 86 D7
Bikoro Dem. Rep. Congo 98 B4
Bikou China 76 E1
Bikramganj India 83 F4
Bilād Banī Bū 'Alī Oman 87 I5
Bilaigarh India 84 D1
Bilara India 82 C4
Bilaspur Chhattisgarh India 83 E5
Bilaspur Himachal Pradesh India 82 D3
Biläsuvar Azer. 91 H3
Bila Tserkva Ukr. 43 F6
Bilauktaung Range mts Myanmar/Thai. 71 B4
Bilbao Spain 57 E2
Bilbays Egypt 90 C5
Bilbeis Egypt see Bilbays
Bilbo Spain see Bilbao
Bilecik Turkey 59 M4
Biłgoraj Poland 43 D6
Bilharamulo Tanz. 98 D4
Bilhaur India 82 E4
Bilhorod-Dnistrovs'kyy Ukr. 59 N1
Bili Dem. Rep. Congo 98 C3
Bilibino Rus. Fed. 65 R3
Bilin Myanmar 70 B3
Bill U.S.A. 126 G4
Billabalong Australia 109 A6
Billabong Creek r. Australia see Moulamein Creek
Billericay U.K. 49 H7
Billiluna Australia 108 D4
Billingham U.K. 48 F4
Billings U.S.A. 126 F3
Billiton i. Indon. see Belitung
Bill of Portland hd U.K. 49 E8
Bill Williams r. U.S.A. 129 F4
Bill Williams Mountain U.S.A. 129 G4
Bilma Niger 96 E3
Bilo r. Rus. Fed. see Belaya
Biloela Australia 110 E5
Bilohirs'k Ukr. 90 D1
Bilohir"ya Ukr. 43 E6
Biloku Guyana 143 G3
Biloli India 84 C2
Bilovods'k Ukr. 43 H6
Biloxi U.S.A. 131 F6
Bilpa Morea Claypan salt flat Australia 110 B5
Bilston U.K. 50 F5
Biltine Chad 97 F3
Bilto Norway 44 L2
Bilugyun Island Myanmar 70 B3
Bilyayivka Ukr. 59 N1
Bilzen Belgium 52 F4
Bima Indon. 108 B2
Bimberi, Mount Australia 112 D5
Bimini Islands Bahamas 133 E7
Bimlipatam India 84 D2
Bināb Iran 88 C2
Bina-Etawa India 82 D4
Binaija, Gunung mt. Indon. 67 E8
Bīnālūd, Kūh-e mts Iran 88 E2
Binboğa Daği mt. Turkey 90 E3
Bincheng China see Binzhou
Binchuan China 76 D3
Bindebango Australia 112 C1
Bindle Australia 112 D1
Bindu Dem. Rep. Congo 99 B4
Bindura Zimbabwe 99 D5
Binefar Spain 57 G3
Binga Zimbabwe 99 C5
Binga, Monte mt. Moz. 99 D5
Bingara Australia 112 E2
Bingaram i. India 84 B4
Bing Bong Australia 110 B2
Bingen am Rhein Germany 53 H5
Bingham U.S.A. 135 K1
Binghamton U.S.A. 135 H2
Bingmei China see Congjiang
Bingöl Turkey 91 F3
Bingol Dağı mt. Turkey 91 F3
Bingxi China see Yushan
Bingzhongluo China 76 C2
Binh Gia Vietnam 70 D2
Binika India 83 E5
Binjai Indon. 71 B7
Bin Mūrkhan well U.A.E. 88 D5
Binnaway Australia 112 D3
Binpur India 83 F5
Bintan i. Indon. 71 D7
Bint Jbeil Lebanon see Bent Jbaïl
Bintulu Sarawak Malaysia 68 E6
Binxian Heilong. China 74 B3
Binxian Shaanxi China 77 F1
Binya Australia 112 C5
Binyang China 77 F4
Bin-Yauri Nigeria 96 D3
Binzhou Guangxi China see Binyang
Binzhou Heilong. China see Binxian
Binzhou Shandong China 73 L5
Bioco i. Equat. Guinea 96 D4
Biograd na Moru Croatia 58 F3
Bioko i. Equat. Guinea see Bioco
Biokovo mts Croatia 58 G3
Biquinhas Brazil 145 B2
Bir India see Bid
Bira Rus. Fed. 74 D2
Bi'r Abū Jady oasis Syria 85 D1
Bīrag, Kūh-e mts Iran 89 F5
Birāk Libya 97 E2
Birakan Rus. Fed. 74 C2
Bi'r al 'Abd Egypt 85 A4
Bi'r al Halbā well Syria 85 D2
Bi'r al Jifjāfah well Egypt 85 A4
Bi'r al Khamsah well Egypt 90 B5
Bi'r al Mālihah well Egypt 85 A5
Bi'r al Mulūsi Iraq 91 F4
Bi'r al Munbatih well Syria 85 D2
Bi'r al Qatrānī well Egypt 90 B5
Bi'r al Ubbayid well Egypt 90 B6
Birandozero Rus. Fed. 42 H3
Bi'r an Nuşf well Egypt see Bi'r an Nuşş
Bi'r an Nuşş well Egypt 90 B5
Bir Anzarane W. Sahara 96 B2
Birao Cent. Afr. Rep. 98 C2
Bi'r ar Rābiyah well Egypt 90 B5
Biratnagar Nepal 83 F4
Bi'r aţ Ţarfāwī well Libya 90 B5
Bi'r Başīrī well Syria 85 C2
Bi'r Baydā' well Egypt 85 B4
Bi'r Baylī well Egypt 90 B5
Bîr Beida well Egypt see Bi'r Baydā'
Bi'r Buţaymān Syria 91 E3
Birch r. Canada 121 H3
Birch Hills Canada 121 J4
Birch Island Canada 120 G5
Birch Lake N.W.T. Canada 120 G2
Birch Lake Ont. Canada 121 M5
Birch Lake Sask. Canada 121 I4
Birch Mountains Canada 120 H3
Birch River U.S.A. 134 E4
Birch Run U.S.A. 134 D2
Bircot Eth. 98 E3
Birdaard Neth. 52 F1
Bîr Dignâsh well Egypt see Bi'r Diqnāsh
Bi'r Diqnāsh well Egypt 90 B5
Bird Island N. Mariana Is see Farallon de Medinilla
Birdseye U.S.A. 129 H2
Birdsville Australia 111 B5
Birecik Turkey 90 E3
Bîr el 'Abd Egypt see Bi'r al 'Abd
Bir el Arbi well Alg. 57 I6
Bîr el Istabl well Egypt see Bi'r Iştabl
Bîr el Khamsa well Egypt see Bi'r al Khamsah
Bîr el Nuşş well Egypt see Bi'r an Nuşş
Bîr el Obeiyid well Egypt see Bi'r al Ubbayid
Bîr el Qatrâni well Egypt see Bi'r al Qaţrānī
Bîr el Râbia well Egypt see Bi'r ar Rābiyah
Birendranagar Nepal see Surkhet
Bir en Natrûn well Sudan 86 C6
Bireun Indon. 71 B6
Bi'r Fādil well Saudi Arabia 88 C6
Bi'r Fajr well Saudi Arabia 90 E5
Bi'r Fu'ād well Egypt 90 B5
Bîr Gifgâfa well Egypt see Bi'r al Jifjāfah
Bi'r Ḩajal well Syria 85 D2
Birhan mt. Eth. 98 D2
Bi'r Ḩasanah well Egypt 85 A4
Bi'r Ḩayzān well Saudi Arabia 90 E6
Bi'r Ibn Hirmās Saudi Arabia see Al Bi'r
Bi'r Ibn Juhayyim Saudi Arabia 88 C6
Birigüi Brazil 145 A3
Bīrīn Syria 85 C2
Bi'r Iştabl well Egypt 90 B5
Bīrjand Iran 88 E3
Bi'r Jubnī well Libya 90 B5
Birkát Hamad well Iraq 91 G5
Birkenfeld Germany 53 H5
Birkenhead U.K. 48 D5
Birkirkara Malta 58 F7
Birksgate Range hills Australia 109 E6
Bîrlad Romania see Bârlad
Bi'r Lahfān well Egypt 85 A4
Birlik Kazakh. see Brlik
Birmal reg. Afgh. 89 H3
Birmingham U.K. 49 F6
Birmingham U.S.A. 133 C5
Bîr Mogreïn Mauritania 96 B2
Bi'r Muhaymid al Wazwaz well Syria 85 D2
Bi'r Nāhid oasis Egypt 90 C5
Birnin-Gwari Nigeria 96 D3
Birnin-Kebbi Nigeria 96 D3
Birnin Konni Niger 96 D3
Birobidzhan Rus. Fed. 74 D2
Bi'r Qaşīr as Sirr well Egypt 90 B5
Birr Rep. of Ireland 51 E4
Bi'r Rawḑ Sālim well Egypt 85 A4
Birrie r. Australia 112 C2
Birrindudu Australia 108 E4
Bîr Rôd Sâlim well Egypt see Bi'r Rawḑ Sālim
Birsay U.K. 50 F1
Bi'r Shalatayn Egypt 86 E5
Bîr Shalatein Egypt see Bi'r Shalatayn
Birsk Rus. Fed. 41 R4
Birstall U.K. 49 F6
Birstein Germany 53 J4
Bir Talhah well Saudi Arabia 88 B6
Birthday Mountain hill Australia 110 C2
Birtle Canada 121 K5
Biru China 76 B2
Birur India 84 B3
Bi'r Usaylīlah well Saudi Arabia 88 B6
Biruxiong China see Biru
Biržai Lith. 45 N8
Bisa India 70 A1
Bisa i. Indon. 69 H7
Bisalpur India 82 D3
Bisau India 82 C3
Bisbee U.S.A. 127 F7
Biscay, Bay of sea France/Spain 56 B4
Biscay Abyssal Plain sea feature N. Atlantic Ocean 148 H3
Biscayne National Park U.S.A. 133 D7
Biscoe Islands Antarctica 152 L2
Biscotasi Lake Canada 122 E5
Biscotasing Canada 122 E5
Bisezhai China 76 D4
Bishan China 76 E2
Bishbek Kyrg. see Bishkek
Bishenpur India see Bishnupur

▶Bishkek Kyrg. 80 D3
Capital of Kyrgyzstan.

Bishnath India 76 B3
Bishnupur Manipur India 83 H4
Bishnupur W. Bengal India 83 F5
Bisho S. Africa 101 H7
Bishop U.S.A. 128 D3
Bishop Auckland U.K. 48 F4
Bishop Lake Canada 120 G1
Bishop's Stortford U.K. 49 H7
Bishopville U.S.A. 133 D5
Bishrī, Jabal hills Syria 85 D2
Bishui Heilong. China 74 A1
Bishui Henan China see Biyang
Biskra Alg. 54 F5
Bislig Phil. 69 H5

▶Bismarck U.S.A. 130 C2
State capital of North Dakota.

Bismarck Archipelago is P.N.G. 69 L7
Bismarck Range mts P.N.G. 69 K7
Bismarck Sea P.N.G. 69 L7
Bismark (Altmark) Germany 53 L2
Bismil Turkey 91 F3
Bismo Norway 44 F6
Bison U.S.A. 130 C2
Bispgården Sweden 44 J5
Bispingen Germany 53 K1
Bissa, Djebel mt. Alg. 57 G5
Bissamcuttak India 84 D2

▶Bissau Guinea-Bissau 96 B3
Capital of Guinea-Bissau.

Bissaula Nigeria 96 E4
Bissett Canada 121 M5
Bistcho Lake Canada 120 G3
Bistrița Romania 59 K1
Bistrița r. Romania 59 L1
Bitburg Germany 52 G5
Bitche France 53 H5
Bithur India 82 E4
Bithynia reg. Turkey 59 M4
Bitkine Chad 97 E3
Bitlis Turkey 91 F3
Bitola Macedonia 59 I4
Bitolj Macedonia see Bitola
Bitonto Italy 58 G4
Bitrān, Jabal hill Saudi Arabia 84 B6
Bitra Par reef India 84 B4
Bitter Creek r. U.S.A. 129 I2
Bitterfeld Germany 53 M3
Bitterfontein S. Africa 100 D6
Bitter Lakes Egypt 90 D5
Bitterroot r. U.S.A. 126 E3
Bitterroot Range mts U.S.A. 126 E3
Bitterwater U.S.A. 128 C3
Bittkau Germany 53 L2
Bitung Indon. 69 H6
Biu Nigeria 96 E3
Biwa-ko l. Japan 75 D6
Biwmaris U.K. see Beaumaris
Biyang China 77 G1
Bīye K'obē Eth. 98 E2
Biysk Rus. Fed. 72 F2
Bizana S. Africa 101 I6
Bizerta Tunisia see Bizerte
Bizerte Tunisia 58 C6
Bīzhanābād Iran 88 E5

▶Bjargtangar hd Iceland 44 [inset]
Most westerly point of Europe.

Bjästa Sweden 44 K5
Bjelovar Croatia 58 G2
Bjerkvik Norway 44 J2
Bjerringbro Denmark 45 F8
Bjørgan Norway 44 G5
Björkliden Sweden 44 K2
Björklinge Sweden 45 J6
Bjorli Norway 44 F5
Björna Sweden 44 K5
Björneborg Fin. see Pori

▶Bjørnøya i. Arctic Ocean 64 C2
Part of Norway.

Bjurholm Sweden 44 K5
Bla Mali 96 C3
Black r. Man. Canada 121 L5
Black r. Ont. Canada 122 E4
Black r. AR U.S.A. 131 F5
Black r. AR U.S.A. 131 F5
Black r. AZ U.S.A. 129 H5
Black r. Vietnam 70 D2
Blackadder Water r. U.K. 50 G5
Blackall Australia 110 D5
Blackbear r. Canada 121 N4
Black Birch Lake Canada 121 J3
Black Bourton U.K. 49 F7
Blackbull Australia 110 C3
Blackburn U.K. 48 E5
Blackbutt Australia 112 F1
Black Butte mt. U.S.A. 128 B2
Black Butte Lake U.S.A. 128 B2
Black Canyon gorge U.S.A. 129 F4
Black Canyon of the Gunnison National Park U.S.A. 129 J2
Black Combe hill U.K. 48 D4
Black Creek watercourse U.S.A. 129 I4
Black Donald Lake Canada 135 G1
Blackdown Tableland National Park Australia 110 E4
Blackduck U.S.A. 130 E2
Blackfalds Canada 120 H4
Blackfoot U.S.A. 126 E4
Black Foot r. U.S.A. 126 E3
Black Forest mts Germany 47 L7
Black Hill hill U.K. 48 F5
Black Hills SD U.S.A. 124 G3
Black Hills SD U.S.A. 126 G3
Black Island Canada 121 L5
Black Lake Canada 121 J3
Black Lake l. Canada 121 J3
Black Lake l. U.S.A. 134 C1
Black Mesa mt. U.S.A. 129 I5
Black Mesa ridge U.S.A. 129 H3
Black Mountain Pak. 89 I3
Black Mountain hill U.K. 49 D7
Black Mountain AK U.S.A. 118 B3
Black Mountain CA U.S.A. 128 E4
Black Mountain KY U.S.A. 134 D5
Black Mountain NM U.S.A. 129 I5
Black Mountains hills U.K. 49 D7
Black Mountains U.S.A. 129 F4
Black Nossob watercourse Namibia 100 D2
Black Pagoda India see Konarka
Blackpool U.K. 48 D5
Black Range mts U.S.A. 129 I5
Black River MI U.S.A. 134 D1
Black River NY U.S.A. 135 H1
Black River Falls U.S.A. 130 F2
Black Rock hill Jordan see 'Unāb, Jabal al
Black Rock Desert U.S.A. 126 D4
Blacksburg U.S.A. 134 E5
Black Sea Asia/Europe 43 H8
Blacks Fork r. U.S.A. 126 F4
Blackshear U.S.A. 133 D6
Blacksod Bay Rep. of Ireland 51 B3
Black Springs U.S.A. 128 D2
Blackstairs Mountains hills Rep. of Ireland 51 F5
Blackstone U.S.A. 135 F5
Black Sugarloaf mt. Australia 112 E3
Black Tickle Canada 123 L3
Blackville Australia 112 E3
Blackwater Australia 110 E4
Blackwater Rep. of Ireland 51 F5
Blackwater r. Rep. of Ireland 51 E5
Blackwater r. Rep. of Ireland/U.K. 51 F3
Blackwater watercourse U.S.A. 131 C5
Blackwater Lake Canada 120 F2
Blackwater Reservoir U.K. 50 E4
Blackwood r. Australia 109 A8
Blackwood National Park Australia 110 D4
Bladensburg National Park Australia 110 C4
Blaenavon U.K. 49 D7
Blagodarnyy Rus. Fed. 91 F1
Blagoevgrad Bulg. 59 J3
Blagoveshchensk Amurskaya Oblast' Rus. Fed. 74 B2
Blagoveshchensk Respublika Bashkortostan Rus. Fed. 41 R4
Blaikiston, Mount Canada 120 H5
Blaine Lake Canada 121 J4
Blair U.S.A. 130 D3
Blair Athol Australia 110 D4
Blair Atholl U.K. 50 F4
Blairgowrie U.K. 50 F4
Blairsden U.S.A. 128 C2
Blairsville U.S.A. 133 D5
Blakang Mati, Pulau i. Sing. see Sentosa
Blakely U.S.A. 133 C6
Blakeney U.K. 49 I6

▶Blanc, Mont mt. France/Italy 56 H4
5th highest mountain in Europe.

Blanca, Bahía b. Arg. 144 D5
Blanca, Sierra mt. U.S.A. 127 G6
Blanca Peak U.S.A. 127 G5
Blanche, Lake salt flat S.A. Australia 111 B6
Blanche, Lake salt flat W.A. Australia 108 C5
Blanchester U.S.A. 134 D4
Blanc Nez, Cap c. France 52 B4
Blanco r. Bol. 142 F6
Blanco U.S.A. 129 J3
Blanco, Cape U.S.A. 126 B4
Blanc-Sablon Canada 123 K4
Bland r. Australia 112 C4
Bland U.S.A. 134 E5
Blanda r. Iceland 44 [inset]
Blandford Forum U.K. 49 E8
Blanding U.S.A. 129 I3
Blanes Spain 57 H3
Blangah, Telok Sing. 71 [inset]
Blangkejeren Indon. 71 B7
Blangpidie Indon. 71 B7
Blankenberge Belgium 52 D3
Blankenheim Germany 52 G4
Blanquilla, Isla i. Venez. 142 F1
Blansko Czech Rep. 47 P6
Blantyre Malawi 99 D5
Blarney Rep. of Ireland 51 D6
Blaufelden Germany 53 J5
Blåviksjön Sweden 44 K4
Blaye France 56 D4
Blayney Australia 112 D4
Blaze, Point Australia 108 E3
Bleckede Germany 53 K1
Bleilochtalsperre resr Germany 53 L4
Blenheim Canada 134 E2
Blenheim N.Z. 113 D5
Blenheim Palace tourist site U.K. 49 F7
Blerick Neth. 52 G3
Blessington Lakes Rep. of Ireland 51 F4
Bletchley U.K. 49 G6
Blida Alg. 57 H5
Blies r. Germany 53 H5
Bligh Water b. Fiji 107 H3
Blind River Canada 122 E5
Bliss U.S.A. 126 E4
Blissfield U.S.A. 134 D3
Blitta Togo 96 D4
Blocher U.S.A. 134 C4
Block Island U.S.A. 135 J3
Block Island Sound sea chan. U.S.A. 135 J3
Bloemfontein S. Africa 101 H5
Bloemhof S. Africa 101 G4
Bloemhof Dam S. Africa 101 G4
Bloemhof Dam Nature Reserve S. Africa 101 G4
Blomberg Germany 53 J3
Blönduós Iceland 44 [inset]
Blongas Indon. 108 B2
Bloods Range mts Australia 109 E6
Bloodsworth Island U.S.A. 135 G4
Bloodvein r. Canada 121 L5
Bloody Foreland pt Rep. of Ireland 51 D2
Bloomer U.S.A. 130 F2
Bloomfield Canada 135 G2
Bloomfield IA U.S.A. 130 E3
Bloomfield IN U.S.A. 134 B4
Bloomfield MO U.S.A. 131 F4
Bloomfield NM U.S.A. 129 J3
Blooming Prairie U.S.A. 130 E3
Bloomington IL U.S.A. 130 F3
Bloomington IN U.S.A. 134 B4
Bloomington MN U.S.A. 130 E2
Bloomsburg U.S.A. 135 G3
Blossburg U.S.A. 135 G3
Blosseville Kyst coastal area Greenland 119 P3
Blouberg S. Africa 101 I2
Blouberg Nature Reserve S. Africa 101 I2
Blountstown U.S.A. 133 C6
Blountville U.S.A. 134 D5
Bloxham U.K. 49 F6
Blue r. Canada 120 D3
Blue watercourse U.S.A. 129 I5
Blue Bell Knoll mt. U.S.A. 129 H2
Blueberry r. Canada 120 F3
Blue Diamond U.S.A. 129 F3
Blue Earth U.S.A. 130 E3
Bluefield VA U.S.A. 132 D4
Bluefield WV U.S.A. 134 E5
Bluefields Nicaragua 137 H6
Blue Hills Turks and Caicos Is 129 F8
Blue Knob hill U.S.A. 135 F3
Blue Mesa Reservoir U.S.A. 129 J2
Blue Mountain hill Canada 123 K4
Blue Mountain India 83 H5
Blue Mountain Lake U.S.A. 135 H2
Blue Mountain Pass Lesotho 101 H5
Blue Mountains Australia 112 D4
Blue Mountains U.S.A. 126 D3
Blue Mountains National Park Australia 112 E4
Blue Nile r. Eth./Sudan 86 D6
also known as Ābay Wenz (Ethiopia), Bahr el Azraq (Sudan)
Bluenose Lake Canada 118 G3
Blue Ridge GA U.S.A. 133 C5
Blue Ridge VA U.S.A. 134 F5
Blue Ridge mts U.S.A. 134 E5
Blue Stack hill Rep. of Ireland 51 D3
Blue Stack Mts hills Rep. of Ireland 51 D3
Bluestone Lake U.S.A. 134 E5
Bluewater U.S.A. 129 J4
Bluff N.Z. 113 B8
Bluff U.S.A. 129 I3
Bluffdale U.S.A. 129 H1
Bluff Island Hong Kong China 73 [inset]
Bluff Knoll mt. Australia 109 B8
Bluffton IN U.S.A. 134 C3
Bluffton OH U.S.A. 134 D3
Blumenau Brazil 145 A4
Blustry Mountain Canada 126 C2
Blyde River Canyon Nature Reserve S. Africa 101 J3
Blyth Canada 134 E2
Blyth England U.K. 48 F3
Blyth England U.K. 48 F5
Blythe U.S.A. 129 F5
Blytheville U.S.A. 131 F5
Bø Norway 45 F7
Bo Sierra Leone 96 B4
Boa Esperança Brazil 145 B3
Bo'ai Henan China 77 G1
Bo'ai Yunnan China 76 E4
Boali Cent. Afr. Rep. 98 B3
Boalsert Neth. see Bolsward
Boane Moz. 101 K4
Boa Nova Brazil 145 C1
Boardman U.S.A. 134 E3
Boatlaname Botswana 101 G2
Boa Viagem Brazil 143 K5
Boa Vista Brazil 142 F3
Boa Vista i. Cape Verde 96 [inset]
Bobadah Australia 112 C4
Bobai China 77 F4
Bobaomby, Tanjona c. Madag. 99 E5
Bobbili India 84 D2
Bobcaygeon Canada 135 F1
Bobo-Dioulasso Burkina 96 C3
Bobotov Kuk mt. Serb. and Mont. see Durmitor
Bobriki Rus. Fed. see Novomoskovsk
Bobrinets Ukr. see Bobrynets'
Bobrov Rus. Fed. 43 I6
Bobrovitsa Ukr. see Bobrovytsya
Bobrovytsya Ukr. 43 F6
Bobruysk Belarus see Babruysk
Bobrynets' Ukr. 43 G6
Bobs Lake Canada 135 G1
Bobuk Sudan 86 D7
Bobures Venez. 142 D2
Boby mt. Madag. 99 E6
Boca de Macareo Venez. 142 F2
Boca do Acre Brazil 142 E5
Boca do Jari Brazil 143 H4
Bocaiúva Brazil 145 C2
Bocaranga Cent. Afr. Rep. 98 B3
Boca Raton U.S.A. 133 D7
Bocas del Toro Panama 137 H7
Bochnia Poland 47 R6
Bocholt Germany 52 G3
Bochum Germany 53 H3
Bochum S. Africa 101 I2
Bockenem Germany 53 K2
Bocoio Angola 99 B5
Bocoyna Mex. 127 G8
Boda Cent. Afr. Rep. 98 B3
Bodalla Australia 112 E6
Bodallin Australia 109 B7
Bodaybo Rus. Fed. 65 M4
Boddam U.K. 50 H3
Bode r. Germany 53 L3
Bodega Head hd U.S.A. 128 B2
Bodélé reg. Chad 97 E3
Boden Sweden 44 L4
Bodenham U.K. 49 E6
Bodensee l. Germany/Switz. see Constance, Lake
Bodenteich Germany 53 K2
Bodenwerder Germany 53 J3
Bodie U.S.A. 128 D2
Bodinayakkanur India 84 C4
Bodmin U.K. 49 C8
Bodmin Moor moorland U.K. 49 C8
Bodø Norway 44 I3
Bodoquena Brazil 143 G7
Bodoquena, Serra da hills Brazil 144 E2
Bodrum Turkey 59 L6
Bodträskfors Sweden 44 L3
Boechout Belgium 52 E3
Boende Dem. Rep. Congo 97 F5
Boerne U.S.A. 131 D6
Boeuf r. U.S.A. 131 F6
Boffa Guinea 96 B3
Bogalay Myanmar see Bogale
Bogale Myanmar 70 A3
Bogale r. Myanmar 70 A4
Bogalusa U.S.A. 131 F6
Bogan r. Australia 112 C2
Bogandé Burkina 96 C3
Bogan Gate Australia 112 C4
Bogani Nani Wartabone National Park Indon. 69 G6
Boğazlıyan Turkey 90 D3
Bogcang Zangbo r. China 83 F3
Bogda Shan mts China 80 G3
Boggabilla Australia 112 E2
Boggabri Australia 112 E3
Boggeragh Mts hills Rep. of Ireland 51 C5
Boghar Alg. 57 H6
Boghari Alg. see Ksar el Boukhari

Bognor Regis U.K. 49 G8
Bogodukhov Ukr. see Bohodukhiv
Bog of Allen reg. Rep. of Ireland 51 E4
Bogong, Mount Australia 112 C6
Bogopol' Rus. Fed. 74 D3
Bogor Indon. 68 D8
Bogoroditsk Rus. Fed. 43 H5
Bogorodsk Rus. Fed. 42 I4
Bogorodskoye *Khabarovskiy Kray* Rus. Fed. 74 F1
Bogorodskoye *Kirovskaya Oblast'* Rus. Fed. 42 K4

▶Bogotá Col. 142 D3
Capital of Colombia and 5th most populous city in South America.

Bogotol Rus. Fed. 64 J4
Bogoyavlenskoye Rus. Fed. see Pervomayskiy
Bogra Bangl. 83 G4
Boguchany Rus. Fed. 65 K4
Boguchar Rus. Fed. 43 I6
Bogué Mauritania 96 B3
Bo Hai g. China 73 L5
Bohain-en-Vermandois France 52 D5
Bohai Wan b. China 66 D4
Bohemia reg. Czech Rep. 47 N6
Bohemian Forest mts Germany see Böhmer Wald
Böhlen Germany 53 M3
Bohlokong S. Africa 101 I5
Böhme r. Germany 53 J2
Böhmer Wald mts Germany 53 M5
Bohmte Germany 53 I2
Bohodukhiv Ukr. 43 G6
Bohol i. Phil. 69 G5
Bohol Sea Phil. 69 G5
Böhöt Mongolia 73 J3
Bohu China 80 G3
Boiaçu Brazil 142 F4
Boichoko S. Africa 100 F5
Boigu Island Australia 69 K8
Boikhutso S. Africa 101 H4
Boileau, Cape Australia 108 C4
Boim Brazil 143 G4
Boipeba, Ilha i. Brazil 145 D1
Bois r. Brazil 145 A2
Bois Blanc Island U.S.A. 132 C2

▶Boise U.S.A. 126 D4
State capital of Idaho.

Boise City U.S.A. 131 C4
Boissevain Canada 121 K5
Boitumelong S. Africa 101 G4
Boizenburg Germany 53 K1
Bojd Iran 88 E3
Bojnūrd Iran 88 E2
Bokaak atoll Marshall Is see Taongi
Bokajan India 83 H4
Bokaro India 83 F5
Bokaro Reservoir India 83 F5
Bokatola Dem. Rep. Congo 98 B4
Boké Guinea 96 B3
Bokele Dem. Rep. Congo 98 C4
Bokhara r. Australia 112 C2
Bo Kheo Cambodia see Bâ Kêv
Boknafjorden sea chan. Norway 45 D7
Bokoko Dem. Rep. Congo 98 C3
Bokoro Chad 97 E3
Bokovskaya Rus. Fed. 43 I6
Bokspits S. Africa 100 E4
Boktor Rus. Fed. 74 E2
Bokurdak Turkm. see Bakhardok
Bol Chad 97 E3
Bolaiti Dem. Rep. Congo 97 F5
Bolama Guinea-Bissau 96 B3
Bolangir India 84 D1
Bolan Pass Pak. 89 G4
Bolbec France 56 E2
Bole China 80 F3
Bole Ghana 96 C4
Boleko Dem. Rep. Congo 98 B4
Bolen Rus. Fed. 74 D2
Bolgar Rus. Fed. 43 K5
Bolgatanga Ghana 96 C3
Bolgrad Ukr. see Bolhrad
Bolhrad Ukr. 59 M2
Boli China 74 C3
Bolia Dem. Rep. Congo 98 B4
Boliden Sweden 44 L4
Bolingbrook U.S.A. 134 A3
Bolintin-Vale Romania 59 K2
Bolívar Peru 142 C5
Bolivar NY U.S.A. 135 F2
Bolivar TN U.S.A. 131 F5
Bolívar, Pico mt. Venez. 142 D2
Bolivia Cuba 133 E8

▶Bolivia country S. America 142 E7
5th largest country in South America.
South America 9, 140–141

Bolkhov Rus. Fed. 43 H5
Bollène France 56 G4
Bollnäs Sweden 45 J6
Bollon Australia 112 C2
Bollstabruk Sweden 44 J5
Bolmen l. Sweden 45 H8
Bolobo Dem. Rep. Congo 98 B4
Bologna Italy 58 D2
Bolognesi Peru 142 D5
Bologoye Rus. Fed. 42 G4
Bolokanang S. Africa 101 G5
Bolomba Dem. Rep. Congo 98 B3
Bolon' Rus. Fed. see Achan
Bolovens, Phouphieng plat. Laos 70 D4
Bolpur India 83 F5
Bolsena, Lago di l. Italy 58 D3
Bol'shakovo Rus. Fed. 45 L9
Bol'shaya Chernigovka Rus. Fed. 41 Q5
Bol'shaya Glushitsa Rus. Fed. 43 K5
Bol'shaya Imandra, Ozero l. Rus. Fed. 44 R3
Bol'shaya Martinovka Rus. Fed. 39 I7
Bol'shaya Tsarevshchina Rus. Fed. see Volzhskiy
Bol'shenarymskoye Kazakh. 80 F2
Bol'shevik, Ostrov i. Rus. Fed. 65 L2
Bol'shezemel'skaya Tundra lowland Rus. Fed. 42 L2
Bol'shiye Barsuki, Peski des. Kazakh. 80 A2
Bol'shiye Chirki Rus. Fed. 42 J3
Bol'shiye Kozly Rus. Fed. 42 H2
Bol'shoy Aluy r. Rus. Fed. 65 Q3
Bol'shoy Begichev, Ostrov i. Rus. Fed. 153 E2
Bol'shoye Murashkino Rus. Fed. 42 J5
Bol'shoy Irgiz r. Rus. Fed. 43 J6
Bol'shoy Kamen' Rus. Fed. 74 D4
Bol'shoy Kavkaz mts Asia/Europe see Caucasus
Bol'shoy Kundysh r. Rus. Fed. 42 J4
Bol'shoy Lyakhovskiy, Ostrov i. Rus. Fed. 65 P2
Bol'shoy Tokmak Kyrg. see Tokmok
Bol'shoy Tokmak Ukr. see Tokmak
Bolsward Neth. 52 F1
Bolton Canada 134 F2
Bolton U.K. 48 E5
Bolu Turkey 59 N4
Boluntay China 83 H1
Boluo China 77 G4
Bolus Head hd Rep. of Ireland 51 B6
Bolvadin Turkey 59 N5
Bolzano Italy 58 D1
Boma Dem. Rep. Congo 99 B4
Bomaderry Australia 112 E5
Bombala Australia 112 D6
Bombay India see Mumbai
Bombay Beach U.S.A. 129 F5
Bomberai, Semenanjung pen. Indon. 69 I7
Bomboma Dem. Rep. Congo 98 B3
Bom Comércio Brazil 142 E5
Bomdila India 83 H4
Bomi China 76 B2
Bomili Dem. Rep. Congo 98 C3
Bom Jardim Brazil 145 D1
Bom Jardim de Goiás Brazil 145 A2
Bom Jesus Brazil 145 A5
Bom Jesus da Gurgueia, Serra do hills Brazil 143 J5
Bom Jesus da Lapa Brazil 145 C1
Bom Jesus do Norte Brazil 145 C3
Bømlo i. Norway 45 D7
Bomokandi r. Dem. Rep. Congo 98 C3
Bom Retiro Brazil 145 A4
Bom Sucesso Brazil 145 B3
Bon, Cap c. Tunisia 58 D6
Bon, Ko i. Thai. 71 B5
Bona Alg. see Annaba
Bona, Mount U.S.A. 120 A2
Bonāb Iran 88 B2
Bon Air U.S.A. 135 G5
Bonaire i. Neth. Antilles 137 K6
Bonanza Peak U.S.A. 126 C2
Bonaparte Archipelago is Australia 108 D3
Bonaparte Lake Canada 120 F5
Bonar Bridge U.K. 50 E3
Bonavista Canada 123 L4
Bonavista Bay Canada 123 L4
Bonchester Bridge U.K. 50 G5
Bondo Dem. Rep. Congo 98 C3
Bondokodi Indon. 68 F8
Bondoukou Côte d'Ivoire 96 C4
Bonduel U.S.A. 134 A1
Bondyuzhskiy Rus. Fed. see Mendeleyevsk
Bône Alg. see Annaba
Bone, Teluk b. Indon. 69 G8
Bönen Germany 53 H3
Bonerate, Kepulauan is Indon. 108 C1
Bo'ness U.K. 50 F4

▶Bonete, Cerro mt. Arg. 144 C3
3rd highest mountain in South America.

Bonga Eth. 98 D3
Bongaigaon India 83 G4
Bongandanga Dem. Rep. Congo 98 C3
Bongani S. Africa 100 F5
Bongao Phil. 68 F5
Bongba China 82 E2
Bong Co l. China 83 G3
Bongo, Massif des mts Cent. Afr. Rep. 98 C3
Bongo, Serra do mts Angola 99 B4
Bongolava mts Madag. 99 E5
Bongor Chad 97 E3
Bông Sơn Vietnam 71 E4
Bonham U.S.A. 131 D5
Bonheiden Belgium 52 E3
Boni Mali 96 C3
Bonifacio Corsica France 56 I6
Bonifacio, Bocche di strait France/Italy see Bonifacio, Strait of
Bonifacio, Bouches de strait France/Italy see Bonifacio, Strait of
Bonifacio, Strait of France/Italy 56 I6

▶Bonin Islands Japan 75 F8
Part of Japan.

▶Bonn Germany 52 H4
Former capital of Germany.

Bonna Germany see Bonn
Bonnåsjøen Norway 44 I3
Bonners Ferry U.S.A. 126 D2
Bonnet, Lac du resr Canada 117 M5
Bonneville France 56 H3
Bonneville Salt Flats U.S.A. 129 G1
Bonnières-sur-Seine France 52 B5
Bonnie Rock Australia 109 B7
Bonnieville U.S.A. 134 C5
Bonnyrigg U.K. 50 F5
Bonnyville Canada 121 I4
Bonobono Phil. 68 F5
Bonom Mhai mt. Vietnam 71 D5
Bononia Italy see Bologna
Bonorva Sardinia Italy 58 C4
Bonshaw Australia 112 E2
Bontebok National Park S. Africa 100 E8
Bonthe Sierra Leone 96 B4
Bontoc Phil. 77 I5
Bontosunggu Indon. 68 F8
Bontrug S. Africa 101 G7
Bonvouloir Islands P.N.G. 110 E1
Bonwapitse Botswana 101 H2
Boo, Kepulauan is Indon. 69 H7
Book Cliffs ridge U.S.A. 129 I2
Booker U.S.A. 131 C4
Boolba Australia 112 D2
Booligal Australia 112 B4
Boomer U.S.A. 134 E4
Boomi Australia 112 D2
Boon U.S.A. 134 C1
Boonah Australia 112 F1
Boone CO U.S.A. 127 G5
Boone IA U.S.A. 130 E3
Boone NC U.S.A. 132 D4
Boone Lake U.S.A. 134 D5
Boones Mill U.S.A. 134 F5
Booneville AR U.S.A. 131 E5
Booneville KY U.S.A. 134 D5
Booneville MS U.S.A. 131 F5
Böön Tsagaan Nuur salt l. Mongolia 80 I2
Boonville CA U.S.A. 128 B2
Boonville IN U.S.A. 134 B4
Boonville MO U.S.A. 130 E4
Boonville NY U.S.A. 135 H2
Boorabin National Park Australia 109 C7
Boorama Somalia 98 E3
Booroorban Australia 112 B5
Boorowa Australia 112 D5
Boort Australia 112 A6
Boothby, Cape Antarctica 152 D2
Boothia, Gulf of Canada 119 J3
Boothia Peninsula Canada 119 I2
Bootle U.K. 48 E5
Booué Gabon 98 B4
Boppard Germany 53 H4
Boqê China 83 G3
Boqueirão, Serra do hills Brazil 143 J6
Bor Czech Rep. 53 M5
Bor Rus. Fed. 42 J4
Bor Sudan 97 G4
Bor Turkey 90 D3
Bor Serb. and Mont. 59 J2
Boraha, Nosy i. Madag. 99 F5
Borah Peak U.S.A. 126 E3
Borai India 84 D1
Borakalalo Nature Reserve S. Africa 101 H3
Boran Kazakh. see Buran
Boraphet, Bung l. Thai. 70 C4
Boraphet, Nong l. Thai. see Boraphet, Bung
Borås Sweden 45 H8
Borasambar India 84 D1
Borāzjān Iran 88 C4
Borba Brazil 143 G4
Borba China 76 C1
Borborema, Planalto da plat. Brazil 143 K5
Borchen Germany 53 I3
Borçka Turkey 91 F2
Bor Dağı mt. Turkey 59 M6
Bordeaux France 56 D4
Borden Island Canada 119 G2
Borden Peninsula Canada 119 J2
Border Ranges National Park Australia 112 F2
Borðeyri Iceland 44 [inset]
Bordj Bou Arréridj Alg. 57 I5
Bordj Bounaama Alg. 57 G6
Bordj Flye Ste-Marie Alg. 96 C2
Bordj Messaouda Alg. 54 F5
Bordj Mokhtar Alg. 96 D2
Bordj Omar Driss Alg. see Bordj Omer Driss
Bordj Omer Driss Alg. 96 D2
Boreas Abyssal Plain sea feature Arctic Ocean 153 H1
Borel r. Canada 123 H2
Borgå Fin. see Porvoo
Borgarfjörður Iceland 44 [inset]
Borgarnes Iceland 44 [inset]
Børgefjell Nasjonalpark nat. park Norway 44 H4
Borger U.S.A. 131 C5
Borgholm Sweden 45 J8
Borgne, Lake b. U.S.A. 131 F6
Borgo San Lorenzo Italy 58 D3
Bori India 84 C1
Bori r. India 82 C5
Borikhan Laos 70 C3
Borislav Ukr. see Boryslav
Borisoglebsk Rus. Fed. 43 I6
Borisov Belarus see Barysaw
Borisovka Rus. Fed. 43 H6
Borispol' Ukr. see Boryspil'
Bo River Post Sudan 97 F4
Borja Peru 142 C4
Borken Germany 52 G3
Borkenes Norway 44 J2
Borkovskaya Rus. Fed. 42 K2
Borkum Germany 52 G1
Borkum i. Germany 52 G1
Borlänge Sweden 45 I6
Borlaug Norway 45 E6
Borlu Turkey 59 M5
Borna Germany 53 M3
Born-Berge hill Germany 53 K3
Borndiep sea chan. Neth. 52 F1
Borne Neth. 52 G2

▶Borneo i. Asia 68 E6
Largest island in Asia and 3rd in the world.
Asia 60–61
World 12–13

Bornholm county Denmark 153 H3
Bornholm i. Denmark 45 I9
Bornova Turkey 59 L5
Borodino Rus. Fed. 64 J3
Borodinskoye Rus. Fed. 45 P6
Borogontsy Rus. Fed. 65 O3
Borohoro Shan mts China 80 F3
Borok-Sulezhskiy Rus. Fed. 42 H4
Boromo Burkina 96 C3
Boron U.S.A. 128 E4
Borondi India 84 D2
Boroughbridge U.K. 48 F4
Borovichi Rus. Fed. 42 G4
Borovoy *Kirovskaya Oblast'* Rus. Fed. 42 K4
Borovoy *Respublika Kareliya* Rus. Fed. 44 R4
Borovoy *Respublika Komi* Rus. Fed. 42 L3
Borpeta India see Barpeta
Borrisokane Rep. of Ireland 51 D5
Borroloola Australia 110 B3
Børsa Norway 44 G5
Borşa Romania 43 E7
Borshchiv Ukr. 43 E6
Borshchovochnyy Khrebet mts Rus. Fed. 73 J3
Bortala China see Bole
Borton U.S.A. 134 B4
Borūjen Iran 88 C4
Borūjerd Iran 88 C3
Borun Iran 88 E3
Borve U.K. 50 C3
Boryslav Ukr. 43 D6
Boryspil' Ukr. 43 F6
Borzna Ukr. 43 G6
Borzya Rus. Fed. 73 L2
Bosanska Dubica Bos.-Herz. 58 G2
Bosanska Gradiška Bos.-Herz. 58 G2
Bosanska Krupa Bos.-Herz. 58 G2
Bosanski Novi Bos.-Herz. 58 G2
Bosansko Grahovo Bos.-Herz. 58 G2
Boscawen Island Tonga see Niuatoputopu
Bose China 76 E4
Boshof S. Africa 101 G5
Boshruyeh Iran 88 E3
Bosna i Hercegovina country Europe see Bosnia-Herzegovina
Bosna Saray Bos.-Herz. see Sarajevo
▶Bosnia-Herzegovina country Europe 58 G2
Europe 5, 38–39
Bosobogolo Pan salt pan Botswana 100 F3
Bosobolo Dem. Rep. Congo 98 B3
Bōsō-hantō pen. Japan 75 F6
Bosporus strait Turkey 59 M4
Bossaga Turkm. see Basaga
Bossangoa Cent. Afr. Rep. 98 B3
Bossembélé Cent. Afr. Rep. 98 B3
Bossier City U.S.A. 131 E5
Bossiesvlei Namibia 100 C3
Bossut, Cape Australia 108 C4
Bostan China 83 F1
Bostān Iran 88 B4
Bostan Pak. 89 G4
Bostāneh, Ra's-e pt Iran 88 D5
Bosten Hu l. China 80 G3
Boston U.K. 49 G6

▶Boston U.S.A. 135 J2
State capital of Massachusetts.

Boston Mountains U.S.A. 131 E5
Boston Spa U.K. 48 F5
Boswell U.S.A. 134 B3
Botad India 82 B5
Botany Bay Australia 112 E4
Botev mt. Bulg. 59 K3
Botevgrad Bulg. 59 J3
Bothaville S. Africa 101 H4
Bothnia, Gulf of Fin./Sweden 45 K6
Bothwell Canada 134 E2
Botkins U.S.A. 134 C3
Botlikh Rus. Fed. 91 G2
Botoşani Romania 43 E7
Botou China 73 L5
Bô Trach Vietnam 70 D3
Botshabelo S. Africa 101 H5
▶Botswana country Africa 99 C6
Africa 7, 94–95
Botte Donato, Monte mt. Italy 58 G5
Bottenviken g. Fin./Sweden see Bothnia, Gulf of
Bottesford U.K. 48 G5
Bottrop Germany 52 G3
Botucatu Brazil 145 A3
Botuporã Brazil 145 C1
Botwood Canada 123 L4
Bouaflé Côte d'Ivoire 96 C4
Bouaké Côte d'Ivoire 96 C4
Bouar Cent. Afr. Rep. 98 B3
Bouârfa Morocco 54 D5
Bouba Ndjida, Parc National de nat. park Cameroon 97 E4
Bouca Cent. Afr. Rep. 98 B3
Boucaut Bay Australia 108 F3
Bouchain France 52 D4
Bouctouche Canada 123 I5
Boudh India 84 E1
Bougaa Alg. 57 I5
Bougainville, Cape Australia 104 D3
Bougainville Island P.N.G. 106 F2
Bougainville Reef Australia 110 D2
Boughessa Mali 96 D3
Bougie Alg. see Bejaïa
Bougouni Mali 96 C3
Bougtob Alg. 54 E5
Bouillon Belgium 52 F5
Bouira Alg. 57 H5
Bou Izakarn Morocco 96 C2
Boujdour W. Sahara 96 B2
Boulder Australia 109 C7
Boulder CO U.S.A. 126 G4
Boulder MT U.S.A. 126 E3
Boulder UT U.S.A. 129 H3
Boulder Canyon gorge U.S.A. 129 F3
Boulder City U.S.A. 129 F4
Boulevard U.S.A. 128 E5
Boulia Australia 110 B4
Boulogne France see Boulogne-sur-Mer
Boulogne-Billancourt France 52 C6
Boulogne-sur-Mer France 52 B4
Boumerdes Alg. 57 H5
Bouna Côte d'Ivoire 96 C4
Bou Naceur, Jbel mt. Morocco 54 D5
Boû Nâga Mauritania 96 B3
Boundary Mountains U.S.A. 135 J1
Boundary Peak U.S.A. 128 D3
Boundiali Côte d'Ivoire 96 C4
Boundji Congo 98 B4
Boun Nua Laos 70 C2
Bountiful U.S.A. 129 H1
Bounty Islands N.Z. 107 H6
Bounty Trough sea feature S. Pacific Ocean 150 H9
Bourail New Caledonia 107 G4
Bourbon reg. France see Bourbonnais
Bourbon terr. Indian Ocean see Réunion
Bourbon U.S.A. 134 B3
Bourbonnais reg. France 56 F3
Bourem Mali 96 C3
Bouressa Mali see Boughessa
Bourg-Achard France 49 H9
Bourganeuf France 56 E4
Bourg-en-Bresse France 56 G3
Bourges France 56 F3
Bourget Canada 135 H1
Bourgogne reg. France see Burgundy
Bourgogne, Canal de France 52 G3
Bourke Australia 112 B3
Bourne U.K. 49 G6
Bournemouth U.K. 49 F8
Bourtoutou Chad 97 F3
Bou Saâda Alg. 57 I6
Bou Salem Tunisia 58 C6
Bouse U.S.A. 129 F5
Bouse Wash watercourse U.S.A. 129 F4
Boussu Belgium 52 D4
Boutilimit Mauritania 96 B3
Bouvet Island terr. S. Atlantic Ocean see Bouvetøya

▶Bouvetøya terr. S. Atlantic Ocean 148 I9
Dependency of Norway.

Bouy France 52 E5
Bova Marina Italy 58 F6
Bovenden Germany 53 J3
Bow r. Alta Canada 121 I5
Bowa China see Muli
Bowbells U.S.A. 130 C1
Bowden U.S.A. 134 F4
Bowditch atoll Tokelau see Fakaofo
Bowen Australia 110 E4
Bowen, Mount Australia 112 D6
Bowenville Australia 112 E1
Bowers Ridge sea feature Bering Sea 150 H2
Bowie Australia 110 D4
Bowie AZ U.S.A. 129 I5
Bowie TX U.S.A. 131 D5
Bow Island Canada 121 I5
Bowkan Iran 88 B2
Bowling Green KY U.S.A. 134 B5
Bowling Green MO U.S.A. 130 F4
Bowling Green OH U.S.A. 134 D3
Bowling Green VA U.S.A. 135 G4
Bowling Green Bay National Park Australia 110 D3
Bowman U.S.A. 130 C2
Bowman, Mount Canada 126 C2
Bowman Island Antarctica 152 F2
Bowman Peninsula Antarctica 152 L2
Bowmore U.K. 50 C5
Bowo China see Bomi
Bowral Australia 112 E5
Bowser Lake Canada 120 D3
Boxberg Germany 53 J5
Box Elder U.S.A. 130 C2
Box Elder r. U.S.A. 130 C2
Boxtel Neth. 52 F3
Boyabat Turkey 90 D2
Boyana tourist site Bulg. 59 J3
Boyang China 77 H2
Boyd r. Australia 112 F2
Boyd Lagoon salt flat Australia 109 D6
Boyd Lake Canada 121 K2
Boydton U.S.A. 135 F5
Boyers U.S.A. 134 F3
Boykins U.S.A. 135 G5
Boyle Canada 121 H4
Boyle Rep. of Ireland 51 D4
Boyne r. Rep. of Ireland 51 F4
Boyne City U.S.A. 134 C1
Boysen Reservoir U.S.A. 126 F4
Boysun Uzbek. see Baysun
Boyuibe Bol. 142 F8
Böyük Qafqaz mts Asia/Europe see Caucasus

▶Bozcaada i. Turkey 59 L5
Most westerly point of Asia.

Bozdağ mt. Turkey 59 L5
Bozdağ mt. Turkey 85 C1
Boz Dağları mts Turkey 59 L5
Bozdoğan Turkey 59 M6
Bozeat U.K. 49 G6
Bozeman U.S.A. 126 F3
Bozen Italy see Bolzano
Bozhou China 77 G1
Bozoum Cent. Afr. Rep. 98 B3
Bozova Turkey 90 E3
Bozqūsh, Kūh-e mts Iran 88 B2
Bozüyük Turkey 59 N5
Bozyazı Turkey 85 A1
Bra Italy 58 B2
Brač i. Croatia 58 G3
Bracadale U.K. 50 C3
Bracadale, Loch b. U.K. 50 C3
Bracara Port. see Braga
Bracciano, Lago di l. Italy 58 E3
Bracebridge Canada 134 F1
Brachet, Lac au l. Canada 123 H4
Bräcke Sweden 44 I5
Brackenheim Germany 53 J5
Brackettville U.S.A. 131 C6
Bracknell U.K. 49 G7
Bradano r. Italy 58 G4
Bradenton U.S.A. 133 D7
Bradford Canada 134 F1
Bradford U.K. 48 F5
Bradford OH U.S.A. 134 C3
Bradford PA U.S.A. 135 F3
Bradley U.S.A. 134 B3
Brady U.S.A. 131 D6
Brady Glacier U.S.A. 120 B3
Brae U.K. 50 [inset]
Braemar U.K. 50 F3
Braga Port. 57 B3
Bragado Arg. 144 D5
Bragança Brazil 143 I4
Bragança Port. 57 C3
Bragança Paulista Brazil 145 B3
Brahin Belarus 43 F6
Brahlstorf Germany 53 K1
Brahmanbaria Bangl. 83 G5
Brahmapur India 84 E2
Brahmaputra r. Asia 83 H4
also known as Dihang (India) or Jamuna (Bangladesh) or Siang (India) or Yarlung Zangbo (China)
Brahmaur India 82 D2
Brăila Romania 59 L2
Braine France 52 D5
Braine-le-Comte Belgium 52 E4
Brainerd U.S.A. 130 E2
Braintree U.K. 49 H7
Braithwaite Point Australia 108 F2
Brak r. S. Africa 101 I2
Brake (Unterweser) Germany 53 I1
Brakel Belgium 52 D4
Brakel Germany 53 J3
Brakwater Namibia 100 C2
Bramfield Australia 109 F8
Bramming Denmark 45 F9
Brämön i. Sweden 44 J5
Brampton Canada 134 F2
Brampton England U.K. 48 E4
Brampton England U.K. 49 I6
Bramsche Germany 53 I2
Bramwell Australia 110 C2
Brancaster U.K. 49 H6
Branch Canada 123 L5
Branco r. Brazil 142 F4
Brandberg mt. Namibia 99 B6
Brandbu Norway 45 G6
Brande Denmark 45 F9
Brandenburg Germany 53 M2
Brandenburg land Germany 53 N2
Brandenburg U.S.A. 134 B5
Brandfort S. Africa 101 H5
Brandis Germany 53 N3
Brandon Canada 121 L5
Brandon U.K. 49 H6
Brandon MS U.S.A. 131 F5
Brandon VT U.S.A. 135 I2
Brandon Head hd Rep. of Ireland 51 B5
Brandon Mountain hill Rep. of Ireland 51 B5
Brandvlei S. Africa 100 E6
Braniewo Poland 47 Q3
Bransfield Strait Antarctica 152 L2
Branson U.S.A. 131 C4
Brantford Canada 134 E2
Branxton Australia 112 E4
Bras d'Or Lake Canada 123 J5
Brasil country S. America see Brazil
Brasil, Planalto do plat. Brazil 143 J7
Brasileia Brazil 142 E6

▶Brasília Brazil 145 B1
Capital of Brazil.

Brasília de Minas Brazil 145 B2
Braslav Belarus see Braslaw
Braslaw Belarus 45 O9
Braşov Romania 59 K2
Brassey, Mount Australia 109 F5
Brassey Range hills Australia 109 C6
Brasstown Bald mt. U.S.A. 133 D5

▶Bratislava Slovakia 47 P6
Capital of Slovakia.

Bratsk Rus. Fed. 72 I1
Bratskoye Vodokhranilishche resr Rus. Fed. 72 I1
Brattleboro U.S.A. 135 I2
Braunau am Inn Austria 47 N6
Braunfels Germany 53 I4
Braunlage Germany 53 K3
Braunsbedra Germany 53 L3
Braunschweig Germany 53 K2
Brava i. Cape Verde 96 [inset]
Brave U.S.A. 134 E4
Bråviken inlet Sweden 45 J7
Bravo, Cerro mt. Bol. 142 F7
Bravo del Norte, Río r. Mex./U.S.A. 127 G7 see Rio Grande
Brawley U.S.A. 129 F5
Bray Rep. of Ireland 51 F4
Bray Island Canada 119 K3
Brazeau r. Canada 120 H4
Brazeau, Mount Canada 120 G4

▶Brazil country S. America 143 G5
Largest country in South America and 5th in the world. Most populous country in South America and 5th in the world.
South America 9, 140–141

Brazil U.S.A. 134 B4
Brazil Basin sea feature S. Atlantic Ocean 148 G7
Brazos r. U.S.A. 131 E6

▶Brazzaville Congo 99 B4
Capital of Congo.

Brčko Bos.-Herz. 58 H2
Bré Rep. of Ireland see Bray
Breadalbane Australia 110 B4
Breaksea Sound inlet N.Z. 113 A7
Bream Bay N.Z. 113 E2
Brechfa U.K. 49 C7
Brechin U.K. 50 G4
Brecht Belgium 52 E3
Breckenridge MI U.S.A. 134 C2
Breckenridge MN U.S.A. 130 D2
Breckenridge TX U.S.A. 131 D5
Břeclav Czech Rep. 47 P6
Brecon U.K. 49 D7
Brecon Beacons reg. U.K. 49 D7
Brecon Beacons National Park U.K. 49 D7
Breda Neth. 52 E3
Bredasdorp S. Africa 100 E8
Bredbo Australia 112 D5
Breddin Germany 53 M2
Bredevoort Neth. 52 G3
Bredviken Sweden 44 I3
Bree Belgium 52 F3
Breed U.S.A. 134 A1
Bregenz Austria 47 L7
Breiðafjörður b. Iceland 44 [inset]
Breiðdalsvík Iceland 44 [inset]
Breidenbach Germany 53 I4
Breien U.S.A. 130 C2
Breitenfelde Germany 53 K1
Breitengüßbach Germany 53 K5
Breiter Luzinsee l. Germany 53 N1
Breivikbotn Norway 44 M1
Breizh reg. France see Brittany
Brejo Velho Brazil 145 C1
Brekstad Norway 44 F5
Bremen Germany 53 I1

Bremen *land* Germany 53 I1
Bremen IN U.S.A. 134 B3
Bremen OH U.S.A. 134 D4
Bremer Bay Australia 109 B8
Bremerhaven Germany 53 I1
Bremersdorp Swaziland *see* Manzini
Bremer Range *hills* Australia 105 C8
Bremm Germany 52 H4
Brenham U.S.A. 131 D6
Brenna Norway 44 H4
Brennero, Passo di *pass* Austria/Italy *see* Brenner Pass
Brennerpaß *pass* Austria/Italy *see* Brenner Pass
Brenner Pass Austria/Italy 58 D1
Brentwood U.K. 49 H7
Brescia Italy 58 B2
Breslau Poland *see* Wrocław
Bresle *r.* France 52 B4
Brésolles, Lac *l.* Canada 123 H3
Bressanone Italy 58 D1
Bressay *i.* U.K. 50 [inset]
Bressuire France 56 D3
Brest Belarus 45 M10
Brest France 56 B2
Brest-Litovsk Belarus *see* Brest
Bretagne *reg.* France *see* Brittany
Breteuil France 52 C4
Brétigny-sur-Orge France 52 C6
Breton Canada 120 H4
Breton Sound *b.* U.S.A. 131 F6
Brett, Cape N.Z. 113 E2
Bretten Germany 53 I5
Bretton U.K. 48 E5
Breuĥ, Pulau *i.* Indon. 71 A6
Brevard U.S.A. 133 D5
Breves Brazil 143 H4
Brewarrina Australia 112 C2
Brewer U.S.A. 132 G2
Brewster NE U.S.A. 130 D3
Brewster OH U.S.A. 134 E3
Brewster, Kap *c.* Greenland *see* Kangikajik
Brewster, Lake *imp. l.* Australia 112 B4
Brewton U.S.A. 133 C6
Breyten S. Africa 101 I4
Breytovo Rus. Fed. 42 H4
Brezhnev Rus. Fed. *see* Naberezhnyye Chelny
Brezno Slovakia 47 Q6
Brezovo Bulg. 59 K3
Brezovo Polje *hill* Croatia 58 G2
Bria Cent. Afr. Rep. 98 C3
Briançon France 56 H4
Brian Head *mt.* U.S.A. 129 G3
Bribbaree Australia 112 C5
Bribie Island Australia 112 F1
Briceni Moldova 43 E6
Brichany Moldova *see* Briceni
Brichen' Moldova *see* Briceni
Bridgend U.K. 49 D7
Bridge of Orchy U.K. 50 E4
Bridgeport CA U.S.A. 128 D2
Bridgeport CT U.S.A. 135 I3
Bridgeport IL U.S.A. 134 B4
Bridgeport NE U.S.A. 130 C3
Bridger Peak U.S.A. 126 G4
Bridgeton U.S.A. 135 H4
Bridgetown Australia 109 B8

▶Bridgetown Barbados 137 M6
  Capital of Barbados.

Bridgetown Canada 123 I5
Bridgeville U.S.A. 135 H4
Bridgewater Canada 123 I5
Bridgewater U.S.A. 135 H2
Bridgnorth U.K. 49 E6
Bridgton U.S.A. 135 J1
Bridgwater U.K. 49 D7
Bridgwater Bay U.K. 49 D7
Bridlington U.K. 48 G4
Bridlington Bay U.K. 48 G4
Bridport Australia 111 [inset]
Bridport U.K. 49 E8
Brie *reg.* France 52 F2
Brie-Comte-Robert France 52 C6
Brieg Poland *see* Brzeg
Briery Knob *mt.* U.S.A. 134 E4
Brig Switz. 56 H3
Brigg U.K. 48 G5
Brigham City U.S.A. 126 E4
Brightlingsea U.K. 49 I7
Brighton Canada 135 G1
Brighton U.K. 49 G8
Brighton CO U.S.A. 126 G5
Brighton MI U.S.A. 134 D2
Brighton NY U.S.A. 135 G2
Brighton WV U.S.A. 134 D4
Brignoles France 56 H5
Brikama Gambia 96 B3
Brillion U.S.A. 134 A1
Brilon Germany 53 I3
Brindisi Italy 58 G4
Brinkley U.S.A. 131 F5
Brion, Île *i.* Canada 123 J5
Brioude France 56 F4
Brisay Canada 123 H3

▶Brisbane Australia 112 F1
  State capital of Queensland and 3rd most populous city in Oceania.

Brisbane Ranges National Park Australia 112 B6
Bristol U.K. 49 E7
Bristol CT U.S.A. 135 I3
Bristol FL U.S.A. 133 C6
Bristol NH U.S.A. 135 J2
Bristol RI U.S.A. 135 J3
Bristol TN U.S.A. 134 D5
Bristol VT U.S.A. 135 I1
Bristol Bay U.S.A. 118 B4
Bristol Channel *est.* U.K. 49 C7
Bristol Lake U.S.A. 129 F4
Britannia Island New Caledonia *see* Maré
British Antarctic Territory *reg.* Antarctica 152 L2
British Columbia *prov.* Canada 120 F5
British Empire Range *mts* Canada 119 J1
British Guiana *country* S. America *see* Guyana

British Honduras *country* Central America *see* Belize

▶British Indian Ocean Territory *terr.*
  Indian Ocean 149 M6
  United Kingdom Overseas Territory.

British Solomon Islands *country*
  S. Pacific Ocean *see* Solomon Islands
Brito Godins Angola *see* Kiwaba N'zogi
Brits S. Africa 101 H3
Britstown S. Africa 100 F6
Brittany *reg.* France 56 C2
Britton U.S.A. 130 D2
Brive-la-Gaillarde France 56 E4
Briviesca Spain 57 E2
Brixham U.K. 49 D8
Brixia Italy *see* Brescia
Brlik Kazakh. 80 D3
Brno Czech Rep. 47 P6
Broach India *see* Bharuch
Broad *r.* U.S.A. 133 D5
Broadalbin U.S.A. 135 H2
Broad Arrow Australia 109 C7
Broad Bay U.K. *see* Tuath, Loch a'
Broadback *r.* Canada 122 F4
Broadford Australia 112 B6
Broadford Rep. of Ireland 51 D5
Broadford U.K. 50 D3
Broad Law *hill* U.K. 50 F5
Broadmere Australia 110 A3
Broad Peak China/Jammu and Kashmir 89 J3
Broad Sound *sea chan.* Australia 110 E4
Broadstairs U.K. 49 I7
Broadus U.S.A. 126 G3
Broadview Canada 121 K5
Broadway U.S.A. 135 F4
Broadwood N.Z. 113 D2
Brochet, Canada 121 K3
Brochet, Lac *l.* Canada 121 K3
Brocken *mt.* Germany 53 K3
Brockman, Mount Australia 108 B5
Brockport NY U.S.A. 135 G2
Brockport PA U.S.A. 135 F3
Brockton U.S.A. 135 J2
Brockville Canada 135 H1
Brockway U.S.A. 135 F3
Brodeur Peninsula Canada 119 J2
Brodhead U.S.A. 134 C5
Brodick U.K. 50 D5
Brodnica Poland 47 Q4
Brody Ukr. 43 E6
Broken Arrow U.S.A. 131 E4
Broken Bay Australia 112 E4
Broken Bow NE U.S.A. 130 D3
Broken Bow OK U.S.A. 131 E5
Brokenhead *r.* Canada 121 L5
Broken Hill Australia 111 C6
Broken Hill Zambia *see* Kabwe
Broken Plateau *sea feature* Indian Ocean 149 O8
Brokopondo Suriname 143 G2
Brokopondo Stuwmeer *resr* Suriname *see* Professor van Blommestein Meer
Bromberg Poland *see* Bydgoszcz
Brome Germany 53 K2
Bromsgrove U.K. 49 E6
Brønderslev Denmark 45 F8
Brønnøysund Norway 44 H4
Bronson FL U.S.A. 133 D6
Bronson MI U.S.A. 134 C3
Brooke U.K. 49 I6
Brookfield U.S.A. 134 A2
Brookhaven U.S.A. 131 F6
Brookings OR U.S.A. 126 B4
Brookings SD U.S.A. 130 D2
Brookline U.S.A. 135 J2
Brooklyn U.S.A. 134 C2
Brooklyn Park U.S.A. 130 E2
Brookneal U.S.A. 135 F5
Brooks Canada 121 I5
Brooks Brook Canada 120 C2
Brooks Range *mts* Canada 118 D3
Brookston U.S.A. 134 B3
Brooksville FL U.S.A. 133 D6
Brooksville KY U.S.A. 134 C4
Brookton Australia 109 B8
Brookville IN U.S.A. 134 C4
Brookville PA U.S.A. 134 F3
Brookville Lake U.S.A. 134 C4
Broom, Loch *inlet* U.K. 50 D3
Broome Australia 108 C4
Brora U.K. 50 F2
Brora *r.* U.K. 50 F2
Brösarp Sweden 45 I9
Brosna *r.* Rep. of Ireland 51 E4
Brosville U.S.A. 134 F5
Brothers *is* India 71 A5
Brough U.K. 48 E4
Brough Ness *pt* U.K. 50 G2
Broughshane U.K. 51 F3
Broughton Islands Australia 112 F4
Brovary Ukr. 43 F6
Brovinia Australia 111 E5
Brovst Denmark 45 F8
Brown City U.S.A. 134 D2
Brown Deer U.S.A. 134 B2
Browne Range *hills* Australia 109 D6
Brownfield U.S.A. 131 C5
Browning U.S.A. 126 E2
Brown Mountain U.S.A. 128 C4
Brownstown U.S.A. 134 B4
Brownsville IN U.S.A. 134 B5
Brownsville PA U.S.A. 134 F3
Brownsville TN U.S.A. 131 F5
Brownsville TX U.S.A. 131 D7
Brownwood U.S.A. 131 D6
Browse Island Australia 108 C3
Bruay-la-Buissière France 52 C4
Bruce Canada 134 E1
Bruce Peninsula Canada 134 E1
Bruce Peninsula National Park Canada 134 E1
Bruce Rock Australia 109 B7
Bruchsal Germany 53 I5
Brück Germany 53 M2
Bruck an der Mur Austria 47 O7
Brue *r.* U.K. 49 E7
Bruges Belgium *see* Brugge
Brugge Belgium 52 D3

Brühl Baden-Württemberg Germany 53 I5
Brühl Nordrhein-Westfalen Germany 52 G4
Bruin KY U.S.A. 134 D4
Bruin PA U.S.A. 134 F3
Bruin Point *mt.* U.S.A. 129 H2
Bruint India 83 I3
Brûk, Wâdi el *watercourse* Egypt *see* Burûk, Wâdi al
Brûlé Canada 120 G4
Brûlé, Lac *l.* Canada 123 J3
Brûly Belgium 52 E5
Brumado Brazil 145 C1
Brumath France 53 H6
Brumunddal Norway 45 G6
Brunau Germany 53 L2
Brundisium Italy *see* Brindisi
Bruneau U.S.A. 126 E4

▶Brunei *country* Asia 68 E6
  6, 62–63

Brunei Brunei *see* Bandar Seri Begawan
Brunette Downs Australia 110 A3
Brunflo Sweden 44 I5
Brunico Italy 58 D1
Brünn Czech Rep. *see* Brno
Brunner, Lake N.Z. 113 C6
Bruno Canada 121 J4
Brunsbüttel Germany *see* Braunschweig
Brunswick GA U.S.A. 133 D6
Brunswick MD U.S.A. 135 G4
Brunswick ME U.S.A. 135 K2
Brunswick, Península de *pen.* Chile 144 B8
Brunswick Bay Australia 108 D3
Brunswick Lake Canada 122 E4
Bruntál Czech Rep. 47 P6
Brunt Ice Shelf Antarctica 152 B2
Bruntville S. Africa 101 J5
Bruny Island Australia 111 [inset]
Brusa Turkey *see* Bursa
Brusenets Rus. Fed. 42 I3
Brushton U.S.A. 135 H1
Brusque Brazil 145 A4
Brussel Belgium *see* Brussels

▶Brussels Belgium 52 E4
  Capital of Belgium.

Bruthen Australia 112 C6
Bruxelles Belgium *see* Brussels
Bruzual Venez. 142 E2
Bryan OH U.S.A. 134 C3
Bryan TX U.S.A. 131 D6
Bryan, Mount *hill* Australia 111 B7
Bryan Coast Antarctica 152 L2
Bryansk Rus. Fed. 43 G5
Bryanskoye Rus. Fed. 91 G1
Bryant Pond U.S.A. 135 J1
Bryantsburg U.S.A. 134 C4
Bryce Canyon National Park U.S.A. 129 G3
Bryce Mountain U.S.A. 129 I5
Brynbuga U.K. *see* Usk
Bryne Norway 45 D7
Bryukhovetskaya Rus. Fed. 43 H7
Brzeg Poland 47 P5
Brześć nad Bugiem Belarus *see* Brest
Bua *r.* Malawi 99 D5
Bu'aale Somalia 98 E3
Buala Solomon Is 107 F2
Bu'ayj *well* Saudi Arabia 88 C5
Bübiyan Island Kuwait 88 C4
Bucak Turkey 59 N6
Bucaramanga Col. 142 D2
Buccaneer Archipelago *is* Australia 108 C4
Buchanan Liberia 96 B4
Buchanan MI U.S.A. 134 B3
Buchanan VA U.S.A. 134 F5
Buchanan, Lake *salt flat* Australia 110 D4
Buchan Gulf Canada 119 K2

▶Bucharest Romania 59 L2
  Capital of Romania.

Büchen Germany 53 K1
Buchen (Odenwald) Germany 53 J5
Buchholz Germany 53 M1
Bucholz in der Nordheide Germany 53 J1
Buchon, Point U.S.A. 128 C4
Buchy France 52 B5
Bucin, Pasul *pass* Romania 59 K1
Buckambool Mountain *hill* Australia 112 B3
Bückeburg Germany 53 J2
Bücken Germany 53 J2
Buckeye U.S.A. 129 G5
Buckhannon U.S.A. 134 E4
Buckhaven U.K. 50 F4
Buckhorn Lake Canada 135 F1
Buckie U.K. 50 G3
Buckingham U.K. 49 G6
Buckingham U.S.A. 135 F5
Buckingham Bay Australia 67 F9
Buckland Tableland *reg.* Australia 110 E5
Buckleboo Australia 109 B8
Buckle Island Antarctica 152 H2
Buckley *watercourse* Australia 110 B4
Buckley Bay Antarctica 152 G2
Bucklin U.S.A. 130 D4
Buckskin Mountains U.S.A. 129 G4
Bucksport U.S.A. 123 H5
Bucks Mountain U.S.A. 128 C2
Bückwitz Germany 53 M2
București Romania *see* Bucharest
Bucyrus U.S.A. 134 D3
Buda-Kashalyova Belarus 43 F5
Budalin Myanmar 70 A2

▶Budapest Hungary 59 H1
  Capital of Hungary.

Budaun India 82 D3
Budawang National Park Australia 112 E5
Budda Australia 112 B3
Budd Coast Antarctica 152 F2
Buddusò Sardinia Italy 58 C4
Bude U.K. 49 C8
Bude U.S.A. 131 F6
Budennovsk Rus. Fed. 91 G1
Buderim Australia 112 F1
Büding Iran 88 E5
Büdingen Germany 53 J4
Budiyah, Jabal *hills* Egypt 85 A5
Budongquan China 83 H2

Budoni *Sardinia* Italy 58 C4
Budū', Sabkhat al *salt pan* Saudi Arabia 88 C6
Budweis Czech Rep. *see* České Budějovice
Buea Cameroon 96 D4
Buëch *r.* France 56 G4
Buellton U.S.A. 128 C4
Buena Park U.S.A. 128 E5
Buena Vista *i.* N. Mariana Is *see* Tinian
Buena Vista CO U.S.A. 126 G5
Buena Vista VA U.S.A. 134 F5
Buendia, Embalse de *resr* Spain 57 E3

▶Buenos Aires Arg. 144 E4
  Capital of Argentina. 2nd most populous city in South America.

Buenos Aires, Lago *l.* Arg./Chile 144 B7
Buerarema Brazil 145 D1
Buet *r.* Canada 123 H1
Búfalo Mex. 131 B7
Buffalo *r.* Canada 120 H2
Buffalo KY U.S.A. 134 C5
Buffalo MO U.S.A. 130 E4
Buffalo NY U.S.A. 135 F2
Buffalo OK U.S.A. 131 D4
Buffalo SD U.S.A. 130 C2
Buffalo TX U.S.A. 131 D6
Buffalo WY U.S.A. 126 G3
Buffalo Head Hills Canada 120 G3
Buffalo Head Prairie Canada 120 G3
Buffalo Hump *mt.* U.S.A. 126 E3
Buffalo Lake *Alta* Canada 121 H4
Buffalo Lake N.W.T. Canada 120 H2
Buffalo Narrows Canada 121 I4
Buffels *watercourse* S. Africa 100 C5
Buffels Drift S. Africa 101 H2
Buftea Romania 59 K2
Bug *r.* Poland 47 S5
Buga Col. 142 C3
Bugaldie Australia 112 D3
Bugdayli Turkm. 88 D2
Buggenhout Belgium 52 E3
Bugojno Bos.-Herz. 58 G2
Bugrino Rus. Fed. 42 K1
Bugt China 74 A2
Bugul'ma Rus. Fed. 41 Q5
Bugun' Kazakh. 80 B2
Bügür China *see* Luntai
Buguruslan Rus. Fed. 41 Q5
Bühäbäd Iran 88 D4
Buhera Zimbabwe 99 D5
Bühl Germany 53 I6
Buhuşi Romania 59 L1
Buick Canada 120 F3
Builth Wells U.K. 49 D6
Bui National Park Ghana 96 C4
Buinsk Rus. Fed. 43 K5
Bu'in Zahrā Iran 88 C3
Buir Nur *l.* Mongolia 73 L3
Buitepos Namibia 100 D2
Bujanovac Serb. and Mont. 59 I3

▶Bujumbura Burundi 98 C4
  Capital of Burundi.

Bukachacha Rus. Fed. 73 L2
Buka Daban *mt.* China 83 G1
Buka Island P.N.G. 106 F2
Bukavu Dem. Rep. Congo 98 C4
Bukhara Uzbek. 89 G2
Bukhoro Uzbek. *see* Bukhara
Bukit Baka - Bukit Raya National Park Indon. 68 E7
Bukit Timah Sing. 71 [inset]
Bukittinggi Indon. 68 C7
Bukkapatnam India 84 C3
Bukoba Tanz. 98 D4
Bükres Romania *see* Bucharest
Bül, Kūh-e *mt.* Iran 88 D4
Bula P.N.G. 69 K8
Bülach Switz. 56 I3
Bulan *i.* Indon. 71 C7
Bulancak Turkey 90 E2
Bulandshahr India 82 D3
Bulanık Turkey 91 F3
Bulava Rus. Fed. 74 F2
Bulawayo Zimbabwe 99 C6
Buldan Turkey 59 M5
Buldana India *see* Buldhana
Buldhana India 84 C1
Buleda *reg.* Pak. 89 F5
Bulembu Swaziland 101 J3
Bulgan *Bulgan* Mongolia 80 J2
Bulgan *Hovd* Mongolia *see* Bürenhayrhan
Bulgar Rus. Fed. *see* Bolgar
▶Bulgaria *country* Europe 59 K3
  Europe 5, 38–39
Bülgariya *country* Europe *see* Bulgaria
Bulkley Ranges *mts* Canada 120 D4
Bullawarra, Lake *salt flat* Australia 112 A1
Bullen *r.* Canada 121 K1
Buller *r.* N.Z. 113 C5
Buller, Mount Australia 112 C6
Bulleringa National Park Australia 110 C3
Bullfinch Australia 109 B7
Bullhead City U.S.A. 129 F4
Bulli Australia 112 E5
Bullion Mountains U.S.A. 128 E4
Bullo *r.* Australia 108 E3
Bulloo *watercourse* Australia 111 C6
Bulloo Downs Australia 111 C6
Bulloo Lake *salt flat* Australia 111 C6
Bully Choop Mountain U.S.A. 128 B1
Bulman Australia 108 F3
Bulman Gorge Australia 108 F3
Bulmer Lake Canada 120 F2
Buloh, Pulau *i.* Sing. 71 [inset]
Buloke, Lake *dry lake* Australia 112 A6
Bulolo P.N.G. 69 L8
Bulsar India *see* Valsad
Bultfontein S. Africa 101 H5
Bulukumba Indon. 69 G8
Bulun Rus. Fed. 65 N2
Bulungu Dem. Rep. Congo 99 C4
Bulungur Uzbek. 89 G2
Bumba Dem. Rep. Congo 98 C3
Bümbah Libya 90 A4
Bumbah, Khalīj *b.* Libya 90 A4
Bumhpa Bum *mt.* Myanmar 70 B1
Buna Dem. Rep. Congo 98 B4

Buna Kenya 98 D3
Bunayyān *well* Saudi Arabia 88 C6
Bunazi Tanz. 98 D4
Bunbeg Rep. of Ireland 51 D2
Bunbury Australia 109 A8
Bunclody Rep. of Ireland 51 F5
Buncrana Rep. of Ireland 51 E2
Bunda Tanz. 98 D4
Bundaberg Australia 110 F5
Bundaleer Australia 112 C2
Bundarra Australia 112 E3
Bundi India 82 C4
Bundjalung National Park Australia 112 F2
Bundoran Rep. of Ireland 51 D3
Bunduqiya Sudan 97 G4
Buner *reg.* Pak. 89 I3
Bungay U.K. 49 I6
Bungendore Australia 112 D5
Bunger Hills Antarctica 152 F2
Bungle Bungle National Park Australia *see* Purnululu National Park
Bungo-suidō *sea chan.* Japan 71 D6
Bunguran, Kepulauan *is* Indon. *see* Natuna, Kepulauan
Bunguran, Pulau *i.* Indon. *see* Natuna Besar
Bunia Dem. Rep. Congo 98 D3
Buninyong Australia 112 A6
Buningonia *well* Australia 109 C7
Bunji Jammu and Kashmir 82 C2
Bunkeya Dem. Rep. Congo 99 C5
Bunnell U.S.A. 133 D6
Bunya Mountains National Park Australia 112 E1
Bünyan Turkey 90 D3
Bunyu *i.* Indon. 68 F6
Buôn Mê Thuôt Vietnam 71 E4
Buorkhaya, Guba *b.* Rus. Fed. 65 O2
Bup *r.* China 83 F3
Buqayq Saudi Arabia *see* Abqaiq
Buqbuq Egypt 90 B5
Bura Kenya 98 D4
Buraan Somalia 98 E2
Buram Sudan 97 F3
Buran Kazakh. 80 G2
Buranhaém Brazil 145 C2
Buranhaém *r.* Brazil 145 D2
Burao Somalia 98 E3
Buraq Syria 85 C3
Buray *r.* India 82 C5
Buraydah Saudi Arabia 86 F4
Burbach Germany 53 I4
Burbank U.S.A. 128 D4
Burcher Australia 112 C4
Burco Somalia *see* Burao
Bürd Mongolia 80 J3
Burdaard Neth. *see* Birdaard
Burdalyk Turkm. 89 G2
Burdekin *r.* Australia 110 D3
Burdigala France *see* Bordeaux
Burdur Turkey 59 N6
Burdur Gölü *l.* Turkey 59 N6
Burdwan India *see* Barddhaman
Burē Eth. 98 D3
Bure *r.* U.K. 49 I6
Bureå Sweden 44 L4
Bureinskiy Khrebet *mts* Rus. Fed. 74 D2
Bürenhayrhan Mongolia 80 H2
Bureya *r.* Rus. Fed. 74 C2
Bureya Range *mts* Rus. Fed. *see* Bureinskiy Khrebet
Bureinski Zapovednik *nature res.* Rus. Fed. 74 D2
Burford Canada 134 E2
Burg Germany 53 L2
Burgas Bulg. 59 L3
Burgaw U.S.A. 133 E5
Burg bei Magdeburg Germany 53 L2
Burgbernheim Germany 53 K5
Burgdorf Germany 53 K2
Burgeo Canada 123 K5
Burgersdorp S. Africa 101 H6
Burgersfort S. Africa 101 J3
Burges, Mount *hill* Australia 109 C7
Burgess Hill U.K. 49 G8
Burghaun Germany 53 J4
Burghausen Germany 47 N6
Burghead U.K. 50 F3
Burgh-Haamstede Neth. 52 D3
Burgio, Serra di *hill* Sicily Italy 58 F6
Burglengenfeld Germany 53 M5
Burgos Mex. 131 D7
Burgos Spain 57 E2
Burgstädt Germany 53 M4
Burgsvik Sweden 45 K8
Burgum Neth. *see* Bergum
Burgundy *reg.* France 56 G3
Burhan Budai Shan *mts* China 80 H4
Burhaniye Turkey 59 L5
Burhanpur India 82 C5
Burhar-Dhanpuri India 83 E5
Buri Brazil 145 A3
Burias *i.* Phil. 69 G4
Burin Canada 123 L5
Buriram Thai. 70 C4
Buritama Brazil 145 A3
Buriti Alegre Brazil 145 A2
Buriti Bravo Brazil 143 J5
Buritirama Brazil 143 J6
Buritis Brazil 145 B1
Burj Pak. 89 G5
Burke U.S.A. 130 D3
Burke Island Antarctica 152 K2
Burke Pass N.Z. *see* Burkes Pass
Burkes Pass N.Z. 113 C7
Burkesville U.S.A. 134 C5
Burketown Australia 110 B3
Burkeville U.S.A. 135 F5
▶Burkina *country* Africa 96 C3
  Africa 7, 94–95
Burkina Faso *country* Africa *see* Burkina
Burk's Falls Canada 122 F5
Burley U.S.A. 126 E4
Burlington Canada 134 F2
Burlington CO U.S.A. 130 C4
Burlington IA U.S.A. 130 F3
Burlington KS U.S.A. 130 E4
Burlington KY U.S.A. 134 C4
Burlington NC U.S.A. 132 E4
Burlington VT U.S.A. 135 I1
Burlington WI U.S.A. 134 A2
Burmantovo Rus. Fed. 41 S3
Burnaby Canada 120 F5

Burnet U.S.A. 131 D6
Burney U.S.A. 128 C1
Burney, Monte *vol.* Chile 144 B8
Burnham U.S.A. 135 G3
Burnie Australia 111 [inset]
Burniston U.K. 48 G4
Burns U.S.A. 126 D4
Burnside *r.* Canada 118 H3
Burnside U.S.A. 134 C5
Burnside, Lake *salt flat* Australia 109 C6
Burns Junction U.S.A. 126 D4
Burns Lake Canada 120 E4
Burntisland U.K. 50 F4
Burnt Lake Canada *see* Brûlé, Lac
Burntwood *r.* Canada 121 L4
Burog Co *l.* China 83 F2
Buron *r.* Canada 123 H2
Burovoy Uzbek. 89 F1
Burqin China 80 G2
Burqu' Jordan 85 D3
Burra Australia 111 B7
Burravoe U.K. 50 [inset]
Burrel Albania 59 I4
Burrel U.S.A. 128 D3
Burren *reg.* Rep. of Ireland 51 C4
Burrendong Reservoir Australia 112 D4
Burren Junction Australia 112 D3
Burrewarra Point Australia 112 E5
Burrinjuck Australia 112 D5
Burrinjuck Reservoir Australia 112 D5
Burro, Serranías del *mts* Mex. 131 C6
Burr Oak Reservoir U.S.A. 134 D4
Burro Creek *watercourse* U.S.A. 129 G4
Burro Peak U.S.A. 129 I5
Burrowa Pine Mountain National Park Australia 112 C6
Burrow Head *hd* U.K. 50 E6
Burrows U.S.A. 134 B3
Burrundie Australia 108 E3
Bursa Turkey 59 M4
Bür Safāga Egypt *see* Bür Safājah
Bür Safājah Egypt 86 D4
Bür Sa'īd Egypt *see* Port Said
Bür Sa'īd *governorate* Egypt *see* Bür Sa'īd
Bür Sa'īd *governorate* Egypt 85 A4
Bursinskoye Vodokhranilishche *resr* Rus. Fed. 74 C2
Bürstadt Germany 53 I5
Bür Sudan Sudan *see* Port Sudan
Burt Lake U.S.A. 132 C2
Burton U.S.A. 134 D2
Burton, Lac *l.* Canada 122 F3
Burtonport Rep. of Ireland 51 D3
Burton upon Trent U.K. 49 F6
Burträsk Sweden 44 L4
Burt Well Australia 109 F5
Buru *i.* Indon. 69 H7
Burûk, Wâdi al *watercourse* Egypt 85 A4
Burullus, Bahra el *lag.* Egypt *see* Burullus, Lake
Burullus, Buhayrat al *lag.* Egypt *see* Burullus, Lake
Burullus, Lake *lag.* Egypt 90 C5
Burultokay China *see* Fuhai
Burün, Ra's *pt* Egypt 85 A4
▶Burundi *country* Africa 98 C4
  Africa 7, 94–95
Burunniy Rus. Fed. *see* Tsagan Aman
Bururi Burundi 98 C4
Burwash Landing Canada 120 B2
Burwick U.K. 50 G2
Buryn' Ukr. 43 G6
Bury St Edmunds U.K. 49 H6
Burzil Pass Jammu and Kashmir 82 C2
Busan S. Korea *see* Pusan
Busanga Dem. Rep. Congo 98 C4
Busby U.S.A. 126 G3
Buseire Syria *see* Al Buşayrah
Bush *r.* U.K. 51 F2
Büshehr Iran 38 C4
Bushêngcaka China 83 E3
Bushenyi Uganda 98 D4
Bushire Iran *see* Büshehr
Bushmills U.K. 51 F2
Bushnell U.S.A. 133 D6
Businga Dem. Rep. Congo 98 C3
Buşrá ash Shām Syria 85 C3
Busse Rus. Fed. 74 B2
Busselton Australia 109 A8
Bussum Neth. 52 F2
Bustillos, Lago *l.* Mex. 127 G7
Busto Arsizio Italy 58 C2
Buta Dem. Rep. Congo 98 C3
Butare Rwanda 98 C4
Butaritari *atoll* Kiribati 150 H5
Bute Australia 111 B7
Bute *i.* U.K. 50 D5
Butedale Canada 120 D4
Butha Buthe Lesotho 101 I5
Butha Qi China *see* Zalantun
Buthidaung Myanmar 70 A2
Butiaba Uganda 98 D3
Butler AL U.S.A. 131 C5
Butler GA U.S.A. 133 C5
Butler IN U.S.A. 134 C3
Butler KY U.S.A. 134 C4
Butler MO U.S.A. 130 E4
Butler PA U.S.A. 134 F3
Butlers Bridge Rep. of Ireland 51 E3
Buton *i.* Indon. 69 G7
Bütow Germany 53 M1
Butte MT U.S.A. 126 E3
Butte NE U.S.A. 130 D3
Buttelstedt Germany 53 L3
Butterworth Malaysia 71 C6
Butterworth S. Africa 101 I7
Buttes, Sierra *mt.* U.S.A. 128 C2
Buttevant Rep. of Ireland 51 D5
Butt of Lewis *hd* U.K. 50 C2
Button Bay Canada 121 M3
Butuan Phil. 69 H5
Butuo China 76 D3
Buturlinovka Rus. Fed. 43 I6
Butwal Nepal 83 E4
Butzbach Germany 53 I4
Buulobarde Somalia 98 E3
Buur Gaabo Somalia 98 E4
Buurhabaka Somalia 98 E3
Buxar India 83 F4
Buxtehude Germany 53 J1
Buxton U.K. 48 F5

Buy Rus. Fed. 42 I4
Buyant Mongolia 80 I2
Buynaksk Rus. Fed. 91 G2
Büyükçekmece Turkey 90 C2
Büyük Egri Dağ mt. Turkey 85 A1
Büyükmenderes r. Turkey 59 L6
Buzancy France 52 E5
Buzău Romania 59 L2
Buzdyak Rus. Fed. 41 Q5
Búzi Moz. 99 D5
Büzmeýin Turkm. see Byuzmeyin
Buzuluk Rus. Fed. 41 Q5
Buzuluk r. Rus. Fed. 43 I6
Buzzards Bay U.S.A. 135 J3
Byakar Bhutan see Jakar
Byala Bulg. 59 K3
Byala Slatina Bulg. 59 J3
Byalynichy Belarus 43 F5
Byarezina r. Belarus 43 F5
Byaroza Belarus 45 N10
Byblos tourist site Lebanon 85 B2
Bydgoszcz Poland 47 Q4
Byelorussia country Europe see Belarus
Byerazino Belarus 43 F5
Byers U.S.A. 126 G5
Byeshankovichy Belarus 43 F5
Byesville U.S.A. 134 E4
Bygland Norway 45 E7
Bykhaw Belarus 43 F5
Bykhov Belarus see Bykhaw
Bykle Norway 45 E7
Bykovo Rus. Fed. 43 J6
Bylas U.S.A. 129 H5
Bylot Island Canada 119 K2
Byramgore Reef India 84 A4
Byrd Glacier Antarctica 152 H1
Byrdstown U.S.A. 134 C5
Byrkjelo Norway 45 E6
Byrock Australia 112 C3
Byron U.S.A. 135 J1
Byron, Cape Australia 112 F2
Byron Bay Australia 112 F2
Byron Island Kiribati see Nikunau
Byrranga, Gory mts Rus. Fed. 65 K2
Byske Sweden 44 L4
Byssa Rus. Fed. 74 C1
Byssa r. Rus. Fed. 74 C1
Bytom Poland 47 Q5
Bytów Poland 47 P3
Byurgyutli Turkm. 88 D2
Byuzmeyin Turkm. 88 E2
Byzantium Turkey see İstanbul

C

Ca, Sông r. Vietnam 70 D3
Caacupé Para. 144 E3
Caatinga Brazil 145 B2
Caazapá Para. 144 E3
Cabaiguán Cuba 133 E8
Caballas Peru 142 C6
Caballococha Peru 142 D4
Cabanaconde Peru 142 D7
Cabanatuan Phil. 69 G3
Cabano Canada 123 H5
Cabdul Qaadir Somalia 98 E2
Cabeceira Rio Manso Brazil 139 G7
Cabeceiras Brazil 145 B1
Cabeza del Buey Spain 57 D4
Cabezas Bol. 142 F7
Cabimas Venez. 142 D1
Cabinda Angola 99 B4
Cabinda prov. Angola 99 B5
Cabinet Inlet Antarctica 152 L2
Cabinet Mountains U.S.A. 126 E2
Cabistra Turkey see Ereğli
Cabo Frio Brazil 145 C3
Cabo Frio, Ilha do i. Brazil 145 C3
Cabonga, Réservoir resr Canada 122 F5
Cabool U.S.A. 131 E4
Caboolture Australia 112 F1
Cabo Orange, Parque Nacional de nat. park Brazil 143 H3
Cabo Pantoja Peru 142 C4
Cabora Bassa, Lake resr Moz. 99 D5
Cabo Raso Arg. 144 C6
Caborca Mex. 127 E7
Cabot Head hd Canada 134 E1
Cabot Strait Canada 123 J5
Cabourg France 49 G9
Cabo Verde country N. Atlantic Ocean see Cape Verde
Cabo Verde, Ilhas do is N. Atlantic Ocean 96 [inset]
Cabo Yubi Morocco see Tarfaya
Cabral, Serra do mts Brazil 145 B2
Cäbrayıl Azer. 91 G3
Cabrera i. Spain 57 H4
Cabri Canada 121 I5
Cabullona Mex. 127 F7
Caçador Brazil 145 A4
Cacagoin China see Qagca
Čačak Serb. and Mont. 59 I3
Caccia, Capo c. Sardinia Italy 58 C4
Cacequi Brazil 144 F3
Cáceres Brazil 143 G7
Cáceres Spain 57 C4
Cache Creek Canada 120 F5
Cache Peak U.S.A. 126 E4
Cacheu Guinea-Bissau 96 B3
Cachi, Nevados de mts Arg. 144 C2
Cachimbo, Serra do hills Brazil 143 H5
Cachoeira Brazil 145 D1
Cachoeira Alta Brazil 145 A2
Cachoeira de Goiás Brazil 145 A2
Cachoeira do Arari Brazil 143 I4
Cachoeiro de Itapemirim Brazil 145 C3
Cacine Guinea-Bissau 96 B3
Caciporé, Cabo c. Brazil 143 H3
Cacolo Angola 99 B5
Cacongo Angola 99 B4
Cactus U.S.A. 131 C4
Caçu Brazil 145 A2
Caculé Brazil 145 C1
Čadca Slovakia 47 Q6
Cadereyta Mex. 131 C7
Cadibarrawirracanna, Lake salt flat Australia 111 A6
Cadillac Canada 121 J5
Cadillac U.S.A. 134 C1
Cadiz Phil. 69 G4
Cádiz Spain 57 C5
Cadiz IN U.S.A. 134 C4
Cadiz KY U.S.A. 132 C4
Cadiz OH U.S.A. 134 E3
Cádiz, Golfo de g. Spain 57 C5
Cadiz Lake U.S.A. 129 F4
Cadomin Canada 120 G4
Cadotte r. Canada 120 G3
Cadotte Lake Canada 120 G3
Caen France 56 D2
Caerdydd U.K. see Cardiff
Caerffili U.K. see Caerphilly
Caerfyrddin U.K. see Carmarthen
Caergybi U.K. see Holyhead
Caernarfon U.K. 49 C5
Caernarfon Bay U.K. 49 C5
Caernarvon U.K. see Caernarfon
Caerphilly U.K. 49 D7
Caesaraugusta Spain see Zaragoza
Caesarea Alg. see Cherchell
Caesarea Cappadociae Turkey see Kayseri
Caesarea Philippi Syria see Bāniyās
Caesarodunum France see Tours
Caesaromagus U.K. see Chelmsford
Caetité Brazil 145 C1
Cafayate Arg. 144 C3
Cafelândia Brazil 145 A3
Caffa Ukr. see Feodosiya
Cagayan de Oro Phil. 69 G5
Cagles Mill Lake U.S.A. 134 B4
Cagli Italy 58 E3
Cagliari Sardinia Italy 58 C5
Cagliari, Golfo di b. Sardinia Italy 58 C5
Cahama Angola 99 B5
Caha Mts hills Rep. of Ireland 51 C6
Cahermore Rep. of Ireland 51 B6
Cahersiveen Rep. of Ireland 51 B6
Cahir Rep. of Ireland 51 E5
Cahirciveen Rep. of Ireland see Cahersiveen
Cahora Bassa, Lago de resr Moz. see Cabora Bassa, Lake
Cahore Point Rep. of Ireland 51 F5
Cahors France 56 E4
Cahuapanas Peru 142 C5
Cahul Moldova 59 M2
Caia Moz. 99 D5
Caiabis, Serra dos hills Brazil 143 G6
Caianda Angola 99 C5
Caiapó r. Brazil 145 A1
Caiapó, Serra do mts Brazil 145 A2
Caiapônia Brazil 145 A2
Caibarién Cuba 133 E8
Cai Bâu, Đao i. Vietnam 70 D2
Caicara Venez. 142 E2
Caicos Islands Turks and Caicos Is 137 J4
Caicos Passage Bahamas/Turks and Caicos Is 133 F8
Caidian China 77 G2
Caiguna Australia 109 D8
Caimodorro mt. Spain 57 F3
Cainnyigoin China 76 D1
Cains Store U.S.A. 134 C5
Caipe Arg. 144 C2
Caird Coast Antarctica 152 B1
Cairngorm Mountains U.K. 50 F3
Cairnryan U.K. 50 D6
Cairns Australia 110 D3
Cairnsmore of Carsphairn hill U.K. 50 E5

▶Cairo Egypt 90 C5
Capital of Egypt and most populous city in Africa.

Cairo U.S.A. 133 C6
Caisleán an Bharraigh Rep. of Ireland see Castlebar
Caiundo Angola 99 B5
Caiwarro Australia 112 B2
Caiyuanzhen China see Shengsi
Caizi Hu l. China 77 H2
Cajamarca Peru 142 C5
Cajati Brazil 145 A4
Cajuru Brazil 145 B3
Caka'lho China see Yanjing
Čakovec Croatia 58 G1
Çal Denizli Turkey 59 M5
Çal Hakkâri Turkey see Çukurca
Cala S. Africa 101 H6
Calabar Nigeria 96 D4
Calabogie Canada 135 G1
Calabria, Parco Nazionale della nat. park Italy 58 G5
Calafat Romania 59 J3
Calagua Mex. 127 F8
Calagurris Spain see Calahorra
Calahorra Spain 57 F2
Calai Angola 99 B5
Calais France 52 B4
Calais U.S.A. 123 I5
Calalasteo, Sierra de mts Arg. 144 C3
Calama Brazil 142 F5
Calama Chile 144 C2
Calamajué Mex. 127 E7
Calamar Col. 142 D1
Calamian Group is Phil. 68 F4
Calamocha Spain 57 F3
Calandula Angola 99 B4
Calang Indon. 71 A6
Calanscio Sand Sea des. Libya 86 B3
Calapan Phil. 69 G4
Călărași Romania 59 L2
Calatayud Spain 57 F3
Calayan i. Phil. 69 G3
Calbayog Phil. 69 G4
Calbe (Saale) Germany 53 L3
Calçoene Brazil 143 H3
Calcutta India see Kolkata
Caldas da Rainha Port. 57 B4
Caldas Novas Brazil 143 I7
Calden Germany 53 J3
Calder r. Canada 120 G1
Caldera Chile 144 B3
Calderyale Australia 110 D5
Caldew r. U.K. 48 E4
Caldwell ID U.S.A. 126 D4
Caldwell KS U.S.A. 131 D4
Caldwell OH U.S.A. 134 E4
Caldwell TX U.S.A. 131 D6
Caledon r. Lesotho/S. Africa 101 H6
Caledon S. Africa 100 D8
Caledon Bay Australia 110 B2
Caledonia Canada 134 F2
Caledonia admin. div. U.K. see Scotland
Caledonia U.S.A. 135 G2
Caleta el Cobre Chile 144 B2
Calexico U.S.A. 129 F5
Calf of Man i. Isle of Man 48 C4
Calgary Canada 120 H5
Calhoun U.S.A. 134 B5
Cali Col. 142 C3
Calicut India 84 B4
Caliente U.S.A. 129 F3
California U.S.A. 134 F3
California state U.S.A. 127 C4
California, Golfo de g. Mex. see California, Gulf of
California, Gulf of Mex. 127 E7
California Aqueduct canal U.S.A. 128 C3
Cälilabad Azer. 91 H3
Calingasta Arg. 144 C4
Calipatria U.S.A. 129 F5
Calistoga U.S.A. 128 B2
Calkiní Mex. 136 F4
Callabonna, Lake salt flat Australia 111 C6
Callabonna Creek watercourse Australia 111 C6
Callaghan, Mount U.S.A. 128 E2
Callan Rep. of Ireland 51 E5
Callan r. U.K. 51 F3
Callander Canada 122 F5
Callander U.K. 50 E4
Callang Phil. 77 I5
Callao Peru 142 C6
Callao U.S.A. 129 G2
Callicoon U.S.A. 135 H3
Calling Lake Canada 120 H4
Callington U.K. 49 C8
Calliope Australia 110 E5
Callipolis Turkey see Gallipoli
Calmar U.S.A. 130 F3
Caloosahatchee r. U.S.A. 133 D7
Caloundra Australia 112 F1
Caltagirone Sicily Italy 58 F6
Caltanissetta Sicily Italy 58 F6
Calucinga Angola 99 B5
Calulo Angola 99 B4
Calunga Angola 99 B5
Caluquembe Angola 99 B5
Caluula Somalia 98 F2
Caluula, Raas pt Somalia 98 F2
Calvert Hills Australia 110 B3
Calvert Island Canada 120 D5
Calvi Corsica France 56 I5
Calvià Spain 57 H4
Calvinia S. Africa 100 D6
Calvo, Monte mt. Italy 58 F4
Cam r. U.K. 49 H6
Camaçari Brazil 145 D1
Camache Reservoir U.S.A. 128 C2
Camachigama r. Canada 122 F5
Camacho Mex. 131 C7
Camacuio Angola 99 B5
Camacupa Angola 99 B5
Camagüey Cuba 137 I4
Camagüey, Archipiélago de is Cuba 137 I4
Camah, Gunung mt. Malaysia 71 C6
Camamu Brazil 145 D1
Camana Peru 142 D7
Camanongue Angola 99 C5
Camapuã Brazil 143 H7
Camaquã Brazil 144 F4
Çamardı Turkey 90 D3
Camargo Bol. 142 E8
Camargue reg. France 56 G5
Camarillo U.S.A. 128 D4
Camarones Arg. 144 C6
Camarones, Bahía b. Arg. 144 C6
Camas r. U.S.A. 126 E4
Ca Mau Vietnam 71 D5
Cambay India see Khambhat
Cambay, Gulf of India see Khambhat, Gulf of
Camberley U.K. 49 G7
▶Cambodia country Asia 71 D4
Asia 6, 62–63
Camboriú Brazil 145 A4
Camborne U.K. 49 B8
Cambrai France 52 D4
Cambria admin. div. U.K. see Wales
Cambrian Mountains hills U.K. 49 D6
Cambridge Canada 134 E2
Cambridge N.Z. 113 E3
Cambridge U.K. 49 H6
Cambridge MA U.S.A. 135 J2
Cambridge MD U.S.A. 135 G4
Cambridge MN U.S.A. 130 E2
Cambridge NY U.S.A. 135 I2
Cambridge OH U.S.A. 134 E3
Cambridge Bay Canada 119 H3
Cambridge City U.S.A. 134 C4
Cambridge Springs U.S.A. 134 E3
Cambrien, Lac l. Canada 123 H2
Cambulo Angola 99 C4
Cambundi-Catembo Angola 99 B5
Cambuquira Brazil 145 B3
Cam Co l. China 83 E2
Camden AL U.S.A. 133 C5
Camden AR U.S.A. 131 E5
Camden NJ U.S.A. 135 H4
Camden NY U.S.A. 135 H2
Camden SC U.S.A. 133 D5
Camdenton U.S.A. 130 E4
Cameia Angola 99 C5
Cameia, Parque Nacional da nat. park Angola 99 C5
Cameron AZ U.S.A. 129 H4
Cameron LA U.S.A. 131 E6
Cameron MO U.S.A. 130 E4
Cameron TX U.S.A. 131 D6
Cameron Highlands mts Malaysia 71 C6
Cameron Hills Canada 120 G3
Cameron Island Canada 119 H2
Cameron Park U.S.A. 128 C2
▶Cameroon country Africa 96 E4
Africa 7, 94–95
Cameroon, Mount vol. Cameroon see Cameroun, Mont
Caméroun country Africa see Cameroon
Cameroun, Mont vol. Cameroon 96 D4
Cametá Brazil 143 I4
Camiña Chile 142 E7
Camiri Bol. 142 F8
Camisea Peru 142 D6
Camocim Brazil 143 J4
Camooweal Australia 110 B3
Camooweal Caves National Park Australia 110 B4
Camorta i. India 81 H10
Campana Mex. 131 C7
Campana, Isla i. Chile 144 A7
Campania Island Canada 120 D4
Campbell S. Africa 100 F5
Campbell, Cape N.Z. 113 E5
Campbell, Mount hill Australia 108 E5
Campbellford Canada 135 G1
Campbell Hill hill U.S.A. 134 D3
Campbell Island N.Z. 150 H9
Campbell Lake Canada 121 J2
Campbell Plateau sea feature S. Pacific Ocean 150 H9
Campbell Range hills Australia 108 D3
Campbell River Canada 120 E5
Campbellsville U.S.A. 134 C5
Campbellton Canada 123 I5
Campbelltown Australia 112 E5
Campbeltown U.K. 50 D5
Campeche Mex. 136 F5
Campeche, Bahía de g. Mex. 136 F5
Camperdown Australia 112 A7
Câmpina Romania 59 K2
Campina Grande Brazil 143 K5
Campinas Brazil 145 B3
Campina Verde Brazil 145 A2
Campo Cameroon 96 D4
Campobasso Italy 58 F4
Campo Belo Brazil 145 B3
Campo Belo do Sul Brazil 145 A4
Campo de Diauarum Brazil 143 H6
Campo Florido Brazil 145 A2
Campo Gallo Arg. 144 D3
Campo Grande Brazil 144 F2
Campo Largo Brazil 145 A4
Campo Maior Brazil 143 J4
Campo Maior Port. 57 C4
Campo Mourão Brazil 144 F2
Campos Brazil 145 C3
Campos Altos Brazil 145 B2
Campos Novos Brazil 145 A4
Campos Sales Brazil 143 J5
Campton U.S.A. 134 D5
Câmpulung Romania 59 K2
Câmpulung Moldovenesc Romania 59 K1
Camp Verde U.S.A. 129 H4
Cam Ranh Vietnam 71 E5
Camrose Canada 121 H4
Camrose U.K. 49 B7
Camsell Lake Canada 121 I2
Camsell Portage Canada 121 I3
Camsell Range mts Canada 120 F2
Camulodunum U.K. see Colchester
Çan Turkey 59 L4
Canaan r. Canada 123 I5
Canaan U.S.A. 135 I2
Canaan Peak U.S.A. 129 H3
Canabrava Brazil 145 B2
Canacona India 84 B3

▶Canada country N. America 118 H4
Largest country in North America and 2nd in the world. 3rd most populous country in North America.
North America 9, 116–117

Canada Basin sea feature Arctic Ocean 153 A1
Canadian U.S.A. 131 C5
Canadian r. U.S.A. 131 E5
Canadian Abyssal Plain sea feature Arctic Ocean 153 A1
Cañadon Grande, Sierra mts Arg. 144 C7
Canaima, Parque Nacional nat. park Venez. 142 F2
Çanakkale Turkey 59 L4
Çanakkale Boğazı strait Turkey see Dardanelles
Canalejas Arg. 144 C5
Cañamares Spain 57 E3
Canandaigua U.S.A. 135 G2
Cananea Mex. 127 F7
Cananéia Brazil 145 B4
Canápolis Brazil 145 A2
Cañar Ecuador 142 C4
Canarias terr. N. Atlantic Ocean see Canary Islands
Canárias, Ilha das i. Brazil 143 J4
Canarias, Islas terr. N. Atlantic Ocean see Canary Islands

▶Canary Islands terr. N. Atlantic Ocean 96 B2
Autonomous Community of Spain.
Africa 7, 94–95

Canaseraga U.S.A. 135 G2
Canastota U.S.A. 135 H2
Canastra, Serra da mts Brazil 145 B2
Canastra, Serra da mts Brazil 145 A1
Canatiba Brazil 145 C1
Canatlán Mex. 131 B7
Canaveral, Cape U.S.A. 133 D6
Cañaveras Spain 57 E3
Canavieiras Brazil 145 D1
Canbelego Australia 112 C3

▶Canberra Australia 112 D5
Capital of Australia.

Cancún Mex. 137 G4
Çandar Turkey see Kastamonu
Çandarlı Turkey 59 L5
Candela Mex. 131 C7
Candela r. Mex. 131 C7
Candelaria Mex. 127 G7
Candia Greece see Iraklion
Cândido de Abreu Brazil 145 A4
Çandır Turkey 90 D2
Candle Lake Canada 121 J4
Candlewood, Lake U.S.A. 135 I3
Cando U.S.A. 130 D1
Candon Phil. 77 I5
Cane r. Australia 108 A5
Canea Greece see Chania
Canela Brazil 145 A5
Canelones Uruguay 144 E4
Cane Valley U.S.A. 134 C5
Cangallo Peru 142 D6
Cangamba Angola 99 B5
Cangandala, Parque Nacional de nat. park Angola 99 B4
Cangbu r. China see Brahmaputra
Cango Caves S. Africa 100 F7
Cangola Angola 99 B4
Cangshan China 77 H1
Canguaretama Brazil 143 K5
Canguçu Brazil 144 F4
Canguçu, Serra do hills Brazil 144 F4
Cangwu China 77 F4
Cangzhou China 73 L5
Caniapiscau Canada 123 H3
Caniapiscau r. Canada 123 H2
Caniapiscau, Lac l. Canada 123 H3
Caniçado Moz. see Guija
Canicattì Sicily Italy 58 E6
Canim Lake Canada 120 F5
Canindé Brazil 143 K4
Canisteo U.S.A. 135 G2
Canisteo r. U.S.A. 135 G2
Canisteo Peninsula Antarctica 152 K2
Cañitas de Felipe Pescador Mex. 131 C8
Çankırı Turkey 90 D2
Canna Australia 109 A7
Canna i. U.K. 50 C3
Cannanore India 84 B4
Cannanore Islands India 84 B4
Cannelton U.S.A. 134 B5
Cannes France 56 H5
Cannock U.K. 49 E6
Cannon Beach U.S.A. 126 C3
Cann River Australia 112 D6
Canoas Brazil 145 A5
Canõas, Rio das r. Brazil 145 A4
Canoeiros Brazil 145 B2
Canoe Lake Canada 121 I4
Canoe Lake l. Canada 121 I4
Canoinhas Brazil 145 A4
Canon City U.S.A. 127 G5
Cañon Largo watercourse U.S.A. 129 J3
Canoona Australia 110 E4
Canora Canada 121 K5
Canowindra Australia 112 D4
Canso Canada 123 J5
Canso, Cape Canada 123 J5
Cantabrian Mountains Spain see Cantábrica, Cordillera
Cantábrica, Cordillera mts Spain 57 D2
Cantábrico, Mar sea Spain 57 C2
Canterbury U.K. 49 I7
Canterbury Bight b. N.Z. 113 C7
Canterbury Plains N.Z. 113 C6
Cần Thơ Vietnam 71 D5
Cantil U.S.A. 128 E4
Canton GA U.S.A. 133 C5
Canton IL U.S.A. 130 F3
Canton MO U.S.A. 130 F3
Canton MS U.S.A. 131 F5
Canton NY U.S.A. 135 H1
Canton OH U.S.A. 134 E3
Canton PA U.S.A. 135 G3
Canton SD U.S.A. 130 D3
Canton TX U.S.A. 131 E5
Canton Island atoll Kiribati see Kanton
Cantuaria U.K. see Canterbury
Canunda National Park Australia 111 C8
Canutama Brazil 142 F5
Canutillo Mex. 131 B7
Canvey Island U.K. 49 H7
Canwood Canada 121 J4
Cany-Barville France 49 H9
Canyon Canada 120 B2
Canyon U.S.A. 131 C5
Canyon City U.S.A. 126 D3
Canyondam U.S.A. 128 C1
Canyon de Chelly National Monument nat. park U.S.A. 129 I3
Canyon Ferry Lake U.S.A. 126 F3
Canyon Lake U.S.A. 129 H5
Canyonlands National Park U.S.A. 129 I2
Canyon Ranges mts Canada 120 E2
Canyons of the Ancients National Monument nat. park U.S.A. 129 I3
Canyonville U.S.A. 126 C4
Cao Bằng Vietnam 70 D2
Caocheng China see Caoxian
Caohai China see Weining
Caohe China see Qichun
Caohu China 80 F3
Caojiahe China see Qichun
Caojian China 76 C3
Cao Nguyên Đắc Lắc plat. Vietnam 71 E4
Caoshi China 74 B4
Caoxian China 77 G1
Caozhou China see Heze
Capac U.S.A. 134 D2
Çapakçur Turkey see Bingöl
Capanaparo r. Venez. 142 E2
Capanema Brazil 143 I4
Capão Bonito Brazil 145 A4
Caparaó, Serra do mts Brazil 145 C3
Cap-aux-Meules Canada 123 J5
Cap-de-la-Madeleine Canada 123 G5
Cape r. Australia 110 D4
Cape Arid National Park Australia 109 C8
Cape Barren Island Australia 111 [inset]
Cape Basin sea feature S. Atlantic Ocean 148 I8
Cape Breton Highlands National Park Canada 123 J5
Cape Breton Island Canada 123 J5
Cape Charles Canada 123 L3
Cape Charles U.S.A. 135 G5
Cape Coast Ghana 96 C4
Cape Coast Castle Ghana see Cape Coast
Cape Cod Bay U.S.A. 135 J3
Cape Cod National Seashore nature res. U.S.A. 135 K3
Cape Coral U.S.A. 133 D7
Cape Crawford Australia 110 A3
Cape Dorset Canada 119 K3
Cape Fanshaw U.S.A. 120 C3
Cape Fear r. U.S.A. 133 E5
Cape George Canada 123 J5
Cape Girardeau U.S.A. 131 F4
Cape Johnson Depth sea feature N. Pacific Ocean 150 E5
Cape Juby Morocco see Tarfaya
Cape Krusenstern National Monument nat. park U.S.A. 118 B3
Capel Australia 109 A8
Cape Le Grand National Park Australia 109 C8
Capelinha Brazil 145 C2
Capella Australia 110 E4
Capelle aan de IJssel Neth. 52 E3
Capelongo Angola see Kuvango
Cape May U.S.A. 135 H4
Cape May Court House U.S.A. 135 H4
Cape May Point U.S.A. 135 H4
Cape Melville National Park Australia 110 D2
Capenda-Camulemba Angola 99 B4
Cape of Good Hope Nature Reserve S. Africa 100 D8
Cape Palmerston National Park Australia 110 E4
Cape Range National Park Australia 108 A5
Cape St George Canada 123 K4

▶Cape Town S. Africa 100 D7
Legislative capital of South Africa.

Cape Tribulation National Park Australia 110 D2
Cape Upstart National Park Australia 110 D3
▶Cape Verde country N. Atlantic Ocean 96 [inset]
Africa 7, 94–95
Cape Verde Basin sea feature N. Atlantic Ocean 148 F5
Cape Verde Plateau sea feature N. Atlantic Ocean 148 F4
Cape Vincent U.S.A. 135 G1
Cape York Peninsula Australia 110 C2
Cap-Haïtien Haiti 137 J5
Capim r. Brazil 143 I4
Capitán Arturo Prat research station Antarctica 152 A2

▶Capitol Hill N. Mariana Is 69 L3
Capital of the Northern Mariana Islands, on Saipan.

Capitol Reef National Park U.S.A. 129 H2
Capivara, Represa resr Brazil 145 A3
Čapljina Bos.-Herz. 58 G3
Cappoquin Rep. of Ireland 51 E5
Capraia, Isola di i. Italy 58 C3
Caprara, Punta pt Sardinia Italy 58 C4
Capri, Isola di i. Italy 58 F4
Capricorn Channel Australia 110 E4
Capricorn Group atolls Australia 110 F4
Caprivi Strip reg. Namibia 99 C5
Cap Rock Escarpment U.S.A. 131 C5
Capsa Tunisia see Gafsa
Captain Cook HI U.S.A. 127 [inset]
Captina r. U.S.A. 134 E4
Capuava Brazil 145 B4
Caquetá r. Col. 142 E4
Caracal Romania 59 K2

▶Caracas Venez. 142 E1
Capital of Venezuela.

Caraguatatuba Brazil 145 B3
Caraí Brazil 145 C2
Carajás Brazil 143 H5
Carajás, Serra dos hills Brazil 143 H5
Carales Sardinia Italy see Cagliari
Caralis Sardinia Italy see Cagliari
Carandaí Brazil 145 C3
Caransebeș Romania 59 J2
Caraquet Canada 123 I5
Caratasca, Laguna de lag. Hond. 137 H5
Caratinga Brazil 145 C2
Carauari Brazil 142 E4
Caravaca de la Cruz Spain 57 F4
Caravelas Brazil 145 D2
Carberry Canada 121 L5
Carbó Mex. 127 F7
Carbonara, Capo c. Sardinia Italy 58 C5
Carbondale CO U.S.A. 129 J2
Carbondale PA U.S.A. 135 H3
Carboneras Mex. 131 D7
Carbonia Sardinia Italy 58 C5
Carbonita Brazil 145 C2
Carcaixent Spain 57 F4
Carcajou Canada 120 G3
Carcajou r. Canada 120 D1
Carcar Phil. 69 G4
Carcassonne France 56 F5
Cardamomes, Chaîne des mts Cambodia/Thai. see Cardamom Range
Cardamom Hills India 84 C4
Cardamom Range mts Cambodia/Thai. 71 C4
Cárdenas Cuba 137 H4
Cárdenas Mex. 136 E4
Cardenyabba watercourse Australia 112 A2
Çardi Turkey see Harmancık
Cardiel, Lago l. Arg. 144 B7

▶Cardiff U.K. 49 D7
Capital of Wales.

Cardiff U.S.A. 135 G4
Cardigan U.K. 49 C6
Cardigan Bay U.K. 49 C6
Cardinal Lake Canada 120 G3
Cardington U.S.A. 134 D3
Cardón, Cerro hill Mex. 127 E8
Cardoso Brazil 145 A3
Cardoso, Ilha do i. Brazil 145 B4
Cardston Canada 120 H5
Careen Lake Canada 121 I3
Carei Romania 59 J1
Carentan France 56 D2
Carey U.S.A. 134 D3
Carey, Lake salt flat Australia 109 C7
Carey Lake Canada 121 K2
Cargados Carajos Islands Mauritius 149 L7
Carhaix-Plouguer France 56 C2
Cariacica Brazil 145 C3
Cariamanga Ecuador 142 C4
Caribbean Sea N. Atlantic Ocean 137 H5
Cariboo Mountains Canada 120 F4

Changbai Shan mts China/N. Korea 74 B4
Chang Cheng research station Antarctica see Great Wall
Changcheng China 77 F5
Changchow Fujian China see Zhangzhou
Changchow Jiangsu China see Changzhou
Changchun China 74 B4
Changchunling China 74 B3
Changde China 77 F2
Changgang China 77 G3
Changge China 77 G1
Changgi-ap pt S. Korea 75 C5
Changgo China 83 F3
Chang Hu l. China 77 G2
Changhua Taiwan 77 I3
Changhŭng S. Korea 75 B6
Changhwa Taiwan see Changhua
Changi Sing. 71 [inset]
Changji China 80 G3
Changjiang China 77 F5
Chang Jiang r. China 77 I2 see Yangtze
Changjiang Kou China see Mouth of the Yangtze
Changjin-ho resr N. Korea 75 B4
Changkiang China see Zhanjiang
Changlang India 83 H4
Changleng China see Xinjian
Changling China 74 A3
Changlung Jammu and Kashmir 87 M3
Changma China 80 I4
Changning Jiangxi China see Xunwu
Changning Sichuan China 76 E2
Changnyŏn N. Korea 75 B5
Ch'ang-pai Shan mts China/N. Korea see Changbai Shan
Changpu China see Suining
Changp'yŏng S. Korea 75 C5
Changsan-got pt N. Korea 75 B5
Changsha China 77 G2
Changshan China 77 H2
Changshi China 76 E3
Changshoujie China 77 G2
Changshu China 77 I2
Changtai China 77 H3
Changteh China see Changde
Changting Fujian China 77 H3
Changting Heilong. China 74 C3
Ch'angwŏn S. Korea 75 C6
Changxing China 77 H2
Changyang China 77 F2
Changyŏn N. Korea 75 B5
Changyuan China 77 G1
Changzhi China 73 K5
Changzhou China 77 H2
Chañi, Nevado de mt. Arg. 144 C2
Chania Greece 59 K7
Chanion, Kolpos b. Greece 59 J7
Chankou China 76 E1
Channahon U.S.A. 134 A3
Channapatna India 84 C3
Channel Islands English Chan. 49 E9
Channel Islands U.S.A. 128 D5
Channel Islands National Park U.S.A. 128 D4
Channel-Port-aux-Basques Canada 123 K5
Channel Rock i. Bahamas 133 E8
Channel Tunnel France/U.K. 49 I7
Channing U.S.A. 131 C5
Chantada Spain 57 C2
Chanthaburi Thai. 71 C4
Chantilly France 52 C5
Chanumla India 71 A5
Chanute U.S.A. 130 E4
Chanuwala Pak. 89 I3
Chany, Ozero salt l. Rus. Fed. 64 I4
Chaohu China 77 H2
Chao Hu l. China 77 H2
Chaor He r. China see Qulin Gol
Chaouèn Morocco 57 D6
Chaowula Shan mt. China 76 C1
Chaoyang Guangdong China 77 H4
Chaoyang Heilong. China see Jiayin
Chaoyang Liaoning China 73 M4
Chaoyangcun China 74 B2
Chaozhong China 74 A2
Chaozhou China 77 H4
Chapada Diamantina, Parque Nacional nat. park Brazil 145 C1
Chapada dos Veadeiros, Parque Nacional da nat. park Brazil 145 B1
Chapais Canada 122 G4
Chapak Guzar Afgh. 89 G2
Chapala, Laguna de l. Mex. 136 D4
Chapayev Kazakh. 78 E1
Chapayevo Kazakh. see Chapayev
Chapayevsk Rus. Fed. 43 K5
Chapecó Brazil 144 F3
Chapecó r. Brazil 144 F3
Chapel-en-le-Frith U.K. 48 F5
Chapelle-lez-Herlaimont Belgium 52 E4
Chapeltown U.K. 48 F5
Chapleau Canada 122 E5
Chaplin Canada 121 J5
Chaplin Lake Canada 121 J5
Chaplygin Rus. Fed. 43 H5
Chapman, Mount Canada 120 G5
Chapmanville U.S.A. 134 D5
Chappell U.S.A. 130 C3
Chappell Islands Australia 111 [inset]
Chapra Bihar India see Chhapra
Chapra Jharkhand India see Chatra
Chapri Pass Afgh. 89 G3
Charagua Bol. 142 F7
Charay Mex. 127 F8
Charcas Mex. 136 D4
Charcot Island Antarctica 152 L2
Chard Canada 121 I4
Chard U.K. 49 E8
Chardara Kazakh. see Shardara
Chardara, Step' plain Kazakh. 80 C3
Chardon U.S.A. 134 E3
Chardzhev Turkm. see Turkmenabat
Chardzhou Turkm. see Turkmenabat
Charef Alg. 57 H6
Charef, Oued watercourse Morocco 54 D5
Charente r. France 56 D4
Chari r. Cameroon/Chad 97 E3
Chārī Iran 88 E4
Chārīkār Afgh. 89 H3
Chariton U.S.A. 130 E3
Chārjew Turkm. see Turkmenabat
Charkayuvom Rus. Fed. 42 L2
Chār Kent Afgh. 89 G2
Charkhlik China see Ruoqiang
Charleroi Belgium 52 E4
Charles, Cape U.S.A. 135 H5
Charlesbourg Canada 123 H5
Charles City IA U.S.A. 130 E3
Charles City VA U.S.A. 135 G5
Charles de Gaulle airport France 52 C5
Charles Hill Botswana 100 E2
Charles Island Galápagos Ecuador see Santa María, Isla
Charles Lake Canada 121 I3
Charles Point Australia 108 E3
Charleston N.Z. 113 C5
Charleston IL U.S.A. 130 F4
Charleston MO U.S.A. 131 F4
Charleston SC U.S.A. 133 E5

▶Charleston WV U.S.A. 134 E4
State capital of West Virginia.

Charleston Peak U.S.A. 129 F3
Charlestown Rep. of Ireland 51 D4
Charlestown IN U.S.A. 134 C4
Charlestown NH U.S.A. 135 I2
Charlestown RI U.S.A. 135 J3
Charles Town U.S.A. 135 G4
Charleville Australia 111 D5
Charleville Rep. of Ireland see Rathluirc
Charleville-Mézières France 52 E5
Charlevoix U.S.A. 134 C1
Charlie Lake Canada 120 F3
Charlotte MI U.S.A. 134 C2
Charlotte NC U.S.A. 133 D5
Charlotte TN U.S.A. 134 B5

▶Charlotte Amalie Virgin Is (U.S.A.) 137 L5
Capital of the U.S. Virgin Islands.

Charlotte Harbor b. U.S.A. 133 D7
Charlotte Lake Canada 120 E4
Charlottesville U.S.A. 135 F4

▶Charlottetown Canada 123 J5
Provincial capital of Prince Edward Island.

Charlton Australia 112 A6
Charlton Island Canada 122 F3
Charron Lake Canada 121 M4
Charsadda Pak. 89 H3
Charshanga Turkm. 89 G2
Charshangngy Turkm. see Charshanga
Charters Towers Australia 110 D4
Chartres France 56 E2
Chas India 83 F5
Chase Canada 120 G5
Chase U.S.A. 134 C2
Chase City U.S.A. 135 F5
Chashmeh Nūrī Iran 88 E3
Chashmeh-ye Ab-e Garm spring Iran 88 E3
Chashmeh-ye Garm Ab spring Iran 88 E3
Chashmeh-ye Magu well Iran 88 E3
Chashmeh-ye Mūkīk spring Iran 88 E3
Chashmeh-ye Palasi Iran 88 D3
Chashmeh-ye Safid spring Iran 88 E3
Chashmeh-ye Shotoran well Iran 88 D3
Chashniki Belarus 43 F5
Chaska U.S.A. 130 E2
Chaslands Mistake c. N.Z. 113 B8
Chasŏng N. Korea 74 B4
Chasseral mt. Switz. 47 K7
Chassiron, Pointe de pt France 56 D3
Chastab, Kūh-e mts Iran 88 D3
Chāt Iran 88 D2
Chatanika U.S.A. 118 D3
Châteaubriant France 56 D3
Château-du-Loir France 56 E3
Châteaudun France 56 E2
Chateaugay U.S.A. 135 H1
Châteauguay Canada 135 I1
Châteauguay r. Canada 123 H2
Châteauguay, Lac l. Canada 123 H2
Châteaulin France 56 B2
Châteaumeillant France 56 F3
Châteauneuf-en-Thymerais France 52 B6
Châteauneuf-sur-Loire France 56 F3
Chateau Pond l. Canada 123 K3
Châteauroux France 56 E3
Château-Salins France 52 G6
Château-Thierry France 52 D5
Chateh Canada 120 G3
Châtelet Belgium 52 E4
Châtellerault France 56 E3
Chatfield U.S.A. 122 B6
Chatham Canada 134 D2
Chatham U.K. 49 H7
Chatham MA U.S.A. 135 K3
Chatham NY U.S.A. 135 I2
Chatham PA U.S.A. 135 H4
Chatham VA U.S.A. 134 F5
Chatham, Isla i. Chile 144 B8
Chatham Island Galápagos Ecuador see San Cristóbal, Isla
Chatham Island N.Z. 107 I6
Chatham Island Samoa see Savai'i
Chatham Islands N.Z. 107 I6
Chatham Rise sea feature S. Pacific Ocean 150 I8
Chatham Strait U.S.A. 120 C3
Châtillon-sur-Seine France 56 G3
Chatkal Range mts Kyrg./Uzbek. 80 D3
Chatom U.S.A. 131 F6
Chatra India 83 F4
Chatra Nepal 83 F4
Chatsworth Canada 134 E1
Chatsworth U.S.A. 135 H4
Chattagam Bangl. see Chittagong
Chattanooga U.S.A. 133 C5
Chattarpur India see Chhatarpur
Chatteris U.K. 49 H6
Chattisgarh state India see Chhattisgarh
Chatturat Thai. 70 C4
Chatyr-Tash Kyrg. 80 E3
Châu Đốc Vietnam 71 D5
Chauhtan India 82 B4
Chauk Myanmar 70 A2
Chaumont France 56 G2
Chauncey U.S.A. 134 D4
Chaungzon Myanmar 70 B3
Chaunskaya Guba b. Rus. Fed. 65 R3
Chauny France 52 D5
Chau Phu Vietnam see Châu Đốc
Chausy Belarus see Chavusy
Chautauqua, Lake U.S.A. 134 F2
Chauter Pak. 89 G4
Chauvin Canada 121 I4
Chavakachcheri Sri Lanka 84 D4
Chaves Port. 57 C3
Chavigny, Lac l. Canada 122 G2
Chavusy Belarus 43 F5
Chawal r. Pak. 89 G4
Chây r. Vietnam 70 D2
Chayatyn, Khrebet ridge Rus. Fed. 74 E1
Chayevo Rus. Fed. 42 H4
Chaykovskiy Rus. Fed. 41 Q4
Chazhegovo Rus. Fed. 42 L3
Chazy U.S.A. 135 I1
Cheadle U.K. 49 F6
Cheaha Mountain hill U.S.A. 133 C5
Cheat r. U.S.A. 134 F4
Cheatham Lake U.S.A. 134 B5
Cheb Czech Rep. 53 M4
Chebba Tunisia 58 D7
Cheboksarskoye Vodokhranilishche resr Rus. Fed. 42 J5
Cheboksary Rus. Fed. 42 J4
Cheboygan U.S.A. 132 C2
Chechen', Ostrov i. Rus. Fed. 91 G2
Chech'ŏn S. Korea 75 C5
Chedabucto Bay Canada 123 J5
Cheddar U.K. 49 E7
Cheduba Myanmar 70 A3
Cheduba Island Myanmar 70 A3
Chée r. France 52 E6
Cheektowaga U.S.A. 135 F2
Cheepie Australia 112 B1
Cheetham, Cape Antarctica 152 H2
Chefoo China see Yantai
Chefornak U.S.A. 118 B3
Chefu Moz. 101 K2
Chegdomyn Rus. Fed. 74 D2
Chegga Mauritania 96 C2
Chegutu Zimbabwe 99 D5
Chehalis U.S.A. 126 C3
Chehar Burj Iran 88 E2
Chehardeh Iran 88 E3
Chehel Chashmeh, Kūh-e hill Iran 88 B3
Chehel Dokhtarān, Kūh-e mt. Iran 89 F4
Chehell'āyeh Iran 88 E4
Cheju S. Korea 75 B6
Cheju-do i. S. Korea 75 B6
Cheju-haehyŏp sea chan. S. Korea 75 B6
Chek Chue Hong Kong China see Stanley
Chekhov Moskovskaya Oblast' Rus. Fed. 43 H5
Chekhov Sakhalinskaya Oblast' Rus. Fed. 74 F3
Chekiang prov. China see Zhejiang
Chekichler Turkm. see Chekishlyar
Chekishlyar Turkm. 88 D2
Chek Lap Kok reg. Hong Kong China 77 [inset]
Chek Mun Hoi Hap Hong Kong China see Tolo Channel
Chekunda Rus. Fed. 74 D2
Chela, Serra da mts Angola 99 B5
Chelan, Lake U.S.A. 126 C2
Cheleken Turkm. 88 D2
Chélif, Oued r. Alg. 57 G5
Cheline Moz. 101 L2
Chelkar Kazakh. see Shalkar
Chełm Poland 43 D6
Chelmer r. U.K. 49 H7
Chełmno Poland 47 Q4
Chelmsford U.K. 49 H7
Chelsea MI U.S.A. 134 C2
Chelsea VT U.S.A. 135 I2
Cheltenham U.K. 49 E7
Chelva Spain 57 F4
Chelyabinsk Rus. Fed. 64 H4
Chelyuskin Rus. Fed. 153 E1
Chemba Moz. 99 D5
Chêm Co l. China 82 D2
Chemenibit Turkm. 89 F3
Chemnitz Germany 53 M4
Chemulpo S. Korea see Inch'ŏn
Chenab r. India/Pak. 82 B3
Chenachane, Oued watercourse Alg. 96 C2
Chendir r. Turkm. see Chandyr
Cheney U.S.A. 126 D3
Cheney Reservoir U.S.A. 130 D4
Chengalpattu India 84 D3
Chengbu China 77 F3
Chengchow China see Zhengzhou
Chengde China 73 L4
Chengdu China 76 E2
Chengele India 76 C2
Chenggong China 76 D3
Chenghai China 77 H4
Cheng Hai l. China 76 D3
Chengjiang China see Taihe
Chengmai China 77 F5
Chengtu China see Chengdu
Chengwu China 77 G1
Chengxian China 76 E1
Chengxiang Chongqing China see Wuxi
Chengxiang Jiangxi China see Quannan
Chengzhong China see Ningming
Cheniu Shan i. China 77 H1
Chenkaladi Sri Lanka 84 D5
Chennai India 84 D3
Chenqian Shan i. China 77 I2
Chenqing China 74 B2
Chenqingqiao China see Chenqing
Chenstokhov Poland see Częstochowa
Chentejn Nuruu mts Mongolia 73 J3
Chenxi China 77 F3
Chenyang China see Chenxi
Chenying China see Wannian
Chenzhou China 77 G3
Cheo Reo Vietnam 71 E4
Chepén Peru 142 C5
Chepes Arg. 144 C4
Chepo Panama 137 I7
Chepstow U.K. 49 E7
Cheptsa r. Rus. Fed. 42 K4
Chequamegon Bay U.S.A. 130 F2
Cher r. France 56 E3
Chera state India see Kerala
Cheraw U.S.A. 133 E5
Cherbaniani Reef India 84 A3
Cherbourg France 56 D2
Cherchell Alg. 57 H5
Cherchen China see Qiemo
Cherdakly Rus. Fed. 43 K5
Cherdyn' Rus. Fed. 41 R3
Chereapani reef India see Byramgore Reef
Cheremkhovo Rus. Fed. 72 I2
Cheremshany Rus. Fed. 74 D3
Cheremukhovka Rus. Fed. 42 K4
Cherepanovo Rus. Fed. 72 E2
Cherepovets Rus. Fed. 42 H4
Cherevkovo Rus. Fed. 42 J3
Chergui, Chott ech imp. l. Alg. 54 D5
Chéria Alg. 58 B7
Cheriton U.S.A. 135 H5
Cheriyam atoll India 84 B4
Cherkassy Ukr. see Cherkasy
Cherkasy Ukr. 43 G6
Cherkessk Rus. Fed. 91 F1
Cherla India 84 D2
Chernaya Rus. Fed. 42 M1
Chernaya r. Rus. Fed. 42 M1
Chernigov Ukr. see Chernihiv
Chernigovka Rus. Fed. 74 D3
Chernihiv Ukr. 43 F6
Cherninivka Ukr. 43 H7
Chernivtsi Ukr. 43 E6
Chernobyl' Ukr. see Chornobyl'
Chernogorsk Rus. Fed. 72 G2
Chernovtsy Ukr. see Chernivtsi
Chernoye More sea Asia/Europe see Black Sea
Chernushka Rus. Fed. 41 R4
Chernyakhiv Ukr. 43 F6
Chernyakhovsk Rus. Fed. 45 L9
Chernyanka Rus. Fed. 43 H6
Chernyayevo Rus. Fed. 74 B1
Chernyshevsk Rus. Fed. 73 L2
Chernyshevskiy Rus. Fed. 65 M3
Chernyshkovskiy Rus. Fed. 43 I6
Chernyye Zemli reg. Rus. Fed. 43 J7
Chernyy Irtysh r. China/Kazakh. see Ertix He
Chernyy Porog Rus. Fed. 42 G3
Chernyy Yar Rus. Fed. 43 J6
Cherokee U.S.A. 130 E3
Cherokee Sound Bahamas 133 E7

▶Cherrapunji India 83 G4
Highest recorded annual rainfall in the world.

Cherry Creek r. U.S.A. 130 C2
Cherry Creek Mountains U.S.A. 129 F1
Cherry Hill U.S.A. 135 H4
Cherry Island Solomon Is 107 G3
Cherry Lake U.S.A. 128 D2
Cherskiy Rus. Fed. 153 C2
Cherskiy Range mts Rus. Fed. see Cherskogo, Khrebet
Cherskogo, Khrebet mts Rus. Fed. 65 P3
Cherskogo, Khrebet mts Rus. Fed. 73 K2
Chertkov Ukr. see Chortkiv
Chertkovo Rus. Fed. 43 I6
Cherven Bryag Bulg. 59 K3
Chervonoarmeyskoye Ukr. see Vil'nyans'k
Chervonoarmiys'k Donets'ka Oblast' Ukr. see Krasnoarmiys'k
Chervonoarmiys'k Rivnens'ka Oblast' Ukr. see Radyvyliv
Chervonograd Ukr. see Chervonohrad
Chervonohrad Ukr. 43 E6
Chervyen' Belarus 43 F5
Cherwell r. U.K. 49 F7
Cherykaw Belarus 43 F5
Chesapeake U.S.A. 135 G5
Chesapeake Bay U.S.A. 135 G4
Chesham U.K. 49 G7
Cheshire Plain U.K. 48 E5
Cheshme 2-y Turkm. 89 F2
Cheshskaya Guba b. Rus. Fed. 42 J2
Cheshtebe Tajik. 89 I2
Cheshunt U.K. 49 G7
Chesnokovka Rus. Fed. see Novoaltaysk
Chester Canada 123 I5
Chester U.K. 48 E5
Chester CA U.S.A. 128 C1
Chester IL U.S.A. 130 F4
Chester MT U.S.A. 126 F2
Chester OH U.S.A. 134 E4
Chester SC U.S.A. 133 D5
Chester r. U.S.A. 135 G4
Chesterfield U.K. 48 F5
Chesterfield U.S.A. 135 G5
Chesterfield, Îles is New Caledonia 107 F3
Chesterfield Inlet Canada 121 N2
Chesterfield Inlet inlet Canada 121 M2
Chester-le-Street U.K. 48 F4
Chestertown MD U.S.A. 135 G4
Chestertown NY U.S.A. 135 I2
Chesterville Canada 135 H1
Chestnut Ridge U.S.A. 134 F3
Chesuncook Lake U.S.A. 132 G2
Chetaïbi Alg. 58 B6
Chéticamp Canada 123 J5
Chetlat i. India 84 B4
Chetumal Mex. 136 G5
Chetwynd Canada 120 F4
Cheung Chau Hong Kong China 77 [inset]
Chevelon Creek r. U.S.A. 129 H4
Cheviot N.Z. 113 D6
Cheviot Hills U.K. 48 E3
Cheviot Range hills Australia 110 C5
Chevreulx r. Canada 122 G3
Cheyenne OK U.S.A. 131 D5

▶Cheyenne WY U.S.A. 126 G4
State capital of Wyoming.

Cheyenne r. U.S.A. 130 C2
Cheyenne Wells U.S.A. 130 C4
Cheyne Bay Australia 109 B8
Cheyur India 84 D3
Chezacut Canada 120 E4
Chhapra India 83 F4
Chhata India 82 D4
Chhatak Bangl. 83 G4
Chhatarpur Jharkhand India 83 F4
Chhatarpur Madhya Pradesh India 82 D4
Chhatr Pak. 89 H4
Chhatrapur India 84 E2
Chhattisgarh state India 83 E5
Chhay Arêng, Stœng r. Cambodia 71 C5
Chhindwara India 82 D5
Chhitkul India 82 D3
Chhukha Bhutan 83 G4
Chi, Lam r. Thai. 71 C4
Chi, Mae Nam r. Thai. 70 D4
Chiai Taiwan 77 I4
Chiamboni Somalia 98 E4
Chiange Angola 99 B5
Chiang Kham Thai. 70 C3
Chiang Khan Thai. 70 C3
Chiang Mai Thai. 70 B3
Chiang Rai Thai. 70 B3
Chiang Saen Thai. 70 C2
Chiari Italy 58 C2
Chiautla Mex. 136 E5
Chiavenno Italy 58 C1
Chiayi Taiwan see Chiai
Chiba Japan 75 F6
Chibi China 77 G2
Chibia Angola 99 B5
Chibizovka Rus. Fed. see Zherdevka
Chiboma Moz. 99 D6
Chibougamau Canada 122 G4
Chibougamau, Lac l. Canada 122 G4
Chibu-Sangaku National Park Japan 75 E5
Chibuto Moz. 101 K3
Chibuzhang Hu l. China 83 G2
Chicacole India see Srikakulam

▶Chicago U.S.A. 134 B3
4th most populous city in North America.

Chic-Chocs, Monts mts Canada 123 I4
Chichagof U.S.A. 120 B3
Chichagof Island U.S.A. 120 C3
Chichak r. Pak. 89 G5
Chichaoua Morocco 54 C5
Chichatka Rus. Fed. 74 A1
Chicheng China see Pengxi
Chichester U.K. 49 G8
Chichester Range mts Australia 108 B5
Chichgarh India 84 D1
Chichibu Japan 75 E6
Chichibu-Tama National Park Japan 75 E6
Chichijima-rettō is Japan 75 F8
Chickasha U.S.A. 131 D5
Chiclana de la Frontera Spain 57 C5
Chiclayo Peru 142 C5
Chico r. Arg. 144 C6
Chico U.S.A. 128 C2
Chicomo Moz. 101 L3
Chicopee U.S.A. 135 I2
Chicoutimi Canada 123 H4
Chicualacuala Moz. 101 J2
Chidambaram India 84 C4
Chidenguele Moz. 101 L3
Chidley, Cape Canada 119 L3
Chido China see Sêndo
Chido S. Korea 75 B6
Chiducuane Moz. 101 L3
Chiefland U.S.A. 133 D6
Chiêm Hoa Vietnam 70 D2
Chiemsee l. Germany 47 N7
Chiengmai Thai. see Chiang Mai
Chiers r. France 52 F5
Chieti Italy 58 F3
Chifeng China 73 L4
Chifre, Serra do mts Brazil 145 C2
Chiganak Kazakh. 80 D2
Chiginagak Volcano, Mount U.S.A. 118 C4
Chigu China 83 G3
Chigubo Moz. 101 K2
Chigu Co l. China 83 G3
Chihli, Gulf of China see Bo Hai
Chihuahua Mex. 127 G7
Chihuahua state Mex. 127 G7
Chiili Kazakh. 80 C3
Chikalda India 82 D5
Chikan China 77 F4
Chikaskia r. U.S.A. 131 D4
Chikhali Kalan Parasia India 82 D5
Chikhli India 84 C1
Chikishlyar Turkm. see Chekishlyar
Chikmagalur India 84 B3
Chikodi India 84 B2
Chilanko r. Canada 120 F4
Chilas Jammu and Kashmir 82 C2
Chilaw Sri Lanka 84 C5
Chilcotin r. Canada 120 F5
Childers Australia 110 F5
Childress U.S.A. 131 C5
▶Chile country S. America 144 B4
South America 9, 140–141
Chile Basin sea feature S. Pacific Ocean 151 O8
Chile Chico Chile 144 B7
Chile Rise sea feature S. Pacific Ocean 151 O8
Chilgir Rus. Fed. 43 J7
Chilhowie U.S.A. 134 E5
Chilia-Nouă Ukr. see Kiliya
Chilik Kazakh. 80 E3
Chilika Lake India 84 E2
Chililabombwe Zambia 99 C5
Chilko r. Canada 120 F4
Chilko Lake Canada 120 E5
Chilkoot Pass Canada/U.S.A. 120 C3
Chilkoot Trail National Historic Site nat. park Canada 120 C3
Chillán Chile 144 B5
Chillicothe MO U.S.A. 130 E4
Chillicothe OH U.S.A. 134 D4
Chilliwack Canada 120 F5
Chil'mamedkum, Peski des. Turkm. 88 D1
Chilo India 82 C4
Chiloé, Isla de i. Chile 144 B6
Chiloé, Isla Grande de i. Chile see Chiloé, Isla de
Chilpancingo Mex. 136 E5
Chilpancingo de los Bravos Mex. see Chilpancingo
Chilpi Jammu and Kashmir 82 C1
Chiltern Hills U.K. 49 G7
Chilton U.S.A. 134 A1
Chiluage Angola 99 C4
Chilubi Zambia 99 C5
Chilung Taiwan 77 I3
Chilwa, Lake Malawi 99 D5
Chimala Tanz. 99 D4
Chimaltenango Guat. 136 F6
Chi Ma Wan Hong Kong China 77 [inset]
Chimay Belgium 52 E4
Chimbas Arg. 144 C4
Chimbay Uzbek. 80 A3
Chimborazo mt. Ecuador 142 C4
Chimbote Peru 142 C5
Chimboy Uzbek. see Chimbay
Chimian Pak. 89 I4
Chimishliya Moldova see Cimişlia
Chimkent Kazakh. see Shymkent
Chimney Rock U.S.A. 129 J3
Chimoio Moz. 99 D5
Chimtargha, Qullai mt. Tajik. 89 H2
Chimtorga, Gora mt. Tajik. see Chimtargha, Qullai

▶China country Asia 72 H5
Most populous country in the world and in Asia. 2nd largest country in Asia and 4th largest in the world.
Asia 6, 62–63

China Mex. 131 D7
China, Republic of country Asia see Taiwan
China Bakir r. Myanmar see To
China Lake CA U.S.A. 128 E4
China Lake ME U.S.A. 135 K1
Chinandega Nicaragua 136 G6
China Point U.S.A. 128 D5
Chinati Peak U.S.A. 131 B6
Chincha Alta Peru 142 C6
Chinchaga r. Canada 120 G3
Chinchilla Australia 112 E1
Chincholi India 84 C2
Chinchorro, Banco sea feature Mex. 137 G5
Chincoteague Bay U.S.A. 135 H5
Chinde Moz. 99 D5
Chindo S. Korea 75 B6
Chin-do i. S. Korea 75 B6
Chindwin r. Myanmar 70 A2
Chinese Turkestan aut. reg. China see Xinjiang Uygur Zizhiqu
Chinghai prov. China see Qinghai
Chingiz-Tau, Khrebet mts Kazakh. 80 E2
Chingleput India see Chengalpattu
Chingola Zambia 99 C5
Chinguar Angola 99 B5
Chinguețți Mauritania 96 B2
Chinhae S. Korea 75 C6
Chinhoyi Zimbabwe 99 D5
Chini India see Kalpa
Chining China see Jining
Chiniot Pak. 89 I4
Chinipas Mex. 127 F8
Chinit, Stœng r. Cambodia 71 D4
Chinju S. Korea 75 C6
Chinle U.S.A. 129 I3
Chinmen Taiwan 77 H3
Chinmen Tao i. Taiwan 77 H3
Chinnamp'o N. Korea see Namp'o
Chinnur India 84 C2
Chino Creek watercourse U.S.A. 129 G4
Chinon France 56 E3
Chinook U.S.A. 126 F2
Chinook Trough sea feature N. Pacific Ocean 150 I3
Chino Valley U.S.A. 129 G4
Chintamani India 84 C3
Chioggia Italy 58 E2
Chios Greece 59 L5
Chios i. Greece 59 K5
Chipata Zambia 99 D5
Chipchihua, Sierra de mts Arg. 144 C6
Chiphu Cambodia 71 D5
Chipindo Angola 99 B5
Chipinga Zimbabwe see Chipinge
Chipinge Zimbabwe 99 D6
Chipley U.S.A. 133 C6
Chipman Canada 123 I5
Chippenham U.K. 49 E7
Chippewa, Lake U.S.A. 130 F2
Chippewa Falls U.S.A. 130 F2
Chipping Norton U.K. 49 F7
Chipping Sodbury U.K. 49 E7
Chipurupalle Andhra Pradesh India 84 D2
Chipurupalle Andhra Pradesh India 84 D2
Chiquilá Mex. 133 C8
Chiquinquira Col. 142 D2
Chir r. Rus. Fed. 43 I6
Chirada India 84 D3
Chirala India 84 D3
Chiras Afgh. 89 G3
Chirchik Uzbek. 80 C3
Chiredzi Zimbabwe 99 D6
Chirfa Niger 96 E2
Chiricahua National Monument nat. park U.S.A. 129 I5
Chiricahua Peak U.S.A. 129 I6
Chirikof Island U.S.A. 118 C4
Chiriquí, Golfo de b. Panama 137 H7
Chiriquí, Volcán de vol. Panama see Barú, Volcán
Chiri-san mt. S. Korea 75 B6
Chirk U.K. 49 D6
Chirnside U.K. 50 G5
Chirripo mt. Costa Rica 137 H7
Chisamba Zambia 99 C5
Chisana r. U.S.A. 120 A2
Chisasibi Canada 122 F3
Chishima-retto is Rus. Fed. see Kuril Islands
Chisholm Canada 120 H4
Chishtian Mandi Pak. 89 I4
Chishui China 76 E2
Chishuihe China 76 E3
Chisimaio Somalia see Kismaayo

▶Chişinău Moldova 59 M1
Capital of Moldova.

Chistopol' Rus. Fed. 42 K5
Chita Rus. Fed. 73 K2
Chitado Angola 99 B5
Chitaldrug India see Chitradurga
Chitalwana India 82 B4
Chitambo Zambia 99 D5
Chita Oblast admin. div. Rus. Fed. see Chitinskaya Oblast'
Chitato Angola 99 C4
Chitek Lake Canada 121 J4
Chitek Lake l. Canada 121 L4
Chitembo Angola 99 B5
Chitina U.S.A. 118 D3

Chitinskaya Oblast' *admin. div.* Rus. Fed. 74 A1
Chitipa Malawi 99 D4
Chitkul India *see* Chhitkul
Chitobe Moz. 99 D6
Chitoor India *see* Chittoor
Chitor India *see* Chittaurgarh
Chitose Japan 74 F4
Chitradurga India 84 C3
Chitrakoot India 82 E4
Chitrakut India *see* Chitrakoot
Chitral Pak. 89 H3
Chitral *r.* Pak. 89 H3
Chitravati *r.* India 84 C3
Chitré Panama 137 H7
Chitrod India 82 B5
Chittagong Bangl. 83 G5
Chittaurgarh India 82 C4
Chittoor India 84 C3
Chittor India *see* Chittoor
Chittorgarh India *see* Chittaurgarh
Chittur India 84 C4
Chitungwiza Zimbabwe 99 D5
Chiu Lung *Hong Kong* China *see* Kowloon
Chiume Angola 99 C5
Chivasso Italy 58 B2
Chívato, Punta *pt* Mex. 127 F8
Chivhu Zimbabwe 99 D5
Chixi China 77 G4
Chizarira National Park Zimbabwe 99 C5
Chizha Vtoraya Kazakh. 43 K6
Chizhou China 77 H2
Chizu Japan 75 D6
Chkalov Rus. Fed. *see* Orenburg
Chkalovsk Rus. Fed. 42 I4
Chkalovskoye Rus. Fed. 74 D3
Chlef Alg. *see* Ech Chélif
Chloride U.S.A. 129 F4
Chlya, Ozero *l.* Rus. Fed. 74 F1
Choa Chu Kang Sing. 71 [inset]
Choa Chu Kang *hill* Sing. 71 [inset]
Chobe National Park Botswana 99 C5
Chodov Czech Rep. 53 M4
Choele Choel Arg. 144 C5
Chogar *r.* Rus. Fed. 74 D1
Chogori Feng *mt.* China/Jammu and Kashmir *see* K2
Chograyskoye Vodokhranilishche *resr* Rus. Fed. 43 J7
Choiseul *i.* Solomon Is 107 F2
Choix Mex. 127 F8
Chojnice Poland 47 P4
Chōkai-san *vol.* Japan 75 F5
Ch'ok'ē *mts* Eth. 98 D2
Ch'ok'ē Mountains Eth. *see* Ch'ok'ē
Chokola *mt.* China 82 E3
Choksum China 83 F3
Chokue Moz. *see* Chókwé
Chokurdakh Rus. Fed. 65 P2
Chókwé Moz. 101 K3
Cho La *pass* China 76 C2
Cholame U.S.A. 128 C4
Chola Shan *mts* China 76 C1
Cholet France 56 D3
Cholpon-Ata Kyrg. 80 E3
Choluteca Hond. 137 G6
Choma Zambia 99 C5
Chomo Ganggar *mt.* China 83 G3
Cho Moi Vietnam 70 D2
Chomo Lhari *mt.* China/Bhutan 83 G4
Chom Thong Thai. 70 B3
Chomutov Czech Rep. 47 N5
Ch'ŏnan S. Korea 75 B5
Chon Buri Thai. 71 C4
Ch'ŏnch'ŏn N. Korea 74 B4
Chone Ecuador 142 B4
Ch'ŏngch'ŏn-gang *r.* N. Korea 75 B5
Ch'ongdo S. Korea 75 C6
Chonggye China *see* Qonggyai
Ch'ŏngjin N. Korea 74 C4
Ch'ŏngju S. Korea 75 B5
Chông Kal Cambodia 71 C4
Chongkü China 76 C2
Chonglong China *see* Zizhong
Chongming Dao *i.* China 77 I2
Chongoroi Angola 99 B5
Chŏngp'yŏng N. Korea 75 B5
Chongqing China 76 E2
Chongqing *municipality* China 76 E2
Chonguene Moz. 101 K3
Chŏngŭp S. Korea 75 B6
Chongyang China 77 G2
Chongyi China 77 G3
Chongzuo China 76 E4
Chŏnju S. Korea 75 B6
Chonogol Mongolia 73 L3
Cho Oyu *mt.* China/Nepal 83 F3
Chopda India 82 C5
Chơ Phươc Hai Vietnam 71 D5
Chor Pak. 89 H5
Chorley U.K. 48 E5
Chornobyl' Ukr. 43 F6
Chornomors'ke Ukr. 59 O2
Chortkiv Ukr. 43 E6
Ch'osan N. Korea 74 B4
Chōshi Japan 75 F6
Chosŏn *country* Asia *see* South Korea
Chosŏn-minjujuŭi-inmin-konghwaguk *country* Asia *see* North Korea
Choszczno Poland 47 O4
Chota Peru 142 C5
Chota Sinchula *hill* India 83 G4
Choteau U.S.A. 126 E3
Choti Pak. 89 H4
Choûm Mauritania 96 B2
Chowchilla U.S.A. 128 C3
Chowghat India 84 B4
Chown, Mount Canada 120 G4
Choybalsan Mongolia 73 K3
Choyr Mongolia 73 J3
Chrétiens, Île aux *i.* Canada *see* Christian Island
Chřiby *hills* Czech Rep. 47 P6
Chrisman U.S.A. 134 B4
Chrissiesmeer S. Africa 101 J4
Christchurch N.Z. 113 D6
Christchurch U.K. 49 F8
Christian, Cape Canada 119 L2
Christiana S. Africa 101 G4
Christiania Norway *see* Oslo
Christian Island Canada 134 E1
Christiansburg U.S.A. 134 E5
Christianshåb Greenland *see* Qasigiannguit
Christie Bay Canada 121 I2
Christie Island Myanmar 71 B5
Christina *r.* Canada 121 I3
Christina, Mount N.Z. 113 B7

▶Christmas Island *terr.* Indian Ocean 68 D9
Australian External Territory.
Asia 6

Christopher, Lake *salt flat* Australia 109 D6
Chrudim Czech Rep. 47 O6
Chrysi *i.* Greece 59 K7
Chrysochou Bay Cyprus 85 A2
Chrysochous, Kolpos *b.* Cyprus *see* Chrysochou Bay
Chu Kazakh. *see* Shu
Chu *r.* Kazakh./Kyrg. 80 C3
Chuadanga Bangl. 83 G5
Chuali, Lago *l.* Moz. 101 K3
Chuanhui China *see* Zhoukou
Chuansha China 77 I2
Chubalung China 76 C2
Chubarovka Ukr. *see* Polohy
Chubartau Kazakh. *see* Barshatas
Chuchkovo Rus. Fed. 43 I5
Chuckwalla Mountains U.S.A. 129 F5
Chudniv Ukr. 43 F6
Chudovo Rus. Fed. 42 F4
Chudskoye, Ozero *l.* Estonia/Rus. Fed. *see* Peipus, Lake
Chugach Mountains U.S.A. 118 D3
Chūgoku-sanchi *mts* Japan 75 D6
Chugqênsumdo China *see* Jigzhi
Chuguchak China *see* Tacheng
Chuguyev Ukr. *see* Chuhuyiv
Chuguyevka Rus. Fed. 74 D3
Chugwater U.S.A. 126 G4
Chuhai China *see* Zhuhai
Chuhuyiv Ukr. 43 H6
Chu-Iliyskiye Gory *mts* Kazakh. 80 D3
Chujiang China *see* Shimen
Chukai Malaysia *see* Cukai
Chukchagirskoye, Ozero *l.* Rus. Fed. 74 E1
Chukchi Abyssal Plain *sea feature* Arctic Ocean 153 B1
Chukchi Peninsula Rus. Fed. *see* Chukotskiy Poluostrov
Chukchi Plateau *sea feature* Arctic Ocean 153 B1
Chukchi Sea Rus. Fed./U.S.A. 65 T3
Chukhloma Rus. Fed. 42 I4
Chukotskiy, Mys *c.* Rus. Fed. 118 A3
Chukotskiy Poluostrov *pen.* Rus. Fed. 65 T3
Chu Lai Vietnam 70 E4
Chulakkurgan Kazakh. *see* Sholakkorgan
Chulaktau Kazakh. *see* Karatau
Chulasa Rus. Fed. 42 J2
Chula Vista U.S.A. 128 E5
Chulucanas Peru 142 B5
Chulung Pass Pak. 82 D2
Chulym Rus. Fed. 64 J4
Chumar Jammu and Kashmir 78 D2
Chumbicha Arg. 144 C3
Chumda China 76 C1
Chumikan Rus. Fed. 65 O4
Chum Phae Thai. 70 C3
Chumphon Thai. 71 B5
Chum Saeng Thai. 70 C4
Chunar India 83 E4
Ch'unch'ŏn S. Korea 75 B5
Chunchura India 83 G5
Chundzha Kazakh. 80 E3
Chunga Zambia 99 C5
Chung-hua Jen-min Kung-ho-kuo *country* Asia *see* China
Chung-hua Min-kuo *country* Asia *see* Taiwan
Ch'ungju S. Korea 75 B5
Chungking China *see* Chongqing
Ch'ungmu S. Korea *see* T'ongyŏng
Chŭngsan N. Korea 75 B5
Chungyang Shanmo *mts* Taiwan 77 I4
Chunskiy Rus. Fed. 72 H1
Chunya *r.* Rus. Fed. 65 K3
Chuôi, Hon *i.* Vietnam 71 D5
Chuosijia China *see* Guanyinqiao
Chupa Rus. Fed. 44 R3
Chūplū Iran 88 B2
Chuquicamata Chile 144 C2
Chur Switz. 56 I3
Churachandpur India 83 H4
Chūrān Iran 88 D4
Churapcha Rus. Fed. 65 O3
Churchill Canada 121 M3
Churchill *r. Man.* Canada 121 M3
Churchill *r. Nfld. and Lab.* Canada 123 J3
Churchill, Cape Canada 121 M3
Churchill Falls Canada 123 J3
Churchill Lake Canada 121 I4
Churchill Mountains Antarctica 152 H1
Churchill Sound *sea chan.* Canada 122 F2
Churchs Ferry U.S.A. 130 D1
Churchville U.S.A. 134 F4
Churia Ghati Hills Nepal 83 F4
Churu India 82 C3
Churubusco U.S.A. 134 C3
Churún-Merú *waterfall* Venez. *see* Angel Falls
Chushul Jammu and Kashmir 82 D2
Chuska Mountains U.S.A. 129 I3
Chusovaya *r.* Rus. Fed. 41 R4
Chusovoy Rus. Fed. 41 R4
Chust Ukr. *see* Khust
Chute-des-Passes Canada 123 H4
Chutia *Assam* India 83 H4
Chutia *Jharkhand* India 83 F5
Chutung Taiwan 77 I3
Chuuk *is* Micronesia 150 G5
Chuxiong China 76 D3
Chüy *r.* Kazakh./Kyrg. *see* Chu
Chư Yang Sin *mt.* Vietnam 71 E4
Chuzhou *Anhui* China 77 H1
Chuzhou *Jiangsu* China 77 H1
Chymyshliya Moldova *see* Cimişlia
Chyulu Hills National Park Kenya 98 D4
Ciadâr-Lunga Moldova *see* Ciadîr-Lunga
Ciadîr-Lunga Moldova 59 M1
Ciamis Indon. 68 D8
Cianjur Indon. 68 D8
Cianorte Brazil 144 F2
Cibecue U.S.A. 129 H4
Cibolo Creek *r.* U.S.A. 131 D6
Cibuta, Sierra *mt.* Mex. 127 F7
Ćićarija *mts* Croatia 58 E2
Cicero U.S.A. 134 B3
Cide Turkey 90 D2
Ciechanów Poland 47 R4
Ciego de Ávila Cuba 137 I4
Ciénaga Col. 142 D1
Ciénega Mex. 131 C7
Ciénega de Flores Mex. 131 C7
Cienfuegos Cuba 137 H4
Cieza Spain 57 F4
Çiftlik Turkey *see* Kelkit
Cifuentes Spain 57 E3
Cigüela *r.* Spain 57 E4
Cihanbeyli Turkey 90 D3
Cijara, Embalse de *resr* Spain 57 D4
Cilacap Indon. 68 D8
Çıldır Turkey 91 F2
Çıldır Gölü *l.* Turkey 91 F2
Çıldıroba Turkey 85 C1
Cilento e del Vallo di Diano, Parco Nazionale del *nat. park* Italy 58 F4
Cili China 77 F2
Cilician Gates *pass* Turkey *see* Gülek Boğazı
Cill Airne Rep. of Ireland *see* Killarney
Cill Chainnigh Rep. of Ireland *see* Kilkenny
Cill Mhantáin Rep. of Ireland *see* Wicklow
Cilo Dağı *mt.* Turkey 91 G3
Çiloy Adası *i.* Azer. 91 H2
Cimarron *CO* U.S.A. 129 J2
Cimarron *KS* U.S.A. 130 C4
Cimarron *NM* U.S.A. 127 G5
Cimarron *r.* U.S.A. 131 D4
Cimişlia Moldova 59 M1
Cimone, Monte *mt.* Italy 58 D2
Cîmpina Romania *see* Câmpina
Cîmpulung Romania *see* Câmpulung
Cîmpulung Moldovenesc Romania *see* Câmpulung Moldovenesc
Cina, Tanjung *c.* Indon. 68 C8
Çınar Turkey 91 F3
Cinaruco-Capanaparo, Parque Nacional *nat. park* Venez. 142 E2
Cinca *r.* Spain 57 G3
Cincinnati U.S.A. 134 C4
Cinco de Outubro Angola *see* Xá-Muteba
Cinderford U.K. 49 E7
Çine Turkey 59 M6
Ciney Belgium 52 F4
Cintalapa Mex. 136 F5
Cinto, Monte *mt.* France 56 I5
Ciping China *see* Jinggangshan
Circeo, Parco Nazionale del *nat. park* Italy 58 E4
Circle *AK* U.S.A. 118 D3
Circle *MT* U.S.A. 126 G3
Circleville *OH* U.S.A. 134 D4
Circleville *UT* U.S.A. 129 G2
Cirebon Indon. 68 D8
Cirencester U.K. 49 F7
Cirò Marina Italy 58 G5
Cirta Alg. *see* Constantine
Cisco U.S.A. 129 I2
Citlaltépetl *vol.* Mex. *see* Orizaba, Pico de
Čitluk Bos.-Herz. 58 G3
Citronelle U.S.A. 131 F6
Citrus Heights U.S.A. 128 C2
Città di Castello Italy 58 E3
Ciucaş, Vârful *mt.* Romania 59 K2
Ciudad Acuña Mex. 131 C6
Ciudad Altamirano Mex. 136 D5
Ciudad Bolívar Venez. 142 F2
Ciudad Camargo Mex. 131 B7
Ciudad Constitución Mex. 136 B3
Ciudad del Carmen Mex. 136 F5
Ciudad Delicias Mex. 131 B6
Ciudad de Panamá Panama *see* Panama City
Ciudad de Valles Mex. 136 E4
Ciudad Flores Guat. *see* Flores
Ciudad Guayana Venez. 142 F2
Ciudad Guerrero Mex. 127 G7
Ciudad Guzmán Mex. 136 D5
Ciudad Juárez Mex. 127 G7
Ciudad Lerdo Mex. 131 C7
Ciudad Mante Mex. 136 E4
Ciudad Obregón Mex. 127 F8
Ciudad Real Spain 57 E4
Ciudad Río Bravo Mex. 131 D7
Ciudad Rodrigo Spain 57 C3
Ciudad Trujillo Dom. Rep. *see* Santo Domingo
Ciudad Victoria Mex. 131 D8
Ciutadella de Menorca Spain 57 H3
Civa Burnu *pt* Turkey 90 E2
Cividale del Friuli Italy 58 E1
Civitanova Marche Italy 58 E3
Civitavecchia Italy 58 D3
Çivril Turkey 59 M5
Cixi China 77 I2
Cizre Turkey 91 F3
Clacton-on-Sea U.K. 49 I7
Clady U.K. 51 E3
Claire, Lake Canada 121 H3
Clairfontaine Alg. *see* El Aouinet
Clamecy France 56 F3
Clane Rep. of Ireland 51 F4
Clanton U.S.A. 133 C5
Clanwilliam Dam S. Africa 100 D7
Clara Rep. of Ireland 51 E4
Clara Island Myanmar 71 B5
Claraville Australia 110 C3
Clare *N.S.W.* Australia 112 A4
Clare *S.A.* Australia 111 B7
Clare *r.* Rep. of Ireland 51 C4
Clare U.S.A. 134 C2
Clarecastle Rep. of Ireland 51 D5
Clare Island Rep. of Ireland 51 B4
Claremont U.S.A. 135 I2
Claremore U.S.A. 131 E4
Claremorris Rep. of Ireland 51 D4
Clarence *r.* Australia 112 F2
Clarence N.Z. 113 D6
Clarence Island Antarctica 152 A2
Clarence Strait Iran *see* Khūran
Clarence Strait U.S.A. 120 C3
Clarence Town Bahamas 133 F8
Clarendon *AR* U.S.A. 131 F5
Clarendon *PA* U.S.A. 134 F3
Clarendon *TX* U.S.A. 131 C5
Clarenville Canada 123 L4
Claresholm Canada 120 H5
Clarie Coast Antarctica *see* Wilkes Coast
Clarinda U.S.A. 130 E3
Clarington U.S.A. 134 E4
Clarion *IA* U.S.A. 130 E3
Clarion *PA* U.S.A. 134 F3
Clarion *r.* U.S.A. 134 F3
Clarión, Isla *i.* Mex. 136 B5
Clark U.S.A. 130 D2
Clark, Mount Canada 120 F1
Clarkdale U.S.A. 129 G4
Clarkebury S. Africa 101 I6
Clarke Range *mts* Australia 110 D4
Clarke River Australia 110 D3
Clarke's Head Canada 123 L4
Clark Mountain U.S.A. 129 F4
Clark Point Canada 134 E1
Clarksburg U.S.A. 134 E4
Clarksdale U.S.A. 131 F5
Clarks Hill U.S.A. 134 B3
Clarksville *AR* U.S.A. 131 E5
Clarksville *TN* U.S.A. 134 B5
Clarksville *TX* U.S.A. 131 E5
Clarksville *VA* U.S.A. 135 F5
Claro *r. Goiás* Brazil 145 A2
Claro *r. Mato Grosso* Brazil 145 A1
Clashmore Rep. of Ireland 51 E5
Claude U.S.A. 131 C5
Claudy U.K. 51 E3
Clavier Belgium 52 F4
Claxton U.S.A. 133 D5
Clay U.S.A. 134 E4
Clayburg U.S.A. 135 I1
Clay Center *KS* U.S.A. 130 D4
Clay Center *NE* U.S.A. 130 D3
Clay City *IN* U.S.A. 134 B4
Clay City *KY* U.S.A. 134 D5
Clayhole Wash *watercourse* U.S.A. 129 G3
Claypool U.S.A. 129 H5
Clay Springs U.S.A. 129 H4
Clayton *DE* U.S.A. 135 H4
Clayton *GA* U.S.A. 133 D5
Clayton *MI* U.S.A. 134 C3
Clayton *MO* U.S.A. 130 F4
Clayton *NM* U.S.A. 131 C4
Clayton *NY* U.S.A. 135 G1
Claytor Lake U.S.A. 134 E5
Clay Village U.S.A. 134 C4
Clear, Cape Rep. of Ireland 51 C6
Clearco U.S.A. 134 E4
Clear Creek Canada 134 E2
Clear Creek *r.* U.S.A. 129 H4
Cleare, Cape U.S.A. 118 D4
Clearfield *PA* U.S.A. 135 F3
Clearfield *UT* U.S.A. 126 E4
Clear Fork Brazos *r.* U.S.A. 131 D5
Clear Hills Canada 120 G3
Clear Island Rep. of Ireland 51 C6
Clear Lake *IA* U.S.A. 130 E3
Clear Lake *SD* U.S.A. 130 D2
Clear Lake *l. CA* U.S.A. 128 B2
Clear Lake *l. UT* U.S.A. 129 G2
Clearmont U.S.A. 126 G3
Clearwater Canada 120 G5
Clearwater *r. Alberta/Saskatchewan* Canada 121 I3
Clearwater *r. Alta* Canada 120 H4
Clearwater U.S.A. 133 D7
Clearwater Lake Canada 121 K4
Clearwater Mountains U.S.A. 126 E3
Cleaton U.S.A. 134 B5
Cleburne U.S.A. 131 D5
Cleethorpes U.K. 48 G5
Clementi Sing. 71 [inset]
Clendenin U.S.A. 134 E4
Clendening Lake U.S.A. 134 E3
Clères France 52 B5
Clerf Lux. *see* Clervaux
Clerke Reef Australia 108 B4
Clermont Australia 110 D4
Clermont France 52 C5
Clermont-en-Argonne France 52 F5
Clermont-Ferrand France 56 F4
Clervaux Lux. 52 G4
Cles Italy 58 D1
Clevedon U.K. 49 E7
Cleveland *MS* U.S.A. 131 F5
Cleveland *OH* U.S.A. 134 E3
Cleveland *TN* U.S.A. 133 C5
Cleveland *UT* U.S.A. 129 H2
Cleveland *WI* U.S.A. 134 B2
Cleveland, Cape Australia 110 D3
Cleveland, Mount U.S.A. 126 E2
Cleveland Heights U.S.A. 134 E3
Cleveland Hills U.K. 48 F4
Cleveleys U.K. 48 D5
Cleves Germany *see* Kleve
Clew Bay Rep. of Ireland 51 C4
Clifden Rep. of Ireland 51 B4
Cliff U.S.A. 129 I5
Cliffoney Rep. of Ireland 51 D3
Clifton Australia 112 E1
Clifton U.S.A. 129 I5
Clifton Beach Australia 110 D3
Clifton Forge U.S.A. 134 F5
Clifton Park U.S.A. 135 I2
Climax Canada 121 I5
Climax U.S.A. 134 C2
Clinch Mountain *mts* U.S.A. 134 D5
Cline River Canada 120 G4
Clinton *B.C.* Canada 120 F5
Clinton *Ont.* Canada 134 E2
Clinton *IA* U.S.A. 130 F3
Clinton *IL* U.S.A. 130 F3
Clinton *IN* U.S.A. 134 B4
Clinton *KY* U.S.A. 131 F4
Clinton *MI* U.S.A. 134 D2
Clinton *MO* U.S.A. 130 E4
Clinton *MS* U.S.A. 131 F5
Clinton *NC* U.S.A. 133 E5
Clinton *OK* U.S.A. 131 D5
Clinton-Colden Lake Canada 121 J1
Clintwood U.S.A. 134 D5

▶Clipperton, Île *terr.* N. Pacific Ocean 151 M5
French Overseas Territory.

Clishham *hill* U.K. 50 C3
Clitheroe U.K. 48 E5
Clive Lake Canada 120 G2
Cliza Bol. 142 E7
Clocolan S. Africa 101 H5
Cloghan Rep. of Ireland 51 E4
Clonakilty Rep. of Ireland 51 D6
Clonbern Rep. of Ireland 51 D4
Cloncurry Australia 110 C4
Cloncurry *r.* Australia 110 C3
Clones Rep. of Ireland 51 E3
Clonmel Rep. of Ireland 51 E5
Clonygowan Rep. of Ireland 51 E4
Cloonbannin Rep. of Ireland 51 C5
Clooneagh Rep. of Ireland 51 E4
Cloppenburg Germany 53 I2
Cloquet U.S.A. 130 E2
Cloquet *r.* U.S.A. 130 E2
Cloud Peak *WY* U.S.A. 124 F3
Cloud Peak *WY* U.S.A. 126 G3
Clova Canada 122 G4
Clover U.S.A. 129 G1
Cloverdale *CA* U.S.A. 128 B2
Cloverdale *IN* U.S.A. 134 B4
Cloverport U.S.A. 134 B5
Clovis *CA* U.S.A. 128 D3
Clovis *NM* U.S.A. 131 C5
Cloyne Canada 135 G1
Cluain Meala Rep. of Ireland *see* Clonmel
Cluanie, Loch *l.* U.K. 50 D3
Cluff Lake Mine Canada 121 I3
Cluj-Napoca Romania 59 J1
Clun U.K. 49 D6
Clunes Australia 112 A6
Cluny Australia 110 B5
Cluses France 56 H3
Cluster Springs U.S.A. 135 F5
Clut Lake Canada 120 G1
Clutterbuck Head *hd* Canada 123 H1
Clutterbuck Hills *hill* Australia 109 D6
Clwydian Range *hills* U.K. 48 D5
Clyde Canada 120 H4
Clyde *r.* U.K. 50 E5
Clyde *NY* U.S.A. 135 G2
Clyde *OH* U.S.A. 134 D3
Clyde, Firth of *est.* U.K. 50 E5
Clydebank U.K. 50 E5
Clyde River Canada 119 L2
Côa *r.* Port. 57 C3
Coachella U.S.A. 128 E5
Coahuila *state* Mex. 131 C7
Coahuila de Zaragoza *state* Mex. *see* Coahuila
Coal *r.* Canada 120 E3
Coal City U.S.A. 134 A3
Coaldale U.S.A. 128 E2
Coalgate U.S.A. 131 D5
Coal Harbour Canada 120 E5
Coalinga U.S.A. 128 C3
Coalport U.S.A. 135 F3
Coal River Canada 120 E3
Coal Valley U.S.A. 129 F3
Coalville U.K. 49 F6
Coalville U.S.A. 129 H1
Coari Brazil 142 F4
Coari *r.* Brazil 142 F4
Coarsegold U.S.A. 128 D3
Coastal Plain U.S.A. 131 E6
Coast Mountains Canada 120 E4
Coast Range *hills* Australia 111 E5
Coast Ranges *mts* U.S.A. 128 B1
Coatbridge U.K. 50 E5
Coatesville U.S.A. 135 H4
Coaticook Canada 135 J1
Coats Island Canada 119 J3
Coats Land *reg.* Antarctica 152 A1
Coatzacoalcos Mex. 136 F5
Cobar Australia 112 B3
Cobargo Australia 112 D6
Cobden Australia 112 A7
Cóbh Rep. of Ireland 51 D6
Cobham *r.* Canada 121 M4
Cobija Bol. 142 E6
Coblenz Germany *see* Koblenz
Cobleskill U.S.A. 135 H2
Cobourg Peninsula Australia 108 F2
Cobra Australia 109 B6
Cobram Australia 112 B5
Coburg Germany 53 K4
Coburg Island Canada 119 K2
Coca Ecuador 142 C4
Coca Spain 57 D3
Cocalinho Brazil 145 A1
Cocanada India *see* Kakinada
Cochabamba Bol. 142 E7
Cochem Germany 53 H4
Cochin India 84 C4
Cochin *reg.* Vietnam 71 D5
Cochinos, Bahía de *b.* Cuba *see* Pigs, Bay of
Cochise U.S.A. 129 I5
Cochise Head *mt.* U.S.A. 129 I5
Cochrane *Alta* Canada 120 H5
Cochrane *Ont.* Canada 122 E4
Cochrane *r.* Canada 121 K3
Cockburn Australia 111 C7
Cockburnspath U.K. 50 G5
Cockburn Town Bahamas 133 F7
Cockburn Town Turks and Caicos Is *see* Grand Turk
Cockermouth U.K. 48 D4
Cocklebiddy Australia 109 D8
Cockscomb *mt.* S. Africa 100 G7
Coco *r.* Hond./Nicaragua 137 H6
Coco, Cayo *i.* Cuba 133 E8
Coco, Isla de *i.* N. Pacific Ocean 137 G7
Cocobeach Gabon 98 A3
Coco Channel India 71 A4
Cocomórachic Mex. 127 G7
Coconino Plateau U.S.A. 129 G4
Cocopara National Park Australia 112 C5
Cocos Brazil 145 B1
Cocos Basin *sea feature* Indian Ocean 149 O5

▶Cocos Islands *terr.* Indian Ocean 68 B9
Australian External Territory.
Asia 6

Cocos Ridge *sea feature* N. Pacific Ocean 151 O5
Cocuy, Sierra Nevada del *mt.* Col. 142 D2
Cod, Cape U.S.A. 135 J3
Codajás Brazil 142 F4
Coderre Canada 121 J5
Codfish Island N.Z. 113 A8
Codigoro Italy 58 E2
Cod Island Canada 123 J2
Codlea Romania 59 K2
Codó Brazil 143 J4
Codsall U.K. 49 E6
Cod's Head *hd* Rep. of Ireland 47 B6
Cody U.S.A. 126 F3
Coeburn U.S.A. 134 D5
Coen Australia 110 C2
Coesfeld Germany 53 H3
Coeur d'Alene U.S.A. 126 D3
Coeur d'Alene Lake U.S.A. 126 D3
Coevorden Neth. 52 G2
Coffee Bay S. Africa 101 I6
Coffeyville U.S.A. 131 E4
Coffin Bay Australia 111 A7
Coffin Bay National Park Australia 111 A7
Coffs Harbour Australia 112 F3
Cofimvaba S. Africa 101 H7
Cognac France 56 D4
Cogo Equat. Guinea 96 D4
Coguno Moz. 101 L3
Cohoes U.S.A. 135 I2
Cohuna Australia 112 B5
Coiba, Isla de *i.* Panama 137 H7
Coigeach, Rubha *pt* U.K. 50 D2
Coihaique Chile 144 B7
Coimbatore India 84 C4
Coimbra Port. 57 B3
Coipasa, Salar de *salt flat* Bol. 142 E7
Coire Switz. *see* Chur
Colac Australia 112 A7
Colair Lake India *see* Kolleru Lake
Colatina Brazil 145 C2
Colbitz Germany 53 L2
Colborne Canada 135 G2
Colby U.S.A. 130 C4
Colchester U.K. 49 H7
Colchester U.S.A. 135 I3
Cold Bay U.S.A. 118 B4
Coldingham U.K. 50 G5
Colditz Germany 53 M3
Cold Lake Canada 121 I4
Cold Lake *l.* Canada 121 I4
Coldspring U.S.A. 131 E6
Coldstream Canada 120 G5
Coldstream U.K. 50 G5
Coldwater Canada 134 F1
Coldwater *KS* U.S.A. 131 D4
Coldwater *MI* U.S.A. 134 C3
Coldwater *r.* U.S.A. 131 F5
Coleambally Australia 112 B5
Colebrook U.S.A. 135 J1
Coleman *r.* Australia 110 C2
Coleman U.S.A. 131 D6
Çölemerik Turkey *see* Hakkâri
Colenso S. Africa 101 I5
Cole Peninsula Antarctica 152 L2
Coleraine Australia 111 C8
Coleraine U.K. 51 F2
Coles, Punta de *pt* Peru 142 D7
Coles Bay Australia 111 [inset]
Colesberg S. Africa 101 G6
Coleville Canada 121 I5
Colfax *CA* U.S.A. 128 C2
Colfax *LA* U.S.A. 131 E6
Colfax *WA* U.S.A. 126 D3
Colhué Huapí, Lago *l.* Arg. 144 C7
Coligny S. Africa 101 H4
Colima Mex. 136 D5
Colima, Nevado de *vol.* Mex. 136 D5
Coll *i.* U.K. 50 C4
Collado Villalba Spain 57 E3
Collarenebri Australia 112 D2
College Station U.S.A. 131 D6
Collerina Australia 112 C2
Collie *N.S.W.* Australia 112 D3
Collie *W.A.* Australia 109 B8
Collier Bay Australia 108 D4
Collier Range National Park Australia 109 B6
Collingwood Canada 134 E1
Collingwood N.Z. 113 D5
Collins U.S.A. 131 F6
Collins Glacier Antarctica 152 E2
Collinson Peninsula Canada 115 H2
Collipulli Chile 144 B5
Collmberg *hill* Germany 53 N3
Collooney Rep. of Ireland 51 D3
Colmar France 56 H2
Colmenar Viejo Spain 57 E3
Colmonell U.K. 50 E5
Colne *r.* U.K. 49 H7
Cologne Germany 52 G4
Coloma U.S.A. 134 B2
Colomb-Béchar Alg. *see* Béchar
Colômbia Brazil 145 A3
Colombia Mex. 131 D7

▶Colombia *country* S. America 142 D3
2nd most populous and 4th largest country in South America.
South America 9, 140–141

Colombian Basin *sea feature* S. Atlantic Ocean 148 C5

▶Colombo Sri Lanka 84 C5
Former capital of Sri Lanka.

Colomiers France 56 E5
Colón *Buenos Aires* Arg. 144 D4
Colón *Entre Ríos* Arg. 144 E4
Colón Cuba 133 D8
Colón Panama 137 I7
Colon U.S.A. 134 C3
Colón, Archipiélago de *is* Ecuador *see* Galapágos Islands
Colona Australia 109 F7
Colonelganj India 83 E4

Colonel Hill Bahamas 133 F8
Colonet, Cabo c. Mex. 127 D7
Colônia r. Brazil 145 D1
Colonia Micronesia 69 J5
Colonia Agrippina Germany see Cologne
Colonia Díaz Mex. 127 F7
Colonia Julia Fenestris Italy see Fano
Colonia Las Heras Arg. 144 C7
Colonial Heights U.S.A. 135 G5
Colonna, Capo c. Italy 58 G5
Colonsay i. U.K. 50 C4
Colorado r. Arg. 144 D5
Colorado r. Mex./U.S.A. 127 E7
Colorado r. U.S.A. 131 D6
Colorado state U.S.A. 126 G5
Colorado City AZ U.S.A. 129 G3
Colorado City TX U.S.A. 131 C5
Colorado Desert U.S.A. 128 E5
Colorado National Monument nat. park U.S.A. 129 I2
Colorado Plateau U.S.A. 129 I3
Colorado River Aqueduct canal U.S.A. 129 F4
Colorado Springs U.S.A. 126 G5
Colossae Turkey see Honaz
Colotlán Mex. 136 D4
Cölpin Germany 53 N1
Colquiri Bol. 142 E7
Colquitt U.S.A. 133 C6
Colson U.S.A. 134 D5
Colsterworth U.K. 49 G6
Colstrip U.S.A. 126 G3
Coltishall U.K. 49 I6
Colton CA U.S.A. 128 E4
Colton NY U.S.A. 135 H1
Colton UT U.S.A. 129 H2
Columbia KY U.S.A. 134 C5
Columbia LA U.S.A. 131 E5
Columbia MD U.S.A. 135 G4
Columbia MO U.S.A. 130 E4
Columbia MS U.S.A. 131 F6
Columbia NC U.S.A. 132 E5
Columbia PA U.S.A. 135 G3
▶Columbia SC U.S.A. 133 D5
State capital of South Carolina.
Columbia TN U.S.A. 132 C5
Columbia r. U.S.A. 126 C3
Columbia, District of admin. dist. U.S.A. 135 G4
Columbia, Mount Canada 120 G4
Columbia, Sierra mts Mex. 123 E7
Columbia City U.S.A. 134 C3
Columbia Lake Canada 120 H5
Columbia Mountains Canada 120 F4
Columbia Plateau U.S.A. 126 D3
Columbine, Cape S. Africa 100 C7
Columbus GA U.S.A. 133 C5
Columbus IN U.S.A. 134 C4
Columbus MS U.S.A. 131 F5
Columbus MT U.S.A. 126 F3
Columbus NC U.S.A. 133 D5
Columbus NE U.S.A. 130 D3
Columbus NM U.S.A. 127 G7
▶Columbus OH U.S.A. 134 D4
State capital of Ohio.
Columbus TX U.S.A. 131 D6
Columbus Grove U.S.A. 134 C3
Columbus Salt Marsh U.S.A. 128 D2
Colusa U.S.A. 128 B2
Colville N.Z. 113 E3
Colville U.S.A. 126 D2
Colville r. U.S.A. 118 C2
Colville Channel N.Z. 113 E3
Colville Lake Canada 118 F3
Colwyn Bay U.K. 48 D5
Comacchio Italy 58 E2
Comacchio, Valli di lag. Italy 58 E2
Comai China 83 G3
Comalcalco Mex. 136 F5
Comanche U.S.A. 131 D6
Comandante Ferraz research station Antarctica 152 A2
Comandante Salas Arg. 144 C4
Comănești Romania 59 L1
Combahee r. U.S.A. 133 D5
Combarbalá Chile 144 B4
Comber U.K. 51 G3
Combermere Bay Myanmar 70 A3
Combles France 52 C4
Combol i. Indon. 71 C7
Combomune Moz. 101 K2
Comboyne Australia 112 F3
Comencho, Lac l. Canada 122 G4
Comendador Dom. Rep. see Elías Piña
Comendador Gomes Brazil 145 A2
Comeragh Mountains hills Rep. of Ireland 51 E5
Comercinho Brazil 145 C2
Cometela Moz. 101 L1
Comfort U.S.A. 131 D6
Comilla Bangl. 83 G5
Comines Belgium 52 C4
Comino, Capo c. Sardinia Italy 58 C4
Comitán de Domínguez Mex. 132 F5
Commack U.S.A. 135 I3
Commentry France 56 F3
Committee Bay Canada 119 J3
Commonwealth Territory admin. div. Australia see Jervis Bay Territory
Como Italy 58 C2
Como, Lago di Italy see Como, Lake
Como, Lake Italy 58 C2
Como Chamling l. China 83 G3
Comodoro Rivadavia Arg. 144 C7
Comores country Africa see Comoros
Comorin, Cape India 84 C4
Comoro Islands country Africa see Comoros
▶Comoros country Africa 99 E5
Africa 7, 94–95
Compiègne France 52 C5
Comprida, Ilha i. Brazil 145 B4
Comrat Moldova 59 M1
Comrie U.K. 50 F4
Comstock U.S.A. 131 C6
Cona China 83 G4
▶Conakry Guinea 96 B4
Capital of Guinea.
Cona Niyeo Arg. 144 C6
Conceição r. Brazil 145 B2
Conceição da Barra Brazil 145 D2
Conceição do Araguaia Brazil 143 I5
Conceição do Mato Dentro Brazil 145 C2
Concepción Chile 144 B5
Concepción Mex. 131 C7
Concepción r. Mex. 127 E7
Concepción Para. 144 E2
Concepción, Punta pt Mex. 127 F8
Concepción de la Vega Dom. Rep. see La Vega
Conception, Point U.S.A. 128 C4
Conception Island Bahamas 129 F8
Conchas U.S.A. 127 G6
Conchas Lake U.S.A. 127 G6
Concho U.S.A. 129 I4
Conchos r. Nuevo León/Tamaulipas Mex. 131 D7
Conchos r. Mex. 131 B6
Concord CA U.S.A. 128 B3
Concord NC U.S.A. 133 D5
▶Concord NH U.S.A. 135 J2
State capital of New Hampshire.
Concord VT U.S.A. 135 J1
Concordia Arg. 144 E4
Concordia Mex. 131 B8
Concordia Peru 142 D4
Concordia S. Africa 100 C5
Concordia KS U.S.A. 130 D4
Concordia KY U.S.A. 134 B4
Concord Peak Afgh. 89 I2
Con Cuông Vietnam 70 D3
Condamine Australia 112 E1
Condamine r. Australia 112 D1
Côn Đao Vietnam 71 D5
Condeúba Brazil 145 C1
Condobolin Australia 112 C4
Condom France 56 E5
Condon U.S.A. 126 C3
Condor, Cordillera del mts Ecuador/Peru 142 C4
Condroz reg. Belgium 52 E4
Conecuh r. U.S.A. 133 C6
Conegliano Italy 58 E2
Conejos Mex. 131 C7
Conejos U.S.A. 127 G5
Conemaugh r. U.S.A. 134 F3
Conestogo Lake Canada 134 E2
Conesus Lake U.S.A. 135 G2
Conflict Group is P.N.G. 110 E1
Confoederatio Helvetica country Europe see Switzerland
Confusion Range mts U.S.A. 129 G2
Congdü China see Nyalam
Conghua China 77 G4
Congjiang China 77 F3
Congleton U.K. 48 E5
▶Congo country Africa 98 B4
Africa 7, 94–95
▶Congo r. Congo/Dem. Rep. Congo 98 B4
2nd longest river and largest drainage basin in Africa.
Formerly known as Zaïre.
Africa 92–93
Congo (Brazzaville) country Africa see Congo
Congo (Kinshasa) country Africa see Congo, Democratic Republic of
▶Congo, Democratic Republic of country Africa 98 C4
3rd largest and 4th most populous country in Africa.
Africa 7, 94–95
Congo, Republic of country Africa see Congo
Congo Basin Dem. Rep. Congo 98 C4
Congo Cone sea feature S. Atlantic Ocean 148 I6
Congo Free State country Africa see Congo, Democratic Republic of
Congonhas Brazil 145 C3
Congress U.S.A. 129 G4
Conimbla National Park Australia 112 D4
Coningsby U.K. 49 G5
Coniston Canada 122 E5
Coniston U.K. 48 D4
Conjuboy Australia 110 D3
Conklin Canada 121 I4
Conn r. Canada 122 F3
Conn, Lough l. Rep. of Ireland 51 C3
Connacht reg. Rep. of Ireland see Connaught
Connaught reg. Rep. of Ireland 51 C4
Conneaut U.S.A. 134 E3
Connecticut state U.S.A. 135 I3
Connemara reg. Rep. of Ireland 51 C4
Connemara National Park Rep. of Ireland 51 C4
Connersville U.S.A. 134 C4
Connolly, Mount Canada 120 C2
Connors Range hills Australia 110 E4
Conoble Australia 112 B4
Conquista Brazil 145 B2
Conrad U.S.A. 126 F2
Conrad Rise sea feature Southern Ocean 149 K9
Conroe U.S.A. 131 E6
Conselheiro Lafaiete Brazil 145 C3
Consett U.K. 48 F4
Consolación del Sur Cuba 133 D8
Côn Sơn i. Vietnam 71 D5
Consort Canada 121 I4
Constance Germany see Konstanz
Constance, Lake Germany/Switz. 47 L7
Constância dos Baetas Brazil 142 F5
Constanța Romania 59 M2
Constantia tourist site Cyprus see Salamis
Constantia Germany see Konstanz
Constantina Spain 57 D5
Constantine Alg. 54 F4
Constantine, Cape U.S.A. 118 C4
Constantinople Turkey see İstanbul
Constitución de 1857, Parque Nacional nat. park Mex. 129 F5
Consul Canada 121 I5
Contact U.S.A. 126 E4
Contagalo Brazil 145 C3
Contamana Peru 142 C5
Contas r. Brazil 145 D1
Contoy, Isla i. Mex. 133 C8
Contria Brazil 145 B2
Contwoyto Lake Canada 121 I1
Convención Col. 142 D2
Convent U.S.A. 131 F6
Conway U.K. see Conwy
Conway AR U.S.A. 131 E5
Conway ND U.S.A. 130 D1
Conway NH U.S.A. 135 J2
Conway SC U.S.A. 133 E5
Conway, Cape Australia 110 E4
Conway, Lake salt flat Australia 111 A6
Conway National Park Australia 110 E4
Conway Reef Fiji see Ceva-i-Ra
Conwy U.K. 48 D5
Conwy r. U.K. 49 D5
Coober Pedy Australia 109 F7
Cooch Behar India see Koch Bihar
Coochbehar India see Koch Bihar
Cook Australia 109 E7
Cook, Cape Canada 120 E5
Cook, Grand Récif de reef New Caledonia 107 G3
Cook, Mount N.Z. see Aoraki
Cookes Peak U.S.A. 127 G6
Cookeville U.S.A. 132 C4
Cookhouse S. Africa 101 G7
Cook Ice Shelf Antarctica 152 H2
Cook Inlet sea chan. U.S.A. 118 C3
▶Cook Islands terr. S. Pacific Ocean 150 J7
Self-governing New Zealand Territory.
Oceania 8, 104–105
Cooksburg U.S.A. 135 H2
Cooks Passage Australia 110 D2
Cookstown U.K. 51 F3
Cook Strait N.Z. 113 E5
Cooktown Australia 110 D2
Coolabah Australia 112 C3
Cooladdi Australia 112 B1
Coolah Australia 112 D3
Coolamon Australia 112 C5
Coolgardie Australia 109 C7
Coolibah Australia 108 E3
Coolidge U.S.A. 129 H5
Cooloola National Park Australia 111 F5
Coolum Beach Australia 111 F5
Cooma Australia 112 D6
Coombah Australia 111 C7
Coonabarabran Australia 112 D3
Coonamble Australia 112 D3
Coondambo Australia 111 A6
Coondapoor India see Kundapura
Coongoola Australia 112 B1
Coon Rapids U.S.A. 130 E2
Cooper Creek watercourse Australia 111 B6
Cooper Mountain Canada 120 G5
Coopernook Australia 112 F3
Cooper's Town Bahamas 133 E7
Cooperstown ND U.S.A. 130 D2
Cooperstown NY U.S.A. 135 H2
Coopracambra National Park Australia 112 D6
Coorabie Australia 109 F7
Coorong National Park Australia 111 B8
Coorow Australia 109 B7
Coosa r. U.S.A. 133 C5
Coos Bay U.S.A. 126 B4
Coos Bay b. U.S.A. 126 E4
Cootamundra Australia 112 D5
Cootehill Rep. of Ireland 51 E3
Cooyar Australia 112 E1
Copala Mex. 136 E5
Cope U.S.A. 130 C4
Copemish U.S.A. 134 C1
▶Copenhagen Denmark 45 H9
Capital of Denmark.
Copenhagen U.S.A. 135 H2
Copertino Italy 58 H4
Copeton Reservoir Australia 112 E2
Cô Pi, Phou mt. Laos/Vietnam 70 D3
Copiapó Chile 144 B3
Copley Australia 111 B6
Copparo Italy 58 D2
Copper Cliff Canada 122 E5
Copper Harbor U.S.A. 132 C2
Coppermine Canada see Kugluktuk
Coppermine r. Canada 120 H1
Coppermine Point Canada 122 D5
Copperton S. Africa 100 F5
Copp Lake Canada 120 H2
Coqên Xizang China 83 F3
Coqên Xizang China see Maindong
Coquilhatville Dem. Rep. Congo see Mbandaka
Coquille i. Micronesia see Pikelot
Coquille U.S.A. 126 B4
Coquimbo Chile 144 B3
Coquitlam Canada 120 F5
Corabia Romania 59 K3
Coração de Jesus Brazil 145 B2
Coracesium Turkey see Alanya
Coraki Australia 112 F2
Coral Bay Australia 109 A5
Coral Harbour Canada 119 J3
Coral Sea S. Pacific Ocean 106 F3
Coral Sea Basin S. Pacific Ocean 150 G6
▶Coral Sea Islands Territory terr. Australia 106 F3
Australian External Territory.
Corangamite, Lake Australia 112 A7
Corat Azer. 91 H2
Corbeny France 52 D5
Corbett Inlet Canada 121 M2
Corbett National Park India 82 D3
Corbie France 52 C5
Corbin U.S.A. 134 C5
Corby U.K. 49 G6
Corcaigh Rep. of Ireland see Cork
Corcoran U.S.A. 128 D3
Corcovado, Golfo de sea chan. Chile 144 B6
Corcyra i. Greece see Corfu
Cordele U.S.A. 133 D6
Cordelia U.S.A. 128 B2
Cordell U.S.A. 131 D5
Cordilheiras, Serra das hills Brazil 143 I5
Cordillera Azul, Parque Nacional nat. park Peru 142 C5
Cordillera de los Picachos, Parque Nacional nat. park Col. 142 D3
Cordillo Downs Australia 111 C5
Cordisburgo Brazil 145 B2
Córdoba Arg. 144 D4
Córdoba Durango Mex. 131 C7
Córdoba Veracruz Mex. 136 E5
Córdoba Spain 57 D5
Córdoba, Sierras de mts Arg. 144 D4
Cordova Spain see Córdoba
Cordova U.S.A. 118 D3
Corduba Spain see Córdoba
Corfu i. Greece 59 H5
Coria Spain 57 C4
Coribe Brazil 145 B1
Coricudgy mt. Australia 112 E4
Corigliano Calabro Italy 58 G5
Coringa Islands Australia 110 E3
Corinium U.K. see Cirencester
Corinth Greece 59 J6
Corinth KY U.S.A. 134 C4
Corinth MS U.S.A. 131 F5
Corinth NY U.S.A. 135 I2
Corinth, Gulf of sea chan. Greece 59 J5
Corinthus Greece see Corinth
Corinto Brazil 145 B2
Cork Rep. of Ireland 51 D6
Corleone Sicily Italy 58 E6
Çorlu Turkey 59 L4
Cormeilles France 49 H9
Cornelia S. Africa 101 I4
Cornélio Procópio Brazil 145 A3
Cornélios Brazil 145 A5
Cornell U.S.A. 130 F2
Corner Brook Canada 123 K4
Corner Inlet b. Australia 112 C7
Corner Seamounts sea feature N. Atlantic Ocean 148 E3
Corneto Italy see Tarquinia
Cornillet, Mont hill France 52 E5
Corning AR U.S.A. 131 F4
Corning CA U.S.A. 128 B2
Corning NY U.S.A. 135 G2
Cornish watercourse Australia 110 D4
Corn Islands is Nicaragua see Maíz, Islas del
Corno, Monte mt. Italy 58 E3
Corno di Campo mt. Italy/Switz. 56 J3
Cornwall Canada 135 H1
Cornwallis Island Canada 119 I2
Cornwall Island Canada 119 I2
Coro Venez. 142 E1
Coroaci Brazil 145 C2
Coroatá Brazil 143 J4
Corofin Rep. of Ireland 51 C5
Coromandel Brazil 145 B2
Coromandel Coast India 84 D4
Coromandel Peninsula N.Z. 113 E3
Coromandel Range hills N.Z. 113 E3
Corona CA U.S.A. 128 E5
Corona NM U.S.A. 127 G6
Coronado U.S.A. 128 E5
Coronado, Bahiá de b. Costa Rica 137 H7
Coronation Canada 121 I4
Coronation Gulf Canada 118 G3
Coronation Island S. Atlantic Ocean 152 A2
Coronda Arg. 144 D4
Coronel Fabriciano Brazil 145 C2
Coronel Oviedo Para. 144 E3
Coronel Pringles Arg. 144 D5
Coronel Suárez Arg. 144 D5
Çorovodë Albania 59 I4
Corowa Australia 112 C5
Corpus Christi U.S.A. 131 D7
Corque Bol. 142 E7
Corral de Cantos mt. Spain 57 D4
Corrales Mex. 131 B7
Corralilla Cuba 133 D8
Corrandibby Range hills Australia 109 A6
Corrente Brazil 143 I6
Corrente r. Bahia Brazil 145 C1
Corrente r. Minas Gerais Brazil 145 A2
Correntes Brazil 143 H7
Correntina Brazil 145 B1
Correntina r. Brazil see Éguas
Corrib, Lough l. Rep. of Ireland 51 C4
Corrientes Arg. 144 E3
Corrientes, Cabo c. Col. 142 C2
Corrientes, Cabo c. Cuba 133 C8
Corrientes, Cabo c. Mex. 136 C4
Corrigin Australia 109 B8
Corris U.K. 49 D6
Corry U.S.A. 134 F3
Corse i. France see Corsica
Corse, Cap c. Corsica France 56 I5
Corsham U.K. 49 E7
Corsica i. France 56 I5
Corsicana U.S.A. 131 D5
Corte Corsica France 56 I5
Cortegana Spain 57 C5
Cortes, Sea of g. Mex. see California, Gulf of
Cortez U.S.A. 129 I3
Cortina d'Ampezzo Italy 58 E1
Cortland U.S.A. 135 G2
Corton U.K. 49 I6
Cortona Italy 58 D3
Coruche Port. 57 B4
Çoruh Turkey see Artvin
Çoruh r. Turkey 91 F2
Çorum Turkey 90 D2
Corumbá Brazil 143 G7
Corumbá r. Brazil 145 A2
Corumbá de Goiás Brazil 145 A1
Corumbaíba Brazil 145 A2
Corumbaú, Ponta pt Brazil 145 D2
Corunna Spain see A Coruña
Corunna U.S.A. 134 C2
Corvallis U.S.A. 126 C3
Corwen U.K. 49 D6
Corydon IA U.S.A. 130 E3
Corydon IN U.S.A. 134 B4
Coryville U.S.A. 135 F3
Cos i. Greece see Kos
Cosentia Italy see Cosenza
Cosenza Italy 58 G5
Coshocton U.S.A. 134 E3
Cosne-Cours-sur-Loire France 56 F3
Costa Blanca coastal area Spain 57 F4
Costa Brava coastal area Spain 57 H3
Costa de la Luz coastal area Spain 57 C5
Costa del Sol coastal area Spain 57 D5
Costa de Miskitos coastal area Nicaragua see Costa de Mosquitos
Costa de Mosquitos coastal area Nicaragua 137 H6
Costa Marques Brazil 142 F6
Costa Rica Brazil 143 H7
▶Costa Rica country Central America 137 H6
North America 9, 116–117
Costa Rica Mex. 136 C4
Costa Verde coastal area Spain 57 C2
Costermansville Dem. Rep. Congo see Bukavu
Costești Romania 59 K2
Costigan Lake Canada 121 J3
Coswig Germany 53 M3
Cotabato Phil. 69 G5
Cotagaita Bol. 142 E8
Cotahuasi Peru 142 D7
Cote, Mount U.S.A. 120 D3
Coteau des Prairies slope U.S.A. 130 D2
Coteau du Missouri slope ND U.S.A. 130 C1
Coteau du Missouri slope SD U.S.A. 130 C2
Côte d'Azur coastal area France 56 H5
▶Côte d'Ivoire country Africa 96 C4
Africa 7, 94–95
Côte Française de Somalis country Africa see Djibouti
Cotentin pen. France 49 F9
Côtes de Meuse ridge France 52 E5
Cothi r. U.K. 49 C7
Cotiaeum Turkey see Kütahya
Cotiella mt. Spain 57 G2
Cotonou Benin 96 D4
Cotopaxi, Volcán vol. Ecuador 142 C4
Cotswold Hills U.K. 49 E7
Cottage Grove U.S.A. 126 C4
Cottbus Germany 47 O5
Cottenham U.K. 49 H6
Cottian Alps mts France/Italy 56 H4
Cottica Suriname 143 H3
Cottiennes, Alpes mts France/Italy see Cottian Alps
Cottonwood AZ U.S.A. 129 G4
Cottonwood CA U.S.A. 128 B1
Cottonwood r. U.S.A. 130 D4
Cottonwood Falls U.S.A. 130 D4
Cotulla U.S.A. 131 D6
Coudersport U.S.A. 135 F3
Couëdic, Cape de Australia 111 B8
Coulee City U.S.A. 126 D3
Coulee Dam U.S.A. 126 D3
Coulman Island Antarctica 152 H2
Coulogne France 52 B4
Coulommiers France 52 D6
Coulonge r. Canada 122 F5
Coulterville U.S.A. 128 C3
Council U.S.A. 126 D3
Council Bluffs U.S.A. 130 E3
Council Grove U.S.A. 130 D4
Councillor Island Australia 111 [inset]
Counselor U.S.A. 129 J3
Coupeville U.S.A. 126 C2
Courageous Lake Canada 121 I1
Courland Lagoon b. Lith./Rus. Fed. 45 L9
Courtenay Canada 120 E5
Courtland U.S.A. 135 G5
Courtmacsherry Rep. of Ireland 51 D6
Courtmacsherry Bay Rep. of Ireland 51 D6
Courtown Rep. of Ireland 51 F5
Courtrai Belgium see Kortrijk
Coushatta U.S.A. 131 E5
Coutances France 56 D2
Coutts Canada 121 I5
Couture, Lac l. Canada 122 G2
Couvin Belgium 52 E4
Cove Fort U.S.A. 129 G2
Cove Island Canada 134 E1
Cove Mountains hills U.S.A. 135 F4
Coventry U.K. 49 F6
Covered Wells U.S.A. 129 G5
Covesville U.S.A. 135 F5
Covilhã Port. 57 C3
Covington GA U.S.A. 133 D5
Covington IN U.S.A. 134 B3
Covington KY U.S.A. 134 C4
Covington LA U.S.A. 131 F6
Covington MI U.S.A. 130 F2
Covington TN U.S.A. 131 F5
Covington VA U.S.A. 134 E5
Cowal, Lake dry lake Australia 112 C4
Cowan, Lake salt flat Australia 109 C7
Cowansville Canada 135 I1
Cowargarzê China 76 C1
Cowcowing Lakes salt flat Australia 109 B7
Cowdenbeath U.K. 50 F4
Cowell Australia 111 B7
Cowes U.K. 49 F8
Cowichan Lake Canada 120 E5
Cowley Australia 112 B1
Cowper Point Canada 119 G2
Cowra Australia 112 D4
Cox r. Australia 110 A2
Coxá r. Brazil 145 B1
Coxen Hole Hond. see Roatán
Coxilha de Santana hills Brazil/Uruguay 144 E4
Coxilha Grande hills Brazil 144 F3
Coxim Brazil 143 H7
Cox's Bazar Bangl. 83 G5
Coyame Mex. 131 B6
Coyhaique Chile see Coihaique
Coyote Lake U.S.A. 128 E4
Coyote Peak hill U.S.A. 129 F5
Cozhê China 83 F2
Cozie, Alpi mts France/Italy see Cottian Alps
Cozumel Mex. 137 G4
Cozumel, Isla de i. Mex. 137 G4
Craboon Australia 112 D4
Cracovia Poland see Kraków
Cracow Australia 110 E5
Cracow Poland see Kraków
Cradle Mountain Lake St Clair National Park Australia 111 [inset]
Cradock S. Africa 101 G7
Craig U.K. 50 D3
Craig AK U.S.A. 120 C4
Craig CO U.S.A. 129 J1
Craigavon U.K. 51 F3
Craigieburn Australia 112 B6
Craig Island Taiwan see Mienhua Yü
Craignure U.K. 50 D4
Craigsville U.S.A. 134 E4
Crail U.K. 50 G4
Crailsheim Germany 53 K5
Craiova Romania 59 J2
Cramlington U.K. 48 F3
Cranberry Lake U.S.A. 135 H1
Cranberry Portage Canada 121 K4
Cranborne Chase for. U.K. 49 E8
Cranbourne Australia 112 B7
Cranbrook Canada 120 H5
Crandon U.S.A. 130 F2
Crane Lake Canada 121 I5
Cranston KY U.S.A. 134 D4
Cranston RI U.S.A. 135 J3
Cranz Rus. Fed. see Zelenogradsk
Crary Ice Rise Antarctica 152 I1
Crary Mountains Antarctica 152 J1
Crater Lake National Park U.S.A. 126 C4
Crater Peak U.S.A. 128 C1
Craters of the Moon National Monument nat. park U.S.A. 126 E4
Crateús Brazil 143 J5
Crato Brazil 143 K5
Crawford CO U.S.A. 129 J2
Crawford NE U.S.A. 130 C3
Crawfordsville U.S.A. 134 B3
Crawfordville FL U.S.A. 133 C6
Crawfordville GA U.S.A. 133 D5
Crawley U.K. 49 G7
Crazy Mountains U.S.A. 126 F3
Creag Meagaidh mt. U.K. 50 E4
Crécy-en-Ponthieu France 52 B4
Credenhill U.K. 49 E6
Crediton U.K. 49 D8
Cree r. Canada 121 J3
Creel Mex. 127 G8
Cree Lake Canada 121 J3
Creemore Canada 134 E1
Creighton Canada 121 K4
Creil France 52 C5
Creil Neth. 52 F2
Crema Italy 58 C2
Cremlingen Germany 53 K2
Cremona Canada 120 H5
Cremona Italy 58 D2
Crépy-en-Valois France 52 C5
Cres i. Croatia 58 F2
Crescent U.S.A. 126 C4
Crescent City CA U.S.A. 126 B4
Crescent City FL U.S.A. 133 D6
Crescent Group is Paracel Is 68 E3
Crescent Head Australia 112 F3
Crescent Junction U.S.A. 129 I2
Crescent Valley U.S.A. 128 E1
Cressy Australia 112 A7
Crest Hill hill Hong Kong China 77 [inset]
Crestline U.S.A. 134 D3
Creston Canada 120 G5
Creston IA U.S.A. 130 E3
Creston WY U.S.A. 126 G4
Crestview U.S.A. 133 C6
Creswick Australia 112 A6
Creta i. Greece see Crete
Crete i. Greece 59 K7
Crete U.S.A. 130 D3
Creus, Cap de c. Spain 57 H2
Creuse r. France 56 E3
Creußen Germany 53 L5
Creutzwald France 52 G5
Creuzburg Germany 53 K3
Crevasse Valley Glacier Antarctica 152 J1
Crewe U.K. 49 E5
Crewe U.S.A. 135 F5
Crewkerne U.K. 49 E8
Crianlarich U.K. 50 E4
Criccieth U.K. 49 C6
Criciúma Brazil 145 A5
Crieff U.K. 50 F4
Criffel hill U.K. 50 F6
Criffell hill U.K. see Criffel
Crikvenica Croatia 58 F2
Crillon, Mount U.S.A. 120 B3
Crimea pen. Ukr. 90 D1
Crimmitschau Germany 53 M4
Crimond U.K. 50 H3
Crisfield U.S.A. 135 H5
Cristalândia Brazil 143 I6
Cristalina Brazil 145 B2
Cristalino r. Brazil see Mariembero
Cristóbal Colón, Pico mt. Col. 142 D1
Crixás Brazil 145 A1
Crixás Açu r. Brazil 145 A1
Crixás Mirim r. Brazil 145 A1
Crna Gora aut. rep. Serb. and Mont. 58 H3
Crni Vrh mt. Serb. and Mont. 59 J2
Črnomelj Slovenia 58 F2
Croagh Patrick hill Rep. of Ireland 51 C4
Croajingolong National Park Australia 112 D6
▶Croatia country Europe 58 G2
Europe 5, 38–39
Crocker, Banjaran mts Malaysia 68 E6
Crockett U.S.A. 131 E6
Crofton KY U.S.A. 134 B5
Crofton NE U.S.A. 130 D3
Croghan U.S.A. 135 H2
Croisilles France 52 C4
Croker, Cape Canada 134 E1
Croker Island Australia 108 F2
Cromarty U.K. 50 E3
Cromarty Firth est. U.K. 50 E3
Cromer U.K. 49 I6
Crook U.K. 48 F4
Crooked Harbour b. Hong Kong China 77 [inset]
Crooked Island Bahamas 133 F8
Crooked Island Hong Kong China 77 [inset]

Crooked Island Passage Bahamas 133 F8
Crookston U.S.A. 130 D2
Crooksville U.S.A. 134 D4
Crookwell Australia 112 D5
Croom Rep. of Ireland 51 D5
Croppa Creek Australia 112 E2
Crosby U.K. 48 D5
Crosby MN U.S.A. 130 E2
Crosby ND U.S.A. 130 C1
Crosbyton U.S.A. 131 C5
Cross Bay Canada 121 M2
Cross City U.S.A. 133 D6
Cross Fell hill U.K. 48 E4
Crossfield Canada 120 H5
Crossgar U.K. 51 G3
Crosshaven Rep. of Ireland 51 D6
Cross Inn U.K. 49 C6
Cross Lake Canada 121 L4
Cross Lake l. Canada 121 L4
Cross Lake l. U.S.A. 135 G2
Crossmaglen U.K. 51 F3
Crossman Peak U.S.A. 129 F4
Crossville U.S.A. 132 C5
Crotch Lake Canada 135 G1
Croton Italy see Crotone
Crotone Italy 58 G5
Crouch r. U.K. 49 H7
Crow r. Canada 120 E3
Crow Agency U.S.A. 126 G3
Crowal watercourse Australia 112 C3
Crowborough U.K. 49 H7
Crowdy Bay National Park Australia 112 F3
Crowell U.S.A. 131 D5
Crowland U.K. 49 G6
Crowley U.S.A. 131 E6
Crowley, Lake U.S.A. 128 D3
Crown Point IN U.S.A. 134 B3
Crownpoint U.S.A. 129 I4
Crown Point NY U.S.A. 135 I2
Crown Prince Olav Coast Antarctica 152 D2
Crown Princess Martha Coast Antarctica 152 B1
Crows Nest Australia 112 F1
Crowsnest Pass Canada 120 H5
Crowsnest Pass pass Canada 120 H5
Crow Wing r. U.S.A. 130 E2
Croydon Australia 110 C3
Crozet U.S.A. 135 F4
Crozet, Îles is Indian Ocean 149 L9
Crozet Basin sea feature Indian Ocean 149 M8
Crozet Plateau sea feature Indian Ocean 149 K8
Crozon France 56 B2
Cruces Cuba 133 D8
Cruden Bay U.K. 50 H3
Cruillas Mex. 131 D7
Crum U.S.A. 134 D5
Crumlin U.K. 51 F3
Crusheen Rep. of Ireland 51 D5
Cruz Alta Brazil 144 F3
Cruz del Eje Arg. 144 D4
Cruzeiro Brazil 145 B3
Cruzeiro do Sul Brazil 142 D5
Cry Lake Canada 120 D3
Crysdale, Mount Canada 120 F4
Crystal U.S.A. 129 I3
Crystal City Canada 121 L5
Crystal City U.S.A. 131 D6
Crystal Falls U.S.A. 130 F2
Crystal Lake U.S.A. 134 A2
Crystal River U.S.A. 133 D6
Csongrád Hungary 59 I1
Cửa Lớn r. Vietnam 71 D5
Cuamba Moz. 99 D5
Cuando r. Angola/Zambia 99 C5
Cuangar Angola 99 B5
Cuango Angola 99 B4
Cuanza r. Angola 99 B4
Cuatro Ciénegas Mex. 131 C7
Cuauhtémoc Mex. 127 G7
Cuba NM U.S.A. 127 G5
Cuba NY U.S.A. 135 F2

▶Cuba country West Indies 137 H4
5th largest island and 5th most populous country in North America.
North America 9, 116–117

Cubal Angola 99 B5
Cubango r. Angola/Namibia 99 C5
Cubatão Brazil 145 B3
Cub Hills Canada 121 J4
Çubuk Turkey 90 D2
Cucapa, Sierra mts Mex. 129 F5
Cuchi Angola 99 B5
Cuchilla Grande hills Uruguay 144 E4
Cucuí Brazil 142 E3
Cucurpe Mex. 127 F7
Cúcuta Col. 142 D2
Cudal Australia 112 D4
Cuddalore India 84 C4
Cuddapah India 84 C3
Cuddeback Lake U.S.A. 128 E4
Cue Australia 109 B6
Cuéllar Spain 57 D3
Cuemba Angola 99 B5
Cuenca Ecuador 142 C4
Cuenca Spain 57 E3
Cuenca, Serranía de mts Spain 57 E3
Cuencamé Mex. 131 C7
Cuernavaca Mex. 136 E5
Cuero U.S.A. 131 D6
Cuervos Mex. 129 F5
Cugir Romania 59 J2
Cuiabá Amazonas Brazil 143 G5
Cuiabá Mato Grosso Brazil 143 G7
Cuiabá r. Brazil 143 G7
Cuihua China see Daguan
Cuijiang China see Ninghua
Cuijk Neth. 52 F3
Cuilcagh hill Rep. of Ireland/U.K. 51 E3
Cuillin Hills U.K. 50 C3
Cuillin Sound sea chan. U.K. 50 C3
Cuilo Angola 99 B4
Cuiluan China 74 C3
Cuité r. Brazil 145 C2
Cuito r. Angola 99 C5
Cuito Cuanavale Angola 99 B5
Cukai Malaysia 71 C6
Çukurca Turkey 88 A2
Çukurova plat. Turkey 85 B1
Cu Lao Cham i. Vietnam 70 E4
Cu Lao Re i. Vietnam 70 E4
Cu Lao Thu i. Vietnam 71 E5
Cu Lao Xanh i. Vietnam 71 E4
Culcairn Australia 112 C5
Culfa Azer. 91 G3
Culgoa r. Australia 112 C2
Culiacán Mex. 136 C4
Culiacán Rosales Mex. see Culiacán
Culion Phil. 69 F4
Culion i. Phil. 68 F4
Cullen U.K. 50 G3
Cullen Point Australia 110 C1
Cullera Spain 57 F4
Cullivoe U.K. 50 [inset]
Cullman U.S.A. 133 C5
Cullybackey U.K. 51 F3
Cul Mòr hill U.K. 50 D2
Culpeper U.S.A. 135 G4
Culuene r. Brazil 143 H6
Culver, Point Australia 109 D8
Culverden N.Z. 113 D6
Cumaná Venez. 142 F1
Cumari Brazil 145 A2
Cumbal, Nevado de vol. Col. 142 C3
Cumberland KY U.S.A. 134 D5
Cumberland MD U.S.A. 135 F4
Cumberland VA U.S.A. 135 F5
Cumberland r. U.S.A. 132 C4
Cumberland, Lake U.S.A. 134 C5
Cumberland Lake Canada 121 K4
Cumberland Mountains U.S.A. 134 D5
Cumberland Peninsula Canada 119 L3
Cumberland Plateau U.S.A. 132 C5
Cumberland Point U.S.A. 130 F2
Cumberland Sound sea chan. Canada 119 L3
Cumbernauld U.K. 50 F5
Cumbres de Majalca, Parque Nacional nat. park Mex. 127 G7
Cumbres de Monterey, Parque Nacional nat. park Mex. 131 C7
Cumbum India 84 C3
Cumlosen Germany 53 L1
Cummings U.S.A. 128 B2
Cummins Australia 111 A7
Cummins Range hills Australia 108 D4
Cumnock Australia 112 D4
Cumnock U.K. 50 E5
Çumra Turkey 90 D3
Cumuruxatiba Brazil 145 D2
Cunagua Cuba see Bolivia
Cunderdin Australia 109 B7
Cunene r. Angola 99 B5
also known as Kunene
Cuneo Italy 58 B2
Cung Sơn Vietnam 71 E4
Cunnamulla Australia 112 B2
Cunningsburgh U.K. 50 [inset]
Cupar U.K. 50 F4
Cupica, Golfo de b. Col. 142 C2
Curaçá Brazil 143 K5
Curaçá r. Brazil 142 D4
Curaçao i. Neth. Antilles 137 K6
Curaray r. Ecuador 142 D4
Curdlawidny Lagoon salt flat Australia 111 B6
Curia Switz. see Chur
Curicó Chile 144 B4
Curitiba Brazil 145 A4
Curitibanos Brazil 145 A4
Curlewis Australia 112 E3
Curnamona Australia 111 B6
Currabubula Australia 112 E3
Currais Novos Brazil 143 K5
Curran U.S.A. 134 D1
Currane, Lough l. Rep. of Ireland 51 B6
Currant U.S.A. 129 F2
Curranyalpa Australia 112 B3
Currawilla Australia 110 C5
Currawinya National Park Australia 112 B2
Currie Australia 106 E5
Currie U.S.A. 129 F1
Currituck U.S.A. 135 G5
Currockbilly, Mount Australia 112 E5
Curtis Channel Australia 110 F5
Curtis Island Australia 110 E4
Curtis Island N.Z. 107 I5
Curuá r. Brazil 143 H5
Curup Indon. 68 C7
Curupira, Serra mts Brazil/Venez. 142 F3
Cururupu Brazil 143 J4
Curvelo Brazil 145 B2
Curwood, Mount hill U.S.A. 130 F2
Cusco Peru 142 D6
Cushendall U.K. 51 F2
Cushendun U.K. 51 F2
Cushing U.S.A. 131 D4
Cusseta U.S.A. 133 C5
Custer MT U.S.A. 126 G3
Custer SD U.S.A. 130 C3
Cut Bank U.S.A. 126 E2
Cuthbert U.S.A. 133 C6
Cuthbertson Falls Australia 108 F3
Cut Knife Canada 121 I4
Cutler Ridge U.S.A. 133 D7
Cuttaburra Creek r. Australia 112 B2
Cuttack India 84 E1
Cuvelai Angola 99 B5
Cuxhaven Germany 47 L4
Cuya Chile 142 D7
Cuyahoga Falls U.S.A. 134 E3
Cuyama U.S.A. 128 D4
Cuyama r. U.S.A. 128 C4
Cuyo Islands Phil. 69 G4
Cuyuni r. Guyana 143 G2
Cuzco Peru see Cusco
Cwmbran U.K. 49 D7
Cyangugu Rwanda 98 C4
Cyclades is Greece 59 K6
Cydonia Greece see Chania
Cygnet U.S.A. 134 D3
Cymru admin. div. U.K. see Wales
Cynthiana U.S.A. 134 C4
Cypress Hills Canada 121 I5
▶Cyprus country Asia 85 A2
Asia 6, 62–63
Cyrenaica reg. Libya 97 F2
Cythera i. Greece see Kythira
Czar Canada 121 I4
Czechia country Europe see Czech Republic

▶Czechoslovakia
Divided in 1993 into the Czech Republic and Slovakia.

▶Czech Republic country Europe 47 O6
Europe 5, 38–39
Czernowitz Ukr. see Chernivtsi
Czersk Poland 47 P4
Częstochowa Poland 47 Q5

D

Đa, Sông r. Vietnam see Black
Da'an China 74 B3
Ḍabāb, Jabal aḍ mt. Jordan 85 B4
Dabakala Côte d'Ivoire 96 C4
Daban China 73 L4
Dabao China 76 D2
Daba Shan mts China 77 F1
Dabba China see Daocheng
Dabein Myanmar 70 B3
Dabhoi India 82 C5
Ḍab'i, Wādī aḍ watercourse Jordan 85 C4
Dabie Shan mts China 77 G2
Dablana India 82 C4
Dabola Guinea 96 B3
Dabqig China 73 J5
Dąbrowa Górnicza Poland 47 Q5
Dabsan Hu salt l. China 83 H1
Dabs Nur l. China 74 A3
Dabu Guangdong China 77 H3
Dabu Guangxi China see Liucheng
Dabusu Pao l. China see Dabs Nur
Dacca Bangl. see Dhaka
Dachau Germany 47 M6
Dachuan China see Dazhou
Dacre Canada 135 G1
Daday Turkey 90 D2
Dade City U.S.A. 133 D6
Dadeville U.S.A. 133 C5
Dādkān Iran 89 F5
Dadong China see Donggang
Dadra India see Achalpur
Dadu Pak. 89 G5
Daegu S. Korea see Taegu
Daejŏn S. Korea see Taejŏn
Daet Phil. 69 G4
Dafang China 76 E3
Dafeng China 77 I1
Dafengman China 74 B4
Dafla Hills India 83 H4
Dafoe Canada 121 J5
Dafoe r. Canada 121 M4
Dagana Senegal 96 B3
Dagcagoin China see Zoigê
Dagcanglhamo China 76 D1
Daghmar Oman 88 E6
Dağlıq Qarabağ aut. reg. Azer. 91 G3
Daglung China 83 G3
Dagö i. Estonia see Hiiumaa
Dagon Myanmar see Rangoon
Daguan China 76 D3
Daguokui Shan hill China 74 C3
Dagupan Phil. 69 G3
Dagxoi Sichuan China see Yidun
Dagxoi Sichuan China see Sowa
Dagzê China 83 G3
Dagzê Co salt l. China 83 F3
Dahadinni r. Canada 120 E2
Dahalach, Isole is Eritrea see Dahlak Archipelago
Dahana des. Saudi Arabia see Ad Dahnā'
Dahe China see Ziyuan
Daheiding Shan mt. China 74 C3
Dahei Shan mts China 74 B4
Daheng China 77 H3
Dahezhen China 74 D3
Da Hinggan Ling mts China 74 A2
Dahlak Archipelago is Eritrea 86 F6
Dahlak Marine National Park Eritrea 86 F6
Daḥl al Furayy well Saudi Arabia 88 B5
Dahlem Germany 52 G4
Dahlenburg Germany 53 K1
Dahm, Ramlat des. Saudi Arabia/Yemen 86 G6
Dahmani Tunisia 58 C7
Dahme Germany 53 N3
Dahn Germany 53 H5
Dahnā' plain Saudi Arabia 88 B5
Dahod India 82 C5
Dahomey country Africa see Benin
Dahongliutan Aksai Chin 82 D2
Dahra Senegal see Dara
Dähre Germany 53 K2
Dahūk Iraq 91 F3
Dai i. Indon. 108 E1
Daik Indon. 68 C7
Daik-u Myanmar 70 B3
Dailekh Nepal 83 E3
Dailly U.K. 50 E5
Daimiel Spain 57 E4
Dainkog China 76 C1
Dainkognubma China 76 C1
Daintree National Park Australia 110 D3
Dairen China see Dalian
Dai-sen vol. Japan 75 D6
Daisetsu-zan National Park Japan 74 F4
Daishan China 77 I2
Daiyun Shan mts China 77 H3
Dajarra Australia 110 B4
Dajin Chuan r. China 76 D2
Da Juh China 83 H1

▶Dakar Senegal 96 B3
Capital of Senegal.

Dākhilah, Wāḥāt ad oasis Egypt 86 C4
Dakhla W. Sahara see Ad Dakhla
Dakhla Oasis oasis Egypt see Dākhilah, Wāḥāt ad
Dak Kon Vietnam 70 D4
Dakoank India 71 A6
Dakol'ka r. Belarus 43 F5
Dakor India 82 C5
Dakoro Niger 96 D3
Dakota City IA U.S.A. 130 E3
Dakota City NE U.S.A. 130 D3
Đakovica Serb. and Mont. 59 I3
Đakovo Croatia 58 H2
Daktuy Rus. Fed. 74 B1
Dala Angola 99 C5
Dalaba Guinea 96 B3
Dalai China see Da'an
Dalain Hob China 80 J3
Dālakī Iran 88 C4
Dalälven r. Sweden 45 J6
Dalaman Turkey 59 M6
Dalandzadgad Mongolia 72 I4
Dalap-Uliga-Darrit Marshall Is see Delap-Uliga-Djarrit
Đa Lat Vietnam 71 E5
Dalatando Angola see N'dalatando
Dalaud India 82 C5
Dalauda India 82 C5
Dalbandin Pak. 89 G4
Dalbeattie U.K. 50 F6
Dalbeg Australia 110 D4
Dalby Australia 112 E1
Dalby Isle of Man 48 C4
Dale Hordaland Norway 45 D6
Dale Sogn og Fjordane Norway 45 D6
Dale City U.S.A. 135 G4
Dale Hollow Lake U.S.A. 134 C5
Dalen Neth. 52 G2
Dalet Myanmar 70 A3
Daletme Myanmar 70 A2
Dalfors Sweden 45 I6
Dalgān Iran 88 E5
Dalgety Australia 112 D6
Dalgety r. Australia 109 A6
Dalhart U.S.A. 131 C4
Dalhousie Canada 123 I4
Dalhousie, Cape Canada 118 F2
Dali Shaanxi China 77 F1
Dali Yunnan China 76 D3
Dalian China 73 M5
Daliang China see Shunde
Daliang Shan mts China 76 D2
Daliji China 77 H1
Dalin China 74 A4
Dalizi China 74 B4
Dalkeith U.K. 50 F5
Dallas OR U.S.A. 126 C3
Dallas TX U.S.A. 131 D5
Dalles City U.S.A. see The Dalles
Dall Island U.S.A. 120 C4
Dalmā i. U.A.E. 88 D5
Dalmacija reg. Bos.-Herz./Croatia see Dalmatia
Dalman India 82 E4
Dalmas, Lac l. Canada 123 H3
Dalmatia reg. Bos.-Herz./Croatia 78 A2
Dalmellington U.K. 50 E5
Dalmeny Canada 121 J4
Dalmi India 83 F5
Dal'negorsk Rus. Fed. 74 D3
Dal'nerechensk Rus. Fed. 74 D3
Dal'niye Zelentsy Rus. Fed. 42 H1
Dalny China see Dalian
Daloa Côte d'Ivoire 96 C4

▶Dalol Eth. 86 F7
Highest recorded annual mean temperature in the world.

Daloloia Group is P.N.G. 110 E1
Dalou Shan mts China 76 E3
Dalqān well Saudi Arabia 88 B5
Dalry U.K. 50 E5
Dalrymple U.K. 50 E5
Dalrymple, Lake Australia 110 D4
Daltenganj India 83 F4
Dalton Canada 122 D4
Dalton S. Africa 101 J5
Dalton GA U.S.A. 133 C5
Dalton MA U.S.A. 135 I2
Dalton PA U.S.A. 135 H3
Daltonganj India see Daltenganj
Dalton-in-Furness U.K. 48 D4
Daludalu Indon. 71 C7
Daluo China 76 D4
Daly r. Australia 108 E3
Daly City U.S.A. 128 B3
Daly River Australia 108 E3
Daly Waters Australia 108 F4
Damagaram Takaya Niger 96 D3
Daman India 84 B1
Daman and Diu union terr. India 84 A1
Damanhūr Egypt see Damanhûr
Damanhûr Egypt 90 C5
Damant Lake Canada 121 J2
Damão India see Daman
Damar i. Indon. 108 E1
Damara Cent. Afr. Rep. 98 B3
Damaraland reg. Namibia 99 B6
Damas Syria see Damascus

▶Damascus Syria 85 C3
Capital of Syria.

Damascus U.S.A. 134 E5
Damaturu Nigeria 96 E3
Damāvand Iran 88 D3
Damāvand, Qolleh-ye mt. Iran 88 D3
Dambulla Sri Lanka 84 D5
Damdy Kazakh. 80 B1
Damghan Iran 88 D2
Damianópolis Brazil 145 B1
Damietta Egypt see Dumyāṭ
Daming Shan mt. China 77 F4
Dāmiyā Jordan 85 B3
Damjong China 76 B1
Damlasu Turkey 85 D1
Dammam Saudi Arabia 86 H4
Damme Belgium 52 D3
Damme Germany 53 I2
Damoh India 82 D5
Damour Lebanon 85 B3
Dampar, Tasik l. Malaysia 71 C7
Dampier Archipelago is Australia 108 B5
Dampier Island P.N.G. see Karkar Island
Dampier Land reg. Australia 108 C4
Dampier Strait P.N.G. 69 L8
Dampir, Selat sea chan. Indon. 69 I7
Damqoq Zangbo r. China see Maquan He
Dam Qu r. China 76 B1
Dâmrei, Chuŏr Phnum mts Cambodia 71 D5
Damroh India 76 B2
Damwâld Neth. see Damwoude
Damwoude Neth. 52 G1
Damxoi China see Comai
Damxung China 83 G3
Ḍānā Jordan 85 B4
Dana Nepal 83 E3
Danakil reg. Africa see Denakil
Danané Côte d'Ivoire 96 C4
Đa Năng Vietnam 70 E3
Đa Nang, Vinh b. Vietnam 70 E3
Danao Phil. 69 G4
Danata Turkm. 88 D2
Danba China 76 D2
Danbury CT U.S.A. 135 I3
Danbury NC U.S.A. 132 D4
Danby U.S.A. 135 I2
Danby Lake U.S.A. 129 F4
Dandaragan Australia 109 A7
Dande Eth. 98 D3
Dandel'dhura Nepal 82 E3
Dandeli India 84 B3
Dandong China 75 B4
Dandot Pak. 89 I3
Dandridge U.S.A. 132 D4
Dane r. U.K. 48 E5
Daneborg Greenland 153 I2
Danese U.S.A. 134 E5
Danfeng China see Shizong
Dangan Liedao i. China 77 G4
Dangara Tajik. see Danghara
Dangbizhen Rus. Fed. 74 C3
Dangchang China 76 E1
Dangchengwan China see Subei
Danger Islands atoll Cook Is see Pukapuka
Danger Point S. Africa 100 D8
Danghara Tajik. 89 H2
Danghe Nanshan mts China 80 H4
Dang La pass China see Tanggula Shankou
Dangla Shan mts China see Tanggula Shan
Dangqên China 83 G3
Dângrêk, Chuŏr Phnum mts Cambodia/Thai. see Phanom Dong Rak, Thiu Khao
Dangriga Belize 136 G5
Dangshan China 77 H1
Dangtu China 77 H2
Daniel's Harbour Canada 123 K4
Daniëlskuil S. Africa 100 F5
Danilov Rus. Fed. 42 I4
Danilovka Rus. Fed. 43 J6
Danilovskaya Vozvyshennost' hills Rus. Fed. 42 H4
Danjiang China see Leishan
Danjiangkou China 77 F1
Danjiangkou Shuiku resr China 77 F1
Danjo-guntō is Japan 75 C6
Dank Oman 88 E6
Dankhar India 82 D2
Dankov Rus. Fed. 43 H5
Danlí Hond. 137 G6
Danmark country Europe see Denmark
Dannebrog Ø i. Greenland see Qillak
Dannenberg (Elbe) Germany 53 L1
Dannenwalde Germany 53 N1
Dannevirke N.Z. 113 F5
Dannhauser S. Africa 101 J5
Dano Burkina 96 C3
Danshui Taiwan see Tanshui
Dansville U.S.A. 135 G2
Danta India 82 C4
Dantan India 83 F5
Dantevada India see Dantewara
Dantewada India see Dantewara
Dantewara India 84 D2
Dantu China 77 H1

▶Danube r. Europe 47 P6
2nd longest river in Europe. Also spelt Donau (Austria/Germany) or Duna (Hungary) or Dunaj (Slovakia) or Dunărea (Romania) or Dunav (Bulgaria/Croatia/Serbia and Montenegro) or Dunay (Ukraine).

Danube Delta Romania/Ukr. 59 M2
Danubyu Myanmar 70 A3
Danville IL U.S.A. 134 B3
Danville IN U.S.A. 134 B4
Danville KY U.S.A. 134 C5
Danville OH U.S.A. 134 D3
Danville PA U.S.A. 135 G3
Danville VA U.S.A. 134 F5
Danville VT U.S.A. 135 I1
Danxian China see Danzhou
Danzhai China 76 E3
Danzhou Guangxi China 77 F3
Danzhou Hainan China 77 F5
Danzig Poland see Gdańsk
Danzig, Gulf of Poland/Rus. Fed. see Gdańsk, Gulf of
Daocheng China 76 D2
Daokou China see Huaxian
Dao Tay Sa is S. China Sea see Paracel Islands
Daoud Alg. see Aïn Beïda
Daoukro Côte d'Ivoire 96 C4
Daozhen China 76 E2
Dapaong Togo 96 D3
Dapeng Wan b. Hong Kong China see Mirs Bay
Daphabum mt. India 83 I4
Daporijo India 83 H4
Dapu China see Liucheng
Da Qaidam Zhen China 80 I4
Daqiao China 76 D3
Daqing China 74 B3
Daqiu China 77 H3
Dāq Mashī Iran 88 E3
Daqq-e Patargān salt flat Iran 89 F3
Daqq-e Tundi, Dasht-e imp. l. Afgh. 89 F3
Daqu Shan i. China 77 I2
Dara Senegal 96 B3
Dar'ā Syria 85 C3
Dāra, Gebel mt. Egypt see Dārah, Jabal
Dārāb Iran 88 D4
Darāgāh Iran 88 D4
Dārah, Jabal mt. Egypt 90 D6
Daraj Libya 96 E1
Dārākūyeh Iran 88 D4
Dārān Iran 88 C3
Đa Răng, Sông r. Vietnam 71 E4
Daraut-Korgon Kyrg. 89 I2
Darazo Nigeria 96 E3
Darband, Kūh-e mt. Iran 88 E4
Darband-e Hajjī Boland Turkm. 89 F2
Darbhanga India 83 F4
Darcang China 76 C1
Dardanelle U.S.A. 131 E5
Dardanelles strait Turkey 59 L4
Dardania prov. Serb. and Mont. see Kosovo
Dardesheim Germany 53 K3
Dardo China see Kangding
Dar el Beida Morocco see Casablanca
Darende Turkey 90 E3

▶Dar es Salaam Tanz. 99 D4
Former capital of Tanzania.

Darfo Boario Terme Italy 58 D2
Dargai Pak. 89 H3
Darganata Turkm. 89 F1
Dargaville N.Z. 113 D2
Dargo Australia 112 C6
Dargo Zangbo r. China 83 F3
Darhan Mongolia 72 J3
Darien U.S.A. 133 D6
Darién, Golfo del g. Col. 142 C2
Darién, Parque Nacional de nat. park Panama 137 I7
Dariga Pak. 89 G5
Darjeeling India see Darjiling
Darjiling India 83 G4
Darkhazīneh Iran 88 C4
Darlag China 76 C1

▶Darling r. Australia 112 B3
2nd longest river in Oceania. Part of the longest (Murray-Darling).

Darling Downs hills Australia 112 D1
Darling Range hills Australia 109 A8
Darlington U.K. 48 F4
Darlington U.S.A. 130 F3
Darlington Point Australia 112 C5
Darlot, Lake salt flat Australia 109 C6
Darłowo Poland 47 P3
Darma Pass China/India 82 E3
Darmstadt Germany 53 I5
Darnah Libya 97 F1
Darnall S. Africa 101 J5
Darnick Australia 112 A4
Darnley, Cape Antarctica 152 E2
Daroca Spain 57 F3
Daroot-Korgon Kyrg. see Daraut-Korgon
Darovskoy Rus. Fed. 42 J4
Darr watercourse Australia 110 C4
Darreh Bīd Iran 88 E3
Darreh-ye Bāhābād Iran 88 D4
Darreh-ye Shahr Iran 88 B3
Darsi India 84 C3
Dart r. U.K. 49 D8
Dartang China see Baqên
Dartford U.K. 49 H7
Dartmoor Australia 111 C8
Dartmoor hills U.K. 49 C8
Dartmoor National Park U.K. 49 D8
Dartmouth Canada 123 J5
Dartmouth U.K. 49 D8
Dartmouth, Lake salt flat Australia 111 D5
Dartmouth Reservoir Australia 112 C6
Darton U.K. 48 F5
Daru P.N.G. 69 K8
Daru Sierra Leone 96 B4
Daruba Indon. 69 H6
Darvaza Turkm. 88 E1
Darvoz, Qatorkŭhi mts Tajik. 89 H2
Darwazgai Afgh. 89 G4
Darwen U.K. 48 E5
Darweshan Afgh. 89 G4

▶Darwin Australia 108 E3
Capital of Northern Territory.

Darwin, Monte mt. Chile 144 C8
Daryācheh-ye Orūmīyeh salt l. Iran see Urmia, Lake
Dar'yalyktakyr, Ravnina plain Kazakh. 80 B2
Dar"yoi Amu r. Asia see Amudar'ya
Dārzīn Iran 88 E4
Dās i. U.A.E. 88 D5
Dasada India 82 B5
Dashennongjia mt. China see Shennong Ding
Dashhowuz Turkm. see Dashoguz
Dashkesan Azer. see Daşkäsän
Dashkhovuz Turkm. see Dashoguz
Dashköpri Turkm. see Tashkepri
Dashoguz Turkm. 87 I1
Dasht Iran 88 E2
Dashtiari Iran 89 F5
Daska Pak. 89 I3
Daşkäsän Azer. 91 G2
Daşoguz Turkm. see Dashoguz
Dasongshu China 76 E3
Daspar mt. Pak. 89 I2
Dassel Germany 53 J3
Dastgardān Iran 88 E3
Datadian Indon. 68 F6
Datça Turkey 59 L6
Date Japan 74 F4
Date Creek watercourse U.S.A. 129 G4
Dateland U.S.A. 129 G5
Datha India 82 C5
Datia India 82 D4
Datian China 77 H3
Datian Ding mt. China 77 F4
Datil U.S.A. 129 J4
Datong Anhui China 77 H2
Datong Heilong. China 74 B3
Datong Shanxi China 73 K4
Datong He r. China 72 I5
Dattapur India 84 C1
Datu, Tanjung c. Indon./Malaysia 71 E7
Daudkandi Bangl. 83 G5
Daugava r. Latvia 45 N8
Daugavpils Latvia 45 O9
Daulatabad India 84 B2
Daulatabad Iran see Malāyer

Daulatpur Bangl. 83 G5
Daun Germany 52 G4
Daungyu r. Myanmar 70 A2
Dauphin Canada 121 K5
Dauphiné reg. France 56 G4
Dauphiné, Alpes du mts France 56 G4
Dauphin Lake Canada 121 L5
Daurie Creek r. Australia 109 A6
Dausa India 82 D4
Dầu Tiếng, Hồ resr Vietnam 71 D5
Dava U.K. 50 F3
Däväçi Azer. 91 H2
Davanagere India see Davangere
Davangere India 84 B3
Davao Phil. 69 H5
Davao Gulf Phil. 69 H5
Dāvarī Iran 88 E5
Dāvarzan Iran 88 E2
Davel S. Africa 101 I4
Davenport IA U.S.A. 130 F3
Davenport WA U.S.A. 126 D3
Davenport Downs Australia 110 C5
Davenport Range hills Australia 108 F5
Daventry U.K. 49 F6
Daveyton S. Africa 101 I4
David Panama 137 H7
David City U.S.A. 130 D3
Davidson Canada 121 J5
Davidson, Mount hill Australia 108 E5
Davis research station Antarctica 152 E2
Davis r. Australia 108 C5
Davis i. Myanmar see Than Kyun
Davis CA U.S.A. 128 C2
Davis WV U.S.A. 134 F4
Davis, Mount hill U.S.A. 134 F4
Davis Bay Antarctica 152 G2
Davis Dam U.S.A. 129 F4
Davis Inlet Canada 123 J3
Davis Sea Antarctica 152 F2
Davis Strait Canada/Greenland 119 M3
Davlekanovo Rus. Fed. 41 Q5
Davos Switz. 56 I3
Davy Lake Canada 121 I3
Dawa Co l. China 83 F3
Dawa Wenz r. Eth. 98 E3
Dawaxung China 83 F3
Dawê China 76 D2
Dawei Myanmar see Tavoy
Dawei r. mouth Myanmar see Tavoy
Dawera i. Indon. 108 E1
Dawna Range mts Myanmar/Thai. 70 B3
Dawna Taungdan mts Myanmar/Thai. see Dawna Range
Dawo China see Maqên
Dawqah Oman 87 H6
Dawson r. Australia 110 E4
Dawson Canada 120 B1
Dawson GA U.S.A. 133 C6
Dawson ND U.S.A. 130 D2
Dawson, Mount Canada 120 G5
Dawson Bay Canada 121 K4
Dawson Creek Canada 120 F4
Dawson Inlet Canada 121 M2
Dawson Range mts Canada 120 A2
Dawsons Landing Canada 120 E5
Dawu Hubei China 77 G2
Dawu Qinghai China see Maqên
Dawu Taiwan see Tawu
Dawukou China see Shizuishan
Dawu Shan hill China 77 G2
Dax France 56 D5
Daxian China see Dazhou
Daxiang Ling mts China 76 D2
Daxin China 76 E4
Daxing Yunnan China see Lüchun
Daxing Yunnan China see Ninglang
Daxing'an Ling mts China see Da Hinggan Ling
Da Xueshan mts China 76 D2
Dayan China see Lijiang
Dayangshu China 74 B2
Dayao China 76 D3
Dayao Shan mts China 77 F4
Daye China 77 G2
Daying China 76 E2
Daying Jiang r. China 76 C3
Dayishan China see Guanyun
Daylesford Australia 112 B6
Daylight Pass U.S.A. 128 E3
Dayong China see Zhangjiajie
Dayr Abū Sa'īd Jordan 85 B3
Dayr az Zawr Syria 91 F4
Dayr Ḥāfir Syria 85 C1
Daysland Canada 121 H4
Dayton OH U.S.A. 134 C4
Dayton TN U.S.A. 132 C5
Dayton VA U.S.A. 135 F4
Dayton WA U.S.A. 126 D3
Daytona Beach U.S.A. 133 D6
Dayu Ling mts China 77 G3
Da Yunhe canal China 77 H1
Dayyina i. U.A.E. 88 D5
Dazhongji China see Dafeng
Dazhou China 76 E2
Dazhou Dao i. China 77 F5
Dazhu China 76 E2
Dazu China 76 E2
Dazu Rock Carvings tourist site China 76 E2
De Aar S. Africa 100 G6
Dead r. Rep. of Ireland 51 D5
Deadman Lake U.S.A. 128 E4
Deadman's Cay Bahamas 133 F8
Dead Mountains U.S.A. 129 F4

▶Dead Sea salt l. Asia 85 B4
Lowest point in the world and in Asia.
Asia 60–61

Deadwood U.S.A. 130 C2
Deakin Australia 109 E7
Deal U.K. 49 I7
Dealesville S. Africa 101 G5
De'an China 77 G2
Dean, Forest of U.K. 49 E7
Deán Funes Arg. 144 D4
Deanuvuotna inlet Norway see Tanafjorden
Dearborn U.S.A. 134 D2
Dearne r. U.K. 48 F5
Deary U.S.A. 126 D3
Dease r. Canada 120 D3
Dease Lake Canada 120 D3
Dease Lake l. Canada 120 D3
Dease Strait Canada 118 H3

▶Death Valley depr. U.S.A. 128 E3
Lowest point in the Americas.
North America 114–115

Death Valley Junction U.S.A. 128 E3
Death Valley National Park U.S.A. 128 E3
Deauville France 56 E2
Deaver U.S.A. 126 F3
De Baai S. Africa see Port Elizabeth
Debao China 76 E4
Debar Macedonia 59 I4
Debden Canada 121 J4
Debenham U.K. 49 I6
De Beque U.S.A. 129 I2
De Biesbosch, Nationaal Park nat. park Neth. 52 E3
Débo, Lac l. Mali 96 C3
Deborah East, Lake salt flat Australia 109 B7
Deborah West, Lake salt flat Australia 109 B7
Debrecen Hungary 59 I1
Debre Markos Eth. 86 E7
Debre Tabor Eth. 86 E7
Debre Zeyit Eth. 98 D3
Decatur AL U.S.A. 133 C5
Decatur GA U.S.A. 133 C5
Decatur IL U.S.A. 130 F4
Decatur IN U.S.A. 134 C3
Decatur MI U.S.A. 134 C2
Decatur MS U.S.A. 131 F5
Decatur TX U.S.A. 131 D5

▶Deccan plat. India 84 C2
Plateau making up most of southern and central India.

Deception Bay Australia 112 F1
Dechang China 76 D3
Děčín Czech Rep. 47 O5
Decker U.S.A. 126 G3
Decorah U.S.A. 130 F3
Dedap i. Indon. see Penasi, Pulau
Dedaye Myanmar 70 A3
Deddington U.K. 49 F7
Dedeğöl Dağları mts Turkey 59 N6
Dedeleben Germany 53 K2
Dedelstorf Germany 53 K2
Dedemsvaart Neth. 52 G2
Dedo de Deus mt. Brazil 145 B4
Dédougou Burkina 96 C3
Dedovichi Rus. Fed. 42 F4
Dedu China see Wudalianchi
Dee r. Rep. of Ireland 51 F4
Dee est. U.K. 48 D5
Dee r. England/Wales U.K. 49 D5
Dee r. Scotland U.K. 50 G3
Deel r. Rep. of Ireland 51 D5
Deel r. Rep. of Ireland 51 F4
Deep Bay Hong Kong China 77 [inset]
Deep Creek Lake U.S.A. 134 F4
Deep Creek Range mts U.S.A. 129 G2
Deep River Canada 122 F5
Deepwater Australia 112 E2
Deeri Somalia 98 E3
Deering U.S.A. 118 B3
Deering, Mount Australia 109 E6
Deer Island U.S.A. 118 B4
Deer Lake Canada 121 M4
Deer Lake l. Canada 121 M4
Deer Lodge U.S.A. 126 E3
Deesa India see Disa
Deeth U.S.A. 126 E4
Defeng China see Liping
Defensores del Chaco, Parque Nacional nat. park Para. 144 D2
Defiance U.S.A. 134 C3
Defiance Plateau U.S.A. 129 I4
Degana India 82 C4
Degeh Bur Eth. 98 E3
Degema Nigeria 96 D4
Deggendorf Germany 53 M6
Degh r. Pak. 89 I4
De Grey r. Australia 108 B5
De Groote Peel, Nationaal Park nat. park Neth. 52 F3
Degtevo Rus. Fed. 43 I6
De Haan Belgium 52 D3
Dehak Iran 89 F4
De Hamert, Nationaal Park nat. park Neth. 52 G3
Deh Bīd Iran 88 D4
Deh-Dasht Iran 88 C4
Dehej India 82 C5
Deheq Iran 88 C3
Dehestān Iran 88 D4
Deh Golān Iran 88 B3
Dehgon Afgh. 89 F3
Dehi Afgh. 89 G3
Dehküyeh Iran 88 D5
Dehlorān Iran 88 B3
De Hoge Veluwe, Nationaal Park nat. park Neth. 52 F2
De Hoop Nature Reserve S. Africa 100 E8
Dehqonobod Uzbek. see Dekhkanabad
Dehra Dun India 82 D3
Dehradun India see Dehra Dun
Dehri India 83 F4
Deh Shū Afgh. 89 F4
Deim Zubeir Sudan 97 F4
Deinze Belgium 52 D4
Deir-ez-Zor Syria see Dayr az Zawr
Dej Romania 59 J1
Deji China see Rinbung
Dejiang China 77 F2
De Jouwer Neth. see Joure
De Kalb IL U.S.A. 130 F3
De Kalb MS U.S.A. 131 F5
De Kalb TX U.S.A. 131 E5
De Kalb Junction U.S.A. 135 H1
De-Kastri Rus. Fed. 74 F2
Dekemhare Eritrea 86 E6
Dekhkanabad Uzbek. 89 G2
Dekina Nigeria 96 D4
Dékoa Cent. Afr. Rep. 98 B3
De Koog Neth. 52 E1
De Kooy Neth. 52 E2
Delaki Indon. 108 D2
Delamar Lake U.S.A. 129 F3
De Land U.S.A. 133 D6
Delano U.S.A. 128 D4
Delano Peak U.S.A. 129 G2

▶Delap-Uliga-Djarrit Marshall Is 150 H5
Capital of the Marshall Islands, on Majuro atoll.

Delārām Afgh. 89 F3
Delareyville S. Africa 101 G4
Delaronde Lake Canada 121 J4
Delavan U.S.A. 122 C6
Delaware U.S.A. 134 D3
Delaware r. U.S.A. 135 H4
Delaware state U.S.A. 135 H4
Delaware, East Branch r. U.S.A. 135 H3
Delaware Bay U.S.A. 135 H4
Delaware Lake U.S.A. 134 D3
Delaware Water Gap National Recreational Area park U.S.A. 135 H3
Delay r. Canada 123 H2
Delbarton U.S.A. 134 D5
Delbrück Germany 53 I3
Delburne Canada 120 H4
Delegate Australia 112 D6
De Lemmer Neth. see Lemmer
Delémont Switz. 56 H3
Delevan CA U.S.A. 128 B2
Delevan NY U.S.A. 135 F2
Delfinópolis Brazil 145 B3
Delft Neth. 52 E2
Delfzijl Neth. 52 G1
Delgada, Point U.S.A. 128 A1
Delgado, Cabo c. Moz. 99 E5
Delhi Canada 134 E2
Delhi China 80 I4
Delhi India 82 D3
Delhi CO U.S.A. 127 G5
Delhi LA U.S.A. 131 F5
Delhi NY U.S.A. 135 H2
Delice Turkey 90 D3
Delice r. Turkey 90 D2
Delījān Iran 88 C3
Déline Canada 120 F1
Delingha China see Delhi
Delisle Canada 121 J5
Delitzsch Germany 53 M3
Delligsen Germany 53 J3
Dell Rapids U.S.A. 130 D3
Dellys Alg. 57 H5
Del Mar U.S.A. 128 E5
Delmenhorst Germany 53 I1
Delnice Croatia 58 F2
Del Norte U.S.A. 127 G5
Delong China see Ande
De-Longa, Ostrova is Rus. Fed. 65 Q2
De Long Islands Rus. Fed. see De-Longa, Ostrova
De Long Mountains U.S.A. 114 B3
De Long Strait Rus. Fed. see Longa, Proliv
Deloraine Canada 121 K5
Delphi U.S.A. 134 B3
Delphos U.S.A. 134 C3
Delportshoop S. Africa 100 G5
Delray Beach U.S.A. 133 D7
Delrey U.S.A. 134 A3
Del Río Mex. 127 F7
Del Rio U.S.A. 131 C6
Delsbo Sweden 45 J6
Delta CO U.S.A. 129 I2
Delta OH U.S.A. 134 C3
Delta UT U.S.A. 129 G2
Delta Downs Australia 110 C3
Delta Junction U.S.A. 118 D3
Deltona U.S.A. 133 D6
Delungra Australia 112 E2
Delvin Rep. of Ireland 51 E4
Delvinë Albania 59 I5
Delwara India 82 C4
Demavend mt. Iran see Damāvand, Qolleh-ye
Demba Dem. Rep. Congo 99 C4
Dembī Dolo Eth. 86 D8
Demerara Guyana see Georgetown
Demerara Abyssal Plain sea feature S. Atlantic Ocean 148 E5
Demidov Rus. Fed. 43 F5
Deming U.S.A. 127 G6
Demirci Turkey 59 M5
Demirköy Turkey 59 L4
Demirtaş Turkey 85 A1
Demmin Germany 47 N4
Demopolis U.S.A. 133 C5
Demotte U.S.A. 134 B3
Dempo, Gunung vol. Indon. 68 C7
Dêmqog Jammu and Kashmir 82 D2
Demta Indon. 69 K7
Dem'yanovo Rus. Fed. 42 J3
De Naawte S. Africa 100 E6
Denakil reg. Africa 98 E2
Denali mt. U.S.A. see McKinley, Mount
Denali National Park and Preserve U.S.A. 118 C3
Denan Eth. 98 E3
Denau Uzbek. 89 G2
Denbigh Canada 135 G1
Denbigh U.K. 48 D5
Den Bosch Neth. see 's-Hertogenbosch
Den Burg Neth. 52 E1
Den Chai Thai. 70 C3
Dendâra Mauritania 96 C3
Dendermonde Belgium 52 E3
Dendi mt. Eth. 98 D3
Dendre r. Belgium 52 E3
Dendron S. Africa 101 I2
Denezhkin Kamen', Gora mt. Rus. Fed. 41 R3
Dêngka China see Têwo
Dêngkagoin China see Têwo
Dengkou China 72 J4
Dêngqên China 76 B2
Dengta China 77 G4
Dengxian China see Dengzhou
Dengzhou China 77 G1
Den Haag Neth. see The Hague
Denham Australia 109 A6
Denham r. Australia 108 E3
Den Ham Neth. 52 G2
Denham Range mts Australia 110 E4
Den Helder Neth. 52 E2
Denholm Canada 121 I4
Denia Spain 57 G4
Denial Bay Australia 111 A7
Deniliquin Australia 112 B5
Denio U.S.A. 126 D4
Denison IA U.S.A. 130 E3
Denison TX U.S.A. 131 D5
Denison, Cape Antarctica 152 G2
Denison Plains Australia 108 E4
Deniyaya Sri Lanka 84 D5
Denizli Turkey 59 M6
Denman Australia 112 E4
Denman Glacier Antarctica 148 F2
Denmark Australia 106 B5
▶Denmark country Europe 45 G8
Europe 5, 38–39
Denmark U.S.A. 134 B1
Denmark Strait Greenland/Iceland 40 A2
Dennis, Lake salt flat Australia 108 E5
Dennison IL U.S.A. 134 B4
Dennison OH U.S.A. 134 E3
Denny U.K. 50 F4
Denow Uzbek. see Denau
Denpasar Indon. 108 A2
Denton MD U.S.A. 135 H4
Denton TX U.S.A. 131 D5
D'Entrecasteaux, Point Australia 109 A8
D'Entrecasteaux, Récifs reef New Caledonia 107 G3
D'Entrecasteaux Islands P.N.G. 106 F2
D'Entrecasteaux National Park Australia 109 A8

▶Denver CO U.S.A. 126 G5
State capital of Colorado.

Denver PA U.S.A. 135 G3
Denys r. Canada 122 F3
Deo India 83 F4
Deoband India 82 D3
Deogarh Jharkhand India see Deoghar
Deogarh Orissa India 83 F5
Deogarh Rajasthan India 82 C4
Deogarh Uttar Pradesh India 82 D4
Deogarh mt. India 83 E5
Deoghar India 83 F4
Deolali India 84 B2
Deoli India 83 F5
Deori Chhattisgarh India 84 D1
Deori Madhya Pradesh India 82 D5
Deoria India 83 E4
Deosai, Plains of Jammu and Kashmir 82 C2
Deosil India 83 E5
De Panne Belgium 52 C3
De Pere U.S.A. 134 A1
Deposit U.S.A. 135 H2
Depsang Point hill Aksai Chin 78 D2
Deputatskiy Rus. Fed. 65 O3
Dêqên Xizang China 83 G3
Dêqên Xizang China 83 G3
Dêqên Xizang China see Dagzê
De Queen U.S.A. 131 E5
Dera Ghazi Khan Pak. 89 H4
Dera Ismail Khan Pak. 89 H4
Derajat reg. Pak. 89 H4
Derawar Fort Pak. 89 H4
Derbent Rus. Fed. 91 H2
Derbesiye Turkey see Şenyurt
Derbur China 74 A2
Derby Australia 108 C4
Derby U.K. 49 F6
Derby CT U.S.A. 135 I3
Derby KS U.S.A. 131 D4
Derby NY U.S.A. 135 F2
Derg r. Rep. of Ireland/U.K. 51 E3
Derg, Lough l. Rep. of Ireland 51 D5
Dergachi Rus. Fed. 43 K6
Dergachi Ukr. see Derhachi
Derhachi Ukr. 43 H6
De Ridder U.S.A. 131 E6
Derik Turkey 91 F3
Derm Namibia 100 D2
Derna Libya see Darnah
Dernberg, Cape Namibia 100 B4
Dêrong China 76 C2
Derravaragh, Lough l. Rep. of Ireland 51 E4
Derry U.K. see Londonderry
Derry U.S.A. 135 J2
Derryveagh Mts hills Rep. of Ireland 51 D3
Dêrub China see Rutög
Derudeb Sudan 86 E6
De Rust S. Africa 100 F7
Derventa Bos.-Herz. 58 G2
Derwent r. England U.K. 48 F6
Derwent r. England U.K. 48 G5
Derwent Water l. U.K. 48 D4
Derweze Turkm. see Darvaza
Derzhavinsk Kazakh. 80 C1
Derzhavinskiy Kazakh. see Derzhavinsk
Desaguadero r. Arg. 144 C4
Désappointement, Îles du is Fr. Polynesia 151 K6
Desatoya Mountains U.S.A. 128 E2
Deschambault Lake Canada 117 K4
Deschutes r. U.S.A. 126 C3
Desē Eth. 98 D2
Deseado Arg. 144 C7
Deseado r. Arg. 144 C7
Desengaño, Punta pt Arg. 144 C7
Deseret U.S.A. 129 G2
Deseret Peak U.S.A. 129 G1
Deseronto Canada 135 G1
Desert Canal Pak. 89 H4
Desert Center U.S.A. 129 F5
Desert Lake U.S.A. 129 F3
Desert View U.S.A. 129 H3
Deshler U.S.A. 134 D3
De Smet U.S.A. 130 D2

▶Des Moines IA U.S.A. 130 E3
State capital of Iowa.

Des Moines NM U.S.A. 131 C4
Des Moines r. U.S.A. 130 F3
Desna r. Rus. Fed./Ukr. 43 F6
Desnogorsk Rus. Fed. 43 G5
Desolación, Isla i. Chile 144 B8
Des Plaines U.S.A. 134 B2
Dessau Germany 53 M3
Dessye Eth. see Desē
Destelbergen Belgium 52 D3
Destruction Bay Canada 153 A2
Desvres France 52 B4
Detah Canada 120 H2
Dete Zimbabwe 99 C5
Detmold Germany 53 I3
Detrital Wash watercourse U.S.A. 129 F3
Detroit U.S.A. 134 D2
Detroit Lakes U.S.A. 130 E2
Dett Zimbabwe see Dete
Deua National Park Australia 108 D5
Deuben Germany 53 M3
Deurne Neth. 52 F3
Deutschland country Europe see Germany
Deutschlandsberg Austria 47 O7
Deutzen Germany 53 M3
Deva Romania 59 J2
Deva U.K. see Chester
Devana U.K. see Aberdeen
Devangere India see Davangere
Devanhalli India 84 C3
Deve Bair pass Bulg./Macedonia see Velbŭzhdki Prokhod
Develi Turkey 90 D3
Deventer Neth. 52 G2
Deveron r. U.K. 50 G3
Devét Skal hill Czech Rep. 47 P6
Devgarh India 84 B2
Devghar India see Deoghar
Devikot India 82 B4
Devil's Bridge U.K. 49 D6
Devil's Gate pass U.S.A. 128 D2
Devil's Lake U.S.A. 130 D1
Devil's Paw mt. U.S.A. 120 C3
Devil's Peak U.S.A. 128 D3
Devil's Point Bahamas 133 F7
Devine U.S.A. 131 D6
Devizes U.K. 49 F7
Devli India 82 C4
Devnya Bulg. 59 L3
Devon r. U.K. 50 F4
Devon Island Canada 119 I2
Devonport Australia 111 [inset]
Devrek Turkey 59 N4
Devrukh India 84 B2
Dewa, Tanjung pt Indon. 71 A7
Dewangiri Bhutan 83 G4
Dewas India 82 D5
De Weerribben, Nationaal Park nat. park Neth. 52 G2
Dewetsdorp S. Africa 101 H5
De Witt AR U.S.A. 131 F5
De Witt IA U.S.A. 130 F3
Dewsbury U.K. 48 F5
Dexing China 77 H2
Dexter ME U.S.A. 135 K1
Dexter MI U.S.A. 134 D2
Dexter MO U.S.A. 131 F4
Dexter NM U.S.A. 127 G6
Dexter NY U.S.A. 135 G1
Deyang China 76 E2
Dey-Dey Lake salt flat Australia 109 E7
Deyhuk Iran 88 E3
Deyong, Tanjung pt Indon. 69 J8
Dêyü Co l. China 83 F2
Deyyer Iran 88 C5
Dez r. Iran 86 G3
Dezadeash Lake Canada 120 B2
Dezfūl Iran 88 C3

▶Dezhneva, Mys c. Rus. Fed. 65 T3
Most easterly point of Asia.

Dezhou Shandong China 73 L5
Dezhou Sichuan China see Dechang
Dezh Shāhpūr Iran see Marīvān
Dhabarau India 83 E4
Dhahab, Wādī adh r. Syria 85 B3
Dhāhiriya West Bank 85 B4
Dhahran Saudi Arabia 88 C5

▶Dhaka Bangl. 83 G5
Capital of Bangladesh and 5th most populous city in Asia.

Dhalbhum reg. India 83 F5
Dhalgaon India 84 B2
Dhamār Yemen 86 F7
Dhamoni India 82 D4
Dhamtari India 84 D1
Dhana Pak. 89 H5
Dhana Sar Pak. 89 H4
Dhanbad India 83 F5
Dhanera India 82 C4
Dhang Range mts Nepal 83 E3
Dhankuta Nepal 83 F4
Dhansia India 82 C3
Dhar India 82 C5
Ḍhar Adrar hills Mauritania 96 B3
Dharampur India 84 B1
Dharan Bazar Nepal 83 F4
Dharashiv India see Osmanabad
Dhari India 82 B5
Dharmapuri India 84 C3
Dharmavaram India 84 C3
Dharmsala Himachal Pradesh India see Dharmshala
Dharmsala Orissa India 83 F5
Dharmshala India 82 D2
Dharnaoda India 82 D4
Ḍhar Oualâta hills Mauritania 96 C3
Ḍhar Tîchît hills Mauritania 96 C3
Dharug National Park Australia 112 E4
Dharur India 84 C2
Dharwad India 84 B3
Dharwar India see Dharwad
Dharwas India 82 D2
Dhasan r. India 82 D4
Dhāt al Ḥājj Saudi Arabia 90 E5
Dhaulagiri mt. Nepal 83 E3
Dhaulpur India see Dholpur
Dhaura India 82 D4
Dhaurahra India 82 E4
Dhawlagiri mt. Nepal see Dhaulagiri
Dhebar Lake India see Jaisamand Lake
Dhekelia Sovereign Base Area military base Cyprus 85 A2
Dhemaji India 83 H4
Dhenkanal India 84 E1
Dhībān Jordan 85 B4
Dhidhimótikhon Greece see Didymoteicho
Dhing India 83 H4
Dhirwāh, Wādī adh watercourse Jordan 85 C4
Dhodhekánisos is Greece see Dodecanese
Dhola India 82 B5
Dholera India 82 C5
Dholpur India 82 D4
Dhomokós Greece see Domokos
Dhone India 84 C3
Dhoraji India 82 B5
Dhori India 82 B5
Dhrangadhra India 82 B5
Dhubāb Yemen 86 F7
Dhubri India 83 G4
Dhuburi India see Dhubri
Dhudial Pak. 89 I3
Dhule India 84 B1
Dhulia India see Dhule
Dhulian India 83 F4
Dhulian Pak. 89 I3
Dhuma India 82 D5
Dhund r. India 82 D4
Dhurwai India 82 D4
Dhuusa Marreeb Somalia 98 E3
Dia i. Greece 59 K7
Diablo, Mount U.S.A. 128 C3
Diablo, Picacho del mt. Mex. 127 E7
Diablo Range mts U.S.A. 128 C3
Diagbe Dem. Rep. Congo 98 C3
Diamante Arg. 144 D4
Diamantina watercourse Australia 110 B5
Diamantina Brazil 145 C2
Diamantina, Chapada plat. Brazil 145 C1
Diamantina Deep sea feature Indian Ocean 149 O8
Diamantina Gates National Park Australia 110 C4
Diamantino Brazil 143 G6
Diamond Islets Australia 110 E3
Diamond Peak U.S.A. 129 F2
Dianbai China 77 F4
Diancang Shan mt. China 76 D3
Dian Chi l. China 76 D3
Diandioumé Mali 96 C3
Diane Bank sea feature Australia 110 E2
Dianjiang China 76 E2
Dianópolis Brazil 143 I6
Dianyang China see Shidian
Diaobingshan China see Tiefa
Diaoling China 74 C3
Diapaga Burkina 96 D3
Diarizos r. Cyprus 85 A2
Diavolo, Mount hill India 71 A4
Diaz Point Namibia 100 B4
Dibaya Dem. Rep. Congo 99 C4
Dibella well Niger 96 E3
Dibeng S. Africa 100 F4
Dibete Botswana 101 H2
Dibrugarh India 83 H4
Dibse Syria see Dibsī
Dibsī Syria 85 D2
Dickens U.S.A. 131 C5
Dickinson U.S.A. 130 C2
Dicle r. Turkey 91 F3 see Tigris
Didēsa Wenz r. Eth. 98 D3
Didiéni Mali 96 C3
Didsbury Canada 120 H5
Didwana India 82 C4
Didymoteicho Greece 59 L4
Die France 56 G4
Dieblich Germany 53 H4
Diébougou Burkina 96 C3
Dieburg Germany 53 I5
Diedenhofen France see Thionville
Diefenbaker, Lake Canada 121 I5
Diego de Almagro, Isla i. Chile 144 A8
Diégo Suarez Madag. see Antsirañana
Diekirch Lux. 52 G5
Diéma Mali 96 C3
Diemel r. Germany 53 J3
Điện Biên Vietnam see Điện Biên Phu
Điện Biên Phu Vietnam 70 C2
Diên Châu Vietnam 70 D3
Diên Khanh Vietnam 71 E4
Diepholz Germany 53 I2
Dieppe France 52 B5
Dierks U.S.A. 131 E5
Di'er Songhua Jiang r. China 74 B3
Diessen Neth. 52 F3
Diest Belgium 52 F4
Dietikon Switz. 56 I3
Diez Germany 53 I4
Diffa Niger 96 E3
Digby Canada 123 I5
Diggi India 82 C4
Diglur India 84 C2
Digne France see Digne-les-Bains
Digne-les-Bains France 56 H4
Digoin France 56 F3
Digos Phil. 69 H5
Digras India 84 C1
Digri Pak. 89 H5
Digul r. Indon. 69 K8
Digya National Park Ghana 96 C4
Dihang r. India 83 H4 see Brahmaputra
Dihōk Iraq see Dahūk
Dihourse, Lac l. Canada 123 I2
Diinsoor Somalia 98 E3
Dijon France 56 G3
Dik Chad 97 E4
Diken India 82 C4
Dikhil Djibouti 86 F7
Dikili Turkey 59 L5
Diklosmta mt. Rus. Fed. 43 J8
Diksal India 84 B2
Diksmuide Belgium 52 C3
Dikson Rus. Fed. 64 J2
Dila Eth. 98 D3
Dilaram Iran 88 E4

▶Dili East Timor 108 D2
Capital of East Timor.

Di Linh Vietnam 71 E5
Dillenburg Germany 53 I4
Dilley U.S.A. 131 D6
Dillingen (Saar) Germany 52 G5
Dillingen an der Donau Germany 47 M6
Dillingham U.S.A. 118 C4
Dillon r. Canada 121 I4
Dillon MT U.S.A. 126 E3

Dillon *SC* U.S.A. 133 E5
Dillwyn U.S.A. 135 F5
Dilolo Dem. Rep. Congo 99 C5
Dilsen Belgium 52 F3
Dimapur India 83 H4
Dimashq Syria *see* Damascus
Dimbokro Côte d'Ivoire 96 C4
Dimboola Australia 111 C8
Dimitrov Ukr. *see* Dymytrov
Dimitrovgrad Bulg. 59 K3
Dimitrovgrad Rus. Fed. 43 K5
Dimitrovo Bulg. *see* Pernik
Dimmitt U.S.A. 131 C5
Dimona Israel 85 B4
Dimpho Pan *salt pan* Botswana 100 E3
Dinagat *i.* Phil. 69 H4
Dinajpur Bangl. 83 G4
Dinan France 56 C2
Dinant Belgium 52 E4
Dinapur India 83 F4
Dinar Turkey 59 N5
Dīnār, Kūh-e *mt.* Iran 88 C4
Dinara Planina *mts* Bos.-Herz./Croatia *see* Dinaric Alps
Dinaric Alps *mts* Bos.-Herz./Croatia 58 G2
Dinbych U.K. *see* Denbigh
Dinbych-y-pysgod U.K. *see* Tenby
Dinder National Park Sudan 97 G3
Dindi *r.* India 84 C2
Dindigul India 84 C4
Dindima Nigeria 96 E3
Dindiza Moz. 101 K2
Dindori India 82 E5
Dingcheng China *see* Dingyuan
Dingelstädt Germany 53 K3
Dingla Nepal 83 F4
Dingle Rep. of Ireland 51 B5
Dingle Bay Rep. of Ireland 51 B5
Dingnan China 77 G3
Dingo Australia 110 E4
Dingolfing Germany 53 M6
Dingping China *see* Linshui
Dingtao China 77 G1
Dinguiraye Guinea 96 B3
Dingwall U.K. 50 E3
Dingxi China 76 E1
Dingyuan China 77 H1
Dinh Lâp Vietnam 70 D2
Dinkelsbühl Germany 53 K5
Dinngyê China 83 F3
Dinokwe Botswana 101 H2
Dinosaur U.S.A. 129 I1
Dinosaur National Monument *nat. park* U.S.A. 129 I1
Dinslaken Germany 52 G3
Dinwiddie U.S.A. 135 G5
Dioïla Mali 96 C3
Dionísio Cerqueira Brazil 144 F3
Diorama Brazil 145 A2
Dioscurias Georgia *see* Sokhumi
Diouloulou Senegal 96 B3
Diourbel Senegal 96 B3
Diphu India 83 H4
Dipkarpaz Cyprus *see* Rizokarpason
Diplo Pak. 89 H5
Dipolog Phil. 69 G5
Dipperu National Park Australia 110 E4
Dipu China *see* Anji
Dir *reg.* Pak. 89 I3
Dirang India 83 H4
Diré Mali 96 C3
Direction, Cape Australia 110 C2
Dirē Dawa Eth. 98 E3
Dirico Angola 99 C5
Dirk Hartog Island Australia 109 A6
Dirranbandi Australia 112 D2
Ḑirs Saudi Arabia 98 E2
Dirschau Poland *see* Tczew
Dirty Devil *r.* U.S.A. 129 H3
Disa India 82 C4
Disang *r.* India 83 H4
Disappointment, Cape S. Georgia 144 I8
Disappointment, Cape U.S.A. 126 B3
Disappointment Islands Fr. Polynesia *see* Désappointement, Îles du
Disappointment, Lake *salt flat* Australia 109 C5
Disappointment Lake Canada 123 J3
Disaster Bay Australia 112 D6
Discovery Bay Australia 111 C8
Disko *i.* Greenland *see* Qeqertarsuaq
Disko Bugt *b.* Greenland *see* Qeqertarsuup Tunua
Dispur India 83 G4
Disputanta U.S.A. 135 G5
Disraëli Canada 123 H5
Diss U.K. 49 I6
Distrito Federal *admin. dist.* Brazil 145 B1
Disūq Egypt 90 C5
Ditloung S. Africa 100 F5
Dittaino *r. Sicily* Italy 58 F6
Diu India 84 A1
Dīvān Darreh Iran 88 B3
Divehi *country* Indian Ocean *see* Maldives
Divi, Point India 84 D3
Divichi Azer. *see* Dāvāçi
Divide Mountain U.S.A. 120 A2
Divinópolis Brazil 145 B3
Divnoye Rus. Fed. 43 I7
Divo Côte d'Ivoire 96 C4
Divriği Turkey 90 E3
Diwana Pak. 89 G5
Diwaniyah Iraq *see* Ad Dīwānīyah
Dixfield U.S.A. 135 J1
Dixon *CA* U.S.A. 128 C2
Dixon *IL* U.S.A. 130 F3
Dixon *KY* U.S.A. 134 B5
Dixon *MT* U.S.A. 126 E3
Dixon Entrance *sea chan.* Canada/U.S.A. 120 C4
Dixonville Canada 120 G3
Dixville Canada 135 J1
Diyadin Turkey 91 F3
Diyarbakır Turkey 91 F3
Diz Pak. 89 F5
Diz Chah Iran 88 D3
Dize Turkey *see* Yüksekova
Dizney U.S.A. 134 D5
Djado Niger 96 E2
Djado, Plateau du Niger 96 E2
Djaja, Puntjak *mt.* Indon. *see* Jaya, Puncak
Djakarta Indon. *see* Jakarta
Djakovica Serb. and Mont. *see* Đakovica
Djakovo Croatia *see* Đakovo
Djambala Congo 98 B4
Djanet Alg. 96 D2
Djarrit-Uliga-Dalap Marshall Is *see* Delap-Uliga-Djarrit
Djelfa Alg. 57 H6
Djéma Cent. Afr. Rep. 98 C3
Djenné Mali 96 C3
Djerdap *nat. park* Serb. and Mont. 59 J2
Djibo Burkina 96 C3
▶Djibouti *country* Africa 86 F7
Africa 7, 94–95

▶Djibouti Djibouti 86 F7
Capital of Djibouti.

Djidjelli Alg. *see* Jijel
Djougou Benin 96 D4
Djoum Cameroon 96 E4
Djourab, Erg du *des.* Chad 97 E3
Djúpivogur Iceland 44 [inset]
Djurås Sweden 45 I6
Djurdjura National Park Alg. 57 I5
Dmitriya Lapteva, Proliv *sea chan.* Rus. Fed. 65 P2
Dmitriyev-L'govskiy Rus. Fed. 43 G5
Dmitriyevsk Ukr. *see* Makiyivka
Dmitrov Rus. Fed. 42 H4
Dmytriyevs'k Ukr. *see* Makiyivka
Dnepr *r.* Rus. Fed. 43 F5 *see* Dnieper
Dneprodzerzhinsk Ukr. *see* Dniprodzerzhyns'k
Dnepropetrovsk Ukr. *see* Dnipropetrovs'k

▶Dnieper *r.* Europe 43 G7
3rd longest river in Europe. Also spelt Dnepr (Rus. Fed.) or Dnipro (Ukraine) or Dnyapro (Belarus).

Dniester *r.* Ukr. 43 F6
also spelt Dnister (Ukraine) *or* Nistru (Moldova)
Dnipro *r.* Ukr. 43 G7 *see* Dnieper
Dniprodzerzhyns'k Ukr. 43 G6
Dnipropetrovs'k Ukr. 43 G6
Dnister *r.* Ukr. 43 F6 *see* Dniester
Dno Rus. Fed. 42 F4
Dnyapro *r.* Belarus 43 F6 *see* Dnieper
Doāb Afgh. 89 G3
Doaba Pak. 89 H3
Doba Chad 97 E4
Doba China *see* Toiba
Dobele Latvia 45 M8
Döbeln Germany 53 N3
Doberai, Jazirah *pen.* Indon. 69 I7
Doberai Peninsula Indon. *see* Doberai, Jazirah
Dobo Indon. 69 I8
Doboj Bos.-Herz. 58 H2
Do Borjī Iran 88 D4
Döbraberg *hill* Germany 53 L4
Dobrich Bulg. 59 L3
Dobrinka Rus. Fed. 43 I5
Dobroye Rus. Fed. 43 H5
Dobrudja *reg.* Romania *see* Dobruja
Dobruja *reg.* Romania 59 L3
Dobrush Belarus 43 F5
Dobryanka Rus. Fed. 41 R4
Dobzha China 83 G3
Doce *r.* Brazil 145 D2
Dochart *r.* U.K. 50 E4
Do China Qala Afgh. 89 H4
Docking U.K. 49 H6
Doctor Hicks Range *hills* Australia 109 D7
Doctor Pedro P. Peña Para. 144 D2
Doda India 82 C2
Doda Betta *mt.* India 84 C4
Dod Ballapur India 84 C3
Dodecanese *is* Greece 59 L7
Dodekanisos *is* Greece *see* Dodecanese
Dodge City U.S.A. 130 C4
Dodgeville U.S.A. 130 F3
Dodman Point U.K. 49 C8

▶Dodoma Tanz. 99 D4
Capital of Tanzania.

Dodsonville U.S.A. 134 D4
Doetinchem Neth. 52 G3
Dog *r.* Canada 122 C4
Dogai Coring *salt l.* China 83 G2
Dogaicoring Qangco *salt l.* China 83 G2
Doğanşehir Turkey 90 E3
Dogên Co *l. Xizang* China *see* Bam Tso
Dogên Co *l. Xizang* China 83 G3
Doghārūn Iran 89 F3
Dog Island Canada 123 J2
Dog Lake *Man.* Canada 121 L5
Dog Lake *Ont.* Canada 122 C4
Dog Lake *Ont.* Canada 122 D4
Dōgo *i.* Japan 75 D5
Dogondoutchi Niger 96 D3
Dog Rocks *is* Bahamas 133 E7
Doğubeyazıt Turkey 91 G3
Doğu Menteşe Dağları *mts* Turkey 59 M6
Dogxung Zangbo *r.* China 83 F3
Do'gyaling China 83 G3

▶Doha Qatar 88 C5
Capital of Qatar.

Dohad India *see* Dahod
Dohazari Bangl. 83 H5
Dohrighat India 83 E4
Doi *i.* Fiji 107 I4
Doi Inthanon National Park Thai. 70 B3
Doi Luang National Park Thai. 70 B3
Doire U.K. *see* Londonderry
Doi Saket Thai. 70 B3
Dois Irmãos, Serra dos *hills* Brazil 143 J5
Dok-dō *i.* N. Pacific Ocean *see* Liancourt Rocks
Dokhara, Dunes de *des.* Alg. 54 F5
Dokka Norway 45 G6
Dokkum Neth. 52 F1
Dokri Pak. 89 H5
Dokshukino Rus. Fed. *see* Nartkala
Dokshytsy Belarus 45 O9
Dokuchayeva, Mys *c.* Rus. Fed. 74 G3
Dokuchayevka Kazakh. *see* Karamendy
Dokuchayevs'k Ukr. 43 H7
Dolak, Pulau *i.* Indon. 69 J8
Dolbenmaen U.K. 49 C6
Dol-de-Bretagne France 56 D2
Dole France 56 G3
Dolgellau U.K. 49 D6
Dolgen Germany 53 N1
Dolgiy, Ostrov *i.* Rus. Fed. 42 L1
Dolgorukovo Rus. Fed. 43 H5
Dolina Ukr. *see* Dolyna
Dolinsk Rus. Fed. 74 F3
Dolisie Congo *see* Loubomo
Dolleman Island Antarctica 152 L2
Dollnstein Germany 53 L6
Dolomites *mts* Italy 58 D2
Dolomiti *mts* Italy *see* Dolomites
Dolomiti Bellunesi, Parco Nazionale delle *nat. park* Italy 58 D1
Dolomitiche, Alpi *mts* Italy *see* Dolomites
Dolonnur China *see* Duolun
Dolo Odo Eth. 98 E3
Dolores Arg. 144 E5
Dolores Uruguay 144 E4
Dolores U.S.A. 129 I3
Dolphin and Union Strait Canada 118 G3
Dolphin Head *hd* Namibia 100 B3
Đô Lương Vietnam 70 D3
Dolyna Ukr. 43 D6
Domaniç Turkey 59 M5
Domar China 80 F5
Domartang China *see* Banbar
Domažlice Czech Rep. 53 M5
Domba China 76 B1
Dom Bākh Iran 88 B3
Dombås Norway 44 F5
Dombóvár Hungary 58 H1
Dombrau Poland *see* Dąbrowa Górnicza
Dombrovitsa Ukr. *see* Dubrovytsya
Dombrowa Poland *see* Dąbrowa Górnicza
Domda China *see* Qingshuihe
Dome Argus *ice feature* Antarctica 152 E1
Dome Charlie *ice feature* Antarctica 152 F2
Dome Creek Canada 120 F4
Dome Rock Mountains U.S.A. 129 F5
Domeyko Chile 144 B3
Domfront France 56 D2
▶Dominica *country* West Indies 137 L5
North America 9, 116–117
Dominicana, República *country* West Indies *see* Dominican Republic
▶Dominican Republic *country* West Indies 137 J5
North America 9, 116–117
Dominion, Cape Canada 119 K3
Dominique *i.* Fr. Polynesia *see* Hiva Oa
Dömitz Germany 53 L1
Dom Joaquim Brazil 145 C2
Dommel *r.* Neth. 52 F3
Domo Eth. 98 E3
Domokos Greece 59 J5
Dompu Indon. 108 B2
Domula China *see* Duomula
Domuyo, Volcán *vol.* Arg. 144 B5
Domville, Mount *hill* Australia 112 E2
Don Mex. 127 F8

▶Don *r.* Rus. Fed. 43 H7
5th longest river in Europe.

Don *r.* U.K. 50 G3
Don, Xé *r.* Laos 70 D4
Donaghadee U.K. 51 G3
Donaghmore U.K. 51 F3
Donald Australia 112 A6
Donaldsonville U.S.A. 131 F6
Donalsonville U.S.A. 133 C6
Doñana, Parque Nacional de *nat. park* Spain 57 C5
Donau *r.* Austria/Germany 47 P6 *see* Danube
Donauwörth Germany 53 K6
Don Benito Spain 57 D4
Doncaster U.K. 48 F5
Dondo Angola 99 B4
Dondo Moz. 99 D5
Dondra Head *hd* Sri Lanka 84 D5
Donegal Rep. of Ireland 51 D3
Donegal Bay Rep. of Ireland 51 D3
Donets'k Ukr. 43 H7
Donetsko-Amrovsiyevka Ukr. *see* Amvrosiyivka
Donets'kyy Kryazh *hills* Rus. Fed./Ukr. 43 H6
Donga *r.* Cameroon/Nigeria 96 D4
Dong'an China 77 F3
Dongane, Lagoa *lag.* Moz. 101 L3
Dongara Australia 109 A7
Dongbo China *see* Mêdog
Dongchuan *Yunnan* China *see* Yao'an
Dongchuan *Yunnan* China 76 D3
Dongco China 83 F2
Dong Co *l.* China 83 F2
Dongfang China 77 F5
Dongfanghong China 74 D3
Dongguan China 75 B5
Donggi Conag *l.* China 76 C1
Donggou China *see* Donggang
Donggu China 77 G3
Dongguan China 77 G4
Dong Hai *sea* N. Pacific Ocean *see* East China Sea
Đông Hới Vietnam 70 D3
Donghuang China *see* Xishui
Dongjiang Shuiku *resr* China 77 G3
Dongjug China 76 B2
Dongkou China 77 F3
Donglan China 76 E3
Dongliao He *r.* China 74 A4
Dongmen China *see* Luocheng
Dongminzhutun China 74 A3
Dongning China 74 C3
Dongo Angola 99 B5
Dongo Dem. Rep. Congo 98 B3
Dongola Sudan 86 D6
Dongou Congo 98 B3
Dong Phraya Yen *esc.* Thai. 70 C4
Dongping *Guangdong* China 77 G4
Dongping *Hunan* China *see* Anhua
Dongpo China *see* Meishan
Dongqiao China 83 G3
Dongshan *Fujian* China 77 H4
Dongshan *Jiangsu* China 77 I2
Dongshan *Jiangxi* China *see* Shangyou
Dongshao China 77 G3
Dongsha Qundao *is* China 68 F2
Dongsheng *Nei Mongol* China 73 K5
Dongsheng *Sichuan* China *see* Shuangliu
Dongshuan China *see* Tangdan
Dongtai China 77 I1
Dongting Hu *l.* China 77 G2
Dongtou China 77 I3
Đông Triều Vietnam 70 D2
Dong Ujimqin Qi China *see* Uliastai
Dông Văn Vietnam 70 D2
Dongxiang China 77 H2
Dongxi Liandao *i.* China 77 H1
Dongxing *Guangxi* China 76 E4
Dongxing *Heilong.* China 74 B3
Dongyang China 77 I2
Dongying China 73 L5
Dongzhi China 77 H2
Donkerbroek Neth. 52 G1
Donnacona Canada 123 H5
Donnellys Crossing N.Z. 113 D2
Donner Pass U.S.A. 128 C2
Donnersberg *hill* Germany 53 H5
Donostia - San Sebastián Spain 57 F2
Donoussa *i.* Greece 59 K6
Donskoye Rus. Fed. 43 I7
Donyztau, Sor *dry lake* Kazakh. 80 A2
Dooagh Rep. of Ireland 51 B4
Doomadgee Australia 110 B3
Doon *r.* U.K. 50 E5
Doon, Loch *l.* U.K. 50 E5
Doonbeg *r.* Rep. of Ireland 51 C5
Doorn Neth. 52 F2
Door Peninsula U.S.A. 134 B1
Doorwerth Neth. 52 F3
Dooxo Nugaaleed *valley* Somalia 98 E3
Doqêmo China 76 B2
Do Qu *r.* China 76 D2
Dor *watercourse* Afgh. 89 F4
Dora U.S.A. 131 C5
Dora, Lake *salt flat* Australia 108 C5
Dorado Mex. 131 B7
Dorah Pass Pak. 89 H2
Doran Lake Canada 121 I2
Dorbiljin China *see* Emin
Dorbod China *see* Taikang
Dorbod Qi China *see* Ulan Hua
Dorchester U.K. 49 E8
Dordabis Namibia 100 C2
Dordogne *r.* France 56 D4
Dordrecht Neth. 52 E3
Dordrecht S. Africa 101 H6
Doreenville Namibia 100 D2
Doré Lake Canada 121 J4
Doré Lake *l.* Canada 121 J4
Dores do Indaiá Brazil 145 B2
Dori *r.* Afgh. 89 G4
Dori Burkina 96 C3
Doring *r.* S. Africa 100 D6
do Rio Manso, Represa *resr* Brazil 143 G6
Dorisvale Australia 108 E3
Dorking U.K. 49 G7
Dormagen Germany 52 G3
Dormans France 52 D5
Dormidontovka Rus. Fed. 74 D3
Dornoch U.K. 50 E3
Dornoch Firth *est.* U.K. 50 E3
Dornum Germany 53 H1
Doro Mali 96 C3
Dorogobuzh Rus. Fed. 43 G5
Dorogorskoye Rus. Fed. 42 J2
Dorohoi Romania 43 E7
Döröö Nuur *salt l.* Mongolia 80 H2
Dorostol Bulg. *see* Silistra
Dorotea Sweden 44 J4
Dorpat Estonia *see* Tartu
Dorre Island Australia 109 A6
Dorrigo Australia 112 F3
Dorris U.S.A. 126 C4
Dorsale Camerounaise *slope* Cameroon/Nigeria 96 E4
Dorset Canada 135 F1
Dorsoidong Co *l.* China 83 G2
Dortmund Germany 53 H3
Dörtyol Turkey 85 C1
Dorum Germany 53 I1
Doruma Dem. Rep. Congo 98 C3
Dorūneh, Kūh-e *mts* Iran 88 E3
Dorval *airport* Canada 122 G5
Dörverden Germany 53 J2
Dorylaeum Turkey *see* Eskişehir
Dos Bahías, Cabo *c.* Arg. 144 C6
Dos de Mayo Peru 142 C5
Doshakh, Koh-i- *mt.* Afgh. *see* Do Shākh, Kūh-e
Do Shākh, Kūh-e *mt.* Afgh. 89 F3
Đo Son Vietnam 70 D2
Dos Palos U.S.A. 128 C3
Dosse *r.* Germany 53 M2
Dosso Niger 96 D3
Dothan U.S.A. 133 C6
Dotsero U.S.A. 129 J2
Douai France 52 D4
Douala Cameroon 96 D4
Douarnenez France 56 B2
Double Headed Shot Cays *is* Bahamas 133 D8
Double Island *Hong Kong* China 77 [inset]
Double Island Point Australia 111 F5
Double Mountain Fork *r.* U.S.A. 131 C5
Double Peak U.S.A. 128 D4
Double Point Australia 110 D3
Double Springs U.S.A. 133 C5
Doubs *r.* France/Switz. 56 G3
Doubtful Sound *inlet* N.Z. 113 A7
Doubtless Bay N.Z. 113 D2
Douentza Mali 96 C3
Dougga *tourist site* Tunisia 58 C6

▶Douglas Isle of Man 48 C4
Capital of the Isle of Man.

Douglas S. Africa 100 F5
Douglas U.K. 50 F5
Douglas *AZ* U.S.A. 127 F7
Douglas *GA* U.S.A. 133 D6
Douglas *WY* U.S.A. 126 G4
Douglas Reef *i.* Japan *see* Okino-Tori-shima
Douglasville U.S.A. 133 C5
Douhudi China *see* Gong'an
Doulatpur Bangl. *see* Daulatpur
Douliu Taiwan *see* Touliu
Doullens France 52 C4
Douna Mali 96 C3
Doune U.K. 50 E4
Doupovské Hory *mts* Czech Rep. 53 N4
Dourada, Serra *hills* Brazil 145 A2
Dourada, Serra *mts* Brazil 145 A1
Dourados Brazil 144 F2
Douro *r.* Port. 57 B3
also known as Duero (Spain)
Doushi China *see* Gong'an
Doushui Shuiku *resr* China 77 G3
Douve *r.* France 49 F9
Douzy France 52 F5
Dove *r.* U.K. 49 F6
Dove Brook Canada 123 K3
Dove Creek U.S.A. 129 I3
Dover U.K. 49 I7

▶Dover *DE* U.S.A. 135 H4
State capital of Delaware.

Dover *NH* U.S.A. 135 J2
Dover *NJ* U.S.A. 135 H3
Dover *OH* U.S.A. 134 E3
Dover *TN* U.S.A. 132 C4
Dover, Strait of France/U.K. 56 E1
Dover-Foxcroft U.S.A. 135 K1
Dovey *r.* U.K. *see* Dyfi
Dovrefjell Nasjonalpark *nat. park* Norway 44 F5
Dowagiac U.S.A. 134 B3
Dowi, Tanjung *pt* Indon. 71 B7
Dowlaiswaram India 84 D2
Dowlatābād Afgh. 89 F3
Dowlatābād *Fārs* Iran 88 C4
Dowlatābād *Fārs* Iran 88 D4
Dowlatābād *Khorāsān* Iran 88 E2
Dowlatābād *Khorāsān* Iran 89 F2
Dowl at Yār Afgh. 89 G3
Downieville U.S.A. 128 C2
Downpatrick U.K. 51 G3
Downsville U.S.A. 135 H2
Dow Rūd Iran 88 C3
Doyle U.S.A. 128 C1
Doylestown U.S.A. 135 H3
Dozdān *r.* Iran 88 E5
Dōzen *is* Japan 75 D5
Dozois, Réservoir *resr* Canada 122 F5
Dozulé France 49 G9
Dracena Brazil 145 A3
Drachten Neth. 52 G1
Drăgănești-Olt Romania 59 K2
Drăgășani Romania 59 K2
Dragonera, Isla *i.* Spain *see* Sa Dragonera
Dragoon U.S.A. 129 H5
Dragsfjärd Fin. 45 M6
Draguignan France 56 H5
Drahichyn Belarus 45 N10
Drake Australia 112 F2
Drake U.S.A. 130 C2
Drakensberg *mts* S. Africa 101 I3
Drake Passage S. Atlantic Ocean 148 D9
Drakes Bay U.S.A. 128 B3
Drama Greece 59 K4
Drammen Norway 45 G7
Drang, Prêk *r.* Cambodia 71 D4
Drangedal Norway 45 F7
Dransfeld Germany 53 J3
Draper, Mount U.S.A. 120 B3
Draperstown U.K. 51 F3
Drapsaca Afgh. *see* Kunduz
Dras Jammu and Kashmir 82 C2
Drasan Pak. 89 I2
Drau *r.* Austria *see* Drava
Drava *r.* Europe 58 H2
also known as Drau (Austria), Drave *or* Drava (Slovenia and Croatia), Dráva (Hungary)
Dráva *r.* Hungary *see* Drava
Drave *r.* Slovenia/Croatia *see* Drava
Drayton Valley Canada 120 H4
Drazinda Pak. 89 H4
Dréan Alg. 58 B6
Dreistelzberge *hill* Germany 53 J4
Drentse Hoofdvaart *canal* Neth. 52 G2
Drepano, Akra *pt* Greece 59 J5
Dresden Canada 134 D2
Dresden Germany 47 N5
Dreux France 52 B6
Drevsjø Norway 45 H6
Drewryville U.S.A. 135 G5
Dri China 76 C2
Driffield U.K. 48 G4
Driftwood U.S.A. 135 F3
Driggs U.S.A. 126 F4
Drillham Australia 112 E1
Drimoleague Rep. of Ireland 51 C6
Drina *r.* Bos.-Herz./Serb. and Mont. 59 H2
Driscoll Island Antarctica 152 J1
Drissa Belarus *see* Vyerkhnyadzvinsk
Drniš Croatia 58 G3
Drobeta - Turnu Severin Romania 59 J2
Drochtersen Germany 53 J1
Drogheda Rep. of Ireland 51 F4
Drogichin Belarus *see* Drahichyn
Drogobych Ukr. *see* Drohobych
Drohobych Ukr. 43 D6
Droichead Átha Rep. of Ireland *see* Drogheda
Droichead Nua Rep. of Ireland *see* Newbridge
Droitwich U.K. *see* Droitwich Spa
Droitwich Spa U.K. 49 E6
Dromedary, Cape Australia 112 E6
Dromod Rep. of Ireland 51 E4
Dromore *Northern Ireland* U.K. 51 E3
Dromore *Northern Ireland* U.K. 51 F3
Dronfield U.K. 48 F5
Dronning Louise Land *reg.* Greenland 153 I1
Dronning Maud Land *reg.* Antarctica *see* Queen Maud Land
Dronten Neth. 52 F2
Druk-Yul *country* Asia *see* Bhutan
Drumheller Canada 121 H5
Drummond *atoll* Kiribati *see* Tabiteuea
Drummond U.S.A. 126 E3
Drummond, Lake U.S.A. 135 G5
Drummond Island Kiribati *see* McKean
Drummond Range *hills* Australia 110 D5
Drummondville Canada 123 G5
Drummore U.K. 50 E6
Drury Lake Canada 120 C2
Druskieniki Lith. *see* Druskininkai
Druskininkai Lith. 45 N10
Druzhina Rus. Fed. 65 P3
Druzhnaya Gorka Rus. Fed. 45 Q7
Dry *r.* Australia 108 F3
Dryanovo Bulg. 59 K3
Dryberry Lake Canada 121 M5
Dryden Canada 121 M5
Dryden U.S.A. 135 G2
Dry Fork *r.* U.S.A. 126 G4
Drygalski Ice Tongue Antarctica 152 H1
Drygalski Island Antarctica 152 F2
Dry Lake U.S.A. 129 F3
Dry Lake *l.* U.S.A. 130 D1
Drymen U.K. 50 E4
Dry Ridge U.S.A. 134 C4
Drysdale *r.* Australia 108 D3
Drysdale River National Park Australia 108 D3
Dry Tortugas *is* U.S.A. 133 D7
Du'an China 77 F4
Duaringa Australia 110 E4
Duarte, Pico *mt.* Dom. Rep. 137 J5
Duartina Brazil 145 A3
Ḑubā Saudi Arabia 86 E4
Dubai U.A.E. 88 D5
Dubakella Mountain U.S.A. 128 B1
Dubawnt *r.* Canada 121 L2
Dubawnt Lake Canada 121 K2
Dubayy U.A.E. *see* Dubai
Dubbo Australia 112 D4

▶Dublin Rep. of Ireland 51 F4
Capital of the Republic of Ireland.

Dublin U.S.A. 133 D5
Dubna Rus. Fed. 42 H4
Dubno Ukr. 43 E6
Dubois *ID* U.S.A. 126 E3
Dubois *IN* U.S.A. 134 B4
Du Bois U.S.A. 135 F3
Dubovka Rus. Fed. 43 J6
Dubovskoye Rus. Fed. 43 I7
Dübrar Pass Azer. 91 H2
Dubréka Guinea 96 B4
Dubris U.K. *see* Dover
Dubrovnik Croatia 58 H3
Dubrovytsya Ukr. 43 E6
Dubuque U.S.A. 130 F3
Dubysa *r.* Lith. 45 M9
Duc de Gloucester, Îles du *is* Fr. Polynesia 151 K7
Duchang China 77 H2
Ducheng China *see* Yunan
Duchesne U.S.A. 129 H1
Duchesne *r.* U.S.A. 129 I1
Duchess Australia 110 B4
Duchess Canada 121 I5
Ducie Island *atoll* Pitcairn Is 151 L7
Duck Bay Canada 121 K4
Duck Creek *r.* Australia 108 B5
Duck Lake Canada 121 J4
Duckwater Peak U.S.A. 129 F2
Đức Trọng Vietnam 71 E5
Dudelange Lux. 52 G5
Duderstadt Germany 53 K3
Dudhi India 83 E4
Dudhwa India 82 E3
Dudinka Rus. Fed. 64 J3
Dudley U.K. 49 E6
Dudleyville U.S.A. 129 H5
Dudna *r.* India 84 C2
Dudu India 82 C4
Duékoué Côte d'Ivoire 96 C4
Duen, Bukit *vol.* Indon. 68 C7
Duero *r.* Spain 57 C3
also known as Douro (Portugal)
Duffel Belgium 52 E3
Dufferin, Cape Canada 122 F2
Duffer Peak U.S.A. 126 D4
Duff Islands Solomon Is 107 G2
Duffreboy, Lac *l.* Canada 123 H2
Dufftown U.K. 50 F3
Dufourspitze *mt.* Italy/Switz. 54 B2
Dufrost, Pointe *pt* Canada 122 F1
Dugi Otok *i.* Croatia 58 F2
Dugi Rat Croatia 58 G3
Du He *r.* China 77 F1
Duida-Marahuaca, Parque Nacional *nat. park* Venez. 142 E3
Duisburg Germany 52 G3
Duiwelskloof S. Africa 101 J2
Dujiangyan China 76 D2
Dukān Dam Iraq 91 G4
Dukathole S. Africa 101 H6
Duke Island U.S.A. 120 D4
Duke of Clarence *atoll* Tokelau *see* Nukunono
Duke of Gloucester Islands Fr. Polynesia *see* Duc de Gloucester, Îles du
Duke of York *atoll* Tokelau *see* Atafu
Duk Fadiat Sudan 97 G4
Dukhovnitskoye Rus. Fed. 43 K5
Duki Pak. 89 H4
Duki Rus. Fed. 74 D2
Duki *r.* Rus. Fed. 74 D2
Dukou China *see* Panzhihua
Dūkštas Lith. 45 O9
Dulac U.S.A. 131 F6
Dulan China 80 I4
Dulce *r.* Arg. 144 D4
Dulce U.S.A. 127 G5
Dul'durga Rus. Fed. 73 K2
Dulhunty *r.* Australia 110 C1
Dulishi Hu *salt l.* China 83 E2
Duliu Jiang *r.* China 77 F3
Dullewala Pak. 89 H4
Dullstroom S. Africa 101 J3
Dülmen Germany 53 H3
Dulmera India 82 C3
Dulovo Bulg. 59 L3
Duluth U.S.A. 130 E2
Dulverton U.K. 49 D7
Dūmā Syria 85 C3
Dumaguete Phil. 69 G5
Dumai Indon. 71 C7
Dumaran *i.* Phil. 68 G4
Dumaresq *r.* Australia 112 E2
Dumas U.S.A. 131 C5
Ḑumayr Syria 85 C3

E

El Dátil Mex. 127 E7
El Desemboque Mex. 127 E7
El Diamante Mex. 131 C6
El'dikan Rus. Fed. 65 O3
El Djezair *country* Africa *see* Algeria
El Djezair Alg. *see* Algiers
El Doctor Mex. 129 F6
Eldon U.S.A. 130 E4
Eldorado Arg. 144 F3
Eldorado Brazil 145 A4
El Dorado Col. 142 D3
El Dorado Mex. 124 F7
El Dorado *AR* U.S.A. 131 E5
El Dorado *KS* U.S.A. 130 D4
Eldorado U.S.A. 131 C6
El Dorado Venez. 142 F2
Eldorado Mountains U.S.A. 129 F4
Eldoret Kenya 98 D3
Elea, Cape Cyprus *see* Elaia, Cape
Eleanor U.S.A. 134 E4
Electric Peak U.S.A. 126 F3
Elefantes *r.* Moz. *see* Olifants
El Eglab *plat.* Alg. 96 C2
El Ejido Spain 57 E5

▶Elemi Triangle *terr.* Africa 98 D3
Disputed territory (Ethiopia/Kenya/Sudan) administered by Kenya.

El Encanto Col. 142 D4
Elend Germany 53 K3
Elephanta Caves *tourist site* India 84 B2
Elephant Butte Reservoir U.S.A. 127 G6
Elephant Island Antarctica 152 A2
Elephant Pass Sri Lanka 84 D4
Elephant Point Bangl. 83 H5
Eleşkirt Turkey 91 F3
El Eulma Alg. 54 F4
Eleuthera *i.* Bahamas 133 E7
Eleven Point *r.* U.S.A. 131 F4
El Fahs Tunisia 58 C6
El Faiyûm Egypt *see* Al Fayyūm
El Fasher Sudan 97 F3
El Ferrol Spain *see* Ferrol
El Ferrol del Caudillo Spain *see* Ferrol
Elfershausen Germany 53 J4
El Fud Eth. 98 E3
El Fuerte Mex. 127 F8
El Gara Egypt *see* Qārah
El Geneina Sudan 97 F3
El Geteina Sudan 86 D7
El Ghardaqa Egypt *see* Al Ghurdaqah
El Ghor *plain* Jordan/West Bank *see* Al Ghawr
Elgin U.K. 50 F3
Elgin *IL* U.S.A. 130 F3
Elgin *ND* U.S.A. 130 C2
Elgin *NV* U.S.A. 129 F3
Elgin *TX* U.S.A. 131 D6
El'ginskiy Rus. Fed. 65 P3
El Gîza Egypt *see* Giza
El Goléa Alg. 54 E5
El Golfo de Santa Clara Mex. 127 E7
Elgon, Mount Kenya/Uganda 78 C6
El Hadjar Alg. 58 B6
El Ḥammâm Egypt *see* Al Ḥammām
El Ḥammâmi *reg.* Mauritania 96 B2
El Ḥank *esc.* Mali/Mauritania 96 C2
El Ḥarra Egypt *see* Al Ḥarrah
El Hazim Jordan *see* Al Hazīm
El Ḥeiz Egypt *see* Al Ḥayz
El Hierro *i.* Canary Is 96 B2
El Homr Alg. 54 E6
El Homra Sudan 86 D7
Eliase Indon. 108 E2
Elías Piña Dom. Rep. 137 J5
Elichpur India *see* Achalpur
Elida U.S.A. 134 C3
Elie U.K. 50 G4
Elila *r.* Dem. Rep. Congo 98 C4
Elim U.S.A. 118 B3
Elimberrum France *see* Auch
Eling China *see* Yinjiang
Elingampangu Dem. Rep. Congo 98 C4
Eliot, Mount Canada 123 J2
Élisabethville Dem. Rep. Congo *see* Lubumbashi
Eliseu Martins Brazil 143 J5
El Iskandarîya Egypt *see* Alexandria
Elista Rus. Fed. 43 J7
Elizabeth *NJ* U.S.A. 135 H3
Elizabeth *WV* U.S.A. 134 E4
Elizabeth, Mount *hill* Australia 108 D4
Elizabeth Bay Namibia 100 B4
Elizabeth City U.S.A. 132 E4
Elizabeth Island Pitcairn Is *see* Henderson Island
Elizabeth Point Namibia 100 B4
Elizabethton U.S.A. 132 D4
Elizabethtown *IL* U.S.A. 130 F4
Elizabethtown *KY* U.S.A. 134 C5
Elizabethtown *NC* U.S.A. 133 E5
Elizabethtown *NY* U.S.A. 135 I1
El Jadida Morocco 54 C5
El Jaralito Mex. 131 B7
El Jem Tunisia 58 D7
Elk *r.* Canada 120 H5
Ełk Poland 47 S4
Elk *r.* U.S.A. 135 H4
El Kaa Lebanon *see* Qaa
El Kab Sudan 86 D6
Elkader U.S.A. 130 F3
El Kala Alg. 58 C6
Elk City U.S.A. 131 D5
Elkedra Australia 110 A4
Elkedra *watercourse* Australia 110 B4
El Kef Tunisia *see* Le Kef
El Kelaâ des Srarhna Morocco 54 C5
Elkford Canada 120 H5
Elk Grove U.S.A. 128 C2
El Khalil West Bank *see* Hebron
El Khandaq Sudan 86 D6
El Khârga Egypt *see* Al Khārijah
El Kharrûba Egypt *see* Al Kharrūbah
Elkhart *IN* U.S.A. 134 C3
Elkhart *KS* U.S.A. 131 C4
El Khartûm Sudan *see* Khartoum
El Khenachich *esc.* Mali *see* El Khnâchîch
El Khnâchîch *esc.* Mali 96 C2
Elkhorn U.S.A. 130 F3
Elkhorn City U.S.A. 134 D5
Elkhovo Bulg. 59 L3
Elki Turkey *see* Beytüşşebap
Elkin U.S.A. 132 D4
Elkins U.S.A. 134 F4
Elk Island National Park Canada 121 H4
Elk Lake Canada 122 E5
Elk Lake *l.* U.S.A. 134 C1
Elkland U.S.A. 135 G3
Elk Mountain U.S.A. 126 G4
Elk Mountains U.S.A. 129 J2
Elko Canada 120 H5
Elko U.S.A. 129 F1
Elk Point Canada 121 I4
Elk Point U.S.A. 130 D3
Elk Springs U.S.A. 129 I1
Elkton *MD* U.S.A. 135 H4
Elkton *VA* U.S.A. 135 F4
El Kûbri Egypt *see* Al Kūbrī
El Kuntilla Egypt *see* Al Kuntillah
Elkview U.S.A. 134 E4
Ellas *country* Europe *see* Greece
Ellaville U.S.A. 133 C5
Ell Bay Canada 121 O1
Ellef Ringnes Island Canada 119 H2
Ellen, Mount U.S.A. 129 H2
Ellenburg Depot U.S.A. 135 I1
Ellendale U.S.A. 130 D2
Ellensburg U.S.A. 126 C3
Ellenville U.S.A. 135 H3
El León, Cerro *mt.* Mex. 131 B7
Ellesmere, Lake N.Z. 113 D6

▶Ellesmere Island Canada 119 J2
4th largest island in North America.

Ellesmere Island National Park Reserve Canada *see* Quttinirpaaq National Park
Ellesmere Port U.K. 48 E5
Ellettsville U.S.A. 134 B4
Ellice *r.* Canada 121 K1
Ellice Island *atoll* Tuvalu *see* Funafuti
Ellice Islands *country* S. Pacific Ocean *see* Tuvalu
Ellicott City U.S.A. 135 G4
Ellijay U.S.A. 133 C5
Ellingen Germany 53 K5
Elliot Australia 108 F4
Elliot S. Africa 101 H6
Elliot, Mount Australia 110 D3
Elliotdale S. Africa 101 I6
Elliot Knob *mt.* U.S.A. 134 F4
Elliot Lake Canada 122 E5
Ellisras S. Africa 101 H2
Elliston U.S.A. 134 E5
Ellon U.K. 50 G3
Ellora Caves *tourist site* India 84 B1
Ellsworth *KS* U.S.A. 130 D4
Ellsworth *ME* U.S.A. 132 G2
Ellsworth *NE* U.S.A. 130 C3
Ellsworth *WI* U.S.A. 130 E2
Ellsworth Land *reg.* Antarctica 152 K1
Ellsworth Mountains Antarctica 152 L1
Ellwangen (Jagst) Germany 53 K6
El Maghreb *country* Africa *see* Morocco
Elmakuz Dağı *mt.* Turkey 85 A1
Elmalı Turkey 59 M6
El Malpais National Monument *nat. park* U.S.A. 129 J4
El Manşûra Egypt *see* Al Manşūrah
El Maţarîya Egypt *see* Al Maţarīyah
El Mazâr Egypt *see* Al Mazār
El Meghaïer Alg. 54 F5
El Milia Alg. 54 F4
El Minya Egypt *see* Al Minyā
Elmira *Ont.* Canada 134 E2
Elmira *P.E.I.* Canada 123 J5
Elmira *MI* U.S.A. 134 C1
Elmira *NY* U.S.A. 135 G2
El Mirage U.S.A. 129 G5
El Moral Spain 57 E5
Elmore Australia 112 B6
El Mreyyé *reg.* Mauritania 96 C3
Elmshorn Germany 53 J1
El Muglad Sudan 86 C7
Elmvale Canada 134 F1
Elnesvågen Norway 44 E5
El Nevado, Cerro *mt.* Col. 142 D3
El Oasis Mex. 129 F5
El Obeid Sudan 86 D7
El Odaiya Sudan 86 C7
El Oro Mex. 131 C7
Elorza Venez. 142 E2
El Oued Alg. 54 F5
Eloy U.S.A. 129 H5
El Palmito Mex. 131 B7
El Paso *IL* U.S.A. 130 F3
El Paso *KS* U.S.A. *see* Derby
El Paso *TX* U.S.A. 127 G7
Elphin U.K. 50 D2
Elphinstone *i.* Myanmar *see* Thayawthadangyi Kyun
El Portal U.S.A. 128 D3
El Porvenir Mex. 131 B6
El Porvenir Panama 137 I7
El Prat de Llobregat Spain 57 H3
El Progreso Hond. 136 G5
El Puerto de Santa María Spain 57 C5
El Qâhira Egypt *see* Cairo
El Qasimiye *r.* Lebanon 85 B3
El Quds Israel/West Bank *see* Jerusalem
El Quşeima Egypt *see* Al Quşaymah
El Quşeir Egypt *see* Al Quşayr
El Qûşîya Egypt *see* Al Qūşīyah
El Regocijo Mex. 131 B8
El Reno U.S.A. 131 D5
Elrose Canada 121 I5
Elsa Canada 120 C2
El Şaff Egypt *see* Aş Şaff
El Sahuaro Mex. 127 E7
El Salado Mex. 131 C7
El Salto Mex. 131 B8
▶El Salvador *country* Central America 136 G6
North America 9, 116–117
El Salvador Chile 144 C3
El Salvador Mex. 131 C7
Elsass *reg.* France *see* Alsace
El Sauz Mex. 127 G7
Else *r.* Germany 53 I2
El Sellûm Egypt *see* As Sallūm
Elsen Nur *l.* China 83 H2
Elsey Australia 108 F3
El Shallûfa Egypt *see* Ash Shallūfah
El Sharana Australia 108 F3
El Shaţţ Egypt *see* Ash Shaţţ
Elsie U.S.A. 134 C2
Elsinore Denmark *see* Helsingør
Elsinore *CA* U.S.A. 128 E5
Elsinore *UT* U.S.A. 129 G2
Elsinore Lake U.S.A. 128 E5
El Sueco Mex. 127 G7
El Suweis Egypt *see* Suez
El Suweis *governorate* Egypt *see* As Suways
El Tama, Parque Nacional *nat. park* Venez. 142 D2
El Tarf Alg. 58 C6
El Teleno *mt.* Spain 57 C2
El Temascal Mex. 131 D7
El Ter *r.* Spain 57 H2
El Thamad Egypt *see* Ath Thamad
El Tigre Venez. 142 F2
Eltmann Germany 53 K5
El'ton Rus. Fed. 43 J6
El'ton, Ozero *l.* Rus. Fed. 43 J6
El Tren Mex. 127 E7
El Tuparro, Parque Nacional *nat. park* Col. 142 E2
El Ţûr Egypt *see* Aţ Ţūr
El Turbio Chile 144 B8
El Uqşur Egypt *see* Luxor
Eluru India 84 D2
Elva Estonia 45 O7
Elvanfoot U.K. 50 F5
Elvas Port. 57 C4
Elverum Norway 45 G6
Elvira Brazil 142 D5
El Wak Kenya 98 E3
El Wâtya *well* Egypt *see* Al Wāţiyah
Elwood *IN* U.S.A. 134 C3
Elwood *NE* U.S.A. 130 D3
El Wuz Sudan 86 D7
Elx Spain *see* Elche-Elx
Elxleben Germany 53 K3
Ely U.K. 49 H6
Ely *MN* U.S.A. 130 F2
Ely *NV* U.S.A. 129 F2
Elyria U.S.A. 134 D3
Elz Germany 53 I4
El Zagâzîg Egypt *see* Az Zaqāzīq
Elze Germany 53 J2
Émaé *i.* Vanuatu 107 G3
Emāmrūd Iran 88 D2
Emām Şaḩeb Afgh. 89 H2
Emām Taqī Iran 88 E2
Emån *r.* Sweden 45 J8
Emas, Parque Nacional das *nat. park* Brazil 143 H7
Emba Kazakh. 80 A2
Emba *r.* Kazakh. 80 A2
Embalenhle S. Africa 101 I4
Embarcación Arg. 144 D2
Embarras Portage Canada 121 I3
Embi Kazakh. *see* Emba
Embira *r.* Brazil *see* Envira
Emborcação, Represa de *resr* Brazil 145 B2
Embrun Canada 135 H1
Embu Kenya 98 D4
Emden Germany 53 H1
Emden Deep *sea feature* N. Pacific Ocean *see* Cape Johnson Depth
Emei China *see* Emeishan
Emeishan China 76 D2
Emei Shan *mt.* China 76 D2
Emerald Australia 110 E4
Emeril Canada 123 I3
Emerita Augusta Spain *see* Mérida
Emerson Canada 121 L5
Emerson U.S.A. 134 D4
Emery U.S.A. 129 H2
Emesa Syria *see* Homs
Emet Turkey 59 M5
eMgwenya S. Africa 101 J3
Emigrant Pass U.S.A. 128 E1
Emigrant Valley U.S.A. 129 F3
eMijindini S. Africa 101 J3
Emi Koussi *mt.* Chad 97 E3
Emile *r.* Canada 120 G2
Emiliano Zapata Mex. 136 F5
Emin China 80 F2
Emine, Nos *pt* Bulg. 59 L3
Eminence U.S.A. 134 C4
Eminska Planina *hills* Bulg. 59 L3
Emirdağ Turkey 59 N5
Emir Dağı *mt.* Turkey 59 N5
Emir Dağları *mts* Turkey 59 N5
Emmaboda Sweden 45 I8
Emmaste Estonia 45 M7
Emmaville Australia 112 E2
Emmeloord Neth. 52 F2
Emmelshausen Germany 53 H4
Emmen Neth. 52 G2
Emmen Switz. 56 I3
Emmerich Germany 52 G3
Emmet Australia 110 D5
Emmetsburg U.S.A. 130 E3
Emmett U.S.A. 126 D4
Emmiganuru India 84 C3
Emo Canada 121 M5
Emona Slovenia *see* Ljubljana
Emory Peak U.S.A. 131 C6
Empalme Mex. 127 F8
Empangeni S. Africa 101 J5
Emperor Seamount Chain *sea feature* N. Pacific Ocean 150 H2
Emperor Trough *sea feature* N. Pacific Ocean 150 H2
Empingham Reservoir U.K. *see* Rutland Water
Emplawas Indon. 108 E2
Empoli Italy 58 D3
Emporia *KS* U.S.A. 130 D4
Emporia *VA* U.S.A. 135 G5
Emporium U.S.A. 135 F3
Empress Canada 121 I5
Empty Quarter *des.* Saudi Arabia *see* Rub' al Khālī
Ems *r.* Germany 53 H1
Emsdale Canada 134 F1
Emsdetten Germany 53 H2
Ems-Jade-Kanal *canal* Germany 53 H1
Emzinoni S. Africa 101 I4
Enafors Sweden 44 H5
Encantadas, Serra das *hills* Brazil 144 F4
Encarnación Para. 144 E3
Enchi Ghana 96 C4
Encinal U.S.A. 131 D6
Encinitas U.S.A. 128 E5
Encino U.S.A. 127 G6
Encruzilhada Brazil 145 C1
Endako Canada 120 E4
Endau-Rompin *nat. park* Malaysia 71 C7
Ende Indon. 108 C2
Endeavour Strait Australia 110 C1
Endeh Indon. *see* Ende
Enderby Canada 120 G5
Enderby *atoll* Micronesia *see* Puluwat
Enderby Land *reg.* Antarctica 152 D2
Endicott U.S.A. 135 G2
Endicott Mountains U.S.A. 118 C3
EnenKio *terr.* N. Pacific Ocean *see* Wake Island
Energodar Ukr. *see* Enerhodar
Enerhodar Ukr. 43 G7
Enewetak *atoll* Marshall Is 150 G5
Enez Turkey 59 L4
Enfe Lebanon 85 B2
Enfião, Ponta do *pt* Angola 99 B5
Enfidaville Tunisia 58 D6
Enfield U.S.A. 132 E4
Engan Norway 44 F5
Engaru Japan 74 F3
Engcobo S. Africa 101 H6
En Gedi Israel 85 B4
Engelhard U.S.A. 132 F5
Engel's Rus. Fed. 43 J6
Engelschmangat *sea chan.* Neth. 52 E1
Enggano *i.* Indon. 68 C8
Enghien Belgium 52 E4
England *admin. div.* U.K. 49 E6
Englee Canada 123 L4
Englehart Canada 122 F5
Englewood *FL* U.S.A. 133 D7
Englewood *OH* U.S.A. 134 C4
English *r.* Canada 121 M5
English U.S.A. 134 B4
English Bazar India *see* Ingraj Bazar
English Channel France/U.K. 49 F9
English Coast Antarctica 152 L2
Engozero Rus. Fed. 42 G2
Enhlalakahle S. Africa 101 J5
Enid U.S.A. 131 D4
Eniwa Japan 74 F4
Eniwetok *atoll* Marshall Is *see* Enewetak
Enjiang China *see* Yongfeng
Enkeldoorn Zimbabwe *see* Chivhu
Enkhuizen Neth. 52 F2
Enköping Sweden 45 J7
Enna *Sicily* Italy 58 F6
Ennadai Lake Canada 121 K2
En Nahud Sudan 86 C7
Ennedi, Massif *mts* Chad 97 F3
Ennell, Lough *l.* Rep. of Ireland 51 E4
Enngonia Australia 112 B2
Enning U.S.A. 130 C2
Ennis Rep. of Ireland 51 D5
Ennis *MT* U.S.A. 126 F3
Ennis *TX* U.S.A. 131 D5
Enniscorthy Rep. of Ireland 51 F5
Enniskillen U.K. 51 E3
Ennistymon Rep. of Ireland 51 C5
En Nâqoûra Lebanon 85 B3
Enns *r.* Austria 47 O6
Eno Fin. 44 Q5
Enoch U.S.A. 129 G3
Enontekiö Fin. 44 M2
Enosburg Falls U.S.A. 135 I1
Enosville U.S.A. 134 B4
Enping China 77 G4
Ens Neth. 52 F2
Ensay Australia 112 C6
Enschede Neth. 52 G2
Ense Germany 53 I3
Ensenada Mex. 127 D7
Enshi China 77 F2
Ensley U.S.A. 133 C6
Entebbe Uganda 98 D3
Enterprise Canada 120 G2
Enterprise *AL* U.S.A. 133 C6
Enterprise *OR* U.S.A. 126 D3
Enterprise *UT* U.S.A. 129 G3
Entre Ríos Bol. 142 F8
Entre Rios Brazil 143 H6
Entre Rios de Minas Brazil 145 B3
Entroncamento Port. 57 B4
Enugu Nigeria 96 D4
Enurmino Rus. Fed. 65 T3
Envira Brazil 142 D5
Envira *r.* Brazil 142 D5
Enyamba Dem. Rep. Congo 98 C4
Eochaill Rep. of Ireland *see* Youghal
Epe Neth. 52 F2
Epéna Congo 98 B3
Épernay France 52 D5
Ephraim U.S.A. 129 H2
Ephrata U.S.A. 135 G3
Epi *i.* Vanuatu 107 G3
Epidamnus Albania *see* Durrës
Épinal France 56 H2
Episkopi Bay Cyprus 85 A2
Episkopis, Kolpos *b.* Cyprus *see* Episkopi Bay
ePitoli S. Africa *see* Pretoria
Epomeo, Monte *hill* Italy 58 E4
Epping U.K. 49 H7
Epping Forest National Park Australia 110 D4
Eppstein Germany 53 I4
Eppynt, Mynydd *hills* U.K. 49 D6
Epsom U.K. 49 G7
Epte *r.* France 52 B5
Eqlīd Iran 88 D4
▶Equatorial Guinea *country* Africa 96 D4
Africa 7, 94–95
Équerdreville-Hainneville France 49 F9
Erac Creek *watercourse* Australia 112 B1
Erandol India 84 B1
Erawadi *r.* Myanmar *see* Irrawaddy
Erawan National Park Thai. 71 B4
Erbaa Turkey 90 E2
Erbendorf Germany 53 M5
Erbeskopf *hill* Germany 52 H5
Ercan *airport* Cyprus 85 A2
Erciş Turkey 91 F3
Erciyes Dağı *mt.* Turkey 90 D3
Érd Hungary 58 H1
Erdaobaihe China *see* Baihe
Erdaogou China 76 B1
Erdao Jiang *r.* China 74 B4
Erdek Turkey 59 L4
Erdemli Turkey 85 B1
Erdenet Mongolia 80 J2
Erdi *reg.* Chad 97 F3
Erdniyevskiy Rus. Fed. 43 J7
Erebus, Mount *vol.* Antarctica 152 H1
Erechim Brazil 144 F3
Ereentsav Mongolia 73 L3
Ereğli *Konya* Turkey 90 D3
Ereğli *Zonguldak* Turkey 59 N4
Erego Moz. *see* Errego
Erei, Monti *mts Sicily* Italy 58 F6
Erementaū Kazakh. *see* Yereymentau
Erenhot China 73 K4
Erepucu, Lago de *l.* Brazil 143 G4
Erevan Armenia *see* Yerevan
Erfurt Germany 53 L4
Erfurt *airport* Germany 53 K4
Ergani Turkey 91 E3
'Erg Chech *des.* Alg./Mali 96 C2
Ergel Mongolia 73 J4
Ergene *r.* Turkey 59 L4
Ērgļi Latvia 45 N8
Ergu China 74 C3
Ergun China 73 M2
Ergun He *r.* China/Rus. Fed. *see* Argun'
Ergun Youqi China *see* Ergun
Ergun Zuoqi China *see* Genhe
Er Hai *l.* China 76 D3
Erhulai China 74 B4
Eriboll, Loch *inlet* U.K. 50 E2
Ericht *r.* U.K. 50 F4
Ericht, Loch *l.* U.K. 50 E4
Erickson Canada 121 L5
Erie *KS* U.S.A. 131 E4
Erie *PA* U.S.A. 134 E2
Erie, Lake Canada/U.S.A. 134 E2
'Erîgât *des.* Mali 96 C3
Erik Eriksenstretet *sea chan.* Svalbard 64 D2
Eriksdale Canada 121 L5
Erimo-misaki *c.* Japan 74 F4
Erin Canada 134 E2
Erinpura Road India 82 C4
Eriskay *i.* U.K. 50 B3
▶Eritrea *country* Africa 86 E6
Africa 7, 94–95
Erlangen Germany 53 L5
Erlangping China 77 F1
Erldunda Australia 109 F6
Erlistoun *watercourse* Australia 109 C6
Erlong Shan *mt.* China 74 C4
Erlongshan Shuiku *resr* China 74 B4
Ermak Kazakh. *see* Aksu
Ermelo Neth. 52 F2
Ermelo S. Africa 101 I4
Ermenek Turkey 85 A1
Ermenek *r.* Turkey 85 A1
Ermont Egypt *see* Armant
Ermoupoli Greece 59 K6
Ernakulam India 84 C4
Erne *r.* Rep. of Ireland/U.K. 51 D3
Ernest Giles Range *hills* Australia 109 C6
Erode India 84 C4
Eromanga Australia 111 C5
Erongo *admin. reg.* Namibia 100 B1
Erp Neth. 52 F3
Erqu China *see* Zhouzhi
Errabiddy Hills Australia 109 A6
Er Rachidia Morocco 54 D5
Er Raoui *des.* Alg. 54 D6
Errego Moz. 99 D5
Er Remla Tunisia 58 D7
Er Renk Sudan 86 D7
Errigal *hill* Rep. of Ireland 51 D2
Errinundra National Park Australia 112 D6
Erris Head *hd* Rep. of Ireland 51 B3
Errol U.S.A. 135 J1
Erromango *i.* Vanuatu 107 G3
Erronan *i.* Vanuatu *see* Futuna
Erseka Albania *see* Ersekë
Ersekë Albania 59 I4
Erskine U.S.A. 130 D2
Ersmark Sweden 44 L5
Ertai China 80 H2
Ertil' Rus. Fed. 43 I6
Ertis *r.* Kazakh./Rus. Fed. *see* Irtysh
Ertix He *r.* China/Kazakh. 80 G2
Ertra *country* Africa *see* Eritrea
Eruh Turkey 91 F3
Erwin U.S.A. 132 D4
Erwitte Germany 53 I3
Erxleben *Sachsen-Anhalt* Germany 53 L2
Erxleben *Sachsen-Anhalt* Germany 53 L2
Eryuan China 76 C3
Erzerum Turkey *see* Erzurum
Erzgebirge *mts* Czech Rep./Germany 53 N4
Erzhan China 74 B2
Erzin Turkey 85 C1
Erzincan Turkey 91 E3
Erzurum Turkey 91 F3
Esa-ala P.N.G. 110 E1
Esan-misaki *pt* Japan 74 F4
Esashi Japan 74 F3
Esbjerg Denmark 45 F9
Esbo Fin. *see* Espoo
Escalante U.S.A. 129 H3
Escalante *r.* U.S.A. 129 H3
Escalante Desert U.S.A. 129 G3
Escalón Mex. 131 B7
Escambia *r.* U.S.A. 133 C6
Escanaba U.S.A. 132 C2
Escárcega Mex. 136 F5
Escatrón Spain 57 F3
Escaut *r.* Belgium 52 D4
Esch Neth. 52 F3
Eschede Germany 53 K2
Eschscholtz *atoll* Marshall Is *see* Bikini
Esch-sur-Alzette Lux. 52 F5
Eschwege Germany 53 K3
Eschweiler Germany 52 G4
Escondido *r.* Mex. 131 C6
Escondido U.S.A. 128 E5
Escudilla *mt.* U.S.A. 129 I5
Escuinapa Mex. 136 C4
Escuintla Guat. 136 F6
Eséka Cameroon 96 E4
Eşen Turkey 59 M6
Esenguly Turkm. 88 D2
Esens Germany 53 H1
Eşfahān Iran 88 C3
Esfarayen, Reshteh-ye *mts* Iran 88 E2
Esfideh Iran 89 E3
Eshan China 76 D3
Eshāqābād Iran 88 E3
Eshkamesh Afgh. 89 H2
Eshkanān Iran 88 D5
Eshowe S. Africa 101 J5
Esikhawini S. Africa 101 K5
Esil Kazakh. *see* Yesil'
Esil *r.* Kazakh./Rus. Fed. *see* Ishim
Esk Australia 112 F1
Esk *r.* Australia 111 [inset]
Esk *r.* U.K. 48 D4
Eskdalemuir U.K. 50 F5
Esker Canada 123 I3
Eskifjörður Iceland 44 [inset]
Eski Gediz Turkey 59 M5
Eskilstuna Sweden 45 J7
Eskimo Lakes Canada 118 E3
Eskimo Point Canada *see* Arviat
Eski Mosul Iraq 91 F3
Eskipazar Turkey 90 D2
Eskişehir Turkey 59 N5
Eski-Yakkabag Uzbek. 89 G2
Esla *r.* Spain 57 C3
Eslāmābād-e Gharb Iran 88 B3
Esler Dağı *mt.* Turkey 59 M6
Eslohe (Sauerland) Germany 53 I3
Eslöv Sweden 45 H9
Esmā'īlī-ye Soflá Iran 88 E4
Eşme Turkey 59 M5
Esmeraldas Ecuador 142 C3
Esmont U.S.A. 135 F5
Esnagami Lake Canada 122 D4
Esnes France 52 D4
Espakeh Iran 89 F5
Espalion France 56 F4
España *country* Europe *see* Spain
Espanola Canada 122 E5
Espanola U.S.A. 131 B4
Espelkamp Germany 53 I2
Esperance Australia 109 C8
Esperance Bay Australia 109 C8
Esperanza *research station* Antarctica 152 A2
Esperanza Arg. 144 B8
Esperanza Mex. 127 F8
Espichel, Cabo *c.* Port. 57 B4
Espigão, Serra do *mts* Brazil 141 A4
Espigüete *mt.* Spain 57 D2
Espinazo Mex. 131 C7
Espinhaço, Serra do *mts* Brazil 145 C2
Espinosa Brazil 145 C1
Espírito Santo Brazil *see* Vila Velha
Espírito Santo *state* Brazil 145 C2
Espíritu Santo *i.* Vanuatu 107 G3
Espíritu Santo, Isla *i.* Mex. 124 E7
Espoo Fin. 45 N5
Espuña *mt.* Spain 57 F5
Esqueda Mex. 127 F7
Esquel Arg. 144 B6
Esquimalt Canada 120 F5
Essaouira Morocco 96 C1
Es Semara W. Sahara 96 B2
Essen Belgium 52 E3

▶Essen Germany 52 H3
5th most populous city in Europe.

Essen (Oldenburg) Germany 53 H2
Essequibo *r.* Guyana 143 G2
Essex Canada 134 D2
Essex *CA* U.S.A. 129 F4
Essex *MD* U.S.A. 135 G4
Essex *NY* U.S.A. 135 I1
Essexville U.S.A. 134 D2
Esslingen am Neckar Germany 53 J6
Esso Rus. Fed. 65 Q4
Essoyla Rus. Fed. 42 G3
Eşţahbān Iran 88 D4
Estância Brazil 143 K6
Estancia U.S.A. 127 G6
Estand, Kūh-e *mt.* Iran 89 F4
Estats, Pic d' *mt.* France/Spain 56 E5
Estcourt S. Africa 101 I5
Este *r.* Germany 53 J1
Estelí Nicaragua 137 G6
Estella Spain 57 E2
Estepa Spain 57 D5
Estepona Spain 57 D5
Esteras de Medinaceli Spain 57 E3
Esterhazy Canada 121 K5
Estero Bay U.S.A. 128 C4
Esteros Para. 144 D2
Estevan Canada 121 K5
Estevan Group *is* Canada 120 D4
Estherville U.S.A. 130 E3
Estill U.S.A. 133 D5
Eston Canada 121 I5
▶Estonia *country* Europe 45 N7
Europe 5, 38–39
Estonskaya S.S.R. *country* Europe *see* Estonia
Estrées-St-Denis France 52 C5
Estrela Brazil 145 A5
Estrela, Serra da *mts* Port. 57 C3
Estrela do Sul Brazil 145 B2
Estrella *mt.* Spain 57 E4
Estrella, Punta *pt* Mex. 127 E7
Estremoz Port. 57 C4
Estrondo, Serra *hills* Brazil 143 I5
Etadunna Australia 111 B6
Etah India 82 D4
Étain France 52 F5
Etamamiou Canada 123 K4
Étampes France 56 F2
Étaples France 52 B4
Etawah *Rajasthan* India 82 D4
Etawah *Uttar Pradesh* India 82 D4
eThandakukhanya S. Africa 101 J4
Ethelbert Canada 121 K5
Ethel Creek Australia 109 C5
E'Thembini S. Africa 100 F5

▶Ethiopia *country* Africa 98 D3
3rd most populous country in Africa.
Africa 7, 94–95

Etimesğut Turkey 90 D3

Etive, Loch inlet U.K. 50 D4
Etna, Mount vol. Sicily Italy 58 F6
Etne Norway 45 D7
Etobicoke Canada 134 F2
Etolin Strait U.S.A. 118 B3
Etorofu-tō i. Rus. Fed. see Iturup, Ostrov
Etosha National Park Namibia 99 B5
Etosha Pan salt pan Namibia 99 B5
Etoumbi Congo 98 B3
Etrek r. Iran/Turkm. see Atrek
Étrépagny France 52 B5
Étretat France 49 H9
Ettelbruck Lux. 52 G5
Etten-Leur Neth. 52 E3
Ettlingen Germany 53 I6
Ettrick Water r. U.K. 50 F5
Euabalong Australia 112 C4
Euboea i. Greece see Evvoia
Eucla Australia 109 E7
Euclid U.S.A. 134 E3
Euclides da Cunha Brazil 143 K6
Eucumbene, Lake Australia 112 D6
Eudistes, Lac des l. Canada 123 I4
Eudora U.S.A. 131 F5
Eudunda Australia 111 B7
Eufaula AL U.S.A. 133 C6
Eufaula OK U.S.A. 131 E5
Eufaula Lake resr U.S.A. 131 E5
Eugene U.S.A. 126 C3
Eugenia, Punta pt Mex. 127 E8
Eugowra Australia 112 D4
Eulo Australia 112 B2
Eumungerie Australia 112 D3
Eungella Australia 110 E4
Eungella National Park Australia 110 E4
Eunice LA U.S.A. 131 E6
Eunice NM U.S.A. 131 C5
Eupen Belgium 52 G4

▶Euphrates r. Asia 91 G5
Longest river in western Asia. Also known as Al Furāt (Iraq/Syria) or Fırat (Turkey).

Eura Fin. 45 M6
Eure r. France 52 B5
Eureka CA U.S.A. 126 B4
Eureka KS U.S.A. 130 D4
Eureka MT U.S.A. 126 E2
Eureka NV U.S.A. 129 F2
Eureka OH U.S.A. 134 D4
Eureka SD U.S.A. 130 D2
Eureka UT U.S.A. 129 G2
Eureka Sound sea chan. Canada 119 J2
Eureka Springs U.S.A. 131 E4
Eureka Valley U.S.A. 128 E3
Euriowie Australia 111 C6
Euroa Australia 112 B6
Eurombah Australia 111 E5
Eurombah Creek r. Australia 111 E5
Europa, Île i. Indian Ocean 99 E6
Europa, Punta de pt Gibraltar see Europa Point
Europa Point Gibraltar 57 D5
Euskirchen Germany 52 G4
Eutaw U.S.A. 133 C5
Eutsuk Lake Canada 120 E4
Eutzsch Germany 53 M3
Eva Downs Australia 108 F4
Evans, Lac l. Canada 122 F4
Evans, Mount U.S.A. 126 G5
Evansburg Canada 120 H4
Evans City U.S.A. 134 E3
Evans Head Australia 112 F2
Evans Head hd Australia 112 F2
Evans Ice Stream Antarctica 152 L1
Evans Strait Canada 121 P2
Evanston IL U.S.A. 134 B2
Evanston WY U.S.A. 126 F4
Evansville Canada 122 E5
Evansville IN U.S.A. 134 B5
Evansville WY U.S.A. 126 G4
Evant U.S.A. 131 D6
Eva Perón Arg. see La Plata
Evart U.S.A. 134 C2
Evaton S. Africa 101 H4
Evaz Iran 88 D5
Evening Shade U.S.A. 131 F4
Evensk Rus. Fed. 65 Q3
Everard, Cape Australia 112 D6
Everard, Lake salt flat Australia 111 A6
Everard, Mount Australia 109 F5
Everard Range hills Australia 109 F6
Everdingen Neth. 52 F3
Everek Turkey see Develi

▶Everest, Mount China/Nepal 83 F4
Highest mountain in the world and in Asia.
Asia 60–61
World 12–13

Everett PA U.S.A. 135 F3
Everett WA U.S.A. 126 C3
Evergem Belgium 52 D3
Everglades swamp U.S.A. 133 D7
Everglades National Park U.S.A. 133 D7
Evergreen U.S.A. 133 C6
Evesham Australia 110 C4
Evesham U.K. 49 F6
Evesham, Vale of valley U.K. 49 F6
Evijärvi Fin. 44 M5
Evje Norway 45 E7
Évora Port. 57 C4
Evoron, Ozero l. Rus. Fed. 74 E2
Évreux France 52 B5
Evros r. Bulgaria see Maritsa
Evros r. Turkey see Meriç
Evrotas r. Greece 59 J6
Évry France 52 C6
Evrychou Cyprus 85 A2
Evrykhou Cyprus see Evrychou
Evvoia i. Greece 59 K5
Ewan Australia 110 D3
Ewaso Ngiro r. Kenya 98 E3
Ewe, Loch b. U.K. 50 D3
Ewing U.S.A. 134 D5
Ewo Congo 98 B4
Exaltación Bol. 142 E6
Excelsior S. Africa 101 H5
Excelsior Mountain U.S.A. 128 D2
Excelsior Mountains U.S.A. 128 D2
Exe r. U.K. 49 D8
Exeter Australia 112 E5
Exeter Canada 134 E2
Exeter U.K. 49 D8
Exeter CA U.S.A. 128 D3
Exeter NH U.S.A. 135 J2
Exeter Lake Canada 121 I1
Exloo Neth. 52 G2
Exminster U.K. 49 D8
Exmoor hills U.K. 49 D7
Exmoor National Park U.K. 49 D7
Exmore U.S.A. 135 H5
Exmouth Australia 108 A5
Exmouth U.K. 49 D8
Exmouth, Mount Australia 112 D3
Exmouth Gulf Australia 108 A5
Exmouth Lake Canada 120 H1
Exmouth Plateau sea feature Indian Ocean 149 P7
Expedition National Park Australia 110 E5
Expedition Range mts Australia 110 E5
Exploits r. Canada 123 L4
Exton U.S.A. 135 H3
Extremadura aut. comm. Spain 57 D4
Exuma Cays is Bahamas 133 E7
Exuma Sound sea chan. Bahamas 133 F7
Eyasi, Lake salt l. Tanz. 98 D4
Eyawadi r. Myanmar see Irrawaddy
Eye U.K. 49 I6
Eyeberry Lake Canada 121 J2
Eyelenoborsk Rus. Fed. 41 S3
Eyemouth U.K. 50 G5
Eyjafjörður inlet Iceland 44 [inset]
Eyl Somalia 98 E3
Eylau Rus. Fed. see Bagrationovsk
Eynsham U.K. 49 F7

▶Eyre, Lake salt lake Australia 111 B6
Largest lake in Oceania and lowest point.
Oceania 102–103

Eyre (North), Lake salt lake Australia 111 B6
Eyre (South), Lake salt lake Australia 111 B6
Eyre Creek watercourse Australia 110 B5
Eyre Mountains N.Z. 113 B7
Eyre Peninsula Australia 111 A7
Eystrup Germany 53 J2
Eysturoy i. Faroe Is 44 [inset]
Ezakheni S. Africa 101 J5
Ezel U.S.A. 134 D5
Ezenzeleni S. Africa 101 I4
Ezequiel Ramos Mexía, Embalse resr Arg. 144 C5
Ezhou China 77 G2
Ezhva Rus. Fed. 42 K3
Ezine Turkey 59 L5
Ezo i. Japan see Hokkaidō
Ezousa r. Cyprus 85 A2

F

Faaborg Denmark see Fåborg
Faadhippolhu Atoll Maldives 84 B5
Faafxadhuun Somalia 98 E3
Fabens U.S.A. 127 G7
Faber, Mount hill Sing. 71 [inset]
Faber Lake Canada 120 G2
Fåborg Denmark 45 G9
Fabriano Italy 58 E3
Faches-Thumesnil France 52 D4
Fachi Niger 96 E3
Fada Chad 97 F3
Fada-N'Gourma Burkina 96 D3
Fadghāmī Syria 91 F4
Fadiffolu Atoll Maldives see Faadhippolhu Atoll
Fadippolu Atoll Maldives see Faadhippolhu Atoll
Faenza Italy 58 D2
Færoerne terr. N. Atlantic Ocean see Faroe Islands
Faeroes terr. N. Atlantic Ocean see Faroe Islands
Făgăraş Romania 59 K2

▶Fagatogo American Samoa 107 I3
Capital of American Samoa.

Fagersta Sweden 45 I7
Fagne reg. Belgium 52 E4
Fagurhólsmýri Iceland 44 [inset]
Fagwir Sudan 86 D8
Fahraj Iran 88 D4
Fā'id Egypt 90 D5
Fairbanks U.S.A. 118 D3
Fairborn U.S.A. 134 C4
Fairbury U.S.A. 130 D3
Fairchance U.S.A. 134 F4
Fairfax U.S.A. 135 G4
Fairfield CA U.S.A. 128 B2
Fairfield IA U.S.A. 130 F3
Fairfield ID U.S.A. 126 E4
Fairfield IL U.S.A. 130 F4
Fairfield OH U.S.A. 134 C4
Fairfield TX U.S.A. 131 D6
Fair Haven U.S.A. 135 I2
Fair Head hd U.K. 51 F2
Fair Isle i. U.K. 50 H1
Fairlee U.S.A. 135 I2
Fairmont MN U.S.A. 130 E3
Fairmont WV U.S.A. 134 E4
Fair Oaks U.S.A. 134 B3
Fairview Australia 110 D2
Fairview Canada 120 G3
Fairview MI U.S.A. 134 C1
Fairview OK U.S.A. 131 D4
Fairview PA U.S.A. 134 E2
Fairview UT U.S.A. 129 H2
Fairview Park Hong Kong China 77 [inset]
Fairweather, Cape U.S.A. 120 B3
Fairweather, Mount Canada/U.S.A. 120 B3
Fais i. Micronesia 69 K5
Faisalabad Pak. 89 I4
Faissault France 52 E5
Faith U.S.A. 130 C2
Faizabad Afgh. see Feyzābād
Faizabad India 83 E4
Fakaofo atoll Tokelau 107 I2
Fakaofo atoll Tokelau see Fakaofo
Fakenham U.K. 49 H6
Fåker Sweden 44 I5
Fakfak Indon. 69 I7
Fakhrabad Iran 88 D4
Fakiragram India 83 G4
Fako vol. Cameroon see Cameroun, Mont
Fal r. U.K. 49 C8
Falaba Sierra Leone 96 B4
Falaise Lake Canada 120 G2
Falam Myanmar 70 A2
Falavarjan Iran 88 C3
Falcon Lake Canada 121 M5
Falcon Lake l. Mex./U.S.A. 131 D7
Falenki Rus. Fed. 42 K4
Falfurrias U.S.A. 131 D7
Falher Canada 120 G4
Falkenberg Germany 53 N3
Falkenberg Sweden 45 H8
Falkenhagen Germany 53 M1
Falkenhain Germany 53 M3
Falkensee Germany 53 N2
Falkenstein Germany 53 M5
Falkirk U.K. 50 F5
Falkland U.K. 50 F4
Falkland Escarpment sea feature S. Atlantic Ocean 148 E9

▶Falkland Islands terr. S. Atlantic Ocean 144 E8
United Kingdom Overseas Territory.
South America 9, 140–141

Falkland Plateau sea feature S. Atlantic Ocean 148 E9
Falkland Sound sea chan. Falkland Is 144 D8
Falköping Sweden 45 H7
Fallbrook U.S.A. 128 E5
Fallieres Coast Antarctica 152 L2
Fallingbostel Germany 53 J2
Fallon U.S.A. 128 D2
Fall River U.S.A. 135 J3
Fall River Pass U.S.A. 126 G4
Falls City U.S.A. 130 E3
Falmouth U.K. 49 B8
Falmouth KY U.S.A. 134 C4
Falmouth VA U.S.A. 135 G4
False r. Canada 123 H2
False Bay S. Africa 100 D8
False Point India 83 F5
Falster i. Denmark 45 G9
Fălticeni Romania 43 E7
Falun Sweden 45 I6
Famagusta Cyprus 85 A2
Famagusta Bay Cyprus see Ammochostos Bay
Fameck France 52 G5
Famenin Iran 88 C3
Fame Range hills Australia 109 C6
Family Lake Canada 121 M5
Family Well Australia 108 D5
Fāmūr, Daryācheh-ye l. Iran 88 C4
Fana Mali 96 C3
Fanad Head hd Rep. of Ireland 47 E2
Fandriana Madag. 99 E6
Fane r. Rep. of Ireland 51 F4
Fang Thai. 70 B3
Fangcheng Guangxi China see Fangchenggang
Fangcheng Henan China 77 G1
Fangchenggang China 77 F4
Fangdou Shan mts China 77 F2
Fangliao Taiwan 77 I4
Fangshan Taiwan 77 I4
Fangxian China 77 F1
Fangzheng China 74 C3
Fankuai China 77 F2
Fankuaidian China see Fankuai
Fanling Hong Kong China 77 [inset]
Fannich, Loch l. U.K. 50 D3
Fannūj Iran 89 E5
Fano Italy 58 E3
Fanshan Anhui China 77 H2
Fanshan Zhejiang China 77 I3
Fan Si Pan mt. Vietnam 70 C2
Fanum Fortunae Italy see Fano
Faqih Aḥmadān Iran 88 C4
Farab Turkm. see Farap
Faraba Mali 96 B3
Faradofay Madag. see Tôlañaro
Farafangana Madag. 99 E6
Farāfirah, Wāḥāt al oasis Egypt 86 C4
Farafra Oasis oasis Egypt see Farāfirah, Wāḥāt al
Farāh Afgh. 89 F3
Faraḥābād Iran see Khezerābād
Farallon de Medinilla i. N. Mariana Is 69 L3
Farallon de Pajaros vol. N. Mariana Is 69 K2
Farallones de Cali, Parque Nacional nat. park Col. 142 C3
Faranah Guinea 96 B3
Farap Turkm. 89 F2
Fararah Oman 87 I5
Farasān, Jazā'ir is Saudi Arabia 86 F6
Faraulep atoll Micronesia 69 K5
Fareham U.K. 49 F8
Farewell, Cape Greenland 119 N3
Farewell, Cape N.Z. 113 D5
Farewell Spit N.Z. 113 D5
Färgelanda Sweden 45 H7
Farghona Uzbek. see Fergana
Fargo U.S.A. 130 D2
Faribault U.S.A. 130 E2
Faribault, Lac l. Canada 123 H2
Faridabad India 82 D3
Faridkot India 82 C3
Faridpur Bangl. 83 G5
Farīmān Iran 89 E3
Farkhar Afgh. see Farkhato
Farkhato Afgh. 89 H2
Farkhor Tajik. 89 H2
Farmahin Iran 88 C3
Farmer Island Canada 122 E2
Farmerville U.S.A. 131 E5
Farmington Canada 120 F4
Farmington ME U.S.A. 135 J1
Farmington MO U.S.A. 130 F4
Farmington NH U.S.A. 135 J2
Farmington NM U.S.A. 129 I3
Farmington Hills U.S.A. 134 D2
Far Mountain Canada 120 E4
Farmville U.S.A. 135 F5
Farnborough U.K. 49 G7
Farne Islands U.K. 48 F3
Farnham U.K. 49 G7
Farnham, Lake salt flat Australia 109 D6
Farnham, Mount Canada 120 G5
Faro Brazil 143 G4
Faro Canada 120 C2
Faro Port. 57 C5
Fårö i. Sweden 45 K8
Faroe - Iceland Ridge sea feature Arctic Ocean 153 I2

▶Faroe Islands terr. N. Atlantic Ocean 44 [inset]
Self-governing Danish Territory.
Europe 5, 38–39

Fårösund Sweden 45 K8
Farquhar Group is Seychelles 99 F5
Farquharson Tableland hills Australia 109 C6
Farrāshband Iran 88 D4
Farr Bay Antarctica 152 F2
Farristown U.S.A. 134 C5
Farrukhabad India see Fatehgarh
Fārsī Afgh. 89 F3
Farsund Norway 45 E7
Fārūj Iran 88 E2
Farwell MI U.S.A. 134 C2
Farwell TX U.S.A. 131 C5
Fasā Iran 88 D4
Fasano Italy 58 G4
Faşikan Geçidi pass Turkey 85 A1
Faßberg Germany 53 K2
Fastiv Ukr. 43 F6
Fastov Ukr. see Fastiv
Fatehabad India 82 C3
Fatehgarh India 82 D4
Fatehpur Rajasthan India 82 C4
Fatehpur Uttar Pradesh India 82 E4
Fatick Senegal 96 B3
Fattoilep atoll Micronesia see Faraulep
Faughan r. U.K. 51 E2
Faulkton U.S.A. 130 D2
Faulquemont France 52 G5
Fauresmith S. Africa 101 G5
Fauske Norway 44 I3
Faust Canada 120 H4
Fawcett Canada 120 H4
Fawley U.K. 49 F8
Fawn r. Canada 121 N4
Faxaflói b. Iceland 44 [inset]
Faxälven r. Sweden 44 J5
Faya Chad 97 E3
Fayette AL U.S.A. 133 C5
Fayette MO U.S.A. 130 E4
Fayette MS U.S.A. 131 F6
Fayette OH U.S.A. 134 C3
Fayetteville AR U.S.A. 131 E4
Fayetteville NC U.S.A. 133 E5
Fayetteville TN U.S.A. 133 C5
Fayetteville WV U.S.A. 134 E4
Fâyid Egypt see Fā'id
Faylakah i. Kuwait 88 C4
Fazao Malfakassa, Parc National de nat. park Togo 96 D4
Fazilka India 82 C3
Fazrān, Jabal hill Saudi Arabia 88 C5
Fdérik Mauritania 96 B2
Fead Group is P.N.G. see Nuguria Islands
Feale r. Rep. of Ireland 51 C5
Fear, Cape U.S.A. 133 E5
Featherston N.Z. 113 E5
Feathertop, Mount Australia 112 C6
Fécamp France 56 E2
Federal District admin. dist. Brazil see Distrito Federal
Federalsburg U.S.A. 135 H4
Federated Malay States country Asia see Malaysia
Fedusar India 82 C4
Fehet Lake Canada 121 M1
Fehmarn i. Germany 47 M3
Fehrbellin Germany 53 M2
Feia, Lagoa lag. Brazil 145 C3
Feicheng China see Feixian
Feijó Brazil 142 D5
Feilding N.Z. 113 E5
Fei Ngo Shan hill Hong Kong China see Kowloon Peak
Feio r. Brazil see Aguapeí
Feira de Santana Brazil 145 D1
Feixi China 77 H2
Feixian China 77 H1
Fejd-el-Abiod pass Alg. 58 B6
Feke Turkey 90 D3
Felanitx Spain 57 H4
Feldberg Germany 53 N1
Feldberg mt. Germany 47 L7
Feldkirch Austria 47 L7
Feldkirchen in Kärnten Austria 47 O7
Felidhu Atoll Maldives 81 D11
Felidu Atoll Maldives see Felidhu Atoll
Felipe C. Puerto Mex. 136 G5
Felixlândia Brazil 145 B2
Felixstowe U.K. 49 I7
Felixton S. Africa 101 J5
Fellowsville U.S.A. 134 F4
Felsina Italy see Bologna
Felton U.S.A. 135 H4
Feltre Italy 58 D1
Femunden l. Norway 44 G5
Femundsmarka Nasjonalpark nat. park Norway 44 H5
Fenaio, Punta del pt Italy 58 D3
Fence Lake U.S.A. 129 I4
Fener Burnu hd Turkey 85 B1
Fénérive Madag. see Fenoarivo Atsinanana
Fengari mt. Greece 59 K4
Fengcheng Fujian China see Lianjiang
Fengcheng Fujian China see Anxi
Fengcheng Fujian China see Yongding
Fengcheng Guangdong China see Xinfeng
Fengcheng Guangxi China see Fengshan
Fengcheng Guizhou China see Tianzhu
Fengcheng Jiangxi China 77 G2
Fenggang Fujian China see Shaxian
Fenggang Guizhou China 76 E3
Fenggang Jiangxi China see Yihuang
Fengguang China 74 B3
Fenghuang China 77 F3
Fengjiaba China see Wangcang
Fengjie China 77 F2
Fengkai China 77 F4
Fenglin Taiwan 77 I4
Fengming Shaanxi China see Qishan
Fengming Sichuan China see Pengshan
Fengqing China 76 C3
Fengshan Fujian China see Luoyuan
Fengshan Guangxi China 76 E3
Fengshan Hubei China see Luotian
Fengshan Yunnan China see Fengqing
Fengshuba Shuiku resr China 77 G3
Fengshui Shan mt. China 74 A1
Fengtongzai Giant Panda Reserve nature res. China 76 D2
Fengxian China 76 E1
Fengxiang Heilong. China see Luobei
Fengxiang Yunnan China see Lincang
Fengyang China 77 H1
Fengyüan Taiwan 77 I3
Fengzhen China 73 K4
Feni Bangl. 83 G5
Feni Islands P.N.G. 106 F2
Fennville U.S.A. 134 B2
Feno, Capo di c. Corsica France 56 I6
Fenoarivo Atsinanana Madag. 99 E5
Fenshui Guan pass China 77 H3
Fenton U.S.A. 134 D2
Fenua Ura atoll Fr. Polynesia see Manuae
Fenyi China 77 G3
Feodosiya Ukr. 90 D1
Fer, Cap de c. Alg. 58 B6
Férai Greece see Feres
Ferdows Iran 88 E3
Fère-Champenoise France 52 D6
Feres Greece 59 L4
Fergana Uzbek. 87 L1
Fergus Canada 134 E2
Fergus Falls U.S.A. 130 D2
Ferguson Lake Canada 121 L2
Fergusson Island P.N.G. 106 F2
Fériana Tunisia 58 C7
Ferijaz Serb. and Mont. see Uroševac
Ferkessédougou Côte d'Ivoire 96 C4
Fermo Italy 58 E3
Fermont Canada 123 I3
Fermoselle Spain 57 C3
Fermoy Rep. of Ireland 51 D5
Fernandina, Isla i. Galápagos Ecuador 142 [inset]
Fernandina Beach U.S.A. 133 D6
Fernando de Magallanes, Parque Nacional nat. park Chile 144 B8
Fernando de Noronha i. Brazil 148 F6
Fernandópolis Brazil 145 A3
Fernando Poó i. Equat. Guinea see Bioco
Fernão Dias Brazil 145 B2
Ferndale U.S.A. 128 A1
Ferndown U.K. 49 F8
Fernlee Australia 112 C2
Fernley U.S.A. 128 D2
Ferns Rep. of Ireland 51 F5
Ferozepore India see Firozpur
Ferrara Italy 58 D2
Ferreira-Gomes Brazil 143 H3
Ferro, Capo c. Sardinia Italy 58 C4
Ferrol Spain 57 B2
Ferron U.S.A. 129 H2
Ferros Brazil 145 C2
Ferryland Canada 123 L5
Ferryville Tunisia see Menzel Bourguiba
Fertő-tavi nat. park Hungary 58 G1
Ferwerd Neth. 52 F1
Ferwert Neth. see Ferwerd
Fès Morocco 54 D5
Feshi Dem. Rep. Congo 99 B4
Fessenden U.S.A. 130 D2
Festus U.S.A. 130 F4
Fété Bowé Senegal 96 B3
Fethard Rep. of Ireland 51 E5
Fethiye Malatya Turkey see Yazıhan
Fethiye Muğla Turkey 59 M6
Fethiye Körfezi b. Turkey 59 M6
Fetisovo Kazakh. 91 I2
Fetlar i. U.K. 50 [inset]
Fettercairn U.K. 50 G4
Feucht Germany 53 L5
Feuchtwangen Germany 53 K5
Feuilles, Rivière aux r. Canada 123 H2
Fevral'sk Rus. Fed. 74 C1
Fevzipaşa Turkey 90 E3
Feyzābād Afgh. 89 H2
Feyzābād Kermān Iran 88 D4
Feyzābād Khorāsān Iran 88 E3
Fez Morocco see Fès
Ffestiniog U.K. 49 D6
Fianarantsoa Madag. 99 E6
Fichē Eth. 98 D3
Fichtelgebirge hills Germany 53 M4
Field U.S.A. 134 D5
Fier Albania 59 H4
Fiery Creek r. Australia 110 B3
Fife Lake U.S.A. 134 C1
Fife Ness pt U.K. 50 G4
Fifield Australia 112 C4
Fifth Meridian Canada 120 H3
Figeac France 56 F4
Figueira da Foz Port. 57 B3
Figueras Spain see Figueres
Figueres Spain 57 H2
Figuig Morocco 54 D5
Figuil Cameroon 97 E4

▶Fiji country S. Pacific Ocean 107 H3
4th most populous and 5th largest country in Oceania.
Oceania 8, 104–105

Fīk' Eth. 98 E3
Filadelfia Para. 144 D2
Filchner Ice Shelf Antarctica 152 A1
Filey U.K. 48 G4
Filibe Bulg. see Plovdiv
Filingué Niger 96 D3
Filipinas country Asia see Philippines
Filippiada Greece 59 I5
Filipstad Sweden 45 I7
Fillan Norway 44 F5
Fillmore CA U.S.A. 128 D4
Fillmore UT U.S.A. 129 G2
Fils r. Germany 53 J6
Filtu Eth. 98 E3
Fimbull Ice Shelf Antarctica 152 C2
Fin Iran 88 C3
Finch Canada 135 H1
Findhorn r. U.K. 50 F3
Fındık Turkey 88 A2
Findlay U.S.A. 134 D3
Fine U.S.A. 135 H1
Finger Lake Canada 121 M4
Finger Lakes U.S.A. 135 G2
Finike Turkey 59 N6
Finike Körfezi b. Turkey 59 N6
Finisterre Spain see Fisterra
Finisterre, Cabo c. Spain see Finisterre, Cape
Finisterre, Cape Spain 57 B2
Finke watercourse Australia 110 A5
Finke, Mount hill Australia 109 F7
Finke Bay Australia 108 E3
Finke Gorge National Park Australia 109 F6
▶Finland country Europe 44 O5
Europe 5, 38–39
Finland, Gulf of Europe 45 M7
Finlay r. Canada 120 E3
Finlay, Mount Canada 120 E3
Finlay Forks Canada 120 F4
Finley U.S.A. 130 D2
Finn r. Rep. of Ireland 51 E3
Finne ridge Germany 53 L3
Finnigan, Mount Australia 110 D2
Finniss, Cape Australia 109 F8
Finnmarksvidda reg. Norway 44 H2
Finnsnes Norway 44 J2
Fins Oman 88 E6
Finschhafen P.N.G. 69 L8
Finspång Sweden 45 I7
Fintona U.K. 51 E3
Fintown Rep. of Ireland 51 D3
Finucane Range hills Australia 110 C4
Fionn Loch l. U.K. 50 D3
Fionnphort U.K. 50 C4
Fiordland National Park N.Z. 113 A7
Fir reg. Saudi Arabia 88 B4
Fırat r. Turkey 90 E3 see Euphrates
Firebaugh U.S.A. 128 C3
Firedrake Lake Canada 121 J2
Firenze Italy see Florence
Fireside Canada 120 E3
Firk, Sha'ib watercourse Iraq 91 G5
Firmat Arg. 144 D4
Firminy France 56 G4
Firmum Italy see Fermo
Firmum Picenum Italy see Fermo
Firovo Rus. Fed. 42 G4
Firozabad India 82 D4
Firozkoh reg. Afgh. 89 G3
Firozpur India 82 C3
First Three Mile Opening sea chan. Australia 110 D2
Fīrūzābād Iran 88 D4
Fīrūzkūh Iran 88 D3
Firyuza Turkm. 88 E2
Fischbach Germany 53 H5
Fischersbrunn Namibia 100 B3
Fish watercourse Namibia 100 C5
Fisher Australia 109 E7
Fisher Bay Antarctica 152 G2
Fisher Glacier Antarctica 152 E2
Fisher River Canada 121 L5
Fishers U.S.A. 134 B4
Fishers Island U.S.A. 135 J3
Fisher Strait Canada 119 J3
Fishguard U.K. 49 C7
Fishing Creek U.S.A. 135 G4
Fishing Lake Canada 121 M4
Fish Lake Canada 120 F2
Fish Point U.S.A. 134 D2
Fish Ponds Hong Kong China 77 [inset]
Fiske, Cape Antarctica 152 L2
Fiskenæsset Greenland see Qeqertarsuatsiaat
Fismes France 52 D5
Fisterra Spain 57 B2
Fisterra, Cabo c. Spain see Finisterre, Cape
Fitchburg U.S.A. 130 F3
Fitri, Lac l. Chad 97 E3
Fitzgerald Canada 121 I3
Fitzgerald U.S.A. 133 D6
Fitzgerald River National Park Australia 109 B8
Fitz Hugh Sound sea chan. Canada 120 D5
Fitz Roy Arg. 144 C7
Fitzroy r. Australia 108 C4
Fitz Roy, Cerro mt. Arg. 144 B7
Fitzroy Crossing Australia 108 D4
Fitzwilliam Island Canada 134 E1
Fiume Croatia see Rijeka
Fivemiletown U.K. 51 E3
Five Points U.S.A. 128 C3
Fizi Dem. Rep. Congo 99 C4
Fizuli Azer. see Füzuli
Flå Norway 45 F6
Flagstaff S. Africa 101 I6
Flagstaff U.S.A. 129 H4
Flagstaff Lake U.S.A. 132 G2
Flaherty Island Canada 122 F2
Flambeau r. U.S.A. 130 F2
Flamborough Head hd U.K. 48 G4
Fläming hills Germany 53 M2
Flaming Gorge Reservoir U.S.A. 126 F4
Flaminksvlei salt pan S. Africa 100 E6
Flanagan r. Canada 121 M4
Flandre reg. France 52 C4
Flannagan Lake U.S.A. 134 D5
Flannan Isles U.K. 50 B2
Flåsjön l. Sweden 44 I4
Flat r. Canada 120 E2
Flat r. U.S.A. 134 C2
Flat Creek Canada 120 B2
Flathead r. U.S.A. 124 E2
Flathead Lake U.S.A. 126 E3
Flatiron mt. U.S.A. 126 E3
Flat Island S. China Sea 68 F4
Flat Lick U.S.A. 134 D5
Flattery, Cape Australia 110 D2
Flattery, Cape U.S.A. 126 B2
Flat Top mt. Canada 120 B2
Flatwillow Creek r. U.S.A. 126 G3

Flatwoods U.S.A. 134 E4
Fleetmark Germany 53 L2
Fleetwood Australia 110 D4
Fleetwood U.K. 48 D5
Fleetwood U.S.A. 135 H3
Flekkefjord Norway 45 E7
Flemingsburg U.S.A. 134 D4
Flemington U.S.A. 135 H3
Flen Sweden 45 J7
Flensburg Germany 47 L3
Flers France 56 D2
Flesherton Canada 134 E1
Fletcher Lake Canada 121 I2
Fletcher Peninsula Antarctica 152 L2
Fleur de Lys Canada 123 K4
Fleur-de-May, Lac l. Canada 123 I4
Flinders r. Australia 110 C3
Flinders Chase National Park Australia 111 B7
Flinders Group National Park Australia 110 D2
Flinders Island Australia 111 [inset]
Flinders Passage Australia 110 E3
Flinders Ranges mts Australia 111 B7
Flinders Ranges National Park Australia 111 B6
Flinders Reefs Australia 110 E3
Flin Flon Canada 121 K4
Flint U.K. 48 D5
Flint U.S.A. 134 D2
Flint r. U.S.A. 133 C6
Flint Island Kiribati 151 J6
Flinton Australia 112 D1
Flisa Norway 45 H6

▶Flissingskiy, Mys c. Rus. Fed. 64 H2
Most easterly point of Europe.

Flixecourt France 52 C4
Flodden U.K. 48 E3
Flöha Germany 53 N4
Flood Range mts Antarctica 152 J1
Flora r. Australia 108 E3
Flora U.S.A. 134 B3
Florac France 56 F4
Florala U.S.A. 133 C6
Florange France 52 G5
Flora Reef Australia 110 D3
Florence Italy 58 D3
Florence AL U.S.A. 133 C5
Florence AZ U.S.A. 129 H5
Florence CO U.S.A. 127 G5
Florence OR U.S.A. 126 B4
Florence SC U.S.A. 133 E5
Florence WI U.S.A. 130 F2
Florence Junction U.S.A. 129 H5
Florencia Col. 142 C3
Florennes Belgium 52 E4
Florentia Italy see Florence
Florentino Ameghino, Embalse resr Arg. 144 C6
Flores r. Arg. 144 E5
Flores Guat. 136 G5
Flores i. Indon. 108 C2
Flores, Laut sea Indon. 108 B1
Flores Island Canada 120 E5
Flores Sea Indon. see Flores, Laut
Floresta Brazil 143 K5
Floresville U.S.A. 131 D6
Floriano Brazil 143 J5
Florianópolis Brazil 145 A4
Florida Uruguay 144 E4
Florida state U.S.A. 133 D6
Florida, Straits of Bahamas/U.S.A. 133 D8
Florida Bay U.S.A. 133 D7
Florida City U.S.A. 133 D7
Florida Islands Solomon Is 107 G2
Florida Keys is U.S.A. 133 D7
Florin U.S.A. 128 C2
Florina Greece 59 I4
Florissant U.S.A. 130 F4
Florø Norway 45 D6
Flour Lake Canada 123 I3
Floyd U.S.A. 134 E5
Floyd, Mount U.S.A. 129 G4
Floydada U.S.A. 131 C5
Fluessen l. Neth. 52 F2
Flushing Neth. see Vlissingen
Fly r. P.N.G. 69 K8
Flying Fish, Cape Antarctica 152 K2
Flying Mountain U.S.A. 129 I6
Flylân i. Neth. see Vlieland
Foam Lake Canada 121 K5
Foča Bos.-Herz. 58 H3
Foça Turkey 59 L5
Fochabers U.K. 50 F3
Focşani Romania 59 L2
Fogang China 77 G4
Foggia Italy 58 F4
Fogi Indon. 69 H7
Fogo i. Cape Verde 96 [inset]
Fogo Island Canada 123 L4
Foinaven hill U.K. 50 E2
Foix France 56 E5
Folda sea chan. Norway 44 I3
Foldereid Norway 44 H4
Foldfjorden sea chan. Norway 44 G4
Folegandros i. Greece 59 K6
Foleyet Canada 122 E4
Foley Island Canada 119 K3
Foligno Italy 58 E3
Folkestone U.K. 49 I7
Folkingham U.K. 49 G6
Folkston U.S.A. 133 D6
Folldal Norway 44 G5
Follonica Italy 58 D3
Folsom Lake U.S.A. 128 C2
Fomboni Comoros 99 E5
Fomento Cuba 133 E8
Fomin Rus. Fed. 43 I7
Fominskaya Rus. Fed. 42 K2
Fominskoye Rus. Fed. 42 I4
Fonda U.S.A. 135 H2
Fond-du-Lac Canada 121 J3
Fond du Lac r. Canada 121 J3
Fond du Lac U.S.A. 134 A2
Fondevila Spain 57 B3
Fondi Italy 58 E4
Fonni Sardinia Italy 58 C4
Fonsagrada Spain see A Fonsagrada
Fonseca, Golfo do b. Central America 136 G6
Fontaine Lake Canada 121 J3
Fontanges Canada 123 H3
Fontas Canada 120 F3
Fontas r. Canada 120 F3
Fonte Boa Brazil 142 E4
Fonteneau, Lac l. Canada 123 J4
Fontur pt Iceland 44 [inset]
Foochow China see Fuzhou
Foot's Bay Canada 134 F1
Foping China 77 F1
Foraker, Mount U.S.A. 118 C3
Foraulep atoll Micronesia see Faraulep
Forbes Australia 112 D4
Forbes, Mount Canada 120 G4
Forchheim Germany 53 L5
Ford r. U.S.A. 132 C2
Ford City U.S.A. 128 D4
Førde Norway 45 D6
Forde Lake Canada 121 L2
Fordham U.K. 49 H6
Fordingbridge U.K. 49 F8
Ford Range mts Antarctica 152 J1
Fords Bridge Australia 112 B2
Fordsville U.S.A. 134 B5
Fordyce U.S.A. 131 E5
Forécariah Guinea 96 B4
Forel, Mont mt. Greenland 119 O3
Foreland hd U.K. 49 F8
Foreland Point U.K. 49 D7
Foremost Canada 126 F2
Foresight Mountain Canada 116 E4
Forest Canada 134 E2
Forest MS U.S.A. 131 F5
Forest OH U.S.A. 134 D3
Forestburg Canada 121 H4
Forest Creek r. Australia 110 C3
Forest Hill Australia 112 C5
Forest Ranch U.S.A. 128 C2
Forestville Canada 123 H4
Forestville CA U.S.A. 128 B2
Forestville MI U.S.A. 134 D2
Forfar U.K. 50 G4
Forgan U.S.A. 131 C4
Forges-les-Eaux France 52 B5
Forillon, Parc National de nat. park Canada 123 I4
Forked River U.S.A. 135 H4
Forks U.S.A. 126 B3
Fork Union U.S.A. 135 F5
Forlì Italy 58 E2
Forman U.S.A. 130 D2
Formby U.K. 48 D5
Formentera i. Spain 57 G4
Formentor, Cap de c. Spain 57 H4
Formerie France 52 B5
Former Yugoslav Republic of Macedonia country Europe see Macedonia
Formiga Brazil 145 B3
Formosa Arg. 144 E3
Formosa country Asia see Taiwan
Formosa Brazil 145 B1
Formosa, Serra hills Brazil 143 G6
Formosa Bay Kenya see Ungwana Bay
Formosa Strait China/Taiwan see Taiwan Strait
Formoso r. Bahia Brazil 145 B1
Formoso r. Tocantins Brazil 145 A1
Fornos Moz. 101 L2
Forres U.K. 50 F3
Forrest Vic. Australia 112 A7
Forrest W.A. Australia 109 E7
Forrestal Range mts Antarctica 152 A1
Forrest City U.S.A. 131 F5
Forrest Lake Canada 121 I3
Forrest Lakes salt flat Australia 109 E7
Fors Sweden 44 J5
Forsayth Australia 110 C3
Forsnäs Sweden 44 M3
Forssa Fin. 45 M6
Forster Australia 112 F4
Forsyth GA U.S.A. 133 D5
Forsyth MT U.S.A. 126 G3
Forsyth Range hills Australia 110 C4
Fort Abbas Pak. 89 I4
Fort Albany Canada 122 E3
Fortaleza Brazil 143 K4
Fort Amsterdam U.S.A. see New York
Fort Archambault Chad see Sarh
Fort Ashby U.S.A. 135 F4
Fort Assiniboine Canada 120 H4
Fort Augustus U.K. 50 E3
Fort Beaufort S. Africa 101 H7
Fort Benton U.S.A. 126 F3
Fort Brabant Canada see Tuktoyaktuk
Fort Bragg U.S.A. 128 B2
Fort Branch U.S.A. 134 B4
Fort Carillon U.S.A. see Ticonderoga
Fort Charlet Alg. see Djanet
Fort Chimo Canada see Kuujjuaq
Fort Chipewyan Canada 121 I3
Fort Collins U.S.A. 126 G4
Fort-Coulonge Canada 122 F5
Fort Crampel Cent. Afr. Rep. see Kaga Bandoro
Fort-Dauphin Madag. see Tôlañaro
Fort Davis U.S.A. 131 C6

▶Fort-de-France Martinique 137 L6
Capital of Martinique.

Fort de Kock Indon. see Bukittinggi
Fort de Polignac Alg. see Illizi
Fort Dodge U.S.A. 130 E3
Fort Duchesne U.S.A. 129 I1
Fort Edward U.S.A. 135 I2
Fortescue r. Australia 108 B5
Forte Veneza Brazil 143 H5
Fort Flatters Alg. see Bordj Omer Driss
Fort Foureau Cameroon see Kousséri
Fort Franklin Canada see Déline
Fort Gardel Alg. see Zaouatallaz
Fort Gay U.S.A. 134 D4
Fort George Canada see Chisasibi
Fort Good Hope Canada 118 F3
Fort Gouraud Mauritania see Fdérik
Forth r. U.K. 50 F4
Forth, Firth of est. U.K. 50 F4
Fort Hertz Myanmar see Putao
Fortification Range mts U.S.A. 129 F2
Fortín General Mendoza Para. 144 D2
Fortín Leonida Escobar Para. 144 D2
Fortín Madrejón Para. 144 E2
Fortín Pilcomayo Arg. 144 D2
Fortín Ravelo Bol. 142 F7
Fortín Sargento Primero Leyes Arg. 144 E2
Fortín Suárez Arana Bol. 142 F7
Fortín Teniente Juan Echauri López Para. 144 D2
Fort Jameson Zambia see Chipata
Fort Johnston Malawi see Mangochi
Fort Kent U.S.A. 132 G2
Fort Lamy Chad see Ndjamena
Fort Laperrine Alg. see Tamanrasset
Fort Laramie U.S.A. 126 G4
Fort Lauderdale U.S.A. 133 D7
Fort Liard Canada 120 F2
Fort Mackay Canada 121 I3
Fort Macleod Canada 120 H5
Fort Madison U.S.A. 130 F3
Fort Manning Malawi see Mchinji
Fort McMurray Canada 121 I3
Fort McPherson Canada 118 E3
Fort Meyers Beach U.S.A. 133 D7
Fort Morgan U.S.A. 130 C3
Fort Munro Pak. 89 H4
Fort Myers U.S.A. 133 D7
Fort Nelson Canada 120 F3
Fort Nelson r. Canada 120 F3
Fort Norman Canada see Tulita
Fort Orange U.S.A. see Albany
Fort Payne U.S.A. 133 C5
Fort Peck U.S.A. 126 G2
Fort Peck Reservoir U.S.A. 126 G3
Fort Pierce U.S.A. 133 D7
Fort Portal Uganda 98 D3
Fort Providence Canada 120 G2
Fort Randall U.S.A. see Cold Bay
Fort Resolution Canada 120 H2
Fortrose N.Z. 113 B8
Fortrose U.K. 50 E3
Fort Rosebery Zambia see Mansa
Fort Rousset Congo see Owando
Fort Rupert Canada see Waskaganish
Fort Sandeman Pak. see Zhob
Fort Saskatchewan Canada 120 H4
Fort Scott U.S.A. 130 E4
Fort Severn Canada 122 D2
Fort-Shevchenko Kazakh. 78 E2
Fort Simpson Canada 120 F2
Fort Smith Canada 121 H2
Fort Smith U.S.A. 131 E5
Fort St James Canada 120 E4
Fort St John Canada 120 F3
Fort Stockton U.S.A. 131 C6
Fort Sumner U.S.A. 127 G6
Fort Supply U.S.A. 131 D4
Fort Thomas U.S.A. 129 I5
Fort Trinquet Mauritania see Bîr Mogreïn
Fortuna U.S.A. 130 C1
Fortune Bay Canada 123 L5
Fort Valley U.S.A. 133 D5
Fort Vermilion Canada 120 G3
Fort Victoria Zimbabwe see Masvingo
Fort Ware Canada see Ware
Fort Wayne U.S.A. 134 C3
Fort William U.K. 50 D4
Fort Worth U.S.A. 131 D5
Fort Yates U.S.A. 130 C2
Fort Yukon U.S.A. 118 D3
Forum Iulii France see Fréjus
Forūr, Jazīreh-ye i. Iran 88 D5
Forvik Norway 44 H4
Foshan China 77 G4
Fo Shek Chau Hong Kong China see Basalt Island
Fossano Italy 58 B2
Fossil U.S.A. 126 C3
Fossil Downs Australia 108 D4
Foster Australia 112 C7
Foster U.S.A. 134 C4
Foster, Mount Canada/U.S.A. 120 C3
Foster Lakes Canada 121 J3
Fostoria U.S.A. 134 D3
Fotadrevo Madag. 99 E6
Fotherby U.K. 48 G5
Fotokol Cameroon 97 E3
Fotuna i. Vanuatu see Futuna
Fougères France 56 D2
Foula i. U.K. 50 [inset]
Foul Island Myanmar 70 A3
Foulness Point U.K. 49 H7
Foul Point Sri Lanka 84 D4
Foumban Cameroon 96 E4
Foundation Ice Stream glacier Antarctica 152 L1
Fount U.S.A. 134 D5
Fountains Abbey (NT) tourist site U.K. 48 F4
Fourches, Mont des hill France 56 G2
Four Corners U.S.A. 128 E4
Fouriesburg S. Africa 101 I5
Fourmies France 52 E4
Fournier, Lac l. Canada 123 I4
Fournoi i. Greece 59 L6
Fourpeaked Mountain U.S.A. 118 C4
Fouta Djallon reg. Guinea 96 B3
Foveaux Strait N.Z. 113 A8
Fowey r. U.K. 49 C8
Fowler CO U.S.A. 127 G5
Fowler IN U.S.A. 134 B3
Fowler Ice Rise Antarctica 152 L1
Fowlers Bay Australia 106 D5
Fowlers Bay b. Australia 109 F8
Fowlerville U.S.A. 134 C2
Fox r. B.C. Canada 120 E3
Fox r. Man. Canada 121 M3
Fox r. U.S.A. 130 F3
Fox Creek Canada 120 G4
Fox Creek U.S.A. 134 C5
Foxdale Isle of Man 48 C4
Foxe Basin g. Canada 119 K3
Foxe Channel Canada 119 J3
Foxe Peninsula Canada 119 K3
Fox Glacier N.Z. 113 C6
Fox Islands U.S.A. 118 B4
Fox Lake Canada 120 H3
Fox Mountain Canada 120 C2
Fox Valley Canada 121 I5
Foyers U.K. 50 E3
Foyle r. Rep. of Ireland/U.K. 51 E3
Foyle, Lough b. Rep. of Ireland/U.K. 51 E2
Foynes Rep. of Ireland 51 C5
Foz de Areia, Represa de resr Brazil 145 A4
Foz do Cunene Angola 99 B5
Foz do Iguaçu Brazil 144 F3
Fraga Spain 57 G3
Frakes, Mount Antarctica 152 K1
Framingham U.S.A. 135 J2
Framnes Mountains Antarctica 152 E2
Franca Brazil 145 B3
Français, Récif des reef New Caledonia 107 G3
Francavilla Fontana Italy 58 G4

▶France country Europe 56 F3
3rd largest and 4th most populous country in Europe.
Europe 5, 38–39

Frances Australia 111 C8
Frances Lake Canada 120 D2
Frances Lake l. Canada 120 D2
Franceville Gabon 98 B4
Francis Canada 121 K5
Francis atoll Kiribati see Beru
Francis, Lake U.S.A. 135 J1
Francisco de Orellana Ecuador see Puerto Francisco de Orellana
Francisco I. Madero Coahuila Mex. 131 C7
Francisco I. Madero Durango Mex. 131 B7
Francisco Zarco Mex. 128 E5
Francistown Botswana 99 C6
Francois Canada 123 K5
François Lake Canada 120 E4
Francois Peron National Park Australia 109 A6
Francs Peak U.S.A. 126 F4
Franeker Neth. 52 F1
Frankenberg Germany 53 N4
Frankenberg (Eder) Germany 53 I3
Frankenhöhe hills Germany 47 M6
Frankenmuth U.S.A. 134 D2
Frankenthal (Pfalz) Germany 53 I5
Frankenwald mts Germany 53 L4
Frankford Canada 135 G1
Frankfort IN U.S.A. 134 B3

▶Frankfort KY U.S.A. 134 C4
State capital of Kentucky.

Frankfort MI U.S.A. 134 B1
Frankfort OH U.S.A. 134 D4
Frankfurt Germany see Frankfurt am Main
Frankfurt am Main Germany 53 I4
Frankfurt an der Oder Germany 47 O4
Frank Hann National Park Australia 109 C8
Frankin Lake U.S.A. 129 F1
Fränkische Alb hills Germany 53 K6
Fränkische Schweiz reg. Germany 53 L5
Frankland, Cape Australia 111 [inset]
Franklin AZ U.S.A. 129 I5
Franklin GA U.S.A. 133 C5
Franklin IN U.S.A. 134 B4
Franklin KY U.S.A. 134 B5
Franklin LA U.S.A. 131 F6
Franklin MA U.S.A. 135 J2
Franklin NC U.S.A. 133 D5
Franklin NE U.S.A. 130 D3
Franklin NH U.S.A. 135 J2
Franklin PA U.S.A. 134 F3
Franklin TN U.S.A. 132 C5
Franklin TX U.S.A. 131 D6
Franklin VA U.S.A. 135 G5
Franklin WV U.S.A. 134 F4
Franklin Bay Canada 153 A2
Franklin D. Roosevelt Lake resr U.S.A. 126 D2
Franklin Furnace U.S.A. 134 D4
Franklin-Gordon National Park Australia 111 [inset]
Franklin Island Antarctica 152 H1
Franklin Mountains Canada 120 F2
Franklin Strait Canada 119 I2
Franklinton U.S.A. 131 F6
Franklinville U.S.A. 135 F2
Frankston Australia 112 B7
Fränsta Sweden 44 J5
Frantsa-Iosifa, Zemlya is Rus. Fed. 64 G2
Franz Canada 122 D4
Franz Josef Glacier N.Z. 113 C6
Frasca, Capo della c. Sardinia Italy 58 C5
Frascati Italy 58 E4
Fraser r. Australia 108 C4
Fraser r. B.C. Canada 120 F5
Fraser r. Nfld. and Lab. Canada 123 J2
Fraser, Mount hill Australia 109 B6
Fraserburg S. Africa 100 E6
Fraserburgh U.K. 50 G3
Fraserdale Canada 122 E4
Fraser Island Australia 110 F5
Fraser Island National Park Australia 110 F5
Fraser Lake Canada 120 E4
Fraser National Park Australia 112 B6
Fraser Plateau Canada 120 E4
Fraser Range hills Australia 109 C8
Frauenfeld Switz. 56 I3
Fray Bentos Uruguay 144 E4
Frazeysburg U.S.A. 134 D3
Frechen Germany 52 G4
Freckleton U.K. 48 E5
Frederic U.S.A. 134 C1
Frederica U.S.A. 135 H4
Fredericia Denmark 45 F9
Frederick MD U.S.A. 135 G4
Frederick OK U.S.A. 131 D5
Frederick Reef Australia 110 F4
Fredericksburg TX U.S.A. 131 D6
Fredericksburg VA U.S.A. 135 G4
Fredericktown U.S.A. 130 F4

▶Fredericton Canada 123 I5
Provincial capital of New Brunswick.

Frederikshåb Greenland see Paamiut
Frederikshavn Denmark 45 G8
Frederiksværk Denmark 45 H9
Fredonia AZ U.S.A. 129 G3
Fredonia KS U.S.A. 131 E4
Fredonia NY U.S.A. 134 F2
Fredonia WI U.S.A. 134 B2
Fredrika Sweden 44 K4
Fredrikshamn Fin. see Hamina
Fredrikstad Norway 45 G7
Freedonyer Peak U.S.A. 128 C1
Freehold U.S.A. 135 H3
Freeland U.S.A. 135 H3
Freeling Heights hill Australia 111 B6
Freel Peak U.S.A. 128 D2
Freels, Cape Canada 123 L4
Freeman U.S.A. 130 D3
Freeman, Lake U.S.A. 134 B3
Freeport FL U.S.A. 133 C6
Freeport IL U.S.A. 130 F3
Freeport TX U.S.A. 131 E6
Freeport City Bahamas 133 E7
Freer U.S.A. 131 D7
Freesoil U.S.A. 134 B1
Free State prov. S. Africa 101 H5

▶Freetown Sierra Leone 96 B4
Capital of Sierra Leone.

Fregenal de la Sierra Spain 57 C4
Fregon Australia 109 F6
Fréhel, Cap c. France 56 C2
Freiberg Germany 53 N4
Freiburg Switz. see Fribourg
Freiburg im Breisgau Germany 47 K6
Freisen Germany 53 H5
Freising Germany 47 M6
Freistadt Austria 47 O6
Fréjus France 56 H5
Fremantle Australia 109 A8
Fremont CA U.S.A. 128 C3
Fremont IN U.S.A. 134 C3
Fremont MI U.S.A. 134 C2
Fremont NE U.S.A. 130 D3
Fremont OH U.S.A. 134 D3
Fremont r. U.S.A. 129 H2
Fremont Junction U.S.A. 129 H2
Frenchburg U.S.A. 134 D5
French Cay i. Turks and Caicos Is 133 F8
French Congo country Africa see Congo

▶French Guiana terr. S. America 143 H3
French Overseas Department.
South America 9, 140–141

French Guinea country Africa see Guinea
French Island Australia 112 B7
French Lick U.S.A. 134 B4
Frenchman r. U.S.A. 126 G2
Frenchman Lake CA U.S.A. 128 C2
Frenchman Lake NV U.S.A. 129 F3
Frenchpark Rep. of Ireland 51 D4
French Pass N.Z. 113 D5

▶French Polynesia terr. S. Pacific Ocean 151 K7
French Overseas Territory.
Oceania 8, 104–105

French Somaliland country Africa see Djibouti

▶French Southern and Antarctic Lands terr. Indian Ocean 149 M8
French Overseas Territory.

French Sudan country Africa see Mali
French Territory of the Afars and Issas country Africa see Djibouti
Frenda Alg. 57 G6
Frentsjer Neth. see Franeker
Freren Germany 53 H2
Fresco r. Brazil 143 H5
Freshford Rep. of Ireland 51 E5
Fresnillo Mex. 136 D4
Fresno U.S.A. 128 D3
Fresno r. U.S.A. 128 C3
Fresno Reservoir U.S.A. 126 F2
Fressel, Lac l. Canada 122 G3
Freu, Cap des c. Spain 57 H4
Freudenberg Germany 53 H4
Freudenstadt Germany 47 L6
Frévent France 52 C4
Frew watercourse Australia 110 A4
Frewena Australia 110 A3
Freycinet Estuary inlet Australia 109 A6
Freycinet Peninsula Australia 111 [inset]
Freyenstein Germany 53 M1
Freyming-Merlebach France 52 G5
Fria Guinea 96 B3
Fria, Cape Namibia 99 B5
Friant U.S.A. 128 D3
Frias Arg. 144 C3
Fribourg Switz. 56 H3
Friday Harbor U.S.A. 126 C2
Friedeburg Germany 53 H1
Friedens U.S.A. 135 F3
Friedland Rus. Fed. see Pravdinsk
Friedrichshafen Germany 47 L7
Friedrichskanal canal Germany 53 L2
Friend U.S.A. 130 D3
Friendly Islands country S. Pacific Ocean see Tonga
Friendship U.S.A. 130 F3
Friesack Germany 53 M2
Friese Wad tidal flat Neth. 52 F1
Friesoythe Germany 53 H1
Frinton-on-Sea U.K. 49 I7
Frio r. U.S.A. 131 D6
Frio watercourse U.S.A. 131 C5
Frisco Mountain U.S.A. 129 G2
Frissell, Mount hill U.S.A. 135 I2
Fritzlar Germany 53 J3
Frjentsjer Neth. see Franeker
Frobisher Bay Canada see Iqaluit
Frobisher Bay b. Canada 119 L3
Frobisher Lake Canada 121 I3
Frohavet b. Norway 44 F5
Frohburg Germany 53 M3
Froissy France 52 C5
Frolovo Rus. Fed. 43 I6
Frome watercourse Australia 111 B6
Frome U.K. 49 E7
Frome r. U.K. 49 E8
Frome, Lake salt flat Australia 111 B6
Frome Downs Australia 111 B6
Fröndenberg Germany 53 H3
Frontera Coahuila Mex. 131 C7
Frontera Tabasco Mex. 136 F5
Fronteras Mex. 127 F7
Front Royal U.S.A. 135 F4
Frosinone Italy 58 E4
Frostburg U.S.A. 135 F4
Frøya i. Norway 44 F5
Fruges France 52 C4
Fruita U.S.A. 129 I2
Fruitland U.S.A. 129 H1
Fruitvale U.S.A. 129 I2
Frunze Kyrg. see Bishkek
Frusino Italy see Frosinone
Fruska Gora nat. park Serb. and Mont. 59 H2
Frýdek-Místek Czech Rep. 47 Q6
Fu'an China 77 H3
Fucheng Anhui China see Fengyang
Fucheng Shaanxi China see Fuxian
Fuchuan China 77 F3
Fuchun Jiang r. China 77 I2
Fude China 77 H3
Fuding China 77 I3
Fudul reg. Saudi Arabia 88 B6
Fuenlabrada Spain 57 E3
Fuerte r. Mex. 127 F8
Fuerte Olimpo Para. 144 E2
Fuerteventura i. Canary Is 96 B2
Fufeng China 76 E1
Fuga i. Phil. 59 G3
Fugong China 76 C3
Fugou China 77 G1
Fuhai China 80 G2
Fuḩaymī Iraq 91 F4
Fujairah U.A.E. 88 E5
Fujeira U.A.E. see Fujairah
Fuji Japan 75 E6
Fujian prov. China 77 H3
Fuji-Hakone-Izu National Park Japan 75 E6
Fujin China 74 C3
Fujinomiya Japan 75 E6
Fuji-san vol. Japan 75 E6
Fujiyoshida Japan 75 E6
Fûka Egypt see Fūkah
Fūkah Egypt 90 B5
Fukien prov. China see Fujian
Fukuchiyama Japan 75 D6
Fukue-jima i. Japan 75 C6
Fukui Japan 75 E5
Fukuoka Japan 75 C6
Fukushima Japan 75 F5
Fukuyama Japan 75 C7
Fûl, Gebel hill Egypt see Fūl, Jabal
Fūl, Jabal hill Egypt 85 A5
Fulchhari Bangl. 83 G4
Fulda Germany 53 J4
Fulda r. Germany 53 J3
Fulham U.K. 49 G7
Fuli China see Jixian
Fuliji China 77 H1
Fuling China 76 E2
Fulitun China see Jixian
Fullerton CA U.S.A. 128 E5
Fullerton NE U.S.A. 130 D3
Fullerton, Cape Canada 121 N2
Fulton IN U.S.A. 134 B3
Fulton MO U.S.A. 130 F4
Fulton MS U.S.A. 131 F5
Fulton NY U.S.A. 135 G2
Fumane Moz. 101 K3
Fumay France 52 E5
Fumin China 76 D3
Funabashi Japan 75 E6
Funafuti atoll Tuvalu 107 H2
Funan China 77 G1

▶Funchal Madeira 96 B1
Capital of Madeira.

Fundão Brazil 145 C2
Fundão Port. 57 C3
Fundi Italy see Fondi
Fundición Mex. 127 F8
Fundy, Bay of g. Canada 123 I5
Fundy National Park Canada 119 I5
Fünen i. Denmark see Fyn
Funeral Peak U.S.A. 128 E3
Fünfkirchen Hungary see Pécs
Fung Wong Shan hill Hong Kong China see Lantau Peak
Funhalouro Moz. 101 L2
Funing Jiangsu China 77 H1
Funing Yunnan China 76 E4
Funiu Shan mts China 77 F1
Funtua Nigeria 96 D3
Funzie U.K. 50 [inset]
Fuqing China 77 H3
Fürgun, Küh-e mt. Iran 88 E5
Furmanov Rus. Fed. 42 I4
Furmanovka Kazakh. see Moyynkum
Furmanovo Kazakh. see Zhalpaktal
Furnas, Represa resr Brazil 145 B3
Furneaux Group is Australia 111 [inset]
Furnes Belgium see Veurne
Furong China see Wan'an
Fürstenau Germany 53 H2
Fürstenberg Germany 53 N1
Fürstenwalde Germany 47 O4
Fürth Germany 53 K5
Furth im Wald Germany 53 M5
Furukawa Japan 75 F5
Fury and Hecla Strait Canada 119 J3
Fusan S. Korea see Pusan
Fushun China 74 A4
Fushuncheng China see Shuncheng
Fusong China 74 B4
Fu Tau Pun Chau i. Hong Kong China 77 [inset]
Futuna i. Vanuatu 107 H3
Futuna Islands Wallis and Futuna Is see Hoorn, Îles de
Fuxian Liaoning China see Wafangdian
Fuxian Shaanxi China 73 J5
Fuxian Hu l. China 76 D3
Fuxin China 73 M4
Fuxing China see Wangmo
Fuxinzhen China see Fuxin
Fuyang Anhui China 77 G1
Fuyang Guangxi China see Fuchuan
Fuyang Zhejiang China 77 H2
Fuying Dao i. China 77 I3
Fuyu Anhui China see Susong
Fuyu Heilong. China 74 B3

Fuyu Jilin China 74 B3
Fuyu Jilin China see Songyuan
Fuyuan Heilong. China 74 D2
Fuyuan Yunnan China 76 E3
Fuyun China 80 G2
Fuzhou Fujian China 77 H3
Fuzhou Jiangxi China 77 H3
Füzuli Azer. 91 G3
Fyn i. Denmark 45 G9
Fyne, Loch inlet U.K. 50 D5

G

Gaaf Atoll Maldives see Huvadhu Atoll
Gaâfour Tunisia 58 C6
Gaalkacyo Somalia 98 E3
Gabakly Turkm. see Kabakly
Gabasumdo China see Tongde
Gabbs U.S.A. 128 E2
Gabbs Valley Range mts U.S.A. 128 D2
Gabd Pak. 89 F5
Gabela Angola 99 B5
Gaberones Botswana see Gaborone
Gabès Tunisia 54 C5
Gabès, Golfe de g. Tunisia 54 G5
Gabo Island Australia 112 D6
▶Gabon country Africa 98 B4 Africa 7, 94–95

▶Gaborone Botswana 101 G3 Capital of Botswana.

Gābrīk Iran 88 E5
Gabrovo Bulg. 59 K3
Gabú Guinea-Bissau 96 B3
Gadag India 84 B3
Gadaisu P.N.G. 110 E1
Gadchiroli India 84 D1
Gäddede Sweden 44 I4
Gadê China 76 C1
Gades Spain see Cádiz
Gadhap Pak. 89 G5
Gadhka India 89 H6
Gadhra India 82 B5
Gadra Pak. 89 H5
Gadsden U.S.A. 133 C5
Gadwal India 84 C2
Gadyach Ukr. see Hadyach
Gæi'dnuvuop'pi Norway 44 M2
Gaer U.K. 49 D7
Găeşti Romania 59 K2
Gaeta Italy 58 E4
Gaeta, Golfo di g. Italy 58 E4
Gaferut i. Micronesia 69 L5
Gaffney U.S.A. 133 D5
Gafsa Tunisia 58 C7
Gagarin Rus. Fed. 43 G5
Gagnoa Côte d'Ivoire 96 C4
Gagnon Canada 123 H4
Gago Coutinho Angola see Lumbala N'guimbo
Gagra Georgia 43 I8
Gaiab watercourse Namibia 100 D5
Gaibanda Bangl. see Gaibandha
Gaibandha Bangl. 83 G4
Gaifi, Wâdi el watercourse Egypt see Jayfi, Wādī al
Gail U.S.A. 131 C5
Gaildorf Germany 53 J6
Gaillac France 56 E5
Gaillimh Rep. of Ireland see Galway
Gaillon France 52 B5
Gaindainqoinkor China see Lhünzhub
Gainesboro U.S.A. 134 C5
Gainesville FL U.S.A. 133 D6
Gainesville GA U.S.A. 133 D5
Gainesville MO U.S.A. 131 E4
Gainesville TX U.S.A. 131 D5
Gainsborough U.K. 48 G5
Gairdner, Lake salt flat Australia 111 A6
Gairloch U.K. 50 D3
Gair Loch b. U.K. 50 D3
Gajah Hutan, Bukit hill Malaysia/Thai. 71 C6
Gajipur India see Ghazipur
Gajol India 83 G4
Gakarosa mt. S. Africa 100 F4
Gala China 83 G3
Galaasiya Uzbek. 89 G2
Gala Co l. China 83 G3
Galâla el Baharîya, Gebel el plat. Egypt see Jalālah al Baḥrīyah, Jabal
Galana r. Kenya 98 E4
Galanta Slovakia 47 P6
Galaosiyo Uzbek. see Galaasiya

▶Galapagos Islands is Ecuador 151 O6 Part of Ecuador. Most westerly point of South America.

Galapagos Rise sea feature Pacific Ocean 151 N6
Galashiels U.K. 50 G5
Galaţi Romania 59 M2
Galatina Italy 58 H4
Gala Water r. U.K. 50 G5
Galax U.S.A. 134 E5
Galaymor Turkm. see Kala-I-Mor
Galbally Rep. of Ireland 51 D5
Galdhøpiggen mt. Norway 45 F6
Galeana Chihuahua Mex. 127 G7
Galeana Nuevo León Mex. 131 C7
Galena AK U.S.A. 118 C3
Galena IL U.S.A. 130 F3
Galena MD U.S.A. 135 H4
Galena MO U.S.A. 131 E4
Galera, Punta pt Chile 144 B6
Galesburg IL U.S.A. 130 F3
Galesburg MI U.S.A. 134 C2
Galeshewe S. Africa 100 G5
Galeton U.S.A. 135 G3
Galey r. Rep. of Ireland 51 C5
Galheirão r. Brazil 145 B1
Galiano Island Canada 120 F5
Galich Rus. Fed. 42 I4
Galichskaya Vozvyshennost' hills Rus. Fed. 42 I4
Galicia aut. comm. Spain 57 C2
Galičica nat. park Macedonia 59 I4
Galilee, Lake salt flat Australia 110 D4
Galilee, Sea of l. Israel 85 B3
Galion U.S.A. 134 D3
Galiuro Mountains U.S.A. 129 H5
Galizia aut. comm. Spain see Galicia
Gallabat Sudan 86 E7
Gallatin MO U.S.A. 130 E4
Gallatin TN U.S.A. 134 B5
Galle Sri Lanka 84 D5
Gallego Rise sea feature Pacific Ocean 151 M6
Gallegos r. Arg. 144 C8
Gallia country Europe see France

▶Gallinas, Punta pt Col. 142 D1 Most northerly point of South America.

Gallipoli Italy 58 H4
Gallipoli Turkey 59 L4
Gallipolis U.S.A. 134 D4
Gällivare Sweden 44 L3
Gällö Sweden 44 I5
Gallo Island U.S.A. 135 G2
Gallo Mountains U.S.A. 129 I4
Gallup U.S.A. 129 I4
Gallyaaral Uzbek. 89 G1
Galmisdale U.K. 50 C4
Galong Australia 112 D5
Galoya Sri Lanka 84 D4
Gal Oya National Park Sri Lanka 84 D5
Galston U.K. 50 E5
Galt U.S.A. 128 C2
Galtat Zemmour W. Sahara 96 B2
Galtee Mountains hills Rep. of Ireland 51 D5
Galtymore hill Rep. of Ireland 46 C4
Galūgāh, Kūh-e mts Iran 88 D4
Galveston IN U.S.A. 134 B3
Galveston TX U.S.A. 131 E6
Galveston Bay U.S.A. 131 E6
Galwa Nepal 83 E3
Galway Rep. of Ireland 51 C4
Galway Bay Rep. of Ireland 51 C4
Gâm r. Vietnam 70 D2
Gamalakhe S. Africa 101 J6
Gamba China 83 G3
Gamba Gabon 98 A4
Gambēla Eth. 98 D3
Gambēla National Park Eth. 98 D3
Gambell U.S.A. 118 A3
Gambella Eth. see Gambēla
▶Gambia, The country Africa 96 B3 Africa 7, 94–95
Gambier, Îles is Fr. Polynesia 147 L7
Gambier Islands Australia 111 B7
Gambier Islands Fr. Polynesia see Gambier, Îles
Gambo Canada 123 L4
Gamboma Congo 98 B4
Gamboola Australia 110 C3
Gamboula Cent. Afr. Rep. 98 B3
Gamda China see Zamtang
Gamlakarleby Fin. see Kokkola
Gamleby Sweden 45 J8
Gammelstaden Sweden 44 M4
Gammon Ranges National Park Australia 111 B6
Gamova, Mys pt Rus. Fed. 74 C4
Gamshadzai Kūh mts Iran 89 F4
Gamtog China 76 C2
Gamud mt. Eth. 98 D3
Gana China 76 D1
Ganado U.S.A. 129 I4
Gananoque Canada 135 G1
Ganāveh Iran 88 C4
Gäncä Azer. 91 G2
Gancheng China 77 F5
Ganda Angola 99 B5
Gandaingoin China 83 G3
Gandajika Dem. Rep. Congo 99 C4
Gandak Dam Nepal 83 E4
Gandari Mountain Pak. 89 H4
Gandava Pak. 89 G4
Gander Canada 123 L4
Ganderkesee Germany 53 I1
Gandesa Spain 57 G3
Gandhidham India 82 B5
Gandhinagar India 82 C5
Gandhi Sagar resr India 82 C4
Gandía Spain 57 F4
Gandzha Azer. see Gäncä
Ganga r. Bangl./India 83 G5 see Ganges
Ganga Cone sea feature Indian Ocean see Ganges Cone
Gangán Arg. 144 C6
Ganganagar India 82 C3
Gangapur India 82 D4
Ganga Sera India 82 B4
Gangaw Myanmar 70 A2
Gangawati India 84 C3
Gangaw Range mts Myanmar 70 B2
Gangca China 80 J4
Gangdisê Shan mts China 83 E3
Ganges r. Bangl./India 83 G5 also known as Ganga
Ganges France 56 F5
Ganges, Mouths of the Bangl./India 83 G5
Ganges Cone sea feature Indian Ocean 149 N4
Gangouyi China 72 J5
Gangra Turkey see Çankırı
Gangtok India 83 G4
Gangu China 76 E1
Gani Indon. 69 H7
Gan Jiang r. China 77 H2
Ganjig China 73 M4
Ganluo China 76 D2
Ganmain Australia 112 C5
Gannan China 74 A3
Gannat France 56 F3
Gannett Peak U.S.A. 126 F4
Ganq China 80 H4
Ganshui China 76 E2
Gansu prov. China 76 D1
Gantheaume Point Australia 108 C4
Gantsevichi Belarus see Hantsavichy
Ganxian China 77 G3
Ganye Nigeria 96 E4
Ganyu China 77 H1
Ganyushkino Kazakh. 41 P6
Ganzhou China 77 G3
Ganzi Sudan 97 G4
Gao Mali 96 C3
Gaocheng China see Litang
Gaocun China see Mayang
Gaohe China see Huaining
Gaohebu China see Huaining
Gaoleshan China see Xianfeng
Gaoliangjian China see Hongze
Gaomutang China 77 F3
Gaoping China 77 G1
Gaotai China 80 I4
Gaoting China see Daishan
Gaotingzhen China see Daishan
Gaoua Burkina 96 C3
Gaoual Guinea 96 B3
Gaoxiong Taiwan see Kaohsiung
Gaoyao China see Zhaoqing
Gaoyou China 77 H1
Gaoyou Hu l. China 77 H1
Gap France 56 H4
Gap Carbon hd Alg. 57 F6
Gapuwiyak Australia 110 A2
Gaqoi China 83 E3
Gar China 82 E2
Gar Pak. 89 F5
Gar' r. Rus. Fed. 74 C1
Gara, Lough l. Rep. of Ireland 51 D4
Garabekevyul Turkm. 89 G2
Garabekewül Turkm. see Garabekevyul
Garabil Belentligi hills Turkm. see Karabil', Vozvyshennost'
Garabogaz Aylagy b. Turkm. see Kara-Bogaz-Gol, Zaliv
Garabogazköl Aylagy b. Turkm. see Kara-Bogaz-Gol, Zaliv
Garabogazköl Bogazy sea chan. Turkm. see Kara-Bogaz-Gol, Proliv
Garāgheh Iran 89 F4
Garagum des. Turkm. see Kara Kumy
Garagum des. Turkm. see Karakum Desert
Garagum Kanaly canal Turkm. see Karakumskiy Kanal
Garah Australia 112 D2
Garalo Mali 96 C3
Garamätnyyaz Turkm. see Karamet-Niyaz
Garamba r. Dem. Rep. Congo 98 C3
Garanhuns Brazil 143 K5
Ga-Rankuwa S. Africa 101 H3
Garapuava Brazil 145 B2
Gárasavvon Sweden see Karesuando
Garautha India 82 D4
Garba China see Jiulong
Garbahaarey Somalia 98 E3
Garba Tula Kenya 98 D3
Garberville U.S.A. 128 B1
Garbo China see Lhozhag
Garbsen Germany 53 J2
Garça Brazil 145 A3
Garco China 83 G2
Garda, Lago di Italy see Garda, Lake
Garda, Lake Italy 58 D2
Garde, Cap de c. Alg. 58 B6
Gardelegen Germany 53 L2
Garden City U.S.A. 130 C4
Garden Hill Canada 121 M4
Garden Mountain U.S.A. 134 E5
Gardeyz Afgh. see Gardēz
Gardēz Afgh. 89 H3
Gardinas Belarus see Hrodna
Gardiner U.S.A. 135 K1
Gardiner, Mount Australia 108 F5
Gardiner Range hills Australia 108 E4
Gardiners Island U.S.A. 135 I3
Gardīz Afgh. see Gardēz
Gardner atoll Micronesia see Faraulep
Gardner U.S.A. 135 J2
Gardner Inlet Antarctica 152 L1
Gardner Island atoll Kiribati see Nikumaroro
Gardner Pinnacles is U.S.A. 150 I4
Gáregasnjárga Fin. see Karigasniemi
Garelochhead U.K. 50 E4
Garet El Djenoun mt. Alg. 96 D2
Gargano, Parco Nazionale del nat. park Italy 58 F4
Gargantua, Cape Canada 122 D5
Gargunsa China see Gar
Gargždai Lith. 45 L9
Garhchiroli India see Gadchiroli
Garhi Madhya Pradesh India 84 C1
Garhi Rajasthan India 82 C5
Garhi Ikhtiar Khan Pak. 89 H4
Garhi Khairo Pak. 89 G4
Garhwa India 83 E4
Gari Rus. Fed. 41 S4
Gariau Indon. 69 I7
Garibaldi, Mount Canada 120 F5
Gariep Dam resr S. Africa 101 G6
Garies S. Africa 100 C6
Garigliano r. Italy 58 E4
Garissa Kenya 98 D4
Garkalne Latvia 45 N8
Garkung Caka l. China 83 F2
Garland U.S.A. 131 D5
Garm Tajik. see Gharm
Garm Āb Iran 89 E3
Garmab Iran 88 E3
Garmī Iran 88 C2
Garmsar Iran 88 D3
Garmsel reg. Afgh. 89 F4
Garner IA U.S.A. 130 E3
Garner KY U.S.A. 134 D5
Garnett U.S.A. 130 E4
Garnpung Lake imp. l. Australia 112 A4
Garo Hills India 83 G4
Garonne r. France 55 D4
Garoowe Somalia 98 E3
Garopaba Brazil 145 A5
Garoua Cameroon 96 E4
Garoua Boulai Cameroon 97 E4
Garqêntang China see Sog
Garré Arg. 144 D5
Garrett U.S.A. 134 C3
Garrison U.S.A. 130 E2
Garruk Pak. 89 G4
Garry r. U.K. 50 E3
Garrychyrla Turkm. see imeni Kerbabayeva
Garry Lake Canada 121 K1
Garrynahine U.K. 50 C2
Garsen Kenya 98 E4
Garshy Turkm. see Karshi
Garsila Sudan 97 F3
Gartar China see Qianning
Garth U.K. 49 D6
Gartog China see Markam
Gartok China see Garyarsa
Gartow Germany 53 L1
Garub Namibia 100 C4
Garvagh U.K. 51 F3
Garve U.K. 50 E3
Garwa India see Garhwa
Garwha India see Garhwa
Gar Xincun China 82 E2
Gary IN U.S.A. 134 B3
Gary WV U.S.A. 134 E5
Garyarsa China 82 E3
Garyi China 76 C2
Garyū-zan mt. Japan 75 D6
Garza García Mex. 131 C7
Garzê China 76 C2
Gasan-Kuli Turkm. see Esenguly
Gasan-Kuliyskiy Zapovednik nature res. Turkm. 88 D2
Gas City U.S.A. 134 C3
Gascogne reg. France see Gascony
Gascogne, Golfe de g. France see Gascony, Gulf of
Gascony reg. France 56 D5
Gascony, Gulf of France 56 C5
Gascoyne r. Australia 109 A6
Gascoyne Junction Australia 109 A6
Gasherbrum I mt. China/Jammu and Kashmir 82 D2
Gashua Nigeria 96 E3
Gask Iran 89 E3
Gaspar Cuba 133 E8
Gaspar, Selat sea chan. Indon. 68 D7
Gaspé Canada 123 I4
Gaspé, Cap c. Canada 123 I4
Gaspé, Péninsule de pen. Canada 123 I4
Gassan vol. Japan 75 F5
Gassaway U.S.A. 134 E4
Gasselte Neth. 52 G2
Gasteiz Spain see Vitoria-Gasteiz
Gastello Rus. Fed. 74 F2
Gaston U.S.A. 135 G5
Gaston, Lake U.S.A. 135 G5
Gastonia U.S.A. 133 D5
Gata, Cabo de c. Spain 57 E5
Gata, Cape Cyprus 85 A2
Gata, Sierra de mts Spain 57 C3
Gataga r. Canada 120 E3
Gatas, Akra c. Cyprus see Gata, Cape
Gatchina Rus. Fed. 45 Q7
Gate City U.S.A. 134 D5
Gatehouse of Fleet U.K. 50 E6
Gatentiri Indon. 69 K8
Gateshead U.K. 48 F4
Gates of the Arctic National Park and Preserve U.S.A. 118 C3
Gatesville U.S.A. 131 D6
Gateway U.S.A. 129 I2
Gatineau Canada 135 H1
Gatineau r. Canada 122 G5
Gatong China see Jomda
Gatooma Zimbabwe see Kadoma
Gatton Australia 112 F1
Gatvand Iran 88 C3
Gatyana S. Africa see Willowvale
Gau i. Fiji 107 H3
Gauer Lake Canada 121 L3
Gauhati India see Guwahati
Gaujas nacionālais parks nat. park Latvia 45 N8
Gaul country Europe see France
Gaula r. Norway 44 G5
Gaume reg. Belgium 52 F5
Gaurama Brazil 145 A4
Gauribidanur India 84 C3
Gauteng prov. S. Africa 101 I4
Gavarr Armenia see Kamo
Gāvbandī Iran 88 D5
Gāvbūs, Kūh-e mts Iran 88 D5

▶Gavdos i. Greece 59 K7 Most southerly point of Europe.

Gavião r. Brazil 145 C1
Gavileh Iran 88 B3
Gav Khūnī Iran 88 D3
Gävle Sweden 45 J6
Gavrilovka Vtoraya Rus. Fed. 43 I5
Gavrilov-Yam Rus. Fed. 42 H4
Gawachab Namibia 100 C4
Gawai Myanmar 76 C3
Gawan India 83 F4
Gawilgarh Hills India 82 D5
Gawler Australia 111 B7
Gawler Ranges hills Australia 111 A7
Gaxun Nur salt l. China 80 J3
Gaya India 83 F4
Gaya Niger 96 D3
Gaya He r. China 74 C4
Gayéri Burkina 96 D3
Gaylord U.S.A. 134 C1
Gayndah Australia 111 E5
Gayny Rus. Fed. 42 L3
Gaysin Ukr. see Haysyn
Gayutino Rus. Fed. 42 H4
Gaz Iran 88 C3

▶Gaza terr. Asia 85 B4 Semi-autonomous region. Asia 6

▶Gaza Gaza 85 B4 Capital of Gaza.

Gaza prov. Moz. 101 K2
Gazan Pak. 89 G4
Gazandzhyk Turkm. 88 D2
Gazanjyk Turkm. see Gazandzhyk
Gaza Strip terr. Asia see Gaza
Gaziantep Turkey 90 E3
Gaziantep prov. Turkey 85 C1
Gazibenli Turkey see Yahyalı
Gazīk Iran 89 F3
Gazimağusa Cyprus see Famagusta
Gazimurskiy Khrebet mts Rus. Fed. 73 L2
Gazimurskiy Zavod Rus. Fed. 73 L2
Gazipaşa Turkey 85 A1
Gazli Uzbek. 89 F1
Gaz Māhū Iran 88 E5
Gbarnga Liberia 96 C4
Gboko Nigeria 96 D4
Gcuwa S. Africa see Butterworth
Gdańsk Poland 47 Q3
Gdańsk, Gulf of Poland/Rus. Fed. 47 Q3
Gdańska, Zatoka g. Poland/Rus. Fed. see Gdańsk, Gulf of
Gdingen Poland see Gdynia
Gdov Rus. Fed. 45 O7
Gdynia Poland 47 Q3
Gearhart Mountain U.S.A. 126 C4
Gearraidh na h-Aibhne U.K. see Garrynahine
Gebe i. Indon. 69 H6
Gebesee Germany 53 K3
Geçitkale Cyprus see Lefkonikon
Gedaref Sudan 86 E7
Gedern Germany 53 J4
Gedinne Belgium 52 E5
Gediz r. Turkey 59 L5
Gedney Drove End U.K. 49 H6
Gedong, Tanjong pt Sing. 71 [inset]
Gedser Denmark 45 G9
Geel Belgium 52 F3
Geelong Australia 112 B7
Geelvink Channel Australia 109 A7
Geel Vloer salt pan S. Africa 100 E5
Gees Gwardafuy c. Somalia see Gwardafuy, Gees
Geeste Germany 53 H2
Geesthacht Germany 53 K1
Ge Hu l. China 77 H2
Geidam Nigeria 96 E3
Geiersberg hill Germany 53 J5
Geikie r. Canada 121 K3
Geilenkirchen Germany 52 G4
Geilo Norway 45 F6
Geiranger Norway 44 E5
Geislingen an der Steige Germany 53 J6
Geisûm, Gezâ'ir is Egypt see Qaysūm, Juzur
Geita Tanz. 98 D4
Geithain Germany 53 M3
Gejiu China 76 D4
Gekdepe Turkm. 88 E2
Gela Sicily Italy 58 F6
Gēladaindong mt. China 83 G2
Geladī Eth. 98 E3
Gelang, Tanjung pt Malaysia 71 C7
Geldern Germany 52 G3
Gelendzhik Rus. Fed. 90 E1
Gelephu Bhutan 83 G4
Gelibolu Turkey see Gallipoli
Gelidonya Burnu pt Turkey see Yardımcı Burnu
Gelincik Dağı mt. Turkey 59 N5
Gelmord Iran 88 E3
Gelnhausen Germany 53 J4
Gelsenkirchen Germany 52 H3
Gemas Malaysia 71 C7
Gemena Dem. Rep. Congo 98 B3
Geminokağı Cyprus see Karavostasi
Gemlik Turkey 59 M4
Gemona del Friuli Italy 58 E1
Gemsa Egypt see Jamsah
Gemsbok National Park Botswana 100 E3
Gemsbokplein well S. Africa 100 E4
Genalē Wenz r. Eth. 98 E3
Genappe Belgium 52 E4
General Acha Arg. 144 D5
General Alvear Arg. 144 C5
General Belgrano II research station Antarctica see Belgrano II
General Bernardo O'Higgins research station Antarctica 152 A2
General Bravo Mex. 131 D7

▶General Carrera, Lago l. Arg./Chile 144 B7 Deepest lake in South America.

General Conesa Arg. 144 D6
General Freire Angola see Muxaluando
General Juan Madariaga Arg. 144 E5
General La Madrid Arg. 144 D5
General Machado Angola see Camacupa
General Pico Arg. 144 D5
General Pinedo Arg. 144 D3
General Roca Arg. 144 C5
General Salgado Brazil 145 A3
General San Martín research station Antarctica see San Martín
General Santos Phil. 69 H5
General Simón Bolívar Mex. 131 C7
General Trías Mex. 127 G7
General Villegas Arg. 144 D5
Genesee U.S.A. 135 G3
Geneseo U.S.A. 135 G2
Geneva S. Africa 101 H4
Geneva Switz. 56 H3
Geneva AL U.S.A. 133 C6
Geneva IL U.S.A. 134 A3
Geneva NE U.S.A. 130 D3
Geneva NY U.S.A. 135 G2
Geneva OH U.S.A. 134 E3
Geneva, Lake France/Switz. 56 H3
Genève Switz. see Geneva
Genf Switz. see Geneva
Gengda China see Gana
Gengma China 76 C4
Gengxuan China see Gengma
Genhe China 74 A2
Genichesk Ukr. see Heniches'k
Genji India 82 C5
Genk Belgium 52 F4
Gennep Neth. 52 F3
Genoa Australia 112 D6
Genoa Italy 58 C2
Genoa, Gulf of Italy 58 C2
Genova Italy see Genoa
Genova, Golfo di Italy see Genoa, Gulf of
Gent Belgium see Ghent
Genthin Germany 53 M2
Gentioux, Plateau de France 56 F4
Genua Italy see Genoa
Geographe Bay Australia 109 A8
Geographical Society Ø i. Greenland 119 P2
Geok-Tepe Turkm. see Gekdepe
Georga, Zemlya i. Rus. Fed. 64 F1
George r. Canada 123 I2
George S. Africa 100 F7
George, Lake Australia 112 D5
George, Lake FL U.S.A. 133 D6
George, Lake NY U.S.A. 135 I2
George Land i. Rus. Fed. see Georga, Zemlya
Georges Mills U.S.A. 135 I2
George Sound inlet N.Z. 113 A7
Georgetown Australia 110 C3

▶George Town Cayman Is 137 H5 Capital of the Cayman Islands.

Georgetown Gambia 96 B3

▶Georgetown Guyana 143 G2 Capital of Guyana.

George Town Malaysia 71 C6
Georgetown DE U.S.A. 135 H4
Georgetown GA U.S.A. 133 C6
Georgetown IL U.S.A. 134 B4
Georgetown KY U.S.A. 134 C4
Georgetown OH U.S.A. 134 D4
Georgetown SC U.S.A. 133 E5
Georgetown TX U.S.A. 131 D6
George VI Sound sea chan. Antarctica 152 L2
George V Land reg. Antarctica 152 G2
George West U.S.A. 131 D6
▶Georgia country Asia 91 F2 Asia 6, 62–63
Georgia state U.S.A. 133 D5
Georgia, Strait of Canada 120 E5
Georgiana U.S.A. 133 C6
Georgian Bay Canada 134 E1
Georgian Bay Islands National Park Canada 134 F1
Georgienne, Baie b. Canada see Georgian Bay
Georgina watercourse Australia 110 B5
Georgiu-Dezh Rus. Fed. see Liski
Georgiyevka Vostochnyy Kazakhstan Kazakh. 80 F2
Georgiyevka Zhambylskaya Oblast' Kazakh. see Korday
Georgiyevsk Rus. Fed. 91 F1
Georgiyevskoye Rus. Fed. 42 J4
Georg von Neumayer research station Antarctica see Neumayer
Gera Germany 53 M4
Geraardsbergen Belgium 52 D4
Geral, Serra mts Brazil 145 A4
Geral de Goiás, Serra hills Brazil 145 B1
Geraldine N.Z. 113 C7
Geral do Paraná, Serra hills Brazil 145 B1
Geraldton Australia 109 A7
Gerar watercourse Israel 85 B4
Gerber U.S.A. 128 B1
Gercüş Turkey 91 F3
Gerede Turkey 90 D2
Gereshk Afgh. 89 G4
Gerik Malaysia 71 C6
Gerlach U.S.A. 128 D1
Gerlachovský štít mt. Slovakia 47 R6
Germaine, Lac l. Canada 123 I3
Germania country Europe see Germany
Germanicea Turkey see Kahramanmaraş
Germansen Landing Canada 120 E4
German South-West Africa country Africa see Namibia
Germantown OH U.S.A. 134 C4
Germantown WI U.S.A. 134 A2

▶Germany country Europe 47 L5 2nd most populous country in Europe. Europe 5, 38–39

Germersheim Germany 53 I5
Gernsheim Germany 53 I5
Gerolstein Germany 52 G4
Gerolzhofen Germany 53 K5
Gerona Spain see Girona
Gerrit Denys is P.N.G. see Lihir Group
Gers r. France 56 E4
Gersfeld (Rhön) Germany 53 J4
Gersoppa India 84 B3
Gerstungen Germany 53 K4
Gerwisch Germany 53 L2
Géryville Alg. see El Bayadh
Gêrzê China 83 F2
Gerze Turkey 90 D2
Gescher Germany 52 H3
Gesoriacum France see Boulogne-sur-Mer
Gessie U.S.A. 134 B3
Gete r. Belgium 52 F4
Gettysburg PA U.S.A. 135 G4
Gettysburg SD U.S.A. 130 D2
Gettysburg National Military Park nat. park U.S.A. 135 G4
Getz Ice Shelf Antarctica 152 J2
Geumpang Indon. 71 B6
Geureudong, Gunung vol. Indon. 71 B6
Geurie Australia 112 D4
Gevaş Turkey 91 F3
Gevgelija Macedonia 59 J4
Gexto Spain see Algorta
Gey Iran see Nīkshahr
Geyikli Turkey 59 L5
Geysdorp S. Africa 101 G4
Geyserville U.S.A. 128 B2
Geyve Turkey 59 N4
Gezīr Iran 88 D5
Ghaap Plateau S. Africa 100 F4
Ghāb, Wādī al r. Syria 85 C2
Ghabāghib Syria 85 C3
Ghabeish Sudan 86 C7
Ghadaf, Wādī al watercourse Jordan 85 C4
Ghadamés Libya see Ghadāmis
Ghadāmis Libya 96 D1
Ghaem Shahr Iran 88 D2
Ghaghara r. India 83 F4
Ghaibi Dero Pak. 89 G5
Ghalend Iran 89 F4
Ghalkarteniz, Solonchak salt marsh Kazakh. 80 B2
Ghallaorol Uzbek. see Gallyaaral
▶Ghana country Africa 96 C4 Africa 7, 94–95
Ghanādah, Rās pt U.A.E. 88 D5

Harry S. Truman Reservoir U.S.A. 130 E4
Har Sai Shan mt. China 76 C1
Harsefeld Germany 53 J1
Harsīn Iran 88 B3
Harşit r. Turkey 90 E2
Hârşova Romania 59 L2
Harstad Norway 44 J2
Harsud India 82 D5
Harsum Germany 53 J2
Hart r. Canada 118 E3
Hart U.S.A. 134 B2
Hartbees watercourse S. Africa 100 E5
Hartberg Austria 47 O7
Harteigan mt. Norway 45 E6
Harter Fell hill U.K. 48 E4

▶Hartford CT U.S.A. 135 I3
State capital of Connecticut.

Hartford KY U.S.A. 134 B5
Hartford MI U.S.A. 134 B2
Hartford City U.S.A. 134 C3
Hartland U.K. 49 C8
Hartland U.S.A. 135 K1
Hartland Point U.K. 49 C7
Hartlepool U.K. 48 F4
Hartley U.S.A. 131 C5
Hartley Zimbabwe see Chegutu
Hartley Bay Canada 120 D4
Hartola Fin. 45 O6
Harts r. S. Africa 101 G5
Härtsfeld hills Germany 53 K6
Harts Range mts Australia 109 F5
Hartsville U.S.A. 134 B5
Hartswater S. Africa 100 G4
Hartville U.S.A. 131 E4
Hartwell U.S.A. 133 D5
Har Us Nuur l. Mongolia 80 H2
Harūz-e Bālā Iran 88 E4
Harvard, Mount U.S.A. 126 G5
Harvey Australia 109 A8
Harvey U.S.A. 130 C2
Harvey Mountain U.S.A. 128 C1
Harwich U.K. 49 I7
Haryana state India 82 D3
Harz hills Germany 47 M5
Har Zin Israel 85 B4
Ḩaşāh, Wādī al watercourse Jordan 85 B4
Ḩaşāh, Wādī al watercourse Jordan/Saudi Arabia 85 C4
Hasalbag China 89 J2
Ḩasanah, Wādī watercourse Egypt 85 A4
Hasan Dağı mts Turkey 90 D3
Hasan Guli Turkm. see Esenguly
Hasankeyf Turkey 91 F3
Hasan Kūleh Afgh. 89 F3
Hasanur India 84 C4
Hasbaïya Lebanon 85 B3
Hasbaya Lebanon see Hasbaïya
Hase r. Germany 53 H2
Haselünne Germany 53 H2
Hashak Iran 89 F5
HaSharon plain Israel 85 B3
Hashtgerd Iran 88 C3
Hashtpar Iran 88 C2
Hashtrud Iran 88 B2
Haskell U.S.A. 131 D5
Haslemere U.K. 49 G7
Hăşmaşul Mare mt. Romania 55 K1
Ḩaşş, Jabal al hills Syria 85 C1
Hassan India 84 C3
Hassayampa watercourse U.S.A. 129 G5
Haßberge hills Germany 53 K4
Hasselt Belgium 52 F4
Hasselt Neth. 52 G2
Hassi Bel Guebbour Alg. 96 D2
Hassi Messaoud Alg. 54 F5
Hässleholm Sweden 45 H8
Hastings Australia 112 B7
Hastings r. Australia 112 F3
Hastings Canada 135 G1
Hastings N.Z. 113 F4
Hastings U.K. 49 H8
Hastings MI U.S.A. 134 C2
Hastings MN U.S.A. 130 E2
Hastings NE U.S.A. 130 D3
Hata India 83 E4
Hatay Turkey see Antakya
Hatay prov. Turkey 85 C1
Hatch U.S.A. 129 G3
Hatches Creek Australia 110 A4
Hatchet Lake Canada 121 K3
Hatfield Australia 112 A4
Hatfield U.K. 48 G5
Hatgal Mongolia 80 J1
Hath India 84 D1
Hat Head National Park Australia 112 F3
Hathras India 82 D4
Ha Tiên Vietnam 71 D5
Ha Tinh Vietnam 70 D3
Hatisar Bhutan see Gelephu
Hatod India 82 C5
Hato Hud East Timor see Hatudo
Hatra Iraq 91 F4
Hattah Australia 111 C7
Hatteras, Cape U.S.A. 133 F5
Hatteras Abyssal Plain sea feature S. Atlantic Ocean 148 D4
Hattfjelldal Norway 44 H4
Hattiesburg U.S.A. 131 F6
Hattingen Germany 53 H3
Hattras Passage Myanmar 71 B4
Hatudo East Timor 108 D2
Hat Yai Thai. 71 C6
Hau Bon Vietnam see Cheo Reo
Haubstadt U.S.A. 134 B4
Haud reg. Eth. 98 E3
Hauge Norway 45 E7
Haugesund Norway 45 D7
Haukeligrend Norway 45 E7
Haukipudas Fin. 44 N4
Haukivesi l. Fin. 44 P5
Haultain r. Canada 121 J4
Hauraki Gulf N.Z. 113 E3
Haut Atlas mts Morocco 54 C5
Haute-Normandie admin. reg. France 52 B5
Haute-Volta country Africa see Burkina
Haut-Folin hill France 56 G3
Hauts Plateaux Alg. 54 D5

▶Havana Cuba 137 H4
Capital of Cuba.

Havana U.S.A. 130 F3
Havant U.K. 49 G8
Havasu, Lake U.S.A. 129 F4
Havel r. Germany 53 L2
Havelange Belgium 52 F4
Havelberg Germany 53 M2
Havelock Canada 135 G1
Havelock N.Z. 113 D5
Havelock Swaziland see Bulembu
Havelock U.S.A. 133 E5
Havelock Falls Australia 108 F3
Havelock Island India 71 A5
Havelock North N.Z. 113 F4
Haverfordwest U.K. 49 C7
Haverhill U.S.A. 135 J2
Haveri India 84 B3
Haversin Belgium 52 F4
Havixbeck Germany 53 H3
Havlíčkův Brod Czech Rep. 47 O6
Havøysund Norway 44 N1
Havran Turkey 59 L5
Havre U.S.A. 126 F2
Havre Aubert, Île du i. Canada 123 J5
Havre Rock i. Kermadec Is 107 I5
Havre-St-Pierre Canada 123 J4
Havza Turkey 90 D2
Hawaii i. HI U.S.A. 127 [inset]
Hawaiian Islands N. Pacific Ocean 150 I4
Hawaiian Ridge sea feature N. Pacific Ocean 150 I4
Hawaii Volcanoes National Park HI U.S.A. 127 [inset]
Ḩawallī Kuwait 88 C4
Hawar i. Bahrain see Ḩuwār
Hawarden U.K. 48 D5
Hawea, Lake N.Z. 113 B7
Hawera N.Z. 113 E4
Hawes U.K. 48 E4
Hawesville U.S.A. 134 B5
Hawi HI U.S.A. 127 [inset]
Hawick U.K. 50 G5
Ḩawīzah, Hawr al imp. l. Iraq 87 G5
Hawkdun Range mts N.Z. 113 B7
Hawke Bay N.Z. 113 F4
Hawkes Bay Canada 123 K4
Hawkins Peak U.S.A. 129 G3
Hawlēr Iraq see Arbīl
Hawley U.S.A. 135 H3
Hawng Luk Myanmar 70 B2
Ḩawrān, Wādī watercourse Iraq 91 F4
Ḩawshah, Jibāl al mts Saudi Arabia 88 B6
Hawston S. Africa 100 D8
Hawthorne U.S.A. 128 D2
Haxat China 74 B3
Haxby U.K. 48 F4
Hay Australia 112 B5
Hay watercourse Australia 110 B5
Hay r. Canada 120 H2
Haya China 72 I4
Hayachine-san mt. Japan 75 F5
Hayastan country Asia see Armenia
Haydān, Wādī al r. Jordan 85 B4
Haydarābad Iran 88 B2
Hayden AZ U.S.A. 129 H5
Hayden CO U.S.A. 129 J1
Hayden IN U.S.A. 134 C4
Hayes r. Man. Canada 121 M3
Hayes r. Nunavut Canada 119 I3
Hayes Halvø pen. Greenland 119 L2
Hayfield Reservoir U.S.A. 129 F5
Hayfork U.S.A. 128 B1
Hayl, Wādī al watercourse Syria 85 C3
Hayl, Wādī al watercourse Syria 85 D2
Hayle U.K. 49 B8
Haymā' Oman 87 I6
Haymana Turkey 90 D3
Haymarket U.S.A. 135 G4
Hay-on-Wye U.K. 49 D6
Hayrabolu Turkey 59 L4
Hay River Canada 118 G3
Hay River Reserve Canada 120 H2
Hays KS U.S.A. 130 D4
Hays MT U.S.A. 126 F2
Ḩays Yemen 86 F7
Haysville U.S.A. 131 D4
Haysyn Ukr. 43 F6
Ḩaytān, Jabal hill Egypt 85 A4
Hayward CA U.S.A. 128 B3
Hayward WI U.S.A. 130 F2
Haywards Heath U.K. 49 G8
Hazar Turkm. see Cheleken
Hazarajat reg. Afgh. 89 G3
Hazard U.S.A. 134 D5
Hazaribag India see Hazaribagh
Hazaribagh India 83 F5
Hazaribagh Range mts India 83 E5
Hazār Masjed, Kūh-e mts Iran 88 E2
Hazebrouck France 52 C4
Hazelton Canada 120 E4
Hazen Strait Canada 119 G2
Hazerswoude-Rijndijk Neth. 52 E2
Hazhdanahr reg. Afgh. 89 G2
Hazleton IN U.S.A. 134 B4
Hazleton PA U.S.A. 135 H3
Hazlett, Lake salt flat Australia 108 E5
Hazrat Sultan Afgh. 89 G2
H. Bouchard Arg. 144 D4
Headford Rep. of Ireland 51 C4
Headingly Australia 110 B4
Head of Bight b. Australia 109 E7
Healdsburg U.S.A. 128 B2
Healesville Australia 112 B6
Healy U.S.A. 118 D3
Heanor U.K. 49 F5

▶Heard and McDonald Islands terr. Indian Ocean 149 M9
Australian External Territory.

Heard Island Indian Ocean 149 M9
Hearne U.S.A. 131 D6
Hearne Lake Canada 121 H2
Hearrenfean Neth. see Heerenveen
Hearst Canada 122 E4
Hearst Island Antarctica 152 L2
Heart r. U.S.A. 130 C2
Heart of Neolithic Orkney tourist site U.K. 50 F1
Heathcote Australia 112 B6
Heathfield U.K. 49 H8
Heathsville U.S.A. 135 G5
Hebbardsville U.S.A. 134 B5
Hebbronville U.S.A. 131 D7
Hebei prov. China 73 L5
Hebel Australia 112 C2
Heber U.S.A. 129 H4
Heber City U.S.A. 129 H1
Heber Springs U.S.A. 131 E5
Hebi China 73 K5
Hebron Canada 123 J2
Hebron U.S.A. 130 D3
Hebron West Bank 85 B4
Hecate Strait Canada 120 D4
Hecheng Jiangxi China see Zixi
Hecheng Zhejiang China see Qingtian
Hechi China 77 F3
Hechuan Chongqing China 76 E2
Hechuan Jiangxi China see Yongxing
Hecla Island Canada 121 L5
Hede China see Sheyang
Hede Sweden 44 H5
Hedemora Sweden 45 I6
He Devil Mountain U.S.A. 126 D3
Hedi Shuiku resr China 77 F4
Heech Neth. see Heeg
Heeg Neth. 52 F2
Heek Germany 52 H2
Heer Belgium 52 E4
Heerde Neth. 52 G2
Heerenveen Neth. 52 F2
Heerhugowaard Neth. 52 E2
Heerlen Neth. 52 F4
Ḩefa Israel see Haifa
Ḩefa, Mifraz Israel see Haifa, Bay of
Hefei China 77 H2
Hefeng China 77 F2
Heflin U.S.A. 133 C5
Hegang China 74 C3
Heho Myanmar 70 B2
Heidan r. Jordan see Haydān, Wādī al
Heidberg hill Germany 53 L3
Heide Germany 47 L3
Heide Namibia 100 C2
Heidelberg Germany 53 I5
Heidelberg S. Africa 101 I4
Heidenheim an der Brenz Germany 53 K6
Heihe China 74 B2
Heilbron S. Africa 101 H4
Heilbronn Germany 53 J5
Heiligenhafen Germany 47 M3
Hei Ling Chau i. Hong Kong China 77 [inset]
Heilongjiang prov. China 74 C3
Heilong Jiang r. China 74 D2
also known as Amur (Rus. Fed.)
Heilong Jiang r. Rus. Fed. see Amur
Heilsbronn Germany 53 K5
Heilungkiang prov. China see Heilongjiang
Heinola Fin. 45 O6
Heinze Islands Myanmar 71 B4
Heirnkut Myanmar 70 A1
Heishi Beihu l. China 83 E2
Heishui China 76 D1
Heisker Islands U.K. see Monach Islands
Heist-op-den-Berg Belgium 52 E3
Heiṭān, Gebel hill Egypt see Ḩaytān, Jabal
Hejaz reg. Saudi Arabia see Hijaz
Hejiang China 76 E2
He Jiang r. China 77 F4
Hejing China 80 G3
Hekimhan Turkey 90 E3
Hekla vol. Iceland 44 [inset]
Hekou Gansu China 72 I5
Hekou Hubei China 77 G2
Hekou Jiangxi China see Yanshan
Hekou Sichuan China see Yajiang
Hekou Yunnan China 76 D4
Helagsfjället mt. Sweden 44 H5
Helam India 76 B3
Helan Shan mts China 72 J5
Helbra Germany 53 L3
Helen atoll Palau 69 I6
Helena AR U.S.A. 131 F5

▶Helena MT U.S.A. 126 E3
State capital of Montana.

Helen Reef Palau 69 I6
Helensburgh U.K. 50 E4
Helen Springs Australia 108 F4
Ḩelez Israel 85 B4
Helgoland i. Germany 47 K3
Helgoländer Bucht g. Germany 47 L3
Heligoland i. Germany see Helgoland
Heligoland Bight g. Germany see Helgoländer Bucht
Heliopolis Lebanon see Ba'albek
Helixi China see Ningguo
Hella Iceland 44 [inset]
Helland Norway 44 J2
Hellas country Europe see Greece
Helleh r. Iran 88 C4
Hellespont strait Turkey see Dardanelles
Hellevoetsluis Neth. 52 E3
Hellhole Gorge National Park Australia 110 D5
Hellín Spain 57 F4
Hellinikon tourist site Greece 86 A3
Hells Canyon gorge U.S.A. 126 D3
Hell-Ville Madag. see Andoany
Helmand r. Afgh. 89 F4
Helmantica Spain see Salamanca
Helmbrechts Germany 53 L4
Helme r. Germany 53 L3
Helmeringhausen Namibia 100 C3
Helmond Neth. 52 F3
Helmsdale U.K. 50 F2
Helmsdale r. U.K. 50 F2
Helmstedt Germany 53 L2
Helong China 74 C4
Helper U.S.A. 129 H2
Helpter Berge hills Germany 53 N1
Helsingborg Sweden 45 H8
Helsingfors Fin. see Helsinki
Helsingør Denmark 45 H8

▶Helsinki Fin. 45 N6
Capital of Finland.

Helston U.K. 49 B8
Helvécia Brazil 145 D2
Helvetic Republic country Europe see Switzerland
Ḩelwân Egypt see Ḩulwān
Hemel Hempstead U.K. 49 G7
Hemet U.S.A. 128 E5
Hemingford U.S.A. 130 C3
Hemlock Lake U.S.A. 135 G2
Hemmingen Germany 53 J2
Hemmingford Canada 135 I1
Hemmoor Germany 53 J1
Hempstead U.S.A. 131 D6
Hemsby U.K. 49 I6
Hemse Sweden 45 K8
Henan China 76 D1
Henan prov. China 77 G1
Henares r. Spain 57 E3
Henashi-zaki pt Japan 75 E4
Henbury Australia 109 F6
Hendek Turkey 59 N4
Henderson KY U.S.A. 134 B5
Henderson NC U.S.A. 132 E4
Henderson NV U.S.A. 129 F3
Henderson NY U.S.A. 135 G2
Henderson TN U.S.A. 131 F5
Henderson TX U.S.A. 131 E5
Henderson Island Pitcairn Is 151 L7
Hendersonville NC U.S.A. 133 D5
Hendersonville TN U.S.A. 134 B5
Henderville atoll Kiribati see Aranuka
Hendon U.K. 49 G7
Hendorābī i. Iran 88 D5
Hendy-Gwyn U.K. see Whitland
Hengām Iran 89 E5
Hengduan Shan mts China 76 C2
Hengelo Neth. 52 G2
Hengfeng China 77 H2
Hengnan China see Hengyang
Hengshan China 74 C3
Heng Shan mt. China 77 G3
Hengshui Hebei China 73 L5
Hengshui Jiangxi China see Chongyi
Hengxian China 77 F4
Hengyang Hunan China 77 G3
Hengyang Hunan China 77 G3
Hengzhou China see Hengxian
Heniches'k Ukr. 43 G7
Henley N.Z. 113 C7
Henley-on-Thames U.K. 49 G7
Henlopen, Cape U.S.A. 135 H4
Hennef (Sieg) Germany 53 H4
Hennenman S. Africa 101 H4
Hennepin U.S.A. 130 F3
Hennessey U.S.A. 131 D4
Hennigsdorf Berlin Germany 53 N2
Henniker U.S.A. 135 J2
Henning U.S.A. 134 B3
Henrietta U.S.A. 131 D5
Henrietta Maria, Cape Canada 122 E3
Henrieville U.S.A. 129 H3
Henrique de Carvalho Angola see Saurimo
Henry, Cape U.S.A. 135 G5
Henry Ice Rise Antarctica 152 A1
Henryk Arctowski research station Antarctica see Arctowski
Henry Kater, Cape Canada 119 L3
Henry Mountains U.S.A. 129 H2
Hensall Canada 134 E2
Henshaw, Lake U.S.A. 128 E5
Hentiesbaai Namibia 100 B2
Henty Australia 112 C5
Henzada Myanmar 70 A3
Heping Guangdong China 77 G3
Heping Guizhou China see Huishui
Heping Guizhou China see Yanhe
Hepo China see Jiexi
Heppner U.S.A. 126 D3
Heptanesus is Greece see Ionian Islands
Hepu China 77 F4
Heqing China 76 D3
Heraclea Turkey see Ereğli
Heraclea Pontica Turkey see Ereğli
Heraklion Greece see Iraklion
Herald Cays atolls Australia 110 E3
Herāt Afgh. 89 F3
Hérault r. France 56 F5
Herbertabad India 71 A5
Herbert Downs Australia 110 B4
Herbert River Falls National Park Australia 110 D3
Herbert Wash salt flat Australia 109 D6
Herborn Germany 53 I4
Herbstein Germany 53 J4
Hercules Dome ice feature Antarctica 152 K1
Herdecke Germany 53 H3
Herdorf Germany 53 H4
Hereford U.K. 49 E6
Hereford U.S.A. 131 C5
Héréhérétué atoll Fr. Polynesia 151 K7
Herent Belgium 52 E4
Herford Germany 53 I2
Heringen (Werra) Germany 53 K4
Herington U.S.A. 130 D4
Heris Iran 88 B2
Herisau Switz. 56 I3
Herkimer U.S.A. 135 H2
Herlen Gol r. China/Mongolia 73 L3
Herlen He r. China/Mongolia see Herlen Gol
Herleshausen Germany 53 K3
Herlong U.S.A. 128 C1
Herm i. Channel Is 49 E9
Hermanas Mex. 131 C7
Herma Ness hd U.K. 50 [inset]
Hermann U.S.A. 130 F4
Hermannsburg Germany 53 K2
Hermanus S. Africa 100 D8
Hermel Lebanon 85 C2
Hermes, Cape S. Africa 101 I6
Hermidale Australia 112 C3
Hermiston U.S.A. 126 D3
Hermitage MO U.S.A. 130 E4
Hermitage PA U.S.A. 134 E3
Hermitage Bay Canada 123 K5
Hermite, Islas is Chile 144 C9
Hermit Islands P.N.G. 69 L7
Hermon, Mount Lebanon/Syria 85 B3
Hermonthis Egypt see Armant
Hermopolis Magna Egypt see Al Ashmūnayn
Hermosa U.S.A. 129 J3
Hermosillo Mex. 127 F7
Hernandarias Para. 144 F3
Hernando U.S.A. 131 F5
Herndon CA U.S.A. 128 D3
Herndon PA U.S.A. 135 G3
Herndon WV U.S.A. 134 E5
Herne Germany 53 H3
Herne Bay U.K. 49 I7
Herning Denmark 45 F8
Heroica Nogales Mex. see Nogales
Heroica Puebla de Zaragoza Mex. see Puebla
Hérouville-St-Clair France 49 G9
Herowābād Iran see Khalkhāl
Herrera del Duque Spain 57 D4
Herrieden Germany 53 K5
Hershey U.S.A. 135 G3
Hertford U.K. 49 G7
Hertzogville S. Africa 101 G5
Herve Belgium 52 F4
Hervé, Lac l. Canada 123 H3
Hervey Islands Cook Is 151 J7
Herzberg Brandenburg Germany 53 M2
Herzberg Brandenburg Germany 53 N3
Herzlake Germany 53 H2
Herzliyya Israel 85 B3
Herzogenaurach Germany 53 K5
Herzsprung Germany 53 M1
Ḩesār Iran 88 C4
Ḩeşār Iran 88 E5
Hesdin France 52 C4
Hesel Germany 53 H1
Heshan China 77 F4
Heshengqiao China 77 G2
Hesperia U.S.A. 128 E4
Hesperus U.S.A. 129 I3
Hesperus Peak U.S.A. 129 I3
Hesquiat Canada 120 E5
Hess r. Canada 120 C2
Heßdorf Germany 53 K5
Hesse land Germany see Hessen
Hesselberg hill Germany 53 K5
Hessen land Germany 53 J4
Hessisch Lichtenau Germany 53 J3
Hess Mountains Canada 120 C2
Het r. Laos 70 D2
Heteren Neth. 52 F3
Hetou China 77 F4
Hettinger U.S.A. 130 C2
Hetton U.K. 48 E4
Hettstedt Germany 53 L3
Heung Kong Tsai Hong Kong China see Aberdeen
Ḩevron West Bank see Hebron
Hexham U.K. 48 E4
Hexian Anhui China 77 H2
Hexian Guangxi China see Hezhou
Heyang China 77 F1
Ḩeydarābād Iran 89 F4
Heydebreck Poland see Kędzierzyn-Koźle
Heysham U.K. 48 E4
Heyshope Dam S. Africa 101 J4
Heyuan China 77 G4
Heywood U.K. 48 E5
Heze China 77 G1
Hezhang China 76 E3
Hezheng China 76 D1
Hezhou China 77 F3
Hezuo China 76 D1
Hezuozhen China see Hezuo
Hialeah U.S.A. 133 D7
Hiawassee U.S.A. 133 D5
Hiawatha U.S.A. 130 E4
Hibbing U.S.A. 130 E2
Hibbs, Point Australia 111 [inset]
Hibernia Reef Australia 108 C3
Hīchān Iran 89 F5
Hicks Bay N.Z. 113 G3
Hicks Lake Canada 121 K2
Hicksville U.S.A. 134 C3
Hico U.S.A. 131 D5
Hidaka-sanmyaku mts Japan 74 F4
Hidalgo Mex. 131 D7
Hidalgo del Parral Mex. 131 B7
Hidrolândia Brazil 145 A2
Hierosolyma Israel/West Bank see Jerusalem
Higashi-suidō sea chan. Japan 75 C6
Higgins U.S.A. 131 C4
Higgins Bay U.S.A. 135 H2
Higgins Lake U.S.A. 134 C1
High Atlas mts Morocco see Haut Atlas
High Desert U.S.A. 126 C4
High Island i. Hong Kong China 77 [inset]
High Island U.S.A. 131 E6
High Island Reservoir Hong Kong China 77 [inset]
Highland Peak CA U.S.A. 128 D2
Highland Peak NV U.S.A. 129 F3
Highlands U.S.A. 135 I3
Highland Springs U.S.A. 135 G5
High Level Canada 120 G3
Highmore U.S.A. 130 D2
High Point U.S.A. 132 E5
High Point hill U.S.A. 135 H3
High Prairie Canada 120 G4
High River Canada 120 H5
Highrock Lake Man. Canada 121 K4
Highrock Lake Sask. Canada 121 J3
High Springs U.S.A. 133 D6
High Tatras mts Poland/Slovakia see Tatra Mountains
High Wycombe U.K. 49 G7
Higuera de Zaragoza Mex. 127 F8
Higüey Dom. Rep. 137 K5
Hiiumaa i. Estonia 45 M7
Hijānah, Buḩayrat al imp. l. Syria 85 C3
Hijaz reg. Saudi Arabia 86 E4
Ḩikmah, Ra's al pt Egypt 90 B5
Hiko U.S.A. 129 F3
Hikone Japan 75 E6
Hikurangi mt. N.Z. 113 G3
Hila Indon. 108 D1
Hilāl, Jabal hill Egypt 85 A4
Hilāl, Ra's al pt Libya 86 B3
Hilary Coast Antarctica 152 H1
Hildale U.S.A. 129 G3
Hildburghausen Germany 53 K4
Hilders Germany 53 K4
Hildesheim Germany 53 J2
Hillah Iraq 91 G4
Hill City U.S.A. 130 D4
Hillegom Neth. 52 E2
Hill End Australia 112 D4
Hillerød Denmark 45 H9
Hillgrove Australia 110 D3
Hill Island Lake Canada 121 I2
Hillman U.S.A. 134 D1
Hillsboro ND U.S.A. 130 D2
Hillsboro NM U.S.A. 127 G6
Hillsboro OH U.S.A. 134 D4
Hillsboro OR U.S.A. 126 C3
Hillsboro TX U.S.A. 131 D5
Hillsdale IN U.S.A. 134 B4
Hillsdale MI U.S.A. 134 C3
Hillside Australia 108 B5
Hillston Australia 112 B4
Hillsville U.S.A. 134 E5
Hilo HI U.S.A. 127 [inset]
Hilton Australia 110 B4
Hilton S. Africa 101 J5
Hilton U.S.A. 135 G2
Hilton Head Island U.S.A. 133 D5
Hilvan Turkey 90 E3
Hilversum Neth. 52 F2
Himachal Pradesh state India 82 D3
Himalaya mts Asia 82 D2
Himalchul mt. Nepal 83 F3
Himanka Fin. 44 M4
Ḩimār, Wādī al watercourse Syria/Turkey 85 D1
Himarë Albania 59 H4
Himatnagar India 82 C5
Himeji Japan 75 D6
Ḩimş Syria see Homs
Ḩimş, Baḩrat resr Syria see Qaţţīnah, Buḩayrat
Hinchinbrook Island Australia 110 D3
Hinckley U.K. 49 F6
Hinckley MN U.S.A. 130 E2
Hinckley UT U.S.A. 129 G2
Hinckley Reservoir U.S.A. 135 H2
Hindaun India 82 D4
Hinderwell U.K. 48 G4
Hindley U.K. 48 E5
Hindman U.S.A. 134 D5
Hindmarsh, Lake dry lake Australia 111 C8
Hindu Kush mts Afgh./Pak. 89 G3
Hindupur India 84 C3
Hines Creek Canada 120 G3
Hinesville U.S.A. 133 D6
Hinganghat India 84 C1
Hingoli India 84 C2
Hinis Turkey 91 F3
Hinnøya i. Norway 44 I2
Hinojosa del Duque Spain 57 D4
Hinsdale U.S.A. 135 I2
Hinte Germany 53 H1
Hinthada Myanmar see Henzada
Hinton Canada 120 G4
Hinton U.S.A. 134 E5
Hiort i. U.K. see St Kilda
Hippolytushoef Neth. 52 E2
Hipponium Italy see Vibo Valentia
Hippo Regius Alg. see Annaba
Hippo Zarytus Tunisia see Bizerte
Hirabit Dağ mt. Turkey 91 G3
Hirakud Dam India 83 E5
Hirakud Reservoir India 83 E5
Hirapur India 82 D4
Hiriyur India 84 C3
Hirosaki Japan 74 F4
Hiroshima Japan 75 D6
Hirschaid Germany 53 L5
Hirschberg Germany 53 L4
Hirschberg mt. Germany 47 M7
Hirschberg Poland see Jelenia Góra
Hirschenstn mt. Germany 53 M6
Hirson France 52 E5
Hîrşova Romania see Hârşova
Hirta is U.K. see St Kilda
Hirtshals Denmark 45 F8
Hisar India 82 C3
Hisar Iran 88 C2
Hisarköy Turkey see Domaniç
Hisarönü Turkey 59 O4
Ḩisb, Sha'īb watercourse Iraq 91 G5
Ḩisbān Jordan 85 B4
Hisiu P.N.G. 69 L8
Hisor Tajik. 89 H2
Hisor Tizmasi mts Tajik./Uzbek. see Gissar Range
Hispalis Spain see Seville
Hispania country Europe see Spain

▶Hispaniola i. Caribbean Sea 137 J4
Consists of the Dominican Republic and Haiti.

Hispur Glacier Jammu and Kashmir 82 C1
Hissar India see Hisar
Hisua India 83 F4
Ḩisyah Syria 85 C2
Hīt Iraq 91 F4
Hitachi Japan 75 F5
Hitachinaka Japan 75 F5
Hitra i. Norway 44 F5
Hitzacker Germany 53 L1
Hiva Oa i. Fr. Polynesia 151 K6
Hixon Canada 120 F4
Hixson Cay reef Australia 110 F4
Hiyon watercourse Israel 85 B4
Hizan Turkey 91 F3
Hjälmaren l. Sweden 45 I7
Hjerkinn Norway 44 F5
Hjo Sweden 45 I7
Hjørring Denmark 45 G8
Hkakabo Razi mt. China/Myanmar 76 C2
Hlaingdet Myanmar 70 B2
Hlako Kangri mt. China see Lhagoi Kangri
Hlane Royal National Park Swaziland 101 J4
Hlatikulu Swaziland 101 J4
Hlegu Myanmar 70 B3
Hlohlowane S. Africa 101 H5
Hlotse Lesotho 101 I5
Hluhluwe-Umfolozi Park nature res. S. Africa 101 J5
Hlukhiv Ukr. 43 G6
Hlung-Tan Myanmar 70 B2
Hlusha Belarus 43 F5
Hlybokaye Belarus 45 O9
Ho Ghana 96 D4

Hòa Binh Vietnam 70 D2
Hoachanas Namibia 100 D2
Hoagland U.S.A. 134 C3
Hoang Liên Son mts Vietnam 70 C2
Hoang Sa is S. China Sea see Paracel Islands
▶Hobart Australia 111 [inset]
State capital of Tasmania.
Hobart U.S.A. 131 D5
Hobbs U.S.A. 131 C5
Hobbs Coast Antarctica 152 J1
Hobe Sound U.S.A. 133 D7
Hobiganj Bangl. see Habiganj
Hobro Denmark 45 F8
Hobyo Somalia 98 E3
Hoceima, Baie d'Al b. Morocco 57 E6
Höchberg Germany 53 J5
Hochfeiler mt. Austria/Italy see Gran Pilastro
Hochfeld Namibia 99 B6
Hochharz nat. park Germany 53 K3
Hô Chi Minh Vietnam see Ho Chi Minh City
Ho Chi Minh City Vietnam 71 D5
Hochschwab mt. Austria 47 O7
Hochschwab mts Austria 47 O7
Hockenheim Germany 53 I5
Ḥôḍ reg. Mauritania 96 C3
Hoddesdon U.K. 49 G7
Hodeidah Yemen 86 F7
Hodgenville U.S.A. 134 C5
Hodgson Downs Australia 108 F3
Hódmezővásárhely Hungary 59 I1
Hodna, Chott el salt l. Alg. 57 I6
Hodo-dan pt N. Korea 75 B5
Hoek van Holland Neth. see Hook of Holland
Hoensbroek Neth. 52 F4
Hoeryŏng N. Korea 74 C4
Hof Germany 53 L4
Hoffman Mountain U.S.A. 135 I2
Hofheim in Unterfranken Germany 53 K4
Hofmeyr S. Africa 101 G6
Höfn Iceland 44 [inset]
Hofors Sweden 45 J6
Hofsjökull ice cap Iceland 44 [inset]
Hofsós Iceland 44 [inset]
Hōfu Japan 75 C6
Hofūf Saudi Arabia see Al Hufūf
Höganäs Sweden 45 H8
Hogan Group is Australia 112 C7
Hogansburg U.S.A. 135 H1
Hogback Mountain U.S.A. 130 C3
Hoge Vaart canal Neth. 52 F2
Hogg, Mount Canada 120 C2
Hoggar plat. Alg. 96 D2
Hog Island U.S.A. 135 H5
Högsby Sweden 45 J8
Hohenloher Ebene plain Germany 53 J5
Hohenmölsen Germany 53 M3
Hohennauen Germany 53 M2
Hohensalza Poland see Inowrocław
Hohenwald U.S.A. 132 C5
Hohenwartetalsperre resr Germany 53 L4
Hoher Dachstein mt. Austria 47 N7
Hohe Rhön mts Germany 53 J4
Hohe Tauern mts Austria 47 N7
Hohe Venn moorland Belgium 52 G4
Hohhot China 73 K4
Hohneck mt. France 56 H2
Hoh Sai Hu l. China 83 H2
Hoh Xil Hu salt l. China 83 G2
Hoh Xil Shan mts China 83 G2
Hôi An Vietnam 70 E4
Hoima Uganda 98 D3
Hôi Xuân Vietnam 70 D2
Hojagala Turkm. see Khodzha-Kala
Hojai India 83 H4
Hojambaz Turkm. see Khodzhambaz
Højryggen mts Greenland 119 M2
Hokitika N.Z. 113 C6
Hokkaidō i. Japan 74 F4
Hokksund Norway 45 F7
Hoktemberyan Armenia 91 G2
Hol Norway 45 F6
Holbæk Denmark 45 G9
Holbeach U.K. 49 H6
Holbrook Australia 112 C5
Holbrook U.S.A. 129 H4
Holden U.S.A. 129 G2
Holdenville U.S.A. 131 D5
Holdrege U.S.A. 130 D3
Holgate U.S.A. 134 C3
Holguín Cuba 137 I4
Höljes Sweden 45 H6
Holland country Europe see Netherlands
Holland MI U.S.A. 134 B2
Holland NY U.S.A. 135 F2
Hollandia Indon. see Jayapura
Hollick-Kenyon Peninsula Antarctica 152 L2
Hollick-Kenyon Plateau Antarctica 152 K1
Hollidaysburg U.S.A. 135 F3
Hollis AK U.S.A. 120 C4
Hollis OK U.S.A. 131 D5
Hollister U.S.A. 128 C3
Holly U.S.A. 134 D2
Hollyhill U.S.A. 134 C5
Holly Springs U.S.A. 131 F5
Hollywood U.S.A. 133 D7
Holm Norway 44 H4
Holman Canada 118 G2
Holmes Reef Australia 110 D3
Holmestrand Norway 45 G7
Holmgard Rus. Fed. see Velikiy Novgorod
Holm Ø i. Greenland see Kiatassuaq
Holmön i. Sweden 44 L5
Holmsund Sweden 44 L5
Ḥolon Israel 85 B3
Holoog Namibia 100 C4
Holothuria Banks reef Australia 108 D3
Holroyd r. Australia 110 C2
Holstebro Denmark 45 F8
Holstein U.S.A. 130 E3
Holsteinsborg Greenland see Sisimiut
Holston r. U.S.A. 132 D4
Holsworthy U.K. 49 C8
Holt U.K. 49 I6
Holt U.S.A. 134 C2
Holton U.S.A. 134 B2
Holwerd Neth. 52 F1
Holwert Neth. see Holwerd
Holycross Rep. of Ireland 51 E5
Holy Cross U.S.A. 118 C3
Holy Cross, Mount of the U.S.A. 126 G5
Holyhead U.K. 48 C5
Holyhead Bay U.K. 48 C5
Holy Island England U.K. 48 F3
Holy Island Wales U.K. 48 C5
Holyoke U.S.A. 130 C3
Holy See Europe see Vatican City
Holywell U.K. 48 D5
Holzhausen Germany 53 M3
Holzkirchen Germany 47 M7
Holzminden Germany 53 J3
Homand Iran 89 E3
Homāyūnshahr Iran see Khomeynīshahr
Homberg (Efze) Germany 53 J3
Hombori Mali 96 C3
Homburg Germany 53 H5
Home Bay Canada 119 L3
Homécourt France 52 F5
Homer GA U.S.A. 133 D5
Homer LA U.S.A. 131 E5
Homer MI U.S.A. 134 C2
Homer NY U.S.A. 135 G2
Homerville U.S.A. 133 D6
Homestead Australia 110 D4
Homnabad India 84 C2
Homoine Moz. 101 L2
Homs Libya see Al Khums
Homs Syria 85 C2
Homyel' Belarus 43 F5
Honan prov. China see Henan
Honavar India 84 B3
Honaz Turkey 59 M6
Hon Chông Vietnam 71 D5
Hondeklipbaai S. Africa 100 C6
Hondo U.S.A. 131 D6
Hondsrug reg. Neth. 52 G1
▶Honduras country Central America 137 G6
5th largest country in Central and North America.
North America 9, 116–117
Hønefoss Norway 45 G6
Honesdale U.S.A. 135 H3
Honey Lake salt l. U.S.A. 128 C1
Honeyoye Lake U.S.A. 135 G2
Honfleur France 56 E2
Hong, Mouths of the Vietnam see Red River, Mouths of the
Hông, Sông r. Vietnam see Red
Hongchuan China see Hongya
Hông Gai Vietnam 70 D2
Hongguo China see Panxian
Honghai Wan b. China 77 G4
Honghe China 76 D4
Hong He r. China 77 G1
Honghu China 77 G2
Hongjiang Hunan China 77 F3
Hongjiang Sichuan China see Wangcang
▶Hong Kong Hong Kong China 77 [inset]
Asia 6, 62–63
Hong Kong aut. reg. China 77 [inset]
Hong Kong Harbour sea chan. Hong Kong China 77 [inset]
Hong Kong Island Hong Kong China 77 [inset]
Hongliuwan China see Aksay
Hongliuyuan China 80 I3
Hongqiao China see Qidong
Hongqizhen China see Tongshi
Hongshi China 74 B4
Hongshui He r. China 76 F4
Honguedo, Détroit d' sea chan. Canada 123 I4
Hongwŏn N. Korea 75 B4
Hongxing China 74 A3
Hongya China 76 D2
Hongyuan China 76 D1
Hongze China 77 H1
Hongze Hu l. China 77 H1
▶Honiara Solomon Is 107 F2
Capital of the Solomon Islands.
Honiton U.K. 49 D8
Honjō Japan 75 F5
Honkajoki Fin. 45 M6
Honningsvåg Norway 44 N1
Honokaa HI U.S.A. 127 [inset]
▶Honolulu HI U.S.A. 127 [inset]
State capital of Hawaii.
▶Honshū i. Japan 75 D6
3rd largest island in Asia.
Honwad India 84 B2
Hood, Mount vol. U.S.A. 126 C3
Hood Point Australia 109 B8
Hood Point P.N.G. 110 D1
Hood River U.S.A. 126 C3
Hoogeveen Neth. 52 G2
Hoogezand-Sappemeer Neth. 48 G1
Hooghly r. mouth India see Hugli
Hooker U.S.A. 131 C4
Hook Head hd Rep. of Ireland 51 F5
Hook of Holland Neth. 52 E3
Hook Reef Australia 110 E3
Hoonah U.S.A. 120 C3
Hooper Bay U.S.A. 153 B2
Hooper Island U.S.A. 135 G4
Hoopeston U.S.A. 134 B3
Hoopstad S. Africa 101 G4
Höör Sweden 45 H9
Hoorn Neth. 52 F2
Hoorn, Îles de is Wallis and Futuna Is 107 I3
Hoosick U.S.A. 135 I2
Hoover Dam U.S.A. 129 F3
Hoover Memorial Reservoir U.S.A. 134 D3
Hopa Turkey 91 F2
Hope Canada 120 F5
Hope r. N.Z. 113 D6
Hope AR U.S.A. 131 E5
Hope IN U.S.A. 134 C4
Hope, Lake salt flat Australia 109 C8
Hope, Point U.S.A. 118 B3
Hopedale Canada 123 J3
Hopefield S. Africa 100 D7
Hopei prov. China see Hebei
Hope Mountains Canada 123 J3
Hope Saddle pass N.Z. 113 D5
Hopes Advance, Baie b. Canada 123 H2
Hopes Advance, Cap c. Canada 119 L3
Hopes Advance Bay Canada see Aupaluk
Hopetoun Australia 111 C7
Hopetown S. Africa 100 G5
Hopewell U.S.A. 135 G5
Hopewell Islands Canada 122 F2
Hopin Myanmar 70 B1
Hopkins r. Australia 111 C8
Hopkins, Lake salt flat Australia 109 E6
Hopkinsville U.S.A. 134 B5
Hopland U.S.A. 128 B2
Hoquiam U.S.A. 126 C3
Hor China 76 D1
Horasan Turkey 91 F2
Hörby Sweden 45 H9
Horgo Mongolia 80 I2
▶Horizon Deep sea feature S. Pacific Ocean 150 I7
2nd deepest point in the world (Tonga Trench).
Horki Belarus 43 F5
Horlick Mountains Antarctica 152 K1
Horlivka Ukr. 43 H6
Hormoz i. Iran 88 E5
Hormoz, Kūh-e mt. Iran 88 D5
Hormuz, Strait of Iran/Oman 88 E5
Horn Austria 47 O6
Horn r. Canada 120 G2
Horn c. Iceland 44 [inset]
▶Horn, Cape Chile 144 C9
Most southerly point of South America.
Hornavan l. Sweden 44 J3
Hornbrook U.S.A. 126 C4
Hornburg Germany 53 K2
Horncastle U.K. 48 G5
Horndal Sweden 45 J6
Horne, Îles de is Wallis and Futuna Is see Hoorn, Îles de
Horneburg Germany 53 J1
Hörnefors Sweden 44 K5
Hornell U.S.A. 135 G2
Hornepayne Canada 122 D4
Hornillos Mex. 127 F8
Hornisgrinde mt. Germany 47 L6
Hornkranz Namibia 100 C2
Horn Mountains Canada 120 F2
Hornos, Cabo de Chile see Horn, Cape
Hornoy-le-Bourg France 52 B5
Horn Peak Canada 120 D2
Hornsby Australia 112 E4
Hornsea U.K. 48 G5
Hornslandet pen. Sweden 45 J6
Horodenka Ukr. 43 E6
Horodnya Ukr. 43 F6
Horodok Khmel'nyts'ka Oblast' Ukr. 43 E6
Horodok L'vivs'ka Oblast' Ukr. 43 D6
Horokanai Japan 74 F3
Horoshiri-dake mt. Japan 74 F4
Horqin Youyi Qianqi China see Ulanhot
Horqin Zuoyi Houqi China see Ganjig
Horqin Zuoyi Zhongqi China see Baokang
Horrabridge U.K. 49 C8
Horrocks Australia 109 A7
Horru China 83 G3
Horse Cave U.S.A. 134 C5
Horsefly Canada 120 F4
Horseheads U.S.A. 135 G2
Horse Islands Canada 123 L4
Horseleap Rep. of Ireland 51 D4
Horsens Denmark 45 F9
Horseshoe Bend Australia 109 F6
Horseshoe Reservoir U.S.A. 129 H4
Horseshoe Seamounts sea feature N. Atlantic Ocean 148 G3
Horsham Australia 111 C8
Horsham U.K. 49 G7
Horšovský Týn Czech Rep. 53 M5
Horst hill Germany 53 J4
Hörstel Germany 53 H2
Horten Norway 45 G7
Hortobágyi nat. park Hungary 59 I1
Horton r. Canada 118 F3
Horwood Lake Canada 122 E4
Hösbach Germany 53 J4
Hose, Pegunungan mts Malaysia 68 E6
Ḥoseynābād Iran 88 B3
Ḥoseynīyeh Iran 88 C4
Hoshab Pak. 89 F5
Hoshangabad India 82 D5
Hoshiarpur India 82 C3
Hospet India 84 C3
Hospital Rep. of Ireland 51 D5
Hosséré Vokre mt. Cameroon 96 E4
Hosta Butte mt. U.S.A. 129 I4
Hotagen r. Sweden 44 I5
Hotahudo East Timor see Hatudo
Hotan China 82 E1
Hotazel S. Africa 100 F4
Hot Creek Range mts U.S.A. 128 E2
Hotgi India 84 C2
Hotham r. Australia 109 B8
Hoting Sweden 44 J4
Hot Springs AR U.S.A. 131 E5
Hot Springs NM U.S.A. see Truth or Consequences
Hot Springs SD U.S.A. 130 C3
Hot Sulphur Springs U.S.A. 126 G4
Hottah Lake Canada 120 G1
Hottentots Bay Namibia 100 B4
Hottentots Point Namibia 100 B4
Houdan France 52 B6
Houffalize Belgium 52 F4
Hougang Sing. 71 [inset]
Houghton MI U.S.A. 130 F2
Houghton NY U.S.A. 135 F2
Houghton Lake U.S.A. 134 C1
Houghton Lake l. U.S.A. 134 C1
Houghton le Spring U.K. 48 F4
Houie Moc, Phou mt. Laos 70 C2
Houlton U.S.A. 132 H2
Houma China 77 F1
Houma U.S.A. 131 F6
Houmen China 77 G4
House Range mts U.S.A. 129 G2
Houston Canada 120 E4
Houston MO U.S.A. 131 F4
Houston MS U.S.A. 131 F5
Houston TX U.S.A. 131 E6
Hout r. S. Africa 101 I2
Houtman Abrolhos is Australia 109 A7
Houton U.K. 50 F2
Houwater S. Africa 100 F6
Hovd Hovd Mongolia 80 H2
Hovd Övörhangay Mongolia 80 J3
Hove U.K. 49 G8
Hoveton U.K. 49 I6
Hovmantorp Sweden 45 I8
Hövsgöl Nuur l. Mongolia 80 J1
Hövüün Mongolia 80 J3
Howar, Wadi watercourse Sudan 86 C6
Howard Australia 110 F5
Howard PA U.S.A. 135 G3
Howard SD U.S.A. 130 D2
Howard WI U.S.A. 134 A1
Howard City U.S.A. 134 C2
Howard Lake Canada 121 J2
Howden U.K. 48 G5
Howe, Cape Australia 112 D6
Howe, Mount Antarctica 152 J1
Howell U.S.A. 134 D2
Howick Canada 135 I1
Howick S. Africa 101 J5
Howland U.S.A. 132 G2
▶Howland Island terr. N. Pacific Ocean 107 I1
United States Unincorporated Territory.
Howlong Australia 112 C5
Howrah India see Haora
Howth Rep. of Ireland 51 F4
Ḥowz well Iran 88 E3
Ḥowz-e Khān well Iran 88 E3
Ḥowz-e Panj Iran 88 E4
Ḥowz-e Panj waterhole Iran 88 D3
Howz i-Mian i-Tak Iran 88 D3
Höxter Germany 53 J3
Hoy i. U.K. 50 F2
Hoya Germany 53 J2
Høyanger Norway 45 E6
Hoyerswerda Germany 47 O5
Høylandet Norway 44 H4
Hoym Germany 53 L3
Höytiäinen l. Fin. 44 P5
Hoyt Peak U.S.A. 129 H1
Hpa-an Myanmar see Pa-an
Hradec Králové Czech Rep. 47 O5
Hradiště hill Czech Rep. 53 N4
Hrasnica Bos.-Herz. 58 H3
Hrazdan Armenia 91 G2
Hrebinka Ukr. 43 G6
Hrodna Belarus 45 M10
Hrvatska country Europe see Croatia
Hrvatsko Grahovo Bos.-Herz. see Bosansko Grahovo
Hsataw Myanmar 70 B3
Hsenwi Myanmar 70 B2
Hsiang Chang i. Hong Kong China see Hong Kong Island
Hsiang Kang Hong Kong China see Hong Kong
Hsi-hseng Myanmar 70 B2
Hsin-chia-p'o country Asia see Singapore
Hsin-chia-p'o Sing. see Singapore
Hsinchu Taiwan 77 I3
Hsinking China see Changchun
Hsinying Taiwan 77 I4
Hsipaw Myanmar 70 B2
Hsi-sha Ch'ün-tao is S. China Sea see Paracel Islands
Hsiyüp'ing Yü i. Taiwan 77 H4
Hsüeh Shan mt. Taiwan 77 I3
Huab watercourse Namibia 99 B6
Huachinera Mex. 127 F7
Huacho Peru 142 C6
Huachuan China 74 C3
Huade China 73 K4
Huadian China 74 B4
Huadu China 77 G4
Hua Hin Thai. 71 B4
Huai'an Jiangsu China 77 H1
Huai'an Jiangsu China see Chuzhou
Huaibei China 77 H1
Huaibin China 77 G1
Huaicheng Guangdong China see Huaiji
Huaicheng Jiangsu China see Chuzhou
Huaidezhen China 74 B4
Huaidian China see Shenqiu
Huai Had National Park Thai. 70 D3
Huaihua China 77 F3
Huaiji China 77 G4
Huai Kha Khaeng Wildlife Reserve nature res. Thai. 70 B4
Huailillas mt. Peru 142 C5
Huainan China 77 H1
Huaining Anhui China 77 H2
Huaining Anhui China see Shipai
Huaiyang China 77 G1
Huaiyin Jiangsu China 77 H1
Huaiyin Jiangsu China see Huai'an
Huaiyuan China 77 H1
Huajialing China 76 E1
Huajuápan de León Mex. 136 E5
Hualapai Peak U.S.A. 129 G4
Hualian Taiwan see Hualien
Hualien Taiwan 77 I3
Huallaga r. Peru 142 C5
Huambo Angola 99 B5
Huanan China 74 C3
Huancane Peru 142 E7
Huancavelica Peru 142 C6
Huancayo Peru 142 C6
Huangbei China 77 G3
Huangcaoba China see Xingyi
Huangchuan China 77 G1
Huanggang China see Huangzhou
Huang Hai sea N. Pacific Ocean see Yellow Sea
Huang He r. China see Yellow River
Huangjiajian China 77 I1
Huangling China 77 F1
Huangliu China 77 F5
Huanglongsi China see Kaifeng
Huangmao Jian mt. China 77 H3
Huangmei China 77 G2
Huangpu China 77 G4
Huangqi China 77 H3
Huangshan China 77 H2
Huangshi China 77 G2
Huangtu Gaoyuan plat. China 73 J5
Huangyan China 77 I2
Huangzhou China 77 G2
Huaning China 76 D3
Huanjiang China 77 F3
Huanren China 74 B4
Huanshan China see Yuhuan
Huánuco Peru 142 C5
Huaping China 76 D3
Huap'ing Yü i. Taiwan 77 I3
Huaqiao China 76 E2
Huaqiaozhen China see Huaqiao
Huaráz Peru 142 C5
Huarmey Peru 142 C6
Huarong China 77 G2
Huascarán, Nevado de mt. Peru 142 C5
Huasco Chile 144 B3
Hua Shan mt. China 77 F1
Huashixia China 76 C1
Huashugou China see Jingtieshan
Huashulinzi China 74 B4
Huatabampo Mex. 127 F8
Huaxian Guangdong China see Huadu
Huaxian Henan China 77 G1
Huayang China see Jixi
Huayin China 77 F1
Huayuan China 77 F2
Huazangsi China see Tianzhu
Hubbard, Mount Canada/U.S.A. 120 B2
Hubbard, Pointe pt Canada 123 I2
Hubbard Lake U.S.A. 134 D1
Hubbart Point Canada 121 M3
Hubei prov. China 77 G2
Hubli India 84 B3
Hückelhoven Germany 52 G3
Hucknall U.K. 49 F5
Huddersfield U.K. 48 F5
Huder China 74 A2
Hudiksvall Sweden 45 J6
Hudson MA U.S.A. 135 J2
Hudson MD U.S.A. 135 G4
Hudson MI U.S.A. 134 C3
Hudson NH U.S.A. 135 J2
Hudson NY U.S.A. 135 I2
Hudson r. U.S.A. 135 I3
Hudson, Baie d' sea Canada see Hudson Bay
Hudson, Détroit d' strait Canada see Hudson Strait
Hudson Bay Canada 121 K4
Hudson Bay sea Canada 119 J4
Hudson Falls U.S.A. 135 I2
Hudson Island Tuvalu see Nanumanga
Hudson Mountains Antarctica 152 K2
Hudson's Hope Canada 120 F3
Hudson Strait Canada 119 K3
Huê Vietnam 70 D3
Huehuetenango Guat. 136 F5
Huehueto, Cerro mt. Mex. 131 B7
Huelva Spain 57 C5
Huentelauquén Chile 144 B4
Huépac Mex. 127 F7
Huércal-Overa Spain 57 F5
Huertecillas Mex. 131 C7
Huesca Spain 57 F2
Huéscar Spain 57 E5
Hughenden Australia 110 D4
Hughes Australia 109 E7
Hughes r. Canada 121 K3
Hughson U.S.A. 128 C3
Hugli r. mouth India 83 F5
Hugo CO U.S.A. 130 C4
Hugo OK U.S.A. 131 E5
Hugo Lake U.S.A. 131 E5
Hugoton U.S.A. 131 C4
Huhehot China see Hohhot
Huhhot China see Hohhot
Huhudi S. Africa 100 G4
Hui'an China 77 H3
Hui'anpu China 72 J5
Huiarau Range mts N.Z. 113 F4
Huib-Hoch Plateau Namibia 100 C4
Huichang China 77 G3
Huicheng Anhui China see Shexian
Huicheng Guangdong China see Huilai
Huidong China 76 D3
Huijbergen Neth. 52 E3
Huila, Nevado de vol. Col. 142 C3
Huilai China 77 H4
Huíla Plateau Angola 99 B5
Huili China 76 D3
Huimanguillo Mex. 136 F5
Huinahuaca Arg. 144 C2
Huinan China see Nanhui
Huining China 76 E1
Huishi China see Huining
Huishui China 76 E3
Huiten Nur l. China 83 G2
Huitong China 77 F3
Huittinen Fin. 45 M6
Huixian Gansu China 76 E1
Huixian Henan China 77 G1
Huiyang China see Huizhou
Huize China 76 D3
Huizhou China 77 G4
Hujirt Mongolia 72 I3
Hujr Saudi Arabia 86 F4
Hukawng Valley Myanmar 70 B1
Hukuntsi Botswana 100 E2
Hulan China 74 B3
Hulan Ergi China 74 A3
Ḥulayfah Saudi Arabia 86 F4
Ḥulayḥilah well Syria 85 D2
Huliao China see Dabu
Hulilan Iran 88 B3
Hulin China 74 D3
Hulin Gol r. China 74 B3
Hull Canada 135 H1
Hull U.K. see Kingston upon Hull
Hull Island atoll Kiribati see Orona
Hultsfred Sweden 45 I8
Hulun China see Hailar
Hulun Nur l. China 73 L3
Ḥulwān Egypt 90 C5
Huma China 74 B2
Humaitá Brazil 142 F5
Humaya r. Mex. 127 G8
Humaym well U.A.E. 88 D6
Humayyār, Jabal hill Saudi Arabia 88 B5
Humber, Mouth of the U.K. 48 H5
Humboldt Canada 121 J4
Humboldt AZ U.S.A. 129 G4
Humboldt NE U.S.A. 130 E3
Humboldt NV U.S.A. 128 D1
Humboldt r. U.S.A. 128 D1
Humboldt Bay U.S.A. 126 B4
Humboldt Range mts U.S.A. 128 D1
Humbolt Salt Marsh U.S.A. 128 E2
Hume r. Canada 120 D1
Humeburn Australia 112 B1
Hu Men sea chan. China 77 G4
Hume Reservoir Australia 112 C5
Humphrey Island atoll Cook Is see Manihiki
Humphreys, Mount U.S.A. 128 D3
Humphreys Peak U.S.A. 129 H4
Hūn Libya 97 E2
Húnaflói b. Iceland 44 [inset]
Hunan prov. China 77 F3
Hundeluft Germany 53 M3
Hunedoara Romania 59 J2
Hünfeld Germany 53 J4
▶Hungary country Europe 55 H2
Europe 5, 38–39
Hungerford Australia 112 B2
Hung Fa Leng hill Hong Kong China see Robin's Nest
Hŭngnam N. Korea 75 B5
Hung Shui Kiu Hong Kong China 77 [inset]
Hưng Yên Vietnam 70 D2
Hunjiang China see Baishan
Huns Mountains Namibia 100 C4
Hunstanton U.K. 49 H6
Hunte r. Germany 53 I1
Hunter r. Australia 112 E4
Hunter Island Australia 111 [inset]
Hunter Island Canada 120 D5
Hunter Island S. Pacific Ocean 107 H4
Hunter Islands Australia 111 [inset]
Huntingburg U.S.A. 134 B4
Huntingdon Canada 135 H1
Huntingdon U.K. 49 G6
Huntingdon PA U.S.A. 135 G3
Huntingdon TN U.S.A. 131 F4
Huntington IN U.S.A. 134 C3
Huntington OR U.S.A. 126 D3
Huntington WV U.S.A. 134 D4
Huntington Beach U.S.A. 128 D5
Huntington Creek r. U.S.A. 129 F1
Huntly N.Z. 113 E3
Huntly U.K. 50 G3
Hunt Mountain U.S.A. 126 G3
Huntsville Canada 134 F1
Huntsville AL U.S.A. 133 C5
Huntsville AR U.S.A. 131 E4
Huntsville TN U.S.A. 134 C5
Huntsville TX U.S.A. 131 E6
Hunza reg. Jammu and Kashmir 82 C1
Huolin He r. China see Hulin Gol
Huolongmen China 74 B2
Hương Khê Vietnam 70 D3
Hương Thuy Vietnam 70 D3
Huonville Australia 111 [inset]
Huoqiu China 77 H1
Huoshan China 77 H2
Huo Shan mt. China see Baima Jian
Huoshao Tao i. Taiwan see Lü Tao
Hupeh prov. China see Hubei
Hupnik r. Turkey 85 C1
Hupu India 76 B2
Ḥūr Iran 88 E4
Hurault, Lac l. Canada 123 H3
Ḥuraydin, Wādī watercourse Egypt 85 A4
Huraysān reg. Saudi Arabia 88 B6
Hurd, Cape Canada 134 E1
Hurd Island Kiribati see Arorae
Hurghada Egypt see Al Ghurdaqah
Hurler's Cross Rep. of Ireland 51 D5
Hurley NM U.S.A. 129 I5
Hurley WI U.S.A. 130 F2
Hurmagai Pak. 89 G4
Huron CA U.S.A. 128 C3
Huron SD U.S.A. 130 D2
▶Huron, Lake Canada/U.S.A. 134 D1
2nd largest lake in North America and 4th in the world.
World 12–13
Hurricane U.S.A. 129 G3
Hursley U.K. 49 F7
Hurst Green U.K. 49 H7
Husain Nika Pak. 89 H4
Húsavík Norðurland eystra Iceland 44 [inset]
Húsavík Vestfirðir Iceland 44 [inset]
Huseyinabat Turkey see Alaca
Huseyinli Turkey see Kızılırmak
Hushan Zhejiang China 77 H2
Hushan Zhejiang China see Cixi
Hushan Zhejiang China see Wuyi
Huşi Romania 59 M1
Huskvarna Sweden 45 I8
Husn Jordan see Al Ḥiṣn
Ḥuṣn Āl 'Abr Yemen 86 G6
Husnes Norway 45 D7
Husum Germany 47 L3
Husum Sweden 44 K5
Hutag Mongolia 80 J2
Hutchinson KS U.S.A. 130 D4
Hutchinson MN U.S.A. 130 E2
Hutch Mountain U.S.A. 129 H4
Hutou China 74 D3
Hutsonville U.S.A. 134 B4
Huttah Kulkyne National Park Australia 111 C7
Hutton, Mount hill Australia 111 E5
Hutton Range hills Australia 109 C6
Huu Đô Vietnam 70 D2
Huvadhu Atoll Maldives 81 D11
Hüvek Turkey see Bozova
Hüvīān, Kūh-e mts Iran 89 E5
Huwār i. Bahrain 88 C5
Huwaytat reg. Saudi Arabia 85 C5
Huxi China 77 G3
Huzhong China 74 A2

Iskitim Rus. Fed. 64 J4
Iskūr r. Bulg. 59 K3
Iskushuban Somalia 98 F2
Isla r. Scotland U.K. 50 F4
Isla r. Scotland U.K. 50 G3
Isla Gorge National Park Australia 110 E5
İslahiye Turkey 90 E3
Islamabad India see Anantnag

▶Islamabad Pak. 89 I3
Capital of Pakistan.

Islamgarh Pak. 89 H5
Islamkot Pak. 89 H5
Island r. Canada 120 F2
Ísland country Europe see Iceland
Island U.S.A. 134 B5
Island Falls U.S.A. 132 G2
Island Lagoon salt flat Australia 111 B6
Island Lake Canada 121 M4
Island Lake l. Canada 121 M4
Island Magee pen. U.K. 51 G3
Island Pond U.S.A. 135 J1
Islands, Bay of N.Z. 113 E2
Islay i. U.K. 50 C5

▶Isle of Man terr. Irish Sea 48 C4
United Kingdom Crown Dependency.
Europe 5

Isle of Wight U.S.A. 135 G5
Isle Royale National Park U.S.A. 130 F2
Ismail Ukr. see Izmayil
Ismâ'ilîya Egypt see Al Ismā'īlīyah
Ismâ'ilîya governorate Egypt see Ismā'īlīyah
Ismā'īlīyah governorate Egypt 85 A4
Ismailly Azer. see İsmayıllı
İsmayıllı Azer. 91 H2
Isojoki Fin. 44 L5
Isoka Zambia 99 D5
Isokylä Fin. 44 O3
Isokyrö Fin. 44 M5
Isola di Capo Rizzuto Italy 58 G5
Ispahan Iran see Eşfahān
Isparta Turkey 59 N6
Isperikh Bulg. 59 L3
Ispikan Pak. 89 F5
İspir Turkey 91 F2
Ispisar Tajik. see Khŭjand
Isplinji Pak. 89 G4
▶Israel country Asia 85 B4
Asia 6, 62–63
Israelite Bay Australia 109 C8
Isra'il country Asia see Israel
Isselburg Germany 52 G3
Issia Côte d'Ivoire 96 C4
Issoire France 56 F4
Issyk-Kul' Kyrg. see Balykchy
Issyk-Kul', Ozero salt l. Kyrg. see Ysyk-Köl
Istalif Afgh. 89 H3

▶İstanbul Turkey 59 M4
2nd most populous city in Europe.

İstanbul Boğazı strait Turkey see Bosporus
Īstgāh-e Eznā Iran 88 C3
Istiaia Greece 59 J5
Istik r. Tajik. 89 I2
Istra pen. Croatia see Istria
Istres France 56 G5
Istria pen. Croatia 58 E2
Iswardi Bangl. see Ishurdi
Itabapoana r. Brazil 145 C3
Itaberá Brazil 145 A3
Itaberaba Brazil 145 C1
Itaberaí Brazil 145 A2
Itabira Brazil 145 C2
Itabirito Brazil 145 C3
Itabuna Brazil 145 D1
Itacajá Brazil 143 I5
Itacarambi Brazil 145 B1
Itacoatiara Brazil 143 G4
Itaetê Brazil 145 C1
Itagmatana Iran see Hamadān
Itaguaçu Brazil 145 C2
Itaí Brazil 145 A3
Itaiópolis Brazil 145 A4
Itäisen Suomenlahden kansallispuisto nat. park Fin. 45 O6
Itaituba Brazil 143 G4
Itajaí Brazil 145 A4
Itajubá Brazil 145 B3
Itajuipe Brazil 145 D1
Italia country Europe see Italy
Italia, Laguna l. Bol. 142 F6

▶Italy country Europe 58 E3
5th most populous country in Europe.
Europe 5, 38–39

Itamarandiba Brazil 145 C2
Itambé Brazil 145 C1
Itambé, Pico de mt. Brazil 145 C2
It Amelân i. Neth. see Ameland
Itampolo Madag. 99 E6
Itanagar India 83 H4
Itanguari r. Brazil 145 B1
Itanhaém Brazil 145 B4
Itanhém Brazil 145 C2
Itanhém r. Brazil 145 D2
Itaobím Brazil 145 C2
Itapaci Brazil 145 A1
Itapajipe Brazil 145 A2
Itapebi Brazil 145 D1
Itapecerica Brazil 145 B3
Itapemirim Brazil 145 C3
Itaperuna Brazil 145 C3
Itapetinga Brazil 145 C1
Itapetininga Brazil 145 A3
Itapeva Brazil 145 A3
Itapeva, Lago l. Brazil 145 A5
Itapicuru Brazil 143 J6
Itapicuru, Serra de hills Brazil 143 I5
Itapicuru Mirim Brazil 143 J4
Itapipoca Brazil 143 K4
Itapira Brazil 145 B3
Itaporanga Brazil 145 A3
Itapuã Brazil 145 A5
Itaqui Brazil 144 E3
Itararé Brazil 145 A4
Itarsi India 82 D5
Itarumã Brazil 145 A2
Itatiba Brazil 145 B3
Itatuba Brazil 142 F5
Itaúna Brazil 145 B3
Itaúnas Brazil 145 D2
Itbayat i. Phil. 69 G2
Itchen Lake Canada 121 H1
Itea Greece 59 J5
Ithaca MI U.S.A. 134 C2
Ithaca NY U.S.A. 135 G2
It Hearrenfean Neth. see Heerenveen
iThekweni S. Africa see Durban
Ith Hils ridge Germany 53 J2
Ithrah Saudi Arabia 85 C4
Itihusa-yama mt. Japan 75 C6
Itilleq Greenland 119 M3
Itimbiri r. Dem. Rep. Congo 98 C3
Itinga Brazil 145 C2
Itiquira Brazil 143 H7
Itiruçu Brazil 145 C1
Itiúba, Serra de hills Brazil 143 K6
Itō Japan 75 E6
iTswane S. Africa see Pretoria
Ittiri Sardinia Italy 58 C4
Ittoqqortoormiit Greenland 119 P2
Itu Brazil 145 B3
Itu Abu Island Spratly Is 68 E4
Ituaçu Brazil 145 C1
Ituberá Brazil 145 D1
Ituí r. Brazil 142 D4
Ituiutaba Brazil 145 A2
Itumbiara Brazil 145 A2
Itumbiara, Barragem resr Brazil 145 A2
Ituni Guyana 143 G2
Itupiranga Brazil 143 I5
Ituporanga Brazil 145 A4
Iturama Brazil 145 A2
Iturbide Mex. 131 D7
Ituri r. Dem. Rep. Congo 98 C3
Iturup, Ostrov i. Rus. Fed. 74 G3
Itutinga Brazil 145 B3
Ituxi r. Brazil 142 F5
Ītyop'ia country Africa see Ethiopia
Itz r. Germany 53 K5
Itzehoe Germany 47 L4
Iuka U.S.A. 131 F5
Iul'tin Rus. Fed. 65 T3
Ivalo Fin. 44 O2
Ivalojoki r. Fin. 44 O2
Ivanava Belarus 45 N10
Ivanhoe Australia 112 B4
Ivanhoe U.S.A. 130 D2
Ivanhoe Lake Canada 121 J2
Ivankiv Ukr. 43 F6
Ivankovtsy Rus. Fed. 74 D2
Ivano-Frankivs'k Ukr. 43 E6
Ivano-Frankovsk Ukr. see Ivano-Frankivs'k
Ivanovka Rus. Fed. 74 B2
Ivanovo Belarus see Ivanava
Ivanovo tourist site Bulg. 59 K3
Ivanovo Rus. Fed. 42 I4
Ivanteyevka Rus. Fed. 43 K5
Ivantsevichi Belarus see Ivatsevichy
Ivatsevichy Belarus 45 N10
Ivaylovgrad Bulg. 59 L4
Ivdel' Rus. Fed. 41 S3
Ivittuut Greenland 119 N3
Iviza i. Spain see Ibiza
Ivory Coast country Africa see Côte d'Ivoire
Ivrea Italy 58 B2
İvrindi Turkey 59 L5
Ivris Ugheltekhili pass Georgia 91 G2
Ivry-la-Bataille France 52 B6
Ivugivik Canada see Ivujivik
Ivujivik Canada 119 K3
Ivyanyets Belarus 45 O10
Ivydale U.S.A. 134 E4
Iwaki Japan 75 F5
Iwaki-san vol. Japan 74 F4
Iwakuni Japan 75 D6
Iwamizawa Japan 74 F4
Iwo Nigeria 96 D4
Iwye Belarus 45 N10
Ixelles Belgium 52 E4
Ixiamas Bol. 142 E6
Ixmiquilpán Mex. 136 E4
Ixopo S. Africa 101 J6
Ixtlán Mex. 136 D4
Ixworth U.K. 49 H6
İyirmi Altı Bakı Komissarı Azer. see 26 Bakı Komissarı
Izabal, Lago de l. Guat. 136 G5
Izberbash Rus. Fed. 91 G2
Izegem Belgium 52 D4
Īzeh Iran 88 C4
Izgal Pak. 89 I3
Izhevsk Rus. Fed. 41 Q4
Izhma Respublika Komi Rus. Fed. 42 L2
Izhma Respublika Komi Rus. Fed. see Sosnogorsk
Izhma r. Rus. Fed. 42 L2
Izmail Ukr. see Izmayil
Izmayil Ukr. 59 M2
İzmir Turkey 59 L5
İzmir Körfezi g. Turkey 59 L5
İzmit Turkey see Kocaeli
İzmit Körfezi b. Turkey 59 M4
Izozog Bol. 142 F7
Izra' Syria 85 C3
Iztochni Rodopi mts Bulg. 59 K4
Izu-hantō pen. Japan 75 E6
Izuhara Japan 75 C6
Izumo Japan 75 D6

▶Izu-Ogasawara Trench sea feature N. Pacific Ocean 150 F3
5th deepest trench in the world.

Izu-shotō is Japan 75 E6
Izyaslav Ukr. 43 E6
Iz"yayu Rus. Fed. 42 M2
Izyum Ukr. 43 H6

J

Jabal Dab Saudi Arabia 88 C6
Jabalón r. Spain 57 D4
Jabalpur India 82 D5
Jabbūl, Sabkhat al salt flat Syria 85 C2
Jabir reg. Oman 88 E6
Jabiru Australia 108 F3
Jablah Syria 85 B2
Jablanica Bos.-Herz. 58 G3
Jaboatão Brazil 143 L5
Jaboticabal Brazil 145 A3
Jabung, Tanjung pt Indon. 68 C7
Jacaraci Brazil 145 C1
Jacareacanga Brazil 143 G5
Jacareí Brazil 145 B3
Jacarézinho Brazil 145 A3
Jáchymov Czech Rep. 53 M4
Jacinto Brazil 145 C2
Jack r. Australia 110 D2
Jack Lake Canada 135 F1
Jackman U.S.A. 132 G2
Jacksboro U.S.A. 131 D5
Jackson Australia 112 D1
Jackson AL U.S.A. 133 C6
Jackson CA U.S.A. 128 C2
Jackson GA U.S.A. 133 D5
Jackson KY U.S.A. 134 D5
Jackson MI U.S.A. 134 C2
Jackson MN U.S.A. 130 E3

▶Jackson MS U.S.A. 131 F5
State capital of Mississippi.

Jackson NC U.S.A. 132 E4
Jackson OH U.S.A. 134 D4
Jackson TN U.S.A. 131 F5
Jackson WY U.S.A. 126 F4
Jackson, Mount Antarctica 152 L2
Jackson Head hd N.Z. 113 B6
Jacksonville AR U.S.A. 131 E5
Jacksonville FL U.S.A. 133 D6
Jacksonville IL U.S.A. 130 F4
Jacksonville NC U.S.A. 133 E5
Jacksonville OH U.S.A. 134 D4
Jacksonville TX U.S.A. 131 E6
Jacksonville Beach U.S.A. 133 D6
Jack Wade U.S.A. 118 D3
Jacmel Haiti 137 J5
Jacobabad Pak. 89 H4
Jacobina Brazil 143 J6
Jacob Lake U.S.A. 129 G3
Jacobsdal S. Africa 100 G5
Jacques-Cartier, Détroit de sea chan. Canada 123 I4
Jacques Cartier, Mont mt. Canada 123 I4
Jacques Cartier Passage Canada see Jacques-Cartier, Détroit de
Jacuí Brazil 145 B3
Jacuípe r. Brazil 143 K6
Jacunda Brazil 143 I4
Jaddangi India 84 D2
Jaddi, Ras pt Pak. 89 F5
Jadebusen b. Germany 53 I1
J. A. D. Jensen Nunatakker nunataks Greenland 119 N3
Jadotville Dem. Rep. Congo see Likasi
Jādū Libya 96 E1
Jaén Spain 57 E5
Ja'farābād Iran 88 E2
Jaffa, Cape Australia 111 B8
Jaffna Sri Lanka 84 C4
Jafr, Qa' al imp. l. Jordan 85 C4
Jagadhri India 82 D3
Jagalur India 84 C3
Jagatsinghapur India see Jagatsinghpur
Jagatsinghpur India 83 F5
Jagdalpur India 84 D2
Jagdaqi China 74 B2
Jagersfontein S. Africa 101 G5
Jaggang China 82 D2
Jaggayyapeta India 84 D2
Jaghīn Iran 88 E5
Jagok Tso salt l. China see Urru Co
Jagsamka China see Luding
Jagst r. Germany 53 J5
Jagtial India 84 C2
Jaguariaíva Brazil 145 A4
Jaguaripe Brazil 145 D1
Jagüey Grande Cuba 133 D8
Jahanabad India see Jehanabad
Jahmah well Iraq 91 G5
Jahrom Iran 88 D4
Jaicós Brazil 143 J5
Jaigarh India 84 B2
Jailolo Gilolo i. Indon. see Halmahera
Jaintapur Bangl. see Jaintiapur
Jaintiapur Bangl. 83 H4
Jaipur India 82 C4
Jaipurhat Bangl. see Joypurhat
Jais India 83 E4
Jaisalmer India 82 B4
Jaisamand Lake India 82 C4
Jaitaran India 82 C4
Jaitgarh hill India 84 C1
Jajapur India see Jajpur
Jajarkot Nepal 87 N4
Jajce Bos.-Herz. 58 G2
Jajnagar state India see Orissa
Jajpur India 83 F5
Jakar Bhutan 83 G4

▶Jakarta Indon. 68 D8
Capital of Indonesia.

Jakes Corner Canada 120 C2
Jakhan India 82 B5
Jakin mt. Afgh. 89 G4
Jakkī Kowr Iran 89 F5
Jäkkvik Sweden 44 J3
Jakliat India 82 C3
Jakobshavn Greenland see Ilulissat
Jakobstad Fin. 44 M5
Jal U.S.A. 131 C5
Jalaid China see Inder
Jalājil Saudi Arabia 88 B5
Jalālābād Afgh. 89 H3
Jalal-Abad Kyrg. 80 D3
Jalālah al Baḩrīyah, Jabal plat. Egypt 90 C5
Jalāmid, Ḩazm al ridge Saudi Arabia 91 E5
Jalandhar India 82 C3
Jalapa Mex. 136 E5
Jalapa Enríquez Mex. see Jalapa
Jalapur Pirwala Pak. 89 H4
Jalasjärvi Fin. 44 M5
Jalaun India 82 D4
Jalawlā' Iraq 91 G4
Jaldak Afgh. 89 G4
Jaldrug India 84 C2
Jales Brazil 145 A3
Jalesar India 82 D4
Jalgaon India 82 C5
Jalībah Iraq 91 G5
Jalingo Nigeria 96 E4
Jallābī Iran 88 E5
Jalna India 84 B2
Jālo Iran 89 F5
Jalón r. Spain 57 F3
Jalor India see Jalore
Jalore India 82 C4
Jalpa Mex. 136 D4
Jalpaiguri India 83 G4
Jālū Libya 97 F2
Jalūlā Iraq see Jalawlā'
Jām reg. Iran 89 F3
▶Jamaica country West Indies 137 I5
North America 9, 116–117
Jamaica Channel Haiti/Jamaica 137 I5
Jamalpur Bangl. 83 G4
Jamalpur India 83 F4
Jamanxim r. Brazil 143 G4
Jambi Indon. 68 C7
Jambin Australia 110 E5
Jambo India 82 C4
Jambuair, Tanjung pt Indon. 67 B6
Jamda India 83 F5
Jamekunte India 84 C2
James r. N. Dakota/S. Dakota U.S.A. 130 D3
James r. VA U.S.A. 135 G5
James, Baie b. Canada see James Bay
Jamesabad Pak. 89 H5
James Bay Canada 122 E3
Jamesburg U.S.A. 135 H3
James Island Galápagos Ecuador see San Salvador, Isla
Jameson Land reg. Greenland 119 P2
James Peak N.Z. 113 B7
James Ranges mts Australia 109 F6
James Ross Island Antarctica 152 A2
James Ross Strait Canada 119 I3
Jamestown Australia 111 B7
Jamestown Canada see Wawa
Jamestown S. Africa 101 H6

▶Jamestown St Helena 148 H7
Capital of St Helena and Dependencies.

Jamestown ND U.S.A. 130 D2
Jamestown NY U.S.A. 134 F2
Jamestown TN U.S.A. 134 C5
Jamkhed India 84 B2
Jammu India 82 C2

▶Jammu and Kashmir terr. Asia 82 D2
Disputed territory (India/Pakistan).
Asia 6, 62–63

Jamnagar India 82 B5
Jampur Pak. 89 H4
Jamrud Pak. 89 H3
Jämsä Fin. 45 N6
Jamsah Egypt 90 D6
Jämsänkoski Fin. 44 N6
Jamshedpur India 83 F5
Jamtari Nigeria 96 E4
Jamui India 83 F4
Jamuna r. Bangl. see Raimangal
Jamuna r. India see Yamuna
Janā i. Saudi Arabia 88 C5
Janāb, Wādī al watercourse Jordan 85 C4
Janakpur India 83 E5
Janaúba Brazil 145 C1
Jand Pak. 89 I3
Jandaia Brazil 145 A2
Jandaq Iran 88 D3
Jandola Pak. 89 H3
Jandowae Australia 112 E1
Janesville CA U.S.A. 128 C1
Janesville WI U.S.A. 130 F3
Jangada Brazil 145 A4
Jangal Iran 88 E3
Jangamo Moz. 101 L3
Jangaon India 84 C2
Jangipur India 83 G4
Jangnga Turkm. see Dzhanga
Jangngai Ri mts China 83 F2
Jänickendorf Germany 53 N2
Jani Khel Pak. 89 H3

▶Jan Mayen terr. Arctic Ocean 153 I2
Part of Norway.

Jan Mayen Fracture Zone sea feature Arctic Ocean 153 I2
Janos Mex. 127 F7
Jans Bay Canada 121 I4
Jansenville S. Africa 100 G7
Januária Brazil 145 B1
Janūb Sīnā' governorate Egypt 85 A5
Janūb Sīnā' governorate Egypt see Janūb Sīnā'
Janzar mt. Pak. 89 F5
Jaodar Pak. 89 F5
▶Japan country Asia 75 D5
Asia 6, 62–63
Japan, Sea of N. Pacific Ocean 75 D5
Japan Alps National Park Japan see Chibu-Sangaku National Park
Japan Trench sea feature N. Pacific Ocean 150 F3
Japiim Brazil 142 D5
Japurá r. Brazil 142 F4
Japvo Mount India 83 H4
Jarābulus Syria 85 D1
Jaraguá Brazil 145 A1
Jaraguá, Serra mts Brazil 145 A4
Jaraguá do Sul Brazil 145 A4
Jarash Jordan 85 B3
Jarboesville U.S.A. see Lexington Park
Jardine River National Park Australia 110 C1
Jardinésia Brazil 145 A2
Jardinópolis Brazil 145 B3
Jargalang China 74 A4
Jargalant Bayanhongor Mongolia 80 I2
Jargalant Dornod Mongolia 73 L3
Jargalant Hovd Mongolia see Hovd
Jari r. Brazil 143 H4
Järna Sweden 45 J7
Jarocin Poland 47 P5
Jarosław Poland 43 D6
Järpen Sweden 44 H5
Jarqŭrghon Uzbek. see Dzharkurgan
Jarrettsville U.S.A. 135 G4
Jarú Brazil 142 F6
Jarud China see Lubei
Järvakandi Estonia 45 N7
Järvenpää Fin. 45 N6

▶Jarvis Island terr. S. Pacific Ocean 150 J6
United States Unincorporated Territory.

Jarwa India 83 E4
Jashpurnagar India 83 F5
Jäsk Iran 88 E5
Jäsk-e Kohneh Iran 88 E5
Jasliq Uzbek. see Zhaslyk
Jasło Poland 43 D6
Jasol India 82 C4
Jason Islands Falkland Is 144 D8
Jason Peninsula Antarctica 152 L2
Jasonville U.S.A. 134 B4
Jasper Canada 118 G4
Jasper AL U.S.A. 133 C5
Jasper FL U.S.A. 133 D6
Jasper GA U.S.A. 133 C5
Jasper IN U.S.A. 134 B4
Jasper NY U.S.A. 135 G2
Jasper TN U.S.A. 133 C5
Jasper TX U.S.A. 131 E6
Jasper National Park Canada 120 G4
Jasrasar India 82 C4
Jaşşān Iraq 91 G4
Jassy Romania see Iaşi
Jastrzębie-Zdrój Poland 47 Q6
Jaswantpura India 82 C4
Jászberény Hungary 59 H1
Jataí Brazil 145 A2
Jatapu r. Brazil 143 G4
Jath India 84 B2
Jati Pak. 89 H5
Jatibonico Cuba 133 E8
Játiva Spain see Xàtiva
Jatoi Pak. 89 H4
Jat Poti Afgh. 89 G4
Jaú Brazil 145 A3
Jaú r. Brazil 142 F4
Jaú, Parque Nacional do nat. park Brazil 142 F4
Jaua Sarisariñama, Parque Nacional nat. park Venez. 142 F3
Jauja Peru 142 C6
Jaunlutriņi Latvia 45 M8
Jaunpiebalga Latvia 45 O8
Jaunpur India 83 E4
Jauri Iran 89 F4
Java Georgia 91 F2

▶Java i. Indon. 108 A1
5th largest island in Asia.

Javaés r. Brazil see Formoso
Javand Afgh. 89 G3
Javari r. Brazil/Peru see Yavari
Java Ridge sea feature Indian Ocean 149 P6
Javarthushuu Mongolia 73 K3
Java Sea Indon. see Jawa, Laut

▶Java Trench sea feature Indian Ocean 149 O6
Deepest point in the Indian Ocean.

Java Trench sea feature Indian Ocean 149 P6
Jävenitz Germany 53 L2
Jävre Sweden 44 L4
Jawa i. Indon. see Java
Jawa, Laut sea Indon. 68 E7
Jawhar India 84 B2
Jawhar Somalia 98 E3
Jawor Poland 47 P5
Jay U.S.A. 131 E4

▶Jaya, Puncak mt. Indon. 69 J7
Highest mountain in Oceania.
Oceania 102–103

Jayakusumu mt. Indon. see Jaya, Puncak
Jayakwadi Sagar l. India 84 B2
Jayantiapur Bangl. see Jaintiapur
Jayapura Indon. 69 K7
Jayawijaya, Pegunungan mts Indon. 69 J7
Jayb, Wādī al watercourse Israel/Jordan 85 B4
Jayfi, Wādī al watercourse Egypt 85 B4
Jaypur India 84 D2
Jayrūd Syria 85 C3
Jayton U.S.A. 131 C5
Jazīreh-ye Shīf Iran 88 C4
Jazminal Mex. 131 C7
Jbail Lebanon 85 B2
J. C. Murphey Lake U.S.A. 134 B3
Jean U.S.A. 129 F4
Jean Marie River Canada 120 F2
Jeannin, Lac l. Canada 123 I2
Jebāl Bārez, Kūh-e mts Iran 88 E4
Jebel, Bahr el r. Sudan/Uganda see White Nile
Jebel Abyad Plateau Sudan 86 C6
Jech Doab lowland Pak. 89 I4
Jedburgh U.K. 50 G5
Jeddah Saudi Arabia 86 E5
Jedeida Tunisia 58 C6
Jeetze r. Germany 53 L1
Jefferson IA U.S.A. 130 E3
Jefferson NC U.S.A. 132 D4
Jefferson OH U.S.A. 134 E3
Jefferson TX U.S.A. 131 E5
Jefferson, Mount U.S.A. 128 E2
Jefferson, Mount vol. U.S.A. 126 C3

▶Jefferson City U.S.A. 130 E4
State capital of Missouri.

Jeffersonville GA U.S.A. 133 D5
Jeffersonville IN U.S.A. 134 C4
Jeffersonville OH U.S.A. 134 D4
Jeffrey's Bay S. Africa 100 G8
Jehanabad India 83 F4
Jeju S. Korea see Cheju
Jejuí Guazú r. Para. 144 E2
Jēkabpils Latvia 45 N8
Jelbart Ice Shelf Antarctica 152 B2
Jelenia Góra Poland 47 O5
Jelep La pass China/India 83 G4
Jelgava Latvia 45 M8
Jellico U.S.A. 134 C5
Jellicoe Canada 122 D4
Jelloway U.S.A. 134 D3
Jemaja i. Indon. 71 D7
Jember Indon. 68 E8
Jempang, Danau l. Indon. 68 F7
Jena Germany 53 L4
Jena U.S.A. 131 E6
Jendouba Tunisia 58 C6
Jengish Chokusu mt. China/Kyrg. see Pobeda Peak
Jenīn West Bank 85 B3
Jenkins U.S.A. 134 D5
Jenne Mali see Djenné
Jenner Canada 121 I5
Jennings r. Canada 120 C3
Jennings U.S.A. 131 E6
Jenolan Caves Australia 112 E4
Jenpeg Canada 121 L4
Jensen U.S.A. 129 I1
Jens Munk Island Canada 119 K3
Jeparit Australia 111 C8
Jequié Brazil 145 C1
Jequitaí r. Brazil 145 B2
Jequitinhonha Brazil 145 C2
Jequitinhonha r. Brazil 145 D1
Jerba, Île de i. Tunisia 54 G5
Jerbar Sudan 97 G4
Jereh Iran 88 C4
Jérémie Haiti 137 J5
Jerez Mex. 136 D4
Jerez de la Frontera Spain 57 C5
Jerggul Norway 44 N2
Jergucat Albania 59 I5
Jericho Australia 110 D4
Jericho West Bank 85 B4
Jerichow Germany 53 M2
Jerid, Chott el salt l. Tunisia 54 F5
Jerilderie Australia 112 B5
Jerimoth Hill hill U.S.A. 135 J3
Jeroaquara Brazil 145 A1
Jerome U.S.A. 126 E4
Jerruck Pak. 89 H5

▶Jersey terr. Channel Is 49 E9
United Kingdom Crown Dependency.
Europe 5, 38–39

Jersey City U.S.A. 135 H3
Jersey Shore U.S.A. 135 G3
Jerseyville U.S.A. 130 F4
Jerumenha Brazil 143 J5

▶Jerusalem Israel/West Bank 85 B4
Capital of Israel (De facto capital. Disputed).

Jervis Bay Australia 112 E5
Jervis Bay b. Australia 112 E5
Jervis Bay Territory admin. div. Australia 112 E5
Jesenice Slovenia 58 F1
Jesenice, Vodní nádrž resr Czech Rep. 53 M4
Jesi Italy 58 E3
Jesselton Sabah Malaysia see Kota Kinabalu
Jessen Germany 53 M3
Jessheim Norway 45 G6
Jessore Bangl. 83 G5
Jesteburg Germany 53 J1
Jesu Maria Island P.N.G. see Rambutyo Island
Jesup U.S.A. 133 D6
Jesús María, Barra spit Mex. 131 D7
Jetmore U.S.A. 130 D4
Jever Germany 53 H1
Jewell Ridge U.S.A. 134 E5
Jewish Autonomous Oblast admin. div. Rus. Fed. see Yevreyskaya Avtonomnaya Oblast'
Jeypur India see Jaypur
Jezzine Lebanon 85 B3
Jhabua India 82 C5
Jhajhar India see Jhajjar
Jhajjar India 82 D3
Jhal Pak. 89 G4
Jhalawar India 82 D4
Jhal Jhao Pak. 89 G5
Jhang Pak. 89 I4
Jhansi India 82 D4
Jhanzi r. India 70 A1
Jhapa Nepal 83 F4
Jharia India 83 F5
Jharkhand state India 83 F5
Jharsuguda India 83 F5
Jhawani Nepal 83 F4
Jhelum r. India/Pak. 89 I4
Jhelum Pak. 89 I3
Jhenaidah Bangl. 83 G5
Jhenaidaha Bangl. see Jhenaidah
Jhenida Bangl. see Jhenaidah
Jhimpir Pak. 89 H5
Jhudo Pak. 89 H5
Jhumritilaiya India 83 F4
Jhund India 82 B5
Jhunjhunun India 82 C3
Jiachuan China 76 E1
Jiachuanzhen China see Jiachuan
Jiading Jiangxi China see Xinfeng
Jiading Shanghai China 77 I2
Jiahe China 77 G3
Jiajiang China 76 D2
Jiamusi China 74 C3
Ji'an Jiangxi China 77 G3
Ji'an Jilin China 74 B4
Jianchuan China 76 C3
Jiande China 77 H2
Jiangbei China see Yubei
Jiangbiancun China 77 G3
Jiangcheng China 76 D4

Jiangcun China 77 F3
Jiangdu China 77 H1
Jiange China see Pu'an
Jianghong China 77 F4
Jiangjin China 76 E2
Jiangjunmiao China 80 G3
Jiangkou Guangdong China see Fengkai
Jiangkou Guizhou China 77 F3
Jiangkou Shaanxi China 76 E1
Jiangling China see Jingzhou
Jiangluozhen China 76 E1
Jiangmen China 77 G4
Jiangna China see Yanshan
Jiangshan China 77 H2
Jiangsi China see Dejiang
Jiangsu prov. China 77 H1
Jiangxi prov. China 77 G3
Jiangxia China 77 G2
Jiangyan China 77 I1
Jiangyin China 77 I2
Jiangyou China 76 E2
Jiangzhesongrong China 83 F3
Jianjun China see Yongshou
Jiankang China 76 D3
Jianli China 77 G2
Jian'ou China 77 H3
Jianping China see Langxi
Jianpur India 83 E4
Jianshe China see Baiyü
Jianshi China 77 F2
Jianshui China 76 D4
Jianshui Hu l. China 83 E2
Jianxing China 76 E2
Jianyang Fujian China 77 H3
Jianyang Sichuan China 76 E2
Jiaochang China 76 D1
Jiaochangba China see Jiaochang
Jiaocheng China see Jiaoling
Jiaohe China 74 B4
Jiaojiang China see Taizhou
Jiaokui China see Yiliang
Jiaoling China 77 H3
Jiaopingdu China 76 D3
Jiaowei China 77 H3
Jiaozuo China 77 G1
Jiasa China 76 D3
Jiashan China see Mingguang
Jia Tsuo La pass China 83 F3
Jiawang China 77 H1
Jiaxian China 77 G1
Jiaxing China 77 I2
Jiayi Taiwan see Chiai
Jiayin China 74 C2
Jiayuguan China 80 I4
Jiazi China 77 H4
Jībūtī country Africa see Djibouti
Jibuti Djibouti see Djibouti
Jiddah Saudi Arabia see Jeddah
Jiddī, Jabal al hill Egypt 85 A4
Jidong China 74 C3
Jiehkkevarri mt. Norway 44 K2
Jieshi China 77 G4
Jieshipu China 77 F4
Jieshi Wan b. China 77 G4
Jiešjávri l. Norway 44 N2
Jiexi China 77 G4
Jiexiu China 73 K5
Jieyang China 77 H4
Jieznas Lith. 45 N9
Jigzhi China 76 D1
Jiḩār, Wādī al watercourse Syria 85 C2
Jihlava Czech Rep. 47 O6
Jija Sarai Afgh. 89 F3
Jijel Alg. 54 F4
Jijiga Eth. 98 E3
Jījīrud Iran 88 C3
Jijü China 76 D2
Jil'ād reg. Jordan 85 B3
Jilf al Kabīr, Haḑabat al plat. Egypt 86 C5
Jilh al 'Ishār plain Saudi Arabia 88 B5
Jilib Somalia 98 E3
Jilin China 74 B4
Jilin prov. China 74 B4
Jilin Hada Ling mts China 74 B4
Jiliu He r. China 74 A2
Jilo India 82 C4
Jilong Taiwan see Chilung
Jīma Eth. 98 D3
Jimda China see Zindo
Jiménez Chihuahua Mex. 131 B7
Jiménez Coahuila Mex. 131 C6
Jiménez Tamaulipas Mex. 131 D7
Jimía, Cerro mt. Hond. 136 G5
Jimsar China 80 G3
Jim Thorpe U.S.A. 135 H3
Jinan China 73 L5
Jin'an China see Songpan
Jinbi China see Dayao
Jinchang China 72 I5
Jincheng Shanxi China 77 G1
Jincheng Sichuan China see Yilong
Jincheng Yunnan China see Wuding
Jinchengjiang China see Hechi
Jinchuan Gansu China see Jinchang
Jinchuan Jiangxi China see Xingan
Jind India 82 D3
Jinding China see Lanping
Jindřichův Hradec Czech Rep. 47 O6
Jin'e China see Longchang
Jingbian China 73 J5
Jingchuan China 76 E1
Jingde China 77 H2
Jingdezhen China 77 H2
Jingellic Australia 112 C5
Jinggangshan China 77 G3
Jinggang Shan hill China 77 G3
Jinggongqiao China 77 H2
Jinggu China 76 D4
Jing He r. China 77 F1
Jinghong China 76 D4
Jingle China 73 K5
Jingmen China 77 G2
Jingpo China 74 C4
Jingpo Hu resr China 74 C4
Jingsha China see Jingzhou
Jingtai China 72 I5
Jingtieshan China 80 I4
Jingxi China 76 E4
Jingxian Anhui China 77 H2
Jingxian Hunan China see Jingzhou
Jingyang China see Jingde
Jingyu China 74 B4
Jingyuan China 72 I5
Jingzhou Hubei China 77 G2
Jingzhou Hubei China 77 G2
Jingzhou Hunan China 77 F3
Jinhe Nei Mongol China 74 A2
Jinhe Yunnan China see Jinping
Jinhu China 77 H1
Jinhua Yunnan China see Jianchuan
Jinhua Zhejiang China 77 H2
Jining Nei Mongol China 73 K4
Jining Shandong China 77 H1
Jinja Uganda 98 D3
Jinjiang Hainan China see Chengmai
Jinjiang Yunnan China 76 D3
Jin Jiang r. China 77 G2
Jinka Eth. 98 D3
Jinmen Taiwan see Chinmen
Jinmen Dao i. Taiwan see Chinmen Tao
Jinmu Jiao pt China 77 F5
Jinning China 76 D3
Jinotepe Nicaragua 137 G6
Jinping Guizhou China 77 F3
Jinping Yunnan China 76 D4
Jinping Yunnan China see Qiubei
Jinping Shan mts China 76 D3
Jinsen S. Korea see Inch'ŏn
Jinsha China 76 E3
Jinsha Jiang r. China 76 E2 see Yangtze
Jinshan Nei Mongol China see Guyang
Jinshan Shanghai China 77 I2
Jinshan Yunnan China see Lufeng
Jinshi Hunan China 77 F2
Jinshi Hunan China see Xinning
Jintur India 84 C2
Jinxi Anhui China see Taihu
Jinxi Jiangxi China 77 H3
Jinxi Liaoning China see Lianshan
Jin Xi r. China 77 H3
Jinxian China 77 H2
Jinxiang China 77 H1
Jinyun China 77 I2
Jinz, Qā' al salt flat Jordan 85 C4
Jinzhai China 77 G2
Jinzhong China 73 K5
Jinzhou China 73 M4
Jinzhu China see Daocheng
Ji-Paraná Brazil 142 F6
Jipijapa Ecuador 142 B4
Ji Qu r. China 76 C2
Jiquiriçá Brazil 145 D1
Jiquitaia Brazil 145 D2
Jirā', Wādī watercourse Egypt 85 A5
Jirānīyāt, Shi'bān al watercourse Saudi Arabia 85 D4
Jirgatol Tajik. 89 H2
Jiri r. India 70 A1
Jīroft Iran 88 E4
Jirriiban Somalia 98 E3
Jirwān Saudi Arabia 88 C6
Jirwan well Saudi Arabia 88 C6
Jishou China 77 F2
Jisr ash Shughūr Syria 85 C2
Jitian China see Lianshan
Jitra Malaysia 71 C6
Jiu r. Romania 59 J3
Jiudding Shan mt. China 76 D2
Jiujiang Jiangxi China 77 G2
Jiujiang Jiangxi China 77 H2
Jiulian China see Mojiang
Jiuling Shan mts China 77 G2
Jiulong Hong Kong China see Kowloon
Jiulong Sichuan China 76 D2
Jiuqian China 77 F3
Jiuquan China 80 I4
Jiuxu China 76 E3
Jiuzhou Jiang r. China 77 F4
Jiwani Pak. 89 F5
Jiwen China 74 A2
Jixi Anhui China 77 H2
Jixi Heilong. China 74 C3
Jixian China 74 C3
Jiyuan China 77 G1
Jīzah, Ahrāmāt al tourist site Egypt see Pyramids of Giza
Jīzān Saudi Arabia 86 F6
Jizzakh Uzbek. see Dzhizak
Joaçaba Brazil 145 A4
Joaíma Brazil 145 C2
João Belo Moz. see Xai-Xai
João de Almeida Angola see Chibia
João Pessoa Brazil 143 L5
João Pinheiro Brazil 145 B2
Joaquin V. González Arg. 144 D3
Job Peak U.S.A. 128 D2
Jocketa Germany 53 M4
Joda India 83 F5
Jodhpur India 82 C4
Jodiya India 82 B5
Joensuu Fin. 44 P5
Jōetsu Japan 75 E5
Jofane Moz. 99 D6
Joffre, Mount Canada 120 H5
Jogbura Nepal 82 E3
Jõgeva Estonia 45 O7
Jogjakarta Indon. see Yogyakarta
Jõgua Estonia 45 O7
Johannesburg S. Africa 101 H4
Johannesburg U.S.A. 128 E4
Johan Peninsula Canada 119 K2
Johi Pak. 89 G5
John Day U.S.A. 126 D3
John Day r. U.S.A. 126 C3
John D'Or Prairie Canada 120 H3
John F. Kennedy airport U.S.A. 135 I3
John H. Kerr Reservoir U.S.A. 135 F5
John Jay, Mount Canada/U.S.A. 120 D3
John o'Groats U.K. 50 F2
Johnson U.S.A. 130 C4
Johnsonburg U.S.A. 135 F3
Johnson City NY U.S.A. 135 H2
Johnson City TN U.S.A. 132 D4
Johnson City TX U.S.A. 131 D6
Johnsondale U.S.A. 128 D4
Johnson Draw watercourse U.S.A. 131 C6
Johnson's Crossing Canada 120 C2
Johnston, Lake salt flat Australia 109 C8
Johnston and Sand Islands terr. N. Pacific Ocean see Johnston Atoll

▶Johnston Atoll terr. N. Pacific Ocean 150 I4
United States Unincorporated Territory.

Johnstone U.K. 50 E5
Johnstone Lake Canada see Old Wives Lake
Johnston Range hills Australia 109 B7
Johnstown Rep. of Ireland 51 E5
Johnstown NY U.S.A. 135 H2
Johnstown PA U.S.A. 135 F3
Johor, Selat strait Malaysia/Sing. 71 [inset]
Johor, Sungai r. Malaysia 71 [inset]
Johor Bahru Malaysia 71 [inset]
Johore Bahru Malaysia see Johor Bahru
Jõhvi Estonia 45 O7
Joinville Brazil 145 A4
Joinville France 56 G2
Joinville Island Antarctica 152 A2
Jokkmokk Sweden 44 K3
Jökulsá r. Iceland 44 [inset]
Jökulsá á Fjöllum r. Iceland 44 [inset]
Jökulsá í Fljótsdal r. Iceland 44 [inset]
Jolfa Iran 88 B2
Joliet U.S.A. 134 A3
Joliet, Lac l. Canada 122 F4
Joliette Canada 123 G5
Jolly Lake Canada 121 H1
Jolo Phil. 69 G5
Jolo i. Phil. 69 G5
Jomda China 76 C2
Jonancy U.S.A. 134 D5
Jonava Lith. 45 N9
Jonê China 76 D1
Jonesboro AR U.S.A. 131 F5
Jonesboro LA U.S.A. 131 E5
Jones Sound sea chan. Canada 119 J2
Jonesville MI U.S.A. 134 C3
Jonesville VA U.S.A. 134 D5
Jonglei Canal Sudan 86 D8
Jönköping Sweden 45 I8
Jonquière Canada 123 H4
Joplin U.S.A. 131 E4
Joppa Israel see Tel Aviv-Yafo
Jora India 82 D4

▶Jordan country Asia 85 C4
Asia 6, 62–63

Jordan r. Asia 85 B4
Jordan U.S.A. 126 G3
Jordan r. U.S.A. 126 D4
Jordânia Brazil 145 C1
Jordet Norway 45 H6
Jorhat India 83 H4
Jork Germany 53 J1
Jorm Afgh. 89 H2
Jörn Sweden 44 L4
Joroinen Fin. 44 O5
Jørpeland Norway 45 E7
Jos Nigeria 96 D4
José de San Martín Arg. 144 B6
Joseph, Lac l. Canada 123 I3
Joseph Bonaparte Gulf Australia 108 E3
Joseph City U.S.A. 129 H4
Joshimath India 82 D3
Joshipur India 84 E1
Joshua Tree National Park U.S.A. 129 F5
Jos Plateau Nigeria 96 D4
Jostedalsbreen Nasjonalpark nat. park Norway 45 E6
Jotunheimen Nasjonalpark nat. park Norway 45 F6
Jouaiya Lebanon 85 B3
Joubertina S. Africa 100 F7
Jouberton S. Africa 101 H4
Joûnié Lebanon 85 B3
Joure Neth. 52 F2
Joutsa Fin. 45 O6
Joutseno Fin. 45 P6
Jouy-aux-Arches France 52 G5
Jovellanos Cuba 133 D8
Jowai India 83 H4
Jowr Deh Iran 88 C2
Jowzak Iran 89 F4
Joy, Mount Canada 120 C2
Joyce's Country reg. Rep. of Ireland 51 C4
Joypurhat Bangl. 83 G4
Juan Aldama Mex. 131 C7
Juancheng China 77 G1
Juan de Fuca Strait Canada/U.S.A. 124 C2
Juan Fernández, Archipiélago is S. Pacific Ocean 151 O8
Juan Fernández Islands S. Pacific Ocean see Juan Fernández, Archipiélago
Juanjuí Peru 142 C5
Juankoski Fin. 44 P5
Juan Mata Ortíz Mex. 127 F7
Juaréz Mex. 131 C7
Juárez, Sierra de mts Mex. 123 D6
Juàzeiro Brazil 143 J5
Juàzeiro do Norte Brazil 143 K5
Juba r. Somalia see Jubba
Juba Sudan 97 G4
Jubany research station Antarctica 152 A2
Jubba r. Somalia 98 E4
Jubbah Saudi Arabia 91 F5
Jubbulpore India see Jabalpur
Jubilee Lake salt flat Australia 109 D7
Juby, Cap c. Morocco 96 B2
Júcar r. Spain 57 F4
Juçara Brazil 145 A1
Juchitán Mex. 136 E5
Jucuruçu Brazil 145 D2
Jucuruçu r. Brazil 145 D2
Judaberg Norway 45 D7
Judaidat al Hamir Iraq 91 F5
Judayyidat 'Ar'ar well Iraq 91 F5
Judenburg Austria 47 O7
Judian China 76 C3
Judith Gap U.S.A. 126 F3
Juegang China see Rudong
Juelsminde Denmark 45 G9
Juerana Brazil 145 D2
Jugar China see Sêrxü
Juigalpa Nicaragua 137 G6
Juillet, Lac l. Canada 123 J3
Juína Brazil 143 G6
Juist i. Germany 52 H1
Juiz de Fora Brazil 145 C3
Julaca Bol. 142 E8
Julesburg U.S.A. 130 C3
Julia Brazil 142 E4
Juliaca Peru 142 D7
Julia Creek Australia 110 C4
Julian U.S.A. 128 E5
Julian, Lac l. Canada 122 F3
Julianadorp Neth. 52 E2
Julian Alps mts Slovenia see Julijske Alpe
Julianatop mt. Indon. see Mandala, Puncak
Juliana Top mt. Suriname 143 G3
Julianehåb Greenland see Qaqortoq
Jülich Germany 52 G4
Julijske Alpe mts Slovenia 58 E1
Julimes Mex. 131 B6
Juliomagus France see Angers
Julius, Lake Australia 110 B4
Jullundur India see Jalandhar
Juma Uzbek. see Dzhuma
Jumbilla Peru 142 C5
Jumilla Spain 57 F4
Jumla Nepal 83 E3
Jümme r. Germany 53 H1
Jumna r. India see Yamuna
Jump r. U.S.A. 130 F2
Junagadh India 82 B5
Junagarh India 84 D2
Junan China 77 H1
Junayfah Egypt 85 A4
Junbuk Iran 88 E3
Junction TX U.S.A. 131 D6
Junction UT U.S.A. 129 G2
Junction City KS U.S.A. 130 D4
Junction City KY U.S.A. 134 C5
Junction City OR U.S.A. 126 C3
Jundiaí Brazil 145 B3
Jundian China 77 F1

▶Juneau AK U.S.A. 120 C3
State capital of Alaska.

Juneau WI U.S.A. 130 F3
Juneau Icefield Canada 120 C3
Junee Australia 112 C5
Jūn el Khudr b. Lebanon 85 B3
Jungar Qi China see Shagedu
Jungfrau mt. Switz. 56 H3
Junggar Pendi basin China 80 G2
Juniata r. U.S.A. 135 G3
Junín Arg. 144 D4
Junín Peru 142 C6
Junior U.S.A. 134 F4
Juniper Mountain U.S.A. 129 I1
Juniper Mountains U.S.A. 129 G4
Junipero Serro Peak U.S.A. 124 C3
Junlian China 76 E2
Junmenling China 77 G3
Juno U.S.A. 131 C6
Junsele Sweden 44 J5
Junshan Hu l. China 77 H2
Junxi China see Datian
Junxian China see Danjiangkou
Ju'nyung China 76 C1
Ju'nyunggoin China see Ju'nyung
Juodupė Lith. 45 N8
Jupiá Brazil 145 A3
Jupiá, Represa resr Brazil 145 A3
Jupiter U.S.A. 133 D7
Juquiá r. Brazil 145 B4
Jur r. Sudan 86 C8
Jura mts France/Switz. 56 G4
Jura i. U.K. 50 D4
Jura, Sound of sea chan. U.K. 50 D5
Jurací Brazil 145 C1
Jurbarkas Lith. 45 M9
Jurf ad Darāwīsh Jordan 85 B4
Jürgenstorf Germany 53 M1
Jurhen Ul mts China 83 G2
Jūrmala Latvia 45 M8
Jurmu Fin. 44 O4
Jurong Sing. 71 [inset]
Jurong, Sungai r. Sing. 71 [inset]
Jurong Island reg. Sing. 71 [inset]
Juruá r. Brazil 142 E4
Juruena r. Brazil 143 G5
Juruti Brazil 143 G4
Jurva Fin. 44 L5
Jūshqān Iran 88 E2
Jūsīyah Syria 85 C2
Justice U.S.A. 134 E5
Jutaí Brazil 142 E5
Jutaí r. Brazil 142 E4
Jüterbog Germany 53 N3
Jutiapa Guat. 136 G6
Juticalpa Hond. 137 G6
Jutis Sweden 44 J3
Jutland pen. Denmark 45 F8
Juuka Fin. 44 P5
Juva Fin. 44 O6
Juwain Afgh. 89 F4
Juye China 77 H1
Jūyom Iran 88 D4
Južnoukrajinsk Ukr. see Yuzhnoukrayinsk
Jwaneng Botswana 100 G3
Jylland pen. Denmark see Jutland
Jyväskylä Fin. 44 N5

K

▶K2 mt. China/Jammu and Kashmir 82 D2
2nd highest mountain in the world and in Asia.
World 12–13

Ka r. Nigeria 96 D3
Kaafu Atoll Maldives see Male Atoll
Kaa-Iya, Parque Nacional nat. park Bol. 142 F7
Kaakhka Turkm. see Kaka
Kaala mt. HI U.S.A. 127 [inset]
Kaapstad S. Africa see Cape Town
Kaarina Fin. 45 M6
Kaarßen Germany 53 L1
Kaarst Germany 52 G3
Kaavi Fin. 44 P5
Kaba China see Habahe
Kabakly Turkm. 89 F2
Kabala Sierra Leone 96 B4
Kabale Uganda 98 C4
Kabalega Falls National Park Uganda see Murchison Falls National Park
Kabalo Dem. Rep. Congo 99 C4
Kabambare Dem. Rep. Congo 99 C4
Kabangu Dem. Rep. Congo 99 C5
Kabanjahe Indon. 71 B7
Kabara i. Fiji 107 I3
Kabarega National Park Uganda see Murchison Falls National Park
Kabaw Valley Myanmar 70 A2
Kabbani r. India 84 C3
Kåbdalis Sweden 44 L3
Kabinakagami r. Canada 122 D4
Kabinakagami Lake Canada 122 D4
Kabinda Dem. Rep. Congo 99 C4
Kabīr r. Syria 85 B2
Kabīrkūh mts Iran 88 B3
Kabo Cent. Afr. Rep. 98 B3
Kābol Afgh. see Kābul
Kabompo r. Zambia 99 C5
Kabongo Dem. Rep. Congo 99 C4
Kabūdeh Iran 89 F3
Kabūd Gonbad Iran 89 E2
Kabūd Rāhang Iran 88 C3

▶Kābul Afgh. 89 H3
Capital of Afghanistan.

Kābul r. Afgh. 89 I3
Kabuli P.N.G. 69 L7
Kabunda Dem. Rep. Congo 99 C5
Kabunduk Indon. 108 B2
Kaburuang i. Indon. 69 H6
Kabūtar Khān Iran 88 E4
Kabwe Zambia 99 C5
Kacha Kuh mts Iran/Pak. 89 F4
Kachalinskaya Rus. Fed. 43 J6
Kachchh, Great Rann of marsh India see Kachchh, Rann of
Kachchh, Gulf of India 82 B5
Kachchh, Rann of marsh India 82 B4
Kachia Nigeria 96 D4
Kachiry Kazakh. 72 D2
Kachkanar Rus. Fed. 41 R4
Kachret'i Georgia 91 G2
Kachug Rus. Fed. 72 J2
Kaçkar Dağı mt. Turkey 91 F2
Kadaingti Myanmar 70 B3
Kadaiyanallur India 84 C4
Kadanai r. Afgh./Pak. 89 G4
Kadan Kyun i. Myanmar 71 B4
Kadavu i. Fiji 107 H3
Kadavu Passage Fiji 107 H3
Kaddam l. India 84 C2
Kade Ghana 96 C4
Kādhimain Iraq see Al Kāẓimīyah
Kadi India 82 C5
Kadıköy Turkey 59 M4
Kadınhanı Turkey 90 D3
Kadiolo Mali 96 C3
Kadiri India 84 C3
Kadirli Turkey 90 E3
Kadirpur Pak. 89 I4
Kadiyevka Ukr. see Stakhanov
Kadmat atoll India 84 B4
Ka-do i. N. Korea 75 B5
Kadok Malaysia 71 C6
Kadoka U.S.A. 130 C3
Kadoma Zimbabwe 99 C5
Kadonkani Myanmar 70 A4
Kadu Myanmar 70 B1
Kadugli Sudan 86 C7
Kaduna Nigeria 96 D3
Kaduna r. Nigeria 96 D4
Kadusam mt. China/India 83 I3
Kaduy Rus. Fed. 42 H4
Kadyy Rus. Fed. 42 I4
Kadzherom Rus. Fed. 42 L2
Kaédi Mauritania 96 B3
Kaélé Cameroon 97 E3
Kaeng Krachan National Park Thai. 71 B4
Kaesŏng N. Korea 75 B5
Kāf Saudi Arabia 85 C4
Kafa Ukr. see Feodosiya
Kafakumba Dem. Rep. Congo 99 C4
Kafan Armenia see Kapan
Kafanchan Nigeria 96 D4
Kafireas, Akra pt Greece 59 K5
Kafiristan reg. Pak. 89 H3
Kafr ash Shaykh Egypt 90 C5
Kafr el Sheikh Egypt see Kafr ash Shaykh
Kafue Zambia 99 C5
Kafue r. Zambia 99 C5
Kafue National Park Zambia 99 C5
Kaga Japan 75 E5
Kaga Bandoro Cent. Afr. Rep. 98 B3
Kagan Pak. 89 I3
Kagan Uzbek. 89 G2
Kagang China 76 D1
Kaganovichabad Tajik. see Kolkhozobod
Kaganovichi Pervyye Ukr. see Polis'ke
Kagarlyk Ukr. see Kaharlyk
Kåge Sweden 44 L4
Kağızman Turkey 91 F2
Kagmar Sudan 86 D7
Kagoshima Japan 75 C7
Kagoshima pref. Japan 75 C7
Kagul Moldova see Cahul
Kahama Tanz. 98 D4
Kaharlyk Ukr. 43 F6
Kaherekoau Mountains N.Z. 113 A7
Kahla Germany 53 L4
Kahnūj Iran 88 E4
Kahoka U.S.A. 130 F3
Kahoolawe i. HI U.S.A. 127 [inset]
Kahperusvaarat mts Fin. 44 L2
Kahramanmaraş Turkey 90 E3
Kahror Pak. 89 H4
Kâhta Turkey 90 E3
Kahuku HI U.S.A. 127 [inset]
Kahuku Point HI U.S.A. 127 [inset]
Kahului i. U.S.A. see Kahoolawe
Kahurangi National Park N.Z. 113 D5
Kahurangi Point N.Z. 113 D5
Kahuta Pak. 89 I3
Kahuzi-Biega, Parc National du nat. park Dem. Rep. Congo 98 C4
Kai, Kepulauan is Indon. 69 I8
Kaiapoi N.Z. 113 D6
Kaibab U.S.A. 129 G3
Kaibab Plateau U.S.A. 129 G3
Kai Besar i. Indon. 69 I8
Kaibito Plateau U.S.A. 129 H3
Kaifeng Henan China 77 G1
Kaifeng Henan China 77 G1
Kaihua Yunnan China see Wenshan
Kaihua Zhejiang China 77 H2
Kaiingveld reg. S. Africa 100 E5
Kaijiang China 76 E2
Kai Kecil i. Indon. 69 I8
Kai Keung Leng Hong Kong China 77 [inset]
Kaikoura N.Z. 113 D6
Kailas mt. China see Kangrinboqê Feng
Kailasahar India see Kailashahar
Kailashahar India 83 H4
Kailas Range mts China see Gangdisê Shan
Kaili China 76 E3
Kailu China 73 M4
Kailua HI U.S.A. 127 [inset]
Kailua Kona HI U.S.A. 127 [inset]
Kaimana Indon. 69 I7
Kaimanawa Mountains N.Z. 113 E4
Kaimar China 76 B1
Kaimur Range hills India 82 E4
Käina Estonia 45 M7
Kainan Japan 75 D6
Kainda Kyrg. see Kayyngdy
Kaindy Kyrg. see Kayyngdy
Kainji Lake National Park Nigeria 96 D4
Kaipara Harbour N.Z. 113 E3
Kaiparowits Plateau U.S.A. 129 H3
Kaiping China 77 G4
Kaipokok Bay Canada 123 K3
Kairana India 82 D3
Kairiru Island P.N.G. 69 K7
Kaironi Indon. 69 I7
Kairouan Tunisia 58 D7
Kaiserslautern Germany 53 H5
Kaiser Wilhelm II Land reg. Antarctica 152 E2
Kaitaia N.Z. 113 D2
Kaitangata N.Z. 113 B8
Kaitawa N.Z. 113 F4
Kaithal India 82 D3
Kaitum Sweden 44 L3
Kaiwatu Indon. 108 D2
Kaiwi Channel HI U.S.A. 127 [inset]
Kaixian China 77 F2
Kaiyang China 76 E3
Kaiyuan Liaoning China 74 B4
Kaiyuan Yunnan China 76 D4
Kajaani Fin. 44 O4
Kajabbi Australia 110 C4
Kajaki Afgh. 89 G3
Kajrān Afgh. 89 G3
Kaka Turkm. 89 E2
Kakabeka Falls Canada 122 C4
Kakadu National Park Australia 108 F3
Kakagi Lake Canada 121 M5
Kakamas S. Africa 100 E5
Kakamega Kenya 98 D3
Kakana India 71 A5
Kakar Pak. 89 G5
Kakata Liberia 96 B4
Kake U.S.A. 120 C3
Kakenge Dem. Rep. Congo 99 C4
Kakerbeck Germany 53 L2
Kakhi Azer. see Qax
Kakhovka Ukr. 59 O1
Kakhovs'ke Vodoskhovyshche resr Ukr. 43 G7
Kakhul Moldova see Cahul
Kākī Iran 88 C4
Kakinada India 84 D2
Kakisa Canada 120 G2
Kakisa r. Canada 120 G2
Kakisa Lake Canada 120 G2
Kakogawa Japan 75 D6
Kakori India 82 E4
Kakshaal-Too mts China/Kyrg. 80 E3
Kaktovik U.S.A. 118 D2
Kakul Pak. 89 I3
Kakwa r. Canada 120 G4
Kala Pak. 89 H4
Kala Tanz. 99 D4
Kalaâ Kebira Tunisia 58 D7
Kalaallit Nunaat terr. N. America see Greenland
Kalabahi Indon. 108 D2
Kalabáka Greece see Kalampaka
Kalabgur India 84 C2
Kalabo Zambia 99 C5
Kalach Rus. Fed. 43 I6
Kalacha Dida Kenya 98 D3
Kalach-na-Donu Rus. Fed. 43 I6
Kaladan r. India/Myanmar 70 A2
Kaladar Canada 135 G1
Ka Lae pt HI U.S.A. 127 [inset]
Kalagwe Myanmar 70 B2
Kalahari Desert Africa 100 F2
Kalahari Gemsbok National Park S. Africa 100 E3
Kalaikhum Tajik. see Qal'aikhum
Kalai-Khumb Tajik. see Qal'aikhum
Kala-I-Mor Turkm. 89 F3
Kalajoki Fin. 44 M4
Kalalé Benin 96 D3
Kalam India 84 C1
Kalam Pak. 89 I3
Kalámai Greece see Kalamata
Kalamare Botswana 101 H2
Kalamaria Greece 59 J4
Kalamata Greece 59 J6
Kalamazoo U.S.A. 134 C2
Kalampaka Greece 59 I5
Kalanchak Ukr. 59 O1
Kalandi Pak. 89 F4
Kalandula Angola see Calandula
Kalannie Australia 109 B7
Kalān Zīād Iran 89 E5
Kalapana HI U.S.A. 127 [inset]
Kalār Iraq 91 G4
Kalasin Thai. 70 C3
Kalāt Afgh. 89 G3
Kalāt Khorāsān Iran see Kabūd Gonbad
Kalāt Sīstān va Balūchestān Iran 89 E5
Kalat Balochistan Pak. 89 G4

Kalat *Balochistan* Pak. 89 G5
Kalat, Küh-e *mt.* Iran 88 E3
Kalaupapa U.S.A. 127 [inset]
Kalaus *r.* Rus. Fed. 43 J7
Kalaw Myanmar 70 B2
Kälbäcär Azer. 91 G2
Kalbarri Australia 109 A6
Kalbarri National Park Australia 109 A6
Kalbe (Milde) Germany 53 L2
Kale Turkey 59 M6
Kalecik Turkey 90 D2
Kalefeld Germany 53 K3
Kaleindaung *inlet* Myanmar 70 A3
Kalemie Dem. Rep. Congo 99 C4
Kalemyo Myanmar 70 A2
Käl-e Namak Iran 88 D3
Kalevala Rus. Fed. 44 Q4
Kalewa Myanmar 70 A2
Kaleybar Iran 88 B2
Kalgan China *see* Zhangjiakou
Kalghatgi India 84 B3
Kalgoorlie Australia 109 C7
Käl Güsheh Iran 88 E4
Kali Croatia 58 F2
Kali *r.* India/Nepal 82 E3
Kaliakra, Nos *pt* Bulg. 59 M3
Kali Gandaki *r.* Nepal 83 F4
Kaligiri India 84 C3
Kalikata India *see* Kolkata
Kalima Dem. Rep. Congo 98 C4
Kalimantan *reg.* Indon. 68 E7
Kálimnos *i.* Greece *see* Kalymnos
Kalinin Rus. Fed. *see* Tver'
Kalinin Adyndaky Tajik. *see* Cheshtebe
Kaliningrad Rus. Fed. 45 L9
Kalinino Armenia *see* Tashir
Kalinino Rus. Fed. 42 I4
Kalininsk Rus. Fed. 43 J6
Kalininskaya Rus. Fed. 43 H7
Kalinjara India 82 C5
Kalinkavichy Belarus 43 F5
Kalinkovichi Belarus *see* Kalinkavichy
Kalisch Poland *see* Kalisz
Kalispell U.S.A. 126 E2
Kalisz Poland 47 Q5
Kalitva *r.* Rus. Fed. 43 I6
Kaliua Tanz. 99 D4
Kaliujar India 82 E4
Kalix Sweden 44 M4
Kalkalighat India 83 H4
Kalkalpen, Nationalpark *nat. park* Austria 47 O7
Kalkan Turkey 59 M6
Kalkaska U.S.A. 134 C1
Kalkfeld Namibia 99 B6
Kalkfonteindam *dam* S. Africa 97 G5
Kalkudah Sri Lanka 84 D5
Kall Germany 52 G4
Kallang *r.* Sing. 71 [inset]
Kallaste Estonia 45 O7
Kallavesi *l.* Fin. 44 O5
Kallsedet Sweden 44 H5
Kallsjön *l.* Sweden 44 H5
Kallur India 84 C2
Kalmar Sweden 45 J8
Kalmarsund *sea chan.* Sweden 45 J8
Kalmit *hill* Germany 53 I5
Kalmükh Qal'eh Iran 88 E2
Kalmunai Sri Lanka 84 D5
Kalmykia *aut. rep.* Rus. Fed. *see* Kalmykiya-Khalm'g-Tangch, Respublika
Kalmykiya-Khalm'g-Tangch, Respublika *aut. rep.* Rus. Fed. 91 G1
Kalmykovo Kazakh. *see* Taypak
Kalmytskaya Avtonomnaya Oblast' *aut. rep.* Rus. Fed. *see* Kalmykiya-khalm'g-Tangch, Respublika
Kalnai India 83 E5
Kalodnaye Belarus 45 O11
Kalol India 82 C5
Kalomo Zambia 99 C5
Kalone Peak Canada 120 E4
Kalpa India 82 D3
Kalpeni *atoll* India 84 B4
Kalpetta India 84 C4
Kalpi India 82 D4
Kaltag U.S.A. 118 C3
Kaltensundheim Germany 53 K4
Kaltukatjara Australia 109 E6
Kalu India 89 I4
Kaluga Rus. Fed. 43 H5
Kalukalukuang *i.* Indon. 68 F8
Kalundborg Denmark 45 G9
Kalush Ukr. 43 E6
Kalvakol India 84 C2
Kälviä Fin. 44 M5
Kal'ya Rus. Fed. 41 R3
Kalyan India 84 B2
Kalyandurg India 87 M7
Kalyansingapuram India 84 D2
Kalyazin Rus. Fed. 42 H4
Kalymnos *i.* Greece 59 L6
Kama Dem. Rep. Congo 98 C4
Kama Myanmar 70 A3

▶Kama *r.* Rus. Fed. 42 L4
4th longest river in Europe.

Kamaishi Japan 75 F5
Kamalia Pak. 89 I4
Kaman Turkey 90 D3
Kamaniskeg Lake Canada 135 G1
Kamanjab Namibia 99 B5
Kamarän *i.* Yemen 86 F6
Kamaran Island Yemen *see* Kamarän
Kamard *reg.* Afgh. 89 G3
Kamarod Pak. 89 F5
Kamaron Sierra Leone 96 B4
Kamashi Uzbek. 89 G2
Kamasin India 82 E4
Kambaiti Myanmar 70 B1
Kambalda Australia 109 C7
Kambam India 84 C4
Kambara *i.* Fiji *see* Kabara
Kambia Sierra Leone 96 B4
Kambing, Pulau *i.* East Timor *see* Ataúro, Ilha de
Kambo-san *mt.* N. Korea *see* Kwanmo-bong
Kambove Dem. Rep. Congo 99 C5
Kambüt Libya 90 B5
Kamchatka, Poluostrov *pen.* Rus. Fed. *see* Kamchatka Peninsula
Kamchatka Basin *sea feature* Bering Sea 150 H2
Kamchatka Peninsula Rus. Fed. 65 Q4
Kamchiya *r.* Bulg. 59 L3
Kameia, Parque Nacional de *nat. park* Angola *see* Cameia, Parque Nacional da
Kamelik *r.* Rus. Fed. 43 K5
Kamen Germany 53 H3
Kamen', Gory *mt.* Rus. Fed. 64 K3
Kamenets-Podol'skiy Ukr. *see* Kam"yanets'-Podil's'kyy
Kamenitsa *mt.* Bulg. 59 J4
Kamenjak, Rt *pt* Croatia 58 E2
Kamenka Kazakh. 41 Q5
Kamenka *Arkhangel'skaya Oblast'* Rus. Fed. 42 J2
Kamenka *Penzenskaya Oblast'* Rus. Fed. 43 J5
Kamenka *Primorskiy Kray* Rus. Fed. 74 E3
Kamenka-Bugskaya Ukr. *see* Kam"yanka-Buz'ka
Kamenka-Strumilovskaya Ukr. *see* Kam"yanka-Buz'ka
Kamen'-na-Obi Rus. Fed. 72 E2
Kamennogorsk Rus. Fed. 45 P6
Kamennomostskiy Rus. Fed. 91 F1
Kamenolomni Rus. Fed. 43 I7
Kamenongue Angola *see* Camanongue
Kamen'-Rybolov Rus. Fed. 74 D3
Kamenskoye Rus. Fed. 65 R3
Kamenskoye Ukr. *see* Dniprodzerzhyns'k
Kamensk-Shakhtinskiy Rus. Fed. 43 I6
Kamensk-Ural'skiy Rus. Fed. 64 H4
Kamet *mt.* China 82 D3
Kamiesberge *mts* S. Africa 100 D6
Kamieskroon S. Africa 100 C6
Kamileroi Australia 110 C3
Kamilukuak Lake Canada 121 K2
Kamina Dem. Rep. Congo 99 C4
Kaminak Lake Canada 121 M2
Kaminuriak Lake Canada *see* Qamanirjuaq Lake
Kamishihoro Japan 74 F4
Kamloops Canada 120 F5
Kamo Armenia 91 G2
Kamoke Pak. 89 I4
Kamonia Dem. Rep. Congo 99 C4

▶Kampala Uganda 98 D3
Capital of Uganda.

Kampar *r.* Indon. 68 C6
Kampar Malaysia 71 C6
Kampara India 84 D1
Kampen Neth. 52 F2
Kampene Dem. Rep. Congo 98 C4
Kamphaeng Phet Thai. 70 B3
Kampinoski Park Narodowy *nat. park* Poland 47 R4
Kâmpóng Cham Cambodia 71 D5
Kâmpóng Chhnăng Cambodia 71 D4
Kâmpóng Khleăng Cambodia 71 D4
Kâmpóng Saôm Cambodia *see* Sihanoukville
Kâmpóng Spœ Cambodia 71 D5
Kâmpóng Thum Cambodia 71 D4
Kâmpóng Trâbêk Cambodia 71 D5
Kâmpôt Cambodia 71 D5
Kampuchea *country* Asia *see* Cambodia
Kamrau, Teluk *b.* Indon. 69 I7
Kamsack Canada 121 K5
Kamskoye Vodokhranilishche *resr* Rus. Fed. 41 R4
Kamsuuma Somalia 98 E3
Kamuchawie Lake Canada 121 K3
Kamuli Uganda 98 D3
Kam"yanets'-Podil's'kyy Ukr. 43 E6
Kam"yanka-Buz'ka Ukr. 43 E6
Kamyanyets Belarus 45 M10
Kämyärän Iran 88 B3
Kamyshin Rus. Fed. 43 J6
Kamyslybas, Ozero *l.* Kazakh. 80 B2
Kamyzyak Rus. Fed. 43 K7
Kamzar Oman 88 E5
Kanaaupscow *r.* Canada 122 F3
Kanab U.S.A. 129 G3
Kanab Creek *r.* U.S.A. 129 G3
Kanairiktok *r.* Canada 123 K3
Kanak Pak. 89 G4
Kananga Dem. Rep. Congo 99 C4
Kanangio, Mount *vol.* P.N.G. 69 L7
Kanangra-Boyd National Park Australia 112 E4
Kanarak India *see* Konarka
Kanarraville U.S.A. 129 G3
Kanas *watercourse* Namibia 100 C4
Kanash Rus. Fed. 42 J5
Kanauj India *see* Kannauj
Kanazawa Japan 75 E5
Kanbalu Myanmar 70 A2
Kanchanaburi Thai. 71 B4
Kanchanjanga *mt.* India/Nepal *see* Kangchenjunga
Kanchipuram India 84 C3
Kand *mt.* Pak. 89 G4
Kanda Pak. 89 G4
Kandahär Afgh. 89 G4
Kandalaksha Rus. Fed. 44 R3
Kandalakshskiy Zaliv *g.* Rus. Fed. 44 R3
Kandang Indon. 71 B7
Kandar Indon. 108 E2
Kandavu *i.* Fiji *see* Kadavu
Kandavu Passage Fiji *see* Kadavu Passage
Kandé Togo 96 D4
Kandhkot Pak. 89 H4
Kandi Benin 96 D3
Kandi India 84 C2
Kandiaro Pak. 89 H5
Kandıra Turkey 59 N4
Kandos Australia 112 D4
Kandreho Madag. 99 E5
Kandrian P.N.G. 69 L8
Kandukur India 84 C3
Kandy Sri Lanka 84 D5
Kandyagash Kazakh. 80 A2
Kane U.S.A. 135 F3
Kane Bassin *b.* Greenland 153 K1
Kaneh *watercourse* Iran 88 D5
Kaneohe *HI* U.S.A. 127 [inset]
Kaneti Pak. 89 G4
Kanevskaya Rus. Fed. 43 H7
Kang Afgh. 89 F4
Kang Botswana 100 F2
Kangaamiut Greenland 119 M3
Kangaarsussuaq *c.* Greenland 119 K2
Kangaba Mali 96 C3
Kangal Turkey 90 E3
Kangän *Büshehr* Iran 88 D5
Kangän *Hormozgan* Iran 88 E5
Kangandala, Parque Nacional de *nat. park* Angola *see* Cangandala, Parque Nacional de
Kangar Malaysia 71 C6
Kangaroo Island Australia 111 B7
Kangaroo Point Australia 110 B3
Kangaslampi Fin. 44 P5
Kangasniemi Fin. 44 O6
Kangävar Iran 88 B3

▶Kangchenjunga *mt.* India/Nepal 83 G4
3rd highest mountain in the world and in Asia.
World 12–13

Kangding China 76 D2
Kangean, Kepulauan *is* Indon. 68 F8
Kangen *r.* Sudan 97 G4
Kangerlussuaq Greenland 119 M3
Kangerlussuaq *inlet* Greenland 119 M3
Kangerlussuaq *inlet* Greenland 153 J2
Kangersuatsiaq Greenland 119 M2
Kangertittivaq *sea chan.* Greenland 119 P2
Kanggye N. Korea 74 B4
Kanghwa S. Korea 75 B5
Kangikajik *c.* Greenland 119 P2
Kangiqsualujjuaq Canada 123 I2
Kangirsuk Canada 123 H1
Kang Krung National Park Thai. 71 B5
Kangle *Gansu* China 76 D1
Kangle *Jiangxi* China *see* Wanzai
Kanglong China 76 C1
Kangmar China 83 F3
Kangnŭng S. Korea 75 C5
Kango Gabon 98 B3
Kangping China 74 A4
Kangri Karpo Pass China/India 83 I3
Kangrinboqê Feng *mt.* China 82 E3
Kangsangdobdê China *see* Xainza
Kangto *mt.* China/India 83 H4
Kangtog China 83 F2
Kangxian China 76 E1
Kanibongan *Sabah* Malaysia 68 F5
Kanifing Gambia 96 B3
Kanigiri India 84 C3
Kanimekh Uzbek. 89 G1
Kanin, Poluostrov *pen.* Rus. Fed. 42 J2
Kanin Nos Rus. Fed. 153 G2
Kanin Nos, Mys *c.* Rus. Fed. 42 I1
Kaninskiy Bereg *coastal area* Rus. Fed. 42 I2
Kanjiroba *mt.* Nepal 83 E3
Kankaanpää Fin. 45 M6
Kankakee U.S.A. 134 B3
Kankan Guinea 96 C3
Kanker India 84 D1
Kankesanturai Sri Lanka 84 D4
Kankossa Mauritania 96 B3
Kanmaw Kyun *i.* Myanmar 71 B5
Kannauj India 82 D4
Kanniya Kumari *c.* India *see* Comorin, Cape
Kannonkoski Fin. 44 N5
Kannur India *see* Cannanore
Kannus Fin. 44 M5
Kano Nigeria 96 D3
Kanonpunt *pt* S. Africa 100 E8
Kanosh U.S.A. 129 G2
Kanovlei Namibia 99 B5
Kanoya Japan 75 C7
Kanpur *Orissa* India 84 E1
Kanpur *Uttar Pradesh* India 82 E4
Kanpur Pak. 89 H4
Kanrach *reg.* Pak. 89 G5
Kansai *airport* Japan 75 D6
Kansas U.S.A. 134 B4
Kansas *r.* U.S.A. 130 E4
Kansas *state* U.S.A. 130 D4
Kansas City *KS* U.S.A. 130 E4
Kansas City *MO* U.S.A. 130 E4
Kansk Rus. Fed. 65 K4
Kansu *prov.* China *see* Gansu
Kantang Thai. 71 B6
Kantara *hill* Cyprus 85 A2
Kantaralak Thai. 71 D4
Kantavu *i.* Fiji *see* Kadavu
Kantchari Burkina 96 D3
Kantemirovka Rus. Fed. 43 H6
Kanthi India 83 F5
Kantishna *r.* U.S.A. 118 C3
Kanton *atoll* Kiribati 107 I2
Kantulong Myanmar 70 B3
Kanturk Rep. of Ireland 51 D5
Kanuku Mountains Guyana 143 G3
Kanur India 84 C3
Kanus Namibia 100 D4
Kanyakubja India *see* Kannauj
KaNyamazane S. Africa 101 J3
Kanye Botswana 101 G3
Kaôh Pring *i.* Cambodia 71 C5
Kaohsiung Taiwan 77 I4
Kaôh Smăch *i.* Cambodia 71 C5
Kaôh Tang *i.* Cambodia 71 C5
Kaokoveld *plat.* Namibia 99 B5
Kaolack Senegal 96 B3
Kaoma Zambia 99 C5
Kaouadja Cent. Afr. Rep. 98 C3
Kapa S. Africa *see* Cape Town
Kapaa *HI* U.S.A. 127 [inset]
Kapaau *HI* U.S.A. 127 [inset]
Kapan Armenia 91 G3
Kapanga Dem. Rep. Congo 99 C4
Kaparhä Iran 88 C4
Kapatu Zambia 99 D4
Kapchagay Kazakh. 80 E3
Kapchagayskoye Vodokhranilishche *resr* Kazakh. 80 E3
Kap Dan Greenland *see* Kulusuk
Kapellen Belgium 52 E3
Kapello, Akra *pt* Greece 59 J6
Kapellskär Sweden 45 K7
Kapelskär Sweden *see* Kapellskär
Kapili *r.* India 83 G4
Kapingamarangi *atoll* Micronesia 150 G5
Kapingamarangi Rise *sea feature* N. Pacific Ocean 150 G5
Kapıorman Dağları *mts* Turkey 59 N4
Kapip Pak. 89 H4
Kapiri Mposhi Zambia 99 C5
Kapisillit Greenland 119 M3
Kapiskau *r.* Canada 122 E3
Kapit *Sarawak* Malaysia 68 E6
Kapiti Island N.Z. 113 E5
Kaplankyr, Chink *hills* Asia 91 I2
Kaplankyrskiy Gosudarstvennyy Zapovednik *nature res.* Turkm. 88 E1
Kapoeta Sudan 97 G4
Kapondai, Tanjung *pt* Indon. 69 G8
Kaposvár Hungary 58 G1
Kappel Germany 53 H5
Kappeln Germany 47 L3
Kapsukas Lith. *see* Marijampolė
Kaptai Bangl. 83 H5
Kapuas *r.* Indon. 68 D7
Kapuriya India 82 C4
Kapurthala India 82 C3
Kapuskasing Canada 122 E4
Kapustin Yar Rus. Fed. 43 J6
Kaputar *mt.* Australia 112 E3
Kaputir Kenya 98 D3
Kapuvár Hungary 58 G1
Kapydzhik, Gora *mt.* Armenia/Azer. *see* Qazangödağ
Kapyl' Belarus 45 O10
Kaqung China 89 J2
Kara India 82 E4
Kara Togo 96 D4
Kara *r.* Turkey 91 F3
Kara Art Pass China/Tajik. 89 I2
Kara-Balta Kyrg. 80 D3
Karabalyk Kazakh. 78 F1
Karabekaul' Turkm. *see* Garabekevyul
Karabiga Turkey 59 L4
Karabil', Vozvyshennost' *hills* Turkm. 89 F2
Kara-Bogaz-Gol, Proliv *sea chan.* Turkm. 91 I2
Kara-Bogaz-Gol, Zaliv *b.* Turkm. 91 I2
Kara-Bogaz-Gol'skiy Zaliv *b.* Turkm. *see* Kara-Bogaz-Gol, Zaliv
Karabük Turkey 90 D2
Karaburun Turkey 59 L5
Karabutak Kazakh. 80 B2
Karacabey Turkey 59 M4
Karacaköy Turkey 59 M4
Karacalı Dağ *mt.* Turkey 91 E3
Karaçal Tepe *mt.* Turkey 85 A1
Karacasu Turkey 59 M6
Karaca Yarımadası *pen.* Turkey 59 N6
Karachayevsk Rus. Fed. 91 F2
Karachev Rus. Fed. 43 G5
Karachi Pak. 89 G5
Karacurun Turkey *see* Hilvan
Karad India 84 B2
Kara Dağ *hill* Turkey 85 D1
Kara Dağ *mt.* Turkey 90 D3
Kara-Dar'ya Uzbek. *see* Payshanba
Kara Deniz *sea* Asia/Europe *see* Black Sea
Karagan Rus. Fed. 74 A1
Karaganda Kazakh. 80 D2
Karagayly Kazakh. 80 E2
Karaginskiy Zaliv *b.* Rus. Fed. 65 R4
Karagiye, Vpadina *depr.* Kazakh. 91 H2
Karagola India 83 F4
Karahallı Turkey 59 M5
Karahasanlı Turkey 90 D3
Karaikal India 84 C4
Karaikkudi India 84 C4
Karaisalı Turkey 90 D3
Karaj Iran 88 C3
Karak Jordan *see* Al Karak
Karakalli Turkey *see* Özalp
Karakax China *see* Moyu
Karakax He *r.* China 82 E1
Karakax Shan *mts* China 82 E2
Karakelong *i.* Indon. 69 H6
Karaki China 82 E1
Karaklis Armenia *see* Vanadzor
Karakoçan Turkey 91 F3
Kara-Köl Kyrg. 79 G2
Karakol Kyrg. 80 E3
Karakoram Pass China/Jammu and Kashmir 82 D2
Karakoram Range *mts* Asia 89 I2
Kara K'orē Eth. 98 D2
Karakorum Range *mts* Asia *see* Karakoram Range
Karaköse Turkey *see* Ağrı
Kara Kul' Kyrg. *see* Kara-Köl
Karakul' Uzbek. 89 F2
Karakul', Ozero *l.* Tajik. *see* Qarokŭl
Kara Kum *des.* Turkm. *see* Kara Kumy
Kara Kum *des.* Turkm. *see* Karakum Desert
Karakum, Peski Kazakh. *see* Karakum Desert
Karakum Desert Kazakh. 78 E2
Karakum Desert Turkm. *see* Kara Kumy
Karakum Desert Turkm. 88 F2
Karakumskiy Kanal *canal* Turkm. 89 F2
Kara Kumy *des.* Turkm. 88 E2
Karakurt Turkey 91 F2
Karakuş Dağı *ridge* Turkey 59 N5
Karal Chad 97 E3
Karala Estonia 45 L7
Karalundi Australia 109 B6
Karama *r.* Indon. 68 F7
Karaman Turkey 90 D3
Karaman *prov.* Turkey 85 A1
Karamanlı Turkey 59 M6
Karamay China 80 F2
Karambar Pass Afgh./Pak. 89 I2
Karamea N.Z. 113 D5
Karamea Bight *b.* N.Z. 113 C5
Karamendy Kazakh. 80 B1
Karamet-Niyaz Turkm. 89 G2
Karamiran China 83 F1
Karamiran Shankou *pass* China 83 F1
Karamürsel Turkey 59 M4
Karamyshevo Rus. Fed. 45 P8
Karän *i.* Saudi Arabia 88 C5
Karangasem Indon. 108 A2
Karanja India 84 C1
Karanjia India 82 E5
Karapınar *Gaziantep* Turkey 85 C1
Karapınar *Konya* Turkey 90 D3
Karas *admin. reg.* Namibia 100 C4
Karasay China 83 E1
Karasburg Namibia 100 D5
Kara Sea Rus. Fed. 64 I2
Kárášjohka Norway 44 N2
Karasjok Norway *see* Kárášjohka
Kara Strait Rus. Fed. *see* Karskiye Vorota, Proliv
Karasu *r.* Syria/Turkey 85 C1
Karasu *Bitlis* Turkey *see* Hizan
Karasu *Sakarya* Turkey 59 N4
Karasu *r.* Turkey 91 F3
Karasubazar Ukr. *see* Bilohirs'k
Karasuk Rus. Fed. 64 I4
Karät Iran 89 F3
Karataş Turkey 85 B1
Karataş Burnu *hd* Turkey *see* Fener Burnu
Karatau Kazakh. 80 D3
Karatau, Khrebet *mts* Kazakh. 80 C3
Karatepe Turkey 85 A1
Karathuri Myanmar 71 B5
Karativu *i.* Sri Lanka 84 C4
Karatsu Japan 75 C6
Karaudanawa Guyana 143 G3
Karaulbazar Uzbek. 89 G2
Karauli India 82 D4
Karavan Kyrg. *see* Kerben
Karavostasi Cyprus 85 A2
Karawang Indon. 68 D8
Karayılan Turkey 85 C1
Karayulgan China 80 F3
Karazhal Kazakh. 80 D2
Karbalā' Iraq 91 G4
Karben Germany 53 I4
Karcag Hungary 59 I1
Karden Germany 53 H4
Kardhítsa Greece *see* Karditsa
Karditsa Greece 59 I5
Kärdla Estonia 45 M7
Karee S. Africa 101 H5
Kareeberge *mts* S. Africa 100 E6
Kareima Sudan 86 D6
Kareli India 82 D5
Karelia *aut. rep.* Rus. Fed. *see* Kareliya, Respublika
Kareliya, Respublika *aut. rep.* Rus. Fed. 44 R5
Karel'skaya A.S.S.R. *aut. rep.* Rus. Fed. *see* Kareliya, Respublika
Karel'skiy Bereg *coastal area* Rus. Fed. 44 R3
Karema Tanz. 99 D4
Karera India 82 D4
Karesuando Sweden 44 M2
Käreyändar Iran 89 F5
Kargalinskaya Rus. Fed. 91 G2
Kargalinski Rus. Fed. *see* Kargalinskaya
Kargapazarı Dağları *mts* Turkey 91 F3
Karghalik China *see* Yecheng
Kargı Turkey 90 D2
Kargil India 82 D2
Kargilik China *see* Yecheng
Kargıpınarı Turkey 85 B1
Kargopol' Rus. Fed. 42 H3
Karholmsbruk Sweden 45 J6
Kari Nigeria 96 E3
Kariän Iran 88 E5
Kariba Zimbabwe 99 C5
Kariba, Lake *resr* Zambia/Zimbabwe 99 C5
Kariba Dam Zambia/Zimbabwe 99 C5
Kariba-yama *vol.* Japan 74 E4
Karibib Namibia 100 B1
Karigasniemi Fin. 44 N2
Karijini National Park Australia 109 B5
Karijoki Fin. 44 L5
Karikachi-tōge *pass* Japan 74 F4
Karikari, Cape N.Z. 113 D2
Karimata, Pulau-pulau *is* Indon. 68 D7
Karimata, Selat *strait* Indon. 68 D7
Karimganj India 83 H4
Karimnagar India 84 C2
Karimun Besar *i.* Indon. 71 C7
Karimunjawa, Pulau-pulau *is* Indon. 68 E8
Káristos Greece *see* Karystos
Karjat *Maharashtra* India 84 B2
Karjat *Maharashtra* India 84 B2
Karkaralinsk Kazakh. 80 E2
Karkar Island P.N.G. 69 L7
Karkh Pak. 89 G5
Karkinits'ka Zatoka *g.* Ukr. 59 O2
Kärkölä Fin. 45 N6
Karkonoski Park Narodowy *nat. park* Czech Rep./Poland *see* Krkonošský národní park
Karksi-Nuia Estonia 45 N7
Karkük Iraq *see* Kirkük
Karlachi Pak. 89 H3
Karlik Shan *mt.* China 80 H3
Karlıova Turkey 91 F3
Karlivka Ukr. 43 G6
Karl Marks, Qullai *mt.* Tajik. 89 I2
Karl-Marx-Stadt Germany *see* Chemnitz
Karlovac Croatia 58 F2
Karlovka Ukr. *see* Karlivka
Karlovo Bulg. 59 K3
Karlovy Vary Czech Rep. 53 M4
Karlsbad Germany 53 I6
Karlsborg Sweden 45 I7
Karlsburg Romania *see* Alba Iulia
Karlshamn Sweden 45 I8
Karlskoga Sweden 45 I7
Karlskrona Sweden 45 I8
Karlsruhe Germany 53 I5
Karlstad Sweden 45 H7
Karlstad U.S.A. 130 D1
Karlstadt Germany 53 J5
Karluk U.S.A. 118 C4
Karlyuk Turkm. 89 G2
Karmala India 84 B2
Karmel, Har *hill* Israel *see* Carmel, Mount
Karmona Spain *see* Córdoba
Karmøy *i.* Norway 45 D7
Karmpur Pak. 89 I4
Karnabchul', Step' *plain* Uzbek. 89 G2
Karnafuli Reservoir Bangl. 83 H5
Karnal India 82 D3
Karnataka *state* India 84 B3
Karnavati India *see* Ahmadabad
Karnes City U.S.A. 131 D6
Karnobat Bulg. 59 L3
Karodi Pak. 89 G5
Karoi Zimbabwe 99 C5
Karokpi Myanmar 70 B4
Karo La *pass* China 83 G3
Karong India 83 H4
Karonga Malawi 99 D4
Karonie Australia 109 C7
Karoo National Park S. Africa 100 F7
Karoo Nature Reserve S. Africa 100 G7
Karoonda Australia 111 B7
Karora Eritrea 86 E6
Káros *i.* Greece *see* Keros
Karossa Indon. 68 F7
Karossa, Tanjung *pt* Indon. 108 B2
Karow Germany 53 M1
Karpasia *pen.* Cyprus 85 B2
Karpas Peninsula Cyprus *see* Karpasia
Karpathos *i.* Greece 59 L7
Karpathou, Steno *sea chan.* Greece 59 L6
Karpaty *mts* Europe *see* Carpathian Mountains
Karpenisi Greece 59 I5
Karpilovka Belarus *see* Aktsyabrski
Karpinsk Rus. Fed. 41 S4
Karpogory Rus. Fed. 42 J2
Karpuz *r.* Turkey 85 A1
Karratha Australia 108 B5
Karroo *plat.* S. Africa *see* Great Karoo
Karrychirla Turkm. *see* imeni Kerbabayeva
Kars Turkey 91 F2
Kärsämäki Fin. 44 N5
Kārsava Latvia 45 O8
Karshi Turkm. 91 I2
Karshi Uzbek. 89 G2
Karshinskaya Step' *plain* Uzbek. 89 G2
Karskiye Vorota, Proliv *strait* Rus. Fed. 64 G3
Karskoye More *sea* Rus. Fed. *see* Kara Sea
Karstädt Germany 53 L1
Karstula Fin. 44 N5
Karsu Turkey 85 C1
Karsun Rus. Fed. 43 J5
Kartal Turkey 59 M4
Kartaly Rus. Fed. 64 H4
Kartayel' Rus. Fed. 42 L2
Karttula Fin. 44 O5
Karumba Australia 110 C3
Karumbhar Island India 82 B5
Karun, Küh-e *hill* Iran 88 C4
Kärün, Rüd-e *r.* Iran 88 C4
Karuni Indon. 108 B2
Karur India 84 C4
Karvia Fin. 44 M5
Karviná Czech Rep. 47 Q6
Karwar India 84 B3
Karyagino Azer. *see* Füzuli
Karymskoye Rus. Fed. 73 K2
Karynzharyk, Peski *des.* Kazakh. 91 I2
Karystos Greece 59 K5
Kaş Turkey 59 M6
Kasa India 84 B2
Kasaba Turkey *see* Turgutlu
Kasabonika Canada 122 C3
Kasabonika Lake Canada 122 C3
Kasaï *r.* Dem. Rep. Congo 98 B4
also known as Kwa
Kasaï, Plateau du Dem. Rep. Congo 99 C4
Kasaji Dem. Rep. Congo 99 C5
Kasama Zambia 99 D5
Kasan Uzbek. 89 G2
Kasane Botswana 99 C5
Kasaragod India 84 B3
Kasargod India *see* Kasaragod
Kasargode India *see* Kasaragod
Kasatkino Rus. Fed. 74 C2
Kasba Lake Canada 121 K2
Kasba Tadla Morocco 54 C5
Kasenga Dem. Rep. Congo 99 C5
Kasengu Dem. Rep. Congo 99 C4
Kasese Dem. Rep. Congo 98 C4
Kasese Uganda 98 D3
Kasevo Rus. Fed. *see* Neftekamsk
Kasganj India 82 D4
Kasha China *see* Gonjo
Kashabowie Canada 122 C4
Käshän Iran 88 C3
Kashary Rus. Fed. 43 I6
Kashechewan Canada 122 E3
Kashgar China *see* Kashi
Kashi China 80 E4
Kashihara Japan 75 D6
Kashima-nada *b.* Japan 75 F5
Kashin Rus. Fed. 42 H4
Kashipur India 82 D3
Kashira Rus. Fed. 43 H5
Kashiwazaki Japan 75 E5
Kashkarantsy Rus. Fed. 42 H2
Kashku'iyeh Iran 88 D4
Käshmar Iran 88 E3
Kashmir *terr.* Asia *see* Jammu and Kashmir
Kashmir, Vale of *reg.* India 82 C2
Kashyukulu Dem. Rep. Congo 99 C4
Kasi India *see* Varanasi
Kasigar Afgh. 89 H3
Kasimov Rus. Fed. 43 I5
Kaskattama *r.* Canada 121 N3
Kaskinen Fin. 44 L5
Kas Klong *i.* Cambodia *see* Kŏng, Kaôh
Kaskö Fin. *see* Kaskinen
Kaslo Canada 120 G5
Kasmere Lake Canada 121 K3
Kasongo Dem. Rep. Congo 99 C4
Kasongo-Lunda Dem. Rep. Congo 99 B4
Kasos *i.* Greece 59 L7
Kaspiy Mangy Oypaty *lowland* Kazakh./Rus. Fed. *see* Caspian Lowland
Kaspiysk Rus. Fed. 91 G2
Kaspiyskiy Rus. Fed. *see* Lagan'
Kaspiyskoye More *l.* Asia/Europe *see* Caspian Sea
Kassa Slovakia *see* Košice
Kassala Sudan 86 E6
Kassandras, Akra *pt* Greece 59 J5
Kassandras, Kolpos *b.* Greece 59 J4
Kassel Germany 53 J3
Kasserine Tunisia 58 C7
Kastag Pak. 89 F5
Kastamonu Turkey 90 D2
Kastellaun Germany 53 H4

Kastelli Greece 59 J7
Kastéllion Greece see Kastelli
Kastellorizon i. Greece see Megisti
Kasterlee Belgium 52 E3
Kastoria Greece 59 I4
Kastornoye Rus. Fed. 43 H6
Kastsyukovichy Belarus 43 G5
Kasulu Tanz. 99 D4
Kasumkent Rus. Fed. 91 H2
Kasungu Malawi 99 D5
Kasungu National Park Malawi 99 D5
Kasur Pak. 89 I4
Katādtlit Nunāt terr. N. America see Greenland
Katahdin, Mount U.S.A. 132 G2
Kataklik Jammu and Kashmir 82 D2
Katako-Kombe Dem. Rep. Congo 98 C4
Katakwi Uganda 98 D3
Katana India 82 C5
Katangi India 82 D5
Katanning Australia 109 B8
Katavi National Park Tanz. 99 D4
Katawaz reg. Afgh. 89 G3
Katchall i. India 71 A6
Katea Dem. Rep. Congo 99 C4
Katerini Greece 59 J4
Katesh Tanz. 99 D4
Kate's Needle mt. Canada/U.S.A. 120 C3
Katete Zambia 99 D5
Katherîna, Gebel mt. Egypt see Kātrīnā, Jabal
Katherine Australia 108 F3
Katherine Gorge National Park Australia see Nitmiluk National Park
Kathi India 89 I6
Kathiawar pen. India 82 B5
Kathihar India see Katihar
Kathiraveli Sri Lanka 84 D4
Kathiwara India 82 C5
Kathleen Falls Australia 108 E3
Kathlehong S. Africa 101 I4

▶Kathmandu Nepal 83 F4
Capital of Nepal.

Kathu S. Africa 100 F4
Kathua India 82 C2
Kati Mali 96 C3
Katihar India 83 F4
Kati-Kati S. Africa 101 H7
Katima Mulilo Namibia 99 C5
Katimik Lake Canada 121 L4
Katiola Côte d'Ivoire 96 C4
Kā Tiritiri o te Moana mts N.Z. see Southern Alps
Katkop Hills S. Africa 100 E6
Katmai National Park and Preserve U.S.A. 118 C4
Katmandu Nepal see Kathmandu
Kato Achaïa Greece 59 I5
Kat O Chau Hong Kong China see Crooked Island
Kat O Hoi b. Hong Kong China see Crooked Harbour
Katoomba Australia 112 E4
Katowice Poland 47 Q5
Katoya India 83 G5
Katrancık Dağı mts Turkey 59 M6
Kātrīnā, Jabal mt. Egypt 90 D5
Katrine, Loch l. U.K. 50 E4
Katrineholm Sweden 45 J7
Katse Dam Lesotho 101 I5
Katsina Nigeria 96 D3
Katsina-Ala Nigeria 96 D4
Katsuura Japan 75 F6
Kattaktoc, Cap c. Canada 123 I2
Kattakurgan Uzbek. 89 G2
Kattamudda Well Australia 108 D5
Kattaqŭrghon Uzbek. see Kattakurgan
Kattasang Hills Afgh. 89 G3
Kattegat strait Denmark/Sweden 45 G8
Kattowitz Poland see Katowice
Katumbar India 82 D4
Katunino Rus. Fed. 42 J4
Katuri Pak. 89 H4
Katwa India see Katoya
Katwijk aan Zee Neth. 52 E2
Katzenbuckel hill Germany 53 J5
Kauai i. U.S.A. 127 [inset]
Kauai Channel U.S.A. 127 [inset]
Kaub Germany 53 H4
Kaufungen Germany 53 J3
Kauhajoki Fin. 44 M5
Kauhava Fin. 44 M5
Kaukauna U.S.A. 134 A1
Kaukkwè Hills Myanmar 70 B1
Kaukonen Fin. 44 N3
Kaula i. HI U.S.A. 127 [inset]
Kaulakahi Channel HI U.S.A. 127 [inset]
Kaumajet Mountains Canada 123 J2
Kaunakakai HI U.S.A. 127 [inset]
Kaunas Lith. 45 M9
Kaunata Latvia 45 O8
Kaundy, Vpadina depr. Kazakh. 91 I2
Kaunia Bangl. 83 G4
Kaura-Namoda Nigeria 96 D3
Kau Sai Chau i. Hong Kong China 77 [inset]
Kaustinen Fin. 44 M5
Kautokeino Norway 44 M2
Kau-ye Kyun i. Myanmar 71 B5
Kavadarci Macedonia 59 J4
Kavak Turkey 90 E2
Kavaklıdere Turkey 59 M6
Kavala Greece 59 K4
Kavalas, Kolpos b. Greece 59 K4
Kavalerovo Rus. Fed. 74 D3
Kavali India 84 D3
Kavār Iran 88 D4
Kavaratti India 84 B4
Kavaratti atoll India 84 B4
Kavarna Bulg. 59 M3
Kavendou, Mont mt. Guinea 96 B3
Kaveri r. India 84 C4
Kavīr Iran 88 C3
Kavīr salt flat Iran 88 D3
Kavīr, Dasht-e des. Iran 88 D3
Kavīr Kūshk well Iran 88 E3
Kavkasioni mts Asia/Europe see Caucasus
Kawa Myanmar 70 B3
Kawagama Lake Canada 135 F1
Kawagoe Japan 75 E6
Kawaguchi Japan 75 E6
Kawaihae HI U.S.A. 127 [inset]
Kawaikini, Mount HI U.S.A. 127 [inset]
Kawakawa N.Z. 113 E2
Kawambwa Zambia 99 C4
Kawana Zambia 99 C5
Kawardha India 82 E5
Kawartha Lakes Canada 135 F1
Kawasaki Japan 75 E6
Kawau Island N.Z. 113 E3
Kawawachikamach Canada 123 I3
Kawdut Myanmar 70 B4
Kawerau N.Z. 113 F4
Kawhia N.Z. 113 E4
Kawhia Harbour N.Z. 113 E4
Kawich Peak U.S.A. 128 E3
Kawich Range mts U.S.A. 128 E3
Kawinaw Lake Canada 121 L4
Kaw Lake U.S.A. 131 D4
Kawlin Myanmar 70 A2
Kawm Umbū Egypt 86 D5
Kawngmeum Myanmar 70 B2
Kawthaung Myanmar 71 B5
Kaxgar China see Kashi
Kaxgar He r. China 80 E4
Kax He r. China 80 F3
Kaxtax Shan mts China 83 E1
Kaya Burkina 96 C3
Kayadibi Turkey 90 E3
Kayan r. Indon. 68 F6
Kayankulam India 84 C4
Kayar India 84 C2
Kaycee U.S.A. 126 G4
Kaydak, Sor dry lake Kazakh. 91 I1
Kaydanovo Belarus see Dzyarzhynsk
Kayembe-Mukulu Dem. Rep. Congo 99 C4
Kayenta U.S.A. 129 H3
Kayes Mali 96 B3
Kaymaz Turkey 59 N5
Kaynar Kazakh. 80 E2
Kaynar Turkey 90 E3
Kayseri Turkey 90 D3
Kayuyu Dem. Rep. Congo 98 C4
Kayyngdy Kyrg. 80 D3
Kazach'ye Rus. Fed. 65 O2
Kazakh Azer. see Qazax
Kazakhskaya S.S.R. country Asia see Kazakhstan
Kazakhskiy Melkosopochnik plain Kazakh. 80 D1
Kazakhskiy Zaliv b. Kazakh. 91 I2

▶Kazakhstan country Asia 78 F2
4th largest country in Asia.
Asia 6, 62–63

Kazakhstan Kazakh. see Aksay
Kazakstan country Asia see Kazakhstan
Kazan r. Canada 121 M2
Kazan' Rus. Fed. 42 K5
Kazandzhik Turkm. see Gazandzhyk
Kazanka r. Rus. Fed. 42 K5
Kazanlı Turkey 85 B1
Kazanlŭk Bulg. 59 K3
Kazan-rettō is Japan see Volcano Islands
Kazatin Ukr. see Kozyatyn

▶Kazbek mt. Georgia/Rus. Fed. 43 J8
4th highest mountain in Europe.

Kaz Dağı mts Turkey 59 L5
Kāzerūn Iran 88 C4
Kazhim Rus. Fed. 42 K3
Kazidi Tajik. see Qozideh
Kazi Magomed Azer. see Qazımämmäd
Kazincbarcika Hungary 43 D6
Kaziranga National Park India 83 H4
Kazret'i Georgia 91 G2
Kaztalovka Kazakh. 41 P6
Kazy Turkm. 88 E2
Kazym r. Rus. Fed. 41 T3
Kazymskiy Mys Rus. Fed. 41 T3
Kea i. Greece 59 K6
Keady U.K. 51 F3
Keams Canyon U.S.A. 129 H4
Kéamu i. Vanuatu see Anatom
Kearney U.S.A. 130 D3
Kearny U.S.A. 129 H5
Keban Turkey 90 E3
Keban Barajı resr Turkey 90 E3
Kébémèr Senegal 96 B3
Kebili Tunisia 54 F5
Kebīr, Nahr al r. Lebanon/Syria 85 B2
Kebkabiya Sudan 97 F3
Kebnekaise mt. Sweden 44 K3
Kebock Head hd U.K. 50 C2
K'ebrī Dehar Eth. 98 E3
Kech reg. Pak. 89 F5
Kechika r. Canada 120 E3
Keçiborlu Turkey 59 N6
Kecskemét Hungary 59 H1
K'eda Georgia 91 F2
Kėdainiai Lith. 45 M9
Kedairu Passage Fiji see Kadavu Passage
Kedgwick Canada 123 I5
Kedian China 77 G2
Kedong China 74 B3
Kedva r. Rus. Fed. 42 L2
Kędzierzyn-Koźle Poland 47 Q5
Keele r. Canada 120 E1
Keele Peak Canada 120 D2
Keeler U.S.A. 128 E3
Keeley Lake Canada 121 I4
Keeling Islands terr. Indian Ocean see Cocos Islands
Keen, Mount hill U.K. 50 G4
Keene CA U.S.A. 128 D4
Keene KY U.S.A. 134 C5
Keene NH U.S.A. 135 I2
Keene OH U.S.A. 134 E3
Keepit, Lake resr Australia 112 E3
Keep River National Park Australia 108 E3
Keerbergen Belgium 52 E3
Keer-weer, Cape Australia 110 C2
Keetmanshoop Namibia 100 D4
Keewatin Canada 121 M5
Kefallinía i. Greece see Cephalonia
Kefallonia i. Greece see Cephalonia
Kefamenanu Indon. 108 D2
Kefe Ukr. see Feodosiya
Keffi Nigeria 96 D4
Keflavík Iceland 44 [inset]
Kegalla Sri Lanka 84 D5
Kegen Kazakh. 80 E3
Keglo, Baie de b. Canada 123 I2
Keg River Canada 120 G3
Kegul'ta Rus. Fed. 43 J7
Kehra Estonia 45 N7
Kehsi Mansam Myanmar 70 B2
Keighley U.K. 48 F5
Keila Estonia 45 N7
Keimoes S. Africa 100 E5
Keitele Fin. 44 O5
Keitele l. Fin. 44 O5
Keith Australia 111 C8
Keith U.K. 50 G3
Keith Arm b. Canada 120 F1
Kejimkujik National Park Canada 123 I5
Kekaha HI U.S.A. 127 [inset]
Kékes mt. Hungary 47 R7
Kekri India 82 C4
K'elafo Eth. 98 E3
Kelai i. Maldives 84 B5
Kelang Malaysia 71 C7
Kelberg Germany 52 G4
Kelheim Germany 53 L6
Kelibia Tunisia 58 D6
Kelifskiy Uzboy marsh Turkm. 89 F2
Kelīrī Iran 88 E5
Kelkheim (Taunus) Germany 53 I4
Kelkit Turkey 91 E2
Kelkit r. Turkey 90 E2
Kéllé Congo 98 B4
Keller Lake Canada 120 F2
Kellett, Cape Canada 118 F2
Kelleys Island U.S.A. 134 D3
Kelliher Canada 121 K5
Kelloselkä Fin. 44 P3
Kells Rep. of Ireland 51 F4
Kells r. U.K. 51 F3
Kelly U.S.A. 134 B5
Kelly Lake Canada 120 E1
Kelly Range hills Australia 109 C6
Kelmė Lith. 45 M9
Kelmis Belgium 52 G4
Kelo Chad 97 E4
Kelowna Canada 120 G5
Kelp Head hd Canada 120 E5
Kelseyville U.S.A. 128 B2
Kelso U.K. 50 G5
Kelso CA U.S.A. 129 F4
Kelso WA U.S.A. 126 C3
Keluang Malaysia 71 C7
Kelvington Canada 121 K4
Kem' Rus. Fed. 42 G2
Kem' r. Rus. Fed. 42 G2
Ke Macina Mali see Massina
Kemah Turkey 90 E3
Kemaliye Turkey 90 E3
Kemalpaşa Turkey 59 L5
Kemano Canada 120 E4
Kembé Cent. Afr. Rep. 98 C3
Kemeneshát hills Hungary 58 G1
Kemer Antalya Turkey 59 N6
Kemer Muğla Turkey 59 M6
Kemer Barajı resr Turkey 59 M6
Kemerovo Rus. Fed. 64 J4
Kemi Fin. 44 N4
Kemijärvi Fin. 44 O3
Kemijärvi l. Fin. 44 O3
Kemijoki r. Fin. 44 N4
Kemiö Fin. see Kimito
Kemir Turkm. 88 D2
Kemmerer U.S.A. 126 F4
Kemnath Germany 53 L5
Kemnay U.K. 50 G3
Kemp Coast reg. Antarctica see Kemp Land
Kempele Fin. 44 N4
Kempen Germany 52 G3
Kempisch Kanaal canal Belgium 52 F3
Kemp Land reg. Antarctica 152 D2
Kemp Peninsula Antarctica 152 A2
Kemp's Bay Bahamas 133 E7
Kempsey Australia 112 F3
Kempt, Lac l. Canada 122 G5
Kempten (Allgäu) Germany 47 M7
Kempton U.S.A. 134 B3
Kempton Park S. Africa 101 I4
Kemptville Canada 135 H1
Kemujan i. Indon. 68 E8
Ken r. India 82 E4
Kenai U.S.A. 118 C3
Kenai Fiords National Park U.S.A. 118 C4
Kenai Mountains U.S.A. 118 C4
Kenamu r. Canada 123 K3
Kenansville U.S.A. 133 E5
Kenâyis, Râs el pt Egypt see Ḥikmah, Ra's al
Kenbridge U.S.A. 135 F5
Kendal U.K. 48 E4
Kendall Australia 112 F3
Kendall, Cape Canada 119 J3
Kendallville U.S.A. 134 C3
Kendari Indon. 69 G7
Kendawangan Indon. 68 E7
Kendégué Chad 97 E3
Kendrapara India 83 F5
Kendraparha India see Kendrapara
Kendrick Peak U.S.A. 129 H4
Kendujhar India see Keonjhar
Kendujhargarh India see Keonjhar
Kendyrli-Kayasanskoye, Plato plat. Kazakh. 91 I2
Kendyrlisor, Solonchak salt l. Kazakh. 91 I2
Kenebri Australia 112 D3
Kenedy U.S.A. 131 D6
Kenema Sierra Leone 96 B4
Keneurgench Turkm. 87 I1
Kenge Dem. Rep. Congo 99 B4
Keng Lap Myanmar 70 C2
Kengtung Myanmar 70 B2
Kenhardt S. Africa 100 E5
Kéniéba Mali 96 B3
Kénitra Morocco 54 C5
Kenmare Rep. of Ireland 51 C6
Kenmare U.S.A. 130 C1
Kenmare River inlet Rep. of Ireland 51 B6
Kenmore U.S.A. 135 F2
Kenn Germany 52 G5
Kenna U.S.A. 131 C5
Kennebec U.S.A. 130 D3
Kennebec r. U.S.A. 132 G2
Kennebunkport U.S.A. 135 J2
Kennedy, Cape U.S.A. see Canaveral, Cape
Kennedy Range National Park Australia 109 A6
Kennedy Town Hong Kong China 77 [inset]
Kenner U.S.A. 131 F6
Kennet r. U.K. 49 G7
Kenneth Range hills Australia 109 B5
Kennett U.S.A. 131 F4
Kennewick U.S.A. 126 D3
Kenn Reef Australia 110 F4
Kenogami r. Canada 122 D4
Keno Hill Canada 120 C2
Kenora Canada 121 M5
Kenosha U.S.A. 134 B2
Kenozero, Ozero l. Rus. Fed. 42 H3
Kent r. U.K. 48 E4
Kent OH U.S.A. 134 E3
Kent TX U.S.A. 131 B6
Kent VA U.S.A. 134 E5
Kent WA U.S.A. 126 C3
Kentani S. Africa 101 I7
Kent Group is Australia 111 [inset]
Kentland U.S.A. 134 B3
Kenton U.S.A. 134 D3
Kent Peninsula Canada 118 H3
Kentucky state U.S.A. 134 C5
Kentucky Lake U.S.A. 131 F4
▶Kenya country Africa 98 D3
Africa 7, 94–95

▶Kenya, Mount Kenya 98 D4
2nd highest mountain in Africa.

Kenyir, Tasik resr Malaysia 71 C6
Keokuk U.S.A. 130 F3
Keoladeo National Park India 82 D4
Keonjhar India 83 F5
Keonjhargarh India see Keonjhar
Keosauqua U.S.A. 130 F3
Keowee, Lake resr U.S.A. 133 D5
Kepina r. Rus. Fed. 42 I2
Keppel Bay Australia 110 E4
Kepsut Turkey 59 M5
Kera India 83 F5
Kerāh Iran 88 E4
Kerala state India 84 B4
Kerang Australia 112 A5
Kerava Fin. 45 N6
Kerba Alg. 57 G5
Kerbela Iraq see Karbalā'
Kerben Kyrg. 80 D3
Kerbi r. Rus. Fed. 74 E1
Kerbodot, Lac l. Canada 123 I3
Kerch Ukr. 90 E1
Kerchem'ya Rus. Fed. 42 L3
Kerema P.N.G. 69 L8
Keremeos Canada 120 G5
Kerempe Burun pt Turkey 90 D2
Keren Eritrea 86 E6
Kerewan Gambia 96 B3
Kergeli Turkm. 88 E2
Kerguélen, Îles is Indian Ocean 149 M9
Kerguelen Islands Indian Ocean see Kerguélen, Îles
Kerguelen Plateau sea feature Indian Ocean 149 M9
Kericho Kenya 98 D4
Kerikeri N.Z. 113 D2
Kerimäki Fin. 44 P6
Kerinci, Gunung vol. Indon. 68 C7
Kerinci Seblat National Park Indon. 68 C7
Kerintji vol. Indon. see Kerinci, Gunung
Keriya He watercourse China 72 E5
Keriya Shankou pass China 83 E2
Kerken Germany 52 G3
Kerkenah, Îles is Tunisia 58 D7
Kerki Turkm. 89 G2
Kerkichi Turkm. 89 G2
Kerkinitis, Limni l. Greece 59 J4
Kérkira i. Greece see Corfu
Kerkouane tourist site Tunisia 58 D6
Kerkyra Greece 59 H5
Kerkyra i. Greece see Corfu
Kerma Sudan 86 D6
Kermadec Islands S. Pacific Ocean 107 I5

▶Kermadec Trench sea feature S. Pacific Ocean 150 I8
4th deepest trench in the world.

Kermān Iran 88 E4
Kerman U.S.A. 128 C3
Kermān Desert Iran 88 E4
Kermānshāh Iran 88 B3
Kermānshāhān Iran 88 D4
Kermine Uzbek. see Navoi
Kermit U.S.A. 131 C6
Kern r. U.S.A. 128 D4
Kernertut, Cap c. Canada 123 I2
Keros i. Greece 59 K6
Keros Rus. Fed. 42 L3
Kérouané Guinea 96 C4
Kerpen Germany 52 G4
Kerr, Cape Antarctica 152 H1
Kerrobert Canada 121 I5
Kerrville U.S.A. 131 D6
Kerry Head hd Rep. of Ireland 51 C5
Kerteminde Denmark 45 G9
Kerulen r. China/Mongolia see Herlen Gol
Kerur India 84 B2
Keryneia Cyprus see Kyrenia
Kerzaz Alg. 96 C2
Kerzhenets r. Rus. Fed. 42 J4
Kesagami Lake Canada 122 E4
Kesälahti Fin. 44 P6
Keşan Turkey 59 L4
Keşap Turkey 43 H8
Kesariya India 83 F4
Kesennuma Japan 75 F5
Keshan China 74 B2
Keshem Afgh. 89 H2
Keshena U.S.A. 134 A1
Keshendeh-ye Bala Afgh. 89 G2
Keshod India 82 B5
Keshvar Iran 88 C3
Keskin Turkey 90 D3
Keskozero Rus. Fed. 42 G3
Kesova Gora Rus. Fed. 42 H4
Kessel Neth. 52 G3
Kestell S. Africa 101 I5
Kesten'ga Rus. Fed. 44 Q4
Kestilä Fin. 44 O4
Keswick Canada 134 F1
Keswick U.K. 48 D4
Keszthely Hungary 58 G1
Ketapang Indon. 68 E7
Ketchikan U.S.A. 120 D4
Keti Bandar Pak. 89 G5
Ketmen', Khrebet mts China/Kazakh. 80 F3
Kettering U.K. 49 G6
Kettering U.S.A. 134 C4
Kettle r. Canada 120 G5
Kettle Creek r. U.S.A. 135 G3
Kettle Falls U.S.A. 126 D2
Kettleman City U.S.A. 128 D3
Kettle River Range mts U.S.A. 126 D2
Keuka U.S.A. 135 G2
Keuka Lake U.S.A. 135 G2
Keumgang, Mount N. Korea see Kumgang-san
Keumsang, Mount N. Korea see Kumgang-san
Keuruu Fin. 44 N5
Kew Turks and Caicos Is 133 F8
Kewanee U.S.A. 130 F3
Kewaunee U.S.A. 134 B1
Keweenaw Bay U.S.A. 130 F2
Keweenaw Peninsula U.S.A. 130 F2
Keweenaw Point U.S.A. 132 C2
Key, Lough l. Rep. of Ireland 51 D3
Keyala Sudan 97 G4
Keyano Canada 123 G3
Keya Paha r. U.S.A. 130 D3
Key Harbour Canada 122 E5
Keyihe China 74 A2
Key Largo U.S.A. 133 D7
Keymir Turkm. see Kemir
Keynsham U.K. 49 E7
Keyser U.S.A. 135 F4
Keystone Lake U.S.A. 131 D4
Keystone Peak U.S.A. 129 H6
Keysville U.S.A. 135 F5
Keytesville U.S.A. 130 E4
Keyvy, Vozvyshennost' hills Rus. Fed. 42 H2
Key West U.S.A. 133 D7
Kez Rus. Fed. 41 Q4
Kezi Zimbabwe 99 C6
Kgalagadi admin. dist. Botswana 100 E3
Kgalazadi admin. dist. Botswana see Kgalagadi
Kgatlen admin. dist. Botswana see Kgatleng
Kgatleng admin. dist. Botswana 101 H3
Kgomofatshe Pan salt pan Botswana 100 E2
Kgoro Pan salt pan Botswana 100 G3
Kgotsong S. Africa 101 H4
Khabab Syria 85 C3
Khabar Iran 88 D4
Khabarikha Rus. Fed. 42 L2
Khabarovsk Rus. Fed. 74 D2
Khabarovskiy Kray admin. div. Rus. Fed. 74 D2
Khabarovsk Kray admin. div. Rus. Fed. see Khabarovskiy Kray
Khabary Rus. Fed. 72 D2
Khabis Iran see Shahdād
Khabody Pass Afgh. 89 F3
Khachmas Azer. see Xaçmaz
Khadar, Jabal mt. Oman 88 E6
Khadro Pak. 89 H5
Khafs Banbān well Saudi Arabia 88 B5
Khagaria India 83 F4
Khagrachari Bangl. 83 G5
Khagrachhari Bangl. see Khagrachari
Khairgarh Pak. 89 H4
Khairpur Punjab Pak. 89 I4
Khairpur Sindh Pak. 89 H5
Khāīz, Kūh-e mt. Iran 88 C4
Khaja Du Koh hill Afgh. 89 G2
Khajuha India 82 E4
Khāk-e Jabbar Afgh. 89 H3
Khakhea Botswana 100 F3
Khakīr Afgh. 89 G3
Khak-rēz Afgh. 89 G4
Khakriz reg. Afgh. 89 G4
Khalach Turkm. 89 G2
Khalajestan reg. Iran 88 C3
Khalatse Jammu and Kashmir 82 D2
Khalifat mt. Pak. 89 G4
Khalīj Surt g. Libya see Sirte, Gulf of
Khalilabad India 83 E4
Khalīlī Iran 88 D5
Khalkabad Turkm. 89 F1
Khalkhāl Iran 88 C2
Khálki i. Greece see Chalki
Khalkís Greece see Chalkida
Khallikot India 84 E2
Khalturin Rus. Fed. see Orlov
Khamar-Daban, Khrebet mts Rus. Fed. 72 I2
Khamaria India 84 D1
Khambhat India 82 C5
Khambhat, Gulf of India 84 A2
Khamgaon India 84 C1
Khamir Yemen 86 F6
Khamis Mushayţ Saudi Arabia 86 F6
Khamkkeut Laos 70 D3
Khamma well Saudi Arabia 88 B5
Khammam India 84 D2
Khammouan Laos see Muang Khammouan
Khamra Rus. Fed. 65 M3
Khamseh reg. Iran 88 C3
Khan Afgh. 89 H3
Khan, Nam r. Laos 70 C3
Khānābād Afgh. 89 H2
Khān al Baghdādī Iraq 91 F4
Khān al Mashāhidah Iraq 91 G4
Khān al Muşallá Iraq 91 G4
Khanapur India 84 B2
Khān ar Raḩbah Iraq 91 G5
Khanasur Pass Iran/Turkey 91 G3
Khanbalik China see Beijing
Khānch Iran 88 B2
Khandu India 89 I6
Khandwa India 82 D5
Khandyga Rus. Fed. 65 O3
Khanewal Pak. 89 H4
Khanh Dương Vietnam 71 E4
Khan Hung Vietnam see Soc Trăng
Khaniá Greece see Chania
Khānī Yek Iran 88 D4
Khanka, Lake China/Rus. Fed. 74 D3
Khanka, Ozero l. China/Rus. Fed. see Khanka, Lake
Khankendi Azer. see Xankändi
Khanna India 82 D3
Khannā, Qā' salt pan Jordan 85 C3
Khanpur Pak. 89 H4
Khān Ruḩābah Iraq see Khān ar Raḩbah
Khansar Pak. 89 H4
Khān Shaykhūn Syria 85 C2
Khantayskoye, Ozero l. Rus. Fed. 64 K3
Khanthabouli Laos see Savannakhét
Khanty-Mansiysk Rus. Fed. 64 H3
Khān Yūnis Gaza 85 B4
Khanzi admin. dist. Botswana see Ghanzi
Khao Ang Rua Nai Wildlife Reserve nature res. Thai. 71 C4
Khao Banthat Wildlife Reserve nature res. Thai. 71 B6
Khao Chum Thong Thai. 71 B5
Khaoen Si Nakarin National Park Thai. 71 B4
Khao Laem National Park Thai. 70 B4
Khao Laem Reservoir Thai. 70 B4
Khao Luang National Park Thai. 71 B5
Khao Pu-Khao Ya National Park Thai. 71 B6
Khao Soi Dao Wildlife Reserve nature res. Thai. 71 C4
Khao Sok National Park Thai. 67 B5
Khao Yai National Park Thai. 71 C4
Khapalu Jammu and Kashmir 80 E4
Khaptad National Park Nepal 82 E3
Kharabali Rus. Fed. 43 J7
Kharagpur Bihar India 83 F4
Kharagpur W. Bengal India 83 F5
Khārān r. Iran 87 I4
Kharari India see Abu Road
Kharda India 84 B2
Khardi India 82 C6
Khardong La pass Jammu and Kashmir see Khardung La
Khardung La pass Jammu and Kashmir 82 D2
Kharez Ilias Afgh. 89 F3
Kharfiyah Iraq 91 G5
Kharga Egypt see Al Khārijah
Kharga r. Rus. Fed. 74 D1
Khârga, El Wâhât el oasis Egypt see Khārijah, Wāḩāt al
Kharga Oasis Egypt see Khārijah, Wāḩāt al
Khārg Islands Iran 88 C4
Khargon India 82 C5
Khari r. Rajasthan India 82 C4
Khari r. Rajasthan India 82 C4
Kharian Pak. 89 I3
Khariar India 84 D1
Khārijah, Wāḩāt al oasis Egypt 86 D5
Kharīm, Gebel hill Egypt see Kharīm, Jabal
Kharīm, Jabal hill Egypt 85 A4
Kharkhara r. India 82 E5
Kharkiv Ukr. 43 H6
Khar'kov Ukr. see Kharkiv
Khār Kūh mt. Iran 88 D4
Kharlovka Rus. Fed. 42 H1
Kharlu Rus. Fed. 44 Q6
Kharmanli Bulg. 59 K4
Kharoti reg. Afgh. 89 H3
Kharovsk Rus. Fed. 42 I4
Kharsia India 83 E5

▶Khartoum Sudan 86 D6
Capital of Sudan.

Kharwar reg. Afgh. 89 H3
Khasardag, Gora mt. Turkm. 88 E2
Khasav'yurt Rus. Fed. 91 G2
Khash Afgh. 89 F4
Khāsh Iran 89 F4
Khash Desert Afgh. 89 F4
Khashgort Rus. Fed. 41 T2
Khashm el Girba Sudan 86 E7
Khashm Şana' Saudi Arabia 90 E6
Khash Rūd r. Afgh. 89 F4
Khashuri Georgia 91 F2
Khasi Hills India 83 G4
Khaskovo Bulg. 59 K4
Khatanga Rus. Fed. 65 L2
Khatanga, Gulf of Rus. Fed. see Khatangskiy Zaliv
Khatangskiy Zaliv b. Rus. Fed. 65 L2
Khatayakha Rus. Fed. 42 M2
Khatinza Pass Pak. 89 H2
Khatmat al Malāha Oman 88 E5
Khatyrka Rus. Fed. 65 S3
Khavda India 82 B5
Khawak Pass Afgh. 89 H3
Khayamnandi S. Africa 101 G6
Khaybar Saudi Arabia 86 E4
Khayelitsha S. Africa 100 D8
Khayrān, Ra's al pt Oman 88 E6
Khê Bo Vietnam 70 D3
Khedrī Iran 88 E3
Khefa Israel see Haifa
Khehuene, Ponta pt Moz. 101 L2
Khemis Miliana Alg. 57 H5
Khemmarat Thai. 70 D3
Khenchela Alg. 58 B7
Khenifra Morocco 54 C5
Kherāmeh Iran 88 D4
Kherrata Alg. 57 I5
Kherreh Iran 88 D5
Khersan r. Iran 88 C4
Kherson Ukr. 59 O1
Kheta r. Rus. Fed. 65 L2
Kheyrābād Iran 88 D4
Khezerābād Iran 88 D2
Khiching India 83 F5
Khilok Rus. Fed. 73 K2
Khilok r. Rus. Fed. 73 J2
Khinganskiy Zapovednik nature res. Rus. Fed. 74 C2
Khinsar Pak. 89 H5
Khíos i. Greece see Chios
Khirbat Isrīyah Syria 85 C2

Khitai Pass Aksai Chin 82 D2
Khīyāv Iran 88 B2
Khiytola Rus. Fed. 45 P6
Khlevnoye Rus. Fed. 43 H5
Khlong, Mae r. Thai. 71 C4
Khlong Saeng Wildlife Reserve nature res. Thai. 71 B5
Khlong Wang Chao National Park Thai. 70 B3
Khlung Thai. 71 C4
Khmel'nik Ukr. see Khmil'nyk
Khmel'nitskiy Ukr. see Khmel'nyts'kyy
Khmel'nyts'kyy Ukr. 43 E6
Khmer Republic country Asia see Cambodia
Khmil'nyk Ukr. 43 E6
Khoai, Hon i. Vietnam 71 D5
Khobda Kazakh. 80 A1
Khobi Georgia 91 F2
Khodā Āfarīd spring Iran 88 E3
Khodzha-Kala Turkm. 88 E2
Khodzhambaz Turkm. 89 G2
Khodzhaolen Turkm. 88 E2
Khodzhapir'yakh, Gora mt. Uzbek. 89 G2
Khodzhent Tajik. see Khŭjand
Khodzheyli Uzbek. 80 A3
Khojand Tajik. see Khŭjand
Khokhowe Pan salt pan Botswana 100 E3
Khokhropar Pak. 89 H5
Khoksar India 82 D2
Kholm Afgh. 89 G2
Kholm Poland see Chełm
Kholm Rus. Fed. 42 F4
Kholmsk Rus. Fed. 74 F3
Kholon Israel see Holon
Khomas admin. reg. Namibia 100 C2
Khomas Highland hills Namibia 100 B2
Khomeyn Iran 88 C3
Khomeynīshahr Iran 88 C3
Khong, Mae Nam r. Laos/Thai. 66 D4 see Mekong
Khonj Iran 88 D5
Khonj, Kūh-e mts Iran 88 D5
Khon Kaen Thai. 70 C3
Khon Kriel Cambodia see Phumĭ Kon Kriel
Khonsa India 83 H4
Khonuu Rus. Fed. 65 P3
Khoper r. Rus. Fed. 43 I6
Khor Rus. Fed. 74 D3
Khor r. Rus. Fed. 74 D3
Khorat Plateau Thai. 70 C3
Khorda India see Khurda
Khordha India see Khurda
Khoreyver Rus. Fed. 42 M2
Khorinsk Rus. Fed. 73 J2
Khorixas Namibia 99 B6
Khormūj, Kūh-e mt. Iran 88 C4
Khorog Tajik. see Khorugh
Khorol Rus. Fed. 74 D3
Khorol Ukr. 43 G6
Khoroslū Dāgh hills Iran 88 B2
Khorramābād Iran 88 C3
Khorramshahr Iran 88 C4
Khorugh Tajik. 89 H2
Khosheutovo Rus. Fed. 43 J7
Khosūyeh Iran 88 D4
Khotan China see Hotan
Khouribga Morocco 54 C5
Khovaling Tajik. 89 H2
Khowrjān Iran 88 D4
Khowrnag, Kūh-e mt. Iran 88 D3
Khowst reg. Afgh./Pak. 89 H3
Khreum Myanmar 70 A2
Khroma r. Rus. Fed. 65 P2
Khromtau Kazakh. 80 A1
Khrushchev Ukr. see Svitlovods'k
Khrysokhou Bay Cyprus see Chrysochou Bay
Khrystynivka Ukr. 43 F6
Khuar Pak. 89 I3
Khudumelapye Botswana 100 G2
Khudzhand Tajik. see Khŭjand
Khufaysah, Khashm al hill Saudi Arabia 88 B6
Khugiana Afgh. see Pirzada
Khuis Botswana 100 E4
Khŭjand Tajik. 80 C3
Khŭjayli Uzbek. see Khodzheyli
Khu Khan Thai. 71 D4
Khulays Saudi Arabia 86 E5
Khulkhuta Rus. Fed. 43 J7
Khulm r. Afgh. 89 G2
Khulna Bangl. 83 G5
Khulo Georgia 91 F2
Khuma S. Africa 101 H4
Khŭm Batheay Cambodia 71 D5
Khunayzīr, Jabal al mts Syria 81 C2
Khūnīk Bālā Iran 88 E3
Khūnīnshahr Iran see Khorramshahr
Khunjerab Pass China/Jammu and Kashmir 82 C1
Khunsar Iran 88 C3
Khun Yuam Thai. 70 B3
Khūr Iran 88 E3
Khūran sea chan. Iran 88 D5
Khurayş Saudi Arabia 86 G4
Khurd, Koh-i- mt. Afgh. 89 G3
Khurda India 84 E1
Khurdha India see Khurda
Khurja India 82 D3
Khurmalik Afgh. 89 F3
Khurmuli Rus. Fed. 74 E2
Khūrrāb Iran 88 D4
Khurz Iran 88 D3
Khushab Pak. 89 I3
Khushalgarh Pak. 89 H3
Khushshah, Wādī al watercourse Jordan/Saudi Arabia 85 C5
Khust Ukr. 43 D6
Khutse Game Reserve nature res. Botswana 100 G2
Khutsong S. Africa 101 H4
Khutu r. Rus. Fed. 74 E2
Khuzdar Pak. 89 G5
Khvāf Iran 89 F3
Khvāf reg. Iran 89 F3
Khvājeh Iran 88 B2
Khvalynsk Rus. Fed. 43 K5
Khvodrān Iran 88 D4
Khvord Nārvan Iran 88 E3
Khvormūj Iran 88 C4
Khvoy Iran 88 B2
Khvoynaya Rus. Fed. 42 G4
Khwaja Amran mt. Pak. 89 G4
Khwaja Muhammad Range mts Afgh. 89 H2
Khyber Pass Afgh./Pak. 89 H3
Kiama Australia 112 E5
Kiamichi r. U.S.A. 131 E5
Kiangsi prov. China see Jiangxi
Kiangsu prov. China see Jiangsu
Kiantajärvi l. Fin. 44 P4
Kīāseh Iran 88 D2
Kiatassuaq i. Greenland 119 M2
Kibaha Tanz. 99 D4
Kibali r. Dem. Rep. Congo 98 C3
Kibangou Congo 98 B4
Kibaya Tanz. 99 D4
Kiboga Uganda 98 D3
Kibombo Dem. Rep. Congo 98 C4
Kibondo Tanz. 98 D4
Kibre Mengist Eth. 97 G4
Kibris country Asia see Cyprus
Kibungo Rwanda 98 D4
Kičevo Macedonia 59 I4
Kichmengskiy Gorodok Rus. Fed. 42 J4
Kiçik Qafqaz mts Asia see Lesser Caucasus
Kicking Horse Pass Canada 116 G5
Kidal Mali 96 D3
Kidderminster U.K. 49 E6
Kidepo Valley National Park Uganda 98 D3
Kidira Senegal 96 B3
Kidmang Jammu and Kashmir 82 D2
Kidnappers, Cape N.Z. 113 F4
Kidsgrove U.K. 49 E5
Kiel Germany 47 M3
Kiel U.S.A. 134 A2
Kiel Canal Germany 47 L3
Kielce Poland 47 R5
Kielder Water resr U.K. 48 E3
Kieler Bucht b. Germany 47 M3
Kienge Dem. Rep. Congo 99 C5
Kierspe Germany 53 H3
▶Kiev Ukr. 43 F6
Capital of Ukraine.
Kiffa Mauritania 96 B3
Kifisia Greece 59 J5
Kifrī Iraq 91 G4
▶Kigali Rwanda 98 D4
Capital of Rwanda.
Kiğı Turkey 91 F3
Kiglapait Mountains Canada 123 J2
Kigoma Tanz. 99 C4
Kihlanki Fin. 44 M3
Kihniö Fin. 44 M5
Kiholo HI U.S.A. 127 [inset]
Kiiminki Fin. 44 N4
Kii-sanchi mts Japan 75 D6
Kii-suidō sea chan. Japan 75 D6
Kikerino Rus. Fed. 45 P7
Kikinda Serb. and Mont. 59 I2
Kikki Pak. 89 F5
Kikládhes is Greece see Cyclades
Kiknur Rus. Fed. 42 J4
Kikonai Japan 74 F4
Kikori P.N.G. 69 K8
Kikori r. P.N.G. 69 K8
Kikwit Dem. Rep. Congo 99 B4
Kilafors Sweden 45 J6
Kilar India 82 D2
Kilauea HI U.S.A. 127 [inset]
Kilauea Crater HI U.S.A. 127 [inset]
Kilchu N. Korea 74 C4
Kilcoole Rep. of Ireland 51 F4
Kilcormac Rep. of Ireland 51 E4
Kilcoy Australia 112 F1
Kildare Rep. of Ireland 51 F4
Kil'dinstroy Rus. Fed. 44 R2
Kilemary Rus. Fed. 42 J4
Kilembe Dem. Rep. Congo 99 B4
Kilfinan U.K. 50 D5
Kilgore U.S.A. 131 E5
Kilham U.K. 48 E3
Kilia Ukr. see Kiliya
Kılıç Dağı mt. Syria/Turkey see Aqra', Jabal al
Kilifi Kenya 98 D4
Kilik Pass China/Jammu and Kashmir 82 C1
▶Kilimanjaro vol. Tanz. 98 D4
Highest mountain in Africa.
Africa 92–93
Kilimanjaro National Park Tanz. 98 D4
Kilinailau Islands P.N.G. 106 F2
Kilindoni Tanz. 99 D4
Kilingi-Nõmme Estonia 45 N7
Kilis Turkey 85 C1
Kilis prov. Turkey 85 C1
Kiliya Ukr. 59 M2
Kilkee Rep. of Ireland 51 C5
Kilkeel U.K. 51 G3
Kilkenny Rep. of Ireland 51 E5
Kilkhampton U.K. 49 C8
Kilkis Greece 59 J4
Killala Rep. of Ireland 51 C3
Killala Bay Rep. of Ireland 51 C3
Killaloe Rep. of Ireland 51 D5
Killam Canada 121 I4
Killarney N.T. Australia 108 E4
Killarney Qld Australia 112 F2
Killarney Canada 122 E5
Killarney Rep. of Ireland 51 C5
Killarney National Park Rep. of Ireland 51 C6
Killary Harbour b. Rep. of Ireland 51 C4
Killbuck U.S.A. 134 E3
Killeen U.S.A. 131 D6
Killenaule Rep. of Ireland 51 E5
Killimor Rep. of Ireland 51 D4
Killin U.K. 50 E4
Killinchy U.K. 51 G3
Killíni mt. Greece see Kyllini
Killinick Rep. of Ireland 51 F5
Killorglin Rep. of Ireland 51 C5
Killurin Rep. of Ireland 51 F5
Killybegs Rep. of Ireland 51 D3
Kilmacrenan Rep. of Ireland 51 E2
Kilmaine Rep. of Ireland 51 C4
Kilmallock Rep. of Ireland 51 D5
Kilmaluag U.K. 50 C3
Kilmarnock U.K. 50 E5
Kilmelford U.K. 50 D4
Kil'mez' Rus. Fed. 42 K4
Kil'mez' r. Rus. Fed. 42 K4
Kilmona Rep. of Ireland 51 D6
Kilmore Australia 112 B6
Kilmore Quay Rep. of Ireland 51 F5
Kilosa Tanz. 99 D4
Kilpisjärvi Fin. 44 L2
Kilrea U.K. 51 F3
Kilrush Rep. of Ireland 51 C5
Kilsyth U.K. 50 E5
Kiltan atoll India 84 B4
Kiltullagh Rep. of Ireland 51 D4
Kilwa Masoko Tanz. 99 D4
Kilwinning U.K. 50 E5
Kim U.S.A. 131 C4
Kimba Australia 109 G8
Kimba Congo 98 B4
Kimball U.S.A. 130 C3
Kimball, Mount U.S.A. 118 D3
Kimbe P.N.G. 106 F2
Kimberley S. Africa 100 G5
Kimberley Plateau Australia 108 D4
Kimberley Range hills Australia 109 B6
Kimch'aek N. Korea 75 C4
Kimch'ŏn S. Korea 75 C5
Kimhae S. Korea 75 C6
Kimhandu mt. Tanz. 99 D4
Kími Greece see Kymi
Kimito Fin. 45 M6
Kimmirut Canada 119 L3
Kimolos i. Greece 59 K6
Kimovsk Rus. Fed. 43 H5
Kimpese Dem. Rep. Congo 99 B4
Kimpoku-san mt. Japan see Kinpoku-san
Kimry Rus. Fed. 42 H4
Kimsquit Canada 120 E4
Kimvula Dem. Rep. Congo 99 B4
Kinabalu, Gunung mt. Sabah Malaysia 68 F5
Kinango Kenya 99 D4
Kinaskan Lake Canada 120 D3
Kinbasket Lake Canada 120 G4
Kinbrace U.K. 50 F2
Kincaid Canada 121 J5
Kincardine Canada 134 E1
Kincardine U.K. 50 F4
Kinchega National Park Australia 111 C7
Kincolith Canada 120 D4
Kinda Dem. Rep. Congo 99 C4
Kindat Myanmar 70 A2
Kinde U.S.A. 134 D2
Kinder Scout hill U.K. 48 F5
Kindersley Canada 121 I5
Kindia Guinea 96 B3
Kindu Dem. Rep. Congo 98 C4
Kinel' Rus. Fed. 43 K5
Kineshma Rus. Fed. 42 I4
Kingaroy Australia 112 E1
King Christian Island Canada 119 H2
King City U.S.A. 128 C3
King Edward VII Land pen. Antarctica see Edward VII Peninsula
Kingfield U.S.A. 135 J1
Kingfisher U.S.A. 131 D5
King George U.S.A. 135 G4
King George, Mount Canada 126 E2
King George Island Antarctica 152 A2
King George Islands Canada 122 F2
King George Islands Fr. Polynesia see Roi Georges, Îles du
King Hill hill Australia 108 C5
Kingisepp Rus. Fed. 45 P7
King Island Australia 111 [inset]
King Island Canada 120 E4
King Island Myanmar see Kadan Kyun
Kingisseppa Estonia see Kuressaare
Kinglake National Park Australia 112 B6
King Leopold and Queen Astrid Coast Antarctica 152 E2
King Leopold Range National Park Australia 108 D4
King Leopold Ranges hills Australia 108 D4
Kingman U.S.A. 129 F4
▶Kingman Reef terr. N. Pacific Ocean 150 J5
United States Unincorporated Territory.
King Mountain Canada 120 D3
King Mountain hill U.S.A. 131 C6
Kingoonya Australia 111 A6
King Peak Antarctica 152 L1
King Peninsula Antarctica 152 K2
Kingri Pak. 89 H4
Kings r. Rep. of Ireland 51 E5
Kings r. CA U.S.A. 128 C3
Kings r. NV U.S.A. 126 D4
King Salmon U.S.A. 118 C4
Kingsbridge U.K. 49 D8
Kingsburg U.S.A. 128 D3
Kings Canyon National Park U.S.A. 128 D3
Kingscliff Australia 112 F2
Kingscote Australia 111 B7
Kingscourt Rep. of Ireland 51 F4
King Sejong research station Antarctica 152 A2
King's Lynn U.K. 49 H6
Kingsmill Group is Kiribati 107 H2
Kingsnorth U.K. 49 H7
King Sound b. Australia 108 C4
Kings Peak U.S.A. 129 H1
Kingsport U.S.A. 132 D4
Kingston Australia 111 [inset]
Kingston Canada 135 G1
▶Kingston Jamaica 137 I5
Capital of Jamaica.
▶Kingston Norfolk I. 107 G4
Capital of Norfolk Island.
Kingston MO U.S.A. 130 E4
Kingston NY U.S.A. 135 H3
Kingston OH U.S.A. 134 D4
Kingston PA U.S.A. 135 H3
Kingston Peak U.S.A. 129 F4
Kingston South East Australia 111 B8
Kingston upon Hull U.K. 48 G5
▶Kingstown St Vincent 137 L6
Capital of St Vincent.
Kingstree U.S.A. 133 E5
Kingsville U.S.A. 131 D7
Kingswood U.K. 49 E7
Kington U.K. 49 D6
Kingungi Dem. Rep. Congo 99 B4
Kingurutik r. Canada 123 J2
Kingussie U.K. 50 E3
King William U.S.A. 135 G5
King William Island Canada 119 I3
King William's Town S. Africa 101 H7
Kingwood TX U.S.A. 131 E6
Kingwood WV U.S.A. 134 F4
Kinloch N.Z. 113 B7
Kinloss U.K. 50 F3
Kinmen Taiwan see Chinmen
Kinmen i. Taiwan see Chinmen Tao
Kinmount Canada 135 F1
Kinna Sweden 45 H8
Kinnegad Rep. of Ireland 51 E4
Kinneret, Yam l. Israel see Galilee, Sea of
Kinniyai Sri Lanka 84 D4
Kinnula Fin. 44 N5
Kinoje r. Canada 122 E3
Kinoosao Canada 121 K3
Kinpoku-san mt. Japan 75 E5
Kinross U.K. 50 F4
Kinsale Rep. of Ireland 51 D6
Kinsale U.S.A. 135 G4
▶Kinshasa Dem. Rep. Congo 99 B4
Capital of the Democratic Republic of Congo and 3rd most populous city in Africa.
Kinsley U.S.A. 130 D4
Kinsman U.S.A. 134 E3
Kinston U.S.A. 133 E5
Kintore U.K. 50 G3
Kintyre pen. U.K. 50 D5
Kinu Myanmar 70 A2
Kinushseo r. Canada 122 E3
Kinyeti mt. Sudan 97 G4
Kinzig r. Germany 53 I4
Kiowa CO U.S.A. 126 G5
Kiowa KS U.S.A. 131 D4
Kipahigan Lake Canada 121 K4
Kiparissía Greece see Kyparissia
Kipawa, Lac l. Canada 122 F5
Kipling Canada 121 K5
Kipling Station Canada see Kipling
Kipnuk U.S.A. 118 B4
Kiptopeke U.S.A. 135 H5
Kipungo Angola see Quipungo
Kipushi Dem. Rep. Congo 99 C5
Kirakira Solomon Is 107 G3
Kirandul India 84 D2
Kirchdorf Germany 53 I2
Kirchheim-Bolanden Germany 53 I5
Kirchheim unter Teck Germany 53 J6
Kircubbin U.K. 51 G3
Kirdimi Chad 97 E3
Kirenga r. Rus. Fed. 73 J1
Kirensk Rus. Fed. 65 L4
Kireyevsk Rus. Fed. 43 H5
Kirghizia country Asia see Kyrgyzstan
Kirghiz Range mts Kazakh./Kyrg. 80 D3
Kirgizskaya S.S.R. country Asia see Kyrgyzstan
Kirgizskiy Khrebet mts Kazakh./Kyrg. see Kirghiz Range
Kirgizstan country Asia see Kyrgyzstan
Kiri Dem. Rep. Congo 98 B4
Kiribati country Pacific Ocean 150 I6
Kırıkhan Turkey 85 C1
Kırıkkale Turkey 90 D3
Kirillov Rus. Fed. 42 H4
Kirillovo Rus. Fed. 74 F3
Kirin China see Jilin
Kirin prov. China see Jilin
Kirinda Sri Lanka 84 D5
Kirinyaga mt. Kenya see Kenya, Mount
Kirishi Rus. Fed. 42 G4
Kirishima-Yaku National Park Japan 75 C7
Kirishima-yama vol. Japan 75 C7
Kiritimati atoll Kiribati 151 J5
Kiriwina Islands P.N.G. see Trobriand Islands
Kırkağaç Turkey 59 L5
Kirk Bulāg Dāgi mt. Iran 88 B2
Kirkby U.K. 48 E5
Kirkby in Ashfield U.K. 49 F5
Kirkby Lonsdale U.K. 48 E4
Kirkby Stephen U.K. 48 E4
Kirkcaldy U.K. 50 F4
Kirkcolm U.K. 50 D6
Kirkcudbright U.K. 50 E6
Kirkenær Norway 45 H6
Kirkenes Norway 44 Q2
Kirkfield Canada 135 F1
Kirkintilloch U.K. 50 E5
Kirkkonummi Fin. 45 N6
Kirkland U.S.A. 129 G4
Kirkland Lake Canada 122 E4
Kırklareli Turkey 59 L4
Kirklin U.S.A. 134 B3
Kirk Michael Isle of Man 48 C4
Kirkoswald U.K. 48 E4
Kirkpatrick, Mount Antarctica 152 H1
Kirksville U.S.A. 130 E3
Kirkūk Iraq 91 G4
Kirkwall U.K. 50 G2
Kirkwood S. Africa 101 G7
Kirman Iran see Kermān
Kirn Germany 53 H5
Kirov Kaluzhskaya Oblast' Rus. Fed. 43 G5
Kirov Kirovskaya Oblast' Rus. Fed. 42 K4
Kirova, Zaliv b. Azer. see Qızılağac Körfäzi
Kirovabad Azer. see Gäncä
Kirovabad Tajik. see Panj
Kirovakan Armenia see Vanadzor
Kirovo Ukr. see Kirovohrad
Kirovo-Chepetsk Rus. Fed. 42 K4
Kirovo-Chepetskiy Rus. Fed. see Kirovo-Chepetsk
Kirovograd Ukr. see Kirovohrad
Kirovohrad Ukr. 43 G6
Kirovsk Leningradskaya Oblast' Rus. Fed. 42 F4
Kirovsk Murmanskaya Oblast' Rus. Fed. 44 R3
Kirovsk Turkm. see Babadaykhan
Kirovs'ke Ukr. 90 D1
Kirovskiy Rus. Fed. 74 D3
Kirovskoye Ukr. see Kirovs'ke
Kırpaşa pen. Cyprus see Karpasia
Kirpili Turkm. 88 E2
Kirriemuir U.K. 50 F4
Kirs Rus. Fed. 42 L4
Kirsanov Rus. Fed. 43 I5
Kırşehir Turkey 90 D3
Kirthar National Park Pak. 89 G5
Kirthar Range mts Pak. 89 G5
Kirtland U.S.A. 129 I3
Kirtorf Germany 53 J4
Kiruna Sweden 44 L3
Kirundu Dem. Rep. Congo 98 C4
Kirwan Escarpment Antarctica 152 B2
Kiryū Japan 75 E5
Kisa Sweden 45 I8
Kisama, Parque Nacional de nat. park Angola see Quiçama, Parque Nacional do
Kisandji Dem. Rep. Congo 99 B4
Kisangani Dem. Rep. Congo 98 C3
Kisantu Dem. Rep. Congo 99 B4
Kisar i. Indon. 108 D2
Kisaran Indon. 71 B7
Kiselevsk Rus. Fed. 72 F2
Kisel'ovka Rus. Fed. 74 E2
Kishanganj India 83 F4
Kishangarh Madhya Pradesh India 82 D4
Kishangarh Rajasthan India 82 B4
Kishangarh Rajasthan India 82 C4
Kishangarh Rajasthan India 82 D4
Kishi Nigeria 96 D4
Kishinev Moldova see Chişinău
Kishkenekol' Kazakh. 79 G1
Kishoreganj Bangl. 83 G4
Kishorganj Bangl. see Kishoreganj
Kisi Nigeria see Kishi
Kisii Kenya 98 D4
Kiska Island U.S.A. 65 S4
Kiskittogisu Lake Canada 121 L4
Kiskitto Lake Canada 121 L4
Kiskunfélegyháza Hungary 59 H1
Kiskunhalas Hungary 59 H1
Kiskunsági nat. park Hungary 59 H1
Kislovodsk Rus. Fed. 91 F2
Kismaayo Somalia 98 E4
Kismayu Somalia see Kismaayo
Kisoro Uganda 97 F5
Kispiox Canada 120 E4
Kispiox r. Canada 120 E4
Kisseraing Island Myanmar see Kanmaw Kyun
Kissidougou Guinea 96 B4
Kissimmee U.S.A. 133 D6
Kissimmee, Lake U.S.A. 133 D7
Kississing Lake Canada 121 K4
Kistendey Rus. Fed. 43 I5
Kistigan Lake Canada 121 M4
Kistna r. India see Krishna
Kisumu Kenya 98 D4
Kisykkamys Kazakh. see Dzhangala
Kita Mali 96 C3
Kitab Uzbek. 89 G2
Kita-Daitō-jima i. Japan 73 O7
Kitaibaraki Japan 75 F5
Kita-Iō-jima vol. Japan 69 K1
Kitakami Japan 75 F5
Kita-Kyūshū Japan 75 C6
Kitale Kenya 98 D3
Kitami Japan 74 F4
Kit Carson U.S.A. 130 C4
Kitchener Canada 134 E2
Kitchigama r. Canada 122 F4
Kitee Fin. 44 Q5
Kitgum Uganda 98 D3
Kíthira i. Greece see Kythira
Kíthnos i. Greece see Kythnos
Kiti, Cape Cyprus see Kition, Cape
Kitimat Canada 120 D4
Kitinen r. Fin. 44 O3
Kition, Cape Cyprus 85 A2
Kitiou, Akra c. Cyprus see Kition, Cape
Kitkatla Canada 120 D4
Kitob Uzbek. see Kitab
Kitsault Canada 120 D4
Kittanning U.S.A. 134 F3
Kittatinny Mountains hills U.S.A. 135 H3
Kittery U.S.A. 135 J2
Kittilä Fin. 44 N3
Kittur India 84 B3
Kitty Hawk U.S.A. 132 F4
Kitui Kenya 98 D4
Kitwanga Canada 120 D4
Kitwe Zambia 99 C5
Kitzbüheler Alpen mts Austria 47 N7
Kitzingen Germany 53 K5
Kitzscher Germany 53 M3
Kiu Lom Reservoir Thai. 70 B3
Kiunga P.N.G. 69 K8
Kiuruvesi Fin. 44 O5
Kivalina U.S.A. 118 B3
Kivijärvi Fin. 44 N5
Kiviõli Estonia 45 O7
Kivu, Lake Dem. Rep. Congo/Rwanda 98 C4
Kiwaba N'zogi Angola 99 B4
Kiwai Island P.N.G. 69 K8
Kiyev Ukr. see Kiev
Kiyevskoye Vodokhranilishche resr Ukr. see Kyyivs'ke Vodoskhovyshche
Kıyıköy Turkey 59 M4
Kizel Rus. Fed. 41 R4
Kizema Rus. Fed. 42 J3
Kızılcadağ Turkey 59 M6
Kızılca Dağ mt. Turkey 90 C3
Kızılcahamam Turkey 90 D2
Kızıldağ mt. Turkey 85 A1
Kızıldağ mt. Turkey 85 B1
Kızıl Dağı mt. Turkey 90 E3
Kızılırmak Turkey 90 D2
Kızılırmak r. Turkey 90 D2
Kızıltepe Turkey 91 F3
Kizil"yurt Rus. Fed. 91 G2
Kızkalesi Turkey 85 B1
Kizlyar Rus. Fed. 91 G2
Kizlyarskiy Zaliv b. Rus. Fed. 91 G1
Kizner Rus. Fed. 42 K4
Kizyl-Arbat Turkm. see Gyzylarbat
Kizyl-Atrek Turkm. see Gyzyletrek
Kjøllefjord Norway 44 O1
Kjøpsvik Norway 44 J2
Kladno Czech Rep. 47 O5
Klagenfurt Austria 47 O7
Klagetoh U.S.A. 129 I4
Klaipėda Lith. 45 L9
Klaksvík Faroe Is 44 [inset]
Klamath U.S.A. 126 B4
Klamath r. U.S.A. 118 F5
Klamath Falls U.S.A. 126 C4
Klamath Mountains U.S.A. 126 C4
Klarälven r. Sweden 45 H7
Klatovy Czech Rep. 47 N6
Klawer S. Africa 100 D6
Klazienaveen Neth. 52 G2
Kleides Islands Cyprus 85 B2
Kleinbegin S. Africa 100 E5
Klein Karas Namibia 100 D4
Klein Nama Land reg. S. Africa see Namaqualand
Klein Roggeveldberge mts S. Africa 100 E7
Kleinsee S. Africa 100 C5
Klemtu Canada 120 D4
Klerksdorp S. Africa 101 H4
Kletnya Rus. Fed. 43 G5
Kletsk Belarus see Klyetsk
Kletskaya Rus. Fed. 43 I6
Kletskiy Rus. Fed. see Kletskaya
Kleve Germany 52 G3
Klidhes Islands Cyprus see Kleides Islands
Klimkovka Rus. Fed. 42 K4
Klimovo Rus. Fed. 43 G5
Klin Rus. Fed. 42 H4
Klingenberg am Main Germany 53 J5
Klingenthal Germany 53 M4
Klingkang, Banjaran mts Indon./Malaysia 68 E6
Klink Germany 53 M1
Klínovec mt. Czech Rep. 53 N4
Klintehamn Sweden 45 K8
Klintsy Rus. Fed. 43 G5
Ključ Bos.-Herz. 58 G2
Kłodzko Poland 47 P5
Klondike r. Canada 120 B1
Klondike Gold Rush National Historical Park nat. park U.S.A. 120 C3
Kloosterhaar Neth. 52 G2
Klosterneuburg Austria 47 P6
Klötze (Altmark) Germany 53 L2
Kluane Lake Canada 120 B2
Kluane National Park Canada 120 B2
Kluang Malaysia see Keluang
Kluczbork Poland 47 Q5
Klukhori Rus. Fed. see Karachayevsk
Klukwan U.S.A. 120 C3
Klupro Pak. 89 H5
Klyetsk Belarus 45 O10
Klyuchevskaya, Sopka vol. Rus. Fed. 65 R4
Klyuchi Rus. Fed. 74 B2
Knåda Sweden 45 I6
Knaresborough U.K. 48 F4
Knee Lake Man. Canada 121 M4
Knee Lake Sask. Canada 121 J4
Knetzgau Germany 53 K5
Knife r. U.S.A. 130 C2
Knight Inlet Canada 120 E5
Knighton U.K. 49 D6
Knights Landing U.S.A. 128 C2
Knightstown U.S.A. 134 C4
Knin Croatia 58 G2
Knittelfeld Austria 47 O7
Knjaževac Serb. and Mont. 59 J3
Knob Lake Canada see Schefferville
Knob Lick U.S.A. 134 C5
Knob Peak hill Australia 108 E3
Knock Rep. of Ireland 51 D4
Knockaboy hill Rep. of Ireland 51 C6
Knockalongy hill Rep. of Ireland 51 D3
Knockalough Rep. of Ireland 51 C5
Knockanaffrin hill Rep. of Ireland 51 E5
Knock Hill hill U.K. 50 G3
Knockmealdown Mts hills Rep. of Ireland 51 D5
Knocknaskagh hill Rep. of Ireland 51 D5
Knokke-Heist Belgium 52 D3
Knorrendorf Germany 53 N1
Knowle U.K. 49 F6
Knowlton Canada 135 I1
Knox IN U.S.A. 134 B3
Knox PA U.S.A. 134 F3
Knox, Cape Canada 120 C4
Knox Coast Antarctica 152 F2
Knoxville GA U.S.A. 133 D5
Knoxville TN U.S.A. 132 D5
Knud Rasmussen Land reg. Greenland 119 L2
Knysna S. Africa 100 F8
Ko, Gora mt. Rus. Fed. 74 E3
Koartac Canada see Quaqtaq
Koba Indon. 68 D7
Kobbfoss Norway 44 P2
Kōbe Japan 75 D6
København Denmark see Copenhagen
Kobenni Mauritania 96 C3
Koblenz Germany 53 H4
Koboldo Rus. Fed. 74 D1
Kobrin Belarus see Kobryn
Kobroör i. Indon. 69 I8
Kobryn Belarus 45 N10
Kobuk Valley National Park U.S.A. 118 C3
K'obulet'i Georgia 91 F2
Kocaeli Turkey 59 M4
Kocaeli Yarımadası pen. Turkey 59 M4
Kočani Macedonia 59 J4
Kocasu r. Turkey 59 M4
Kočevje Slovenia 58 F2
Koch Bihar India 83 G4
Kocher r. Germany 53 J5
Kochevo Rus. Fed. 41 Q4
Kochi India see Cochin
Kōchi Japan 75 D6
Koçhisar Turkey see Kızıltepe

Kualasimpang Indon. 71 B6
Kuala Terengganu Malaysia 71 C6
Kualatungal Indon. 68 C7
Kuamut Sabah Malaysia 68 F5
Kuandian China 74 B4
Kuantan Malaysia 71 C7
Kuba Azer. see Quba
Kuban' r. Rus. Fed. 43 H7
Kubār Syria 91 E4
Kubaybāt Syria 85 C2
Kubaysah Iraq 91 F4
Kubenskoye, Ozero l. Rus. Fed. 42 H4
Kubrat Bulg. 59 L3
Kubuang Indon. 68 F6
Kuchaman Road India 89 I5
Kuchema Rus. Fed. 42 I2
Kuching Sarawak Malaysia 68 E6
Kucing Sarawak Malaysia see Kuching
Kuçovë Albania 59 H4
Kuda India 82 B5
Kudal India 84 B3
Kudap Indon. 71 C7
Kudat Sabah Malaysia 68 F5
Kudligi India 84 C3
Kudremukh mt. India 84 B3
Kudus Indon. 68 E8
Kudymkar Rus. Fed. 41 Q4
Kueishan Tao i. Taiwan 77 I3
Kufstein Austria 47 N7
Kugaaruk Canada 119 J3
Kugesi Rus. Fed. 42 J4
Kugka Lhai China 83 G3
Kugluktuk Canada 118 G3
Kugmallit Bay Canada 153 A2
Kūh, Ra's-al- pt Iran 88 E5
Kūhak Iran 89 F5
Kuhanbokano mt. China 83 E3
Kuhbier Germany 53 M1
Kūhdasht Iran 88 B3
Kūhīn Iran 88 C2
Kūhīrī Iran 89 F5
Kuhmo Fin. 44 P4
Kuhmoinen Fin. 45 N6
Kūhpāyeh mt. Iran 88 E4
Kūhrān, Kūh-e mt. Iran 88 E5
Kühren Germany 53 M3
Kui Buri Thai. 71 B4
Kuis Namibia 100 C3
Kuiseb watercourse Namibia 100 B2
Kuitan China 77 G4
Kuito Angola 99 B5
Kuitun China see Kuytun
Kuiu Island U.S.A. 120 C3
Kuivaniemi Fin. 44 N4
Kujang N. Korea 75 B5
Kuji Japan 75 F4
Kujū-san vol. Japan 75 C6
Kukālār, Kūh-e hill Iran 88 C4
Kukan Rus. Fed. 74 D2
Kukës Albania 59 I3
Kukesi Albania see Kukës
Kukmor Rus. Fed. 42 K4
Kukshi India 82 C5
Kukunuru India 84 D2
Kukurtli Turkm. 88 E2
Kūl r. Iran 88 D5
Kula Turkey 59 M5
Kulaisila India 83 F5
Kula Kangri mt. China/Bhutan 79 G3
Kulandy Kazakh. 80 A2
Kulaneh reg. Pak. 89 F5
Kular Rus. Fed. 65 O2
Kuldīga Latvia 45 L8
Kuldja China see Yining
Kul'dur Rus. Fed. 74 C2
Kule Botswana 100 E2
Kulebaki Rus. Fed. 43 I5
Kulen Cambodia 71 D4
Kulgera Australia 109 F6
Kulikovo Rus. Fed. 42 J3
Kulim Malaysia 71 C6
Kulin Australia 109 B8
Kulja Australia 109 B7
Kulkyne watercourse Australia 112 B3
Kullu India 82 D3
Kulmbach Germany 53 L4
Kŭlob Tajik. 89 H2
Kuloy Rus. Fed. 42 I3
Kuloy r. Rus. Fed. 42 I2
Kulp Turkey 91 F3
Kul'sary Kazakh. 78 E2
Külsheim Germany 53 J5
Kulu India see Kullu
Kulu Turkey 90 D3
Kulunda Rus. Fed. 72 D2
Kulundinskaya Step' plain Kazakh./Rus. Fed. 72 D2
Kulundinskoye, Ozero salt l. Rus. Fed. 72 D2
Kulusuk Greenland 119 O3
Kulwin Australia 111 C7
Kulyab Tajik. see Kŭlob
Kuma r. Rus. Fed. 43 J7
Kumagaya Japan 75 E5
Kumai, Teluk b. Indon. 68 E7
Kumalar Dağı mts Turkey 59 N5
Kumamoto Japan 75 C6
Kumano Japan 75 E6
Kumanovo Macedonia 59 I3
Kumara Rus. Fed. 74 B2
Kumasi Ghana 96 C4
Kumayri Armenia see Gyumri
Kumba Cameroon 96 D4
Kumbakonam India 84 C4
Kumbe Indon. 69 K8
Kümbet Turkey 59 N5
Kumbharli Ghat mt. India 84 B2
Kumbla India 84 B3
Kumchuru Botswana 100 F2
Kum-Dag Turkm. see Gumdag
Kumdah Saudi Arabia 86 G5
Kumel well Iran 88 D3
Kumeny Rus. Fed. 42 K4
Kumertau Rus. Fed. 64 G4
Kumgang-san mt. N. Korea 71 C5
Kumguri India 83 G4
Kumhwa S. Korea 75 B5
Kumi S. Korea 75 C5
Kumi Uganda 97 G4
Kumkurgan Uzbek. 89 G2
Kumla Sweden 45 I7
Kumlu Turkey 85 C1
Kummersdorf-Alexanderdorf Germany 53 N2
Kumo Nigeria 96 E3
Kŭmŏ-do i. S. Korea 75 B6
Kumon Range mts Myanmar 70 B1
Kumphawapi Thai. 70 C3
Kums Namibia 100 D5
Kumta India 84 B3
Kumu Dem. Rep. Congo 98 C3
Kumukh Rus. Fed. 91 G2
Kumul China see Hami
Kumund India 84 D1
Kumylzhenskaya Rus. Fed. see Kumylzhenskiy
Kumylzhenskiy Rus. Fed. 43 I6
Kun r. Myanmar 70 B3
Kunar r. Afgh. 89 H3
Kunashir, Ostrov i. Rus. Fed. 70 G3
Kunashirskiy Proliv sea chan. Japan/Rus. Fed. see Nemuro-kaikyō
Kunchaung Myanmar 70 B2
Kunchuk Tso salt l. China 83 E2
Kunda Estonia 45 O7
Kunda India 83 E4
Kundapura India 84 B3
Kundelungu, Parc National de nat. park Dem. Rep. Congo 99 C5
Kundelungu Ouest, Parc National de nat. park Dem. Rep. Congo 99 C5
Kundia India 82 C4
Kundur i. Indon. 68 C6
Kunduz Afgh. 89 H2
Kunene r. Angola see Cunene
Kuneneng admin. dist. Botswana see Kweneng
Künes China see Xinyuan
Kungälv Sweden 45 G8
Kunghit Island Canada 120 D4
Kungrad Uzbek. 80 A3
Kungsbacka Sweden 45 H8
Kungshamn Sweden 45 G7
Kungu Dem. Rep. Congo 98 B3
Kungur mt. China see Kongur Shan
Kungur Rus. Fed. 41 R4
Kunhing Myanmar 70 B2
Kuni r. India 84 C2
Kūnīch Iran 88 E5
Kunié i. New Caledonia see Pins, Île des
Kunigai India 84 C3
Kunimi-dake mt. Japan 75 C6
Kunlavav India 82 B5
Kunlong Myanmar 70 B2
Kunlun Shan mts China 82 D1
Kunlun Shankou pass China 79 H2
Kunming China 76 D3
Kunsan S. Korea 75 B6
Kunshan China 77 I2
Kununurra Australia 108 E3
Kunwak r. Canada 121 L2
Kun'ya Rus. Fed. 42 F4
Kunyang Yunnan China see Jinning
Kunyang Zhejiang China see Pingyang
Kunya-Urgench Turkm. see Keneurgench
Künzelsau Germany 53 J5
Künzels-Berg hill Germany 53 L3
Kuocang Shan mts China 77 I2
Kuohijärvi l. Fin. 45 N6
Kuolayarvi Rus. Fed. 44 P3
Kuopio Fin. 44 O5
Kuortane Fin. 44 M5
Kupa r. Croatia/Slovenia 58 G2
Kupang Indon. 108 C2
Kupari India 83 F5
Kupiškis Lith. 45 N9
Kupreanof Island U.S.A. 120 C3
Kupwara India 82 C2
Kup"yans'k Ukr. 43 H6
Kuqa China 80 F3
Kür r. Georgia 91 G2
also known as Kur (Russian Federation), Kura
Kur r. Rus. Fed. 74 D2
also known as Kür (Georgia), Kura
Kuragino Rus. Fed. 72 G2
Kurakh Rus. Fed. 43 J8
Kurama Range mts Asia 87 K1
Kuraminskiy Khrebet mts Asia see Kurama Range
Kūrān Dap Iran 89 E5
Kurashiki Japan 75 D6
Kurasia India 83 E5
Kurayn i. Saudi Arabia 88 C5
Kurayoshi Japan 75 D6
Kurchatov Rus. Fed. 43 G6
Kurchum Kazakh. 80 F2
Kürdämir Azer. 91 H2
Kŭrdzhali Bulg. 59 K4
Kure Japan 75 D6
Küre Turkey 90 D2
Kure Atoll U.S.A. 150 I4
Kuressaare Estonia 45 M7
Kurgal'dzhino Kazakh. see Korgalzhyn
Kurgal'dzhinskiy Kazakh. see Korgalzhyn
Kurgan Rus. Fed. 64 H4
Kurganinsk Rus. Fed. 91 F1
Kurgannaya Rus. Fed. see Kurganinsk
Kurgantyube Tajik. see Qŭrghonteppa
Kuri Afgh. 89 H2
Kuri India 82 B4
Kuria Muria Islands Oman see Ḥalāniyāt, Juzur al
Kuridala Australia 110 C4
Kurigram Bangl. 83 G4
Kurikka Fin. 44 M5
Kuril Basin sea feature Sea of Okhotsk 150 F2
Kuril Islands Rus. Fed. 74 H3
Kurilovka Rus. Fed. 43 K6
Kuril'sk Rus. Fed. 74 G3
Kuril'skiye Ostrova is Rus. Fed. see Kuril Islands
Kuril Trench sea feature N. Pacific Ocean 150 F3
Kurkino Rus. Fed. 43 H5
Kurmashkino Kazakh. see Kurchum
Kurmuk Sudan 86 D7
Kurnool India 84 C3
Kuroiso Japan 75 F5
Kurort Schmalkalden Germany 53 K4
Kurovskiy Rus. Fed. 74 B1
Kurow N.Z. 113 C7
Kurram Pak. 89 H3
Kurri Kurri Australia 112 E4
Kursavka Rus. Fed. 91 F1
Kürshim Kazakh. see Kurchum
Kurshskiy Zaliv b. Lith./Rus. Fed. see Courland Lagoon
Kuršių marios b. Lith./Rus. Fed. see Courland Lagoon
Kursk Rus. Fed. 43 H6
Kurskaya Rus. Fed. 91 G1
Kurskiy Zaliv b. Lith./Rus. Fed. see Courland Lagoon
Kurşunlu Turkey 90 D2
Kurtalan Turkey 91 F3
Kurtoğlu Burnu pt Turkey 59 M6
Kurtpınar Turkey 85 B1
Kurucaşile Turkey 90 D2
Kuruçay Turkey 90 E3
Kurukshetra India 82 D3
Kuruktag mts China 80 G3
Kuruman S. Africa 100 F4
Kuruman watercourse S. Africa 100 E4
Kurume Japan 75 C6
Kurumkan Rus. Fed. 73 K2
Kurunegala Sri Lanka 84 D5
Kurupam India 84 D2
Kurush, Jebel hills Sudan 86 D5
Kur'ya Rus. Fed. 41 R3
Kuryk Kazakh. 91 H2
Kuşadası Turkey 59 L6
Kuşadası Körfezi b. Turkey 59 L6
Kusaie atoll Micronesia see Kosrae
Kusary Azer. see Qusar
Kuşcenneti nature res. Turkey 85 B1
Kuschke Nature Reserve S. Africa 101 I3
Kusel Germany 53 H5
Kuş Gölü l. Turkey 59 L4
Kushalgarh India 82 C5
Kushchevskaya Rus. Fed. 43 H7
Kushimoto Japan 75 D6
Kushiro Japan 74 G4
Kushka Turkm. see Gushgy
Kushkopola Rus. Fed. 42 J3
Kushmurun Kazakh. 78 F1
Kushtagi India 84 C3
Kushtia Bangl. 83 G5
Kushtih Iran 89 E4
Kuskan Turkey 85 A1
Kuskokwim r. U.S.A. 118 B3
Kuskokwim Bay U.S.A. 118 B4
Kuskokwim Mountains U.S.A. 118 C3
Kuşluyan Turkey see Gölköy
Kusŏng N. Korea 75 B5
Kustanay Kazakh. see Kostanay
Küstence Romania see Constanța
Küstenkanal canal Germany 53 H1
Kustia Bangl. see Kushtia
Kut Iran 88 C4
Kut, Ko i. Thai. 71 C5
Küt 'Abdollāh Iran 88 C4
Kutacane Indon. 71 B7
Kütahya Turkey 59 M5
K'ut'aisi Georgia 91 F2
Kut-al-Imara Iraq see Al Kūt
Kutan Rus. Fed. 91 G1
Kutanibong Indon. 71 B7
Kutaraja Indon. see Banda Aceh
Kutayfat Ţurayf vol. Saudi Arabia 85 D4
Kutch, Gulf of India see Kachchh, Gulf of
Kutch, Rann of marsh India see Kachchh, Rann of
Kutchan Japan 74 F4
Kutina Croatia 58 G2
Kutjevo Croatia 58 G2
Kutkai Myanmar 70 B2
Kutno Poland 47 Q4
Kutru India 84 D2
Kutu Dem. Rep. Congo 98 B4
Kutubdia Island Bangl. 83 G5
Kutum Sudan 97 F3
Kutztown U.S.A. 135 H3
Kuujjua r. Canada 118 G2
Kuujjuaq Canada 123 H2
Kuujjuarapik Canada 122 F3
Kuuli-Mayak Turkm. 88 D1
Kuusamo Fin. 44 P4
Kuusankoski Fin. 45 O6
Kuvango Angola 99 B5
Kuvshinovo Rus. Fed. 42 G4
▶Kuwait country Asia 88 B4
Asia 6, 62–63

▶Kuwait Kuwait 88 B4
Capital of Kuwait.

Kuwajleen atoll Marshall Is see Kwajalein
Kuybyshev Novosibirskaya Oblast' Rus. Fed. 64 I4
Kuybyshev Respublika Tatarstan Rus. Fed. see Bolgar
Kuybyshev Samarskaya Oblast' Rus. Fed. see Samara
Kuybysheve Ukr. 43 H7
Kuybyshevka-Vostochnaya Rus. Fed. see Belogorsk
Kuybyshevskoye Vodokhranilishche resr Rus. Fed. 43 K5
Kuyeda Rus. Fed. 41 R4
Kuygan Kazakh. 80 D2
Kuytun China 80 F3
Kuytun Rus. Fed. 72 I2
Kuyucak Turkey 59 M6
Kuzino Rus. Fed. 41 R4
Kuznechnoye Rus. Fed. 45 P6
Kuznetsk Rus. Fed. 43 J5
Kuznetsovo Rus. Fed. 74 E3
Kuznetsovs'k Ukr. 43 E6
Kuzovatovo Rus. Fed. 43 J5
Kvænangen sea chan. Norway 44 L1
Kvaløya i. Norway 44 K2
Kvalsund Norway 44 M1
Kvarnerić sea chan. Croatia 58 F2
Kvitøya ice feature Svalbard 64 E2
Kwa r. Dem. Rep. Congo see Kasaï
Kwabhaca S. Africa see Mount Frere
Kwadelen atoll Marshall Is see Kwajalein
Kwajalein atoll Marshall Is 150 H5
Kwale Nigeria 96 D4
KwaMashu S. Africa 101 J5
KwaMhlanga S. Africa 101 I3
Kwa Mtoro Tanz. 99 D4
Kwangch'ŏn S. Korea 75 B5
Kwangchow China see Guangzhou
Kwangju S. Korea 75 B6
Kwangsi Chuang Autonomous Region aut. reg. China see Guangxi Zhuangzu Zizhiqu
Kwangtung prov. China see Guangdong
Kwanmo-bong mt. N. Korea 74 C4
Kwanobuhle S. Africa 101 G7
KwaNojoli S. Africa 101 G7
Kwanonqubela S. Africa 101 H7
Kwanonzame S. Africa 100 G6
Kwanza r. Angola see Cuanza
Kwatinidubu S. Africa 101 H7
KwaZamokhule S. Africa 101 I4
Kwazamukucinga S. Africa 100 G7
Kwazamuxolo S. Africa 100 G6
KwaZanele S. Africa 101 I4
KwaZulu-Natal prov. S. Africa 97 J5
Kweichow prov. China see Guizhou
Kweiyang China see Guiyang
Kwekwe Zimbabwe 99 C5
Kweneng admin. dist. Botswana 100 G2
Kwenge r. Dem. Rep. Congo 99 B4
Kwetabohigan r. Canada 122 E4
Kwezi-Naledi S. Africa 101 H6
Kwidzyn Poland 47 Q4
Kwikila P.N.G. 69 L8
Kwilu r. Angola/Dem. Rep. Congo 99 B4
Kwo Chau Kwan To is Hong Kong China see Ninepin Group
Kwoka mt. Indon. 69 I7
Kyabra Australia 111 C5
Kyabram Australia 112 B6
Kyadet Myanmar 70 A2
Kyaikkami Myanmar 70 B3
Kyaiklat Myanmar 70 A3
Kyaikto Myanmar 70 B3
Kyakhta Rus. Fed. 72 J2
Kyalite Australia 112 A5
Kyancutta Australia 109 F8
Kyangin Myanmar 70 B3
Kyangngoin China 76 B2
Kyaukhnyat Myanmar 70 B3
Kyaukkyi Myanmar 70 B3
Kyaukme Myanmar 70 B2
Kyaukpadaung Myanmar 70 A2
Kyaukpyu Myanmar 70 A3
Kyaukse Myanmar 70 B2
Kyauktaw Myanmar 70 A2
Kyaunggon Myanmar 70 A3
Kybartai Lith. 45 M9
Kyebogyi Myanmar 70 B3
Kyêbxang Co l. China 83 G2
Kyeikdon Myanmar 70 B3
Kyeikywa Myanmar 70 B3
Kyeintali Myanmar 70 A3
Kyela Tanz. 99 D4
Kyelang India 82 D2
Kyidaunggan Myanmar 70 B3
Kyiv Ukr. see Kiev
Kyklades is Greece see Cyclades
Kyle Canada 121 I5
Kyle of Lochalsh U.K. 50 D3
Kyll r. Germany 52 G5
Kyllini mt. Greece 59 J6
Kymi Greece 59 K5
Kymis, Akra pt Greece 59 K5
Kyneton Australia 112 B6
Kynuna Australia 110 C4
Kyoga, Lake Uganda 98 D3
Kyōga-misaki pt Japan 75 D6
Kyogle Australia 112 F2
Kyong Myanmar 70 B2
Kyŏngju S. Korea 75 C6
Kyonpyaw Myanmar 70 A3
Kyōto Japan 75 D6
Kyparissia Greece 59 I6
Kypros country Asia see Cyprus
Kypshak, Ozero salt l. Kazakh. 79 F1
Kyra Rus. Fed. 73 K3
Kyra Panagia i. Greece 59 K5
Kyrenia Cyprus 85 A2
Kyrenia Mountains Cyprus see Pentadaktylos Range
Kyrgyz Ala-Too mts Kazakh./Kyrg. see Kirghiz Range
▶Kyrgyzstan country Asia 80 D3
Asia 6, 62–63
Kyritz Germany 53 M2
Kyrksæterøra Norway 44 F5
Kyrta Rus. Fed. 41 R3
Kyssa Rus. Fed. 42 J2
Kytalyktakh Rus. Fed. 65 O3
Kythira i. Greece 59 J6
Kythnos i. Greece 59 K6
Kyunglung China 82 E3
Kyunhla Myanmar 70 A2
Kyun Pila i. Myanmar 71 B5
Kyuquot Canada 120 E5
Kyurdamir Azer. see Kürdämir
Kyūshū i. Japan 75 C7
Kyushu-Palau Ridge sea feature N. Pacific Ocean 150 F4
Kyustendil Bulg. 59 J3
Kywebwe Myanmar 70 B3
Kywong Australia 112 C5
Kyyev Ukr. see Kiev
Kyyiv Ukr. see Kiev
Kyyivs'ke Vodoskhovyshche resr Ukr. 43 F6
Kyyjärvi Fin. 44 N5
Kyzyl Rus. Fed. 80 H1
Kyzyl-Art, Pereval pass Kyrg./Tajik. see Kyzylart Pass
Kyzylart Pass Kyrg./Tajik. 89 I2
Kyzyl-Burun Azer. see Siyäzän
Kyzyl-Kiya Kyrg. see Kyzyl-Kyya
Kyzylkum, Peski des. Kazakh./Uzbek. see Kyzylkum Desert
Kyzylkum Desert Kazakh./Uzbek. 80 B3
Kyzyl-Kyya Kyrg. 80 D3
Kyzyl-Mazhalyk Rus. Fed. 80 H1
Kyzylorda Kazakh. 80 C3
Kyzylrabot Tajik. see Qizilrabot
Kyzylsay Kazakh. 91 I2
Kyzylysor Kazakh. 91 H1
Kyzylzhar Kazakh. 80 C2
Kzyl-Dzhar Kazakh. see Kyzylzhar
Kzyl-Orda Kazakh. see Kyzylorda
Kzyltu Kazakh. see Kishkenekol'

L

Laagri Estonia 45 N7
Laam Atoll Maldives see Hadhdhunmathi Atoll
La Angostura, Presa de resr Mex. 136 F5
Laanila Fin. 44 O2
Laascaanood Somalia 98 E3
La Ascensión, Bahía de b. Mex. 137 G5
Laasgoray Somalia 98 E2

▶Laâyoune W. Sahara 96 B2
Capital of Western Sahara.

La Babia Mex. 131 C6
La Bahía, Islas de is Hond. 137 G5
La Baie Canada 123 H4
La Baleine, Grande Rivière de r. Canada 122 F3
La Baleine, Petite Rivière de r. Canada 122 F3
La Baleine, Rivière à r. Canada 123 I2
La Banda Arg. 144 D3
La Barge U.S.A. 126 F4
Labasa Fiji 107 H3
La Baule-Escoublac France 56 C3
Labazhskoye Rus. Fed. 42 L2
Labe r. Czech Rep. see Elbe
Labé Guinea 96 B3
La Belle U.S.A. 133 D7
La Bénoué, Parc National de nat. park Cameroon 97 E4
Laberge, Lake Canada 120 C2
Labian, Tanjung pt Malaysia 68 F5
La Biche, Lac l. Canada 121 H4
Labinsk Rus. Fed. 91 F1
Labis Malaysia 71 C7
La Boquilla Mex. 131 B7
La Boucle du Baoulé, Parc National de nat. park Mali 96 C3
Labouheyre France 56 D4
Laboulaye Arg. 144 D4
Labrador reg. Canada 123 J3
Labrador City Canada 123 I3
Labrador Sea Canada/Greenland 119 M3
Labrang China see Xiahe
Lábrea Brazil 142 F5
Labuan Malaysia 68 F5
Labudalin China see Ergun
Labuhanbilik Indon. 71 C7
Labuhanruku Indon. 71 B7
Labuna Indon. 69 H7
Labutta Myanmar 70 A3
Labyrinth, Lake salt flat Australia 111 A6
Labytnangi Rus. Fed. 64 H3
Laç Albania 59 H4
La Cabrera, Sierra de mts Spain 57 C2
La Cadena Mex. 131 B7
Lac Allard Canada 123 J4
La Calle Alg. see El Kala
La Cañiza Spain see A Cañiza
La Capelle France 52 D5
La Carlota Arg. 144 D4
La Carolina Spain 57 E4
Lăcăuți, Vârful mt. Romania 59 L2
Laccadive, Minicoy and Amindivi Islands union terr. India see Lakshadweep
Laccadive Islands India 84 B4
Lac du Bonnet Canada 121 L5
Lacedaemon Greece see Sparti
La Ceiba Hond. 137 G5
Lacepede Bay Australia 111 B8
Lacepede Islands Australia 108 C4
Lacha, Ozero l. Rus. Fed. 42 H3
Lachendorf Germany 53 K2
Lachine U.S.A. 134 D1

▶Lachlan r. Australia 112 A5
5th longest river in Oceania.

La Chorrera Panama 137 I7
Lachute Canada 122 G5
Laçın Azer. 91 G3
La Ciotat France 56 G5
Lac La Biche Canada 121 I4
Lac la Martre Canada see Wha Ti
Lacolle Canada 135 I1
La Colorada Sonora Mex. 127 F7
La Colorada Zacatecas Mex. 131 C8
Lacombe Canada 120 H4
La Comoé, Parc National de nat. park Côte d'Ivoire 96 C4
Laconi Sardinia Italy 58 C5
Laconia U.S.A. 135 J2
La Corey Canada 121 I4
La Coruña Spain see A Coruña
La Corvette, Lac de l. Canada 122 G3
La Coubre, Pointe de pt France 56 D4
La Crete Canada 120 G3
La Crosse KS U.S.A. 130 D4
La Crosse VA U.S.A. 135 F5
La Crosse WI U.S.A. 130 F3
La Cruz Mex. 136 C4
Lac Thiên Vietnam 71 E4
La Cuesta Mex. 131 C6
La Culebra, Sierra de mts Spain 57 C3
La Cygne U.S.A. 130 E4
Ladainha Brazil 145 C2
Ladakh reg. Jammu and Kashmir 82 D2
Ladakh Range mts India 82 D2
Ladang, Ko i. Thai. 71 B6
La Demajagua Cuba 133 D8
La Demanda, Sierra de mts Spain 57 E2
La Déroute, Passage de strait Channel Is/France 49 E9
Ladik Turkey 90 D2
Lādīz Iran 89 F4
Ladnun India 82 C4

▶Ladoga, Lake Rus. Fed. 45 Q6
2nd largest lake in Europe.

Ladong China 77 F3
Ladozhskoye Ozero l. Rus. Fed. see Ladoga, Lake
Ladrones terr. N. Pacific Ocean see Northern Mariana Islands
Ladu mt. India 83 H4
Ladue r. Canada/U.S.A. 120 A2
Ladva-Vetka Rus. Fed. 42 G3
Ladybank U.K. 50 F4
Ladybrand S. Africa 101 H5
Lady Frere S. Africa 101 H6
Lady Grey S. Africa 101 H6
Ladysmith S. Africa 101 I5
Ladysmith U.S.A. 130 F2
Ladzhanurges Georgia see Lajanurpekhi
Lae P.N.G. 69 L8
Laem Ngop Thai. 71 C4
Lærdalsøyri Norway 45 E6
La Esmeralda Bol. 142 F8
Læsø i. Denmark 45 G8
Lafayette Alg. see Bougaa
Lafayette AL U.S.A. 133 C5
Lafayette IN U.S.A. 134 B3
Lafayette LA U.S.A. 131 E6
Lafayette TN U.S.A. 134 B5
Lafé Cuba 133 C8
La Fère France 52 D5
Laferte r. Canada 120 G2
La Ferté-Gaucher France 52 D6
La-Ferté-Milon France 52 D5
La Ferté-sous-Jouarre France 52 D6
Lafia Nigeria 96 D4
Lafiagi Nigeria 96 D4
Laflamme r. Canada 122 F4
Lafleche Canada 121 J5
La Flèche France 56 D3
La Follette U.S.A. 134 C5
La Forest, Lac l. Canada 123 H3
Laforge Canada 123 G3
Laforge r. Canada 123 G3
La Frégate, Lac de l. Canada 122 G3
Lāft Iran 88 D5
Laful India 71 A6
La Galissonnière, Lac l. Canada 123 J4

▶La Galite i. Tunisia 58 C6
Most northerly point of Africa.

La Galite, Canal de sea chan. Tunisia 58 C6
La Gallega Mex. 131 B7
Lagan' Rus. Fed. 43 J7
Lagan r. U.K. 51 G3
La Garamba, Parc National de nat. park Dem. Rep. Congo 98 C3
Lagarto Brazil 143 K6
Lage Germany 53 I3
Lågen r. Norway 45 G7
Lage Vaart canal Neth. 52 F2
Lagg U.K. 50 D5
Laggan U.K. 50 E3
Lagh Bor watercourse Kenya/Somalia 98 E3
Laghouat Alg. 54 E5
Lagkor Co salt l. China 83 F2
La Gloria Mex. 131 D7
Lago Agrio Ecuador see Nueva Loja
Lagoa Santa Brazil 145 C2
Lagoa Vermelha Brazil 145 A5
Lagodekhi Georgia 91 G2
Lagolândia Brazil 145 A1
La Gomera i. Canary Is 96 B2
La Gonâve, Île de i. Haiti 137 J5
Lagong i. Indon. 71 E7

▶Lagos Nigeria 96 D4
Former capital of Nigeria. 2nd most populous city in Africa.

Lagos Port. 57 B5
Lagosa Tanz. 99 C4
La Grande r. Canada 122 F3
La Grande U.S.A. 126 D3
La Grande 2, Réservoir resr Canada 122 F3
La Grande 3, Réservoir resr Canada 122 G3
La Grande 4, Réservoir resr Que. Canada 123 G3
Lagrange Australia 108 C4
La Grange CA U.S.A. 128 C3
La Grange GA U.S.A. 133 C5
Lagrange U.S.A. 134 C3
La Grange KY U.S.A. 132 C4
La Grange TX U.S.A. 131 D6
La Gran Sabana plat. Venez. 138 F2
La Grita Venez. 142 D2
La Guajira, Península de pen. Col. 142 D1
Laguna Brazil 145 A5
Laguna Dam U.S.A. 129 F5
Laguna Mountains U.S.A. 128 E5
Lagunas Chile 144 C2
Laguna San Rafael, Parque Nacional nat. park Chile 144 B7
Laha China 74 B2
La Habana Cuba see Havana
La Habra U.S.A. 128 E5
Lahad Datu Sabah Malaysia 68 F5
La Hague, Cap de c. France 56 D2
Laharpur India 82 E4
Lahat Indon. 68 C7
Lahe Myanmar 70 A1
Lahemaa rahvuspark nat. park Estonia 45 N7
La Hève, Cap de c. France 49 H9
Lahewa Indon. 71 B7
Laḩij Yemen 86 F7
Lāhījān Iran 88 C2
Lahn r. Germany 53 H4
Lahnstein Germany 53 H4
Laholm Sweden 45 H8
Lahontan Reservoir U.S.A. 128 D2
Lahore Pak. 89 I4
Lahri Pak. 89 H4
Lahti Fin. 45 N6
Laï Chad 97 E4
Lai'an China 77 H1
Laibach Slovenia see Ljubljana
Laibin China 77 F4
Laidley Australia 112 F1
Laifeng China 77 F2
L'Aigle France 56 E2
Laihia Fin. 44 M5
Lai-hka Myanmar 70 B2
Lai-Hsak Myanmar 70 B2
Laimakuri India 83 H4
Laingsburg S. Africa 100 E7
Laingsburg U.S.A. 134 C2

Loyalty Islands New Caledonia see Loyauté, Îles
Loyang China see Luoyang
Loyauté, Îles is New Caledonia 107 G4
Loyev Belarus see Loyew
Loyew Belarus 43 F6
Lozère, Mont mt. France 56 F4
Loznica Serb. and Mont. 59 H2
Lozova Ukr. 43 H6
Lozovaya Ukr. see Lozova
Lua r. Dem. Rep. Congo 98 B3
Luacano Angola 99 C5
Lu'an China 77 H2
Luân Châu Vietnam 70 C2
Luanchuan China 77 F1

▶Luanda Angola 99 B4
Capital of Angola.

Luang, Khao mt. Thai. 71 B5
Luang, Thale lag. Thai. 71 C6
Luang Namtha Laos see Louang Namtha
Luang Phrabang, Thiu Khao mts Laos/Thai. 70 C3
Luang Prabang Laos see Louangphrabang
Luanhaizi China 76 B1
Luanshya Zambia 99 C5
Luanza Dem. Rep. Congo 99 C4
Luao Angola see Luau
Luarca Spain 57 C2
Luashi Dem. Rep. Congo 99 C5
Luau Angola 99 C5
Luba Equat. Guinea 96 D4
Lubaczów Poland 43 D6
Lubalo Angola 99 B4
Lubānas ezers l. Latvia 45 O8
Lubang Islands Phil. 68 F4
Lubango Angola 99 B5
Lubao Dem. Rep. Congo 99 C4
Lubartów Poland 43 D6
Lübbecke Germany 53 I2
Lubbeskolk salt pan S. Africa 100 D5
Lubbock U.S.A. 131 C5
Lübbow Germany 53 L2
Lübeck Germany 47 M4
Lubeck U.S.A. 134 E4
Lubefu Dem. Rep. Congo 99 C4
Lubei China 73 M4
Lüben Poland see Lubin
Lubersac France 56 E4
Lubin Poland 47 P5
Lublin Poland 43 D6
Lubnān country Asia see Lebanon
Lubnān, Jabal mts Lebanon see Liban, Jebel
Lubny Ukr. 43 G6
Lubok Antu Sarawak Malaysia 64 E6
Lübtheen Germany 53 L1
Lubudi Dem. Rep. Congo 99 C4
Lubuklinggau Indon. 68 C7
Lubukpakam Indon. 71 B7
Lubuksikaping Indon. 68 C6
Lubumbashi Dem. Rep. Congo 99 C5
Lubutu Dem. Rep. Congo 98 C4
Lübz Germany 53 M1
Lucala Angola 99 B4
Lucan Canada 134 E2
Lucan Rep. of Ireland 51 F4
Lucania, Mount Canada 120 A2
Lucapa Angola 99 C4
Lucas U.S.A. 134 B5
Lucasville U.S.A. 134 D4
Lucca Italy 58 D3
Luce Bay U.K. 50 E6
Lucedale U.S.A. 131 F6
Lucélia Brazil 145 A3
Lucena Phil. 69 G4
Lucena Spain 57 D5
Lučenec Slovakia 47 Q6
Lucera Italy 58 F4
Lucerne Switz. 56 I3
Lucerne Valley U.S.A. 128 E4
Lucero Mex. 127 G7
Luchegorsk Rus. Fed. 74 D3
Lucheng Guangxi China see Luchuan
Lucheng Sichuan China see Kangding
Luchuan China 77 F4
Lüchun China 76 D4
Lucipara, Kepulauan is Indon. 69 H8
Łuck Ukr. see Luts'k
Luckeesarai India see Lakhisarai
Luckenwalde Germany 53 N2
Luckhoff S. Africa 100 G5
Lucknow Canada 134 E2
Lucknow India 82 E4
Lücongpo China 77 F2
Lucrecia, Cabo c. Cuba 137 I4
Lucusse Angola 99 C5
Lucy Creek Australia 110 B4
Lüda China see Dalian
Lüdenscheid Germany 53 H3
Lüderitz Namibia 100 B4
Ludewa Tanz. 99 D5
Ludhiana India 82 C3
Ludian China 76 D3
Luding China 76 D2
Ludington U.S.A. 134 B2
Ludlow U.K. 49 E6
Ludlow U.S.A. 128 E4
Ludogorie reg. Bulg. 59 L3
Ludowici U.S.A. 133 D6
Ludvika Sweden 45 I6
Ludwigsburg Germany 53 J6
Ludwigsfelde Germany 53 N2
Ludwigshafen am Rhein Germany 53 I5
Ludwigslust Germany 53 L1
Ludza Latvia 45 O8
Luebo Dem. Rep. Congo 99 C4
Luena Angola 99 B5
Luena Flats plain Zambia 99 C5
Lüeyang China 76 E1
Lufeng Guangdong China 77 G4
Lufeng Yunnan China 76 D3
Lufkin U.S.A. 131 E6
Lufu China see Shilin
Luga Rus. Fed. 45 P7
Luga r. Rus. Fed. 45 P7
Lugano Switz. 56 I3
Lugansk Ukr. see Luhans'k
Lugau Germany 53 M4
Lügde Germany 53 J3
Lugdunum France see Lyon
Lugg r. U.K. 49 E6
Luggudontsen mt. China 83 G3
Lugo Italy 58 D2
Lugo Spain 57 C2
Lugoj Romania 59 I2
Luhans'k Ukr. 43 H6
Luhe China 77 H1
Luhe r. Germany 53 K1
Luḩfi, Wādī watercourse Jordan 85 C3
Luhit r. China/India see Zayü Qu
Luhit r. India 83 H4
Luhua China see Heishui
Luhuo China 76 D2
Luhyny Ukr. 43 F6
Luia Angola 99 C4
Luiana Angola 99 C5
Luichow Peninsula China see Leizhou Bandao
Luik Belgium see Liège
Luimneach Rep. of Ireland see Limerick
Luiro r. Fin. 44 O3
Luis Echeverría Álvarez Mex. 128 E5
Luitpold Coast Antarctica 152 A1
Luiza Dem. Rep. Congo 99 C4
Lujiang China 77 H2
Lüjing China 76 E1
Lukackek Rus. Fed. 74 D1
Lukapa Angola see Lucapa
Lukavac Bos.-Herz. 58 H2
Lukenga, Lac l. Dem. Rep. Congo 99 C4
Lukenie r. Dem. Rep. Congo 98 B4
Lukh r. Rus. Fed. 42 I4
Lukhovitsy Rus. Fed. 43 H5
Luk Keng Hong Kong China 77 [inset]
Lukou China see Zhuzhou
Lukovit Bulg. 59 K3
Łuków Poland 43 D6
Lukoyanov Rus. Fed. 43 J5
Lukusuzi National Park Zambia 99 D5
Luleå Sweden 44 M4
Luleälven r. Sweden 44 M4
Lüleburgaz Turkey 59 L4
Luliang China 76 D3
Lüliang Shan mts China 73 K5
Lulimba Dem. Rep. Congo 99 C4
Luling U.S.A. 131 D6
Lulonga r. Dem. Rep. Congo 98 B3
Luluabourg Dem. Rep. Congo see Kananga
Lülung China 83 F3
Lumachomo China 83 F3
Lumajang Indon. 68 E8
Lumajangdong Co salt l. China 82 E2
Lumbala Moxico Angola see Lumbala Kaquengue
Lumbala Moxico Angola see Lumbala N'guimbo
Lumbala Kaquengue Angola 99 C5
Lumbala N'guimbo Angola 99 C5
Lumberton U.S.A. 133 E5
Lumbini Nepal 83 E4
Lumbis Indon. 68 F6
Lumbrales Spain 57 C3
Lumezzane Italy 58 D2
Lumi P.N.G. 69 K7
Lumphăt Cambodia 71 D4
Lumpkin U.S.A. 133 C5
Lumsden Canada 121 J5
Lumsden N.Z. 113 B7
Lumut Malaysia 71 C6
Lumut, Tanjung pt Indon. 68 D7
Luna U.S.A. 129 I5
Lunan China see Shilin
Lunan Bay U.K. 50 G4
Lunan Lake Canada 121 M1
Lunan Shan mts China 76 D3
Luna Pier U.S.A. 134 D3
Lund Pak. 89 H5
Lund Sweden 45 H9
Lund NV U.S.A. 129 F2
Lund UT U.S.A. 129 G2
Lundar Canada 121 L5
Lundy Island U.K. 49 C7
Lune r. Germany 53 I1
Lune r. U.K. 48 E4
Lüneburg Germany 53 K1
Lüneburger Heide reg. Germany 53 K1
Lünen Germany 53 H3
Lunenburg U.S.A. 135 F5
Lunéville France 56 H2
Lunga r. Zambia 99 C5
Lungdo China 83 E2
Lunggar China 83 E3
Lung Kwu Chau i. Hong Kong China 77 [inset]
Lungleh India see Lunglei
Lunglei India 83 H5
Lungmari mt. China 83 F3
Lungmu Co salt l. China 82 E2
Lungnaquilla Mountain hill Rep. of Ireland 51 F5
Lungwebungu r. Zambia 99 C5
Lunh Nepal 83 E3
Luni India 82 C4
Luni r. India 82 B4
Luni r. Pak. 89 H4
Luninets Belarus see Luninyets
Luning U.S.A. 128 D2
Luninyets Belarus 45 O10
Lunkaransar India 82 C3
Lunkha India 82 C3
Lünne Germany 53 H2
Lunsar Sierra Leone 96 B4
Lunsklip S. Africa 101 I3
Luntai China 80 F3
Luobei China 74 C3
Luobuzhuang China 80 G4
Luocheng Fujian China see Hui'an
Luocheng Guangxi China 77 F3
Luodian China 76 E3
Luoding China 77 F4
Luodou Sha i. China 77 F4
Luohe China 77 G1
Luo He r. China 77 G1
Luonan China 77 F1
Luoning China 77 F1
Luoping China 76 E3
Luotian China 77 G2
Luoto Fin. 44 M5
Luoxiao Shan mts China 77 G3
Luoxiong China see Luoping
Luoyang Guangdong China see Boluo
Luoyang Henan China 77 G1
Luoyang Zhejiang China see Taishun
Luoyuan China 77 H3
Luozigou China 74 C4
Lupane Zimbabwe 99 C5
Lupanshui China 76 E3
L'Upemba, Parc National de nat. park Dem. Rep. Congo 95 C4
Lupeni Romania 59 J2
Lupilichi Moz. 99 D5
Lupton U.S.A. 129 I4
Luqiao China see Luding
Luqu China 76 D1
Lu Qu r. China see Tao He
Luquan China 70 C1
Luray U.S.A. 135 F4
Luremo Angola 99 B4
Lurgan U.K. 51 F3
Luring China see Oma
Lúrio Moz. 99 E5
Lurio r. Moz. 99 E5

▶Lusaka Zambia 99 C5
Capital of Zambia.

Lusambo Dem. Rep. Congo 99 C4
Lusancay Islands and Reefs P.N.G. 106 F2
Lusangi Dem. Rep. Congo 99 C4
Luseland Canada 121 I4
Lush, Mount hill Australia 108 D4
Lushi China 77 F1
Lushnja Albania see Lushnjë
Lushnjë Albania 59 H4
Lushui China 76 C3
Lushuihe China 74 B4
Lüsi China 77 I1
Lusikisiki S. Africa 101 I6
Lusk U.S.A. 126 G4
Luso Angola see Luena
Lussvale Australia 112 C1
Lut, Bahrat salt l. Asia see Dead Sea
Lut, Dasht-e des. Iran 88 E4
Lü Tao i. Taiwan 77 I4
Lutetia France see Paris
Lüt-e Zangī Aḩmad des. Iran 88 E4
Luther U.S.A. 134 C1
Luther Lake Canada 134 E2
Lutherstadt Wittenberg Germany 53 M3
Luton U.K. 49 G7
Łutselk'e Canada 121 I2
Luts'k Ukr. 43 E6
Luttelgeest Neth. 52 F2
Luttenberg Neth. 52 G2
Lutto r. Fin./Rus. Fed. see Lotta
Lutz U.S.A. 133 D6
Lützelbach Germany 53 J5
Lützow-Holm Bay Antarctica 152 D2
Lutzputs S. Africa 100 E5
Lutzville S. Africa 100 D6
Luumäki Fin. 45 O6
Luuq Somalia 98 E3
Luverne AL U.S.A. 133 C6
Luverne MN U.S.A. 130 D3
Luvuei Angola 99 C5
Luvuvhu r. S. Africa 101 J2
Luwero Uganda 98 D3
Luwingu Zambia 99 C5
Luwuk Indon. 69 G7
▶Luxembourg country Europe 52 G5
Europe 5, 38–39

▶Luxembourg Lux. 52 G5
Capital of Luxembourg.

Luxemburg country Europe see Luxembourg
Luxeuil-les-Bains France 56 H3
Luxi Hunan China 77 F2
Luxi Yunnan China 76 C3
Luxi Yunnan China 76 D3
Luxolweni S. Africa 101 G6
Luxor Egypt 86 D4
Luyi China 77 G1
Luyksgestel Neth. 52 F3
Luza Rus. Fed. 42 J3
Luza r. Rus. Fed. 42 J3
Luza r. Rus. Fed. 42 M2
Luzern Switz. see Lucerne
Luzhai China 77 F3
Luzhang China see Lushui
Luzhi China 76 E3
Luzhou China 76 E2
Luziânia Brazil 145 B2
Luzon i. Phil. 69 G3
Luzon Strait Phil. 69 G2
Luzy France 56 F3
L'viv Ukr. 43 E6
L'vov Ukr. see L'viv
Lwów Ukr. see L'viv
Lyady Rus. Fed. 45 P7
Lyakhavichy Belarus 45 O10
Lyakhovichi Belarus see Lyakhavichy
Lyallpur Pak. see Faisalabad
Lyamtsa Rus. Fed. 42 H2
Lycia reg. Turkey 59 M6
Lyck Poland see Ełk
Lycksele Sweden 44 K4
Lycopolis Egypt see Asyūţ
Lydd U.K. 49 H8
Lydda Israel see Lod
Lyddan Island Antarctica 152 B2
Lydenburg S. Africa 101 J3
Lydia reg. Turkey 59 L5
Lydney U.K. 49 E7
Lyel'chytsy Belarus 43 F6
Lyell, Mount U.S.A. 128 D3
Lyell Brown, Mount hill Australia 109 E5
Lyell Island Canada 120 D4
Lyepyel' Belarus 45 P9
Lykens U.S.A. 135 G3
Lyman U.S.A. 126 F4
Lyme Bay U.K. 49 E8
Lyme Regis U.K. 49 E8
Lymington U.K. 49 F8
Lynchburg OH U.S.A. 134 D4
Lynchburg TN U.S.A. 132 C5
Lynchburg VA U.S.A. 134 F5
Lynchville U.S.A. 135 J1
Lyndhurst N.S.W. Australia 112 D4
Lyndhurst Qld Australia 110 D3
Lyndhurst S.A. Australia 111 B6
Lyndon Australia 109 A5
Lyndon r. Australia 109 A5
Lyndonville U.S.A. 135 I1
Lyne r. U.K. 48 D4
Lyness U.K. 50 F2
Lyngdal Norway 45 E7
Lynn U.K. see King's Lynn
Lynn IN U.S.A. 134 C3
Lynn MA U.S.A. 135 J2
Lynndyl U.S.A. 129 G2
Lynn Lake Canada 121 K3
Lynton U.K. 49 D7
Lynx Lake Canada 121 J2
Lyon France 56 G4
Lyon r. U.K. 50 F4
Lyon Mountain U.S.A. 135 I1
Lyons Australia 109 F7
Lyons France see Lyon
Lyons GA U.S.A. 133 D5
Lyons NY U.S.A. 135 G2
Lyons Falls U.S.A. 135 H2
Lyozna Belarus 43 F5
Lyra Reef P.N.G. 106 F2
Lys r. France 52 D4
Lysekil Sweden 45 G7
Lyskovo Rus. Fed. 42 J4
Lys'va Rus. Fed. 41 R4
Lysychans'k Ukr. 43 H6
Lysyye Gory Rus. Fed. 43 J6
Lytham St Anne's U.K. 48 D5
Lytton Canada 120 F5
Lyuban' Belarus 45 P10
Lyubertsy Rus. Fed. 41 N4
Lyubeshiv Ukr. 43 E6
Lyubim Rus. Fed. 42 I4
Lyubytino Rus. Fed. 42 G4
Lyudinovo Rus. Fed. 43 G5
Lyunda r. Rus. Fed. 42 J4
Lyzha r. Rus. Fed. 42 M2

M

Ma r. Myanmar 70 B2
Ma, Nam r. Laos 70 C2
Ma'agan Israel 85 B3
Maale Maldives see Male
Maale Atholhu atoll Maldives see Male Atoll
Maalhosmadulu Atholhu Uthuruburi atoll Maldives see North Maalhosmadulu Atoll
Maalhosmadulu Atoll Maldives 84 B5
Ma'ān Jordan 85 B4
Maan Turkey see Nusratiye
Maaninka Fin. 44 O5
Maaninkavaara Fin. 44 P3
Ma'anshan China 77 H2
Maardu Estonia 45 N7
Maarianhamina Fin. see Mariehamn
Ma'arrat an Nu'mān Syria 85 C2
Maarssen Neth. 52 F2
Maas r. Neth. 52 E3
also known as Meuse (Belgium/France)
Maaseik Belgium 52 F3
Maasin Phil. 69 G4
Maasmechelen Belgium 52 F4
Maas-Schwalm-Nette nat. park Germany/Neth. 52 F3
Maastricht Neth. 52 F4
Maaza Plateau Egypt 90 C6
Maba Guangdong China see Qujiang
Maba Jiangsu China 77 H1
Mabai China see Maguan
Mabalane Moz. 101 K2
Mabana Dem. Rep. Congo 98 C3
Mabaruma Guyana 142 G2
Mabein Myanmar 70 B2
Mabel Creek Australia 109 F7
Mabel Downs Australia 108 D4
Mabella Canada 122 C4
Mabel Lake Canada 120 G5
Maberly Canada 135 G1
Mabian China 76 D2
Mablethorpe U.K. 48 H5
Mabopane S. Africa 101 I3
Mabote Moz. 101 L2
Mabou Canada 123 J5
Mabrak, Jabal mt. Jordan 85 B4
Mabuasehube Game Reserve nature res. Botswana 100 F3
Mabule Botswana 100 G3
Mabutsane Botswana 100 F3
Macá, Monte mt. Chile 144 B7
Macadam Plains Australia 109 B6
Macaé Brazil 145 C3
Macajuba Brazil 145 C1
Macaloge Moz. 99 D5
MacAlpine Lake Canada 119 H3
Macamic Canada 122 F4
Macandze Moz. 101 K2
Macao China see Macau
Macao aut. reg. China see Macau
Macapá Brazil 143 H3
Macará Ecuador 142 C4
Macarani Brazil 145 C1
Macas Ecuador 142 C4
Macassar Indon. see Makassar
Macau Brazil 143 K5
Macau China 77 G4
Macau aut. reg. China 77 G4
Macaúba Brazil 143 H6
Macauley Island N.Z. 107 I5
Macau Special Administrative Region aut. reg. China see Macau
Maccaretane Moz. 101 K3
Macclenny U.S.A. 133 D6
Macclesfield U.K. 48 E5
Macdiarmid Canada 122 C4
Macdonald, Lake salt flat Australia 109 E5
Macdonald Range hills Australia 108 D3
Macdonnell Ranges mts Australia 109 E5
MacDowell Lake Canada 121 M4
Macduff U.K. 50 G3
Macedo de Cavaleiros Port. 57 C3
Macedon mt. Australia 112 B6
Macedon country Europe see Macedonia
▶Macedonia country Europe 59 I4
Europe 5, 38–39
Maceió Brazil 143 K5
Macenta Guinea 96 C4
Macerata Italy 58 E3
Macfarlane, Lake salt flat Australia 111 B7
Macgillycuddy's Reeks mts Rep. of Ireland 51 C6
Machachi Ecuador 142 C4
Machaila Moz. 101 K2
Machakos Kenya 98 D4
Machala Ecuador 142 C4
Machali China see Madoi
Machanga Moz. 99 D6
Machar Marshes Sudan 86 D8
Machattie, Lake salt flat Australia 110 B5
Machatuine Moz. 101 K3
Machault France 52 E5
Machaze Moz. see Chitobe
Macheng China 77 G2
Macherla India 84 C2
Machhagan India 83 F5
Machias ME U.S.A. 132 H2
Machias NY U.S.A. 135 F2
Machilipatnam India 84 D2
Machiques Venez. 142 D1
Māch Kowr Iran 89 F5
Machrihanish U.K. 50 D5
Machu Picchu tourist site Peru 142 D6
Machynlleth U.K. 49 D6
Macia Moz. 101 K3
Macias Nguema i. Equat. Guinea see Bioco
Măcin Romania 59 M2
Macintyre r. Australia 112 E2
Macintyre Brook r. Australia 112 E2
Mack U.S.A. 129 I2
Maçka Turkey 91 E2
Mackay Australia 110 E4
MacKay r. Canada 121 I3
Mackay U.S.A. 126 E3
Mackay, Lake salt flat Australia 108 E5
MacKay Lake Canada 121 I2
Mackenzie r. Australia 110 E4
Mackenzie Canada 120 F4
Mackenzie r. Canada 120 F2
Mackenzie Guyana see Linden
Mackenzie atoll Micronesia see Ulithi
Mackenzie Bay Antarctica 152 E2
Mackenzie Bay Canada 118 E3
Mackenzie Highway Canada 120 G2
Mackenzie King Island Canada 119 G2
Mackenzie Mountains Canada 120 C1

▶Mackenzie-Peace-Finlay r. Canada 118 E3
2nd longest river in North America.

Mackillop, Lake salt flat Australia see Yamma Yamma, Lake
Mackintosh Range hills Australia 109 D6
Macklin Canada 121 I4
Macksville Australia 112 F3
Maclean Australia 112 F2
Maclear S. Africa 101 I6
MacLeod Canada see Fort Macleod
MacLeod, Lake imp. l. Australia 109 A6
Macmillan r. Canada 120 C2
Macmillan Pass Canada 120 D2
Macomb U.S.A. 130 F3
Macomer Sardinia Italy 58 C4
Mâcon France 56 G3
Macon GA U.S.A. 133 D5
Macon MO U.S.A. 130 E4
Macon MS U.S.A. 131 F5
Macon OH U.S.A. 134 D4
Macondo Angola 99 C5
Macoun Lake Canada 121 K3
Macpherson Robertson Land reg. Antarctica see Mac. Robertson Land
Macpherson's Strait India 71 A5
Macquarie r. Australia 112 C3
Macquarie, Lake b. Australia 112 E4

▶Macquarie Island S. Pacific Ocean 150 G9
Part of Australia. Most southerly point of Oceania.

Macquarie Marshes Australia 112 C3
Macquarie Mountain Australia 112 D4
Macquarie Ridge sea feature S. Pacific Ocean 150 G9
MacRitchie Reservoir Sing. 71 [inset]
Mac. Robertson Land reg. Antarctica 152 E2
Macroom Rep. of Ireland 51 D6
Macumba Australia 111 A5
Macumba watercourse Australia 111 B5
Macuzari, Presa resr Mex. 127 F8
Mādabā Jordan 85 B4
Madadeni S. Africa 101 J4

▶Madagascar country Africa 99 E6
Largest island in Africa and 4th in the world.
Africa 7, 92–93, 94–95
World 12–13

Madagascar Basin sea feature Indian Ocean 149 L7
Madagascar Ridge sea feature Indian Ocean 149 K8
Madagasikara country Africa see Madagascar
Madakasira India 84 C3
Madama Niger 97 E2
Madan Bulg. 59 K4
Madanapalle India 84 C3
Madang P.N.G. 69 L8
Madaoua Niger 96 D3
Madaripur Bangl. 83 G5
Madau Turkm. 88 D2
Madaw Turkm. see Madau
Madawaska Canada 135 G1
Madawaska r. Canada 135 G1
Madaya Myanmar 70 B2
Madded India 84 D2

▶Madeira r. Brazil 142 G4
4th longest river in South America.

▶Madeira terr. N. Atlantic Ocean 96 B1
Autonomous Region of Portugal.
Africa 7 94–95

Madeira, Arquipélago da terr. N. Atlantic Ocean see Madeira
Maden Turkey 91 E3
Madera Mex. 127 F7
Madera U.S.A. 128 C3
Madgaon India 84 B3
Madha India 84 B2
Madhavpur India 82 B5
Madhepura India 83 F4
Madhipura India see Madhepura
Madhubani India 83 F4
Madhya Pradesh state India 82 D5
Madibogo S. Africa 101 G4
Madidi r. Bol. 142 E6
Madikeri India 84 B3
Madikwe Game Reserve nature res. S. Africa 101 H3
Madill U.S.A. 131 D5
Madīnat ath Thawrah Syria 85 D2
Madingo-Kayes Congo 99 B4
Madingou Congo 99 B4
Madison FL U.S.A. 133 D6
Madison GA U.S.A. 133 D5
Madison IN U.S.A. 134 C4
Madison ME U.S.A. 135 K1
Madison NE U.S.A. 130 D3
Madison SD U.S.A. 130 D2
Madison VA U.S.A. 135 F4

▶Madison WI U.S.A. 130 F3
State capital of Wisconsin.

Madison WV U.S.A. 134 E4
Madison r. U.S.A. 126 F3
Madison Heights U.S.A. 134 F5
Madisonville KY U.S.A. 134 B5
Madisonville TX U.S.A. 131 E6
Madiun Indon. 68 E8
Madley, Mount hill Australia 109 C6
Madoc Canada 135 G1
Mado Gashi Kenya 98 D3
Madoi China 76 C1
Madona Latvia 45 O8
Madpura India 82 B4
Madra Dağı mts Turkey 59 L5
Madrakah Saudi Arabia 86 E5
Madrakah, Ra's c. Oman 87 I6
Madras India see Chennai
Madras state India see Tamil Nadu
Madras U.S.A. 126 C3
Madre, Laguna lag. Mex. 131 D7
Madre, Laguna lag. U.S.A. 131 D7
Madre de Dios r. Peru 142 E6
Madre de Dios, Isla i. Chile 144 A8
Madre del Sur, Sierra mts Mex. 136 D5
Madre Mountain U.S.A. 129 J4
Madre Occidental, Sierra mts Mex. 127 F7
Madre Oriental, Sierra mts Mex. 131 C7

▶Madrid Spain 57 E3
Capital of Spain.

Madridejos Spain 57 E4
Madruga Cuba 133 D8
Madugula India 84 D2
Madura i. Indon. 68 E8
Madura, Selat sea chan. Indon. 68 E8
Madurai India 84 C4
Madurantakam India 84 C3
Madvār, Kūh-e mt. Iran 88 D4
Madvezh'ya vol. Rus. Fed. 74 H3
Madwas India 83 E4
Maé i. Vanuatu see Émaé
Maebashi Japan 75 E5
Mae Hong Son Thai. 70 B3
Mae Ping National Park Thai. 70 B3
Mae Ramat Thai. 70 B3
Mae Sai Thai. 70 B2
Mae Sariang Thai. 70 B3
Mae Sot Thai. 70 B3
Mae Suai Thai. 70 B3
Mae Tuen Wildlife Reserve nature res. Thai. 70 B3
Maevatanana Madag. 99 E5
Maéwo i. Vanuatu 107 G3
Mae Wong National Park Thai. 70 B4
Mae Yom National Park Thai. 70 C3
Mafeking Canada 121 K4
Mafeking S. Africa see Mafikeng
Mafeteng Lesotho 101 H5
Maffra Australia 112 C6
Mafia Island Tanz. 99 D4
Mafikeng S. Africa 101 G3
Mafinga Tanz. 99 D4
Mafra Brazil 145 A4
Mafraq Jordan see Al Mafraq
Magabeni S. Africa 101 J6
Magadan Rus. Fed. 65 Q4
Magadi Kenya 98 D4
Magaiza Moz. 101 K2
Magallanes Chile see Punta Arenas
Magallanes, Estrecho de Chile see Magellan, Strait of
Magangue Col. 142 D2
Mağara Dağı mt Turkey 85 A1
Magaramkent Rus. Fed. 91 H2
Magaria Niger 96 D3
Magarida P.N.G. 110 E1
Magas Rus. Fed. 91 G2
Magazine Mountain hill U.S.A. 131 E5
Magdagachi Rus. Fed. 74 B1
Magdalena Bol. 142 F6
Magdalena r. Col. 142 D1
Magdalena Baja California Sur Mex. 127 E8
Magdalena Sonora Mex. 127 F7
Magdalena r. Mex. 127 F7
Magdalena, Bahía b. Mex. 136 B4
Magdalena, Isla i. Chile 144 B6
Magdeburg Germany 53 L2
Magdelaine Cays atoll Australia 110 E3

Magellan, Strait of Chile 144 B8
Magellan Seamounts sea feature N. Pacific Ocean 150 F4
Magenta, Lake salt flat Australia 109 B8
Magerøya i. Norway 44 N1
Maggiorasca, Monte mt. Italy 58 C2
Maggiore, Lago Italy see Maggiore, Lake
Maggiore, Lake Italy 58 C2
Maghâgha Egypt see Maghāghah
Maghāghah Egypt 90 C5
Maghama Mauritania 96 B3
Maghâra, Gebel hill Egypt see Maghārah, Jabal
Maghārah, Jabal hill Egypt 85 A4
Maghera U.K. 51 F3
Magherafelt U.K. 51 F3
Maghnia Alg. 57 F6
Maghor Afgh. 89 F3
Maghull U.K. 48 E5
Magilligan Point U.K. 51 F2
Magma U.S.A. 129 H5
Magna Grande mt. Sicily Italy 58 F6
Magnetic Island Australia 110 D3
Magnetic Passage Australia 110 D3
Magnetity Rus. Fed. 44 R2
Magnitogorsk Rus. Fed. 64 G4
Magnolia AR U.S.A. 131 E5
Magnolia MS U.S.A. 131 F6
Magny-en-Vexin France 52 B5
Mago Rus. Fed. 74 F1
Màgoé Moz. 99 D5
Magog Canada 135 I1
Mago National Park Eth. 98 D3
Magosa Cyprus see Famagusta
Magpie r. Canada 123 I4
Magpie, Lac l. Canada 123 I4
Magta' Lahjar Mauritania 96 B3
Magu Tanz. 98 D4
Magu, Khrebet mts Rus. Fed. 74 E1
Maguan China 76 E4
Magude Moz. 101 K3
Magueyal Mex. 131 C7
Magura Bangl. 83 G5
Maguse Lake Canada 121 M2
Magway Myanmar see Magwe
Magwe Myanmar 70 A2
Magyar Köztársaság country Europe see Hungary
Magyichaung Myanmar 70 A2
Mahābād Iran 88 B2
Mahabharat Range mts Nepal 83 F4
Mahaboobnagar India see Mahbubnagar
Mahad India 84 B2
Mahadeo Hills India 82 D5
Mahaffey U.S.A. 135 F3
Mahajan India 82 C3
Mahajanga Madag. 99 E5
Mahakam r. Indon. 68 F7
Mahalapye Botswana 101 H2
Mahale Mountains National Park Tanz. 99 C4
Mahalevona Madag. 99 E5
Mahallāt Iran 88 C3
Māhān Iran 88 E4
Mahanadi r. India 84 E1
Mahanoro Madag. 99 E5
Maha Oya Sri Lanka 84 D5
Maharashtra state India 84 B2
Maha Sarakham Thai. 70 C3
Mahasham, Wâdi el watercourse Egypt see Muhashsham, Wādī al
Mahaxai Laos 70 D3
Mahbubabad India 84 D2
Mahbubnagar India 84 C2
Mahd adh Dhahab Saudi Arabia 86 F5
Mahdia Alg. 57 G6
Mahdia Guyana 143 G2
Mahdia Tunisia 58 D7
Mahe China 76 E1
Mahé i. Seychelles 149 L6
Mahendragiri mt. India 84 E2
Mahenge Tanz. 99 D4
Mahesana India 82 C5
Mahi r. India 82 C5
Mahia Peninsula N.Z. 113 F4
Mahilyow Belarus 43 F5
Mahim India 84 B2
Mah Jān Iran 88 D4
Mahlabatini S. Africa 101 J5
Mahlsdorf Germany 53 L2
Mahmudabad Iran 88 D2
Maḥmūd-e 'Erāqī Afgh. see Maḥmūd-e Rāqī
Maḥmūd-e Rāqī Afgh. 89 H3
Mahnomen U.S.A. 130 D2
Maho Sri Lanka 84 D5
Mahoba India 82 D4
Maholi India 82 E4
Mahón Spain 57 I4
Mahony Lake Canada 120 E1
Mahrauni India 82 D4
Mahrès Tunisia 58 D7
Māhrūd Iran 89 F3
Mahsana India see Mahesana
Mahudaung mts Myanmar 70 A2
Mahukona HI U.S.A. 127 [inset]
Mahur India 84 C2
Mahuva India 82 B5
Mahwa India 82 D4
Mahya Dağı mt. Turkey 59 L4
Mai i. Vanuatu see Émaé
Maiaia Moz. see Nacala
Maibang India 70 A1
Maicao Col. 142 D1
Maicasagi r. Canada 122 F4
Maicasagi, Lac l. Canada 122 F4
Maichen China 77 F4
Maidenhead U.K. 49 G7
Maidstone Canada 121 I4
Maidstone U.K. 49 H7
Maiduguri Nigeria 96 E3
Maiella, Parco Nazionale della nat. park Italy 58 F3
Mai Gudo mt. Eth. 98 D3
Maigue r. Rep. of Ireland 51 D5
Maihar India 82 E4
Maiji Shan mt. China 76 E1
Maikala Range hills India 82 E5
Maiko r. Dem. Rep. Congo 98 C3
Mailan Hill mt. India 83 E5
Mailly-le-Camp France 52 E6
Mailsi Pak. 89 I4
Main r. Germany 53 I4
Main r. U.K. 51 F3
Main Brook Canada 123 L4
Mainburg Germany 53 L6
Main Channel lake channel Canada 134 E1
Maindargi India 84 C2
Mai-Ndombe, Lac l. Dem. Rep. Congo 98 B4
Main-Donau-Kanal canal Germany 53 K5
Maindong China 83 F3
Main Duck Island Canada 135 G2
Maine state U.S.A. 135 K1
Maine, Gulf of Canada/U.S.A. 135 K2
Mainé Hanari, Cerro hill Col. 142 D4
Maïné-Soroa Niger 96 E3
Maingkaing Myanmar 70 A1
Maingkwan Myanmar 70 B1
Maingy Island Myanmar 71 B4
Mainhardt Germany 53 J5
Mainkung China 76 C2
Mainland i. Scotland U.K. 50 F1
Mainland i. Scotland U.K. 50 [inset]
Mainleus Germany 53 L4
Mainoru Australia 108 F3
Mainpat reg. India 83 E5
Mainpuri India 82 D4
Main Range National Park Australia 112 F2
Maintenon France 52 B6
Maintirano Madag. 99 E5
Mainz Germany 53 I4
Maio i. Cape Verde 96 [inset]
Maipú Arg. 144 E5
Maiskhal Island Bangl. 83 G5
Maisons-Laffitte France 52 C6
Maitengwe Botswana 99 C6
Maitland N.S.W. Australia 112 E4
Maitland S.A. Australia 111 B7
Maitland r. Australia 108 B5
Maitri research station Antarctica 152 C2
Maiwo i. Vanuatu see Maéwo
Maiyu, Mount hill Australia 108 E4
Maíz, Islas del is Nicaragua 137 H6
Maizar Pak. 89 H3
Maizuru Japan 75 D6
Maja Jezercë mt. Albania 59 H3
Majene Indon. 68 F7
Majestic U.S.A. 134 D5
Majhūd well Saudi Arabia 88 C6
Majī Eth. 98 D3
Majiang Guangxi China 77 F4
Majiang Guizhou China 76 E3
Majiazi China 74 B2
Majōl country N. Pacific Ocean see Marshall Islands
Major, Puig mt. Spain 57 H4
Majorca i. Spain 57 H4
Mājro atoll Marshall Is see Majuro
Majunga Madag. see Mahajanga
Majuro atoll Marshall Is 150 H5
Majwemasweu S. Africa 101 H5
Makabana Congo 98 B4
Makale Indon. 69 F7

▶Makalu mt. China/Nepal 83 F4
5th highest mountain in the world and in Asia.
World 12–13

Makalu Barun National Park Nepal 83 F4
Makanchi Kazakh. 80 F2
Makanpur India 82 E4
Makari Mountain National Park Tanz. see Mahale Mountains National Park
Makarov Rus. Fed. 74 F2
Makarov Basin sea feature Arctic Ocean 153 B1
Makarska Croatia 58 G3
Makarwal Pak. 89 H3
Makar'ye Rus. Fed. 42 K4
Makar'yev Rus. Fed. 42 I4
Makasar, Selat strait Indon. see Makassar, Selat
Makassar Indon. 68 F8
Makassar, Selat strait Indon. 68 F7
Makassar Strait Indon. see Makassar, Selat
Makat Kazakh. 78 E2
Makatini Flats lowland S. Africa 101 K4
Makedonija country Europe see Macedonia
Makeni Sierra Leone 96 B4
Makete Tanz. 99 D4
Makeyevka Ukr. see Makiyivka
Makgadikgadi depr. Botswana 99 C6
Makgadikgadi Pans National Park Botswana 99 C6
Makhachkala Rus. Fed. 91 G2
Makhad Pak. 89 H3
Makhado S. Africa see Louis Trichardt
Makhāzin, Kathīb al des. Egypt 85 A4
Makhâzin, Kathib el des. Egypt see Makhāzin, Kathīb al
Makhazine, Barrage El dam Morocco 57 D6
Makhmūr Iraq 91 F4
Makhtal India 84 C2
Makin atoll Kiribati see Butaritari
Makindu Kenya 98 D4
Makinsk Kazakh. 79 G1
Makira i. Solomon Is see San Cristobal
Makiyivka Ukr. 43 H6
Makkah Saudi Arabia see Mecca
Makkovik Canada 123 K3
Makkovik, Cape Canada 123 K3
Makkum Neth. 52 F1
Makó Hungary 59 I1
Makokou Gabon 98 B3
Makopong Botswana 100 F3
Makotipoko Congo 97 E5
Makran reg. Iran/Pak. 89 F5
Makrana India 82 C4
Makran Coast Range mts Pak. 89 F5
Makri India 84 D2
Maksatikha Rus. Fed. 42 G4
Maksi India 82 D5
Maksimovka Rus. Fed. 74 E3
Maksotag Iran 89 F4
Maksudangarh India 82 D5
Mākū Iran 88 B2
Makunguwiro Tanz. 99 D5
Makurdi Nigeria 96 D4
Makwassie S. Africa 101 G4
Mal India 83 G4
Mala Rep. of Ireland see Mallow
Mala i. Solomon Is see Malaita
Malå Sweden 44 K4
Mala, Punta pt Panama 137 H7
Malabar Coast India 84 B3

▶Malabo Equat. Guinea 96 D4
Capital of Equatorial Guinea.

Malaca Spain see Málaga
Malacca Malaysia see Melaka
Malacca, Strait of Indon./Malaysia 71 B6
Malad City U.S.A. 126 E4
Maladzyechna Belarus 45 O9
Malá Fatra nat. park Slovakia 47 Q6
Málaga Spain 57 D5
Malaga U.S.A. 131 B5
Malagasy Republic country Africa see Madagascar
Malaita i. Solomon Is 107 G2
Malakal Sudan 86 D8
Malakanagiri India see Malkangiri
Malakheti Nepal 82 E3
Malakula i. Vanuatu 107 G3
Malan, Ras pt Pak. 89 G5
Malang Indon. 68 E8
Malangana Nepal see Malangwa
Malange Angola see Malanje
Malangwa Nepal 83 F4
Malanje Angola 99 B4
Malappuram India 84 C4
Mälaren l. Sweden 45 J7
Malargüe Arg. 144 C5
Malartic Canada 122 F4
Malaspina Glacier U.S.A. 120 A3
Malatya Turkey 90 E3
Malavalli India 84 C3

▶Malawi country Africa 99 D5
Africa 7, 94–95

Malawi, Lake Africa see Nyasa, Lake
Malawi National Park Zambia see Nyika National Park
Malaya pen. Malaysia see Peninsular Malaysia
Malaya Pera Rus. Fed. 42 L2
Malaya Vishera Rus. Fed. 42 G4
Malaybalay Phil. 69 H5
Malāyer Iran 88 C3
Malay Peninsula Asia 71 B4
Malay Reef Australia 110 E3

▶Malaysia country Asia 68 D5
Asia 6, 62–63

Malaysia, Semenanjung pen. Malaysia see Peninsular Malaysia
Malazgirt Turkey 91 F3
Malbon Australia 110 C4
Malbork Poland 47 Q3
Malborn Germany 52 G5
Malchin Germany 47 N4
Malcolm Australia 109 C7
Malcolm, Point Australia 109 C8
Malcolm Island Myanmar 71 B5
Maldegem Belgium 52 D3
Malden U.S.A. 131 F4
Malden Island Kiribati 151 J6

▶Maldives country Indian Ocean 81 D10
Asia 6, 62–63

Maldon Australia 112 B6
Maldon U.K. 49 H7
Maldonado Uruguay 144 F4

▶Male Maldives 81 D11
Capital of the Maldives.

Maleas, Akra pt Greece 59 J6
Male Atoll Maldives 81 D11
Malebogo S. Africa 101 G5
Malegaon Maharashtra India 84 B1
Malegaon Maharashtra India 84 C2
Malé Karpaty hills Slovakia 47 P6
Malek Siāh, Kūh-e mt. Afgh. 89 F4
Malele Dem. Rep. Congo 99 B4
Maler Kotla India 82 C3
Maleševske Planine mts Bulg./Macedonia 59 J4
Malgobek Rus. Fed. 91 G2
Malgomaj l. Sweden 44 J4
Malḥa, Naqb mt. Egypt see Māliḥah, Naqb
Malhada Brazil 145 C1
Malheur r. U.S.A. 126 D3
Malheur Lake U.S.A. 126 D4

▶Mali country Africa 96 C3
Africa 7, 94–95

Mali Dem. Rep. Congo 98 C4
Mali Guinea 96 B3
Maliana East Timor 108 D2
Malianjing China 80 I3
Māliḥah, Naqb mt. Egypt 85 A5
Malik Naro mt. Pak. 89 F4
Mali Kyun i. Myanmar 71 B4
Malili Indon. 69 G7
Malin Ukr. see Malyn
Malindi Kenya 98 E4
Malines Belgium see Mechelen
Malin Head hd Rep. of Ireland 51 E2
Malin More Rep. of Ireland 51 D3
Malipo China 76 E4
Mali Raginac mt. Croatia 58 F2
Malita Phil. 69 H5
Malka r. Rus. Fed. 91 G2
Malkangiri India 84 D2
Malkapur India 84 C2
Malkara Turkey 59 L4
Mal'kavichy Belarus 45 O10
Malko Tŭrnovo Bulg. 59 L4
Mallacoota Australia 112 D6
Mallacoota Inlet b. Australia 112 D6
Mallaig U.K. 50 D4
Mallani reg. India 89 H5
Mallawī Egypt 90 C5
Mallee Cliffs National Park Australia 111 C7
Mallery Lake Canada 121 L1
Mallét Brazil 145 A4
Mallorca i. Spain see Majorca
Mallow Rep. of Ireland 51 D5
Mallowa Well Australia 108 D5
Mallwyd U.K. 49 D6
Malm Norway 44 G4
Malmberget Sweden 44 L3
Malmédy Belgium 52 G4
Malmesbury S. Africa 100 D7
Malmesbury U.K. 49 E7
Malmö Sweden 45 H9
Malmyzh Rus. Fed. 42 K4
Maloca Brazil 143 G3
Malone U.S.A. 135 H1
Malonje mt. Tanz. 99 D4
Maloshuyka Rus. Fed. 42 H3
Malosmadulu Atoll Maldives see Maalhosmadulu Atoll
Måløy Norway 44 D6
Maloyaroslavets Rus. Fed. 43 H5
Malozemel'skaya Tundra lowland Rus. Fed. 42 K2
Malpelo, Isla de i. N. Pacific Ocean 137 H8
Malprabha r. India 84 C2

▶Malta country Europe 58 F7
Europe 5, 38–39

Malta Latvia 45 O8
Malta ID U.S.A. 126 E4
Malta MT U.S.A. 126 G2
Malta Channel Italy/Malta 58 F6
Maltahöhe Namibia 100 C3
Maltby U.K. 48 F5
Maltby le Marsh U.K. 48 H5
Malton U.K. 48 G4
Malukken is Indon. see Moluccas
Maluku is Indon. see Moluccas
Maluku, Laut sea Indon. 69 H6
Ma'lūlā, Jabal mts Syria 85 C3
Malung Sweden 45 H6
Maluti Mountains Lesotho 101 I5
Malu'u Solomon Is 107 G2
Malvan India 84 B2
Malvasia Greece see Monemvasia
Malvern U.K. see Great Malvern
Malvern U.S.A. 131 E5
Malvérnia Moz. see Chicualacuala
Malvinas, Islas terr. S. Atlantic Ocean see Falkland Islands
Malyn Ukr. 43 F6
Malyy Anyuy r. Rus. Fed. 65 R3
Malyye Derbety Rus. Fed. 43 J7
Malyy Kavkaz mts Asia see Lesser Caucasus
Malyy Lyakhovskiy, Ostrov i. Rus. Fed. 65 P2
Malyy Uzen' r. Kazakh./Rus. Fed. 43 K6
Mama r. Rus. Fed. 65 P3
Mamadysh Rus. Fed. 42 K5
Mamafubedu S. Africa 101 I4
Mamatān Nāvar l. Afgh. 89 G4
Mamba China 76 B2
Mambai Brazil 145 B1
Mambasa Dem. Rep. Congo 98 C3
Mamburao Phil. 69 G4
Mamelodi S. Africa 101 I3
Mamfe Cameroon 96 D4
Mamison Pass Georgia/Rus. Fed. 91 F2
Mamit India 83 H5
Mammoth U.S.A. 129 H5
Mammoth Cave National Park U.S.A. 134 B5
Mammoth Reservoir U.S.A. 128 D3
Mamonas Brazil 145 C1
Mamoré r. Bol./Brazil 142 E6
Mamou Guinea 96 B3
Mampikony Madag. 99 E5
Mampong Ghana 96 C4
Mamuju Indon. 68 F7
Mamuno Botswana 100 E2
Man Côte d'Ivoire 96 C4
Man India 84 B2
Man r. India 84 B2
Man U.S.A. 134 E5

▶Man, Isle of terr. Irish Sea 48 C4
United Kingdom Crown Dependency.
Europe 5

Manacapuru Brazil 142 F4
Manacor Spain 57 H4
Manado Indon. 69 G6

▶Managua Nicaragua 137 G6
Capital of Nicaragua.

Manakara Madag. 99 E6
Manakau mt. N.Z. 113 D6
Manākhah Yemen 86 F6

▶Manama Bahrain 88 C5
Capital of Bahrain.

Manamadurai India 84 C4
Mana Maroka National Park S. Africa 101 H5
Manamelkudi India 84 C4
Manam Island P.N.G. 69 L7
Mananara Avaratra Madag. 99 E5
Manangoora Australia 110 B3
Mananjary Madag. 99 E6
Manantali, Lac de l. Mali 96 B3
Manantenina Madag. 99 E6
Mana Pass China/India 82 D3
Mana Pools National Park Zimbabwe 99 C5

▶Manapouri, Lake N.Z. 113 A7
Deepest lake in Oceania.

Manasa India 82 C4
Manas He r. China 80 G2
Manas Hu l. China 80 G2
Manāṣīr reg. U.A.E. 88 D6
Manaslu mt. Nepal 83 F3
Manassas U.S.A. 135 G4
Manastir Macedonia see Bitola
Manas Wildlife Sanctuary nature res. Bhutan 83 G4
Man-aung Myanmar see Cheduba
Man-aung Kyun i. Myanmar see Cheduba Island
Manaus Brazil 142 F4
Manavgat Turkey 90 C3
Manbazar India 83 F5
Manbij Syria 85 C1
Manby U.K. 48 H5
Mancelona U.S.A. 134 C1
Manchar India 84 B2
Manchester U.K. 48 E5
Manchester CT U.S.A. 135 I3
Manchester IA U.S.A. 130 F3
Manchester KY U.S.A. 134 D5
Manchester MD U.S.A. 135 G4
Manchester MI U.S.A. 134 C2
Manchester NH U.S.A. 135 J2
Manchester OH U.S.A. 134 D4
Manchester TN U.S.A. 132 C5
Manchester VT U.S.A. 135 I2
Mancılık Turkey 90 E3
Mand Pak. 89 F5
Mand, Rūd-e r. Iran 88 C4
Manda Tanz. 99 D4
Manda, Jebel mt. Sudan 97 F4
Manda, Parc National de nat. park Chad 97 E4
Mandabe Madag. 99 E6
Mandai Sing. 71 [inset]
Mandal Afgh. 89 F3
Mandal Norway 45 E7

▶Mandala, Puncak mt. Indon. 69 K7
3rd highest mountain in Oceania.

Mandalay Myanmar 70 B2
Mandale Myanmar see Mandalay
Mandalgovĭ Mongolia 72 J3
Mandalī Iraq 91 G4
Mandalt China 73 K4
Mandan U.S.A. 130 C2
Mandas Sardinia Italy 58 C5
Mandasa India 84 E2
Mandasor India see Mandsaur
Mandav Hills India 82 B5
Mandera Kenya 98 E3
Manderfield U.S.A. 129 G2
Manderscheid Germany 52 G4
Mandeville Jamaica 137 I5
Mandeville N.Z. 113 B7
Mandha India 82 B4
Mandhoúdhion Greece see Mantoudi
Mandi India 82 D3
Mandiana Guinea 96 C3
Mandi Burewala Pak. 89 I4
Mandié Moz. 99 D5
Mandini S. Africa 101 J5
Mandira Dam India 83 F5
Mandla India 82 E5
Mandleshwar India 82 C5
Mandrael India 82 D4
Mandritsara Madag. 99 E5
Mandsaur India 82 C4
Mandurah Australia 109 A8
Manduria Italy 58 G4
Mandvi India 82 B5
Mandya India 84 C3
Manerbio Italy 58 D2
Manevychi Ukr. 43 E6
Manfalūṭ Egypt 90 C6
Manfredonia Italy 58 F4
Manfredonia, Golfo di g. Italy 58 G4
Manga Brazil 145 C1
Manga Burkina 96 C3
Mangabeiras, Serra das hills Brazil 143 I6
Mangai Dem. Rep. Congo 98 B4
Mangaia i. Cook Is 151 J7
Mangakino N.Z. 113 E4
Mangalagiri India 84 D2
Mangaldai India 70 A1
Mangaldoi India see Mangaldai
Mangalia Romania 59 M3
Mangalmé Chad 97 E3
Mangalore India 84 B3
Mangaon India 84 B2
Mangareva Islands Fr. Polynesia see Gambier, Îles
Mangaung Free State S. Africa 97 H5
Mangaung Free State S. Africa see Bloemfontein
Mangawan India 83 E4
Ma'ngê China see Luqu
Mangea i. Cook Is see Mangaia
Mangghyshlaq Kazakh. see Mangystau
Mangghystaū Kazakh. see Mangystau
Mangghystaū admin. div. Kazakh. see Mangistauskaya Oblast'
Mangghyt Uzbek. see Mangit
Manghit Uzbek. see Mangit
Mangin Range mts Myanmar see Mingin Range
Mangistau Kazakh. see Mangystau
Mangistauskaya Oblast' admin. div. Kazakh. 91 I2
Mangit Uzbek. 80 B3
Mangla Bangl. see Mongla
Mangla China see Guinan
Mangla Pak. 89 I3
Manglaqiongtuo China see Guinan
Mangnai China 80 H4
Mangnai Zhen China 80 H4
Mangochi Malawi 99 D5
Mangoky r. Madag. 99 E6
Mangole i. Indon. 69 H7
Mangoli India 84 B2
Mangotsfield U.K. 49 E7
Mangqystaū Shyghanaghy b. Kazakh. see Mangyshlakskiy Zaliv
Mangra China see Guinan
Mangral India 82 B5
Mangrul India 84 C1
Mangshi China see Luxi
Mangualde Port. 57 C3
Manguéni, Plateau du Niger 96 E2
Mangui China 74 A2
Mangula Zimbabwe see Mhangura
Mangum U.S.A. 131 D5
Mangyshlak Kazakh. see Mangystau
Mangyshlak, Poluostrov pen. Kazakh. 91 H1
Mangyshlak Oblast admin. div. Kazakh. see Mangistauskaya Oblast'
Mangyshlakskaya Oblast' admin. div. Kazakh. see Mangistauskaya Oblast'
Mangyshlakskiy Zaliv b. Kazakh. 91 H1
Mangystau Kazakh. 91 H2
Manhã Brazil 145 B1
Manhattan U.S.A. 130 D4
Manhica Moz. 101 K3
Manhoca Moz. 101 K4
Manhuaçu Brazil 145 C3
Manhuaçu r. Brazil 145 C2
Mani China 83 F2
Mania r. Madag. 99 E5
Maniago Italy 58 E1
Manicouagan Canada 123 H4
Manicouagan r. Canada 123 H4
Manicouagan, Réservoir resr Canada 123 H4
Manic Trois, Réservoir resr Canada 123 H4
Manīfah Saudi Arabia 88 C5
Maniganggo China 76 C2
Manigotagan Canada 121 L5
Manihiki atoll Cook Is 150 J6
Maniitsoq Greenland 119 M3
Manikchhari Bangl. 83 H5
Manikgarh India see Rajura

▶Manila Phil. 69 G4
Capital of the Philippines.

Manila U.S.A. 126 F4
Manildra Australia 112 D4
Manilla Australia 112 E3
Maningrida Australia 108 F3
Manipur India see Imphal
Manipur state India 83 H4
Manisa Turkey 59 L5
Manistee U.S.A. 134 B1
Manistee r. U.S.A. 134 B1
Manistique U.S.A. 132 C2
Manitoba prov. Canada 121 L4
Manitoba, Lake Canada 121 L5
Manito Lake Canada 121 I4
Manitou Canada 121 L5
Manitou, Lake U.S.A. 134 B3
Manitou Beach U.S.A. 135 G2
Manitou Falls Canada 121 M5
Manitou Islands U.S.A. 134 B1
Manitoulin Island Canada 122 E5
Manitouwadge Canada 122 D4
Manitowoc U.S.A. 134 B1
Maniwaki Canada 122 G5
Manizales Col. 142 C2
Manja Madag. 99 E6
Manjarabad India 84 B3
Manjeri India 84 C4
Manjhand Pak. 89 H5
Manjhi India 83 F4
Manjra r. India 84 C2
Man Kabat Myanmar 70 B1
Mankaiana Swaziland see Mankayane
Mankato KS U.S.A. 130 D4
Mankato MN U.S.A. 130 E2
Mankayane Swaziland 101 J4
Mankera Pak. 89 H4
Mankono Côte d'Ivoire 96 C4
Mankota Canada 121 J5
Manley Hot Springs U.S.A. 118 C3
Manmad India 84 B1
Mann r. Australia 108 F3
Mann, Mount Australia 109 E6
Manna Indon. 68 C7
Man Na Myanmar 70 B2
Mannahill Australia 111 B7
Mannar Sri Lanka 84 C4
Mannar, Gulf of India/Sri Lanka 84 C4
Manneru r. India 84 D3
Mannessier, Lac l. Canada 123 H3
Mannheim Germany 53 I5
Mannicolo Islands Solomon Is see Vanikoro Islands
Manning r. Australia 112 F3
Manning Canada 120 G3
Manning U.S.A. 133 D5
Mannington U.S.A. 134 E4
Manningtree U.K. 49 I7
Mann Ranges mts Australia 109 E6
Mannsville KY U.S.A. 134 C5
Mannsville NY U.S.A. 135 G2
Mannu, Capo c. Sardinia Italy 58 C4
Mannville Canada 121 I4
Man-of-War Rocks is U.S.A. see Gardner Pinnacles
Manoharpur India 82 D4
Manohar Thana India 82 D4
Manokotak U.S.A. 118 C4
Manokwari Indon. 69 I7
Manoron Myanmar 71 B5
Manosque France 56 G5
Manouane r. Canada 123 H4
Manouane, Lac l. Canada 123 H4
Man Pan Myanmar 70 B2
Manp'o N. Korea 74 B4
Manra i. Kiribati 107 I2
Manresa Spain 57 G3
Mansa Gujarat India 82 C5
Mansa Punjab India 82 C3
Mansa Zambia 99 C5
Mansa Konko Gambia 96 B3
Man Sam Myanmar 70 B2
Mansehra Pak. 87 L3
Mansel Island Canada 119 K3
Mansfield Australia 112 C6
Mansfield U.K. 49 F5
Mansfield LA U.S.A. 131 E5
Mansfield OH U.S.A. 134 D3
Mansfield PA U.S.A. 135 G3
Mansfield, Mount U.S.A. 135 I1
Man Si Myanmar 70 B1
Mansi Myanmar 70 A1
Manso r. Brazil see Mortes, Rio das
Manta Ecuador 142 B4
Mantaro r. Peru 142 D6
Manteca U.S.A. 128 C3
Mantena Brazil 145 C2
Manteo U.S.A. 132 F5
Mantes-la-Jolie France 52 B6
Mantiqueira, Serra da mts Brazil 145 B3
Manton U.S.A. 134 C1
Mantoudi Greece 59 J5
Mantova Italy see Mantua
Mäntsälä Fin. 45 N6
Mänttä Fin. 44 N5
Mantua Cuba 133 C8
Mantua Italy 58 D2
Mantuan Downs Australia 110 D5
Manturovo Rus. Fed. 42 J4

Mäntyharju Fin. 45 O6
Mäntyjärvi Fin. 44 O3
Manú Peru 142 D6
Manu, Parque Nacional nat. park Peru 142 D6
Manuae atoll Fr. Polynesia 151 J7
Manua Islands American Samoa 107 I3
Manuel Ribas Brazil 145 A4
Manuel Vitorino Brazil 145 C1
Manuelzinho Brazil 143 H5
Manui i. Indon. 69 G7
Manukau N.Z. 113 E3
Manukau Harbour N.Z. 113 E3
Manunda watercourse Australia 111 B7
Manusela National Park Indon. 69 H7
Manus Island P.N.G. 69 L7
Manvi India 84 C3
Many U.S.A. 131 E6
Manyana Botswana 101 G3
Manyas Turkey 59 L4
Manyas Gölü l. Turkey see Kuş Gölü
Manych-Gudilo, Ozero l. Rus. Fed. 43 I7
Many Island Lake Canada 121 I5
Manyoni Tanz. 99 D4
Manzai Pak. 89 H3
Manzanares Spain 57 E4
Manzanillo Cuba 137 I4
Manzanillo Mex. 136 D5
Manzhouli China 73 L3
Manzini Swaziland 101 J4
Mao Chad 97 E3
Maó Spain see Mahón
Maoba Guizhou China 76 E3
Maoba Hubei China 77 F2
Maocifan China 77 G2
Mao'ergai China 76 D1
Maoke, Pegunungan mts Indon. 69 J7
Maokeng S. Africa 101 H4
Maokui Shan mt. China 74 A4
Maolin China 74 A4
Maoming China 77 F4
Ma On Shan hill Hong Kong China 77 [inset]
Maopi T'ou c. Taiwan 77 I4
Maopora i. Indon. 108 D1
Maotou Shan mt. China 76 D3
Mapai Moz. 101 J2
Mapam Yumco l. China 83 E3
Mapanza Zambia 99 C5
Maphodi S. Africa 101 G6
Mapimí Mex. 131 C7
Mapimí, Bolsón de des. Mex. 131 B7
Mapin i. Phil. 68 F5
Mapinhane Moz. 101 L2
Mapiri Bol. 142 E7
Maple r. MI U.S.A. 134 C2
Maple r. ND U.S.A. 130 D2
Maple Creek Canada 121 I5
Maple Heights U.S.A. 134 E3
Maple Peak U.S.A. 129 I5
Mapmakers Seamounts sea feature N. Pacific Ocean 150 H4
Mapoon Australia 110 C1
Mapor i. Indon. 71 D7
Mapoteng Lesotho 101 H5
Maprik P.N.G. 69 K7
Mapuera r. Brazil 143 G4
Mapulanguene Moz. 101 K3

▶Maputo Moz. 101 K3
Capital of Mozambique.

Maputo prov. Moz. 101 K3
Maputo r. Moz./S. Africa 101 K4
Maputo, Baía de b. Moz. 101 K4
Maputsoe Lesotho 101 H5
Maqanshy Kazakh. see Makanchi
Maqar an Na'am well Iraq 91 F5
Maqat Kazakh. see Makat
Maqên China 76 D1
Maqên Kangri mt. China 76 C1
Maqnā Saudi Arabia 90 D5
Maqteïr reg. Mauritania 96 B2
Maqu China 76 D1
Ma Qu r. China see Yellow River
Maquan He r. China 83 F3
Maquela do Zombo Angola 99 B4
Maquinchao Arg. 144 C6
Mar r. Pak. 89 G5
Mar, Serra do mts Rio de Janeiro/São Paulo Brazil 145 B3
Mar, Serra do mts Rio Grande do Sul/Santa Catarina Brazil 145 A5
Mara r. Canada 121 I1
Mara India 83 E5
Mara S. Africa 101 I2
Maraã Brazil 142 E4
Maraba Brazil 143 I5
Maraboon, Lake resr Australia 110 E4
Maracá, Ilha de i. Brazil 143 H3
Maracaibo Venez. 142 D1
Maracaibo, Lago de Venez. see Maracaibo, Lake
Maracaibo, Lake Venez. 142 D2
Maracaju Brazil 144 E2
Maracaju, Serra de hills Brazil 144 E2
Maracanda Uzbek. see Samarkand
Maracás Brazil 145 C1
Maracás, Chapada de hills Brazil 145 C1
Maracay Venez. 142 E1
Marādah Libya 97 E2
Maradi Niger 96 D3
Marāgheh Iran 88 B2
Marahuaca, Cerro mt. Venez. 142 E3
Marajó, Baía de est. Brazil 143 I4
Marajó, Ilha de i. Brazil 143 H4
Marakele National Park S. Africa 101 H3
Maralal Kenya 98 D3
Maralbashi China see Bachu
Maralinga Australia 109 E7
Maralwexi China see Bachu
Maramasike i. Solomon Is 107 G2
Maramba Zambia see Livingstone
Marambio research station Antarctica 152 A2
Maran Malaysia 71 C7
Maran mt. Pak. 89 G4
Marana U.S.A. 129 H5
Marand Iran 88 B2
Marandellas Zimbabwe see Marondera
Marang Malaysia 71 C6
Marang Myanmar 71 B5
Maranhão r. Brazil 145 A1
Maranoa r. Australia 112 D1
Marañón r. Peru 142 D4
Marão Moz. 101 L3
Marão mt. Port. 57 C3
Mara Rosa Brazil 145 A1
Maraş Turkey see Kahramanmaraş
Marathon Canada 122 D4
Marathon FL U.S.A. 133 D7
Marathon NY U.S.A. 135 G2
Marathon TX U.S.A. 131 C6
Maratua i. Indon. 68 F6
Maraú Brazil 145 D1
Maravillas Creek watercourse U.S.A. 131 C6
Mărăzä Azer. 91 H2
Marbella Spain 57 D5
Marble Bar Australia 108 B5
Marble Canyon U.S.A. 129 H3
Marble Canyon gorge U.S.A. 129 H3
Marble Hall S. Africa 101 I3
Marble Hill U.S.A. 131 F4
Marble Island Canada 121 N2
Marbul Pass Jammu and Kashmir 82 C2
Marburg S. Africa 101 J6
Marburg Slovenia see Maribor
Marburg an der Lahn Germany 53 I4
Marca, Ponta do pt Angola 99 B5
Marcali Hungary 58 G1
Marcelino Ramos Brazil 145 A4
March U.K. 49 H6
Marche reg. France 56 E3
Marche-en-Famenne Belgium 52 F4
Marchena Spain 57 D5
Marchinbar Island Australia 110 B1
Mar Chiquita, Lago l. Arg. 144 D4
Marchtrenk Austria 47 O6
Marco U.S.A. 133 D7
Marcoing France 52 D4
Marcona Peru 142 C7
Marcopeet Islands Canada 122 F2
Marcus Baker, Mount U.S.A. 118 D3
Marcy, Mount U.S.A. 135 I1
Mardan Pak. 89 I3
Mar del Plata Arg. 144 E5
Mardīan Afgh. 89 G2
Mardın Turkey 91 F3
Maré i. New Caledonia 107 G4
Maree, Loch l. U.K. 50 D3
Mareh Iran 89 E5
Marengo IA U.S.A. 130 E3
Marengo IN U.S.A. 134 B4
Marevo Rus. Fed. 42 G4
Marfa U.S.A. 131 B6
Marganets Ukr. see Marhanets'
Margao India see Madgaon
Margaret r. Australia 108 D4
Margaret watercourse Australia 111 B6
Margaret, Mount hill Australia 108 B5
Margaret Lake Alta Canada 120 H3
Margaret Lake N.W.T. Canada 120 G1
Margaret River Australia 109 A8
Margaretville U.S.A. 135 H2
Margarita, Isla de i. Venez. 142 F1
Margaritovo Rus. Fed. 74 D4
Margate U.K. 49 I7
Margherita, Lake Eth. see Abaya, Lake

▶Margherita Peak Dem. Rep. Congo/Uganda 98 C3
3rd highest mountain in Africa.

Marghilon Uzbek. see Margilan
Margilan Uzbek. 80 D3
Mārgo, Dasht-i des. Afgh. see Mārgow, Dasht-e
Margog Caka l. China 83 F2
Mārgow, Dasht-e des. Afgh. 89 F4
Margraten Neth. 52 F4
Marguerite Canada 120 F4
Marguerite, Pic mt. Dem. Rep. Congo/Uganda see Margherita Peak
Marguerite Bay Antarctica 152 L2
Margyang China 83 G3
Marhaj Khalīl Iraq 91 G4
Marhanets' Ukr. 43 G7
Marhoum Alg. 54 D5
Mari Myanmar 70 B1
Maria atoll Fr. Polynesia 151 J7
María Elena Chile 144 C2
Maria Island Australia 110 A2
Maria Island Myanmar 71 B5
Maria Island National Park Australia 111 [inset]
Mariala National Park Australia 111 D5
Mariana Brazil 145 C3
Marianao Cuba 133 D8
Mariana Ridge sea feature N. Pacific Ocean 150 F4

▶Mariana Trench sea feature N. Pacific Ocean 150 F5
Deepest trench in the world.

Mariani India 83 H4
Mariánica, Cordillera mts Spain see Morena, Sierra
Marian Lake Canada 120 G2
Marianna AR U.S.A. 131 F5
Marianna FL U.S.A. 133 C6
Mariano Machado Angola see Ganda
Mariánské Lázně Czech Rep. 53 M5
Marias r. U.S.A. 126 F3
Marías, Islas is Mex. 136 C4

▶Mariato, Punta pt Panama 137 H7
Most southerly point of North America.

Maria van Diemen, Cape N.Z. 113 D2
Ma'rib Yemen 86 G6
Maribor Slovenia 58 F1
Marica r. Bulg. see Maritsa
Maricopa AZ U.S.A. 129 G5
Maricopa CA U.S.A. 128 D4
Maricopa Mountains U.S.A. 129 G5
Maridi Sudan 97 F4
Marie Byrd Land reg. Antarctica 152 J1
Marie-Galante i. Guadeloupe 133 L5
Mariehamn Fin. 45 K6
Mariembero r. Brazil 145 A1
Marienbad Czech Rep. see Mariánské Lázně
Marienberg Germany 53 N4
Marienburg Poland see Malbork
Marienhafe Germany 53 H1
Mariental Namibia 100 C3
Marienwerder Poland see Kwidzyn
Mariestad Sweden 45 H7
Mariet r. Canada 122 F2
Marietta GA U.S.A. 133 C5
Marietta OH U.S.A. 134 E4
Marietta OK U.S.A. 131 D5
Marignane France 56 G5
Marii, Mys pt Rus. Fed. 66 G2
Mariinsk Rus. Fed. 64 J4
Mariinskiy Posad Rus. Fed. 42 J4
Marijampolė Lith. 45 M9
Marília Brazil 145 A3
Marillana Australia 108 B5
Marimba Angola 99 B4
Marín Spain 57 B2
Marina U.S.A. 128 C3
Marina di Gioiosa Ionica Italy 58 G5
Mar''ina Gorka Belarus see Mar''ina Horka
Mar''ina Horka Belarus 45 P10
Marinduque i. Phil. 69 G4
Marinette U.S.A. 134 B1
Maringá Brazil 145 A3
Maringa r. Dem. Rep. Congo 98 B3
Maringo U.S.A. 134 D3
Marinha Grande Port. 57 B4
Marion AL U.S.A. 133 C5
Marion AR U.S.A. 131 F5
Marion IL U.S.A. 130 F4
Marion IN U.S.A. 134 C3
Marion KS U.S.A. 130 D4
Marion MI U.S.A. 134 C1
Marion NY U.S.A. 135 G2
Marion OH U.S.A. 134 D3
Marion SC U.S.A. 133 E5
Marion VA U.S.A. 134 E5
Marion, Lake U.S.A. 133 D5
Marion Reef Australia 110 F3
Maripa Venez. 142 E2
Mariposa U.S.A. 128 D3
Marisa Indon. 69 G6
Mariscal Estigarribia Para. 144 D2
Maritime Alps mts France/Italy 56 H4
Maritime Kray admin. div. Rus. Fed. see Primorskiy Kray
Maritimes, Alpes mts France/Italy see Maritime Alps
Maritsa r. Bulg. 59 L4
also known as Evros (Greece), Marica (Bulgaria), Meriç (Turkey)
Marittime, Alpi mts France/Italy see Maritime Alps
Mariupol' Ukr. 43 H7
Mariusa nat. park Venez. 142 F2
Marīvān Iran 88 B3
Marjan Afgh. see Wazi Khwa
Marjayoûn Lebanon 85 B3
Marka Somalia 98 E3
Markala Mali 96 C3
Markam China 76 C2
Markaryd Sweden 45 H8
Markdale Canada 134 E1
Marken S. Africa 101 I2
Markermeer l. Neth. 52 F2
Market Deeping U.K. 49 G6
Market Drayton U.K. 49 E6
Market Harborough U.K. 49 G6
Markethill U.K. 51 F3
Market Weighton U.K. 48 G5
Markha r. Rus. Fed. 65 M3
Markham Canada 134 F2
Markit China 80 E4
Markkleeberg Germany 53 M3
Markleeville U.S.A. 128 D2
Marklohe Germany 53 J2
Markog Qu r. China 76 D1
Markounda Cent. Afr. Rep. 98 B3
Markovo Rus. Fed. 65 S3
Markranstädt Germany 53 M3
Marks Rus. Fed. 43 J6
Marks U.S.A. 131 F5
Marksville U.S.A. 131 E6
Marktheidenfeld Germany 53 J5
Marktredwitz Germany 53 M4
Marl Germany 52 H3
Marla Australia 109 F6
Marlborough Downs hills U.K. 49 F7
Marle France 52 D5
Marlette U.S.A. 134 D2
Marlin U.S.A. 131 D6
Marlinton U.S.A. 134 E4
Marlo Australia 112 D6
Marmagao India 84 B3
Marmande France 56 E4
Marmara, Sea of g. Turkey 59 M4
Marmara Denizi g. Turkey see Marmara, Sea of
Marmara Gölü l. Turkey 59 M5
Marmarica reg. Libya 90 B5
Marmaris Turkey 59 M6
Marmarth U.S.A. 130 C2
Marmet U.S.A. 134 E4
Marmion, Lake salt l. Australia 109 C7
Marmion Lake Canada 121 N5
Marmolada mt. Italy 58 D1
Marne r. France 52 C6
Marne-la-Vallée France 52 C6
Marnitz Germany 53 L1
Maroantsetra Madag. 99 E5
Maroc country Africa see Morocco
Marol Jammu and Kashmir 82 D2
Marol Pak. 89 I4
Maroldsweisach Germany 53 K4
Maromokotro mt. Madag. 99 E5
Marondera Zimbabwe 99 D5
Maroochydore Australia 112 F1
Maroonah Australia 109 A5
Maroon Peak U.S.A. 126 G5
Marosvásárhely Romania see Târgu Mureş
Maroua Cameroon 97 E3
Marovoay Madag. 99 E5
Marqādah Syria 91 F4
Mar Qu r. China see Markog Qu
Marquard S. Africa 101 H5
Marquesas Islands Fr. Polynesia 151 K6
Marquesas Keys is U.S.A. 133 D7
Marquês de Valença Brazil 145 C3
Marquette U.S.A. 132 C2
Marquez U.S.A. 131 D6
Marquion France 52 D4
Marquise France 52 B4
Marquises, Îles is Fr. Polynesia see Marquesas Islands
Marra Australia 112 A3
Marra r. Australia 112 C3
Marra, Jebel mt. Sudan 97 F3
Marracuene Moz. 101 K3
Marrakech Morocco 54 C5
Marrakesh Morocco see Marrakech
Marrangua, Lagoa l. Moz. 101 L3
Marra Plateau Sudan 97 F3
Marrar Australia 112 C5
Marrawah Australia 111 [inset]
Marree Australia 111 B6
Marrowbone U.S.A. 134 C5
Marruecos country Africa see Morocco
Marrupa Moz. 99 D5
Marryat Australia 109 F6
Marsá al 'Alam Egypt 86 D4
Marsa 'Alam Egypt see Marsá al 'Alam
Marsa al Burayqah Libya 97 E1
Marsabit Kenya 98 D3
Marsala Sicily Italy 58 E6
Marsá Maṭrūḥ Egypt 90 B5
Marsberg Germany 53 I3
Marsciano Italy 58 E3
Marsden Australia 112 C4
Marsden Canada 121 I4
Marsdiep sea chan. Neth. 52 E2
Marseille France 56 G5
Marseilles France see Marseille
Marsfjället mt. Sweden 44 I4
Marshall watercourse Australia 110 B4
Marshall AR U.S.A. 131 E5
Marshall IL U.S.A. 134 B4
Marshall MI U.S.A. 134 C2
Marshall MN U.S.A. 130 E2
Marshall MO U.S.A. 130 E4
Marshall TX U.S.A. 131 E5
▶Marshall Islands country N. Pacific Ocean 150 H5
Oceania 8, 104–105
Marshalltown U.S.A. 130 E3
Marshfield MO U.S.A. 131 E4
Marshfield WI U.S.A. 130 F2
Marsh Harbour Bahamas 133 E7
Mars Hill U.S.A. 132 H2
Marsh Island U.S.A. 131 F6
Marsh Peak U.S.A. 129 I1
Marsh Point Canada 121 M3
Marsing U.S.A. 126 D4
Märsta Sweden 45 J7
Marsyaty Rus. Fed. 41 S3
Martaban Myanmar 70 B3
Martaban, Gulf of Myanmar 70 B3
Martapura Indon. 68 E7
Marten River Canada 122 F5
Marte R. Gómez, Presa resr Mex. 131 D7
Martha's Vineyard i. U.S.A. 135 J3
Martigny Switz. 56 H3
Martim Vaz, Ilhas is S. Atlantic Ocean see Martin Vas, Ilhas
Martin r. Canada 120 F2
Martin Slovakia 47 Q6
Martin MI U.S.A. 134 C2
Martin SD U.S.A. 130 C3
Martinez Lake U.S.A. 129 F5
Martinho Campos Brazil 145 B2

▶Martinique terr. West Indies 137 L6
French Overseas Department.
North America 9, 116–117

Martinique Passage Dominica/Martinique 137 L5
Martin Peninsula Antarctica 152 K2
Martinsburg U.S.A. 135 G4
Martins Ferry U.S.A. 134 E3
Martinsville IL U.S.A. 134 B4
Martinsville IN U.S.A. 134 B4
Martinsville VA U.S.A. 134 F5

▶Martin Vas, Ilhas is S. Atlantic Ocean 148 G7
Most easterly point of South America.

Martin Vaz Islands S. Atlantic Ocean see Martin Vas, Ilhas
Martök Kazakh. see Martuk
Marton N.Z. 113 E5
Martorell Spain 57 G3
Martos Spain 57 E5
Martuk Kazakh. 78 E1
Martuni Armenia 91 G2
Maruf Afgh. 89 G4
Maruim Brazil 143 K6
Marukhis Ugheltekhili pass Georgia/Rus. Fed. 91 F2
Marulan Australia 112 D5
Marusthali reg. India 89 H5
Marvast Iran 88 D4
Marv Dasht Iran 88 D4
Marvejols France 56 F4
Marvine, Mount U.S.A. 129 H2
Marwayne Canada 121 I4
Mary r. Australia 108 E3
Mary Turkm. 89 F2
Maryborough Qld Australia 111 F5
Maryborough Vic. Australia 112 A6
Marydale S. Africa 100 F5
Mary Frances Lake Canada 121 J2
Mary Lake Canada 121 K2
Maryland state U.S.A. 135 G4
Maryport U.K. 48 D4
Mary's Harbour Canada 123 L3
Marysvale U.S.A. 129 G2
Marysville CA U.S.A. 128 C2
Marysville KS U.S.A. 130 D4
Marysville OH U.S.A. 134 D3
Maryvale N.T. Australia 109 F6
Maryvale Qld Australia 110 D3
Maryville MO U.S.A. 130 E3
Maryville TN U.S.A. 132 D5
Marzagão Brazil 145 A2
Marzahna Germany 53 M2
Masada tourist site Israel 85 B4
Masāhūn, Kūh-e mt. Iran 88 D4
Masai Steppe plain Tanz. 99 D4
Masaka Uganda 98 D4
Masakhane S. Africa 101 H6
Masalembu Besar i. Indon. 68 E8
Masallı Azer. 91 H3
Masan S. Korea 75 C6
Masasi Tanz. 99 D5
Masavi Bol. 142 F7
Masbate Phil. 69 G4
Masbate i. Phil. 69 G4
Mascara Alg. 57 G6
Mascarene Basin sea feature Indian Ocean 149 L7
Mascarene Plain sea feature Indian Ocean 149 L7
Mascarene Ridge sea feature Indian Ocean 149 L6
Mascote Brazil 145 D1
Masein Myanmar 70 A2
Masela Indon. 108 E2
Masela i. Indon. 108 E2

▶Maseru Lesotho 101 H5
Capital of Lesotho.

Mashai Lesotho 101 I5
Mashan China 77 F4
Masherbrum mt. Jammu and Kashmir 82 D2
Mashhad Iran 89 E2
Mashket r. Pak. 89 F5
Mashki Chah Pak. 89 F4
Masi Norway 44 M2
Masiáca Mex. 127 F8
Masibambane S. Africa 101 H6
Masīlah, Wādī al watercourse Yemen 86 H6
Masilo S. Africa 101 H5
Masi-Manimba Dem. Rep. Congo 99 B4
Masindi Uganda 98 D3
Masinyusane S. Africa 100 F6
Masira, Gulf of Oman see Maşīrah, Khalīj
Maşīrah, Jazīrat i. Oman 87 I5
Maşīrah, Khalīj b. Oman 87 I6
Masira Island Oman see Maşīrah, Jazīrat
Masjed Soleymān Iran 88 C4
Mask, Lough l. Rep. of Ireland 51 C4
Maskūtān Iran 89 E5
Maslovo Rus. Fed. 41 S3
Masoala, Tanjona c. Madag. 99 F5
Mason MI U.S.A. 134 C2
Mason OH U.S.A. 134 C4
Mason TX U.S.A. 131 D6
Mason, Lake salt flat Australia 109 B6
Mason Bay N.Z. 113 A8
Mason City U.S.A. 130 E3
Masontown U.S.A. 134 F4
Masqaṭ Oman see Muscat
Masqaṭ reg. Oman see Muscat
'Masrūg well Oman 88 D6
Massa Italy 58 D2
Massachusetts state U.S.A. 135 I2
Massachusetts Bay U.S.A. 135 J2
Massadona U.S.A. 129 I1
Massafra Italy 58 G4
Massakory Chad 97 E3
Massa Marittimo Italy 58 D3
Massangena Moz. 99 D6
Massango Angola 99 B4
Massawa Eritrea 86 E6
Massawippi, Lac l. Canada 135 I1
Massena U.S.A. 135 H1
Massenya Chad 97 E3
Masset Canada 120 C4
Massieville U.S.A. 134 D4
Massif Central mts France 56 F4
Massilia France see Marseille
Massillon U.S.A. 134 E3
Massina Mali 96 C3
Massinga Moz. 101 L2
Massingir Moz. 101 K2
Massingir, Barragem de resr Moz. 101 K2
Masson Island Antarctica 152 F2
Mastchoh Tajik. 89 H2
Masterton N.Z. 113 E5
Masticho, Akra pt Greece 59 L5
Mastung Pak. 78 F4
Mastūrah Saudi Arabia 86 E5
Masty Belarus 45 N10
Masuda Japan 75 C6
Masuku Gabon see Franceville
Masulipatam India see Machilipatnam
Masulipatnam India see Machilipatnam
Masuna i. American Samoa see Tutuila
Masvingo Zimbabwe 99 D6
Masvingo prov. Zimbabwe 101 J1
Maswa Tanz. 98 D4
Maswaar i. Indon. 69 I7
Maşyāf Syria 85 C2
Mat, Hon i. Vietnam 70 D3
Mat, Nam r. Laos 70 D3
Mata Myanmar 70 B1
Matabeleland South prov. Zimbabwe 101 I1
Matachewan Canada 122 E5
Matadi Dem. Rep. Congo 99 B4
Matador U.S.A. 131 C5
Matagalpa Nicaragua 137 G6
Matagami Canada 122 F4
Matagami, Lac l. Canada 122 F4
Matagorda Island U.S.A. 131 D6
Matak i. Indon. 71 D7
Matakana Island N.Z. 113 F3
Matala Angola 99 B5
Maṭālī', Jabal hill Saudi Arabia 91 F6
Matam Senegal 96 B3
Matamey Niger 96 D3
Matamoras U.S.A. 135 H3
Matamoros Coahuila Mex. 131 C7
Matamoros Tamaulipas Mex. 131 D7
Matandu r. Tanz. 99 D4
Matane Canada 123 I4
Matanzas Cuba 137 H4
Matapan, Cape pt Greece see Tainaro, Akra
Matapédia, Lac l. Canada 123 I4
Maṭār well Saudi Arabia 88 B5
Matara Sri Lanka 84 D5
Mataram Indon. 108 B2
Matarani Peru 142 D7
Mataranka Australia 108 F3
Mataripe Brazil 145 D1
Mataró Spain 57 H3
Matasiri i. Indon. 68 F7
Matatiele S. Africa 101 I6
Matatila Dam India 82 D4
Mataura N.Z. 113 B8

▶Matā'utu Wallis and Futuna Is 107 I3
Capital of Wallis and Futuna.

Mata-Utu Wallis and Futuna Is see Matā'utu
Matawai N.Z. 113 F4
Matay Kazakh. 80 E2
Matcha Tajik. see Mastchoh
Mategua Bol. 142 F5
Matehuala Mex. 131 C8
Matemanga Tanz. 99 D5
Matera Italy 58 G4
Mateur Tunisia 58 C6
Mathaji India 82 B4
Matheson Canada 122 E4
Mathews U.S.A. 135 G5
Mathis U.S.A. 131 D6
Mathoura Australia 112 B5
Mathura India 82 D4
Mati Phil. 69 H5
Matiali India 83 G4
Matias Cardoso Brazil 145 C1
Matías Romero Mex. 136 E5
Matimekosh Canada 123 I3
Matin India 83 E5
Matinenda Lake Canada 122 E5
Matizi China 76 D1
Matla r. India 83 G5
Matlabas r. S. Africa 101 H2
Matli Pak. 89 H5
Matlock U.K. 49 F5
Mato, Cerro mt. Venez. 142 E2
Matobo Hills Zimbabwe 99 C6
Mato Grosso Brazil 142 G7
Mato Grosso state Brazil 145 A1
Mato Grosso, Planalto do plat. Brazil 143 H7
Matopo Hills Zimbabwe see Matobo Hills
Matos Costa Brazil 145 A4
Matosinhos Port. 57 B3
Mato Verde Brazil 145 C1
Maṭraḥ Oman 88 E6
Matroosberg mt. S. Africa 100 D7
Matsesta Rus. Fed. 91 E2
Matsue Japan 75 D6
Matsumoto Japan 75 E5
Matsu Tao i. Taiwan 77 I3
Matsuyama Japan 75 D6
Mattagami r. Canada 122 E4
Mattamuskeet, Lake U.S.A. 132 E5
Mattawa Canada 122 F5
Matterhorn mt. Italy/Switz. 58 B2
Matterhorn mt. U.S.A. 126 E4
Matthew Town Bahamas 137 J4
Maṭṭī, Sabkhat salt pan Saudi Arabia 88 D6
Mattoon U.S.A. 130 F4
Matturai Sri Lanka see Matara
Matuku i. Fiji 107 H3
Matumbo Angola 99 B5
Maturín Venez. 142 F2
Matusadona National Park Zimbabwe 99 C5
Matwabeng S. Africa 101 H5
Maty Island P.N.G. see Wuvulu Island
Mau India see Maunath Bhanjan
Maúa Moz. 99 D5
Maubeuge France 52 D4
Maubin Myanmar 70 A3
Ma-ubin Myanmar 70 B1
Maubourguet France 56 E5
Mauchline U.K. 50 E5
Maudaha India 82 E4
Maude Australia 111 D7
Maud Seamount sea feature S. Atlantic Ocean 148 I10
Mau-é-ele Moz. see Marão
Maués Brazil 143 G4
Maughold Head hd Isle of Man 48 C4
Maug Islands N. Mariana Is 69 L2
Maui i. HI U.S.A. 127 [inset]
Maukkadaw Myanmar 70 A2
Maulbronn Germany 53 I6
Maule r. Chile 144 B5
Maulvi Bazar Bangl. see Moulvibazar
Maumee U.S.A. 134 D3
Maumee Bay U.S.A. 134 D3
Maumere Indon. 108 C2
Maumturk Mts hills Rep. of Ireland 51 C4
Maun Botswana 99 C5
Mauna Kea vol. HI U.S.A. 127 [inset]
Mauna Loa vol. HI U.S.A. 127 [inset]
Maunath Bhanjan India 83 E4
Maunatlala Botswana 101 H2
Maungaturoto N.Z. 113 E3
Maungdaw Myanmar 70 A2
Maungmagan Islands Myanmar 71 B4
Maurepas, Lake U.S.A. 131 F6
Mauriac France 56 F4
Maurice country Indian Ocean see Mauritius
Maurice, Lake salt flat Australia 109 E7
Maurik Neth. 52 F3
▶Mauritania country Africa 96 B3
Africa 7, 94–95
Mauritanie country Africa see Mauritania
▶Mauritius country Indian Ocean 149 L7
Africa 7, 94–95
Maurs France 56 F4
Mauston U.S.A. 130 F3
Mava Dem. Rep. Congo 98 C3
Mavago Moz. 99 D5
Mavan, Kūh-e hill Iran 88 E3
Mavanza Moz. 101 L2
Mavinga Angola 99 C5
Mavrovo nat. park Macedonia 59 I4
Mavume Moz. 101 L2
Mavuya S. Africa 101 H6
Ma Wan i. Hong Kong China 77 [inset]
Māwān, Khashm hill Saudi Arabia 88 B6
Mawana India 82 D3
Mawanga Dem. Rep. Congo 99 B4
Ma Wang Dui tourist site China 77 G2
Mawei China 77 H3

Mawjib, Wādī al r. Jordan 85 B4
Mawkmai Myanmar 70 B2
Mawlaik Myanmar 70 A2
Mawlamyaing Myanmar see Moulmein
Mawlamyine Myanmar see Moulmein
Mawqaq Saudi Arabia 91 F6
Mawson research station Antarctica 152 E2
Mawson Coast Antarctica 152 E2
Mawson Escarpment Antarctica 152 E2
Mawson Peninsula Antarctica 152 H2
Maw Taung mt. Myanmar 71 B5
Mawza Yemen 86 F7
Maxán Arg. 144 C3
Maxhamish Lake Canada 120 F3
Maxia, Punta mt. Sardinia Italy 58 C5
Maxixe Moz. 101 L2
Maxmo Fin. 44 M5
May, Isle of i. U.K. 50 G4
Maya r. Rus. Fed. 65 O3
Mayaguana i. Bahamas 133 F8
Mayaguana Passage Bahamas 133 F8
Mayagüez Puerto Rico 137 K5
Mayahi Niger 96 D3
Mayakovskiy, Qullai mt. Tajik. 89 H2
Mayakovskogo, Pik mt. Tajik. see Mayakovskiy, Qullai
Mayama Congo 98 B4
Maya Mountains Belize/Guat. 136 G5
Mayan China see Mayanhe
Mayang China 77 F3
Mayanhe China 76 E1
Mayar hill U.K. 50 F4
Maybeury U.S.A. 134 E5
Maybole U.K. 50 E5
Maych'ew Eth. 98 D2
Maydān Shahr Afgh. see Meydān Shahr
Maydh Somalia 86 G7
Maydos Turkey see Eceabat
Mayen Germany 53 H4
Mayenne France 56 D2
Mayenne r. France 56 D3
Mayer U.S.A. 129 G4
Mayêr Kangri mt. China 83 F2
Mayersville U.S.A. 131 F5
Mayerthorpe Canada 120 H4
Mayfield N.Z. 113 C6
Mayi He r. China 74 C3
Maykop Rus. Fed. 91 F1
Maymyo Myanmar 70 B2
Mayna Respublika Khakasiya Rus. Fed. 64 K4
Mayna Ul'yanovskaya Oblast' Rus. Fed. 43 J5
Mayni India 84 B2
Maynooth Canada 135 G1
Mayo Canada 120 C2
Mayo U.S.A. 133 D6
Mayo Alim Cameroon 96 E4
Mayoko Congo 98 B4
Mayo Lake Canada 120 C2
Mayo Landing Canada see Mayo
Mayor, Puig mt. Spain see Major, Puig
Mayor Island N.Z. 113 F3
Mayor Pablo Lagerenza Para. 144 D1

▶Mayotte terr. Africa 99 E5
French Territorial Collectivity.
Africa 7, 94–95

Mayskiy Amurskaya Oblast' Rus. Fed. 74 C1
Mayskiy Kabardino-Balkarskaya Respublika Rus. Fed. 91 G2
Mays Landing U.S.A. 135 H4
Mayson Lake Canada 121 J3
Maysville U.S.A. 134 D4
Mayumba Gabon 98 B4
Mayum La pass China 83 E3
Mayuram India 84 C4
Mayville MI U.S.A. 134 D2
Mayville ND U.S.A. 130 D2
Mayville NY U.S.A. 134 F2
Mayville WI U.S.A. 134 A2
Mazabuka Zambia 99 C5
Mazaca Turkey see Kayseri
Mazagan Morocco see El Jadida
Mazar China 82 D1
Mazar, Koh-i- mt. Afgh. 89 G3
Mazara, Val di valley Sicily Italy 58 E6
Mazara del Vallo Sicily Italy 58 E6
Mazār-e Sharīf Afgh. 89 G2
Mazārī' reg. U.A.E. 88 D6
Mazatán Mex. 127 F7
Mazatlán Mex. 136 C4
Mazatzal Peak U.S.A. 129 H4
Mazdaj Iran 91 H4
Mažeikiai Lith. 45 M8
Mazīm Oman 88 E6
Mazocahui Mex. 127 F7
Mazocruz Peru 142 E7
Mazomora Tanz. 99 D4
Mazu Dao i. Taiwan see Matsu Tao
Mazunga Zimbabwe 99 C6
Mazyr Belarus 43 F5
Mazzouna Tunisia 58 C7

▶Mbabane Swaziland 101 J4
Capital of Swaziland.

Mbahiakro Côte d'Ivoire 96 C4
Mbaïki Cent. Afr. Rep. 98 B3
Mbakaou, Lac de l. Cameroon 96 E4
Mbala Zambia 99 D4
Mbale Uganda 98 D3
Mbalmayo Cameroon 96 E4
Mbam r. Cameroon 96 E4
Mbandaka Dem. Rep. Congo 98 B4
M'banza Congo Angola 99 B4
Mbarara Uganda 97 G5
Mbari r. Cent. Afr. Rep. 98 C3
Mbaswana S. Africa 101 K4
Mbemkuru r. Tanz. 99 D4
Mbeya Tanz. 99 D4
Mbinga Tanz. 99 D5
Mbini Equat. Guinea 96 D4
Mbizi Zimbabwe 99 D6
Mboki Cent. Afr. Rep. 98 C3
Mbomo Congo 98 B3
Mbouda Cameroon 96 E4
Mbour Senegal 96 B3
Mbout Mauritania 96 B3
Mbozi Tanz. 99 D4
Mbrès Cent. Afr. Rep. 98 B3
Mbuji-Mayi Dem. Rep. Congo 99 C4
Mbulu Tanz. 98 D4
Mburucuyá Arg. 144 E3
McAdam Canada 123 I5
McAlester U.S.A. 131 E5
McAlister mt. Australia 112 D5
McAllen U.S.A. 131 D7
McArthur r. Australia 110 B2
McArthur U.S.A. 134 D4
McArthur Mills Canada 135 G1
McBain U.S.A. 134 C1
McBride Canada 120 F4
McCall U.S.A. 126 D3
McCamey U.S.A. 131 C6
McCammon U.S.A. 126 E4
McCauley Island Canada 120 D4
McClintock, Mount Antarctica 152 H1
McClintock Channel Canada 119 H2
McClintock Range hills Australia 108 D4
McClure, Lake U.S.A. 128 C3
McClure Strait Canada 118 G2
McClusky U.S.A. 130 C2
McComb U.S.A. 131 F6
McConaughy, Lake U.S.A. 130 C3
McConnellsburg U.S.A. 135 G4
McConnelsville U.S.A. 134 E4
McCook U.S.A. 130 C3
McCormick U.S.A. 133 D5
McCrea r. Canada 120 H2
McCreary Canada 121 L5
McDame Canada 120 D3
McDermitt U.S.A. 126 D4
McDonald Islands Indian Ocean 149 M9
McDonald Peak U.S.A. 126 E3
McDonough U.S.A. 133 C5
McDougall's Bay S. Africa 100 C5
McDowell Peak U.S.A. 129 H5
McFarland U.S.A. 128 D4
McGill U.S.A. 129 F2
McGivney Canada 123 I5
McGrath AK U.S.A. 118 C3
McGrath MN U.S.A. 130 E2
McGraw U.S.A. 135 G2
McGregor r. Canada 120 F4
McGregor S. Africa 100 D7
McGregor, Lake Canada 120 H5
McGregor Range hills Australia 111 C5
McGuire, Mount U.S.A. 126 E3
Mchinga Tanz. 99 D4
Mchinji Malawi 99 D5
McIlwraith Range hills Australia 110 C2
McInnes Lake Canada 121 M4
McIntosh U.S.A. 130 C2
McKay Range hills Australia 108 C5
McKean i. Kiribati 107 I2
McKee U.S.A. 134 C5
McKenzie r. U.S.A. 126 C3
McKinlay r. Australia 110 C4

▶McKinley, Mount U.S.A. 118 C3
Highest mountain in North America.
North America 114–115

McKinney U.S.A. 131 D5
McKittrick U.S.A. 128 D4
McLaughlin U.S.A. 130 C2
McLeansboro U.S.A. 130 F4
McLennan Canada 120 G4
McLeod r. Canada 120 H4
McLeod Bay Canada 121 I2
McLeod Lake Canada 120 F4
McLoughlin, Mount U.S.A. 126 C4
McMillan, Lake U.S.A. 131 B5
McMinnville OR U.S.A. 126 C3
McMinnville TN U.S.A. 132 C5
McMurdo research station Antarctica 152 H1
McMurdo Sound b. Antarctica 152 H1
McNary U.S.A. 129 I4
McNaughton Lake Canada see Kinbasket Lake
McPherson U.S.A. 130 D4
McQuesten r. Canada 120 B2
McRae U.S.A. 133 D5
McTavish Arm b. Canada 120 G1
McVeytown U.S.A. 135 G3
McVicar Arm b. Canada 120 F1
Mdantsane S. Africa 101 H7
M'Daourouch Alg. 58 B6
Mê, Hon i. Vietnam 70 D3
Mead, Lake resr U.S.A. 129 F3
Meade U.S.A. 131 C4
Meade r. U.S.A. 118 C2
Meadow Australia 109 A6
Meadow SD U.S.A. 130 C2
Meadow UT U.S.A. 129 G2
Meadow Lake Canada 121 I4
Meadville MS U.S.A. 131 F6
Meadville PA U.S.A. 134 E3
Meaford Canada 134 E1
Meaken-dake vol. Japan 74 G4
Mealhada Port. 57 B3
Mealy Mountains Canada 123 K3
Meandarra Australia 112 D1
Meander River Canada 120 G3
Meaux France 52 C6
Mecca Saudi Arabia 86 E5
Mecca CA U.S.A. 128 E5
Mecca OH U.S.A. 134 E3
Mechanic Falls U.S.A. 135 J1
Mechanicsville U.S.A. 135 G5
Mechelen Belgium 52 E3
Mechelen Neth. 52 F4
Mecherchar i. Palau see Eil Malk
Mecheria Alg. 54 D5
Mechernich Germany 52 G4
Mecitözü Turkey 90 D2
Meckenheim Germany 52 H4
Mecklenburger Bucht b. Germany 47 M3
Mecklenburg-Vorpommern land Germany 53 M1
Mecklenburg - West Pomerania land Germany see Mecklenburg-Vorpommern
Meda r. Australia 108 C4
Meda Port. 57 C3
Medak India 84 C2
Medan Indon. 71 B7
Medanosa, Punta pt Arg. 144 C7
Médanos de Coro, Parque Nacional nat. park Venez. 142 E1
Medawachchiya Sri Lanka 84 D4
Médéa Alg. 57 H5
Medebach Germany 53 I3
Medellín Col. 142 C2
Meden r. U.K. 48 G5
Medenine Tunisia 54 G5
Mederdra Mauritania 96 B3
Medford NY U.S.A. 135 I3
Medford OK U.S.A. 131 D4
Medford OR U.S.A. 126 C4
Medford WI U.S.A. 130 F2
Medgidia Romania 59 M2
Media U.S.A. 135 H4
Mediaș Romania 59 K1
Medicine Bow r. U.S.A. 126 G4
Medicine Bow Mountains U.S.A. 126 G4
Medicine Bow Peak U.S.A. 126 G4
Medicine Hat Canada 121 I5
Medicine Lake U.S.A. 126 G2
Medicine Lodge U.S.A. 131 D4
Medina Brazil 145 C2
Medina Saudi Arabia 86 E5
Medina ND U.S.A. 130 D2
Medina NY U.S.A. 135 F2
Medina OH U.S.A. 134 E3
Medinaceli Spain 57 E3
Medina del Campo Spain 57 D3
Medina de Rioseco Spain 57 D3
Medina Lake U.S.A. 131 D6
Medinipur India 83 F5
Mediolanum Italy see Milan
Mediterranean Sea 54 K5
Mednyy, Ostrov i. Rus. Fed. 150 H2
Médoc reg. France 56 D4
Mêdog China 76 B2
Medora U.S.A. 130 C2
Medstead Canada 121 I4
Meduro atoll Marshall Is see Majuro
Medvedevo Rus. Fed. 42 J4
Medveditsa r. Rus. Fed. 43 I6
Medvednica mts Croatia 58 F2
Medvezh'i, Ostrova is Rus. Fed. 65 R2
Medvezh'ya, Gora mt. Rus. Fed. 74 E3
Medvezh'yegorsk Rus. Fed. 42 G3
Medway r. U.K. 49 H7
Meekatharra Australia 109 B6
Meeker CO U.S.A. 129 J1
Meeker OH U.S.A. 134 D3
Meelpaeg Reservoir Canada 123 K4
Meemu Atoll Maldives see Mulaku Atoll
Meerane Germany 53 M4
Meerlo Neth. 52 G3
Meerut India 82 D3
Mega Escarpment Eth./Kenya 98 D3
Megalopoli Greece 59 J6
Megamo Indon. 69 I7
Mégantic, Lac l. Canada 123 H5
Megara Greece 59 J5
Megezez mt. Eth. 98 D3

▶Meghalaya state India 83 G4
Highest mean annual rainfall in the world.

Meghasani mt. India 83 F5
Meghri Armenia 91 G3
Megin Turkm. 88 E2
Megisti i. Greece 59 M6
Megri Armenia see Meghri
Mehamn Norway 44 O1
Mehar Pak. 89 G5
Meharry, Mount Australia 109 B5
Mehbubnagar India see Mahbubnagar
Mehdia Tunisia see Mahdia
Meherpur Bangl. 83 G5
Meherrin U.S.A. 135 F5
Meherrin r. U.S.A. 135 G5
Mehlville U.S.A. 130 F4
Mehrakān salt marsh Iran 88 D5
Mehrān Hormozgan Iran 88 D5
Mehrān Īlām Iran 88 B3
Mehren Germany 52 G4
Mehriz Iran 88 D4
Mehsana India see Mahesana
Mehtar Lām Afgh. 89 H3
Meia Ponte r. Brazil 145 A2
Meicheng China see Minqing
Meiganga Cameroon 97 E4
Meighen Island Canada 119 I2
Meigu China 76 D2
Meihekou China 74 B4
Meikeng China 77 G3
Meikle r. Canada 120 G3
Meikle Says Law hill U.K. 50 G5
Meiktila Myanmar 70 A2
Meilin China see Ganxian
Meilleur r. Canada 120 E2
Meilu China 77 F4
Meine Germany 53 K2
Meinersen Germany 53 K2
Meiningen Germany 53 K4
Meishan Anhui China see Jinzhai
Meishan Sichuan China 76 D2
Meishan Shuiku resr China 77 G2
Meißen Germany 47 N5
Meister r. Canada 120 D2
Meitan China 76 E3
Meixi China 74 C3
Meixian China see Meizhou
Meixing China see Xiaojin
Meizhou China 77 H3
Mej r. India 82 D4
Mejicana mt. Arg. 144 C3
Mejillones Chile 144 B2
Mékambo Gabon 98 B3
Mek'elē Eth. 98 D2
Mekelle Eth. see Mek'elē
Mékhé Senegal 96 B3
Mekhtar Pak. 89 H4
Meknassy Tunisia 58 C7
Meknès Morocco 54 C5
Mekong r. Xizang/Yunnan China 72 C2
Mekong r. Laos/Thai. 70 D4
also known as Mae Nam Khong (Laos/Thailand)
Mekong, Mouths of the Vietnam 71 D5
Mekoryuk U.S.A. 118 B3
Melaka Malaysia 71 C7
Melanau, Gunung hill Indon. 71 E7
Melanesia is Pacific Ocean 150 G6
Melanesian Basin sea feature Pacific Ocean 150 G5

▶Melbourne Australia 112 B6
State capital of Victoria. 2nd most populous city in Oceania.

Melbourne U.S.A. 133 D6
Melby U.K. 50 [inset]
Meldorf Germany 47 L3
Melekess Rus. Fed. see Dimitrovgrad
Melenki Rus. Fed. 43 I5
Melet Turkey see Mesudiye
Mélèzes, Rivière aux r. Canada 123 H2
Melfa U.S.A. 135 H5
Mélfi Chad 97 E3
Melfi Italy 58 F4
Melfort Canada 121 J4
Melhus Norway 44 G5
Meliadine Lake Canada 121 M2
Melide Spain 57 C2

▶Melilla N. Africa 57 E6
Spanish Territory.

Melimoyu, Monte mt. Chile 144 B6
Meliskerke Neth. 52 D3
Melita Canada 121 K5
Melitene Turkey see Malatya
Melitopol' Ukr. 43 G7
Melk Austria 47 O6
Melka Guba Eth. 98 D3
Melksham U.K. 49 E7
Mellakoski Fin. 44 N3
Mellansel Sweden 44 K5
Melle Germany 53 I2
Mellerud Sweden 45 H7
Mellette U.S.A. 130 D2
Mellid Spain see Melide
Mellilia N. Africa see Melilla
Mellor Glacier Antarctica 152 E2
Mellrichstadt Germany 53 K4
Mellum i. Germany 53 I1
Melmoth S. Africa 101 J5
Mel'nichoye Rus. Fed. 74 D3
Melo Uruguay 144 F4
Meloco Moz. 99 D5
Melolo Indon. 108 C2
Melozitna r. U.S.A. 118 C3
Melrhir, Chott salt l. Alg. 54 F5
Melrose Australia 109 C6
Melrose U.K. 50 G5
Melrose U.S.A. 130 E2
Melsungen Germany 53 J3
Melton Australia 112 B6
Melton Mowbray U.K. 49 G6
Melun France 56 F2
Melville Canada 121 K5
Melville, Cape Australia 110 D2
Melville, Lake Canada 123 K3
Melville Bugt b. Greenland see Qimusseriarsuaq
Melville Island Australia 108 E2
Melville Island Canada 119 H2
Melville Peninsula Canada 119 J3
Melvin U.S.A. 134 A3
Melvin, Lough l. Rep. of Ireland/U.K. 51 D3
Mêmar Co salt l. China 83 E2
Memba Moz. 99 E5
Memberamo r. Indon. 69 J7
Memel Lith. see Klaipėda
Memel S. Africa 101 I4
Memmelsdorf Germany 53 K5
Memmingen Germany 47 M7
Mempawah Indon. 68 D6
Memphis tourist site Egypt 90 C5
Memphis MI U.S.A. 134 D2
Memphis TN U.S.A. 131 F5
Memphis TX U.S.A. 131 C5
Memphrémagog, Lac l. Canada 135 I1
Mena Ukr. 43 G6
Mena U.S.A. 131 E5
Menado Indon. see Manado
Ménaka Mali 96 D3
Menard U.S.A. 131 D6
Menasha U.S.A. 134 A1
Mendanha Brazil 145 C2
Mendarik i. Indon. 71 D7
Mende France 56 F4
Mendefera Eritrea 86 E7
Mendeleyev Ridge sea feature Arctic Ocean 153 B1
Mendeleyevsk Rus. Fed. 42 L5
Mendenhall U.S.A. 131 F6
Mendenhall, Cape U.S.A. 118 B4
Mendenhall Glacier U.S.A. 120 C3
Méndez Mex. 131 D7
Mendī Eth. 98 D3
Mendi P.N.G. 69 K8
Mendip Hills U.K. 49 E7
Mendocino U.S.A. 128 B2
Mendocino, Cape U.S.A. 128 A1
Mendocino, Lake U.S.A. 128 B2
Mendooran Australia 112 D3
Mendota CA U.S.A. 128 C3
Mendota IL U.S.A. 130 F3
Mendoza Arg. 144 C4
Menemen Turkey 59 L5
Ménerville Alg. see Thenia
Mengban China 76 D4
Mengcheng China 77 H1
Menghai China 76 D4
Mengjin China 77 G1
Mengla China 76 D4
Menglang China see Lancang
Menglie China see Jiangcheng
Mengyang China see Mingshan
Mengzi China 76 D4
Menihek Canada 123 I3
Menihek Lakes Canada 123 I3
Menindee Australia 111 C7
Menindee Lake Australia 111 C7
Ménistouc, Lac l. Canada 123 I3
Menkere Rus. Fed. 65 N3
Mennecy France 52 C6
Menominee U.S.A. 134 B1
Menomonee Falls U.S.A. 134 A2
Menomonie U.S.A. 130 F2
Menongue Angola 99 B5
Menorca i. Spain see Minorca
Mentawai, Kepulauan is Indon. 68 B7
Mentawai, Selat sea chan. Indon. 68 C7
Menteroda Germany 53 K3
Mentmore U.S.A. 129 I4
Menton France 56 H5
Mentone U.S.A. 131 C6
Menuf Egypt see Minūf
Menzel Bourguiba Tunisia 58 C6
Menzelet Barajı resr Turkey 90 E3
Menzelinsk Rus. Fed. 41 Q4
Menzel Temime Tunisia 58 D6
Menzies Australia 109 C7
Menzies, Mount Antarctica 148 E2
Meobbaai b. Namibia 100 B3
Meoqui Mex. 131 B6
Meppel Neth. 52 G2
Meppen Germany 53 H2
Mepuze Moz. 101 K2
Meqheleng S. Africa 101 H5
Mequon U.S.A. 134 B2
Merak Indon. 68 D8
Meråker Norway 44 G5
Merano Italy 58 D1
Meratswe r. Botswana 100 G2
Merauke Indon. 69 K8
Merca Somalia see Marka
Mercantour, Parc National du nat. park France 56 H4
Merced U.S.A. 128 C3
Merced r. U.S.A. 128 C3
Mercedes Arg. 144 E3
Mercedes Uruguay 144 E4
Mercer ME U.S.A. 135 K1
Mercer PA U.S.A. 134 E3
Mercer WI U.S.A. 130 F2
Mercês Brazil 145 C3
Mercury Islands N.Z. 113 E3
Mercy, Cape Canada 119 L3
Merdenik Turkey see Göle
Mere Belgium 52 D4
Mere U.K. 49 E7
Meredith U.S.A. 135 J2
Meredith, Lake U.S.A. 131 C5
Merefa Ukr. 43 H6
Merga Oasis Sudan 86 C6
Mergui Myanmar 71 B4
Mergui Archipelago is Myanmar 71 B5
Meriç r. Turkey 59 L4
also known as Evros (Greece), Marica, Maritsa (Bulgaria)
Mérida Mex. 136 G4
Mérida Spain 57 C4
Mérida Venez. 142 D2
Mérida, Cordillera de mts Venez. 142 D2
Meriden U.S.A. 135 I3
Meridian MS U.S.A. 131 F5
Meridian TX U.S.A. 131 D6
Mérignac France 56 D4
Merijärvi Fin. 44 N4
Merikarvia Fin. 45 L6
Merimbula Australia 112 D6
Merín, Laguna l. Brazil/Uruguay see Mirim, Lagoa
Meringur Australia 111 C7
Merir i. Palau 69 I6
Merjayoun Lebanon see Marjayoûn
Merkel U.S.A. 131 C5
Merluna Australia 110 C2
Mermaid Reef Australia 108 B4
Meron, Har mt. Israel 85 B3
Merowe Sudan 86 D6
Mêrqung Co l. China 83 F3
Merredin Australia 109 B7
Merrick hill U.K. 50 E5
Merrickville Canada 135 H1
Merrill MI U.S.A. 134 C2
Merrill WI U.S.A. 130 F2
Merrill, Mount Canada 120 E2
Merrillville U.S.A. 134 B3
Merriman U.S.A. 130 C3
Merritt Canada 120 F5
Merritt Island U.S.A. 133 D6
Merriwa Australia 112 E4
Merrygoen Australia 112 D3
Mersa Fatma Eritrea 86 F7
Mersa Maṭrûḥ Egypt see Marsá Maṭrūḥ
Mersch Lux. 52 G5
Merseburg (Saale) Germany 53 L3
Mersey est. U.K. 48 E5
Mersin Turkey see İçel
Mersing Malaysia 71 C7
Mērsrags Latvia 45 M8
Merta India 82 C4
Merthyr Tydfil U.K. 49 D7
Mértola Port. 57 C5
Mertz Glacier Antarctica 152 G2
Mertz Glacier Tongue Antarctica 152 G2
Mertzon U.S.A. 131 C6
Méru France 52 C5

▶Meru vol. Tanz. 98 D4
4th highest mountain in Africa.

Merui Pak. 89 F4
Merv Turkm. see Mary
Merweville S. Africa 100 E7
Merzifon Turkey 90 D2
Merzig Germany 52 G5
Merz Peninsula Antarctica 152 L2
Mesa AZ U.S.A. 129 H5
Mesa NM U.S.A. 127 G6
Mesabi Range hills U.S.A. 130 E2
Mesagne Italy 58 G4
Mesa Negra mt. U.S.A. 129 J4
Mesara, Ormos b. Greece 59 K7
Mesa Verde National Park U.S.A. 129 I3
Meschede Germany 53 I3
Mese Myanmar 70 B3
Meselefors Sweden 44 J4
Mesgouez Lake Canada 122 G4
Meshed Iran see Mashhad
Meshkān Iran 88 E2
Meshra'er Req Sudan 86 C8
Mesick U.S.A. 134 C1
Mesimeri Greece 59 J4
Mesolongi Greece 59 I5
Mesolóngion Greece see Mesolongi
Mesopotamia reg. Iraq 91 F4
Mesquita Brazil 145 C2
Mesquite NV U.S.A. 129 F3
Mesquite TX U.S.A. 131 D5
Mesquite Lake U.S.A. 129 F4
Messaad Alg. 54 E5
Messana Sicily Italy see Messina
Messina Sicily Italy 58 F5
Messina S. Africa 101 J2
Messina, Strait of Italy 58 F5
Messina, Stretta di Italy see Messina, Strait of
Messini Greece 59 J6
Messiniakos Kolpos b. Greece 59 J6
Mesta r. Bulg. 59 K4
Mesta r. Greece see Nestos
Mestghanem Alg. see Mostaganem
Mestlin Germany 53 L1
Meston, Akra pt Greece 59 K5
Mestre Italy 58 E2
Mesudiye Turkey 90 E2
Meta r. Col./Venez. 142 E2
Métabetchouan Canada 123 H4
Meta Incognita Peninsula Canada 119 L3
Metairie U.S.A. 131 F6
Metallifere, Colline mts Italy 58 D3
Metán Arg. 144 C3
Meteghan Canada 123 I5
Meteor Depth sea feature S. Atlantic Ocean 148 G9
Methoni Greece 59 I6
Methuen U.S.A. 135 J2
Methven U.K. 50 F4
Metionga Lake Canada 122 C4
Metković Croatia 58 G3
Metlaoui Tunisia 54 F5
Metoro Moz. 99 D5
Metro Indon. 68 D8
Metropolis U.S.A. 131 F4
Metsada tourist site Israel see Masada
Metter U.S.A. 133 D5
Mettet Belgium 52 E4
Mettingen Germany 53 H2
Mettler U.S.A. 128 D4
Mettur India 84 C4
Metu Eth. 98 D3
Metz France 52 G5
Metz U.S.A. 134 C3
Meulaboh Indon. 71 B6
Meureudu Indon. 71 B6
Meuse r. Belgium/France 52 F3
also known as Maas (Netherlands)
Meuselwitz Germany 53 M3
Mevagissey U.K. 49 C8
Mêwa China 76 D1
Mexia U.S.A. 131 D6
Mexiana, Ilha i. Brazil 143 I3
Mexicali Mex. 129 F5
Mexican Hat U.S.A. 129 I3
Mexican Water U.S.A. 129 I3

▶Mexico country Central America 136 D4
2nd most populous and 3rd largest country in Central and North America.
North America 9, 116–117

México Mex. see Mexico City
Mexico ME U.S.A. 135 J1
Mexico MO U.S.A. 130 F4
Mexico NY U.S.A. 135 G2
Mexico, Gulf of Mex./U.S.A. 125 H6

▶Mexico City Mex. 136 E5
Capital of Mexico. Most populous city in North America and 2nd in the world.

Meybod Iran 88 D3
Meydanī, Ra's-e pt Iran 88 E5
Meydān Shahr Afgh. 89 H3
Meyenburg Germany 53 M1
Meyersdale U.S.A. 134 F4
Meymaneh Afgh. 89 G3
Meymeh Iran 88 C3
Meynypil'gyno Rus. Fed. 153 C2
Mezada tourist site Israel see Masada
Mezdra Bulg. 59 J3
Mezen' Rus. Fed. 42 J2
Mezen' r. Rus. Fed. 42 J2
Mézenc, Mont mt. France 56 G4
Mezenskaya Guba b. Rus. Fed. 42 I2
Mezhdurechensk Kemerovskaya Oblast' Rus. Fed. 72 F2
Mezhdurechensk Respublika Komi Rus. Fed. 42 K3
Mezhdurechnye Rus. Fed. see Shali
Mezhdusharskiy, Ostrov i. Rus. Fed. 64 G2
Mezitli Turkey 85 B1
Mezőtúr Hungary 59 I1
Mežvidi Latvia 45 O8
Mhàil, Rubh' a' pt U.K. 50 C5
Mhangura Zimbabwe 99 D5
Mhlume Swaziland 101 J4
Mhow India 82 C5
Mi r. Myanmar 83 H5
Miahuatlán Mex. 136 E5
Miajadas Spain 57 D4
Miamere Cent. Afr. Rep. 98 B3
Miami AZ U.S.A. 129 H5
Miami FL U.S.A. 133 D7
Miami OK U.S.A. 131 E4
Miami Beach U.S.A. 133 D7
Miancaowan China 76 C1
Mīāndehī Iran 88 E3
Miandowāb Iran 88 B2
Miandrivazo Madag. 99 E5
Mīāneh Iran 88 B2
Miang, Phu mt. Thai. 70 C3
Miani India 89 I4
Miani Hor b. Pak. 89 G5
Mianjoi Afgh. 89 G3
Mianning China 76 D2
Mianwali Pak. 89 H3
Mianxian China 76 E1
Mianyang Hubei China see Xiantao
Mianyang Shaanxi China see Mianxian
Mianyang Sichuan China 76 E2
Mianzhu China 76 E2
Miaoli Taiwan 77 I3
Miarinarivo Madag. 99 E5
Miarritze France see Biarritz
Miass Rus. Fed. 64 H4
Mica Creek Canada 120 G4
Mica Mountain U.S.A. 129 H5
Micang Shan mts China 76 E1
Michalovce Slovakia 43 D6

Moldoveanu, Vârful mt. Romania 59 K2
Moldovei de Sud, Cîmpia plain Moldova 59 M1
Molega Lake Canada 123 I5
Molen r. S. Africa 101 I4
Mole National Park Ghana 96 C4
Molepolole Botswana 101 G3
Molėtai Lith. 45 N9
Molfetta Italy 58 G4
Molière Alg. see Bordj Bounaama
Molihong Shan mt. China see Morihong Shan
Molina de Aragón Spain 57 F3
Moline U.S.A. 131 D4
Molkom Sweden 45 H7
Mollagara Turkm. see Mollakara
Mollakara Turkm. 88 D2
Mol Len mt. India 83 H4
Möllenbeck Germany 53 N1
Mollendo Peru 142 D7
Mölln Germany 53 K1
Mölnlycke Sweden 45 H8
Molochnyy Rus. Fed. 44 R2
Molodechno Belarus see Maladzyechna
Molodezhnaya research station Antarctica 152 D2
Molokai i. HI U.S.A. 127 [inset]
Moloma r. Rus. Fed. 42 K4
Molong Australia 112 D4
Molopo watercourse Botswana/S. Africa 100 E5
Molotov Rus. Fed. see Perm'
Molotovsk Kyrg. see Kayyngdy
Molotovsk Arkhangel'skaya Oblast' Rus. Fed. see Severodvinsk
Molotovsk Kirovskaya Oblast' Rus. Fed. see Nolinsk
Moloundou Cameroon 97 E4
Molson Lake Canada 121 L4
Molu i. Indon. 69 I8
Moluccas is Indon. 69 H7
Molucca Sea sea Indon. see Maluku, Laut
Moma Moz. 99 D5
Momba Australia 112 A3
Mombaça Brazil 143 K5
Mombasa Kenya 98 D4
Mombetsu Hokkaidō Japan see Monbetsu
Mombetsu Hokkaidō Japan see Monbetsu
Mombi New India 83 H4
Mombum Indon. 69 J8
Momchilgrad Bulg. 59 K4
Momence U.S.A. 134 B3
Momi, Ra's pt Yemen 87 H7
Mompós Col. 142 D2
Møn i. Denmark 45 H9
Mon India 83 H4
Mona terr. Irish Sea see Isle of Man
Mona U.S.A. 129 H2
Monaca U.S.A. 134 E3
Monach, Sound of sea chan. U.K. 50 B3
Monach Islands U.K. 50 B3
▶Monaco country Europe 56 H5
Europe 5, 38–39
Monaco Basin sea feature N. Atlantic Ocean 148 G4
Monadhliath Mountains U.K. 50 E3
Monaghan Rep. of Ireland 51 F3
Monahans U.S.A. 131 C6
Mona Passage Dom. Rep./Puerto Rico 137 K5
Monapo Moz. 99 E5
Monar, Loch l. U.K. 50 D3
Monarch Mountain Canada 120 E5
Monarch Pass U.S.A. 127 G5
Mona Reservoir U.S.A. 129 H2
Monashee Mountains Canada 120 G5
Monastir Macedonia see Bitola
Monastir Tunisia 58 D7
Monastyrishche Ukr. see Monastyryshche
Monastyryshche Ukr. 43 F6
Monbetsu Hokkaidō Japan 74 F3
Monbetsu Hokkaidō Japan 74 F4
Moncalieri Italy 58 B2
Monchegorsk Rus. Fed. 44 R3
Mönchengladbach Germany 52 G3
Monchique Port. 57 B5
Moncks Corner U.S.A. 133 D5
Monclova Mex. 131 C7
Moncouche, Lac l. Canada 123 H4
Moncton Canada 123 I5
Mondego r. Port. 57 B3
Mondlo S. Africa 101 J4
Mondo Chad 97 E3
Mondovì Italy 58 B2
Mondragone Italy 58 E4
Mondy Rus. Fed. 72 I2
Monemvasia Greece 59 J6
Monessen U.S.A. 134 F3
Moneta U.S.A. 126 G4
Moneygall Rep. of Ireland 51 E5
Moneymore U.K. 51 F3
Monfalcone Italy 58 E2
Monfalut Egypt see Manfalūṭ
Monforte Spain 57 C2
Monga Dem. Rep. Congo 98 C3
Mongala r. Dem. Rep. Congo 98 B3
Mongar Bhutan 83 G4
Mongbwalu Dem. Rep. Congo 98 D3
Mông Cai Vietnam 70 D2
Mongers Lake salt flat Australia 109 B7
Mong Hang Myanmar 70 B2
Mong Hkan Myanmar 70 C2
Mong Hpayak Myanmar 70 B2
Mong Hsat Myanmar 70 B2
Mong Hsawk Myanmar 70 B2
Mong Hsu Myanmar 70 B2
Monghyr India see Munger
Mong Kung Myanmar 70 B2
Mong Kyawt Myanmar 70 B3
Mongla Bangl. 83 G5
Mong Lin Myanmar 70 C2
Mong Loi Myanmar 70 C2
Mong Long Myanmar 70 B2
Mong Nai Myanmar 70 B2
Mong Nawng Myanmar 70 B2
Mongo Chad 97 E3
▶Mongolia country Asia 72 I3
Asia 6, 62–63
Mongol Uls country Asia see Mongolia
Mongonu Nigeria 96 E3
Mongora Pak. 89 I3
Mongour hill U.K. 50 G4
Mong Pan Myanmar 70 B2
Mong Ping Myanmar 70 B2
Mong Pu Myanmar 70 B2
Mong Pu-awn Myanmar 70 B2
Mong Si Myanmar 70 B2
Mongu Zambia 99 C5
Mong Un Myanmar 70 C2
Mong Yai Myanmar 70 B2
Mong Yang Myanmar 70 B2
Mong Yawn Myanmar 70 B2
Mong Yawng Myanmar 70 C2
Mönh Hayrhan Uul mt. Mongolia 80 H2
Moniaive U.K. 50 F5
Monitor Mountain U.S.A. 128 E2
Monitor Range mts U.S.A. 128 E2
Monivea Rep. of Ireland 51 D4
Monkey Bay Malawi 99 D5
Monkira Australia 110 C5
Monkton Canada 134 E2
Monmouth U.K. 49 E7
Monmouth U.S.A. 130 F3
Monmouth Mountain Canada 120 F5
Monnow r. U.K. 49 E7
Mono, Punta del pt Nicaragua 137 H6
Mono Lake U.S.A. 128 D2
Monolithos Greece 59 L6
Monomoy Point U.S.A. 135 J3
Monon U.S.A. 134 B3
Monopoli Italy 58 G4
Monreal del Campo Spain 57 F3
Monreale Sicily Italy 58 E5
Monroe IN U.S.A. 134 C3
Monroe LA U.S.A. 131 E5
Monroe MI U.S.A. 134 D3
Monroe NC U.S.A. 133 D5
Monroe WI U.S.A. 130 F3
Monroe Center U.S.A. 130 F2
Monroe Lake U.S.A. 134 B4
Monroeton U.S.A. 135 G3
▶Monrovia Liberia 96 B4
Capital of Liberia.
Mons Belgium 52 D4
Monschau Germany 52 G4
Monselice Italy 58 D2
Montabaur Germany 53 H4
Montagu S. Africa 100 E7
Montague Canada 123 J5
Montague MI U.S.A. 134 B2
Montague TX U.S.A. 131 D5
Montague Range hills Australia 109 B6
Montalto mt. Italy 58 F5
Montalto Uffugo Italy 58 G5
Montana Bulg. 59 J3
Montana state U.S.A. 126 F3
Montargis France 56 F3
Montauban France 56 E4
Montauk U.S.A. 135 J3
Montauk Point U.S.A. 135 J3
Mont-aux-Sources mt. Lesotho 101 I5
Montbard France 56 G3
Montblanc Spain 57 G3
Montblanch Spain see Montblanc
Montbrison France 56 G4
Montceau-les-Mines France 56 G3
Montcornet France 52 E5
Mont-de-Marsan France 56 D5
Montdidier France 52 C5
Monte Alegre Brazil 143 H4
Monte Alegre de Goiás Brazil 145 B1
Monte Alegre de Minas Brazil 145 A2
Monte Azul Brazil 145 C1
Monte Azul Paulista Brazil 145 A3
Montebello Canada 122 G5
Montebello Islands Australia 104 A5
Montebelluna Italy 58 E2
Monte-Carlo Monaco 56 H5
Monte Christo S. Africa 101 H2
Monte Cristi Dom. Rep. 137 J5
Monte Dourado Brazil 143 H4
Monte Falterona, Campigna e delle Foreste Casentinesi, Parco Nazionale del nat. park Italy 58 D3
Montego Bay Jamaica 137 I5
Montélimar France 56 G4
Monte Lindo r. Para. 144 E2
Montello U.S.A. 130 F3
Montemorelos Mex. 131 D7
Montemor-o-Novo Port. 57 B4
Montenegro aut. rep. Serb. and Mont. see Crna Gora
Montepulciano Italy 58 D3
Monte Quemado Arg. 144 D3
Montereau-faut-Yonne France 56 F2
Monterey Mex. see Monterrey
Monterey CA U.S.A. 128 C3
Monterey VA U.S.A. 134 F4
Monterey Bay U.S.A. 128 B3
Montería Col. 142 C2
Monteros Arg. 144 C3
Monterrey Baja California Mex. 129 F5
Monterrey Nuevo León Mex. 131 C7
Montervary hd Rep. of Ireland 51 C6
Montesano U.S.A. 126 C3
Montesano sulla Marcellana Italy 58 F4
Monte Santo Brazil 143 K6
Monte Santu, Capo di c. Sardinia Italy 58 C4
Montes Claros Brazil 145 C2
Montesilvano Italy 58 F3
Montevarchi Italy 58 D3
▶Montevideo Uruguay 144 E4
Capital of Uruguay.
Montevideo U.S.A. 130 E2
Montezuma U.S.A. 130 E3
Montezuma Creek U.S.A. 129 I3
Montezuma Peak U.S.A. 128 E3
Montfort Neth. 52 F3
Montgomery U.K. 49 D6
▶Montgomery AL U.S.A. 133 C5
State capital of Alabama.
Montgomery WV U.S.A. 134 E4
Montgomery Islands Australia 108 C3
Monthey Switz. 56 H3
Monticello AR U.S.A. 131 F5
Monticello FL U.S.A. 133 D6
Monticello IN U.S.A. 134 B3
Monticello KY U.S.A. 134 C5
Monticello MO U.S.A. 130 F3
Monticello NY U.S.A. 135 H3
Monticello UT U.S.A. 129 I3
Montignac France 56 E4
Montignies-le-Tilleul Belgium 52 E4
Montigny-lès-Metz France 52 G5
Montilla Spain 57 D5
Monti Sibillini, Parco Nazionale dei nat. park Italy 58 E3
Montividiu Brazil 145 A2
Montivilliers France 49 H9
Mont-Joli Canada 123 H4
Mont-Laurier Canada 122 G5
Montluçon France 56 F3
Montmagny Canada 123 H5
Montmédy France 52 F5
Montmirail France 52 D6
Montmorillon France 56 E3
Montmort-Lucy France 52 D6
Monto Australia 110 E5
Montour Falls U.S.A. 135 G2
Montoursville U.S.A. 135 G3
Montpelier ID U.S.A. 126 F4
▶Montpelier VT U.S.A. 135 I1
State capital of Vermont.
Montpellier France 56 F5
Montréal Canada 122 G5
Montreal r. Ont. Canada 122 D5
Montreal r. Ont. Canada 122 F5
Montreal Lake Canada 121 J4
Montreal Lake l. Canada 121 J4
Montreal River Canada 122 D5
Montreuil France 52 B4
Montreux Switz. 56 H3
Montrose well S. Africa 100 E4
Montrose U.K. 50 G4
Montrose CO U.S.A. 129 J2
Montrose PA U.S.A. 135 H3
Montross U.S.A. 135 G4
Monts, Pointe des pt Canada 123 I4
▶Montserrat terr. West Indies 137 L5
United Kingdom Overseas Territory.
North America 9, 116–117
Mont-St-Aignan France 49 I9
Montviel, Lac l. Canada 123 H3
Monument Valley reg. U.S.A. 129 H3
Monywa Myanmar 70 A2
Monza Italy 58 C2
Monze, Cape pt Pak. see Muari, Ras
Monzón Spain 57 G3
Mooi r. S. Africa 101 J5
Mooifontein Namibia 100 C4
Mookane Botswana 101 H2
Mookgopong S. Africa see Naboomspruit
Moolawatana Australia 111 B6
Moomba Australia 111 C6
Moomin Creek r. Australia 112 D2
Moonaree Australia 111 A6
Moonbi Range mts Australia 112 E3
Moonda Lake salt flat Australia 111 C5
Moonie Australia 112 E1
Moonie r. Australia 112 D2
Moora Australia 109 B7
Mooraberree Australia 110 C5
Moorcroft U.S.A. 126 G3
Moore r. Australia 109 A7
Moore U.S.A. 126 F3
Moore, Lake salt flat Australia 109 B7
Moore Embayment b. Antarctica 152 H1
Moorefield U.S.A. 135 F4
Moore Haven U.S.A. 133 D7
Moore Reef Australia 110 E3
Moore Reservoir U.S.A. 135 J1
Moore River National Park Australia 109 A7
Moores Island Bahamas 133 E7
Moorfoot Hills U.K. 50 F5
Moorhead U.S.A. 130 D2
Moorman U.S.A. 134 B5
Moornanyah Lake imp. l. Australia 112 A4
Mooroopna Australia 112 B6
Moorreesburg S. Africa 100 D7
Moorrinya National Park Australia 110 D4
Moose r. Canada 122 E4
Moose Factory Canada 122 E4
Moosehead Lake U.S.A. 132 G2
Moose Jaw Canada 121 J5
Moose Jaw r. Canada 121 J5
Moose Lake U.S.A. 130 E2
Mooselookmeguntic Lake U.S.A. 135 J1
Moose Mountain Creek r. Canada 121 K5
Moosilauke, Mount U.S.A. 135 J1
Moosomin Canada 121 K5
Moosonee Canada 122 E4
Mootwingee National Park Australia 111 C6
Mopane S. Africa 101 I2
Mopeia Moz. 99 D5
Mopipi Botswana 99 C6
Mopti Mali 96 C3
Moqor Afgh. 89 G3
Moquegua Peru 142 D7
Mora Cameroon 97 E3
Mora Spain 57 E4
Mora Sweden 45 I6
Mora MN U.S.A. 130 E2
Mora NM U.S.A. 127 G6
Mora r. U.S.A. 127 G6
Moradabad India 82 D3
Morada Nova Brazil 143 K5
Moraine Lake Canada 121 J1
Moraleda, Canal sea chan. Chile 144 B6
Moram India 84 C2
Moramanga Madag. 99 E5
Moran U.S.A. 126 F4
Moranbah Australia 110 E4
Morang Nepal see Biratnagar
Morar, Loch l. U.K. 50 D4
Morari, Tso l. Jammu and Kashmir 82 D2
Moratuwa Sri Lanka 84 C5
Morava reg. Czech Rep. 47 P5
Moravia U.S.A. 135 G2
Morawa Australia 109 A7
Moray Firth b. U.K. 50 E3
Moray Range hills Australia 108 E3
Morbach Germany 52 H5
Morbeng S. Africa see Soekmekaar
Morbi India 82 B5
Morcenx France 56 D4
Morcillo Mex. 131 B7
Mordaga China 73 M2
Mor Dağı mt. Turkey 91 G3
Morden Canada 121 L5
Mordovo Rus. Fed. 43 I5
Moreau r. U.S.A. 130 C2
Moreau, South Fork r. U.S.A. 130 C2
Morecambe U.K. 48 E4
Morecambe Bay U.K. 48 D4
Moree Australia 112 D2
Morehead P.N.G. 69 K8
Morehead U.S.A. 134 D4
Morehead City U.S.A. 137 I2
Moreland U.S.A. 134 C5
More Laptevykh sea Rus. Fed. see Laptev Sea
Morelia Mex. 136 D5
Morella Australia 110 C4
Morella Spain 57 F3
Morelos Mex. 127 G8
Morena India 82 D4
Morena, Sierra mts Spain 57 C5
Morenci AZ U.S.A. 129 I5
Morenci MI U.S.A. 134 C3
Moreni Romania 59 K2
Moreno Mex. 127 F7
Moreno Valley U.S.A. 128 E5
Moresby, Mount Canada 120 C4
Moresby Island Canada 120 C4
Moreswe Pan salt pan Botswana 100 G2
Moreton Bay Australia 112 F1
Moreton-in-Marsh U.K. 49 F7
Moreton Island Australia 112 F1
Moreton Island National Park Australia 112 F1
Moreuil France 52 C5
Morez France 56 H3
Morfou Cyprus 85 A2
Morfou Bay Cyprus 85 A2
Morgan U.S.A. 126 F4
Morgan City U.S.A. 131 F6
Morgan Hill U.S.A. 128 C3
Morganton U.S.A. 132 D5
Morgantown KY U.S.A. 134 B5
Morgantown WV U.S.A. 134 F4
Morgenzon S. Africa 101 I4
Morges Switz. 56 H3
Morhar r. India 83 F4
Mori China 80 H3
Mori Japan 74 F4
Moriah, Mount U.S.A. 129 F2
Moriarty's Range hills Australia 112 B2
Morice Lake Canada 120 E4
Morichal Col. 142 D3
Morihong Shan mt. China 74 B4
Morija Lesotho 101 H5
Morin Dawa China see Nirji
Moringen Germany 53 J3
Morioka Japan 75 F5
Moris Mex. 127 F7
Morisset Australia 112 E4
Moriyoshi-zan vol. Japan 75 F5
Morjärv Sweden 44 M3
Morjen r. Pak. 89 F4
Morki Rus. Fed. 42 K4
Morlaix France 56 C2
Morley U.K. 48 F5
Mormam Flat Dam U.S.A. 129 H5
Mormant France 52 C6
Mormon Lake U.S.A. 129 H4
Mormugao India see Marmagao
Morne Diablotins vol. Dominica 137 L5
Morney watercourse Australia 110 C5
Mornington, Isla i. Chile 144 A7
Mornington Abyssal Plain sea feature S. Atlantic Ocean 148 C9
Mornington Island Australia 110 B3
Mornington Peninsula National Park Australia 112 B7
Moro Pak. 89 G5
Moro U.S.A. 126 C3
Morobe P.N.G. 69 L8
▶Morocco country Africa 96 C1
Africa 7, 94–95
Morocco U.S.A. 134 B3
Morococala mt. Bol. 142 E7
Morogoro Tanz. 99 D4
Moro Gulf Phil. 69 G5
Morojaneng S. Africa 101 H5
Morokweng S. Africa 100 F4
Morombe Madag. 99 E6
Morón Cuba 133 E8
Mörön Mongolia 80 J2
Morondava Madag. 99 E6
Morón de la Frontera Spain 57 D5
▶Moroni Comoros 99 E5
Capital of the Comoros.
Moroni U.S.A. 129 H2
Moron Us He r. China see Tongtian He
Morotai i. Indon. 69 H6
Moroto Uganda 98 D3
Morozovsk Rus. Fed. 43 I6
Morpeth Canada 134 E2
Morpeth U.K. 48 F3
Morphou Cyprus see Morfou
Morrill U.S.A. 134 C5
Morrilton U.S.A. 131 E5
Morrin Canada 121 H5
Morrinhos Brazil 145 A2
Morris Canada 121 L5
Morris IL U.S.A. 130 F3
Morris MN U.S.A. 130 E2
Morris PA U.S.A. 135 G3
▶Morris Jesup, Kap c. Greenland 153 I1
Most northerly point of North America.
Morrison U.S.A. 130 F3
Morristown AZ U.S.A. 129 G5
Morristown NJ U.S.A. 135 H3
Morristown NY U.S.A. 135 H1
Morristown TN U.S.A. 132 D4
Morrisville U.S.A. 135 H2
Morro Brazil 145 B2
Morro Bay U.S.A. 128 C4
Morro d'Anta Brazil 145 D2
Morro do Chapéu Brazil 143 J5
Morro Grande hill Brazil 143 H4
Morrosquillo, Golfo de b. Col. 142 C2
Morrumbene Moz. 101 L2
Morschen Germany 53 J3
Morse Canada 121 J5
Morse U.S.A. 131 C4
Morse, Cape Antarctica 152 G2
Morse Reservoir U.S.A. 134 B3
Morshanka Rus. Fed. 43 I5
Morshansk Rus. Fed. see Morshanka
Morsott Alg. 58 C7
Mort watercourse Australia 110 C4
Mortagne-au-Perche France 56 E2
Mortagne-sur-Sèvre France 56 D3
Mortara Italy 58 C2
Mortehoe U.K. 49 C7
Morteros Arg. 144 D4
Mortes, Rio das r. Brazil 145 A1
Mortimer's Bahamas 133 F8
Mortlake Australia 112 A7
Mortlock Islands Micronesia 150 G5
Mortlock Islands P.N.G. see Tauu Islands
Morton U.K. 49 G6
Morton TX U.S.A. 131 C5
Morton WA U.S.A. 126 C3
Morton National Park Australia 112 E5
Morundah Australia 112 C5
Morupule Botswana 101 H2
Moruroa atoll Fr. Polynesia see Mururoa
Moruya Australia 112 E5
Morven Australia 111 D5
Morven hill U.K. 50 F2
Morvern reg. U.K. 50 D4
Morvi India see Morbi
Morwara India 82 B4
Morwell Australia 112 C7
Morzhovets, Ostrov i. Rus. Fed. 42 I2
Mosbach Germany 53 J5
Mosborough U.K. 48 F5
Mosby U.S.A. 126 G3
▶Moscow Rus. Fed. 42 H5
Capital of the Russian Federation and 3rd most populous city in Europe.
Moscow ID U.S.A. 126 D3
Moscow PA U.S.A. 135 H3
Moscow University Ice Shelf Antarctica 152 G2
Mosel r. Germany 53 H4
Moselebe watercourse Botswana 100 F3
Moselle r. France 52 G5
Möser Germany 53 L2
Moses, Mount U.S.A. 128 E1
Moses Lake U.S.A. 126 D3
Mosgiel N.Z. 113 C7
Moshaweng watercourse S. Africa 100 F4
Moshchnyy, Ostrov i. Rus. Fed. 45 O7
Moshi Tanz. 98 D4
Mosh'yuga Rus. Fed. 42 L2
Mosi-oa-Tunya waterfall Zambia/Zimbabwe see Victoria Falls
Mosjøen Norway 44 H4
Moskal'vo Rus. Fed. 74 F1
Moskenesøy i. Norway 44 H3
Moskva Rus. Fed. see Moscow
Moskva Tajik. 89 H2
Mosonmagyaróvár Hungary 47 P7
Mosquera Col. 142 C3
Mosquero U.S.A. 127 G6
Mosquito r. Brazil 145 C1
Mosquito Creek Lake U.S.A. 134 E3
Mosquito Lake Canada 121 K2
Moss Norway 45 G7
Mossâmedes Angola see Namibe
Mossat U.K. 50 G3
Mossburn N.Z. 113 B7
Mosselbaai S. Africa see Mossel Bay
Mossel Bay S. Africa 100 F8
Mossel Bay b. S. Africa 100 F8
Mossgiel Australia 112 B4
Mossman Australia 110 D3
Mossoró Brazil 143 K5
Moss Vale Australia 112 E5
Mossy r. Canada 121 K4
Most Czech Rep. 47 N5
Mostaganem Alg. 57 G6
Mostar Bos.-Herz. 58 G3
Mostoos Hills Canada 121 I4
Mostovskoy Rus. Fed. 91 F1
Mosty Belarus see Masty
Mosul Iraq 91 F3
Møsvatnet l. Norway 45 F7
Motala Sweden 45 I7
Motaze Moz. 101 K3
Motetema S. Africa 101 I3
Moth India 82 D4
Motherwell U.K. 50 F5
Motian Ling hill China 74 A4
Motihari India 83 F4
Motilla del Palancar Spain 57 F4
Motiti Island N.Z. 113 F3
Motokwe Botswana 100 F3
Motril Spain 57 E5
Motru Romania 59 J2
Mott U.S.A. 130 C2
Motu Ihupuku i. N.Z. see Campbell Island
Motul Mex. 136 G4
Mouaskar Alg. see Mascara
Mouding China 76 D3
Moudjéria Mauritania 96 B3
Moudros Greece 59 K5
Mouhijärvi Fin. 45 M6
Mouila Gabon 98 B4
Moulamein Australia 112 B5
Moulamein Creek r. Australia 112 A5
Moulavibazar Bangl. see Moulvibazar
Mould Bay Canada 118 G2
Moulèngui Binza Gabon 98 B4
Moulins France 56 F3
Moulmein Myanmar 70 B3
Moulouya, Oued r. Morocco 54 D4
Moultrie U.S.A. 133 D6
Moultrie, Lake U.S.A. 133 E5
Moulvibazar Bangl. 83 G4
Mound City KS U.S.A. 130 E4
Mound City SD U.S.A. 130 C2
Moundou Chad 97 E4
Moundsville U.S.A. 134 E4
Moŭng Roessei Cambodia 71 C4
Mount Abu India 82 C4
Mountain r. Canada 120 D1
Mountainair U.S.A. 127 G6
Mountain Brook U.S.A. 133 C5
Mountain City U.S.A. 134 E5
Mountain Home AR U.S.A. 131 E4
Mountain Home ID U.S.A. 126 E4
Mountain Home UT U.S.A. 129 H1
Mountain Lake Park U.S.A. 134 F4
Mountain View U.S.A. 131 E5
Mountain Zebra National Park S. Africa 101 G7
Mount Airy U.S.A. 134 E5
Mount Aspiring National Park N.Z. 113 B7
Mount Assiniboine Provincial Park Canada 120 H5
Mount Ayliff S. Africa 101 I6
Mount Ayr U.S.A. 130 E3
Mount Bellew Rep. of Ireland 51 D4
Mount Buffalo National Park Australia 112 C6
Mount Carmel U.S.A. 134 B4
Mount Carmel Junction U.S.A. 129 G3
Mount Cook National Park N.Z. 113 C6
Mount Coolon Australia 110 D4
Mount Darwin Zimbabwe 99 D5
Mount Denison Australia 108 F5
Mount Desert Island U.S.A. 132 G2
Mount Dutton Australia 111 A5
Mount Eba Australia 111 A6
Mount Elgon National Park Uganda 98 D3
Mount Fletcher S. Africa 101 I6
Mount Forest Canada 134 E2
Mount Frankland National Park Australia 109 B8
Mount Frere S. Africa 101 I6
Mount Gambier Australia 111 C8
Mount Gilead U.S.A. 134 D3
Mount Hagen P.N.G. 69 K8
Mount Holly U.S.A. 135 H4
Mount Hope Australia 112 B4
Mount Hope U.S.A. 134 E5
Mount Howitt Australia 111 C5
Mount Isa Australia 110 B4
Mount Jackson U.S.A. 135 F4
Mount Jewett U.S.A. 135 F3
Mount Joy U.S.A. 135 G3
Mount Kaputar National Park Australia 112 E3
Mount Keith Australia 109 C6
Mount Lofty Range mts Australia 111 B7
Mount Magnet Australia 109 B7
Mount Manara Australia 112 A4
Mount McKinley National Park U.S.A. see Denali National Park and Preserve
Mount Meadows Reservoir U.S.A. 128 C1
Mountmellick Rep. of Ireland 51 E4
Mount Moorosi Lesotho 101 H6
Mount Morgan Australia 110 E4
Mount Morris MI U.S.A. 134 D2
Mount Morris NY U.S.A. 135 G2
Mount Murchison Australia 112 A3
Mount Nebo U.S.A. 134 E4
Mount Olivet U.S.A. 134 C4
Mount Pearl Canada 123 L5
Mount Pleasant Canada 123 I5
Mount Pleasant IA U.S.A. 130 F3
Mount Pleasant MI U.S.A. 134 C2
Mount Pleasant TX U.S.A. 131 E5
Mount Pleasant UT U.S.A. 129 H2
Mount Rainier National Park U.S.A. 126 C3
Mount Remarkable National Park Australia 111 B7
Mount Revelstoke National Park Canada 120 G5
Mount Robson Provincial Park Canada 120 G4
Mount Rogers National Recreation Area park U.S.A. 134 E5
Mount Sanford Australia 108 E4
Mount's Bay U.K. 49 B8
Mount Shasta U.S.A. 126 C4
Mountsorrel U.K. 49 F6
Mount Sterling U.S.A. 134 D4
Mount St Helens National Volcanic Monument nat. park U.S.A. 126 C3
Mount Swan Australia 110 A4
Mount Union U.S.A. 135 G3
Mount Vernon Australia 109 B6
Mount Vernon IL U.S.A. 130 F4
Mount Vernon IN U.S.A. 132 C4
Mount Vernon KY U.S.A. 134 C5
Mount Vernon MO U.S.A. 131 E4
Mount Vernon OH U.S.A. 134 D3
Mount Vernon TX U.S.A. 131 E5
Mount Vernon WA U.S.A. 126 C2
Mount William National Park Australia 111 [inset]
Mount Willoughby Australia 109 F6
Moura Australia 110 E5
Moura Brazil 142 F4
Moura Port. 57 C4
Mourdi, Dépression du depr. Chad 97 F3
Mourdiah Mali 96 C3
Mourne r. U.K. 51 E3
Mourne Mountains hills U.K. 51 F3
Mousa i. U.K. 50 [inset]
Mouscron Belgium 52 D4
Mousgougou Chad 98 B2
Moussafoyo Chad 97 E4
Moussoro Chad 97 E3
Moutamba Congo 98 B4
Mouth of the Yangtze China 77 I2
Moutong Indon. 69 G6
Mouy France 52 C5
Mouydir, Monts du plat. Alg. 96 D2
Mouzon France 52 F5
Movas Mex. 127 F7
Mowbullan, Mount Australia 112 E1
Moxey Town Bahamas 133 E7
Moy r. Rep. of Ireland 51 C3
Moyale Eth. 98 D3
Moyen Atlas mts Morocco 54 C5
Moyen Congo country Africa see Congo
Moyeni Lesotho 101 H6
Moynalyk Rus. Fed. 80 I1
Moynaq Uzbek. see Muynak
Moyo i. Indon. 108 B2
Moyobamba Peru 142 C5
Moyock U.S.A. 135 G5

Moyola r. U.K. 51 F3
Moyu China 82 D1
Moyynkum Kazakh. 80 D3
Moyynkum, Peski des. Kazakh. 80 C3
Moyynty Kazakh. 80 D2
▶Mozambique country Africa 99 D6
Africa 7, 94–95
Mozambique Channel Africa 99 E6
Mozambique Ridge sea feature Indian Ocean 149 K7
Mozdok Rus. Fed. 91 G2
Mozdūrān Iran 89 F2
Mozhaysk Rus. Fed. 43 H5
Mozhga Rus. Fed. 42 L4
Mozhnābād Iran 89 F3
Mozo Myanmar 76 B4
Mozyr' Belarus see Mazyr
Mpaathutlwa Pan salt pan Botswana 100 E3
Mpanda Tanz. 99 D4
Mpen India 83 I4
Mpika Zambia 99 D5
Mpolweni S. Africa 101 J5
Mporokoso Zambia 99 D4
Mpulungu Zambia 99 D4
Mpumalanga prov. S. Africa 101 I4
Mpunde mt. Tanz. 99 D4
Mpwapwa Tanz. 99 D4
Mqanduli S. Africa 101 I6
Mqinvartsveri mt. Georgia/Rus. Fed. see Kazbek
Mrewa Zimbabwe see Murehwa
Mrkonjić-Grad Bos.-Herz. 58 G2
M'Saken Tunisia 58 D7
Mshinskaya Rus. Fed. 45 P7
M'Sila Alg. 57 I6
Msta r. Rus. Fed. 42 F4
Mstislavl' Belarus see Mstsislaw
Mstsislaw Belarus 43 F5
Mtelo Kenya 98 D3
Mtoko Zimbabwe see Mutoko
Mtorwi Tanz. 99 D4
Mtsensk Rus. Fed. 43 H5
Mts'ire Kavkasioni Asia see Lesser Caucasus
Mtubatuba S. Africa 101 K5
Mtunzini S. Africa 101 J5
Mtwara Tanz. 99 E5
Mu r. Myanmar 70 A2
Mu'āb, Jibāl reg. Jordan see Moab
Muanda Dem. Rep. Congo 99 B4
Muang Ham Laos 70 D2
Muang Hiam Laos 70 C2
Muang Hinboun Laos 70 D3
Muang Hôngsa Laos 70 C3
Muang Khammouan Laos 70 D3
Muang Khi Laos 70 C3
Muang Không Laos 71 D4
Muang Khoua Laos 70 C2
Muang Lamam Laos see Ban Phon
Muang Mok Laos 70 D3
Muang Ngoy Laos 70 C2
Muang Ou Nua Laos 70 C2
Muang Pakbeng Laos 70 C3
Muang Paktha Laos 70 C2
Muang Pakxan Laos see Muang Xaignabouri
Muang Phalan Laos 68 D3
Muang Phin Laos 70 D3
Muang Phôn-Hông Laos 70 C3
Muang Sam Sip Thai. 70 D4
Muang Sing Laos 70 C2
Muang Soum Laos 70 C3
Muang Souy Laos 70 C3
Muang Thadua Laos 70 C3
Muang Thai country Asia see Thailand
Muang Va Laos 70 C2
Muang Vangviang Laos 70 C3
Muang Xaignabouri Laos 70 C3
Muang Xaignabouri Laos 70 C3
Muang Xay Laos 70 C2
Muang Xon Laos 70 C2
Muar Malaysia 71 C7
Muarabungo Indon. 68 C7
Muarateweh Indon. 68 E7
Muari, Ras pt Pak. 89 G5
Mu'ayqil, Khashm al hill Saudi Arabia 88 C5
Mubarek Uzbek. 89 G2
Mubarraz well Saudi Arabia 91 F5
Mubende Uganda 98 D3
Mubi Nigeria 96 E3
Muborak Uzbek. see Mubarek
Mubur i. Indon. 71 D7
Mucajaí, Serra do mts Brazil 138 F3
Mucalic r. Canada 123 I2
Muccan Australia 108 C5
Much Germany 53 H4
Muchinga Escarpment Zambia 99 D5
Muchuan China 76 D2
Muck i. U.K. 50 C4
Mucojo Moz. 99 E5
Muconda Angola 99 C5
Mucubela Moz. 99 D5
Mucugê Brazil 145 C1
Mucur Turkey 90 D3
Mucuri Brazil 145 D2
Mucuri r. Brazil 145 D2
Mudabidri India 84 B3
Mudan China see Heze
Mudanjiang China 74 C3
Mudan Jiang r. China 74 C3
Mudan Ling mts China 74 B4
Mudanya Turkey 59 M4
Mudaybī Oman 88 E6
Mudaysīsāt, Jabal al hill Jordan 85 C4
Muddus nationalpark nat. park Sweden 44 K3
Muddy r. U.S.A. 129 F3
Muddy Gap Pass U.S.A. 126 G4
Muddy Peak U.S.A. 129 F3
Mūd-e Dahanāb Iran 88 E3
Mudersbach Germany 53 H4
Mudgal India 84 C3
Mudgee Australia 112 D4
Mudhol India 84 B2
Mudigere India 84 B3
Mudjatik r. Canada 121 J3
Mud Lake U.S.A. 128 E3
Mudraya country Africa see Egypt
Mudurnu Turkey 59 N4
Mud'yuga Rus. Fed. 42 H3
Mueda Moz. 99 D5
Mueller Range hills Australia 108 D4
Muertos Cays is Bahamas 133 D7
Muftyuga Rus. Fed. 42 J2
Mufulira Zambia 99 C5
Mufumbwe Zambia 99 C5
Mufu Shan mts China 77 G2
Muğan Düzü lowland Azer. 91 H3
Mugarripug China 83 F2
Mughalbhin Pak. see Jati
Mughal Kot Pak. 89 H4
Mughal Sarai India 83 E4
Mūghār Iran 88 D3
Mughayrā' Saudi Arabia 85 C5
Mughayrā' well Saudi Arabia 88 B5
Muğla Turkey 59 M6
Mugodzhary, Gory mts Kazakh. 80 A2
Mugxung China 76 B1
Mūḩ, Sabkhat imp. l. Syria 85 D2
Muhammad Ashraf Pak. 89 H5
Muhammad Qol Sudan 86 E5
Muhammarah Iran see Khorramshahr
Muhashsham, Wādī al watercourse Egypt 85 B4
Muḩaysh, Wādī al watercourse Jordan 85 C5
Muhaysin Syria 85 D1
Mühlanger Germany 53 M3
Mühlberg Germany 53 N3
Mühlhausen (Thüringen) Germany 53 K3
Mühlig-Hofmann Mountains Antarctica 152 C2
Muhos Fin. 44 N4
Muḩradah Syria 85 C2
Muhri Pak. 89 G4
Mui Bai Bung c. Vietnam see Mui Ca Mau
Mui Ba Lang An pt Vietnam 70 E4
Mui Ca Mau c. Vietnam 71 D5
Mui Dinh hd Vietnam 71 E5
Mui Đôc pt Vietnam 70 D3
Muié Angola 99 C5
Mui Kê pt Vietnam 71 E5
Mui Nây pt Vietnam 71 E4
Muineachán Rep. of Ireland see Monaghan
Muine Bheag Rep. of Ireland 51 F5
Muir U.S.A. 134 C2
Muirkirk U.K. 50 E5
Muir of Ord U.K. 50 E3
Mui Ron hd Vietnam 70 D3
Muite Moz. 99 D5
Muji China 82 D1
Muju S. Korea 75 B5
Mukacheve Ukr. 43 D6
Mukachevo Ukr. see Mukacheve
Mukah Sarawak Malaysia 68 E6
Mukalla Yemen 86 G7
Mukandwara India 82 D4
Mukdahan Thai. 70 D3
Mukden China see Shenyang
Muketei r. Canada 122 D3
Mukhen Rus. Fed. 74 E2
Mukhino Rus. Fed. 74 B1
Mukhtuya Rus. Fed. see Lensk
Mukinbudin Australia 109 B7
Mu Ko Chang Marine National Park Thai. 71 C5
Mukojima-rettō is Japan 75 F8
Mukry Turkm. 89 G2
Muktsar India 82 C3
Mukutawa r. Canada 121 L4
Mukwonago U.S.A. 134 A2
Mula r. India 84 B2
Mulakatholhu atoll Maldives see Mulaku Atoll
Mulaku Atoll Maldives 81 D11
Mulan China 74 C3
Mulanje, Mount Malawi 99 D5
Mulapula, Lake salt flat Australia 111 B6
Mulatos Mex. 127 F7
Mulayḩ Saudi Arabia 88 B5
Mulayḩah, Jabal hill U.A.E. 88 D5
Mulayz, Wādī al watercourse Egypt 85 A4
Mulchatna r. U.S.A. 118 C3
Mulde r. Germany 53 M3
Mule Creek NM U.S.A. 129 I5
Mule Creek WY U.S.A. 126 G4
Mulegé Mex. 127 E8
Mules i. Indon. 108 C2
Muleshoe U.S.A. 131 C5
Mulga Park Australia 109 E6
Mulgathing Australia 109 F7
Mulhacén mt. Spain 57 E5
Mülhausen France see Mulhouse
Mülheim an der Ruhr Germany 52 G3
Mulhouse France 56 H3
Muli China 76 D3
Muli Rus. Fed. see Vysokogorniy
Mulia Indon. 69 J7
Muling Heilong. China 74 C3
Muling Heilong. China 74 C3
Muling He r. China 74 D3
Mull i. U.K. 50 D4
Mull, Sound of sea chan. U.K. 50 C4
Mullaghcleevaun hill Rep. of Ireland 51 F4
Mullaittivu Sri Lanka 84 D4
Mullaley Australia 112 D3
Mullengudgery Australia 112 C3
Mullens U.S.A. 134 E5
Muller watercourse Australia 108 F5
Muller, Pegunungan mts Indon. 68 E6
Mullett Lake U.S.A. 134 C1
Mullewa Australia 109 A7
Mullica r. U.S.A. 135 H4
Mullingar Rep. of Ireland 51 E4
Mullion Creek Australia 112 D4
Mull of Galloway c. U.K. 50 E6
Mull of Kintyre hd U.K. 50 D5
Mull of Oa hd U.K. 50 C5
Mullumbimby Australia 112 F2
Mulobezi Zambia 99 C5
Mulshi Lake India 84 B2
Multai India 82 D5
Multan Pak. 89 H4
Multia Fin. 44 N5
Multien reg. France 52 C6
Mulug India 84 C2
▶Mumbai India 84 B2
2nd most populous city in Asia and 5th in the world.
Mumbil Australia 112 D4
Mumbwa Zambia 99 C5
Muminabad Tajik. see Leningrad
Mū'minobod Tajik. see Leningrad
Mun, Mae Nam r. Thai. 70 D4
Muna i. Indon. 69 G8
Muna Mex. 136 G4
Muna r. Rus. Fed. 65 N3
Munabao Pak. 89 H5
Munaðarnes Iceland 44 [inset]
Münchberg Germany 53 L4
München Germany see Munich
München-Gladbach Germany see Mönchengladbach
Münchhausen Germany 53 I4
Muncho Lake Canada 120 E3
Muncie U.S.A. 134 C3
Muncoonie West, Lake salt flat Australia 110 B5
Muncy U.S.A. 135 G3
Munda Pak. 89 H4
Mundel Lake Sri Lanka 84 C5
Mundesley U.K. 49 I6
Mundford U.K. 49 H6
Mundiwindi Australia 109 C5
Mundra India 82 B5
Mundrabilla Australia 106 C5
Munds Park U.S.A. 129 H4
Mundubbera Australia 111 E5
Mundwa India 82 C4
Munfordville U.S.A. 134 C5
Mungallala Australia 111 D5
Mungana Australia 110 D3
Mungári Moz. 99 D5
Mungbere Dem. Rep. Congo 98 C3
Mungeli India 83 E5
Munger India 83 F4
Mu Nggava i. Solomon Is see Rennell
Mungindi Australia 112 D2
Mungla Bangl. see Mongla
Mungo Angola 99 B5
Mungo, Lake Australia 112 A4
Mungo National Park Australia 112 A4
Munich Germany 47 M6
Munising U.S.A. 132 C2
Munjpur India 82 B5
Munkács Ukr. see Mukacheve
Munkedal Sweden 45 G7
Munkelva Norway 44 P2
Munkfors Sweden 45 H7
Munkhafaḑ al Qaţţārah depr. Egypt see Qattara Depression
Munku-Sardyk, Gora mt. Mongolia/Rus. Fed. 72 I2
Münnerstadt Germany 53 K4
Munnik S. Africa 101 I2
Munroe Lake Canada 121 L3
Munsan S. Korea 75 B5
Münster Hessen Germany 53 I5
Münster Niedersachsen Germany 53 K2
Münster Nordrhein-Westfalen Germany 53 H3
Munster reg. Rep. of Ireland 51 D5
Münsterland reg. Germany 53 H3
Muntadgin Australia 109 B7
Munyal-Par sea feature India see Bassas de Pedro Padua Bank
Munzur Vadisi Milli Parkı nat. park Turkey 55 L4
Muojärvi l. Fin. 44 P4
Mương Lam Vietnam 70 D3
Mương Nhie Vietnam 70 C2
Muong Sai Laos see Muang Xay
Muonio Fin. 44 M3
Muonioälven r. Fin./Sweden 44 M3
Muonionjoki r. Fin./Sweden see Muonioälven
Mupa, Parque Nacional da nat. park Angola 99 B5
Muping China see Baoxing
Muqaynimah well Saudi Arabia 88 C6
Muqdisho Somalia see Mogadishu
Muquem Brazil 145 A1
Muqui Brazil 145 C3
Mur r. Austria 47 P7
also known as Mura (Croatia/Slovenia)
Mura r. Croatia/Slovenia see Mur
Murai, Tanjong pt Sing. 71 [inset]
Murai Reservoir Sing. 71 [inset]
Murakami Japan 75 E5
Murallón, Cerro mt. Chile 144 B7
Muramvya Burundi 98 C4
Murashi Rus. Fed. 42 K4
Murat r. Turkey 91 E3
Muratlı Turkey 59 L4
Muraysah, Ra's al pt Libya 90 B5
Murchison watercourse Australia 109 A6
Murchison, Mount Antarctica 152 H2
Murchison, Mount hill Australia 109 B6
Murchison Falls National Park Uganda 98 D3
Murcia Spain 57 F5
Murcia aut. comm. Spain 57 F5
Murdo U.S.A. 130 C3
Murehwa Zimbabwe 99 D5
Mureşul r. Romania 59 I1
Muret France 56 E5
Murewa Zimbabwe see Murehwa
Murfreesboro AR U.S.A. 131 E5
Murfreesboro TN U.S.A. 132 C5
Murg r. Germany 53 I6
Murgab Tajik. see Murghob
Murgab Turkm. see Murgap
Murgab r. Turkm. see Murgap
Murgap Turkm. 89 F2
Murgap r. Turkm. 87 J2
Murghab r. Afgh. 89 F3
Murghab reg. Afgh. 89 F3
Murgha Kibzai Pak. 89 H4
Murghob Tajik. 89 I2
Murgh Pass Afgh. 89 H3
Murgon Australia 111 E5
Murgoo Australia 109 B6
Muri India 83 F5
Muriaé Brazil 145 C3
Murid Pak. 89 G4
Muriege Angola 99 C4
Müritz l. Germany 53 M1
Müritz, Nationalpark nat. park Germany 53 N1
Murmansk Rus. Fed. 44 R2
Murmanskaya Oblast' admin. div. Rus. Fed. 42 H2
Murmanskiy Bereg coastal area Rus. Fed. 42 G1
Murmansk Oblast admin. div. Rus. Fed. see Murmanskaya Oblast'
Muro, Capo di c. Corsica France 56 I6
Murom Rus. Fed. 42 I5
Muroran Japan 74 F4
Muros Spain 57 B2
Muroto Japan 75 D6
Muroto-zaki pt Japan 75 D6
Murphy ID U.S.A. 126 D4
Murphy NC U.S.A. 133 D5
Murphysboro U.S.A. 130 F4
Murrah reg. Saudi Arabia 88 C6
Murrah al Kubrá, Al Buḩayrah al l. Egypt see Great Bitter Lake
Murrah aş Şughrá, Al Buḩayrah al l. Egypt see Little Bitter Lake
Murra Murra Australia 112 C2
Murrat el Kubra, Buheirat l. Egypt see Great Bitter Lake
Murrat el Sughra, Buheirat l. Egypt see Little Bitter Lake
▶Murray r. S.A. Australia 111 B7
3rd longest river in Oceania. Part of the longest (Murray-Darling).
Murray r. W.A. Australia 109 A8
Murray KY U.S.A. 131 F4
Murray UT U.S.A. 129 H1
Murray, Lake P.N.G. 69 K8
Murray, Lake U.S.A. 133 D5
Murray, Mount Canada 120 D2
Murray Bridge Australia 111 B7
▶Murray-Darling r. Austr. 106 E5
Longest river and largest drainage basin in Oceania.
Oceania 102–103
Murray Downs Australia 108 F5
Murray Range hills Australia 109 E6
Murraysburg S. Africa 100 F6
Murray Sunset National Park Australia 111 C7
Murrhardt Germany 53 J6
Murrieta U.S.A. 128 E5
Murringo Australia 112 D5
Murrisk reg. Rep. of Ireland 51 C4
Murroogh Rep. of Ireland 51 C4
▶Murrumbidgee r. Australia 112 A5
4th longest river in Oceania.
Murrumburrah Australia 112 D5
Murrurundi Australia 112 E3
Mursan India 82 D4
Murshidabad India 83 G4
Murska Sobota Slovenia 58 G1
Mürt Iran 89 F5
Murtoa Australia 111 C8
Murua i. P.N.G. see Woodlark Island
Murud India 84 B2
Murud, Gunung mt. Indon. 68 F6
Murunkan Sri Lanka 84 D4
Murupara N.Z. 113 F4
Mururoa atoll Fr. Polynesia 151 K7
Murviedro Spain see Sagunto
Murwara India 82 E5
Murwillumbah Australia 112 F2
Murzechirla Turkm. 89 F2
Murzūq Libya 97 E2
Mürzzuschlag Austria 47 O7
Muş Turkey 91 F3
Mūsā, Khowr-e b. Iran 88 C4
Musa Khel Bazar Pak. 89 H4
Musala mt. Bulg. 59 J3
Musala i. Indon. 71 B7
Musan N. Korea 74 C4
Musandam Peninsula Oman/U.A.E. 88 E5
Mūsá Qal'eh, Rūd-e r. Afgh. 89 G3
Musay'īd Qatar see Umm Sa'id
▶Muscat Oman 88 E6
Capital of Oman.
Muscat reg. Oman 88 E5
Muscat and Oman country Asia see Oman
Muscatine U.S.A. 130 F3
Musgrave Australia 110 C2
Musgrave Harbour Canada 123 L4
Musgrave Ranges mts Australia 109 E6
Mushāsh al Kabid well Jordan 85 C5
Mushayyish, Wādī al watercourse Jordan 85 C4
Mushie Dem. Rep. Congo 98 B4
Mushkaf Pak. 89 G4
Music Mountain U.S.A. 129 G4
Musinia Peak U.S.A. 129 H2
Muskeg r. Canada 120 F2
Muskeget Channel U.S.A. 135 J3
Muskegon MI U.S.A. 132 C3
Muskegon MI U.S.A. 134 B2
Muskegon r. U.S.A. 134 B2
Muskegon Heights U.S.A. 134 B2
Muskeg River Canada 120 G4
Muskogee U.S.A. 131 E5
Muskoka, Lake Canada 134 F1
Muskrat Dam Lake Canada 121 N4
Musmar Sudan 86 E6
Musoma Tanz. 98 D4
Musquanousse, Lac l. Canada 123 J4
Musquaro, Lac l. Canada 123 J4
Mussau Island P.N.G. 69 L7
Musselburgh U.K. 50 F5
Musselkanaal Neth. 52 H2
Musselshell r. U.S.A. 126 G3
Mussende Angola 99 B5
Mustafakemalpaşa Turkey 59 M4
Mustjala Estonia 45 M7
Mustvee Estonia 45 O7
Musu-dan pt N. Korea 74 C4
Muswellbrook Australia 112 E4
Mūţ Egypt 86 C4
Mut Turkey 85 A1
Mutá, Ponta do pt Brazil 145 D1
Mutare Zimbabwe 99 D5
Mutayr reg. Saudi Arabia 88 B5
Mutina Italy see Modena
Muting Indon. 69 K8
Mutis Col. 142 C2
Mutnyy Materik Rus. Fed. 42 L2
Mutoko Zimbabwe 99 D5
Mutsamudu Comoros 99 E5
Mutsu Japan 74 F4
Muttaburra Australia 110 D4
Muttonbird Islands N.Z. 113 A8
Mutton Island Rep. of Ireland 51 C5
Muttukuru India 84 D3
Muttupet India 84 C4
Mutum Brazil 145 C2
Mutunópolis Brazil 145 A1
Mutur Sri Lanka 84 D4
Mutusjärvi r. Fin. 44 O2
Muurola Fin. 44 N3
Mu Us Shamo des. China 73 J5
Muxaluando Angola 99 B4
Muxi China see Muchuan
Muxima Angola 99 B4
Muyezerskiy Rus. Fed. 44 R5
Muyinga Burundi 98 D4
Muynak Uzbek. 80 A3
Mŭynoq Uzbek. see Muynak
Muyumba Dem. Rep. Congo 99 C4
Muyunkum, Peski des. Kazakh. see Moyynkum, Peski
Muyuping China 77 F2
Muzaffarabad Pak. 89 I3
Muzaffargarh Pak. 89 H4
Muzaffarnagar India 82 D3
Muzaffarpur India 83 F4
Muzamane Moz. 101 K2
Muzhi Rus. Fed. 41 S2
Mūzīn Iran 89 F5
Muzon, Cape U.S.A. 120 C4
Múzquiz Mex. 131 C7
Muztag mt. China 82 E2
Muz Tag mt. China 83 F1
Muztagata mt. China 89 I2
Muztor Kyrg. see Toktogul
Mvadi Gabon 98 B3
Mvolo Sudan 97 F4
Mvuma Zimbabwe 99 D5
Mwanza Malawi 99 D5
Mwanza Tanz. 98 D4
Mweelrea hill Rep. of Ireland 51 C4
Mweka Dem. Rep. Congo 99 C4
Mwene-Ditu Dem. Rep. Congo 99 C4
Mwenezi Zimbabwe 99 D6
Mwenga Dem. Rep. Congo 98 C4
Mweru, Lake Dem. Rep. Congo/Zambia 99 C4
Mweru Wantipa National Park Zambia 99 C4
Mwimba Dem. Rep. Congo 99 C4
Mwinilunga Zambia 99 C5
Myadaung Myanmar 70 B2
Myadzyel Belarus 45 O9
Myajlar India 82 B4
Myall Lakes National Park Australia 112 F4
Myanaung Myanmar 70 A3
▶Myanmar country Asia 70 A2
Asia 6, 62–63
Myauk-U Myanmar see Myohaung
Myaungmya Myanmar 70 A3
Myawadi Thai. 70 B3
Mybster U.K. 50 F2
Myebon Myanmar 70 A2
Myede Myanmar 70 A3
Myeik Myanmar see Mergui
Myingyan Myanmar 70 A2
Myinkyado Myanmar 70 B2
Myinmoletkat mt. Myanmar 71 B4
Myitkyina Myanmar 70 B1
Myitson Myanmar 70 B2
Myitta Myanmar 71 B4
Myittha Myanmar 70 B2
Mykolayiv Ukr. 59 O1
Mykonos i. Greece 59 K6
Myla Rus. Fed. 42 K2
Myla r. Rus. Fed. 42 K2
Mylae Sicily Italy see Milazzo
Mylasa Turkey see Milas
Mymensing Bangl. see Mymensingh
Mymensingh Bangl. 83 G4
Mynämäki Fin. 45 M6
Myohaung Myanmar 70 A2
Myŏnggan N. Korea 74 C4
Myory Belarus 45 O9
Mýrdalsjökull ice cap Iceland 44 [inset]
Myre Norway 44 I2
Myrheden Sweden 44 L4
Myrhorod Ukr. 43 G6
Myrnam Canada 121 I4
Myronivka Ukr. 43 F6
Myrtle Beach U.S.A. 133 E5
Myrtleford Australia 112 C6
Myrtle Point U.S.A. 126 B4
Mys Articheskiy c. Rus. Fed. 153 E1
Mysia reg. Turkey 59 L5
Mys Lazareva Rus. Fed. see Lazarev
Myślibórz Poland 47 O4
My Son Sanctuary tourist site Vietnam 70 E4
Mysore India 84 C3
Mysore state India see Karnataka
Mys Shmidta Rus. Fed. 65 T3
Mysy Rus. Fed. 42 L3
My Tho Vietnam 71 D5
Mytilene i. Greece see Lesbos
Mytilini Greece 59 L5
Mytilini Strait Greece/Turkey 59 L5
Mytishchi Rus. Fed. 42 H5
Myton U.S.A. 129 H1
Myyeldino Rus. Fed. 42 L3
Mzamomhle S. Africa 101 H6
Mže r. Czech Rep. 53 M5
Mzimba Malawi 99 D5
Mzuzu Malawi 99 D5

N

Naab r. Germany 53 M5
Naalehu HI U.S.A. 127 [inset]
Naantali Fin. 45 M6
Naas Rep. of Ireland 51 F4
Naba Myanmar 70 B1
Nababeep S. Africa 100 C5
Nababganj Bangl. see Nawabganj
Nabadwip India see Navadwip
Nabarangapur India 84 D2
Nabarangpur India see Nabarangapur
Nabari Japan 75 E6
Nabatîyé et Tahta Lebanon 85 B3
Nabatiyet et Tahta Lebanon see Nabatîyé et Tahta
Nabberu, Lake salt flat Australia 109 C6
Nabburg Germany 53 M5
Naberera Tanz. 99 D4
Naberezhnyye Chelny Rus. Fed. 41 Q4
Nabesna U.S.A. 120 A2
Nabeul Tunisia 58 D6
Nabha India 82 D3
Nabil'skiy Zaliv lag. Rus. Fed. 74 F2
Nabire Indon. 69 J7
Nabi Younés, Ras en pt Lebanon 85 B3
Nāblus West Bank 85 B3
Naboomspruit S. Africa 101 I3
Nabq Reserve nature res. Egypt 90 D5
Nābulus West Bank see Nāblus
Nacala Moz. 99 E5
Nachalovo Rus. Fed. 43 K7
Nachicapau, Lac l. Canada 123 I2
Nachingwea Tanz. 99 D5
Nachna India 82 B4
Nachuge India 71 A5
Nacimiento Reservoir U.S.A. 128 C4
Naco U.S.A. 127 F7
Nacogdoches U.S.A. 131 E6
Nada China see Danzhou
Nadaleen r. Canada 120 C2
Nådendal Fin. see Naantali
Nadezhdinskoye Rus. Fed. 74 D2
Nadiad India 82 C5
Nadol India 82 C4
Nador Morocco 57 E6
Nadqān, Qalamat well Saudi Arabia 88 C6
Nadūshan Iran 88 D3
Nadvirna Ukr. 43 E6
Nadvoitsy Rus. Fed. 42 G3
Nadvornaya Ukr. see Nadvirna
Nadym Rus. Fed. 64 I3
Næstved Denmark 45 G9
Nafarroa aut. comm. Spain see Navarra
Nafas, Ra's an mt. Egypt 85 B5
Nafha, Har hill Israel 85 B4
Nafpaktos Greece 59 I5
Nafplio Greece 59 J6
Naftalan Azer. 91 G2
Naft-e Safid Iran 88 C4
Naft-e Shāh Iran see Naft Shahr
Naft Shahr Iran 88 B3
Nafūd ad Daḩl des. Saudi Arabia 88 B6
Nafūd al Ghuwayţah des. Saudi Arabia 85 D5
Nafūd al Jur'ā des. Saudi Arabia 88 B5
Nafūd as Sirr des. Saudi Arabia 88 B5
Nafūd as Surrah des. Saudi Arabia 88 A6
Nafūd Qunayfidhah des. Saudi Arabia 88 B5
Nafūsah, Jabal hills Libya 96 E1
Nafy Saudi Arabia 86 F4
Nag, Co l. China 83 G2
Naga Phil. 69 G4
Nagagami r. Canada 122 D4
Nagagami Lake Canada 122 D4
Nagahama Japan 75 D6
Naga Hills India 83 H4
Naga Hills state India see Nagaland
Nagaland state India 83 H4
Nagamangala India 84 C3
Nagambie Australia 112 B6
Nagano Japan 75 E5
Nagaoka Japan 75 E5
Nagaon India 83 H4
Nagapatam India see Nagapattinam
Nagapattinam India 84 C4
Nagar Himachal Pradesh India 87 M3
Nagar Karnataka India 84 B3
Nagaram India 84 D2
Nagari Hills India 84 C3
Nagarjuna Sagar Reservoir India 84 C2
Nagar Parkar Pak. 89 H5
Nagasaki Japan 75 C6
Nagato Japan 75 C6
Nagaur India 82 C4
Nagbhir India 84 C1
Nagda India 82 C5
Nageezi U.S.A. 129 J3
Nagercoil India 84 C4
Nagha Kalat Pak. 89 G5
Nag' Ḩammâdi Egypt see Naj' Ḩammādī
Nagina India 82 D3
Nagold r. Germany 53 I6
Nagong Chu r. China see Parlung Zangbo
Nagorno-Karabakh aut. reg. Azer. see Dağlıq Qarabağ
Nagornyy Karabakh aut. reg. Azer. see Dağlıq Qarabağ
Nagorsk Rus. Fed. 42 K4
Nagoya Japan 75 E6
Nagpur India 82 D5
Nagqu China 76 B2
Nag Qu r. China 76 B2
Nagurskoye Rus. Fed. 64 F1
Nagyatád Hungary 58 G1
Nagybecskerek Serb. and Mont. see Zrenjanin
Nagyenyed Romania see Aiud
Nagykanizsa Hungary 58 G1
Nagyvárad Romania see Oradea
Naha Japan 73 N7
Nahan India 82 D3
Nahanni Butte Canada 120 F2
Nahanni National Park Canada 120 E2
Nahanni Range mts Canada 120 F2
Naharāyim Jordan 85 B3
Nahariyya Israel 85 B3
Nahāvand Iran 88 C3
Nahr Dijlah r. Iraq/Syria 91 G5 see Tigris
Nahuel Huapi, Parque Nacional nat. park Arg. 144 B6
Nahunta U.S.A. 133 D6
Naica Mex. 131 B7
Nai Ga Myanmar 76 C3
Naij Tal China 83 H2

Orlik Rus. Fed. 72 H2
Orlov Rus. Fed. 42 K4
Orlov Gay Rus. Fed. 43 K6
Orlovskiy Rus. Fed. 43 I7
Orly airport France 52 C6
Ormara Pak. 89 G5
Ormara, Ras hd Pak. 89 G5
Ormiston Canada 121 J5
Ormoc Phil. 69 G4
Ormskirk U.K. 48 E5
Ormstown Canada 135 I1
Ornach Pak. 89 G5
Ornain r. France 52 E6
Orne r. France 56 D2
Ørnes Norway 44 H3
Örnsköldsvik Sweden 44 K5
Orobie, Alpi mts Italy 58 C1
Orobo, Serra do hills Brazil 145 C1
Orodara Burkina 96 C3
Orofino U.S.A. 126 D3
Oro Grande U.S.A. 128 E4
Orogrande U.S.A. 127 G6
Orol Dengizi salt l. Kazakh./Uzbek. see Aral Sea
Oromocto Canada 123 I5
Oromocto Lake Canada 123 I5
Oron Israel 85 B4
Orona atoll Kiribati 107 I2
Orono U.S.A. 132 G2
Orontes r. Asia 90 E3 see 'Āṣī, Nahr al
Orontes r. Lebanon/Syria 85 C2
Oroqen Zizhiqi China see Alihe
Oroquieta Phil. 69 G5
Orós, Açude resr Brazil 143 K5
Orosei, Golfo di b. Sardinia Italy 58 C4
Orosháza Hungary 59 I1
Oroville U.S.A. 128 C2
Oroville, Lake U.S.A. 128 C2
Orqohan China 74 A2
Orr U.S.A. 130 E1
Orsa Sweden 45 I6
Orsha Belarus 43 F5
Orshanka Rus. Fed. 42 J4
Orsk Rus. Fed. 64 G4
Ørsta Norway 44 E5
Orta Toroslar plat. Turkey 85 A1
Ortegal, Cabo c. Spain 57 C2
Orthez France 56 D5
Ortigueira Spain 57 C2
Ortiz Mex. 127 F7
Ortles mt. Italy 58 D1
Orton U.K. 48 E4
Ortona Italy 58 F3
Ortonville U.S.A. 130 D2
Ortospana Afgh. see Kābul
Orulgan, Khrebet mts Rus. Fed. 65 N3
Orumbo Namibia 100 C2
Orūmīyeh Iran see Urmia
Oruro Bol. 142 E7
Orūzgān Afgh. 89 G3
Orvieto Italy 58 E3
Orville Coast Antarctica 152 L1
Orwell OH U.S.A. 134 E3
Orwell VT U.S.A. 135 I2
Oryol Rus. Fed. see Orel
Os Norway 44 G5
Osa Rus. Fed. 41 R4
Osa, Península de pen. Costa Rica 137 H7
Osage IA U.S.A. 130 E3
Osage WV U.S.A. 134 E4
Osage WY U.S.A. 126 G3
Ōsaka Japan 75 D6
Osakarovka Kazakh. 80 D1
Osawatomie U.S.A. 130 E4
Osborne U.S.A. 130 D4
Osby Sweden 45 H8
Osceola IA U.S.A. 130 E3
Osceola MO U.S.A. 130 E4
Osceola NE U.S.A. 130 D3
Oschatz Germany 53 N3
Oschersleben (Bode) Germany 53 L2
Oschiri Sardinia Italy 58 C4
Ösel i. Estonia see Hiiumaa
Osetr r. Rus. Fed. 43 H5
Ōse-zaki pt Japan 75 C6
Osgoode Canada 135 H1
Osgood Mountains U.S.A. 126 D4
Osh Kyrg. 80 D3
Oshakati Namibia 99 B5
Oshawa Canada 135 F2
Oshika-hantō pen. Japan 75 F5
Ō-shima i. Japan 74 E4
Ō-shima i. Japan 75 E6
Oshkosh NE U.S.A. 130 C3
Oshkosh WI U.S.A. 134 A1
Oshmyany Belarus see Ashmyany
Oshnovīyeh Iran 88 B2
Oshogbo Nigeria 96 D4
Oshtorān Kūh mt. Iran 88 C3
Oshwe Dem. Rep. Congo 98 B4
Osijek Croatia 58 H2
Osilinka r. Canada 120 E3
Osimo Italy 58 E3
Osipenko Ukr. see Berdyans'k
Osipovichi Belarus see Asipovichy
Osiyan India 82 C4
Osizweni S. Africa 101 J4
Osječenica mts Bos.-Herz. 58 G2
Ösjön l. Sweden 44 I5
Oskaloosa U.S.A. 130 E3
Oskarshamn Sweden 45 J8
Öskemen Kazakh. see Ust'-Kamenogorsk

▶Oslo Norway 45 G7
Capital of Norway.

Oslofjorden sea chan. Norway 41 G7
Osmanabad India 84 C2
Osmancık Turkey 90 D2
Osmaneli Turkey 59 M4
Osmaniye Turkey 90 E3
Osmannagar India 84 C2
Os'mino Rus. Fed. 45 P7
Osnabrück Germany 53 I2
Osnaburg atoll Fr. Polynesia see Mururoa
Osogbo Nigeria see Oshogbo
Osogovska Planina mts Bulg./Macedonia 59 J3
Osogovske Planine mts Bulg./Macedonia see Osogovska Planina
Osogovski Planini mts Bulg./Macedonia see Osogovska Planina
Osorno Chile 144 B6
Osorno Spain 57 D2
Osoyoos Canada 120 G5
Osøyri Norway 45 D6
Osprey Reef Australia 110 D2
Oss Neth. 52 F3
Ossa, Mount Australia 111 [inset]
Osseo U.S.A. 122 C5
Ossineke U.S.A. 134 D1
Ossining U.S.A. 135 I3
Ossipee U.S.A. 135 J2
Ossipee Lake U.S.A. 135 J2
Oßmannstedt Germany 53 L3
Ossokmanuan Lake Canada 123 I3
Ossora Rus. Fed. 65 R4
Ostashkov Rus. Fed. 42 G4
Ostbevern Germany 53 H2
Oste r. Germany 53 J1
Ostend Belgium 52 C3
Ostende Belgium see Ostend
Osterburg (Altmark) Germany 53 L2
Österbymo Sweden 45 I8
Österdalälven l. Sweden 45 H6
Østerdalen valley Norway 45 G5
Osterfeld Germany 53 L3
Osterholz-Scharmbeck Germany 53 I1
Osterode am Harz Germany 53 K3
Österreich country Europe see Austria
Östersund Sweden 44 I5
Osterwieck Germany 53 K3
Ostfriesische Inseln Germany see East Frisian Islands
Ostfriesland reg. Germany 53 H1
Östhammar Sweden 45 K6
Ostrava Czech Rep. 47 Q6
Ostróda Poland 47 Q4
Ostrogozhsk Rus. Fed. 43 H6
Ostrov Czech Rep. 53 M4
Ostrov Rus. Fed. 45 P8
Ostrovets Poland see Ostrowiec Świętokrzyski
Ostrovskoye Rus. Fed. 42 I4
Ostrov Vrangelya i. Rus. Fed. see Wrangel Island
Ostrów Poland see Ostrów Wielkopolski
Ostrowiec Poland see Ostrowiec Świętokrzyski
Ostrowiec Świętokrzyski Poland 43 D6
Ostrów Mazowiecka Poland 47 R4
Ostrowo Poland see Ostrów Wielkopolski
Ostrów Wielkopolski Poland 47 P5
O'Sullivan Lake Canada 122 D4
Osŭm r. Bulg. 59 K3
Ōsumi-shotō is Japan 75 C7
Osuna Spain 57 D5
Oswego KS U.S.A. 131 E4
Oswego NY U.S.A. 135 G2
Oswestry U.K. 49 D6
Otago Peninsula N.Z. 113 C7
Otahiti i. Fr. Polynesia see Tahiti
Otaki N.Z. 113 E5
Otanmäki Fin. 44 O4
Otaru Japan 74 F4
Otavi Namibia 99 B5
Ōtawara Japan 75 F5
Otdia atoll Marshall Is see Wotje
Otelnuc, Lac l. Canada 123 H2
Otematata N.Z. 113 C7
Otepää Estonia 45 O7
Otgon Tenger Uul mt. Mongolia 80 I2
Otinapa Mex. 131 B7
Otira N.Z. 113 C6
Otis U.S.A. 130 C3
Otish, Monts hills Canada 123 H4
Otjinene Namibia 99 B6
Otjiwarongo Namibia 99 B6
Otjozondjupa admin. reg. Namibia 100 C1
Otley U.K. 48 F5
Otorohanga N.Z. 113 E4
Otoskwin r. Canada 121 N5
Otpan, Gora hill Kazakh. 91 H1
Otpor Rus. Fed. see Zabaykal'sk
Otradnoye Rus. Fed. see Otradnyy
Otradnyy Rus. Fed. 43 K5
Otranto Italy 58 H4
Otranto, Strait of Albania/Italy 58 H4
Otrogovo Rus. Fed. see Stepnoye
Otrozhnyy Rus. Fed. 65 S3
Otsego Lake U.S.A. 135 H2
Ōtsu Japan 75 D6
Otta Norway 45 F6

▶Ottawa Canada 135 H1
Capital of Canada.

Ottawa r. Canada 122 G5
also known as Rivière des Outaouais
Ottawa IL U.S.A. 130 F3
Ottawa KS U.S.A. 130 E4
Ottawa OH U.S.A. 134 C3
Ottawa Islands Canada 122 E2
Otter r. U.K. 49 D8
Otterbein U.S.A. 134 B3
Otterburn U.K. 48 E3
Otter Rapids Canada 122 E4
Ottersberg Germany 53 J1
Ottignies Belgium 52 E4
Ottumwa U.S.A. 130 E3
Ottweiler Germany 53 H5
Otukpo Nigeria 96 D4
Oturkpo Nigeria see Otukpo
Otuzco Peru 142 C5
Otway, Cape Australia 112 A7
Otway National Park Australia 112 A7
Ouachita r. U.S.A. 131 F6
Ouachita, Lake U.S.A. 131 E5
Ouachita Mountains Arkansas/Oklahoma U.S.A. 125 I5
Ouachita Mountains Arkansas/Oklahoma U.S.A. 131 E5
Ouadda Cent. Afr. Rep. 98 C3
Ouaddaï reg. Chad 97 F3

▶Ouagadougou Burkina 96 C3
Capital of Burkina.

Ouahigouya Burkina 96 C3
Ouahran Alg. see Oran
Ouaka r. Cent. Afr. Rep. 98 B3
Oualâta Mauritania 96 C3
Ouallam Niger 96 D3
Ouanda-Djailé Cent. Afr. Rep. 94 C3
Ouando Cent. Afr. Rep. 98 C3
Ouango Cent. Afr. Rep. 98 C3
Ouara r. Cent. Afr. Rep. 98 C3
Ouarâne reg. Mauritania 96 C2
Ouargaye Burkina 96 D3
Ouargla Alg. 54 F5
Ouarogou Burkina see Ouargaye
Ouarzazate Morocco 54 C5
Oubangui r. Cent. Afr. Rep./Dem. Rep. Congo see Ubangi
Oubergpas pass S. Africa 100 G7
Oudenaarde Belgium 52 D4
Oudtshoorn S. Africa 100 F7
Oud-Turnhout Belgium 52 E3
Oued Tlélat Alg. 57 F6
Oued Zem Morocco 54 C5
Oued Zénati Alg. 58 B6
Ouessant, Île d' i. France 56 B2
Ouesso Congo 98 B3
Ouezzane Morocco 57 D6
Oughter, Lough l. Rep. of Ireland 51 E3
Ouguati Namibia 100 B1
Ouistreham France 49 G9
Oujda Morocco 57 F6
Oujeft Mauritania 96 B3
Oulainen Fin. 44 N4
Oulangan kansallispuisto nat. park Fin. 44 P3
Ouled Djellal Alg. 57 I6
Ouled Farès Alg. 57 G5
Ouled Naïl, Monts des mts Alg. 57 H6
Oulu Fin. 44 N4
Oulujärvi l. Fin. 44 O4
Oulujoki r. Fin. 44 N4
Oulunsalo Fin. 44 N4
Oulx Italy 58 B2
Oum-Chalouba Chad 97 F3
Oum el Bouaghi Alg. 58 B7
Oum-Hadjer Chad 97 E3
Ounasjoki r. Fin. 44 N3
Oundle U.K. 49 G6
Oungre Canada 121 K5
Ounianga Kébir Chad 97 F3
Oupeye Belgium 52 F4
Our r. Lux. 52 G5
Ouray CO U.S.A. 129 J2
Ouray UT U.S.A. 129 I1
Ourcq r. France 52 D5
Ourense Spain 57 C2
Ouricuri Brazil 143 J5
Ourinhos Brazil 145 A3
Ouro r. Brazil 145 A1
Ouro Preto Brazil 145 C3
Ourthe r. Belgium 52 F4
Ous Rus. Fed. 41 S3
Ouse r. England U.K. 48 G5
Ouse r. England U.K. 49 H8
Outaouais, Rivière des r. Canada 122 G5
see Ottawa
Outardes r. Canada 123 H4
Outardes Quatre, Réservoir resr Canada 123 H4
Outer Hebrides is U.K. 50 B3
Outer Mongolia country Asia see Mongolia
Outer Santa Barbara Channel U.S.A. 128 D5
Outjo Namibia 99 B6
Outlook Canada 121 J5
Outokumpu Fin. 44 P5
Out Skerries is U.K. 50 [inset]
Ouvéa atoll New Caledonia 107 G4
Ouyanghai Shuiku resr China 77 G3
Ouyen Australia 111 C7
Ouzel r. U.K. 49 G6
Ovace, Punta d' mt. Corsica France 56 I6
Ovacık Turkey 85 A1
Ovada Italy 58 C2
Ovalle Chile 144 B4
Ovamboland reg. Namibia 99 B5
Ovan Gabon 98 B3
Ovar Port. 57 B3
Overath Germany 53 H4
Överkalix Sweden 44 M3
Overlander Roadhouse Australia 109 A6
Overland Park U.S.A. 130 E4
Overton U.S.A. 129 F3
Övertorneå Sweden 44 M3
Överum Sweden 45 J8
Overveen Neth. 52 E2
Ovid CO U.S.A. 130 C3
Ovid NY U.S.A. 135 G2
Oviedo Spain 57 D2
Ovoot Mongolia 73 K3
Øvre Anarjokka Nasjonalpark nat. park Norway 44 N2
Øvre Dividal Nasjonalpark nat. park Norway 44 K2
Øvre Rendal Norway 45 G6
Ovruch Ukr. 43 F6
Ovsyanka Rus. Fed. 74 B1
Owando Congo 98 B4
Owa Rafa i. Solomon Is see Santa Ana
Owasco Lake U.S.A. 135 G2
Owase Japan 75 E6
Owatonna U.S.A. 130 E2
Owbeh Afgh. 89 F3
Owego U.S.A. 135 G2
Owel, Lough l. Rep. of Ireland 51 E4
Owen Island Myanmar 71 B5
Owenmore r. Rep. of Ireland 51 C3
Owenmore r. Rep. of Ireland 51 D3
Owenreagh r. U.K. 51 E3
Owen River N.Z. 113 D5
Owens r. U.S.A. 128 E3
Owensboro U.S.A. 134 B5
Owen Sound Canada 134 E1
Owen Sound inlet Canada 134 E1
Owen Stanley Range mts P.N.G. 69 L8
Owenton U.S.A. 134 C4
Owerri Nigeria 96 D4
Owikeno Lake Canada 120 E5
Owingsville U.S.A. 134 D4
Owl r. Canada 121 M3
Owl Creek Mountains U.S.A. 126 F4
Owo Nigeria 96 D4
Owosso U.S.A. 134 C2
Owyhee U.S.A. 126 D4
Owyhee r. U.S.A. 126 D4
Owyhee Mountains U.S.A. 126 D4
Öxarfjörður b. Iceland 44 [inset]
Oxbow Canada 121 K5
Ox Creek r. U.S.A. 130 C1
Oxelösund Sweden 45 J7
Oxford N.Z. 113 D6
Oxford U.K. 49 F7
Oxford IN U.S.A. 134 B3
Oxford MA U.S.A. 135 J2
Oxford MD U.S.A. 135 G4
Oxford MS U.S.A. 131 F5
Oxford NC U.S.A. 132 E4
Oxford NY U.S.A. 135 H2
Oxford OH U.S.A. 134 C4
Oxford House Canada 121 M4
Oxford Lake Canada 121 M4
Oxley Australia 112 B5
Oxleys Peak Australia 112 E3
Oxley Wild Rivers National Park Australia 112 F3
Ox Mountains hills Rep. of Ireland see Slieve Gamph
Oxnard U.S.A. 128 D4
Oxtongue Lake Canada 135 F1
Oxus r. Asia see Amudar'ya
Øya Norway 44 H3
Oyama Japan 75 E5
Oyem Gabon 98 B3
Oyen Canada 121 I5
Oygon Mongolia 80 I2
Oykel r. U.K. 50 E3
Oyo Nigeria 96 D4
Oyonnax France 56 G3
Oyster Rocks is India 84 B3
Oyten Germany 53 J1
Oytograk China 83 E1
Oyukludağı mt. Turkey 85 A1
Özalp Turkey 91 G3
Ozamiz Phil. 69 G5
Ozark AL U.S.A. 133 C6
Ozark AR U.S.A. 131 E5
Ozark MO U.S.A. 131 E4
Ozark Plateau U.S.A. 131 E4
Ozarks, Lake of the U.S.A. 130 E4
O'zbekiston country Asia see Uzbekistan
Özen Kazakh. see Kyzylsay
Ozernovskiy Rus. Fed. 65 Q4
Ozernyy Rus. Fed. 43 G5
Ozerpakh Rus. Fed. 74 F1
Ozersk Rus. Fed. 45 M9
Ozerskiy Rus. Fed. 74 F3
Ozery Rus. Fed. 43 H5
Ozeryane Rus. Fed. 74 C2
Ozieri Sardinia Italy 58 C4
Ozinki Rus. Fed. 43 K6
Oznachennoye Rus. Fed. see Sayanogorsk
Ozona U.S.A. 131 C6
Ozuki Japan 75 C6

P

Paamiut Greenland 119 N3
Pa-an Myanmar 70 B3
Paanopa i. Kiribati see Banaba
Paarl S. Africa 100 D7
Paatsjoki r. Europe see Patsoyoki
Paballelo S. Africa 100 E5
P'abal-li N. Korea 74 C4
Pabbay i. U.K. 50 B3
Pabianice Poland 47 Q5
Pabianitz Poland see Pabianice
Pabna Bangl. 83 G4
Pabradė Lith. 45 N9
Pab Range mts Pak. 89 G5
Pacaás Novos, Parque Nacional nat. park Brazil 142 F6
Pacaraimã, Serra mts S. America see Pakaraima Mountains
Pacasmayo Peru 142 C5
Pachagarh Bangl. see Panchagarh
Pacheco Chihuahua Mex. 127 F7
Pacheco Zacatecas Mex. 131 C7
Pachikha Rus. Fed. 42 J3
Pachino Sicily Italy 58 F6
Pachmarhi India 82 D5
Pachor India 82 D5
Pachora India 84 B1
Pachpadra India 82 C4
Pachuca Mex. 136 E4
Pachuca de Soto Mex. see Pachuca
Pacific-Antarctic Ridge sea feature S. Pacific Ocean 151 J9
Pacific Grove U.S.A. 128 C3

▶Pacific Ocean 150–147
Largest ocean in the world.

Pacific Rim National Park Canada 120 E5
Pacitan Indon. 68 E8
Packsaddle Australia 111 C6
Pacoval Brazil 143 H4
Pacuí r. Brazil 145 B2
Paczków Poland 47 P5
Padali Rus. Fed. see Amursk
Padampur India 82 C3
Padang Indon. 68 C7
Padang i. Indon. 71 C7
Padang Endau Malaysia 71 C7
Padangpanjang Indon. 68 C7
Padangsidimpuan Indon. 71 B7
Padany Rus. Fed. 42 G3
Padatha, Kūh-e mt. Iran 88 C3
Padaung Myanmar 70 A3
Padcaya Bol. 142 F8
Padderborn-Lippstadt airport Germany 53 I3
Paden City U.S.A. 134 E4
Paderborn Germany 53 I3
Padeşu, Vârful mt. Romania 59 J2
Padibyu Myanmar 70 B2
Padilla Bol. 142 F7
Padjelanta nationalpark nat. park Sweden 44 J3
Padova Italy see Padua
Padrão, Ponta pt Angola 99 B4
Padrauna India 83 F4
Padre Island U.S.A. 131 D7
Padstow U.K. 49 C8
Padsvillye Belarus 45 O9
Padua India 84 D2
Padua Italy 58 D2
Paducah KY U.S.A. 131 F4
Paducah TX U.S.A. 131 C5
Padum Jammu and Kashmir 82 D2
Paegam N. Korea 74 C4
Paektu-san mt. China/N. Korea see Baotou Shan
Paengnyŏng-do i. S. Korea 75 B5
Pafos Cyprus see Paphos
Pafuri Moz. 101 J2
Pag Croatia 58 F2
Pag i. Croatia 58 F2
Paga Indon. 108 C2
Pagadian Phil. 69 G5
Pagai Selatan i. Indon. 68 C7
Pagalu i. Equat. Guinea see Annobón
Pagan i. N. Mariana Is 69 L3
Pagasitikos Kolpos b. Greece 59 J5
Pagatan Indon. 68 F7
Page U.S.A. 129 H3
Paget, Mount S. Georgia 144 I8
Paget Cay reef Australia 110 F3
Pagon i. N. Mariana Is see Pagan
Pagosa Springs U.S.A. 127 G5
Pagqên China see Gadê
Pagwa River Canada 122 D4
Pagwi P.N.G. 69 K7
Pahala HI U.S.A. 127 [inset]
Pahang r. Malaysia 71 C7
Pahlgam Jammu and Kashmir 82 C2
Pahoa HI U.S.A. 127 [inset]
Pahokee U.S.A. 133 D7
Pahra Kariz Afgh. 89 F3
Pahranagat Range mts U.S.A. 129 F3
Pahrump U.S.A. 129 F3
Pahuj r. India 82 D4
Pahute Mesa plat. U.S.A. 128 E3
Pai Thai. 70 B3
Paicines U.S.A. 128 C3
Paide Estonia 45 N7
Paignton U.K. 49 D8
Päijänne l. Fin. 45 N6
Paikü Co l. China 83 F3
Pailin Cambodia 71 C4
Pailolo Channel HI U.S.A. 127 [inset]
Paimio Fin. 45 M6
Painel Brazil 145 A4
Painesville U.S.A. 134 E3
Pains Brazil 145 B3
Painted Desert U.S.A. 129 H3
Painted Rock Dam U.S.A. 129 G5
Paint Hills Canada see Wemindji
Paint Rock U.S.A. 131 D6
Paintsville U.S.A. 134 D5
Paisley U.K. 50 E5
Paita Peru 142 B5
Paitou China 77 I2
Paiva Couceiro Angola see Quipungo
Paizhou China 77 G2
Pajala Sweden 44 M3
Paka Malaysia 71 C6
Pakala India 84 C3
Pakanbaru Indon. see Pekanbaru
Pakangyi Myanmar 70 A2
Pakaraima Mountains Guyana 142 G3
Pakaraima Mountains S. America 142 F3
Pakaur India 83 F4
Pakesley Canada 122 E5
Pakhachi Rus. Fed. 65 R3
Pakhoi China see Beihai
Paki Nigeria 96 D3

▶Pakistan country Asia 89 H4
4th most populous country in Asia.
Asia 6, 62–63

Pakkat Indon. 71 B7
Paknampho Thai. see Nakhon Sawan
Pakokku Myanmar 70 A2
Pakowki Lake imp. l. Canada 121 I5
Pakpattan Pak. 89 I4
Pak Phanang Thai. 71 C5
Pak Phayun Thai. 71 C6
Pakruojis Lith. 45 M9
Paks Hungary 58 H1
Pakse Laos see Pakxé
Pak Tam Chung Hong Kong China 77 [inset]
Pak Thong Chai Thai. 70 C4
Pakur India see Pakaur
Pakxé Laos 70 D4
Pakxeng Laos 70 C2
Pala Chad 97 E4
Pala Myanmar 71 B4
Palaestinia reg. Asia see Palestine
Palaiochora Greece 59 J7
Palaiseau France 52 C6
Palakkad India see Palghat
Palakkat India see Palghat
Palamakoloi Botswana 100 F2
Palamau India see Palamu
Palamós Spain 57 H3
Palamu India 83 F5
Palana Rus. Fed. 65 Q4
Palandur India 84 D1
Palangān, Kūh-e mts Iran 89 F4
Palangkaraya Indon. 68 E7
Palani India 84 C4
Palanpur India 82 C4
Palantak Pak. 89 G5
Palapye Botswana 101 H2
Palatka Rus. Fed. 65 Q3
Palatka U.S.A. 133 D6
▶Palau country N. Pacific Ocean 69 I5
Asia 6, 62–63
Palau Islands Palau 69 I5
Palauk Myanmar 71 B4
Palaw Myanmar 71 B4
Palawan i. Phil. 68 F5
Palawan Passage strait Phil. 68 F5
Palawan Trough sea feature N. Pacific Ocean 150 D5
Palayankottai India 84 C4
Palchal Lake India 84 D2
Paldiski Estonia 45 N7
Palekh Rus. Fed. 42 I4
Palembang Indon. 68 C7
Palena Chile 144 B6
Palencia Spain 57 D2
Palermo Sicily Italy 58 E5
Palestine reg. Asia 85 B3
Palestine U.S.A. 131 E6
Paletwa Myanmar 70 A2
Palezgir Pak. 89 H4
Palghat India 84 C4
Palgrave, Mount hill Australia 109 A5
Palhoca Brazil 145 A4
Pali Chhattisgarh India 84 D1
Pali Maharashtra India 84 B2
Pali Rajasthan India 82 C4

▶Palikir Micronesia 150 G5
Capital of Micronesia.

Palinuro, Capo c. Italy 58 F4
Paliouri, Akra pt Greece 59 J5
Palisade U.S.A. 129 I2
Paliseul Belgium 52 F5
Palitana India 82 B5
Palivere Estonia 45 M7
Palk Bay Sri Lanka 84 C4
Palkino Rus. Fed. 45 P8
Palkonda Range mts India 84 C3
Palk Strait India/Sri Lanka 84 C4
Palla Bianca mt. Austria/Italy see Weißkugel
Pallamallawa Australia 112 E2
Pallas Green Rep. of Ireland 51 D5
Pallas ja Ounastunturin kansallispuisto nat. park Fin. 44 M2
Pallasovka Rus. Fed. 43 J6
Pallavaram India 84 D3
Palliser, Cape N.Z. 113 E5
Palliser, Îles is Fr. Polynesia 151 K7
Palliser Bay N.Z. 113 E5
Pallu India 82 C3
Palma r. Brazil 145 B1
Palma del Río Spain 57 D5
Palma de Mallorca Spain 57 H4
Palmaner India 84 C3
Palmares Brazil 143 K5
Palmares do Sul Brazil 145 A5
Palmas Paraná Brazil 145 A4
Palmas Tocantins Brazil 143 I6
Palmas, Cape Liberia 96 C4
Palm Bay U.S.A. 133 D7
Palmdale U.S.A. 128 D4
Palmeira Brazil 145 A4
Palmeira das Missões Brazil 144 F3
Palmeira dos Índios Brazil 143 K5
Palmeirais Brazil 143 J5
Palmeiras Brazil 145 C1
Palmeirinhas, Ponta das pt Angola 99 B4
Palmer research station Antarctica 152 L2
Palmer r. Australia 110 C3
Palmer watercourse Australia 109 F6
Palmer U.S.A. 118 D3
Palmer Land reg. Antarctica 152 L2
Palmerston N.T. Australia 108 E3
Palmerston N.T. Australia see Darwin
Palmerston Canada 134 E2
Palmerston atoll Cook Is 107 J3
Palmerston N.Z. 113 C7
Palmerston North N.Z. 113 E5
Palmerton U.S.A. 135 H3
Palmerville Australia 110 D2
Palmetto Point Bahamas 133 E7
Palmi Italy 58 F5
Palmira Col. 142 C3
Palmira Cuba 133 D8
Palm Springs U.S.A. 128 E5
Palmyra Syria see Tadmur
Palmyra MO U.S.A. 130 F4
Palmyra PA U.S.A. 135 G3
Palmyra VA U.S.A. 135 F5

▶Palmyra Atoll terr. N. Pacific Ocean 150 J5
United States Unincorporated Territory.

Palmyras Point India 83 F5
Palni Hills India 84 C4
Palo Alto U.S.A. 128 B3
Palo Blanco Mex. 131 C7
Palo Chino watercourse Mex. 127 E7
Palo Duro watercourse U.S.A. 131 C5
Paloich Sudan 86 D7
Palojärvi Fin. 44 M2
Palojoensuu Fin. 44 M2
Palomaa Fin. 44 O2
Palomar Mountain U.S.A. 128 E5
Paloncha India 84 D2
Palo Pinto U.S.A. 131 D5
Palopo Indon. 69 G7
Palos, Cabo de c. Spain 57 F5
Palo Verde U.S.A. 129 F5
Paltamo Fin. 44 O4
Palu Indon. 68 F7
Palu i. Indon. 108 C2
Palu Turkey 91 E3
Pal'vart Turkm. 89 G2
Palwal India 82 D3
Palwancha India see Paloncha
Palyeskaya Nizina marsh Belarus/Ukr. see Pripet Marshes
Pambarra Moz. 101 L1
Pambula Australia 112 D6
Pamidi India 84 C3
Pamiers France 56 E5
Pamir mts Asia 89 I2
Pamlico Sound sea chan. U.S.A. 133 E5
Pamouscachiou, Lac l. Canada 123 H4
Pampa U.S.A. 131 C5
Pampa de Infierno Arg. 144 D3
Pampas reg. Arg. 144 D5
Pampeluna Spain see Pamplona
Pamphylia reg. Turkey 59 N6
Pamplin U.S.A. 135 F5
Pamplona Col. 142 D2
Pamplona Spain 57 F2
Pampow Germany 53 L1
Pamukova Turkey 59 N4
Pamzal Jammu and Kashmir 82 D2
Pana U.S.A. 130 F4
Panaca U.S.A. 129 F3
Panache, Lake Canada 122 E5
Panagyurishte Bulg. 59 K3
Panaitan i. Indon. 68 D8
Panaji India 84 B3
▶Panama country Central America 137 H7
North America 9, 116–117

▶Panama i. Indon. 108 C2
Most southerly point of Asia.

Panamá Panama see Panama City

Pequeña, Punta pt Mex. 127 E8
Pequop Mountains U.S.A. 129 F1
Peradeniya Sri Lanka 84 D5
Pera Head hd Australia 110 C2
Perak i. Malaysia 71 B6
Perales del Alfambra Spain 57 F3
Perambalur India 84 C4
Perämeren kansallispuisto nat. park Fin. 44 N4
Peräseinäjoki Fin. 44 M5
Percé Canada 123 I4
Percival Lakes salt flat Australia 108 D5
Percy U.S.A. 135 J1
Percy Isles Australia 110 E4
Percy Reach l. Canada 135 G1
Perdizes Brazil 145 B2
Perdu, Lac l. Canada 123 H4
Peregrebnoye Rus. Fed. 41 T3
Pereira Col. 142 C3
Pereira Barreto Brazil 145 A3
Pereira de Eça Angola see Ondjiva
Pere Marquette r. U.S.A. 134 B2
Peremul Par reef India 84 B4
Peremyshlyany Ukr. 43 E6
Perenjori Australia 109 B7
Pereslavl'-Zalesskiy Rus. Fed. 42 H4
Pereslavskiy Natsional'nyy Park nat. park Rus. Fed. 42 H4
Pereyaslavka Rus. Fed. 74 D3
Pereval Klukhorskiy pass Rus. Fed. 91 F2
Pereyaslav-Khmel'nitskiy Ukr. see Pereyaslav-Khmel'nyts'kyy
Pereyaslav-Khmel'nyts'kyy Ukr. 43 F6
Perforated Island Thai. see Bon, Ko
Pergamino Arg. 144 D4
Perhentian Besar, Pulau i. Malaysia 71 C6
Perho Fin. 44 N5
Péribonca, Lac l. Canada 123 H4
Perico Arg. 144 C2
Pericos Mex. 127 G8
Peridot U.S.A. 129 H5
Périgueux France 56 E4
Perijá, Parque Nacional nat. park Venez. 142 D2
Perija, Sierra de mts Venez. 138 D2
Periyar India see Erode
Perkasie U.S.A. 135 H3
Perlas, Punta de pt Nicaragua 137 H6
Perleberg Germany 53 L1
Perm' Rus. Fed. 41 R4
Permas Rus. Fed. 42 J4
Pernambuco Brazil see Recife
Pernambuco Abyssal Plain sea feature S. Atlantic Ocean 148 G6
Pernatty Lagoon salt flat Australia 111 B6
Pernem India 84 B3
Pernik Bulg. 59 J3
Pernov Estonia see Pärnu
Perojpur Bangl. see Pirojpur
Peron Islands Australia 108 E3
Péronne France 52 C5
Perpignan France 56 F5
Perranporth U.K. 49 B8
Perrégaux Alg. see Mohammadia
Perris U.S.A. 128 E5
Perros-Guirec France 56 C2
Perrot, Île i. Canada 135 I1
Perry FL U.S.A. 133 D6
Perry GA U.S.A. 133 D5
Perry MI U.S.A. 134 C2
Perry OK U.S.A. 131 D4
Perry Lake U.S.A. 130 E4
Perryton U.S.A. 131 C4
Perryville AK U.S.A. 118 C4
Perryville MO U.S.A. 130 F4
Perseverancia Bol. 142 F6
Pershore U.K. 49 E6
Persia country Asia see Iran
Persian Gulf Asia see The Gulf
Pertek Turkey 91 E3

▶Perth Australia 109 A7
State capital of Western Australia. 4th most populous city in Oceania.

Perth Canada 135 G1
Perth U.K. 50 F4
Perth Amboy U.S.A. 135 H3
Perth-Andover Canada 123 I5
Perth Basin sea feature Indian Ocean 149 P7
Pertominsk Rus. Fed. 42 H2
Pertunmaa Fin. 45 O6
Pertusato, Capo c. Corsica France 56 I6
Peru atoll Kiribati see Beru

▶Peru country S. America 142 D6
3rd largest and 4th most populous country in South America.
South America 9, 140–141

Peru IL U.S.A. 130 F3
Peru IN U.S.A. 134 B3
Peru NY U.S.A. 135 I1
Peru-Chile Trench sea feature S. Pacific Ocean 151 O6
Perugia Italy 58 E3
Peruru India 84 C3
Perusia Italy see Perugia
Péruwelz Belgium 52 D4
Pervomaysk Rus. Fed. 43 I5
Pervomays'k Ukr. 43 F6
Pervomayskiy Kazakh. 80 F1
Pervomayskiy Arkhangel'skaya Oblast' Rus. Fed. see Novodvinsk
Pervomayskiy Tambovskaya Oblast' Rus. Fed. 43 I5
Pervomays'kyy Ukr. 43 H6
Pervorechenskiy Rus. Fed. 65 R3
Pesaro Italy 58 E3
Pescadores is Taiwan see P'enghu Ch'üntao
Pescara Italy 58 F3
Pescara r. Italy 58 F3
Peschanokopskoye Rus. Fed. 39 I7
Peschanoye Rus. Fed. see Yashkul'
Peschanyy, Mys pt Kazakh. 87 H2
Pesha r. Rus. Fed. 42 J2
Peshanjan Afgh. 89 F3
Peshawar Pak. 89 H3
Peshkopi Albania 59 I4
Peshtera Bulg. 59 K3
Peski Turkm. 89 F2
Peski Karakumy des. Turkm. see Karakum Desert
Peskovka Rus. Fed. 42 L4
Pesnica Slovenia 58 F1
Pessac France 56 D4
Pessin Germany 53 M2
Pestovo Rus. Fed. 42 G4
Pestravka Rus. Fed. 43 K5
Petah Tiqwa Israel 85 B3
Petäjävesi Fin. 44 N5
Petaling Jaya Malaysia 71 C7
Petalion, Kolpos sea chan. Greece 59 K5
Petaluma U.S.A. 128 B2
Pétange Lux. 52 F5
Petatlán Mex. 136 D5
Petauke Zambia 99 D5
Petenwell Lake U.S.A. 130 F2
Peterbell Canada 122 E4
Peterborough Australia 111 B7
Peterborough Canada 135 F1
Peterborough U.K. 49 G6
Peterborough U.S.A. 135 J2
Peterculter U.K. 50 G3
Peterhead U.K. 50 H3
Peter I Island Antarctica 152 K2
Peter I Øy i. Antarctica see Peter I Island
Peter Lake Canada 121 M2
Peterlee U.K. 48 F4
Petermann Bjerg nunatak Greenland 119 P2
Petermann Ranges mts Australia 109 E6
Peter Pond Lake Canada 121 I4
Peters, Lac l. Canada 123 H2
Petersberg Germany 53 J4
Petersburg AK U.S.A. 120 C3
Petersburg IL U.S.A. 130 F4
Petersburg IN U.S.A. 134 B4
Petersburg NY U.S.A. 135 I2
Petersburg VA U.S.A. 135 G5
Petersburg WV U.S.A. 134 F4
Petersfield U.K. 49 G7
Petershagen Germany 53 I2
Petersville U.S.A. 118 C3
Peter the Great Bay Rus. Fed. see Petra Velikogo, Zaliv
Peth India 84 B2
Petilia Policastro Italy 58 G5
Petit Atlas mts Morocco see Anti Atlas
Petitcodiac Canada 123 I5
Petitjean Morocco see Sidi Kacem
Petit Lac Manicouagan l. Canada 123 I3
Petit Mécatina r. Nfld. and Lab./Que. Canada 123 K4
Petit Mécatina, Île du i. Canada 123 K4
Petit Morin r. France 52 D6
Petitot r. Canada 120 F2
Petit Saut Dam resr Fr. Guiana 143 H3
Petit St-Bernard, Col du pass France 56 H4
Peto Mex. 136 G4
Petoskey U.S.A. 132 C2
Petra tourist site Jordan 85 B4
Petra Velikogo, Zaliv b. Rus. Fed. 74 C4
Petre, Point Canada 135 G2
Petrich Bulg. 59 J4
Petrified Forest National Park U.S.A. 129 I4
Petrikau Poland see Piotrków Trybunalski
Petrikov Belarus see Pyetrykaw
Petrinja Croatia 58 G2
Petroaleksandrovsk Uzbek. see Turtkul'
Petrograd Rus. Fed. see St Petersburg
Petrokhanski Prokhod pass Bulg. 59 J3
Petrokov Poland see Piotrków Trybunalski
Petrolia Canada 134 D2
Petrolia U.S.A. 128 A1
Petrolina Brazil 143 J5
Petrolina de Goiás Brazil 145 A2
Petropavl Kazakh. see Petropavlovsk
Petropavlovsk Kazakh. 79 F1
Petropavlovsk Rus. Fed. see Petropavlovsk-Kamchatskiy
Petropavlovsk-Kamchatskiy Rus. Fed. 65 Q4
Petrópolis Brazil 145 C3
Petroșani Romania 59 J2
Petrovsk Rus. Fed. 43 J5
Petrovskoye Rus. Fed. see Svetlograd
Petrovsk-Zabaykal'skiy Rus. Fed. 73 J2
Petrozavodsk Rus. Fed. 42 G3
Petrus Steyn S. Africa 101 I4
Petrusville S. Africa 100 G6
Petsamo Rus. Fed. see Pechenga
Pettau Slovenia see Ptuj
Petten Neth. 52 E2
Pettigo U.K. 51 E3
Petukhovo Rus. Fed. 64 H4
Petushki Rus. Fed. 42 H5
Petzeck mt. Austria 47 N7
Peuetsagu, Gunung vol. Indon. 71 B6
Peureula Indon. 71 B6
Pevek Rus. Fed. 65 S3
Pêxung China 76 B1
Pey Ostān Iran 88 E3
Peza r. Rus. Fed. 42 J2
Pezinok Slovakia 47 P6
Pezu Pak. 89 H3
Pfälzer Wald hills Germany 49 H5
Pforzheim Germany 53 I6
Pfungstadt Germany 53 I5
Phagwara India 82 C3
Phahameng Free State S. Africa 101 H5
Phahameng Limpopo S. Africa 101 I3
Phalaborwa S. Africa 101 J2
Phalodi India 82 C4
Phalsund India 82 B4
Phalta India 83 G5
Phaluai, Ko i. Thai. 71 B5
Phalut Peak India/Nepal 83 G4
Phan Thai. 70 B3
Phanat Nikhom Thai. 71 C4
Phangan, Ko i. Thai. 71 C5
Phang Hoei, San Khao mts Thai. 70 C3
Phangnga Thai. 71 B5
Phanom Dong Rak, Thiu Khao mts Cambodia/Thai. 71 D4
Phan Rang Vietnam 71 E5
Phan Thiêt Vietnam 71 E5
Phapon Myanmar see Pyapon
Phat Diêm Vietnam 70 D2
Phatthalung Thai. 71 C6
Phayam, Ko i. Thai. 71 B5
Phayao Thai. 70 B3
Phayuhakhiri Thai. 70 C4
Phek India 83 H4
Phelps Lake Canada 121 K3
Phen Thai. 70 C3
Phenix U.S.A. 135 F5
Phenix City U.S.A. 133 C5
Phet Buri Thai. 71 B4
Phetchabun Thai. 70 C3
Phiafai Laos 70 D4
Phichai Thai. 70 C3
Phichit Thai. 70 C3
Philadelphia Jordan see 'Ammān
Philadelphia Turkey see Alaşehir
Philadelphia MS U.S.A. 131 F5
Philadelphia NY U.S.A. 135 H1
Philadelphia PA U.S.A. 135 H4
Philip U.S.A. 130 C2
Philip Atoll Micronesia see Sorol
Philippeville Alg. see Skikda
Philippeville Belgium 52 E4
Philippi U.S.A. 134 E4
Philippi, Lake salt flat Australia 110 B5
Philippine Neth. 52 D3
Philippine Basin sea feature N. Pacific Ocean 150 E4
▶Philippines country Asia 69 G4
Asia 6, 62–63
Philippine Sea N. Pacific Ocean 69 G3

▶Philippine Trench sea feature N. Pacific Ocean 150 E4
3rd deepest trench in the world.

Philippolis S. Africa 101 G6
Philippopolis Bulg. see Plovdiv
Philippsburg Germany 53 I5
Philipsburg MT U.S.A. 126 E3
Philipsburg PA U.S.A. 135 F3
Philip Smith Mountains U.S.A. 118 D3
Philipstown S. Africa 100 G6
Phillip Island Australia 112 B7
Phillips ME U.S.A. 135 J1
Phillips WI U.S.A. 130 F2
Phillipsburg U.S.A. 130 D4
Phillips Range hills Australia 108 D4
Philmont U.S.A. 135 I2
Philomelium Turkey see Akşehir
Phiritona S. Africa 101 H4
Phitsanulok Thai. 70 C3

▶Phnom Penh Cambodia 71 D5
Capital of Cambodia.

Phnum Pénh Cambodia see Phnom Penh
Pho, Laem pt Thai. 71 C5
Phoenicia U.S.A. 135 H2

▶Phoenix U.S.A. 127 E6
State capital of Arizona.

Phoenix Island Kiribati see Rawaki
Phoenix Islands Kiribati 107 I2
Phon Thai. 70 C4
Phong Nha Vietnam 70 D3
Phôngsali Laos 70 C2
Phong Saly Laos see Phôngsali
Phong Thô Vietnam 70 C2
Phon Phisai Thai. 70 C3
Phon Thong Thai. 70 C3
Phosphate Hill Australia 110 C4
Phrae Thai. 70 C3
Phra Nakhon Si Ayutthaya Thai. see Ayutthaya
Phrao Thai. 70 B3
Phra Saeng Thai. 71 B5
Phrom Phiram Thai. 70 C3
Phsar Ream Cambodia 71 C5
Phuchong-Nayoi National Park Thai. 71 D4
Phu Cuong Vietnam see Thu Dâu Môt
Phu Hôi Vietnam 71 E4
Phuket Thai. 71 B6
Phuket, Ko i. Thai. 71 B6
Phu-khieo Wildlife Reserve nature res. Thai. 70 C3
Phulabani India see Phulbani
Phulbani India 84 E1
Phulchhari Ghat Bangl. see Fulchhari
Phulji Pak. 89 G5
Phu Lôc Vietnam 70 D3
Phu Luang National Park Thai. 70 C3
Phu Ly Vietnam 70 D2
Phumĭ Bŏeng Mealea Cambodia 71 D4
Phumĭ Chhlong Cambodia 71 D4
Phumĭ Kaôh Kŏng Cambodia 71 C5
Phumĭ Kon Kriel Cambodia 71 C4
Phumĭ Mlu Prey Cambodia 71 D4
Phumĭ Moŭng Cambodia 71 C4
Phumĭ Prêk Kak Cambodia 71 D4
Phumĭ Sâmraông Cambodia 71 C4
Phumĭ Trâm Kak Cambodia 71 D5
Phumĭ Veal Renh Cambodia 71 C5
Phu My Vietnam 71 E4
Phung Hiêp Vietnam 71 D5
Phu Phac Mo mt. Vietnam 70 C2
Phu Phan National Park Thai. 70 C3
Phu Quôc, Đao i. Vietnam 71 C5
Phu Tho Vietnam 70 D2
Phu Vinh Vietnam see Tra Vinh
Piaca Brazil 143 I5
Piacenza Italy 58 C2
Piacouadie, Lac l. Canada 123 H4
Piagochioui r. Canada 122 F3
Piai, Tanjung pt Malaysia 71 C7
Pian r. Australia 112 D3
Pianosa, Isola i. Italy 58 D3
Piatra Neamț Romania 59 L1
Piave r. Italy 58 E2
Pibor Post Sudan 97 G4
Pic r. Canada 122 D4
Picacho U.S.A. 129 I5
Picachos, Cerro dos mt. Mex. 127 E7
Picardie admin. reg. France 52 C5
Picardie reg. France see Picardy
Picardy admin. reg. France see Picardie
Picardy reg. France 52 B5
Picauville France 49 F9
Picayune U.S.A. 131 F6
Piceance Creek r. U.S.A. 129 I1
Pichanal Arg. 144 D2
Pichhor India 82 D4
Pichilemu Chile 144 B4
Pichilingue Mex. 136 B4
Pickens U.S.A. 134 E4
Pickering Canada 134 F2
Pickering U.K. 48 G4
Pickering, Vale of valley U.K. 48 G4
Pickle Lake Canada 119 I4
Pico da Neblina, Parque Nacional do nat. park Brazil 142 E3
Picos Brazil 143 J5
Pico Truncado Arg. 144 C7
Picton Australia 112 E5
Picton Canada 135 G2
Picton N.Z. 113 E5
Pictou Canada 123 J5
Picture Butte Canada 121 H5
Pidarak Pak. 89 F5
Pidurutalagala mt. Sri Lanka 84 D5
Piedade Brazil 145 B3
Piedra de Águila Arg. 144 B6
Piedras, Punta pt Arg. 144 E5
Piedras Blancas Point U.S.A. 128 C4
Piedras Negras Mex. 131 C6
Pie Island Canada 122 C4
Pieksämäki Fin. 44 O5
Pielavesi Fin. 44 O5
Pielinen l. Fin. 44 P5
Pieljekaise nationalpark nat. park Sweden 44 J3
Pienaarsrivier S. Africa 101 I3
Pieniński Park Narodowy nat. park Poland 47 R6
Pieninský nat. park Slovakia 47 R6
Pierce U.S.A. 130 D3
Pierce Lake Canada 121 M4
Pierceland Canada 121 I4
Pierceton U.S.A. 134 C3
Pieria mts Greece 59 J4
Pierowall U.K. 50 G1
Pierpont U.S.A. 134 E3

▶Pierre U.S.A. 130 C2
State capital of South Dakota.

Pierrelatte France 56 G4
Pietermaritzburg S. Africa 101 J5
Pietersaari Fin. see Jakobstad
Pietersburg S. Africa 101 I2
Pie Town U.S.A. 129 I4
Pietra Spada, Passo di pass Italy 58 G5
Piet Retief S. Africa 101 J4
Pietrosa mt. Romania 59 K1
Pigeon U.S.A. 134 D2
Pigeon Bay Canada 134 D3
Pigeon Lake Canada 120 H4
Piggott U.S.A. 131 F4
Pigg's Peak Swaziland 101 J3
Pigs, Bay of Cuba 133 D8
Pihij India 82 C5
Pihkva järv l. Estonia/Rus. Fed. see Pskov, Lake
Pihlajavesi l. Fin. 44 P6
Pihlava Fin. 45 L6
Pihtipudas Fin. 44 N5
Piippola Fin. 44 N4
Piispajärvi Fin. 44 P4
Pikalevo Rus. Fed. 42 G4
Pike U.S.A. 134 E4
Pike Bay Canada 134 E1
Pikelot i. Micronesia 69 L5
Pikes Peak U.S.A. 126 G5
Piketon U.S.A. 134 D4
Pikeville KY U.S.A. 134 D5
Pikeville TN U.S.A. 132 C5
Pikinni atoll Marshall Is see Bikini
Piła Poland 47 P4
Pilanesberg National Park S. Africa 101 H3
Pilar Arg. 144 E4
Pilar Para. 144 E3
Pilar de Goiás Brazil 145 A1
Pilaya r. Bol. 142 F8
Pilcomayo r. Bol./Para. 142 F8
Piler India 84 C3
Pili, Cerro mt. Chile 144 C2
Pilibangan India 82 C3
Pilibhit India 82 D3
Pilipinas country Asia see Philippines
Pillau Rus. Fed. see Baltiysk
Pillcopata Peru 142 D6
Pilliga Australia 112 D3
Pillsbury, Lake U.S.A. 128 B2
Pil'na Rus. Fed. 42 J5
Pil'nya, Ozero l. Rus. Fed. 42 M1
Pilões, Serra dos mts Brazil 145 B2
Pílos Greece see Pylos
Pilot Knob mt. U.S.A. 126 E3
Pilot Peak U.S.A. 128 E2
Pilot Station U.S.A. 118 B3
Pilsen Czech Rep. see Plzeň
Piltene Latvia 45 L8
Pil'tun, Zaliv lag. Rus. Fed. 74 F1
Pilu Pak. 89 H5
Pima U.S.A. 129 I5
Pimenta Bueno Brazil 142 F6
Pimento U.S.A. 134 B4
Pimpalner India 84 B1
Pin r. India 82 D2
Pin r. Myanmar 70 A2
Pinahat India 82 D4
Pinaleno Mountains U.S.A. 129 H5
Pinamar Arg. 144 E5
Pinang Malaysia see George Town
Pinang i. Malaysia 71 C6
Pınarbaşı Turkey 90 E3
Pinar del Río Cuba 137 H4
Pınarhisar Turkey 59 L4
Piñas Ecuador 142 C4
Pincher Creek Canada 120 H5
Pinckneyville U.S.A. 130 F4
Pinconning U.S.A. 134 D2
Pińczów Poland 47 R5
Pindaí Brazil 145 C1
Pindamonhangaba Brazil 145 B3
Pindar Australia 109 A7
Pindaré r. Brazil 143 J4
Píndhos Óros mts Greece see Pindus Mountains
Pindos mts Greece see Pindus Mountains
Pindrei India 82 E5
Pindus Mountains Greece 59 I5
Pine watercourse Australia 111 C7
Pine r. MI U.S.A. 134 C1
Pine r. MI U.S.A. 134 C2
Pine Bluff U.S.A. 131 E5
Pine Bluffs U.S.A. 126 G4
Pine Creek Australia 108 E3
Pine Creek r. U.S.A. 135 G3
Pinecrest U.S.A. 128 C2
Pinedale NM U.S.A. 129 I4
Pinedale WY U.S.A. 126 F4
Pine Dock Canada 121 L5
Pine Falls Canada 121 L5
Pine Flat Lake U.S.A. 128 D3
Pinega Rus. Fed. 42 I2
Pinega r. Rus. Fed. 42 I2
Pinegrove Australia 109 A6
Pine Grove U.S.A. 135 G3
Pine Hills CA U.S.A. 128 E4
Pine Hills FL U.S.A. 133 D6
Pinehouse Lake Canada 121 J4
Pinehouse Lake l. Canada 121 J4
Pineimuta r. Canada 121 N4
Pineios r. Greece 59 J5
Pine Island Bay Antarctica 151 N10
Pine Island Glacier Antarctica 152 K1
Pine Islands FL U.S.A. 133 D7
Pine Islands FL U.S.A. 133 D7
Pine Knot U.S.A. 134 C5
Pineland U.S.A. 131 E6
Pine Mountain U.S.A. 128 C4
Pine Peak U.S.A. 129 G4
Pine Point Canada 120 H2
Pine Point pt Canada 120 H2
Pineridge U.S.A. 128 D3
Pine Ridge U.S.A. 130 C3
Pinerolo Italy 58 B2
Pines, Isle of i. Cuba see La Juventud, Isla de
Pines, Isle of i. New Caledonia see Pins, Île des
Pinetop U.S.A. 129 I4
Pinetown S. Africa 101 J5
Pine Valley U.S.A. 135 G2
Pineville KY U.S.A. 134 D5
Pineville MO U.S.A. 131 E4
Pineville WV U.S.A. 134 E5
Ping, Mae Nam r. Thai. 70 C4
Ping'an China 72 I5
Ping'anyi China see Ping'an
Pingba China 76 E3
Pingbian China 76 D4
Ping Dao i. China 77 H1
Pingdingbu China see Guyuan
Pingdingshan China 77 G1
Pingdong Taiwan see P'ingtung
Pingdu Jiangxi China see Anfu
Pingdu Shandong China 73 L5
Pinggang China 74 B4
Pinghe China 77 H3
Pinghu China see Pingtang
Pingjiang China 77 G2
Pingjinpu China 76 E2
Pingle China 77 F3
Pingli China 77 F1
Pingliang China 76 E1
Pinglu China 77 F1
Pingma China see Tiandong
Pingnan China 77 H3
Pingqiao China 77 G1
Pingshan Sichuan China 76 E2
Pingshan Yunnan China see Luquan
Pingshi China 77 G3
Pingtan China 77 H3
Pingtan Dao i. China see Haitan Dao
Pingtang China 76 E3
P'ingtung Taiwan 77 I4
Pingxi China see Yuping
Pingxiang Guangxi China 76 E4
Pingxiang Jiangxi China 77 G3
Pingyang Heilong. China 74 B2
Pingyang Zhejiang China 77 I3
Pingyi China 77 H1
Pingyu China 77 G1
Pingyuanjie China 76 D4
Pingzhai China 77 F3
Pinhal Brazil 145 B3
Pinheiro Brazil 143 I4
Pinhoe U.K. 49 D8
Pini i. Indon. 68 B6
Piniós r. Greece see Pineios
Pinjin Australia 109 C7
Pink Mountain Canada 120 F3
Pinlaung Myanmar 70 B2
Pinlebu Myanmar 70 A1
Pinnacle hill U.S.A. 135 F4
Pinnacles National Monument nat. park U.S.A. 128 C3
Pinnau r. Germany 53 J1
Pinneberg Germany 53 J1
Pinnes, Akra pt Greece 59 K4
Pinos, Isla de i. Cuba see La Juventud, Isla de
Pinos, Mount U.S.A. 128 D4
Pinotepa Nacional Mex. 136 E5
Pins, Île des i. New Caledonia 107 G4
Pins, Pointe aux pt Canada 134 E2
Pinsk Belarus 45 O10
Pinta, Sierra hill U.S.A. 129 G5
Pintada Creek watercourse U.S.A. 127 G6
Pintados Chile 144 C2
Pintura U.S.A. 129 G3
Pioche U.S.A. 129 F3
Piodi Dem. Rep. Congo 99 C4
Pioneer Mountains U.S.A. 126 E3
Pioner, Ostrov i. Rus. Fed. 64 K2
Pionerskiy Kaliningradskaya Oblast' Rus. Fed. 45 L9
Pionerskiy Khanty-Mansiyskiy Avtonomnyy Okrug Rus. Fed. 41 S3
Pionki Poland 47 R5
Piopio N.Z. 113 E4
Piopiotahi inlet N.Z. see Milford Sound
Piorini, Lago l. Brazil 142 F4
Piotrków Trybunalski Poland 47 Q5
Pipa Dingzi mt. China 74 C4
Pipar India 82 C4
Pipar Road India 82 C4
Piperi i. Greece 59 K5
Piper Peak U.S.A. 128 E3
Pipestone Canada 121 K5
Pipestone r. Canada 121 N4
Pipestone U.S.A. 130 D3
Pipli India 82 C3
Pipmuacan, Réservoir resr Canada 123 H4
Piqua U.S.A. 134 C3
Piquiri r. Brazil 145 A4
Pira Benin 96 D4
Piracanjuba Brazil 145 A2
Piracicaba Brazil 145 B3
Piracicaba r. Brazil 145 C2
Piraçununga Brazil 145 B3
Piracuruca Brazil 143 J4
Piraeus Greece 59 J6
Piraí do Sul Brazil 145 A4
Piráievs Greece see Piraeus
Piraju Brazil 145 A3
Pirajuí Brazil 145 A3
Pirallahı Adası Azer. 91 H2
Piranhas Bahia Brazil 145 C1
Piranhas Goiás Brazil 143 H7
Piranhas r. Rio Grande do Norte Brazil 143 K5
Piranhas r. Brazil 145 A2
Pirapora Brazil 145 B2
Piraube, Lac l. Canada 123 H4
Pirawa India 82 D4
Pirenópolis Brazil 145 A1
Pires do Rio Brazil 145 A2
Pirgos Greece see Pyrgos
Pirin nat. park Bulg. 59 J4
Pirineos mts Europe see Pyrenees
Piripiri Brazil 143 J4
Pirlerkondu Turkey see Taşkent
Pirmasens Germany 53 H5
Pirojpur Bangl. 83 G5
Pir Panjal Pass Jammu and Kashmir 82 C2
Pir Panjal Range mts India/Pak. 89 I3
Piryatin Ukr. see Pyryatyn
Pirzada Afgh. 89 G4
Pisa Italy 58 D3
Pisae Italy see Pisa
Pisagua Chile 142 D7
Pisang, Kepulauan is Indon. 69 I7
Pisaurum Italy see Pesaro
Pisco Peru 142 C6
Písek Czech Rep. 47 O6
Pisha China see Ningnan
Pishan China 82 D1
Pīshīn Iran 80 B6
Pishin Pak. 89 G4
Pishin Lora r. Pak. 89 G4
Pishpek Kyrg. see Bishkek
Pisidia reg. Turkey 90 C3

▶Pissis, Cerro Arg. 144 C3
4th highest mountain in South America.

Pisté Mex. 136 G4
Pisticci Italy 58 G4
Pistoia Italy 58 D3
Pistoriae Italy see Pistoia
Pisuerga r. Spain 57 D3
Pita Guinea 96 B3
Pitaga Canada 123 I3
Pitanga Brazil 145 A4
Pitangui Brazil 145 B2
Pitar India 82 B5
Pitarpunga Lake imp. l. Australia 112 A5
Pitcairn, Henderson, Ducie and Oeno Islands terr. S. Pacific Ocean see Pitcairn Islands
Pitcairn Island Pitcairn Is 151 L7

▶Pitcairn Islands terr. S. Pacific Ocean 151 L7
United Kingdom Overseas Territory.
Oceania 8, 104–105

Piteå Sweden 44 L4
Piteälven r. Sweden 44 L4
Pitelino Rus. Fed. 43 I5
Piterka Rus. Fed. 43 J6
Pitești Romania 59 K2
Pithoragarh India 82 E3
Pithira India 82 D5
Pitiquito Mex. 127 E7
Pitkyaranta Rus. Fed. 42 F3
Pitlochry U.K. 50 F4
Pitong China see Pixian
Pitsane Siding Botswana 101 G3
Pitti i. India 84 B4
Pitt Island Canada 120 D4
Pitt Island N.Z. 107 I6
Pitt Islands Solomon Is see Vanikoro Islands
Pittsboro U.S.A. 131 F5
Pittsburg KS U.S.A. 131 E4
Pittsburg TX U.S.A. 131 E5
Pittsburgh U.S.A. 134 F3
Pittsfield MA U.S.A. 135 I2
Pittsfield ME U.S.A. 135 K1
Pittsfield VT U.S.A. 135 I2
Pittston U.S.A. 135 H3
Pittsworth Australia 112 E1
Pitz Lake Canada 121 L2
Piumhí Brazil 145 B3
Piura Peru 142 B5
Piute Mountains U.S.A. 129 F4
Piute Peak U.S.A. 128 D4
Piute Reservoir U.S.A. 129 G2
Piuthan Nepal 83 E3
Pivabiska r. Canada 122 E4
Pivka Slovenia 58 F2
Pixariá mt. Greece see Pyxaria
Pixian China 76 D2
Pixley U.S.A. 128 D4
Piz Bernina mt. Italy/Switz. 58 C1
Piz Buin mt. Austria/Switz. 47 M7
Pizhanka Rus. Fed. 42 K4
Pizhi Nigeria 96 D4
Pizhma Rus. Fed. 42 J4
Pizhma r. Rus. Fed. 42 K4
Pizhma r. Rus. Fed. 42 L2
Pizhou China 77 H1
Placentia Canada 123 L5
Placentia Italy see Piacenza
Placentia Bay Canada 123 L5
Placerville CA U.S.A. 128 C2
Placerville CO U.S.A. 129 I2
Placetas Cuba 133 E8
Plácido de Castro Brazil 142 E6
Plain Dealing U.S.A. 131 E5

Plainfield CT U.S.A. 135 J3
Plainfield IN U.S.A. 134 B4
Plainfield VT U.S.A. 135 I1
Plains KS U.S.A. 131 C4
Plains TX U.S.A. 131 C5
Plainview U.S.A. 131 C5
Plainville IN U.S.A. 134 B4
Plainville KS U.S.A. 130 D4
Plainwell U.S.A. 134 C2
Plaka, Akra *pt* Greece 59 L7
Plakoti, Cape Cyprus 85 B2
Plamondon Canada 121 H4
Planá Czech Rep. 53 M5
Plana Cays *is* Bahamas 133 F8
Planada U.S.A. 128 C3
Planaltina Brazil 145 B1
Plane *r.* Germany 53 M2
Plankinton U.S.A. 130 D3
Plano U.S.A. 131 D5
Planura Brazil 145 A3
Plaquemine U.S.A. 131 F6
Plasencia Spain 57 C3
Plaster City U.S.A. 129 F5
Plaster Rock Canada 123 I5
Plastun Rus. Fed. 74 E3
Platani *r. Sicily* Italy 58 E6
Platberg *mt.* S. Africa 101 I5

▶Plateau Antarctica
Lowest recorded annual mean temperature in the world.
World 16-17

Plateau of Tibet China 83 F2
Platina U.S.A. 128 B1
Platinum U.S.A. 153 B3
Plato Col. 142 D2
Platte *r.* U.S.A. 130 E3
Platte City U.S.A. 130 E4
Plattling Germany 53 M6
Plattsburgh U.S.A. 135 I1
Plattsmouth U.S.A. 130 E3
Plau Germany 53 M1
Plauen Germany 53 M4
Plauer See *l.* Germany 53 M1
Plavsk Rus. Fed. 43 H5
Playa Noriega, Lago *l.* Mex. 127 F7
Playas Ecuador 142 B4
Playas Lake U.S.A. 129 I6
Plây Cu Vietnam 71 E4
Pleasant, Lake U.S.A. 129 G5
Pleasant Bay U.S.A. 135 K3
Pleasant Grove U.S.A. 129 H1
Pleasant Hill Lake U.S.A. 134 D3
Pleasanton U.S.A. 131 D6
Pleasant Point N.Z. 113 C7
Pleasantville U.S.A. 135 H4
Pleasure Ridge Park U.S.A. 134 C4
Pleaux France 56 F4
Pledger Lake Canada 122 E4
Plei Doch Vietnam 71 D4
Pleinfeld Germany 53 K5
Pleiße *r.* Germany 53 M3
Plenty *watercourse* Australia 110 B5
Plenty, Bay of *g.* N.Z. 113 F3
Plentywood U.S.A. 126 G2
Plesetsk Rus. Fed. 42 I3
Pleshchentsy Belarus *see* Plyeshchanitsy
Pletipi, Lac *l.* Canada 123 H4
Plettenberg Germany 53 H3
Plettenberg Bay S. Africa 100 F8
Pleven Bulg. 59 K3
Plevna Bulg. *see* Pleven
Pljevlja Serb. and Mont. 59 H3
Płock Poland 47 Q4
Pločno *mt.* Bos.-Herz. 58 G3
Plodovoye Rus. Fed. 42 F3
Ploemeur France 56 C3
Ploești Romania *see* Ploiești
Ploiești Romania 59 L2
Plomb du Cantal *mt.* France 56 F4
Ploskoye Rus. Fed. *see* Stanovoye
Płoty Poland 47 O4
Ploudalmézeau France 56 B2
Plouzané France 56 B2
Plovdiv Bulg. 59 K3
Plover Cove Reservoir Hong Kong China 77 [inset]
Plozk Poland *see* Płock
Plum U.S.A. 134 F3
Plumridge Lakes *salt flat* Australia 109 D7
Plungė Lith. 45 L9
Plutarco Elías Calles, Presa *resr* Mex. 127 F7
Pluto, Lac *l.* Canada 123 H3
Plyeshchanitsy Belarus 45 O9
Ply Huey Wati, Khao *mt.* Myanmar/Thai. 70 B3

▶Plymouth Montserrat 137 L5
Capital of Montserrat, largely abandoned in 1997 owing to volcanic activity.

Plymouth U.K. 49 C8
Plymouth CA U.S.A. 128 C2
Plymouth IN U.S.A. 134 B3
Plymouth MA U.S.A. 135 J3
Plymouth NC U.S.A. 132 E5
Plymouth NH U.S.A. 135 J2
Plymouth WI U.S.A. 134 B2
Plymouth Bay U.S.A. 135 J3
Plynlimon *hill* U.K. 49 D6
Plyussa Rus. Fed. 45 P7
Plzeň Czech Rep. 47 N6
Pô Burkina 96 C3
Po *r.* Italy 58 E2
Pô, Parc National de *nat. park* Burkina 96 C3
Pobeda Peak China/Kyrg. 80 F3
Pobedy, Pik *mt.* China/Kyrg. *see* Pobeda Peak
Pocahontas U.S.A. 131 F4
Pocatello U.S.A. 126 E4
Pochala Sudan 97 G4
Pochayiv Ukr. 43 E6
Pochep Rus. Fed. 43 G5
Pochinki Rus. Fed. 43 J5
Pochinok Rus. Fed. 43 G5
Pochutla Mex. 136 E5
Pocking Germany 47 N6
Pocklington U.K. 48 G5
Poções Brazil 145 C1
Pocomoke City U.S.A. 135 H4
Pocomoke Sound *b.* U.S.A. 135 H5
Poconé Brazil 143 G7
Pocono Mountains *hills* U.S.A. 135 H3
Pocono Summit U.S.A. 135 H3
Poços de Caldas Brazil 145 B3
Podanur India 84 C4
Poddor'ye Rus. Fed. 42 F4
Podgorenskiy Rus. Fed. 43 H6
Podgorica Serb. and Mont. 59 H3
Podgornoye Rus. Fed. 64 J4
Podile India 84 C3
Podișul Transilvaniei *plat.* Romania *see* Transylvanian Basin
Podkamennaya Tunguska *r.* Rus. Fed. 65 K3
Podocarpus, Parque Nacional *nat. park* Ecuador 142 C4
Podol'sk Rus. Fed. 43 H5
Podporozh'ye Rus. Fed. 42 G3
Podujevë Serb. and Mont. *see* Podujevo
Podujevo Serb. and Mont. 59 I3
Podz' Rus. Fed. 42 K3
Poelela, Lagoa *l.* Moz. 101 L3
Poeppel Corner *salt flat* Australia 111 B5
Poetovio Slovenia *see* Ptuj
Pofadder S. Africa 100 D5
Pogar Rus. Fed. 43 G5
Poggibonsi Italy 58 D3
Poggio di Montieri *mt.* Italy 58 D3
Pogradec Albania 59 I4
Pogranichnik Afgh. 89 F3
Po Hai *g.* China *see* Bo Hai
P'ohang S. Korea 75 C5
Pohnpei *atoll* Micronesia 150 G5
Pohri India 82 D4
Poi India 83 H4
Poiana Mare Romania 59 J3
Poinsett, Cape Antarctica 152 F2
Point Arena U.S.A. 128 B2
Point au Fer Island U.S.A. 131 F6
Pointe a la Hache U.S.A. 131 F6
Pointe-à-Pitre Guadeloupe 137 L5
Pointe-Noire Congo 99 B4
Point Hope U.S.A. 118 B3
Point Lake Canada 120 H1
Point of Rocks U.S.A. 126 F4
Point Pelee National Park Canada 134 D3
Point Pleasant NJ U.S.A. 135 H3
Point Pleasant WV U.S.A. 134 D4
Poitiers France 56 E3
Poitou *reg.* France 56 E3
Poix-de-Picardie France 52 B5
Pojuca *r.* Brazil 145 D1
Pokaran India 82 B4
Pokataroo Australia 112 D2
Pokcha Rus. Fed. 41 R3
Pokhara Nepal 83 E3
Pokhvistnevo Rus. Fed. 41 Q5
Pok Liu Chau *i.* Hong Kong China *see* Lamma Island
Poko Dem. Rep. Congo 98 C3
Pokosnoye Rus. Fed. 72 I1
Pokran Pak. 89 G5
P'ok'r Kovkas *mts* Asia *see* Lesser Caucasus
Pokrovka *Chitinskaya Oblast'* Rus. Fed. 74 A1
Pokrovka *Primorskiy Kray* Rus. Fed. 74 C4
Pokrovsk *Respublika Sakha (Yakutiya)* Rus. Fed. 65 N3
Pokrovsk *Saratovskaya Oblast'* Rus. Fed. *see* Engel's
Pokrovskoye Rus. Fed. 43 H7
Pokshen'ga *r.* Rus. Fed. 42 J3
Pol India 82 C5
Pola Croatia *see* Pula
Polacca Wash *watercourse* U.S.A. 129 H4
Pola de Lena Spain 57 D2
Pola de Siero Spain 57 D2
▶Poland *country* Europe 40 J5
Europe 5, 38–39
Poland NY U.S.A. 135 H2
Poland OH U.S.A. 134 E3
Polar Plateau Antarctica 152 A1
Polatlı Turkey 90 D3
Polatsk Belarus 45 P9
Polavaram India 84 D2
Polcirkeln Sweden 44 L3
Pol-e Fāsā Iran 88 D4
Pole-Khatum Iran 89 F2
Pol-e Khomrī Afgh. 89 H3
Pol-e Safid Iran 88 D2
Polessk Rus. Fed. 45 L9
Poles'ye *marsh* Belarus/Ukr. *see* Pripet Marshes
Polgahawela Sri Lanka 84 D5
Poli Cyprus *see* Polis
Políaigos *i.* Greece *see* Polyaigos
Police Poland 47 O4
Policoro Italy 58 G4
Poligny France 56 G3
Políkastron Greece *see* Polykastro
Polillo Islands Phil. 69 G3
Polis Cyprus 85 A2
Polis'ke Ukr. 43 F6
Polis'kyy Zapovidnyk *nature res.* Ukr. 43 F6
Politovo Rus. Fed. 42 K2
Políyiros Greece *see* Polygyros
Polkowice Poland 47 P5
Pollachi India 84 C4
Pollard Islands U.S.A. *see* Gardner Pinnacles
Polle Germany 53 J3
Pollino, Monte *mt.* Italy 58 G5
Pollino, Parco Nazionale del *nat. park* Italy 58 G5
Pollock Pines U.S.A. 128 C2
Pollock Reef Australia 109 C8
Polmak Norway 44 O1
Polnovat Rus. Fed. 41 T3
Polo Fin. 44 P4
Poloat *atoll* Micronesia *see* Puluwat
Pologi Ukr. *see* Polohy
Polohy Ukr. 43 H7
Polonne Ukr. 43 E6
Polonnoye Ukr. *see* Polonne
Polotsk Belarus *see* Polatsk
Polperro U.K. 49 C8
Polska *country* Europe *see* Poland
Polson U.S.A. 126 E3
Polta *r.* Rus. Fed. 42 I2
Poltava Ukr. 43 G6
Poltoratsk Turkm. *see* Ashgabat
Põltsamaa Estonia 45 N7
Polunochnoye Rus. Fed. 41 S3
Põlva Estonia 45 O7
Polvadera U.S.A. 127 G6
Polvijärvi Fin. 44 P5
Polyaigos *i.* Greece 59 K6
Polyanovgrad Bulg. *see* Karnobat
Polyarnyy *Chukotskiy Avtonomnyy Okrug* Rus. Fed. 65 S3
Polyarnyy *Murmanskaya Oblast'* Rus. Fed. 44 R2
Polyarnyye Zori Rus. Fed. 44 R3
Polyarnyy Ural *mts* Rus. Fed. 41 S2
Polygyros Greece 59 J4
Polykastro Greece 59 J4
Polynesia *is* Pacific Ocean 150 I6
Polynésie Française *terr.* S. Pacific Ocean *see* French Polynesia
Pom Indon. 69 J7
Pomarkku Fin. 45 M6
Pombal *Pará* Brazil 143 H4
Pombal *Paraíba* Brazil 143 K5
Pombal Port. 57 B4
Pomene Moz. 101 L2
Pomeroy S. Africa 101 J5
Pomeroy U.K. 51 F3
Pomeroy OH U.S.A. 134 D4
Pomeroy WA U.S.A. 126 D3
Pomezia Italy 58 E4
Pomfret S. Africa 100 F3
Pomona Namibia 100 B4
Pomona U.S.A. 128 E4
Pomorie Bulg. 59 L3
Pomorska, Zatoka *b.* Poland 47 O3
Pomorskie, Pojezierze *reg.* Poland 47 O4
Pomorskiy Bereg *coastal area* Rus. Fed. 42 G2
Pomorskiy Proliv *sea chan.* Rus. Fed. 42 K1
Pomos Point Cyprus 85 A2
Pomo Tso *l.* China *see* Puma Yumco
Pomou, Akra *pt* Cyprus *see* Pomos Point
Pomozdino Rus. Fed. 42 L3
Pompain China 76 B2
Pompano Beach U.S.A. 133 D7
Pompei Italy 58 F4
Pompéia Brazil 145 A3
Pompey France 52 G6
Pompeyevka Rus. Fed. 74 C2
Ponape *atoll* Micronesia *see* Pohnpei
Ponask Lake Canada 121 M4
Ponazyrevo Rus. Fed. 42 J4
Ponca City U.S.A. 131 D4
Ponce Puerto Rico 137 K5
Ponce de Leon Bay U.S.A. 133 D7
Poncheville, Lac *l.* Canada 122 F4
Pondicherry India 84 C4
Pondicherry *union terr.* India 84 C4
Pondichéry India *see* Pondicherry
Pond Inlet Canada 153 K2
Ponds Bay Canada *see* Pond Inlet
Ponente, Riviera di *coastal area* Italy 58 B3
Poneto U.S.A. 134 C3
Ponferrada Spain 57 C2
Pongara, Pointe *pt* Gabon 98 A3
Pongaroa N.Z. 113 F5
Pongo *watercourse* Sudan 97 F4
Pongola *r.* S. Africa 101 K4
Pongolapoort Dam *l.* S. Africa 101 J4
Ponnagyun Myanmar 70 A2
Ponnaivar *r.* India 84 C4
Ponnampet India 84 B3
Ponnani India 84 B4
Ponnyadaung Range *mts* Myanmar 70 A2
Pono Indon. 69 I8
Ponoka Canada 120 H4
Ponoy *r.* Rus. Fed. 42 I2
Pons *r.* Canada 123 H2

▶Ponta Delgada Arquipélago dos Açores 148 G3
Capital of the Azores.

Ponta Grossa Brazil 145 A4
Pontal Brazil 145 A3
Pontalina Brazil 145 A2
Pont-à-Mousson France 52 G6
Ponta Porã Brazil 144 E2
Pontarfynach U.K. *see* Devil's Bridge
Pont-Audemer France 49 H9
Pontault-Combault France 52 C6
Pontax *r.* Canada 122 F4
Pontchartrain, Lake U.S.A. 131 F6
Pont-de-Loup Belgium 52 E4
Ponte Alta do Norte Brazil 143 I6
Ponte de Sor Port. 57 B4
Ponte Firme Brazil 145 B2
Pontefract U.K. 48 F5
Ponteix Canada 121 J5
Ponteland U.K. 48 F3
Ponte Nova Brazil 145 C3
Pontes-e-Lacerda Brazil 143 G7
Pontevedra Spain 57 B2
Ponthierville Dem. Rep. Congo *see* Ubundu
Pontiac IL U.S.A. 130 F3
Pontiac MI U.S.A. 134 D2
Pontiae *is* Italy *see* Ponziane, Isole
Pontianak Indon. 68 D7
Pontine Islands *is* Italy *see* Ponziane, Isole
Pont-l'Abbé France 56 B3
Pontoise France 52 C5
Ponton *watercourse* Australia 105 C7
Ponton Canada 121 L4
Pontotoc U.S.A. 131 F5
Pont-Ste-Maxence France 52 C5
Pontypool U.K. 49 D7
Pontypridd U.K. 49 D7
Ponza, Isola di *i.* Italy 58 E4
Ponziane, Isole *is* Italy 58 E4
Poochera Australia 109 F8
Poole U.K. 49 F8
Poole U.S.A. 134 B5
Poolowanna Lake *salt flat* Australia 111 B5
Poona India *see* Pune
Pooncarie Australia 111 C7
Poonch India *see* Punch
Poopelloe, Lake *salt l.* Australia 112 B3
Poopó, Lago de *l.* Bol. 142 E7
Poor Knights Islands N.Z. 113 E2
Popayán Col. 142 C3
Poperinge Belgium 52 C4
Popigay *r.* Rus. Fed. 65 L2
Popiltah Australia 111 C7
Popilta Lake *imp. l.* Australia 111 C7
Poplar *r.* Canada 121 L4
Poplar U.S.A. 126 G2
Poplar Bluff U.S.A. 131 F4
Poplar Camp U.S.A. 134 E5
Poplarville U.S.A. 131 F6

▶Popocatépetl, Volcán *vol.* Mex. 136 E5
5th highest mountain in North America.

Popokabaka Dem. Rep. Congo 99 B4
Popondetta P.N.G. 69 L8
Popovichskaya Rus. Fed. *see* Kalininskaya
Popovo Bulg. 59 L3
Popovo Polje *plain* Bos.-Herz. 58 G3
Poppberg *hill* Germany 53 L5
Poppenberg *hill* Germany 53 K3
Poprad Slovakia 47 R6
Poquoson U.S.A. 135 G5
Porali *r.* Pak. 89 G5
Porangahau N.Z. 113 F5
Porangatu Brazil 145 A1
Porbandar India 82 B5
Porcher Island Canada 120 D4
Porcos *r.* Brazil 145 B1
Porcupine, Cape Canada 123 K3
Porcupine Abyssal Plain *sea feature* N. Atlantic Ocean 148 G2
Porcupine Gorge National Park Australia 110 D4
Porcupine Hills Canada 121 K4
Porcupine Mountains U.S.A. 130 F2
Poreč Croatia 58 E2
Porecatu Brazil 145 A3
Poretskoye Rus. Fed. 43 J5
Pori Fin. 45 L6
Porirua N.Z. 113 E5
Porkhov Rus. Fed. 45 P8
Porlamar Venez. 142 F1
Pormpuraaw Australia 110 C2
Pornic France 56 C3
Poronaysk Rus. Fed. 74 F2
Porong China *see* Baingoin
Poros Greece 59 J6
Porosozero Rus. Fed. 42 G3
Porpoise Bay Antarctica 152 G2
Porsangen *sea chan.* Norway 44 N1
Porsangerhalvøya *pen.* Norway 44 N1
Porsgrunn Norway 45 F7
Porsuk *r.* Turkey 59 N5
Portadown U.K. 51 F3
Portaferry U.K. 51 G3
Portage MI U.S.A. 134 C2
Portage PA U.S.A. 135 F3
Portage WI U.S.A. 130 F3
Portage Lakes U.S.A. 134 E3
Portage la Prairie Canada 121 L5
Portal U.S.A. 130 C1
Port Alberni Canada 120 E5
Port Albert Australia 112 C7
Portalegre Port. 57 C4
Portales U.S.A. 131 C5
Port-Alfred Canada *see* La Baie
Port Alfred S. Africa 101 H7
Port Alice Canada 120 E5
Port Allegany U.S.A. 135 F3
Port Allen U.S.A. 131 F6
Port Alma Australia 110 E4
Port Angeles U.S.A. 126 C2
Port Antonio Jamaica 137 I5
Portarlington Rep. of Ireland 51 E4
Port Arthur Australia 111 [inset]
Port Arthur U.S.A. 131 E6
Port Askaig U.K. 50 C5
Port Augusta Australia 111 B7

▶Port-au-Prince Haiti 137 J5
Capital of Haiti.

Port Austin U.S.A. 134 D1
Port aux Choix Canada 123 K4
Portavogie U.K. 51 G3
Port Beaufort S. Africa 100 E8
Port Blair India 71 A5
Port Bolster Canada 134 F1
Portbou Spain 57 H2
Port Burwell Canada 134 E2
Port Campbell Australia 112 A7
Port Campbell National Park Australia 112 A7
Port Carling Canada 134 F1
Port-Cartier Canada 123 I4
Port Chalmers N.Z. 113 C7
Port Charlotte U.S.A. 133 D7
Port Clements Canada 120 C4
Port Clinton U.S.A. 134 D3
Port Credit Canada 134 F2
Port-de-Paix Haiti 137 J5
Port Dickson Malaysia 71 C7
Port Douglas Australia 110 D3
Port Edward Canada 120 D4
Port Edward S. Africa 101 J6
Porteira Brazil 143 G4
Porteirinha Brazil 145 C1
Portel Brazil 143 H4
Port Elgin Canada 134 E1
Port Elizabeth S. Africa 101 G7
Port Ellen U.K. 50 C5
Port Erin Isle of Man 48 C4
Porter Lake *N.W.T.* Canada 121 J2
Porter Lake *Sask.* Canada 121 J3
Porter Landing Canada 120 D3
Porterville S. Africa 100 D7
Porterville U.S.A. 128 D3
Port Étienne Mauritania *see* Nouâdhibou
Port Everglades U.S.A. *see* Fort Lauderdale
Port Fitzroy N.Z. 113 E3
Port Francqui Dem. Rep. Congo *see* Ilebo
Port-Gentil Gabon 98 A4
Port Glasgow U.K. 50 E5
Port Harcourt Nigeria 96 D4
Port Harrison Canada *see* Inukjuak
Porthcawl U.K. 49 D7
Port Hedland Australia 108 B5
Port Henry U.S.A. 135 I1
Port Herald Malawi *see* Nsanje
Porthleven U.K. 49 B8
Porthmadog U.K. 49 C6
Port Hope Canada 135 F2
Port Hope Simpson Canada 123 L3
Port Hueneme U.S.A. 128 D4
Port Huron U.S.A. 134 D2
Portimão Port. 57 B5
Port Jackson Australia *see* Sydney
Port Jackson *inlet* Australia 112 E4
Port Keats Australia *see* Wadeye
Port Klang Malaysia *see* Pelabuhan Kelang
Port Láirge Rep. of Ireland *see* Waterford
Portland *N.S.W.* Australia 112 D4
Portland *Vic.* Australia 111 C8
Portland IN U.S.A. 134 C3
Portland ME U.S.A. 135 J2
Portland MI U.S.A. 134 C2
Portland OR U.S.A. 126 C3
Portland TN U.S.A. 134 B5
Portland, Isle of *pen.* U.K. 49 E8
Portland Bill *hd* U.K. *see* Bill of Portland
Portland Creek Pond *l.* Canada 123 K4
Portland Roads Australia 110 C2
Port-la-Nouvelle France 56 F5
Portlaoise Rep. of Ireland 51 E4
Port Lavaca U.S.A. 131 D6
Portlaw Rep. of Ireland 51 E5
Portlethen U.K. 50 G3
Port Lincoln Australia 111 A7
Port Loko Sierra Leone 96 B4

▶Port Louis Mauritius 149 L7
Capital of Mauritius.

Port-Lyautrey Morocco *see* Kénitra
Port Macquarie Australia 112 F3
Portmadoc U.K. *see* Porthmadog
Port McNeill Canada 120 E5
Port-Menier Canada 123 I4

▶Port Moresby P.N.G. 69 L8
Capital of Papua New Guinea.

Portnaguran U.K. 50 C2
Portnahaven U.K. 50 C5
Port nan Giúran U.K. *see* Portnaguran
Port Neill Australia 111 B7
Port Ness U.K. 50 C2
Portneuf *r.* Canada 123 H4
Port Nis U.K. *see* Port Ness
Port Noarlunga Australia 111 B7
Port Nolloth S. Africa 100 C5
Port Norris U.S.A. 135 H4
Port-Nouveau-Québec Canada *see* Kangiqsualujjuaq
Porto Port. *see* Oporto
Porto Acre Brazil 142 E5
Porto Alegre Brazil 145 A5
Porto Alexandre Angola *see* Tombua
Porto Amboim Angola 99 B5
Porto Amélia Moz. *see* Pemba
Porto Artur Brazil 143 G6
Porto Belo Brazil 145 A4
Porto de Moz Brazil 143 H4
Porto de Santa Cruz Brazil 145 C1
Porto dos Gaúchos Óbidos Brazil 143 G6
Porto Esperança Brazil 143 G7
Porto Esperidião Brazil 143 G7
Portoferraio Italy 58 D3
Porto Franco Brazil 143 I5

▶Port of Spain Trin. and Tob. 137 L6
Capital of Trinidad and Tobago.

Porto Grande Brazil 143 H3
Portogruaro Italy 58 E2
Porto Jofre Brazil 143 G7
Portola U.S.A. 128 C2
Portomaggiore Italy 58 D2
Porto Mendes Brazil 144 F2
Porto Murtinho Brazil 144 E2
Porto Nacional Brazil 143 I6

▶Porto-Novo Benin 96 D4
Capital of Benin.

Porto Novo Cape Verde 96 [inset]
Porto Primavera, Represa *resr* Brazil 144 F2
Port Orchard U.S.A. 126 C3
Port Orford U.S.A. 126 B4
Porto Rico Angola 99 B4
Porto Santo, Ilha de *i.* Madeira 96 B1
Porto Seguro Brazil 145 D2
Porto Tolle Italy 58 E2
Porto Torres *Sardinia* Italy 58 C4
Porto União Brazil 145 A4
Porto-Vecchio *Corsica* France 56 I6
Porto Velho Brazil 142 F5
Portoviejo Ecuador 142 B4
Porto Wálter Brazil 142 D5
Portpatrick U.K. 50 D6
Port Perry Canada 135 F1
Port Phillip Bay Australia 112 B7
Port Pirie Australia 111 B7
Port Radium Canada *see* Echo Bay
Portreath U.K. 49 B8
Portree U.K. 50 C3
Port Rexton Canada 123 L4
Port Royal U.S.A. 135 G4
Port Royal Sound *inlet* U.S.A. 133 D5
Portrush U.K. 51 F2
Port Safaga Egypt *see* Bûr Safâjah
Port Said Egypt 85 A4
Portsalon Rep. of Ireland 51 E2
Port Sanilac U.S.A. 134 D2
Port Severn Canada 134 F1
Port Shepstone S. Africa 101 J6
Port Simpson Canada *see* Lax Kw'alaams
Portsmouth U.K. 49 F8
Portsmouth NH U.S.A. 135 J2
Portsmouth OH U.S.A. 134 D4
Portsmouth VA U.S.A. 135 G5
Portsoy U.K. 50 G3
Port Stanley Falkland Is *see* Stanley
Port Stephens *b.* Australia 112 F4
Portstewart U.K. 51 F2
Port St Joe U.S.A. 133 C6
Port St Lucie City U.S.A. 133 D7
Port St Mary Isle of Man 48 C4
Port Sudan Sudan 86 E6
Port Swettenham Malaysia *see* Pelabuhan Kelang
Port Talbot U.K. 49 D7
Porttipahdan tekojärvi *l.* Fin. 44 O2
Port Townsend U.S.A. 126 C2
▶Portugal *country* Europe 57 C4
Europe 5, 38–39
Portugália Angola *see* Chitato
Portuguese East Africa *country* Africa *see* Mozambique
Portuguese Guinea *country* Africa *see* Guinea-Bissau
Portuguese Timor *country* Asia *see* East Timor
Portuguese West Africa *country* Africa *see* Angola
Portumna Rep. of Ireland 51 D4
Portus Herculis Monoeci *country* Europe *see* Monaco
Port-Vendres France 56 F5

▶Port Vila Vanuatu 107 G3
Capital of Vanuatu.

Portville U.S.A. 135 F2
Port Vladimir Rus. Fed. 44 R2
Port Waikato N.Z. 113 E3
Port Washington U.S.A. 134 B2
Port William U.K. 50 E6
Porvenir Bol. 142 E6
Porvenir Chile 144 B8
Porvoo Fin. 45 N6
Posada Spain 57 D2
Posada de Llanera Spain *see* Posada
Posadas Arg. 144 E3
Posen Poland *see* Poznań
Posen U.S.A. 134 D1
Poseyville U.S.A. 134 B4
Poshekhon'ye Rus. Fed. 42 H4
Poshekhon'ye-Volodarsk Rus. Fed. *see* Poshekhon'ye
Posht-e Badam Iran 88 D3
Poshteh-ye Chaqvīr *hill* Iran 88 E4
Posht-e Kūh *mts* Iran 88 B3
Posht-e Rūd-e Zamindavar *reg.* Afgh. *see* Zamīndāvar
Posht Kūh *hill* Iran 88 C2
Posio Fin. 44 P3
Poso Indon. 69 G7
Posof Turkey 91 F2
Posŏng S. Korea 75 B6
Possession Island Namibia 100 B4
Pößneck Germany 53 L4
Post U.S.A. 131 C5
Postavy Belarus *see* Pastavy
Poste-de-la-Baleine Canada *see* Kuujjuarapik
Postmasburg S. Africa 100 F5
Poston U.S.A. 129 F4
Postville Canada 123 K3
Postville U.S.A. 130 F3
Post Weygand Alg. 96 D2
Postysheve Ukr. *see* Krasnoarmiys'k
Pota Indon. 108 C2
Pótam Mex. 127 F8
Poté Brazil 145 C2
Poteau U.S.A. 131 E5
Potegaon India 84 D2
Potentia Italy *see* Potenza
Potenza Italy 58 F4
Potgietersrus S. Africa 101 I3
Poth U.S.A. 131 D6
P'ot'i Georgia 91 F2
Potikal India 84 D2
Potiraguá Brazil 145 D1
Potiskum Nigeria 96 E3
Potlatch U.S.A. 126 D3
Pot Mountain U.S.A. 126 E3
Po Toi *i.* Hong Kong China 77 [inset]
Potomac *r.* U.S.A. 135 G4
Potosí Bol. 142 E7
Potosi U.S.A. 130 F4
Potosi Mountain U.S.A. 129 F4
Potrerillos Chile 144 C3
Potrero del Llano Mex. 131 B6
Potsdam Germany 53 N2
Potsdam U.S.A. 135 H1
Potter U.S.A. 130 C3
Potterne U.K. 49 E7
Potters Bar U.K. 49 G7
Potter Valley U.S.A. 128 B2
Pottstown U.S.A. 135 H3
Pottsville U.S.A. 135 G3
Pottuvil Sri Lanka 84 D5
Potwar *reg.* Pak. 89 I3
Pouch Cove Canada 123 L5
Poughkeepsie U.S.A. 135 I3
Poulin de Courval, Lac *l.* Canada 123 H4
Poulton-le-Fylde U.K. 48 E5
Pouso Alegre Brazil 145 B3
Poŭthĭsăt Cambodia 71 C4
Poŭthĭsăt, Stœng *r.* Cambodia 71 D4
Považská Bystrica Slovakia 47 Q6
Povenets Rus. Fed. 42 G3
Poverty Bay N.Z. 113 F4
Povlen *mt.* Serb. and Mont. 59 H2
Póvoa de Varzim Port. 57 B3
Povorino Rus. Fed. 43 I6
Povorotnyy, Mys *hd* Rus. Fed. 74 D4
Poway U.S.A. 128 E5
Powder *r.* U.S.A. 126 G3
Powder, South Fork *r.* U.S.A. 126 G4
Powder River U.S.A. 126 G4
Powell *r.* U.S.A. 134 D5
Powell, Lake *resr* U.S.A. 129 H3
Powell Lake Canada 120 E5
Powell Mountain U.S.A. 128 D2
Powell Point Bahamas 133 E7
Powell River Canada 120 E5
Powhatan AR U.S.A. 131 F4
Powhatan VA U.S.A. 135 G5
Powo China 76 C1
Pōwrize Turkm. *see* Firyuza
Poxoréu Brazil 143 H7
Poyang China *see* Boyang
Poyang Hu *l.* China 77 H2
Poyan Reservoir Sing. 71 [inset]
Poyarkovo Rus. Fed. 74 C2
Pozantı Turkey 90 D3

Požarevac Serb. and Mont. 59 I2
Poza Rica Mex. 136 E4
Pozdeyevka Rus. Fed. 74 C2
Požega Croatia 58 G2
Požega Serb. and Mont. 59 I3
Pozharskoye Rus. Fed. 74 D3
Poznań Poland 47 P4
Pozoblanco Spain 57 D4
Pozo Colorado Para. 144 E2
Pozsony Slovakia see Bratislava
Pozzuoli Italy 58 F4
Prabumulih Indon. 68 C7
Prachatice Czech Rep. 47 O6
Prachi r. India 83 F6
Prachin Buri Thai. 71 C4
Prachuap Khiri Khan Thai. 71 B5
Prades France 56 F5
Prado Brazil 145 D2

▶Prague Czech Rep. 47 O5
Capital of the Czech Republic.

Praha Czech Rep. see Prague

▶Praia Cape Verde 96 [inset]
Capital of Cape Verde.

Praia do Bilene Moz. 101 K3
Prainha Brazil 143 H4
Prairie Australia 110 D4
Prairie r. U.S.A. 130 E2
Prairie Dog Town Fork r. U.S.A. 131 C5
Prairie du Chien U.S.A. 130 F3
Prairie River Canada 121 K4
Pram, Khao mt. Thai. 71 B5
Pran r. Thai. 71 C4
Pran Buri Thai. 71 B4
Prapat Indon. 71 B7
Prasonisi, Akra pt Greece 59 L7
Prata Brazil 145 A2
Prata r. Brazil 145 A2
Prat de Llobregat Spain see El Prat de Llobregat
Prathes Thai country Asia see Thailand
Prato Italy 58 D3
Pratt U.S.A. 130 D4
Prattville U.S.A. 133 C5
Pravdinsk Rus. Fed. 45 L9
Praya Indon. 108 B2
Preah, Prêk r. Cambodia 71 D4
Preăh Vihear Cambodia 71 D4
Preble U.S.A. 135 G2
Prechistoye *Smolenskaya Oblast'* Rus. Fed. 43 G5
Prechistoye *Yaroslavskaya Oblast'* Rus. Fed. 42 I4
Precipice National Park Australia 110 E5
Preeceville Canada 121 K5
Pregolya r. Rus. Fed. 45 L9
Preiļi Latvia 45 O8
Prelate Canada 121 I5
Premer Australia 112 D3
Prémery France 56 F3
Premnitz Germany 53 M2
Prentiss U.S.A. 131 F6
Prenzlau Germany 47 N4
Preparis Island Cocos Is 68 A4
Preparis North Channel Cocos Is 68 A4
Preparis South Channel Cocos Is 68 A4
Přerov Czech Rep. 47 P6
Presa San Antonio Mex. 131 C7
Prescelly Mts hills U.K. see Preseli, Mynydd
Prescott Canada 135 H1
Prescott AR U.S.A. 131 E5
Prescott AZ U.S.A. 129 G4
Prescott Valley U.S.A. 129 G4
Preseli, Mynydd hills U.K. 49 C7
Preševo Serb. and Mont. 59 I3
Presidencia Roque Sáenz Peña Arg. 144 D3
Presidente Dutra Brazil 143 J5
Presidente Eduardo Frei research station Antarctica 152 A2
Presidente Hermes Brazil 142 F6
Presidente Olegário Brazil 145 B2
Presidente Prudente Brazil 145 A3
Presidente Venceslau Brazil 145 A3
Presidio U.S.A. 131 B6
Preslav Bulg. see Veliki Preslav
Prešov Slovakia 43 D6
Prespa, Lake Europe 59 I4
Prespansko Ezero l. Europe see Prespa, Lake
Prespes nat. park Greece 59 I4
Prespës, Liqeni i l. Europe see Prespa, Lake
Presque Isle ME U.S.A. 132 G2
Presque Isle MI U.S.A. 134 D1
Pressburg Slovakia see Bratislava
Presteigne U.K. 49 D6
Preston U.K. 48 E5
Preston ID U.S.A. 126 F4
Preston MN U.S.A. 130 E3
Preston MO U.S.A. 130 E4
Preston, Cape Australia 108 B5
Prestonpans U.K. 50 G5
Prestonsburg U.S.A. 134 D5
Prestwick U.K. 50 E5
Preto r. *Bahia* Brazil 143 J6
Preto r. *Minas Gerais* Brazil 145 B2
Preto r. Brazil 145 D1

▶Pretoria S. Africa 101 I3
Official capital of South Africa.

Pretoria-Witwatersrand-Vereeniging prov. S. Africa see Gauteng
Pretzsch Germany 53 M3
Preussisch-Eylau Rus. Fed. see Bagrationovsk
Preußisch Stargard Poland see Starogard Gdański
Preveza Greece 59 I5
Prewitt U.S.A. 129 I4
Prey Vêng Cambodia 71 D5
Priaral'skiye Karakumy, Peski des. Kazakh. 80 B2
Priargunsk Rus. Fed. 73 L2
Pribilof Islands U.S.A. 118 A4
Priboj Serb. and Mont. 59 H3
Price r. Australia 108 E3
Price NC U.S.A. 134 F5
Price UT U.S.A. 129 H2
Price r. U.S.A. 129 H2
Price Island Canada 120 D4
Prichard AL U.S.A. 131 F6
Prichard WV U.S.A. 134 D4
Pridorozhnoye Rus. Fed. see Khulkhuta
Priekule Latvia 45 L8
Priekuļi Latvia 45 N8
Prienai Lith. 45 M9
Prieska S. Africa 100 F5
Prievidza Slovakia 47 Q6
Prignitz reg. Germany 53 M1
Prijedor Bos.-Herz. 58 G2
Prijepolje Serb. and Mont. 59 H3
Prikaspiyskaya Nizmennost' lowland Kazakh./Rus. Fed. see Caspian Lowland
Prilep Macedonia 59 I4
Priluki Ukr. see Pryluky
Přimda Czech Rep. 53 M5
Primero de Enero Cuba 133 E8
Primorsk Rus. Fed. 45 P6
Primorsk Ukr. see Prymors'k
Primorskiy Kray admin. div. Rus. Fed. 74 D3
Primorsko-Akhtarsk Rus. Fed. 43 H7
Primo Tapia Mex. 128 E5
Primrose Lake Canada 121 I4
Prims r. Germany 52 G5
Prince Albert Canada 121 J4
Prince Albert S. Africa 100 F7
Prince Albert Mountains Antarctica 152 H1
Prince Albert National Park Canada 121 J4
Prince Albert Peninsula Canada 118 G2
Prince Albert Road S. Africa 100 E7
Prince Alfred, Cape Canada 118 F2
Prince Alfred Hamlet S. Africa 100 D7
Prince Charles Island Canada 119 K3
Prince Charles Mountains Antarctica 152 E2
Prince Edward Island prov. Canada 123 J5

▶Prince Edward Islands Indian Ocean 149 K9
Part of South Africa.

Prince Edward Point Canada 135 G2
Prince Frederick U.S.A. 135 G4
Prince George Canada 120 F4
Prince Harald Coast Antarctica 152 D2
Prince of Wales, Cape U.S.A. 118 B3
Prince of Wales Island Australia 110 C1
Prince of Wales Island Canada 119 I2
Prince of Wales Island U.S.A. 120 C4
Prince of Wales Strait Canada 118 G2
Prince Patrick Island Canada 118 G2
Prince Regent Inlet sea chan. Canada 119 I2
Prince Rupert Canada 120 D4
Princess Anne U.S.A. 135 H4
Princess Astrid Coast Antarctica 152 C2
Princess Charlotte Bay Australia 110 C2
Princess Elizabeth Land reg. Antarctica 152 E2
Princess Mary Lake Canada 121 L1
Princess Ragnhild Coast Antarctica 152 C2
Princess Royal Island Canada 120 D4
Princeton Canada 120 F5
Princeton CA U.S.A. 128 B2
Princeton IL U.S.A. 130 F3
Princeton IN U.S.A. 134 B4
Princeton MO U.S.A. 130 E3
Princeton NJ U.S.A. 135 H3
Princeton WV U.S.A. 134 E5
Prince William Sound b. U.S.A. 118 D3
Príncipe i. São Tomé and Príncipe 96 D4
Prineville U.S.A. 126 C3
Prins Harald Kyst coastal area Antarctica see Prince Harald Coast
Prinzapolca Nicaragua 137 H6
Priozersk Rus. Fed. 45 Q6
Priozyorsk Rus. Fed. see Priozersk
Pripet r. Belarus/Ukr. 43 F6
also spelt Pryp"yat' (Ukraine) or Prypyats' (Belarus)
Pripet Marshes Belarus/Ukr. 43 E6
Prirechnyy Rus. Fed. 44 Q2
Prishtinë Serb. and Mont. see Priština
Priština Serb. and Mont. 59 I3
Pritzier Germany 53 L1
Pritzwalk Germany 53 M1
Privas France 56 G4
Privlaka Croatia 58 F2
Privolzhsk Rus. Fed. 42 I4
Privolzhskaya Vozvyshennost' hills Rus. Fed. 43 J6
Privolzhskiy Rus. Fed. 43 J6
Privolzh'ye Rus. Fed. 43 K5
Priyutnoye Rus. Fed. 43 I7
Prizren Serb. and Mont. 59 I3
Probolinggo Indon. 68 E8
Probstzella Germany 53 L4
Probus U.K. 49 C8
Proddatur India 84 C3
Professor van Blommestein Meer resr Suriname 143 G3
Progreso Hond. see El Progreso
Progreso Mex. 131 C7
Progress Rus. Fed. 74 C2
Project City U.S.A. 126 C4
Prokhladnyy Rus. Fed. 91 G2
Prokop'yevsk Rus. Fed. 72 F2
Prokuplje Serb. and Mont. 59 I3
Proletarsk Rus. Fed. 43 I7
Proletarskaya Rus. Fed. see Proletarsk
Prome Myanmar see Pyè
Promissão Brazil 145 A3
Promissão, Represa resr Brazil 145 A3
Prophet r. Canada 120 F3
Prophet River Canada 120 F3
Propriá Brazil 143 K6
Proskurov Ukr. see Khmel'nyts'kyy
Prosser U.S.A. 126 D3
Protem S. Africa 100 E8
Provadiya Bulg. 59 L3
Prøven Greenland see Kangersuatsiaq
Provence reg. France 56 G5
Providence KY U.S.A. 134 B5
Providence MD U.S.A. see Annapolis

▶Providence RI U.S.A. 135 J3
State capital of Rhode Island.

Providence, Cape N.Z. 113 A8
Providencia, Isla de i. Caribbean Sea 137 H6
Provideniya Rus. Fed. 65 T3
Provincetown U.S.A. 135 J2
Provo U.S.A. 129 H1
Provost Canada 121 I4
Prudentópolis Brazil 145 A4
Prudhoe Bay U.S.A. 118 D2
Prüm Germany 52 G4
Prüm r. Germany 52 G5
Prunelli-di-Fiumorbo *Corsica* France 56 I5
Pruntytown U.S.A. 134 E4
Prusa Turkey see Bursa
Prushkov Poland see Pruszków
Pruszków Poland 47 R4
Prut r. Europe 43 F7
Prydz Bay Antarctica 152 E2
Pryelbrusskiy Natsional'nyy Park nat. park Rus. Fed. 43 I8
Pryluky Ukr. 43 G6
Prymors'k Ukr. 43 H7
Prymors'ke Ukr. see Sartana
Pryp"yat' r. Ukr. 43 F6 see Pripet
Prypyats' r. Belarus 41 L5 see Pripet
Przemyśl Poland 43 D6
Przheval'sk Kyrg. see Karakol
Psara i. Greece 59 K5
Pskov Rus. Fed. 45 P8
Pskov, Lake Estonia/Rus. Fed. 45 O7
Pskov Oblast admin. div. Rus. Fed. see Pskovskaya Oblast'
Pskovskaya Oblast' admin. div. Rus. Fed. 45 P8
Pskovskoye Ozero l. Estonia/Rus. Fed. see Pskov, Lake
Ptolemaïda Greece 59 I4
Ptolemais Israel see 'Akko
Ptuj Slovenia 58 F1
Pua Thai. 70 C3
Puaka hill Sing. 71 [inset]
Pu'an *Guizhou* China 76 E3
Pu'an *Sichuan* China 76 E2
Puan S. Korea 75 B6
Pucallpa Peru 142 D5
Pucheng *Fujian* China 77 H3
Pucheng *Shaanxi* China 77 F1
Puchezh Rus. Fed. 42 I4
Puch'ŏn S. Korea 75 B5
Puck Poland 47 Q3
Pudai watercourse Afgh. see Dor
Pūdanū Iran 88 D3
Pudasjärvi Fin. 44 O4
Pudimoe S. Africa 100 G4
Pudozh Rus. Fed. 42 H3
Pudsey U.K. 48 F5
Pudu China see Suizhou
Puduchcheri India see Pondicherry
Pudukkottai India 84 C4
Puebla *Baja California* Mex. 129 F5
Puebla *Puebla* Mex. 136 E5
Puebla de Sanabria Spain 57 C2
Puebla de Zaragoza Mex. see Puebla
Pueblo U.S.A. 127 G5
Pueblo Yaqui Mex. 127 F8
Puelches Arg. 144 C5
Puelén Arg. 144 C5
Puente-Genil Spain 57 D5
Pu'er China 76 D4
Puerco watercourse U.S.A. 129 H4
Puerto Acosta Bol. 142 E7
Puerto Alegre Bol. 142 F6
Puerto Ángel Mex. 136 E5
Puerto Armuelles Panama 137 H7
Puerto Ayacucho Venez. 142 E2
Puerto Bahía Negra Para. see Bahía Negra
Puerto Baquerizo Moreno *Galápagos* Ecuador 142 [inset]
Puerto Barrios Guat. 136 G5
Puerto Cabello Venez. 142 E1
Puerto Cabezas Nicaragua 137 H6
Puerto Carreño Col. 142 E2
Puerto Casado Para. 144 E2
Puerto Cavinas Bol. 142 E6
Puerto Coig Arg. 144 C8
Puerto Cortés Mex. 136 B4
Puerto de Lobos Mex. 127 E7
Puerto Escondido Mex. 136 E5
Puerto Francisco de Orellana Ecuador see Coca
Puerto Frey Bol. 142 F6
Puerto Génova Bol. 142 E6
Puerto Guarani Para. 144 E2
Puerto Heath Bol. 142 E6
Puerto Huitoto Col. 142 D3
Puerto Inírida Col. 142 E3
Puerto Isabel Bol. 143 G7
Puerto Leguízamo Col. 142 D4
Puerto Lempira Hond. 137 H5
Puerto Libertad Mex. 127 E7
Puerto Limón Costa Rica 137 H6
Puertollano Spain 57 D4
Puerto Lobos Arg. 144 C6
Puerto Madryn Arg. 144 C6
Puerto Maldonado Peru 142 E6
Puerto Máncora Peru 142 B4
Puerto México Mex. see Coatzacoalcos
Puerto Montt Chile 144 B6
Puerto Natales Chile 144 B8
Puerto Nuevo Col. 142 E2
Puerto Peñasco Mex. 127 E7
Puerto Pirámides Arg. 144 D6
Puerto Plata Dom. Rep. 137 J5
Puerto Portillo Peru 142 D5
Puerto Prado Peru 142 D6
Puerto Princesa Phil. 68 F5
Puerto Rico Arg. 144 E3
Puerto Rico Bol. 142 E6

▶Puerto Rico terr. West Indies 137 K5
United States Commonwealth.
North America 9, 116–117

▶Puerto Rico Trench sea feature Caribbean Sea 148 D4
Deepest trench in the Atlantic Ocean.

Puerto Santa Cruz Arg. 144 C8
Puerto Sastre Para. 144 E2
Puerto Saucedo Bol. 142 F6
Puerto Suárez Bol. 143 G7
Puerto Supe Peru 142 C6
Puerto Vallarta Mex. 136 C4
Puerto Victoria Peru 142 D5
Puerto Visser Arg. 144 C7
Puerto Yartou Chile 144 B8
Puerto Ybapobó Para. 144 E2
Pugachev Rus. Fed. 43 K5
Pugal India 82 C3
Puge China 76 D3
Pūhāl-e Khamīr, Kūh-e mts Iran 88 D5
Puhiwaero c. N.Z. see South West Cape
Puigmal mt. France/Spain 56 F5
Pui O Wan b. Hong Kong China 77 [inset]
Puji China see Puge
Pukaki, Lake N.Z. 113 C7
Pukapuka atoll Cook Is 107 J3
Pukaskwa National Park Canada 122 D4
Pukatawagan Canada 121 K4
Pukchin N. Korea 75 B4
Pukch'ŏng N. Korea 75 C4
Pukekohe N.Z. 113 E3
Puketeraki Range mts N.Z. 113 D6
Pukeuri Junction N.Z. 113 C7
Puksubaek-san mt. N. Korea 74 B4
Pula China see Nyingchi
Pula Croatia 58 E2
Pula *Sardinia* Italy 58 C5
Pulap atoll Micronesia 69 L5
Pulaski NY U.S.A. 135 G2
Pulaski VA U.S.A. 134 E5
Pulaski WI U.S.A. 134 A1
Pulheim Germany 52 G3
Pulicat Lake inlet India 84 D3
Pulivendla India 84 C3
Pulkkila Fin. 44 N4
Pullman U.S.A. 126 D3
Pulo Anna i. Palau 69 I6
Pulozero Rus. Fed. 44 R2
Púlpito, Punta pt Mex. 127 F8
Pulu China 82 E1
Pülümür Turkey 91 E3
Pulusuk atoll Micronesia 69 L5
Puluwat atoll Micronesia 69 L5
Pulwama India 89 I3
Pumasillo, Cerro mt. Peru 142 D6
Puma Yumco l. China 83 G3
Pumiao China see Yongning
Puná, Isla i. Ecuador 142 B4
Punakha Bhutan 83 G4
Punch India 82 C2
Punchaw Canada 120 F4
Punda Maria S. Africa 101 J2
Pundri India 82 D3
Pune India 84 B2
P'ungsan N. Korea 74 C4
Puning China 77 H4
Punjab state India 82 C3
Punjab prov. Pak. 89 H4
Punmah Glacier China/Jammu and Kashmir 82 D2
Puno Peru 142 D7
Punta, Cerro de mt. Puerto Rico 137 K5
Punta Abreojos Mex. 127 E8
Punta Alta Arg. 144 D5
Punta Arenas Chile 144 B8
Punta Balestrieri mt. Italy 58 C4
Punta del Este Uruguay 144 F5
Punta Delgada Arg. 144 D6
Punta Gorda Belize 136 G5
Punta Gorda U.S.A. 133 D7
Punta Norte Arg. 144 D6
Punta Prieta Mex. 127 E7
Puntarenas Costa Rica 137 H6
Punxsutawney U.S.A. 135 F3
Puokio Fin. 44 O4
Puolanka Fin. 44 O4
Puqi China see Chibi
Pur r. Rus. Fed. 64 I3
Puracé, Volcán de vol. Col. 142 C3
Purcell U.S.A. 131 D5
Purcell Mountains Canada 120 G5
Purgatoire r. U.S.A. 130 C4
Puri India 84 E2
Purmerend Neth. 52 E2
Purna r. *Maharashtra* India 82 D5
Purna r. *Maharashtra* India 84 C2
Purnea India see Purnia
Purnia India 83 F4
Purnululu National Park Australia 108 E4
Pursat Cambodia see Poŭthĭsăt
Puruliya India 83 F5

▶Purus r. Peru 142 F4
3rd longest river in South America.

Puruvesi l. Fin. 44 P6
Purwodadi Indon. 68 E8
Puryŏng N. Korea 74 C4
Pusad India 84 C2
Pusan S. Korea 75 C6
Pusatlı Dağı mt. Turkey 85 A1
Pushchino Rus. Fed. 43 H5
Pushemskiy Rus. Fed. 42 J3
Pushkin Rus. Fed. 45 Q7
Pushkino Azer. see Biläsuvar
Pushkinskaya, Gora mt. Rus. Fed. 74 F3
Pushkinskiye Gory Rus. Fed. 45 P8
Pusht-i-Rud reg. Afgh. see Zamīndāvar
Pustoshka Rus. Fed. 42 F4
Pusur r. Bangl. 83 G5
Putahow Lake Canada 121 K3
Putain Indon. 108 D2
Putao Myanmar 70 B1
Puteoli Italy see Pozzuoli
Puthein Myanmar see Bassein
Putian China 77 H3
Puting China see De'an
Puting, Tanjung pt Indon. 68 E7
Putlitz Germany 53 M1
Putna r. Romania 59 L2
Putney U.S.A. 135 I2
Putoi i. Hong Kong China see Po Toi
Putorana, Gory mts Rus. Fed. 153 E2

▶Putrajaya Malaysia 71 C7
Joint capital of Malaysia, with Kuala Lumpur.

Putre Chile 142 E7
Putsonderwater S. Africa 100 E5
Puttalam Sri Lanka 84 C4
Puttalam Lagoon Sri Lanka 84 C4
Puttelange-aux-Lacs France 52 G5
Putten Neth. 52 F2
Puttershoek Neth. 52 E3
Puttgarden Germany 47 M3
Putumayo r. Col. 142 D4
also known as Içá (Peru)
Putuo China see Shenjiamen
Puumala Fin. 45 P6
Puuwai HI U.S.A. 127 [inset]
Puvurnituq Canada 122 F1
Puyallup U.S.A. 126 C3
Puyang China 77 G1
Puy de Sancy mt. France 56 F4
Puyehue, Parque Nacional nat. park Chile 144 B6
Puysegur Point N.Z. 113 A8
Puzla Rus. Fed. 42 L3
Pweto Dem. Rep. Congo 99 C4
Pwinbyu Myanmar 70 A2
Pwllheli U.K. 49 C6
Pyal'ma Rus. Fed. 42 G3
Pyalo Myanmar 70 A3
Pyamalaw r. Myanmar 70 A4
Pyandzh Tajik. see Panj
Pyaozero, Ozero l. Rus. Fed. 44 Q3
Pyaozerskiy Rus. Fed. 44 Q4
Pyapali India 84 C3
Pyapon Myanmar 70 A3
Pyasina r. Rus. Fed. 64 J2
Pyatigorsk Rus. Fed. 91 F1
Pyatikhatki Ukr. see P"yatykhatky
P"yatykhatky Ukr. 43 G6
Pyay Myanmar see Pyè
Pychas Rus. Fed. 42 L4
Pyè Myanmar 70 A3
Pye, Mount hill N.Z. 113 B8
Pyetrykaw Belarus 43 F5
Pygmalion Point India 71 A6
Pyhäjoki Fin. 44 N4
Pyhäjoki r. Fin. 44 N4
Pyhäntä Fin. 44 O4
Pyhäsalmi Fin. 44 N5
Pyhäselkä l. Fin. 44 P5
Pyi Myanmar see Pyè
Pyin Myanmar see Pyè
Pyingaing Myanmar 70 A2
Pyinmana Myanmar 70 B3
Pyle U.K. 49 D7
Pyl'karamo Rus. Fed. 64 J3
Pylos Greece 59 I6
Pymatuning Reservoir U.S.A. 134 E3
Pyŏktong N. Korea 74 B4
P'yŏnggang N. Korea 75 B5
P'yŏnghae S. Korea 75 C5
P'yŏngsong N. Korea 75 B5
P'yŏngt'aek S. Korea 75 B5

▶P'yŏngyang N. Korea 75 B5
Capital of North Korea.

Pyramid Hill Australia 112 B6
Pyramid Lake U.S.A. 128 D1
Pyramid Peak U.S.A. 129 J1
Pyramid Range mts U.S.A. 128 D2
Pyramids of Giza tourist site Egypt 90 C5
Pyrénées mts Europe see Pyrenees
Pyrenees mts Europe 57 H2
Pyrénées Occidentales, Parc National des nat. park France/Spain 56 D5
Pyrgos Greece 59 I6
Pyryatyn Ukr. 43 G6
Pyrzyce Poland 47 O4
Pyshchug Rus. Fed. 42 J4
Pytalovo Rus. Fed. 45 O8
Pyu Myanmar 70 B3
Pyxaria mt. Greece 59 J5

Q

Qaa Lebanon 85 C2
Qaanaaq Greenland see Thule
Qabātiya West Bank 85 B3
Qabnag China 76 B2
Qabqa China see Gonghe
Qacentina Alg. see Constantine
Qacha's Nek Lesotho 101 I6
Qādes Afgh. 89 F3
Qādisīyah, Sadd dam Iraq 91 F4
Qadisiyah Dam Iraq see Qādisīyah, Sadd
Qa'emabad Iran 89 F4
Qagan China 73 L3
Qagan Nur China 73 K4
Qagan Nur l. China 74 B3
Qagan Us *Nei Mongol* China 73 K4
Qagan Us *Qinghai* China see Dulan
Qagbasêrag China 76 B2
Qagca China 76 C1
Qagcaka China 83 E2
Qagchêng China see Xiangcheng
Qahremānshahr Iran see Kermānshāh
Qaidam He r. China 83 H1
Qaidam Pendi basin China 80 H4
Qainaqangma China 83 G2
Qaisar Afgh. 89 G3
Qaisar, Koh-i- mt. Afgh. see Qeyşār, Kūh-e
Qakar China 82 E1
Qal'a Beni Hammad tourist site Alg. 57 I6
Qalā Diza Iraq 91 G3
Qalagai Afgh. 89 H3
Qala-i-Kang Afgh. see Kang
Qal'aikhum Tajik. 89 H2
Qala Jamal Afgh. 89 F3
Qalansīyah Yemen 87 H7
Qala Shinia Takht Afgh. 89 G3
Qalāt Afgh. see Kalāt
Qal'at al Ḥiṣn Syria 85 C2
Qal'at al Mu'aẓẓam Saudi Arabia 90 E6
Qal'at Bīshah Saudi Arabia 86 F5
Qal'at Muqaybirah, Jabal mt. Syria 85 D2
Qal'eh Dāgh mt. Iran 88 B2
Qal'eh Tirpul Afgh. 89 F3
Qal'eh-ye Bost Afgh. 89 G4
Qal'eh-ye Now Afgh. 89 F3
Qal'eh-ye Shūrak well Iran 88 E3
Qalhāt Oman 88 E6
Qalīb Bāqūr well Iraq 91 G5
Qalluviartuuq, Lac l. Canada 122 G2
Qalyūb Egypt 90 C5
Qalyûb Egypt see Qalyūb
Qamalung China 76 C1
Qamanirjuaq Lake Canada 121 M2
Qamanittuaq Canada see Baker Lake
Qamashi Uzbek. see Kamashi
Qamata S. Africa 101 H6
Qamdo China 76 C2
Qanāt as Suways canal Egypt see Suez Canal
Qandahar Afgh. see Kandahār
Qandarānbāshī, Kūh-e mt. Iran 88 B2
Qandyaghash Kazakh. see Kandyagash
Qangzê China 82 D3
Qapan Iran 88 D2
Qapshagay Kazakh. see Kapchagay
Qapshagay Bögeni resr Kazakh. see Kapchagayskoye Vodokhranilishche
Qapugtang China see Zadoi
Qaqortoq Greenland 119 N3
Qara Āghach r. Iran see Mand, Rūd-e
Qarabutaq Kazakh. see Karabutak
Qaraçala Azer. 88 C2
Qara Ertis r. China/Kazakh. see Ertix He
Qaraghandy Kazakh. see Karaganda
Qaraghayly Kazakh. see Karagayly
Qārah Egypt 90 B5
Qārah Saudi Arabia 91 F5
Qarah Bāgh Afgh. 89 H3
Qarak China 89 J2
Qaraqum des. Turkm. see Kara Kumy
Qaraqum des. Turkm. see Karakum Desert
Qara Quzi Iran 88 D2
Qarasu Azer. 91 H2
Qara Şū Chāy r. Syria/Turkey see Karasu
Qara Tarai mt. Afgh. 89 G3
Qarataū Kazakh. see Karatau
Qarataū Zhotasy mts Kazakh. see Karatau, Khrebet
Qara Tikan Iran 88 C2
Qarazhal Kazakh. see Karazhal
Qardho Somalia 98 E3
Qareh Chāy r. Iran 88 C3
Qareh Sū r. Iran 88 B2
Qareh Tekān Iran 89 F2
Qarhan China 83 H1
Qarkilik China see Ruoqiang
Qarn al Kabsh, Jabal mt. Egypt 90 D5
Qarnayn i. U.A.E. 88 D5
Qarnein i. U.A.E. see Qarnayn
Qarn el Kabsh, Gebel mt. Egypt see Qarn al Kabsh, Jabal
Qarokŭl l. Tajik. 89 I2
Qarqan China see Qiemo
Qarqan He r. China 80 G4
Qarqaraly Kazakh. see Karkaralinsk
Qarshi Uzbek. see Karshi
Qarshi Chŭli plain Uzbek. see Karshinskaya Step'
Qartaba Lebanon 85 B2
Qārūh, Jazīrat i. Kuwait 88 C4
Qārūn, Birkat l. Egypt 90 C5
Qârûn, Birket l. Egypt see Qārūn, Birkat
Qaryat al Gharab Iraq 91 G5
Qaryat al Ulyā Saudi Arabia 88 B5
Qasa Murg mts Afgh. 89 F3
Qāsemābād Iran 88 E3
Qash Qai reg. Iran 88 C4
Qasigiannguit Greenland 119 M3
Qaşr al Azraq Jordan 85 C4
Qaşr al Farāfirah Egypt 90 B6
Qaşr al Kharānah Jordan 85 C4
Qaşr al Khubbāz Iraq 91 F4
Qaşr 'Amrah tourist site Jordan 85 C4
Qaşr Burqu' tourist site Jordan 85 C3
Qaşr-e Shīrīn Iran 88 B3
Qasr Farâfra Egypt see Qaşr al Farāfirah
Qassimiut Greenland 119 N3
Qaṭanā Syria 85 C3
▶Qatar country Asia 88 C5
Asia 6, 62–63
Qaṭmah Syria 85 C1
Qaṭrūyeh Iran 88 D4
Qaṭṭāfī, Wādī al watercourse Jordan 85 C4
Qaṭṭâra, Râs esc. Egypt see Qaṭṭārah, Ra's
Qattara Depression Egypt 90 B5
Qaṭṭārah, Ra's esc. Egypt 90 B5
Qaṭṭīnah, Buḥayrat resr Syria 81 C2
Qax Azer. 91 G2
Qāyen Iran 88 E3
Qaynar Kazakh. see Kaynar
Qaysīyah, Qā' al imp. l. Jordan 85 C4
Qaysūm, Juzur is Egypt 90 D6
Qayyārah Iraq 91 F4
Qazangödağ mt. Armenia/Azer. 91 G3
Qazaq Shyghanaghy b. Kazakh. see Kazakhskiy Zaliv
Qazaqstan country Asia see Kazakhstan
Qazax Azer. 86 G1
Qazi Ahmad Pak. 89 H5
Qazımämmäd Azer. 91 H2
Qazvīn Iran 88 C2
Qeisûm, Gezâ'ir is Egypt see Qaysūm, Juzur
Qeisum Islands Egypt see Qaysūm, Juzur
Qena Egypt see Qinā
Qeqertarsuaq Greenland 119 M3
Qeqertarsuaq i. Greenland 119 M3
Qeqertarsuatsiaat Greenland 119 M3
Qeqertarsuup Tunua b. Greenland 119 M3
Qeshm Iran 88 E5
Qeydār Iran 88 C2
Qeydū Iran 88 C3
Qeys i. Iran 88 D5
Qeyşār, Kūh-e mt. Afgh. 89 G3
Qezel Owzan, Rūdkhāneh-ye r. Iran 88 C2
Qezi'ot Israel 85 B4
Qian'an China 74 B3
Qian Gorlos China see Qianguozhen
Qianguozhen China 74 B3

Qianjiang Chongqing China 77 F2
Qianjiang Hubei China 77 G2
Qianjin Heilong. China 74 D3
Qianjin Jilin China 74 C3
Qianning China 76 D2
Qianqihao China 74 A3
Qian Shan mts China 74 A4
Qianxi China 76 E3
Qiaocheng China see Bozhou
Qiaojia China 76 D3
Qiaoshan China see Huangling
Qiaowa China see Muli
Qiaowan China 80 I3
Qiaozhuang China see Qingchuan
Qibā' Saudi Arabia 91 G6
Qibing S. Africa 101 H5
Qichun China 77 G2
Qidong China 77 G3
Qidukou China 76 B1
Qiemo China 80 G4
Qijiang China 76 E2
Qijiaojing China 80 H3
Qikiqtarjuaq Canada 119 L3
Qila Ladgasht Pak. 89 F5
Qila Saifullah Pak. 89 H4
Qilian China 80 J4
Qilian Shan mts China 80 I4
Qillak i. Greenland 119 O3
Qiman Tag mts China 83 G1
Qimusseriarsuaq b. Greenland 119 L2
Qinā Egypt 86 D4
Qin'an China 76 E1
Qincheng China see Nanfeng
Qing'an China 74 B3
Qingchuan China 76 E1
Qingdao China 73 M5
Qinggang China 74 B3
Qinggil China see Qinghe
Qinghai prov. China 76 B1
Qinghai Hu salt l. China 80 J4
Qinghai Nanshan mts China 80 I4
Qinghe Heilong. China 74 C3
Qinghe Xinjiang China 80 H2
Qinghecheng China 74 B4
Qinghua China see Bo'ai
Qingjiang Jiangsu China see Huai'an
Qingjiang Jiangxi China see Zhangshu
Qing Jiang r. China 77 F2
Qingkou China see Ganyu
Qinglan China 77 F5
Qingliu China 77 H3
Qinglung China 83 G3
Qingpu China 77 I2
Qingquan China see Xishui
Qingshan China see Wudalianchi
Qingshui China 76 E1
Qingshuihe Nei Mongol China 73 K5
Qingshuihe Qinghai China 76 C1
Qingtian China 77 I2
Qingyang Anhui China 77 H2
Qingyang Jiangsu China see Sihong
Qingyuan Gansu China see Weiyuan
Qingyuan Guangdong China 77 G4
Qingyuan Guangxi China see Yizhou
Qingyuan Liaoning China 74 B4
Qingyuan Zhejiang China 77 H3
Qingzang Gaoyuan plat. China see Plateau of Tibet
Qingzhen China 76 E3
Qinhuangdao China 73 L5
Qinjiang China see Shicheng
Qin Ling mts China 76 E1
Qinshui China 77 G1
Qinting China see Lianhua
Qinzhou China 77 F4
Qionghai China 77 F5
Qiongjiexue China see Qonggyai
Qionglai China 76 D2
Qionglai Shan mts China 76 D2
Qiongxi China see Hongyuan
Qiongzhong China 77 F5
Qiongzhou Haixia strait China see Hainan Strait
Qiqian China 74 A1
Qiqihar China 74 A3
Qīr Iran 88 D4
Qira China 82 E1
Qîraîya, Wâdi watercourse Egypt see Qurayyah, Wādī
Qiryat Israel 85 B3
Qiryat Shemona Israel 85 B3
Qishan China 76 E1
Qishon r. Israel 85 B3
Qitab ash Shāmah vol. crater Saudi Arabia 85 C4
Qitaihe China 74 C3
Qiubei China 76 E3
Qiujin China 77 G2
Qixing He r. China 74 D3
Qiyang China 77 F3
Qizhou Liedao i. China 77 F5
Qızılağac Körfäzi b. Azer. 88 C2
Qizil-Art, Aghbai pass Kyrg./Tajik. see Kyzylart Pass
Qizilqum des. Kazakh./Uzbek. see Kyzylkum Desert
Qizilrabot Tajik. 89 I2
Qogir Feng mt. China/Jammu and Kashmir see K2
Qog Qi China see Sain Us
Qom Iran 88 C3
Qomdo China see Qumdo
Qomisheh Iran see Shahrezā
Qomolangma Feng mt. China/Nepal see Everest, Mount
Qomsheh Iran see Shahrezā
Qonāq, Kūh-e hill Iran 88 C3
Qondūz Afgh. see Kunduz
Qonggyai China 83 G3
Qong Muztag mt. China 83 E2
Qongrat Uzbek. see Kungrad
Qoornoq Greenland 119 M3
Qoqek China see Tacheng
Qorghalzhyn Kazakh. see Korgalzhyn
Qornet es Saouda mt. Lebanon 85 C2
Qorowulbozor Uzbek. see Karaulbazar
Qorveh Iran 88 B3
Qosh Tepe Iraq 91 F3
Qostanay Kazakh. see Kostanay
Qoubaiyat Lebanon 85 C2
Qowowuyag mt. China/Nepal see Cho Oyu
Qozideh Tajik. 89 H2
Quabbin Reservoir U.S.A. 135 I2
Quadra Island Canada 120 E5
Quadros, Lago dos l. Brazil 145 A5
Quaidabad Pak. 89 H3
Quail Mountains U.S.A. 128 E4
Quairading Australia 109 B8
Quakenbrück Germany 53 H2
Quakertown U.S.A. 135 H3
Quambatook Australia 112 A5
Quambone Australia 112 C3
Quamby Australia 110 C4
Quanah U.S.A. 131 D5
Quanbao Shan mt. China 77 F1
Quan Dao Hoang Sa is S. China Sea see Paracel Islands
Quân Đao Nam Du i. Vietnam 71 D5
Quan Dao Truong Sa is S. China Sea see Spratly Islands
Quang Ngai Vietnam 70 E4
Quang Tri Vietnam 70 D3
Quan Long Vietnam see Ca Mau
Quannan China 77 G3
Quan Phu Quoc i. Vietnam see Phu Quôc, Đao
Quantock Hills U.K. 49 D7
Quanwan Hong Kong China see Tsuen Wan
Quanzhou Fujian China 77 H3
Quanzhou Guangxi China 77 F3
Qu'Appelle r. Canada 121 K5
Quaqtaq Canada 119 L3
Quarry Bay Hong Kong China 77 [inset]
Quartu Sant'Elena Sardinia Italy 58 C5
Quartzite Mountain U.S.A. 128 E3
Quartzsite U.S.A. 129 F5
Quba Azer. 91 H2
Quchan Iran 88 E2
Qudaym Syria 85 D2
Queanbeyan Australia 112 D5

▶Québec Canada 123 H5
Provincial capital of Québec.

Québec prov. Canada 135 I1
Quebra Anzol r. Brazil 145 B2
Quedlinburg Germany 53 L3
Queen Adelaide Islands Chile see La Reina Adelaida, Archipiélago de
Queen Anne U.S.A. 135 H4
Queen Bess, Mount Canada 122 B2
Queen Charlotte Canada 120 C4
Queen Charlotte Islands Canada 120 C4
Queen Charlotte Sound sea chan. Canada 120 D5
Queen Charlotte Strait Canada 120 E5
Queen Creek U.S.A. 129 H5
Queen Elizabeth Islands Canada 119 H2
Queen Elizabeth National Park Uganda 98 C4
Queen Mary Land reg. Antarctica 152 F2
Queen Maud Gulf Canada 115 H3
Queen Maud Land reg. Antarctica 152 C2
Queen Maud Mountains Antarctica 152 J1
Queenscliff Australia 112 B7
Queensland state Australia 112 B1
Queenstown Australia 111 [inset]
Queenstown N.Z. 113 B7
Queenstown Rep. of Ireland see Cóbh
Queenstown S. Africa 101 H6
Queenstown Sing. 71 [inset]
Queets U.S.A. 126 B3
Queimada, Ilha i. Brazil 143 H4
Quelimane Moz. 99 D5
Quellón Chile 144 B6
Quelpart Island S. Korea see Cheju-do
Quemado U.S.A. 129 I4
Quemoy i. Taiwan see Chinmen Tao
Que Que Zimbabwe see Kwekwe
Querétaro Mex. 136 D4
Querétaro de Arteaga Mex. see Querétaro
Querfurt Germany 53 L3
Querobabi Mex. 127 F7
Quesnel Canada 120 F4
Quesnel Lake Canada 120 F4
Quetta Pak. 89 G4
Quetzaltenango Guat. 136 F6
Queuco Chile 144 B5
Quezaltenango Guat. see Quetzaltenango

▶Quezon City Phil. 69 G4
Former capital of the Philippines.

Qufu China 77 H1
Quibala Angola 99 B5
Quibaxe Angola 99 B4
Quibdó Col. 142 C2
Quiberon France 56 C3
Quiçama, Parque Nacional do nat. park Angola 99 B4
Qui Châu Vietnam 70 D3
Quiet Lake Canada 120 C2
Quilengues Angola 99 B5
Quillabamba Peru 142 D6
Quillacollo Bol. 142 E7
Quillan France 56 F5
Quill Lakes Canada 121 J5
Quilmes Arg. 144 E4
Quilon India 84 C4
Quilpie Australia 112 B1
Quilpué Chile 144 B4
Quimbele Angola 99 B4
Quimilí Arg. 144 D3
Quimper France 56 B3
Quimperlé France 56 C3
Quinag hill U.K. 50 D2
Quincy CA U.S.A. 128 C2
Quincy FL U.S.A. 133 C6
Quincy IL U.S.A. 130 F4
Quincy IN U.S.A. 134 B4
Quincy MA U.S.A. 135 J2
Quincy MI U.S.A. 134 C3
Quincy OH U.S.A. 134 D3
Quines Arg. 144 C4
Quinga Moz. 99 E5
Qui Nhon Vietnam 71 E4
Quinn Canyon Range mts U.S.A. 129 F3
Quinto Spain 57 F3
Quionga Moz. 99 E5
Quipungo Angola 99 B5
Quirima Angola 99 B5
Quirindi Australia 112 E3
Quirinópolis Brazil 145 A2
Quissanga Moz. 99 E5
Quissico Moz. 101 L3
Quitapa Angola 99 B5
Quitilipi Arg. 144 D3
Quitman GA U.S.A. 133 D6
Quitman MS U.S.A. 131 F5

▶Quito Ecuador 142 C4
Capital of Ecuador.

Quitovac Mex. 127 E7
Quixadá Brazil 143 K4
Quixeramobim Brazil 143 K5
Qujiang Guangdong China 77 G3
Qujiang Sichuan China see Quxian
Qujie China 77 F4
Qujing China 76 D3
Qulandy Kazakh. see Kulandy
Qulbān Layyah well Iraq 88 B4
Qulin Gol r. China 74 A3
Qulsary Kazakh. see Kul'sary
Qulyndy Zhazyghy plain Kazakh./Rus. Fed. see Kulundinskaya Step'
Qulzum, Baḩr al Egypt see Suez Bay
Qumar He r. China 72 G6
Qumarheyan China 80 H4
Qumarlêb China see Sêrwolungwa
Qumarrabdün China 76 B1
Qumbu S. Africa 101 I6
Qumdo China 76 B2
Qumqŭrghon Uzbek. see Kumkurgan
Qumrha S. Africa 101 H7
Qumulangma mt. China/Nepal see Everest, Mount
Qunayy well Saudi Arabia 88 B6
Qundüz Afgh. see Kunduz
Qŭnghirot Uzbek. see Kungrad
Quntamari China 83 G2
Qu'nyido China 76 C2
Quoich r. Canada 121 M1
Quoich, Loch l. U.K. 50 D3
Quoile r. U.K. 51 G3
Quoin Point S. Africa 100 D8
Quoxo r. Botswana 100 G2
Qŭqon Uzbek. see Kokand
Qurama, Qatorkŭhi mts Asia see Kurama Range
Qurama Tizmasi mts Asia see Kurama Range
Qurayyah, Wādī watercourse Egypt 85 B4
Qurayyat al Milḩ l. Jordan 85 C4
Qŭrghonteppa Tajik. 89 H2
Qusar Azer. 91 H2
Qushan China see Beichuan
Qŭshrabot Uzbek. see Koshrabad
Qusmuryn Kazakh. see Kushmurun
Qusum China 82 D2
Quthing Lesotho see Moyeni
Quttinirpaaq National Park Canada 119 K1
Quwayq, Nahr r. Syria/Turkey 85 C2
Quxar China see Lhazê
Quxian Sichuan China 76 E2
Quxian Zhejiang China see Quzhou
Quyang China see Jingzhou
Quyghan Kazakh. see Kuygan
Quynh Lưu Vietnam 70 D3
Quyon Canada 135 G1
Qüyün Eshek i. Iran 88 B2
Quzhou China 77 H2
Qypshaq Köli salt l. Kazakh. see Kypshak, Ozero
Qyrghyz Zhotasy mts Kazakh./Kyrg. see Kirghiz Range
Qyteti Stalin Albania see Kuçovë
Qyzylorda Kazakh. see Kyzylorda
Qyzylqum des. Kazakh./Uzbek. see Kyzylkum Desert
Qyzyltū Kazakh. see Kishkenekol'
Qyzylzhar Kazakh. see Kyzylzhar

R

Raa Atoll Maldives see North Maalhosmadulu Atoll
Raab r. Austria 47 P7
Raab Hungary see Győr
Raahe Fin. 44 N4
Rääkkylä Fin. 44 P5
Raalte Neth. 52 G2
Raanujärvi Fin. 44 N3
Raasay i. U.K. 50 C3
Raasay, Sound of sea chan. U.K. 50 C3
Raba Indon. 108 B2
Rabang China 82 E2
Rabat Gozo Malta see Victoria
Rabat Malta 58 F7

▶Rabat Morocco 54 C5
Capital of Morocco.

Rabaul P.N.G. 106 F2
Rabbath Ammon Jordan see 'Ammān
Rabbit r. Canada 120 E3
Rabbit Flat Australia 108 E5
Rabbitskin r. Canada 120 F2
Rābigh Saudi Arabia 86 E5
Rabnabad Islands Bangl. 83 G5
Râbniţa Moldova see Rîbniţa
Rabocheostrovsk Rus. Fed. 42 G2
Racaka China see Riwoqê
Raccoon Cay i. Bahamas 133 F8
Race, Cape Canada 123 L5
Race Point U.S.A. 135 J2
Rachaïya Lebanon 85 B3
Rachal U.S.A. 131 D7
Rachaya Lebanon see Rachaïya
Rachel U.S.A. 129 F3
Rach Gia Vietnam 71 D5
Rach Gia, Vinh b. Vietnam 71 D5
Racibórz Poland 47 Q5
Racine WI U.S.A. 134 B2
Racine WV U.S.A. 134 E4
Rădăuţi Romania 43 E7
Radcliff U.S.A. 134 C5
Radde Rus. Fed. 74 C2
Radford U.S.A. 134 E5
Radisson Que. Canada 122 F3
Radisson Sask. Canada 121 J4
Radlinski, Mount Antarctica 152 K1
Radnevo Bulg. 59 K3
Radom Poland 47 R5
Radom Sudan 97 F4
Radomir Bulg. 59 J3
Radom National Park Sudan 97 F4
Radomsko Poland 47 Q5
Radoviš Macedonia 90 A2
Radstock U.K. 49 E7
Radstock, Cape Australia 109 F8
Radun' Belarus 45 N9
Radviliškis Lith. 45 M9
Radyvyliv Ukr. 43 E6
Rae Bareli India 82 E4
Rae-Edzo Canada 120 G2
Rae Lakes Canada 120 G1
Raeside, Lake salt flat Australia 109 C7
Raetihi N.Z. 113 E4
Rāf hill Saudi Arabia 91 E5
Rafaela Arg. 144 D4
Rafaḩ Gaza see Rafiaḩ
Rafaï Cent. Afr. Rep. 98 C3
Rafḩā' Saudi Arabia 91 F5
Rafiaḩ Gaza 85 B4
Rafsanjān Iran 88 D4
Raft r. U.S.A. 126 E4
Raga Sudan 97 F4
Rägelin Germany 53 M1
Ragged, Mount hill Australia 109 C8
Ragged Island Bahamas 133 F8
Rāgh Afgh. 89 H2
Rago Nasjonalpark nat. park Norway 44 J3
Ragösen Germany 53 M2
Ragueneau Canada 123 H4
Raguhn Germany 53 M3
Ragusa Croatia see Dubrovnik
Ragusa Sicily Italy 58 F6
Ra'gyagoinba China 76 D1
Raha Indon. 69 G7
Rahachow Belarus 43 F5
Rahad r. Sudan 86 D7
Rahaeng Thai. see Tak
Rahden Germany 53 I2
Rahimyar Khan Pak. 89 H4
Rahovec Serb. and Mont. see Orahovac
Rahuri India 84 B2
Rai, Hon i. Vietnam 71 D5
Raiatea i. Fr. Polynesia 151 J7
Raibu i. Indon. see Air
Raichur India 84 C2
Raiganj India 83 G4
Raigarh Chhattisgarh India 83 E5
Raigarh Orissa India 84 D2
Raijua i. Indon. 108 C2
Railroad Pass U.S.A. 128 E2
Railroad Valley U.S.A. 129 F2
Raimangal r. Bangl. 83 G5
Raimbault, Lac l. Canada 123 H3
Rainbow Lake Canada 120 G3
Raine Island Australia 110 D1
Rainelle U.S.A. 134 E5
Raini r. Pak. 89 H4
Rainier, Mount vol. U.S.A. 126 C3
Rainy r. Canada/U.S.A. 121 M5
Rainy Lake Canada/U.S.A. 125 I2
Rainy River Canada 121 M5
Raipur Chhattisgarh India 83 E5
Raipur W. Bengal India 83 F5
Raisen India 82 D5
Raisio Fin. 45 M6
Raismes France 52 D4
Raitalai India 82 D5
Raivavae i. Fr. Polynesia 151 K7
Raiwind Pak. 89 I4
Raja, Ujung pt Indon. 71 B7
Rajaampat, Kepulauan is Indon. 69 H7
Rajahmundry India 84 D2
Raja-Jooseppi Fin. 44 P2
Rajanpur Pak. 89 H4
Rajapalaiyam India 84 C4
Rajapur India 84 B2
Rajasthan state India 82 C4
Rajasthan Canal India 82 C3
Rajauri India see Rajouri
Rajevadi India 84 B2
Rajgarh India 82 D4
Rájijovsset Fin. see Raja-Jooseppi
Rajkot India 82 B5
Raj Mahal India 82 C4
Rajmahal Hills India 83 F4
Rajnandgaon India 82 E5
Rajouri India 82 C2
Rajpipla India 82 C5
Rajpur India 82 C5
Rajpura India 82 D3
Rajputana Agency state India see Rajasthan
Rajsamand India 82 C4
Rajshahi Bangl. 83 G4
Rājū Syria 85 C1
Rajula India 84 A1
Rajur India 84 C1
Rajura India 84 C2
Raka China 83 F3
Rakan, Ra's pt Qatar 88 C5
Rakaposhi mt. Jammu and Kashmir 82 C1
Raka Zangbo r. China see Dogxung Zangbo
Rakhiv Ukr. 43 E6
Rakhni Pak. 89 H4
Rakhshan r. Pak. 89 F5
Rakitnoye Belgorodskaya Oblast' Rus. Fed. 43 G6
Rakitnoye Primorskiy Kray Rus. Fed. 74 D3
Rakiura i. N.Z. see Stewart Island
Rakke Estonia 45 O7
Rakkestad Norway 45 G7
Rakni r. Pak. 89 H4
Rakovski Bulg. 59 K3
Rakushechnyy, Mys pt Kazakh. 91 H2
Rakvere Estonia 45 O7

▶Raleigh U.S.A. 132 E5
State capital of North Carolina.

Ralston U.S.A. 135 G3
Ram r. Canada 120 F2
Ramagiri India 84 E2
Ramah U.S.A. 129 I4
Ramalho, Serra do hills Brazil 145 B1
Ramallah West Bank 85 B4
Ramanagaram India 84 C3
Ramanathapuram India 84 C4
Ramapo Deep sea feature N. Pacific Ocean 150 F3
Ramapur India 84 D1
Ramas, Cape India 84 B3
Ramatlabama S. Africa 101 G3
Rambhapur India 82 C5
Rambouillet France 52 B6
Rambutyo Island P.N.G. 69 L7
Rame Head hd Australia 112 D6
Rame Head hd U.K. 49 C8
Rameshki Rus. Fed. 42 H4
Ramezān Kalak Iran 89 F5
Ramgarh Jharkhand India 83 F5
Ramgarh Madhya Pradesh India 82 E5
Ramgarh Rajasthan India 82 B4
Ramgarh Rajasthan India 82 C3
Ramgul reg. Afgh. 89 H3
Rāmhormoz Iran 88 C4
Ramingining Australia 108 F3
Ramitan Uzbek. see Romitan
Ramla Israel 85 B4
Ramlat Rabyānah des. Libya see Rebiana Sand Sea
Ramm, Jabal mts Jordan 85 B5
Ramnad India see Ramanathapuram
Râmnicu Sărat Romania 59 L2
Râmnicu Vâlcea Romania 59 K2
Ramon' Rus. Fed. 43 H6
Ramona U.S.A. 128 E5
Ramos r. Mex. 131 B7
Ramotswa Botswana 101 G3
Rampart of Genghis Khan tourist site Asia 73 K3
Rampur India 82 D3
Rampur Boalia Bangl. see Rajshahi
Ramree Myanmar 70 A3
Ramree Island Myanmar 70 A3
Ramsele Sweden 44 J5
Ramsey Isle of Man 48 C4
Ramsey U.K. 49 G6
Ramsey U.S.A. 135 H3
Ramsey Bay Isle of Man 48 C4
Ramsey Island U.K. 49 B7
Ramsey Lake Canada 122 E5
Ramsgate U.K. 49 I7
Rāmshir Iran 88 C4
Ramsing mt. India 83 H3
Ramu Bangl. 83 H5
Ramusio, Lac l. Canada 123 J3
Ramygala Lith. 45 N9
Ranaghat India 83 G5
Ranai i. U.S.A. see Lanai
Rana Pratap Sagar resr India 78 C4
Ranapur India 82 C5
Ranasar India 82 B4
Rancagua Chile 144 B4
Rancharia Brazil 145 A3
Rancheria Canada 120 D2
Rancheria r. Canada 120 D2
Ranchi India 83 F5
Ranco, Lago l. Chile 144 B6
Rand Australia 112 C5
Randalstown U.K. 51 F3
Randers Denmark 45 G8
Randijaure l. Sweden 44 K3
Randolph ME U.S.A. 135 K1
Randolph UT U.S.A. 126 F4
Randolph VT U.S.A. 135 I2
Randsjö Sweden 44 H5
Råneå Sweden 44 M4
Ranérou Senegal 96 B3
Ranfurly N.Z. 113 C7
Rangae Thai. 71 C6
Rangamati Bangl. 83 H5
Rangapara North India 83 H4
Rangeley Lake U.S.A. 135 J1
Rangely U.S.A. 129 I1
Ranger Lake Canada 122 E5
Rangiora N.Z. 113 D6
Rangitata r. N.Z. 113 C7
Rangitikei r. N.Z. 113 E5
Rangke China see Zamtang
Rangkŭl Tajik. 89 I2
Rangôn Myanmar see Rangoon

▶Rangoon Myanmar 70 B3
Capital of Myanmar.

Rangoon r. Myanmar 70 B3
Rangpur Bangl. 83 G4
Rangsang i. Indon. 71 C7
Rangse Myanmar 70 A1
Ranibennur India 84 B3
Raniganj India 83 F5
Ranipur Pak. 89 H5
Raniwara India 82 C4
Rankin U.S.A. 131 C6
Rankin Inlet Canada 121 M2
Rankin's Springs Australia 112 C4
Ranna Estonia 45 O7
Rannes Australia 110 E5
Rannoch, L. U.K. 50 E4
Ranong Thai. 71 B5
Ranot Thai. 71 C6
Ranpur India 82 B5
Ranrkan Pak. 89 H4
Rānsa Iran 88 C3
Ransby Sweden 45 H6
Rantasalmi Fin. 44 P5
Rantau i. Indon. 71 C7
Rantauprapat Indon. 71 B7
Rantoul U.S.A. 134 A3
Rantsila Fin. 44 N4
Ranua Fin. 44 O4
Ŗanya Iraq 91 G3
Ranyah, Wādī watercourse Saudi Arabia 86 F5
Rao Go mt. Laos/Vietnam 70 D3
Raohe China 74 D3
Raoul Island Kermadec Is 107 I4
Rapa i. Fr. Polynesia 151 K7
Rapa-iti i. Fr. Polynesia see Rapa
Rapallo Italy 58 C2
Rapar India 82 B5
Raphoe Rep. of Ireland 51 E3
Rapidan r. U.S.A. 135 G4
Rapid City U.S.A. 130 C2
Rapid River U.S.A. 132 C2
Rapla Estonia 45 N7
Rapur Andhra Pradesh India 84 C3
Rapur Gujarat India 82 B5
Raqqa Syria see Ar Raqqah
Raquette Lake U.S.A. 135 H2
Rara National Park Nepal 83 E3
Raritan Bay U.S.A. 135 H3
Raroia atoll Fr. Polynesia 151 K7
Rarotonga i. Cook Is 151 J7
Ras India 82 C4
Rasa, Punta pt Arg. 144 D6
Ra's ad Daqm Oman 87 I6
Ra's al Ḩikmah Egypt 90 B5
Ras al Khaimah U.A.E. see Ra's al Khaymah
Ra's al Khaymah U.A.E. 88 D5
Ra's an Naqb Jordan 85 B4
Ras Dashen mt. Eth. see Ras Dejen

▶Ras Dejen mt. Eth. 98 D2
5th highest mountain in Africa.

Raseiniai Lith. 45 M9
Râs el Hikma Egypt see Ra's al Ḩikmah
Ra's Ghārib Egypt 90 D5
Rashad Sudan 86 D7
Rashîd Egypt see Rashīd
Rashīd Egypt 90 C5
Rashīd Qala Afgh. 89 G4
Rashm Iran 88 D3
Rasht Iran 88 C2
Raskam mts China 82 C1
Ras Koh mt. Pak. 89 G4
Raskoh mts Pak. 89 G4
Raso, Cabo c. Arg. 144 C6
Raso da Catarina hills Brazil 143 K5
Rason Lake salt flat Australia 109 D7
Rasony Belarus 45 P9
Rasra India 83 E4
Rasshua, Ostrov i. Rus. Fed. 73 S3
Rass Jebel Tunisia 58 D6
Rasskazovo Rus. Fed. 43 I5
Rastatt Germany 53 I6
Rastede Germany 53 I1
Rastow Germany 53 L1
Rasūl watercourse Iran 88 D5
Rasul Pak. 89 I3
Ratae U.K. see Leicester
Rätan Sweden 44 I5
Ratanda S. Africa 101 I4
Ratangarh India 82 C3
Rätansbyn Sweden 44 I5
Rat Buri Thai. 71 B4
Rathangan Rep. of Ireland 51 F4
Rathbun Lake U.S.A. 130 E3
Rathdowney Rep. of Ireland 51 E5
Rathdrum Rep. of Ireland 51 F5
Rathedaung Myanmar 70 A2
Rathenow Germany 53 M2
Rathfriland U.K. 51 F3
Rathkeale Rep. of Ireland 51 D5
Rathlin Island U.K. 51 F2
Rathluirc Rep. of Ireland 51 D5
Ratibor Poland see Racibórz
Ratingen Germany 52 G3
Ratisbon Germany see Regensburg
Ratiya India 82 C3
Rat Lake Canada 121 L3
Ratlam India 82 C5
Ratnagiri India 84 B2
Ratnapura Sri Lanka 84 D5
Ratne Ukr. 43 E6
Ratno Ukr. see Ratne
Raton U.S.A. 127 G5
Rattray Head hd U.K. 50 H3
Rättvik Sweden 45 I6
Ratz, Mount Canada 120 C3
Ratzeburg Germany 53 K1
Raub Malaysia 71 C7
Rauðamýri Iceland 44 [inset]
Raudhatain Kuwait 88 B4
Rauenstein Germany 53 L4
Raufarhöfn Iceland 44 [inset]
Raukumara Range mts N.Z. 113 F4
Raul Soares Brazil 145 C3
Rauma Fin. 45 L6
Raurkela India 83 F5
Rauschen Rus. Fed. see Svetlogorsk
Rausu Japan 74 G3
Rautavaara Fin. 44 P5
Rautjärvi Fin. 45 P6
Ravānsar Iran 88 B3
Rāvar Iran 88 E4
Ravat Kyrg. 89 H2
Ravels Belgium 52 E3
Ravena U.S.A. 135 I2
Ravenglass U.K. 48 D4
Ravenna Italy 58 E2
Ravenna NE U.S.A. 130 D3
Ravenna OH U.S.A. 134 E3
Ravensburg Germany 47 L7
Ravenshoe Australia 110 D3
Ravenswood Australia 110 D4
Ravi r. Pak. 89 H4
Ravnina Maryyskaya Oblast' Turkm. 89 F2
Ravnina Maryyskaya Oblast' Turkm. 89 F2
Rāwah Iraq 91 F4
Rawaki i. Kiribati 107 I2
Rawalpindi Pak. 89 I3
Rawalpindi Lake Canada 120 H1
Ŗawāndiz Iraq 91 G3
Rawi, Ko i. Thai. 71 B6
Rawicz Poland 47 P5
Rawlinna Australia 109 D7
Rawlins U.S.A. 126 G4
Rawlinson Range hills Australia 109 E6
Rawnina Turkm. see Ravnina
Rawson Arg. 144 C5
Rawu China 76 C2
Raxón, Cerro mt. Guat. 136 G5
Ray, Cape Canada 123 K5
Raya, Bukit mt. Indon. 68 E7
Rayachoti India 84 C3
Rayadurg India 84 C3
Rayagada India 84 D2
Rayagarha India see Rayagada
Rayak Lebanon 85 C3
Raychikhinsk Rus. Fed. 74 C2
Raydah Yemen 86 F6

Rayes Peak U.S.A. 128 D4
Rayevskiy Rus. Fed. 41 Q5
Rayleigh U.K. 49 H7
Raymond U.S.A. 135 J2
Raymond Terrace Australia 112 E4
Raymondville U.S.A. 131 D7
Raymore Canada 121 J5
Rayner Glacier Antarctica 152 D2
Rayong Thai. 71 C4
Raystown Lake U.S.A. 135 F3
Raz, Pointe du pt France 56 B2
Razan Iran 88 C3
Răzān Iran 88 C3
Razani Pak. 89 H3
Razāzah, Buḩayrat ar l. Iraq 91 F4
Razdan Armenia see Hrazdan
Razdel'naya Ukr. see Rozdil'na
Razdol'noye Rus. Fed. 74 C4
Razeh Iran 88 C3
Razgrad Bulg. 59 L3
Razim, Lacul lag. Romania 59 M2
Razisi China 76 D1
Razlog Bulg. 59 J4
Razmak Pak. 89 H3
Raz"yezd 3km Rus. Fed. see Novyy Urgal
Ré, Île de i. France 56 D3
Reading U.K. 49 G7
Reading MI U.S.A. 134 C3
Reading OH U.S.A. 134 C4
Reading PA U.S.A. 135 H3
Reagile S. Africa 101 H3
Realicó Arg. 144 D5
Réalmont France 56 F5
Reăng Kesei Cambodia 71 C4
Reate Italy see Rieti
Rebais France 52 D6
Rebecca, Lake salt flat Australia 109 C7
Rebiana Sand Sea des. Libya 97 F2
Reboly Rus. Fed. 44 Q5
Rebrikha Rus. Fed. 72 E2
Rebun-tō i. Japan 74 F3
Recherche, Archipelago of the is Australia 109 C8
Rechitsa Belarus see Rechytsa
Rechna Doab lowland Pak. 89 I4
Rechytsa Belarus 43 F5
Recife Brazil 143 L5
Recife, Cape S. Africa 101 G8
Recklinghausen Germany 53 H3
Reconquista Arg. 144 E3
Recreo Arg. 144 C3
Rectorville U.S.A. 134 D4
Red r. Australia 110 C3
Red r. Canada 120 E3
Red r. Canada/U.S.A. 130 D1
Red r. TN U.S.A. 134 B5
Red r. U.S.A. 131 F6
Red r. Vietnam 70 D2
Redang i. Malaysia 71 C6
Red Bank NJ U.S.A. 135 H3
Red Bank TN U.S.A. 133 C5
Red Basin China see Sichuan Pendi
Red Bay Canada 123 K4
Redberry Lake Canada 121 J4
Red Bluff U.S.A. 128 B1
Red Bluff Lake U.S.A. 131 C6
Red Butte mt. U.S.A. 129 G4
Redcar U.K. 48 F4
Redcliff Canada 126 F2
Redcliffe, Mount hill Australia 109 C7
Red Cliffs Australia 111 C7
Red Cloud U.S.A. 130 D3
Red Deer Canada 120 H4
Red Deer r. Alberta/Saskatchewan Canada 121 I5
Red Deer r. Man./Sask. Canada 121 K4
Red Deer Lake Canada 121 K4
Reddersburg S. Africa 101 H5
Redding U.S.A. 128 B1
Redditch U.K. 49 F6
Rede r. U.K. 48 E3
Redenção Brazil 143 H5
Redeyef Tunisia 58 C7
Redfield U.S.A. 130 D2
Red Granite Mountain Canada 120 B2
Red Hills U.S.A. 131 D4
Red Hook U.S.A. 135 I3
Red Indian Lake Canada 123 K4
Redkey U.S.A. 134 C3
Redkino Rus. Fed. 42 H4
Redknife r. Canada 120 G2
Red Lake Canada 121 M5
Red Lake U.S.A. 129 G4
Red Lake r. U.S.A. 130 D2
Red Lake Falls U.S.A. 121 L6
Red Lakes U.S.A. 130 E1
Redlands U.S.A. 128 E4
Red Lion U.S.A. 135 G4
Red Lodge U.S.A. 126 F3
Redmesa U.S.A. 129 I3
Redmond OR U.S.A. 126 C3
Redmond UT U.S.A. 129 H2
Red Oak U.S.A. 130 E3
Redonda Island Canada 120 E5
Redondo Port. 57 C4
Redondo Beach U.S.A. 128 D5
Red Peak U.S.A. 126 E3
Red River, Mouths of the Vietnam 70 D2
Red Rock Canada 122 C4
Red Rock AZ U.S.A. 129 H5
Redrock U.S.A. 129 I5
Red Rock PA U.S.A. 135 G3
Redrock Lake Canada 120 H1
Red Sea Africa/Asia 86 D4
Redstone r. Canada 120 E1
Red Sucker Lake Canada 121 M4
Reduzum Neth. see Roordahuizum
Redwater Canada 120 H4
Redway U.S.A. 128 B1
Red Wing U.S.A. 130 E2
Redwood City U.S.A. 128 B3
Redwood Falls U.S.A. 130 E2
Redwood National Park U.S.A. 126 B4
Redwood Valley U.S.A. 128 B2
Ree, Lough l. Rep. of Ireland 51 E4
Reed U.S.A. 134 B5
Reed City U.S.A. 134 C2
Reedley U.S.A. 128 D3
Reedsport U.S.A. 126 B4
Reedsville U.S.A. 134 E4
Reedville U.S.A. 135 G5
Reedy U.S.A. 134 E4
Reedy Glacier Antarctica 152 J1
Reefton N.Z. 113 C6
Rees Germany 52 G3
Reese U.S.A. 134 D2
Reese r. U.S.A. 128 E1
Refahiye Turkey 90 E3
Refugio U.S.A. 131 D6
Regen Germany 53 N6
Regen r. Germany 53 M5
Regência Brazil 145 D2
Regensburg Germany 53 M5
Regenstauf Germany 53 M5
Reggane Alg. 96 D2
Reggio Calabria Italy see Reggio di Calabria
Reggio Emilia-Romagna Italy see Reggio nell'Emilia
Reggio di Calabria Italy 58 F5
Reggio Emilia Italy see Reggio nell'Emilia
Reggio nell'Emilia Italy 58 D2
Reghin Romania 59 K1
Regi Afgh. 89 G3

►Regina Canada 121 J5
Provincial capital of Saskatchewan.

Régina Fr. Guiana 143 H3
Registān reg. Afgh. 89 G4
Registro Brazil 144 G2
Registro do Araguaia Brazil 145 A1
Regium Lepidum Italy see Reggio nell'Emilia
Regozero Rus. Fed. 44 Q4
Rehau Germany 53 M4
Rehburg (Rehburg-Loccum) Germany 53 J2
Rehli India 82 D5
Rehoboth Namibia 100 C2
Rehoboth Bay U.S.A. 135 H4
Rehovot Israel 85 B4
Reibell Alg. see Ksar Chellala
Reibitz Germany 53 M3
Reichenbach Germany 53 M4
Reichshoffen France 53 H6
Reid Australia 109 E7
Reidh, Rubha pt U.K. 50 D3
Reidsville U.S.A. 132 E4
Reigate U.K. 49 G7
Reiley Peak U.S.A. 129 H5
Reims France 52 E5
Reinbek Germany 53 K1
Reindeer r. Canada 121 K4
Reindeer Island Canada 121 L4
Reindeer Lake Canada 121 K3
Reine Norway 44 H3
Reinosa Spain 57 D2
Reinsfeld Germany 52 G5
Reiphólsfjöll hill Iceland 44 [inset]
Reisaelva r. Norway 44 L2
Reisa Nasjonalpark nat. park Norway 44 M2
Reisjärvi Fin. 44 N5
Reitz S. Africa 101 I4
Rekapalle India 84 D2
Reken Germany 52 H3
Reliance Canada 121 I2
Relizane Alg. 57 G6
Rellano Mex. 131 B7
Rellingen Germany 53 J1
Remagen Germany 53 H4
Remarkable, Mount hill Australia 111 B7
Remedios Cuba 133 E8
Remeshk Iran 88 E5
Remhoogte Pass Namibia 100 C2
Remi France see Reims
Remmel Mountain U.S.A. 126 C2
Remscheid Germany 53 H3
Rena Norway 45 G6
Renaix Belgium see Ronse
Renam Myanmar 76 C3
Renapur India 84 C2
Rendsburg Germany 47 L3
René-Levasseur, Île i. Canada 123 H4
Renews Canada 123 L5
Renfrew Canada 135 G1
Renfrew U.K. 50 E5
Rengali Reservoir India 83 F5
Rengat Indon. 68 C7
Rengo Chile 144 B4
Ren He r. China 77 F1
Renheji China 77 G2
Renhua China 77 G3
Reni Ukr. 59 M2
Renick U.S.A. 134 E5
Renland reg. Greenland see Tuttut Nunaat
Rennell i. Solomon Is 107 G3
Rennerod Germany 53 I4
Rennes France 56 D2
Rennick Glacier Antarctica 152 H2
Rennie Canada 121 M5
Reno r. Italy 58 E2
Reno U.S.A. 128 D2
Renovo U.S.A. 135 G3
Rensselaer U.S.A. 134 B3
Renswoude Neth. 52 F2
Renton U.S.A. 126 C3
Réo Burkina 96 C3
Reo Indon. 108 C2
Repalle India 84 D2
Repetek Turkm. 89 F2
Repetekskiy Zapovednik nature res. Turkm. 89 F2
Repolka Rus. Fed. 45 P7
Republic U.S.A. 126 D2
Republican r. U.S.A. 130 D4
►Republic of Ireland country Europe 51 E4
Europe 5, 38–39

►Republic of South Africa country Africa 100 F5
5th most populous country in Africa.
Africa 7, 94–95

Repulse Bay b. Australia 110 E4
Repulse Bay Canada 119 J3
Requena Peru 142 D5
Requena Spain 57 F4
Reşadiye Turkey 90 E2
Reserva Brazil 145 A4
Reserve U.S.A. 129 I5
Reshi China 77 F2
Reshteh-ye Alborz mts Iran see Elburz Mountains
Resistencia Arg. 144 E3
Reşiţa Romania 59 I2
Resolute Bay Canada 119 I2
Resolution Island Canada 119 L3
Resolution Island N.Z. 113 A7
Resplendor Brazil 145 C2
Restigouche r. Canada 123 I5
Resülayn Turkey see Ceylanpınar
Retalhuleu Guat. 136 F6
Retezat, Parcul Naţional nat. park Romania 59 J2
Retford U.K. 48 G5
Rethel France 52 E5
Rethem (Aller) Germany 53 J2
Réthimnon Greece see Rethymno
Rethymno Greece 59 K7
Retreat Australia 110 C5
Reuden Germany 53 M2

►Réunion terr. Indian Ocean 149 L7
French Overseas Department.
Africa 7, 94–95

Reus Spain 57 G3
Reusam, Pulau i. Indon. 71 B7
Reutlingen Germany 47 L6
Reval Estonia see Tallinn
Revda Rus. Fed. 44 S3
Revel Estonia see Tallinn
Revel France 56 F5
Revelstoke Canada 120 G5
Revigny-sur-Ornain France 52 E6
Revillagigedo, Islas is Mex. 136 B5
Revillagigedo Island U.S.A. 120 D4
Revin France 52 E5
Revivim Israel 85 B4
Revolyutsii, Pik mt. Tajik. see Revolyutsiya, Qullai
Revolyutsiya, Qullai mt. Tajik. 89 I2
Rewa India 82 E4
Rewari India 82 D3
Rexburg U.S.A. 126 F4
Rexton Canada 123 I5
Reyes, Point U.S.A. 128 B2
Reyhanlı Turkey 85 C1
Reykir Iceland 44 [inset]
Reykjanes Ridge sea feature N. Atlantic Ocean 148 F2
Reykjanestá pt Iceland 44 [inset]

►Reykjavík Iceland 44 [inset]
Capital of Iceland.

Reyneke, Ostrov i. Rus. Fed. 74 E1
Reynoldsburg U.S.A. 134 D4
Reynolds Range mts Australia 108 F5
Reynosa Mex. 131 D7
Rezā Iran 88 D3
Reẕā'īyeh Iran see Urmia
Reẕā'īyeh, Daryācheh-ye salt l. Iran see Urmia, Lake
Rēzekne Latvia 45 O8
Rezvān Iran 89 F4
Reẕvāndeh Iran see Reẕvānshahr
Reẕvānshahr Iran 88 C2
Rhaeader Gwy U.K. see Rhayader
Rhayader U.K. 49 D6
Rheda-Wiedenbrück Germany 53 I3
Rhede Germany 52 G3
Rhegium Italy see Reggio di Calabria
Rheims France see Reims
Rhein r. Germany 53 G3 see Rhine
Rheine Germany 53 H2
Rheinland-Pfalz land Germany 53 H5
Rheinsberg Germany 53 M1
Rheinstetten Germany 53 I6
Rhemilès well Alg. 96 C2
Rhin r. France 53 I6 see Rhine
Rhine r. Germany 53 G3
also spelt Rhein (Germany) or Rhin (France)
Rhinebeck U.S.A. 135 I3
Rhinelander U.S.A. 130 F2
Rhineland-Palatinate land Germany see Rheinland-Pfalz
Rhinkanal canal Germany 53 M2
Rhinow Germany 53 M2
Rhiwabon U.K. see Ruabon
Rho Italy 58 C2
Rhode Island state U.S.A. 135 J3
Rhodes Greece 59 M6
Rhodes i. Greece 59 M6
Rhodesia country Africa see Zimbabwe
Rhodes Peak U.S.A. 126 E3
Rhodope Mountains Bulg./Greece 59 J4
Rhodus i. Greece see Rhodes
Rhône r. France/Switz. 56 G5
Rhum i. U.K. see Rum
Rhuthun U.K. see Ruthin
Rhydaman U.K. see Ammanford
Rhyl U.K. 48 D5
Riachão Brazil 143 I5
Riacho Brazil 145 C2
Riacho de Santana Brazil 145 C1
Riacho dos Machados Brazil 145 C1
Rialma Brazil 145 A1
Rialto U.S.A. 128 E4
Riasi Jammu and Kashmir 82 C2
Riau, Kepulauan is Indon. 68 C6
Ribadeo Spain 57 C2
Ribadesella Spain 57 D2
Ribas do Rio Pardo Brazil 144 F2
Ribat Afgh. 89 H2
Ribat-i-Shur waterhole Iran 88 E3
Ribáuè Moz. 99 D5
Ribble r. U.K. 48 E5
Ribblesdale valley U.K. 48 E4
Ribe Denmark 45 F9
Ribécourt-Dreslincourt France 52 C5
Ribeira r. Brazil 145 B4
Ribeirão Preto Brazil 145 B3
Ribemont France 52 D5
Ribérac France 56 E4
Riberalta Bol. 142 E6
Rîbniţa Moldova 43 F7
Ribnitz-Damgarten Germany 47 N3
Říčany Czech Rep. 47 O6
Rice U.S.A. 135 F5
Rice Lake Canada 135 F1
Richards Bay S. Africa 101 K5
Richards Inlet Antarctica 152 H1
Richards Island Canada 118 E3
Richardson r. Canada 121 I3
Richardson U.S.A. 131 D5
Richardson Island Canada 120 G1
Richardson Lakes U.S.A. 135 J1
Richardson Mountains Canada 118 E3
Richardson Mountains N.Z. 113 B7
Richfield U.S.A. 129 G2
Richfield Springs U.S.A. 135 H2
Richford NY U.S.A. 135 G2
Richford VT U.S.A. 135 I1
Richgrove U.S.A. 128 D4
Richland U.S.A. 126 D3
Richland Center U.S.A. 130 F3
Richmond N.S.W. Australia 112 E4
Richmond Qld Australia 110 C4
Richmond Canada 135 H1
Richmond N.Z. 113 D5
Richmond Kwazulu-Natal S. Africa 101 J5
Richmond N. Cape S. Africa 100 F6
Richmond U.K. 48 F4
Richmond CA U.S.A. 128 B3
Richmond IN U.S.A. 134 C4
Richmond KY U.S.A. 134 C5
Richmond MI U.S.A. 134 D2
Richmond MO U.S.A. 130 E4
Richmond TX U.S.A. 131 E6

►Richmond VA U.S.A. 135 G5
State capital of Virginia.

Richmond Dale U.S.A. 134 D4
Richmond Hill U.S.A. 133 D6
Richmond Range hills Australia 112 F2
Richtersveld National Park S. Africa 100 C5
Richvale U.S.A. 128 C2
Richwood U.S.A. 134 E4
Rico U.S.A. 129 I3
Ricomagus France see Riom
Riddell Nunataks Antarctica 152 E2
Rideau Lakes Canada 135 G1
Ridge r. Canada 122 D4
Ridgecrest U.S.A. 128 E4
Ridge Farm U.S.A. 134 B4
Ridgeland MS U.S.A. 131 F5
Ridgeland SC U.S.A. 133 D5
Ridgetop U.S.A. 134 B5
Ridgetown Canada 134 E2
Ridgeway OH U.S.A. 134 D3
Ridgeway VA U.S.A. 134 F5
Ridgway CO U.S.A. 129 J2
Ridgway PA U.S.A. 135 F3
Riding Mountain National Park Canada 121 K5
Riecito Venez. 142 E1
Riemst Belgium 52 F4
Riesa Germany 53 N3
Riesco, Isla i. Chile 144 B8
Riet watercourse S. Africa 100 E6
Rietavas Lith. 45 L9
Rietfontein S. Africa 100 E4
Rieti Italy 58 E3
Rifā'ī, Tall mt. Jordan/Syria 85 C3
Rifeng China see Lichuan
Rifle U.S.A. 129 J2
Rifstangi pt Iceland 44 [inset]
Rift Valley Lakes National Park Eth. see Abijatta-Shalla National Park

►Rīga Latvia 45 N8
Capital of Latvia.

Riga, Gulf of Estonia/Latvia 45 M8
Rigain Pünco l. China 83 F2
Rīgān Iran 88 E4
Rīgas jūras līcis b. Estonia/Latvia see Riga, Gulf of
Rigby U.S.A. 126 F4
Rīgestān reg. Afgh. see Registān
Rigolet Canada 123 K3
Rigside U.K. 50 F5
Riia laht b. Estonia/Latvia see Riga, Gulf of
Riihimäki Fin. 45 N6
Riiser-Larsen Ice Shelf Antarctica 152 B2
Riito Mex. 129 F5
Rijau Nigeria 96 D3
Rijeka Croatia 58 F2
Rikā, Wādī ar watercourse Saudi Arabia 88 B6
Rikitgaib Indon. 71 B6
Rikor India 76 B2
Rikuchū-kaigan National Park Japan 75 F5
Rikuzen-takata Japan 75 F5
Rila mts Bulg. 59 J3
Rila China 83 F3
Riley U.S.A. 126 D4
Rileyville U.S.A. 135 F4
Rillieux-la-Pape France 56 G4
Rillito U.S.A. 129 H5
Rimah, Wādī al watercourse Saudi Arabia 86 F4
Rimavská Sobota Slovakia 47 R6
Rimbey Canada 120 H4
Rimini Italy 58 E2
Rîmnicu Sărat Romania see Râmnicu Sărat
Rîmnicu Vîlcea Romania see Râmnicu Vâlcea
Rimouski Canada 123 H4
Rimpar Germany 53 J5
Rimsdale, Loch l. U.K. 50 E2
Rinbung China 83 G3
Rincão Brazil 145 A3
Rindal Norway 44 F5
Ringarooma Bay Australia 111 [inset]
Ringas India 82 C4
Ringe Germany 52 G2
Ringebu Norway 45 G6
Ringhkung Myanmar 76 C2
Ringkøbing Denmark 45 F8
Ringsend U.K. 51 F2
Ringsted Denmark 45 G9
Ringtor China 83 E3
Ringvassøy i. Norway 44 K2
Ringwood Australia 112 B6
Ringwood U.K. 49 F8
Rinjani, Gunung vol. Indon. 68 F8
Rinns Point U.K. 50 C5
Rinqênzê China 83 G3
Rinteln Germany 53 J2
Rio Azul Brazil 145 A4
Riobamba Ecuador 142 C4
Rio Blanco U.S.A. 129 J2
Rio Bonito Brazil 145 C3
Rio Branco Brazil 142 E6
Rio Branco, Parque Nacional do nat. park Brazil 142 F3
Río Bravo, Parque Internacional del nat. park Mex. 131 C6
Rio Brilhante Brazil 144 F2
Rio Casca Brazil 145 C3
Rio Claro Brazil 145 B3
Río Colorado Arg. 144 D5
Río Cuarto Arg. 144 D4
Rio das Pedras Moz. 101 L2
Rio de Contas Brazil 145 C1

►Rio de Janeiro Brazil 145 C3
3rd most populous city in South America. Former capital of Brazil.

Rio de Janeiro state Brazil 145 C3

►Río de la Plata-Paraná r. S. America 144 E4
2nd longest river in South America.

Rio Dell U.S.A. 128 A1
Rio do Sul Brazil 145 A4
Río Gallegos Arg. 144 C8
Río Grande Arg. 144 C8
Rio Grande Brazil 144 F4
Río Grande Mex. 131 C8
Rio Grande r. Mex./U.S.A. 127 G5
also known as Río Bravo del Norte
Rio Grande City U.S.A. 131 D7
Rio Grande do Sul state Brazil 145 A5
Rio Grande Rise sea feature S. Atlantic Ocean 148 F8
Ríohacha Col. 142 D1
Río Hondo, Embalse resr Arg. 144 C3
Rioja Peru 142 C5
Río Lagartos Mex. 133 B8
Rio Largo Brazil 143 K5
Riom France 56 F4
Rio Mulatos Bol. 142 E7
Río Muni reg. Equat. Guinea 96 E4
Río Negro, Embalse del resr Uruguay 144 E4
Rioni r. Georgia 91 F2
Rio Novo Brazil 145 C3
Rio Pardo de Minas Brazil 145 C1
Rio Preto Brazil 145 C3
Rio Preto, Serra do hills Brazil 145 B2
Rio Rancho U.S.A. 127 G6
Río Tigre Ecuador 142 C4
Riou Lake Canada 121 J3
Rio Verde Brazil 145 A2
Rio Verde de Mato Grosso Brazil 143 H7
Rio Vista U.S.A. 128 C2
Ripky Ukr. 43 F6
Ripley England U.K. 48 F4
Ripley England U.K. 49 F5
Ripley NY U.S.A. 134 F2
Ripley OH U.S.A. 134 D4
Ripley WV U.S.A. 134 E4
Ripoll Spain 57 H2
Ripon U.K. 48 F4
Ripon U.S.A. 128 C3
Ripu India 83 G4
Risca U.K. 49 D7
Rishiri-tō i. Japan 74 F3
Rishon Le Ẕiyyon Israel 85 B4
Rish Pish Iran 89 F5
Rising Sun IN U.S.A. 134 C4
Rising Sun MD U.S.A. 135 G4
Risle r. France 49 H9
Risør Norway 45 F7
Rissa Norway 44 F5
Ristiina Fin. 45 O6
Ristijärvi Fin. 44 P4
Ristikent Rus. Fed. 44 Q2
Risum China 82 D2
Ritchie S. Africa 100 G5
Ritchie's Archipelago is India 71 A4
Ritscher Upland mts Antarctica 152 B2
Ritsem Sweden 44 J3
Ritter, Mount U.S.A. 128 D3
Ritterhude Germany 53 I1
Ritzville U.S.A. 126 D3
Riu, Laem pt Thai. 71 B5
Riva del Garda Italy 58 D2
Rivas Nicaragua 137 G6
Rivera Arg. 144 D5
Rivera Uruguay 144 E4
River Cess Liberia 96 C4
Riverhead U.S.A. 135 I3
Riverhurst Canada 121 J5
Riverina Australia 109 C7
Riverina reg. Australia 112 B5
Riversdale S. Africa 100 E8
Riverside S. Africa 101 I6
Riverside U.S.A. 128 E5
Rivers Inlet Canada 120 E5
Riversleigh Australia 110 B3
Riverton N.Z. 113 B8
Riverton VA U.S.A. 135 F4
Riverton WY U.S.A. 126 F4
Riverview Canada 123 I5
Rivesaltes France 56 F5
Riviera Beach U.S.A. 133 D7
Rivière-du-Loup Canada 123 H5
Riviere-Pentecote Canada 123 I4
Riviere-Pigou Canada 123 I4
Rivne Ukr. 43 E6
Rivungo Angola 99 C5
Riwaka N.Z. 113 D5
Riwoqê China 76 C2

►Riyadh Saudi Arabia 86 G5
Capital of Saudi Arabia.

Riyan India 89 I5
Riza well Iran 88 D3
Rize Turkey 91 F2
Rizhao Shandong China 77 H1
Rizhao Shandong China 77 H1
Rizokarpaso Cyprus see Rizokarpason
Rizokarpason Cyprus 85 B2
Rīzū well Iran 88 E3
Rīzū'īyeh Iran 88 E4
Rjukan Norway 45 F7
Rjuvbrokkene mt. Norway 45 E7
Rkîz Mauritania 96 B3
Roa Norway 45 G6
Roachdale U.S.A. 134 B4
Roach Lake U.S.A. 129 F4
Roade U.K. 49 G6
Roads U.S.A. 134 D4

►Road Town Virgin Is (U.K.) 137 L5
Capital of the British Virgin Islands.

Roan Norway 44 G4
Roan Fell hill U.K. 50 G5
Roan High Knob mt. U.S.A. 132 D4
Roanne France 56 G3
Roanoke IN U.S.A. 134 C3
Roanoke VA U.S.A. 134 F5
Roanoke r. U.S.A. 132 E4
Roanoke Rapids U.S.A. 132 E4
Roan Plateau U.S.A. 129 I2
Roaring Spring U.S.A. 135 F3
Roaringwater Bay Rep. of Ireland 51 C6
Roatán Hond. 137 G5
Röbäck Sweden 44 L5
Robat r. Afgh. 89 F4
Robāṭe Tork Iran 88 C3
Robāţ Karīm Iran 88 C3
Robāt-Sang Iran 88 E3
Robb Canada 120 G4
Robbins Island Australia 111 [inset]
Robbinsville U.S.A. 133 D5
Robe Australia 111 B8
Robe r. Australia 108 A5
Robe r. Rep. of Ireland 51 C4
Röbel Germany 53 M1
Robert Glacier Antarctica 152 D2
Robert Lee U.S.A. 131 C6
Roberts U.S.A. 126 E4
Roberts, Mount Australia 112 F2
Robertsburg U.S.A. 134 E4
Roberts Butte mt. Antarctica 152 H2
Roberts Creek Mountain U.S.A. 128 E2
Robertsfors Sweden 44 L4
Robertsganj India 83 E4
Robertson S. Africa 100 D7
Robertson, Lac l. Canada 123 K4
Robertson Bay Antarctica 152 H2
Robertson Island Antarctica 152 A2
Robertson Range hills Australia 109 C5
Robertsport Liberia 96 B4
Roberval Canada 123 G4
Robhanais, Rubha hd U.K. see Butt of Lewis
Robin Hood's Bay U.K. 48 G4
Robin's Nest hill Hong Kong China 77 [inset]
Robinson Canada 120 C2
Robinson U.S.A. 134 B4
Robinson Range hills Australia 109 B6
Robinson River Australia 110 B3
Robles Pass U.S.A. 129 H5
Roblin Canada 121 K5
Robsart Canada 121 I5
Robson, Mount Canada 120 G4
Robstown U.S.A. 131 D7
Roby U.S.A. 131 C5
Roçadas Angola see Xangongo
Rocca Busambra mt. Sicily Italy 58 E6
Rocha Uruguay 144 F4
Rochdale U.K. 48 E5
Rochechouart France 56 E4
Rochefort Belgium 52 F4
Rochefort France 56 D4
Rochefort, Lac l. Canada 123 G2
Rochegda Rus. Fed. 42 I3
Rochester Australia 112 B6
Rochester U.K. 49 H7
Rochester IN U.S.A. 134 B3
Rochester MN U.S.A. 130 E2
Rochester NH U.S.A. 135 J2
Rochester NY U.S.A. 135 G2
Rochford U.K. 49 H7
Rochlitz Germany 53 M3
Roc'h Trévezel hill France 56 C2
Rock r. Canada 120 E2
Rockall i. N. Atlantic Ocean 40 D4
Rockall Bank sea feature N. Atlantic Ocean 148 G2
Rock Creek Canada 120 B1
Rock Creek U.S.A. 134 E3
Rock Creek r. U.S.A. 126 G2
Rockdale U.S.A. 131 D6
Rockefeller Plateau Antarctica 152 J1
Rockford AL U.S.A. 133 C5
Rockford IL U.S.A. 130 F3
Rockford MI U.S.A. 134 C2
Rockglen Canada 121 J5
Rockhampton Australia 110 E4
Rockhampton Downs Australia 108 F4
Rock Hill U.S.A. 133 D5
Rockingham Australia 109 A8
Rockingham U.S.A. 133 E5
Rockingham Bay Australia 110 D3
Rockinghorse Lake Canada 121 H1
Rock Island Canada 135 I1
Rock Island U.S.A. 130 F3
Rocklake U.S.A. 130 D1
Rockland MA U.S.A. 135 J2
Rockland ME U.S.A. 132 G2
Rocknest Lake Canada 120 H1
Rockport IN U.S.A. 134 B5
Rockport TX U.S.A. 131 D7
Rock Rapids U.S.A. 130 D3
Rock River U.S.A. 126 G4
Rock Sound Bahamas 133 E7
Rock Springs MT U.S.A. 126 G3
Rocksprings U.S.A. 131 C6
Rock Springs WY U.S.A. 126 F4
Rockstone Guyana 143 G2
Rockville CT U.S.A. 135 I3
Rockville IN U.S.A. 134 B4
Rockville MD U.S.A. 135 G4
Rockwell City U.S.A. 130 E3
Rockwood MI U.S.A. 134 D2
Rockwood PA U.S.A. 134 F4
Rockyford Canada 120 H5
Rocky Harbour Canada 123 K4
Rocky Hill U.S.A. 134 D4
Rocky Island Lake Canada 122 E5
Rocky Lane Canada 120 G3
Rocky Mount U.S.A. 134 F5

Rocky Mountain House Canada 120 H4
Rocky Mountain National Park U.S.A. 126 G4
Rocky Mountains Canada/U.S.A. 124 F3
Rocourt-St-Martin France 52 D5
Rocroi France 52 E5
Rodberg Norway 45 F6
Rødbyhavn Denmark 45 G9
Roddickton Canada 123 L4
Rodeio Brazil 145 A4
Rodel U.K. 50 C3
Roden Neth. 52 G1
Rödental Germany 53 L4
Rodeo Arg. 144 C4
Rodeo Mex. 131 B7
Rodeo U.S.A. 127 F7
Rodez France 56 F4
Ródhos i. Greece see Rhodes
Rodi i. Greece see Rhodes
Roding Germany 53 M5
Rodney, Cape U.S.A. 118 B3
Rodniki Rus. Fed. 42 I4
Rodolfo Sanchez Toboada Mex. 127 D7
Rodopi Planina mts Bulg./Greece see Rhodope Mountains
Rodos Greece see Rhodes
Rodos i. Greece see Rhodes
Rodosto Turkey see Tekirdağ
Rodrigues Island Mauritius 149 M7
Roe r. U.K. 51 F2
Roebourne Australia 108 B5
Roebuck Bay Australia 108 C4
Roedtan S. Africa 101 I3
Roe Plains Australia 109 D7
Roermond Neth. 52 F3
Roeselare Belgium 52 D4
Roes Welcome Sound sea chan. Canada 119 J3
Rogachev Belarus see Rahachow
Rogätz Germany 53 L2
Rogers U.S.A. 131 E4
Rogers, Mount U.S.A. 134 E5
Rogers City U.S.A. 134 D1
Rogers Lake U.S.A. 128 E4
Rogerson U.S.A. 126 E4
Rogersville U.S.A. 134 D5
Roggan r. Canada 122 F3
Roggan, Lac l. Canada 122 F3
Roggeveen Basin sea feature S. Pacific Ocean 151 O8
Roggeveld plat. S. Africa 100 E7
Roggeveldberge esc. S. Africa 100 E7
Roghadal U.K. see Rodel
Rognan Norway 44 I3
Rögnitz r. Germany 53 K1
Rogue r. U.S.A. 126 B4
Roha India 84 B2
Rohnert Park U.S.A. 128 B2
Rohrbach in Oberösterreich Austria 47 N6
Rohrbach-lès-Bitche France 53 H5
Rohri Pak. 89 H5
Rohtak India 82 D3
Roi Et Thai. 70 C3
Roi Georges, Îles du is Fr. Polynesia 151 K6
Rois-Bheinn hill U.K. 50 D4
Roisel France 52 D5
Roja Latvia 45 M8
Rojas Arg. 144 D4
Rokeby Australia 110 C2
Rokeby National Park Australia 110 C2
Rokiškis Lith. 45 N9
Roknäs Sweden 44 L4
Rokytne Ukr. 43 E6
Rolagang China 83 G2
Rola Kangri mt. China 83 G2
Rolândia Brazil 145 A3
Rolim de Moura Brazil 142 F6
Roll AZ U.S.A. 129 G5
Roll IN U.S.A. 134 C3
Rolla MO U.S.A. 130 F4
Rolla ND U.S.A. 130 D1
Rollag Norway 45 F6
Rolleston Australia 110 E5
Rolleville Bahamas 133 F8
Rolling Fork U.S.A. 131 F5
Rollins U.S.A. 126 E3
Roma Australia 111 E5
Roma i. Indon. 108 D1
Roma Italy see Rome
Roma Lesotho 101 H5
Roma Sweden 45 K8
Romain, Cape U.S.A. 133 E5
Romaine r. Canada 123 J4
Roman Romania 59 L1
Română, Câmpia plain Romania 59 J2
Romanche Gap sea feature S. Atlantic Ocean 148 G6
Romanet, Lac l. Canada 123 I2
▶Romania country Europe 59 K2
Europe 5, 38–39
Roman-Kosh mt. Ukr. 90 D1
Romano, Cape U.S.A. 133 D7
Romanovka Rus. Fed. 73 K2
Romans-sur-Isère France 56 G4
Romanzof, Cape U.S.A. 118 B3
Rombas France 52 G5
Romblon Phil. 69 G4

▶Rome Italy 58 E4
Capital of Italy.

Rome GA U.S.A. 133 C5
Rome ME U.S.A. 135 K1
Rome NY U.S.A. 135 H2
Rome TN U.S.A. 134 B5
Rome City U.S.A. 134 C3
Romeo U.S.A. 134 D2
Romford U.K. 49 H7
Romilly-sur-Seine France 56 F2
Romitan Uzbek. 89 G2
Romney U.S.A. 135 F4
Romney Marsh reg. U.K. 49 H7
Romny Ukr. 43 G6
Rømø i. Denmark 45 F9
Romodanovo Rus. Fed. 43 J5
Romorantin-Lanthenay France 56 E3
Rompin r. Malaysia 71 C7
Romsey U.K. 49 F8
Romulus U.S.A. 134 D2
Ron India 84 B3
Rona i. U.K. 50 D1
Ronas Hill hill U.K. 50 [inset]
Roncador, Serra do hills Brazil 143 H6
Roncador Reef Solomon Is 107 F2
Ronda Spain 57 D5
Ronda, Serranía de mts Spain 57 D5
Rondane Nasjonalpark nat. park Norway 45 F6
Rondon Brazil 144 F2
Rondonópolis Brazil 143 H7
Rondout Reservoir U.S.A. 135 H3
Rongcheng Anhui China see Qingyang
Rongcheng Guangxi China see Rongxian
Rongcheng Hubei China see Jianli
Rong Chu r. China 83 G3
Rongelap atoll Marshall Is 150 H5
Rongjiang Guizhou China 77 F3
Rongjiang Jiangxi China see Nankang
Rongjiawan China see Yueyang
Rongklang Range mts Myanmar 70 A2
Rongmei China see Hefeng
Rongshui China 77 F3
Rongwo China see Tongren
Rongxian China 77 F4
Rongyul China 76 C2
Rongzhag China see Danba
Rönlap atoll Marshall Is see Rongelap
Rønne Denmark 45 I9
Ronneby Sweden 45 I8
Ronne Entrance strait Antarctica 152 L2
Ronne Ice Shelf Antarctica 152 L1
Ronnenberg Germany 53 J2
Ronse Belgium 52 D4
Roodeschool Neth. 52 G1
Rooke Island P.N.G. see Umboi
Roordahuizum Neth. 52 F1
Roorkee India 82 D3
Roosendaal Neth. 52 E3
Roosevelt AZ U.S.A. 129 H5
Roosevelt UT U.S.A. 129 I1
Roosevelt, Mount Canada 120 E3
Roosevelt Island Antarctica 152 I1
Root r. Canada 120 F2
Root r. U.S.A. 130 F3
Ropar India see Rupnagar
Roper r. Australia 110 A2
Roper Bar Australia 108 F3
Roquefort France 56 D4
Roraima, Mount Guyana 142 F2
Rori India 82 C3
Rori Indon. 69 J7
Røros Norway 44 G5
Rørvik Norway 44 G4
Rosa, Punta pt Mex. 127 F8
Rosalia U.S.A. 126 D3
Rosamond U.S.A. 128 D4
Rosamond Lake U.S.A. 128 D4
Rosario Arg. 144 D4
Rosário Brazil 143 J4
Rosario Baja California Mex. 127 E7
Rosario Coahuila Mex. 131 C7
Rosario Sinaloa Mex. 136 C4
Rosario Sonora Mex. 124 F6
Rosario Zacatecas Mex. 131 C7
Rosario Venez. 142 D1
Rosário do Sul Brazil 144 F4
Rosário Oeste Brazil 143 G6
Rosarito Baja California Mex. 127 E7
Rosarito Baja California Mex. 128 E5
Rosarito Baja California Sur Mex. 127 F8
Rosarno Italy 58 F5
Roscoff France 56 C2
Roscommon Rep. of Ireland 51 D4
Roscommon U.S.A. 134 C1
Roscrea Rep. of Ireland 51 E5
Rose r. Australia 110 A2
Rose, Mount U.S.A. 128 D2
Rose Atoll American Samoa see Rose Island

▶Roseau Dominica 137 L5
Capital of Dominica.

Roseau U.S.A. 130 E1
Roseau r. U.S.A. 130 D1
Roseberth Australia 111 B5
Rose Blanche Canada 123 K5
Rosebud r. Canada 120 H5
Rosebud U.S.A. 126 G3
Roseburg U.S.A. 126 C4
Rose City U.S.A. 134 C1
Rosedale U.S.A. 131 F5
Rosedale Abbey U.K. 48 G4
Roseires Reservoir Sudan 86 D7
Rose Island atoll American Samoa 107 J3
Rosenberg U.S.A. 131 E6
Rosendal Norway 45 E7
Rosendal S. Africa 101 H5
Rosenheim Germany 47 N7
Rose Peak U.S.A. 129 I5
Rose Point Canada 120 D4
Roseto degli Abruzzi Italy 58 F3
Rosetown Canada 121 J5
Rosetta Egypt see Rashīd
Rose Valley Canada 121 K4
Roseville CA U.S.A. 128 C2
Roseville MI U.S.A. 134 D2
Roseville OH U.S.A. 134 D4
Rosewood Australia 112 F1
Roshchino Rus. Fed. 45 P6
Rosh Pinah Namibia 100 C4
Roshtkala Tajik. see Roshtqal'a
Roshtqal'a Tajik. 89 H2
Rosignano Marittimo Italy 58 D3
Roșiori de Vede Romania 59 K2
Roskilde Denmark 45 H9
Roskruge Mountains U.S.A. 129 H5
Roslavl' Rus. Fed. 43 G5
Roslyakovo Rus. Fed. 44 R2
Roslyatino Rus. Fed. 42 J4
Ross N.Z. 113 C6
Ross, Mount hill N.Z. 113 E5
Rossano Italy 58 G5
Rossan Point Rep. of Ireland 51 D3
Ross Barnett Reservoir U.S.A. 131 F5
Ross Bay Junction Canada 123 I3
Ross Carbery Rep. of Ireland 51 C6
Ross Dependency reg. Antarctica 152 I2
Rosseau, Lake Canada 134 F1
Rossel Island P.N.G. 110 F1
Ross Ice Shelf Antarctica 152 I1
Rossignol, Lac l. Canada 122 G3
Rössing Namibia 100 B2
Ross Island Antarctica 152 H1
Rossiyskaya Sovetskaya Federativnaya Sotsialisticheskaya Respublika country Asia/Europe see Russian Federation
Rossland Canada 120 G5
Rosslare Rep. of Ireland 51 F5
Rosslare Harbour Rep. of Ireland 51 F5
Roßlau Germany 53 M3
Rosso Mauritania 96 B3
Ross-on-Wye U.K. 49 E7
Rossony Belarus see Rasony
Rossosh' Rus. Fed. 43 H6
Ross River Canada 120 C2
Ross Sea Antarctica 152 H1
Roßtal Germany 53 K5
Røssvatnet l. Norway 44 I4
Rossville U.S.A. 134 B3
Roßwein Germany 53 N3
Rosswood Canada 120 D4
Rostāq Afgh. 89 H2
Rostāq Iran 88 D5
Rosthern Canada 121 J4
Rostock Germany 47 N3
Rostov Rus. Fed. 42 H4
Rostov-na-Donu Rus. Fed. 43 H7
Rostov-on-Don Rus. Fed. see Rostov-na-Donu
Rosvik Sweden 44 L4
Roswell U.S.A. 127 G6
Rota i. N. Mariana Is 69 L4
Rot am See Germany 53 K5
Rotch Island Kiribati see Tamana
Rote i. Indon. 108 C2
Rotenburg (Wümme) Germany 53 J1
Roth Germany 53 L5
Rothaargebirge hills Germany 53 I4
Rothbury U.K. 48 F3
Rothenburg ob der Tauber Germany 53 K5
Rother r. U.K. 49 G8
Rothera research station Antarctica 152 L2
Rotherham U.K. 48 F5
Rothes U.K. 50 F3
Rothesay U.K. 50 D5
Rothwell U.K. 49 G6
Roti Indon. 108 C2
Roti i. Indon. see Rote
Roto Australia 112 B4
Rotomagus France see Rouen
Rotomanu N.Z. 113 C6
Rotondo, Monte mt. Corsica France 56 I5
Rotorua N.Z. 113 F4
Rotorua, Lake N.Z. 113 F4
Röttenbach Germany 53 L5
Rottendorf Germany 53 K5
Rottenmann Austria 47 O7
Rotterdam Neth. 52 E3
Rottleberode Germany 53 K3
Rottnest Island Australia 109 A8
Rottweil Germany 47 L6
Rotuma i. Fiji 107 H3
Rotumeroog i. Neth. 52 G1
Rotung India 76 B2
Rötviken Sweden 44 I5
Rötz Germany 53 M5
Roubaix France 52 D4
Rouen France 52 B5
Rough River Lake U.S.A. 134 B5
Roulers Belgium see Roeselare
Roumania country Europe see Romania
Roundeyed Lake Canada 123 H3
Round Hill hill U.K. 48 F4
Round Mountain Australia 112 F3
Round Rock AZ U.S.A. 129 I3
Round Rock TX U.S.A. 131 D6
Roundup U.S.A. 126 F3
Rousay i. U.K. 50 F1
Rouses Point U.S.A. 135 I1
Rouxville S. Africa 101 H6
Rouyn Canada 122 F4
Rovaniemi Fin. 44 N3
Roven'ki Rus. Fed. 43 H6
Rovereto Italy 58 D2
Rôviĕng Tbong Cambodia 71 D4
Rovigo Italy 58 D2
Rovinj Croatia 58 E2
Rovno Ukr. see Rivne
Rovnoye Rus. Fed. 43 J6
Rovuma r. Moz./Tanz. see Ruvuma
Rowena Australia 112 D2
Rowley Island Canada 119 K3
Rowley Shoals sea feature Australia 108 B4
Równe Ukr. see Rivne
Roxas Mindoro Phil. 69 G4
Roxas Palawan Phil. 68 F4
Roxas Panay Phil. 69 G4
Roxboro U.S.A. 132 E4
Roxburgh N.Z. 113 B7
Roxburgh Island Cook Is see Rarotonga
Roxby Downs Australia 111 B6
Roxo, Cabo c. Senegal 96 B3
Roy MT U.S.A. 126 F3
Roy NM U.S.A. 127 G5
Royal Canal Rep. of Ireland 51 E4
Royal Chitwan National Park Nepal 83 F4
Royale, Île i. Canada see Cape Breton Island
Royale, Isle i. U.S.A. 130 F1
Royal Natal National Park S. Africa 101 I5
Royal National Park Australia 112 E5
Royal Oak U.S.A. 134 D2
Royal Suklaphanta National Park Nepal 82 E3
Royan France 56 D4
Roye France 52 C5
Roy Hill Australia 108 B5
Royston U.K. 49 G6
Rozdil'na Ukr. 59 N1
Rozivka Ukr. 43 H7
Rtishchevo Rus. Fed. 43 I5
Ruabon U.K. 49 D6
Ruaha National Park Tanz. 99 D4
Ruahine Range mts N.Z. 113 F5
Ruanda country Africa see Rwanda
Ruapehu, Mount vol. N.Z. 113 E4
Ruapuke Island N.Z. 113 B8
Ruatoria N.Z. 113 G3
Ruba Belarus 43 F5

▶Rub' al Khālī des. Saudi Arabia 86 G6
Largest uninterrupted stretch of sand in the world.

Rubaydā reg. Saudi Arabia 88 C5
Rubtsovsk Rus. Fed. 80 F1
Ruby U.S.A. 118 C3
Ruby Dome mt. U.S.A. 129 F1
Ruby Mountains U.S.A. 129 F1
Rubys Inn U.S.A. 129 G3
Ruby Valley U.S.A. 129 F1
Rucheng China 77 G3
Ruckersville U.S.A. 135 F4
Rudall River National Park Australia 108 C5
Rudarpur India 83 E4
Ruda Śląska Poland 47 Q5
Rudauli India 83 E4
Rūdbār Iran 88 C2
Rudkøbing Denmark 45 G9
Rudnaya Pristan' Rus. Fed. 74 D3
Rudnichnyy Rus. Fed. 42 L4
Rudnik Ingichka Uzbek. see Ingichka
Rudnya Smolenskaya Oblast' Rus. Fed. 43 F5
Rudnya Volgogradskaya Oblast' Rus. Fed. 43 J6
Rudnyy Kazakh. 78 F1
Rudolf, Lake salt l. Eth./Kenya see Turkana, Lake

▶Rudol'fa, Ostrov i. Rus. Fed. 64 G1
Most northerly point of Europe.

Rudolph Island Rus. Fed. see Rudol'fa, Ostrov
Rudolstadt Germany 53 L4
Rudong China 77 I1
Rūdsar Iran 88 C2
Rue France 52 B4
Rufiji r. Tanz. 99 D4
Rufino Arg. 144 D4
Rufisque Senegal 96 B3
Rufrufua Indon. 69 I7
Rufunsa Zambia 99 C5
Rugao China 77 I1
Rugby U.K. 49 F6
Rugby U.S.A. 130 C1
Rugeley U.K. 49 F6
Rügen i. Germany 47 N3
Rugged Mountain Canada 120 E5
Rügland Germany 53 K5
Ruḥayyat al Ḥamr'ā' waterhole Saudi Arabia 88 B5
Ruhengeri Rwanda 98 C4
Ruhnu i. Estonia 45 M8
Ruhr r. Germany 53 G3
Ruhuna National Park Sri Lanka 84 D5
Rui'an China 77 I3
Rui Barbosa Brazil 145 C1
Ruicheng China 77 F1
Ruijin China 77 G3
Ruili China 76 C3
Ruin Point Canada 121 P2
Ruipa Tanz. 99 D4
Ruiz Mex. 136 C4
Ruiz, Nevado del vol. Col. 142 C3
Rujaylah, Ḥarrat ar lava field Jordan 85 C3
Rūjiena Latvia 45 N8
Ruk is Micronesia see Chuuk
Rukanpur Pak. 89 I4
Rukumkot Nepal 83 E3
Rukwa, Lake Tanz. 99 D4
Rulin China see Chengbu
Rulong China see Xinlong
Rum i. U.K. 50 C4
Rum, Jebel mts Jordan see Ramm, Jabal
Ruma Serb. and Mont. 59 H2
Rumāh Saudi Arabia 86 G4
Rumania country Europe see Romania
Rumbek Sudan 97 F4
Rumberpon i. Indon. 69 I7
Rum Cay i. Bahamas 133 F8
Rum Jungle Australia 108 E3
Rummānā hill Syria 85 D3
Rumphi Malawi 99 D5
Runan China 77 G1
Runaway, Cape N.Z. 113 F3
Runcorn U.K. 48 E5
Rundu Namibia 99 B5
Rundvik Sweden 44 K5
Rŭng, Kaôh i. Cambodia 71 C5
Rungwa Tanz. 99 D4
Rungwa r. Tanz. 99 D4
Runheji China 77 H1
Runing China see Runan
Runton Range hills Australia 109 C5
Ruokolahti Fin. 45 P6
Ruoqiang China 80 G4
Rupa India 83 H4
Rupat i. Indon. 71 C7
Rupert r. Canada 122 F4
Rupert ID U.S.A. 126 E4
Rupert WV U.S.A. 134 E5
Rupert Bay Canada 122 F4
Rupert Coast Antarctica 152 J1
Rupert House Canada see Waskaganish
Rupnagar India 82 D3
Rupshu reg. Jammu and Kashmir 82 D2
Ruqqād, Wādī ar watercourse Israel 85 B3
Rural Retreat U.S.A. 134 E5
Rusaddir N. Africa see Melilla
Rusape Zimbabwe 99 D5
Ruschuk Bulg. see Ruse
Ruse Bulg. 59 K3
Rusera India 83 F4
Rush U.S.A. 134 D4
Rush Creek r. U.S.A. 130 C4
Rushden U.K. 49 G6
Rushinga Zimbabwe 99 D5
Rushville IL U.S.A. 130 F3
Rushville IN U.S.A. 134 C4
Rushville NE U.S.A. 130 C3
Rushworth Australia 112 B6
Rusk U.S.A. 131 E6
Russell Man. Canada 121 K5
Russell Ont. Canada 135 H1
Russell N.Z. 113 E2
Russell KS U.S.A. 130 D4
Russell PA U.S.A. 134 F3
Russell Bay Antarctica 152 J2
Russell Lake Man. Canada 121 K3
Russell Lake N.W.T. Canada 120 H2
Russell Lake Sask. Canada 121 J3
Russell Range hills Australia 109 C8
Russell Springs U.S.A. 134 C5
Russellville AR U.S.A. 131 E5
Russellville KY U.S.A. 134 B5
Rüsselsheim Germany 53 I4
Russia country Asia/Europe see Russian Federation
Russian r. U.S.A. 128 B2

▶Russian Federation country Asia/Europe 64 I3
Largest country in the world, Europe and Asia. Most populous country in Europe and 5th in Asia.
Asia 6, 62–63
Europe 5, 38–39

Russian Soviet Federal Socialist Republic country Asia/Europe see Russian Federation
Russkiy, Ostrov i. Rus. Fed. 74 C4
Russkiy Kameshkir Rus. Fed. 43 J5
Rust'avi Georgia 91 G2
Rustburg U.S.A. 134 F5
Rustenburg S. Africa 101 H3
Ruston U.S.A. 131 E5
Rutanzige, Lake Dem. Rep. Congo/Uganda see Edward, Lake
Ruteng Indon. 108 C2
Ruth U.S.A. 129 F2
Rüthen Germany 53 I3
Rutherglen Australia 112 C6
Ruther Glen U.S.A. 135 G5
Ruthin U.K. 49 D5
Ruthiyai India 82 D4
Ruth Reservoir U.S.A. 128 B1
Rutka r. Rus. Fed. 42 J4
Rutland U.S.A. 135 I2
Rutland Water resr U.K. 49 G6
Rutledge Lake Canada 121 I2
Rutog Xizang China 76 B2
Rutög China 82 D2
Rutog Xizang China 83 F3
Rutul Rus. Fed. 91 G2
Ruukki Fin. 44 N4
Ruvuma r. Moz./Tanz. 99 E5
also known as Rovuma
Ruwayshid, Wādī watercourse Jordan 85 C3
Ruwayṭah, Wādī watercourse Jordan 85 C5
Ruweis U.A.E. 88 D5
Ruwenzori National Park Uganda see Queen Elizabeth National Park
Ruza Rus. Fed. 42 H5
Ruzayevka Kazakh. 78 F1
Ruzayevka Rus. Fed. 43 J5
Ruzhou China 77 G1
Ružomberok Slovakia 47 Q6
▶Rwanda country Africa 98 C4
Africa 7, 94–95
Ryābād Iran 88 D2
Ryan, Loch b. U.K. 50 D5
Ryazan' Rus. Fed. 43 H5
Ryazhsk Rus. Fed. 43 I5
Rybachiy, Poluostrov pen. Rus. Fed. 44 R2
Rybach'ye Kyrg. see Balykchy
Rybinsk Rus. Fed. 42 H4
Rybinskoye Vodokhranilishche resr Rus. Fed. 42 H4
Rybnik Poland 47 Q5
Rybnitsa Moldova see Rîbnița
Rybnoye Rus. Fed. 43 H5
Rybreka Rus. Fed. 42 G3
Ryd Sweden 45 I8
Rydberg Peninsula Antarctica 152 L2
Ryde U.K. 49 F8
Rye U.K. 49 H8
Rye r. U.K. 48 G4
Rye Bay U.K. 49 H8
Ryegate U.S.A. 126 F3
Rye Patch Reservoir U.S.A. 128 D1
Rykovo Ukr. see Yenakiyeve
Ryl'sk Rus. Fed. 43 G6
Rylstone Australia 112 D4
Ryn-Peski des. Kazakh. 41 P6
Ryukyu Islands Japan 75 B8
Ryūkyū-rettō is Japan see Ryukyu Islands
Ryukyu Trench sea feature N. Pacific Ocean 150 E4
Rzeszów Poland 43 D6
Rzhaksa Rus. Fed. 43 I5
Rzhev Rus. Fed. 42 G4

S

Sa'ādah al Barṣā' pass Saudi Arabia 85 C5
Sa'ādatābād Iran 88 D4
Saal an der Donau Germany 53 L6
Saale r. Germany 53 L3
Saalfeld Germany 53 L4
Saanich Canada 120 F5
Saar land Germany see Saarland
Saar r. Germany 52 G5
Saarbrücken Germany 52 G5
Saaremaa i. Estonia 45 M7
Saarenkylä Fin. 44 N3
Saargau reg. Germany 52 G5
Saarijärvi Fin. 44 N5
Saari-Kämä Fin. 44 O3
Saarikoski Fin. 44 L2
Saaristomeren kansallispuisto nat. park Fin. see Skärgårdshavets nationalpark
Saarland land Germany 52 G5
Saarlouis Germany 52 G5
Saatlı Azer. 91 H3
Saatly Azer. see Saatlı
Sab'a Egypt see Saba'ah
Saba'ah Egypt 85 A4
Sab' Ābār Syria 85 C3
Šabac Serb. and Mont. 59 H2
Sabadell Spain 57 H3
Sabae Japan 75 E6
Sabak Malaysia 71 C7
Sabalana i. Indon. 68 F8
Sabalana, Kepulauan is Indon. 68 F8
Sabana, Archipiélago de is Cuba 137 H4
Sabang Indon. 71 A6
Şabanözü Turkey 90 D2
Sabará Brazil 145 C2
Sabastiya West Bank 85 B3
Sab'atayn, Ramlat as des. Yemen 86 G6
Sabaudia Italy 58 E4
Sabaya Bol. 142 E7
Sabdê China 76 D2
Sabelo S. Africa 100 F6
Ṣabḥā Jordan 85 C3
Sabhā Libya 97 E2
Ṣabḥā' Saudi Arabia 88 B6
Sabhrai India 82 B5
Sabi r. India 82 D3
Sabi r. Moz./Zimbabwe see Save
Sabie Moz. 101 K3
Sabie r. Moz./S. Africa 101 K3
Sabie S. Africa 101 J3
Sabina U.S.A. 134 D4
Sabinal Mex. 127 G7
Sabinal, Cayo i. Cuba 133 E8
Sabinas Mex. 131 C7
Sabinas r. Mex. 131 C7
Sabinas Hidalgo Mex. 131 C7
Sabine r. U.S.A. 131 E6
Sabine Lake U.S.A. 131 E6
Sabine Pass U.S.A. 131 E6
Sabini, Monti mts Italy 58 E3
Sabirabad Azer. 91 H2
Sabkhat al Bardawīl Reserve nature res. Egypt see Lake Bardawil Reserve
Sable, Cape Canada 123 I6
Sable, Cape U.S.A. 133 D7
Sable, Lac du l. Canada 123 I3
Sable Island Canada 123 K6
Sabon Kafi Niger 96 D3
Sabrina Coast Antarctica 152 F2
Sabugal Port. 57 C3
Sabzawar Afgh. see Shīndand
Sabzevār Iran 88 E2
Sabzvārān Iran see Jīroft
Sacalinul Mare, Insula i. Romania 59 M2
Sacaton U.S.A. 129 H5
Sac City U.S.A. 130 E3
Săcele Romania 59 K2
Sachigo r. Canada 121 N4
Sachigo Lake Canada 121 M4
Sachin India 82 C5
Sach'on S. Korea 75 C6
Sach Pass India 82 D2
Sachsen land Germany 53 N3
Sachsen-Anhalt land Germany 53 L2
Sachsenheim Germany 53 J6
Sachs Harbour Canada 118 F2
Sacirsuyu r. Syria/Turkey see Sājūr, Nahr
Sackpfeife hill Germany 53 I4
Sackville Canada 123 I5
Saco ME U.S.A. 135 J2
Saco MT U.S.A. 126 G2
Sacramento Brazil 145 B2

▶Sacramento U.S.A. 128 C2
State capital of California.

Sacramento r. U.S.A. 128 C2
Sacramento Mountains U.S.A. 127 G6
Sacramento Valley U.S.A. 128 B1
Sada S. Africa 101 H7
Sádaba Spain 57 F2
Sá da Bandeira Angola see Lubango
Ṣadad Syria 85 C2
Ṣa'dah Yemen 86 F6
Sadao Thai. 71 C6
Saddat al Hindīyah Iraq 91 G4
Saddleback Mesa mt. U.S.A. 131 C5
Saddle Hill hill Australia 110 D2
Saddle Peak hill India 71 A4
Sa Đec Vietnam 71 D5
Sadêng China 76 B2
Sadieville U.S.A. 134 C4
Sadīj watercourse Iran 88 E5
Sadiola Mali 96 B3
Sadiqabad Pak. 89 H4
Sad Istragh mt. Afgh./Pak. 89 I2
Sa'dīyah, Hawr as imp. l. Iraq 91 G4
Sa'dīyat i. U.A.E. 88 D5
Sado r. Port. 57 B4
Sadoga-shima i. Japan 75 E5
Sadot Egypt see Sadūt
Sadovoye Rus. Fed. 43 J7
Sa Dragonera i. Spain 57 H4
Sadras India 84 D3
Sadūt Egypt 85 B4
Sadût Egypt see Sadūt
Sæby Denmark 45 G8
Saena Julia Italy see Siena
Safad Israel see Ẕefat
Safayal Maqūf well Iraq 91 G5
Safed Khirs mts Afgh. 89 H2
Safed Koh mts Afgh. 89 G3
Safed Koh mts Afgh./Pak. 89 H3
Saffānīyah, Ra's as pt Saudi Arabia 88 C4
Säffle Sweden 45 H7
Safford U.S.A. 129 I5
Saffron Walden U.K. 49 H6
Safi Morocco 54 C5
Safīdār, Kūh-e mt. Iran 88 D4
Safīd Kūh mts Afgh. see Paropamisus
Safid Sagak Iran 89 F3
Safiras, Serra das mts Brazil 145 C2
Şāfītā Syria 85 C2
Safonovo Arkhangel'skaya Oblast' Rus. Fed. 42 K2
Safonovo Smolenskaya Oblast' Rus. Fed. 43 G5
Safrā' al Asyāḥ esc. Saudi Arabia 88 A5
Safrā' as Sark esc. Saudi Arabia 86 F4
Safranbolu Turkey 90 D2
Saga China 83 F3
Saga Japan 75 C6
Saga Kazakh. 80 B1
Sagaing Myanmar 70 A2
Sagami-nada g. Japan 75 E6
Sagamore U.S.A. 134 F3
Saganthit Kyun i. Myanmar 71 B4
Sagar Karnataka India 84 B3
Sagar Karnataka India 84 C2
Sagar Madhya Pradesh India 82 D5
Sagaredzho Georgia see Sagarejo
Sagarejo Georgia 91 G2
Sagar Island India 83 G5

Sagarmatha National Park Nepal 83 F4
Sagastyr Rus. Fed. 65 N2
Sagavanirktok r. U.S.A. 118 D2
Sage U.S.A. 126 F4
Saggi, Har mt. Israel 85 B4
Saghand Iran 88 D3
Saginaw U.S.A. 134 D2
Saginaw Bay U.S.A. 134 D2
Saglek Bay Canada 123 J2
Saglouc Canada see Salluit
Sagone, Golfe de b. Corsica France 56 I5
Sagres Port. 57 B5
Sagthale India 82 C5
Saguache U.S.A. 127 G5
Sagua la Grande Cuba 137 H4
Saguaro Lake U.S.A. 129 H5
Saguaro National Park U.S.A. 129 H5
Saguenay r. Canada 123 H4
Sagunt Spain see Sagunto
Sagunto Spain 57 F4
Saguntum Spain see Sagunto
Sahagún Spain 57 D2
Sahand, Kūh-e mt. Iran 88 B2

▶Sahara des. Africa 96 D3
Largest desert in the world.

Şahara el Gharbîya des. Egypt see Western Desert
Şahara el Sharqîya des. Egypt see Eastern Desert
Saharan Atlas mts Alg. see Atlas Saharien
Saharanpur India 82 D3
Sahara Well Australia 108 C5
Saharsa India 83 F4
Sahaswan India 82 D3
Sahat, Kūh-e hill Iran 88 D3
Sahatwar India 83 F4
Şahbuz Azer. 91 G3
Sahdol India see Shahdol
Sahebganj India see Sahibganj
Sahebgunj India see Sahibganj
Saheira, Wâdi el watercourse Egypt see Suhaymī, Wādī as
Sahel reg. Africa 96 C3
Sahibganj India 83 F4
Sahiwal Pak. 89 I4
Sahlābād Iran 89 E3
Şaḩm Oman 88 E5
Şaḩneh Iran 88 B3
Şaḩrā al Ḩijārah reg. Iraq 91 G5
Sahuaripa Mex. 127 F7
Sahuayo Mex. 136 D4
Sahuteng China see Zadoi
Sa Huynh Vietnam 71 E4
Sahyadri mts India see Western Ghats
Sahyadriparvat Range hills India 84 B1
Sai r. India 83 E4
Sai Buri Thai. 71 C6
Saïda Alg. 57 G6
Saïda Lebanon see Sidon
Sai Dao Tai, Khao mt. Thai. 71 C4
Saïdia Morocco 57 E6
Sa'īdīyeh Iran see Solţānīyeh
Saidpur Bangl. 83 G4
Saiha India 83 H5
Saihan Tal China 73 K4
Saijō Japan 75 D6
Saikai National Park Japan 75 C6
Saiki Japan 75 C6
Sai Kung Hong Kong China 77 [inset]
Sailana India 82 C5
Saimaa l. Fin. 45 P6
Saimbeyli Turkey 90 E3
Saindak Pak. 89 F4
Sa'īndezh Iran 88 B2
Sa'īn Qal'eh Iran see Sa'īndezh
St Abb's Head hd U.K. 50 G5
St Agnes U.K. 49 B8
St Agnes i. U.K. 49 A9
St Alban's Canada 123 L5
St Albans U.K. 49 G7
St Albans VT U.S.A. 135 I1
St Albans WV U.S.A. 134 E4
St Alban's Head hd U.K. 49 E8
St Albert Canada 120 H4
St Aldhelm's Head hd U.K. see St Alban's Head
St-Amand-les-Eaux France 52 D4
St-Amand-Montrond France 56 F3
St-Amour France 56 G3
St-André, Cap pt Madag. see Vilanandro, Tanjona
St Andrews U.K. 50 G4
St Andrew Sound inlet U.S.A. 133 D6
St Anne U.S.A. 134 B3
St Ann's Bay Jamaica 137 I5
St Anthony Canada 123 L4
St Anthony U.S.A. 126 F4
St-Arnaud Alg. see El Eulma
St Arnaud Australia 112 A6
St Arnaud Range mts N.Z. 113 D6
St-Arnoult-en-Yvelines France 52 B6
St-Augustin Canada 123 K4
St Augustin r. Canada 123 K4
St Augustine U.S.A. 133 D6
St Austell U.K. 49 C8
St-Avertin France 56 E3
St-Avold France 52 G5
St Barbe Canada 123 K4
St-Barthélemy i. West Indies 137 L5
St Bees U.K. 48 D4
St Bees Head hd U.K. 48 D4
St Bride's Bay U.K. 49 B7
St-Brieuc France 56 C2
St Catharines Canada 134 F2
St Catherines Island U.S.A. 133 D6
St Catherine's Point U.K. 49 F8
St-Céré France 56 E4
St-Chamond France 56 G4
St Charles ID U.S.A. 126 F4
St Charles MD U.S.A. 135 G4
St Charles MI U.S.A. 134 C2
St Charles MO U.S.A. 130 F4
St-Chély-d'Apcher France 56 F4
St Christopher and Nevis country West Indies see St Kitts and Nevis
St Clair r. Canada/U.S.A. 134 D2
St Clair, Lake Canada/U.S.A. 134 D2
St-Claude France 56 G3
St Clears U.K. 49 C7
St Cloud U.S.A. 130 E2
St Croix r. U.S.A. 122 B5
St Croix Falls U.S.A. 130 E2
St David U.S.A. 129 H6
St David's Head hd U.K. 49 B7
St-Denis France 52 C6

▶St-Denis Réunion 149 L7
Capital of Réunion.

St-Denis-du-Sig Alg. see Sig
St-Dié France 56 H2
St-Dizier France 52 E6
St-Domingue country West Indies see Haiti
Ste-Anne Canada 121 L5
Ste-Anne, Lac l. Canada 123 I4
St Elias, Cape U.S.A. 118 D4

▶St Elias, Mount U.S.A. 120 A2
4th highest mountain in North America.

St Elias Mountains Canada 120 A2
Ste-Marguerite r. Canada 123 I4
Ste-Marie, Cap c. Madag. see Vohimena, Tanjona
Sainte-Marie, Île i. Madag. see Boraha, Nosy
Ste-Maxime France 56 H5
Sainte Rose du Lac Canada 121 L5
Saintes France 56 D4
Sainte Thérèse, Lac l. Canada 120 F1
St-Étienne France 56 G4
St-Étienne-du-Rouvray France 52 B5
St-Fabien Canada 123 H4
St-Félicien Canada 123 G4
Saintfield U.K. 51 G3
St-Florent Corsica France 56 I5
St-Florent-sur-Cher France 56 F3
St Floris, Parc National nat. park Cent. Afr. Rep. 98 C3
St-Flour France 56 F4
St Francesville U.S.A. 131 F6
St Francis U.S.A. 130 C4
St Francis r. U.S.A. 131 F5
St Francis Isles Australia 109 F8
St-François r. Canada 123 G5
St-François, Lac l. Canada 123 H5
St-Gaudens France 56 E5
St George Australia 112 D2
St George r. Australia 110 D3
St George AK U.S.A. 118 B4
St George SC U.S.A. 133 D5
St George UT U.S.A. 129 G3
St George, Point U.S.A. 126 B4
St George Head hd Australia 112 E5
St George Island U.S.A. 118 B4
St George Ranges hills Australia 108 D4
St-Georges Canada 123 H5

▶St George's Grenada 137 L6
Capital of Grenada.

St George's Bay Nfld. and Lab. Canada 123 K4
St George's Bay N.S. Canada 123 J5
St George's Channel P. N.G. 106 F2
St George's Channel Rep. of Ireland/U.K. 51 F6
St Gotthard Hungary see Szentgotthárd
St Gotthard Pass Switz. 56 I3
St Govan's Head hd U.K. 49 C7
St Helen U.S.A. 134 C1
St Helena U.S.A. 128 B2
St Helena i. S. Atlantic Ocean 148 H7

▶St Helena and Dependencies terr. S. Atlantic Ocean 148 H7
United Kingdom Overseas territory. Consists of St Helena, Ascension, Tristan da Cunha and Gough Island.
Africa 7

St Helena Bay S. Africa 100 D7
St Helens Australia 111 [inset]
St Helens U.K. 48 E5
St Helens U.S.A. 126 C3
St Helens, Mount vol. U.S.A. 126 C3
St Helens Point Australia 111 [inset]

▶St Helier Channel Is 49 E9
Capital of Jersey.

Sainthiya India 83 F5
St-Hubert Belgium 52 F4
St-Hyacinthe Canada 123 G5
St Ignace U.S.A. 132 C2
St Ignace Island Canada 122 D4
St Ishmael U.K. 49 C7
St Ives England U.K. 49 B8
St Ives England U.K. 49 G6
St-Jacques, Cap Vietnam see Vung Tau
St-Jacques-de-Dupuy Canada 122 F4
St James MN U.S.A. 130 E3
St James MO U.S.A. 130 F4
St James, Cape Canada 120 D5
St-Jean r. Canada 123 I4
St-Jean, Lac l. Canada 123 G4
St-Jean-d'Acre Israel see 'Akko
St-Jean-d'Angély France 56 D4
St-Jean-de-Monts France 56 C3
St-Jean-sur-Richelieu Canada 135 I1
St-Jérôme Canada 122 G5
St Joe r. U.S.A. 126 D3
Saint John Canada 123 I5
St John U.S.A. 130 D4
St John r. U.S.A. 132 H2
St John, Cape Canada 123 L4
St John Bay Canada 123 K4
St John Island Canada 123 K4

▶St John's Antigua and Barbuda 137 L5
Capital of Antigua and Barbuda.

▶St John's Canada 123 L5
Provincial capital of Newfoundland and Labrador.

St Johns AZ U.S.A. 129 I4
St Johns MI U.S.A. 134 C2
St Johns OH U.S.A. 134 C3
St Johns r. U.S.A. 133 D6
St Johnsbury U.S.A. 135 I1
St John's Chapel U.K. 48 E4
St Joseph IL U.S.A. 134 A3
St Joseph LA U.S.A. 131 F6
St Joseph MI U.S.A. 134 B2
St Joseph MO U.S.A. 130 E4
St Joseph r. U.S.A. 134 C3
St Joseph, Lake Canada 121 N5
St-Joseph-d'Alma Canada see Alma
St Joseph Island Canada 122 E5
St-Junien France 56 E4
St Just U.K. 49 B8
St-Just-en-Chaussée France 52 C5
St Keverne U.K. 49 B8
St Kilda i. U.K. 40 E4
St Kilda is U.K. 46 C2
▶St Kitts and Nevis country West Indies 137 L5
North America 9, 116–117
St-Laurent inlet Canada see St Lawrence
St-Laurent, Golfe du g. Canada see St Lawrence, Gulf of
St-Laurent-du-Maroni Fr. Guiana 143 H2
St Lawrence Canada 123 L5
St Lawrence inlet Canada 123 H4
St Lawrence, Cape Canada 123 J5
St Lawrence, Gulf of Canada 123 J4
St Lawrence Island U.S.A. 118 B3
St Lawrence Islands National Park Canada 135 H1
St Lawrence Seaway sea chan. Canada/U.S.A. 135 H1
St-Léonard Canada 123 G5
St Leonard U.S.A. 135 G4
St Lewis r. Canada 123 K3
St-Lô France 56 D2
St-Louis Senegal 96 B3
St Louis MI U.S.A. 134 C2
St Louis MO U.S.A. 130 F4
St Louis r. U.S.A. 122 B5
▶St Lucia country West Indies 137 L6
North America 9, 116–117
St Lucia, Lake S. Africa 101 K5
St Lucia Estuary S. Africa 101 K5
St Luke's Island Myanmar see Zadetkale Kyun
St Magnus Bay U.K. 50 [inset]
St-Maixent-l'École France 56 D3
St-Malo France 56 C2
St-Malo, Golfe de g. France 56 C2
St-Marc Haiti 137 J5
St Maries U.S.A. 126 D3
St Marks S. Africa 101 H7
St Mark's S. Africa see Cofimvaba

▶St-Martin i. West Indies 137 L5
Dependency of Guadeloupe (France). The southern part of the island is the Dutch territory of Sint Maarten.

St Martin, Cape S. Africa 100 C7
St Martin, Lake Canada 121 L5
St Martin's i. U.K. 49 A9
St Martin's Island Bangl. 70 A2
St Mary Peak Australia 111 B6
St Mary Reservoir Canada 120 H5
St Mary's Canada 134 E2
St Mary's U.K. 50 G2
St Mary's i. U.K. 49 A9
St Marys PA U.S.A. 135 F3
St Marys WV U.S.A. 134 E4
St Marys r. U.S.A. 134 C3
St Mary's, Cape Canada 123 L5
St Mary's Bay Canada 123 L5
St Marys City U.S.A. 135 G4
St Matthew Island U.S.A. 118 A3
St Matthews U.S.A. 134 C4
St Matthew's Island Myanmar see Zadetkyi Kyun
St Matthias Group is P. N.G. 69 L7
St Maurice r. Canada 123 G5
St Mawes U.K. 49 B8
St-Médard-en-Jalles France 56 D4
St Meinrad U.S.A. 134 B4
St Michaels U.S.A. 135 G4
St Michael's Bay Canada 123 L3
St-Mihiel France 52 F6
St-Nazaire France 56 C3
St Neots U.K. 49 G6
St-Nicolas Belgium see Sint-Niklaas
St-Nicolas, Mont hill Lux. 52 G5
St-Nicolas-de-Port France 56 H2
St-Omer France 52 C4
Saintonge reg. France 56 D4
St-Pacôme Canada 123 H5
St-Palais France 56 D5
St Paris U.S.A. 134 D3
St Pascal Canada 123 H5
St Paul r. Canada 123 K4
St-Paul atoll Fr. Polynesia see Hereheretue
St Paul AK U.S.A. 118 A4

▶St Paul MN U.S.A. 130 E2
State capital of Minnesota.

St Paul NE U.S.A. 130 D3
St-Paul, Île i. Indian Ocean 149 N8
St Paul Island U.S.A. 118 A4
St Peter and St Paul Rocks is N. Atlantic Ocean see São Pedro e São Paulo

▶St Peter Port Channel Is 49 E9
Capital of Guernsey.

St Peter's Nova Scotia Canada 123 J5
St Peters P.E.I. Canada 123 J5
St Petersburg Rus. Fed. 45 Q7
St Petersburg U.S.A. 133 D7
St-Pierre mt. France 56 G5

▶St-Pierre St Pierre and Miquelon 123 L5
Capital of St Pierre and Miquelon.

▶St Pierre and Miquelon terr. N. America 123 K5
French Territorial Collectivity.
North America 9, 116–117

St-Pierre-d'Oléron France 56 D4
St-Pierre-le-Moûtier France 56 F3
St-Pol-sur-Ternoise France 52 C4
St-Pourçain-sur-Sioule France 56 F3
St-Quentin France 52 D5
St Regis U.S.A. 126 E3
St Regis Falls U.S.A. 135 H1
St-Rémi Canada 135 I1
St-Saëns France 52 B5
St Sebastian Bay S. Africa 100 E8
St Siméon Canada 123 H5
St Simons Island U.S.A. 133 D6
St Theresa Point Canada 121 M4
St Thomas Canada 134 E2
St-Trond Belgium see Sint-Truiden
St-Tropez France 56 H5
St-Tropez, Cap de c. France 56 H5
St-Vaast-la-Hougue France 49 F9
St-Valery-en-Caux France 49 H9
St-Véran France 56 H4
St Vincent U.S.A. 130 D1
St Vincent country West Indies see St Vincent and the Grenadines
St Vincent, Cape Australia 111 [inset]
St Vincent, Cape Port. see São Vicente, Cabo de
St Vincent, Gulf Australia 111 B7
▶St Vincent and the Grenadines country West Indies 137 L6
North America 9, 116–117
St Vincent Passage St Lucia/St Vincent 137 L6
St-Vith Belgium 52 G4
St Walburg Canada 121 I4
St Williams Canada 134 E2
St-Yrieix-la-Perche France 56 E4
Sain Us China 72 J4
Saioa mt. Spain 57 F2
Saipal mt. Nepal 82 E3
Saipan i. N. Mariana Is 69 L3
Sai Pok Liu Hoi Hap Hong Kong China see West Lamma Channel
Saiteli Turkey see Kadınhanı
Saitlai Myanmar 70 A2
Saittanulkki hill Fin. 44 N3
Sai Yok National Park Thai. 71 B4
Sajam Indon. 69 I7
Sajama, Nevado mt. Bol. 142 E7
Sājir Saudi Arabia 88 B5
Sājūr, Nahr r. Syria/Turkey 85 D1
Sajzī Iran 88 D3
Sak watercourse S. Africa 100 E5
Sakaide Japan 75 D6
Sakākah Saudi Arabia 91 F5
Sakakawea, Lake U.S.A. 130 C2
Sakami Canada 122 G3
Sakami r. Canada 122 F3
Sakami Lake Canada 122 F3
Sakar mts Bulg. 59 L4
Sakaraha Madag. 99 E6
Sak'art'velo country Asia see Georgia
Sakarya Turkey 59 N4
Sakarya r. Turkey 59 N4
Sakassou Côte d'Ivoire 96 C4
Sakata Japan 75 E5
Sakchu N. Korea 75 B4
Sakesar Pak. 89 I3
Sakhalin i. Rus. Fed. 74 F2
Sakhalin Oblast admin. div. Rus. Fed. see Sakhalinskaya Oblast'
Sakhalinskaya Oblast' admin. div. Rus. Fed. 74 F2
Sakhalinskiy Zaliv b. Rus. Fed. 74 F1
Sakhi India 82 C3
Sakhile S. Africa 101 I4
Sakht-Sar Iran 88 C2
Şāki Azer. 91 G2
Saki Nigeria see Shaki
Saki Ukr. see Saky
Šakiai Lith. 45 M9
Sakir mt. Pak. 89 G4
Sakishima-shotō is Japan 73 M8
Sakoli India 82 D5
Sakon Nakhon Thai. 70 D3
Sakrivier S. Africa 100 E6
Sakura Japan 75 F6
Saky Ukr. 90 D1
Säkylä Fin. 45 M6
Sal i. Cape Verde 96 [inset]
Sal r. Rus. Fed. 43 I7
Sala Sweden 45 J7
Salaberry-de-Valleyfield Canada 135 H1
Salacgrīva Latvia 45 N8
Sala Consilina Italy 58 F4
Salada, Laguna salt l. Mex. 129 F5
Saladas Arg. 144 E3
Salado r. Buenos Aires Arg. 144 E5
Salado r. Santa Fé Arg. 144 D4
Salado r. Mex. 131 D7
Salaga Ghana 96 C4
Salairskiy Kryazh ridge Rus. Fed. 72 E2
Salajwe Botswana 100 G2
Şalālah Oman 87 H6
Salamanca Mex. 136 D4
Salamanca Spain 57 D3
Salamanca U.S.A. 135 F2
Salamanga Moz. 101 K4
Salamantica Spain see Salamanca
Salamat, Bahr r. Chad 97 E4
Salāmī Iran 89 E3
Salamina i. Greece 59 J6
Salamis tourist site Cyprus 85 A2
Salamís i. Greece see Salamina
Salamīyah Syria 85 C2
Salamonie r. U.S.A. 134 C3
Salamonie Lake U.S.A. 134 C3
Salang Tunnel Afgh. 89 H3
Salantai Lith. 45 L8
Salar de Pocitos Arg. 144 C2
Salari Pak. 89 G5
Salas Spain 57 C2
Salaspils Latvia 45 N8
Salawati i. Indon. 69 I7
Salawin, Mae Nam r. China/Myanmar see Salween
Salaya India 82 B5
Salayar i. Indon. 69 G8

▶Sala y Gómez, Isla i. S. Pacific Ocean 151 M7
Most easterly point of Oceania

Salazar Angola see N'dalatando
Salbris France 56 F3
Šalčininkai Lith. 45 N9
Salcombe U.K. 49 D8
Saldae Alg. see Bejaïa
Saldaña Spain 57 D2
Saldanha S. Africa 100 C7
Saldanha Bay S. Africa 100 C7
Saldus Latvia 45 M8
Sale Australia 112 C7
Saleh, Teluk b. Indon. 68 F8
Şāleḩābād Iran 88 C3
Salekhard Rus. Fed. 64 H3
Salem India 84 C4
Salem AR U.S.A. 131 F4
Salem IL U.S.A. 130 F4
Salem IN U.S.A. 134 B4
Salem MA U.S.A. 135 J2
Salem MO U.S.A. 130 F4
Salem NJ U.S.A. 135 H4
Salem NY U.S.A. 135 I2
Salem OH U.S.A. 134 E3

▶Salem OR U.S.A. 126 C3
State capital of Oregon.

Salem SD U.S.A. 130 D3
Salem VA U.S.A. 134 E5
Salen Scotland U.K. 50 D4
Salen Scotland U.K. 50 D4
Salerno Italy 58 F4
Salerno, Golfo di g. Italy 58 F4
Salernum Italy see Salerno
Salford U.K. 48 E5
Salgótarján Hungary 47 Q6
Salgueiro Brazil 143 K5
Salian Afgh. 89 F4
Salibabu i. Indon. 69 H6
Salida U.S.A. 127 G5
Salies-de-Béarn France 56 D5
Salihli Turkey 59 M5
Salihorsk Belarus 45 O10
Salima Malawi 99 D5
Salina KS U.S.A. 130 D4
Salina UT U.S.A. 129 H2
Salina, Isola i. Italy 58 F5
Salina Cruz Mex. 136 E5
Salinas Brazil 145 C2
Salinas Ecuador 142 B4
Salinas Mex. 136 D4
Salinas r. Mex. 131 D7
Salinas U.S.A. 128 C3
Salinas r. U.S.A. 128 C3
Salinas, Cabo de c. Spain see Ses Salines, Cap de
Salinas, Ponta das pt Angola 99 B5
Salinas Peak U.S.A. 127 G6
Saline U.S.A. 134 D2
Saline r. U.S.A. 130 D4
Saline Valley depr. U.S.A. 128 E3
Salinópolis Brazil 143 I4
Salinosó Lachay, Punta pt Peru 142 C6
Salisbury U.K. 49 F7
Salisbury MD U.S.A. 135 H4
Salisbury NC U.S.A. 132 D5
Salisbury Zimbabwe see Harare
Salisbury Plain U.K. 49 E7
Şalkhad Syria 85 C3
Salla Fin. 44 P3
Sallisaw U.S.A. 131 E5
Salluit Canada 153 K2
Sallum, Khalīj as b. Egypt 90 B5
Sallyana Nepal 83 E3
Salmās Iran 88 B2
Salmi Rus. Fed. 42 F3
Salmo Canada 120 G5
Salmon U.S.A. 126 E3
Salmon r. U.S.A. 126 D3
Salmon Arm Canada 120 G5
Salmon Falls Creek r. U.S.A. 126 E4
Salmon Gums Australia 109 C8
Salmon Reservoir U.S.A. 135 H2
Salmon River Mountains U.S.A. 126 E3
Salmtal Germany 52 G5
Salo Fin. 45 M6
Salome U.S.A. 129 G5
Salon India 82 E4
Salon-de-Provence France 56 G5
Salonica Greece see Thessaloniki
Salonika Greece see Thessaloniki
Salpausselkä reg. Fin. 45 N6
Salqīn Syria 85 C1
Salses, Étang de l. France see Leucate, Étang de
Sal'sk Rus. Fed. 43 I7
Salsomaggiore Terme Italy 58 C2
Salt Jordan see As Salț
Salt watercourse S. Africa 100 F7
Salt r. U.S.A. 129 G5
Salta Arg. 144 C2
Saltaire U.K. 48 F5
Saltash U.K. 49 C8
Saltcoats U.K. 50 E5
Saltee Islands Rep. of Ireland 51 F5
Saltfjellet Svartisen Nasjonalpark nat. park Norway 44 I3
Saltfjorden sea chan. Norway 44 H3
Salt Fork Arkansas r. U.S.A. 131 D4
Salt Fork Lake U.S.A. 134 E3
Saltillo Mex. 131 C7
Salt Lake India 89 I5

▶Salt Lake City U.S.A. 129 H1
State capital of Utah.

Salt Lick U.S.A. 134 D4
Salto Brazil 145 B3
Salto Uruguay 144 E4
Salto da Divisa Brazil 145 D2
Salto Grande Brazil 145 A3
Salton Sea salt l. U.S.A. 129 F5
Salto Santiago, Represa de resr Brazil 144 F3
Salt Range hills Pak. 89 I3
Salt River Canada 121 H2
Saluda U.S.A. 135 G5
Salûm Egypt see As Sallūm
Salûm, Khalîg el b. Egypt see Sallum, Khalīj as
Saluq, Kūh-e mt. Iran 88 E2
Salur India 84 D2
Saluzzo Italy 58 B2
Salvador Brazil 145 D1
Salvador country Central America see El Salvador
Salvador, Lake U.S.A. 131 F6
Salvaleón de Higüey Dom. Rep. see Higüey
Salvation Creek r. U.S.A. 129 H2
Salwah Saudi Arabia 98 F1
Salwah, Dawḩat b. Qatar/Saudi Arabia 88 C5
Salween r. China/Myanmar 76 C5
also known as Mae Nam Khong or Mae Nam Salawin or Nu Jiang (China) or Thanlwin (Myanmar)
Salyan Azer. 91 H3
Salyan Nepal see Sallyana
Sal'yany Azer. see Salyan
Salyersville U.S.A. 134 D5
Salzbrunn Namibia 100 C3
Salzburg Austria 47 N7
Salzgitter Germany 53 K2
Salzhausen Germany 53 K1
Salzkotten Germany 53 I3
Salzmünde Germany 53 L3
Salzwedel Germany 53 L2
Sam India 82 B4
Samae San, Ko i. Thai. 71 C4
Samagaltay Rus. Fed. 80 H1
Samāh well Saudi Arabia 88 B4
Samaida Iran see Someydeh
Samaixung China 83 E2
Samakhixai Laos see Attapu
Samalanga Indon. 71 B6
Samalayuca Mex. 127 G7
Samalkot India 84 D2
Samālūț Egypt 90 C5
Samâlût Egypt see Samālūț
Samana Cay i. Bahamas 133 F8
Samanala mt. Sri Lanka see Adam's Peak
Samandağı Turkey 85 B1
Samangān Afgh. see Āybak
Samangān Iran 89 F3
Samani Japan 74 F4
Samanlı Dağları mts Turkey 59 M4
Samar Kazakh. see Samarskoye
Samar i. Phil. 69 H4
Samara Rus. Fed. 43 K5
Samara r. Rus. Fed. 41 Q5
Samarga Rus. Fed. 74 E3
Samarinda Indon. 68 F7
Samarka Rus. Fed. 74 D3
Samarkand Uzbek. 89 G2
Samarkand, Pik mt. Tajik. see Samarqand, Qullai
Samarobriva France see Amiens
Samarqand Uzbek. see Samarkand
Samarqand, Qullai mt. Tajik. 89 H2
Sāmarrā' Iraq 91 F4
Samarskoye Kazakh. 80 F2
Samasata Pak. 89 H4
Samastipur India 83 F4
Şamaxı Azer. 91 H2
Samba Jammu and Kashmir 82 C2
Sambaliung mts Indon. 68 F6
Sambalpur India 83 E5
Sambar, Tanjung pt Indon. 68 E7
Sambas Indon. 71 E7
Sambat Ukr. see Kiev
Sambava Madag. 99 F5
Sambha India 83 G4
Sambhajinagar India see Aurangabad
Sambhal India 82 D3
Sambhar Lake India 82 C4
Sambir Ukr. 43 D6
Sambito r. Brazil 143 J5
Sâmbor Cambodia 71 D4
Sambor Ukr. see Sambir
Samborombón, Bahía b. Arg. 144 E5
Sambre r. Belgium/France 52 E4
Samch'ŏk S. Korea 75 C5
Samch'ŏnp'o S. Korea see Sach'on
Same Tanz. 98 D4
Samer France 52 B4
Sami India 82 B5
Samīrah Saudi Arabia 86 F4
Samirum Iran see Yazd-e Khvāst
Samjiyŏn N. Korea 74 C4
Şāmkir Azer. 91 G2
Şamnan va Damghan reg. Iran 88 D3
Sam Neua Laos see Xam Nua
▶Samoa country S. Pacific Ocean 107 I3
Oceania 8, 104–105
Samoa Basin sea feature S. Pacific Ocean 150 I7
Samoa i Sisifo country S. Pacific Ocean see Samoa
Samobor Croatia 58 F2
Samoded Rus. Fed. 42 I3
Samokov Bulg. 59 J3
Šamorín Slovakia 47 P6
Samos i. Greece 59 L6
Samosir i. Indon. 71 B7
Samothrace i. Greece see Samothraki
Samothraki i. Greece 59 K4
Samoylovka Rus. Fed. 43 I6
Sampê China see Xiangcheng
Sampit Indon. 68 E7
Sampit, Teluk b. Indon. 68 E7
Sam Rayburn Reservoir U.S.A. 131 E6
Samrong Cambodia see Phumĭ Sâmraông
Samsang China 83 E3
Sam Sao, Phou mts Laos/Vietnam 70 C2
Samson U.S.A. 133 C6
Sâm Sơn Vietnam 70 D3
Samsun Turkey 90 E2
Samti Afgh. 89 H2
Samui, Ko i. Thai. 71 C5
Samut Prakan Thai. 71 C4
Samut Sakhon Thai. 71 C4
Samut Songkhram Thai. 71 C4
Samyai China 83 G3
San Mali 96 C3
San, Phou mt. Laos 70 C3
San, Tônlé r. Cambodia 71 D4

▶Şan'ā' Yemen 86 F6
Capital of Yemen.

Sanaa Yemen see Şan'ā'
Sanae research station Antarctica 152 B2
San Agostín U.S.A. see St Augustine
San Agustin, Cape Phil. 69 H5
San Agustin, Plains of U.S.A. 129 I5

Sanak Island U.S.A. 118 B4
Sanandaj Iran 88 B3
San Andreas U.S.A. 128 C2
San Andrés, Isla de i. Caribbean Sea 137 H6
San Andres Mountains U.S.A. 127 G6
San Angelo U.S.A. 131 C6
San Antonio Chile 144 B4
San Antonio NM U.S.A. 127 G6
San Antonio TX U.S.A. 131 D6
San Antonio r. U.S.A. 131 D6
San Antonio, Cabo c. Cuba 137 H4
San Antonio Abad Spain 57 G4
San Antonio del Mar Mex. 127 D7
San Antonio Oeste Arg. 144 D6
San Antonio Reservoir U.S.A. 128 C4
San Augustín de Valle Fértil Arg. 144 C4
San Augustine U.S.A. 131 E6
San Benedetto del Tronto Italy 58 E3
San Benedicto, Isla i. Mex. 136 B5
San Benito U.S.A. 131 D7
San Benito r. U.S.A. 128 C3
San Benito Mountain U.S.A. 128 C3
San Bernardino U.S.A. 128 E4
San Bernardino Mountains U.S.A. 128 E4
San Bernardo Chile 144 B4
San Blas Mex. 127 F8
San Blas, Cape U.S.A. 133 C6
San Borja Bol. 142 E6
Sanbornville U.S.A. 135 J2
Sanbu China see Kaiping
San Buenaventura Mex. 131 C7
San Carlos Chile 144 B5
San Carlos Equat. Guinea see Luba
San Carlos Coahuila Mex. 131 C6
San Carlos Tamaulipas Mex. 131 D7
San Carlos U.S.A. 129 H5
San Carlos Venez. 142 E2
San Carlos de Bariloche Arg. 144 B6
San Carlos de Bolívar Arg. 144 D5
San Carlos Lake U.S.A. 129 H5
Sancha China 76 E1
Sanchahe China see Fuyu
Sancha He r. China 76 E3
Sanchi India 82 D5
San Chien Pau mt. Laos 70 C2
Sanchor India 82 B4
San Clemente U.S.A. 128 E5
San Clemente Island U.S.A. 128 D5
Sanclêr U.K. see St Clears
San Cristóbal Arg. 144 D4
San Cristobal i. Solomon Is 107 G3
San Cristóbal Venez. 142 D2
San Cristóbal, Isla i. Galápagos Ecuador 142 [inset]
San Cristóbal de las Casas Mex. 136 F5
Sancti Spíritus Cuba 137 I4
Sand r. S. Africa 101 J2
Sandagou Rus. Fed. 74 D4
Sanda Island U.K. 50 D5
Sandakan Sabah Malaysia 68 F5
Sândăn Cambodia 71 D4
Sandane Norway 44 E6
Sandanski Bulg. 59 J4
Sandaré Mali 96 B3
Sandau Germany 53 M2
Sanday i. U.K. 50 G1
Sandbach U.K. 49 E5
Sandborn U.S.A. 134 B4
Sand Cay reef India 84 B4
Sandefjord Norway 45 G7
Sandercock Nunataks Antarctica 152 D2
Sanders U.S.A. 129 I4
Sandersleben Germany 53 L3
Sanderson U.S.A. 131 C6
Sandfire Roadhouse Australia 108 C4
Sand Fork U.S.A. 134 E4
Sandgate Australia 112 F1
Sandhead U.K. 50 E6
Sand Hill r. U.S.A. 130 D2
Sand Hills U.S.A. 130 C3
Sandia Peru 142 E6
San Diego Mex. 131 B6
San Diego CA U.S.A. 128 E5
San Diego TX U.S.A. 131 D7
San Diego, Sierra mts Mex. 127 F7
Sandıklı Turkey 59 N5
Sandila India 82 E4
Sand Lake Canada 122 D5
Sand Lake l. Canada 121 M5
Sandnes Norway 45 D7
Sandnessjøen Norway 44 H3
Sandoa Dem. Rep. Congo 99 C4
Sandomierz Poland 43 D6
San Donà di Piave Italy 58 E2
Sandover watercourse Australia 110 B4
Sandovo Rus. Fed. 42 H4
Sandoway Myanmar 70 A3
Sandown U.K. 49 F8
Sandoy i. Faroe Is 44 [inset]
Sand Point U.S.A. 118 B4
Sandpoint U.S.A. 126 D2
Sandray i. U.K. 50 B4
Sandringham Australia 110 B5
Şandrul Mare, Vârful mt. Romania 59 L1
Sandsjö Sweden 45 I6
Sandspit Canada 120 D4
Sand Springs U.S.A. 131 D4
Sand Springs Salt Flat U.S.A. 128 D2
Sandstone Australia 109 B6
Sandstone U.S.A. 130 E2
Sandu Guizhou China 76 E3
Sandu Hunan China 77 G3
Sandur Faroe Is 44 [inset]
Sandusky MI U.S.A. 134 D2
Sandusky OH U.S.A. 134 D3
Sandveld mts S. Africa 100 D6
Sandverhaar Namibia 100 C4
Sandvika Akershus Norway 45 G7
Sandvika Nord-Trøndelag Norway 44 H5
Sandviken Sweden 45 J6
Sandwich Bay Canada 123 K3
Sandwich Island Vanuatu see Éfaté
Sandwich Islands N. Pacific Ocean see Hawaiian Islands
Sandwick U.K. 50 [inset]
Sandwip Bangl. 83 G5
Sandy U.S.A. 129 H1
Sandy r. U.S.A. 135 K1
Sandy Bay Canada 121 K4
Sandy Cape Qld Australia 110 F5
Sandy Cape Tas. Australia 111 [inset]
Sandy Hook U.S.A. 134 D4
Sandy Hook pt U.S.A. 135 H3
Sandy Island Australia 108 C3
Sandykachi Turkm. 89 F2
Sandykgachy Turkm. see Sandykachi
Sandykly Gumy des. Turkm. see Sundukli, Peski
Sandy Lake Alta Canada 120 H4
Sandy Lake Ont. Canada 121 M4
Sandy Lake l. Canada 121 M4
Sandy Springs U.S.A. 133 C5
San Estanislao Para. 144 E2
San Esteban, Isla i. Mex. 127 E7
San Felipe Chile 144 B4
San Felipe Baja California Mex. 127 E7
San Felipe Chihuahua Mex. 127 G8
San Felipe Venez. 142 E1
San Felipe, Cayos de is Cuba 133 D8
San Felipe de Puerto Plata Dom. Rep. see Puerto Plata
San Fernando Chile 144 B4
San Fernando Mex. 131 D7
San Fernando watercourse Mex. 127 E7
San Fernando Phil. 69 G3
San Fernando Spain 57 C5
San Fernando Trin. and Tob. 137 L6
San Fernando U.S.A. 128 D4
San Fernando de Apure Venez. 142 E2
San Fernando de Atabapo Venez. 142 E3
San Fernando de Monte Cristi Dom. Rep. see Monte Cristi
Sanford FL U.S.A. 133 D6
Sanford ME U.S.A. 135 J2
Sanford MI U.S.A. 134 C2
Sanford NC U.S.A. 132 E5
Sanford, Mount U.S.A. 118 D3
Sanford Lake U.S.A. 134 C2
San Francisco Arg. 144 D4
San Francisco U.S.A. 128 B3
San Francisco, Cabo de c. Ecuador 142 B3
San Francisco, Passo de pass Arg./Chile 144 C3
San Francisco Bay inlet U.S.A. 128 B3
San Francisco del Oro Mex. 131 B7
San Francisco de Paula, Cabo c. Arg. 144 C7
San Francisco Javier Spain 57 G4
San Gabriel, Punta pt Mex. 127 E7
San Gabriel Mountains U.S.A. 128 D4
Sangachaly Azer. see Sanqaçal
Sangameshwar India 84 B2
Sangamon r. U.S.A. 130 F3
Sangan, Koh-i- mt. Afgh. see Sangān, Kūh-e
Sangān, Kūh-e mt. Afgh. 89 G3
Sangar Rus. Fed. 65 N3
Sangareddi India 84 C2
Sangareddy India see Sangareddi
San Gavino Monreale Sardinia Italy 58 C5
Sangay, Parque Nacional nat. park Ecuador 142 C4
Sangbur Afgh. 89 F3
Sangeang i. Indon. 108 B2
Sanger U.S.A. 128 D3
Sangerfield U.S.A. 135 H2
Sangerhausen Germany 53 L3
Sang-e Surakh Iran 88 E2
Sanggarmai China 76 D1
Sanggau Indon. 68 E6
Sangilen, Nagor'ye mts Rus. Fed. 80 I1
San Giovanni in Fiore Italy 58 G5
Sangir India 82 C5
Sangir i. Indon. 69 H6
Sangir, Kepulauan is Indon. 69 G6
Sangiyn Dalay Mongolia 72 I3
Sangkapura Indon. 68 E8
Sangkulirang Indon. 68 F6
Sangli India 84 B2
Sangmai China see Dêrong
Sangmélima Cameroon 96 E4
Sangngagqoiling China 76 B2
Sango Zimbabwe 99 D6
Sangole India 84 B2
San Gorgonio Mountain U.S.A. 128 E4
Sangpi China see Xiangcheng
Sangre de Cristo Range mts U.S.A. 127 G5
Sangrur India 82 C3
Sangu r. Bangl. 83 G5
Sanguem India 84 B3
Sangutane r. Moz. 101 K3
Sangzhi China 77 F2
Sanhe China see Sandu
San Hipólito, Punta pt Mex. 127 E8
Sanhūr Egypt 90 C5
Sanhûr Egypt see Sanhūr
San Ignacio Beni Bol. 142 E6
San Ignacio Santa Cruz Bol. 142 F7
San Ignacio Santa Cruz Bol. 142 F7
San Ignacio Baja California Mex. 127 E7
San Ignacio Durango Mex. 131 C7
San Ignacio Sonora Mex. 127 F7
San Ignacio Para. 144 E3
San Ignacio, Laguna l. Mex. 127 E8
Sanikiluaq Canada 122 F2
Sanin-kaigan National Park Japan 75 D6
San Jacinto U.S.A. 128 E5
San Jacinto Peak U.S.A. 128 E5
San Javier Bol. 142 F7
Sanjeli India 82 C5
Sanjiang Guangdong China see Liannan
Sanjiang Guangxi China 77 F3
Sanjiang Guizhou China see Jinping
Sanjiangkou China 74 A4
Sanjiaocheng China see Haiyan
Sanjiaoping China 77 F2
Sanjō Japan 75 E5
San Joaquin r. U.S.A. 128 C2
San Joaquin Valley U.S.A. 128 C3
San Jon U.S.A. 131 C5
San Jorge, Golfo de g. Arg. 144 C7
San Jorge, Golfo de g. Spain see Sant Jordi, Golf de

▶San José Costa Rica 137 H7
Capital of Costa Rica.

San Jose Phil. 69 G3
San Jose CA U.S.A. 128 C3
San Jose NM U.S.A. 127 G6
San Jose watercourse U.S.A. 129 J4
San José, Isla i. Mex. 136 B4
San José de Amacuro Venez. 142 F2
San José de Bavicora Mex. 127 G7
San Jose de Buenavista Phil. 69 G4
San José de Chiquitos Bol. 142 F7
San José de Comondú Mex. 127 F8
San José de Gracia Mex. 127 E8
San Joséde la Brecha Mex. 127 F8
San José del Cabo Mex. 136 C4
San José del Guaviare Col. 142 D3
San José de Mayo Uruguay 144 E4
San José de Raíces Mex. 131 C7
San Juan Arg. 144 C4
San Juan r. Costa Rica/Nicaragua 137 H6
San Juan mt. Cuba 133 D8
San Juan Mex. 127 G8
San Juan r. Mex. 131 D7

▶San Juan Puerto Rico 137 K5
Capital of Puerto Rico.

San Juan U.S.A. 129 J5
San Juan r. U.S.A. 129 H3
San Juan, Cabo c. Arg. 144 D8
San Juan, Cabo c. Equat. Guinea 96 D4
San Juan Bautista Para. 144 E3
San Juan Bautista de las Misiones Para. see San Juan Bautista
San Juan de Guadalupe Mex. 131 C7
San Juan de los Morros Venez. 142 E2
San Juan Mountains U.S.A. 129 J3
San Juan y Martínez Cuba 129 D8
San Julián Arg. 144 C7
San Justo Arg. 144 D4
Sankari Drug India 84 C4
Sankh r. India 81 F7
Sankhu India 82 C3
Sankra Chhattisgarh India 84 D1
Sankra Rajasthan India 82 B4
Sankt Augustin Germany 53 H4
Sankt Gallen Switz. 56 I3
Sankt-Peterburg Rus. Fed. see St Petersburg
Sankt Pölten Austria 47 O6
Sankt Veit an der Glan Austria 47 O7
Sankt Vith Belgium see St-Vith
Sankt Wendel Germany 53 H5
Sanku Jammu and Kashmir 82 D2
Şanlıurfa Turkey 90 E3
Şanlıurfa prov. Turkey 85 D1
San Lorenzo Arg. 144 D4
San Lorenzo Beni Bol. 142 E7
San Lorenzo Tarija Bol. 142 F8
San Lorenzo Ecuador 142 C3
San Lorenzo mt. Spain 57 E2
San Lorenzo, Cerro mt. Arg./Chile 144 B7
San Lorenzo, Isla i. Mex. 127 E7
Sanlúcar de Barrameda Spain 57 C5
San Lucas Baja California Sur Mex. 127 E8
San Lucas Baja California Sur Mex. 136 C4
San Lucas, Serranía de mts Col. 142 D2
San Luis Arg. 144 C4
San Luis AZ U.S.A. 129 F5
San Luis AZ U.S.A. 129 H5
San Luis CO U.S.A. 131 B4
San Luís, Isla i. Mex. 127 E7
San Luisito Mex. 127 E7
San Luis Obispo U.S.A. 128 C4
San Luis Obispo Bay U.S.A. 128 C4
San Luis Potosí Mex. 136 D4
San Luis Reservoir U.S.A. 128 C3
San Luis Río Colorado Mex. 129 F5
San Manuel U.S.A. 129 H5
San Marcial, Punta pt Mex. 127 F8
San Marcos U.S.A. 131 D6
San Marcos, Isla i. Mex. 127 E8
▶San Marino country Europe 58 E3
Europe 5, 38–39

▶San Marino San Marino 58 E3
Capital of San Marino.

San Martín research station Antarctica 152 L2
San Martín Catamarca Arg. 144 C3
San Martín Mendoza Arg. 144 C4
San Martín, Lago l. Arg./Chile 144 B7
San Martín de los Andes Arg. 144 B6
San Mateo U.S.A. 128 B3
San Mateo Mountains U.S.A. 129 J4
San Matías Bol. 143 G7
San Matías, Golfo g. Arg. 144 D6
Sanmen China 77 I2
Sanmen Wan b. China 77 I2
Sanmenxia China 77 F1
San Miguel El Salvador 136 G6
San Miguel U.S.A. 128 C4
San Miguel r. U.S.A. 129 I2
San Miguel de Huachi Bol. 142 E7
San Miguel de Tucumán Arg. 144 C3
San Miguel do Araguaia Brazil 145 A1
San Miguel Island U.S.A. 128 C4
Sanming China 77 H3
Sanndatti India 84 B3
Sanndraigh i. U.K. see Sandray
Sannicandro Garganico Italy 58 F4
San Nicolás Durango Mex. 131 B7
San Nicolás Tamaulipas Mex. 131 D7
San Nicolas Island U.S.A. 128 D5
Sannieshof S. Africa 101 G4
Sanniquellie Liberia 96 C4
Sanok Poland 43 D6
San Pablo Bol. 142 E8
San Pablo Phil. 69 G4
San Pablo de Manta Ecuador see Manta
San Pedro Arg. 144 D2
San Pedro Bol. 142 F7
San Pedro Chile 144 C2
San-Pédro Côte d'Ivoire 96 C4
San Pedro Baja California Sur Mex. 124 E7
San Pedro Chihuahua Mex. 127 G7
San Pedro Para. see San Pedro de Ycuamandyyú
San Pedro watercourse U.S.A. 129 H5
San Pedro, Sierra de mts Spain 57 C4
San Pedro Channel U.S.A. 128 D5
San Pedro de Arimena Col. 142 D3
San Pedro de Atacama Chile 144 C2
San Pedro de las Colonias Mex. 131 C7
San Pedro de Macorís Dom. Rep. 137 K5
San Pedro de Ycuamandyyú Para. 144 E2
San Pedro Martir, Parque Nacional nat. park Mex. 127 E7
San Pedro Sula Hond. 136 G5
San Pierre U.S.A. 134 B3
San Pietro, Isola di i. Sardinia Italy 58 C5
San Pitch r. U.S.A. 129 H2
Sanqaçal Azer. 91 H2
Sanquhar U.K. 50 F5
Sanquianga, Parque Nacional nat. park Col. 142 C3
San Quintín, Cabo c. Mex. 127 D7
San Rafael Arg. 144 C4
San Rafael CA U.S.A. 128 B3
San Rafael NM U.S.A. 129 J4
San Rafael r. U.S.A. 129 H2
San Rafael Knob mt. U.S.A. 125 H2
San Rafael Mountains U.S.A. 128 C4
San Ramón Bol. 142 F6
Sanrao China 77 H3
San Remo Italy 58 B3
San Roque Spain 57 B2
San Roque, Punta pt Mex. 127 E8
San Saba U.S.A. 131 D6
San Salvador i. Bahamas 133 F7

▶San Salvador El Salvador 136 G6
Capital of El Salvador.

San Salvador, Isla i. Galápagos Ecuador 142 [inset]
San Salvador de Jujuy Arg. 144 C2
Sansanné-Mango Togo 96 D3
San Sebastián Arg. 144 C8
San Sebastián Spain see Donostia - San Sebastián
San Sebastián de los Reyes Spain 57 E3
Sansepolcro Italy 58 E3
San Severo Italy 58 F4
San Simon U.S.A. 129 I5
Sanski Most Bos.-Herz. 58 G2
Sansoral Islands Palau see Sonsorol Islands
Sansui China 77 F3
Santa r. Peru 142 C5
Santa Ana Bol. 142 E7
Santa Ana El Salvador 136 G6
Santa Ana Mex. 127 F7
Santa Ana i. Solomon Is 107 G3
Santa Ana U.S.A. 128 E5
Santa Ana de Yacuma Bol. 142 E6
Santa Anna U.S.A. 131 D6
Santa Bárbara Brazil 145 C2
Santa Bárbara Cuba see La Demajagua
Santa Bárbara Mex. 131 B7
Santa Barbara U.S.A. 128 D4
Santa Bárbara, Ilha i. Brazil 145 D2
Santa Barbara Channel U.S.A. 128 C4
Santa Bárbara d'Oeste Brazil 145 B3
Santa Barbara Island U.S.A. 128 D5
Santa Catalina, Gulf of U.S.A. 128 E5
Santa Catalina, Isla i. Mex. 127 F8
Santa Catalina de Armada Spain 57 B2
Santa Catalina Island U.S.A. 124 D5
Santa Catarina state Brazil 145 A4
Santa Catarina Baja California Mex. 127 E7
Santa Catarina Nuevo León Mex. 131 C7
Santa Catarina, Ilha de i. Brazil 145 A4
Santa Clara Col. 142 E4
Santa Clara Cuba 137 I4
Santa Clara Mex. 131 B6
Santa Clara CA U.S.A. 128 C3
Santa Clara UT U.S.A. 129 G3
Santa Clarita U.S.A. 128 D4
Santa Clotilde Peru 142 D4
Santa Comba Angola see Waku-Kungo
Santa Croce, Capo c. Sicily Italy 58 F6
Santa Cruz Bol. 142 F7
Santa Cruz Brazil 143 K5
Santa Cruz Costa Rica 142 A1
Santa Cruz U.S.A. 128 B3
Santa Cruz watercourse U.S.A. 129 G5
Santa Cruz, Isla i. Galápagos Ecuador 142 [inset]
Santa Cruz, Isla i. Mex. 127 F8
Santa Cruz Cabrália Brazil 145 D2
Santa Cruz de Goiás Brazil 145 A2
Santa Cruz de la Palma Canary Is 96 B2
Santa Cruz del Sur Cuba 137 I4
Santa Cruz de Moya Spain 57 F4

▶Santa Cruz de Tenerife Canary Is 96 B2
Joint capital of the Canary Islands.

Santa Cruz do Sul Brazil 144 F3
Santa Cruz Island U.S.A. 128 D4
Santa Cruz Islands Solomon Is 107 G3
Santa Elena, Bahía de b. Ecuador 142 B4
Santa Elena, Cabo c. Costa Rica 137 G6
Santa Elena, Punta pt Ecuador 142 B4
Santa Eudóxia Brazil 145 B3
Santa Eufemia, Golfo di g. Italy 58 G5
Santa Fé Arg. 144 D4
Santa Fé Cuba 133 D8

▶Santa Fe U.S.A. 127 G6
State capital of New Mexico.

Santa Fé de Bogotá Col. see Bogotá
Santa Fé de Minas Brazil 145 B2
Santa Fé do Sul Brazil 145 A3
Santa Helena Brazil 143 I4
Santa Helena de Goiás Brazil 145 A2
Santai Sichuan China 76 E2
Santai Yunnan China 76 D3
Santa Inês Brazil 143 I4
Santa Inés, Isla i. Chile 152 L3
Santa Isabel Arg. 144 C5
Santa Isabel Equat. Guinea see Malabo
Santa Isabel i. Solomon Is 107 F2
Santa Juliana Brazil 145 B2
Santalpur India 82 B5
Santa Lucia Range mts U.S.A. 128 C3
Santa Margarita U.S.A. 128 C4
Santa Margarita, Isla i. Mex. 136 B4
Santa María Arg. 144 C3
Santa Maria Amazonas Brazil 143 G4
Santa Maria Rio Grande do Sul Brazil 144 F3
Santa Maria Cape Verde 96 [inset]
Santa María r. Mex. 127 G7
Santa María Peru 142 D4
Santa Maria U.S.A. 128 C4
Santa Maria r. U.S.A. 129 G4
Santa Maria, Cabo de c. Moz. 101 K4
Santa Maria, Cabo de c. Port. 57 C5
Santa Maria, Chapadão de hills Brazil 145 B1
Santa María, Isla i. Galápagos Ecuador 142 [inset]
Santa Maria, Serra de hills Brazil 145 B1
Santa Maria da Vitória Brazil 145 B1
Santa María de Cuevas Mex. 131 B7
Santa Maria do Suaçuí Brazil 145 C2
Santa Maria Island Vanuatu 107 G3
Santa Maria Madalena Brazil 145 C3
Santa Maria Mountains U.S.A. 129 G4
Santa Marta Col. 142 D1
Santa Marta, Cabo de c. Angola 99 B5
Santa Marta Grande, Cabo de c. Brazil 145 A5
Santa Maura i. Greece see Lefkada
Santa Monica U.S.A. 128 D4
Santa Monica, Pico mt. Mex. 127 E8
Santa Monica Bay U.S.A. 128 D5
Santan Indon. 68 F7
Santana Brazil 145 C1
Santana r. Brazil 145 A2
Santana do Araguaia Brazil 143 H5
Santander Spain 57 E2
Santa Nella U.S.A. 128 C3
Santanilla, Islas is Caribbean Sea see Swan Islands
Santan Mountain hill U.S.A. 129 H5
Sant'Antioco Sardinia Italy 58 C5
Sant'Antioco, Isola di i. Sardinia Italy 58 C5
Santapilly India 84 D2
Santaquin U.S.A. 129 H2
Santa Quitéria Brazil 143 J4
Santarém Brazil 143 H4
Santarém Port. 57 B4
Santa Rita Mex. 131 C7
Santa Rosa Arg. 144 D5
Santa Rosa Acre Brazil 142 D5
Santa Rosa Rio Grande do Sul Brazil 144 F3
Santa Rosa Mex. 131 C7
Santa Rosa CA U.S.A. 128 B2
Santa Rosa NM U.S.A. 127 G6
Santa Rosa de Copán Hond. 136 G6
Santa Rosa de la Roca Bol. 142 F7
Santa Rosa Island U.S.A. 128 C5
Santa Rosalía Mex. 127 E8
Santa Rosa Range mts U.S.A. 126 D4
Santa Rosa Wash watercourse U.S.A. 129 G5
Santa Sylvina Arg. 144 D3
Santa Teresa Australia 109 F6
Santa Teresa r. Brazil 145 A1
Santa Teresa Mex. 131 D7
Santa Vitória Brazil 145 A2
Santa Ynez r. U.S.A. 128 C4
Santa Ysabel i. Solomon Is see Santa Isabel
Santee U.S.A. 128 E5
Santee r. U.S.A. 133 E5
Santiago Brazil 144 F3
Santiago i. Cape Verde 96 [inset]

▶Santiago Chile 144 B4
Capital of Chile.

Santiago Dom. Rep. 137 J5
Santiago Panama 137 H7
Santiago Phil. 69 G3
Santiago de Compostela Spain 57 B2
Santiago de Cuba Cuba 137 I4
Santiago del Estero Arg. 144 D3
Santiago de los Caballeros Dom. Rep. see Santiago
Santiago de Veraguas Panama see Santiago
Santiaguillo, Laguna de l. Mex. 131 B7
Santianna Point Canada 121 P2
Santipur India see Shantipur
Sant Jordi, Golf de g. Spain 57 G3
Santo Amaro Brazil 145 D1
Santo Amaro de Campos Brazil 145 C3
Santo Anastácio Brazil 145 A3
Santo André Brazil 145 B3
Santo Angelo Brazil 144 F3

▶Santo Antão i. Cape Verde 96 [inset]
Most westerly point of Africa.

Santo Antônio Brazil 142 F4
Santo Antônio r. Brazil 145 C2
Santo António São Tomé and Príncipe 96 D4
Santo Antônio, Cabo c. Brazil 145 D1
Santo Antônio da Platina Brazil 145 A3
Santo Antônio de Jesus Brazil 145 D1
Santo Antônio do Içá Brazil 142 E4
Santo Corazón Bol. 143 G7
Santo Domingo Cuba 133 D8

▶Santo Domingo Dom. Rep. 137 K5
Capital of the Dominican Republic.

Santo Domingo Baja California Mex. 127 E7
Santo Domingo Baja California Sur Mex. 127 F8
Santo Domingo country West Indies see Dominican Republic
Santo Domingo de Guzmán Dom. Rep. see Santo Domingo
Santo Hipólito Brazil 145 B2
Santorini i. Greece see Thira
Santos Brazil 145 B3
Santos Dumont Brazil 145 C3
Santos Plateau sea feature S. Atlantic Ocean 148 E7
Santo Tomás Mex. 127 E7
Santo Tomás Peru 142 D6
Santo Tomé Arg. 144 E3
Sanup Plateau U.S.A. 129 G3
San Valentín, Cerro mt. Chile 144 B7
San Vicente El Salvador 136 G6
San Vicente Mex. 127 D7
San Vicente de Baracaldo Spain see Barakaldo
San Vicente de Cañete Peru 142 C6
San Vincenzo Italy 58 D3
San Vito, Capo c. Sicily Italy 58 E5
Sanwer India 82 C5
Sanya China 77 F5
Sanyuan China 77 F1
Sanza Pombo Angola 99 B4
Sao, Phou mt. Laos 70 C3
São Bernardo do Campo Brazil 145 B3
São Borja Brazil 144 E3
São Carlos Brazil 145 B3
São Domingos Brazil 145 B1
São Felipe, Serra de hills Brazil 145 B1
São Félix Bahia Brazil 145 D1
São Félix Mato Grosso Brazil 143 H6
São Félix Pará Brazil 143 H5
São Fidélis Brazil 145 C3
São Francisco Brazil 145 B1

▶São Francisco r. Brazil 145 C1
5th longest river in South America.

São Francisco, Ilha de i. Brazil 145 A4
São Francisco de Paula Brazil 145 A5
São Francisco de Sales Brazil 145 A2
São Francisco do Sul Brazil 145 A4
São Gabriel Brazil 144 F4
São Gonçalo Brazil 145 C3
São Gonçalo do Abaeté Brazil 145 B2
São Gonçalo do Sapucaí Brazil 145 B3
São Gotardo Brazil 145 B2
São João, Ilhas de is Brazil 143 J4
São João da Barra Brazil 145 C3
São João da Boa Vista Brazil 145 B3
São João da Madeira Port. 57 B3
São João da Ponte Brazil 145 B1
São João del Rei Brazil 145 B3
São João do Paraíso Brazil 145 C1
São Joaquim Brazil 145 A5
São Joaquim da Barra Brazil 145 B3
São José Amazonas Brazil 142 E4
São José Santa Catarina Brazil 145 A4
São José do Rio Preto Brazil 145 A3
São José dos Campos Brazil 145 B3
São José dos Pinhais Brazil 145 A4
São Leopoldo Brazil 145 A5
São Lourenço Brazil 145 B3
São Lourenço r. Brazil 143 G7
São Luís Brazil 143 J4
São Luís Brazil 143 G4
São Luís de Montes Belos Brazil 145 A2
São Manuel Brazil 145 A3
São Marcos r. Brazil 145 B2
São Mateus Brazil 145 D2
São Mateus do Sul Brazil 145 A4
São Miguel i. Arquipélago dos Açores 148 G3
São Miguel r. Brazil 145 B2
São Miguel do Tapuio Brazil 143 J5
Saône r. France 56 G4
Saoner India 82 D5
São Nicolau i. Cape Verde 96 [inset]

▶São Paulo Brazil 145 B3
Most populous city in South America and 3rd in the world.

São Paulo state Brazil 145 A3
São Paulo de Olivença Brazil 142 E4
São Pedro da Aldeia Brazil 145 C3
São Pedro e São Paulo is N. Atlantic Ocean 148 G5
São Pires r. Brazil see Teles Pires
São Raimundo Nonato Brazil 143 J5
São Romão Amazonas Brazil 142 E5
São Romão Minas Gerais Brazil 145 B2
São Roque Brazil 145 B3
São Roque, Cabo de c. Brazil 143 K5
São Salvador Angola see M'banza Congo
São Salvador do Congo Angola see M'banza Congo
São Sebastião Brazil 145 B3
São Sebastião, Ilha do i. Brazil 145 B3
São Sebastião do Paraíso Brazil 145 B3
São Sebastião dos Poções Brazil 145 B1
São Simão Minas Gerais Brazil 143 H7
São Simão São Paulo Brazil 145 B3
São Simão, Barragem de resr Brazil 145 A2
São Tiago i. Cape Verde see Santiago

▶São Tomé São Tomé and Príncipe 96 D4
Capital of São Tomé and Príncipe.

São Tomé i. São Tomé and Príncipe 96 D4
São Tomé, Cabo de c. Brazil 145 C3
São Tomé, Pico de mt. São Tomé and Príncipe 96 D4
▶São Tomé and Príncipe country Africa 96 D4
Africa 7, 94–95
Saoura, Oued watercourse Alg. 54 D6
São Vicente Brazil 145 B3
São Vicente i. Cape Verde 96 [inset]
São Vicente, Cabo de c. Port. 57 B5
Sapanca Turkey 59 N4
Sapaul India see Supaul
Şaphane Dağı mt. Turkey 59 N5
Sapo National Park Liberia 96 C4
Sapouy Burkina 96 C3
Sapozhok Rus. Fed. 43 I5
Sappa Creek r. U.S.A. 130 D3
Sapporo Japan 74 F4
Sapulpa U.S.A. 131 D4
Sapulut Sabah Malaysia 68 F6
Saputang China see Zadoi
Sāqī Iran 88 E3
Saqqez Iran 88 B2
Sarā Iran 88 B2
Sarāb Iran 88 B2
Sara Buri Thai. 71 C4
Saradiya India 82 B5
Saragossa Spain see Zaragoza
Saragt Akhal'skaya Oblast' Turkm. 89 F2
Saragt Akhal'skaya Oblast' Turkm. see Sarakhs
Saraguro Ecuador 142 C4
Sarahs Turkm. see Sarakhs
Sarai Afgh. 89 G3
Sarai Sidhu Pak. 89 I4

223

224

Shmidta, Ostrov i. Rus. Fed. 64 K1
Shmidta, Poluostrov pen. Rus. Fed. 74 F1
Shoal Lake Canada 121 K5
Shoals U.S.A. 134 B4
Shōbara Japan 75 D6
Shoh Tajik. 89 H2
Shohi Pass Pak see Tal Pass
Shokanbetsu-dake mt. Japan 74 F4
Sholakkorgan Kazakh. 80 C3
Sholapur India see Solapur
Sholaqorghan Kazakh. see Sholakkorgan
Shomba r. Rus. Fed. 44 R4
Shomvukva Rus. Fed. 42 K3
Shona Ridge sea feature S. Atlantic Ocean 148 I9
Shonzha Kazakh. see Chundzha
Shor India 82 D2
Shorap Pak. 89 G5
Shorapur Ind a 84 C2
Shorawak reg. Afgh. 89 G4
Shorewood IL U.S.A. 134 A3
Shorewood WI U.S.A. 134 B2
Shorkot Pak. 89 I4
Shorkozakhly, Solonchak salt flat Turkm. 91 J2
Shoshone CA U.S.A. 128 E4
Shoshone ID U.S.A. 126 E4
Shoshone r. U.S.A. 126 F3
Shoshone Mountains U.S.A. 128 E2
Shoshone Peak U.S.A. 128 E3
Shoshong Botswana 101 H2
Shoshoni U.S.A. 126 F4
Shostka Ukr. 43 G6
Shouyang Shan mt. China 77 F1
Showak Sudan 86 E7
Show Low U.S.A. 129 H4
Shoyna Rus. Fed. 42 J2
Shpakovskoye Rus. Fed. 91 F1
Shpola Ukr. 43 F6
Shqipëria country Europe see Albania
Shreve U.S.A. 134 D3
Shreveport U.S.A. 131 E5
Shrewsbury U.K. 49 E6
Shri Lanka country Asia see Sri Lanka
Shri Mohangarh India 82 B4
Shrirampur India 83 G5
Shu Kazakh. 80 D3
Shū r. Kazakh./Kyrg. see Chu
Shu'ab, Ra's pt Yemen 87 H7
Shuajingsi China 76 D1
Shuangbai China 76 D3
Shuangcheng Fujian China see Zherong
Shuangcheng Heilong. China 74 B3
Shuanghe China 77 G2
Shuanghechang China 76 E2
Shuanghedagang China 74 C2
Shuangjiang Guizhou China see Jiangkou
Shuangjiang Hunan China see Tongdao
Shuangjiang Yunnan China see Eshan
Shuangliao China 74 A4
Shuangliu China 76 D2
Shuangpai China 77 F3
Shuangshipu China see Fengxian
Shuangxi China see Shunchang
Shuangyang China 74 B4
Shuangyashan China 74 C3
Shubarkuduk Kazakh. 80 A2
Shubayh well Saudi Arabia 85 D4
Shugozero Rus. Fed. 42 G4
Shuicheng China see Lupanshui
Shuidong China see Dianbai
Shuijing China 76 E1
Shuikou China 77 F3
Shuikouguan China 76 E4
Shuikoushan China 77 G3
Shuluocheng China see Zhuanglang
Shuizhai China see Wuhua
Shulan China 74 B3
Shumagin Islands U.S.A. 118 B4
Shumba Zimbabwe 99 C5
Shumen Bulg. 59 L3
Shumerlya Rus. Fed. 42 J5
Shumilina Belarus 43 F5
Shumyachi Rus. Fed. 43 G5
Shunchang China 77 H3
Shuncheng China 74 A4
Shunde China 77 G4
Shuoxian China see Shuozhou
Shuozhou China 73 K5
Shuqrah Yemen 86 G7
Shūr r. Iran 88 D4
Shūr r. Iran 89 F3
Shūr watercourse Iran 88 D5
Shur watercourse Iran 88 E3
Shūr, Rūd-e watercourse Iran 88 E4
Shūr Āb watercourse Iran 88 D4
Shurchi Uzbek. 89 G2
Shūrjestān Iran 88 D4
Shūrū Iran 89 F4
Shuryshkarskiy Sor, Ozero l. Rus. Fed. 41 T2
Shūsh Iran 88 C3
Shusha Azer. see Şuşa
Shushtar Iran 88 C3
Shutar Khun Pass Afgh. 89 G3
Shutfah, Qalamat well Saudi Arabia 88 D6
Shuwaysh, Tall ash hill Jordan 85 C4
Shuya Ivanovskaya Oblast' Rus. Fed. 42 I4
Shuya Respublika Kareliya Rus. Fed. 42 G3
Shuyskoye Rus. Fed. 42 I4
Shwebo Myanmar 70 A2
Shwedwin Myanmar 70 A1
Shwegun Myanmar 70 B3
Shwegyin Myanmar 70 B3
Shweudaung mt. Myanmar 70 B2
Shyghanaq Kazakh. see Chiganak
Shymkent Kazakh. 80 C3
Shyok Jammu and Kashmir 82 D2
Shypuvate Ukr. 43 H6
Shyroke Ukr. 43 G7
Sia Indon. 69 I8
Siabu Indon. 71 B7
Siahan Range mts Pak. 89 F5
Siāh Chashmeh Iran 88 B2
Siahgird Afgh. 89 G2
Siah Koh mts Afgh. 89 G3
Sialkot Pak. 89 I3
Siam country Asia see Thailand
Sian China see Xi'an
Sian Rus. Fed. 74 B1
Siang r. India see Brahmaputra
Siantan i. Indon. 71 D7
Siargao i. Phil. 69 H5
Siau i. Indon. 69 H6
Šiauliai Lith. 45 M9
Siazan' Azer. see Siyäzän
Si Bai, Lam r. Thai. 70 D4
Sibasa S. Africa 101 J2
Sibayi, Lake S. Africa 101 K4
Sibda China 76 C2
Šibenik Croatia 58 F3
Siberia reg. Rus. Fed. 65 M3
Siberut i. Indon. 68 B7
Siberut, Selat sea chan. Indon. 68 B7
Sibi Pak. 89 G4
Sibidiri P.N.G. 69 K8
Sibigo Indon. 71 A7
Sibiloi National Park Kenya 98 D3
Sibir' reg. Rus. Fed. see Siberia
Sibiti Congo 98 B4
Sibiu Romania 59 K2
Sibley U.S.A. 130 E3
Siboa Indon. 69 G6
Sibolga Indon. 71 B7
Siborongborong Indon. 71 B7
Sibsagar India 83 H4
Sibu Sarawak Malaysia 68 E6
Sibut Cent. Afr. Rep. 98 B3
Sibuyan i. Phil. 69 G4
Sibuyan Sea Phil. 69 G4
Sicamous Canada 120 G5
Sicca Veneria Tunisia see Le Kef
Siccus watercourse Australia 111 B6
Sicheng Anhui China see Sixian
Sicheng Guangxi China see Lingyun
Sichon Thai. 71 B5
Sichuan prov. China 76 D2
Sichuan Pendi basin China 76 E2
Sicié, Cap c. France 56 G5
Sicilia i. Italy see Sicily
Sicilian Channel Italy/Tunisia 58 E6
Sicily i. Italy 58 F5
Sicuani Peru 142 D6
Siddhapur India 82 C5
Siddipet India 84 C2
Sideros, Akra pt Greece 59 L7
Sidesaviwa S. Africa 100 F7
Sidhauli India 82 E4
Sidhi India 83 E4
Sidhpur India see Siddhapur
Sidi Aïssa Alg. 57 H6
Sidi Ali Alg. 57 G5
Sīdī Barrānī Egypt 90 B5
Sidi Bel Abbès Alg. 57 F6
Sidi Bennour Morocco 54 C5
Sidi Bou Sa'id Tunisia see Sidi Bouzid
Sidi Bouzid Tunisia 58 C7
Sidi el Barrâni Egypt see Sīdī Barrānī
Sidi El Hani, Sebkhet de salt pan Tunisia 58 D7
Sidi Ifni Morocco 96 B2
Sidi Kacem Morocco 54 C5
Sidikalang Indon. 71 B7
Sidi Khaled Alg. 54 E5
Sid Lake Canada 121 J2
Sidlaw Hills U.K. 50 F4
Sidley, Mount Antarctica 152 J1
Sidli India 83 G4
Sidmouth U.K. 49 D8
Sidney IA U.S.A. 130 E3
Sidney MT U.S.A. 126 G3
Sidney NE U.S.A. 130 C3
Sidney OH U.S.A. 134 C3
Sidney Lanier, Lake U.S.A. 133 D5
Sidoktaya Myanmar 70 A2
Sidon Lebanon 85 B3
Sidr Egypt see Sudr
Siedlce Poland 43 D5
Sieg r. Germany 53 H4
Siegen Germany 53 I4
Siĕmréab Cambodia 71 C4
Siem Reap Cambodia see Siĕmréab
Si'en China see Huanjiang
Siena Italy 58 D3
Sieradz Poland 47 Q5
Sierra Blanca U.S.A. 127 G7
Sierra Colorada Arg. 144 C6
Sierra Grande Arg. 144 C6
▶Sierra Leone country Africa 96 B4
Africa 7, 94–95
Sierra Leone Basin sea feature N. Atlantic Ocean 148 G5
Sierra Leone Rise sea feature N. Atlantic Ocean 148 G5
Sierra Madre Mountains U.S.A. 128 C4
Sierra Mojada Mex. 131 C7
Sierra Nevada, Parque Nacional nat. park Venez. 142 D2
Sierra Nevada de Santa Marta, Parque Nacional nat. park Col. 142 D1
Sierraville U.S.A. 128 C2
Sierra Vista U.S.A. 127 F7
Sierre Switz. 56 H3
Sievi Fin. 44 N5
Sifang Ling mts China 76 E4
Sifangtai China 74 B3
Sifenī Eth. 98 E2
Sifnos i. Greece 59 K6
Sig Alg. 57 F6
Siggup Nunaa pen. Greenland 119 M2
Sighetu Marmației Romania 43 D7
Sighișoara Romania 59 K1
Siglap Sing. 71 [inset]
Sigli Indon. 71 A6
Siglufjörður Iceland 44 [inset]
Signal de Botrange hill Belgium 52 G4
Signal de la Ste-Baume mt. France 56 G5
Signal Peak U.S.A. 129 F5
Signy-l'Abbaye France 52 E5
Sigourney U.S.A. 130 E3
Sigri, Akra pt Greece 59 K5
Sigsbee Deep sea feature G. of Mexico 151 N4
Sigüenza Spain 57 E3
Siguiri Guinea 96 C3
Sigulda Latvia 45 N8
Sigurd U.S.A. 129 H2
Sihanoukville Cambodia 71 C5
Sihaung Myauk Myanmar 70 A2
Sihawa India 84 D1
Sihong China 77 H1
Sihora India 82 E5
Sihui China 77 G4
Siikajoki Fin. 44 N4
Siilinjärvi Fin. 44 O5
Siirt Turkey 91 F3
Sijawal Pak. 82 B4
Sika India 82 B5
Sikaka Saudi Arabia see Sakākah
Sikandra Rao India 82 D4
Sikanni Chief Canada 120 F3
Sikanni Chief r. Canada 120 F3
Sikar India 82 C4
Sikaram mt. Afgh. 89 H3
Sikasso Mali 96 C3
Sikaw Myanmar 70 B2
Sikeston U.S.A. 131 F4
Sikhote-Alin' mts Rus. Fed. 74 D4
Sikhote-Alinskiy Zapovednik nature res. Rus. Fed. 74 E3
Sikinos i. Greece 59 K6
Sikkim state India 83 G4
Siksjö Sweden 44 J4
Sil r. Spain 57 C2
Şila' i. Saudi Arabia 90 D6
Šilalė Lith. 45 M9
Si Lanna National Park Thai. 70 B3
Silas U.S.A. 131 F6
Silavatturai Sri Lanka 84 C4
Silawaih Agam vol. Indon. 71 A6
Silberberg hill Germany 53 J1
Silchar India 83 H4
Şile Turkey 59 M4
Šileru r. India 84 D2
Silesia reg. Czech Rep./Poland 47 P5
Sileti r. Kazakh. 72 C2
Siletiteniz, Ozero salt l. Kazakh. 79 G1
Silgadi Nepal see Silgarhi
Silgarhi Nepal 82 E3
Silghat India 83 H4
Siliana Tunisia 58 C6
Silifke Turkey 85 A1
Siliguri India see Shiliguri
Siling Co salt l. China 83 G3
Silipur India 82 D4
Silistra Bulg. 59 L2
Silistria Bulg. see Silistra
Silivri Turkey 59 M4
Siljan l. Sweden 45 I6
Silkeborg Denmark 45 F8
Sillajhuay mt. Chile 142 E7
Sillamäe Estonia 45 O7
Sille Turkey 90 D3
Silli India 83 F5
Sillod India 84 B1
Silobela S. Africa 101 J4
Silsby Lake Canada 121 M4
Silt U.S.A. 129 J2
Siltaharju Fin. 44 O3
Sīlūp r. Iran 89 F5
Šilutė Lith. 45 L9
Silvan Turkey 91 F3
Silvânia Brazil 145 A2
Silvassa India 84 B1
Silver Bank Passage Turks and Caicos Is 137 J4
Silver Bay U.S.A. 130 F2
Silver City Canada 120 B2
Silver City NM U.S.A. 129 I5
Silver City NV U.S.A. 128 D2
Silver Creek r. U.S.A. 129 H4
Silver Lake U.S.A. 126 C4
Silver Lake l. U.S.A. 128 E4
Silvermine Mts hills Rep. of Ireland 51 D5
Silver Peak Range mts U.S.A. 128 E3
Silver Spring U.S.A. 135 G4
Silver Springs U.S.A. 128 D2
Silverthrone Mountain Canada 120 E5
Silvertip Mountain Canada 120 F5
Silverton U.K. 49 D8
Silverton CO U.S.A. 129 J3
Silverton TX U.S.A. 131 C5
Sima China 83 G3
Simanggang Sarawak Malaysia see Sri Aman
Simao China 76 D4
Simàrd, Lac l. Canada 122 F5
Simaria India 83 F4
Simav Turkey 59 M5
Simav Dağları mts Turkey 59 M5
Simba Dem. Rep. Congo 98 C3
Simbirsk Rus. Fed. see Ul'yanovsk
Simcoe Canada 134 E2
Simcoe, Lake Canada 134 F1
Simdega India 84 E1
Simēn mts Eth. 98 D2
Simēn Mountains Eth. see Simēn
Simeulue i. Indon. 71 B7
Simeulue Reserve nature res. Indon. 71 A7
Simferopol' Ukr. 90 D1
Simi i. Greece see Symi
Simikot Nepal 83 E3
Similan, Ko i. Thai. 71 B5
Simi Valley U.S.A. 128 D4
Simla India see Shimla
Simla U.S.A. 126 G5
Şimleu Silvaniei Romania 59 J1
Simmerath Germany 52 G4
Simmern (Hunsrück) Germany 53 H5
Simmesport U.S.A. 131 F6
Simms U.S.A. 126 F3
Simojärvi l. Fin. 44 O3
Simon Mex. 131 C7
Simonette r. Canada 120 G4
Simon Wash watercourse U.S.A. 129 I5
Simoom Sound Canada 120 E5
Simoon Sound Canada see Simoom Sound
Simpang Indon. 68 C7
Simpang Mangayau, Tanjung pt Malaysia 68 F5
Simplício Mendes Brazil 143 J5
Simplon Pass Switz. 56 I3
Simpson Canada 121 J5
Simpson U.S.A. 126 F2
Simpson Desert Australia 110 B5
Simpson Desert National Park Australia 110 B5
Simpson Desert Regional Reserve nature res. Australia 111 B5
Simpson Islands Canada 121 H2
Simpson Park Mountains U.S.A. 128 E2
Simpson Peninsula Canada 119 J3
Simrishamn Sweden 45 I9
Simushir, Ostrov i. Rus. Fed. 73 S3
Sina r. India 84 B2
Sinabang Indon. 71 B7
Sinabung vol. Indon. 71 B7
Sinai pen. Egypt 85 A5
Sinai, Mont hill France 52 E5
Sinai al Janûbîya governorate Egypt see Janūb Sīnā'
Sinai ash Shamâlîya governorate Egypt see Shamāl Sīnā'
Si Nakarin Reservoir Thai. 70 B4
Sinaloa state Mex. 127 F8
Sinalunga Italy 58 D3
Sinan China 77 F3
Sinancha Rus. Fed. see Cheremshany
Sinbo Myanmar 70 B1
Sinbyubyin Myanmar 71 B4
Sinbyugyun Myanmar 70 A2
Sincan Turkey 90 E3
Sincelejo Col. 142 C2
Sinchu Taiwan see T'aoyüan
Sinclair Mills Canada 120 F4
Sincora, Serra do hills Brazil 145 C1
Sind r. India 82 D4
Sind Pak. see Thul
Sind prov. Pak. see Sindh
Sinda Rus. Fed. 74 E2
Sindari India 82 B4
Sindelfingen Germany 53 I6
Sindh prov. Pak. 89 H5
Sindhuli Garhi Nepal 83 F4
Sindhulimadi Nepal see Sindhuli Garhi
Sındırgı Turkey 59 M5
Sindor Rus. Fed. 42 K3
Sindou Burkina 96 C3
Sindri India 83 F5
Sind Sagar Doab lowland Pak. 89 H4
Sinel'nikovo Ukr. see Synel'nykove
Sines Port. 57 B5
Sines, Cabo de c. Port. 57 B5
Sinettä Fin. 44 N3
Sinfra Côte d'Ivoire 96 C4
Sing Myanmar 70 B2
Singa Sudan 86 D7
Singanallur India 84 C4
▶Singapore country Asia 71 [inset]
Asia 6, 62–63

▶Singapore Sing. 71 [inset]
Capital of Singapore.

Singapore r. Sing. 71 [inset]
Singapore, Strait of Indon./Sing. 71 [inset]
Singapura country Asia see Singapore
Singapura Sing. see Singapore
Singapuram India 84 D2
Singaraja Indon. 108 A2
Sing Buri Thai. 70 C4
Singhampton Canada 134 E1
Singhana India 82 C3
Singida Tanz. 99 D4
Singidunum Serb. and Mont. see Belgrade
Singkaling Hkamti Myanmar 70 A1
Singkawang Indon. 68 D6
Singkep i. Indon. 68 C7
Singkil Indon. 71 B7
Singkuang Indon. 71 B7
Singleton Australia 112 E4
Singleton, Mount hill N.T. Australia 108 E5
Singleton, Mount hill W.A. Australia 109 B7
Singora Thai. see Songkhla
Sin'gosan N. Korea see Kosan
Singra India 83 G4
Singri India 83 H4
Singu Myanmar 76 B4
Singwara India 84 D1
Sin'gye N. Korea 75 B5
Sinhala country Asia see Sri Lanka
Sinhkung Myanmar 70 B1
Sining China see Xining
Siniscola Sardinia Italy 58 C4
Sinj Croatia 58 G3
Sinjai Indon. 69 G8
Sinjār, Jabal mt. Iraq 91 F3
Sinkat Sudan 86 E6
Sinkiang aut. reg. China see Xinjiang Uygur Zizhiqu
Sinkiang Uighur Autonomous Region aut. reg. China see Xinjiang Uygur Zizhiqu
Sinmi-do i. N. Korea 75 B5
Sinn Germany 53 I4
Sinnamary Fr. Guiana 143 H2
Sinn Bishr, Gebel hill Egypt see Sinn Bishr, Jabal
Sinn Bishr, Jabal hill Egypt 85 A5
Sinneh Iran see Sanandaj
Sinoia Zimbabwe see Chinhoyi
Sinop Brazil 143 G6
Sinop Turkey 90 D2
Sinope Turkey see Sinop
Sinp'a N. Korea 74 B4
Sinp'o N. Korea 75 C4
Sinsang N. Korea 75 B5
Sinsheim Germany 53 I5
Sintang Indon. 68 E6
Sint Eustatius i. Neth. Antilles 137 L5
Sint-Laureins Belgium 52 D3

▶Sint Maarten i. Neth. Antilles 137 L5
Part of the Netherlands Antilles. The northern part of the island is the French territory of St Martin.

Sint-Niklaas Belgium 52 E3
Sinton U.S.A. 131 D6
Sintra Port. 57 B4
Sint-Truiden Belgium 52 F4
Sinŭiju N. Korea 75 B4
Sinzig Germany 53 H4
Siófok Hungary 58 H1
Sioma Ngwezi National Park Zambia 99 C5
Sion Switz. 56 H3
Sion Mills U.K. 51 E3
Siorapaluk Greenland 119 K2
Sioux Center U.S.A. 125 H3
Sioux City U.S.A. 130 D3
Sioux Falls U.S.A. 130 D3
Sioux Lookout Canada 121 N5
Siphaqeni S. Africa see Flagstaff
Siping China 74 B4
Sipiwesk Canada 121 L4
Sipiwesk Lake Canada 121 L4
Siple, Mount Antarctica 152 J2
Siple Coast Antarctica 152 I1
Siple Island Antarctica 152 J2
Siponj Tajik. see Bartang
Sipsey r. U.S.A. 131 F5
Sipura i. Indon. 68 B7
Siq, Wādī as watercourse Egypt 85 A5
Sir r. Pak. 89 H6
Sir, Dar"yoi r. Asia see Syrdar'ya
Sira India 84 C3
Sira r. Norway 45 E7
Şīr Abū Nu'āyr i. U.A.E. 88 D5
Siracusa Sicily Italy see Syracuse
Siraha Nepal see Sirha
Sirajganj Bangl. 83 G4
Sir Alexander, Mount Canada 120 F4
Şiran Turkey 91 E2
Sirbāl, Jabal mt. Egypt 90 D5
Şīr Banī Yās i. U.A.E. 88 D5
Sircilla India see Sirsilla
Sirdaryo r. Asia see Syrdar'ya
Sirdaryo Uzbek. see Syrdar'ya
Sirdingka China see Lhari
Sir Edward Pellew Group is Australia 110 B2
Sirha Nepal 83 F4
Sirḩān, Wādī as watercourse Jordan/Saudi Arabia 85 C4
Sirik, Tanjung pt Malaysia 68 E6
Siri Kit Dam Thai. 70 C3
Sirína i. Greece see Syrna
Sirjā Iran 89 F5
Sir James MacBrien, Mount Canada 120 E2
Sīrjān Iran 88 D4
Sīrjān salt flat Iran 88 D4
Sirkazhi India 84 C4
Sirmilik National Park Canada 119 K2
Şırnak Turkey 91 F3
Sirohi India 82 C4
Sirombu Indon. 71 B7
Sironj India 82 D4
Síros i. Greece see Syros
Sirpur India 84 C2
Sirretta Peak U.S.A. 128 D4
Sīrrī, Jazīreh-ye i. Iran 88 D5
Sirsa India 82 C3
Sir Sandford, Mount Canada 120 G5
Sirsi Karnataka India 84 B3
Sirsi Madhya Pradesh India 82 D4
Sirsi Uttar Pradesh India 82 D3
Sirsilla India 84 C2
Sirte Libya 97 E1
Sirte, Gulf of Libya 97 E1
Sir Thomas, Mount hill Australia 109 E6
Siruguppa India 84 C3
Sirur India 84 B2
Şirvan Turkey 91 F3
Sirvel India 84 C3
Širvintai Lith. see Širvintos
Širvintos Lith. 45 N9
Sīrwān r. Iraq 91 G4
Sir Wilfrid Laurier, Mount Canada 120 G4
Sis Turkey see Kozan
Sisak Croatia 58 G2
Sisaket Thai. 70 D4
Siscia Croatia see Sisak
Sishen S. Africa 100 F4
Sishilipu China 76 E1
Sishuang Liedao is China 77 I3
Sisian Armenia 91 G3
Sisimiut Greenland 119 M3
Sisipuk Lake Canada 121 K4
Sisŏphŏn Cambodia 71 C4
Sissano P.N.G. 69 K7
Sisseton U.S.A. 130 D2
Sistān reg. Iran 89 F4
Sīstan, Daryācheh-ye marsh Afgh./Iran 89 F4
Sisteron France 56 G4
Sisters is India 71 A5
Sīt Iran 88 E5
Sitamarhi India 83 F4
Sitang China see Sinan
Sitapur India 82 E4
Siteia Greece 59 L7
Siteki Swaziland 101 J4
Sithonia pen. Greece 59 J4
Sitía Greece see Siteia
Sitidgi Lake Canada 118 E3
Sitila Moz. 101 L2
Siting China 76 E3
Sítio do Mato Brazil 145 C1
Sitka U.S.A. 120 C3
Sitka National Historical Park nat. park U.S.A. 120 C3
Sitra oasis Egypt see Sitrah
Sitrah oasis Egypt 90 B5
Sittang r. Myanmar 70 B3
Sittard Neth. 52 F4
Sittaung Myanmar 70 A1
Sittaung r. Myanmar see Sittang
Sittensen Germany 53 J1
Sittingbourne U.K. 49 H7
Sittoung r. Myanmar see Sittang
Sittwe Myanmar 70 A2
Situbondo Indon. 68 E8
Siumpu i. Indon. 69 G8
Siuri India 83 F5
Sivaganga India 84 C4
Sivakasi India 84 C4
Sivaki Rus. Fed. 74 B1
Sivan India see Siwan
Sivas Turkey 90 E3
Sivaslı Turkey 59 M5
Siverek Turkey 91 E3
Siverskiy Rus. Fed. 45 Q7
Sivers'kyy Donets' r. Rus. Fed./Ukr. see Severskiy Donets
Sivomaskinskiy Rus. Fed. 41 S2
Sivrice Turkey 91 E3
Sivrihisar Turkey 59 N5
Sivukile S. Africa 101 I4
Sīwa Egypt see Sīwah
Sīwah Egypt 90 B5
Sīwah, Wāḩāt oasis Egypt 90 B5
Siwalik Range mts India/Nepal 82 D3
Siwan India 83 F4
Siwana India 82 C4
Siwa Oasis oasis Egypt see Sīwah, Wāḩāt
Sixian China 77 H1
Sixmilecross U.K. 51 E3
Siyabuswa S. Africa 101 I3
Siyäzän Azer. 91 H2
Sīyunī Iran 88 D3
Sizhan China 74 B2
Siziwang Qi China see Ulan Hua
Sjælland i. Denmark see Zealand
Sjenica Serb. and Mont. 59 I3
Sjöbo Sweden 45 H9
Sjøvegan Norway 44 J2
Skadarsko Jezero nat. park Serb. and Mont. 59 H3
Skadovs'k Ukr. 59 O1
Skaftafell nat. park Iceland 40 [inset]
Skaftárós r. mouth Iceland 44 [inset]
Skagafjörður inlet Iceland 44 [inset]
Skagen Denmark 45 G8
Skagerrak strait Denmark/Norway 45 F8
Skagit r. U.S.A. 126 C2
Skagway U.S.A. 153 A3
Skaidi Norway 44 N1
Skaland Norway 44 J2
Skalmodal Sweden 44 I4
Skanderborg Denmark 45 F8
Skaneateles Lake U.S.A. 135 G2
Skara Sweden 45 H7
Skardarsko Jezero l. Albania/Serb. and Mont. see Scutari, Lake
Skardu Jammu and Kashmir 82 C2
Skärgårdshavets nationalpark nat. park Fin. 45 L7
Skarnes Norway 45 G6
Skarżysko-Kamienna Poland 47 R5
Skaulo Sweden 44 L3
Skawina Poland 47 Q6
Skeena r. Canada 120 D4
Skeena Mountains Canada 120 D3
Skegness U.K. 48 H5
Skellefteå Sweden 44 L4
Skellefteälven r. Sweden 44 L4
Skelleftehamn Sweden 44 L4
Skellig Rocks is Rep. of Ireland 51 B6
Skelmersdale U.K. 48 E5
Skerries Rep. of Ireland 51 F4
Ski Norway 45 G7
Skiathos i. Greece 59 J5
Skibbereen Rep. of Ireland 51 C6
Skibotn Norway 44 L2
Skiddaw hill U.K. 48 D4
Skien Norway 45 F7
Skiermûntseach Neth. see Schiermonnikoog
Skiermûntseach i. Neth. see Schiermonnikoog
Skierniewice Poland 47 R5
Skikda Alg. 58 B6
Skipsea U.K. 48 G5
Skipton Australia 112 A6
Skipton U.K. 48 E5
Skirlaugh U.K. 48 G5
Skíros i. Greece see Skyros
Skive Denmark 45 F8
Skjern Denmark 45 F9
Skjolden Norway 45 E6
Skobelev Uzbek. see Fergana
Skobeleva, Pik mt. Kyrg. 89 I2
Skodje Norway 44 E5
Skoganvarre Norway 44 N2
Skokie U.S.A. 134 B2
Skomer Island U.K. 49 B7
Skopelos i. Greece 59 J5
Skopin Rus. Fed. 43 H5

▶Skopje Macedonia 59 I4
Capital of Macedonia.

Skoplje Macedonia see Skopje
Skövde Sweden 45 H7
Skovorodino Rus. Fed. 74 A1
Skowhegan U.S.A. 135 K1
Skrunda Latvia 45 M8
Skukum, Mount Canada 120 C2
Skukuza S. Africa 101 J3
Skull Valley U.S.A. 129 G4
Skuodas Lith. 45 L8
Skurup Sweden 45 H9
Skutskär Sweden 45 J6
Skvyra Ukr. 43 F6
Skye i. U.K. 50 C3
Skylge i. Neth. see Terschelling
Skyring, Seno b. Chile 144 B8
Skyros Greece 59 K5
Skyros i. Greece 59 K5
Skytrain Ice Rise Antarctica 152 L1
Slættaratindur hill Faroe Is 44 [inset]
Slagelse Denmark 45 G9
Slagnäs Sweden 44 K4
Slane Rep. of Ireland 51 F4
Slaney r. Rep. of Ireland 51 F5
Slantsy Rus. Fed. 45 P7
Slapovi Krke nat. park Croatia 58 F3
Slashers Reefs Australia 110 D3
Slatina Croatia 58 G2
Slatina Romania 59 K2
Slaty Fork U.S.A. 134 E4
Slava Rus. Fed. 74 C1
Slave r. Canada 121 H2
Slave Coast Africa 96 D4
Slave Lake Canada 120 H4
Slave Point Canada 120 H2
Slavgorod Belarus see Slawharad
Slavgorod Rus. Fed. 72 D2
Slavkovichi Rus. Fed. 45 P8
Slavonska Požega Croatia see Požega
Slavonski Brod Croatia 58 H2
Slavuta Ukr. 43 E6
Slavutych Ukr. 43 F6
Slavyanka Rus. Fed. 74 C4
Slavyansk Ukr. see Slov"yans'k
Slavyanskaya Rus. Fed. see Slavyansk-na-Kubani
Slavyansk-na-Kubani Rus. Fed. 90 E1
Slawharad Belarus 43 F5
Sławno Poland 47 P3
Slayton U.S.A. 130 E3
Sleaford U.K. 49 G5
Slea Head hd Rep. of Ireland 51 B5
Sleat Neth. see Sloten
Sleat, Sound of sea chan. U.K. 50 D3
Sled Lake Canada 121 J4

Sleeper Islands Canada 122 F2
Sleeping Bear Dunes National Lakeshore *nature res.* U.S.A. 134 B1
Slessor Glacier Antarctica 152 B1
Slick Rock U.S.A. 129 I2
Slide Mountain U.S.A. 135 H3
Slieve Bloom Mts *hills* Rep. of Ireland 51 E5
Slieve Car *hill* Rep. of Ireland 51 C3
Slieve Donard *hill* U.K. 51 G3
Slieve Gamph *hills* Rep. of Ireland 51 C4
Slievekimalta *hill* Rep. of Ireland 51 D5
Slieve Mish Mts *hills* Rep. of Ireland 51 B5
Slieve Snaght *hill* Rep. of Ireland 51 E2
Sligachan U.K. 50 C3
Sligeach Rep. of Ireland *see* Sligo
Sligo Rep. of Ireland 51 D3
Sligo U.S.A. 134 F3
Sligo Bay Rep. of Ireland 51 D3
Slinger U.S.A. 134 A2
Slippery Rock U.S.A. 134 E3
Slite Sweden 45 K8
Sliven Bulg. 59 L3
Sloan U.S.A. 129 F4
Sloat U.S.A. 128 C2
Sloboda Rus. Fed. *see* Ezhva
Slobodchikovo Rus. Fed. 42 K3
Slobodskoy Rus. Fed. 42 K4
Slobozia Romania 59 L2
Slochteren Neth. 52 G1
Slonim Belarus 45 N10
Slootdorp Neth. 52 E2
Sloten Neth. 52 F2
Slough U.K. 49 G7
▶Slovakia *country* Europe 40 J6
Europe 5, 38–39
▶Slovenia *country* Europe 58 F2
Europe 5, 38–39
Slovenija *country* Europe *see* Slovenia
Slovenj Gradec Slovenia 58 F1
Slovensko *country* Europe *see* Slovakia
Slovenský raj *nat. park* Slovakia 47 R6
Slov"yans'k Ukr. 43 H6
Słowiński Park Narodowy *nat. park* Poland 47 P3
Sluch *r.* Ukr. 43 E6
Słupsk Poland 47 P3
Slussfors Sweden 44 J4
Slutsk Belarus 45 O10
Slyne Head *hd* Rep. of Ireland 51 B4
Slyudyanka Rus. Fed. 72 I2
Small Point U.S.A. 135 K2
Smallwood Reservoir Canada 119 I3
Smalyavichy Belarus 45 P9
Smalyenskaya Wzwyshsha *hills* Belarus/Rus. Fed. *see* Smolensko-Moskovskaya Vozvyshennost'
Smarhon' Belarus 45 O9
Smeaton Canada 121 J4
Smederevo Serb. and Mont. 59 I2
Smederevska Palanka Serb. and Mont. 59 I2
Smela Ukr. *see* Smila
Smethport U.S.A. 135 F3
Smidovich Rus. Fed. 74 D2
Smila Ukr. 43 F6
Smilde Neth. 52 G2
Smiltene Latvia 45 N8
Smirnykh Rus. Fed. 74 F2
Smith Canada 120 H4
Smith Center U.S.A. 130 D4
Smithfield S. Africa 101 H6
Smithfield *NC* U.S.A. 132 E5
Smithfield *UT* U.S.A. 126 F4
Smith Glacier Antarctica 152 K1
Smith Island India 71 A4
Smith Island *MD* U.S.A. 135 G4
Smith Island *VA* U.S.A. 135 H5
Smith Mountain Lake U.S.A. 134 F5
Smith River Canada 120 E3
Smiths Falls Canada 135 G1
Smithton Australia 111 [inset]
Smithtown Australia 112 F3
Smithville *OK* U.S.A. 131 E5
Smithville *WV* U.S.A. 134 E4
Smoke Creek Desert U.S.A. 128 D1
Smoky Bay Australia 109 F8
Smoky Cape Australia 112 F3
Smoky Falls Canada 122 E4
Smoky Hill *r.* U.S.A. 130 C4
Smoky Hills *KS* U.S.A. 124 H4
Smoky Hills *KS* U.S.A. 130 D4
Smoky Lake Canada 121 H4
Smoky Mountains U.S.A. 126 E4
Smøla *i.* Norway 44 E5
Smolenka Rus. Fed. 43 K6
Smolensk Rus. Fed. 43 G5
Smolensk-Moscow Upland *hills* Belarus/Rus. Fed. *see* Smolensko-Moskovskaya Vozvyshennost'
Smolensko-Moskovskaya Vozvyshennost' *hills* Belarus/Rus. Fed. 43 G5
Smolevichi Belarus *see* Smalyavichy
Smolyan Bulg. 59 K4
Smooth Rock Falls Canada 122 E4
Smoothrock Lake Canada 122 C4
Smoothstone Lake Canada 121 J4
Smørfjord Norway 44 N1
Smorgon' Belarus *see* Smarhon'
Smyley Island Antarctica 152 L2
Smyrna Turkey *see* İzmir
Smyrna U.S.A. 135 H4
Smyth Island *atoll* Marshall Is *see* Taongi
Snæfell *mt.* Iceland 44 [inset]
Snaefell *hill* Isle of Man 48 C4
Snag Canada 120 A2
Snake *r.* Canada 120 C1
Snake *r.* U.S.A. 126 D3
Snake Island Australia 112 C7
Snake Range *mts* U.S.A. 129 F2
Snake River Canada 120 F3
Snake River Plain U.S.A. 126 E4
Snare *r.* Canada 120 G2
Snare Lake Canada 121 J3
Snare Lakes Canada *see* Wekweti
Snares Islands N.Z. 107 G6
Snåsa Norway 44 H4
Sneedville U.S.A. 134 D5
Sneek Neth. 52 F1
Sneem Rep. of Ireland 51 C6
Sneeuberge *mts* S. Africa 100 G6
Snegamook Lake Canada 123 J3
Snegurovka Ukr. *see* Tetiyiv
Snelling U.S.A. 128 C3
Snettisham U.K. 49 H6
Snezhnogorsk Rus. Fed. 64 J3
Snežnik *mt.* Slovenia 58 F2
Sniečkus Lith. *see* Visaginas
Snihurivka Ukr. 43 G7
Snits Neth. *see* Sneek
Snizort, Loch *b.* U.K. 50 C3
Snoqualmie Pass U.S.A. 126 C3
Snøtinden *mt.* Norway 44 H3
Snoul Cambodia *see* Snuŏl
Snover U.S.A. 134 D2
Snovsk Ukr. *see* Shchors
Snowbird Lake Canada 121 K2
Snowcrest Mountain Canada 120 G5
Snowdon *mt.* U.K. 49 C5
Snowdonia National Park U.K. 49 D6
Snowdrift Canada *see* Łutselk'e
Snowdrift *r.* Canada 121 I2
Snowflake U.S.A. 129 H4
Snow Hill U.S.A. 135 H4
Snow Lake Canada 121 K4
Snowville U.S.A. 126 E4
Snow Water Lake U.S.A. 129 F1
Snowy *r.* Australia 112 D6
Snowy Mountain U.S.A. 135 H2
Snowy Mountains Australia 112 C6
Snowy River National Park Australia 112 D6
Snug Corner Bahamas 133 F8
Snug Harbour *Nfld. and Lab.* Canada 123 L3
Snug Harbour *Ont.* Canada 134 E1
Snuŏl Cambodia 71 D4
Snyder U.S.A. 131 C5
Soalala Madag. 99 E5
Soalara Madag. 99 E6
Soanierana-Ivongo Madag. 99 E5
Soan-kundo *is* S. Korea 75 B6
Soavinandriana Madag. 99 E5
Sobat *r.* Sudan 86 D8
Sobernheim Germany 53 H5
Sobger *r.* Indon. 69 K7
Sobinka Rus. Fed. 42 I5
Sobradinho, Barragem de *resr* Brazil 143 J6
Sobral Brazil 143 J4
Sochi Rus. Fed. 91 E2
Sŏch'ŏn S. Korea 75 B5
Society Islands Fr. Polynesia 151 J7
Socorro Brazil 145 B3
Socorro Col. 142 D2
Socorro U.S.A. 127 G6
Socorro, Isla *i.* Mex. 136 B5
Socotra *i.* Yemen 87 H7
Soc Trăng Vietnam 71 D5
Socuéllamos Spain 57 E4
Soda Lake *CA* U.S.A. 128 D4
Soda Lake *CA* U.S.A. 128 E4
Sodankylä Fin. 44 O3
Soda Plains Aksai Chin 82 D2
Soda Springs U.S.A. 126 F4
Söderhamn Sweden 45 J6
Söderköping Sweden 45 J7
Södertälje Sweden 45 J7
Sodiri Sudan 86 C7
Sodo Eth. 98 D3
Södra Kvarken *strait* Fin./Sweden 45 K6
Sodus U.S.A. 135 G2
Soë Indon. 69 G8
Soekarno, Puntjak *mt.* Indon. *see* Jaya, Puncak
Soekmekaar S. Africa 101 I2
Soerabaia Indon. *see* Surabaya
Soerendonk Neth. 52 F3
Soest Germany 53 I3
Soest Neth. 52 F2
Sofala Australia 112 D4
▶Sofia Bulg. 59 J3
Capital of Bulgaria.
Sofiya Bulg. *see* Sofia
Sofiyevka Ukr. *see* Vil'nyans'k
Sofiysk *Khabarovskiy Kray* Rus. Fed. 74 D1
Sofiysk *Khabarovskiy Kray* Rus. Fed. 74 E2
Sofporog Rus. Fed. 44 Q4
Sofra Kalesi *tourist site* Turkey 85 A1
Sōfu-gan *i.* Japan 75 F7
Sog China 76 B2
Soğanlı Dağları *mts* Turkey 91 E2
Sogda Rus. Fed. 74 D2
Sögel Germany 53 H2
Sogma China 82 E2
Søgne Norway 45 E7
Sognefjorden *inlet* Norway 45 D6
Sogruma China 76 D1
Söğüt Turkey 59 N4
Söğüt Dağı *mts* Turkey 59 M6
Soh Iran 88 C3
Sohâg Egypt *see* Sawhāj
Sohagpur India 82 D5
Soham U.K. 49 H6
Sohan *r.* Pak. 89 H3
Sohano P.N.G. 106 F2
Sohar Oman *see* Şuḩār
Sohawal India 82 E4
Sohela India 83 E5
Sohng Gwe, Khao *hill* Myanmar/Thai. 71 B4
Sŏho-ri N. Korea 75 C4
Sohŭksan-do *i.* S. Korea 75 B6
Soignies Belgium 52 E4
Soila China 76 C2
Soini Fin. 44 N5
Soissons France 52 D5
Sojat India 82 C4
Sojat Road India 82 C4
Sok *r.* Rus. Fed. 43 K5
Sokal' Ukr. 43 E6
Sokch'o S. Korea 75 C5
Söke Turkey 59 L6
Sokh Tajik. 89 H2
Sokhor, Gora *mt.* Rus. Fed. 72 J2
Sokhumi Georgia 91 F2
Sokiryany Ukr. *see* Sokyryany
Sokodé Togo 96 D4
Soko Islands *Hong Kong* China 77 [inset]
Sokol Rus. Fed. 42 I4
Sokolo Mali 96 C3
Sokolov Czech Rep. 53 M4
Sokoto Nigeria 96 D3
Sokoto *r.* Nigeria 96 D3
Sokyryany Ukr. 43 E6
Sola Cuba 133 E8
Sola *i.* Tonga *see* Ata
Solan India 82 D3
Solana Beach U.S.A. 128 E5
Solander Island N.Z. 113 A8
Solapur India 84 B2
Soldotna U.S.A. 118 C3
Soledad U.S.A. 128 C3
Soledade Brazil 144 F3
Solenoye Rus. Fed. 43 I7
Solfjellsjøen Norway 44 H3
Solginskiy Rus. Fed. 42 I3
Solhan Turkey 91 F3
Soligalich Rus. Fed. 42 I4
Soligorsk Belarus *see* Salihorsk
Solihull U.K. 49 F6
Solikamsk Rus. Fed. 41 R4
Sol'-Iletsk Rus. Fed. 64 G4
Solimões *r.* S. America *see* Amazon
Solingen Germany 52 H3
Solitaire Namibia 100 B2
Sol-Karmala Rus. Fed. *see* Severnoye
Şollar Azer. 91 H2
Sollefteå Sweden 44 J5
Söllichau Germany 53 M3
Solling *hills* Germany 53 J3
Sollstedt Germany 53 K3
Sollum, Gulf of Egypt *see* Sallum, Khalīj as
Solms Germany 53 I4
Solnechnogorsk Rus. Fed. 42 H4
Solnechnyy *Amurskaya Oblast'* Rus. Fed. 74 A1
Solnechnyy *Khabarovskiy Kray* Rus. Fed. 74 E2
Solok Indon. 68 C7
Solomon U.S.A. 129 I5
Solomon, North Fork *r.* U.S.A. 130 D4
▶Solomon Islands *country* S. Pacific Ocean 107 G2
4th largest and 5th most populous country in Oceania.
Oceania 8, 104–105
Solomon Sea S. Pacific Ocean 106 F2
Solon U.S.A. 135 K1
Solon Springs U.S.A. 130 F2
Solor *i.* Indon. 108 C2
Solor, Kepulauan *is* Indon. 108 C2
Solothurn Switz. 56 H3
Solovetskiye Ostrova *is* Rus. Fed. 42 G2
Solov'yevsk Rus. Fed. 74 B1
Šolta *i.* Croatia 58 G3
Solṭānābād *Kermān* Iran 88 E4
Solṭānābād *Khorāsān* Iran 89 E3
Solṭānābād Iran 88 C3
Solṭānīyeh Iran 88 C2
Soltau Germany 53 J2
Sol'tsy Rus. Fed. 42 F4
Solvay U.S.A. 135 G2
Sölvesborg Sweden 45 I8
Solway Firth *est.* U.K. 50 F6
Solwezi Zambia 99 C5
Soma Turkey 59 L5
Somain France 52 D4
▶Somalia *country* Africa 98 E3
Africa 7, 94–95
Somali Basin *sea feature* Indian Ocean 149 L6
Somali Republic *country* Africa *see* Somalia
Sombo Angola 99 C4
Sombor Serb. and Mont. 59 H2
Sombrero Channel India 71 A6
Sombrio, Lago do *l.* Brazil 145 A5
Somero Fin. 45 M6
Somerset *KY* U.S.A. 134 C5
Somerset *MI* U.S.A. 134 C2
Somerset *OH* U.S.A. 134 D4
Somerset *PA* U.S.A. 134 F4
Somerset, Lake Australia 112 F1
Somerset East S. Africa 101 G7
Somerset Island Canada 119 I2
Somerset Reservoir U.S.A. 135 I2
Somerset West S. Africa 100 D8
Somersworth U.S.A. 135 J2
Somerton U.S.A. 129 F5
Somerville *NJ* U.S.A. 135 H3
Somerville *TN* U.S.A. 131 F5
Someydeh Iran 88 B3
Somme *r.* France 52 B4
Sommen *l.* Sweden 45 I7
Sömmerda Germany 53 L3
Sommet, Lac du *l.* Canada 123 H3
Somnath India 82 B5
Somutu Myanmar 70 B1
Son *r.* India 83 F4
Sonag China *see* Zêkog
Sonapur India 84 D1
Sonar *r.* India 82 D4
Sŏnch'ŏn N. Korea 75 B5
Sønderborg Denmark 45 F9
Sondershausen Germany 53 K3
Søndre Strømfjord Greenland *see* Kangerlussuaq
Søndre Strømfjord *inlet* Greenland *see* Kangerlussuaq
Sondrio Italy 58 C1
Sonepat India *see* Sonipat
Sonepur India *see* Sonapur
Songbai China *see* Shennongjia
Songbu China 77 G2
Sông Cau Vietnam 71 E4
Songcheng China *see* Xiapu
Sông Da, Hô *resr* Vietnam 70 D2
Songea Tanz. 99 D5
Songhua Hu *resr* China 74 B4
Songhua Jiang *r.* *Heilongjiang/Jilin* China 74 D3
Songhua Jiang *r.* *Jilin* China *see* Di'er Songhua Jiang
Songjiang China 77 I2
Songjianghe China 74 B4
Sŏngjin N. Korea *see* Kimch'aek
Songkan China 76 E2
Songkhla Thai. 71 C6
Songling China *see* Ta'erqi
Songlong Myanmar 70 B2
Sŏngnam S. Korea 75 B5
Songnim N. Korea 75 B5
Songo Angola 99 B4
Songo Moz. 99 D5
Songpan China 76 D1
Songshan China *see* Ziyun
Song Shan *mt.* China 77 G1
Songtao China 77 F2
Songxi China 77 H3
Songxian China 77 G1
Songyuan *Fujian* China *see* Songxi
Songyuan *Jilin* China 74 B3
Songzi China 77 F2
Sonid Youqi China *see* Saihan Tal
Sonid Zuoqi China *see* Mandalt
Sonipat India 82 D3
Sonkajärvi Fin. 44 O5
Sonkovo Rus. Fed. 42 H4
Sơn La Vietnam 70 C2
Sonmiani Pak. 89 G5
Sonmiani Bay Pak. 89 G5
Sonneberg Germany 53 L4
Sono *r.* *Minas Gerais* Brazil 145 B2
Sono *r.* *Tocantins* Brazil 143 I5
Sonoma U.S.A. 128 B2
Sonoma Peak U.S.A. 128 E1
Sonora *r.* Mex. 127 F7
Sonora *state* Mex. 127 F7
Sonora *CA* U.S.A. 128 C3
Sonora *KY* U.S.A. 134 C5
Sonora *TX* U.S.A. 131 C6
Sonoran Desert U.S.A. 129 G5
Sonoran Desert National Monument *nat. park* U.S.A. 127 E6
Sonqor Iran 88 B3
Sonsonate El Salvador 136 G6
Sonsorol Islands Palau 69 I5
Sơn Tây Vietnam 70 D2
Sonwabile S. Africa 101 I6
Soochow China *see* Suzhou
Soomaaliya *country* Africa *see* Somalia
Sopi, Tanjung *pt* Indon. 69 H6
Sopo *watercourse* Sudan 97 F4
Sopot Bulg. 59 K3
Sopot Poland 47 Q3
Sop Prap Thai. 70 B3
Sopron Hungary 58 G1
Sopur Jammu and Kashmir 82 C2
Sora Italy 58 E4
Sorab India 84 B3
Sorada India 84 E2
Söråker Sweden 44 J5
Sŏrak-san *mt.* S. Korea 75 C5
Sorak-san National Park S. Korea 75 C5
Sorel Canada 123 G5
Soreq *r.* Israel 85 B4
Sorgun Turkey 90 D3
Sorgun *r.* Turkey 85 B1
Soria Spain 57 E3
Sorkh, Kūh-e *mts* Iran 88 D3
Sorkhān Iran 88 E4
Sorkheh Iran 88 D3
Sørli Norway 44 H4
Soro India 83 F5
Soroca Moldova 43 F6
Sorocaba Brazil 145 B3
Soroki Moldova *see* Soroca
Sorol *atoll* Micronesia 69 K5
Sorong Indon. 69 I7
Soroti Uganda 98 D3
Sørøya *i.* Norway 44 M1
Sorraia *r.* Port. 57 B4
Sørreisa Norway 44 K2
Sorrento Italy 58 F4
Sorsele Sweden 44 J4
Sorsogon Phil. 69 G4
Sortavala Rus. Fed. 44 Q6
Sortland Norway 44 I2
Sortopolovskaya Rus. Fed. 42 K3
Sorvizhi Rus. Fed. 42 K4
Sŏsan S. Korea 75 B5
Sosenskiy Rus. Fed. 43 G5
Soshanguve S. Africa 101 I3
Sosna *r.* Rus. Fed. 43 H5
Sosneado *mt.* Arg. 144 C4
Sosnogorsk Rus. Fed. 42 L3
Sosnovka *Arkhangel'skaya Oblast'* Rus. Fed. 42 J3
Sosnovka *Kaliningradskaya Oblast'* Rus. Fed. 41 K5
Sosnovka *Murmanskaya Oblast'* Rus. Fed. 42 I2
Sosnovka *Tambovskaya Oblast'* Rus. Fed. 43 I5
Sosnovo Rus. Fed. 45 Q6
Sosnovo-Ozerskoye Rus. Fed. 73 K2
Sosnovyy Rus. Fed. 44 R4
Sosnovyy Bor Rus. Fed. 45 P7
Sosnowiec Poland 47 Q5
Sosnowitz Poland *see* Sosnowiec
Sos'va *Khanty-Mansiyskiy Avtonomnyy Okrug* Rus. Fed. 41 S3
Sos'va *Sverdlovskaya Oblast'* Rus. Fed. 41 S4
Sotang China 76 B2
Sotara, Volcán *vol.* Col. 142 C3
Sotkamo Fin. 44 P4
Sotteville-lès-Rouen France 52 B5
Souanké Congo 98 B3
Soubré Côte d'Ivoire 96 C4
Souderton U.S.A. 135 H3
Soufflenheim France 53 H6
Soufli Greece 59 L4
Soufrière St Lucia 137 L6
Soufrière *vol.* St Vincent 137 L6
Sougueur Alg. 57 G6
Souillac France 56 E4
Souilly France 52 F5
Souk Ahras Alg. 58 B6
Souk el Arbaâ du Rharb Morocco 54 C5
Sŏul S. Korea *see* Seoul
Soulac-sur-Mer France 56 D4
Soulom France 56 D5
Sounding Creek *r.* Canada 121 I4
Souni Cyprus 85 A2
Soûr Lebanon *see* Tyre
Soure Brazil 143 I4
Sour el Ghozlane Alg. 57 H5
Souris Canada 121 K5
Souris *r.* Canada 121 L5
Souriya *country* Asia *see* Syria
Sousa Brazil 143 K5
Sousa Lara Angola *see* Bocoio
Sousse Tunisia 58 D7
Soustons France 56 D5
▶South Africa, Republic of *country* Africa 100 F5
5th most populous country in Africa.
Africa 7, 94–95
Southampton Canada 134 E1
Southampton U.K. 49 F8
Southampton U.S.A. 135 I3
Southampton, Cape Canada 119 J3
Southampton Island Canada 119 J3
South Andaman *i.* India 71 A5
South Anna *r.* U.S.A. 135 G5
South Anston U.K. 48 F5
South Aulatsivik Island Canada 123 J2
South Australia *state* Australia 106 D5
South Australian Basin *sea feature* Indian Ocean 149 P8
Southaven U.S.A. 131 F5
South Baldy *mt.* U.S.A. 127 G6
South Bank U.K. 48 F4
South Bass Island U.S.A. 134 D3
South Bend *IN* U.S.A. 134 B3
South Bend *WA* U.S.A. 126 C3
South Bluff *pt* Bahamas 133 F8
South Boston U.S.A. 135 F5
South Brook Canada 123 K4
South Cape *pt* U.S.A. *see* Ka Lae
South Carolina *state* U.S.A. 133 D5
South Charleston *OH* U.S.A. 134 D4
South Charleston *WV* U.S.A. 134 E4
South China Sea N. Pacific Ocean 68 F4
South Coast Town Australia *see* Gold Coast
South Dakota *state* U.S.A. 130 C2
South Downs *hills* U.K. 49 G8
South-East *admin. dist.* Botswana 101 G3
South East Cape Australia 111 [inset]
Southeast Cape U.S.A. 118 B3
Southeast Indian Ridge *sea feature* Indian Ocean 149 N8
South East Isles Australia 109 C8
Southeast Pacific Basin *sea feature* S. Pacific Ocean 151 M10
South East Point Australia 112 C7
Southend Canada 121 K3
Southend U.K. 50 D5
Southend-on-Sea U.K. 49 H7
Southern *admin. dist.* Botswana 100 G3
Southern Alps *mts* N.Z. 113 C6
Southern Cross Australia 109 B7
Southern Indian Lake Canada 121 L3
Southern Lau Group *is* Fiji 107 I3
Southern National Park Sudan 97 F4
Southern Ocean 152 C2
Southern Pines U.S.A. 133 E5
Southern Rhodesia *country* Africa *see* Zimbabwe
Southern Uplands *hills* U.K. 50 E5
South Esk *r.* U.K. 50 F4
South Esk Tableland *reg.* Australia 108 D4
Southey Canada 121 J5
Southfield U.S.A. 134 D2
South Fiji Basin *sea feature* S. Pacific Ocean 150 H7
South Fork U.S.A. 128 B1
South Geomagnetic Pole (2004) Antarctica 152 F1
South Georgia *i.* S. Atlantic Ocean 144 I8
▶South Georgia and South Sandwich Islands *terr.* S. Atlantic Ocean 144 I8
United Kingdom Overseas Territory.
South Harris *pen.* U.K. 50 B3
South Haven U.S.A. 134 B2
South Henik Lake Canada 121 L2
South Hill U.S.A. 135 F5
South Honshu Ridge *sea feature* N. Pacific Ocean 150 F3
South Indian Lake Canada 121 L3
South Island India 84 B4
▶South Island N.Z. 113 D7
2nd largest island in Oceania.
South Junction Canada 121 M5
▶South Korea *country* Asia 75 B5
Asia 6, 62–63
South Lake Tahoe U.S.A. 128 C2
South Luangwa National Park Zambia 99 D5
South Magnetic Pole (2004) Antarctica 152 G2
South Mills U.S.A. 135 G5
Southminster U.K. 49 H7
South Mountains *hills* U.S.A. 135 G4
South New Berlin U.S.A. 135 H2
South Orkney Islands S. Atlantic Ocean 148 F10
South Paris U.S.A. 135 J1
South Platte *r.* U.S.A. 130 C3
South Point Bahamas 133 F8
South Pole Antarctica 152 C1
Southport *Qld* Australia 112 F1
Southport *Tas.* Australia 111 [inset]
Southport U.K. 48 D5
Southport U.S.A. 135 G2
South Portland U.S.A. 135 J2
South Ronaldsay *i.* U.K. 50 G2
South Royalton U.S.A. 135 I2
South Salt Lake U.S.A. 129 H1
South Sand Bluff *pt* S. Africa 101 J6
South Sandwich Islands S. Atlantic Ocean 148 G9
South Sandwich Trench *sea feature* S. Atlantic Ocean 148 G9
South San Francisco U.S.A. 128 B3
South Saskatchewan *r.* Canada 121 J4
South Seal *r.* Canada 121 L3
South Shetland Islands Antarctica 152 A2
South Shetland Trough *sea feature* S. Atlantic Ocean 152 L2
South Shields U.K. 48 F3
South Sinai *governorate* Egypt *see* Janūb Sīnā'
South Solomon Trench *sea feature* S. Pacific Ocean 150 G6
South Taranaki Bight *b.* N.Z. 113 E4
South Tasman Rise *sea feature* Southern Ocean 150 F9
South Tent *mt.* U.S.A. 129 H2
South Tons *r.* India 83 E4
South Twin Island Canada 122 F3
South Tyne *r.* U.K. 48 E4
South Uist *i.* U.K. 50 B3
South Wellesley Islands Australia 110 B3
South-West Africa *country* Africa *see* Namibia
South West Cape N.Z. 113 A8
South West Entrance *sea chan.* P.N.G. 110 E1
Southwest Indian Ridge *sea feature* Indian Ocean 149 K8
South West National Park Australia 111 [inset]
Southwest Pacific Basin *sea feature* S. Pacific Ocean 150 I8
Southwest Peru Ridge *sea feature* S. Pacific Ocean *see* Nazca Ridge
South West Rocks Australia 112 F3
South Whitley U.S.A. 134 C3
South Wichita *r.* U.S.A. 131 D5
South Windham U.S.A. 135 J2
Southwold U.K. 49 I6
Southwood National Park Australia 112 E1
Soutpansberg *mts* S. Africa 101 I2
Souttouf, Adrar *mts* W. Sahara 96 B2
Soverato Italy 58 G5
Sovetsk *Kaliningradskaya Oblast'* Rus. Fed. 45 L9
Sovetsk *Kirovskaya Oblast'* Rus. Fed. 42 K4
Sovetskaya Gavan' Rus. Fed. 74 F2
Sovetskiy *Khanty-Mansiyskiy Avtonomnyy Okrug* Rus. Fed. 41 S3
Sovetskiy *Leningradskaya Oblast'* Rus. Fed. 45 P6
Sovetskiy *Respublika Mariy El* Rus. Fed. 42 K4
Sovetskoye *Chechenskaya Respublika* Rus. Fed. *see* Shatoy
Sovetskoye *Stavropol'skiy Kray* Rus. Fed. *see* Zelenokumsk
Sovyets'kyy Ukr. 90 D1
Sowa China 76 C2
Soweto S. Africa 101 H4
Sōya-kaikyō *strait* Japan/Rus. Fed. *see* La Pérouse Strait
Sōya-misaki *c.* Japan 74 F3
Soyana *r.* Rus. Fed. 42 I2
Soyma *r.* Rus. Fed. 42 K2
Soyopa Mex. 127 F7
Sozh *r.* Europe 43 F6
Sozopol Bulg. 59 L3
Spa Belgium 52 F4
▶Spain *country* Europe 57 E3
4th largest country in Europe.
Europe 5, 38–39
Spalato Croatia *see* Split
Spalatum Croatia *see* Split
Spalding U.K. 49 G6
Spanish Canada 122 E5
Spanish Fork U.S.A. 129 H1
Spanish Guinea *country* Africa *see* Equatorial Guinea
Spanish Netherlands *country* Europe *see* Belgium
Spanish Sahara *terr.* Africa *see* Western Sahara
Spanish Town Jamaica 137 I5
Sparks U.S.A. 128 D2
Sparta Greece *see* Sparti
Sparta *GA* U.S.A. 133 D5
Sparta *KY* U.S.A. 134 C4
Sparta *MI* U.S.A. 134 C2
Sparta *NC* U.S.A. 134 E5
Sparta *TN* U.S.A. 132 C5
Spartanburg U.S.A. 133 D5
Sparti Greece 59 J6
Spartivento, Capo *c.* Italy 58 G6
Spas-Demensk Rus. Fed. 43 G5
Spas-Klepiki Rus. Fed. 43 I5
Spassk-Dal'niy Rus. Fed. 74 D3
Spassk-Ryazanskiy Rus. Fed. 43 I5
Spata (Eleftherios Venizelos) *airport* Greece 59 J6
Spatha, Akra *pt* Greece 59 J7
Spearman U.S.A. 131 C4
Speedway U.S.A. 134 B4
Spence Bay Canada *see* Taloyoak
Spencer *IA* U.S.A. 130 E3
Spencer *ID* U.S.A. 126 E3
Spencer *IN* U.S.A. 134 B4
Spencer *NE* U.S.A. 130 D3
Spencer *WV* U.S.A. 134 E4
Spencer, Cape U.S.A. 120 B3
Spencer Bay Namibia 100 B3
Spencer Gulf *est.* Australia 111 B7
Spencer Range *hills* Australia 108 E3
Spennymoor U.K. 48 F4
Sperrin Mountains *hills* U.K. 51 E3
Sperryville U.S.A. 135 F4
Spessart *reg.* Germany 53 J5
Spetsai *i.* Greece *see* Spetses
Spetses *i.* Greece 59 J6
Spey *r.* U.K. 50 F3
Speyer Germany 53 I5
Spezand Pak. 89 G4
Spice Islands Indon. *see* Moluccas
Spijk Neth. 52 G1
Spijkenisse Neth. 52 E3
Spilimbergo Italy 58 E1
Spilsby U.K. 48 H5
Spīn Būldak Afgh. 89 G4
Spintangi Pak. 89 H4
Spirit Lake U.S.A. 130 E3
Spirit River Canada 120 G4
Spirovo Rus. Fed. 42 G4
Spišská Nová Ves Slovakia 43 D6
Spiti *r.* India 82 D3
▶Spitsbergen *i.* Svalbard 64 C2
5th largest island in Europe.
Spittal an der Drau Austria 47 N7
Spitzbergen *i.* Svalbard *see* Spitsbergen
Split Croatia 58 G3
Split Lake Canada 121 L3

Split Lake l. Canada 121 L3
Spokane U.S.A. 126 D3
Spoletium Italy see Spoleto
Spoleto Italy 58 E3
Spóng Cambodia 71 D4
Spoon r. U.S.A. 130 F3
Spooner U.S.A. 130 F2
Spornitz Germany 53 L1
Spotsylvania U.S.A. 135 G4
Spotted Horse U.S.A. 126 G3
Spranger, Mount Canada 120 F4
Spratly Islands S. China Sea 68 E4
Spray U.S.A. 126 D3
Spree r. Germany 47 N4
Sprimont Belgium 52 F4
Springbok S. Africa 100 C5
Springdale Canada 123 L4
Springdale U.S.A. 134 C4
Springe Germany 53 J2
Springer U.S.A. 127 G5
Springerville U.S.A. 129 I4
Springfield CO U.S.A. 130 C4

▶Springfield IL U.S.A. 130 F4
State capital of Illinois.

Springfield KY U.S.A. 134 C5
Springfield MA U.S.A. 135 I2
Springfield MO U.S.A. 131 E4
Springfield OH U.S.A. 134 D4
Springfield OR U.S.A. 126 C3
Springfield TN U.S.A. 134 B5
Springfield VT U.S.A. 135 I2
Springfield WV U.S.A. 135 F4
Springfontein S. Africa 101 G6
Spring Glen U.S.A. 129 H2
Spring Grove U.S.A. 134 A2
Springhill Canada 123 I5
Spring Hill U.S.A. 133 D6
Springhouse Canada 120 F5
Spring Mountains U.S.A. 129 F3
Springs Junction N.Z. 113 D6
Springsure Australia 110 E5
Spring Valley MN U.S.A. 130 E3
Spring Valley NY U.S.A. 135 H3
Springview U.S.A. 130 D3
Springville CA U.S.A. 128 D3
Springville NY U.S.A. 135 F2
Springville PA U.S.A. 135 H3
Springville UT U.S.A. 129 H1
Sprowston U.K. 49 I6
Spruce Grove Canada 120 H4
Spruce Knob mt. U.S.A. 132 E4
Spruce Mountain CO U.S.A. 129 I2
Spruce Mountain NV U.S.A. 129 F1
Spurn Head hd U.K. 48 H5
Spuzzum Canada 120 F5
Squam Lake U.S.A. 135 J2
Square Lake U.S.A. 123 H5
Squillace, Golfo di g. Italy 58 G5
Squires, Mount hill Australia 109 D6
Srbija aut. rep. Serb. and Mont. 59 I3
Srbinje Bos.-Herz. see Foča
Srê Âmběl Cambodia 71 C5
Srebrenica Bos.-Herz. 58 H2
Sredets Burgas Bulg. 59 L3
Sredets Sofiya-Grad Bulg. see Sofia
Sredinnyy Khrebet mts Rus. Fed. 65 Q4
Sredna Gora mts Bulg. 59 J3
Srednekolymsk Rus. Fed. 65 Q3
Sredne-Russkaya Vozvyshennost' hills Rus. Fed. see Central Russian Upland
Sredne-Sibirskoye Ploskogor'ye plat. Rus. Fed. see Central Siberian Plateau
Sredneye Kuyto, Ozero l. Rus. Fed. 44 Q4
Sredniy Ural mts Rus. Fed. 41 R4
Srednogorie Bulg. 59 K3
Srednyaya Akhtuba Rus. Fed. 43 J6
Sreepur Bangl. see Sripur
Sre Khtum Cambodia 71 D4
Srê Noy Cambodia 71 D4
Sretensk Rus. Fed. 73 L2
Sri Aman Sarawak Malaysia 68 E6
Sriharikota Island India 84 D3

▶Sri Jayewardenepura Kotte Sri Lanka 84 C5
Capital of Sri Lanka.

Srikakulam India 84 E2
Sri Kalahasti India 84 C3
▶Sri Lanka country Asia 84 D5
Asia 6, 62–63
Srinagar India 82 C2
Sri Pada mt. Sri Lanka see Adam's Peak
Sripur Bangl. 83 G4
Srirangam India 84 C4
Sri Thep tourist site Thai. 70 C3
Srivardhan India 84 B2
Staaten r. Australia 110 C3
Staaten River National Park Australia 110 C3
Stabroek Guyana see Georgetown
Stade Germany 53 J1
Staden Belgium 52 D4
Stadskanaal Neth. 52 G2
Stadtallendorf Germany 53 J4
Stadthagen Germany 53 J2
Stadtilm Germany 53 L4
Stadtlohn Germany 52 G3
Stadtoldendorf Germany 53 J3
Stadtroda Germany 53 L4
Staffa i. U.K. 50 C4
Staffelberg hill Germany 53 L4
Staffelstein Germany 53 K4
Stafford U.K. 49 E6
Stafford U.S.A. 135 G4
Stafford Creek Bahamas 133 E7
Stafford Springs U.S.A. 135 I3
Stagg Lake Canada 120 H2
Staicele Latvia 45 N8
Staines U.K. 49 G7
Stakhanov Ukr. 43 H6
Stakhanovo Rus. Fed. see Zhukovskiy
Stalbridge U.K. 49 E8
Stalham U.K. 49 I6
Stalin Bulg. see Varna
Stalinabad Tajik. see Dushanbe
Stalingrad Rus. Fed. see Volgograd
Staliniri Georgia see Ts'khinvali
Stalino Ukr. see Donets'k
Stalinogorsk Rus. Fed. see Novomoskovsk
Stalinogród Poland see Katowice
Stalinsk Rus. Fed. see Novokuznetsk
Stalowa Wola Poland 43 D6
Stamboliyski Bulg. 59 K3
Stamford Australia 110 C4
Stamford U.K. 49 G6
Stamford CT U.S.A. 135 I3
Stamford NY U.S.A. 135 H2
Stampalia i. Greece see Astypalaia
Stampriet Namibia 100 D3
Stamsund Norway 44 H2
Stanardsville U.S.A. 135 F4
Stanberry U.S.A. 130 E3
Stancomb-Wills Glacier Antarctica 152 B1
Standard Canada 120 H5
Standdaarbuiten Neth. 52 E3
Standerton S. Africa 101 I4
Standish U.S.A. 134 D2
Stanfield U.S.A. 129 H5
Stanford KY U.S.A. 134 C5
Stanford MT U.S.A. 126 F3
Stanger S. Africa 101 J5
Stanislaus r. U.S.A. 128 C3
Stanislav Ukr. see Ivano-Frankivs'k
Stanke Dimitrov Bulg. see Dupnitsa
Staňkov Czech Rep. 53 N5
Stanley Australia 111 [inset]
Stanley Hong Kong China 77 [inset]

▶Stanley Falkland Is 144 E8
Capital of the Falkland Islands.

Stanley U.K. 48 F4
Stanley ID U.S.A. 126 E3
Stanley KY U.S.A. 134 B5
Stanley ND U.S.A. 130 C1
Stanley VA U.S.A. 135 F4
Stanley, Mount hill N.T. Australia 108 E5
Stanley, Mount hill Tas. Australia 111 [inset]
Stanley, Mount Dem. Rep. Congo/Uganda see Margherita Peak
Stanleyville Dem. Rep. Congo see Kisangani
Stann Creek Belize see Dangriga
Stannington U.K. 48 F3
Stanovoye Rus. Fed. 43 H5
Stanovoye Nagor'ye mts Rus. Fed. 73 L1
Stanovoy Khrebet mts Rus. Fed. 65 N4
Stansmore Range hills Australia 108 E5
Stanthorpe Australia 112 E2
Stanton U.K. 49 H6
Stanton KY U.S.A. 134 D5
Stanton MI U.S.A. 134 C2
Stanton ND U.S.A. 130 C2
Stanton TX U.S.A. 131 C5
Stapleton U.S.A. 130 C3
Starachowice Poland 47 R5
Stara Planina mts Bulg./Serb. and Mont. see Balkan Mountains
Staraya Russa Rus. Fed. 42 F4
Stara Zagora Bulg. 59 K3
Starbuck Island Kiribati 151 J6
Star City U.S.A. 134 B3
Starcke National Park Australia 110 D2
Stargard in Pommern Poland see Stargard Szczeciński
Stargard Szczeciński Poland 47 O4
Staritsa Rus. Fed. 42 G4
Starke U.S.A. 133 D6
Starkville U.S.A. 131 F5
Star Lake U.S.A. 135 H1
Starnberger See l. Germany 47 M7
Starobel'sk Ukr. see Starobil's'k
Starobil's'k Ukr. 43 H6
Starogard Gdański Poland 47 Q4
Starokonstantinov Ukr. see Starokostyantyniv
Starokostyantyniv Ukr. 43 E6
Starominskaya Rus. Fed. 43 H7
Staroshcherbinovskaya Rus. Fed. 43 H7
Star Peak U.S.A. 128 D1
Start Point U.K. 49 D8
Starve Island Kiribati see Starbuck Island
Staryya Darohi Belarus 43 F5
Staryye Dorogi Belarus see Staryya Darohi
Staryy Kayak Rus. Fed. 65 L2
Staryy Oskol Rus. Fed. 43 H6
Staßfurt Germany 53 L3
State College U.S.A. 135 G3
State Line U.S.A. 131 F6
Staten Island Arg. see Los Estados, Isla de
Statenville U.S.A. 133 D6
Statesboro U.S.A. 133 D5
Statesville U.S.A. 132 D5
Statia i. Neth. Antilles see Sint Eustatius
Station U.S.A. 134 C4
Station Nord Greenland 153 I1
Stauchitz Germany 53 N3
Staufenberg Germany 53 I4
Staunton U.S.A. 134 F4
Stavanger Norway 45 D7
Staveley U.K. 48 F5
Stavropol' Rus. Fed. 91 F1
Stavropol Kray admin. div. Rus. Fed. see Stavropol'skiy Kray
Stavropol'-na-Volge Rus. Fed. see Tol'yatti
Stavropol'skaya Vozvyshennost' hills Rus. Fed. 91 F1
Stavropol'skiy Kray admin. div. Rus. Fed. 91 F1
Stayner Canada 134 E1
Stayton U.S.A. 126 C3
Steadville S. Africa 101 I5
Steamboat Springs U.S.A. 126 G4
Stearns U.S.A. 134 C5
Stebbins U.S.A. 118 B3
Steele Island Antarctica 152 L2
Steelville U.S.A. 130 F4
Steen r. Canada 120 G3
Steenderen Neth. 52 G2
Steenkampsberge mts S. Africa 101 J3
Steen River Canada 120 G3
Steens Mountain U.S.A. 126 D4
Steenstrup Gletscher glacier Greenland see Sermersuaq
Steenvoorde France 52 C4
Steenwijk Neth. 52 G2
Stefansson Island Canada 119 H2
Stegi Swaziland see Siteki
Steigerwald mts Germany 53 K5
Stein Germany 53 L5
Steinach Germany 53 L4
Steinaker Reservoir U.S.A. 129 I1
Steinbach Canada 121 L5
Steinfeld (Oldenburg) Germany 53 I2
Steinfurt Germany 53 H2
Steinhausen Namibia 99 B6
Steinheim Germany 53 J3
Steinkjer Norway 44 G4
Steinkopf S. Africa 100 C5
Steinsdalen Norway 44 G4
Stella S. Africa 100 G4
Stella Maris Bahamas 133 F8
Stellenbosch S. Africa 100 D7
Stello, Monte mt. Corsica France 56 I5
Stelvio, Parco Nazionale dello nat. park Italy 58 D1
Stenay France 52 F5
Stendal Germany 53 L2
Stenhousemuir U.K. 50 F4
Stenungsund Sweden 45 G7
Steornabhagh U.K. see Stornoway
Stepanakert Azer. see Xankändi
Stephens, Cape N.Z. 113 D5
Stephens City U.S.A. 135 F4
Stephens Lake Canada 121 M3
Stephenville U.S.A. 131 D5
Stepnoy Rus. Fed. see Elista
Stepnoye Rus. Fed. 43 J6
Sterkfontein Dam resr S. Africa 101 I5
Sterkstroom S. Africa 101 H6
Sterlet Lake Canada 121 I1
Sterlibashevo Rus. Fed. 41 R5
Sterling S. Africa 100 E6
Sterling CO U.S.A. 130 C3
Sterling IL U.S.A. 130 F3
Sterling MI U.S.A. 134 C1
Sterling UT U.S.A. 129 H2
Sterling City U.S.A. 131 C6
Sterling Heights U.S.A. 134 D2
Sterlitamak Rus. Fed. 64 G4
Stettin Poland see Szczecin
Stettler Canada 121 H4
Steubenville KY U.S.A. 134 C5
Steubenville OH U.S.A. 134 E3
Stevenage U.K. 49 G7
Stevenson U.S.A. 126 C3
Stevenson Lake Canada 121 L4
Stevens Point U.S.A. 130 F2
Stevens Village U.S.A. 118 D3
Stevensville MI U.S.A. 134 B2
Stevensville PA U.S.A. 135 G3
Stewart Canada 120 D4
Stewart r. Canada 120 B2
Stewart, Isla i. Chile 144 B8
Stewart Crossing Canada 120 B2
Stewart Island N.Z. 113 A8
Stewart Islands Solomon Is 107 G2
Stewart Lake Canada 119 J3
Stewarton U.K. 50 E5
Stewarts Point U.S.A. 128 B2
Stewiacke Canada 123 J5
Steynsburg S. Africa 101 G6
Steyr Austria 47 O6
Steytlerville S. Africa 100 G7
Stiens Neth. 52 F1
Stif Alg. see Sétif
Stigler U.S.A. 131 E5
Stikine r. Canada 120 C3
Stikine Plateau Canada 120 D3
Stikine Strait U.S.A. 120 C3
Stilbaai S. Africa 100 E8
Stiles U.S.A. 134 A1
Stillwater MN U.S.A. 130 E2
Stillwater OK U.S.A. 131 D4
Stillwater Range mts U.S.A. 128 D2
Stillwell U.S.A. 134 B3
Stilton U.K. 49 G6
Stilwell U.S.A. 131 E5
Stinnett U.S.A. 131 C5
Štip Macedonia 59 J4
Stirling Australia 108 F5
Stirling Canada 135 G1
Stirling U.K. 50 F4
Stirling Creek r. Australia 108 E4
Stirling Range National Park Australia 109 B8
Stittsville Canada 135 H1
Stjørdalshalsen Norway 44 G5
Stockbridge U.S.A. 134 C2
Stockerau Austria 47 P6
Stockheim Germany 53 L4

▶Stockholm Sweden 45 K7
Capital of Sweden.

Stockinbingal Australia 112 C5
Stockport U.K. 48 E5
Stockton CA U.S.A. 128 C3
Stockton KS U.S.A. 130 D4
Stockton MO U.S.A. 130 E4
Stockton UT U.S.A. 129 G1
Stockton Lake U.S.A. 130 E4
Stockton-on-Tees U.K. 48 F4
Stockville U.S.A. 130 C3
Stod Czech Rep. 53 N5
Stœng Trêng Cambodia 71 D4
Stoer, Point of U.K. 50 D2
Stoke-on-Trent U.K. 49 E5
Stokesley U.K. 48 F4
Stokes Point Australia 111 [inset]
Stokes Range hills Australia 108 E4
Stokkseyri Iceland 44 [inset]
Stokkvågen Norway 44 H3
Stokmarknes Norway 44 I2
Stolac Bos.-Herz. 58 G3
Stolberg (Rheinland) Germany 52 G4
Stolbovoy Rus. Fed. 153 G2
Stolbtsy Belarus see Stowbtsy
Stolin Belarus 45 O11
Stollberg Germany 53 M4
Stolp Poland see Słupsk
Stolzenau Germany 53 J2
Stone U.K. 49 E6
Stoneboro U.S.A. 134 E3
Stonecliffe Canada 122 F5
Stonecutters' Island pen. Hong Kong China 77 [inset]
Stonehaven U.K. 50 G4
Stonehenge Australia 110 C5
Stonehenge tourist site U.K. 49 F7
Stoner U.S.A. 129 I3
Stonewall Canada 121 L5
Stonewall Jackson Lake U.S.A. 134 E4
Stony Creek U.S.A. 135 G5
Stony Lake Canada 121 L3
Stony Point U.S.A. 135 G2
Stony Rapids Canada 121 J3
Stony River U.S.A. 118 C3
Stooping r. Canada 122 E3
Stora Lulevatten l. Sweden 44 K3
Stora Sjöfallets nationalpark nat. park Sweden 44 J3
Storavan l. Sweden 44 K4
Store Bælt sea chan. Denmark see Great Belt
Støren Norway 44 G5
Storfjordbotn Norway 44 O1
Storforshei Norway 44 I3
Storjord Norway 44 I3
Storkerson Peninsula Canada 119 H2
Storm Bay Australia 111 [inset]
Stormberg S. Africa 101 H6
Storm Lake U.S.A. 130 E3
Stornosa mt. Norway 44 E6
Stornoway U.K. 50 C2
Storozhevsk Rus. Fed. 42 L3
Storozhynets' Ukr. 43 E6
Storrs U.S.A. 135 I3
Storseleby Sweden 44 J4
Storsjön l. Sweden 44 I5
Storskrymten mt. Norway 44 F5
Storslett Norway 44 L2
Stortemelk sea chan. Neth. 52 F1
Storuman Sweden 44 J4
Storuman l. Sweden 44 J4
Storvik Sweden 45 J6
Storvorde Denmark 45 G8
Storvreta Sweden 45 J7
Story U.S.A. 126 G3
Stotfold U.K. 49 G6
Stoughton Canada 121 K5
Stour r. England U.K. 49 F6
Stour r. England U.K. 49 F8
Stour r. England U.K. 49 I7
Stour r. England U.K. 49 I7
Stourbridge U.K. 49 E6
Stourport-on-Severn U.K. 49 E6
Stout Lake Canada 121 M4
Stowbtsy Belarus 45 O10
Stowe U.S.A. 135 I1
Stowmarket U.K. 49 H6
Stoyba Rus. Fed. 74 C1
Strabane U.K. 51 E3
Stradbally Rep. of Ireland 51 E4
Stradbroke U.K. 49 I6
Stradella Italy 58 C2
Strakonice Czech Rep. 47 N6
Stralsund Germany 47 N3
Strand S. Africa 100 D8
Stranda Norway 44 E5
Strangford U.K. 51 G3
Strangford Lough inlet U.K. 51 G3
Strangways r. Australia 108 F3
Stranraer U.K. 50 D6
Strasbourg France 56 H2
Strasburg Germany 53 N1
Strasburg U.S.A. 135 F4
Strassburg France see Strasbourg
Stratford Australia 112 C6
Stratford Canada 134 E2
Stratford CA U.S.A. 128 D3
Stratford TX U.S.A. 131 C4
Stratford-upon-Avon U.K. 49 F6
Strathaven U.K. 50 E5
Strathmore Canada 120 H5
Strathmore r. U.K. 50 E2
Strathnaver Canada 120 F4
Strathroy Canada 134 E2
Strathspey valley U.K. 50 F3
Strathy U.K. 50 F2
Stratton U.K. 49 C8
Stratton U.S.A. 135 J1
Stratton Mountain U.S.A. 135 I2
Straubing Germany 53 M6
Straumnes pt Iceland 44 [inset]
Strawberry U.S.A. 129 H4
Strawberry Mountain U.S.A. 126 D3
Strawberry Reservoir U.S.A. 129 H1
Streaky Bay Australia 109 F8
Streaky Bay b. Australia 109 F8
Streator U.S.A. 130 F3
Street U.K. 49 E7
Streetsboro U.S.A. 134 E3
Strehaia Romania 59 J2
Strehla Germany 53 N3
Streich Mound hill Australia 109 C7
Strelka Rus. Fed. 65 Q3
Strel'na r. Rus. Fed. 42 H2
Strenči Latvia 45 N8
Streymoy i. Faroe Is 44 [inset]
Stříbro Czech Rep. 53 M5
Strichen U.K. 50 G3
Strimonas r. Greece 59 J4
also known as Struma (Bulgaria)
Stroeder Arg. 144 D6
Strokestown Rep. of Ireland 51 D4
Stroma, Island of U.K. 50 F2
Stromboli, Isola i. Italy 58 F5
Stromness S. Georgia 144 I8
Stromness U.K. 50 F2
Strömstad Sweden 45 G7
Strömsund Sweden 44 I5
Strongsville U.S.A. 134 E3
Stronsay i. U.K. 50 G1
Stroud Australia 112 E4
Stroud U.K. 49 E7
Stroud Road Australia 112 E4
Stroudsburg U.S.A. 135 H3
Struer Denmark 45 F8
Struga Macedonia 59 I4
Strugi-Krasnyye Rus. Fed. 45 P7
Struis Bay S. Africa 100 E8
Strullendorf Germany 53 K5
Struma r. Bulg. 59 J4
also known as Strimonas (Greece)
Strumble Head hd U.K. 49 B6
Strumica Macedonia 59 J4
Struthers U.S.A. 134 E3
Stryama r. Bulg. 59 K3
Strydenburg S. Africa 100 F5
Stryn Norway 44 E6
Stryy Ukr. 43 D6
Strzelecki, Mount hill Australia 108 F5
Strzelecki Regional Reserve nature res. Australia 111 B6
Stuart FL U.S.A. 133 D7
Stuart NE U.S.A. 130 D3
Stuart VA U.S.A. 134 E5
Stuart Lake Canada 120 E4
Stuart Range hills Australia 111 A6
Stuarts Draft U.S.A. 134 F4
Stuart Town Australia 112 D4
Stuchka Latvia see Aizkraukle
Stučka Latvia see Aizkraukle
Studholme Junction N.Z. 113 C7
Studsviken Sweden 44 K5
Stukley, Lac l. Canada 135 I1
Stung Treng Cambodia see Stœng Trêng
Stupart r. Canada 121 M4
Stupino Rus. Fed. 43 H5
Sturge Island Antarctica 152 H2
Sturgeon r. Ont. Canada 122 F5
Sturgeon r. Sask. Canada 121 J4
Sturgeon Bay b. Canada 121 L4
Sturgeon Bay U.S.A. 134 B1
Sturgeon Bay Canal lake channel U.S.A. 134 B1
Sturgeon Falls Canada 122 F5
Sturgeon Lake Ont. Canada 121 N5
Sturgeon Lake Ont. Canada 135 F1
Sturgis MI U.S.A. 134 C3
Sturgis SD U.S.A. 130 C2
Sturt, Mount hill Australia 111 C6
Sturt Creek watercourse Australia 108 D4
Sturt National Park Australia 111 C6
Sturt Stony Desert Australia 111 C6
Stutterheim S. Africa 101 H7
Stuttgart Germany 53 J6
Stuttgart U.S.A. 131 F5
Stykkishólmur Iceland 44 [inset]
Styr r. Belarus/Ukr. 43 E5
Suaçuí Grande r. Brazil 145 C2
Suai East Timor 108 D2
Suakin Sudan 86 E6
Suao Taiwan 77 I3
Suaqui Grande Mex. 127 F7
Suau P.N.G. 110 E1
Subačius Lith. 45 N9
Subankhata India 83 G4
Subarnapur India see Sonapur
Sūbāshī Iran 88 C3
Subay reg. Saudi Arabia 88 B5
Şubayḩah Saudi Arabia 85 D4
Subei China 80 H4
Subi Besar i. Indon. 71 E7
Subi Kecil i. Indon. 71 E7
Sublette U.S.A. 131 C4
Subotica Serb. and Mont. 59 H1
Success, Lake U.S.A. 128 D3
Succiso, Alpi di mts Italy 58 D2
Suceava Romania 43 E7
Suchan Rus. Fed. see Partizansk
Suck r. Rep. of Ireland 51 D4
Suckling, Mount P.N.G. 110 E1
Suckow Germany 53 L1

▶Sucre Bol. 142 E7
Legislative capital of Bolivia.

Suczawa Romania see Suceava
Sud, Grand Récif du reef New Caledonia 107 G4
Suda Rus. Fed. 42 H4
Sudak Ukr. 90 D1

▶Sudan country Africa 97 F3
Largest country in Africa.
Africa 7, 94–95

Suday Rus. Fed. 42 I4
Sudayr reg. Saudi Arabia 88 B5
Sudbury Canada 122 E5
Sudbury U.K. 49 H6
Sudd swamp Sudan 86 C8
Sude r. Germany 53 K1
Sudest Island P.N.G. see Tagula Island
Sudetenland mts Czech Rep./Poland see Sudety
Sudety mts Czech Rep./Poland 47 O5
Sudislavl' Rus. Fed. 42 I4
Sudlersville U.S.A. 135 H4
Süd-Nord-Kanal canal Germany 52 H2
Sudogda Rus. Fed. 42 I5
Sudr Egypt 85 A5
Suðuroy i. Faroe Is 44 [inset]
Sue watercourse Sudan 97 F4
Sueca Spain 57 F4
Suez Egypt 85 A5
Suez, Gulf of Egypt 85 A5
Suez Bay Egypt 85 A5
Suez Canal Egypt 85 A4
Suffolk U.S.A. 135 G5
Sugarbush Hill hill U.S.A. 130 F2
Sugarloaf Mountain U.S.A. 135 J1
Sugarloaf Point Australia 112 F4
Sugun China 80 E4
Sūhāj Egypt see Sawhāj
Şuḩār Oman 88 E5
Suhaymī, Wādī as watercourse Egypt 85 A4
Sühbaatar Mongolia 72 J2
Suheli Par i. India 84 B4
Suhl Germany 53 K4
Suhlendorf Germany 53 K2
Suhul reg. Saudi Arabia 88 B6
Suhūl al Kidan plain Saudi Arabia 88 D6
Şuhut Turkey 59 N5
Sui Pak. 89 H4
Sui, Laem pt Thai. 71 B5
Suibin China 74 C3
Suid-Afrika country Africa see Republic of South Africa
Suide China 73 K5
Suidzhikurmsy Turkm. see Madau
Suifenhe China 74 C3
Suihua China 74 B3
Suileng China 74 B3
Suining Hunan China 77 F3
Suining Jiangsu China 77 H1
Suining Sichuan China 76 E2
Suippes France 52 E5
Suir r. Rep. of Ireland 51 E5
Suisse country Europe see Switzerland
Sui Vehar Pak. 89 H4
Suixi China 77 H1
Suixian Henan China 77 G1
Suixian Hubei China see Suizhou
Suiyang Guizhou China 76 E3
Suiyang Henan China 77 G1
Suiza country Europe see Switzerland
Suizhong China 73 M4
Suizhou China 77 G2
Sujangarh India 82 C4
Sujawal Pak. 89 H5
Suk atoll Micronesia see Pulusuk
Sukabumi Indon. 68 D8
Sukagawa Japan 75 F5
Sukarnapura Indon. see Jayapura
Sukarno, Puncak mt. Indon. see Jaya, Puncak
Sukchŏn N. Korea 75 B5
Sukhinichi Rus. Fed. 43 G5
Sukhona r. Rus. Fed. 42 J3
Sukhothai Thai. 70 B3
Sukhumi Georgia see Sokhumi
Sukhum-Kale Georgia see Sokhumi
Sukkertoppen Greenland see Maniitsoq
Sukkozero Rus. Fed. 42 G3
Sukkur Pak. 89 H5
Sukma India 84 D2
Sukpay Rus. Fed. 74 E3
Sukpay r. Rus. Fed. 74 E3
Sukri r. India 82 C4
Sukri r. India 82 C4
Suktel r. India 84 D1
Sukun i. Indon. 108 C2
Sula i. Norway 45 D6
Sula r. Rus. Fed. 42 K2
Sula, Kepulauan is Indon. 69 H7
Sulaiman Range mts Pak. 89 H4
Sulak Rus. Fed. 91 G2
Sūlār Iran 88 C4
Sula Sgeir i. U.K. 50 C1
Sulawesi i. Indon. see Celebes
Sulaymān Beg Iraq 91 G4
Sulayyimah Saudi Arabia 88 B6
Sulci Sardinia Italy see Sant'Antioco
Sulcis Sardinia Italy see Sant'Antioco
Suledeh Iran 88 C2
Sule Skerry i. U.K. 50 E1
Sule Stack i. U.K. 50 E1
Sulingen Germany 53 I2
Sulitjelma Norway 44 J3
Sulkava Fin. 44 P6
Sullana Peru 142 B4
Sullivan IL U.S.A. 130 F4
Sullivan IN U.S.A. 134 B4
Sullivan Bay Canada 120 E5
Sullivan Island Myanmar see Lanbi Kyun
Sullivan Lake Canada 121 I5
Sulmo Italy see Sulmona
Sulmona Italy 58 E3
Sulphur LA U.S.A. 131 E6
Sulphur OK U.S.A. 131 D5
Sulphur r. U.S.A. 131 E5
Sulphur Springs U.S.A. 131 E5
Sultan Canada 122 E5
Sultan, Koh-i- mts Pak. 89 F4
Sultanabad India see Osmannagar
Sultanabad Iran see Arāk
Sultan Dağları mts Turkey 59 N5
Sultanıye Turkey see Karapınar
Sultanpur India 83 E4
Sulu Archipelago is Phil. 69 G5
Sulu Basin sea feature N. Pacific Ocean 150 E5
Sülüklü Turkey 90 D3
Sülüktü Kyrg. 89 H2
Sulusaray Turkey 90 E3
Sulu Sea N. Pacific Ocean 68 F5
Suluvvaulik, Lac l. Canada 123 G2
Sulyukta Kyrg. see Sülüktü
Sulzbach-Rosenberg Germany 53 L5
Sulzberger Bay Antarctica 152 I1
Sumāil Oman 88 E6
Sumampa Arg. 144 D3
Sumapaz, Parque Nacional nat. park Col. 142 D3
Sūmār Iran 88 B3
Sumatera i. Indon. see Sumatra

▶Sumatra i. Indon. 71 B7
2nd largest island in Asia.

Šumava nat. park Czech Rep. 47 N6
Sumba i. Indon. 108 C2
Sumba, Selat sea chan. Indon. 108 B2
Sumbar r. Turkm. 88 D2
Sumbawa i. Indon. 108 B2
Sumbawabesar Indon. 108 B2
Sumbawanga Tanz. 99 D4
Sumbe Angola 99 B5
Sumbu National Park Zambia 99 D4
Sumburgh U.K. 50 [inset]
Sumburgh Head hd U.K. 50 [inset]
Sumdo China 76 D2
Sumdum, Mount U.S.A. 120 C3
Sume'eh Sarā Iran 88 C2
Sumeih Sudan 86 C8
Sumenep Indon. 68 E8
Sumgait Azer. see Sumqayıt
Sumisu-jima i. Japan 73 Q6
Summēl Iraq 91 F3
Summer Beaver Canada 122 C3
Summerford Canada 123 L4
Summer Island U.S.A. 132 C2
Summer Isles U.K. 50 D2
Summerland Canada 120 G5
Summersville U.S.A. 134 E4
Summit Lake Canada 120 F4
Summit Mountain U.S.A. 128 E2
Summit Peak U.S.A. 127 G5
Sumnal Aksai Chin 82 D2
Sumner N.Z. 113 D6
Sumner, Lake N.Z. 113 D6
Sumon-dake mt. Japan 75 E5
Šumperk Czech Rep. 47 P6
Sumpu Japan see Shizuoka
Sumqayıt Azer. 91 H2
Sumskiy Posad Rus. Fed. 42 G2
Sumter U.S.A. 133 D5
Sumur Jammu and Kashmir 82 D2
Sumy Ukr. 43 G6
Sumzom China 76 C2
Suna Rus. Fed. 42 K4
Sunaj India 82 D4

Teploye Rus. Fed. 43 H5
Teploye Ozero Rus. Fed. see Teploozersk
Tepoca, Cabo c. Mex. 127 E7
Tepopa, Punta pt Mex. 127 E7
Tequila Mex. 136 D4
Téra Niger 96 D3
Teramo Italy 58 E3
Terang Australia 112 A7
Ter Apel Neth. 52 H2
Teratani r. Pak. 89 H4
Tercan Turkey 91 F3
Terebovlya Ukr. 43 E6
Terekty Kazakh. 80 G2
Teresa Cristina Brazil 145 A4
Tereshka r. Rus. Fed. 43 J6
Teresina Brazil 143 J5
Teresina de Goias Brazil 145 B1
Teresita Col. 142 E3
Teresópolis Brazil 145 C3
Teressa Island India 71 A5
Terezinha Brazil 143 H3
Tergeste Italy see Trieste
Tergnier France 52 D5
Teriberka Rus. Fed. 44 S2
Termez Uzbek. 89 G2
Termini Imerese Sicily Italy 58 E6
Términos, Laguna de lag. Mex. 136 F5
Termit-Kaoboul Niger 96 E3
Termiz Uzbek. see Termez
Termo U.S.A. 128 C1
Termoli Italy 58 F4
Termonde Belgium see Dendermonde
Tern r. U.K. 49 E6
Ternate Indon. 69 H6
Terneuzen Neth. 52 D3
Terney Rus. Fed. 74 E3
Terni Italy 58 E3
Ternopil' Ukr. 43 E6
Ternopol' Ukr. see Ternopil'
Terpeniya, Mys c. Rus. Fed. 74 G2
Terpeniya, Zaliv g. Rus. Fed. 74 F2
Terra Alta U.S.A. 134 F4
Terra Bella U.S.A. 128 D4
Terrace Canada 120 D4
Terrace Bay Canada 122 D4
Terra Firma S. Africa 100 F3
Terråk Norway 44 H4
Terralba Sardinia Italy 58 C5
Terra Nova Bay Antarctica 152 H1
Terra Nova National Park Canada 123 L4
Terre Adélie reg. Antarctica see Adélie Land
Terrebonne Bay U.S.A. 131 F6
Terre Haute U.S.A. 134 B4
Terre-Neuve prov. Canada see Newfoundland and Labrador
Terre-Neuve-et-Labrador prov. Canada see Newfoundland and Labrador
Terres Australes et Antarctiques Françaises terr. Indian Ocean see French Southern and Antarctic Lands
Terry U.S.A. 126 G3
Terschelling i. Neth. 52 F1
Terskiy Bereg coastal area Rus. Fed. 42 H2
Tertenia Sardinia Italy 58 C5
Terter Azer. see Tärtär
Teruel Spain 57 F3
Terutao National Park Thai. 71 B6
Tervola Fin. 44 N3
Tešanj Bos.-Herz. 58 G2
Teseney Eritrea 86 E6
Tesha r. Rus. Fed. 43 I5
Teshekpuk Lake U.S.A. 118 C2
Teshio Japan 74 F3
Teshio-gawa r. Japan 74 F3
Teslin Canada 120 C2
Teslin r. Canada 120 C2
Teslin Lake Canada 120 C2
Tesouras r. Brazil 145 A1
Tessalit Mali 96 D2
Tessaoua Niger 96 D3
Tessolo Moz. 101 L1
Test r. U.K. 49 F8
Testour Tunisia 58 C6
Tetachuck Lake Canada 120 E4
Tetas, Punta pt Chile 144 B2
Tete Moz. 99 D5
Te Teko N.Z. 113 F4
Teteriv r. Ukr. 43 F6
Teterow Germany 47 N4
Tetiyev Ukr. see Tetiyiv
Tetiyiv Ukr. 43 F6
Tetlin U.S.A. 120 A2
Tetlin Lake U.S.A. 120 A2
Tetney U.K. 48 G5
Teton r. U.S.A. 126 F3
Tétouan Morocco 57 D6
Tetovo Macedonia 59 I3
Tetpur India 82 B5
Tetuán Morocco see Tétouan
Tetulia Bangl. 83 G4
Tetulia sea chan. Bangl. 83 G5
Tetyukhe Rus. Fed. see Dal'negorsk
Tetyukhe-Pristan' Rus. Fed. see Rudnaya Pristan'
Tetyushi Rus. Fed. 43 K5
Teuco r. Arg. 144 D2
Teufelsbach Namibia 100 C2
Teunom Indon. 71 A6
Teunom r. Indon. 71 A6
Teutoburger Wald hills Germany 53 I2
Teuva Fin. 44 L5
Tevere r. Italy see Tiber
Teverya Israel see Tiberias
Teviot r. U.K. 50 G5
Te Waewae Bay N.Z. 113 A8
Te Waipounamu i. N.Z. see South Island
Tewane Botswana 101 H2
Tewantin Australia 111 F5
Tewkesbury U.K. 49 E7
Têwo China 76 D1
Texarkana AR U.S.A. 131 E5
Texarkana TX U.S.A. 131 E5
Texas Australia 112 E2
Texas state U.S.A. 131 D6
Texel i. Neth. 52 E1
Texhoma U.S.A. 131 C4
Texoma, Lake U.S.A. 131 D5
Teyateyaneng Lesotho 101 H5
Teykovo Rus. Fed. 42 I4
Teza r. Rus. Fed. 42 I4
Tezpur India 83 H4
Tezu India 83 I4
Tha, Nam r. Laos 70 C2
Thaa Atoll Maldives see Kolhumadulu Atoll
Tha-anne r. Canada 121 M2
Thabana-Ntlenyana mt. Lesotho 101 I5
Thaba Nchu S. Africa 101 H5
Thaba Putsoa mt. Lesotho 101 H5
Thaba-Tseka Lesotho 101 I5
Thabazimbi S. Africa 101 H3
Thab Lan National Park Thai. 71 C4
Tha Bo Laos 70 C3
Thabong S. Africa 101 H4
Thabyedaung Myanmar 76 C4
Thade r. Myanmar 70 A3
Thagyettaw Myanmar 71 B4
Tha Hin Thai. see Lop Buri
Thai Binh Vietnam 70 D2
▶Thailand country Asia 70 C4
Asia 6, 62–63
Thailand, Gulf of Asia 71 C5
Thai Muang Thai. 71 B5
Thai Nguyên Vietnam 70 D2
Thaj Saudi Arabia 88 C5
Thakurgaon Bangl. 83 G4
Thakurtola India 82 E5
Thal Germany 53 K4
Thala Tunisia 58 C7
Thalang Thai. 71 B5
Thalassery India see Tellicherry
Thal Desert Pak. 89 H4
Thale (Harz) Germany 53 L3
Thaliparamba India see Taliparamba
Thallon Australia 112 D2
Thalo Pak. 89 G4
Thamaga Botswana 101 G3
Thamar, Jabal mt. Yemen 86 G7
Thamarīt Oman 87 H6
Thame r. U.K. 49 F7
Thames r. Ont. Canada 125 K3
Thames r. Ont. Canada 134 D2
Thames N.Z. 113 E3
Thames est. U.K. 49 H7
Thames r. U.K. 49 H7
Thamesford Canada 134 E2
Thana India see Thane
Thanatpin Myanmar 70 B3
Thandwè Myanmar see Sandoway
Thane India 84 B2
Thanet, Isle of pen. U.K. 49 I7
Thăng Binh Vietnam 70 E4
Thangoo Australia 108 C4
Thangra Jammu and Kashmir 82 D2
Thanh Hoa Vietnam 70 D3
Thanh Tri Vietnam 71 D5
Thanjavur India 84 C4
Than Kyun i. Myanmar 71 B5
Thanlwin r. China/Myanmar see Salween
Thanlyin Myanmar see Syriam
Thaolintoa Lake Canada 121 L2
Tha Pla Thai. 70 C3
Thap Put Thai. 71 B5
Thapsacus Syria see Dibsī
Thap Sakae Thai. 71 B5
Tharabwin Myanmar 71 B4
Tharad India 82 B4
Thar Desert India/Pak. 89 H5
Thargomindah Australia 112 A1
Tharrawaw Myanmar 70 A3
Tharthār, Buḩayrat ath l. Iraq 91 F4
Tharwānīyyah U.A.E. 88 D6
Thasos i. Greece 59 K4
Thatcher U.S.A. 129 I5
Thât Khê Vietnam 70 D2
Thât Nôt Vietnam 71 D5
Thaton Myanmar 70 B3
Thaungdut Myanmar 70 A1
Tha Uthen Thai. 70 D3
Thayawthadangyi Kyun i. Myanmar 71 B4
Thayetmyo Myanmar 70 A3
Thazi Magwe Myanmar 70 A3
Thazi Mandalay Myanmar 83 I5
The Aldermen Islands N.Z. 113 F3
Theba U.S.A. 129 G5
▶The Bahamas country West Indies 133 E7
North America 9, 116–117
Thebes Greece see Thiva
The Bluff Bahamas 133 E7
The Broads nat. park U.K. 49 I6
The Brothers is Hong Kong China 77 [inset]
The Calvados Chain is P.N.G. 110 F1
The Cheviot hill U.K. 48 E3
The Dalles U.S.A. 126 C3
Thedford U.S.A. 130 C3
The Entrance Australia 112 E4
The Faither stack U.K. 50 [inset]
The Fens reg. U.K. 49 G6
▶The Gambia country Africa 96 B3
Africa 7, 94–95
Thegon Myanmar 70 A3
The Grampians mts Australia 111 C8
The Great Oasis oasis Egypt see Khārijah, Wāḩāt al
The Grenadines is St Vincent 137 L6
The Gulf Asia 88 C4
▶The Hague Neth. 52 E2
Seat of government of the Netherlands.
The Hunters Hills N.Z. 113 C7
Thekulthili Lake Canada 121 I2
The Lakes National Park Australia 112 C6
Thelon r. Canada 121 L1
The Lynd Junction Australia 110 D3
Themar Germany 53 K4
Thembalihle S. Africa 101 I4
The Minch sea chan. U.K. 50 C2
The Naze c. Norway see Lindesnes
The Needles stack U.K. 49 F8
Theni India 84 C4
Thenia Alg. 57 H5
Theniet El Had Alg. 57 H6
The North Sound sea chan. U.K. 50 G1
Theodore Australia 110 E5
Theodore Canada 121 K5
Theodore Roosevelt Lake U.S.A. 129 H5
Theodore Roosevelt National Park U.S.A. 130 C2
Theodosia Ukr. see Feodosiya
The Old Man of Coniston hill U.K. 48 D4
The Paps hill Rep. of Ireland 51 C5
The Pas Canada 121 K4
The Pilot mt. Australia 112 D6
Thera i. Greece see Thira
Thérain r. France 52 C5
Theresa U.S.A. 135 H1
Thermaïkos Kolpos g. Greece 59 J4
Thermopolis U.S.A. 126 F4
The Rock Australia 112 C5
Thérouanne France 52 C4
The Salt Lake salt flat Australia 111 C6
▶The Settlement Christmas I. 68 D9
Capital of Christmas Island.
The Skaw spit Denmark see Grenen
The Slot sea chan. Solomon Is see New Georgia Sound
The Solent strait U.K. 49 F8
Thessalon Canada 122 E5
Thessalonica Greece see Thessaloniki
Thessaloniki Greece 59 J4
The Storr hill U.K. 50 C3
Thet r. U.K. 49 H6
The Terraces hills Australia 109 C7
Thetford U.K. 49 H6
Thetford Mines Canada 123 H5
Thetkethaung r. Myanmar 70 A4
The Triangle mts Myanmar 70 B1
The Trossachs hills U.K. 50 E4
The Twins Australia 111 A6
Theva-i-Ra reef Fiji see Ceva-i-Ra
▶The Valley Anguilla 137 L5
Capital of Anguilla.
Thevenard Island Australia 108 A5
Thévenet, Lac l. Canada 123 H2
Theveste Alg. see Tébessa
The Wash b. U.K. 49 H6
The Weald reg. U.K. 49 H7
The Woodlands U.S.A. 131 E6
Thibodaux U.S.A. 131 F6
Thicket Portage Canada 121 L4
Thief River Falls U.S.A. 130 D1
Thiel Neth. see Tiel
Thiel Mountains Antarctica 152 K1
Thielsen, Mount U.S.A. 126 C4
Thielt Belgium see Tielt
Thiérache reg. France 52 D5
Thiers France 56 F4
Thiès Senegal 96 B3
Thika Kenya 98 D4
Thiladhunmathi Atoll Maldives 84 B5
Thiladunmathi Atoll Maldives see Thiladhunmathi Atoll
Thimbu Bhutan see Thimphu
▶Thimphu Bhutan 83 G4
Capital of Bhutan.
Thionville France 52 G5
Thira i. Greece 59 K6
Thirsk U.K. 48 F4
Thirty Mile Lake Canada 121 L2
Thiruvananthapuram India see Trivandrum
Thiruvannamalai India see Tiruvannamalai
Thiruvarur India 84 C4
Thiruvattiyur India see Tiruvottiyur
Thisted Denmark 45 F8
Thistle Creek Canada 120 B2
Thistle Lake Canada 121 I1
Thityabin Myanmar 70 A2
Thiu Khao Luang Phrabang mts Laos/Thai. see Luang Phrabang, Thiu Khao
Thiva Greece 59 J5
Thívai Greece see Thiva
Thlewiaza r. Canada 121 M2
Thoa r. Canada 121 I2
Thô Chu, Đao i. Vietnam 71 C5
Thoen Thai. 76 C5
Thoeng Thai. 70 C3
Thohoyandou S. Africa 101 J2
Tholen Neth. 52 E3
Tholen i. Neth. 52 E3
Tholey Germany 52 H5
Thomas Hill Reservoir U.S.A. 130 E4
Thomas Hubbard, Cape Canada 119 I1
Thomaston CT U.S.A. 135 I3
Thomaston GA U.S.A. 133 C5
Thomastown Rep. of Ireland 51 E5
Thomasville AL U.S.A. 133 C6
Thomasville GA U.S.A. 133 D6
Thommen Belgium 52 G4
Thompson Canada 121 L4
Thompson r. Canada 120 F5
Thompson U.S.A. 129 I2
Thompson r. U.S.A. 124 I4
Thompson Falls U.S.A. 126 E3
Thompson Peak U.S.A. 127 G6
Thompson's Falls Kenya see Nyahururu
Thompson Sound Canada 120 E5
Thomson U.S.A. 133 D5
Thon Buri Thai. 71 C4
Thonokied Lake Canada 121 I1
Thôn Sơn Hai Vietnam 71 E5
Thoothukudi India see Tuticorin
Thoreau U.S.A. 129 I4
Thorn Neth. 52 F3
Thorn Poland see Toruń
Thornaby-on-Tees U.K. 48 F4
Thornapple r. U.S.A. 134 C2
Thornbury U.K. 49 E7
Thorne U.K. 48 G5
Thorne U.S.A. 128 D2
Thornton r. Australia 110 B3
Thorold Canada 134 F2
Thorshavnfjella reg. Antarctica see Thorshavnheiane
Thorshavnheiane reg. Antarctica 152 C2
Thota-ea-Moli Lesotho 101 H5
Thouars France 56 D3
Thoubal India 83 H4
Thourout Belgium see Torhout
Thousand Islands Canada/U.S.A. 135 G1
Thousand Lake Mountain U.S.A. 129 H2
Thousand Oaks U.S.A. 128 D4
Thousandsticks U.S.A. 134 D5
Thrace reg. Europe 59 L4
Thraki reg. Europe see Thrace
Thrakiko Pelagos sea Greece 59 K4
Three Gorges Project resr China 77 F2
Three Hills Canada 120 H5
Three Hummock Island Australia 111 [inset]
Three Kings Islands N.Z. 113 D2
Three Oaks U.S.A. 134 B3
Three Pagodas Pass Myanmar/Thai. 70 B4
Three Points, Cape Ghana 96 C4
Three Rivers U.S.A. 134 C3
Three Sisters mt. U.S.A. 126 C3
Three Springs Australia 109 A7
Thrissur India see Trichur
Throckmorton U.S.A. 131 D5
Throssell, Lake salt flat Australia 109 D6
Throssel Range hills Australia 108 C5
Thrushton National Park Australia 112 C1
Thubun Lakes Canada 121 I2
Thu Dâu Môt Vietnam 71 D5
Thuddungra Australia 112 D5
Thuin Belgium 52 E4
Thul Pak. 89 H4
Thulaythawāt Gharbī, Jabal hill Syria 85 D2
Thule Greenland 119 L2
Thun Switz. 56 H3
Thunder Bay Canada 119 J5
Thunder Bay b. U.S.A. 134 D1
Thunder Creek r. Canada 121 J5
Thüngen Germany 53 J5
Thung Salaeng Luang National Park Thai. 70 C3
Thung Song Thai. 71 B5
Thung Yai Naresuan Wildlife Reserve nature res. Thai. 70 B4
Thüringen land Germany 53 K3
Thüringer Becken reg. Germany 53 L3
Thüringer Wald mts Germany 53 K4
Thuringia land Germany see Thüringen
Thuringian Forest mts Germany see Thüringer Wald
Thurles Rep. of Ireland 51 E5
Thurn, Pass Austria 47 N7
Thursday Island Australia 110 C1
Thurso U.K. 50 F2
Thurso r. U.K. 50 F2
Thurston Island Antarctica 152 K2
Thurston Peninsula i. Antarctica see Thurston Island
Thüster Berg hill Germany 53 J2
Thuthukudi India see Tuticorin
Thwaite U.K. 48 E4
Thwaites Glacier Tongue Antarctica 152 K1
Thyatira Turkey see Akhisar
Thyborøn Denmark 45 F8
Thymerais reg. France 52 B6
Tianchang China 77 H1
Tiancheng China see Chongyang
Tianchi China see Lezhi
Tiandeng China 76 E4
Tiandong China 76 E4
T'ianet'i Georgia 91 G2
Tianfanjie China 77 H2
Tianjin China 73 L5
Tianjin municipality China 73 L5
Tianjun China 80 I4
Tianlin China 76 E3
Tianma China see Changshan
Tianmen China 77 G2
Tianqiaoling China 74 C4
Tianquan China 76 D2
Tianshan China 73 M4
Tian Shan mts China/Kyrg. see Tien Shan
Tianshui China 76 E1
Tianshuihai Aksai Chin 82 D2
Tiantai China 77 I2
Tiantang China see Yuexi
Tianyang China 76 E4
Tianzhou China see Tianyang
Tianzhu Gansu China 72 I5
Tianzhu Guizhou China 77 F3
Tiaret Alg. 57 G6
Tiassalé Côte d'Ivoire 96 C4
Tibagi Brazil 145 A4
Tibal, Wādī watercourse Iraq 91 F4
Tibati Cameroon 96 E4
Tibba Pak. 89 H4
Tibé, Pic de mt. Guinea 96 C4
Tiber r. Italy 58 E4
Tiberias Israel 85 B3
Tiberias, Lake Israel see Galilee, Sea of
Tiber Reservoir U.S.A. 126 F2
Tibesti mts Chad 97 E2
Tibet aut. reg. China see Xizang Zizhiqu
Tibi India 89 I4
Tibooburra Australia 111 C6
Tibrikot Nepal 83 E3
Tibro Sweden 45 I7
Tibur Italy see Tivoli
Tiburón, Isla i. Mex. 127 E7
Ticehurst U.K. 49 H7
Tichborne Canada 135 G1
Tichégami r. Canada 123 G4
Tîchît Mauritania 96 C3
Tichla W. Sahara 96 B2
Ticinum Italy see Pavia
Ticonderoga U.S.A. 135 I2
Ticul Mex. 136 G4
Tidaholm Sweden 45 H7
Tiddim Myanmar 70 A2
Tiden India 71 A6
Tidjikja Mauritania 96 B3
Tiefa China 74 A4
Tiel Neth. 52 F3
Tieli China 74 B3
Tieling China 74 A4
Tielongtan Aksai Chin 82 D2
Tielt Belgium 52 D4
Tienen Belgium 52 E4
Tien Shan mts China/Kyrg. 72 D4
Tientsin municipality China see Tianjin
Tiên Yên Vietnam 70 D2
Tierp Sweden 45 J6
Tierra Amarilla U.S.A. 127 G5
▶Tierra del Fuego, Isla Grande de i. Arg./Chile 144 C8
Largest island in South America.
South America 138–139
Tierra del Fuego, Parque Nacional nat. park Arg. 144 C8
Tiétar r. Spain 57 D4
Tiétar, Valle de valley Spain 57 D3
Tietê r. Brazil 145 A3
Tieyon Australia 109 F6
Tiffin U.S.A. 134 D3
Tiflis Georgia see T'bilisi
Tifton U.S.A. 133 D6
Tiga Reservoir Nigeria 96 D3
Tigen Kazakh. 91 H1
Tigh Āb Iran 89 F5
Tigheciului, Dealurile hills Moldova 59 M2
Tighina Moldova 59 M1
Tigiria India 84 E1
Tignère Cameroon 96 E4
Tignish Canada 123 I5
Tigranocerta Turkey see Siirt
Tigre r. Venez. 142 F2
Tigris r. Asia 91 G5
also known as Dicle (Turkey) or Nahr Dijlah (Iraq/Syria)
Tigrovaya Balka Zapovednik nature res. Tajik. 89 H2
Tiguidit, Falaise de esc. Niger 96 D3
Tīh, Gebel el plat. Egypt see Tīh, Jabal at
Tīh, Jabal at plat. Egypt 85 A5
Tijuana Mex. 128 E5
Tikamgarh India 82 D4
Tikanlik China 80 G3
Tikhoretsk Rus. Fed. 43 I7
Tikhvin Rus. Fed. 42 G4
Tikhvinskaya Gryada ridge Rus. Fed. 42 G4
Tiki Basin sea feature S. Pacific Ocean 151 L7
Tikokino N.Z. 113 F4
Tikopia i. Solomon Is 107 G3
Tikrīt Iraq 91 F4
Tikse Jammu and Kashmir 82 D2
Tiksheozero, Ozero l. Rus. Fed. 44 R3
Tiksi Rus. Fed. 65 N2
Tiladummati Atoll Maldives see Thiladhunmathi Atoll
Tilaiya Reservoir India 83 F4
Tilbeşar Ovasi plain Turkey 85 C1
Tilbooroo Australia 112 B1
Tilburg Neth. 52 F3
Tilbury Canada 134 D2
Tilbury U.K. 49 H7
Tilcara Arg. 144 C2
Tilden U.S.A. 131 D6
Tilemsès Niger 96 D3
Tilemsi, Vallée du watercourse Mali 96 D3
Tilhar India 82 D4
Tilimsen Alg. see Tlemcen
Tilin Myanmar 70 A2
Tillabéri Niger 96 D3
Tillamook U.S.A. 126 C3
Tillanchong Island India 71 A5
Tillia Niger 96 D3
Tillicoultry U.K. 50 F4
Tillsonburg Canada 134 E2
Tillyfourie U.K. 50 G3
Tilonia India 89 I5
Tilos i. Greece 59 L6
Tilothu India 83 F4
Tilpa Australia 112 B3
Tilsit Rus. Fed. see Sovetsk
Tilt r. U.K. 50 F4
Tilton IL U.S.A. 134 B3
Tilton NH U.S.A. 135 J2
Tim Rus. Fed. 43 H6
Ţimā Egypt 86 D4
Timah, Bukit hill Sing. 71 [inset]
Timakara i. India 84 B4
Timanskiy Kryazh ridge Rus. Fed. 42 K2
Timar Turkey 91 F3
Timaru N.Z. 113 C7
Timashevsk Rus. Fed. 43 H7
Timashevskaya Rus. Fed. see Timashevsk
Timbedgha Mauritania 96 C3
Timber Creek Australia 106 D3
Timber Mountain U.S.A. 128 E3
Timberville U.S.A. 135 F4
Timbuktu Mali 96 C3
Timétrine reg. Mali 96 C3
Timiaouine Alg. 96 D2
Timimoun Alg. 54 E6
Timirist, Râs pt Mauritania 96 B3
Timiskaming, Lake Canada see Témiscamingue, Lac
Timişoara Romania 59 I2
Timmins Canada 122 E4
Timms Hill hill U.S.A. 130 F2
Timon Brazil 143 J5
Timor i. East Timor/Indon. 108 D2
Timor-Leste country Asia see East Timor
Timor Loro Sae country Asia see East Timor
Timor Sea Australia/Indon. 106 C3
Timor Timur country Asia see East Timor
Timperley Range hills Australia 109 C6
Timrå Sweden 44 J5
Tīn, Ra's at pt Libya 90 A4
Ţīna, Khalīg el b. Egypt see Ţīnah, Khalīj at
Tinah Syria 85 D1
Ţīnah, Khalīj aţ b. Egypt 85 A4
Tin Can Bay Australia 111 F5
Tindivanam India 84 C3
Tindouf Alg. 54 C6
Ti-n-Essako Mali 96 D3
Tinggi i. Malaysia 71 D7
Tingha Australia 112 E2
Tingis Morocco see Tangier
Tingo Maria Peru 142 C5
Tingréla Côte d'Ivoire see Tengréla
Tingsryd Sweden 45 I8
Tingvoll Norway 44 F5
Tingwall U.K. 50 F1
Tingzhou China see Changting
Tinharé, Ilha de i. Brazil 145 D1
Tinh Gia Vietnam 70 D3
Tinian i. N. Mariana Is 69 L4
Tini Heke is N.Z. see Snares Islands
Tinnelvelly India see Tirunelveli
Tinogasta Arg. 144 C3
Tinos Greece 59 K6
Tinos i. Greece 59 K6
Tinqueux France 52 D5
Tinrhert, Plateau du Alg. 96 D2
Tinsukia India 83 H4
Tintagel U.K. 49 C8
Ţînţâne Mauritania 96 B3
Tintina Arg. 144 D3
Tintinara Australia 111 C7
Tioga U.S.A. 130 C1
Tioman i. Malaysia 71 D7
Tionesta U.S.A. 134 F3
Tionesta Lake U.S.A. 134 F3
Tipasa Alg. 57 H5
Tiphsah Syria see Dibsī
Tipperary Rep. of Ireland 51 D5
Tipton CA U.S.A. 128 D3
Tipton IA U.S.A. 130 F3
Tipton IN U.S.A. 134 B3
Tipton MO U.S.A. 130 E4
Tipton, Mount U.S.A. 129 F4
Tiptop U.S.A. 134 E5
Tip Top Hill hill Canada 122 D4
Tiptree U.K. 49 H7
Tiptur India 84 C3
Tipturi India see Tiptur
Tiracambu, Serra do hills Brazil 143 I4
Tirah reg. Pak. 89 H3
▶Tirana Albania 59 H4
Capital of Albania.
Tiranë Albania see Tirana
Tirano Italy 58 D1
Tirari Desert Australia 111 B5
Tiraspol Moldova 59 M1
Tiraz Mountains Namibia 100 C4
Tire Turkey 59 L5
Tirebolu Turkey 91 E2
Tiree i. U.K. 50 C4
Tîrgovişte Romania see Târgovişte
Tîrgu Jiu Romania see Târgu Jiu
Tîrgu Mureş Romania see Târgu Mureş
Tîrgu Neamţ Romania see Târgu Neamţ
Tîrgu Secuiesc Romania see Târgu Secuiesc
Tiri Pak. 89 G4
Tirich Mir mt. Pak. 89 H2
Tirlemont Belgium see Tienen
Tirna r. India 84 C2
Tîrnăveni Romania see Târnăveni
Tirnavos Greece see Tyrnavos
Tiros Brazil 145 B2
Tirourda, Col de pass Alg. 57 I5
Tirreno, Mare sea France/Italy see Tyrrhenian Sea
Tirso r. Sardinia Italy 58 C5
Tirthahalli India 84 B3
Tiruchchendur India 84 C4
Tiruchchirappalli India 84 C4
Tiruchengodu India 84 C4
Tirunelveli India 84 C4
Tirupati India 84 C3
Tiruppattur Tamil Nadu India 84 C3
Tiruppattur Tamil Nadu India 84 C4
Tiruppur India 84 C4
Tiruttani India 84 C3
Tirutturaippundi India 84 C4
Tiruvallur India 84 C3
Tiruvannamalai India 84 C3
Tiruvottiyur India 84 D3
Tiru Well Australia 108 D5
Tisa r. Serb. and Mont. 59 I2
also known as Tisza (Hungary), Tysa (Ukraine)
Tisdale Canada 121 J4
Tishomingo U.S.A. 131 D5
Tīsīyah Syria 85 C3
Tissemsilt Alg. 57 G6
Tisza r. Hungary see Tisa
Titalya Bangl. see Tetulia
Titan Dome ice feature Antarctica 152 H1
Titao Burkina 96 C3
Tit-Ary Rus. Fed. 65 N2
Titawin Morocco see Tétouan
Titicaca, Lago Bol./Peru see Titicaca, Lake
▶Titicaca, Lake Bol./Peru 142 E7
Largest lake in South America.
South America 138–139
Titiea mt. N.Z. see Aspiring, Mount
Titlagarh India 84 D1
Titograd Serb. and Mont. see Podgorica
Titova Mitrovica Serb. and Mont. see Kosovska Mitrovica
Titov Drvar Bos.-Herz. 58 G2
Titovo Užice Serb. and Mont. see Užice
Titovo Velenje Slovenia see Velenje
Titov Veles Macedonia see Veles
Titov Vrbas Yugo. see Vrbas
Ti Tree Australia 108 F5
Titu Romania 59 K2
Titusville FL U.S.A. 133 D6
Titusville PA U.S.A. 134 F3
Tiu Chung Chau i. Hong Kong China 77 [inset]
Tiumpain, Rubha an hd U.K. see Tiumpan Head
Tiumpan Head hd U.K. 50 C2
Tiva watercourse Kenya 98 D4
Tivari India 82 C4
Tiverton Canada 134 E1
Tiverton U.K. 49 D8
Tivoli Italy 58 E4
Ţīwī Oman 88 E6
Ti-ywa Myanmar 71 B4
Tizi El Arba hill Alg. 57 H5
Tizimín Mex. 136 G4
Tizi N'Kouilal pass Alg. 57 I5
Tizi Ouzou Alg. 57 I5
Tiznap He r. China 82 D1
Tiznit Morocco 96 C2
Tiztoutine Morocco 57 E6
Tjaneni Swaziland 101 J3
Tjappsåive Sweden 44 K4
Tjeukemeer l. Neth. 52 F2
Tjirebon Indon. see Cirebon
Tjolotjo Zimbabwe see Tsholotsho
Tjorhom Norway 45 E7
Tkibuli Georgia see Tqibuli
Tlahualilo Mex. 131 C7
Tlaxcala Mex. 136 E5
Tl'ell Canada 120 D4
Tlemcen Alg. 57 F6
Thakalatlou S. Africa 100 F5
Tlholong S. Africa 101 I5
Tlokweng Botswana 101 G3
Tlyarata Rus. Fed. 91 G2

To *r.* Myanmar 70 B3
Toad *r.* Canada 120 E3
Toad River Canada 120 E3
Toamasina Madag. 99 E5
Toana *mts* U.S.A. 129 F1
Toano U.S.A. 135 G5
Toa Payoh Sing. 71 [inset]
Toba China 76 C2
Toba, Danau *l.* Indon. 71 B7
Toba, Lake Indon. *see* **Toba, Danau**
Toba and Kakar Ranges *mts* Pak. 89 G4
Toba Gargaji Pak. 89 I4
Tobago *i.* Trin. and Tob. 137 L6
Tobelo Indon. 69 H6
Tobermorey Australia 110 B4
Tobermory Australia 112 A1
Tobermory Canada 134 E1
Tobermory U.K. 50 C4
Tobi *i.* Palau 69 I6
Tobin, Lake *salt flat* Australia 108 D5
Tobin, Mount U.S.A. 128 E1
Tobin Lake Canada 121 K4
Tobin Lake *l.* Canada 121 K4
Tobi-shima *i.* Japan 75 E5
Tobol *r.* Kazakh./Rus. Fed. 78 F1
Tobol'sk Rus. Fed. 64 H4
Tô Bong Vietnam 71 E4
Tobruk Libya *see* **Tubruq**
Tobseda Rus. Fed. 42 L1
Tobyl *r.* Kazakh./Rus. Fed. *see* **Tobol**
Tobysh *r.* Rus. Fed. 42 K2
Tocache Nuevo Peru 142 C5
Tocantinópolis Brazil 143 I5
Tocantins *r.* Brazil 145 A1
Tocantins *state* Brazil 145 A1
Tocantinzinha *r.* Brazil 145 A1
Toccoa U.S.A. 133 D5
Tochi *r.* Pak. 89 H3
Töcksfors Sweden 45 G7
Tocopilla Chile 144 B2
Tocumwal Australia 112 B5
Tod, Mount Canada 120 G5
Todd *watercourse* Australia 110 A5
Todi Italy 58 E3
Todoga-saki *pt* Japan 75 F5
Todos Santos Mex. 136 B4
Toe Head *hd* U.K. 50 B3
Tofino Canada 120 E5
Toft U.K. 50 [inset]
Tofua *i.* Tonga 107 I3
Togatax China 82 E2
Togian *i.* Indon. 69 G7
Togian, Kepulauan *is* Indon. 69 G7
Togliatti Rus. Fed. *see* **Tol'yatti**
▶**Togo** *country* Africa 96 D4
Africa 7, 94–95
Togtoh China 73 K4
Togton He *r.* China 83 H2
Togton Heyan China *see* **Tanggulashan**
Tohatchi U.S.A. 129 I4
Toholampi Fin. 44 N5
Toiba China 83 G3
Toibalewe India 71 A5
Toijala Fin. 45 M6
Toili Indon. 69 G7
Toi-misaki *pt* Japan 75 C7
Toivakka Fin. 44 O5
Toiyabe Range *mts* U.S.A. 128 E2
Tojikiston *country* Asia *see* **Tajikistan**
Tok U.S.A. 120 A2
Tokar Sudan 86 E6
Tokara-rettō *is* Japan 75 C7
Tokarevka Rus. Fed. 43 I6
Tokat Turkey 90 E2
Tŏkchok-to *i.* S. Korea 75 B5
Tokdo *i.* N. Pacific Ocean *see* **Liancourt Rocks**

▶**Tokelau** *terr.* S. Pacific Ocean 107 I2
New Zealand Overseas Territory.
Oceania 8, 104–105

Tokmak Kyrg. *see* **Tokmok**
Tokmak Ukr. 43 G7
Tokmok Kyrg. 80 E3
Tokomaru Bay N.Z. 113 G4
Tokoroa N.Z. 113 E4
Tokoza S. Africa 101 I4
Toksun China 80 G3
Tok-tō *i.* N. Pacific Ocean *see* **Liancourt Rocks**
Toktogul Kyrg. 80 D3
Tokto-ri *i.* N. Pacific Ocean *see* **Liancourt Rocks**
Tokur Rus. Fed. 74 D1
Tokushima Japan 75 D6
Tokuyama Japan 75 C6

▶**Tōkyō** Japan 75 E6
Capital of Japan. Most populous city in the world and in Asia.

Tokzār Afgh. 89 G3
Tolaga Bay N.Z. 113 G4
Tôlañaro Madag. 99 E6
Tolbo Mongolia 80 H2
Tolbukhin Bulg. *see* **Dobrich**
Tolbuzino Rus. Fed. 74 B1
Toledo Brazil 144 F2
Toledo Spain 57 D4
Toledo *IA* U.S.A. 130 E3
Toledo *OH* U.S.A. 134 D3
Toledo *OR* U.S.A. 126 C3
Toledo, Montes de *mts* Spain 57 D4
Toledo Bend Reservoir U.S.A. 131 E6
Toletum Spain *see* **Toledo**
Toliara Madag. 99 E6
Tolitoli Indon. 69 G6
Tol'ka Rus. Fed. 64 J3
Tolleson U.S.A. 129 G5
Tollimarjon Uzbek. *see* **Talimardzhan**
Tolmachevo Rus. Fed. 45 P7
Tolo Dem. Rep. Congo 98 B4
Tolo Channel Hong Kong China 77 [inset]
Tolochin Belarus *see* **Talachyn**
Tolo Harbour *b.* Hong Kong China 77 [inset]
Tolosa France *see* **Toulouse**
Tolosa Spain 57 E2
Toluca Mex. 136 E5
Toluca de Lerdo Mex. *see* **Toluca**
Tol'yatti Rus. Fed. 43 K5
Tom' *r.* Rus. Fed. 74 B2
Tomah U.S.A. 130 F3
Tomakomai Japan 74 F4
Tomales U.S.A. 128 B2
Tomali Indon. 69 G7
Tomamae Japan 74 F3
Tomanivi *mt.* Fiji 107 H3
Tomar Brazil 142 F4
Tomar Port. 57 B4
Tomari Rus. Fed. 74 F3
Tomarza Turkey 90 D3
Tomaszów Lubelski Poland 43 D6
Tomaszów Mazowiecki Poland 47 R5
Tomatin U.K. 50 F3
Tomatlán Mex. 136 C5
Tomazina Brazil 145 A3
Tombador, Serra do *hills* Brazil 143 G6
Tombigbee *r.* U.S.A. 133 C6
Tomboco Angola 99 B4
Tombouctou Mali *see* **Timbuktu**
Tombstone U.S.A. 127 F7
Tombua Angola 99 B5
Tom Burke S. Africa 101 H2
Tomdibuloq Uzbek. *see* **Tamdybulak**
Tome Moz. 101 L2
Tomelilla Sweden 45 H9
Tomelloso Spain 57 E4
Tomi Romania *see* **Constanța**
Tomingley Australia 112 D4
Tomini, Teluk *g.* Indon. 69 G7
Tominian Mali 96 C3
Tomintoul U.K. 50 F3
Tomislavgrad Bos.-Herz. 58 G3
Tomkinson Ranges *mts* Australia 109 E6
Tømmerneset Norway 44 I3
Tommot Rus. Fed. 65 N4
Tomo *r.* Col. 142 E2
Tomóchic Mex. 127 G7
Tomortei China 73 K4
Tompkinsville U.S.A. 134 C5
Tom Price Australia 108 B5
Tomra China 83 F3
Tomsk Rus. Fed. 64 J4
Toms River U.S.A. 135 H4
Tomtabacken *hill* Sweden 45 I8
Tomtor Rus. Fed. 65 P3
Tomur Feng *mt.* China/Kyrg. *see* **Pobeda Peak**
Tomuzlovka *r.* Rus. Fed. 43 J7
Tom White, Mount U.S.A. 118 D3
Tonalá Mex. 136 F5
Tonantins Brazil 142 E4
Tonb-e Bozorg, Jazīreh-ye *i.* The Gulf *see* **Greater Tunb**
Tonb-e Küchek, Jazīreh-ye *i.* The Gulf *see* **Lesser Tunb**
Tonbridge U.K. 49 H7
Tondano Indon. 69 G6
Tønder Denmark 45 F9
Tondi India 84 C4
Tone *r.* U.K. 49 E7
Toney Mountain Antarctica 152 K1
▶**Tonga** *country* S. Pacific Ocean 107 I4
Oceania 8, 104–105
Tongaat S. Africa 101 J5
Tongariro National Park N.Z. 113 E4
Tongatapu Group *is* Tonga 107 I4

▶**Tonga Trench** *sea feature* S. Pacific Ocean 150 I7
2nd deepest trench in the world.

Tongbai Shan *mts* China 77 G1
Tongcheng China 77 H2
T'ongch'ŏn N. Korea 75 B5
Tongchuan *Shaanxi* China 77 F1
Tongchuan *Sichuan* China *see* **Santai**
Tongdao China 77 F3
Tongde China 76 D1
Tongduch'ŏn S. Korea 75 B5
Tongeren Belgium 52 F4
Tonggu China 77 G2
Tonggu Zui *pt* China 77 F5
Tonghae S. Korea 75 C5
Tonghai China 76 D3
Tonghe China 74 C3
Tonghua *Jilin* China 74 B4
Tonghua *Jilin* China 74 B4
Tongi Bangl. *see* **Tungi**
Tongjiang *Heilong.* China 74 D3
Tongjiang *Sichuan* China 76 E2
Tongking, Gulf of China/Vietnam 70 E2
Tongle China *see* **Leye**
Tongliang China 76 E2
Tongliao China 73 M4
Tongling China 77 H2
Tonglu China 77 H2
Tongo Australia 112 A3
Tongo Lake *salt flat* Australia 112 A3
Tongren *Guizhou* China 77 F3
Tongren *Qinghai* China 76 D1
Tongres Belgium *see* **Tongeren**
Tongsa Bhutan *see* **Trongsa**
Tongshan China 77 H1
Tongshi China 77 F5
Tongta Myanmar 70 B2
Tongtian He *r. Qinghai* China 76 B1
Tongtian He *r. Qinghai* China 76 C1 *see* **Yangtze**
Tongue U.K. 50 E2
Tongue *r.* U.S.A. 126 G3
Tongue of the Ocean *sea chan.* Bahamas 133 E7
Tongxin China 72 J5
T'ongyŏng S. Korea 75 C6
Tongzi China 76 E2
Tónichi Mex. 127 F7
Tonk India 82 C4
Tonkābon Iran 88 C2
Tonkin *reg.* Vietnam 70 D2
Tônle Repou *r.* Laos 71 D4
Tônlé Sab *l.* Cambodia *see* **Tonle Sap**

▶**Tonle Sap** *l.* Cambodia 71 C4
Largest lake in Southeast Asia.

Tonopah *AZ* U.S.A. 129 G5
Tonopah *NV* U.S.A. 128 E2
Tønsberg Norway 45 G7
Tonstad Norway 45 E7
Tonto Creek *watercourse* U.S.A. 129 H5
Tonvarjeh Iran 88 E3
Tonzang Myanmar 70 A2
Tonzi Myanmar 70 A1
Toobeah Australia 112 D2
Toobli Liberia 96 C4
Tooele U.S.A. 129 G1
Toogoolawah Australia 112 F1
Tooma *r.* Australia 112 D6
Toompine Australia 112 B1
Toora Australia 112 C7
Tooraweenah Australia 112 D3
Toorberg *mt.* S. Africa 100 G7
Toowoomba Australia 112 E1
Tooxin Somalia 98 F2
Top Afgh. 89 H3
Top Boğazı Geçidi *pass* Turkey 85 C1

▶**Topeka** U.S.A. 130 E4
State capital of Kansas.

Topia Mex. 127 G8
Töplitz Germany 53 M2
Topoľčany Slovakia 47 Q6
Topolobampo Mex. 127 F8
Topolovgrad Bulg. 59 L3
Topozero, Ozero *l.* Rus. Fed. 44 R4
Topsfield U.S.A. 132 H2
Tor Eth. 97 G4
Tor Baldak *mt.* Afgh. 89 G4
Torbalı Turkey 59 L5
Torbat-e Heydarīyeh Iran 88 E3
Torbat-e Jām Iran 89 F3
Torbay Bay Australia 109 B8
Torbert, Mount U.S.A. 118 C3
Torbeyevo Rus. Fed. 43 I5
Torch *r.* Canada 121 K4
Tordesillas Spain 57 D3
Tordesilos Spain 57 F3
Töre Sweden 44 M4
Torelló Spain 57 H2
Torenberg *hill* Neth. 52 F2
Toretam Kazakh. *see* **Baykonyr**
Torgau Germany 53 M3
Torghay Kazakh. *see* **Turgay**
Torgun *r.* Rus. Fed. 43 J6
Torhout Belgium 52 D3
Torino Italy *see* **Turin**
Tori-shima *i.* Japan 75 F7
Torit Sudan 97 G4
Torkamān Iran 88 B2
Torkovichi Rus. Fed. 42 F4
Tornado Mountain Canada 120 H5
Torneå Fin. *see* **Tornio**
Torneälven *r.* Sweden 44 N4
Torneträsk *l.* Sweden 44 K2
Torngat, Monts *mts* Canada *see* **Torngat Mountains**
Torngat Mountains Canada 123 I2
Tornio Fin. 44 N4
Toro Spain 57 D3
Toro, Pico del *mt.* Mex. 131 C7
Torom Rus. Fed. 74 D1

▶**Toronto** Canada 134 F2
Provincial capital of Ontario and 5th most populous city in North America.

Toro Peak U.S.A. 128 E5
Toropets Rus. Fed. 42 F4
Tororo Uganda 98 D3
Toros Dağları *mts* Turkey *see* **Taurus Mountains**
Torphins U.K. 50 G3
Torquay Australia 112 B7
Torquay U.K. 49 D8
Torrance U.S.A. 128 D5
Torrão Port. 57 B4
Torre *mt.* Port. 57 C3
Torreblanca Spain 57 G3
Torre Blanco, Cerro *mt.* Mex. 127 E6
Torrecerredo *mt.* Spain 57 D2
Torre del Greco Italy 58 F4
Torre de Moncorvo Port. 57 C3
Torrelavega Spain 57 D2
Torremolinos Spain 57 D5

▶**Torrens, Lake** *imp. l.* Australia 111 B6
2nd largest lake in Oceania.

Torrens Creek Australia 110 D4
Torrent Spain 57 F4
Torrente Spain *see* **Torrent**
Torreón Mex. 131 C7
Torres Brazil 145 A5
Torres Mex. 127 F7
Torres del Paine, Parque Nacional *nat. park* Chile 144 B8
Torres Islands Vanuatu 107 G3
Torres Novas Port. 57 B4
Torres Strait Australia 106 E2
Torres Vedras Port. 57 B4
Torreta, Sierra *hill* Spain 57 G4
Torrevieja Spain 57 F5
Torrey U.S.A. 129 H2
Torridge *r.* U.K. 49 C8
Torridon, Loch *b.* U.K. 50 D3
Torrijos Spain 57 D4
Torrington Australia 112 E2
Torrington *CT* U.S.A. 132 F3
Torrington *WY* U.S.A. 126 G4
Torsby Sweden 45 H6

▶**Tórshavn** Faroe Is 44 [inset]
Capital of the Faroe Islands.

Tortilla Flat U.S.A. 129 H5
Törtköl Uzbek. *see* **Turtkul'**
Tortolì *Sardinia* Italy 58 C5
Tortona Italy 58 C2
Tortosa Spain 57 G3
Tortum Turkey 91 F2
Torūd Iran 88 D3
Torugart, Pereval *pass* China/Kyrg. *see* **Turugart Pass**
Torul Turkey 91 E2
Toruń Poland 47 Q4
Tory Island Rep. of Ireland 51 D2
Tory Sound *sea chan.* Rep. of Ireland 51 D2
Torzhok Rus. Fed. 42 G4
Tosa Japan 75 D6
Tosbotn Norway 44 H4
Tosca S. Africa 100 F3
Toscano, Arcipelago *is* Italy 58 C3
Tosham India 82 C3
Tōshima-yama *mt.* Japan 75 F4
Toshkent Uzbek. *see* **Tashkent**
Tosno Rus. Fed. 42 F4
Toson Hu *l.* China 83 I1
Tostado Arg. 144 D3
Tostedt Germany 53 J1
Tosya Turkey 90 D2
Totapola *mt.* Sri Lanka 84 D5
Tôtes France 52 B5
Tot'ma Rus. Fed. 42 I4
Totness Suriname 143 G2
Tottenham Australia 112 C4
Totton U.K. 49 F8
Tottori Japan 75 D6
Touba Côte d'Ivoire 96 C4
Touba Senegal 96 B3
Toubkal, Jbel *mt.* Morocco 54 C5
Toubkal, Parc National *nat. park* Morocco 54 C5
Touboro Cameroon 97 E4
Tougan Burkina 96 C3
Touggourt Alg. 54 F5
Tougué Guinea 96 B3
Touil Mauritania 96 B3
Toul France 52 F6
Touliu Taiwan 77 I4
Toulon France 56 G5
Toulon U.S.A. 130 F3
Toulouse France 56 E5
Toumodi Côte d'Ivoire 96 C4
Toungoo Myanmar 70 B3
Toupai China 77 F3
Tourane Vietnam *see* **Đa Năng**
Tourcoing France 52 D4
Tourgis Lake Canada 121 J1
Tourlaville France 49 F9
Tournai Belgium 52 D4
Tournon-sur-Rhône France 56 G4
Tournus France 58 A1
Touros Brazil 143 K5
Tours France 56 E3
Toussidé, Pic *mt.* Chad 97 E2
Toussoro, Mont *mt.* Cent. Afr. Rep. 93 C3
Toutai China 74 B3
Touwsrivier S. Africa 100 E7
Toužim Czech Rep. 53 M4
Tovarkovo Rus. Fed. 43 G5
Tovil'-Dora Tajik. *see* **Tavildara**
Tovuz Azer. 91 G2
Towada Japan 74 F4
Towak Mountain *hill* U.S.A. 118 B3
Towanda U.S.A. 135 G3
Towaoc U.S.A. 129 I3
Towcester U.K. 49 G6
Tower Rep. of Ireland 51 D6
Towner U.S.A. 130 C1
Townes Pass U.S.A. 128 E3
Townsend U.S.A. 126 F3
Townsend, Mount Australia 112 D6
Townshend Island Australia 110 E4
Townsville Australia 110 D3
Towot Sudan 97 G4
Towr Kham Afgh. 89 H3
Towson U.S.A. 135 G4
Towyn U.K. *see* **Tywyn**
Toy U.S.A. 128 D1
Toyah U.S.A. 131 C6
Toyama Japan 75 E5
Toyama-wan *b.* Japan 75 E5
Toyohashi Japan 75 E6
Toyokawa Japan 75 E6
Toyonaka Japan 75 D6
Toyooka Japan 75 D6
Toyota Japan 75 E6
Tozanlı Turkey *see* **Almus**
Tozê Kangri *mt.* China 83 E2
Tozeur Tunisia 54 F5
Tozi, Mount U.S.A. 118 C3
Tqibuli Georgia 91 F2
Traben Germany 52 H5
Trâblous Lebanon *see* **Tripoli**
Trabotivište Macedonia 59 J4
Trabzon Turkey 91 E2
Tracy *CA* U.S.A. 128 C3
Tracy *MN* U.S.A. 130 E2
Trading *r.* Canada 122 C4
Traer U.S.A. 130 E3
Trafalgar U.S.A. 134 B4
Trafalgar, Cabo *c.* Spain 57 C5
Traffic Mountain Canada 120 D2
Trail Canada 120 G5
Tràille, Rubha na *pt* U.K. 50 D5
Traill Island Greenland *see* **Traill Ø**
Traill Ø *i.* Greenland 119 P2
Trainor Lake Canada 120 F2
Trajectum Neth. *see* **Utrecht**
Trakai Lith. 45 N9
Tra Khuc, Sông *r.* Vietnam 70 E4
Trakiya *reg.* Europe *see* **Thrace**
Trakt Rus. Fed. 42 K3
Trakya *reg.* Europe *see* **Thrace**
Tralee Rep. of Ireland 51 C5
Tralee Bay Rep. of Ireland 51 C5
Trá Lí Rep. of Ireland *see* **Tralee**
Tramandaí Brazil 145 A5
Tramán Tepuí *mt.* Venez. 142 F2
Trá Mhór Rep. of Ireland *see* **Tramore**
Tramore Rep. of Ireland 51 E5
Tranås Sweden 45 I7
Trancas Arg. 144 C3
Trancoso Brazil 145 D2
Tranemo Sweden 45 H8
Tranent U.K. 50 G5
Trang Thai. 71 B6
Trangan *i.* Indon. 108 F1
Trangie Australia 112 C4
Transantarctic Mountains Antarctica 152 H2
Trans Canada Highway Canada 121 H5
Transylvanian Alps *mts* Romania 59 J2
Transylvanian Basin *plat.* Romania 59 K1
Trapani *Sicily* Italy 58 E5
Trapezus Turkey *see* **Trabzon**
Trapper Peak U.S.A. 126 E3
Trappes France 52 C6
Traralgon Australia 112 C7
Trashigang Bhutan 83 G4
Trasimeno, Lago *l.* Italy 58 E3
Trasvase, Canal de Spain 57 E4
Trat Thai. 71 C4
Traunsee *l.* Austria 47 N7
Traunstein Germany 47 N7
Travellers Lake *imp. l.* Australia 111 C7
Travers, Mount N.Z. 113 D6
Traverse City U.S.A. 134 C1
Tra Vinh Vietnam 71 D5
Travnik Bos.-Herz. 58 G2
Trbovlje Slovenia 58 F1
Tre, Hon *i.* Vietnam 71 E4
Treasury Islands Solomon Is 106 F2
Trebbin Germany 53 N2
Trebević *nat. park* Bos.-Herz. 58 H3
Třebíč Czech Rep. 47 O6
Trebinje Bos.-Herz. 58 H3
Trebišov Slovakia 43 D6
Trebizond Turkey *see* **Trabzon**
Trebnje Slovenia 58 F2
Trebur Germany 53 I5
Tree Island India 84 B4
Trefaldwyn U.K. *see* **Montgomery**
Treffurt Germany 53 K3
Treffynnon U.K. *see* **Holywell**
Trefyclawdd U.K. *see* **Knighton**
Trefynwy U.K. *see* **Monmouth**
Tregosse Islets and Reefs Australia 110 E3
Treinta y Tres Uruguay 144 F4
Trelew Arg. 144 C6
Trelleborg Sweden 45 H9
Trélon France 52 E4
Tremblant, Mont *hill* Canada 122 G5
Trembleur Lake Canada 120 E4
Tremiti, Isole *is* Italy 58 F3
Tremont U.S.A. 135 G3
Tremonton U.S.A. 126 E4
Tremp Spain 57 G2
Trenance U.K. 49 B8
Trenary U.S.A. 132 C2
Trenche *r.* Canada 123 G5
Trenčín Slovakia 47 Q6
Trendelburg Germany 53 J3
Trêng Cambodia 71 C4
Trenque Lauquén Arg. 144 D5
Trent Italy *see* **Trento**
Trent *r.* U.K. 49 G5
Trento Italy 58 D1
Trenton Canada 135 G1
Trenton *FL* U.S.A. 133 D6
Trenton *GA* U.S.A. 133 C5
Trenton *KY* U.S.A. 134 B5
Trenton *MO* U.S.A. 130 E3
Trenton *NC* U.S.A. 133 E5
Trenton *NE* U.S.A. 130 C3

▶**Trenton** *NJ* U.S.A. 135 H3
State capital of New Jersey.

Treorchy U.K. 49 D7
Trepassey Canada 123 L5
Tres Arroyos Arg. 144 D5
Tresco *i.* U.K. 49 A9
Três Corações Brazil 145 B3
Tres Esquinas Col. 142 C3
Tres Forcas, Cabo *c.* Morocco *see* **Trois Fourches, Cap des**
Três Lagoas Brazil 145 A3
Três Marias, Represa *resr* Brazil 145 B2
Tres Picachos, Sierra *mts* Mex. 127 G7
Tres Picos, Cerro *mt.* Arg. 144 D5
Três Pontas Brazil 145 B3
Tres Puntas, Cabo *c.* Arg. 144 C7
Três Rios Brazil 145 C3
Tretten Norway 45 G6
Tretyy Severnyy Rus. Fed. *see* **3-y Severnyy**
Treuchtlingen Germany 53 K6
Treuenbrietzen Germany 53 M2
Treungen Norway 45 F7
Treves Germany *see* **Trier**
Treviglio Italy 58 C2
Treviso Italy 58 E2
Trevose Head *hd* U.K. 49 B8
Tri An, Hô *resr* Vietnam 71 D5
Triánda Greece *see* **Trianta**
Triangle U.S.A. 135 G4
Trianta Greece 59 M6
Tribal Areas *admin. div.* Pak. 89 H3
Tri Brata, Gora *hill* Rus. Fed. 74 F1
Tribune U.S.A. 130 C4
Tricase Italy 58 H5
Trichinopoly India *see* **Tiruchchirappalli**
Trichur India 84 C4
Tricot France 52 C5
Trida Australia 112 B4
Tridentum Italy *see* **Trento**
Trier Germany 52 G5
Trieste Italy 58 E2
Trieste, Golfo di *g.* Europe *see* **Trieste, Gulf of**
Trieste, Gulf of Europe 58 E2
Triglav *mt.* Slovenia 58 E1
Triglavski Narodni Park *nat. park* Slovenia 58 E1
Trikala Greece 59 I5
Tríkkala Greece *see* **Trikala**

▶**Trikora, Puncak** *mt.* Indon. 69 J7
2nd highest mountain in Oceania.

Trim Rep. of Ireland 51 F4
Trincomalee Sri Lanka 84 D4
Trindade Brazil 145 A2
Trindade, Ilha da *i.* S. Atlantic Ocean 148 G7
Trinidad Bol. 142 F6
Trinidad Cuba 137 I4
Trinidad *i.* Trin. and Tob. 137 L6
Trinidad Uruguay 144 E4
Trinidad U.S.A. 127 G5
Trinidad *country* West Indies *see* **Trinidad and Tobago**
▶**Trinidad and Tobago** *country* West Indies 137 L6
North America 9, 116–117
Trinity U.S.A. 131 E6
Trinity *r. CA* U.S.A. 128 B1
Trinity *r. TX* U.S.A. 131 E6
Trinity Bay Canada 123 L5
Trinity Islands U.S.A. 118 C4
Trinity Range *mts* U.S.A. 128 D1
Trinkat Island India 71 A5
Trionto, Capo *c.* Italy 58 G5
Tripa *r.* Indon. 71 B7
Tripkau Germany 53 L1
Tripoli Greece 59 J6
Tripoli Lebanon 85 B2

▶**Tripoli** Libya 97 E1
Capital of Libya.

Trípolis Greece *see* **Tripoli**
Tripolis Lebanon *see* **Tripoli**
Tripunittura India 84 C4
Tripura *state* India 83 G5

▶**Tristan da Cunha** *i.* S. Atlantic Ocean 148 H8
Dependency of St Helena.

Trisul *mt.* India 82 D3
Triton Canada 123 L4
Triton Island *atoll* Paracel Is 68 E3
Trittau Germany 53 K1
Trittenheim Germany 52 G5
Trivandrum India 84 C4
Trivento Italy 58 F4
Trnava Slovakia 47 P6
Trobriand Islands P.N.G. 106 F2
Trochu Canada 120 H5
Trofors Norway 44 H4
Trogir Croatia 58 G3
Troia Italy 58 F4
Troisdorf Germany 53 H4
Trois Fourches, Cap des *c.* Morocco 57 E6
Trois-Ponts Belgium 52 F4
Trois-Rivières Canada 123 G5
Troitsko-Pechorsk Rus. Fed. 41 R3
Troitskoye *Altayskiy Kray* Rus. Fed. 72 E2
Troitskoye *Khabarovskiy Kray* Rus. Fed. 74 E2
Troitskoye *Respublika Kalmykiya - Khalm'g-Tangch* Rus. Fed. 43 J7
Trollhättan Sweden 45 H7
Trombetas *r.* Brazil 143 G4
Tromelin, Île *i.* Indian Ocean 149 L7
Tromelin Island Micronesia *see* **Fais**
Tromen, Volcán *vol.* Arg. 144 B5
Tromie *r.* U.K. 50 E3
Trompsburg S. Africa 101 G6
Tromsø Norway 44 K2
Trona U.S.A. 128 E4
Tronador, Monte *mt.* Arg. 144 B6
Trondheim Norway 44 G5
Trondheimsfjorden *sea chan.* Norway 44 F5
Trongsa Bhutan 83 G4
Troödos, Mount Cyprus 85 A2
Troödos Mountains Cyprus 85 A2
Troon U.K. 50 E5
Tropeiros, Serra dos *hills* Brazil 145 B1
Tropic U.S.A. 129 G3
Tropic of Cancer 131 B8
Tropic of Capricorn 110 G4
Trosh Rus. Fed. 42 L2
Trostan *hill* U.K. 51 F2
Trout *r. B.C.* Canada 120 E3
Trout *r. N.W.T.* Canada 120 G2
Trout Lake *Alta* Canada 120 H3
Trout Lake *N.W.T.* Canada 120 F2
Trout Lake *l. N.W.T.* Canada 120 F2
Trout Lake *l. Ont.* Canada 121 M5
Trout Peak U.S.A. 126 F3
Trout Run U.S.A. 135 G3
Trouville-sur-Mer France 49 H9
Trowbridge U.K. 49 E7
Troy *tourist site* Turkey 59 L5
Troy *AL* U.S.A. 133 C6
Troy *KS* U.S.A. 130 E4
Troy *MI* U.S.A. 134 D2
Troy *MO* U.S.A. 130 F4
Troy *MT* U.S.A. 126 E2
Troy *NH* U.S.A. 135 I2
Troy *NY* U.S.A. 135 I2
Troy *OH* U.S.A. 134 C3
Troy *PA* U.S.A. 135 G3
Troyan Bulg. 59 K3
Troyes France 56 G2
Troy Lake U.S.A. 128 E4
Troy Peak U.S.A. 129 F2
Trstenik Serb. and Mont. 59 I3
Truc Giang Vietnam *see* **Bên Tre**
Trucial Coast *country* Asia *see* **United Arab Emirates**
Trucial States *country* Asia *see* **United Arab Emirates**
Trud Rus. Fed. 42 G4
Trufanovo Rus. Fed. 42 J2
Trujillo Hond. 137 G5
Trujillo Peru 142 C5
Trujillo Spain 57 D4
Trujillo Venez. 142 D2
Trujillo, Monte *mt.* Dom. Rep. *see* **Duarte, Pico**
Truk *is* Micronesia *see* **Chuuk**
Trulben Germany 53 H5
Trumbull, Mount U.S.A. 129 G3
Trumon Indon. 71 B7
Trundle Australia 112 C4
Trung Hiệp Vietnam 70 D4
Trung Khanh Vietnam 70 D2
Truong Sa *is* S. China Sea *see* **Spratly Islands**
Truro Canada 123 J5
Truro U.K. 49 B8
Truskmore *hill* Rep. of Ireland 51 D3
Trutch Canada 120 F3
Truth or Consequences U.S.A. 127 G6
Trutnov Czech Rep. 47 O5
Truuli Peak U.S.A. 118 C4
Truva *tourist site* Turkey *see* **Troy**
Trypiti, Akra *pt* Greece 59 K7
Trysil Norway 45 H6
Trzebiatów Poland 47 O3
Tsagaannuur Mongolia 80 G2
Tsagaan-Uul Mongolia *see* **Sharga**
Tsagan Aman Rus. Fed. 43 J7
Tsagan-Nur Rus. Fed. 43 J7
Tsaidam Basin China *see* **Qaidam Pendi**
Tsaka La *pass* China/Jammu and Kashmir 82 D2
Tsalenjikha Georgia 91 F2
Tsangbo *r.* China *see* **Brahmaputra**
Tsangpo *r.* China *see* **Brahmaputra**
Tsaratanana, Massif du *mts* Madag. 99 E5

Umbeara Australia 109 F6
Umboi i. P.N.G. 69 L8
Umeå Sweden 44 L5
Umeälven r. Sweden 44 L5
Umfolozi r. S. Africa 101 K5
Umfreville Lake Canada 121 M5
Umhlanga Rocks S. Africa 101 J5
Umiiviip Kangertiva inlet Greenland 119 N3
Umingmaktok Canada 153 L2
Umirzak Kazakh. 91 H2
Umiujaq Canada 122 F2
Umkomaas S. Africa 101 J6
Umlaiteng India 83 H4
Umlazi S. Africa 101 J5
Umm ad Daraj, Jabal mt. Jordan 85 B3
Umm al 'Amad Syria 85 C2
Umm al Jamājim well Saudi Arabia 88 B5
Umm al Qaiwain U.A.E. see Umm al Qaywayn
Umm al Qaywayn U.A.E. 88 D5
Umm ar Raqabah, Khabrat imp. l. Saudi Arabia 85 C5
Umm at Qalbān Saudi Arabia 91 F6
Umm az Zumūl well Oman 88 D6
Umm Bāb Qatar 88 C5
Umm Bel Sudan 86 C7
Umm Keddada Sudan 86 C7
Umm Lajj Saudi Arabia 86 E4
Umm Nukhaylah hill Saudi Arabia 85 D5
Umm Qaşr Iraq 91 G5
Umm Quşur i. Saudi Arabia 90 D6
Umm Ruwaba Sudan 86 D7
Umm Sa'ad Libya 90 B5
Umm Sa'id Qatar 88 C5
Umm Shugeira Sudan 86 C7
Umm Wa'āl hill Saudi Arabia 85 D4
Umm Wazīr well Saudi Arabia 88 B6
Umnak Island U.S.A. 118 B4
Um Phang Wildlife Reserve nature res. Thai. 70 B4
Umpqua r. U.S.A. 126 B4
Umpulo Angola 99 B5
Umraniye Turkey 59 N5
Umred India 84 C1
Umri India 82 D4
Umtali Zimbabwe see Mutare
Umtata S. Africa 101 I6
Umtentweni S. Africa 101 J6
Umuahia Nigeria 96 D4
Umuarama Brazil 144 F2
Umvuma Zimbabwe see Mvuma
Umzimkulu S. Africa 101 I6
Una r. Bos.-Herz./Croatia 58 G2
Una Brazil 145 D1
Una India 82 D3
'Unāb, Jabal al hill Jordan 85 C5
'Unāb, Wādī al watercourse Jordan 85 C4
Unaí Brazil 145 B2
Unai Pass Afgh. 89 H3
Unalaska Island U.S.A. 118 B4
Unapool U.K. 50 D2
'Unayzah Saudi Arabia 86 F4
'Unayzah, Jabal hill Iraq 91 E4
Uncia Bol. 142 E7
Uncompahgre Peak U.S.A. 129 J2
Uncompahgre Plateau U.S.A. 129 I2
Undara National Park Australia 110 D3
Underberg S. Africa 101 I5
Underbool Australia 111 C7
Underwood U.S.A. 134 C4
Undur Indon. 69 I7
Unecha Rus. Fed. 43 G5
Ungama Bay Kenya see Ungwana Bay
Ungarie Australia 112 C4
Ungava, Baie d' b. Canada see Ungava Bay
Ungava, Péninsule d' pen. Canada 122 G1
Ungava Bay Canada 123 I2
Ungava Peninsula Canada see Ungava, Péninsule d'
Ungeny Moldova see Ungheni
Unggi N. Korea 74 C4
Ungheni Moldova 59 L1
Unguana Moz. 101 L2
Unguja i. Tanz. see Zanzibar Island
Unguz, Solonchakovyye Vpadiny salt flat Turkm. 88 E2
Üngüz Angyrsyndaky Garagum des. Turkm. see Zaunguzskiye Karakumy
Ungvár Ukr. see Uzhhorod
Ungwana Bay Kenya 98 E4
Uni Rus. Fed. 42 K4
União Brazil 143 J4
União da Vitória Brazil 145 A4
União dos Palmares Brazil 143 K5
Unimak Island U.S.A. 118 B4
Unini r. Brazil 142 F4
Union MO U.S.A. 130 F4
Union WV U.S.A. 134 E5
Union, Mount U.S.A. 129 G4
Union City OH U.S.A. 134 C3
Union City PA U.S.A. 134 F3
Union City TN U.S.A. 131 F4
Uniondale S. Africa 100 F7
Unión de Reyes Cuba 133 D8

▶Union of Soviet Socialist Republics
Divided in 1991 into 15 independent nations: Armenia, Azerbaijan, Belarus, Estonia, Georgia, Kazakhstan, Kyrgyzstan, Latvia, Lithuania, Moldova, the Russian Federation, Tajikistan, Turkmenistan, Ukraine and Uzbekistan.

Union Springs U.S.A. 133 C5
Uniontown U.S.A. 134 F4
Unionville U.S.A. 135 G3
▶United Arab Emirates country Asia 88 D6
Asia 6, 62–63
United Arab Republic country Africa see Egypt

▶United Kingdom country Europe 46 G3
3rd most populous country in Europe.
Europe 5, 38–39

United Provinces state India see Uttar Pradesh

▶United States of America country N. America 124 F3
Most populous country in North America and 3rd in the world. 3rd largest country in the world and 2nd in North America.
North America 9, 116–117

United States Range mts Canada 119 L1
Unity Canada 121 I4
Unjha India 82 C5
Unna Germany 53 H3
Unnao India 82 E4
Ŭnp'a N. Korea 75 B5
Unsan N. Korea 75 B4
Ŭnsan N. Korea 75 B5
Unst i. U.K. 50 [inset]
Unstrut r. Germany 53 L3
Untari India 83 E4
Untor, Ozero l. Rus. Fed. 41 T3
Unuk r. Canada/U.S.A. 120 D3
Unuli Horog China 83 G2
Unzen-dake vol. Japan 75 C6
Unzha Rus. Fed. 42 J4
Upalco U.S.A. 129 H1
Upar Ghat reg. India 83 F5
Upemba, Lac l. Dem. Rep. Congo 99 C4
Uperbada India 83 F5
Upernavik Greenland 119 M2
Upington S. Africa 100 E5
Upland U.S.A. 128 E4
Upleta India 82 B5
Upoloksha Rus. Fed. 44 Q3
Upolu i. Samoa 107 I3
Upper Arlington U.S.A. 134 D3
Upper Arrow Lake Canada 120 G5
Upper Chindwin Myanmar see Mawlaik
Upper Fraser Canada 120 F4
Upper Garry Lake Canada 121 K1
Upper Hutt N.Z. 113 E5
Upper Klamath Lake U.S.A. 126 C4
Upper Lough Erne l. U.K. 51 E3
Upper Marlboro U.S.A. 135 G4
Upper Mazinaw Lake Canada 135 G1
Upper Missouri Breaks National Monument nat. park U.S.A. 130 A2
Upper Peirce Reservoir Sing. 71 [inset]
Upper Red Lake U.S.A. 130 E1
Upper Sandusky U.S.A. 134 D3
Upper Saranac Lake U.S.A. 135 H1
Upper Seal Lake Canada see Iberville, Lac d'
Upper Tunguska r. Rus. Fed. see Angara
Upper Volta country Africa see Burkina
Upper Yarra Reservoir Australia 112 B6
Uppinangadi India 84 B3
Uppsala Sweden 45 J7
Upsala Canada 122 C4
Upshi Jammu and Kashmir 82 D2
Upton U.S.A. 135 J2
'Uqayqah, Wādī watercourse Jordan 85 B4
'Uqayribāt Syria 85 C2
Uqlat al 'Udhaybah well Iraq 91 G5
Uqturpan China see Wushi
Uracas vol. N. Mariana Is see Farallon de Pajaros
Urad Houqi China see Sain Us
Ūrāf Iran 88 E4
Urakawa Japan 74 F4
Ural hill Australia 112 C4
Ural r. Kazakh./Rus. Fed. 78 E2
Uralla Australia 112 E3
Ural Mountains Rus. Fed. 41 S2
Ural'sk Kazakh. 78 E1
Ural'skaya Oblast' admin. div. Kazakh. see Zapadnyy Kazakhstan
Ural'skiye Gory mts Rus. Fed. see Ural Mountains
Ural'skiy Khrebet mts Rus. Fed. see Ural Mountains
Urambo Tanz. 99 D4
Uran India 84 B2
Urana Australia 112 C5
Urana, Lake Australia 112 C5
Urandangi Australia 110 B4
Urandi Brazil 145 C1
Uranium City Canada 121 I3
Uranquity Australia 112 C5
Uraricoera r. Brazil 142 F3
Urartu country Asia see Armenia
Ura-Tyube Tajik. see Üroteppa
Uravakonda India 84 C3
Uravan U.S.A. 129 I2
Urawa Japan 75 E6
'Urayf an Nāqah, Jabal hill Egypt 85 B4
Uray'irah Saudi Arabia 88 C5
'Urayq ad Duḥūl des. Saudi Arabia 88 B5
'Urayq Sāqān des. Saudi Arabia 88 B5
Urbana IL U.S.A. 130 F3
Urbana OH U.S.A. 134 D3
Urbino Italy 58 E3
Urbinum Italy see Urbino
Urbs Vetus Italy see Orvieto
Urdoma Rus. Fed. 42 K3
Urdyuzhskoye, Ozero l. Rus. Fed. 42 K2
Urdzhar Kazakh. 80 F2
Ure r. U.K. 48 F4
Ureki Georgia 91 F2
Uren' Rus. Fed. 42 J4
Urengoy Rus. Fed. 64 I3
Uréparapara i. Vanuatu 107 G3
Urewera National Park N.Z. 113 F4
Urfa Turkey see Şanlıurfa
Urfa prov. Turkey see Şanlıurfa
Urga Mongolia see Ulan Bator
Urgal r. Rus. Fed. 74 D2
Urganch Uzbek. see Urgench
Urgench Uzbek. 80 B3
Ürgüp Turkey 90 D3
Urgut Uzbek. 89 G2
Urho China 80 G2
Urho Kekkosen kansallispuisto nat. park Fin. 44 O2
Urie r. U.K. 50 G3
Uril Rus. Fed. 74 C2
Urisino Australia 112 A2
Urjala Fin. 45 M6
Urk Neth. 52 F2
Urkan Rus. Fed. 74 B1
Urkan r. Rus. Fed. 74 B1
Urla Turkey 59 L5
Urlingford Rep. of Ireland 51 E5
Urluk Rus. Fed. 73 J2
Urmā aş Şughrá Syria 85 C1
Urmai China 83 F3
Urmia Iran 88 B2
Urmia, Lake salt l. Iran 88 B2
Urmston Road sea chan. Hong Kong China 77 [inset]
Uromi Nigeria 96 D4
Uroševac Serb. and Mont. 59 I3
Urosozero Rus. Fed. 42 G3
Üroteppa Tajik. 89 H2
Urru Co salt l. China 83 F3
Urt Moron China 80 H4
Uruáchic Mex. 124 F6
Uruaçu Brazil 145 A1
Uruana Brazil 145 A1
Uruapan Baja California Mex. 127 D7
Uruapan Michoacán Mex. 136 D5
Urubamba r. Peru 142 D6
Urucara Brazil 143 G4
Urucu r. Brazil 142 F4
Uruçuca Brazil 145 D1
Uruçuí Brazil 143 J5
Uruçuí, Serra do hills Brazil 143 I5
Urucuia Brazil 145 B2
Urucurituba Brazil 143 G4
Uruguai r. Arg./Uruguay see Uruguay
Uruguaiana Brazil 144 E3
Uruguay r. Arg./Uruguay 144 E4
also known as Uruguai
▶Uruguay country S. America 144 E4
South America 9, 140–141
Uruhe China 74 B2
Urumchi China see Ürümqi
Ürümqi China 80 G3
Urundi country Africa see Burundi
Urup, Ostrov i. Rus. Fed. 73 S3
Urusha Rus. Fed. 74 A1
Urutaí Brazil 145 A2
Uryl' Kazakh. 80 G2
Uryupino Rus. Fed. 73 M2
Uryupinsk Rus. Fed. 43 I6
Ürzhar Kazakh. see Urdzhar
Urzhum Rus. Fed. 42 K4
Urziceni Romania 59 L2
Usa Japan 75 C6
Usa r. Rus. Fed. 42 M2
Uşak Turkey 59 M5
Usakos Namibia 100 B1
Usarp Mountains Antarctica 152 H2
Usborne, Mount hill Falkland Is 144 E8
Ushakova, Ostrov i. Rus. Fed. 64 I1
Ushant i. France see Ouessant, Île d'
Üsharal Kazakh. see Ucharal
Ush-Bel'dyr Rus. Fed. 72 H2
Ushtobe Kazakh. 80 E2
Ush-Tyube Kazakh. see Ushtobe
Ushuaia Arg. 144 C8
Ushumun Rus. Fed. 74 B1
Usingen Germany 53 I4
Usinsk Rus. Fed. 41 R2
Usk U.K. 49 E7
Usk r. U.K. 49 E7
Uskhodni Belarus 45 O10
Uskoplje Bos.-Herz. see Gornji Vakuf
Üsküdar Turkey 59 M4
Uslar Germany 53 J3
Usman' Rus. Fed. 43 H5
Usmanabad India see Osmanabad
Usmas ezers l. Latvia 45 M8
Usogorsk Rus. Fed. 42 K3
Usol'ye-Sibirskoye Rus. Fed. 72 I2
Uspenovka Rus. Fed. 74 B1
Ussel France 56 F4
Ussuri r. China/Rus. Fed. 74 D2
Ussuriysk Rus. Fed. 74 C4
Ust'-Abakanskoye Rus. Fed. see Abakan
Usta Muhammad Pak. 89 H4
Ust'-Balyk Rus. Fed. see Nefteyugansk
Ust'-Donetskiy Rus. Fed. 43 I7
Ust'-Dzheguta Rus. Fed. 91 F1
Ust'-Dzhegutinskaya Rus. Fed. see Ust'-Dzheguta
Ustica, Isola di i. Sicily Italy 58 E5
Ust'-Ilimsk Rus. Fed. 65 L4
Ust'-Ilimskiy Vodokhranilishche resr Rus. Fed. 65 L4
Ust'-Ilych Rus. Fed. 41 R3
Ústí nad Labem Czech Rep. 47 O5
Ustinov Rus. Fed. see Izhevsk
Üstirt plat. Kazakh./Uzbek. see Ustyurt Plateau
Ustka Poland 47 P3
Ust'-Kamchatsk Rus. Fed. 65 R4
Ust'-Kamenogorsk Kazakh. 80 F2
Ust'-Kan Rus. Fed. 80 F1
Ust'-Koksa Rus. Fed. 80 G1
Ust'-Kulom Rus. Fed. 42 L3
Ust'-Kut Rus. Fed. 65 L4
Ust'-Kuyga Rus. Fed. 65 O2
Ust'-Labinsk Rus. Fed. 91 E1
Ust'-Labinskaya Rus. Fed. see Ust'-Labinsk
Ust'-Lyzha Rus. Fed. 42 M2
Ust'-Maya Rus. Fed. 65 O3
Ust'-Nera Rus. Fed. 65 P3
Ust'-Ocheya Rus. Fed. 42 K3
Ust'-Olenek Rus. Fed. 65 M2
Ust'-Omchug Rus. Fed. 65 P3
Ust'-Ordynskiy Rus. Fed. 72 I2
Ust'-Penzhino Rus. Fed. see Kamenskoye
Ust'-Port Rus. Fed. 64 J3
Ustrem Rus. Fed. 41 T3
Ust'-Tsil'ma Rus. Fed. 42 L2
Ust'-Uda Rus. Fed. 72 I2
Ust'-Umalta Rus. Fed. 74 D2
Ust'-Undurga Rus. Fed. 73 L2
Ust'-Ura Rus. Fed. 42 J3
Ust'-Urgal Rus. Fed. 74 D2
Ust'-Usa Rus. Fed. 42 M2
Ust'-Vayen'ga Rus. Fed. 42 I3
Ust'-Voya Rus. Fed. 41 R3
Ust'-Vyyskaya Rus. Fed. 42 J3
Ust'ya r. Rus. Fed. 42 I3
Ust'ye Rus. Fed. 42 H4
Ustyurt, Plato plat. Kazakh./Uzbek. see Ustyurt Plateau
Ustyurt Plateau Kazakh./Uzbek. 78 E2
Ustyurt Platosi plat. Kazakh./Uzbek. see Ustyurt Plateau
Ustyuzhna Rus. Fed. 42 H4
Usulután El Salvador 136 G6
Usumbura Burundi see Bujumbura
Usvyaty Rus. Fed. 42 F5
Utah state U.S.A. 126 F5
Utah Lake U.S.A. 129 H1
Utajärvi Fin. 44 O4
Utashinai Rus. Fed. see Yuzhno-Kuril'sk
'Utaybah, Buḥayrat al imp. l. Syria 85 C3
Utena Lith. 45 N9
Uterlai India 82 B4
Uthai Thani Thai. 70 C4
Uthal Pak. 89 G5
'Uthmānīyah Syria 85 C2
Utiariti Brazil 143 G6
Utica NY U.S.A. 135 H2
Utica OH U.S.A. 134 D3
Utiel Spain 57 F4
Utikuma Lake Canada 120 H4
Utlwanang S. Africa 101 G4
Utrecht Neth. 52 F2
Utrecht S. Africa 101 J4
Utrera Spain 57 D5
Utsjoki Fin. 44 O2
Utsunomiya Japan 75 E5
Utta Rus. Fed. 43 J7
Uttaradit Thai. 70 C3
Uttarakhand state India see Uttaranchal
Uttaranchal state India 82 D3
Uttar Kashi India see Uttarkashi
Uttarkashi India 82 D3
Uttar Pradesh state India 82 D4
Uttoxeter U.K. 49 F6
Uttranchal state India see Uttaranchal
Utubulak China 80 G2
Utupua i. Solomon Is 107 G3
Uummannaq Greenland see Dundas
Uummannaq Fjord inlet Greenland 153 J2
Uummannarsuaq c. Greenland see Farewell, Cape
Uurainen Fin. 44 N5
Uusikaarlepyy Fin. see Nykarleby
Uusikaupunki Fin. 45 L6
Uutapi Namibia 99 B5
Uva Rus. Fed. 42 L4
Uvalde U.S.A. 131 D6
Uval Karabaur hills Kazakh./Uzbek. 91 I2
Uval Muzbel' hills Kazakh. 91 I2
Uvarovo Rus. Fed. 43 I6
Uvéa atoll New Caledonia see Ouvéa
Uvinza Tanz. 99 D4
Uvs Nuur salt l. Mongolia 80 H1
Uwajima Japan 75 D6
'Uwayrid, Ḥarrat al lava field Saudi Arabia 86 E4
Uwaysiţ well Saudi Arabia 85 D4
Uweinat, Jebel mt. Sudan 86 C5
Uwi i. Indon. 71 D7
Uxbridge Canada 134 F1
Uxbridge U.K. 49 G7
Uxin Qi China see Dabqig
Uyaly Kazakh. 80 B3
Uyar Rus. Fed. 72 G1
Üydzin Mongolia 72 J4
Uyo Nigeria 96 D4
Uyu Chaung r. Myanmar 70 A1
Uyuni Bol. 142 E8
Uyuni, Salar de salt flat Bol. 138 E8
Uza r. Rus. Fed. 43 J5
▶Uzbekistan country Asia 80 B3
Asia 6, 62–63
Üzbekiston country Asia see Uzbekistan
Uzbekskaya S.S.R. country Asia see Uzbekistan
Uzbek S.S.R. country Asia see Uzbekistan
Uzen' Kazakh. see Kyzylsay
Uzhgorod Ukr. see Uzhhorod
Uzhhorod Ukr. 43 D6
Užhorod Ukr. see Uzhhorod
Užice Serb. and Mont. 59 H3
Uzlovaya Rus. Fed. 43 H5
Üzümlü Turkey 59 M6
Uzun Uzbek. 89 H2
Uzunköprü Turkey 59 L4
Uzynkair Kazakh. 80 B3

V

Vaaf Atoll Maldives see Felidhu Atoll
Vaajakoski Fin. 44 N5
Vaal r. S. Africa 101 F5
Vaala Fin. 44 O4
Vaalbos National Park S. Africa 100 G5
Vaal Dam S. Africa 101 I4
Vaalwater S. Africa 101 I3
Vaasa Fin. 44 L5
Vaavu Atoll Maldives see Felidhu Atoll
Vabkent Uzbek. 89 G1
Vác Hungary 47 Q7
Vacaria Brazil 145 A5
Vacaria, Campo da plain Brazil 145 A5
Vacaville U.S.A. 128 C2
Vachon r. Canada 123 H1
Vad Rus. Fed. 42 J5
Vad r. Rus. Fed. 43 I5
Vada India 84 B2
Vadla Norway 45 E7
Vadodara India 82 C5
Vadsø Norway 44 P1

▶Vaduz Liechtenstein 56 I3
Capital of Liechtenstein.

Værøy i. Norway 44 H3
Vaga r. Rus. Fed. 42 I3
Vågåmo Norway 45 F6
Vaganski Vrh mt. Croatia 58 F2
Vágar i. Faroe Is 44 [inset]
Vägsele Sweden 44 K4
Vágur Faroe Is 44 [inset]
Váh r. Slovakia 47 Q7
Vähäkyrö Fin. 44 M5

▶Vaiaku Tuvalu 107 H2
Capital of Tuvalu, on Funafuti atoll.

Vaida Estonia 45 N7
Vaiden U.S.A. 131 F5
Vail U.S.A. 124 F4
Vailly-sur-Aisne France 52 D5
Vaitupu i. Tuvalu 107 H2
Vajrakarur India see Kanur
Vakhsh Tajik. 89 H2
Vakhsh r. Tajik. 89 H2
Vakhshstroy Tajik. see Vakhsh
Vakīlābād Iran 88 E4
Valbo Sweden 45 J6
Valcheta Arg. 144 C6
Valdai Hills Rus. Fed. see Valdayskaya Vozvyshennost'
Valday Rus. Fed. 42 G4
Valdayskaya Vozvyshennost' hills Rus. Fed. 42 G4
Valdecañas, Embalse de resr Spain 57 D4
Valdemārpils Latvia 45 M8
Valdemarsvik Sweden 45 J7
Valdepeñas Spain 57 E4
Val-de-Reuil France 52 B5

▶Valdés, Península pen. Arg. 144 D6
Lowest point in South America.
South America 138–139

Valdez U.S.A. 118 D3
Valdivia Chile 144 B5
Val-d'Or Canada 122 F4
Valdosta U.S.A. 133 D6
Valdres valley Norway 45 F6
Vale Georgia 91 F2
Vale U.S.A. 126 D3
Valemount Canada 120 G4
Valença Brazil 145 D1
Valence France 56 G4
Valencia Spain 57 F4
València Spain see Valencia
Valencia reg. Spain 57 F4
Valencia Venez. 142 E1
Valencia, Golfo de g. Spain 57 G4
Valencia de Don Juan Spain 57 D2
Valencia Island Rep. of Ireland 51 B6
Valenciennes France 52 D4
Valensole, Plateau de France 56 H5
Valentia Spain see Valencia
Valentin Rus. Fed. 74 D4
Valentine U.S.A. 130 C3
Våler Norway 45 G6
Valera Venez. 142 D2
Vale Verde Brazil 145 D2
Val Grande, Parco Nazionale della nat. park Italy 58 C1
Valjevo Serb. and Mont. 59 H2
Valka Latvia 45 O8
Valkeakoski Fin. 45 N6
Valkenswaard Neth. 52 F3
Valky Ukr. 43 G6
Valkyrie Dome ice feature Antarctica 152 D1
Valladolid Mex. 136 G4
Valladolid Spain 57 D3
Vallard, Lac l. Canada 123 H3
Vall de Uxó Spain 57 F4
Valle Norway 45 E7
Vallecillos Mex. 131 D7
Vallecito Reservoir U.S.A. 129 J3
Valle de la Pascua Venez. 142 E2
Valledupar Col. 142 D1
Vallée-Jonction Canada 123 H5
Valle Fértil, Sierra de mts Arg. 144 C4
Valle Grande Bol. 142 F7
Valle Hermoso Mex. 131 D7
Vallejo U.S.A. 128 B2
Vallenar Chile 144 B3

▶Valletta Malta 58 F7
Capital of Malta.

Valley r. Canada 121 L5
Valley U.K. 48 C5
Valley City U.S.A. 130 D2
Valleyview Canada 120 G4
Valls Spain 57 G3
Val Marie Canada 121 J5
Valmiera Latvia 45 N8
Valmy U.S.A. 128 E1
Valnera mt. Spain 57 E2
Valognes France 49 F9
Valona Albania see Vlorë
Valozhyn Belarus 45 O9
Val-Paradis Canada 122 F4
Valparai India 84 C4
Valparaíso Chile 144 B4
Valparaiso U.S.A. 134 B3
Valpoi India 84 B3
Valréas France 56 G4
Vals, Tanjung c. Indon. 69 J8
Valsad India 84 B1
Valspan S. Africa 100 G4
Val'tevo Rus. Fed. 42 J2
Valtimo Fin. 44 P5
Valuyevka Rus. Fed. 43 I7
Valuyki Rus. Fed. 43 H6
Vammala Fin. 45 M6
Van Turkey 91 F3
Van, Lake salt l. Turkey 91 F3
Vanadzor Armenia 91 G2
Van Buren AR U.S.A. 131 E5
Van Buren MO U.S.A. 131 F4
Van Buren OH U.S.A. see Kettering
Vanceburg U.S.A. 134 D4
Vanch Tajik. see Vanj
Vancleve U.S.A. 134 D5
Vancouver Canada 120 F5
Vancouver U.S.A. 126 C3
Vancouver, Mount Canada/U.S.A. 120 B2
Vancouver Island Canada 120 E5
Vanda Fin. see Vantaa
Vandalia IL U.S.A. 130 F4
Vandalia OH U.S.A. 134 C4
Vandekerckhove Lake Canada 121 K3
Vanderbijlpark S. Africa 101 H4
Vanderbilt U.S.A. 134 C1
Vandergrift U.S.A. 134 F3
Vanderhoof Canada 120 E4
Vanderkloof Dam resr S. Africa 100 G6
Vanderlin Island Australia 110 B2
Vanderwagen U.S.A. 129 I4
Van Diemen, Cape N.T. Australia 108 E2
Van Diemen, Cape Qld Australia 110 B3
Van Diemen Gulf Australia 108 F2
Van Diemen's Land state Australia see Tasmania
Vändra Estonia 45 N7
Väner, Lake Sweden see Vänern

▶Vänern l. Sweden 45 H7
4th largest lake in Europe.

Vänersborg Sweden 45 H7
Vangaindrano Madag. 99 E6
Van Gölü salt l. Turkey see Van, Lake
Van Horn U.S.A. 127 G7
Vanikoro Islands Solomon Is 107 G3
Vanimo P.N.G. 69 K7
Vanino Rus. Fed. 74 F2
Vanivilasa Sagara resr India 84 C3
Vaniyambadi India 84 C3
Vanj Tajik. 89 H2
Vanna i. Norway 44 K1
Vännäs Sweden 44 K5
Vannes France 56 C3
Vannes, Lac l. Canada 123 I3
Vannovka Kazakh. see Turar Ryskulov
Van Rees, Pegunungan mts Indon. 69 J7
Vanrhynsdorp S. Africa 100 D6
Vansant U.S.A. 134 D5
Vansbro Sweden 45 I6
Vansittart Island Canada 119 J3
Van Starkenborgh Kanaal canal Neth. 52 G1
Vantaa Fin. 45 N6
Van Truer Tableland reg. Australia 109 C6
Vanua Lava i. Vanuatu 107 G3
Vanua Levu i. Fiji 107 H3
▶Vanuatu country S. Pacific Ocean 107 G3
Oceania 8, 104–105
Van Wert U.S.A. 134 C3
Vanwyksvlei S. Africa 100 E6
Vanwyksvlei l. S. Africa 100 E6
Vân Yên Vietnam 70 D2
Van Zylsrus S. Africa 100 F4
Varadero Cuba 133 D8
Varahi India 82 B5
Varakļāni Latvia 45 O8
Varalé Côte d'Ivoire 96 C4
Varāmīn Iran 88 C3
Varanasi India 83 E4
Varandey Rus. Fed. 42 M1
Varangerfjorden sea chan. Norway 44 P1
Varanger Halvøya pen. Norway 41 L1
Varangerhalvøya pen. Norway 44 P1
Varaždin Croatia 58 G1
Varberg Sweden 45 H8
Vardar r. Macedonia 59 J4
Varde Denmark 45 F9
Vardenis Armenia 91 G2
Vardø Norway 44 Q1
Varel Germany 53 I1
Varėna Lith. 45 N9
Varese Italy 58 C2
Varfolomeyevka Rus. Fed. 74 D3
Vårgårda Sweden 45 H7
Varginha Brazil 145 B3
Varik Neth. 52 F3
Varillas Chile 144 B2
Varkana Iran see Gorgān
Varkaus Fin. 44 O5
Varna Bulg. 59 L3
Värnamo Sweden 45 I8
Värnäs Sweden 45 H6
Varnavino Rus. Fed. 42 J4
Várnjárg pen. Norway see Varangerhalvøya
Varpaisjärvi Fin. 44 O5
Várpalota Hungary 58 H1
Varsaj Afgh. 89 H2
Varsh, Ozero l. Rus. Fed. 42 J2
Varto Turkey 91 F3
Várzea da Palma Brazil 145 B2
Vasa Fin. see Vaasa
Vasai India 84 B2
Vashka r. Rus. Fed. 42 J2
Vasht Iran see Khāsh
Vasilkov Ukr. see Vasyl'kiv
Vasknarva Estonia 45 O7
Vaslui Romania 59 L1
Vassar U.S.A. 134 D2
Vas-Soproni-síkság hills Hungary 58 G1
Vastan Turkey see Gevaş
Västerås Sweden 45 J7
Västerdalälven r. Sweden 45 I6
Västerfjäll Sweden 44 J3
Västerhaninge Sweden 45 K7
Västervik Sweden 45 J8
Vasto Italy 58 F3
Vasyl'kiv Ukr. 43 F6
Vatan France 56 E3
Vaté i. Vanuatu see Éfaté
Vatersay i. U.K. 50 B4
Vathar India 84 B2
Vathí Greece see Vathy
Vathy Greece 59 L6

▶Vatican City Europe 58 E4
Independent papal state, the smallest country in the world.
Europe 5, 38–39

Vaticano, Città del Europe see Vatican City
Vatnajökull ice cap Iceland 40 [inset]
Vatoa i. Fiji 107 I3
Vatra Dornei Romania 59 K1
Vätter, Lake Sweden see Vättern
Vättern l. Sweden 45 I7
Vaughn U.S.A. 127 G6
Vaupés r. Col. 142 E3
Vauquelin r. Canada 122 F3
Vauvert France 56 G5
Vauxhall Canada 121 H5
Vavatenina Madag. 99 E5
Vava'u Group is Tonga 107 I3
Vavitao i. Fr. Polynesia see Raivavae
Vavoua Côte d'Ivoire 96 C4
Vavozh Rus. Fed. 42 K4
Vavuniya Sri Lanka 84 D4
Vawkavysk Belarus 45 N10
Växjö Sweden 45 I8
Vây, Đao i. Vietnam 71 C5
Vayenga Rus. Fed. see Severomorsk
Vazante Brazil 145 B2
Vazáš Sweden see Vittangi
Veaikevárri Sweden see Svappavaara
Veal Vêng Cambodia 71 C4

235

Wittlich Germany 52 G5
Wittmund Germany 53 H1
Wittstock Germany 53 M1
Witu Islands P.N.G. 69 L7
Witvlei Namibia 100 D2
Witzenhausen Germany 53 J3
Wivenhoe, Lake Australia 112 F1
Władysławowo Poland 47 Q3
Włocławek Poland 47 Q4
Wobkent Uzbek. see Vabkent
Wodonga Australia 112 C6
Wœrth France 53 H6
Wohlthat Mountains Antarctica 152 C2
Woippy France 52 G5
Wōjjā atoll Marshall Is see Wotje
Wokam i. Indon. 69 I8
Woken He r. China 74 C3
Wokha India 83 H4
Woking U.K. 49 G7
Wokingham watercourse Australia 110 C4
Wokingham U.K. 49 G7
Woko National Park Australia 112 E3
Wolcott IN U.S.A. 134 B3
Wolcott NY U.S.A. 135 G2
Woldegk Germany 53 N1
Wolea atoll Micronesia see Woleai
Woleai atoll Micronesia 69 K5
Wolf r. Canada 120 C2
Wolf r. TN U.S.A. 131 F5
Wolf r. WI U.S.A. 130 F2
Wolf Creek MT U.S.A. 126 E3
Wolf Creek OR U.S.A. 126 C4
Wolf Creek Pass U.S.A. 127 G5
Wolfen Germany 53 M3
Wolfenbüttel Germany 53 K2
Wolfhagen Germany 53 J3
Wolf Lake Canada 120 D2
Wolf Point U.S.A. 126 G2
Wolfsberg Austria 47 O7
Wolfsburg Germany 53 K2
Wolfstein Germany 53 H5
Wolfville Canada 123 I5
Wolgast Germany 47 N3
Wolin Poland 47 O4
Wollaston Lake Canada 121 K3
Wollaston Lake l. Canada 121 K3
Wollaston Peninsula Canada 118 G3
Wollemi National Park Australia 112 E4
Wollongong Australia 112 E5
Wolmaransstad S. Africa 101 G4
Wolmirstedt Germany 53 L2
Wolong Reserve nature res. China 76 D2
Wolseley Australia 111 C8
Wolseley S. Africa 100 D7
Wolsey U.S.A. 130 D2
Wolsingham U.K. 48 F4
Wolvega Neth. 52 G2
Wolvega Neth. see Wolvega
Wolverhampton U.K. 49 E6
Wolverine U.S.A. 134 C1
Wommelgem Belgium 52 E3
Womrather Höhe hill Germany 53 H5
Wonarah Australia 110 B3
Wondai Australia 111 E5
Wongalarroo Lake salt l. Australia 112 B3
Wongarbon Australia 112 D4
Wong Chuk Hang Hong Kong China 77 [inset]
Wong Leng hill Hong Kong China 77 [inset]
Wong Wan Chau Hong Kong China see Double Island
Wŏnju S. Korea 75 B5
Wonowon Canada 120 F3
Wŏnsan N. Korea 75 B5
Wonthaggi Australia 112 B7
Wonyulgunna, Mount hill Australia 109 B6
Woocalla Australia 111 B6
Wood, Mount Canada 120 A2
Woodbine GA U.S.A. 133 D6
Woodbine NJ U.S.A. 135 H4
Woodbridge U.K. 49 I6
Woodbridge U.S.A. 135 G4
Wood Buffalo National Park Canada 120 H3
Woodburn U.S.A. 126 C3
Woodbury NJ U.S.A. 135 H4
Woodbury TN U.S.A. 131 G5
Wooded Bluff hd Australia 112 F2
Wood Lake Canada 121 K4
Woodlake U.S.A. 128 D3
Woodland CA U.S.A. 128 C2
Woodland PA U.S.A. 135 F3
Woodland WA U.S.A. 126 C3
Woodlands Sing. 71 [inset]
Woodlark Island P.N.G. 106 F2
Woodridge Canada 121 L5
Woodroffe watercourse Australia 110 B4
Woodroffe, Mount Australia 109 E6
Woodruff UT U.S.A. 126 F4
Woodruff WI U.S.A. 130 F2
Woods, Lake salt flat Australia 108 F4
Woods, Lake of the Canada/U.S.A. 125 I2
Woodsfield U.S.A. 134 E4
Woodside Australia 112 C7
Woodstock N.B. Canada 123 I5
Woodstock Ont. Canada 134 E2
Woodstock IL U.S.A. 130 F3
Woodstock VA U.S.A. 135 F4
Woodstock VT U.S.A. 135 I2
Woodsville U.S.A. 135 I1
Woodville Canada 135 F1
Woodville MS U.S.A. 131 F6
Woodville OH U.S.A. 134 D3
Woodville TX U.S.A. 131 E6
Woodward U.S.A. 131 D4
Woody U.S.A. 128 D4
Wooler U.K. 48 E3
Woolgoolga Australia 112 F3
Wooli Australia 112 F2
Woollard, Mount Antarctica 152 K1
Woollett, Lac l. Canada 122 G4
Woolyeenyer Hill hill Australia 109 C8
Woomera Australia 111 B6
Woomera Prohibited Area Australia 109 F7
Woonsocket RI U.S.A. 135 J2
Woonsocket SD U.S.A. 130 D2
Woorabinda Australia 110 E5
Wooramel r. Australia 109 A6
Wooster U.S.A. 134 E3
Worbis Germany 53 K3
Worbody Point Australia 110 C2
Worcester S. Africa 100 D7
Worcester U.K. 49 E6
Worcester MA U.S.A. 135 J2
Worcester NY U.S.A. 135 H2
Wörgl Austria 47 N7
Workai i. Indon. 69 I8
Workington U.K. 48 D4
Worksop U.K. 48 F5
Workum Neth. 52 F2
Worland U.S.A. 126 G3
Wörlitz Germany 53 M3
Wormerveer Neth. 52 E2
Worms Germany 53 I5
Worms Head hd U.K. 49 C7
Wortel Namibia 100 C2
Wörth am Rhein Germany 53 I5
Worthing U.K. 49 G8
Worthington IN U.S.A. 134 B4
Worthington MN U.S.A. 130 E3
Wotje atoll Marshall Is 150 H5
Wotu Indon. 69 G7
Woudrichem Neth. 52 E3
Woustviller France 52 H5
Wowoni i. Indon. 69 G7
Wozrojdeniye Oroli i. Uzbek. see Vozrozhdeniya, Ostrov
Wrangel Island Rus. Fed. 65 T2
Wrangell Island U.S.A. 120 C3
Wrangell Mountains U.S.A. 153 B3
Wrangell-St Elias National Park and Preserve U.S.A. 120 A2
Wrath, Cape U.K. 50 D2
Wray U.S.A. 130 C3
Wreake r. U.K. 49 F6
Wreck Point S. Africa 100 C5
Wreck Reef Australia 110 F4
Wrecsam U.K. see Wrexham
Wrestedt Germany 53 K2
Wrexham U.K. 49 E5
Wrightmyo India 71 A5
Wrightson, Mount U.S.A. 127 F7
Wrightwood U.S.A. 128 E4
Wrigley Canada 120 F2
Wrigley U.S.A. 134 D4
Wrigley Gulf Antarctica 152 J2
Wrocław Poland 47 P5
Września Poland 47 P4
Wu'an China see Changtai
Wubin Australia 109 B7
Wuchang Heilong. China 74 B3
Wuchang Hubei China see Jiangxia
Wuchow China see Wuzhou
Wuchuan Guangdong China see Meilu
Wuchuan Guizhou China 76 E2
Wudalianchi China 74 B2
Wudām 'Alwā Oman 88 E6
Wudang Shan mt. China 77 F1
Wudaoliang China 76 B1
Wuding China 76 D3
Wudinna Australia 109 F8
Wudu China 76 E1
Wufeng Hubei China 77 F2
Wufeng Yunnan China see Zhenxiong
Wugang China 77 F3
Wuhai China 72 J5
Wuhan China 77 G2
Wuhe China 77 H1
Wuhu China 77 H2
Wuhua China 77 G4
Wuhubei China 77 H2
Wūjang China 82 D2
Wu Jiang r. China 76 E2
Wujin Jiangsu China see Changzhou
Wujin Sichuan China see Xinjin
Wukari Nigeria 96 D4
Wulang China 76 B2
Wuli China 76 B1
Wulian Feng mts China 76 D2
Wuliang Shan mts China 76 D3
Wuliaru i. Indon. 108 E1
Wuli Jiang r. China 77 F4
Wuling Shan mts China 77 F2
Wulong China 76 E2
Wulongji China see Huaibin
Wulur Indon. 108 E1
Wumeng Shan mts China 76 D3
Wuming China 77 F4
Wümme r. Germany 53 I1
Wundwin Myanmar 70 B2
Wungda China 76 D2
Wuning China 77 G2
Wünnenberg Germany 53 I3
Wunnummin Lake Canada 119 J4
Wunsiedel Germany 53 M4
Wunstorf Germany 53 J2
Wupatki National Monument nat. park U.S.A. 129 H4
Wuping China 77 H3
Wuppertal Germany 53 H3
Wuppertal S. Africa 100 D7
Wuqi China 73 J5
Wuqia China 80 D4
Wuquan China see Wuyang
Wuranga Australia 109 B7
Wurno Nigeria 96 D3
Würzburg Germany 53 J5
Wurzen Germany 53 M3
Wushan Chongqing China 77 F2
Wushan Gansu China 76 E1
Wu Shan mts China 77 F2
Wushi Guangdong China 77 F4
Wushi Xinjiang China 80 E3
Wüstegarten hill Germany 53 J3
Wusuli Jiang r. China/Rus. Fed. see Ussuri
Wuvulu Island P.N.G. 69 K7
Wuwei China 72 I5
Wuxi Chongqing China 77 F2
Wuxi Hunan China see Luxi
Wuxi Hunan China see Qiyang
Wuxi Jiangsu China 77 I2
Wuxia China see Wushan
Wuxian China see Suzhou
Wuxing China see Huzhou
Wuxu China 77 F4
Wuxuan China 77 F4
Wuxue China 77 G2
Wuyang Guizhou China see Zhenyuan
Wuyang Henan China 77 G1
Wuyang Zhejiang China see Wuyi
Wuyi China 77 H2
Wuyiling China 74 C2
Wuyi Shan mts China 77 H3
Wuyuan Jiangxi China 77 H2
Wuyuan Nei Mongol China 73 J4
Wuyuan Zhejiang China see Haiyan
Wuyun China see Jinyun
Wuzhi Shan mts China 77 F5
Wuzhong China 72 J5
Wuzhou China 77 F4
Wyalkatchem Australia 109 B7
Wyalong Australia 112 C4
Wyandra Australia 112 B1
Wyangala Reservoir Australia 112 D4
Wyara, Lake salt flat Australia 112 B2
Wycheproof Australia 112 A6
Wylliesburg U.S.A. 135 F5
Wyloo Australia 108 B5
Wylye r. U.K. 49 F7
Wymondham U.K. 49 I6
Wymore U.S.A. 130 D3
Wynbring Australia 109 F7
Wyndham Australia 108 E3
Wyndham-Werribee Australia 112 B6
Wynne U.S.A. 131 F5
Wynyard Canada 121 J5
Wyola Lake salt flat Australia 109 E7
Wyoming U.S.A. 134 C2
Wyoming state U.S.A. 126 G4
Wyoming Peak U.S.A. 126 F4
Wyoming Range mts U.S.A. 126 F4
Wyong Australia 112 E4
Wyperfeld National Park Australia 111 C7
Wysox U.S.A. 135 G3
Wyszków Poland 47 R4
Wythall U.K. 49 F6
Wytheville U.S.A. 134 E5
Wytmarsum Neth. see Witmarsum

X

Xaafuun Somalia 98 F2

▶Xaafuun, Raas pt Somalia 86 H7
Most easterly point of Africa.

Xabyaisamba China 76 C2
Xaçmaz Azer. 91 H2
Xago China 83 G3
Xagquka China 76 B2
Xaidulla China 82 D1
Xaignabouri Laos see Muang Xaignabouri
Xainza China 83 G3
Xai-Xai Moz. 101 K3
Xalapa Mex. see Jalapa
Xambioa Brazil 143 I5
Xam Nua Laos 70 D2
Xá-Muteba Angola 99 B4
Xan r. Laos 70 C3
Xanagas Botswana 100 E2
Xangda China see Nangqên
Xangdin Hural China 73 K4
Xangdoring China 83 E2
Xangongo Angola 99 B5
Xankändi Azer. 91 G3
Xanlar Azer. 91 G2
Xanthi Greece 59 K4
Xarag China 83 I1
Xarardheere Somalia 98 E3
Xátiva Spain 57 F4
Xavantes, Serra dos hills Brazil 143 I6
Xaxa China 83 F2
Xayar China 80 F3
Xela Guat. see Quetzaltenango
Xelva Spain see Chelva
Xenia U.S.A. 134 D4
Xero Potamos r. Cyprus see Xeros
Xeros r. Cyprus 85 A2
Xhora S. Africa see Elliotdale
Xiabole Shan mt. China 74 B2
Xiachuan Dao i. China 77 G4
Xiaguan China see Dali
Xiahe China 76 D1
Xiamen China 77 H3
Xi'an China 77 F1
Xianfeng China 77 F2
Xiangcheng Sichuan China 76 C2
Xiangcheng Yunnan China see Xiangyun
Xiangfan China 77 G1
Xiangfeng China see Laifeng
Xianggang Hong Kong China see Hong Kong
Xianggang Tebie Xingzhengqu aut. reg. China see Hong Kong
Xiangjiang China see Huichang
Xiangkhoang Laos 70 C3
Xiangkhoang Plateau Laos 70 C3
Xiangkou China see Wulong
Xiangning China 73 K5
Xiangquan He r. China see Langqên Zangbo
Xiangride China 83 I2
Xiangshan China see Menghai
Xiangshui China 77 H1
Xiangshuiba China 77 F3
Xiangtan China 77 G3
Xiangxiang China 77 G3
Xiangyang China see Xiangfan
Xiangyang Hu l. China 83 G2
Xiangyin China 77 G2
Xiangyun China 76 D3
Xianju China 77 I2
Xianning China 77 G2
Xiannümiao China see Jiangdu
Xianshui He r. China 76 D2
Xiantao China 77 G2
Xianxia Ling mts China 77 H3
Xianyang China 77 F1
Xiaocaohu China 80 G3
Xiaodong China 77 F4
Xiaodongliang China 76 C1
Xiao'ergou China 74 A2
Xiaogan China 77 G2
Xiaogang China see Dongxiang
Xiao Hinggan Ling mts China 74 B2
Xiaojin China 76 D2
Xiaonanchuan China 83 H2
Xiaosanjiang China 77 G3
Xiaoshan China 77 I2
Xiao Shan mts China 77 F1
Xiaoshi China see Benxi
Xiao Surmang China 76 C1
Xiaotao China 77 H3
Xiaoxi China see Pinghe
Xiaoxian China 77 H1
Xiaoxiang Ling mts China 76 D2
Xiaoxita China see Yichang
Xiapu China 77 I3
Xiaqiong China see Batang
Xiashan China see Zhanjiang
Xiayang China see Yanling
Xiayanjing China see Yanjing
Xiayingpan Guizhou China see Luzhi
Xiayingpan Guizhou China see Lupanshui
Xiayukou China 77 F1
Xiazhuang China see Linshu
Xibdê China 76 C2
Xibing China 77 H3
Xibu China see Dongshan
Xichang China 76 D3
Xichou China 76 E4
Xichuan China 77 F1
Xide China 76 D2
Xidu China see Hengyang
Xiemahe' China 77 F2
Xieng Khouang Laos see Xiangkhoang
Xieyang Dao i. China 77 F4
Xifeng Gansu China 76 E1
Xifeng Guizhou China 76 E3
Xifeng Liaoning China 74 B4
Xifengzhen China see Xifeng
Xigazê China 83 G3
Xihan Shui r. China 76 E1
Xi He r. China 76 E2
Xi Jiang r. China 77 G4
Xijir China 83 G2
Xijir Ulan Hu salt l. China 83 G2
Xiliao He r. China 74 A4
Xilin China 76 E3
Xilinhot China 73 L4
Ximiao China 80 J3
Xin'an Anhui China see Lai'an
Xin'an Guizhou China see Anlong
Xin'an Henan China 77 G1
Xin'anjiang China 77 H2
Xin'anjiang Shuiku resr China 77 H2
Xinavane Moz. 101 K3
Xin Barag Zuoqi China see Amgalang
Xincai China 77 G1
Xinchang Jiangxi China see Yifeng
Xinchang Zhejiang China 77 I2
Xincheng Fujian China see Gutian
Xincheng Guangdong China see Xinxing
Xincheng Guangxi China 77 F3
Xincheng Sichuan China see Zhaojue
Xincun China see Dongchuan
Xindi Guangxi China 77 F4
Xindi Hubei China see Honghu
Xindian China 74 B3
Xindu Guangxi China 77 F4
Xindu Sichuan China see Luhuo
Xindu Sichuan China 76 E2
Xinduqiao China 76 D2
Xinfeng Guangdong China 77 G3
Xinfeng Jiangxi China 77 G3
Xinfengjiang Shuiku resr China 77 G4
Xing'an Guangxi China 77 F3
Xingan China 77 G3
Xing'an Shaanxi China see Ankang
Xingba China see Lhünzê
Xingguo Gansu China see Qin'an
Xingguo Hubei China see Yangxin
Xingguo Jiangxi China 77 G3
Xinghai China 80 I4
Xinghua China 77 H1
Xinghua Wan b. China 77 H3
Xingkai China 74 D3
Xingkai Hu l. China/Rus. Fed. see Khanka, Lake
Xinglong China 74 B2
Xinglongzhen Gansu China 76 E1
Xinglongzhen Heilong. China 74 B3
Xingning Guangdong China 77 G3
Xingning Hunan China 77 G3
Xingou China 77 G2
Xingping China 77 F1
Xingqênggoin China 76 D2
Xingren China 76 E3
Xingsagoinba China 76 D1
Xingshan Guizhou China see Majiang
Xingshan Hubei China 77 F2
Xingtai China 73 K5
Xingu r. Brazil 143 H4
Xingu, Parque Indígena do res. Brazil 143 H6
Xinguara Brazil 143 H5
Xingye China 77 F4
Xingyi China 76 E3
Xinhua Guangdong China see Huadu
Xinhua Hunan China 77 F3
Xinhua Yunnan China see Qiaojia
Xinhua Yunnan China see Funing
Xinhuang China 77 F3
Xinhui China 77 G4
Xining China 72 I5
Xinjian China 77 G2
Xinjiang China 77 F1
Xinjiang aut. reg. China see Xinjiang Uygur Zizhiqu
Xinjiangkou China see Songzi
Xinjiang Uygur Zizhiqu aut. reg. China 82 E1
Xinjie Qinghai China 76 D1
Xinjie Yunnan China 76 C3
Xinjie Yunnan China 76 D4
Xinjin China 76 D2
Xinjing China see Jingxi
Xinkai He r. China 74 A4
Xinling China see Badong
Xinlitun China 74 B2
Xinlong China 76 D2
Xinmi China 77 G1
Xinning Gansu China see Ningxian
Xinning Hunan China 77 F3
Xinning Jiangxi China see Wuning
Xinning Sichuan China see Kaijiang
Xinping China 76 D3
Xinqiao China 77 G1
Xinqing China 74 C2
Xinquan China 77 H3
Xinshan China see Anyuan
Xinshiba China see Ganluo
Xinsi China 76 E1
Xintai China 73 L5
Xintanpu China 77 G2
Xintian China 77 G3
Xinxiang China 77 G1
Xinxing China 77 G4
Xinyang Henan China 77 G1
Xinyang Henan China see Pingqiao
Xinye China 77 G1
Xinyi Guangdong China 77 F4
Xinyi Jiangsu China 77 H1
Xinying China 77 F5
Xinying Taiwan see Hsinying
Xinyu China 77 G3
Xinyuan Qinghai China see Tianjun
Xinyuan Xinjiang China 80 F3
Xinzhangfang China 74 A2
Xinzhou Guangxi China see Longlin
Xinzhou Hubei China 77 G2
Xinzhou Shanxi China 73 K5
Xinzhu Taiwan see Hsinchu
Xinzo de Limia Spain 57 C2
Xiongshan China see Zhenghe
Xiongshi China see Guixi
Xiongzhou China see Nanxiong
Xiping Henan China 77 F1
Xiping Henan China 77 G1
Xiqing Shan mts China 76 D1
Xique Xique Brazil 143 J6
Xisa China see Xichou
Xisha Qundao is S. China Sea see Paracel Islands
Xishuangbanna reg. China 76 D4
Xishui Guizhou China 76 E2
Xishui Hubei China 77 G2
Xitianmu Shan mt. China 77 H2
Xiugu China see Jinxi
Xi Ujimqin Qi China see Bayan Ul Hot
Xiuning China 77 H2
Xiushan Chongqing China 77 F2
Xiushan Yunnan China see Tonghai
Xiushui China 77 G2
Xiuwen China 76 E3
Xiuwu China 77 G1
Xiuying China 77 F4
Xiwu China 76 C1
Xixabangma Feng mt. China 83 F3
Xixia China 77 F1
Xixiang China 76 E1
Xixiu China see Anshun
Xixón Spain see Gijón-Xixón
Xiyang Dao i. China 77 I3
Xiyang Jiang r. China 76 E3
Xizang aut. reg. China see Xizang Zizhiqu
Xizang Gaoyuan plat. China see Plateau of Tibet
Xizang Zizhiqu aut. reg. China 83 G3
Xom An Lôc Vietnam 71 D5
Xom Duc Hanh Vietnam 71 D5
Xorkol China 80 H4
Xuancheng China 77 H2
Xuan'en China 77 F2
Xuanhua China 73 L4
Xuân Lôc Vietnam 71 D5
Xuanwei China 76 E3
Xuanzhou China see Xuancheng
Xuchang China 77 G1
Xucheng China see Xuwen
Xuddur Somalia 98 E3
Xuefeng China see Mingxi
Xuefeng Shan mts China 77 F3
Xue Shan mts China 76 C3
Xugui China 80 I4
Xuguit Qi China see Yakeshi
Xujiang China see Guangchang
Xümatang China 76 C1
Xunde Qundao is Paracel Is see Amphitrite Group
Xungba China see Xangdoring
Xungmai China 83 G3
Xunhe China 74 C2
Xun He r. China 74 C2
Xun Jiang r. China 77 F4
Xunwu China 77 G3
Xunyi China 77 F1
Xuru Co salt l. China 83 F3
Xuwen China 68 E2
Xuyên Môc Vietnam 71 D5
Xuyi China 77 H1
Xuyong China 76 E2
Xuzhou China see Tongshan

Y

Ya'an China 76 D2
Yabanabat Turkey see Kızılcahamam
Yabēlo Eth. 98 D3
Yablonovyy Khrebet mts Rus. Fed. 73 J2
Yabrīn reg. Saudi Arabia 88 C6
Yabuli China 74 C3
Yacha China see Baisha
Yacheng China 77 F5
Yachi He r. China 76 E3
Yacuma r. Bol. 142 E6
Yadgir India 84 C2
Yadrin Rus. Fed. 42 J5
Yaeyama-rettō is Japan 73 M8
Yafa Israel see Tel Aviv-Yafo
Yagaba Ghana 96 C3
Yağda Turkey see Erdemli
Yaghan Basin sea feature S. Atlantic Ocean 148 D9
Yagman Turkm. 88 D2
Yagmo China 83 F3
Yagodnoye Rus. Fed. 65 P3
Yagodnyy Rus. Fed. 74 E2
Yagoua Cameroon 97 E3
Yagra China 83 E3
Yagradagzê Shan mt. China 76 B1
Yaguajay Cuba 133 E8
Yaha Thai. 71 C6
Yahk Canada 120 G5
Yahualica Mex. 136 D4
Yahyalı Turkey 85 L4
Yai Myanmar see Ye
Yai, Khao mt. Thai. 71 B4
Yaizu Japan 75 E6
Yajiang China 76 D2
Yakacık Turkey 85 C1
Yakeshi China 73 M3
Yakhab waterhole Iran 88 E3
Yakhehal Afgh. 89 G4
Yakima U.S.A. 126 C3
Yakima r. U.S.A. 126 D3
Yakmach Pak. 89 F4
Yako Burkina 96 C3
Yakovlevka Rus. Fed. 74 D3
Yaku-shima i. Japan 75 C7
Yakutat U.S.A. 120 B3
Yakutat Bay U.S.A. 120 A3
Yakutsk Rus. Fed. 65 N3
Yakymivka Ukr. 43 G7
Yala Thai. 71 C6
Yalai China 83 F3
Yala National Park Sri Lanka see Ruhuna National Park
Yalan Dünya Mağarası tourist site Turkey 85 A1
Yale Canada 120 F5
Yale U.S.A. 134 D2
Yalgoo Australia 109 B7
Yalleroi Australia 110 D5
Yaloké Cent. Afr. Rep. 98 B3
Yalova Turkey 59 M4
Yalta Ukr. 90 D1
Yalu Jiang r. China/N. Korea 74 B4
Yalujiang Kou r. mouth China/N. Korea 75 B5
Yalvaç Turkey 59 N5
Yamagata Japan 75 F5
Yamaguchi Japan 75 C6
Yamal, Poluostrov pen. Rus. Fed. see Yamal Peninsula
Yam Alin', Khrebet mts Rus. Fed. 74 D1
Yamal Peninsula Rus. Fed. 64 H2
Yamanie Falls National Park Australia 110 D3
Yamba Australia 112 F2
Yamba Lake Canada 121 I1
Yambarran Range hills Australia 108 E3
Yambi, Mesa de hills Col. 142 D3
Yambio Sudan 97 F4
Yambol Bulg. 59 L3
Yamdena i. Indon. 108 E1
Yamethin Myanmar 70 B2

▶Yamin, Puncak mt. Indon. 69 J7
4th highest mountain in Oceania.

Yamkanmardi India 84 B2
Yamkhad Syria see Aleppo
Yamm Rus. Fed. 45 P7
Yamma Yamma, Lake salt flat Australia 111 C5

▶Yamoussoukro Côte d'Ivoire 96 C4
Capital of Côte d'Ivoire.

Yampa r. U.S.A. 129 I1
Yampil' Ukr. 43 F6
Yampol' Ukr. see Yampil'
Yamuna r. India 82 E4
Yamunanagar India 82 D3
Yamzho Yumco l. China 83 G3
Yana r. Rus. Fed. 65 O2
Yanam India 84 D2
Yan'an China 73 J5
Yanaoca Peru 142 D6
Yanaon India see Yanam
Yanaul Rus. Fed. 41 Q4
Yanbu' al Baḩr Saudi Arabia 86 E5
Yanceyville U.S.A. 132 E4
Yancheng Henan China 77 G1
Yancheng Jiangsu China 77 I1
Yanchep Australia 109 A7
Yanco Australia 112 C5
Yanco Creek r. Australia 112 B5
Yanco Glen Australia 111 C6
Yanda watercourse Australia 112 B3
Yandama Creek watercourse Australia 111 C6
Yandao China see Yingjing
Yandoon Myanmar 70 A3
Yandun China 80 H3
Yanfolila Mali 96 C3
Ya'ngamdo China 76 B2
Yangbi China 76 C3
Yangcheng Guangdong China see Yangshan
Yangcheng Shanxi China 77 G1
Yangchuan China see Suiyang
Yangchun China 77 F4
Yangcun China 77 G4
Yangdok N. Korea 75 B5
Yang Hu l. China 83 F2
Yangikishlak Uzbek. 80 C3
Yangi-Nishan Uzbek. 89 G2
Yangi Qal'eh Afgh. 89 H2
Yangirabad Uzbek. 89 G1
Yangiyul' Uzbek. 80 C3
Yangjiajiang China 77 G2
Yangjiang China 77 F4
Yangming China see Heping
Yangôn Myanmar see Rangoon
Yangping China 77 F2
Yangquan China 73 K5
Yangshan China 77 G3
Yang Talat Thai. 70 C3
Yangtouyan China 76 D3

▶Yangtze r. China 76 E2
Longest river in Asia and 3rd in the world. Also known as Chang Jiang or Jinsha Jiang or Tongtian He or Yangtze Kiang or Zhi Qu.
Asia 60–61
World 12–13

Yangtze Kiang r. China see Yangtze
Yangudi Rassa National Park Eth. 98 E2
Yangweigang China 77 H1
Yangxi China 77 F4
Yangxian China 76 E1
Yangxin China 77 G2
Yangyang S. Korea 75 C5
Yangzhou Jiangsu China 77 H1
Yangzhou Shaanxi China see Yangxian
Yanhe China 77 F3
Yanhuqu China 83 E2
Yanishpole Rus. Fed. 42 G3
Yanis"yarvi, Ozero l. Rus. Fed. 44 Q5
Yanji China 74 C4
Yanjiang China see Ziyang
Yanjin Henan China 77 G1
Yanjin Yunnan China 76 E2
Yanjing Sichuan China see Yanyuan
Yanjing Xizang China 76 C2
Yanjing Yunnan China see Yanjin
Yankara National Park Nigeria 96 E4

Yankton U.S.A. 130 D3
Yanling Hunan China 77 G3
Yanling Sichuan China see Weiyuan
Yannina Greece see Ioannina
Yano-Indigirskaya Nizmennost' lowland Rus. Fed. 65 P2
Yanovski, Mount U.S.A. 120 C3
Yanrey r. Australia 109 A5
Yanshan Jiangxi China 77 H2
Yanshan Yunnan China 76 E4
Yanshi China 77 G1
Yanshiping China 76 B1
Yanskiy Zaliv g. Rus. Fed. 65 O2
Yantabulla Australia 112 B2
Yantai China 73 M5
Yanting China 76 E2
Yantongshan China 74 B4
Yantou China 77 I2
Yanwa China 76 C3
Yany-Kurgan Kazakh. see Zhanakorgan
Yanyuan China 76 D3
Yao Chad 97 E3
Yao'an China 76 D3
Yaodu China see Dongzhi
Yaoli China 77 H2

▶Yaoundé Cameroon 96 E4
Capital of Cameroon.

Yaoxian China 77 F1
Yaoxiaoling China 74 B2
Yao Yai, Ko i. Thai. 71 B6
Yap i. Micronesia 69 J5
Yapen i. Indon. 69 J7
Yappar r. Australia 110 C3
Yap Trench sea feature N. Pacific Ocean 150 F5
Yaqui r. Mex. 127 F8
Yar Rus. Fed. 42 L4
Yaradzha Turkm. see Yaradzhi
Yaradzhi Turkm. 88 E2
Yaraka Australia 110 D5
Yarangüme Turkey see Tavas
Yaransk Rus. Fed. 42 J4
Yardea Australia 111 A7
Yardımcı Burnu pt Turkey 59 N6
Yardımlı Azer. 91 H3
Yardymly Azer. see Yardımlı
Yare r. U.K. 49 I6
Yarega Rus. Fed. 42 L3

▶Yaren Nauru 107 G2
Capital of Nauru.

Yarensk Rus. Fed. 42 K3
Yariga-take mt. Japan 75 E5
Yarīm Yemen 86 F7
Yarımca Turkey see Körfez
Yarkand China see Shache
Yarkant China see Shache
Yarkant He r. China 80 E4
Yarker Canada 135 G1
Yarkhun r. Pak. 89 I2
Yarlung Zangbo r. China 76 B2 see Brahmaputra
Yarmouth Canada 123 I6
Yarmouth England U.K. 49 F8
Yarmouth England U.K. see Great Yarmouth
Yarmouth U.S.A. 135 J2
Yarmuk r. Asia 85 B3
Yarnell U.S.A. 129 G4
Yaroslavl' Rus. Fed. 42 H4
Yaroslavskiy Rus. Fed. 74 D3
Yarra r. Australia 112 B6
Yarra Junction Australia 112 B6
Yarram Australia 112 C7
Yarraman Australia 112 E1
Yarrawonga Australia 112 B6
Yarra Yarra Lakes salt flat Australia 109 A7
Yarronvale Australia 112 B1
Yarrowmere Australia 110 D4
Yartö Tra La pass China 83 H3
Yartsevo Krasnoyarskiy Kray Rus. Fed. 64 J3
Yartsevo Smolenskaya Oblast' Rus. Fed. 43 G5
Yarumal Col. 142 C2
Yarwa China 76 C2
Yarzhong China 76 C2
Yaş Romania see Iaşi
Yasawa Group is Fiji 107 H3
Yashilkŭl l. Tajik. 89 I2
Yashkul' Rus. Fed. 43 J7
Yasin Jammu and Kashmir 82 C1
Yasnogorsk Rus. Fed. 43 H5
Yasny Rus. Fed. 74 C1
Yasothon Thai. 70 D4
Yass Australia 112 D5
Yass r. Australia 112 D5
Yassı Burnu c. Cyprus see Plakoti, Cape
Yāsūj Iran 88 C4
Yasuní, Parque Nacional nat. park Ecuador 142 C4
Yatağan Turkey 59 M6
Yaté New Caledonia 107 G4
Yates r. Canada 120 H2
Yates Center U.S.A. 130 E4
Yathkyed Lake Canada 121 L2
Yatsushiro Japan 75 C6
Yaṭṭa West Bank 85 B4
Yatton U.K. 49 E7
Yauca Peru 142 D7
Yau Tong b. Hong Kong China 77 [inset]
Yavan Tajik. see Yovon
Yavari r. Brazil/Peru 142 E4
also known as Javari (Brazil/Peru)
Yávaros Mex. 127 F8
Yavatmal India 84 C1
Yavi Turkey 91 F3
Yaví, Cerro mt. Venez. 142 E2
Yavoriv Ukr. 43 D6
Yavuzlu Turkey 85 C1
Yawatongguzlangar China 83 E1
Yaw Chaung r. Myanmar 76 B4
Yaxian China see Sanya
Yay Myanmar see Ye
Yayladağı Turkey 85 C2
Yazd Iran 88 D4
Yazdān Iran 89 F3
Yazd-e Khvāst Iran 88 D4
Yazıhan Turkey 90 E3
Yazoo City U.S.A. 131 F5
Y Bala U.K. see Bala
Yding Skovhøj hill Denmark 47 L3
Ydra i. Greece 59 J6
Y Drenewydd U.K. see Newtown
Ye Myanmar 70 B4
Yea Australia 112 B6
Yealmpton U.K. 49 D8
Yebawmi Myanmar 70 A1
Yebbi-Bou Chad 97 E2
Yecheng China 80 E4
Yécora Mex. 127 F7
Yedashe Myanmar 70 B3
Yedatore India 84 C3
Yedi Burun Başı pt Turkey 59 M6
Yeeda River Australia 108 C4
Yefremov Rus. Fed. 43 H5
Yêgainnyin China see Henan
Yeghegnadzor Armenia 91 G3
Yegindykol' Kazakh. 80 C1
Yegorlykskaya Rus. Fed. 43 I7
Yegorova, Mys pt Rus. Fed. 74 E3
Yegor'yevsk Rus. Fed. 43 H5
Yei Sudan 97 G4
Yei r. Sudan 97 G4
Yeji China 77 G2
Yejiaji China see Yeji
Yekaterinburg Rus. Fed. 64 H4
Yekaterinodar Rus. Fed. see Krasnodar
Yekaterinoslav Ukr. see Dnipropetrovs'k
Yekaterinoslavka Rus. Fed. 74 C2
Yekhegnadzor Armenia see Yeghegnadzor
Ye Kyun i. Myanmar 70 A3
Yelabuga Khabarovskiy Kray Rus. Fed. 74 D2
Yelabuga Respublika Tatarstan Rus. Fed. 42 K5
Yelan' Rus. Fed. 43 I6
Yelan' r. Rus. Fed. 43 I6
Yelandur India 84 C3
Yelantsy Rus. Fed. 72 J2
Yelarbon Australia 112 E2
Yelbarsli Turkm. 89 F2
Yelenovskiye Kar'yery Ukr. see Dokuchayevs'k
Yelets Rus. Fed. 43 H5
Yélimané Mali 96 B3
Yelizavetgrad Ukr. see Kirovohrad
Yelkhovka Rus. Fed. 43 K5
Yell i. U.K. 50 [inset]
Yellabina Regional Reserve nature res. Australia 109 F7
Yellandu India 84 D2
Yellapur India 84 B3

▶Yellow r. China 77 G1
4th longest river in Asia.

Yellowhead Pass Canada 120 G4

▶Yellowknife Canada 120 H2
Capital of Northwest Territories.

Yellowknife r. Canada 120 H2
Yellow Mountain hill Australia 112 C4
Yellow Sea N. Pacific Ocean 73 N5
Yellowstone r. U.S.A. 130 C2
Yellowstone Lake U.S.A. 126 F3
Yellowstone National Park U.S.A. 126 F3
Yell Sound strait U.K. 50 [inset]
Yeloten Turkm. 89 F2
Yelovo Rus. Fed. 41 Q4
Yel'sk Belarus 43 F6
Yelva r. Rus. Fed. 42 K3
Yematan China 76 C1
▶Yemen country Asia 86 G6
Asia 6, 62–63
Yemetsk Rus. Fed. 42 I3
Yemişenbükü Turkey see Taşova
Yemmiganur India see Emmiganuru
Yemtsa Rus. Fed. 42 I3
Yemva Rus. Fed. 42 K3
Yena Rus. Fed. 44 Q3
Yenagoa Nigeria 96 D4
Yenakiyeve Ukr. 43 H6
Yenakiyevo Ukr. see Yenakiyeve
Yenangyat Myanmar 70 A2
Yenangyaung Myanmar 70 A2
Yenanma Myanmar 70 A3
Yenda Australia 112 C5
Yêndum China see Zhag'yab
Yengisar China 80 E4
Yengo National Park Australia 112 E4
Yenice Turkey 59 L5
Yenidamlar Turkey see Demirtaş
Yenihan Turkey see Yıldızeli
Yenije-i-Vardar Greece see Giannitsa
Yenişehir Greece see Larisa
Yenişehir Turkey 59 M4
Yenisey r. Rus. Fed. 64 J2

▶Yenisey-Angara-Selenga r. Rus. Fed. 64 J2
3rd longest river in Asia.

Yeniseysk Rus. Fed. 64 K4
Yeniseyskiy Kryazh ridge Rus. Fed. 64 K4
Yeniseyskiy Zaliv inlet Rus. Fed. 153 F2
Yeniyol Turkey see Borçka
Yên Minh Vietnam 70 D2
Yenotayevka Rus. Fed. 43 J7
Yeola India 84 B1
Yeo Lake salt flat Australia 109 D6
Yeotmal India see Yavatmal
Yeoval Australia 112 D4
Yeovil U.K. 49 E8
Yeo Yeo r. Australia see Bland
Yeppoon Australia 110 E4
Yeraliyev Kazakh. see Kuryk
Yerbent Turkm. 88 E2
Yerbogachen Rus. Fed. 65 L3
Yercaud India 84 C4

▶Yerevan Armenia 91 G2
Capital of Armenia.

Yereymentau Kazakh. 80 D1
Yergara India 84 C2
Yergeni hills Rus. Fed. 43 J7
Yergoğu Romania see Giurgiu
Yeriḥo West Bank see Jericho
Yerilla Australia 109 C7
Yerington U.S.A. 128 D2
Yerköy Turkey 90 D3
Yerla r. India 84 B2
Yermak Kazakh. see Aksu
Yermakovo Rus. Fed. 74 B1
Yermak Plateau sea feature Arctic Ocean 153 H1
Yermentau Kazakh. see Yereymentau
Yermo Mex. 131 B7
Yermo U.S.A. 128 E4
Yerofey Pavlovich Rus. Fed. 74 A1
Yeroham Israel 85 B4
Yerres r. France 52 C6
Yersa r. Rus. Fed. 42 L2
Yershov Rus. Fed. 43 K6
Yertsevo Rus. Fed. 42 I3
Yerupaja mt. Peru 142 C6
Yerushalayim Israel/West Bank see Jerusalem
Yeruslan r. Rus. Fed. 43 J6
Yesagyo Myanmar 70 A2
Yesan S. Korea 75 B5
Yesil' Kazakh. 78 F1
Yeşilhisar Turkey 90 D3
Yeşilırmak r. Turkey 90 E2
Yeşilova Burdur Turkey 59 M6
Yeşilova Yozgat Turkey see Sorgun
Yessentuki Rus. Fed. 91 F1
Yessey Rus. Fed. 65 L3
Yes Tor hill U.K. 49 C8
Yêtatang China see Baqên
Yetman Australia 112 E2
Yeu Myanmar 70 A2
Yeu, Île d' i. France 56 C3
Yevdokimovskoye Rus. Fed. see Krasnogvardeyskoye
Yevlakh Azer. see Yevlax
Yevlax Azer. 91 G2
Yevpatoriya Ukr. 90 D1
Yevreyskaya Avtonomnaya Oblast' admin. div. Rus. Fed. 74 D2
Yexian China see Laizhou
Yeyik China 83 E1
Yeysk Rus. Fed. 43 H7
Yeyungou China 80 G3
Yezhou China see Jianshi
Yezhuga r. Rus. Fed. 42 J2
Yezo i. Japan see Hokkaidō
Yezyaryshcha Belarus 42 F5
Y Fenni U.K. see Abergavenny
Y Fflint U.K. see Flint
Y Gelli Gandryll U.K. see Hay-on-Wye
Yialí i. Greece see Gyali
Yi'allaq, Gebel mt. Egypt see Yu'alliq, Jabal
Yialousa Cyprus see Aigialousa
Yi'an China 74 B3
Yianisádha i. Greece see Gianysada
Yiannitsá Greece see Giannitsa
Yibin Sichuan China 76 E2
Yibin Sichuan China 76 E2
Yibug Caka salt l. China 83 F2
Yichang Hubei China 77 F2
Yichang Hubei China 77 F2
Yicheng Henan China see Zhumadian
Yicheng Hubei China 77 G2
Yicheng Shanxi China 77 F1
Yichun Heilong. China 74 C3
Yichun Jiangxi China 77 G3
Yidu China see Zhicheng
Yidun China 76 C2
Yifeng China 77 G2
Yi He r. Henan China 77 G1
Yi He r. Shandong China 77 H1
Yihuang China 77 H3
Yijun China 77 F1
Yilaha China 74 B2
Yilan China 74 C3
Yilan Taiwan see Ilan
Yıldız Dağları mts Turkey 59 L4
Yıldızeli Turkey 90 E3
Yilehuli Shan mts China 74 A2
Yiliang China 76 E3
Yilong Heilong. China 74 B3
Yilong Sichuan China 76 E2
Yilong Yunnan China see Shiping
Yilong Hu l. China 76 D4
Yimianpo China 74 C3
Yinbaing Myanmar 70 B3
Yincheng China see Dexing
Yinchuan China 72 J5
Yindarlgooda, Lake salt flat Australia 109 C7
Yingcheng China 77 G2
Yingde China 77 G3
Yinggehai China 77 F5
Yinggen China see Qiongzhong
Ying He r. China 77 H1
Yingjing China 76 D2
Yingkou China 73 M4
Yingshan China 77 G2
Yingtan China 77 H2
Yining Jiangxi China see Xiushui
Yining Xinjiang China 80 F3
Yinjiang China 77 F3
Yinkeng China see Yinkengxu
Yinkengxu China 77 G3
Yinmabin Myanmar 70 A2
Yinnyein Myanmar 70 B3
Yin Shan mts China 73 J4
Yinxian China see Ningbo
Yipinglang China 76 D3
Yiquan China see Meitan
Yirga Alem Eth. 98 D3
Yirol Sudan 97 G4
Yisa China see Honghe
Yishan Guangxi China see Yizhou
Yishan Jiangsu China see Guanyun
Yishui China 73 L5
Yishun Sing. 71 [inset]
Yithion Greece see Gytheio
Yitiaoshan China see Jingtai
Yitong He r. China 74 B3
Yi Tu, Nam r. Myanmar 70 B2
Yitulihe China 74 A2
Yiwu China 76 D4
Yixing China 77 H2
Yiyang China 77 G2
Yizheng China 77 H1
Yizhou China 77 F3
Yizra'el country Asia see Israel
Yläne Fin. 45 M6
Ylihärmä Fin. 44 M5
Yli-Ii Fin. 44 N4
Yli-Kärppä Fin. 44 N4
Ylikiiminki Fin. 44 O4
Yli-Kitka l. Fin. 44 P3
Ylistaro Fin. 44 M5
Ylitornio Fin. 44 M3
Ylivieska Fin. 44 N4
Ylöjärvi Fin. 45 M6
Ymer Ø i. Greenland 119 P2
Ynys Enlli i. U.K. see Bardsey Island
Ynys Môn i. U.K. see Anglesey
Yoakum U.S.A. 131 D6
Yoder U.S.A. 134 C3
Yogan, Cerro mt. Chile 144 B8
Yogyakarta Indon. 68 E8
Yoho National Park Canada 120 G5
Yokadouma Cameroon 97 E4
Yokkaichi Japan 75 E6
Yoko Cameroon 96 E4
Yokohama Japan 75 E6
Yokosuka Japan 75 E6
Yokote Japan 75 F5
Yola Nigeria 96 E4
Yolo U.S.A. 128 C2
Yolombo Dem. Rep. Congo 98 C4
Yolöten Turkm. see Yeloten
Yoluk Mex. 133 C8
Yom, Mae Nam r. Thai. 70 C4
Yomou Guinea 96 C4
Yomuka Indon. 69 J8
Yonaguni-jima i. Japan 77 I3
Yŏnan N. Korea 75 B5
Yonezawa Japan 75 F5
Yong'an Chongqing China see Fengjie
Yong'an Fujian China 77 H3
Yongbei China see Yongsheng
Yongcong China 77 F3
Yongding Fujian China 77 H3
Yongding Yunnan China see Yongren
Yongding Yunnan China see Fumin
Yongfeng China 77 G3
Yongfu China 77 F3
Yŏnghŭng N. Korea 75 B5
Yŏnghŭng-man b. N. Korea 75 B5
Yŏngil-man b. S. Korea 75 C6
Yongjing Guizhou China see Xifeng
Yongjing Liaoning China see Xifeng
Yŏngju S. Korea 75 C5
Yongkang Yunnan China 76 C3
Yongkang Zhejiang China 77 I2
Yongle China see Zhen'an
Yongning Guangxi China 77 F4
Yongning Jiangxi China see Tonggu
Yongning Sichuan China see Xuyong
Yongping China 76 C3
Yongqing China see Qingshui
Yongren China 76 D3
Yongsheng China 76 D3
Yongshou China 77 F1
Yongshun China 77 F2
Yongtai China 77 H3
Yongxi China see Nayong
Yongxing Hunan China 77 G3
Yongxing Jiangxi China 77 G3
Yongxiu China 77 G2
Yongyang China see Weng'an
Yongzhou China 77 F3
Yonkers U.S.A. 135 I3
Yopal Col. 142 D2
Yopurga China 80 E4
Yordu Jammu and Kashmir 82 C2
York Australia 109 B7
York Canada 134 F2
York U.K. 48 F5
York AL U.S.A. 131 F5
York NE U.S.A. 130 D3
York PA U.S.A. 135 G4
York, Cape Australia 110 C1
York, Kap c. Greenland see Innaanganeq
York, Vale of valley U.K. 48 F4
Yorke Peninsula Australia 111 B7
Yorkshire Dales National Park U.K. 48 E4
Yorkshire Wolds hills U.K. 48 G5
Yorkton Canada 121 K5
Yorktown U.S.A. 135 G5
Yorkville U.S.A. 130 F3
Yorosso Mali 96 C3
Yosemite U.S.A. 134 C5
Yosemite National Park U.S.A. 128 D3
Yoshkar-Ola Rus. Fed. 42 J4
Yos Sudarso i. Indon. see Dolak, Pulau
Yŏsu S. Korea 75 B6
Yotvata Israel 85 B5
Youbou Canada 120 E5
Youghal Rep. of Ireland 51 E6
Young Australia 112 D5
Young U.S.A. 129 H4
Younghusband, Lake salt flat Australia 111 B6
Younghusband Peninsula Australia 111 B7
Young Island Antarctica 152 H2
Youngstown Canada 121 I5
Youngstown U.S.A. 134 E3
You Shui r. China 77 F2
Youssoufia Morocco 54 C5
Youvarou Mali 96 C3
Youxi China 77 H3
Youxian China 77 G3
Youyang China 77 F2
Youyi China 74 C3
Youyi Feng mt. China/Rus. Fed. 80 G2
Yovon Tajik. 89 H2
Yowah watercourse Australia 112 B2
Yozgat Turkey 90 D3
Ypres Belgium see Ieper
Yreka U.S.A. 126 C4
Yrghyz Kazakh. see Irgiz
Yr Wyddfa mt. U.K. see Snowdon
Yser r. France 52 C4
also known as IJzer (Belgium)
Ysselsteyn Neth. 52 F3
Ystad Sweden 45 H9
Ystwyth r. U.K. 49 C6
Ysyk-Köl Kyrg. see Balykchy

▶Ysyk-Köl salt l. Kyrg. 80 E3
5th largest lake in Asia.

Ythan r. U.K. 50 G3
Y Trallwng U.K. see Welshpool
Ytyk-Kyuyel' Rus. Fed. 65 O3
Yu'alliq, Jabal mt. Egypt 85 A4
Yuan'an China 77 F2
Yuanbao Shan mt. China 77 F3
Yuanjiang Hunan China 77 G2
Yuanjiang Yunnan China 76 D4
Yuan Jiang r. Hunan China 77 F2
Yuan Jiang r. Yunnan China 76 D4
Yuanjiazhuang China see Foping
Yuanlin China 74 A2
Yuanling China 77 F2
Yuanma China see Yuanmou
Yuanmou China 76 D3
Yuanquan China see Anxi
Yuanshan China see Lianping
Yuanyang China see Xinjie
Yub'ā i. Saudi Arabia 90 D6
Yuba City U.S.A. 128 C2
Yubei China 76 E2
Yuben' Tajik. 89 I2
Yucatán pen. Mex. 136 F5
Yucatan Channel Cuba/Mex. 137 G4
Yucca U.S.A. 129 F4
Yucca Lake U.S.A. 128 E3
Yucca Valley U.S.A. 128 E4
Yucheng Henan China 77 G1
Yucheng Sichuan China see Ya'an
Yuci China see Jinzhong
Yudi Shan mt. China 74 A1
Yudu China 77 G3
Yuelai China see Huachuan
Yueliang Pao l. China 74 A3
Yuendumu Australia 108 E5
Yuen Long Hong Kong China 77 [inset]
Yueqing China 77 I2
Yuexi China 77 H2
Yueyang Hunan China 77 G2
Yueyang Hunan China 77 G2
Yueyang Sichuan China see Anyue
Yug r. Rus. Fed. 42 J3
Yugan China 77 H2
Yugorsk Rus. Fed. 41 S3
Yugoslavia country Europe see Serbia and Montenegro
Yuhang China 77 I2
Yuhu China see Eryuan
Yuhuan China 77 I2
Yuin Australia 109 B6
Yu Jiang r. China 77 F4
Yukagirskoye Ploskogor'ye plat. Rus. Fed. 65 Q3
Yukamenskoye Rus. Fed. 42 L4
Yukarı Sakarya Ovaları plain Turkey 59 N5
Yukarısarıkaya Turkey 90 D3

▶Yukon r. Canada/U.S.A. 120 B2
5th longest river in North America.

Yukon Crossing Canada 120 B2
Yukon Territory admin. div. Canada 120 C2
Yüksekova Turkey 91 G3
Yulara Australia 109 E6
Yule r. Australia 108 B5
Yuleba Australia 112 D1
Yulee U.S.A. 133 D6
Yulin Guangxi China 77 F4
Yulin Shaanxi China 73 J5
Yulong Xueshan mt. China 76 D3
Yuma AZ U.S.A. 129 F5
Yuma CO U.S.A. 130 C3
Yuma Desert U.S.A. 129 F5
Yumen China 80 I4
Yumenguan China 80 H3
Yumurtalık Turkey 85 B1
Yuna Australia 109 A7
Yunak Turkey 90 C3
Yunan China 77 F4
Yunaska Island U.S.A. 118 A4
Yuncheng China 77 F1
Yundamindera Australia 109 C7
Yunfu China 77 G4
Yungas reg. Bol. 142 E7
Yungui Gaoyuan plat. China 76 D3
Yunhe Jiangsu China see Pizhou
Yunhe Yunnan China see Heqing
Yunhe Zhejiang China 77 H2
Yunjinghong China see Jinghong
Yunkai Dashan mts China 77 F4
Yünlin Taiwan see Touliu
Yunling China see Yunxiao
Yun Ling mts China 76 C3
Yunlong China 76 C3
Yunmeng China 77 G2
Yunmenling China see Junmenling
Yunnan prov. China 76 D3
Yunta Australia 111 B7
Yunt Dağı mt. Turkey 85 A1
Yunxi Hubei China 77 F1
Yunxi Sichuan China see Yanting
Yunxian Hubei China 77 F1
Yunxian Yunnan China 76 D3
Yunxiao China 77 H4
Yunyang Chongqing China 77 F2
Yunyang Henan China 77 G1
Yuping Guizhou China see Libo
Yuping Guizhou China 77 F3
Yuping Yunnan China see Pingbian
Yuqing China 76 E3
Yurayqir National Park Australia 112 F2
Yurba Co l. China 83 F2
Yürekli Turkey 85 B1
Yurga Rus. Fed. 64 J4
Yuriria Mex. 136 D4
Yurungkax He r. China 82 E1
Yur'ya Rus. Fed. 42 K4
Yur'yakha r. Rus. Fed. 42 L2
Yuryev Estonia see Tartu
Yur'yevets Rus. Fed. 42 I4
Yur'yev-Pol'skiy Rus. Fed. 42 H4
Yushan China 77 H2
Yü Shan mt. Taiwan 77 I4
Yushino Rus. Fed. 42 L1
Yushkozero Rus. Fed. 44 R4
Yushu Jilin China 74 B3
Yushu Qinghai China 76 C1
Yushuwan China see Huaihua
Yusufeli Turkey 91 F2
Yus'va Rus. Fed. 41 Q4
Yuta West Bank see Yaṭṭa
Yutai China 77 H1
Yutan China see Ningxiang
Yuxi Guizhou China see Daozhen
Yuxi Hubei China 77 F2
Yuxi Yunnan China 76 D3
Yuyangguan China 77 F2
Yuyao China 77 I2
Yuzawa Japan 75 F5
Yuzha Rus. Fed. 42 I4
Yuzhno-Kamyshovyy Khrebet ridge Rus. Fed. 74 F3
Yuzhno-Kuril'sk Rus. Fed. 74 G3
Yuzhno-Muyskiy Khrebet mts Rus. Fed. 73 K1
Yuzhno-Sakhalinsk Rus. Fed. 74 F3
Yuzhno-Sukhokumsk Rus. Fed. 91 G1
Yuzhnoukrayinsk Ukr. 43 F7
Yuzhnyy Rus. Fed. see Adyk
Yuzhou Chongqing China see Chongqing
Yuzhou Henan China 77 G1
Yuzovka Ukr. see Donets'k
Yverdon Switz. 56 H3
Yvetot France 56 E2
Ywamun Myanmar 70 A2

Z

Zaamin Uzbek. 89 H2
Zaandam Neth. 52 E2
Zab, Monts du mts Alg. 57 I6
Zabānābād Iran 88 E3
Zabaykal'sk Rus. Fed. 73 L3
Zabid Yemen 86 F7
Zābol Iran 89 F4
Zacapa Guat. 136 G5
Zacatecas Mex. 136 D4
Zacatecas state Mex. 131 C8
Zacharo Greece 59 I6
Zacoalco Mex. 136 D4
Zacynthus i. Greece see Zakynthos
Zadar Croatia 58 F2
Zadetkale Kyun i. Myanmar 71 B5
Zadetkyi Kyun i. Myanmar 71 B5
Zadi Myanmar 71 B4
Zadoi China 76 B1
Zadonsk Rus. Fed. 43 H5
Zadran reg. Afgh. 89 H3
Za'farâna Egypt see Za'farānah
Za'farānah Egypt 90 D5
Zafer Adaları is Cyprus see Kleides Islands
Zafer Burnu c. Cyprus see Apostolos Andreas, Cape
Zafora i. Greece 59 L6
Zafra Spain 57 C4
Zagazig Egypt see Az Zaqāzīq
Zaghdeh well Iran 88 E3
Zaghouan Tunisia 58 D6
Zagorsk Rus. Fed. see Sergiyev Posad

▶Zagreb Croatia 58 F2
Capital of Croatia.

Zagros, Kūhhā-ye mts Iran see Zagros Mountains
Zagros Mountains Iran 88 B3
Zagunao China see Lixian
Za'gya Zangbo r. China 83 G3
Zāhedān Iran 89 F4
Zaḥlah Lebanon see Zahlé
Zahlé Lebanon 85 B3
Zähmet Turkm. see Zakhmet
Ẓahrān Saudi Arabia 86 F6
Zahrez Chergui salt pan Alg. 57 H6
Zahrez Rharbi salt pan Alg. 57 H6
Zainlha China see Xiaojin
Zainsk Rus. Fed. see Novyy Zay
Zaire country Africa see Congo, Democratic Republic of
Zaïre r. Congo/Dem. Rep. Congo see Congo
Zaječar Serb. and Mont. 59 J3
Zaka Zimbabwe 99 D6
Zakamensk Rus. Fed. 80 J1
Zakataly Azer. see Zaqatala
Zakháro Greece see Zacharo
Zakhmet Turkm. 89 F2
Zākhō Iraq 91 F3
Zakhodnyaya Dzvina r. Europe see Zapadnaya Dvina
Zákinthos i. Greece see Zakynthos
Zakopane Poland 47 Q6
Zakouma, Parc National de nat. park Chad 97 E3
Zakwaski, Mount Canada 120 F5
Zakynthos Greece 59 I6
Zakynthos i. Greece 59 I6
Zala China 76 B2
Zalaegerszeg Hungary 58 G1
Zalai-domsag hills Hungary 58 G1
Zalamea de la Serena Spain 57 D4
Zalantun China 74 A3
Zalari Rus. Fed. 72 I2
Zalău Romania 59 J1
Zaleski U.S.A. 134 D4
Ẓalim Saudi Arabia 86 F5
Zalingei Sudan 97 F3
Ẓalmā, Jabal aẓ mt. Saudi Arabia 86 E4
Zama City Canada 120 G3
Zambeze r. Africa 99 C5 see Zambezi

▶Zambezi r. Africa 99 C5
4th longest river in the world. Also known as Zambeze.

Zambezi Zambia 99 C5
▶Zambia country Africa 99 C5
Africa 7, 54–95
Zamboanga Phil. 69 G5
Zamfara watercourse Nigeria 96 D3
Zamīndāvar reg. Afgh. 89 F4
Zamkog China see Zamtang
Zamora Ecuador 142 C4
Zamora Spain 57 D3
Zamora de Hidalgo Mex. 136 D5
Zamość Poland 43 D6
Zamost'ye Poland see Zamość
Zamtang China 76 D1
Zamuro, Sierra del mts Venez. 142 F3

Zanaga Congo 98 B4
Zancle Sicily Italy see Messina
Zandamela Moz. 101 L3
Zandvliet Belgium 52 E3
Zanesville U.S.A. 134 D4
Zangguy China 82 D1
Zangsêr Kangri mt. China 83 F2
Zangskar reg. Jammu and Kashmir see Zanskar
Zangskar Mountains India see Zanskar Mountains
Zanjān Iran 88 C2
Zanjān Rūd r. Iran 88 B2
Zannah, Jabal az hill U.A.E. 88 D5
Zanskar reg. Jammu and Kashmir 82 D2
Zanskar Mountains India 82 D2
Zante i. Greece see Zakynthos
Zanthus Australia 109 C7
Zanughān Iran 88 E3
Zanzibar Tanz. 99 D4
Zanzibar Island Tanz. 99 D4
Zaoshi Hubei China 77 G2
Zaoshi Hunan China 77 G3
Zaouatallaz Alg. 96 D2
Zaouet el Kahla Alg. see Bordj Omer Driss
Zaoyang China 77 G1
Zaoyangzhan China 77 G1
Zaozernyy Rus. Fed. 65 K4
Zaozhuang China 77 H1
Zapadnaya Dvina r. Europe 42 F5 also known as Dvina or Zakhodnyaya Dzvina. English form Western Dvina
Zapadnaya Dvina Rus. Fed. 42 G4
Zapadni Rodopi mts Bulg. 59 J4
Zapadno-Kazakhstanskaya Oblast' admin. div. Kazakh. see Zapadnyy Kazakhstan
Zapadno-Sakhalinskiy Khrebet mts Rus. Fed. 74 F2
Zapadno-Sibirskaya Nizmennost' plain Rus. Fed. see West Siberian Plain
Zapadno-Sibirskaya Ravnina plain Rus. Fed. see West Siberian Plain
Zapadnyy Chink Ustyurta esc. Kazakh. 91 I2
Zapadnyy Chink Ustyurta esc. Kazakh. 91 I2
Zapadnyy Kazakhstan admin. div. Kazakh. 41 Q6
Zapadnyy Kil'din Rus. Fed. 44 S2
Zapadnyy Sayan reg. Rus. Fed. 72 F2
Zapata U.S.A. 131 D7
Zapata, Península de pen. Cuba 133 D8
Zapiga Chile 142 E7
Zapolyarnyy Rus. Fed. 44 Q2
Zapol'ye Rus. Fed. 42 H4
Zaporizhzhya Ukr. 43 G7
Zaporozh'ye Ukr. see Zaporizhzhya
Zapug China 82 E2
Zaqatala Azer. 91 G2
Zaqên China 76 B1
Za Qu r. China 76 C2
Zaqungngomar mt. China 83 G2
Zara China see Moinda
Zara Croatia see Zadar
Zara Turkey 90 E3
Zarafshan Uzbek. 80 B3
Zarafshon Uzbek. see Zarafshan
Zarafshon, Qatorkŭhi mts Tajik. 89 G2
Zaragoza Spain 57 F3
Zarand Iran 88 E4
Zarang China 82 D3
Zaranikh Reserve nature res. Egypt 85 B4
Zaranj Afgh. 89 F4
Zarasai Lith. 45 O9
Zárate Arg. 144 E4
Zaraysk Rus. Fed. 43 H5
Zaraza Venez. 142 E2
Zarbdar Uzbek. 89 H1
Zärdab Azer. 43 J8
Zarechensk Rus. Fed. 44 Q3
Zāreh Iran 88 C3
Zarembo Island U.S.A. 120 C3
Zargun mt. Pak. 89 G4
Zari Afgh. 89 G3
Zaria Nigeria 96 D3
Zarichne Ukr. 43 E6
Zarifête, Col des pass Alg. 57 F6
Zaring China see Liangdaohe
Zarinsk Rus. Fed. 72 E2
Zarmardan Afgh. 89 F3
Zarneh Iran 88 B3
Zărnești Romania 59 K2
Zarqā' Jordan see Az Zarqā'
Zarqā', Nahr az r. Jordan 85 B3
Zarubino Rus. Fed. 74 C4
Żary Poland 47 O5
Zarzis Tunisia 54 G5
Zasheyek Rus. Fed. 44 Q3
Zaskar reg. Jammu and Kashmir see Zanskar
Zaskar Range mts India see Zanskar Mountains
Zaslawye Belarus 45 O9
Zastron S. Africa 101 H6
Za'tarī, Wādī az watercourse Jordan 85 C3
Zaterechnyy Rus. Fed. 43 J7
Zauche reg. Germany 53 M2
Zaunguzskiye Karakumy des. Turkm. 88 E1
Zavalla U.S.A. 131 E6
Zavetnoye Rus. Fed. 43 I7
Zavety Il'icha Rus. Fed. 74 F2
Zavidoviči Bos.-Herz. 58 H2
Zavitaya Rus. Fed. see Zavitinsk
Zavitinsk Rus. Fed. 74 C2
Zavolzhsk Rus. Fed. 42 I4
Zavolzh'ye Rus. Fed. see Zavolzhsk
Závora, Ponta pt Moz. 101 L3
Zawiercie Poland 47 Q5
Zawīlah Libya 97 E2
Zāwīyah, Jabal az hills Syria 85 C2
Zawr, Ra's az pt Saudi Arabia 88 C5
Zaydī, Wādī az watercourse Syria 85 C3
Zaysan Kazakh. 80 F2
Zaysan, Lake Kazakh. 80 F2
Zaysan, Ozero l. Kazakh. see Zaysan, Lake
Zayü China 76 C2
Zayü Qu r. China/India 83 I3
Žďár nad Sázavou Czech Rep. 47 O6
Zdolbuniv Ukr. 43 E6
Zdolbunov Ukr. see Zdolbuniv
Zealand i. Denmark 45 G9
Zēbāk Afgh. 82 B1
Zebulon U.S.A. 134 D5
Zedelgem Belgium 52 D3
Zeebrugge Belgium 52 D3
Zeeland U.S.A. 134 B2
Zeerust S. Africa 101 H3
Zefat Israel 85 B3
Zehdenick Germany 53 N2
Zeil, Mount Australia 109 F5
Zeil am Main Germany 53 K4
Zeist Neth. 52 F2
Zeitz Germany 53 M3
Zêkog China 76 D1
Zela Turkey see Zile
Zelennik Rus. Fed. 42 J3
Zelenoborsk Rus. Fed. 41 S3
Zelenoborskiy Rus. Fed. 44 R3
Zelenodol'sk Rus. Fed. 42 K5
Zelenogorsk Rus. Fed. 45 P6
Zelenograd Rus. Fed. 42 H4
Zelenogradsk Rus. Fed. 45 L9
Zelenokumsk Rus. Fed. 91 F1
Zelentsovo Rus. Fed. 42 J4
Zelenyy, Ostrov i. Rus. Fed. 74 G4
Zell am See Austria 47 N7
Zellingen Germany 53 J5
Zelzate Belgium 52 D3
Žemaitijos nacionalinis parkas nat. park Lith. 45 L8
Zêmdasam China 76 D1
Zemetchino Rus. Fed. 43 I5
Zémio Cent. Afr. Rep. 98 C3
Zemmora Alg. 57 G6
Zempoaltépetl, Nudo de mt. Mex. 136 E5
Zengcheng China 77 G4
Zenica Bos.-Herz. 58 G2
Zenifim watercourse Israel 85 B4
Zennor U.K. 49 B8
Zenta Serb. and Mont. see Senta
Zenzach Alg. 57 H6
Zeravshanskiy Khrebet mts Tajik. see Zarafshon, Qatorkŭhi
Zerbst Germany 53 M3
Zerenike Reserve nature res. Egypt see Zaranikh Reserve
Zerf Germany 52 G5
Zernien Germany 53 K1
Zernitz Germany 53 M2
Zernograd Rus. Fed. 43 I7
Zernovoy Rus. Fed. see Zernograd
Zêtang China see Nêdong
Zetel Germany 53 H1
Zeulenroda Germany 53 L4
Zeven Germany 53 J1
Zevenaar Neth. 52 G3
Zevgari, Cape Cyprus 85 A2
Zeya Rus. Fed. 74 B1
Zeya r. Rus. Fed. 74 B2
Zeydar Iran 88 E2
Zeydī Iran 89 F5
Zeyskiy Zapovednik nature res. Rus. Fed. 74 B1
Zeysko-Bureinskaya Vpadina depr. Rus. Fed. 74 C2
Zeyskoye Vodokhranilishche resr Rus. Fed. 74 B1
Zeytin Burnu c. Cyprus see Elaia, Cape
Zêzere r. Port. 57 B4
Zgharta Lebanon 85 B2
Zghorta Lebanon see Zgharta
Zgierz Poland 47 Q5
Zhabdün China see Zhongba
Zhabinka Belarus 45 N10
Zhaggo China see Luhuo
Zhaglag China 76 C1
Zhag'yab China 76 C2
Zhaksy Sarysu watercourse Kazakh. see Sarysu
Zhalanash Kazakh. see Damdy
Zhalpaktal Kazakh. 41 P6
Zhalpaqtal Kazakh. see Zhalpaktal
Zhaltyr Kazakh. 80 C1
Zhambyl Karagandinskaya Oblast' Kazakh. 80 D2
Zhambyl Zhambylskaya Oblast' Kazakh. see Taraz
Zhamo China see Bomi
Zhanakorgan Kazakh. 80 C3
Zhanaozen Kazakh. 73 E2
Zhanatas Kazakh. 80 C3
Zhanbei China 74 B2
Zhangaözen Kazakh. see Zhanaozen
Zhanga Qazan Kazakh. see Novaya Kazanka
Zhangaqorghan Kazakh. see Zhanakorgan
Zhangatas Kazakh. see Zhanatas
Zhangbei China 73 K4
Zhangcheng China see Yongtai
Zhangcunpu China 77 H1
Zhangde China see Anyang
Zhangdian China see Zibo
Zhanggu China see Danba
Zhangguangcai Ling mts China 74 C3
Zhanghua Taiwan see Changhua
Zhangjiabang China 77 G2
Zhangjiajie China 77 F2
Zhangjiakou China 73 K4
Zhangjiang China see Taoyuan
Zhangjiapan China see Jingbian
Zhangla China 76 D1
Zhangling China 74 A1
Zhanglou China 77 H1
Zhangping China 77 H3
Zhangqiangzhen China 74 A4
Zhangqiao China 77 H1
Zhangshu China 77 G2
Zhangxian China 76 E1
Zhangye China 80 J4
Zhangzhou China 77 H3
Zhanhe China see Zhanbei
Zhanibek Kazakh. 41 P6
Zhanjiang China 77 F4
Zhanjiang Bei China see Chikan
Zhao'an China 77 H4
Zhaodong China 74 B3
Zhaojue China 76 D2
Zhaoliqiao China 77 G2
Zhaoping China 77 F3
Zhaoqing China 77 G4
Zhaotong China 76 D3
Zhaoyuan China 74 B3
Zhaozhou China 74 B3
Zhari Namco salt l. China 83 F3
Zharkamys Kazakh. 80 A2
Zharkent Kazakh. 80 E3
Zharkovskiy Rus. Fed. 42 G5
Zharma Kazakh. 80 F2
Zhashkiv Ukr. 43 F6
Zhashkov Ukr. see Zhashkiv
Zhaslyk Uzbek. 91 J2
Zhaxi China see Weixin
Zhaxi Co salt l. China 83 F2
Zhaxigang China 82 D2
Zhaxizê China 76 C2
Zhaxizong China 83 F3
Zhayü China 76 C2
Zhayyq r. Kazakh./Rus. Fed. see Ural
Zhdanov Ukr. see Mariupol'
Zhdanovsk Azer. see Beyläqan
Zhedao China see Lianghe
Zhêhor China 76 D2
Zhejiang prov. China 77 I2
Zhelaniya, Mys c. Rus. Fed. 64 H2
Zheleznodorozhnyy Rus. Fed. see Yemva
Zheleznodorozhnyy Uzbek. see Kungrad
Zheleznogorsk Rus. Fed. 43 G5
Zhelou China see Ceheng
Zheltyye Vody Ukr. see Zhovti Vody
Zhem Kazakh. see Emba
Zhemgang Bhutan 83 G4
Zhen'an China 77 F1
Zhenba China 76 E1
Zhenghe China 77 H3
Zhengjiatun China see Shuangliao
Zhengning China 77 F1
Zhengyang China 77 G1
Zhengyangguan China 77 H1
Zhengzhou China 77 G1
Zhenhai China 77 I2
Zhenjiang China see Dantu
Zhenjiangguan China 76 D1
Zhenlai China 74 A3
Zhenning China 76 E3
Zhenping China 77 F2
Zhenxiong China 76 E3
Zhenyang China see Zhengyang
Zhenyuan China 77 F3
Zherdevka Rus. Fed. 43 I6
Zherong China 77 H3
Zheshart Rus. Fed. 42 K3
Zhetikara Kazakh. see Zhitikara
Zhêxam China 83 F3
Zhexi Shuiku resr China 77 F2
Zhezkazgan Kazakh. 80 C2
Zhezqazghan Kazakh. see Zhezkazgan
Zhicheng Hubei China 77 F2
Zhicheng Zhejiang China see Changxing
Zhidoi China 76 B1
Zhifang China see Jiangxia
Zhigalovo Rus. Fed. 72 J2
Zhigansk Rus. Fed. 65 N3
Zhigung China 83 G3
Zhijiang Hubei China 77 F2
Zhijiang Hunan China 70 E1
Zhijin China 76 E3
Zhilong China see Yangxi
Zhi Qu r. China see Yangtze
Zhitikara Kazakh. 78 F1
Zhitkovichi Belarus see Zhytkavichy
Zhitkur Rus. Fed. 43 J6
Zhitomir Ukr. see Zhytomyr
Zhīvār Iran 88 B3
Zhiziluo China 76 C3
Zhlobin Belarus 43 F5
Zhmerinka Ukr. see Zhmerynka
Zhmerynka Ukr. 43 F6
Zhob Pak. 89 H4
Zhob r. Pak. 89 H3
Zhong'an China see Fuyuan
Zhongba Guangdong China 77 G4
Zhongba Sichuan China see Jiangyou
Zhongba Xizang China 83 F3
Zhongdian China 76 C3
Zhongduo China see Youyang
Zhongguo country Asia see China
Zhongguo Renmin Gongheguo country Asia see China
Zhonghe China see Xiushan
Zhongping China see Huize
Zhongshan research station Antarctica 152 E2
Zhongshan Guangdong China 77 G4
Zhongshan Guangxi China 77 F3
Zhongshan Guizhou China see Lupanshui
Zhongshu Yunnan China see Luliang
Zhongshu Yunnan China see Luxi
Zhongtai China see Lingtai
Zhongtiao Shan mts China 77 F1
Zhongwei China 72 J5
Zhongxin Guangdong China 77 G3
Zhongxin Yunnan China see Zhongdian
Zhongxin Yunnan China see Huaping
Zhongxingji China 77 H2
Zhongyaozhan China 74 B2
Zhongyicun China 76 D3
Zhongyuan China 77 F5
Zhongzhai China 76 E1
Zhosaly Kazakh. see Dzhusaly
Zhoujiajing China 72 I5
Zhoukou Henan China 77 G1
Zhoukou Sichuan China see Peng'an
Zhouning China 77 H3
Zhoushan China 77 I2
Zhoushan Dao i. China 77 I2
Zhoushan Qundao is China 77 I2
Zhouzhi China 77 F1
Zhovti Vody Ukr. 43 G6
Zhuanghe China 75 A5
Zhuanglang China 76 E1
Zhubgyügoin China 76 C1
Zhudong Taiwan see Chutung
Zhugla China 76 B2
Zhugqu China 76 E1
Zhuhai China 77 G4
Zhuji Henan China see Shangqiu
Zhuji Zhejiang China 77 I2
Zhujing China see Jinshan
Zhukeng China 77 G4
Zhukovka Rus. Fed. 43 G5
Zhukovskiy Rus. Fed. 43 H5
Zhumadian China 77 G1
Zhuokeji China 76 D2
Zhushan Hubei China 77 F1
Zhushan Hubei China see Xuan'en
Zhuxi China 77 F1
Zhuxiang China 77 H1
Zhuyang China see Dazhu
Zhuzhou Hunan China 77 G3
Zhuzhou Hunan China 77 G3
Zhydachiv Ukr. 43 E6
Zhympity Kazakh. 41 Q5
Zhytkavichy Belarus 45 O10
Zhytomyr Ukr. 43 F6
Zīā'ābād Iran 88 C3
Žiar nad Hronom Slovakia 47 Q6
Zībā salt pan Saudi Arabia 85 D4
Zibo China 73 L5
Zicheng China see Zijin
Zidi Pak. 89 G5
Ziel, Mount Australia see Zeil, Mount
Zielona Góra Poland 47 O5
Ziemelkursas augstiene hills Latvia 45 M8
Zierenberg Germany 53 J3
Ziesar Germany 53 M2
Ziftá Egypt 90 C5
Zīghan Libya 97 F2
Zigong China 76 E2
Ziguey Chad 97 E3
Ziguinchor Senegal 96 B3
Žīguri Latvia 45 O8
Zihuatanejo Mex. 136 D5
Zijin China 77 G4
Zijpenberg hill Neth. 52 G2
Ziketan China see Xinghai
Zile Turkey 90 D2
Žilina Slovakia 47 Q6
Zillah Libya 97 E2
Zima Rus. Fed. 72 I2
Zimba Zambia 99 C5
▶Zimbabwe country Africa 99 C5 Africa 7, 94–95
Zimi Sierra Leone see Zimmi
Zimmerbude Rus. Fed. see Svetlyy
Zimmi Sierra Leone 96 B4
Zimnicea Romania 59 K3
Zimniy Bereg coastal area Rus. Fed. 42 H2
Zimovniki Rus. Fed. 43 I7
Zimrīn Syria 85 B2
Zin watercourse Israel 85 B4
Zin Pak. 89 H4
Zinave, Parque Nacional de nat. park Moz. 99 D6
Zinder Niger 96 D3
Zindo China 76 D2
Ziniaré Burkina 96 C3
Zinjibār Yemen 86 G7
Zinoyevsk Ukr. see Kirovohrad
Zion U.S.A. 134 B2
Zion National Park U.S.A. 129 G3
Zionz Lake Canada 121 N5
Zippori Israel 85 B3
Ziqudukou China 76 B1
Zirc Hungary 58 G1
Zirkel, Mount U.S.A. 126 G4
Zirkūh i. U.A.E. 88 D5
Zirndorf Germany 53 K5
Ziro India 83 H4
Zirreh Afgh. 89 F4
Zīr Rūd Iran 88 C4
Zi Shui r. China 73 K7
Zistersdorf Austria 47 P6
Zitácuaro Mex. 136 D5
Zito China see Lhorong
Zitong China 76 E2
Zittau Germany 47 O5
Zixi China 77 H3
Zixing China see Xingning
Ziyang Jiangxi China see Wuyuan
Ziyang Shaanxi China 77 F1
Ziyang Sichuan China 76 E2
Ziyaret Dağı hill Turkey 85 B1
Ziyuan China 77 F3
Ziyun China 76 E3
Ziz, Oued watercourse Morocco 54 D5
Zizhong China 76 E2
Zlatoustovsk Rus. Fed. 74 D1
Zlín Czech Rep. 47 P6
Zmeinogorsk Rus. Fed. 80 F1
Zmiyevka Rus. Fed. 43 H5
Znamenka Rus. Fed. 43 I5
Znamenka Ukr. see Znam"yanka
Znam"yanka Ukr. 43 G6
Znojmo Czech Rep. 47 P6
Zoar S. Africa 100 E7
Zoetermeer Neth. 52 E2
Zogainrawar China see Huashixia
Zogang China 76 C2
Zogqên China 76 C1
Zoigê China 76 D1
Zoji La pass Jammu and Kashmir 82 C2
Zola S. Africa 101 H7
Zolder Belgium 52 F3
Zolochev Kharkivs'ka Oblast' Ukr. see Zolochiv
Zolochev L'vivs'ka Oblast' Ukr. see Zolochiv
Zolochiv Kharkivs'ka Oblast' Ukr. 43 G6
Zolochiv L'vivs'ka Oblast' Ukr. 43 E6
Zolotonosha Ukr. 43 G6
Zolotoye Rus. Fed. 43 J6
Zolotukhino Rus. Fed. 43 H5
▶Zomba Malawi 99 D5 Former capital of Malawi.
Zombor Serb. and Mont. see Sombor
Zomin Uzbek. see Zaamin
Zongga China see Gyirong
Zongo Dem. Rep. Congo 98 B3
Zonguldak Turkey 59 N4
Zongxoi China 83 G3
Zörbig Germany 53 M3
Zorgho Burkina 96 C3
Zorgo Burkina see Zorgho
Zorn r. France 53 I6
Żory Poland 47 Q5
Zossen Germany 53 N2
Zottegem Belgium 52 D4
Zouar Chad 97 E2
Zoucheng China 77 H1
Zouérat Mauritania 96 B2
Zousfana, Oued watercourse Alg. 54 D5
Zoushi China 77 F2
Zouxian China see Zoucheng
Zrenjanin Serb. and Mont. 59 I2
Zschopau Germany 53 N4
Zschopau r. Germany 53 N3
Zschornewitz Germany 53 M3
Zubālah, Birkat waterhole Saudi Arabia 91 F5
Zubillaga Arg. 144 D5
Zubova Polyana Rus. Fed. 43 I5
Zubtsov Rus. Fed. 42 G4
Zuénoula Côte d'Ivoire 96 C4
Zug Switz. 56 I3
Zugdidi Georgia 91 F2
Zugspitze mt. Austria/Germany 47 M7
Zugu Nigeria 96 D3
Zuider Zee l. Neth. see IJsselmeer
Zuidhorn Neth. 52 G1
Zuid-Kennemerland Nationaal Park nat. park Neth. 52 E2
Zuitai China see Kangxian
Zuitaizi China see Kangxian
Zuitou China see Taibai
Zújar r. Spain 57 D4
Zülpich Germany 52 G4
Zumba Ecuador 142 C4
Zunheboto India 83 H4
Zuni U.S.A. 129 I4
Zuni watercourse U.S.A. 129 I4
Zuni Mountains U.S.A. 129 I4
Zunyi Guizhou China 76 E3
Zunyi Guizhou China 76 E3
Zuo Jiang r. China/Vietnam 70 E2
Županja Croatia 58 H2
Zūrābād Āzarbāyjān-e Gharbī Iran 88 B2
Zūrābād Khorāsān Iran 89 F3
Zürich Switz. 56 I3
Zurmat reg. Afgh. 89 H3
Zuru Nigeria 96 D3
Zurzuna Turkey see Çıldır
Zutphen Neth. 52 G2
Zuwārah Libya 96 E1
Zuyevka Rus. Fed. 42 K4
Zūzan Iran 89 E3
Zvishavane Zimbabwe 99 D6
Zvolen Slovakia 47 Q6
Zvornik Bos.-Herz. 59 H2
Zwedru Liberia 96 C4
Zweeloo Neth. 52 G2
Zweibrücken Germany 53 H5
Zweletemba S. Africa 100 D7
Zwelitsha S. Africa 101 H7
Zwethau Germany 53 N3
Zwettl Austria 47 O6
Zwickau Germany 53 M4
Zwochau Germany 53 M3
Zwolle Neth. 52 G2
Zwönitz Germany 53 M4
Zyablovo Rus. Fed. 42 L4
Zygi Cyprus 85 A2
Zyryan Kazakh. see Zyryanovsk
Zyryanka Rus. Fed. 65 Q3
Zyryanovsk Kazakh. 80 F2
Zyyi Cyprus see Zygi

Acknowledgements

Maps and data

General

Maps designed and created by HarperCollins Reference, Glasgow, UK, www.bartholomewmaps.com
Cross-sections (pp36–37, 60–61, 92–93, 102–103, 114–115, 138–139) and globes (pp14–15, 146–147): Geo-Innovations, Llandudno, UK, www.geoinnovations.co.uk

The publishers would like to thank all national survey departments, road, rail and national park authorities, statistical offices and national place name committees throughout the world for their valuable assistance, and in particular the following:
British Antarctic Survey, Cambridge, UK
Tony Champion, Professor of Population Geography, University of Newcastle upon Tyne, UK
Mr P J M Geelan, London, UK

International Boundary Research Unit, University of Durham, UK
The Meteorological Office, Bracknell, Berkshire, UK
Permanent Committee on Geographical Names for British Official Use, London, UK

Data

Bathymetric data: The GEBCO Digital Atlas published by the British Oceanographic Data Centre on behalf of IOC and IHO, 1994
Earthquakes data (pp14–15): United States Geological Survey (USGS) National Earthquakes Information Center, Denver, USA
Coral reefs data (p18): UNEP World Conservation Monitoring Centre, Cambridge, UK and World Resources Institute (WRI), Washington DC, USA
Desertification data (p18): U.S. Department of Agriculture Natural Resources Conservation Service

Population data (pp20–21): Center for International Earth Science Information Network (CIESIN), Columbia University; International Food Policy Research Institute (IFPRI); and World Resources Institute (WRI). 2000. Gridded Population of the World (GPW), Version 2. Palisades, NY: CIESIN, Columbia University. http://sedac.ciesin.columbia.edu/plue/gpw
Company sales figures (p29): Reprinted by permission of Forbes Magazine © 2004 Forbes Inc.
Terrorism data (p31): Rand-MIPT Terrorist Incident Database (Rand Corporation, Santa Monica, Ca and Oklahoma City National Memorial Institute for the Prevention of Terrorism, 2003) db.mipt.org/mipt_rand.cfm
Antarctica (p152): Antarctic Digital Database (versions 1 and 2), © Scientific Committee on Antarctic Research (SCAR), Cambridge, UK (1993, 1998)

Photographs and images

Page	Image	Satellite/Sensor	Credit
5	The Alps	MODIS	MODIS/NASA
	Amsterdam	IKONOS	Space Imaging Europe/Science Photo Library
	Italy	AVHRR	Earth Satellite Corporation/Science Photo Library
6	Ganges Delta	SPOT	CNES, 1987 Distribution Spot Image/Science Photo Library
	Cyprus	MODIS	MODIS/NASA
	Indian subcontinent	AVHRR	Earth Satellite Corporation/Science Photo Library
7	Victoria Falls		Roger De La Harpe, Gallo Images/CORBIS
	Sinai Peninsula	Shuttle	NASA
8	Mt Cook		Mike Schroder/Still Pictures
	Bora Bora	SPOT	CNES, Distribution Spot Image/Science Photo Library
	Ayers Rock		ImageState
	Sydney	IKONOS	IKONOS satellite imagery provided by Space Imaging, Thornton, Colorado, www.spaceimaging.com
9	The Pentagon	IKONOS	IKONOS satellite imagery provided by Space Imaging, Thornton, Colorado, www.spaceimaging.com
	Panama Canal	Landsat	Clifton-Campbell Imaging Inc. www.tmarchive.com
	Cuba	MODIS	MODIS/NASA
10–11	Dili	SPOT	CNES, Distribution Spot Image/Science Photo Library
	Vatican City	IKONOS	IKONOS satellite imagery provided by Space Imaging, Thornton, Colorado, www.spaceimaging.com
12–13	Greenland	MODIS	MODIS/NASA
	Nile Valley	MODIS	MODIS/NASA
14–15	Bam		Fatih Saribas/Reuters/CORBIS
	Mt Etna		Bernhard Edmaier/Science Photo Library
16–17	Tropical Cyclone Dina	MODIS	MODIS/NASA/GSFC
	Annual precipitation map	Microwave infrared	NASA/Goddard Space Flight Centre
	Climate change maps		Met. Office, Hadley Centre for Climate Prediction and Research
18–19	Snow and ice		Klaus Andrews/Still Pictures
	Urban		Ron Giling/Still Pictures
	Forest		Wolfgang Kaehler/CORBIS
	Barren/Shrubland		Simon Fraser/Science Photo Library
20–21	Kuna Indians		Royalty-Free/CORBIS
	Masai Village		Yann Arthus-Bertrand/CORBIS
22–23	Los Angeles	SRTM/Landsat 5	NASA

Page	Image	Satellite/Sensor	Credit
	Tōkyō		Cities Revealed aerial photography © The GeoInformation Group, 1998
24–25	International telecommunications traffic map		© PriMetrica, Inc. www.telegeography.com and www.primetrica.com
	Internet topology		CAIDA/Science Photo Library
26–27	Health care facilities		John Cole/Science Photo Library
	Education		Moacyr Lopes Junior/UNEP/Still Pictures
28–29	Sudan Village		Mark Edwards/Still Pictures
	The City		London Aerial Photo Library/CORBIS
30–31	Egypt/Gaza border		Marc Schlossman/Panos Pictures
	Spratly Islands	IKONOS	IKONOS satellite imagery provided by Space Imaging, Thornton, Colorado, www.spaceimaging.com
	İstanbul		Getty Images
32–33	Water		Harmut Schwarzbach/Still Pictures
	Drugs		Getty Images
	Aids		Friedrich Stark/Still Pictures
34–35	Aral Sea	Landsat	Data available from the U.S. Geological Survey, EROS Data Center, Sioux Falls, SD
	Abu Dhabi 1972	Landsat	Science Photo Library
	Abu Dhabi 2000	IKONOS	IKONOS satellite imagery provided by Space Imaging, Thornton, Colorado, www.spaceimaging.com
	3 Gorges Dam Before		Wolfgang Kaehler/CORBIS
	3 Gorges Dam Construction		Reuters/CORBIS
	Mesopotamian marshlands		NASA/EROS Data Center
36–37	Iceland	MODIS	MODIS/NASA
	Danube delta	MODIS	MODIS/NASA
	Caucasus	MODIS	MODIS/NASA
38–39	Paris	IKONOS	Space Imaging Europe/Science Photo Library
	Bosporus	SPOT	CNES, 1991 Distribution Spot Image/Science Photo Library
	Belgrade	SIR-C/X-SAR	NASA JPL
60–61	Kamchatka Peninsula	MODIS	MODIS/NASA
	Caspian Sea	MODIS	MODIS/NASA
	Yangtze	MODIS	MODIS/NASA
62–63	Timor	MODIS	MODIS/NASA
	Beijing	IKONOS	IKONOS satellite imagery provided by Space Imaging, Thornton, Colorado, www.spaceimaging.com

Page	Image	Satellite/Sensor	Credit
	Gaza/Egypt/Israel border	Shuttle	Digital image ©1996 CORBIS; Original image courtesy of NASA/CORBIS
92–93	Congo	Shuttle	NASA
	Lake Victoria	MODIS	MODIS/NASA
	Kilimanjaro	Landsat	USGS/NASA
94–95	Cape Verde	MODIS	MODIS/NASA
	Cairo	IKONOS	IKONOS satellite imagery provided by Space Imaging, Thornton, Colorado, www.spaceimaging.com
	Cape Town	IKONOS	IKONOS satellite imagery provided by Space Imaging, Thornton, Colorado, www.spaceimaging.com
102–103	Lake Eyre	Shuttle	NASA
	New Caledonia and Vanuatu	SeaWiFS	Image provided by ORBIMAGE © Orbital Imaging Corporation and processing by NASA Goddard Space Flight Center.
	Banks Peninsula		Institute of Geological and Nuclear Sciences, New Zealand
104–105	Wellington		NZ Aerial Mapping Ltd www.nzam.com
	Tasmania	SeaWiFS	Image provided by ORBIMAGE © Orbital Imaging Corporation and processing by NASA Goddard Space Flight Center.
	Tahiti and Moorea	SPOT	CNES, Distribution Spot Image/Science Photo Library
114–115	Mississippi	ASTER	ASTER/NASA
	Grand Canyon	SPOT	CNES, 1996 Distribution Spot Image/Science Photo Library
	Yucatan	MODIS	MODIS/NASA
116–117	The Bahamas	MODIS	MODIS/NASA
	El Paso	Shuttle	NASA
	Washington DC		US Geological Society/Science Photo Library
138–139	Lake Titicaca	Shuttle	NASA
	Tierra del Fuego	MODIS	MODIS/NASA
	Amazon/Rio Negro	Terra/MISR	NASA
140–141	Galapagos Islands	SPOT	CNES, 1988 Distribution Spot Image/Science Photo Library
	Falkland Islands	MODIS	MODIS/NASA
	Rio de Janeiro	SPOT	Earth Satellite Corporation/Science Photo Library
146–147	Antarctica	AVHRR	NRSC Ltd/Science Photo Library
	Novaya Zemlya	Landsat ETM	NASA